barbri®

First Year Review

Table of Contents

To be used in conjunction with the Fall 2011 and Spring 2012 semesters

Civil Procedure

CIVIL PROCEDURE

TABLE OF CONTENTS

INTRODUCTION

This outline is designed to acquaint you with commonly tested areas within the fields of federal jurisdiction and procedure. These are: personal jurisdiction, subject matter jurisdiction, venue, discovery, pleading and motion practice, and joinder of multiple parties.

A. PERSONAL JURISDICTION

Personal jurisdiction refers to the ability of a court to exercise power over a particular defendant or item of property. It may be categorized as in personam, in rem, or quasi in rem. The primary limitations on a court's power to exercise personal jurisdiction are found in the United States Constitution and state statutes.

B. SUBJECT MATTER JURISDICTION

The subject matter jurisdiction of the federal courts is limited to that authorized by the Constitution as implemented by federal statute and decisional law. In general, it may be categorized as follows:

1. Diversity of Citizenship Jurisdiction

Diversity of citizenship jurisdiction under 28 U.S.C. section 1332 is grounded historically in the desire to protect out-of-state parties from local prejudice. Its main requirement is that there be complete diversity between opposing parties. Each plaintiff must be of diverse citizenship from each defendant. Also, the amount in controversy must exceed $75,000.

2. Federal Question Jurisdiction

Federal question jurisdiction under section 1331 presents fewer specific difficulties. The principal problem in this area is to determine when an action "arises under" federal law. A secondary problem is to know what types of actions are within the exclusive jurisdiction of the federal courts under other specific statutes.

3. Removal Jurisdiction

Removal jurisdiction allows defendants to remove an action brought in a state court to a federal court if the federal court would have had original jurisdiction over the action.

4. Supplemental Jurisdiction

The doctrine of supplemental jurisdiction is codified under section 1367 and includes, under a single name, the concepts of "ancillary" and "pendent" jurisdiction. In any form, supplemental jurisdiction allows a federal court to entertain certain claims over which it would have no independent basis of subject matter jurisdiction, *i.e.*, claims that do not satisfy diversity or federal question jurisdiction requirements. It is important to note that supplemental jurisdiction operates only after a claim has invoked federal subject matter jurisdiction, after the case is properly in federal court. Supplemental jurisdiction operates to bring additional claims into that case that arise from the same transaction or occurrence as the original claim, but it cannot be used to get the case into federal court in the first instance.

C. VENUE

Venue is the designation of the proper district in which to bring an action. Venue will depend on the nature of the jurisdiction (*i.e.*, whether federal question or diversity of citizenship), and on the nature of the parties (*i.e.*, whether corporate or natural persons).

D. DISCOVERY

Discovery issues principally revolve around the scope of the examination allowed in discovery, the uses of depositions at trial, and the available methods of enforcing discovery rights.

E. MULTIPLE PARTIES

Multiple party questions concern whether various types of joinder are permitted under federal law and, if so, whether there is a jurisdictional basis for a particular attempted joinder. The majority of the issues that arise in this area are grounded in the interpretation or application of statutes and the Federal Rules of Civil Procedure ("Federal Rules"), and also require knowledge of subject matter jurisdictional bases, especially supplemental jurisdiction.

I. PERSONAL JURISDICTION

A. OVERVIEW

There are two branches of jurisdiction: subject matter jurisdiction and personal jurisdiction. ***Subject matter jurisdiction*** involves the court's power over a particular ***type of case***. ***Personal jurisdiction*** involves the ability of a court having subject matter jurisdiction to exercise power over a ***particular defendant or item of property***. This section discusses personal jurisdiction.

1. Limitations on Personal Jurisdiction

Limitations on a court's personal jurisdiction arise from two sources: state statutes and the United States Constitution. An exercise of personal jurisdiction must not exceed the limitations of either source.

a. Statutory Limitations

States have the power to decide over whom their courts may exercise jurisdiction. Therefore, the first place to look to determine whether the court has properly exercised personal jurisdiction is state law. If no state statute grants the court the power over the parties before the court, then the court lacks personal jurisdiction. On the other hand, an exercise of jurisdiction will not be proper merely because it comports with a state statute; it must also be within the limitations set by the Constitution (below).

b. Constitutional Limitations

The Due Process Clause of the Constitution places two restrictions on the exercise of personal jurisdiction. First, the defendant must have such contacts with the forum state that the exercise of jurisdiction would be fair and reasonable. Second, the defendant must be given appropriate notice of the action and an opportunity to be heard. Note that these requirements are the outer limits to which a state may reach in exercising jurisdiction over a person. A state statute cannot exceed these constitutional boundaries, but is not required to exercise the full limit of constitutional power. Thus, in evaluating jurisdiction over a person, both constitutional and statutory limitations must be considered.

c. Personal Jurisdiction in Federal Courts

The main jurisdictional problem in state courts arises when the defendant over whom power is sought lives in another state. Since the federal borders encompass all states, one might expect that federal courts would encounter problems of personal jurisdiction only when the defendants were foreign nationals. However, Rule 4 of the Federal Rules provides that, absent some special federal provision, each federal court must analyze personal jurisdiction ***as if it were a court of the state in which it is located***. Thus, in nearly every case, the assessment of whether the court has personal jurisdiction over the defendant will be exactly the same in federal court as it is in state court.

2. Three Types of Personal Jurisdiction

a. In Personam Jurisdiction

In personam jurisdiction exists when the forum has power over the person of a particular defendant. (Jurisdiction over a plaintiff is generally not an issue because the plaintiff accedes to the court's jurisdiction by bringing suit in that court.) In these cases, the court may render a money judgment against the defendant or may order the defendant

to perform acts or refrain from acting. Such a judgment creates a personal obligation on the defendant and is entitled to full faith and credit in all other states; *i.e.,* if a defendant is ordered to pay a sum of money to a plaintiff, the plaintiff may enforce the judgment against the defendant's property in any other state where that property is located.

b. **In Rem Jurisdiction**

In rem jurisdiction exists when the court has power to adjudicate the rights of all persons in the world with respect to a ***particular item*** of property. This jurisdiction is limited to situations where the property is located within the physical borders of the state and where it is necessary for the state to be able to bind all persons regarding the property's ownership and use. This occurs with respect to actions for condemnation (eminent domain cases), forfeiture of property to the state (*e.g.,* when the property is used for the unlawful transportation of narcotics), and settlement of decedents' estates.

c. **Quasi In Rem Jurisdiction**

One type of quasi in rem jurisdiction exists when the court has power to determine whether particular individuals own specific property within the court's control. Unlike in rem jurisdiction, however, it does not permit the court to determine the rights of all persons in the world with respect to the property. A second type of quasi in rem jurisdiction permits the court to adjudicate disputes other than ownership based on the presence of the defendant's property in the forum (*see* E.2.a.2), *infra,* regarding applicable constitutional limitations).

1) **Defendant Is Not Bound Personally**

The basis of a court's power to exercise quasi in rem jurisdiction is the property within the state. (*See* E., *infra.*) The judgment does not bind the defendant ***personally*** and cannot be enforced against any other property belonging to the defendant.

B. STATUTORY LIMITATIONS ON IN PERSONAM JURISDICTION

Each state is free to prescribe its own statutory bases for personal jurisdiction. Of course, the exercise of jurisdiction in a given case must also satisfy the constitutional requirements. (*See* C., *infra.*) Most states have statutes granting their courts in personam jurisdiction in the following four situations:

(i) Where the defendant is present in the forum state and is personally served with process;

(ii) Where the defendant is domiciled in the forum state;

(iii) Where the defendant consents to jurisdiction; and

(iv) Where the defendant has committed acts bringing him within the forum state's long arm statutes.

Each of these bases of in personam jurisdiction will be discussed in detail below.

1. **Physical Presence at Time of Personal Service**

Most states grant their courts in personam jurisdiction over any defendant who can be served with process within the borders of the state, no matter how long he was present (*i.e.,* even if merely passing through). The Supreme Court has upheld this type of jurisdiction, allowing a transient defendant to be served with process for a cause of action unrelated to his brief presence in the state. [Burnham v. Superior Court, 495 U.S. 604 (1990)]

2. **State Law Exceptions to Traditional Rule**
Even though jurisdiction through presence at the time of service has been upheld under the Constitution, state statutes and court decisions have limited the power of their courts in certain situations.

a. **Service by Fraud or Force Invalid**
If a plaintiff brings a defendant into a state by fraud or force to serve process, most courts will find the service invalid. [*See, e.g.,* Copas v. Anglo-American Provision Co., 73 Mich. 541 (1889)]

b. **Immunity of Parties and Witnesses**
Most states likewise grant immunity from personal jurisdiction to nonresidents who are present in the state solely to take part in a judicial proceeding, or who are passing through the state on their way to a judicial proceeding elsewhere.

3. **Domicile**
Most states grant their courts in personam jurisdiction over persons who are domiciliaries of the state, even when the defendant is not physically within the state when served with process.

a. **Defined**
Domicile refers to the place where a person maintains her permanent home. If a person has legal capacity, her domicile is the place she has chosen through presence (even for a moment), coupled with the intention to make that place her home. If a person lacks capacity, domicile is determined by law (*e.g.,* infant is domiciliary of custodial parent's home state).

b. **Citizenship**
A United States citizen, even though domiciled abroad, is subject to personal jurisdiction in the United States. The scope of this basis for jurisdiction is unclear, because states have never attempted to enact laws or rules enabling their courts to obtain jurisdiction solely on the basis of citizenship. However, the power of federal courts to subpoena a United States citizen domiciled abroad to return to the United States to give testimony has been upheld by the Supreme Court.

4. **Consent**
Virtually every state provides for in personam jurisdiction through the defendant's consent. Such consent may be express or implied or through the making of a general appearance.

a. **Express Consent**
A party's express consent to the jurisdiction of local courts, whether given before or after suit is commenced, serves as a sufficient basis for in personam jurisdiction.

1) **By Contract**
A person can, by contract, give advance consent to jurisdiction in the event a suit is brought against him.

2) **By Appointment of Agent to Accept Service of Process**
A person can, by contract, appoint an agent in a particular state to receive service in that state in an action against him. The terms of the contract determine the extent of the agent's power and, thus, the scope of the jurisdiction conferred.

a) **Appointment Required by State**
When the state heavily regulates a type of business (*e.g.,* sale of securities) to protect its citizens, it can require a nonresident engaged in that business to appoint an agent for service of process in the state. *Note:* The state cannot require every nonresident businessperson to appoint such an agent, because the state lacks power to exclude individuals from the state. However, a state can require nonresident corporations to make such an appointment before doing business in the state.

b. **Implied Consent**
When the state has substantial reason to regulate the in-state activity of a nonresident of the state, it may provide that by engaging in such activity, the nonresident thereby appoints a designated state official as his agent for service of process. Thus, for example, the Supreme Court has upheld statutes that use such implied consent to subject a nonresident motorist to jurisdiction in any state in which he has an accident. [Hess v. Pawloski, 274 U.S. 352 (1927)]

c. **Voluntary Appearance**
A defendant may consent to jurisdiction by a voluntary appearance, *i.e.,* by contesting the case without challenging personal jurisdiction. Generally, any sort of appearance provides a sufficient basis for jurisdiction, but many states allow ***"special appearances"*** through which a defendant can object to the court's exercise of jurisdiction. The defendant usually must make this special appearance—by stating grounds for his objection to jurisdiction—in his initial pleading to the court; otherwise, the defendant will be deemed to have consented to jurisdiction.

5. **Long Arm Statutes**
Most states also grant their courts in personam jurisdiction over nonresidents who perform or cause to be performed certain acts within the state. In personam jurisdiction is granted regardless of whether the defendant is served within or outside the forum, but is limited to causes of action arising from the acts performed within the state.

a. **Unlimited Long Arm Statutes**
A few states, such as California, have long arm statutes that give their courts power over any person or property over which the state can constitutionally exercise jurisdiction. (*See* C., *infra.*) These are known as unlimited long arm statutes.

b. **Limited (or Specific) Long Arm Statutes**
Most states, however, have long arm statutes that specify in detail the situations in which their courts can exercise jurisdiction.

1) **Limitations in Tort Cases**
Some statutes permit jurisdiction when a "tort" occurs within the state, while

others require a "tortious act." The latter language has caused problems where an out-of-state manufacturer puts his products into the stream of commerce knowing that some items will end up in the forum state. When the gravamen of the complaint is negligent manufacture, some courts have read "tortious act" narrowly and confined jurisdiction to the place of manufacture; others have read it to mean "the place the tort occurred," interpreting that to be the place of injury.

2) **Limitations in Contract Cases**
Many statutes permit jurisdiction if the cause of action arises out of the "transaction of business" in the state. Some states require the defendant or his agent to have been physically present in the state at the time the transaction took place, but others have taken a broader view—*e.g.,* New York has upheld jurisdiction over a California resident who made telephone bids from California on paintings being sold in New York.

3) **Limitations in Property Actions**
Many state statutes permit jurisdiction over a nonresident defendant when the cause of action arises from ownership of property within the state—as in the case of a tort action based on negligent maintenance of realty or a contract action regarding the sale of the property. Some statutes include chattels, while others are confined to realty.

4) **Limitations in Marital Dissolution Cases**
All states provide that when a married couple last lived together in the state and one spouse then abandons the other, the remaining spouse may obtain personal jurisdiction over the absent spouse for divorce or legal separation proceedings. States vary on whether the plaintiff spouse must be living in the state at the time of abandonment (or other cause for dissolution) or whether jurisdiction may be acquired whenever the plaintiff has acquired domicile in the state.

C. CONSTITUTIONAL LIMITATIONS ON IN PERSONAM JURISDICTION

Once it is determined that a state has a statute that allows the court to exercise in personam jurisdiction over the parties before it, the constitutionality of the exercise must next be determined. As noted above, there are two components of the constitutional aspect: contacts with the forum and notice.

1. Sufficient Contacts with the Forum: Contact and Fairness

a. Traditional Rule: Physical Power

Traditionally, jurisdiction over a person (or res) was a consequence of the state's physical power to carry out its judgment; *i.e.,* it was based on the power to arrest the person to force compliance with a judgment. Accordingly, the Supreme Court upheld exercises of jurisdiction whenever the defendant was served with process within the forum state. [*See* Pennoyer v. Neff, 95 U.S. 714 (1878)] The Court later expanded the states' physical power to extend not only to those defendants who were served within the state, but also to those defendants who consented to the state's power or who were domiciled in the state, regardless of where they were served.

b. Modern Due Process Standard: Contact and Fairness

The concept of power by which a state could enforce its judgments was greatly expanded by the Supreme Court in *International Shoe Co. v. Washington,* 326 U.S. 310 (1945). No longer was power controlled solely by whether one of the traditional bases of presence, residence, or consent was present. Instead, the focus became whether sufficient minimum contacts exist between the defendant and the forum so that maintenance of the suit against the defendant does not offend "traditional notions of fair play and substantial justice." The Supreme Court has listed a series of factors by which to assess the constitutionality of personal jurisdiction. In general, the factors fall under two headings: contact and fairness.

1) Contact

International Shoe requires that the defendant have "such minimum contacts" with the forum that the exercise of jurisdiction would be fair and reasonable. In considering whether there are such contacts, a court will look to two factors: purposeful availment and foreseeability.

a) Purposeful Availment

Defendant's contact with the forum must result from her purposeful availment with that forum. The contacts cannot be accidental. Defendant must reach out to the forum in some way, such as to make money there or to use the roads there. The court must find that through these contacts the defendant ***purposefully availed*** herself "of the privilege of conducting activities within the forum state, thus invoking the benefits and protections of its laws." [Hanson v. Denckla, 357 U.S. 235 (1958)]

Examples: 1) Defendants, Michigan residents, entered into a franchise contract with a Florida corporation. The agreement required, among other things, that fees be sent to the franchisor's home office in Florida, and provided that Florida law would govern any dispute. The Court held that the defendants could be sued in Florida; their contact with Florida resulted from their purposeful availment of that state. [Burger King v. Rudzewicz, 471 U.S. 462 (1985)]

2) Defendant manufactures widgets in Alabama and markets them to customers in Mississippi. Plaintiff, a resident of Mississippi, purchases a widget from Defendant. Defendant accepts the order and ships the widget to Plaintiff in Mississippi. If the widget explodes and injures Plaintiff, she can probably sue Defendant in Mississippi. Defendant purposefully availed itself of the market in Mississippi. [*See* International Shoe Co. v. Washington, *supra*]

Compare: 1) Father, in New York, agreed to give up custody of Daughter to Mother in California. Mother sued Father in California for additional support. Father's only contact with California was letting Daughter go there. The Court held that California could not obtain in personam jurisdiction over Father because, in acting in the interest of family harmony, Father could not be said to have purposefully availed himself of the benefits and

protections of California laws. [Kulko v. Superior Court, 436 U.S. 84 (1978)]

2) Defendant, a New York car dealer, was sued in Oklahoma based on an injury that Plaintiff received from an accident in Oklahoma. The only basis for jurisdiction over Defendant was the sale of the allegedly defective car in New York by Defendant, who knew no more than that any vehicle sold might be driven elsewhere. The Court found that there was no purposeful availment of the privileges or protections of Oklahoma. [World-Wide Volkswagen Corp. v. Woodson, 444 U.S. 286 (1980)]

(1) "Stream of Commerce" Cases

There is great difficulty, however, in assessing purposeful availment in a "stream of commerce" case—*e.g.,* Defendant manufactures valves in State A and sells them to a heater manufacturer in State B. The heater manufacturer incorporates Defendant's valves into its heaters and sells them to customers in States C, D, and E. If a valve explodes and injures Plaintiff in State E, can it be said that Defendant (who acted in State A and sold only to State B) purposefully availed itself of State E? The Supreme Court faced this type of fact pattern in *Asahi Metal Industry Co. v. Superior Court,* 480 U.S. 102 (1987), and failed to resolve it definitively. Four justices opined that placing the item in the stream of commerce, with the knowledge that it would end up in a particular forum, constituted purposeful availment. Four other justices opined that there would also have to be a showing that the defendant took some additional step to avail itself of the forum. Not surprisingly, lower courts have reached varying conclusions on such fact patterns.

(2) Internet Cases

The Supreme Court has not set out a specific test or standard for assessing purposeful availment based on the defendant's Internet activity. Many courts will look at the degree of Internet activity to determine whether the defendant is subject to personal jurisdiction; *e.g.*, does defendant have a passive website that only allows people to view content, an active website that allows people to order and download products, or something in between? The maintenance of a website for only informational purposes, ***without more activity in the forum***, is probably insufficient to exercise jurisdiction over the defendant for all causes of action (*i.e.*, general jurisdiction), but it probably is sufficient for a claim arising from the maintenance of the website itself and brought under the state's long arm statute (thus invoking specific jurisdiction) if the defendant is specifically targeting readers in the forum. On the other hand, maintenance of an active website alone is probably sufficient even for an exercise of general jurisdiction (*i.e.*, a claim unrelated to the website activities) if the defendant is conducting significant business in the jurisdiction. For defendants with websites in between the two extremes (*e.g.*, a defendant with a website that allows the user to submit and request information and place orders but does not have downloads) courts will closely scrutinize the level of business activity to determine

if the defendant should be deemed "present" in the forum for all causes of action. As with passive sites, specific jurisdiction hinges on whether the defendant was purposefully directing his activities to the forum. [*See, e.g.*, Snowney v. Harrah's Entertainment, Inc., 35 Cal. 4th 1054 (2006)—Nevada hotel subject to personal jurisdiction in California when it specifically targeted California consumers by providing rate information to and accepting reservations on its website, by touting its proximity to California, and by providing driving directions from California]

b) Foreseeability

In addition to purposeful availment, the contact requirement of *International Shoe* requires that it be foreseeable that the defendant's activities make her amenable to suit in the forum. The defendant must know or reasonably anticipate that her activities in the forum render it foreseeable that she may be "haled into court" there.

Example: A national magazine is probably subject to in personam jurisdiction for libel cases in every state in which the magazine is marketed. Its publishers may reasonably anticipate causing injury in every state in which the magazine is sold, and thus should reasonably anticipate being haled into court in each state. [Keeton v. Hustler Magazine, 465 U.S. 770 (1984); Calder v. Jones, 465 U.S. 783 (1984)]

2) Fairness

In addition to the defendant's having relevant contacts with the forum, *International Shoe* requires that the exercise of jurisdiction not offend "traditional notions of fair play and substantial justice." The Court has listed several factors relevant to assessing whether jurisdiction would be fair. It is possible that an especially strong showing of fairness might make up for a lesser amount of contact (although minimum contacts are always required).

a) Relatedness of Claim to Contact

One important factor is whether the claim asserted against the defendant arises in some way from the defendant's contacts with the forum. If it does, the court is more likely to find that jurisdiction is fair and reasonable. This assessment requires the court to determine the nature and quality of the defendant's contacts with the state. Some authorities consider this factor to be part of the "contact" assessment; others consider it, as we do here, to be part of the "fairness and reasonableness" assessment. The important point is that you address the issue in your answer, whether under the contact prong or the fairness prong of the analysis.

(1) Claim Arising from Activity in the State (Specific Jurisdiction)

If the defendant's in-state activity is less than systematic or continuous (*e.g.,* isolated acts), in personam jurisdiction over the defendant will be proper only for causes of action arising from ***that in-state activity***; *i.e.,* the court will have "specific jurisdiction."

(2) Systematic and Continuous Activity in the State (General Jurisdiction)

If the defendant engages in systematic and continuous activity in the

forum state, the court could find this activity a sufficient basis for exercising in personam jurisdiction for ***any*** cause of action against the defendant, whether the cause of action arose from the in-state activity or from activity outside the state; *i.e.,* the court will have "general jurisdiction." However, casual, occasional, or indirect activities in the state are not sufficient bases for this general in personam jurisdiction.

Examples: 1) Statutes that grant in personam jurisdiction on the defendant's mere domicile, residence, or doing of business in the state would generally be valid since these constitute systematic and continuous activity in the forum.

2) Due process requirements for personal jurisdiction were not satisfied in Texas in a wrongful death case against a Colombian corporation whose contacts with the forum state consisted of only one trip to Texas by the corporation's chief executive officer to negotiate a contract, acceptance of checks drawn on a Texas bank, and purchases of helicopters and equipment from a Texas manufacturer and related helicopter training trips. The claims were not related to the defendant's activities in Texas, and defendant's contacts with Texas were not so continuous and systematic as to justify general jurisdiction. [Helicopteros Nacionales de Colombia v. Hall, 466 U.S. 408 (1984)]

b) **Convenience**

A defendant will often complain that the forum is inconvenient. The Supreme Court has emphasized, however, that the Constitution does not require that the forum be the best of several alternatives. The forum is constitutionally acceptable unless it is "so gravely difficult and inconvenient that a party is unfairly put at a severe disadvantage in comparison to his opponent." [Burger King v. Rudzewicz, *supra*] This is a very difficult standard to meet, and the defendant usually will not be able to meet it simply by showing that the plaintiff has superior economic resources.

c) **Forum State's Interest**

The forum may have a legitimate interest in providing redress for its residents.

Examples: 1) Decedent, a California resident, purchased a life insurance policy by mail from a Texas company. Decedent regularly mailed his premiums from California to the Texas company, which had no other contacts with California. In a suit brought by the beneficiary of the life insurance policy, the Supreme Court held that California had personal jurisdiction over the Texas company. Among other things, the Court noted that California had a strong interest in protecting its citizens from alleged misfeasance by insurance companies. [McGee v. International Insurance Co., 355 U.S. 220 (1957)]

2) Asahi, a Japanese manufacturer of tire valves, shipped valves to a Taiwanese manufacturer of motorcycle tire tubes.

The valves were incorporated into tires and sold in California, where a resident was injured by a defective tire. The Taiwanese manufacturer was sued in a California court, where it sought to implead Asahi. The main case was settled, leaving only the indemnity claim by the tire manufacturer against Asahi pending. *Held:* Even though Asahi placed the defective goods in the stream of commerce knowing that some would be used in California, exercise of jurisdiction by the California court would be unreasonable considering the severe burdens of Asahi in defending in a foreign legal system, the slight interest of the Taiwanese manufacturer and California in the exercise of jurisdiction, and the international interest in not subjecting an alien corporation to United States jurisdiction. [Asahi Metal Industry Co. v. Superior Court, *supra*]

d) Other Factors

The Supreme Court has listed other factors relevant to the assessment of whether the exercise of jurisdiction would be fair and reasonable, but has not discussed these factors in detail: (i) the plaintiff's interest in obtaining convenient and effective relief, (ii) the interstate judicial system's interest in obtaining the most efficient resolution of controversies, and (iii) the shared interest of the states in furthering fundamental substantive social policies.

2. Notice

In addition to the requirement that the defendant have such minimum contacts with the forum to render the exercise of jurisdiction there fair and reasonable, due process also requires that a ***reasonable method be used to notify the defendant of a pending lawsuit*** so that she may have an opportunity to appear and be heard. Due process requires that notice be "reasonably calculated, under all the circumstances, to apprise interested parties of the pendency of the action and afford them an opportunity to present their objections." [Dusenbery v. United States, 534 U.S. 161 (2002)—*quoting* Mullane v. Central Hanover Bank & Trust Co., 339 U.S. 306 (1950)]

a. Traditional Methods of Personal Service Satisfy Due Process Notice Requirements

Any of the traditional methods of personal service satisfy due process notice requirements. These include personal delivery to the defendant; leaving papers with a responsible person at the defendant's residence or place of business; delivery to an agent appointed to accept service; or delivery by registered mail, return receipt requested. (*See* VII.B., *infra,* for discussion of methods of service of process.)

b. Requirement that Agent Notify Defendant

If an agent is appointed by contract, in a case where the plaintiff chose the agent for his own benefit, or the agent is appointed by operation of law (as under a nonresident motor vehicle statute), the failure of the agent to notify the defendant will prohibit jurisdiction—since the defendant will in fact be deprived of an opportunity to be heard. (This is not true when the defendant voluntarily selects his own agent, since any failure of the agent can and will be attributed to the principal.)

c. Requirements for Cases Involving Multiple Parties or Unknown Parties

In *Mullane v. Central Hanover Bank & Trust Co., supra,* an action was brought against a number of trust beneficiaries scattered throughout the world. The Supreme Court held that the Constitution did not require personal service on each beneficiary since the cost would have been prohibitive. However, every beneficiary had to be notified by the ***best practical means*** available. Thus, those whose addresses were known or could reasonably be ascertained had to be notified by ordinary mail, while those whose names or addresses were unknown could be notified by publication. Such methods of notice are valid only if all defendants have substantially identical interests.

d. Knowledge that Notice by Mail Was Not Received

Although *Mullane v. Central Hanover Bank & Trust Co., supra,* does not require actual notice, if a party knows that the notice by mail was not received, he may not proceed in the face of such knowledge if practicable alternatives to apprise the defendant of the action exist.

Example: In *Jones v. Flowers*, 547 U.S. 220 (2006), the state sent a certified letter to a homeowner to inform him that he was delinquent on taxes and that failure to pay would make his property subject to public sale. By statute, the taxpayer was required to keep his address updated. The letter was returned "unclaimed," after which the state took no further steps (such as using first class mail or posting notice on the property) to notify the taxpayer. The Court held that taking no further steps to provide notice with the knowledge that notice had not been received violated due process.

D. IN REM JURISDICTION

As stated in I.A.2.b., *supra*, in rem actions adjudicate rights of all persons with respect to property located in the state. An in rem judgment does not bind the parties personally, but is binding as to the disposition of the property in the state.

1. Statutory Limitations

Most states have statutes providing for in rem jurisdiction in actions for condemnation, title registration, confiscation of property (such as vehicles used to transport narcotics), forfeiture of a vessel, distribution of the assets of an estate, and a grant of divorce when only the complaining spouse is present and subject to personal jurisdiction. In the last case, the "property" is the marital status of the complainant.

2. Constitutional Limitations

a. Nexus

In in rem actions the basis of jurisdiction is the presence of the property in the state. The state has a great interest in adjudicating the rights of all the world regarding this property. Therefore, the presence of the property in the state is constitutionally sufficient for the exercise of jurisdiction over the property.

1) No Jurisdiction If Property Not Located in State

A court has no in rem power over property outside the state; *e.g.,* in settling a decedent's estate, the court has no in rem power over property in other jurisdictions.

2) No Jurisdiction If Property Brought in by Fraud or Force

The exercise of in rem power is prohibited when the property is brought into the state by fraud or force.

b. Notice

The early view held that attachment of property, when supplemented by publication

of notice in a local newspaper or by posting of notice on the property, would give all interested persons sufficient notice of the action. However, such procedures are no longer adequate, and the requirements of *Mullane v. Central Hanover Bank & Trust Co., supra,* apply to in rem actions. Thus, persons whose interests are affected and whose addresses are known must at least be notified by ordinary mail. [Walker v. City of Hutchinson, 352 U.S. 112 (1956)]

E. QUASI IN REM JURISDICTION

Quasi in rem jurisdiction permits a court without in personam jurisdiction to determine certain disputes between a plaintiff and defendant regarding property when the property is located in the forum state. (*See* I.A.2.c., *supra.*)

1. Statutory Limitations

Most states provide for two types of quasi in rem jurisdiction. The first type (type I) involves disputes between parties over their rights in property within the state. The second type (type II) involves disputes ***unrelated*** to the in-state property and has been severely limited by the Supreme Court. In quasi in rem cases, the plaintiff is unable to obtain personal jurisdiction over the defendant, but the defendant has property in the state that the plaintiff attaches. The court then adjudicates the dispute between the parties on the basis of its power over the property. Since the court's sole basis of jurisdiction is the property, any judgment against the defendant can be satisfied only out of that property.

2. Constitutional Limitations

a. Nexus

Before 1977, a state clearly had power over all persons and property found within its borders. A defendant with no other connections with the state could be sued in the state for ***any*** dispute simply because he owned property there. However, in 1977, the Supreme Court held that the minimum contacts standard is applicable to ***every*** exercise of jurisdiction. The Court further found that the mere presence of property within a state is not itself sufficient to permit a court to exercise quasi in rem jurisdiction over property in a quasi in rem action. [Shaffer v. Heitner, 433 U.S. 186 (1977)—quasi in rem jurisdiction is proper only when minimum contacts exist making exercise of jurisdiction fair and just]

1) Quasi In Rem Type I

Thus, when the dispute involves the rights of the parties in the property itself (quasi in rem type I), jurisdiction based upon the presence of the property in the state is proper. The close connection between the litigation and the property provides the necessary minimum contacts.

2) Quasi In Rem Type II

When the dispute is unrelated to the ownership of property (quasi in rem type II), jurisdiction cannot be based solely on the presence of property in the forum state; there must be minimum contacts between the defendant and the forum. However, if the defendant has minimum contacts with the forum, it is also likely that a court could exercise ***in personam*** jurisdiction over a defendant under the forum's long arm statute, thus removing the limit on recovery to the defendant's in-state property. As a result, use of quasi in rem jurisdiction type II will be rare.

Example: A, a Maine resident, flies to Ohio and enters into a contract with B, an Ohio resident. All performance is to occur in Ohio. A flies home. B breaches. A does not want to fly to Ohio to sue B, but he discovers that B has a boat docked in Maine. Traditionally, A could have sued on his contract claim in Maine by attaching the boat (his remedy being limited by the value of the boat). Today, he would have to show minimum contacts between B and Maine.

3) **Procedural Requirements**
To obtain quasi in rem jurisdiction, a plaintiff must "bring the asset before the court" by attachment (or garnishment). This will inhibit the sale or mortgage of the defendant's interest, since a new owner must take subject to the decision of the court. Serious questions have been raised as to whether such a pretrial interference with a defendant's property rights is constitutional unless the defendant is afforded a hearing on the necessity of such procedures. Most commentators think the process is valid, but the Supreme Court has thus far avoided the issue.

b. **Notice**
As in in rem cases, quasi in rem cases require the best practical notice. Therefore, posting of notice or notice by publication will be insufficient where the addresses of persons affected by the action are known or reasonably ascertainable.

II. DIVERSITY OF CITIZENSHIP JURISDICTION

Section 1332: Diversity of Citizenship; Amount in Controversy

(a) The district courts shall have original jurisdiction of all civil actions where the matter in controversy exceeds the sum or value of $75,000, exclusive of interest and costs, and is between—

(1) citizens of different States;
(2) citizens of a State and citizens or subjects of a foreign state;
(3) citizens of different States and in which citizens or subjects of a foreign state are additional parties; and
(4) a foreign state . . . as plaintiff and citizens of a State or of different States.

For the purposes of this section, section 1335, and section 1441, an alien admitted to the United States for permanent residence shall be deemed to be a citizen of the State in which such alien is domiciled.

(b) . . .

(c) For the purposes of this section and section 1441 of this title—

(1) a corporation shall be deemed to be a citizen of any State by which it has been incorporated and of the State where it has its principal place of business. . . .

> (2) the legal representative of the estate of a decedent shall be deemed to be a citizen only of the same State as the decedent, and the legal representative of an infant or incompetent shall be deemed to be a citizen only of the same State as the infant or incompetent.
>
> (d) . . .
>
> (e) The word "States," as used in this section, includes the Territories, the District of Columbia, and the Commonwealth of Puerto Rico.

The federal courts have been given subject matter jurisdiction over controversies between citizens of different states, even though the controversies do not involve questions of federal substantive law, in order to protect an out-of-state party from possible local bias in state courts.

A. DIVERSITY AMONG THE PARTIES

1. Complete Diversity When Action Is Commenced

a. Multiple Parties—Complete Diversity

Every plaintiff must be of diverse citizenship from every defendant. If one defendant and one plaintiff are co-citizens of the same state, there is no diversity jurisdiction. This is the rule of "complete diversity."

Example: A, B, and C bring an action against X, Y, and Z. A and B are citizens of New York; X and Y are citizens of Florida; and C and Z are citizens of Texas. Since no diversity exists between C and Z, the requirement of ***complete*** diversity is not satisfied, and, as structured, the case cannot be brought in federal court under diversity jurisdiction.

1) But Note

The rule of complete diversity does not require that every party be of diverse citizenship from every other party. It requires only that no plaintiff be a co-citizen with any defendant. Thus, two plaintiffs who are both citizens of Missouri may invoke diversity of citizenship jurisdiction against three defendants, all three of whom are citizens of Kansas.

2) Interpleader Exception

a) Federal Interpleader Statute—Minimal Diversity

The federal interpleader statute [28 U.S.C. §1335] requires only that among the parties there be "two or more adverse claimants, of diverse citizenship." Thus, "minimal diversity" is sufficient to confer jurisdiction under the statute. If there is diversity between ***any two*** of the claimants, all other claimants may be citizens of the same state. (Also, section 1335 only requires that the money or property at issue be valued at $500 or more.)

b) **Interpleader Under Federal Rules—Complete Diversity**
Interpleader pursuant to Rule 22 of the Federal Rules, on the other hand, requires the usual diversity between all the plaintiffs (stakeholders) and all the defendants (claimants).

b. **"Alienage" Jurisdiction**
Most bar exam questions in this general area involve basic diversity of citizenship jurisdiction, in which the dispute involves "citizens of different states," as discussed immediately above. However, section 1332(a)(2) grants subject matter jurisdiction over "alienage" cases, in which the dispute is between a citizen of a state, on the one hand, and an "alien"—meaning a citizen or subject of a foreign country. Alienage is occasionally tested on bar exams.

Examples: 1) A, a citizen of Venezuela, sues B, a citizen of New York. This dispute would invoke alienage jurisdiction (assuming the amount in controversy requirement was also met), because it is between a citizen of a state and a citizen of a foreign country.

2) A, a citizen of Venezuela, sues B, a citizen of France. This dispute would ***not*** invoke alienage jurisdiction, because it is ***not*** between a citizen of a state and a citizen of a foreign country. There is no citizen of a state involved here.

c. **Diversity When Action Is Commenced**
Diversity of citizenship (or alienage) must exist as of the time the suit is instituted. [Grupo Dataflux v. Atlas Global Group, 541 U.S. 567 (2004)] It need not exist at the time the cause of action arose, and it is not defeated if, after commencement of the action, a party later becomes a citizen of the same state as one of his opponents.

2. **Questions of Citizenship**

a. **State Citizenship of an Individual—Domicile**
The determination of the state of citizenship of a natural person depends on the permanent home to which he intends to return. The concept is the same, except in name, as domicile. A new state citizenship may be established by (i) ***physical presence*** in a new place and (ii) the ***intention to remain there***, *i.e.,* no present intent to go elsewhere. The citizenship of a child is that of her parents. In most cases, the citizenship of a party will be determined by the court, but it may be left to the jury.

b. **Citizenship of a Corporation—Possible Multiple Citizenships**
For diversity purposes, a corporation's citizenship is defined by 28 U.S.C. section 1332. Under this statute, a corporation is deemed to be a citizen of ***every*** state in which it is incorporated and the ***one*** state in which it has its principal place of business. The Supreme Court has held that a corporation's "principal place of business" is the state from which the corporation's high level officers direct, control, and coordinate the corporation's activities (*i.e.,* its "nerve center," which will usually be the corporation's headquarters). [Hertz Corp. v. Friend, 130 S. Ct. 1181 (2010)] Thus, many corporations have ***two*** citizenships—their state of incorporation ***and*** the state in which their principal place of business is located. Although rare, it also is possible for a corporation to have ***more than two*** state citizenships because a corporation may be incorporated

in more than one state. It is impossible, however, for a corporation to have more than one principal place of business. If an opposing party is a citizen of any of the corporate party's states of citizenship, there is no diversity.

1) **Special Rule for Direct Actions**
The rules of corporate citizenship are subject to a special rule in direct action cases. When a plaintiff sues an insurer on a policy or contract of liability insurance, and does not also join the insured, the insurer (whether incorporated or not) is treated as a citizen of all of the following: (i) the state in which the insurer is incorporated (if it is), (ii) the state in which the insurer has its principal place of business, and (iii) the state of which the ***insured*** is a citizen.

2) **Corporations Chartered in Foreign Countries**
A corporation is deemed a citizen of the foreign country of incorporation and is therefore an ***alien for diversity purposes***. All of the circuits that have reached the issue have also held that when a foreign corporation has its principal place of business in this country, it is also a citizen of the state in which that principal place of business is located. [*See, e.g.,* Jerguson v. Blue Dot Investment, Inc., 659 F.2d 31 (5th Cir. 1981)]

c. **Unincorporated Associations**

1) **Citizenship**
In claims based on federal law for or against an unincorporated association, the association has entity capacity, but the question of its citizenship is normally irrelevant because the court will have federal question jurisdiction. When diversity jurisdiction is involved, an unincorporated association:

(i) May sue or be sued in its own name if local state law so permits; or

(ii) Is an aggregate of individuals if local state law follows the common law rule.

In either case, the unincorporated association's citizenship is that of ***each and every one*** of its members.

2) **Class Action**
If the association is large, a class action is possible. If a class action is brought, the relevant citizenship is that of the ***named members*** who sue or are sued on behalf of the members of the association. (*See* f., *infra.*)

3) **Partnerships**
The citizenship of a general partnership is that of each and every general partner, and the citizenship of a limited partnership is that of each and every partner, both limited and general. [Carden v. Arkoma Associates, 494 U.S. 185 (1990)]

4) **Limited Liability Companies**
Although limited liability companies ("LLCs") are formed in a manner similar to corporations, they are treated as unincorporated associations for citizenship purposes. Thus, an LLC is a citizen of all states of which its members are citizens. [*See, e.g.,* Belleville Catering Co. v. Champaign Market Place LLC, 350 F.3d 691 (7th Cir. 2003)]

d. **Business Trusts**

The ***trustees*** of a business trust are the real parties in interest and their citizenship, not that of the individual shareholders, determines whether there is diversity. [Navarro Savings v. Lee, 446 U.S. 458 (1980)]

e. **Suits Brought by Legal Representatives**

A legal representative of an infant, an incompetent, or an estate of a decedent is deemed to be a citizen of the same state as the infant, incompetent, or decedent.

f. **Class Actions**

If suit is brought by several named persons on behalf of a class under Rule 23, diversity is determined on the basis of the citizenship of the ***named members*** of the class who are suing. Thus, there is considerable room for maneuvering to create diversity if the class has members who are citizens of several different states. The Class Action Fairness Act (*see* VII.F.2.d., *infra*) also expands the federal court's jurisdiction over class actions.

g. **Nonresident United States Citizens**

A United States citizen ***domiciled abroad*** is not a citizen of any state and also is not an alien. (Alien status depends on nationality, not domicile.)

h. **Aliens Admitted for Permanent Residence**

An alien admitted to the United States for permanent residence is deemed to be a citizen of the state in which the alien is domiciled. [28 U.S.C. §1332(a)] Nevertheless, it is generally accepted that at least one party to the suit must be a natural-born or naturalized United States citizen in order for jurisdiction under section 1332 to be proper. [*See* Saadeh v. Farouki, 107 F.3d 52 (D.C. Cir. 1997)]

3. **Collusion and Devices to Create or Defeat Diversity**

The federal court does not have jurisdiction if a party "by assignment or otherwise, has been improperly or collusively made or joined to invoke jurisdiction." [28 U.S.C. §1359]

a. **Assignment of Claims**

The assignment of a claim to another party for collection only is clearly within this section. [Kramer v. Caribbean Mills, Inc., 394 U.S. 823 (1969)] Thus, the assignment would be ignored in determining whether diversity exists. *But note:* There is no collusion if an absolute assignment of a claim is made and the assignor retains no interest in the assigned claim.

b. **Class Actions**

No rule prevents achieving diversity by the adroit selection of named plaintiffs to bring a proper class action on behalf of others. The naming of only members of the class who are not co-citizens of the defendants will create diversity even though other unnamed members of the class are co-citizens who would defeat diversity if named.

c. **Voluntary Change of State Citizenship**

A plaintiff can create diversity by changing his state citizenship after the cause of action accrued but before suit is commenced, but the change must be genuine. In other words,

a true change of citizenship can create or destroy diversity. The party's ***motive*** for changing citizenship is ***irrelevant***.

d. Defeating Diversity to Prevent Removal

No rule prevents manipulation in choice of a representative or assignment of a claim to defeat diversity (and thus prevent removal from state to federal court). On the other hand, fraudulent joinder of an in-state defendant to defeat diversity is no bar to removal.

4. Realignment According to Interest

a. May Create or Destroy Diversity

In determining whether diversity exists, the court will look beyond the nominal designation of the parties in the pleadings and realign them according to their true interests in the dispute. Thus, realignment may create diversity or destroy it.

b. Shareholder Derivative Actions

Taking the view that the shareholder's alignment of the corporation as a party plaintiff or defendant is not controlling insofar as diversity jurisdiction is affected by the citizenship of the corporation, the federal courts have established the rule (at least when alignment of the corporation in a shareholder's derivative suit is not specifically provided for by state law) that the corporation is to be aligned as a party ***defendant.*** Federal diversity jurisdiction is determined in accordance with that alignment when, with respect to the claim sought to be enforced by the shareholder's derivative suit, the corporation is "antagonistic" to the shareholder. [*See* Smith v. Sperling, 354 U.S. 91 (1957)]

5. Ancillary ("Supplemental") Jurisdiction

Occasionally, a claim may be joined that could not, by itself, invoke federal question jurisdiction or diversity jurisdiction (because, for example, it is a state claim between parties who are citizens of the same state or because it does not involve the requisite amount in controversy). (*See* B., *infra.*) The court may nonetheless entertain such claims under the doctrine of ancillary jurisdiction, now codified under the rubric "supplemental" jurisdiction, if they arise from a common nucleus of operative fact as the claim that invoked federal subject matter jurisdiction. The common nucleus test is usually considered to mean that the claims must arise from the same transaction or occurrence, although there is some authority that it is even broader than that.

6. Subsequent Addition of Parties

The Federal Rules permit numerous methods by which additional parties not originally named may become involved in an action. A claim by or against an additional party, like any claim in federal court, must satisfy some basis of federal subject matter jurisdiction, such as diversity of citizenship or federal question. If the claim does not satisfy either of those, and it arises from a common nucleus of operative fact (*see* above), the party asserting the claim might invoke supplemental jurisdiction.

a. Restriction on the Use of Supplemental Jurisdiction in Diversity Cases

For cases based ***solely*** on diversity, supplemental jurisdiction may not be used to support:

(i) Claims by plaintiffs against persons made parties under Rules 14 (impleader), 19 (compulsory joinder), 20 (permissive joinder), or 24 (intervention);

(ii) Claims by persons proposed to be joined as plaintiffs under Rule 19; and

(iii) Claims by persons seeking to intervene as plaintiffs under Rule 24.

[28 U.S.C. §1367(b)]

b. Intervention of Right

Intervention of right is given under Rule 24(a) where the intervenor claims an interest relating to the property or transaction that is the subject of the action and the disposition of the action may adversely affect that interest. Traditionally, intervention of right has not required any showing of independent jurisdiction; the intervenor's claim was considered to be within the court's ancillary jurisdiction if the requirements for intervention of right were met. Under the supplemental jurisdiction statute, however, there is no ancillary jurisdiction for claims by or against intervenors. Thus, such a claim could proceed only if there were an independent basis of jurisdiction, *e.g.,* diversity or federal question.

c. Permissive Intervention

Under Rule 24(b), permissive intervention may be permitted in the court's discretion when the intervenor's action and the main action have a claim or defense involving a ***common question of law or fact***. The claim by a permissive intervenor must invoke either diversity of citizenship or federal question jurisdiction.

d. Substitution of Parties

Substitution under Rule 25 involves changes in parties to a lawsuit necessitated by death, incompetency, etc., of an original party after an action has been commenced. The citizenship of the substituted party is disregarded; that of the original party controls. Substitution should be distinguished from an ***amendment*** that allows "replacement" of an original party by the party in whom or against whom the action properly lies. A "replacement" party must be diverse to the party or parties on the opposing side.

Example: A v. B. A dies and the administrator of his estate is substituted as plaintiff. Jurisdiction is not destroyed even though B and the administrator are co-citizens. However, if A sues B and subsequently discovers that C—not B—is the proper defendant, an amendment to the complaint by which B is replaced by C must show that diversity exists between A and C.

e. Third-Party Practice—Impleader

A third-party claim under Rule 14 is the joinder by the defendant in the original action (who is usually called the third-party plaintiff) of another person not originally a party to the action (who is called the third-party defendant). The impleader claim asserts that the third-party defendant is or may be liable to the defendant for all or part of the plaintiff's claim against the defendant. In other words, an impleader claim is for indemnity or contribution.

Example: P sues D for $500,000 for personal injuries allegedly inflicted by joint tortfeasors D and X. Applicable law provides that joint tortfeasors have

a right of contribution against each other. D may implead X into the pending case. D is seeking to deflect her liability on P's claim, in part, to X. (If X owed D indemnity for some reason, then D could implead X to deflect her entire liability on the underlying claim to X.)

Under Rule 14, after the third-party defendant is impleaded, he may assert a claim against the plaintiff in the pending case if the claim arises from the same transaction or occurrence as the underlying suit. In addition, under Rule 14, after the third-party defendant is impleaded, the plaintiff may assert a claim against him if it arises from the same transaction or occurrence as the underlying suit.

1) Subject Matter Jurisdiction Required

Of course, every claim asserted in federal court must have a basis of subject matter jurisdiction.

Examples: 1) P, a citizen of Illinois, sues D, a citizen of Wisconsin, asserting a state law claim of more than $75,000. Thus, the case invokes diversity of citizenship jurisdiction and is properly brought in federal court. Now D impleads X, who is also a citizen of Illinois, on an indemnity claim of more than $75,000. That claim invokes diversity of citizenship jurisdiction, because it is asserted by a citizen of Wisconsin (D) against a citizen of Illinois (X) and exceeds $75,000. The fact that P is also a citizen of Illinois is irrelevant; the claim is not by or against her, so her citizenship does not affect the impleader claim. If P wanted to assert a claim against X in this situation, however, there would not be diversity because P and X are co-citizens of Illinois. In addition, the claim would not invoke supplemental jurisdiction, because in diversity of citizenship cases, the supplemental jurisdiction statute cannot be used to override the complete diversity rule (*see* III.D., *infra*). Thus, unless the claim by P against X invoked federal question jurisdiction, it could not be asserted in the pending case; it would have to be asserted in state court.

2) P, a citizen of Alabama, sues D, a citizen of Maine, asserting a state law claim of more than $75,000. Thus, the case invokes diversity of citizenship jurisdiction and is properly brought in federal court. Now D impleads X, who is also a citizen of Maine, on a state law contribution claim. The impleader claim does not invoke diversity of citizenship jurisdiction, because it is asserted by a citizen of Maine (D) against another citizen of Maine (X). It does not invoke federal question jurisdiction because it is based on state law. The claim invokes the ancillary form of supplemental jurisdiction, however, because it arises from the same nucleus of common fact as the underlying case and is asserted by the defendant, not the plaintiff, thus avoiding the restriction on the use of supplemental jurisdiction in 28 U.S.C. section 1367(b).

f. Cross-Claims

Rule 13(g) allows a party to assert a claim in a pending case against a co-party, but only if the claim arises from the ***same transaction or occurrence*** as the underlying dispute. So, in a lawsuit of A v. B and C, a claim by B against C (or C against B) that arises from the same transaction or occurrence as the underlying case would be a cross-claim.

1) **Subject Matter Jurisdiction Required**
Cross-claims, like all claims in federal court, must invoke subject matter jurisdiction. Therefore, after determining that a cross-claim would be filed, assess whether that claim could invoke diversity of citizenship or federal question jurisdiction. If so, the claim may be asserted in federal court. ***However***, if a cross-claim does not invoke diversity of citizenship or federal question jurisdiction, the cross-claim could nonetheless be asserted in federal court through the ancillary form of supplemental jurisdiction.

B. JURISDICTIONAL AMOUNT: IN EXCESS OF $75,000

Actions brought in a federal court under the diversity statute must meet the jurisdictional amount requirement. The matter in controversy must be ***in excess of $75,000,*** exclusive of interest and costs. [28 U.S.C. §1332] The amount is determined from what is claimed in the complaint, disregarding potential defenses or counterclaims. Usually, all that is necessary is a ***good faith allegation*** that the amount of the damages or injuries in controversy ***exceeds***, exclusive of interest and costs, the sum of $75,000. Good faith means that there must be a legally tenable possibility that recovery will exceed the jurisdictional amount. The complaint can be dismissed only if it appears there is no legal possibility of a recovery exceeding the jurisdictional amount. Jurisdiction is not retroactively defeated by the fact that the amount actually recovered is less than the jurisdictional amount.

1. What Is "In Controversy"?

a. Collateral Consequences of the Judgment

Does the collateral effect of the judgment sought by the plaintiff bring into controversy the value of other claims that may be governed by the judgment? The Supreme Court has held that the collateral effects of a judgment may ***not*** be considered.

Examples: 1) If an insured asserts a claim for installments due under a disability policy, only the installments due may be considered, even though the judgment may control the insured's rights to payment of future installments. However, if the insurance company sues to cancel the contract for fraud, the value of the entire contract is brought into controversy.

2) If a bondholder sues to collect amounts due on coupons that have matured, only the amount of the coupons is in controversy, even though the judgment will determine the validity of the entire bond issue. However, if the issuer of the bonds seeks a declaratory judgment that the bonds are properly issued, the value of the entire bond issue would be in controversy.

b. Interest and Costs

The statute excludes interest and costs in determining the jurisdictional amount. However, attorneys' fees that are recoverable by contract or by statute are considered

part of the matter in controversy rather than as costs. Similarly, interest that constitutes a part of the claim itself, as distinguished from interest payable by virtue of a delay in payment, is part of the jurisdictional amount.

Example: Plaintiff sues on a three-year note with face value of $70,000 and interest at 5% (an additional $10,500). Since the interest on the note is part of the claim, the jurisdictional amount is satisfied. [*See, e.g.,* Brainin v. Melikian, 396 F.2d 153 (3d Cir. 1968)] But if the interest accrued between maturity and filing, the additional interest after maturity is not part of the claim.

c. Equitable Relief

There may be difficulty calculating an amount in controversy for a claim for equitable relief, given that the claimant does not seek money damages. For example, suppose P sues D for an injunction ordering D to remove part of D's house that blocks P's view. What is the value of the injunction and, therefore, the claim? Some courts look at the issue from the ***plaintiff's viewpoint***, and ask what the value of the harm caused by the blocked view is. Other courts look at the issue from the ***defendant's viewpoint***, and ask what it would cost the defendant to comply with the injunction if it were ordered. Some courts conclude that the amount in controversy requirement is satisfied if the amount under ***either*** test—plaintiff's viewpoint or defendant's viewpoint—exceeds $75,000.

d. Punitive Damages

If a punitive damage claim is permitted under state substantive law, it may be used in making the dollar amount requirement because there is "no legal certainty" that the amount will not be recovered.

2. Aggregation of Separate Claims

a. One Plaintiff Against One Defendant

For purposes of meeting the jurisdictional amount, the plaintiff may aggregate all her claims against a single defendant. This aggregation is permitted regardless of whether the claims are legally or factually related to each other.

b. One Plaintiff Against Several Defendants

A plaintiff who has an action against several defendants cannot aggregate claims based on separate liabilities. Thus, if P had a claim of $50,000 against D-1 and a separate claim of $30,000 against D-2, she may not aggregate those claims. Note, however, that there is no aggregation problem if plaintiff asserts a joint claim against multiple defendants. With a joint claim, courts look to the total value of the claim.

Example: P sues alleged joint tortfeasors X, Y, and Z for damages of $76,000. This claim satisfies the amount in controversy requirement. Because this is a claim based on ***joint liability,*** any of the three defendants might be held liable for the total amount of the claim. This is not a case of trying to aggregate three separate claims. Because of joint liability, courts see this as one claim. Because it exceeds $75,000, it meets the amount requirement.

c. Several Plaintiffs Against One Defendant

Several plaintiffs can aggregate their claims only where they are seeking "to enforce a single title or right in which they have a common or undivided interest . . . . "

Example: If joint owners of real estate file suit to quiet title, the right asserted is held jointly and the amount in controversy is the total value of the land. However, if several victims of the same accident sue for personal injuries, their claims are separate and distinct from one another and aggregation is not allowed.

This rule has special importance in class actions, in which the rule is that the claims of the class members cannot be aggregated if their rights are "separate" rather than "joint" or "common." [Snyder v. Harris, 394 U.S. 332 (1969)]

3. Supplemental Jurisdiction over Claims Not Exceeding $75,000 in Diversity Cases

Claims that do not meet the amount in controversy requirement for diversity of citizenship jurisdiction may invoke supplemental jurisdiction if they arise from a common nucleus of operative fact (which includes the concept of the "same transaction or occurrence") as a claim that invoked diversity of citizenship. However, the supplemental jurisdiction ***cannot*** be used to override the complete diversity rule. [Exxon Mobil Corp. v. Allapattah Services, 545 U.S. 546 (2005)]

Example: P-1, a citizen of California, asserts a claim for $100,000 against D, a citizen of Arizona. That claim invokes diversity of citizenship jurisdiction. In the same case, P-2 asserts a claim against the same D for $50,000. The claims by P-1 and P-2 arise from the same transaction and are based on state law. The claim by P-2 cannot invoke diversity of citizenship jurisdiction because it does not exceed $75,000. Nonetheless, the claim by P-2 can be heard in federal court under supplemental jurisdiction.

Compare: P-1, a citizen of California, asserts a claim for $100,000 against D, a citizen of Arizona. That claim invokes diversity of citizenship jurisdiction. In the same case, P-2, a citizen of Arizona, asserts a claim against the same D for $100,000. The claim by P-1 and the claim by P-2 arise from the same transaction and are based on state law. The claim by P-2 cannot invoke diversity of citizenship jurisdiction because it is by a citizen of Arizona against a citizen of Arizona, and supplemental jurisdiction cannot override the complete diversity requirement. Thus, that claim may be asserted only in state court.

4. Counterclaims

A defendant's counterclaim [*see* Fed. R. Civ. P. 13] cannot be combined with the plaintiff's claim to reach the jurisdictional amount; *e.g.,* if the plaintiff claims $20,000, there is no jurisdictional amount even though the defendant counterclaims for $100,000. Does a counterclaim itself have to meet the requirements of the jurisdictional amount?

a. Compulsory Counterclaim Need Not Meet Jurisdictional Amount

A compulsory counterclaim (arising out of the ***same*** transaction or occurrence) does not need to meet the jurisdictional amount requirement. The court has ***ancillary*** (supplemental) jurisdiction over such a counterclaim just as it does over a third-party claim under Rule 14 impleader.

b. Permissive Counterclaim Must Meet Jurisdictional Amount

A defendant's permissive counterclaim (arising out of an ***unrelated*** transaction) must have an independent jurisdictional basis, and thus ***must meet the jurisdictional amount*** requirement.

c. **No Removal to Federal Court Based on Counterclaim**

A plaintiff who claims $75,000 or less in a state court action who is met with a counterclaim for more than $75,000 may not remove the suit to federal court, regardless of whether the counterclaim is compulsory or permissive, because removal is permitted only to defendants. The weight of authority also holds that in a situation where the plaintiff has not met the jurisdictional amount, the ***defendant*** who must assert a compulsory counterclaim in the state suit ***may not remove*** the action, even though the counterclaim is over $75,000 and there is complete diversity. Thus, a plaintiff with a small claim can require a defendant with a large claim to litigate it in state court simply by being the first to file. *But note:* Even though this is the ***traditional rule***, there is a ***trend allowing removal***.

C. *ERIE* DOCTRINE AND THE LAW APPLIED UNDER DIVERSITY JURISDICTION

A federal court, in the exercise of its diversity jurisdiction, is required to apply the ***substantive law of the state*** in which it is sitting, including that state's conflict of law rules. [Erie Railroad v. Tompkins, 304 U.S. 64 (1938); Klaxon Co. v. Stentor Electric Manufacturing Co., 313 U.S. 487 (1941)] However, the federal courts apply ***federal procedural law*** in diversity cases.

1. **Is There a Federal Directive on Point?**

To determine whether federal law should be applied, the first question to ask is whether there is a federal law (*e.g.*, statute, Federal Rule of Civil Procedure) on point. If there is, the federal law will apply, provided that it is valid.

Example: Federal Rule 4 permits substituted service of process. Suppose that state law (of the state in which the federal court sits) does not permit substituted service. The court will apply the Federal Rule, because it is on point and is valid. A Federal Rule of Civil Procedure is valid if it is "arguably procedural." [Hanna v. Plumer, 380 U.S. 460 (1965)]

a. **Caution**

Sometimes it is difficult to determine whether a federal directive is on point. For example, Federal Rule 3 provides that a case is commenced when the complaint is filed. Many people thought that the rule thus was a directive that the statute of limitations would be tolled from the date of filing the complaint. The Supreme Court held, however, that Rule 3 did not address tolling at all, and thus did not constitute a federal directive on the tolling question. [Walker v. Armco Steel, 446 U.S. 740 (1980)]

b. **Recent Application**

In *Shady Grove Orthopedic Associates v. Allstate Insurance Co.*, 130 S. Ct. 1431 (2010), a plaintiff brought a diversity jurisdiction class action under a New York law for recovery of interest on claims paid late by insurance companies. A New York statute would have denied class action status to claims seeking such recovery. A majority of the Court held that Federal Rule 23 governed regarding class action status and refused to apply the New York statute. Under the Rules Enabling Act, a Federal Rule is valid if it deals with "practice or procedure" and does not "abridge, enlarge, or modify" a substantive right. A majority in *Shady Grove* concluded that Rule 23 is valid. Only four Justices concluded, however, that in determining a Rule's validity, the court looks only at the Federal Rule, and not to the state law to be displaced by it.

2. **If There Is No Federal Directive on Point, Is the Issue Substance or Procedure?**
If there is no federal directive on point, can a federal judge refuse to follow state law on a particular issue? The answer depends on whether the law on that issue is substantive or procedural. If it is a matter of substance, the federal judge must follow state law in a diversity case. If it is a matter of procedure, the federal judge may ignore state law.

a. **Some Situations Are Clearly Established**
In some instances, the characterization as substance or procedure is well established. For example, the Supreme Court has established that ***statutes of limitations and rules for tolling statutes of limitations*** are substantive for *Erie* purposes; therefore, a federal judge in a diversity case must follow state law on those issues. [Guaranty Trust Co. v. York, 326 U.S. 99 (1945)] ***Choice of law rules*** are also substantive for *Erie* purposes, and a federal judge in a diversity case must follow state law on that issue as well. [Klaxon v. Stentor Electric Manufacturing Co., 313 U.S. 487 (1941)] Finally, of course, ***elements of a claim or defense*** are substantive.

b. **Law Is Unclear in Other Situations**
Outside these areas, when there is no federal directive on point, it is often difficult to determine whether an issue is substantive or procedural for *Erie* purposes. The Supreme Court has given different "tests" at different times on this point, and has failed to integrate the tests comprehensively. One such test is ***outcome determination***, which holds that an issue is substantive if it substantially affects the outcome of the case. [Guaranty Trust Co. v. York, *supra*] Another test is ***balance of interests***, in which the court weighs whether the state or federal judicial system has the greater interest in having its rule applied. [Byrd v. Blue Ridge Electric Cooperative, Inc., 356 U.S. 525 (1958)] Yet another test is ***forum shopping deterrence***, which directs that the federal judge should follow state law on the issue if failing to do so would cause litigants to flock to federal court. [Hanna v. Plumer, *supra*]

3. **Statutes Involving Both Substance and Procedure**
Sometimes, a state statute or rule may be both substantive ***and*** procedural. In one case, the state tort reform law relaxed the standard for granting a new trial, making it easier to grant a new trial than under the basic federal standard. Also, the state ***appellate*** court was charged with the responsibility to consider whether a new trial should be ordered. In a diversity case under this state law, the standard for granting a new trial was held to be substantive, so the federal court had to apply the state standard for granting a new trial. However, the requirement that the appellate court consider whether a new trial should be ordered was held to be procedural, so a federal ***trial*** court would determine whether a new trial should be ordered, using the aforementioned state standard, rather than an appellate court. [Gasperini v. Center for Humanities, Inc., 518 U.S. 415 (1996)—in diversity case, federal trial court applied New York "excessive damages" standard for new trial rather than federal "shock the conscience" standard]

4. **Interpreting State Law**
The federal court is bound to apply the substantive state law that would be applied by the highest court of the state. If the state courts have not decided the issue that is before the federal court, or if the decisions on point are old and no longer current with the decisions of other jurisdictions, the federal court may consider the law of other jurisdictions in reaching its decision. However, the focus of the federal court is to ***determine what decision the highest court of the state would reach*** if confronted with the issue.

a. **De Novo Review of District Court's Decision**
On appeal, the federal appellate court reviews the federal trial judge's decision as to state law ***de novo***. [*See* Salve Regina College v. Russell, 499 U.S. 225 (1991)]

b. **Subsequent State Court Decisions**
If the highest state court renders a decision on an issue after the federal court has made its determination, the decision of the district court may be changed to conform to the new decision of the highest state court until the disposition of the final federal appeal. [*See* Thomas v. American Home Products, Inc., 519 U.S. 913 (1996)]

D. EXCEPTIONS TO DIVERSITY OF CITIZENSHIP JURISDICTION

For historical reasons, even though the requirements for diversity of citizenship jurisdiction are satisfied, federal courts will not exercise jurisdiction over domestic relations or probate proceedings.

1. Domestic Relations

The federal court will not take jurisdiction over actions "involving the issuance of a divorce, alimony or child custody decree." [Akenbrandt v. Richards, 504 U.S. 689 (1992)] Note that this exception is quite narrow. Federal courts may maintain actions upon state court decrees, such as those for alimony. They also may hear cases involving intra-family torts. They refuse only cases involving issuance of decrees of divorce, alimony, or child custody.

2. Probate Proceedings

Federal courts will not entertain cases to probate a decedent's estate. To fall within this exception to diversity of citizenship jurisdiction, however, the claim asserted ***must involve actual probate or annulment of a will or seek to reach property in the custody of a state probate court***. [Marshall v. Marshall, 547 U.S. 293 (2006)]

Example: The federal court had jurisdiction over a claim for damages for alleged tortious interference with testator's efforts to create a trust benefiting the plaintiff (who was Anna Nicole Smith). [Marshall v. Marshall, *supra*]

E. MULTIPARTY, MULTIFORUM TRIAL JURISDICTION ACT

The Multiparty, Multiforum Trial Jurisdiction Act applies to accidents meeting the statutory definition. The principal points are these:

1. Requirements

a. **The Action**
The Act grants jurisdiction to federal district courts of civil actions that (i) arise "from a ***single accident,*** (ii) ***where at least 75 natural persons have died*** in the accident (iii) ***at a discrete location***." [28 U.S.C. §1369(a)]

b. **Minimal Diversity**
Such jurisdiction attaches based on ***minimal diversity of citizenship***; thus, all that is required is that at least one plaintiff be of diverse citizenship from at least one defendant.

c. **One Additional Condition**
In addition, however, ***one of three other conditions*** must be satisfied: either (i) a defendant "resides" in a different state from the place where "a substantial part" of the accident took place (even if the defendant also resides where the accident took place); (ii) any two defendants "reside" in different states; or (iii) substantial parts of the accident took place in different states.

2. **Intervention**
Anyone "with a claim arising from the accident" is ***permitted to intervene*** as a plaintiff, even if she could not have maintained an action in the district where the case is pending. [28 U.S.C. §1369(d)]

3. **Service of Process**
Finally, the Act provides for ***nationwide service of process***. [28 U.S.C. §1697]

III. FEDERAL QUESTION JURISDICTION

> **Section 1331: Federal Question**
>
> The district courts shall have original jurisdiction of all civil actions ***arising under the Constitution, laws or treaties of the United States. . . .***

It is difficult to formulate a summary of the case holdings as to when an action "arises under" federal law. The best one can do, perhaps, is the following: A case arises under federal law if the plaintiff is alleging a right or interest that is substantially founded on federal law, which consists of federal common law, federal constitutional law, federal statutory law, treaty law, and federal administrative regulations.

A. FEDERAL QUESTION MUST APPEAR IN THE COMPLAINT
The federal question must appear as part of the ***plaintiff's cause of action*** as set out in a well-pleaded complaint. It is therefore sometimes necessary to determine whether certain allegations are proper in pleading the cause of action, and whether the federal element is essential to the plaintiff's case.

1. **Defendant's Answer or Defense Is Irrelevant**
The content of the defendant's answer is not relevant; the existence of a defense based on federal law will not give federal question jurisdiction. Likewise, the court may not look to a counterclaim asserted by the defendant to determine whether the plaintiff's complaint states a federal question claim. [Holmes Group, Inc. v. Vornado Air Circulation System, Inc., 535 U.S. 826 (2002)]

2. **Anticipation of a Defense**
Similarly, a complaint does not raise a federal question if it does so only in anticipation of some defense.
Example: A sues B for specific performance of a contract and alleges that B's refusal to perform is based on B's erroneous belief that federal law prohibits his performance. No federal question jurisdiction exists because the federal question presented by the plaintiff's complaint is merely in anticipation of B's defense. [Louisville & Nashville Railroad v. Mottley, 211 U.S. 149 (1908)]

B. IMPLIED FEDERAL RIGHT OF ACTION

It is not essential that the federal statute expressly provide for a civil cause of action for an alleged violation. Thus, federal question jurisdiction was held to exist in an action involving an alleged violation of the Fourth and Fifth Amendments [Bell v. Hood, 327 U.S. 678 (1946)] and an alleged violation of the Securities Exchange Acts of 1934 [J. I. Case v. Borak, 377 U.S. 426 (1964)], although neither the Constitution nor the act involved created a "remedy" for the wrongs complained of. However, not all federal provisions creating duties are held to create an implied private right of action. [Cort v. Ash, 422 U.S. 66 (1975)]

C. FEDERAL CORPORATIONS

Federal question jurisdiction does not arise merely from the fact that a corporate party was incorporated by an act of Congress ***unless*** the United States ***owns more than one-half*** of the corporation's capital stock, in which case it is treated as a federal agency that can sue or be sued on that basis in federal court. [28 U.S.C. §1349]

D. PENDENT (SUPPLEMENTAL) JURISDICTION OVER STATE CLAIMS

As previously discussed (*supra,* II.A.5.), claims asserted by parties other than the plaintiff can invoke supplemental jurisdiction in any case that arises from the same transaction or occurrence as the original claim, whether it got into federal court by diversity of citizenship or federal question jurisdiction.

1. Pendent Claims

In some cases, the plaintiff will have both federal and state claims against the defendant. Although there may be no diversity, the federal court has ***discretion*** to exercise pendent jurisdiction over the claim based on state law if the two claims "derive from a common nucleus of operative fact" and are such that a plaintiff "would ordinarily be expected to try them all in one judicial proceeding." [United Mine Workers of America v. Gibbs, 383 U.S. 715 (1966)] Essentially, this means that the two claims must arise from the same transaction or occurrence. The supplemental jurisdiction statute [28 U.S.C. §1367(a)] adopts this standard for the grant of supplemental jurisdiction.

Example: P, a citizen of Arkansas, asserts two claims against D, who is also a citizen of Arkansas, in federal court. Importantly, both claims arise from the same transaction or occurrence. Claim #1 is for violation of a federal statute, and thus invokes federal question jurisdiction. Claim #2 is based on state law, and thus does not invoke federal question jurisdiction (because it is based on state, not federal, law). Also, Claim #2 does not invoke diversity of citizenship (because P and D are citizens of the same state). Nonetheless, Claim #2 invokes supplemental jurisdiction because it arises from the same transaction or occurrence as the claim that invoked federal question jurisdiction.

a. Effect of Dismissal of Federal Claim on Pendent Claim

The court may exercise pendent jurisdiction over the state claim even though the federal claim is dismissed on the merits. However, the state claim should probably also be dismissed (without prejudice) if the federal claim is dismissed before trial. Indeed, the supplemental jurisdiction statute provides that the court may refuse supplemental jurisdiction if the federal claim is dismissed, if the state claims are complex or novel, or if the state claims predominate substantially over federal claims. Note also that a federal court may not award relief against a state official based solely on a state law claim. [Pennhurst State School & Hospital v. Halderman, 465 U.S. 89 (1984)]

2. Pendent Parties

Pendent parties jurisdiction is relevant in cases in which the plaintiff sues more than one defendant, there is federal jurisdiction over the claim against one defendant, and the claim against the second defendant does not invoke federal question or diversity of citizenship jurisdiction. Under the supplemental jurisdiction statute, the claim against the second defendant might invoke supplemental jurisdiction if it arises from the same nucleus of common fact as the claim against the first defendant.

Example: P asserts a federal question claim against D-1 and joins a transactionally related state law (not federal question) claim against D-2. P and D-2 are citizens of the same state. The claim against D-2 does not invoke federal question jurisdiction (because it is based upon state law) and does not invoke diversity of citizenship jurisdiction (because P and D-2 are citizens of the same state). The claim against D-2 invokes supplemental jurisdiction, however, because it arises from the same transaction or occurrence as the claim that invoked federal question jurisdiction and is asserted by the plaintiff in a federal question case.

Conversely, pendent parties jurisdiction can arise when multiple plaintiffs assert claims against one defendant.

Example: P-1 asserts a federal question claim against D. In the same case, P-2 asserts a state law claim against D. P-2 and D are citizens of the same state. The claim by P-2 invokes supplemental jurisdiction if it arises from the same transaction or occurrence as the federal question claim by P-1 against D.

Note: Remember that, ***in a diversity case***, supplemental jurisdiction can be used by a plaintiff to support a claim that fails to meet the amount in controversy requirement for diversity of citizenship jurisdiction, but that supplemental jurisdiction ***cannot*** be used to override the complete diversity rule (*see* II.A.3., *supra*).

E. SPECIFIC STATUTORY GRANTS

1. Amount in Controversy

There is no amount in controversy requirement in federal question cases, with the narrow exception for cases brought against defendants ***other than*** the United States, its agencies, or employees under section 23(a) of the Consumer Product Safety Act. That section authorizes action by any person who sustains injury by reason of a knowing violation of a consumer product safety rule, or any other rule issued by the Commission. In such actions, at least $10,000 must be in controversy. [15 U.S.C. §2072]

2. Exclusive Jurisdiction

Congress has expressly provided that the jurisdiction of the federal courts shall be exclusive of state courts in:

a. **Bankruptcy Proceedings** [28 U.S.C. §1334]

b. **Patent and Copyright Cases** [28 U.S.C. §1338]

c. **Many Cases Where United States Is Involved**

Cases involving fines, penalties, or forfeitures under the laws of the United States;

crimes against the United States; tort suits against the United States; or customs review. (Because of the doctrine of sovereign immunity, there is no jurisdiction in the courts to hear lawsuits against the United States unless the United States has consented to be sued.)

d. **Cases with Consuls and Vice-Consuls as Defendants** [28 U.S.C. §1351]

e. **Antitrust Cases**
Although 28 U.S.C. section 1337 does not expressly make federal jurisdiction exclusive in actions arising under laws regulating interstate commerce, the federal antitrust statutes are interpreted to place the remedy exclusively in the federal courts. [Freeman v. Bee Machine Co., 319 U.S. 448 (1943)]

f. **Admiralty Cases—Caveat**
28 U.S.C. section 1333 grants exclusive jurisdiction in cases of admiralty and maritime jurisdiction, but since the same section has a clause "saving to suitors in all cases all other remedies," the result is that federal jurisdiction is exclusive only in limitation of liability proceedings and in maritime actions in rem.

g. **Foreign State—Caveat**
28 U.S.C. section 1441(d) permits a foreign state (or agency thereof), if sued in state court, to remove the action to federal court.

h. **Postal Matters** [28 U.S.C. §1339]

i. **Internal Revenue** [28 U.S.C. §1340]

j. **Securities Exchange Act** [15 U.S.C. §78aa]

IV. VENUE

Section 1391: Venue Generally

(a) A civil action wherein jurisdiction is founded ***only on diversity*** of citizenship may, except as otherwise provided by law, be brought only in (i) a judicial district where any defendant resides, if all defendants reside in the same State, (ii) a judicial district in which a substantial part of the events or omissions giving rise to the claim occurred, or a substantial part of property that is the subject of the action is situated, or (iii) a judicial district in which any defendant is subject to personal jurisdiction at the time the action is commenced, if there is no district in which the action may otherwise be brought.

(b) A civil action wherein jurisdiction is ***not*** founded ***solely on diversity*** of citizenship may, except as otherwise provided by law, be brought only in (i) a judicial district where any defendant resides, if all defendants reside in the same State, (ii) a judicial district in which a substantial part of the events or omissions giving rise to the claim occurred, or a substantial part of property that is the subject of the action is situated, or (iii) a judicial district in which any defendant may be found, if there is no district in which the action may otherwise be brought.

(c) For purposes of venue under this chapter, a ***defendant*** that is a ***corporation*** shall be deemed to reside in ***any judicial district in which it is subject to personal jurisdiction*** at the time the action is commenced. In a State which has more than one judicial district and in which a defendant that is a corporation is subject to personal jurisdiction at the time an action is commenced, such corporation shall be deemed to reside in any district in that State within which its contacts would be sufficient to subject it to personal jurisdiction if that district were a separate State, and, if there is no such district, the corporation shall be deemed to reside in the district within which it has the most significant contacts.

(d) An alien may be sued in any district.

Section 1392: Defendants or Property in Different Districts in Same State

(a) Any civil action, not of a local nature, against defendants residing in different districts in the same State may be brought in ***any of such districts***.

Section 1404: Change of Venue

(a) For the convenience of parties and witnesses, in the interest of justice, a district court may transfer any civil action to any other district or division ***where it might have been brought***.

Section 1406: Cure or Waiver of Defects

(a) The district court of a district in which is filed a case laying venue in the wrong division or district shall ***dismiss***, or if it be in the interest of justice, ***transfer*** such case to any district or division in which it could have been brought.

(b) Nothing in this chapter shall impair the jurisdiction of a district court of any matter involving a party who does not interpose timely and sufficient objection to the venue.

Federal venue rules determine the judicial district in which an action within the jurisdiction of federal courts may be brought.

A. SUBJECT MATTER JURISDICTION DISTINGUISHED

Subject matter jurisdiction and venue are very often confused. Subject matter jurisdiction is the ***power*** of the court to adjudicate the matter before it. Venue relates to the ***proper district*** in which to bring the action. Subject matter jurisdiction is a question of power or authority; venue is a question of convenience. Subject matter jurisdiction cannot be conferred by agreement; venue can be. A court can have subject matter jurisdiction without having proper venue.

Example: Smith, a citizen of Georgia, brings a personal injury suit arising in Florida against Jones, a citizen of New York. Suit is brought in the federal district court in California. The amount in controversy exceeds $75,000. Under section 1332, the district court has diversity jurisdiction, but venue is improper because section 1391, the general venue statute quoted above, requires that actions founded solely on diversity be brought in a district satisfying one of the requisites of section 1391(a).

B. GENERAL RULES

1. General Rules for Most Civil Actions

Venue in civil actions in the federal courts is proper in:

(i) A judicial district where ***any defendant resides***, if all defendants reside in the same state;

(ii) A judicial district in which ***a substantial part of the events or omissions giving rise to the claim occurred***, or ***a substantial part of property that is the subject of the action is situated***; or

(iii) If there is no district anywhere in the United States which satisfies (i) or (ii),

i. For actions based ***solely on diversity***, a judicial district in which ***any defendant is subject to personal jurisdiction at the time the action is commenced***; or

ii. For actions ***not based solely on diversity***, a judicial district in which ***any defendant may be found***.

[28 U.S.C. §1391]

2. Actions Involving Both Diversity and a Federal Question

If an action satisfies the jurisdictional requirements for both federal question and diversity jurisdiction, the venue provisions for ***federal question*** cases govern, because such a suit is not "based solely on diversity."

3. Special Venue Provisions

There are many venue provisions applicable only to specified types of actions. Two worth noting are:

a. An alien may be sued in any district [28 U.S.C. §1391(d)]; and

b. Where the defendant is the United States or an agency thereof, or an officer, employee, etc., of the United States acting in his official capacity, a civil action may be brought where: (i) a defendant resides; (ii) a substantial part of the events or omissions giving rise to the action occurred, or a substantial part of property that is the subject of the action is situated; or (iii) the plaintiff resides if no real property is involved in the action [28 U.S.C. §1391(e)].

C. RESIDENCE

1. Individuals

Residence for federal venue purposes is usually determined by a ***person's domicile***. Therefore, a person who maintains two homes usually will be deemed to reside only in the district of his domicile. It is possible, however, for a domiciliary of one state to reside for venue purposes in a different state.

2. Corporations

For purposes of venue, a corporation is deemed to reside in ***any judicial district in which it is subject to personal jurisdiction*** at the time the action is commenced. If a state has more than one judicial district, the corporation is deemed to reside in any district in the state within which the corporation's contacts would be sufficient to subject the corporation to personal jurisdiction if the district were a state; if there is no such district, the corporation is deemed to reside in the district within which it has the most significant contacts. [28 U.S.C. §1391(c)]

3. **Unincorporated Associations**
For venue purposes, an unincorporated association "resides" where it does business. [Denver & Rio Grande Western Railroad v. Brotherhood of Railroad Trainmen, 387 U.S. 556 (1967)—union could be sued in Colorado where doing business]

D. VENUE IN "LOCAL ACTIONS"

A "local action" (*e.g.,* an in rem action relating to real property) must be brought in the district where the property that is the subject matter of the action is located. Section 1392(b) provides that where the property is located in more than one district in the same state, venue is proper in any such district.

E. IMPROPER VENUE MAY BE WAIVED

Unlike jurisdiction over the subject matter, venue may be waived by the parties. Venue is considered to be waived unless timely objection (in a pre-pleading motion or, where no such motion is made, in the answer) is made to the improper venue.

F. TRANSFER

1. **Original Venue Proper**
Section 1404(a) allows transfer to another district where the action ***"might have been brought"*** even though venue has been properly laid in the court before which the motion to transfer is made. The policy behind section 1404 is that while venue may be correct, the parties or the witnesses might be greatly inconvenienced by the trial in the original forum. By balancing the relative convenience offered by the alternative forums, the original court has discretion to transfer the action to a court in which the action "might have been brought" in conformity with the rules governing: (i) subject matter jurisdiction, (ii) in personam jurisdiction over the defendant, and (iii) where venue is proper.

a. **Effect of Forum Selection Clause**
The presence of a ***forum selection clause*** in a contract, by which the parties have specified a particular forum as the appropriate place for litigation, ***is a factor*** to be considered along with convenience and the interest of justice in deciding whether to transfer the case. [Stewart Organization, Inc. v. Ricoh Corp., 487 U.S. 22 (1988)]

2. **Original Venue Improper**
Section 1406(a) is designed for situations where the venue is improper and the alternative to transfer is dismissal of the action. The standard for transfer is ***"the interest of justice."*** Transfer is more appropriate than dismissal except in extraordinary circumstances. The transferee forum must have subject matter jurisdiction and in personam jurisdiction over the defendant, and venue must be proper. Some courts have held that section 1406(a) applies when the original court is a proper venue but lacks personal jurisdiction over the defendant. This view seems contrary to the language and purpose of the statute.

3. Original Court Lacks Personal Jurisdiction

The Supreme Court has held that the original court's lack of personal jurisdiction over the defendant does not affect its power to transfer a case under section 1404(a). [Goldlawr, Inc. v. Heiman, 369 U.S. 463 (1962)] There is also authority to support the conclusion that the same is true in transfers under section 1406(a). [*See, e.g.,* United States v. Berkowitz, 328 F.2d 358 (3d Cir. 1964)]

G. LAW APPLICABLE UPON TRANSFER

1. Original Venue Proper

A transfer solely on convenience grounds (under section 1404(a)) carries to the transferee court the originally applicable (under *Erie*) rules (including choice of law); *i.e.,* the law of the state in which the transferor court sat. This is true even where the plaintiff initiates a transfer for convenience after initially choosing the inconvenient forum. [Ferens v. Deere Co., 494 U.S. 516 (1990)]

Example: P sued D in a federal district court in Pennsylvania. Upon the transfer to Massachusetts, the district court judge there must apply the law that would have been applied in Pennsylvania. [Van Dusen v. Barrack, 376 U.S. 612 (1964)]

2. Original Venue Improper

A transfer on the ground that the original choice of venue was improper (under section 1406(a)) generally results in a change of the law applicable under *Erie; i.e.,* the law of the state in which the transferee court sits.

Example: P sued D in the federal district court in Maryland. Upon transfer to New York under section 1406(a), the law applied in the transferee court (New York) would be its own law.

V. REMOVAL JURISDICTION

Section 1441: Actions Removable Generally

(a) Except as otherwise expressly provided by Act of Congress, any civil action brought in a State court of which the district courts of the United States have ***original jurisdiction***, may be ***removed by the defendant*** or the defendants, to the district court of the United States for the district and division embracing the place where such action is pending. For purposes of removal under this chapter, the citizenship of defendants sued under fictitious names shall be disregarded.

(b) Any civil action of which the district courts have original jurisdiction founded on a claim or right arising under the Constitution, treaties or laws of the United States shall be removable without regard to the citizenship or residence of the parties. Any other such action shall be removable ***only if none*** of the parties in interest properly joined and served as ***defendants is a citizen of the State in which such action is brought***.

(c) Whenever a separate and independent claim or cause of action within the jurisdiction conferred by section 1331 of this title [federal question jurisdiction], is joined with one or more otherwise nonremovable claims or causes of action, ***the entire case may be removed*** and the district court may determine all issues therein, or, in its discretion, may remand all matters not otherwise within its original jurisdiction.

Section 1446: Procedure for Removal

(a) A defendant or defendants desiring to remove any civil action or criminal prosecution from a State court shall file in the district court of the United States for the district and division within which such action is pending a notice of removal signed pursuant to Rule 11 of the Federal Rules of Civil Procedure and containing a short and plain statement of the grounds for removal, together with a copy of all process, pleadings, and orders served upon such defendant or defendants in such action.

(b) The notice of removal of a civil action or proceeding shall be filed within ***30 days*** after receipt by the defendant, through service or otherwise, of a copy of the initial pleading setting forth the claim for relief upon which such action or proceeding is based, or within ***30 days*** after the service of summons upon the defendant if such initial pleading has been filed in court and is not required to be served on the defendant, whichever period is shorter.

If the case stated by the initial pleading is not removable, a notice of removal may be filed within ***30 days*** after receipt by the defendant, through service or otherwise, of a copy of an amended pleading, motion, order, or other paper from which it may first be ascertained that the case is one which is or has become removable, except that a case may ***not*** be removed on the basis of jurisdiction conferred by section 1332 of this title ***more than 1 year after commencement of the action***.

Section 1447: Procedure After Removal Generally

(c) If at any time before final judgment it appears that the district court lacks subject matter jurisdiction, the case shall be ***remanded***. An order remanding the case may require payment of just costs and any actual expenses, including attorney fees, incurred as a result of the removal. . . .

(d) An order remanding a case to the State court from which it was removed is not reviewable on appeal or otherwise. . . .

A. ORIGINAL JURISDICTION NECESSARY

Under section 1441(a), a defendant can only remove an action that could have originally been brought by the plaintiff in the federal courts.

1. When

The prevailing rule is that removal is tested only as of the date of removal. Some courts held

under the statute as it existed before 1989 that original jurisdiction must have existed both at the time the suit was instituted in the state court and at the time of removal. [*In re* Carter, 618 F.2d 1093 (5th Cir. 1980)]

2. **Federal Defense Insufficient**
A defendant cannot remove on the ground that she has a defense grounded in federal law, since the existence of a federal defense is insufficient to confer original federal question jurisdiction under section 1331.

3. **State Court Need Not Have Had Jurisdiction**
By statute, the federal court ***may*** hear and decide a claim in a removed civil action even where the state court had no jurisdiction because the action is exclusively federal. [28 U.S.C. §1441(e)] Formerly, the federal court was required to dismiss.

B. ONLY DEFENDANT MAY REMOVE; ALL MUST SEEK REMOVAL
Only defendants can exercise the right of removal. Thus, a plaintiff cannot remove on the ground that a counterclaim against him could have been brought independently in a federal court. If there is more than one defendant, ***all defendants*** must join in the removal. Thus, if some defendants are precluded under section 1446(b) from removing because of delay, or refuse to join in the removal, removal is not authorized. (*Note:* The Class Action Fairness Act relaxes this rule for some class actions. *See* VII.F.2.d., *infra.*)

C. VENUE
Venue for an action removed under section 1441(a) lies in the federal district court "embracing the place where such [state] action is pending." Note that in removal cases section 1441(a) determines proper venue, not section 1391(a). Thus, in a properly removed case, venue is proper in the federal court of the state where the case was pending, even if venue would have been improper had the plaintiff originally filed the action in the federal district court of that state.

Example: Linda, a citizen of State A, sues Jim, a citizen of State B, in the state court in State Z in the amount of $2 million for negligent acts Jim committed in State B. Jim may remove the case to the federal district court of State Z because the court has diversity jurisdiction and Jim is not a citizen of State Z. Although under section 1391(a) venue would have been improper if Linda had filed her case in the State Z federal district court, under section 1441(a) venue is proper in the federal district court of State Z because it "embraces the place" where the state court action was pending.

D. DEFENDANT MAY REMOVE SEPARATE AND INDEPENDENT FEDERAL QUESTION CLAIM
If there are multiple claims or multiple parties, under 28 U.S.C. section 1441(c), a defendant may remove a ***whole case*** if it contains "a separate and independent claim or cause of action" within federal question jurisdiction. The federal district court may then retain the whole case, or sever and remand the matters not within its original jurisdiction.

E. DISMISSAL OF NONDIVERSE PARTY ALLOWS REMOVAL
If no federal question is involved and diversity does not exist because a party is a co-citizen of an opposing party, removal will be permitted if the nondiverse parties are thereafter dismissed from the action and there is complete diversity between the remaining parties, subject to the limitations discussed below.

1. Limitations on Removal in Diversity of Citizenship Cases

a. Defendant Citizen of Forum State

When the jurisdiction of the federal court is based on diversity and one of the defendants is a citizen of the state in which the state action was brought, the action is not removable.

Example: Jones, a citizen of State A, sues Brown, a citizen of State B, and Smith, a citizen of State C, in the state court in State B. Although diversity jurisdiction would have existed originally (assuming the jurisdictional amount had been met), Brown and Smith cannot remove. Had Jones brought the action in the state court in State A, Brown and Smith could remove. [28 U.S.C. §1441(b)]

When the original jurisdiction of the district court would have been based on a federal question, the defendants can remove without regard to the citizenship of the parties.

b. One Year Rule

A case may not be removed on the basis of diversity of citizenship jurisdiction more than one year after it was commenced in state court. [28 U.S.C. §1446(b)] Note also that a case must be removed no later than 30 days after the defendant discovers, through service of an amended pleading, order, etc., that the case has become removable (*see* F.2., *infra*). Because most cases will be removable, if at all, at commencement of the action, the one year deadline generally will not be difficult to meet. The provision may be important, however, if the case is not removable at the outset, but becomes removable later. The one year rule does not apply to removals based on federal question jurisdiction.

Examples: 1) A (a citizen of State A) sues B (a citizen of State B) in state court in State A, seeking damages of $100,000. The case is removable at its commencement, since the case meets the requirements of diversity of citizenship jurisdiction and no defendant is a citizen of the forum. B must remove the case within 30 days of being served with process.

2) P (a citizen of State A) sues D1 (a citizen of State B) and D2 (a citizen of State A) in state court in State C, seeking damages of $250,000. The case is not removable at its commencement, since it does not satisfy the complete diversity rule for diversity of citizenship jurisdiction. However, if P later voluntarily dismisses the claim against D2, the case becomes removable. D1 must then remove within 30 days. But if more than a year has passed since the state case was commenced, D1 cannot remove on the basis of diversity of citizenship. This rule has been criticized, since it permits P to join a defendant who destroys diversity jurisdiction, wait a year and a day, dismiss the claim against that defendant, and thus thwart the diverse defendant's ability to remove the case to federal court.

Note: The Fifth Circuit court has held that the one year limitation in section 1446(b) may be equitably extended when the plaintiff fraudulently joins a party in order to defeat diversity. [Tedford v. Warner-Lambert Co., 327 F.3d 423 (5th Cir. 2003)] However, the applicability of this theory beyond the Fifth Circuit is unlikely. [*See, e.g.,* Caudill v. Ford Motor Co., 271 F. Supp. 2d 1324 (N.D. Okla. 2003)]

F. PROCEDURE FOR REMOVAL

1. Notice of Removal

A defendant seeking removal must file a notice of removal—containing a short and plain statement of the grounds for removal and signed under Rule 11—in the federal district court in the district and division within which the action is pending. A copy of the notice should be sent to the other parties ***and*** to the state court. Once this is done, the state court can no longer deal with the case. If the state court attempts to do so, the federal court can enjoin the state court's action.

2. Thirty Day Rule

A defendant must file a notice of removal within 30 days "after receipt by the defendant, through service or otherwise, of a copy of the initial pleading." [28 U.S.C. §1446(b)] The "through service or otherwise" language is intended to address different state approaches to the order of filing a case and serving process. For instance, in some states, the defendant is served with a summons but not a copy of the complaint. For such defendants, the 30 day removal period would start to run upon formal receipt of the complaint.

Example: P files an action against B in state court. P faxes a "courtesy copy" of the complaint to B, but does not have formal process (a summons and complaint) served for two weeks. D removes the case within 30 days after being served with process, but more than 30 days after receiving the faxed copy of the complaint. Was removal timely? Yes. The 30 days ran from service of process on the defendant. [Murphy Brothers v. Michetti Pipe Stringing, Inc., 526 U.S. 344 (1999)]

Section 1446(b) also allows a defendant to file a notice of removal within 30 days of receipt of an amended pleading, motion, order, or other court paper that shows that a nonremovable case (or an apparently nonremovable case) is in fact removable. This provision is significant in states that either prohibit the plaintiff from alleging or do not require the plaintiff to allege a specific amount of damages. In such cases, the 30 day window to remove may begin much later than after the service of the initial pleading. [*See, e.g.,* Yonkosky v. Hicks, 409 F. Supp. 2d 149 (W.D.N.Y. 2005)—in accordance with state law, original complaint did not state damages; plaintiff's later filing of demand for relief months later far exceeding the $75,000 threshold started 30 day window to remove]

3. Procedure After Removal

After removal, the case proceeds according to the federal rules of procedure. Repleading is not necessary unless the court so orders. If the defendant has not answered, she must answer or present the other defenses or objections available to her under the Federal Rules within 21 days after being served, or within seven days after filing the petition for removal, whichever period is longer. Amendments may be made to pleadings filed before removal.

4. Right to Jury Trial

a. Demand for Jury Trial

The right to a jury trial in a case removed to a federal court may be waived unless a timely demand for a jury trial is filed. If, at the time of removal, all necessary pleadings have been served, a trial by jury will be granted to a party so entitled. The removing party must file a demand for jury trial within 14 days after the notice of removal is filed.

The nonremoving party must file for jury trial within 14 days after service on her of the notice of filing for removal.

b. **Demand Not Required**
A party who, ***prior to removal***, has made an express demand for trial by jury in accordance with state law, need not make a demand after removal. In addition, if ***state law*** applicable in the court from which the case is removed does not require the parties to make an express demand in order to claim trial by jury, they need not make such demand after removal unless the court directs they do so.

5. **Remand**
A plaintiff can file a motion to have the case remanded (sent back) to the state court. If the plaintiff bases this motion on a defect other than subject matter jurisdiction (*e.g.,* a defect in removal procedures), it must be brought within 30 days of removal. The court must remand, however, whenever it is shown that there was no federal subject matter jurisdiction. If the court erroneously fails to remand, but the subject matter defect is cured before trial begins, failure to remand does not require that the federal judgment be vacated. [Caterpillar Inc. v. Lewis, 519 U.S. 61 (1996)] The federal court has discretion to remand a case to state court once all federal claims have been resolved, leaving only state claims over which there would be no diversity jurisdiction. [Carnegie-Mellon University v. Cohill, 484 U.S. 343 (1988)] Appellate review of remand orders is generally barred [28 U.S.C. §1447(d)]; however, appeal is allowed where a case involving civil rights is remanded to state court. Remand orders can also be reviewed by means of a mandamus if the remand represented a refusal to exercise plainly proper jurisdiction. [Thermtron v. Hermansdorfer, 423 U.S. 336 (1976)]

a. **Subject Matter Jurisdiction Generally Considered First**
Ordinarily, a federal court will determine whether it has subject matter jurisdiction before it considers the merits of the case. [Steel Co. v. Citizens for Better Environment, 523 U.S. 83 (1998)] However, the Supreme Court has held that a federal court could address the issue of personal jurisdiction before assessing subject matter jurisdiction. The circumstances of the case were unusual, however, in that the defendant removed on a novel theory attempting to invoke a rarely used basis of subject matter jurisdiction, and whether that basis was met would have been an issue of first impression. On the other hand, the personal jurisdiction issue was relatively uncomplicated and presented no difficult issue of state law. In these circumstances, the court did not abuse its discretion by addressing personal jurisdiction first. [Ruhrgas AG v. Marathon Oil Co., 526 U.S. 574 (1999)]

G. SPECIFIC TYPES OF ACTIONS

1. **Removable**
Statutes allow removal of certain actions against ***federal officers*** when they were allegedly acting under color of law [28 U.S.C. §1442] and ***federal employees*** for torts by motor vehicle committed in the scope of employment [28 U.S.C. §2679(d)]; actions involving ***international banking***; and criminal or civil actions where the defendant will be denied a right protected under federal ***civil rights*** statutes [28 U.S.C. §1443], but only if the denial is inevitable under state law [Georgia v. Rachel, 384 U.S. 780 (1966)]. Not all of these special types of cases could have been brought originally in the federal courts.

2. Nonremovable

Actions under the Federal Employers Liability Act ("FELA") and the Jones Act are not removable; nor are actions for less than $10,000 against carriers for losses to certain shipments in interstate commerce, workers' compensation proceedings [28 U.S.C. §1445], or actions under the Fair Labor Standards Act. The plaintiff thus has the option to bring these cases in state court.

a. All Writs Act Not a Basis for Removal

Some courts permitted removal of a case under the All Writs Act, 28 U.S.C. section 1651 (permitting federal courts to "issue all writs necessary or appropriate in aid of their respective jurisdictions and agreeable to the usages and principles of law"), even if the case did not invoke federal subject matter jurisdiction. However, the Supreme Court held that the All Writs Act does not provide an independent basis for removal jurisdiction; a case thus must satisfy some independent basis of subject matter jurisdiction, such as diversity of citizenship or federal question jurisdiction. [Syngenta Crop Protection, Inc. v. Henson, 537 U.S. 28 (2002)]

VI. CONFLICT OF JURISDICTION BETWEEN STATE AND FEDERAL COURTS

A. FULL FAITH AND CREDIT EXTENDED TO FEDERAL COURTS

The Constitution's Full Faith and Credit Clause is applicable only where a state court judgment is sought to be enforced in another state. However, an implementing federal statute provides that this Clause is extended to the federal courts. Therefore, recognition of judgments is required between state and federal courts ***and*** between federal courts.

B. INJUNCTIONS AGAINST PENDING STATE PROCEEDINGS

Potentially, a case also could be filed in state court by one party and in federal court by the other party. In such a case, federal court is prohibited from enjoining ***pending*** state court proceedings unless ***expressly*** authorized by statute (*e.g.,* the interpleader provision expressly authorizes injunctions against state court proceedings), or "where necessary in aid of its jurisdiction, or to protect or effectuate its judgments." [28 U.S.C. §2283] The case coming to a final decision first will have preclusive effect on the other. (*See* X.B., *infra.*)

C. INJUNCTIONS AGAINST THREATENED STATE CRIMINAL PROSECUTIONS

Threatened state criminal prosecutions (*i.e.,* where state court proceedings have not already been instituted) will be enjoined only when necessary ***to prevent irreparable harm*** which is clear and imminent ***and*** where ***appellate remedies in the criminal case are clearly inadequate to provide relief***. Such injunctions are almost invariably denied, except where a federal right of free speech or assembly or a federally protected civil right is threatened by the state criminal proceeding, and it is shown that the prosecution is in bad faith or is for the purpose of harassment. Relief by declaratory judgment will ordinarily be denied if an injunction would be denied.

D. INJUNCTIONS AGAINST STATE TAX PROCEDURES

28 U.S.C. section 1341 prohibits injunctions against the assessment, levy, or collection of state taxes "where there is a plain, speedy and efficient remedy . . . in the courts of such State." [*See* Rosewell v. LaSalle National Bank, 450 U.S. 503 (1980)]

E. THE DOCTRINE OF ABSTENTION

Unless the doctrine of abstention applies, nothing prohibits the federal court from hearing a case that is pending in state court.

1. Policy of Abstention

Under certain circumstances the federal courts will retain jurisdiction over a suit involving ***a challenge to the constitutionality of a state law*** but abstain from deciding the question until a decision has been made by the state courts on the meaning of the state law. A determinative interpretation of the state law may obviate the federal constitutional question. The considerations that have led federal courts to refrain from deciding a challenge to the constitutionality of a state law include:

(i) Possible unnecessary friction with the state, particularly when a state regulatory plan based on predominantly local factors is in issue;

(ii) Possible error in the construction of an unclear state law; and

(iii) Reluctance to decide constitutional questions unnecessarily (where the state court might construe the state statute in such a way that it would be constitutional).

Note that in cases where abstention would be proper, the federal courts ordinarily should stay the federal action rather than dismiss it.

2. Federal Intervention in Certain Cases

If the challenged state statute is "flagrantly and patently violative of express constitutional prohibitions in every clause, sentence and paragraph, and in whatever manner and against whomever an effort might be made to apply it" [Huffman v. Pursue, Ltd., 420 U.S. 592 (1975)], then "the federal court need not stay its hand in the face of pending state proceedings" [Moore v. Sims, 442 U.S. 415 (1979)].

Federal intervention on constitutional grounds may occur if the federal plaintiff can demonstrate:

a. Great and immediate irreparable injury;

b. Bad faith in the prosecution of the state action; or

c. Harassment or other unusual circumstances calling for federal equitable relief.

VII. THE FEDERAL RULES OF CIVIL PROCEDURE

A. COMMENCEMENT OF THE ACTION

Rule 3 provides that an action is commenced by ***filing a complaint*** with the court. Federal courts may adopt local rules to permit filing by fax or other electronic means. Filing a complaint before the statute of limitations has run will satisfy the statute of limitations in federal question cases and in diversity cases where the state rule is similar. However, the Supreme Court has held that a state rule that an action is commenced for purposes of the statute of limitations ***only upon service of process*** must be applied in diversity cases. [Walker v. Armco Steel Corp., 446 U.S. 740 (1980)]

B. SERVICE OF PROCESS

1. Who May Serve

Rule 4 authorizes any person who is at least 18 years old and not a party to the action to serve the summons and complaint (together known as "process"). A party may request that service be made by a United States marshal or by another person appointed by the court for that purpose.

2. How Service Is Made

Generally, Rule 4 provides that: (i) personal service, (ii) service left at the defendant's usual place of abode with one of suitable age and discretion residing therein, or (iii) service upon an authorized agent of the defendant, is valid. Alternatively, service may be made under state rules or by mail under the waiver of service provision of Rule 4(d).

a. Service Under State Rules

Rule 4 provides that service may alternatively be made as provided by the rules of the state in which the federal court sits or the state in which service is to be effected, regardless of whether the action is founded on diversity of citizenship jurisdiction. Hence, federal courts can use state long arm provisions.

b. Waiver of Service (Service by Mail)

The plaintiff may also request the defendant to waive service of process. To request a waiver of service, the plaintiff must mail the defendant certain items, the most important of which are a formal request to waive service (that also informs the defendant of the consequences of failing to waive service), two copies of the waiver form, and a copy of the complaint. The defendant generally has 30 days (60 days if outside the United States) from the date that the request was sent to return the waiver.

1) Effect of Waiver

A defendant who waives formal service of process has ***60 days*** (90 days if outside the United States) from the date the request was sent, instead of the usual 21 days (*see* E.3.b., *infra*) to answer the complaint. The waiver of service does ***not*** waive the defendant's right to object to venue and jurisdiction.

2) Effect of Failure to Waive

If the defendant does not waive service of process, the plaintiff must serve him using one of the methods described in 2., *supra*. However, a defendant who is located in the United States is liable for the cost of such service if he does not have good cause for failing to waive service.

3. Parties Served Outside State

The court will acquire personal jurisdiction over parties served outside the state:

a. Under statute and rules for extraterritorial service of the state in which the federal court sits (domiciliaries, long arm jurisdiction, and in rem jurisdiction);

b. If they are third-party defendants [Fed. R. Civ. P. 14] or required to be joined for just adjudication [Fed. R. Civ. P. 19], if served within 100 miles from the place where the summons was issued (but within the United States);

c. If out-of-state service is permitted by federal statute (*e.g.,* interpleader); and

d. ***For cases that involve a federal question***, when a defendant is served with process (or waiver thereof), provided that the defendant is ***not subject to general jurisdiction in any state court***, that the defendant has ***sufficient contacts with the United States*** to warrant the application of federal law, and that the exercise of jurisdiction ***is not prohibited by statute.***

4. Parties Served in Foreign Country

Unless a federal law provides differently, a court will acquire personal jurisdiction over a party served in a foreign country:

a. As provided in an ***international agreement***;

b. In absence of an agreement, as provided by ***the foreign country's law or as directed by a foreign official*** in response to a letter of request (but the method must be reasonably calculated to provide notice);

c. Unless it is prohibited by the foreign country's law, ***by personal service or by mail***, signed return receipt requested. (However, a corporation may not be served by personal service, and a minor or incompetent person may not be served by either of these methods); or

d. ***Any method the court orders*** (so long as the method is not prohibited by international agreement).

5. Immunity from Process

The federal courts recognize the immunity from service of process of parties, witnesses, and attorneys who enter a state to appear in another action. In addition, if a party was induced by the plaintiff's fraud or deceit to enter a state so that he could be served, the service is invalid and the court does not acquire personal jurisdiction.

C. EXTENSION OF TIME PERIODS

Rule 6(b) gives the district court power to extend the period within which actions under the Federal Rules must be performed. However, certain time periods may never be extended. The following motions must be filed, with no extensions, ***within 28 days after entry of judgment***: a renewed motion for judgment as a matter of law, a motion to amend judgment, a motion for a new trial, a motion to amend findings of fact in a nonjury case, and a grant of a new trial on the court's initiative.

D. INTERLOCUTORY INJUNCTIONS

An interlocutory injunction is an equitable remedy by which a person is ordered to act or to refrain from acting in a specified manner. Interlocutory injunctions are granted to maintain the status quo until a trial on the merits may be held.

1. Preliminary Injunction

A preliminary injunction is sought by a party prior to a trial on the merits of the complaint. A preliminary injunction may not be issued without notice to the adverse party. [Fed. R. Civ. P. 65(a)]

2. **Temporary Restraining Order**
A temporary restraining order ("TRO") is granted by a court when it is necessary to prevent irreparable injury to a party, and the injury will result before a preliminary injunction hearing can be held.

a. **Requirements for Ex Parte Temporary Restraining Orders**
Generally, notice of the hearing for the issuance of the TRO must be given before a TRO is issued. However, a court may grant a TRO ***without notice of the hearing to the adverse party*** if three requirements are met [Fed. R. Civ. P. 65(b), (c)]:

1) **Specific Facts Showing Immediate and Irreparable Injury**
The moving party must give specific facts in an affidavit or in the verified complaint to establish that immediate and irreparable injury will result to the moving party before the adverse party can be heard in opposition.

2) **Efforts to Give Notice**
The moving party must certify in writing all efforts she made to give notice of the hearing to the adverse party and the reasons why notice should not be required.

3) **Security**
The moving party must provide some security, the amount of which is determined by the court, to pay for any costs and damages incurred by the adverse party if he was wrongfully enjoined or restrained. The United States, its officers, and its agencies are not required to give security.

b. **Notice of Hearing vs. Actual Notice**
Although a TRO may be issued without notice of the hearing, due process requires that a person must receive actual notice (through service of process or otherwise) of the TRO (or any other injunction for that matter) before he may be held in contempt for violating it. [*See* Fed. R. Civ. P. 65(d)]

c. **Discretion of Court**
Even if the above requirements are met, the court still has discretion whether to issue the TRO. The court may look at the likelihood that the plaintiff will prevail on the merits of the complaint. Also, the court may weigh the injury anticipated by the moving party against the harm caused by issuing the TRO.

d. **Time Limit**
The TRO will expire within 14 days unless the restrained party consents to an extension or good cause is shown for an extension.

E. PLEADINGS
Pleadings serve the function of giving ***notice*** to the opposing parties.

1. **Complaint**
Each claim for relief should contain:

(i) A short statement of the grounds for the court's jurisdiction;

(ii) A short statement of the claim showing that the pleader is entitled to relief; and

(iii) A demand for judgment for relief, which may be in the alternative.

The federal pleading rules generally require only that a pleader put the other side on notice of the claim being asserted; detailed assertions of facts underlying the claim generally are not required. However, the Supreme Court in recent years has required that the plaintiff state facts supporting a ***plausible*** (not just possible) claim. [Bell Atlantic Corp. v. Twombly, 550 U.S. 544 (2007); Ashcroft v. Iqbal, 129 S. Ct. 1937 (2009)]

2. **Pre-Answer Motions**

a. **Rule 12(b)**
Prior to filing an answer, the defendant may, if he chooses, file a motion and raise any or all of the following defenses:

(i) Lack of subject matter jurisdiction;

(ii) Lack of personal jurisdiction;

(iii) Improper venue;

(iv) Insufficient process;

(v) Insufficient service of process;

(vi) Failure to state a claim upon which relief can be granted (*i.e.,* even if plaintiff's allegations are taken as true, relief could not be granted); or

(vii) Failure to join a party needed for a just adjudication (includes necessary and indispensable parties).

The first defense may be raised at any time—even for the first time ***on appeal***. The defendant must raise defenses (ii) through (v) ***at the time he files a motion or his answer***—whichever is first. If he does not, the defendant waives these defenses. The last two defenses (if limited to failure to join an "indispensable party") can be made ***at any time prior to trial or "at trial."*** The defendant may choose not to file a motion and instead raise these defenses in his answer.

b. **Motion for More Definite Statement**
A party may move for a more definite statement ***before responding*** (by filing an answer or reply) to a pleading (a complaint) that is so vague or ambiguous that a responsive pleading cannot reasonably be framed. The opposing party has 14 days after notice of an order to obey unless the court fixes a different time. If not obeyed, the court may strike the pleading or issue any other appropriate order. [Fed. R. Civ. P. 12(e)]

c. **Motion to Strike**
Before responding to a pleading or, if no responsive pleading is permitted, within 21 days after service of the pleading, a party may move to have stricken any insufficient defense, or any redundant, immaterial, impertinent, or scandalous matter. Such motion may also be made upon the court's initiative at any time. [Fed. R. Civ. P. 12(f)]

And note: An objection of failure to state a legal defense to a claim is not waived merely because a Rule 12(f) motion is not made. Such a defense can be made by motion for judgment on the pleadings, or at the trial. [Fed. R. Civ. P. 12(h)]

3. Answer

a. Must Contain Denials or Admissions and Any Affirmative Defenses

The answer must contain a ***specific*** denial or admission of each averment of the complaint, or a ***general*** denial with specific admissions to certain averments. Where the defendant is without knowledge or information sufficient to form a belief, a statement to that effect constitutes a denial. A ***failure to deny*** constitutes an ***admission.*** The answer must also state any ***affirmative defenses*** the defendant may have, such as statute of limitations, Statute of Frauds, res judicata, etc.

b. Time

If no Rule 12 motion is made, a defendant who was formally served with a summons and complaint must present an answer within ***21 days*** after service; a defendant to whom the complaint was mailed and who waives formal service must answer within ***60 days*** after the request for waiver was mailed to her. If a Rule 12 motion is made and the court does not fix another time, the responsive pleading is to be served within ***14 days*** of the court's denial or postponement of the motion. The answer is due within ***14 days*** of service of a more definite statement if the court grants a Rule 12(e) motion (*see* 2.b., *supra.*) The same timing rules apply to answers to counterclaims and cross-claims.

c. Counterclaims

Claims that the defendant may have against the plaintiff may be pleaded in the answer as counterclaims. If a counterclaim arises out of the ***same transaction or occurrence*** as one of the plaintiff's claims, it is a ***compulsory*** counterclaim and must be pleaded or it will be barred. Any other counterclaim is permissive and may be asserted even though there is no connection at all between it and the plaintiff's claim.

d. Effect of Failure to Answer—Default and Default Judgment

A ***default*** is simply a notation in the case file by the clerk that there has been no answer filed within the time permitted by the rules. A ***default judgment*** is a judgment, with the same effect as any other judgment, that is entered because the defendant did not oppose the case.

1) Default

If a party against whom a judgment for relief is sought has failed to plead or otherwise defend, and that fact is made to appear by affidavit or otherwise, the clerk must enter the default of that party. Once the default has been entered, the party may not proceed with the action until the default has been set aside by the court. [Fed. R. Civ. P. 55]

2) Default Judgment

A defendant against whom a default is entered loses the right to contest liability. However, the amount of damages must still be determined before a default judgment may be entered, and the defaulting party can be heard at the hearing for damages. A default judgment may be entered against a minor or incompetent person only if she has a personal representative who has appeared in the case.

a) **Default Judgment Entered by the Clerk**
On request of the plaintiff, supported by an affidavit as to the amount due, the clerk may sign and enter judgment for that amount and costs against the defendant if: (i) the plaintiff's claim against the defaulted defendant is for a ***sum certain***; (ii) the default was entered because the ***defendant failed to appear***; and (iii) the defaulted defendant is ***not an infant or incompetent person***. [Fed. R. Civ. P. 55(b)(1)]

3) **Notice Required**
The clerk or the party must give notice to all parties who have appeared and to the defaulted party after the entry of a default. In addition, if the defendant has "appeared," even though he has not answered, he must be notified of the request for a default judgment by first-class mail at least seven days before the hearing on the application for a default judgment. Appearance includes any actual formal appearance before the court and any other action that clearly indicates that the defendant intends to contest the case on the merits (*e.g.,* the defendant's continued settlement negotiations). [Fed. R. Civ. P. 55(b)(2)]

4) **Setting Aside a Default or a Default Judgment**
An entry of default may be set aside for "good cause shown," or a default judgment may be set aside as provided in Rule 60 (relief from judgments) (*see* VIII.A., *infra*).

4. **Inconsistent Claims or Defenses**
A party may set out as many alternative claims or defenses as he may have regardless of consistency.

5. **Special Pleading**
The general rule of pleading is for short and plain statements, but there are certain rules for special circumstances. [*See* Fed. R. Civ. P. 9] Note that in some of these situations (notably concerning fraud, mistake, and special damages), the Federal Rules require a party to state more detail than simply a short and plain statement. These situations requiring greater specificity are narrow, however, and the Supreme Court has emphasized that courts have no power to impose such rigorous pleading requirements outside the areas addressed by Federal Rule or statute. [Swierkiewicz v. Sorema N.A., 534 U.S. 506 (2002)—lower court erred by requiring detailed pleading of employment discrimination claim; Leatherman v. Tarrant County, 507 U.S. 163 (1993)—lower court erred by requiring detailed pleading of civil rights case against municipality]

a. **Capacity**
Capacity or authority to sue or be sued ***need not be alleged***. A person wishing to challenge a party's capacity has the duty to raise the issue by specific negative averment, including such particulars as are within his knowledge.

b. **Fraud or Mistake**
Circumstances that establish fraud or mistake must be stated with ***particularity***. By

statute (the Private Securities Litigation Reform Act), plaintiffs in federal securities fraud cases must plead with particularity facts relating to the defendant's acting with the required scienter.

c. **Conditions of the Mind**
Malice, intent, knowledge, or other conditions of the mind may be averred ***generally***.

d. **Conditions Precedent**
The performance of conditions precedent may be alleged ***generally***. Denial of performance or occurrence must be made specifically and with particularity.

e. **Official Document or Act**
When dealing with an official document or act, it is ***sufficient*** to aver that it was issued or the act was ***done in compliance with the law***.

f. **Judgment**
It is ***not necessary to aver jurisdiction*** when a domestic or foreign court or a board or officer renders a judgment or decision.

g. **Timing**
Time and place averments are ***material*** for the purpose of testing the sufficiency of a pleading.

h. **Special Damages**
Elements of special damages must be ***specifically*** stated.

6. **Reply**
A reply ***by the plaintiff*** to the defendant's answer is required ***only*** if the court orders the plaintiff to file one. A plaintiff need not reply to an affirmative defense; he is deemed to deny or avoid the allegation of the defense. [Fed. R. Civ. P. 7, 12]

7. **Amendment and Supplemental Pleadings**

a. **Amendment**
As a matter of course, a pleading may be amended ***once*** within 21 days of serving it or, if the pleading is one to which a responsive pleading is required, 21 days after service of a responsive pleading or a pre-answer motion. Thereafter, a pleading may be amended only by the written consent of the adverse party or by leave of the court upon motion. Leave of the court is "freely given when justice so requires." [Fed. R. Civ. P. 15]

1) **Relation Back**
Amendments relate back to the date that the original pleading was filed if the conduct, transaction, or occurrence set forth in the amendment was set forth or attempted to be set forth in the original pleading. Amendments also relate back if relation back is permitted by the law that provides the statute of limitations applicable to the action. [Fed. R. Civ. P. 15(c)]

2) **Changing Party**
An amendment changing the party or the naming of the party against whom a

claim is asserted relates back if the amendment ***concerns the same conduct, transaction, or occurrence*** as the original pleading ***and*** if, within 120 days after filing the complaint (and such additional time as the court may order upon showing of good cause), the party to be brought in by amendment:

(i) Has ***received such notice of the action that she will not be prejudiced in maintaining her defense*** on the merits; and

(ii) Knew or should have known that, ***but for a mistake concerning the proper party's identity***, the action would have been brought against her.

[Fed. R. Civ. P. 15(c)(1)(C)] The Supreme Court has emphasized that it is the knowledge of the party to be brought in by amendment (not of the plaintiff) that is relevant. [Krupski v. Costa Crociere S.p.A., 130 S. Ct. 2485 (2010)]

3) Conform to Evidence

A pleading may be amended during or after trial, or even after judgment, to conform to the evidence, reflect an issue actually tried by the express or implied consent of the parties, or permit the raising of new issues at trial. However, a party may not raise a new claim or defense for which the opposing party had no opportunity to prepare and which would result in prejudice in maintaining his action or defense. [Fed. R. Civ. P. 15(b)]

4) Due Process Limitation

Amendments to pleadings must satisfy due process. For example, in *Nelson v. Adams U.S.A. Inc.,* 529 U.S. 460 (2000), the trial court permitted a post-verdict amendment to add a defendant, and simultaneously entered judgment against that new defendant. The Supreme Court held that this procedure violated the new defendant's due process rights. The Federal Rules are meant to provide an opportunity for an added defendant to respond to a claim, and do not permit such "swift passage from pleading to judgment in the pleader's favor."

b. Supplemental Pleadings

Supplemental pleadings relate to matters ***occurring after*** the date of the original pleading. The permission of the court, upon motion, is required. Permission may be granted even though the original pleading is defective in its statement of a claim for relief or a defense. [Fed. R. Civ. P. 15(d)]

8. Rule 11

a. Certification upon Presenting Paper to Court

In federal civil cases, the attorney (or unrepresented party), by presenting to the court a pleading, written motion, or other paper, certifies that to the best of her knowledge, information, and belief formed after an inquiry reasonable under the circumstances:

(i) The paper is not presented for any ***improper purpose*** (harassment, delay, etc.);

(ii) The legal contentions therein are ***warranted by existing law*** or a nonfrivolous argument for the ***modification of existing law*** or the establishment of a new law;

(iii) The allegations and factual contentions either have, or upon further investigation or discovery are likely to have, ***evidentiary support***; and

(iv) Denials of factual contentions are ***warranted on the evidence*** or, where specified, are reasonably based on a lack of information and belief.

The certification applies anew each time an attorney or unrepresented party "later advocates" a position contained in a pleading, motion, etc. Thus, a paper that was not sanctionable when first presented may become sanctionable if the attorney or party later advocating a position contained in the paper has since learned that the position no longer has merit.

b. Sanctions

The court has discretion to impose sanctions, "limited to what is sufficient to deter repetition of such conduct," against a party who presents a paper to the court in violation of the above requirements, either on the court's own initiative or on motion of the opposing party. When appropriate, sanctions may be imposed against parties, attorneys, or law firms, and may consist of nonmonetary directives or monetary penalties including payment of expenses and attorneys' fees incurred because of the improper paper.

1) Court's Initiative

A court on its own initiative may enter an order describing the matter that appears to violate Rule 11 and direct the proponent to show cause why sanctions should not be imposed.

2) Party's Motion

A party who believes that his opponent has presented a paper in violation of Rule 11 may serve a motion for sanctions on the party. If the party does not withdraw or correct the matter within 21 days, the moving party may then file the motion for sanctions with the court.

F. JOINDER

1. Joinder of Parties

a. Capacity

An individual's capacity to sue or be sued is determined by the law of her domicile; the capacity of an organization (*e.g.,* an association or partnership) is determined by the law of the state where the federal court sits, except that a partnership or unincorporated association always has capacity where a substantive federal right is asserted by or against it.

b. Compulsory Joinder

Under Rule 19, a party should be joined if: (i) complete relief cannot be given to existing parties in her absence; (ii) disposition in her absence may impair her ability to protect her interest in the controversy; ***or*** (iii) her absence would expose existing parties to a substantial risk of double or inconsistent obligations. (*See* 1) and 2), *infra.*) *But note:* The Supreme Court has held that a joint tortfeasor subject to joint and several liability is not a person needed for just adjudication. [Temple v. Synthes Corp., 498 U.S. 5 (1990)]

1) **Must Be Joined If Feasible**
When a compulsory party is amenable to process ***and*** her joinder will not destroy diversity or venue, she ***must*** be joined. There is no supplemental jurisdiction over claims by or against persons joined under Rule 19.

2) **When Joinder Is Not Feasible**
When joinder is not feasible (*i.e.,* the compulsory party is not subject to process, objects to venue, or would destroy diversity jurisdiction), the court ***must decide whether the action can proceed in the party's absence or must be dismissed.*** The court must consider these four factors:

(i) Whether the judgment in the party's absence would ***prejudice her or the existing parties***;

(ii) Whether the ***prejudice can be reduced*** in shaping the judgment;

(iii) Whether a ***judgment*** in the party's absence would be ***adequate***; and

(iv) Whether the ***plaintiff will be deprived of an adequate remedy*** if the action is dismissed.

The cases have shown a preference for dismissal if there is a state forum in which all the parties may be joined in practice as well as in theory.

c. **Permissive Joinder—Requirements**
Parties may join as plaintiffs or be joined as defendants whenever:

(i) Some claim is made by each plaintiff and against each defendant relating to or arising out of the ***same series of occurrences or transactions; and***

(ii) There is a ***question of fact or law common*** to all the parties.

Example: It is very common for all persons injured in an automobile accident to join as plaintiffs. The common issue is the defendant's negligence; the other issues of contributory negligence and damages are tried individually for each plaintiff.

The court is given wide discretion to order separate trials where joinder would be unfair to a party not sufficiently involved in all the claims.

2. **Joinder of Claims**
The policy of the Federal Rules is to permit the adjudication of all claims between the parties and all claims arising out of a single transaction. A plaintiff can join any number and type of claims against a defendant; when multiple plaintiffs or multiple defendants are involved, it is essential only that at least one of the claims arise out of a transaction in which all were involved.

a. **Successive Claims**
Rule 18(b) permits the plaintiff to join two claims when success on the first is a prerequisite to the second, such as a claim for money damages and a suit to set aside a conveyance that was fraudulent because of the debt asserted in the first claim.

b. Jurisdiction

When jurisdiction is based on the diversity of citizenship between the plaintiff and defendant, the plaintiff may aggregate all claims she has against the defendant to satisfy the jurisdictional amount. When jurisdiction is based on a "federal question" claim, a nonfederal claim can be joined only if it is regarded as part of the same case or controversy as the federal claim, *i.e.,* the "pendent" jurisdiction test of state and federal claims arising from a "common nucleus of operative fact."

Example: Plaintiffs claimed that the defendant appropriated plaintiffs' literary work in such a way as to (i) infringe federal law copyright, and (ii) constitute state law unfair competition. There was federal pendent jurisdiction over the state claim. [Hurn v. Oursler, 289 U.S. 238 (1933)]

c. Class Actions

1) Prerequisites

Rule 23 takes a functional approach to the class action device. Named representatives will be permitted to sue on behalf of a class if:

a) The class is so ***numerous*** that joinder of all members is ***impracticable***;

b) There are ***questions of law or fact*** common to the class;

c) The ***named parties' interests are typical*** of the class;

d) The named representatives will ensure the ***fair and adequate representation*** of the interests of absent members of the class [Fed. R. Civ. P. 23(a)]; and

e) The action meets ***any*** of the following requirements of Rule 23(b):

(1) Separate actions by class members would create a ***risk of inconsistent results*** or, as a practical matter, ***would impair the interests of other absent members of the class***; or

(2) A defendant has acted or refused to act on grounds applicable to the class and ***injunctive or declaratory relief is appropriate*** for the class as a whole (*e.g.,* most civil rights actions); or

(3) There are ***questions of fact or law common to members*** of the class that ***predominate*** over individual issues and a class action is superior to the alternative methods of adjudication.

2) Consideration in Treating Case as a Class Action

The court should determine at an early practicable time whether the action may be maintained as a class action, *i.e.,* whether to "certify" a class, but may determine at any time thereafter that the action is not an appropriate one for class action treatment. In determining whether to treat the case as a class action, the court should consider, inter alia, the following factors: (i) the interest of individual control, (ii) the extent and nature of litigation elsewhere on the same subject, (iii) the desirability of having the whole package in this court, and (iv) the difficulties in managing the class action.

a) **Court Must Define Class Claims, Issues, or Defenses**
The court, in certifying a class, must "define the class and the class claims, issues, or defenses."

b) **Appointment of Class Counsel**
The court must appoint class counsel for every certified class and expressly mandates that the attorney must fairly and adequately represent the interests of the class. [Fed. R. Civ. P. 23(g)(1)]

3) **Effect of Judgment**
All members of a class will be ***bound*** by the judgment rendered in a class action ***except*** those in a "common question" class action [Fed. R. Civ. P. 23(b)(3); *see* (3), *supra*] who notify the court that they do not wish to be bound ("opting out"). Members of Rule 23(b)(1) and 23(b)(2) classes cannot opt out. Note, however, that if the substantive claim of the individual representing the class is mooted, this ***does not*** render the class action moot. [United States Parole Commission v. Geraghty, 445 U.S. 388 (1980)—release from prison of named plaintiff in class action suit challenging parole procedure did not moot entire class action suit]

a) **Personal Jurisdiction Over Absent Class Members Not Required**
The due process/minimum contacts requirements that must be met for the assertion of personal jurisdiction need not be satisfied to bind absent members of the plaintiff class in a Rule 23(b)(3) ("common question") suit who chose not to opt out. [Phillips Petroleum Co. v. Shutts, 472 U.S. 797 (1985)] This allows a state or federal court to bind persons to a class action judgment under Rule 23(b)(3) even though they have no contact at all with the state.

4) **Notice**

a) **Notice Required in Common Question Suits**
Notice to all members of the class ***of the pendency*** of the class action is required under Rule 23 only in ***"common question" suits*** [Fed. R. Civ. P. 23(b)(3)], so that class members can opt out. The notice must state (i) the nature of the action, (ii) the definition of the class, (iii) the class claims, issues, or defenses, and (iv) the binding effect of a class judgment.

b) **Notice Discretionary in Other Types of Class Action Suits**
Notice to members of the class of the pendency of the class action in other class suits is discretionary with the court. [*See* Eisen v. Carlisle & Jacquelin, 417 U.S. 156 (1974); Oppenheimer v. Sanders, 437 U.S. 340 (1978)]

Note: Notice of ***dismissal or compromise*** is a separate notice. It must be given to class members of all types of class actions if the case is dismissed or settled. (*See* 6), *infra*.)

5) **Jurisdiction**

a) **Diversity Action**
In class actions founded on diversity, only the ***citizenship of the named representatives*** of the class is taken into account to establish diversity. The

Supreme Court held that the same rule applies for determining if the amount in controversy requirement is satisfied in a class action that invokes diversity of citizenship—so long as the ***representative's*** claim exceeds $75,000, the class action may proceed in federal court ***even if class members' claims do not exceed $75,000***. [Exxon Mobil Corp. v. Allapattah Services, II.B.3., *supra*] The claims by the class members that do not exceed $75,000 invoke supplemental jurisdiction.

b) Federal Question Action

If the class asserts a claim arising under federal law, it can invoke federal question jurisdiction. In that sort of case, of course, the citizenship of the parties and the amount in controversy are irrelevant. (*See* III., *supra.*)

6) Court Approval

The court must approve the dismissal or settlement of a class action. The class must satisfy the requirements for certification under Rule 23(a) and (b) before a court can approve a class settlement (*see* 1), above). [Amchem Products, Inc. v. Windsor, 521 U.S. 591 (1997)]

a) Notice of Dismissal or Settlement

Moreover, notice of the proposed dismissal or settlement must be given to all members of the class in a manner as directed by the court. [Fed. R. Civ. P. 23(e)] This notice is required in all types of class actions, unless the judgment will not bind the class. The purpose of notice to class members is to allow them to object to the proposed dismissal or settlement when the court holds a "fairness hearing" to determine whether to approve the dismissal or settlement. (*See* below.)

b) Procedures for Settlements of Class Action Suits

Rule 23(e) requires a settlement hearing (usually called a "fairness hearing") if the judgment will bind the class and permits settlement only if the court finds the terms to be fair, reasonable, and adequate. The court must make a finding supporting its conclusion that the settlement meets that standard. Parties seeking approval of a settlement must inform the court of any collateral agreements made in connection with the class settlement.

(1) "Opt Out" Provision

The court may refuse to approve a settlement of a Rule 23(b)(3) class action if members are not provided a new opportunity to opt out. Thus, members who received notice of the pendency of the class action (*see* 4), above) but refused to opt out may be permitted a second opportunity to opt out, essentially to reject the terms of the settlement and proceed on their own.

c) Appeal of Approval of Settlement

A class member who objects to the approval of settlement may bring an appeal of the approval of settlement. [Devlin v. Scardelletti, 536 U.S. 1 (2002)]

7) Appeal of Class Action Certification Decision

Although a court's order granting or denying the certification of a class is not a final judgment in the case, a party may seek review of the decision in the court of appeals under Rule 23(f). (*See* IX.C.6., *infra*.)

d. Class Action Fairness Act

The Class Action Fairness Act ("CAFA") relaxes federal jurisdictional requirements for ***some*** class actions in an effort to make it easier for class action plaintiffs to file in federal court and for class action defendants to remove class actions from state to federal court. (Congress had concluded that some state courts had certified class actions inappropriately and that greater access to federal courts would protect defendants from such perceived abuses.)

1) Subject Matter Jurisdiction Under the CAFA

Under the CAFA, subject matter jurisdiction is established if:

a) ***Any*** class member (not just the representative, but anyone in the plaintiff class) is of diverse citizenship from ***any*** defendant;

b) The amount in controversy ***in the aggregate*** (*i.e.*, adding all the class claims together) ***exceeds $5 million***; and

c) There are at least ***100 members*** in the proposed class or classes.

2) Removal Under the CAFA

Additionally, in a case falling under the CAFA, ***any*** defendant, rather than ***all*** defendants, may remove the case from state to federal court. Moreover, there is no in-state defendant limitation on removal—the case may be removed under the CAFA even if a defendant is a citizen of the forum.

3) Excluded Actions

a) Primary Defendants Are States or Governmental Entities

There is no federal court jurisdiction under the CAFA if the primary defendants are states, state officials, or other governmental entities against whom the court may be foreclosed from ordering relief.

b) Claims Based on Securities Laws or Regarding Corporate Governance

There is no federal court jurisdiction under the CAFA over a class action that ***solely*** involves a claim under ***federal securities laws***, or that relates to the ***internal affairs of a corporation and is based on the laws of the state of incorporation***.

4) Local Considerations May Defeat Jurisdiction

The CAFA has some provisions designed to defeat federal jurisdiction in class actions that are relatively local in nature. These provisions contain some unclear terms.

a) Mandatory Decline of Jurisdiction

A district court ***must*** decline jurisdiction provided by the CAFA if: (i) ***more than two-thirds*** of the members of the proposed plaintiff class ***are citizens of the state in which the action was filed***; (ii) ***a defendant*** from whom

"significant relief" is sought is ***a citizen of that state***; and (iii) the ***"principal injuries"*** were incurred ***in the state in which the action was filed***.

b) **Discretionary Decline of Jurisdiction**
A district court ***may*** decline jurisdiction provided by the CAFA if ***more than one-third but less than two-thirds*** of the proposed plaintiff class are ***citizens of the state in which the action was filed*** and the ***"primary defendants" are also citizens of that state***. In that case, the court considers a variety of factors, including whether the claims involve matters of national interest, whether the claims will be governed by the law of the state in which it was filed, and whether the state has a "distinct nexus" with the class members, the alleged harm, or the defendants.

5) **Protections Under the CAFA**
The CAFA adds a number of protections that apply to settlements in ***all*** class actions in federal court.

a) **Coupon Settlements**
Sometimes, class action settlements provide that the class members are to receive coupons good for purchase of further goods or services from the defendant. The court may approve such a settlement only after ***holding a hearing*** and ***making a finding that the settlement is fair***, and it may also require that ***unclaimed coupons be distributed to charitable organizations***. If attorneys' fees in such cases are to be based on the value of the settlement to the class, they must be limited to the value of the coupons actually redeemed by class members, rather than the total amount available to class members. Alternatively, attorneys' fees can be based on the amount of time class counsel reasonably expended on the action.

b) **Protection Against Loss by Class Members**
In some consumer class actions, some class members have actually lost money, because attorneys' fee awards required them to pay the lawyers more than they received from the settlement. A court may approve a settlement that would have that effect only if it makes a written finding that nonmonetary benefits to the class member ***substantially outweigh*** the monetary loss.

c) **Protection Against Discrimination Based on Geographic Location**
The court may not approve a settlement that provides larger payouts for some class members than others solely because the benefitted class members are located closer to the court.

d) **Notification of Federal and State Officials**
Settling defendants are required to give notice of proposed settlements to identified federal and state officials. Final approval of the proposed settlement may not be issued until at least 90 days after the notice is served. A class member who demonstrates that required notice was not provided may choose not to be bound by the settlement.

e. **Shareholder Derivative Suits**

1) **Minority Shareholder Allegations**
Under Rule 23.1, a minority shareholder, suing on behalf of other minority shareholders to enforce some right of the corporation which the corporation refuses to assert, ***must allege*** in a ***verified*** complaint that:

(i) She was ***a shareholder at the time*** of the transaction complained of (or received her shares thereafter by operation of law);

(ii) The action is not a ***collusive*** effort to confer jurisdiction on the court that it would otherwise lack; and

(iii) She made a ***demand on the directors*** and, if required by state law, on the shareholders, or the reasons why she did not make such demands. For this requirement, facts must be pleaded with particularity.

Rule 23.1, like Rule 23, requires that the class representative be able to fairly and adequately represent the class.

2) **Corporation Named as Defendant**
The corporation must be named as a defendant if those who control the corporation are antagonistic to the action sought by the plaintiffs. If not so named, the court will align the corporation as a defendant to reflect the antagonism.

3) **Jurisdictional Amount and Venue**
The judgment runs to the corporation; therefore, the jurisdictional amount looks to the damages allegedly suffered by the corporation. By statute, venue is proper wherever the corporation could have sued the same defendants (*i.e.,* usually in the state of its incorporation). [28 U.S.C. §1401]

4) **Court Approval**
The court must approve the dismissal or settlement of a derivative suit.

f. **Interpleader**

1) **Purpose Is to Avoid Double Liability**
Interpleader permits a person in the position of a stakeholder to require two or more claimants to litigate among themselves to determine which, if any, has the valid claim where separate actions might result in double liability on a single obligation. Interpleader is available under Rule 22 and under the Federal Interpleader Statute. [28 U.S.C. §1335]

2) **Rights of Plaintiff Stakeholder**
The plaintiff stakeholder does not have to admit liability to any claimant and the claims do not have to have common origin. Once the court has allowed interpleader, a trial by jury is available to determine the issues of fact.

3) **Jurisdiction**

a) **Rule 22 Interpleader**
If Rule 22 interpleader is relied on, the normal rules as to subject matter

jurisdiction apply. Therefore, there must be either a federal question claim, or complete diversity between the stakeholder and the claimants and more than $75,000 in controversy.

b) **Federal Interpleader Statute**
Under the Federal Interpleader Statute, on the other hand, the jurisdictional requirements are less restrictive. The federal statute permits jurisdiction where the amount in controversy is $500 or more and where there is diversity between ***any two*** contending claimants. Venue lies where any claimant resides, and process may be served anywhere in the United States under the statute (but not under Rule 22). The plaintiff stakeholder must deposit the amount in controversy (or a bond) with the court.

g. **Intervention**
Intervention may be granted to a party of right or permissively.

1) **Intervention of Right**
Intervention of right is available whenever the applicant claims an interest in the property or transaction that is the subject matter of the action, and the disposition of the action without her may impair her ability to protect that interest (unless her interest is already represented). The possible *stare decisis* effect of a judgment may be sufficient "interest" to authorize intervention of right. Traditionally, intervention of right invoked ancillary jurisdiction, so that no independent basis of subject matter jurisdiction was required over claims by or against the intervenor of right. Under the supplemental jurisdiction statute, however, it appears that there is ***no*** supplemental (ancillary) jurisdiction over claims by or against one seeking to intervene in a diversity action. The United States has a right of intervention in all cases where the constitutionality of a United States statute is raised.

2) **Permissive Intervention**
Permissive intervention is available when the applicant's claim or defense and the main action have a question of fact or law in common; no direct personal or pecuniary interest is required. A claim in permissive intervention must not destroy complete diversity (if it does, intervention will be denied), and ***must be supported by its own jurisdictional ground***.

3) **Caveat**
In all cases of intervention, the application must be timely, a matter within the court's discretion.

h. **Third-Party Practice (Impleader)**

1) **Claims for Indemnity or Contribution**
A defending party may implead a nonparty, but only if the nonparty is or may be liable to her for any part of a judgment that the plaintiff may recover against her. Usually, such an impleader claim will be for indemnity or contribution. If the indemnity or contribution claim by the defending party against the third-party defendant does not meet the requirements for diversity of citizenship or federal question jurisdiction, it will invoke supplemental (ancillary) jurisdiction, because

such claims will meet ***the "common nucleus of operative fact" requirement of supplemental (ancillary) jurisdiction***. (*See* II.A.5., 6.e., *supra*.) Thus, the defending party may assert an indemnity or contribution claim in federal court even if there is no diversity between the defending party and the third-party defendant and the third-party claim is based on state law. Furthermore, ***venue need not be proper*** for the third-party defendant.

2) Non-Indemnity or Non-Contribution Claims

As part of the third-party complaint, the third-party plaintiff (*i.e.*, the original defending party) may join ***other*** (non-indemnity or non-contribution) claims she may have against the third-party defendant. ***If these other claims cannot invoke diversity of citizenship or federal question jurisdiction, they would also need to invoke supplemental (ancillary) jurisdiction*** (*see* II.A.5., 6.e., *supra*), although it is less likely that the "common nucleus" test could be met.

3) Severance of Third-Party Claims

In any event, ***even if jurisdiction exists***, the court ***may sever any third-party claim*** to be tried separately ***if it is just to do so*** (*e.g.*, if addition of those claims would lead to unfair prejudice to one of the parties).

4) Response of Impleaded Party

After he is joined by the third-party complaint, the third-party defendant may assert defenses to the plaintiff's original claim, as well as defenses to the third-party liability asserted against him.

5) Impleading Insurance Companies

In some states, a defendant may not implead its own insurance company, but if the insurance company denies coverage and refuses to defend, then the defendant may implead the company and have that issue decided in the same case.

i. Cross-Claims

Co-parties may assert claims against each other that arise out of the same transaction or occurrence as the main action by filing cross-claims. Since a cross-claim is, by definition, transactionally related to the existing action, it is commonly considered to come within the court's ancillary (supplemental) jurisdiction at least if the claim is by a defendant against a co-defendant.

G. DUTY OF DISCLOSURE; DISCOVERY

1. Disclosure Requirements

Rule 26 requires parties to disclose certain information to other parties without waiting for a discovery request. However, Rule 26 also has provisions allowing stipulation of the parties or court order to modify some disclosure requirements.

a. Types of Disclosure Required

Before making her disclosures, a party has an obligation to make a reasonable inquiry into the facts of the case. Rule 26 requires parties to disclose all information "then reasonably available" that is not privileged or protected as work product. A party is not relieved from her obligation to disclose merely because she has failed to complete her

investigation or because another party has not made his disclosures or has made inadequate disclosures. Three types of disclosure are required: ***initial*** disclosures, disclosure of ***expert testimony***, and ***pretrial*** disclosures.

1) **Initial Disclosures**
Without waiting for a discovery request, a party must provide to other parties (unless stipulation or court order provides otherwise):

(i) The names, addresses, and telephone numbers of individuals likely to have discoverable information that the disclosing party may use to support its claims or defenses, unless solely for impeachment;

(ii) Copies or descriptions of documents, electronically stored information, and tangible things that are in the disclosing party's possession or control and that the disclosing party may use to support its claims or defenses, unless solely for impeachment;

(iii) A computation of damages claimed by the disclosing party and copies of materials upon which the computation is based; and

(iv) Copies of insurance agreements under which an insurer might be liable for all or part of any judgment that might be entered.

These disclosures must be made ***within 14 days*** after the meeting of the parties required by Rule 26(f) (discussed at H.1., *infra*) unless a different time is set by court order or by stipulation.

a) **Exemptions from Initial Disclosure Requirement**
Initial disclosures are not required in particular types of cases, such as actions to review an administrative record, actions to enforce an arbitration award, pro se litigation brought by prisoners, actions to quash or enforce subpoenas, or habeas corpus petitions. [Fed. R. Civ. P. 26(a)(1)(B)]

2) **Disclosure of Expert Testimony**
A party must also disclose to other parties the identities of expert witnesses expected to be used at trial. This disclosure generally must be accompanied by a report prepared and signed by each expert witness stating her qualifications, the opinions to be expressed, and the basis for those opinions. This disclosure must be made at the time directed by the court or, in the absence of any directions or any stipulations among the parties, at least 90 days before trial; if the evidence is intended solely to rebut another party's disclosure of expert testimony, it must be made within 30 days after disclosure of the evidence being rebutted.

3) **Pretrial Disclosures**
At least 30 days before trial, a party must disclose to the other parties and file with the court a list of the witnesses she expects to call at trial, the witnesses she will call if the need arises, the witnesses whose testimony will be presented by means of a deposition and a transcript of pertinent portions of the deposition, and a list of documents or exhibits she expects to offer or might offer if needed. Within 14 days

after this disclosure, a party may serve objections to use of the depositions at trial and to the admissibility of disclosed documents and exhibits. Such objections are waived if not made at this point, except for objections that the evidence is irrelevant, prejudicial, or confusing under Federal Rules of Evidence 402 and 403.

2. **Discovery of Electronically Stored Data**

The Rules require parties to discuss the discovery and preservation of electronically stored data and to report to the court on those discussions. Electronically stored information need not be produced if the responding party identifies it as from a source not reasonably accessible because of undue burden or cost. On motion to compel or for a protective order, that party must show to the court's satisfaction that its assertion is justified. Even then, the court may order the information produced for good cause, but it may also impose conditions such as cost-shifting or cost-sharing. [Fed. R. Civ. P. 26(b)(2)(B)]

a. **Format for Producing Electronic Documents**

A requesting party may specify the form or forms for producing electronically stored information, and the responding party must use that form unless it objects (but the party must still produce other items to which it has no objections). The court will determine if the objection is valid. If the request does not specify the form for producing electronically stored information, the responding party may use any form in which the information is maintained or a form that is reasonably usable by the requesting party. [Fed. R. Civ. P. 34(b)]

b. **Safe Harbor Provision**

Rule 37(e) creates a safe harbor that would forbid sanctions against parties who lost information in the ordinary course of operating an electronic information system. The party would have to have taken reasonable steps to save the information, however, after it became clear that it would be discoverable in the litigation.

3. **Scope of Disclosure and Discovery**

a. **In General**

Discovery may be had of ***"any nonprivileged matter that is relevant to any party's claim or defense."*** "Any matter" encompasses both documentary evidence and individuals with knowledge of any discoverable matter. Furthermore, as long as the information sought is reasonably calculated to lead to the discovery of admissible evidence, it is not required that the information itself be admissible at trial. [Fed. R. Civ. P. 26(b)(1)]

Note: The requirement that the information sought be relevant to a claim or defense is narrower than a previous provision that the information be "relevant to the subject matter involved in the pending action." Henceforth, this broader scope is appropriate only if the court so orders, for good cause shown.

b. **Trial Preparation Materials**

Work product of a party or a representative of a party (*e.g.*, a lawyer) made ***in anticipation of litigation*** is discoverable only upon showing ***"substantial need"*** and to ***avoid***

"undue hardship" in obtaining materials in an alternative way. If the court orders the disclosure of work product, it must take steps to avoid the disclosure of mental impressions, conclusions, opinions, or legal theories of the disclosing party. However, a party may obtain, without a court order and without showing need and hardship, a copy of any statement previously made by ***that party***. Draft reports and disclosures of experts identified in required disclosures are work product. Confidential communications between such experts and counsel for the party are generally protected under the lawyer-client privilege, except for communications relating to the expert's compensation or to facts or data the attorney provided to the expert. [Fed. R. Civ. P. 26(b)]

1) Procedure for Claiming Privilege

When a party claims that certain discoverable information is privileged trial preparation material, he still must disclose the existence of, but not the content of, the information to the opposing party so that the opposing party may assess the claim of privilege.

2) Inadvertent Disclosure of Trial Preparation Materials

If a party inadvertently discloses trial preparation material to opposing parties, he may still invoke a claim of privilege by notifying the opposing parties of the inadvertent disclosure and the basis for the claim of privilege. Once so notified, the opposing party may not use or disclose the trial preparation material until the claim of privilege is resolved, and he must take reasonable steps to retrieve the material if he disclosed it to others before being notified of the privilege.

c. Experts

A party may depose experts who are expected to be called at trial (***testifying experts***). The opinions of experts who are retained in anticipation of litigation but who are not expected to testify at trial (***consulting experts***) may be discovered only upon a showing of exceptional circumstances under which it is impracticable to obtain facts or opinions by other means. [Fed. R. Civ. P. 26(b)(4)]

d. Protective Orders

Protective orders may be obtained under Rule 26(c) to limit the nature and scope of examination or to terminate examination if discovery is abused.

e. Supplementation of Disclosures and Discovery Responses

A party ***must*** timely supplement required disclosures and prior responses to interrogatories, requests for production, or requests for admissions if she learns that the information disclosed was materially incomplete or incorrect and the new information has not been made known to the other party in discovery or in writing. The duty to supplement also applies to an expert's reports and information from any deposition of an expert. [Fed. R. Civ. P. 26(e)]

4. Types of Discovery

a. Pre-Action Depositions

Prior to a lawsuit being filed, or while an appeal is pending, a potential party or party to an appeal may ask the court to order the deposition of any person in order ***to perpetuate***

her testimony. To obtain the order prior to trial, the potential party must file a verified petition in the federal court for the judicial district in which ***any expected adverse party resides***.

1) **Contents of Petition**
The request for a court order is included within the petition itself. The petition also must show that, among other things, the petitioner ***expects to be a party*** to an action cognizable in a court in the United States but is ***presently unable*** to bring it or cause it to be brought. All expected adverse parties must be named.

2) **Notice and Appointed Counsel**
At least ***21 days*** before the hearing date for the court order, the potential party must serve each expected adverse party with a copy of the petition and a notice of hearing. The manner of service is the same as for an original petition (*see* VII.B., *supra*). If the expected adverse party cannot be so served, the court must appoint counsel for that party.

3) **Court Order**
If the court finds that ordering a deposition may prevent a failure or delay of justice, it will issue an order that specifies the person being deposed, the subject matter of the deposition, and the manner of the deposition.

b. **Discovery of Documents and Things; Orders for Physical and Mental Examinations**

1) **Oral Deposition of a Witness, Including a Party-Witness**
A common form of discovery is the oral deposition under Rule 30. If the deponent is not available at trial, it may be used in lieu of her appearance as a witness. The deposition may be recorded by sound, sound and visual, or stenographic means. Depositions may be taken by telephone or through other remote electronic devices. All parties may pose questions to the deponent. A party may not take more than ***10 depositions,*** nor may she depose the same person more than once, without leave of court or stipulation of the parties. A deposition may not exceed "one day of seven hours" absent court order or stipulation to the contrary.

a) **Compulsory Appearance of Witnesses**

(1) **Subpoena Not Needed for Parties**
It is not necessary to serve a subpoena on an adverse party or an officer, director, or managing agent of a party to compel appearance; the notice of deposition is sufficient to compel attendance. For organizations, the notice may name the organization and state with "reasonable particularity" the matters to be covered. The organization then designates individuals to testify. [Fed. R. Civ. P. 30(b)(6), 37]

(2) **Nonparties Should Be Subpoenaed**
If the witness to be deposed is not a party to the action, he should be subpoenaed. The subpoena may be served by any person who is not a party and is not less than 18 years old. Service is made by delivering a copy of the subpoena with any necessary fees to the person named in

the subpoena. A nonparty organization may be required by subpoena to designate individuals to testify, as in (1), *supra*. [Fed. R. Civ. P. 30(b)(6), 45(b)]

(3) Costs When Notifying Party Fails to Attend

When the party who notices the deposition does not appear (in person or by an attorney) to take the deposition, and the other party does appear, the latter can obtain his costs of attending, including reasonable attorneys' fees.

2) Deposition of Witnesses on Written Questions

Rule 31 provides for written questions to witnesses (including parties) and is designed to facilitate the depositions of witnesses living a great distance from the parties. All parties can pose questions to the deponent. A party may not take more than ***10 depositions,*** nor may she depose the same person more than once, without leave of court or stipulation of the parties.

3) Interrogatories to the Parties

Rule 33 provides for written interrogatories to other parties and written answers by the party to whom the interrogatories are directed. The party must respond not only with facts which she herself knows, but also with facts that are available to her. The party may also be asked to give opinions, even on the application of law to facts. Initially, the requesting party may not serve more than ***25 interrogatories including subparts*** without court order or stipulation, and leave may be granted to serve additional ones.

4) Production of Physical Material; Inspection

Rule 34 provides (i) for the production by a ***party*** (or, if accompanied by a subpoena, a nonparty) of physical material, including documents, relevant to the pending action; and (ii) that a party be required to permit entry onto land for relevant testing.

5) Physical and Mental Examinations

a) Order for Examination

Rule 35 provides for an independent physical or mental examination of a party when that party's physical or mental condition is in controversy. Such exam is available only if ordered by the court, on showing of good cause. Traditionally, this rule has allowed exams only by "physicians." Now, however, it allows exams by a "suitably licensed or certified examiner," which would include, for example, doctors, dentists, occupational therapists, and any others required to be licensed and qualified to comment on a physical or mental condition.

b) Report of Findings

The person examined may request a copy of the examiner's report, but if that person so requests or takes a deposition of the examiner, she waives any privilege and must produce, upon demand, copies of her own doctor's reports of any other examinations of the same condition.

6) **Requests for Admission**
Any party may serve on any other party a written request for admission as to the truth or genuineness of any matter or document described in the request. The matters will be considered admitted unless the party upon whom the request was served returns a sworn statement denying the truth of the matters set forth in the request, or explaining why she cannot admit or deny them. Alternatively, the party upon whom the request was served can file written objections to those requests that she has a legal basis for not answering. A party may be asked to admit matters that are genuine issues for trial. The admission is for the purpose of the pending action only and may not be used against the party in any other proceeding. [Fed. R. Civ. P. 36]

5. **Enforcing Disclosure and Discovery**

a. **Motion to Compel and Sanctions for Violation of Order to Compel**

1) **Motion to Compel Disclosures and Discovery**
If a party fails to provide discovery or provides incomplete discovery (including disclosures and answers to interrogatories and deposition questions), the other party may move to compel discovery. A motion to compel must certify that the moving party has made a good faith attempt to obtain the discovery. [Fed. R. Civ. P. 37]

2) **Sanctions for Violation of Order to Compel**
If a party fails to comply with an order to provide discovery, the court may: (i) order the matters to be treated as admitted; (ii) prohibit the party from supporting or opposing designated claims or defenses; (iii) strike pleadings, stay or dismiss the action, or render a default judgment; or (iv) hold the delinquent party or witness in contempt (but the contempt sanction may not be used for refusal to submit to a physical or mental examination). The court may also assess reasonable expenses incurred because of the refusal, including attorneys' fees. [Fed. R. Civ. P. 37(b)]

b. **Immediate Sanction**
If a party fails to attend his own deposition or fails to provide ***any*** answers to interrogatories, a party may move for ***immediate sanctions*** (as opposed to moving to compel discovery). The motion must certify that the moving party has made a good faith attempt to obtain the answers. In response to a motion for immediate sanctions, the court may make such orders in regard to the failure as are "just," including: (i) ordering the matters to be treated as admitted; (ii) prohibiting the party from supporting or opposing designated claims or defenses; and (iii) striking pleadings, staying or dismissing the action, or rendering a default judgment. [Fed. R. Civ. P. 37(d)]

c. **Automatic Sanction**
The Rules also provide for an ***automatic sanction*** against a party who "without substantial justification" fails to disclose information as required under Rule 26, or who fails to supplement or amend discovery responses under Rule 26(e) (*see* 3.e.,

supra). Rule 37 provides that the party who fails to make required disclosures will not be permitted to use the information withheld as evidence at trial, at a hearing, or on a motion, unless such failure was "harmless." The court may impose other appropriate sanctions, including: (i) ordering the matters to be treated as admitted; (ii) prohibiting the party from supporting or opposing designated claims or defenses; (iii) striking pleadings, staying or dismissing the action, or rendering a default judgment; and (iv) informing the jury of the failure to make the disclosure. [Fed. R. Civ. P. 37(c)]

Note: Apparently, the failure to make required disclosures under Rule 26 may result in either a motion to compel or automatic sanctions.

6. Use of Depositions at Trial or Hearing

Subject to the rules of evidence, a deposition may be used (at trial or in a hearing) against any party who was present at the deposition or had notice of it:

(i) ***To impeach*** the testimony of the deponent as a witness;

(ii) For any purpose if the court finds that the deponent (including a party-deponent) is ***dead,*** at a distance greater than ***100 miles*** from the place of trial (unless the absence was procured by the party offering the deposition), or ***unable to testify*** because of age, sickness, etc.; or

(iii) For any purpose if the ***deponent is an adverse party***.

[Fed. R. Civ. P. 32]

7. Errors and Irregularities in Depositions

Rule 32 governs the waiver of errors and irregularities in the taking of depositions.

a. As to Notice

Errors and irregularities relating to the notice of deposition are waived unless written objection is promptly served on the party giving notice.

b. As to Manner of Taking

Errors of any kind which could have been obviated if promptly presented are waived unless ***seasonable*** objection is made at the time of taking the deposition (applies to form of questions, oath, conduct of parties, etc.).

c. As to Completion and Return

Errors and irregularities as to the completion and return of the deposition are waived unless a motion to suppress is made with reasonable promptness after the error was or should have been discovered (applies to signing, sealing, certification, and transmittal).

d. As to Form of Written Questions

Objections to the form of written questions are waived unless served on the party propounding them within the time for serving succeeding questions and within five days after service of the last questions authorized.

H. PRETRIAL CONFERENCES

1. **Rule 26(f) Conference of Parties—Planning for Discovery**
As soon as practicable, and in any event at least 21 days before a scheduling conference is held or the scheduling order required by Rule 16(b) is due (*see* below), the parties must confer to consider their ***claims and defenses,*** the ***possibility of settlement, initial disclosures,*** and a ***discovery plan.*** The parties must submit to the court a proposed discovery plan within 14 days after the conference addressing the timing and form of required disclosures, the subjects on which discovery may be needed, the timing of and limitations on discovery, and relevant orders that may be required of the court.

2. **Rule 16(b) Scheduling Conference**
The court must (except in classes of cases exempted by local rule) hold a scheduling conference among the parties or counsel. The conference may be held by telephone, mail, or other suitable means. The court must, within 90 days after the appearance of a defendant and within 120 days after the complaint has been served on a defendant, enter a scheduling order limiting the time for ***joinder***, ***motions***, and ***discovery***. The order may also include dates for ***pretrial conferences***, ***a trial date***, and ***any other appropriate matters***. This schedule cannot be modified except by leave of court upon a showing of good cause. [Fed. R. Civ. P. 16(b)]

3. **Pretrial Conferences**
The court may also hold pretrial conferences as necessary to expedite trial and foster settlement. A ***final pretrial conference***, if any, is held as close to the time of trial as reasonable, and is for the purpose of formulating a plan for the trial, including the admission of evidence. This conference is to be attended by at least one of the lawyers for each side who will actually be conducting the trial, and by any unrepresented parties. After a pretrial conference, an order must be entered that ***controls the subsequent course of events*** in the case. Thus, the final pretrial conference order is a blueprint for the trial, usually listing witnesses to be called, evidence to be presented, factual and legal issues needing resolution, and like matters. It is thus said to supersede the pleadings and may be modified only for good cause.

4. **Sanctions**
A party or counsel may be sanctioned for failure to attend a conference or obey an order entered pursuant to a conference, for being substantially unprepared to participate in a conference, or for acting in bad faith. The court has a broad range of available sanctions including contempt, striking pleadings, and prohibiting the introduction of evidence. In addition, the court shall require the disobedient party or counsel to pay expenses incurred (including attorneys' fees) by other parties, unless the court finds that circumstances make such an award unjust.

I. ALTERNATIVE DISPUTE RESOLUTION

Alternative dispute resolution ("ADR") is a process in which a neutral person resolves a dispute or helps the parties to resolve their dispute. Examples of these processes include contractual arbitration, judicial arbitration, and mediation.

1. **Contractual Arbitration**
The Federal Arbitration Act ("FAA") governs written arbitration agreements involving interstate or international commerce and preempts conflicting state law. [9 U.S.C. §§1 *et seq.*]

a. Procedure

A written agreement to arbitrate a dispute is valid and enforceable unless a contractual ground for revocation exists (*e.g.*, fraud in the inducement of the arbitration clause, illegality, or unconscionability). Court proceedings are stayed until the arbitration proceedings are completed. The appointment of the arbitrator usually will be provided for in the arbitration agreement. At the arbitration proceeding, the arbitrator can subpoena witnesses and require them to bring documentary evidence to the hearing. After the arbitrator renders the award, a party can move to have the court confirm the award. The opposing party may move to vacate the arbitration award on the grounds below. If the award is confirmed, it is considered to be final and binding, and it is enforceable as a court judgment.

1) Judicial Review of Award

An arbitration award may be vacated, even on appeal, on narrow statutory grounds, such as ***fraud, evident partiality of the arbitrator, the arbitrator's refusal to delay proceedings for sufficient cause, or not following the arbitration agreement to such a degree as to affect the outcome.*** A party may also move to modify the award ***to correct miscalculations, to modify awards that go beyond the scope of the arbitration agreement, or to correct minor imperfections of form***. Additionally, an arbitration award also may be overturned when it represents a ***manifest disregard of the law***, a judicially created and extremely deferential standard that requires the complaining party to show that the arbitrator knew the applicable law but chose to disregard it.

2. Judicial Arbitration

"Judicial arbitration" is a dispute-resolution process conducted by a neutral person under the auspices of the court in an attempt to resolve the action without trial. Judicial arbitration may be employed by federal courts under local district court rules. At the federal level, participation in arbitration procedures is voluntary, and even then certain actions (cases involving a violation of constitutional rights, certain civil rights actions, and cases alleging an amount in controversy of more than $150,000) may not be referred to ADR even if the parties consent. Within 30 days of the arbitration award, a party may reject the award and request trial de novo. Any evidence that the case was arbitrated is generally excluded. [28 U.S.C. §§654 *et seq.*]

3. Mediation

Mediation involves the use of a neutral person to help parties to a dispute reach a mutually acceptable agreement. The mediator does not have decisionmaking power; his role is to facilitate the process by which the parties reach their own voluntary agreement. In federal court, mediation is accomplished by local district rule. By local rule, mediation may be made mandatory for certain cases. [28 U.S.C. §§651, 652]

J. TRIAL

1. Jury Trial Problems

Rule 38 requires a party who desires a jury trial (on some or all fact issues) to file a written demand with the court and serve it on the parties. (Such demand may be indorsed upon a pleading of the party.) Failure to make such a demand within 14 days after the service of the pleading in which the jury-triable issue arose constitutes a ***waiver*** by that party of any right to trial by jury. A court may, within its discretion, order a trial by jury if the plaintiff's waiver was not intentional. In the absence of compelling reasons to the contrary, a court should grant relief from waiver if the issue is one normally tried by a jury. [Cox v. Masland & Sons, Inc., 607 F.2d 138 (5th Cir. 1979)] A jury demand may be withdrawn only if ***all*** parties consent.

a. **Right to Jury Trial**

The Seventh Amendment preserves the right to a jury trial in federal courts of facts in all "suits of common law" where the amount in controversy exceeds $20. The distinction is historical and turns initially on whether the claim or relief was available at law or in equity in 1791. The Supreme Court has demonstrated a clear ***preference for jury trial*** in doubtful cases by holding that:

1) If legal and equitable claims are joined in one action involving common fact issues, the ***legal claim should be tried first to the jury*** and then the equitable claim to the court (the jury's finding on fact issues will bind the court in the equitable claim);

2) If a procedure formerly available only in equity, such as a class suit, interpleader, or derivative action, is now permitted under the Federal Rules for determining a "legal" claim, a ***jury should try the fact issues***;

3) If damages are claimed as part of an action seeking an injunction, the defendant ***cannot be denied a jury on the damages issues*** on the ground that they are "incidental" to the equitable relief; and

4) If a new claim is created that did not exist at common law, a right to a jury trial will exist if the claim is similar to a claim for common law rights and remedies, unless the statute creating the right provides otherwise. [*See, e.g.,* Feltner v. Columbia Pictures Television, Inc., 523 U.S. 340 (1998)—statutory damages under Copyright Act to be tried to jury]

b. **Jury Trials in Diversity Cases**

1) **Right to a Jury Trial**

The federal court ***must permit a jury trial*** in any diversity "suit at common law" even though the state court would deny a jury (the Seventh Amendment prevails over *Erie*); and a federal court will generally ***follow the federal practice*** of submitting issues of fact to the jury even though the state law assigns the issue to the court. [Byrd v. Blue Ridge Electric Cooperative, Inc., II.C.2.b., *supra*] If the state rule requires submission of a fact issue to the jury, the federal court may nonetheless direct a verdict under the usual standards or otherwise follow a federal practice that calls for the court to be the trier of fact. Likewise, state law is disregarded in determining the sufficiency of the evidence to create a jury issue; *i.e.,* the directed verdict standards are always federal.

2) **Motion for New Trial Based on Excessiveness of Verdict**

The Supreme Court has required federal trial courts to apply a state standard when

considering a motion for a new trial based on excessiveness of the verdict. [Gasperini v. Center for Humanities, Inc., II.C.3., *supra*] Under the Seventh Amendment, federal appellate review of whether a trial court properly denied a motion to set aside a verdict as excessive is limited to whether the trial court abused its discretion in denying the motion. In contrast, a jury's determination of the amount of a punitive damage award is reviewed de novo on appeal. [Cooper Industries, Inc. v. Leatherman Tool Group, Inc., 532 U.S. 424 (2001)]

c. **Jury Size and Composition**

In federal civil cases, a jury must have at least six and not more than 12 jurors. [Fed. R. Civ. P. 48] There is no provision for alternate jurors. A juror may be excused for good cause (*e.g.,* illness) without causing a mistrial, so long as at least six jurors participate in reaching the verdict. The verdict must be unanimous unless the parties agree to the contrary. A race-neutral reason is required in exercising peremptory strikes of potential jury members from the panel. [Edmonson v. Leesville Concrete Co., 500 U.S. 614 (1991)] In cases in which the government is a litigant, peremptory challenges must be used for a gender-neutral reason. [J.E.B. v. Alabama, 511 U.S. 127 (1994)] Because striking potential jurors significantly involves the state, this holding will undoubtedly be extended to litigation completely between private parties.

d. **Jury Instructions**

At the close of the evidence, or sooner at the court's direction, a party may file proposed instructions. ***Objections*** to giving or failing to give instructions must be made ***before the jury retires*** to consider a verdict. [Fed. R. Civ. P. 51]

e. **Jury Verdicts**

The trial court has discretion to decide the type of verdict to be used. [Fed. R. Civ. P. 49] Jurors cannot decide a verdict by flipping a coin or averaging (although averaging may be proper as a starting point for discussion).

1) **General Verdict**

In a general verdict, the jury finds for the plaintiff or defendant and gives the amount of damages or relief due. A general verdict implies that all essential issues were found in favor of the prevailing party.

2) **Special Verdict**

In a special verdict, the jury is asked to make a finding on all material conclusions of fact, and the court applies the law. The procedure for a special verdict is to submit to the jury a series of questions regarding each ultimate fact. The court then makes legal conclusions based on those facts. Each question must deal with a single fact only and must not assume the existence of facts in dispute. A party waives objections to the form of the questions if she does not object when they are given. If the court fails, on request, to submit an issue to the jury, the case will be reversed unless the omission was harmless. If no request was made, a jury trial on the issue is generally held to be waived, and the court will decide it. [*See* Fed. R. Civ. P. 49]

3) **General Verdict with Special Interrogatories**

In a general verdict with interrogatories, the jury is asked to give a general verdict

and also to answer specific questions concerning certain ultimate facts in the case. The purpose is to ensure that the jury properly considered the important issues. Interrogatories must be submitted with the general verdict to test the verdict's validity. [*See* Fed. R. Civ. P. 49(b)]

4) **Jury Deliberations**

Jurors may take into the jury room ***all papers or exhibits in evidence and their own notes***. Instructions, pleadings, or other matters are generally improper for use in the jury room, except when they are formally admitted into evidence. A jury may not engage in experiments in the jury room, and jurors may not make private studies of documents or items outside of the jury room. Jurors may not view property or places involved in the case, except by court order. Jurors ***must not communicate with any nonjuror*** regarding the trial; in fact, ***any*** private communication between jurors and counsel or parties is serious misconduct that may lead to a new trial. It is error for a juror, in the jury room, to state facts not in evidence; however, jurors are entitled to evaluate evidence presented in light of their general knowledge and experience.

5) **Erroneous Verdicts**

Inconsistent determinations are erroneous if they are irreconcilable (*e.g.,* when a verdict is rendered against a person vicariously liable and the principal wrongdoer is exonerated). Additionally, when a verdict shows on its face that the jury failed to follow the court's instructions, the verdict may be set aside, and either the jury will be asked to reconsider its verdict or a new trial will be ordered. Any clear compromise verdict falls within this category, as does any verdict that simply finds for the plaintiff "for actual damages suffered."

a) **Correctable Errors**

Correctable errors must be raised by the aggrieved party or they are waived. It is an abuse of discretion for the court to refuse a request that the jury be told to reconsider an improper verdict that can be corrected. A jury may completely change its verdict when redeliberation is ordered. The court may not coerce the jury when ordering redeliberation.

6) **Juror Misconduct**

A new trial is appropriate if the juror ***gave false testimony on voir dire or concealed material facts relating to his qualifications to serve***. A verdict will not be set aside if the alleged misconduct was harmless. ***Nonjurors*** may give evidence of misconduct ***except*** as to declarations of jurors to them. Under Federal Rule of Evidence 606(b), a juror may not testify as to any matter occurring during deliberations, except on the question of whether extraneous prejudicial information was improperly brought to the jury's attention, or whether any outside influence was brought to bear on any juror.

2. **Consolidation and Separate Trials**

Rule 42(a) allows the court to consolidate actions then before it when the actions have a common question of law or fact. Rule 42(b) allows the court to order separate trials of any claim, cross-claim, counterclaim, or other issues when such separation will foster judicial economy.

3. Involuntary Dismissals

On the defendant's motion, a court may order an involuntary dismissal against a plaintiff for failure to: (i) prosecute; (ii) comply with the Federal Rules; or (iii) comply with a court order. [Fed. R. Civ. P. 41(b)] An involuntary dismissal is with prejudice, meaning that it operates as adjudication on the merits, unless the court orders otherwise.

4. Voluntary Dismissals

The plaintiff can give up his case voluntarily by way of a voluntary dismissal, either without leave of court or with leave of court. [Fed. R. Civ. P. 41(a)]

a. Without Leave of Court

If the defendant has not answered or filed a motion for summary judgment, the plaintiff may dismiss her case. She may also voluntarily dismiss on stipulation with the other parties. The plaintiff is charged with costs only if she files the action again after the voluntary dismissal. Furthermore, a voluntary dismissal is without prejudice, unless the plaintiff has previously filed and dismissed a case involving the same claim. Dismissal could be with prejudice, however, if such was a condition of the parties' settlement.

b. With Leave of Court

When a voluntary dismissal without leave of court is not available (*i.e.,* there has been an answer, motion, or previous dismissal), the court has discretion to grant dismissal on such terms and conditions as the court deems proper. The dismissal is without prejudice unless the court specifies otherwise. ***If there is a counterclaim pending in the action, there can be no dismissal over the defendant's objection unless the counterclaim remains pending.***

5. Summary Judgment

a. Standard

Summary judgment shall be granted if, from the pleadings, affidavits, and discovery materials, it appears that there is ***no genuine dispute of material fact*** and the moving party is entitled to judgment as a matter of law. [Fed. R. Civ. P. 56] The court may not decide disputed fact issues on a motion for summary judgment; if there is a disputed material fact, the case must go to trial.

b. Applicable to All Civil Actions

Rule 56 applies to all parties and civil actions that are subject to the Federal Rules including actions by and against the United States, and to all types of claims that appear in a civil action (counterclaim, cross-claim, declaratory judgment, injunction, and interpleader).

c. Time

Unless local rule or court order dictates otherwise, a party may file a motion for summary judgment any time until 30 days after close of all discovery. [Fed. R. Civ. P. 56(b)] If a motion is premature, the court may defer ruling on it.

d. Partial

Summary judgment may be partial (as well as complete).

Example: Summary judgment may be rendered on the issue of liability alone although there is a genuine issue as to the amount of damages.

e. **Support**
The motion may be supported or opposed with affidavits or other declarations made under penalty of perjury, depositions, pleadings, admissions, answers to interrogatories, or other materials in the record.

f. **Affidavits**

1) Affidavits or declarations must: (i) be made on ***personal knowledge***; (ii) set forth such facts as would be ***admissible*** in evidence; and (iii) show the affiant is ***competent to testify***.

2) A party ***may object*** that the material cited to support or dispute a fact ***cannot be presented in a form that would be admissible*** in evidence.

3) If a party fails to support an assertion of fact or fails properly to address another party's assertion of fact, the court may ***consider the fact undisputed*** for purposes of the motion, ***grant summary judgment*** if appropriate, ***give an opportunity to address the fact***, or issue any other appropriate order.

4) When the party opposing the motion shows by affidavit or declaration that he cannot present facts, he ***may state the reasons*** for their unavailability or declarations. The court may then ***deny*** the motion, ***order a continuance*** to permit affidavits to be obtained or depositions to be taken, or ***make such other order*** as is just.

5) When affidavits or declarations are made in ***bad faith***, the court may:

a) Order the party using them to ***reimburse*** the other party for those expenses that the affidavits caused him, including attorneys' fees.

b) Adjudge in ***contempt*** the offending party or attorney.

g. **Nonappealability**
The denial of a motion for summary judgment is generally not appealable.

h. **Relationship to Motion to Dismiss**
A motion pursuant to Rule 12(b)(6) to dismiss a complaint for failure to state a claim upon which relief can be granted differs from a motion for summary judgment in that the former is addressed only to the ***legal sufficiency of the complaint***.

i. **Relationship to Motion for Judgment on the Pleadings**
Similarly, a motion for judgment on the pleadings presents the moving party's contention that ***on the face of the pleadings***, he is entitled to judgment. Theoretically, matters outside the pleadings are irrelevant to a decision on either of these motions. However, a party making such a motion and accompanying it with an affidavit or other matters outside the pleadings may in reality be making a motion for summary judgment, putting the wrong label on the motion. The court is expressly authorized to treat such a motion as one for summary judgment and to conduct subsequent proceedings thereon in accordance with the rule on summary judgment, giving the parties full opportunity to present material made relevant by that rule.

6. **Motion for Judgment as a Matter of Law (Formerly Directed Verdict)**
Historically, a judge could direct a particular verdict whenever the evidence—viewed in the light most favorable to the party against whom the verdict was directed (including legitimate inferences in that party's favor) and without considering the credibility of witnesses—was such that reasonable persons could come to only one conclusion. Today, this can be done pursuant to a party's ***motion for judgment as a matter of law*** ("JMOL"). The motion may be made by any party any time before submission of the case to the jury, and the moving party must specify the judgment sought and the law and facts on which it is entitled to judgment. The motion may be granted only after the nonmoving party ***"has been fully heard"*** on the matter. To grant the motion, the court must find that ***"a reasonable jury would not have a legally sufficient basis*** to find for the party on that issue." [Fed. R. Civ. P. 50(a)]

7. **Renewed Motion for Judgment as a Matter of Law (Formerly Judgment Notwithstanding the Verdict ("JNOV"))**
Historically, a party against whom judgment was entered could move for JNOV if the judgment was based upon a verdict that reasonable persons could not have reached and if the moving party had sought a directed verdict at the close of all the evidence. Now, the motion for JNOV is called a ***renewed motion for judgment as a matter of law***. It must be filed no later than 28 days after entry of judgment and the party making the renewed motion must have moved for judgment as a matter of law ***at some time during the trial***. In theory, a party may raise only those issues raised in the motion for a JMOL. The standard is the same as for the motion for judgment as a matter of law. [Fed. R. Civ. P. 50(b)]

8. **Motion for New Trial**
A motion for a new trial must be filed no later than 28 days after judgment is entered. Within that period, the court may order a new trial on its own motion. [Fed. R. Civ. P. 59]

a. **Reasons for Granting New Trial**
The court may grant a new trial because of an error during the trial (usually going to the admissibility of evidence or the propriety of the instructions), because the verdict is against the weight of the evidence (limited to cases where the judge finds the verdict seriously erroneous), because of juror misconduct, or because the verdict is excessive or inadequate.

1) **Remittitur**
If the trial judge believes that the jury's compensatory damages award is so excessive as to "shock the conscience" (or in a diversity case if the award meets the state standard for excessiveness), the judge may order a new trial or may offer the alternative of remittitur. When offered remittitur, the plaintiff is given the choice between accepting an award less than that given her by the jury or submitting to a new trial. Note that the court cannot simply lower the award given by the jury. It must offer the plaintiff the alternative of a lower award or a new trial. [Hetzel v. Prince Williams County, 523 U.S. 208 (1998)]

2) **Additur**
If the trial judge believes that the jury's compensatory damages are inadequate, she may ***not*** offer the defendant the choice of accepting a higher award or submitting

to a new trial. "Additur" has been held to violate the Seventh Amendment (which is not applicable to the states). However, inadequate damages may be a basis for a new trial.

b. **Renewed Motion for Judgment as a Matter of Law with Motion for New Trial**
When a renewed motion for judgment as a matter of law and a motion for a new trial are made ***in the alternative*** and the renewed motion is granted, the court must rule hypothetically on the new trial motion so that no remand is required if the judgment on the merits ruling is subsequently reversed on appeal.

9. **Effect of Failure to Move for a Renewed Judgment as a Matter of Law or for a New Trial**
If a party fails to move for either a renewed judgment as a matter of law or for a new trial on the basis of insufficiency of the evidence, that party is precluded from raising the question of evidentiary sufficiency on appeal, to support either judgment as a matter of law or a new trial. [Unitherm Food Systems, Inc. v. Swift-Eckrich, Inc., 546 U.S. 394 (2006)]

10. **Judgment on Partial Findings**
In a ***nonjury*** trial, the judge may enter a judgment as a matter of law against a party on any issue whenever there are ***sufficient facts to resolve the issue***, provided that the ***party has been fully heard*** on the issue. If the issue is dispositive of a claim or defense, the judge may enter judgment as a matter of law against a party on that claim or defense. The judge may also wait until the close of all evidence to render judgment. Because the judge is acting as the trier of fact, she decides issues of disputed facts, and she may consider the credibility of witnesses. The judgment must be supported by findings of fact and conclusions of law. [Fed. R. Civ. P. 52]

VIII. ATTACK ON THE JUDGMENT AT THE TRIAL COURT LEVEL

A. RELIEF FROM JUDGMENT OR ORDER

1. **Clerical Mistakes**
A clerical error is one arising from oversight or omission, and may occur in judgments, orders, or other parts of the record. The court can correct clerical errors ***on its own motion or the motion of any party***. [Fed. R. Civ. P. 60(a)] There is no time limit for the correction of clerical errors, and the court order correcting the error dates back to the time judgment was entered. As a result, the battle over what constitutes a clerical error is acute.

2. **Defendant Not Personally Notified**
A defendant over whom personal jurisdiction was necessary and acquired, but who did not in fact have knowledge of the pendency of the action, may enter an appearance within one year after the final judgment. If the defendant shows reasons justifying relief from the judgment and innocent third persons will not be prejudiced, the court may relieve the defendant from the judgment for which personal jurisdiction was necessary, on payment of costs and on conditions the court deems just.

3. **Other Grounds for Relief from Judgment**
On motion and just terms, the court may relieve a party from a final judgment or order on the following grounds:

(i) ***Mistake, inadvertence, surprise, or excusable neglect***;

(ii) ***Newly discovered evidence*** that by due diligence ***could not have been discovered*** in time to move for a new trial;

(iii) ***Fraud, misrepresentation, or other misconduct*** of an adverse party;

(iv) The judgment is ***void***;

(v) The judgment has been ***satisfied, released, or discharged***; a ***prior judgment*** on which it is based has been ***reversed or otherwise vacated***; or it is ***no longer equitable*** that the judgment should have prospective application; or

(vi) ***Any other reason*** justifying relief from the operation of the judgment.

For grounds (i), (ii), and (iii), the motion must be made within one year; for the other grounds, the motion must be made within a reasonable time. [Fed. R. Civ. P. 60(b)] *Note:* Ground (iv) does not apply simply because the judgment was erroneous; such errors are to be remedied on appeal. Ground (iv) applies only if there was a fundamental flaw such as lack of jurisdiction or deprivation of due process by failure to give notice or opportunity to be heard. [United Student Aid Funds, Inc. v. Espinoza, 130 S. Ct. 1367 (2010)]

B. INDEPENDENT ACTION IN EQUITY TO SET ASIDE THE JUDGMENT

A court, in its discretion, may entertain an independent action to relieve a party from a judgment or order, to grant relief to a defendant not actually personally notified of the action, or to set aside a judgment for fraud on the court. The plaintiff must show that he is likely to win if a new action is allowed. The only advantage of an independent action is that it will not be barred by the specific time limits outlined in A., above. However, the aggrieved party must act promptly once he knows or should know of the ground for relief. An independent action will be rejected if a motion to set aside the judgment has been rejected on the merits.

IX. FINAL JUDGMENT AND APPELLATE REVIEW

A. JUDGMENT

1. Relief that May Be Given

Except in default cases, the court is not limited to the demand for relief in the pleadings and may give ***any relief*** that is appropriate based on the evidence. Thus, damages may exceed the plaintiff's demand and an injunction may be entered although not requested. Interest on a money judgment is awarded at the rate provided under state law from the date of judgment.

2. Judgment on Multiple Claims or Parties

When multiple claims or multiple parties are involved in an action, the court may enter a final judgment as to fewer than all of the claims or parties only upon (i) an express determination that there is no just reason for delay, and (ii) an express direction for the entry of judgment. ***Unless*** the trial judge makes such an ***express determination***, the order determining the merits of fewer than all of the claims or dismissing fewer than all of the parties

is ***not a final judgment and is not appealable***. This is in accord with the traditional policy against piecemeal appeals. [Fed. R. Civ. P. 54(b)]

3. **Final Decision on Merits May Be Valid Despite Lack of Subject Matter Jurisdiction**
Occasionally, lack of subject matter jurisdiction is not raised until the decision is final and all appeals are completed. The question then is whether the decision may be collaterally attacked—*i.e.,* be set aside in an independent proceeding or treated as invalid in a later case. The factors that must be balanced in making this determination are: (i) lack of jurisdiction is clear; (ii) jurisdiction depends on a question of law, not fact; (iii) the court is of limited, not general, jurisdiction; (iv) the question of jurisdiction was not litigated; and (v) strong policy exists against the court acting beyond its jurisdiction.

B. TIME FOR APPEALS

Under Rules 3 and 4 of the Federal Rules of Appellate Procedure, an appeal may be taken by filing a notice of appeal with the district court ***within 30 days*** from the entry of the judgment appealed from (60 days where the United States is a party to the action). However, if a ***timely*** renewed motion for judgment as a matter of law (formerly a motion for JNOV) or motion for new trial is made, or if a motion to set aside or amend the judgment is made within 28 days of judgment, the running of the 30 days is terminated. Upon the entry of an order based on such post-trial motions, a new 30-day period begins to run. However, a notice of appeal filed during the pendency of such a post-trial motion will become effective on final disposition of the motion by the trial court. Upon a showing of excusable neglect, made within 30 days after the time to appeal has expired, the district court may extend the time for filing a notice of appeal by 30 days from the time it would otherwise have run, or 14 days from the date of the order granting the extension, whichever is later.

C. REVIEWABLE ORDER

Generally, ***only final orders*** are reviewable on appeal. A final order is one that disposes of the whole case on its merits, by rendering final judgment not only as to all the parties but as to all causes of action involved. [Cunningham v. Hamilton County, 527 U.S. 198 (1999)—order imposing sanctions on attorney is not a final order even when the attorney no longer represents a party to the case] However, certain interlocutory orders are ***also reviewable***:

1. **Interlocutory Orders as of Right**

a. **Injunction**
A party may appeal as of right any order granting, continuing, modifying, refusing, dissolving, or refusing to dissolve or modify an injunction.

b. **Receivers**
A party may appeal as of right any order appointing a receiver, or refusing to wind up or take steps to accomplish purposes of receiverships (*e.g.,* directing sales or other disposals of property).

c. **Admiralty**
An order finding liability but leaving damages to be assessed later in admiralty cases may be appealed.

d. **Patent Infringement**
A patent infringement order where only an accounting is wanting may be appealed.

e. **Property Possession**
A party may appeal as of right any order whereby possession of property is changed or affected, such as orders dissolving writs of attachment and the like.

2. **Interlocutory Appeals Act**
Review under the Interlocutory Appeals Act [28 U.S.C. §1292] is ***discretionary*** and may be available when: (i) the trial judge certifies that the interlocutory order involves a controlling question of law, as to which there is substantial ground for difference of opinion, and immediate appeal from the order may materially advance the ultimate termination of the litigation; and (ii) the court of appeals then agrees to allow the appeal. A party obtaining such a certificate from the trial judge must, within ***10 days,*** apply to the court of appeals, where two out of three judges must agree with the trial judge.

3. **Fewer than All Claims or Parties**
(*See* A.2., *supra.*)

4. **Collateral Order Rule**
If the claim or issue is separable from and collateral to the main suit and is too important to require deferring appellate review, it may be classified as a judgment in a separate ("collateral") proceeding and thus be appealable. [Puerto Rico Aqueduct & Sewer Authority v. Metcalf & Eddy, Inc., 506 U.S. 139 (1993)—governmental entity's claim of Eleventh Amendment immunity from suit denied; issue appealable immediately under collateral order rule because failure to permit interlocutory appeal would effectively eviscerate Eleventh Amendment immunity from suit in federal court by requiring entity to litigate to final judgment before appealing]

5. **Orders Made Appealable (or Nonappealable) by Writ**
In exceptional cases, nearly all jurisdictions allow some circumvention of the final judgment rule through the appellate writs of mandamus and prohibition. Mandamus commands a trial judge to act, and prohibition commands the judge to refrain from acting. The writs are available only if an appeal will be insufficient to correct a problem and the trial court's actions constitute a serious abuse of power that must be immediately corrected.

6. **Certification of Class Actions**
A district court's order granting or denying certification of a class action can be appealed within 14 days of entry of the order. [Fed. R. Civ. P. 23(f)] The court of appeals has complete discretion in deciding whether to hear the appeal. If the court decides to hear the appeal, proceedings are ***not stayed*** at the district court unless the district court or court of appeals so orders.

D. **STAY PENDING APPEAL**
Stays are governed generally by Rule 62.

1. **Execution**
No execution on judgments is allowed for 14 days after entry except injunctions or receiverships, which are not held up unless otherwise ordered by a court.

2. **Enforceability**
Judgments are ***enforceable during pendency of post-trial motions unless*** a court otherwise orders in its discretion and on such conditions for the security of the adverse party as are proper.

3. **Bond**
A supersedeas bond is required in sufficient size to satisfy the judgment, costs, interest, and damages for delay, should the appeal be dismissed or affirmed. Upon filing such a bond, an appellant has a stay pending appeal—unless the order was for an injunction or receivership.

4. **Injunction Order**

   a. **Power of Trial Court**
   When appeal is taken from an interlocutory or final judgment granting, dissolving, or denying an injunction, the court may suspend, modify, restore, or grant an injunction during the pendency of the appeal upon such bond as it considers proper for the security of the adverse party.

   b. **Power of Appellate Court**
   An appellate court has similar power to grant a stay or injunction pending appeal, or to vacate one granted by the trial court, or to make any order appropriate to preserve the status quo or the effectiveness of the judgment subsequently to be entered. Ordinarily such a stay or injunction pending appeal must be sought in the trial court before the appellate court will entertain it.

E. SUPREME COURT JURISDICTION
The Supreme Court has direct appeal jurisdiction from any order granting or denying an injunction in any proceeding required to be heard by a three-judge court. [28 U.S.C. §1253]

1. **Court of Appeals Cases**
Cases in the courts of appeals may be reviewed by the Supreme Court:

   (i) ***By certiorari*** granted upon petition of any party to any civil or criminal case, before or after rendition of judgment or decree; or

   (ii) ***By certification*** by the court of appeals of any question of law in any civil or criminal case as to which it desires instructions. Upon such certification, the Supreme Court may give binding instructions or may require the entire record to be sent to it for decision of the entire case.

   [28 U.S.C. §1254]

2. **Cases from Highest State Court**
Final judgments rendered by the highest court of a state in which decision could be had may be reviewed by the Supreme Court ***by certiorari*** in the following circumstances:

   (i) Where the validity of a ***treaty or federal statute*** is drawn into question; or

   (ii) Where the validity of a ***state statute*** is drawn into question on the ground that it is repugnant to the federal Constitution or to a treaty or federal statute; or

   (iii) Where any ***title***, ***right***, ***privilege***, ***or immunity*** is claimed under the federal Constitution or treaty or federal statute.

   [28 U.S.C. §1257] Only the Supreme Court may hear appeals coming from the state court system.

X. EFFECTS OF JUDGMENT ON FUTURE CASES

A. RES JUDICATA (CLAIM PRECLUSION)

1. Definition

Once a ***final*** judgment ***on the merits*** has been rendered on a particular cause of action, the claimant is barred by res judicata (also called claim preclusion) from asserting the ***same cause*** of action in a later lawsuit.

2. Terminology Used to Describe Effect—"Merger" and "Bar"

When the ***claimant wins*** the earlier lawsuit, the cause of action is said to have been "***merged***" into the judgment. When the ***defendant wins,*** the claimant is said to be "***barred***" by the earlier adverse judgment. Both terms simply mean that the ***claimant cannot sue again*** on the same cause.

3. Requirements for "Merger" and "Bar"

Before merger or bar apply, it must be shown that (i) the earlier judgment is a valid, final judgment "***on the merits***"; (ii) the cases are brought by the ***same claimant*** against the ***same defendant***; and (iii) the ***same*** "***cause of action***" (or "claim") is involved in the later lawsuit.

4. Valid, Final Judgment "On the Merits"

Res judicata (claim preclusion) flows from the entry in an earlier case of a valid, final judgment "on the merits." A judgment is valid as long as it is not void (*e.g.*, for lack of subject matter jurisdiction). Whether a judgment is final for these purposes is generally the same as whether it is final for purposes of taking an appeal. (*See* IX.C., *supra.*) Usually, the more difficult issue is whether the valid, final judgment is considered "on the merits" for res judicata purposes. Often, a judgment will be based on actual litigation between the parties, but it can also be a default judgment entered as a penalty against a party (such as a dismissal for willful violation of discovery orders) or an involuntary dismissal closely related to the merits (such as for failure to state a claim upon which relief may be granted). In contrast, other involuntary dismissals not involving the merits (such as those based on lack of jurisdiction, improper venue, or failure to join an indispensable party) are not a judgment on the merits and do not have claim preclusive effect. Although Federal Rule 41(b) indicates that all dismissals are to operate "as an adjudication on the merits" unless based on jurisdiction, improper venue, or failure to join an indispensable party, the Supreme Court has held that Rule 41(b) does ***not*** govern whether the judgment is "on the merits" for res judicata purposes. [Semtek, Inc. v. Lockheed Martin Corp., 531 U.S. 497 (2001)] Thus, jurisdictions may take different views of whether a particular dismissal—*e.g.*, dismissal because the statute of limitations has run—is deemed "on the merits" for res judicata purposes.

5. Same Claimant Versus Same Defendant

Res judicata applies only if the earlier case and the latter case are brought by the same claimant against the same defendant. It is not enough that the same litigants were also parties in the previous case; they must have been in the same configuration of one asserting a claim against the other.

Examples: 1) In Case One, A sues Z to recover damages for personal injuries suffered in an automobile collision between the two. A valid, final judgment on the merits is entered. Now A sues Z again, this time to recover damages for property damage inflicted in the same wreck. Assuming that both cases involve the same "cause of action" (discussed immediately below), res judicata would apply, because both cases were brought by A against Z.

2) In Case One, A sues Z to recover damages for personal injuries suffered in an automobile collision between the two. A valid, final judgment on the merits is entered. Now Z sues A to recover for her personal injuries suffered in the same wreck. Res judicata ***does not apply.*** Here, the second case is brought ***by Z against A, while the first case was brought by A against Z.*** *Note:* Z may be barred from asserting her claim because of the compulsory counterclaim rule, but not because of res judicata. The compulsory counterclaim rule requires a defending party to assert against the claimant ***in the pending case*** any claims arising from the same transaction or occurrence as the claimant's claim. (*See* VII.E.3.c., *supra.*)

6. "Cause of Action"

While various tests have been used to define "cause of action," the modern approach is to require assertion of all claims arising out of the same transaction or occurrence that is the subject matter of a claim asserted by the claimant.

a. Common Examples

1) Accidents

The claimant seeks to recover separate damages from the same accident in separate actions. The claimant may not seek damages for neck injuries in one action and leg injuries in another. Likewise, most courts would not permit the claimant to sue for personal injuries and property damage in separate actions. However, if the claimant is insured for property damage and, after payment of the claim, the claimant assigns her cause of action for property damage to the insurance company, most courts would consider the property damage claim and personal injury claim as two separate causes of action.

2) Installment Obligations

In the situation of a series of obligations, such as installment payments on a debt or lease, the claimant is required to sue on all installments due at the time of suit, but not later installments. But if the contract has an acceleration clause that makes all installments due if earlier ones are not paid, the claimant must sue for all installments (unless the acceleration clause is optional and the claimant elects not to exercise the option). This rule does not apply if the installment obligations are represented by separate notes; in such cases, suit as each note comes due represents suit on a separate cause of action.

B. COLLATERAL ESTOPPEL (ISSUE PRECLUSION)

1. Definition

A judgment binds the plaintiff or defendant (or their privies) in subsequent actions on different causes of action between them (or their privies) as to ***issues actually litigated*** and ***essential to the judgment*** in the first action. This conclusive effect of the first judgment is called collateral estoppel, or issue preclusion. Note that collateral estoppel is narrower than

res judicata. Res judicata focuses on something relatively large—the scope of a "***cause of action***." If it applies, the result is usually to bar the claimant from asserting a second case. Collateral estoppel, in contrast, focuses on something relatively narrow—***an issue*** that was litigated and determined in the first case, and that is relevant in a second case. With collateral estoppel, the issue is deemed established in the second case without need to proffer evidence on it.

2. Requirements

a. First Case Ended in a Valid, Final Judgment on the Merits

This requirement is the same as was just discussed above regarding res judicata. (*See* A.4., *supra.*)

b. Issue Actually Litigated and Determined

The issue on which collateral estoppel applies must actually have been litigated and determined in the previous case. Thus, if a ***default*** or ***consent*** judgment is entered, there is generally no collateral estoppel as to the fact issues that would have been tried had the case gone forward.

c. Issue Was Essential to the Judgment

1) It must be clear exactly how the issue was decided by the trier of fact.

Example: P sues for personal injuries based on D's negligence. D pleads contributory negligence as a defense. If the jury renders a general verdict for D, the decision will have no collateral estoppel effect in a subsequent case involving either P or D's negligence, because there is no way of knowing whether the jury found that D was not negligent or that P was contributorily negligent, or both.

Compare: However, if the jury found for P for the full amount of his injuries, it clearly had to decide that D was negligent and P was not. Thus, both issues could have collateral estoppel effect in a later case.

2) The judgment must depend on the issue of fact decided.

Example: If, in a personal injury action, the jury specially finds that neither P nor D was negligent—thereby rendering a verdict for D—the finding that P was not negligent was ***not*** essential to judgment and will have no collateral estoppel effect in a later suit.

3) Note that the "essential fact" rule tends to reduce the number of cases in which collateral estoppel can be applied, thus eliminating some of the burden from the first suit.

d. Due Process and Mutuality Considerations

1) *Against* Whom Is Collateral Estoppel Used?

Collateral estoppel may be asserted ***only against*** someone who was a party (or in privity with a party) to the previous case (the case in which the issue was actually litigated and determined). This requirement is imposed by due process, and thus is the rule in every jurisdiction.

2) ***By* Whom Is Collateral Estoppel Used?**
Under the traditional "mutuality" rule, only someone who was a party (or in privity with a party) in the previous case can use collateral estoppel. This requirement is not imposed by due process, however, and has been subject to modification in certain circumstances to allow nonparties to take advantage of a prior judgment, as discussed in D., below.

C. RES JUDICATA AND COLLATERAL ESTOPPEL IN SPECIAL SITUATIONS

1. Judgments for Specific Performance

Rules of bar and collateral estoppel apply in actions brought for specific performance and the like. However, ***merger does not apply*** because such a judgment, unlike one for money, cannot be enforced by bringing a suit on the judgment. Thus, if the defendant fails to obey the first judgment, the claimant may sue again.

2. In Rem Judgments

If a court exercises in rem jurisdiction over some property or status within its control, and if proper notice has been given to all interested persons, the judgment as to title or status is ***binding on all persons***.

3. Quasi In Rem Judgments

A quasi in rem judgment determines the rights of the parties only in the specific property before the court. ***No personal judgment*** is granted against anyone, and ***no other property is affected***.

D. WHICH PERSONS ARE BOUND BY A JUDGMENT?

1. Parties Are Bound

Parties are persons named as parties who have the power to control the action or who, if they lack capacity, are represented by guardians. ***Nonparties*** normally are ***not bound***. Even where the lawsuit raises an issue as to performance or rights, nonparties normally are not bound by the judgment; *e.g.,* an assignor who has no control over the suit and no interest in the outcome, or an employee who allegedly was negligent, where the suit is filed only against the employer.

2. Privies to Parties Are Bound

Persons who control the litigation and who will be affected by the outcome are bound by collateral estoppel as to ***all issues litigated***. For example, if the owner of a patent assumes control of an infringement suit brought by her licensee against a competitor, and the court holds the patent invalid, the owner is barred on that issue should she sue the same competitor. The owner has had her day in court.

Persons whose interests are represented are bound. ***Beneficiaries*** are bound by an action brought or defended on their behalf by the fiduciary, provided the fiduciary is operating within her authority. ***Holders of future interests*** are bound. ***Unborn or unascertained*** persons having future interests in property are bound by judgments as to the property if their interests are identical to those of parties to the action, or if a special representative is appointed for them. This rule reflects public policy favoring free marketability of property. ***Members of a class*** are bound by a valid class action judgment. ***Successors in interest***

are bound. ***Transferees of property*** are in privity with prior owners and thus are bound by a prior judgment concerning the property. This rule protects the public as to security of titles.

Note, however, that one is not barred from asserting a claim simply because she is asserting the same claim that a previous claimant has already litigated.

Example: Citizen A sues to challenge a tax as unconstitutional and loses. Citizen B is not barred from suing to challenge the same tax on the same basis unless Citizen A and Citizen B are in privity or Citizen A represented Citizen B in bringing the first suit. [Richards v. Jefferson County, 517 U.S. 793 (1996)]

In ***vicarious liability*** situations (master-servant, principal-agent, insurer-insured) a judgment exonerating either generally is held to preclude an action on the same claim against the other.

Example: P sues Principal claiming injuries as a result of Agent's negligence. P alleges Agent was acting in the course and scope of agency at the time of harm. A judgment in favor of Principal on the ground that Agent was not negligent would in some jurisdictions preclude suing Agent thereafter on the theory that Agent was negligent in causing the harm. If P first sued Agent and Agent was found not negligent, P should thereafter be barred from suing Principal for the negligence of Agent causing the harm.

3. Strangers May Take Advantage of Collateral Estoppel in Certain Circumstances

While persons who are neither parties nor privies cannot be bound by a judgment, such persons may be able to take advantage of, or to assert, collateral estoppel (issue preclusion).

a. Traditional "Mutuality" Rules

Since a judgment cannot be used ***against*** a person who was not a party (because such use would violate due process rights), that person has traditionally been barred from ***taking advantage*** of the judgment—even though this may make little sense in a specific case, and even though this is not required by due process.

b. Exceptions to Mutuality When Judgment Used as a Shield

When a nonparty wishes to utilize a prior judgment ***to avoid liability*** in a subsequent suit, there are often compelling reasons for allowing her to do so. For example, if P unsuccessfully sues a person primarily liable (*e.g.,* a servant), P's later suit against a person secondarily liable (*e.g.,* against the master for the servant's acts) will be barred by collateral estoppel in virtually all courts. Similarly, if P unsuccessfully sues a person secondarily liable, there is little reason why the person primarily liable should be subjected to a separate suit, and most courts so hold.

Note: This rule does not apply if the first suit was or could have been decided solely on the ground that the defendant was ***not*** secondarily liable (*e.g.,* where the defendant claims no master-servant relationship exists).

c. Exceptions to Mutuality When Judgment Used as a Sword

1) Collateral Estoppel Generally Unavailable to Nonparty Plaintiffs

Courts have been very reluctant to permit a nonparty to use a judgment to aid him (as a plaintiff) to obtain relief. For example, suppose one of many passengers in a public vehicle successfully sues the driver for injuries received in an accident, and other passengers wish to utilize the judgment to establish liability. While a few courts have permitted such use, others refuse. They fear a situation in which 10 plaintiffs each sue and lose, and the 11th plaintiff wins, and all other potential plaintiffs seek to ignore the first 10 suits and rely solely on the 11th; application of collateral estoppel in such a situation is considered unfair and demeaning to the legal system.

2) **Courts Should Consider Fairness to Defendant**
The United States Supreme Court, in *Parklane Hosiery Co. v. Shore,* 439 U.S. 322 (1979), upheld the use of collateral estoppel as a sword. In the first action, brought by the Securities and Exchange Commission, the defendant was held to have violated the federal securities laws. The second suit, brought by a private plaintiff against the same defendant, alleged damages resulting from the same violation established in the first action. The Court allowed the latter plaintiff to rely on collateral estoppel to establish the existence of the violation since under all the circumstances it was fair to the defendant to do so. *Note:* Nonmutual collateral estoppel cannot be used against the United States. [United States v. Mendoza, 464 U.S. 154 (1984)]

d. **Present Status of Mutuality**
In jurisdictions where the mutuality principle has been eroded, a ***four-part test*** is usually applied to determine whether a stranger may rely on a prior judgment:

(i) Was the issue decided in the first case ***identical*** to that in the second?

(ii) Was there a final judgment on the ***merits***?

(iii) Did the party against whom the judgment is to be used have a ***fair opportunity to be heard*** on the critical issue?

(iv) Is the posture of the case such that it would ***not*** be ***unfair or inequitable*** to a party to apply collateral estoppel?

If ***all*** these questions are answered affirmatively, collateral estoppel will normally be upheld. A court may find, however, that a party has not had a fair opportunity to be heard if the first case was insignificant (*e.g.,* brought for $200), while the second is more substantial (*e.g.,* brought for $200,000).

E. WHICH CHOICE OF LAW RULES APPLY TO PRECLUSION QUESTIONS?

Preclusion questions—whether claim preclusion or issue preclusion—always involve at least two cases. One case has gone to a valid, final judgment on the merits. Preclusion law determines whether that judgment (in "case one") precludes litigation of any matters in a pending case ("case two"). (By the way, note that "case one" was not necessarily filed first; it is "case one" because it went to judgment first.) A choice of law issue arises when case two is brought in a different jurisdiction than case one; *i.e.,* what law does the court in case two use to determine whether the judgment in case one is entitled to claim or issue preclusion?

1. **Case One Decided in State Court**
When case one has been decided in state court, the court in case two (whether state or federal) generally will apply the claim or issue preclusion law of the jurisdiction that decided case one.
Example: Judgment is entered in a case in Kansas. A second case is brought in Missouri. To decide whether that case is subject to claim or issue preclusion, the judge in Missouri should generally apply Kansas law on claim or issue preclusion.

2. **Case One Decided in Federal Court Under Diversity Jurisdiction**
What if case one was decided in a federal court under diversity jurisdiction? Here, the Supreme Court held that the court in case two should apply federal law (because a federal court decided case one). However, it also held that usually the federal law in such an instance would be the state law of the state in which the federal court sat.
Example: After plaintiff files suit in a California state court, defendant removes the case to federal court based on diversity jurisdiction. Plaintiff's federal court case is then dismissed under Rule 41(b) (involuntary dismissal) because it is barred by California's statute of limitations. Plaintiff files the same claims in state court in Maryland (which has a longer statute of limitations). In determining whether to dismiss the case under claim preclusion, the Maryland state court should look to federal law. But federal law would adopt the California law (unless "state law is incompatible with federal interests"). Because California law would allow the plaintiff to file in a jurisdiction with a longer statute of limitations, the Maryland court should not dismiss under claim preclusion. [Semtek, Inc. v. Lockheed Martin Corp., A.4., *supra*]

REVIEW QUESTIONS

INTRODUCTORY NOTE

The true/false questions that follow are intended to serve as both a substantive review and a diagnostic test. Respond to the questions quickly and compare your answers with those found at the end of this section. This will allow you to identify areas in which you may need further review.

FILL IN ANSWER

PERSONAL JURISDICTION

1. Plaintiff sues Defendant in a court in Alabama, asking for damages for personal injuries suffered when a motor manufactured by Defendant blew up. Defendant's motion to dismiss for lack of personal jurisdiction will be denied if an Alabama statute clearly authorizes jurisdiction over Defendant on the sole basis that:

    a. Defendant formally appointed an agent in Alabama to receive process for any case involving personal injuries caused by Defendant's motors. ________

    b. Defendant was born in Alabama and lived there until two years ago, when he moved permanently to Wisconsin. ________

    c. Defendant was served with process while driving through Alabama. ________

    d. Plaintiff's injury, which took place in Wisconsin, was caused by a defective motor manufactured by Defendant in Alabama. ________

    e. Plaintiff's injury occurred in Alabama, and was caused by a defective motor made by Defendant in California for use in California by the California government (unknown to Defendant, California sold the motor to Plaintiff at an auction of used state equipment). ________

    f. Defendant is the sole owner of a large, financially successful clothing store in Alabama. ________

2. Plaintiff and Defendant are both citizens of Illinois. Plaintiff wishes to sue Defendant in a federal court on a $1 million claim. Therefore, Plaintiff moves permanently to Iowa just before filing suit. Immediately after suit is filed, Defendant moves permanently to Iowa and files a motion to dismiss. The motion should be granted. ________

3. The governor of Florida claims that Smokey Co., by emitting certain pollutants from its smokestack, is endangering the lives and property of 4,000 Florida residents. Smokey Co. has filed suit in a Florida court against the 4,000 residents, requesting a declaration that it is not liable for damages for pollution. Jurisdiction over all the defendants is proper if:

a. Detailed notice of the suit appears in a local newspaper delivered to the homes of each defendant. ________

b. One thousand of the defendants, chosen at random, are personally served, and a notice was published in the local paper. ________

c. Detailed notice of the suit is posted at 100-foot intervals throughout the area where the defendants all live. ________

d. A letter giving detailed notice of the suit is sent by ordinary mail to each defendant. ________

4. Plaintiff sues Defendant in a Michigan court for breach of a land sale contract negotiated and to be performed in Michigan. Plaintiff can obtain jurisdiction in the case:

a. Even though legislation in Michigan purports to prohibit jurisdiction in such cases. ________

b. On the basis that Defendant has a bank account in Michigan, provided that the bank account is attached in accordance with a Michigan statute. ________

c. If the action is brought to declare that Plaintiff and not Defendant is the owner of the realty involved in the land sale agreement. ________

SUBJECT MATTER JURISDICTION

5. Plaintiff, a citizen of Indiana, sues Defendant, a citizen of Nevada, and Co-Defendant, a citizen of California, in a federal court. The amount of the claim exceeds $75,000. Either Co-Defendant or Defendant could successfully move to dismiss for lack of jurisdiction. ________

6. Plaintiff Co. is incorporated in Delaware and has its principal place of business in California. It brings three separate suits, each in a federal court, and each demanding over $75,000 in damages. The suits are brought respectively against a citizen of Delaware, a citizen of California, and an American citizen who lives abroad in France. Each of the three defendants may successfully move to dismiss the suit against her for lack of jurisdiction. ________

7. Plaintiff, a citizen of Maine, sues Defendant, a citizen of Canada, and Co-Defendant, a citizen of Germany, in a federal court, asking for $40,000 damages from each. A motion to dismiss for lack of jurisdiction by Defendant or by Co-Defendant will be granted. ________

8. Plaintiff sued Defendant in a federal district court for damages of $80,000 due to a breach of contract. Jurisdiction was based on diversity of citizenship. Defendant filed a counterclaim against Plaintiff for $2,000 alleging that Plaintiff negligently damaged Defendant's automobile. The court should strike the counterclaim. ________

9. Plaintiff sues Defendant in a federal court of Alabama. Jurisdiction is based on diversity of citizenship.

   a. The court must apply the substantive law as set forth by a 10-year-old decision of an intermediate appellate court in Alabama (the only state decision on point) rather than a substantially different law more recently adopted by courts of other states on the same issue. ________

   b. The court cannot allow pretrial discovery of documents pursuant to Federal Rule 34 when the Alabama legislature has enacted a bill prohibiting such discovery in the courts of Alabama. ________

10. Plaintiff brings suit in a federal court for breach of contract. Plaintiff alleges as the basis for jurisdiction that Defendant will claim that a federal statute bars enforcement of the contract. Defendant's motion to dismiss for lack of jurisdiction should be denied. ________

11. Plaintiff brings suit in a federal court under the federal copyright act. He joins a claim based on identical facts under the state unfair competition laws. The court, on motion for summary judgment, dismisses the federal claim. The court must also dismiss the state claim. ________

VENUE; REMOVAL

12. Plaintiff, a resident of the Northern District of California, sues Defendant, a resident of the Southern District of New York, for injuries suffered in Utah, which has but one federal court district. Federal venue would be proper in any one of the three mentioned districts. ________

13. Plaintiff, a citizen of California, filed a suit against Defendant, a citizen of Oregon, in a federal court in Wyoming. Jurisdiction was based on diversity of citizenship. The cause of action involved an auto collision in California close to the California-Nevada border. All of the witnesses live and work in Nevada, where both Plaintiff and Defendant were hospitalized and treated for their injuries.

   a. A timely venue challenge by Defendant will be successful. ________

   b. The case cannot be transferred to the Nevada federal court. ________

14. Plaintiff, a citizen of the Central District of California, brings a federal antitrust action against Defendant Corporation. Defendant Corporation does business in Arizona and is licensed to do business in Utah, but has no contacts with California. Federal venue would be proper in the Central District of California or in the federal district court in Arizona or Utah. ________

15. Plaintiff, a citizen of California, sues Defendant, a citizen of Nevada, in a Nevada state court, on an $80,000 claim.

a. Defendant can have the claim tried in federal court by removing it. ________

b. Defendant could not remove had the action been initiated in a California state court. ________

RULES OF CIVIL PROCEDURE

16. A challenge based on lack of subject matter jurisdiction is waived if not made prior to trial. ________

17. Plaintiff alleged in a complaint that Defendant gave Plaintiff a vicious dirty look, causing Plaintiff to suffer severe physical and mental injury. Defendant answered, denying that the look was vicious.

    a. Just prior to trial, Defendant moved to dismiss the complaint for failure to state a claim. The motion should be denied as untimely. ________

    b. Along with the above motion, Defendant moved to dismiss on the ground that the complaint, on its face, showed that the statute of limitations had run prior to the time the complaint was filed. The motion will be denied as untimely. ________

    c. Along with the above motions, Defendant moved to dismiss the action for improper venue. The motion should be dismissed as untimely. ________

18. A pleading which is filed late is usually attacked by a motion to strike and not by a motion to dismiss. ________

19. In some courts, a pleading may not be attacked because it contains vague or uncertain allegations unless the opposing party is required to file a responsive pleading. ________

20. Plaintiff sues Defendant on a claim for negligence. In his answer, Defendant alleges "Defendant's defense is that the whole problem was Plaintiff's own fault." Plaintiff's motion for a more definite statement of Defendant's defense will normally be permitted in almost all jurisdictions. ________

21. Plaintiff filed suit against Defendant, alleging that (i) Defendant was the owner of a certain automobile, (ii) Defendant loaned the vehicle to Driver, (iii) Driver negligently drove the vehicle through a red light, striking Plaintiff, and (iv) as a result Plaintiff suffered personal injuries of $75,000 and damage to personal property of $4,250.

    a. Defendant filed an answer admitting allegation (i) and denying the remaining allegations on the basis of lack of information or belief. Plaintiff may successfully claim that Defendant has admitted all of the allegations in the complaint. ________

    b. Defendant filed an answer, admitting every allegation but (iii) as to which Defendant said, "Defendant neither admits nor denies that Driver was negligent but puts Plaintiff to his proof on the issue." In most jurisdictions, Plaintiff may successfully claim Defendant has admitted Driver's negligence. ________

c. Defendant filed an answer admitting every allegation but (iv), as to which Defendant alleged, "Plaintiff has suffered neither personal injuries nor damage to personal property in the sum of $4,250." Plaintiff may successfully claim that Defendant has admitted that Plaintiff suffered all the damages alleged in his complaint. ________

22. Plaintiff alleged in a complaint against Defendant that Defendant entered Plaintiff's land without permission and struck Plaintiff with his fist, causing severe personal injury. Defendant answered, denying generally the allegations in Plaintiff's complaint. At trial, Defendant seeks to introduce evidence as to the matters listed below. Plaintiff objects to the introduction of evidence on each matter. Plaintiff's objection should be upheld as to Defendant's evidence:

a. That Defendant owned the land in question. ________

b. That Defendant struck Plaintiff in self-defense. ________

c. That Plaintiff and Defendant entered into a contract settling the case. ________

d. That Plaintiff's injuries occurred when he slipped during a mountain climbing expedition. ________

23. Plaintiff sues Defendant for breach of contract. Defendant has a claim against Plaintiff for injuries occurring in a fight. Defendant may assert his claim as a counterclaim in Plaintiff's action. ________

24. Plaintiff sues Defendant for breach of an installment contract. Defendant has a claim against Plaintiff for Plaintiff's breach regarding a prior installment of the same contract. Defendant runs the risk of losing her claim if she fails to raise it as a counterclaim to Plaintiff's action. ________

25. Plaintiff sued Defendant in an auto accident case. Regarding damages, Plaintiff alleged only that he "suffered severe and permanent physical injuries in the amount of $76,000." At trial, Defendant's objection will be upheld to each of the following items of evidence sought to be introduced by Plaintiff:

a. As a result of the accident, Plaintiff broke his right arm. ________

b. As a result of the accident, Plaintiff incurred medical expenses for setting his broken arm. ________

c. As a result of the accident, Plaintiff suffered severe pain due to a broken arm and the treatment for it. ________

26. Alfred Johnson filed suit against Wilhelm P. Smith, alleging that on February 1, 2007, "Smith negligently drove his car into plaintiff, causing plaintiff serious physical injury." At trial, plaintiff introduced evidence to show defendant's negligence and plaintiff's resulting personal injury. In addition, the evidence showed the facts listed below. Defendant moved to dismiss the action as brought against the wrong person. Plaintiff moved to amend his complaint to conform to the proof. Plaintiff ***must*** be permitted to amend his complaint to reflect that:

    a. Wilhelm P. Smith is actually named Wilhelm P. Smythe. ________

    b. As a consequence of the accident, plaintiff suffered damages of $2,000 due to the destruction of personal property he was carrying. ________

    c. Shortly before the accident occurred, defendant had improperly induced plaintiff's employer to discharge plaintiff. ________

27. Plaintiff sued Dr. Defendant, alleging that Dr. Defendant negligently performed an operation on Plaintiff, causing Plaintiff permanent injuries to his legs. Dr. Defendant was personally served in the action. Shortly before trial, and after the statute of limitations had run, Plaintiff learned that his injuries were due to improper postoperative care by Dr. Co-Defendant, who shares Dr. Defendant's office and who does all the follow-up care after Dr. Defendant's surgery.

    a. Plaintiff may successfully amend this complaint to allege that his injuries were due to negligent postoperative care. ________

    b. Plaintiff may successfully amend to join Dr. Co-Defendant as a defendant in the case. ________

28. Plaintiff sues Defendant to enjoin Defendant from constructing a building, alleging that Defendant's methods of construction violate air pollution laws. Defendant is under contract to Owner to erect the building on Owner's land. The court may not proceed with the case unless Owner is joined as a party. ________

29. Plaintiff makes a single contract with three brothers, all of whom are professional athletes, to handle their financial affairs for a 15-year period. One brother sues Plaintiff for a declaration that the contract is void as against public policy. The court may not proceed with the action unless the other two brothers are joined as parties. ________

30. Larry, a pedestrian, was struck by an automobile driven by Mo. Mo stopped his car to render aid. Shortly thereafter, a car driven by Curly hit the rear of Mo's car, knocking it over onto Larry, causing Larry further injuries. Larry may not join Mo and Curly as defendants in a single action. ________

31. Plaintiff is a passenger in a car driven by Co-Plaintiff, when it is struck by another car driven by Defendant. Plaintiff and Co-Plaintiff both wish to sue Defendant for personal injuries received in the collision. Plaintiff and Co-Plaintiff cannot join their claims in a single lawsuit. ________

32. Plaintiff has a claim for breach of a written contract against Defendant. Prior to filing suit, Plaintiff purchases from Gardener and Janitor claims that each of them has against Defendant. These latter claims are for the reasonable value of gardening and janitorial services. Plaintiff may not join all three of the claims against Defendant in a single lawsuit in federal court. ________

33. Plaintiff sues on behalf of herself, as a photographer, and all other photographers who work in New York City, to enjoin enforcement of a New York City ordinance requiring all photographers to obtain a special license. Only 15 photographers are known to work in New York City. The court should uphold New York City's motion requiring Plaintiff to bring the action solely on her own behalf. ________

34. Plaintiff lives in a subdivision built by Defendant. Several years after her house was built, Plaintiff noted several serious cracks that resulted from Defendant's improper filling of the land before building. Plaintiff sued Defendant on behalf of herself and all other homeowners in the subdivision for damages due to Defendant's neglect. Defendant moves to require Plaintiff to bring the action solely on her own behalf. Under modern rules, the court is not required to grant Defendant's motion. ________

35. Plaintiff owns a Zilch automobile. Plaintiff sues the Zilch Company on behalf of himself and all other Zilch car owners, alleging that all Zilch cars have parts that deteriorate at an unusually rapid rate, causing an unnatural drop-off in the car's value. Zilch Company makes a deal with Plaintiff. It pays Plaintiff $10,000 for his trouble and sets up a fund whereby all other Zilch owners can collect $250 if they apply within one year. Plaintiff then consents to the entry of judgment for Zilch in the action. Several months later Tom, a Zilch owner, sues Zilch for damages due to the rapid deterioration of his vehicle. Zilch defends on the ground that Tom is barred by the prior suit. Zilch's defense will be upheld. ________

36. Plaintiff filed suit against Retailer and Wholesaler, alleging that he was injured when a defective auto tire, which was supplied to Retailer by Wholesaler and thereafter bought by Plaintiff from Retailer, blew out on the highway.

    a. Retailer files a cross-claim against Wholesaler, alleging that if Retailer is liable to Plaintiff, Wholesaler must indemnify Retailer. Wholesaler's motion to strike this cross-claim should be granted. ________

    b. Wholesaler files an impleader against a new party, Manufacturer, alleging that Manufacturer, as the tire manufacturer, should indemnify Wholesaler if Wholesaler is in any way held liable for Plaintiff's injuries. Wholesaler's motion to strike the impleader should be granted. ________

37. Plaintiff sues Defendant for personal injuries arising out of an auto accident.

a. Plaintiff seeks to discover from Defendant what Defendant learned from a police officer concerning statements made to the officer by Eyewitness concerning which of the parties was at fault. Such statements to Defendant are clearly hearsay and could not be introduced at trial. The court should nevertheless permit pretrial discovery of the statements. ________

b. Plaintiff wishes to know in which order Defendant will call his defense witnesses. Plaintiff should be permitted to discover such information. ________

c. Plaintiff wishes to know whether Defendant is insured, and, if so, the exact extent of the coverage. Many courts will permit such discovery. ________

d. Defendant is self-insured. Plaintiff wishes to know the extent of Defendant's assets. Courts that permit discovery of insurance policy limits will normally allow discovery in such a case. ________

e. Plaintiff has confided in his minister concerning the cause of the accident and the extent of his injuries. Such information is privileged; hence the minister cannot be called to testify at trial. However, the evidence is relevant; therefore, Defendant can use pretrial discovery to learn what Plaintiff told the minister. ________

38. Plaintiff sues Defendant for trespass. Defendant claims the property in question belongs to him, not to Plaintiff.

a. After suit was filed, Plaintiff took a statement from each of two persons, Sherlock and Jacques, who had inspected a deed under which Defendant claims title to the property. Shortly thereafter, Sherlock took a job in Thailand; Jacques still lives nearby. Under modem discovery rules, Defendant can obtain a copy of Sherlock's statement but not that of Jacques. ________

b. After a considerable search, Defendant's attorney located an old deed that could provide a missing link in Plaintiff's chain of title. The attorney immediately put the deed in her file on the case. Under modern discovery rules, Plaintiff can inspect the document. ________

c. Defendant spoke to an investigator hired by Plaintiff's attorney. The investigator wrote down a summary of Defendant's remarks which Defendant then signed. Defendant may obtain a copy of this statement. ________

d. Defendant hired a handwriting expert to examine the deed under which Defendant claims title and several other deeds upon which Plaintiff relies. Shortly thereafter, the deed upon which Defendant relies was lost; the other deeds were returned to Plaintiff. Plaintiff now seeks to examine the report of the handwriting expert. Defendant argues that since he will not call the handwriting expert to testify, discovery should be denied. The court should uphold Defendant's argument. ________

39. Rotto Drink Company sues Coca-Cola, alleging that Coca-Cola stole its formula from Rotto. Rotto seeks to discover the Coca-Cola formula, stating that it has no other way to prove that the two formulas are identical. Coca-Cola claims that Rotto merely wishes to blackmail Coca-Cola, knowing that if discovery is required, Coca-Cola will default rather than reveal such a well-kept secret. The court must permit Rotto to see the formula. _________

40. Interrogatories can usually be served on any party, whether or not adverse, but not on a nonparty. _________

41. As a general rule, one party cannot discover documents or other items in the custody of another party, without obtaining a court order granted only upon a showing of good cause. _________

42. In most jurisdictions, there is no way to force a nonparty to permit inspection of documents or other items in his control. _________

43. One party can have her own doctor examine an opposing party's mental or physical condition, but only upon a court order based on a showing of good cause. _________

44. Plaintiff sued Defendant for personal injuries received in an industrial accident. Plaintiff voluntarily submitted to a physical examination by Defendant's doctor.

    a. After the examination, Plaintiff demanded a copy of the doctor's report. Under modern discovery rules, Plaintiff is entitled to receive it. _________

    b. Thereafter, Defendant demanded copies of reports of all of Plaintiff's doctors relating to Plaintiff's alleged injuries. These reports are confidential, and Plaintiff does not have to turn them over to Defendant. _________

45. Plaintiff contracted to buy a number of electric motors from Defendant. Plaintiff installed the motors in tool and die machinery that Plaintiff then sold to various customers. After receiving many complaints concerning the operation of the motors, Plaintiff sued Defendant for breach of contract. Defendant denied that the motors were defective.

    a. Plaintiff sent Defendant a request to admit that many customers had found the motors to be unsatisfactory. Defendant can refuse to answer since the request calls for knowledge that Defendant normally would not have. _________

    b. Plaintiff sent Defendant a request to admit that the motors were defective. Defendant can refuse to answer since the request involves a crucial issue in dispute on the pleadings. _________

    c. Plaintiff sent Defendant a request to admit that the motors did not meet specifications called for in the contract between Plaintiff and Defendant.

Defendant can refuse to answer on the ground that the request calls for a legal conclusion. ________

46. A party who responds to a request to admit by admitting the proposition in question will not normally be permitted to introduce evidence at trial to contradict the admission. ________

47. If a party refuses to respond to a valid request for discovery, the party seeking discovery can obtain a court order requiring such a response to be made. ________

48. If a party refuses to obey a court order for discovery, the court must dismiss his action if he is a plaintiff or enter a default judgment against him if he is a defendant. ________

49. Plaintiff sued Defendant for injuries received in an automobile collision.

    a. Plaintiff took Defendant's deposition. Plaintiff can introduce the deposition at trial only if Defendant takes the stand and makes statements contrary to those in the deposition. ________

    b. Under no circumstances may Defendant's attorney introduce Defendant's own deposition. ________

    c. Plaintiff took the deposition of an eyewitness to the collision. If the eyewitness dies prior to trial, or is out of the area and not subject to subpoena, either Plaintiff or Defendant may introduce the eyewitness's deposition. ________

50. Plaintiff sued Defendant for personal injuries. Defendant answered, denying the allegations of liability and damages. At the conclusion of a pretrial conference, the court issued a pretrial order stating that the sole unresolved issue was the extent of Plaintiff's injuries. At trial, Defendant will not be permitted to introduce evidence tending to show that he was not liable. ________

51. Plaintiff owns a tract of land on which she grows flowers for commercial use. Defendant's trucks have frequently run over a corner of Plaintiff's land, destroying the crops. If Plaintiff sues Defendant to recover damages, Plaintiff will be entitled to a jury trial; if Plaintiff sues only to enjoin Defendant's trucks from further intrusions onto Plaintiff's land, Plaintiff will not be able to demand a jury. ________

52. Plaintiff and Defendant were involved in an automobile collision in which Defendant was injured. Plaintiff filed an action against Defendant, asking for a declaration that Plaintiff is not liable for Defendant's injuries. Plaintiff is entitled to a jury trial on his case. ________

53. Plaintiff sues Defendant in federal court to force Defendant to remove a new building that covers a portion of Plaintiff's property. In addition, Plaintiff sues for $2,000 in damages allegedly incurred because of the trespass. Assuming subject matter jurisdiction is present, Defendant has a clear right to a jury trial. ________

54. Plaintiff brings an action to reform a contract with Defendant, alleging fraud by Defendant. In the same action Plaintiff claims that Defendant's fraud has already resulted in very substantial damages far in excess of the value of the contract. In some courts, at least, Defendant may insist that the issue of fraud be tried before a jury. ________

55. The right to a jury trial is waived by a party who fails to make a timely demand. ________

56. Plaintiff sues Shortline Railroad for injuries received in a collision between Plaintiff's auto and Shortline's train. The accident occurred at a grade crossing; Plaintiff claims that Shortline's engineer was negligent in failing to blow the train whistle or ring the bell upon approaching the crossing. Plaintiff's only evidence as to liability consists of the testimony of 12 people who live in an apartment house located close to the crossing. These witnesses all testified that they were in their apartments at the time of the accident and that they heard the sounds of the crash. They further testified that they had no recollection of hearing the whistle or bell prior to the collision. On cross-examination each witness stated that he or she had no particular reason for listening for the train, or its whistle and bell, and that trains pass the area at least 25 times every day. At the conclusion of Plaintiff's case, Shortline made a motion for judgment as a matter of law (directed verdict). The court must deny the motion. ________

57. Plaintiff sued Defendant for failure to pay on a note. Defendant generally denied the allegations in the complaint. At trial Plaintiff produced the note, the authenticity of which was acknowledged by Defendant. Plaintiff then testified that Defendant had made none of the payments. Defendant's cross-examination in no way shook Plaintiff's testimony. Defendant did not present any witnesses who contradicted Plaintiff's testimony. The trial court granted a motion for judgment as a matter of law (directed verdict) for Plaintiff. Defendant appealed, arguing that for purposes of the directed verdict, Plaintiff's testimony had to be considered untrue. An appellate court would clearly not uphold the directed verdict. ________

58. In federal court, a renewed motion for judgment as a matter of law (judgment N.O.V.) is appropriate only if the moving party had previously moved for a judgment as a matter of law (directed verdict). ________

59. A trial judge may not grant a new trial on a ground that would not justify reversal by an appellate court. ________

60. Plaintiff sued Defendant for damages to her property due to an alleged trespass. The evidence was uncontradicted that Plaintiff suffered $12,000 damages. However, the evidence was closely divided on whether the damage was caused by Defendant or by someone else. The jury awarded a verdict of $6,000. Plaintiff moved for a new trial solely on the issue of damages. The court should deny the motion and offer to grant a new trial on the entire case. ________

61. Defendant moves for summary judgment on the basis of the affidavits of 20 independent eyewitnesses, all persons of integrity in the community, who swear to facts showing that Defendant is not liable. Plaintiff files one counteraffidavit, her own, in which she swears to facts directly contradicting Defendant's witnesses. The court may grant summary judgment, although it does not have to do so. ________

62. If one party files a motion for summary judgment, accompanied by affidavits, the motion must be granted unless the opposing party submits counteraffidavits in response thereto. ________

63. Plaintiff files suit for property damage allegedly caused by Defendant. Defendant moves for summary judgment on the basis of the affidavit of an independent eyewitness who swears that the damage was done by Xavier. Plaintiff files no counteraffidavits, but, at the hearing on the motion, supplies proof that the independent eyewitness died a few days after he made his affidavit. Modern summary judgment rules clearly require the court to deny Defendant's motion. ________

FINAL JUDGMENT AND APPELLATE REVIEW

64. Plaintiff filed suit against Defendant seeking to enjoin Defendant from further encroachments on Plaintiff's property. Defendant defaulted, and Plaintiff moved for a default judgment. At the hearing on the motion, the court found that an injunction would be a harsh and unnecessary remedy under the circumstances and, instead, awarded Plaintiff $10,000 damages for past encroachments. On appeal, the court's award will be set aside. ________

65. Plaintiff files suit against Bob Bankrupt and Wally Wealthy in a court that follows the final judgment rule as generally applied in most jurisdictions. Wally, the only defendant who is solvent and from whom money damages can be collected, successfully moves for his dismissal from the action. In most courts, there is a procedure by which Plaintiff can appeal Wally's dismissal before proceeding with the case against Bob. ________

66. Plaintiff sues Defendant for breach of contract. Defendant seeks pretrial discovery of documents vital to the decision in the case. Plaintiff's refusal to produce the documents is erroneously upheld by the trial judge. Before proceeding any further, Defendant could appeal the ruling on discovery. ________

EFFECTS OF JUDGMENT ON FUTURE CASES

67. Plaintiff's building collapsed, causing $100,000 damages. Defendant Insurance had issued a policy on the building covering all damages, regardless of cause, "excepting losses due directly or indirectly to fire." Plaintiff sued on the policy. Defendant admitted Plaintiff's allegation that the amount of damages was $100,000 but denied that it had issued a policy and alleged, as an affirmative defense, that the damage was due to fire. At trial, Plaintiff's evidence as to issuance of the policy was not refuted. Defendant did, however, put in considerable

evidence attempting to show that the collapse was due to fire. The jury found for Defendant and a judgment was entered accordingly. Plaintiff then brought a second suit against Defendant on a fire insurance policy. Defendant denied Plaintiff's allegations that the damages amounted to $100,000, or that the building collapse had resulted from fire. The trial court properly held:

a. The first suit established $100,000 as the amount of Plaintiff's loss. ________

b. The first suit established that the damage was the result of fire. ________

68. Plaintiff, acting as trustee of certain funds, brought suit against Defendant, a stockbroker, alleging that Defendant had embezzled some of the trust corpus. A trial was held and a decision rendered for Defendant. A few months later, in accordance with the trust instrument, the funds were distributed to Bob, the major beneficiary. Bob then brought suit against Defendant, re-alleging the same acts of embezzlement as charged in Plaintiff's suit. The court should grant Defendant's motion to dismiss based on the first decision. ________

69. A bus, owned and operated by Transit Company, was involved in a collision with a truck.

a. Ed, one of the injured bus passengers, sued the bus driver, Ralph, for negligence. The verdict was for Ralph. Ed then sued Transit, alleging that Ralph was negligent. The court should grant Transit's motion to dismiss based on the decision in the first suit. ________

b. Ed sues Ralph, the bus driver, and wins. Ed may utilize the decision against Ralph to establish Ralph's negligence in Ed's subsequent suit against Transit. ________

c. Ed sues Transit on the basis of Ralph's negligence, and Ralph is held not negligent. In a subsequent negligence suit by Ed against Ralph, Ralph can use the decision in the first suit to establish that he was not liable. ________

d. Ed sues Transit on the basis of Ralph's negligence and Ed wins. In a subsequent suit by Ed against Ralph, Ed can use the first decision to establish Ralph's negligence. ________

e. Ed sues Transit for $2,000, on the basis of Ralph's negligence, and wins a judgment for that amount. Alice, another injured bus passenger, brings a suit for $100,000, alleging the same facts of liability as did Ed. Alice may rely on the decision in Ed's case to establish Transit's liability. ________

ANSWERS TO REVIEW QUESTIONS

Ques. No.	Answer	Explanation
1.a.	***TRUE***	A party can consent to personal jurisdiction over him by appointing an agent to accept service.
b.	***FALSE***	The state where a person is domiciled can exercise jurisdiction over him. However, a person has but one domicile, and here it has been changed to Wisconsin.
c.	***TRUE***	Presence at the time of service has traditionally been a valid basis for personal jurisdiction.
d.	***TRUE***	Under the "minimum contacts" doctrine, the place where the defective motor was manufactured could assert jurisdiction over the manufacturer.
e.	***FALSE***	Defendant had no contacts with Alabama. There was no reason for Defendant to foresee that its motor would arrive in Alabama where it might cause injury.
f.	***TRUE***	Defendant may be sued in Alabama where he engages in systematic and continuous activity, even though Plaintiff's cause did not arise from that activity.
2.	***FALSE***	Diversity is always decided as of the time suit is filed, not when the cause arises of after the case is commenced.
3.a.	***FALSE***	Newspaper publication will not meet minimum constitutional requirements of notice for persons whose names and addresses are known. The best practical means of actual notice is required; here, a letter sent to each person by ordinary mail would probably suffice.
b.	***FALSE***	Random selection of persons to be notified is insufficient to justify jurisdiction over others whose addresses are known.
c.	***FALSE***	Posting notice on property is insufficient to notify owners whose names and addresses are known, even as to actions directly involving the property.
d.	***TRUE***	When a large number of persons are identically involved, and personal delivery or registered mail to each would require great expense, notice to each by ordinary mail is sufficient.
4.a.	***FALSE***	Even though a state may constitutionally assert jurisdiction in a case, it is not required to do so.
b.	***FALSE***	Mere location of Defendant's property in a state can no longer serve as the basis of quasi in rem jurisdiction in that state. There must be minimum contacts

between the state and the cause of action for which such jurisdiction is asserted.

c. ***TRUE*** Quasi in rem jurisdiction is proper in actions to settle disputes as to title to property since a state has an important interest in matters involving ownership of property within its borders.

5. ***FALSE*** The court has jurisdiction when, as here, complete diversity exists; *i.e.,* no defendant is from the same state as Plaintiff, and the amount in controversy exceeds $75,000.

6. ***TRUE*** A corporation is a citizen of every state in which it is incorporated and the one state in which it has its principal place of business. Therefore, there is no diversity between the corporation and citizens of Delaware or California. The third defendant is not a citizen of any state, nor is she an alien. There is no provision for diversity between a citizen of a state and a citizen of the United States living abroad.

7. ***TRUE*** Although diversity exists in a case in which one party is a citizen of a state and the others are foreign citizens, there is an additional requirement in diversity cases that the amount in controversy between each plaintiff and each defendant exceed $75,000.

8. ***TRUE*** In federal courts, unless a counterclaim arises from the same transaction o occurrence as set forth in plaintiff's complaint, the counterclaim can only be maintained if there is independent federal jurisdiction over it. Although the parties are diverse, the amount Defendant alleged to be in controversy does not exceed $75,000.

9.a. ***FALSE*** The federal court is bound, under *Erie Railroad v. Tompkins,* to apply the same substantive state law as would ***currently*** be applied by the highest state court. This means the federal court should consider the lower state court decision and decisions outside the state to determine what position the highest state court would adopt.

b. ***FALSE*** *Erie* does not apply to matters that are "procedural" in nature. Discovery is simply a procedural method of gathering evidence for purposes of narrowing the issues and eliciting the truth in preparation for trial. It does not impinge on substantive law, which determines whether, on the facts proved, Plaintiff or Defendant should prevail.

10. ***FALSE*** There is no basis for federal subject matter jurisdiction. The action does not arise out of a federal question merely because Plaintiff anticipates Defendant will rely on a federal defense.

11. ***FALSE*** Under the rules of supplemental jurisdiction, a federal court obtains jurisdiction over state claims based on the same facts as federal claims. If the federa claim was not frivolous, the court may retain the state claim even though th federal claim fails or is settled.

12. ***FALSE*** Venue would not be proper in the Northern District of California. In a diversity case, venue is proper in a district where defendant resides or the cause of the action arose, but not where plaintiff resides (unless defendant is subject to personal jurisdiction in plaintiff's district).

13.a. ***TRUE*** Venue is clearly improper in Wyoming because defendant does not reside there and no events giving rise to the claim occurred there.

b. ***TRUE*** Under federal statutes, transfer of venue, either because current venue is improper or because a more appropriate forum exists, is limited to those districts where the action "might have been brought" originally. Nevada does not qualify for the same reason Wyoming does not.

14. ***FALSE*** Plaintiff cannot sue in the Central District of California. In federal question cases such as the one here, venue is proper in a district where defendant resides or where the claim arose. Thus, Defendant Corporation could be sued in the federal district court in Arizona or Utah because a corporation is deemed to reside, for purposes of venue, in any judicial district in which it is subject to personal jurisdiction at the time the action is commenced. This was not the case in California; therefore, Plaintiff may not sue in that district.

15.a. ***FALSE*** Generally a defendant can remove a case if federal subject matter jurisdiction existed when the action was filed; but there is an exception where the basis for jurisdiction is diversity of citizenship and the action is brought in the home state of one of the defendants.

b. ***FALSE*** The action could be removed since diversity jurisdiction existed when the suit was filed and defendant is not from California.

16. ***FALSE*** Such a challenge can be made at any time even on appeal. In some cases, it has been held to be a valid basis for collateral attack.

17.a. ***FALSE*** A motion to dismiss (or a demurrer) for failure to set forth a valid claim is timely when raised anytime before trial or at trial.

b. ***TRUE*** Although the general rule is that the complaint can be dismissed at any time before trial or at trial if on its face it shows a complete defense, the statute of limitations is held by some courts to be a disfavored defense that results in special treatment. The defense is held waived unless raised at the earliest opportunity (but the court has discretion to permit an amendment of the answer to raise this defense).

c. ***TRUE*** This is a plea in abatement. If not raised at the earliest opportunity (*e.g.,* time of the answer or prior thereto), it is waived (no amendment of answer permitted).

18. ***TRUE*** The motion to dismiss is used to attack the insufficiency of the pleading. The motion to strike is used to reach technical defects and to eliminate irrelevant allegations.

19.	***TRUE***	This is the rule in federal courts. In some states, such an attack can be made even if no responsive pleading is required.
20.	***FALSE***	In most jurisdictions, including the federal courts, such a motion is allowed only if necessary to permit a response to the challenged pleading. Therefore (since no response to Defendant's defense is required), the motion will be denied. In those jurisdictions that allow the motion even when a response is not required, the motion would be granted because the defense is vague.
21.a.	***FALSE***	Such a denial is improper as to allegation (ii) since it involves a matter that Defendant is presumed to know. But such a denial may well be appropriate for the remaining allegations.
b.	***TRUE***	This is an evasive denial that is treated as an admission.
c.	***FALSE***	Defendant has properly denied the amount of personal injuries. However, Defendant is guilty of alleging a "negative pregnant" by specifically denying the $4,250 figure. In some jurisdictions this would constitute an admission that some damages to Plaintiff's personal property were suffered.
22.a.	***FALSE***	Evidence that Defendant owned the land is proper. It directly contradicts Plaintiff's allegation of ownership and is admissible under a denial.
b.	***TRUE***	Self-defense is an affirmative defense which must be pleaded by Defendant before he can introduce evidence thereon.
c.	***TRUE***	A contract of settlement is also an affirmative defense.
d.	***FALSE***	Evidence that Plaintiff suffered his injuries other than at the hands of Defendant directly contradicts Plaintiff's case and hence comes in under Defendant's denial.
23.	***TRUE***	Most courts allow defendant to counterclaim for any claim he has against Plaintiff, regardless of its nature.
24.	***TRUE***	In most jurisdictions, Defendant ***must*** raise as a counterclaim any claim she has against Plaintiff that arises from the same transaction or occurrence as Plaintiff's claim or she will be barred from asserting it later in an independent action. "Same transaction or occurrence" is usually given a fairly broad interpretation, thus encompassing Defendant's claim in this case. (It should be noted that in some jurisdictions there is no compulsory counterclaim rule.)
25.a.	***FALSE***	The fact that Plaintiff broke his arm is provable as part of general damages flowing from an accident. No special pleading is required.
b.	***TRUE***	Medical expenses are special damages that must be specifically pleaded, or they cannot be proved at trial.

c. ***FALSE*** Pain and suffering are general damages that normally flow from injury.

26.a. ***TRUE*** This is an immaterial variance, with no harm to defendant. Thus, Smythe's motion should be dismissed.

b. ***FALSE*** This is a material variance between the pleading and proof; however, the alteration involves the same general subject matter as the original complaint. Thus, it is within the discretion of the court whether or not to grant the amendment. The amendment should be granted only on the condition that defendant have time to gather and present evidence. If, as a result of plaintiff's failure to plead his property damages in the original complaint, defendant has lost valuable evidence on the matter, the amendment can be refused.

c. ***FALSE*** This is a completely different claim from the one pleaded. Unless defendant has, in fact, fully litigated the matter, the amendment should be denied.

27.a. ***TRUE*** The amendment here seeks only to broaden the case ***against Dr. Defendant***. Assuming Plaintiff's delay in altering his claims caused no special prejudice, in most jurisdictions Plaintiff will be permitted to amend, ***and the amendment will relate back*** to the time the original complaint was filed so as to overcome a statute of limitations defense. An amendment relates back when it arises from the same transaction or occurrences set forth in the original pleading. Most courts give a broad interpretation to "transaction or occurrence" for this purpose, and thus would include the amendment in question.

b. ***FALSE*** In most jurisdictions an amendment to join a new party is not permitted after the limitations period has run. The federal rule, however, permits such an amendment if the proposed new defendant knew of the action prior to the running of the period and knew that he would have been named as a defendant had it not been for Plaintiff's error. In the present case, service on Dr. Defendant might be considered notice to Dr. Co-Defendant in light of their close relationship. But because of the error in stating the nature of the cause, it is somewhat difficult to say that Dr. Co-Defendant should have known he was the proper defendant.

28. ***TRUE*** Since a verdict for Plaintiff will necessarily and directly affect Owner's interests, Owner is a necessary party to the action.

29. ***FALSE*** The two brothers are necessary, but not indispensable, parties. This means that they must be joined if such joinder is possible and will not unduly complicate the case. But the case may proceed without them since a decision as to one brother can be rendered without binding the other two.

30. ***FALSE*** Plaintiffs or defendants may be joined if the claims by or against them arise from the same transaction or occurrence and raise a common question of law or fact. The courts give a very broad interpretation to "same transaction or occurrence" for joinder purposes, clearly encompassing these facts.

31. ***FALSE*** Under the Federal Rules and many state courts, as long as joinder of parties is proper (which it is here—same transaction and common question), joinder of claims is also proper.

32. ***FALSE*** Under the Federal Rules, Plaintiff may join all claims he has against Defendant.

33. ***FALSE*** This is a classic case where a class action is appropriate since the issues presented and relief sought are identical for all members of the class. The fact that only a few persons are involved should not prevent the action since nothing would be gained by requiring ordinary joinder or separate actions.

34. ***TRUE*** Under modern rules the court balances the value to be achieved by a class action—such as a single trial on common, vital issues—against the problems that may ensue, such as confusion when each individual plaintiff has to prove his own damages.

35. ***FALSE*** One requirement for the maintenance of a valid class action is that the representative fairly and adequately protect the interests of the class. Moreover, class actions cannot be dismissed or settled without some form of notice to the members. Both of these factors are missing in the present case; hence, Tom cannot be bound by the prior suit.

36.a. ***FALSE*** One defendant may cross-claim against a co-party on any claim arising out of the same transaction or occurrence as plaintiff's claim. This includes claims for indemnity.

b. ***FALSE*** A claim of indemnity can be brought even against an outsider.

37.a. ***TRUE*** A party may discover any information reasonably calculated to lead to admissible evidence, even if the information itself is not admissible at trial.

b. ***FALSE*** Such information is not relevant to the issues. It deals solely with Defendant's trial tactics and is not discoverable.

c. ***TRUE*** The Federal Rules require initial disclosure of copies of insurance agreements under which an insurer might be liable for all or part of any judgment that might be entered.

d. ***FALSE*** Such information is not considered relevant under any discovery rules.

e. ***FALSE*** Privileged information is not discoverable. The purpose of a privilege is to prevent required disclosure of confidential information at any time.

38.a. ***TRUE*** The statements are the work product of Plaintiff's attorney. They can be discovered only upon a strong showing of need. Such need exists only with respect to Sherlock, who is unavailable.

b. ***TRUE*** The work product doctrine does not permit evidence to be hidden, even if that evidence is located by an attorney in preparation for trial.

c. ***TRUE*** A party is permitted to obtain a copy of his own statement. This is a special exception to the work product rule.

d. ***FALSE*** Normally a party cannot obtain the report of an adverse party's expert unless the expert will be called to testify. An exception applies, however, when the party seeking discovery cannot obtain expert information of his own. Therefore, the report should be made available, but only insofar as it relates to the deed that was lost.

39. ***FALSE*** A court can issue protective orders to prevent injustice or harassment through discovery. Assuming that it finds Rotto's claim to be in good faith, the court cannot deny all disclosure. It can, however, order both Rotto and Coca-Cola to disclose their formulas to a neutral arbiter, sworn to secrecy, who shall then report to the court on whether the formulas are substantially identical. If not, further discovery may be denied.

40. ***TRUE*** However, a few jurisdictions allow interrogatories to be served only on adverse parties.

41. ***FALSE*** Many courts, including the federal courts, have dropped this court-order requirement.

42. ***FALSE*** The party seeking discovery may take the deposition of the nonparty. In connection therewith, a subpoena duces tecum can be obtained requiring the deponent to produce the items to be inspected.

43. ***TRUE*** Court control is considered vital to protect parties from abuse.

44.a. ***TRUE*** The examined party may obtain a copy of the medical report, even when he voluntarily agrees to an examination.

b. ***FALSE*** By demanding a copy of the report of Defendant's doctor, Plaintiff waives any privilege he has with regard to reports of his own doctors and must provide Defendant with copies thereof.

45.a. ***FALSE*** Defendant must respond on the basis of what it knows or what a reasonable investigation would reveal. Then, if Defendant cannot admit or deny, Defendant may say so and explain why.

b. ***FALSE*** Defendant must respond by admitting or denying, or explaining why it cannot do either.

c. ***FALSE*** This is a request for a factual conclusion. Defendant may deny the statement if it believes it to be false, but Defendant cannot refuse to answer.

46. ***TRUE*** In most jurisdictions, admission of an issue eliminates that issue from trial. A few courts have held, however, that such an admission is merely evidence that can be refuted by contradictory evidence.

47. ***TRUE*** An order requiring response is the first sanction for refusal to respond.

48. ***FALSE*** The court may do so, but it has a wide variety of other sanctions available.

49.a. ***FALSE*** One party's deposition may be introduced by an adverse party for any purpose. However, a party may not introduce the deposition of a nonparty witness who is available to be called at trial but who does not testify.

b. ***FALSE*** If any witness, including a party, is unavailable at trial—*e.g.,* not subject to service of subpoena or too ill to attend—his deposition may be introduced into evidence by either side.

c. ***TRUE*** This assumes, however, that the party seeking to use the deposition has not procured the eyewitness's absence from the area.

50. ***TRUE*** The pretrial order supersedes the pleadings.

51. ***TRUE*** In most jurisdictions a right to a jury trial exists only in cases that historically would be tried in an action at law as opposed to a suit in equity.

52. ***TRUE*** The court must look to the basic substance of any case to see if a jury trial is appropriate. The underlying relief involved here is a declaration that Plaintiff is not liable in damages, a defensive posture that historically would be taken only in a court of law where a jury trial was available on demand.

53. ***TRUE*** This is a case where both legal and equitable issues exist. The equitable issues clearly predominate. Many jurisdictions would therefore treat this case as solely one in equity without a right to a jury trial. These courts recognize the "clean-up" doctrine under which equity courts, in the interest of economy, can grant incidental legal relief. Federal courts do not recognize the "clean-up" doctrine and therefore would grant a jury trial on the legal aspects of the case.

54. ***TRUE*** When a case involves both legal and equitable issues, and the "clean-up" doctrine does not apply, then there is a right to jury trial on the legal issues. The problem is whether the legal or equitable part of the case is tried first, because on a common law issue (such as fraud, here), once a trier of fact makes a determination, the issue is conclusively decided. In some jurisdictions, including the federal courts, the right to a jury trial is considered so important that whenever common law issues exist, the jury must be permitted to make the first decision.

55. ***TRUE*** Failure to make timely demand results in waiver.

56. ***FALSE*** In deciding whether to grant a motion for judgment as a matter of law (directed verdict), the court must look to all the evidence in the light most favorable to the responding party. Nevertheless, at least if that party has the burden of proof, there must be more than a "scintilla" of evidence in that party's favor. Here, the evidence for Plaintiff is so weak and insubstantial that a court may legitimately determine that no reasonable person could find for Plaintiff.

57. ***FALSE*** Under the usual rule—*i.e.,* that the court must consider all evidence in the light most favorable to the party against whom a verdict would be directed—the court should treat Plaintiff's testimony as untrue, and a motion for judgment as a matter of law (directed verdict) would have to be denied. However, some courts have granted directed verdicts for such a party where his evidence is clear, convincing, and uncontradicted. Such result is arguably called for here, unless the position is taken that Plaintiff's testimony on his own behalf is so unreliable that it must be discounted in these circumstances.

58. ***TRUE*** In most jurisdictions, if a judgment as a matter of law (directed verdict) was not first requested, the trial judge can only grant a new trial.

59. ***FALSE*** The trial judge has discretion to grant a new trial for a broad range of reasons, many of which would be insufficient to justify a reversal.

60. ***TRUE*** The decision to grant a new trial on the damages issue alone is normally within the court's discretion, but only when the jury has erred in its evaluation. Here, it is apparent that the jury has not erred in evaluating Plaintiff's damages but has compromised the damages because of its uncertainty concerning liability. In such circumstances, the court should grant a new trial on the entire case.

61. ***FALSE*** Summary judgment must be denied. The court may not, at this stage, determine which of the witnesses are telling the truth.

62. ***FALSE*** Only where the moving party's affidavits are sufficient to support a summary judgment, if uncontradicted, does the opposing party have the burden to submit counteraffidavits.

63. ***TRUE*** Affidavits are to be made on personal knowledge and must show that the affiant could testify to the facts at trial. If the eyewitness were still alive, summary judgment would be appropriate.

64. ***TRUE*** In default cases, the prayer for relief limits the plaintiff's recovery.

65. ***TRUE*** If the trial court makes an express determination that there is no just reason for delay and makes an express direction for the entry of judgment, many courts allow an immediate appeal.

66. ***FALSE*** Most jurisdictions follow the final judgment rule; therefore, the trial court's decision on a discovery matter would not be appealable.

67.a. ***FALSE*** The issue was not actually litigated. Defendant conceded the issue in the pleadings.

b. ***FALSE*** The issue of the cause of the fire was not necessarily essential to the judgment since the jury could have determined not to believe Plaintiff's evidence as to the existence of the policy. If, however, the evidence showing the existence of the policy was such that reasonable persons could not disbelieve it, some

courts might hold that the decision must be assumed to have been made on the basis that the damage was due to fire.

68. ***TRUE*** Plaintiff as trustee had the power to sue Defendant on behalf of the trust. The decision in such a case is binding on the beneficiaries.

69.a. ***TRUE*** Most courts today permit a party who can only be liable vicariously because of the acts of another person to utilize the exoneration of that other person. Ed had every chance to establish his case against Ralph.

b. ***FALSE*** Transit had no opportunity to litigate the first case. Ralph may have failed to properly defend, and Transit cannot be bound by Ralph's inadequate defense.

c. ***TRUE*** The considerations are the same as in a. above. However, the common law mutuality rule would have prohibited use of the first judgment because Ed could not have used a decision against Transit to establish Ralph's liability in a subsequent suit against Ralph.

d. ***FALSE*** Ralph was not a party and had no opportunity or duty to defend in the first suit. Ralph cannot be bound by possible tactical errors made by Transit's counsel during the trial of the case.

e. ***FALSE*** The significance of Ed's case differs markedly from Alice's case. Transit may not feel that it is necessary or prudent to put forward a full defense to Ed's action where only a small amount is involved or where other tactical considerations dictate a low level of defense. It would then be very unfair to bind Transit in the suit by Alice. Some courts would not permit use of the first decision even if the first case had involved large sums, either because there is a lack of mutuality, or because they do not allow use of collateral estoppel as a sword, or because they feel that the nature of the case makes it unfair to do so.

ESSAY EXAM QUESTIONS

INTRODUCTORY NOTE

The essay questions that follow have been selected to provide you with an opportunity to experience how the substantive law you have been reviewing may be tested in the hypothetical essay examination question context. These sample essay questions are a valuable self-diagnostic tool designed to enable you to enhance your issue-spotting ability and practice your exam writing skills.

It is suggested that you approach each question as though under actual examination conditions. The time allowed for each question is 60 minutes. You should spend 15 to 20 minutes spotting issues, underlining key facts and phrases, jotting notes in the margins, and outlining your answer. ***If*** you organize your thoughts well, 40 minutes will be more than adequate for writing them down. Should you prefer to forgo the actual writing involved on these questions, be sure to give yourself no more time for issue-spotting than you would on the actual examination.

The BARBRI technique for writing a well-organized essay answer is to (i) spot the issues in a question and then (ii) analyze and discuss each issue using the "CIRAC" method:

C — State your ***conclusion*** first. (In other words, you must think through your answer ***before*** you start writing.)
I — State the ***issue*** involved.
R — Give the ***rule(s)*** of law involved.
A — ***Apply*** the rule(s) of law to the facts.
C — Finally, restate your ***conclusion***.

After completing (or outlining) your own analysis of each question, compare it with the BARBRI model answer provided herein. A passing answer does ***not*** have to match the model one, but it should cover most of the issues presented and the law discussed and should ***apply the law to the facts*** of the question. Use of the CIRAC method results in the best answer you can write.

EXAM QUESTION NO. 1

Plaintiff filed a complaint in the United States District Court in State X, alleging in substance the following:

Plaintiff resides in State X; the shopping area nearest to plaintiff's residence is in State Y. Plaintiff read, in a national magazine, an advertisement for an electrical device called "Warnem" which, when installed in a home in accordance with instructions, was designed to sound an alarm bell and turn on the lights if an intruder entered the premises. "Warnem" was manufactured by defendant, Warnem Corporation, incorporated and having its company headquarters in State W; it sells the "Warnem" device f.o.b. its plant in State W to retailers throughout the United States. Plaintiff purchased a "Warnem" from a retailer in State Y and installed it in his home in State X in accordance with instructions. While the "Warnem" was installed and plaintiff was asleep in his home, intruders entered the home and destroyed a rare antique vase worth $5,000. The device failed to function. Plaintiff claims damages of $5,000 for the value of the vase and $100,000 for mental anguish resulting from its loss.

The summons and complaint, issued by the district court in State X, was served on Warnem by personal delivery to the president of the corporation at the corporate office in State W.

You have been consulted by Warnem Corporation. Your research into State X law establishes that the Supreme Court of State X has recently held that there can be no recovery of damages for mental anguish from unintentional conduct unless there has been an impact. What are the various motions that you might make or pleadings that you might file prior to filing an answer in the case, and how would you expect the court to rule on each? Discuss.

EXAM QUESTION NO. 2

Company, a manufacturer incorporated and with its plant and offices in State X, asks Bookkeeper, an accountant of State Y, to prepare a financial statement for publication with a nationwide issue of Company's securities. Company mails its books to State Y, where Bookkeeper prepares a favorable report, negligently failing to discover that Company has fraudulently concealed several million dollars of debts. Company mails the report from State X to stockbrokers in every state. Investor, a resident and businessperson of State Z, reads the report in State Z and in reliance thereon purchases in State Z a number of shares of Company stock. He is later compelled by the economic instability of Company to sell the shares in Colorado at a loss.

Investor sues both Company and Bookkeeper for damages in a State Z court, serving both defendants by registered mail, return receipt requested, in their home states in accordance with a Colorado statute.

Both Bookkeeper and Company appear specially and move to dismiss for lack of jurisdiction over the person. How should the court rule on the motions? Discuss.

EXAM QUESTION NO. 3

Ped is a resident of State A. Driver is a resident of State D. Health is a corporation incorporated in State H with its company headquarters in State A. Ped was injured when struck by a motor vehicle being operated by Driver in State A. Ped was hospitalized in the Health hospital and his injuries were aggravated, allegedly as a result of the hospital's negligence.

Ped sued Driver and Health in state court in State A, claiming damages in the sum of $100,000 and alleging that he was uncertain as to which defendant was responsible for his damages.

(1) Upon Health's timely notice of removal, the case was removed to the United States District Court in State A. Thereafter Ped moved to have the case remanded to the state court in State A. That motion was granted.

(2) After remand, Health demurred on the grounds of misjoinder of parties defendant and improper joinder of several causes of action. The demurrer was overruled.

(3) Both Health and Driver filed answers denying liability and damages. Ped then filed timely requests for admissions, asking that each defendant admit liability, reserving for trial only the issue of damages. Both defendants filed timely objections on the grounds that the requests called for legal conclusions. The objections were sustained.

(4) Following a jury trial, a verdict was returned in favor of Ped and against both defendants in the sum of $43,652.89. Ped moved for a new trial on the issue of damages or, in the alternative, on all issues. He supported his motion by the affidavits of five jurors that stated that: (a) immediately after entering the jury room, the jurors took a ballot on the issue of whether Ped should recover and the vote was 12 to zero in favor of Ped and against both defendants; (b) then each juror wrote down his idea of the amount of the recovery, the figures were totaled, divided by 12, and the result was $43,652.89; and (c) all jurors then agreed that their verdict would be $43,652.89. Based upon defendants' objections, the court refused to consider the affidavits and denied Ped's motion for a new trial.

Discuss the correctness of the court's rulings, setting forth the arguments that might reasonably be made in support of and in opposition to each of the following:

(1) Health's motion to remand;
(2) Health's demurrer;
(3) Ped's requests for admissions; and
(4) Ped's motion for a new trial.

EXAM QUESTION NO. 4

Valco is a corporation incorporated in State B with its principal place of business in State A. It manufactures pressure valves for use on compressed air tanks. It purchases from Mity, a corporation, the "collars" affixed to the pressure valves, which are used to attach the valve to the air tank. Mity is incorporated and has its sole place of business in State A.

The Valco pressure valve on a piece of machinery owned by Peter and Quincy, and used by them in State C, exploded. Peter and Quincy were seriously injured. At all times Peter was a resident of State C. At the time of the explosion, Quincy was a resident of State A, but after the accident he moved to State B, where he now lives.

Peter and Quincy wish to assert claims against Valco and Mity on the theory that the valve exploded because of a defective "collar." Valco has informed Peter and Quincy that it will claim as a defense that a written notice recalling the valves had been sent to them, and to all other users of this model valve, and that Peter and Quincy ignored the notice.

(1) If Peter, as sole plaintiff, institutes an action against Valco, as sole defendant, in United States District Court in State C, may Valco object to the failure to join Mity as a defendant? May Valco bring Mity into the case as a defendant and, if so, how? Discuss.

(2) If Peter and Quincy institute an action against Valco and Mity in United States District Court in State C for $100,000 damages each, what issues might be raised as to joinder of parties plaintiff, joinder of parties defendant, joinder of causes of action, jurisdiction over the defendants, and jurisdiction over the subject matter? How should the trial court rule on each issue? Discuss.

(3) If an action by Peter, as sole plaintiff, against Valco and Mity is commenced and tried in United States District Court in State A, should the trial court apply State A law, State C law, or federal law on the two issues of (a) whether plaintiff must plead freedom from contributory fault, and (b) who has the burden of persuasion on the issue of contributory fault? Discuss.

ANSWERS TO ESSAY EXAM QUESTIONS

ANSWER TO EXAM QUESTION NO. 1

Motion to Dismiss for Lack of Subject Matter Jurisdiction

The district court's power to hear and determine this case turns on whether it has ***jurisdiction over the subject matter,*** otherwise the suit must be dismissed. Since the facts present no "federal question," jurisdiction must proceed based on diversity of citizenship, which requires that all plaintiffs be of diverse citizenship from all defendants, and that there be more than $75,000 in controversy.

Clearly, the diversity element is met (plaintiff residing in State X and Warnem a resident of State W); however, it is debatable whether the amount in controversy exceeds $75,000. The jurisdictional amount is ordinarily determined from the prayer of the complaint, subject to a good faith limitation that there be some reasonable expectation of recovery in excess of $75,000. If it appears to a legal certainty that recovery cannot go above $75,000, the action must be dismissed.

Although plaintiff's complaint alleges $105,000 in damages, $100,000 of this is for mental anguish, and the recent decision of the State X Supreme Court indicates that those damages are not recoverable (no impact). Since a federal court sitting in a diversity case must apply the same substantive law as would the highest court of the state in which it is sitting [Erie v. Tompkins], the court in this case is apparently bound by the State X decision. This would require disregarding the $100,000 claim for mental anguish, with the result that there will be a lack of subject matter jurisdiction and the case must be dismissed.

Motion to Dismiss for Lack of Personal Jurisdiction

Since plaintiff is seeking to recover money damages from Warnem ("in personam" action), there must be a showing of some constitutionally sufficient contact between Warnem and State X to subject the company to the court's personal jurisdiction. Assuming State X statutes empower its courts to exercise jurisdiction up to the constitutional limits, the question is whether those limits would be exceeded in Warnem's case.

Constitutional limits are couched in terms of fair play and substantial justice and require a finding of some purposeful forum-related activity by the defendant. Here, even though Warnem manufactured its alarm device in State W, it advertises and sells the product nationally. Hence, it was logically put on notice that the alarm could theoretically be purchased and cause an adverse effect in any state in the country. Having sought out a national market, Warnem should reasonably be held to answer in the courts of the place where the device was used.

Warnem might argue that it should not be held subject to State X's jurisdiction, on the theory that it sells outright to retailers f.o.b. its State W plant and cannot be responsible for persons like plaintiff who purchase in one state for use in another. Rather, Warnem should be liable at most only in those states where its retailers are located. Nonetheless, this is a weak argument at best: It is a commonplace fact that people who live near a border may purchase nationally advertised products in one state for use in another.

Therefore, on balance, a motion to dismiss should fail, with the result that jurisdiction over Warnem will be upheld.

ANSWER TO EXAM QUESTION NO. 2

Does the State Z Statute Provide an Adequate Basis for Asserting Personal Jurisdiction over Company and Bookkeeper? The question does not set forth the provisions of the State Z statute, and

mere notice to a nonresident outside the state is not sufficient to establish personal jurisdiction. Assuming, however, that State Z has enacted a long arm statute, the court could assert jurisdiction over nonresident individuals and corporations as to causes of action arising out of, among other things, the transaction of business or the commission of a tortious act within the state. Here, since Investor is bringing suit on a tort theory, apparently the "tortious act" part of the statute is being relied on to establish jurisdiction.

Has a Tortious Act Been Committed Within State Z so that the Statute Is Applicable?

Company: Company's fraudulent concealment of its debts was a misrepresentation committed in each state to which it mailed the report and offered its securities for sale. It had a duty to disclose its debts to prospective purchasers, not merely to Bookkeeper. Thus, since the report was sent to State Z and Investor purchased shares in reliance thereon, both the wrongful act (failure to disclose) and the injury to Investor (loss on resale) occurred in State Z, and the statute is applicable.

Bookkeeper: Bookkeeper's negligent failure to discover the concealed debts occurred in State Y, while investor's injury occurred in State Z. In this situation—where an act is done outside the state that causes injury within the state—the cases are in conflict as to whether the long arm statute applies. Some courts have adopted the "place of effect" theory, holding that a tortious act occurs "within" the state if injury occurs there and defendant should have known that his acts might take effect there. Other courts insist that the defendant must be shown to have acted while (physically) within the state.

If State Z follows the "place of effect" approach, Bookkeeper comes within the statute because he was told that his financial statement was for nationwide issue and thus should have known that his act would affect investors in State Z. However, if State Z follows the "place of act" approach, the statute would not apply to Bookkeeper—since he "acted" in State Y—and, hence, there would be no basis for asserting jurisdiction over him.

(*Note:* Since Bookkeeper knew his report would be circulated to every state in the Union, he might also arguably fit within the "doing business" part of the statute even if the "commission of a tortious act" part were held not applicable.)

Has Adequate Notice Been Given to the Nonresidents? The defendants, Company and Bookkeeper, were served by registered mail in their home states in accordance with a statute of State Z. Service by registered mail, return receipt requested, is reasonably calculated to provide the defendant with actual notice of the action. As a result, service by mail, return receipt requested, is constitutional, and thus adequate.

Does the State Z Statute, as Applied to this Case, Meet Constitutional Standards for Personal Jurisdiction?

Company: The Court in *International Shoe v. Washington* set forth the "minimum contacts" approach for testing whether a state can constitutionally assert personal jurisdiction over a nonresident: It must appear that there are sufficient minimum contacts between the defendant and the forum state such that the "maintenance of suit locally does not offend traditional notions of fair play and substantial justice." The modern interpretation of this test merely requires a showing that defendant purposefully engaged in forum-related activity and that the quality of that activity makes it reasonable to expect him to appear and defend. [Hanson v. Denckla; McGee v. International Life]

In this case (as indicated above), Company has committed a tortious act in State Z that injured a local resident. Moreover, it purposefully entered the State Z marketplace by mailing its financial report and offering its securities for sale there. These two factors combined establish constitutionally sufficient contacts for the exercise of personal jurisdiction over Company. Therefore, Company's motion to dismiss should be denied.

Bookkeeper: Should it be held that Bookkeeper has not committed a tort within the state, the State Z long arm statute would not apply and the constitutional question need not be reached. However, if it is concluded that Bookkeeper ***has*** committed a tort within the state, the argument made for jurisdiction over Company applies to him as well. It is immaterial that Bookkeeper is not a corporation because the minimum contacts test applies to ***any*** nonresident defendant. Bookkeeper's knowledge that his report would be circulated nationwide and his probable expectation of a fee for a job that would have consequences in State Z establish the type of purposeful forum-related activity required under the Due Process Clause. Hence, a finding of an adequate basis for personal jurisdiction would be proper, and Bookkeeper's motion to dismiss should be denied.

ANSWER TO EXAM QUESTION NO. 3

(1) Removal to Federal Court and Motion to Remand

Cases within a state court's jurisdiction that could have been brought originally in federal court can generally be ***removed*** to federal court at defendant's request. In this instance, however, removal was improperly granted on two grounds.

The only possible basis for federal jurisdiction over the case is ***diversity of citizenship*** (no federal question presented), but the "diversity" element requires that no plaintiff be a citizen of the same state as any defendant. Here, Ped is a citizen of State A, and Health is a citizen not only of State H (state of incorporation), but also of State A, where it has its company headquarters. Therefore, diversity did ***not exist*** and there was no removal jurisdiction.

Moreover, even if diversity had existed, removal is not permitted where any defendant is a citizen of the state where the action was filed, the theory being that local residents have no basis for fearing a biased forum. Thus, since Ped brought suit in State A, where Health is a citizen, removal should have been prohibited.

Where an action is improperly removed, the appropriate remedy is a ***remand*** back to the state court; and therefore, the federal court acted correctly.

(2) Joinder of Defendants

Today, federal and most state courts have extremely liberal joinder rules. Defendants can be joined where the claim against them arises from the same transaction or series of transactions and involves at least one common question of law or fact.

Both criteria are met here: There are common questions of negligence law, and aggravation of an injury during treatment is considered part of the same series of events as the original injury. Health's demurrer on the ground of misjoinder of parties was therefore appropriately overruled.

Joinder of Claims

In those few states that still follow the stricter standard for joinder, joinder of claims is restricted by a rule requiring that all causes joined affect every party to the action. Since a claim for damages against Driver does not affect Health, and vice versa, if the State A court is bound to follow this rule, the demurrer should have been granted (defect appears on face of complaint).

Modern rules, on the other hand, abolish all restrictions on joinder of claims. Once defendants are properly joined, plaintiff can join as many claims as he has against any of them, regardless of subject matter relationship. Hence, assuming the State A court follows this liberal rule, it was correct in overruling the demurrer.

(3) **Ped's Requests for Admissions**

Any party may serve on any other party a written request to admit the truth of any relevant matter, the purpose being to narrow the issues. Generally, the answering party cannot object solely because the requested admission calls for a legal conclusion, as long as the legal conclusion relates to the facts of the case. Thus, for example, it is proper to ask the adverse party to admit that he was "negligent."

Arguably, however, in this case the request to admit "liability" was improper because it calls for a final legal conclusion. On the other hand, it seems logical that the form of the request should not govern, and since requesting an admission of liability really only calls for an admission of negligence, objections to the requests should not have been sustained. Nonetheless, this court might well be sitting in a jurisdiction that does not permit requests as to ***ultimate issues***. If this is the case, Ped's requests were inappropriate and discovery was properly withheld.

(4) **Motion for New Trial**

Misconduct in jury deliberations is ground for a new trial in whole or in part. One form of such misconduct is the use of ***"quotient verdicts"***—that is, where the jurors agree ***beforehand*** that the measure of recovery will be arrived at by totaling the amount favored by each juror and dividing that total by 12 (number of jurors). A quotient, however, can be used as a starting point for discussion, and here the jurors agreed to the quotient after it was derived; therefore, the verdict is probably proper.

Even if the verdict were improper, however, it is not clear that it could be impeached by use of the juror's own affidavits. A few states allow submission of such affidavits to prove any improper influence on the verdict. However, many states—as well as the Federal Rules—do ***not*** permit juror testimony as to matters occurring during deliberation, so that the quotient verdict apparently could not be attacked by the affidavits used here. Assuming State A follows this restrictive position, the court's refusal to consider Ped's evidence in support of his motion was proper, so that there could be no basis for ordering a new trial.

In the event it is held that it was error, to refuse use of the affidavits, a new trial on the damages issue should result. Moreover, it is arguable that a new trial on ***liability*** is also called for since the jurors spent no time in deliberation and apparently did not take their duties seriously. Although in some courts juror affidavits are not allowed to show lack of deliberation, once accepted on a proper ground (quotient verdict), logically the full text should be considered to prove that an entire new trial is warranted.

ANSWER TO EXAM QUESTION NO. 4

(1) ***Peter v. Valco***

Joinder of Defendants: Whether Valco has ground for challenging Peter's failure to join Mity turns on compulsory joinder rules. Traditionally, courts distinguished between "indispensable" and "necessary" parties. A person is indispensable if his interests are nonseverable from the pending case, and thus must be joined or the suit will be dismissed for lack of subject matter jurisdiction. A necessary party ought to be joined if possible, but since his interests are severable, the court can render an effective judgment without his joinder.

Under the modern approach—represented by the Federal Rules—the court will require joinder of any person who has a ***material interest*** in the case and whose absence would result in ***substantial prejudice*** either to himself or to those parties already before the court.

Applying both the modern and traditional approaches to this case, it does not appear that Mity's joinder is required. Its interests are not in danger because a determination in the present suit will not bind Mity in the future; and although Valco might suffer tactical disadvantages by the absence of Mity as co-defendant, this is not ground for compelling joinder. Valco can protect itself from possible inconsistent liability by impleading Mity (*see* below).

Hence, joinder of Mity is not compulsory and an objection by Valco should be overruled.

Impleader: Where a stranger to a pending lawsuit may be liable for all or part of plaintiff's claim against defendant (*i.e.,* defendant has a potential right to indemnification), that third party can be brought into the suit by ***impleader.*** The major purpose is to avoid two trials with possible inconsistent verdicts.

Here, since it is likely that the underlying cause of the explosion was Mity's fault (allegedly defective "collar"), Valco would have a valid claim for indemnification, and can implead Mity. Moreover, the fact that both Valco and Mity are citizens of A, and hence not diverse, does not destroy the court's jurisdiction. A third-party claim is deemed ***supplemental*** to the main claim and has no effect on jurisdiction.

(2) ***Peter and Quincy v. Valco and Mity***

Joinder of Parties: The liberal Federal Rules allow joinder of plaintiffs and defendants, provided that any right by or against them arises from the same transaction or series of transactions, and that there is at least one question of law or fact common to all.

In this case there are many common questions (*e.g.,* both plaintiffs injured by same defective pressure valve) and the "same transaction" requirement is met by the fact that one single incident caused the harm. Hence, joinder on both sides is warranted.

Joinder of Claims: There is no problem with joinder of causes of action because the Federal Rules have abolished all restrictions. As long as joinder of parties is proper (as here), any claims can be united in a single action, regardless of subject matter relationship. Therefore, any objections to joinder should be overruled.

Jurisdiction over Defendants: Assuming State C has a long arm statute that would give a state court jurisdiction over Valco and Mity, the federal court will follow it, and the only problem is whether application of the statute would violate due process. Under the standard established in *International Shoe v. Washington,* it need only appear that there are sufficient ***minimum contacts*** between the defendants and the forum state such that the maintenance of suit locally does "not offend traditional notions of fair play and substantial justice."

In this case, injury occurred in State C, and if evidence shows that Valco and Mity had reason to foresee that their product would be used there, most courts would find sufficient contacts on the theory that defendant's knowledge that his product might have an adverse effect in the forum state makes it reasonable to hold him answerable there. Here, jurisdiction over Valco should be easily upheld since the fact that it sent plaintiffs a warning in State C implies it knew they were using the product there. And, unless Mity had legitimate ground to believe that the tanks were used only locally in A or B, it is likely that jurisdiction over Mity will also be upheld.

Jurisdiction over Subject Matter: Since no federal question is presented, jurisdiction can only be based on ***diversity of citizenship***—which requires that more than $75,000 be in controversy and that no plaintiff be a citizen of the same state as any defendant.

Here, there is ***not*** complete diversity between the parties. Since citizenship for diversity purposes is determined ***when the suit is filed***, Quincy and Valco are both citizens of B (state of Valco's incorporation and Quincy's residence when suit commenced). Therefore, the court has no power to decide the case and must dismiss for lack of subject matter jurisdiction.

(3) ***Peter v. Valco and Mity***

What Law Applies? Should Peter alone sue Valco and Mity there would be complete diversity. In diversity cases, a federal court is bound to apply the law of the state in which it is sitting on all

substantive matters [Erie v. Tompkins]; however, federal procedural rules control where state procedural rules differ.

Questions of pleading (here, whether plaintiff must plead freedom from contributory fault) clearly involve the mechanics of the federal court system, and as such, the Federal Rules apply.

Burden of persuasion, on the other hand, involves basic policy considerations regarding the substance of the case, so that the federal court must follow *Erie* and apply the same law as would the highest court in State A. Hence, if State A would apply its own law, so would the district court, but if on conflict of law principles State C law would govern (place of injury), the federal court would similarly be bound thereby.

Constitutional Law

CONSTITUTIONAL LAW

TABLE OF CONTENTS

PART ONE: POWERS OF THE FEDERAL GOVERNMENT

I. THE JUDICIAL POWER

A. ARTICLE III

The federal government is a government of limited powers, which means that for federal action to be legitimate, it must be authorized. The Constitution is the instrument that authorizes the federal government to act. Thus, whenever a question involves action by an entity of the federal government, the action will be valid only if it is authorized by the Constitution. The Constitution authorizes a federal court system in Article III, which provides that federal courts shall have judicial power over all "***cases and controversies***":

1. Arising under the Constitution, laws, or treaties of the United States;
2. Of admiralty and maritime jurisdiction;
3. In which the United States is a party;
4. Between two or more states;
5. Between a state and citizens of another state;
6. Between citizens of different states;
7. Between citizens of the same state claiming lands under grants of different states; and
8. Between a state or citizens thereof and foreign states, citizens, or subjects.

B. POWER OF JUDICIAL REVIEW

1. Review of Other Branches of Federal Government

The Constitution does not explicitly state that the Supreme Court may determine the constitutionality of acts of other branches of government. However, judicial review of other branches of the federal government was established in *Marbury v. Madison,* 5 U.S. 137 (1803) (per Marshall, C.J.); the Constitution is "law" and it is the province and duty of the judiciary to declare what the law is.

a. Separation of Powers and Finality of Court Decisions

The Constitution separates governmental powers among the branches of government. This separation of powers doctrine prohibits the legislature from interfering with the courts' final judgments.

Example: The Supreme Court inferred a limitations period under an ambiguous federal securities law. Because new Supreme Court rulings generally apply to all pending cases, the limitations period imposed by the Court resulted in the dismissal of many pending cases as time-barred. Congress amended the securities law to provide (i) a different limitations period and (ii) a special motion for reinstating the cases dismissed as time-barred by the Supreme Court's ruling. The Supreme Court held that the statute providing for the reinstatement of the dismissed cases violated the separation of powers doctrine under the Constitution. [Plaut v. Spendthrift Farm, Inc., 514 U.S. 211 (1995)]

1) **Caution**

When determining whether federal legislation impairs the finality of a decision of the United States Supreme Court, be careful to scrutinize the facts. For example, states have limited power to regulate interstate commerce, while the federal government has plenary power to do so. Thus, a decision that a state lacked the power to enact a particular regulation of commerce does not necessarily prevent Congress from adopting a regulation similar to the state regulation that was struck down. There is no interference with the finality of the Court's decision, because of the difference in standards.

2. **Federal Review of State Acts**

Federal review of state acts (executive, legislative, or judicial) was established by the Marshall Court in a series of decisions. Clear basis exists here in the Supremacy Clause of Article VI, which states that the Constitution, Laws, and Treaties of the United States take precedence over state laws and that the judges of the state courts must follow federal law, anything in the constitution or laws of any state to the contrary notwithstanding. [Fletcher v. Peck, 10 U.S. 87 (1810)]

C. FEDERAL COURTS

Only the actions of Article III courts are the subject of our outline, but you should know that there are two types of federal courts.

1. **Article III Courts**

Article III courts are those established by Congress pursuant to the provisions of Article III, Section 1. Although Congress has plenary power to delineate the jurisdictional limits, both original and appellate, of these courts, it is bound by the standards of judicial power set forth in Article III as to subject matter, parties, and the requirement of "case or controversy." Thus, Congress cannot require these courts to render advisory opinions or perform administrative or nonjudicial functions.

2. **Article I Courts**

Congress has created certain other courts, however, by way of implementing its various legislative powers; *e.g.,* United States Tax Court, courts of the District of Columbia. Judges of such Article I courts do not have life tenure or protection from salary decrease as do Article III court judges. Article I courts are sometimes vested with ***administrative as well as judicial*** functions, and the congressional power to create such "hybrid" courts has been sustained by the Supreme Court. [Glidden v. Zdanok, 370 U.S. 530 (1962)]

a. **Limitation**

Congress may not take cases of the type traditionally heard by Article III courts and assign jurisdiction over them to Article I courts. [Northern Pipeline Construction Co. v. Marathon Pipeline Co., 458 U.S. 50 (1982)—broad grant of jurisdiction to bankruptcy courts, including jurisdiction over contract claims, violates Article III]

D. JURISDICTION OF THE SUPREME COURT

1. Original (Trial) Jurisdiction

Under Article III, Section 2, the Supreme Court has original jurisdiction "in all cases affecting Ambassadors, other public Ministers and Consuls, and those in which a State shall be a Party." This provision is self-executing: Congress may ***neither restrict nor enlarge*** the Supreme Court's original jurisdiction, but Congress may give concurrent jurisdiction to lower federal courts and has done so regarding all cases except those between states.

2. Appellate Jurisdiction

Article III, Section 2 further provides that "in all other Cases before mentioned [*i.e.,* arising under the Constitution, Act of Congress, or treaty], the Supreme Court shall have appellate jurisdiction, both as to Law and Fact, with such Exceptions, and under such Regulations as the Congress shall make."

a. Statutory Application of Appellate Jurisdiction

Congress has provided two methods for invoking Supreme Court appellate jurisdiction: ***appeal*** (where jurisdiction is mandatory), and ***certiorari*** (where jurisdiction is within the Court's discretion). Very few cases fall within the Court's mandatory appeal jurisdiction; thus, appellate jurisdiction is almost completely discretionary.

1) Writ of Certiorari (Discretionary)

The Supreme Court has complete discretion to hear cases that come to it by writ of certiorari. A case will be heard if four justices agree to hear it. The following cases may be heard by certiorari:

a) Cases from the ***highest state courts*** where (i) the constitutionality of a federal statute, federal treaty, or state statute is called into question; or (ii) a state statute allegedly violates federal law [28 U.S.C. §1257]; and

b) All cases from ***federal courts of appeals*** [28 U.S.C. §1254].

2) Appeal (Mandatory)

The Supreme Court must hear those few cases that come to it by appeal. Appeal is available only as to decisions made by three-judge federal district court panels that grant or deny injunctive relief. [28 U.S.C. §1253]

b. Limitations on Statutory Regulation

Ex parte McCardle, 74 U.S. 506 (1868), has been read as giving Congress full power to regulate and limit the Supreme Court's appellate jurisdiction. However, ***possible*** limitations on such congressional power have been suggested:

1) Congress may eliminate certain avenues for Supreme Court review as long as it does not eliminate all avenues. For example, in *McCardle,* two statutes had allowed the Supreme Court to grant habeas corpus to federal prisoners. The Supreme Court upheld the constitutionality of the repeal of one of the statutes because the other statute remained as an avenue for Supreme Court habeas corpus review.

2) Although Congress may eliminate Supreme Court review of certain cases within the federal judicial power, it must permit jurisdiction to remain in ***some*** lower federal court.

3) If Congress were to deny ***all*** Supreme Court review of an alleged violation of constitutional rights—or go even further and deny a hearing before any federal judge on such a claim—this would violate due process of law.

E. CONSTITUTIONAL AND SELF-IMPOSED LIMITATIONS ON EXERCISE OF FEDERAL JURISDICTION—POLICY OF "STRICT NECESSITY"

Even if a federal court has jurisdiction over the subject matter of a case, it still might refuse to hear the case. Whether the court will hear the case (*i.e.,* whether the case is justiciable) depends on whether a "case or controversy" is involved, and on whether other limitations on jurisdiction are present.

1. No Advisory Opinions

The Supreme Court's interpretation of the "case and controversy" requirement in Article III bars rendition of "advisory" opinions. Thus, federal courts will not render decisions in ***moot*** cases, ***collusive*** suits, or cases involving challenges to governmental legislation or policy whose enforcement is neither actual nor threatened.

a. Compare—Declaratory Judgments

Federal courts can hear actions for declaratory relief. A case or controversy will exist if there is an actual dispute between parties having adverse legal interest. Complainants must show that they have engaged in (or wish to engage in) specific conduct and that the challenged action poses a ***real and immediate danger*** to their interests. However, the federal courts will not determine the constitutionality of a statute if it has never been enforced and there is no real fear that it ever will be. [Poe v. Ulman, 367 U.S. 497 (1961)—anticontraceptive law not enforced for 80 years despite open public sales]

2. Ripeness—Immediate Threat of Harm

A plaintiff generally is not entitled to review of a state law before it is enforced (*i.e.,* may not obtain a declaratory judgment). Thus, a federal court will not hear a case unless the plaintiff has been harmed or there is an immediate threat of harm.

3. Mootness

A federal court will not hear a case that has become moot; a ***real, live controversy*** must exist ***at all stages of review***, not merely when the complaint is filed. [*See, e.g.,* De Funis v. Odegaard, 416 U.S. 312 (1974)—dismissing as moot a white law student's challenge to state's affirmative action program, since the student, although originally passed over for minority applicants with allegedly poorer records, had been admitted to law school while litigation was pending, was about to graduate by the time the case reached the Supreme Court, and would receive the same law degree whether or not the affirmative action program was invalidated]

a. Exception—Capable of Repetition But Evading Review

Where there is a reasonable expectation that the same complaining party will be subjected to the same action again and would again be unable to resolve the issue because of the short duration of the action (*i.e.,* where the controversy is capable of repetition yet evading review), the controversy will not be deemed moot. [*See* Weinstein v. Bradford, 423 U.S. 147 (1975)]

Examples: 1) Issue concerns events of short duration (*e.g.,* pregnancy, elections, divorce actions); and

2) Defendant voluntarily stops the offending practice, but is free to resume it.

b. Class Actions

A class representative may continue to pursue a class action even though the representative's controversy has become moot, as long as the claims of others in the class are still viable. [United States Parole Commission v. Geraghty, 445 U.S. 388 (1980)]

c. Distinguish Ripeness

Ripeness and mootness are related concepts in that the court will not hear a case unless there is a live controversy. Ripeness bars consideration of claims ***before*** they have been developed; mootness bars their consideration ***after*** they have been resolved.

4. Standing

The Supreme Court will not decide a constitutional challenge to a government action unless the person who is challenging the government action has "standing" to raise the constitutional issue. A person has standing only if she can demonstrate a concrete stake in the outcome of the controversy.

a. Components

A plaintiff will be able to show a sufficient stake in the controversy only if she can show an ***injury in fact***—caused by the government—that will be ***remedied*** by a decision in her favor (*i.e.,* causation and redressability).

1) Injury

To have standing, a person must be able to assert that she is injured by a government action or that the government has made a clear threat to cause injury to her if she fails to comply with a government law, regulation, or order. Some ***specific injury*** must be alleged, and it ***must be more*** than the merely theoretical injury that all persons suffer by seeing their government engage in unconstitutional actions.

Example: A Communist Party member would have standing to challenge a statute making it a crime to be a member of the Communist Party because the member's freedom of association is directly infringed, but a non-Party member would have no standing.

a) Injury Need Not Be Economic

The injury does not always have to be economic. In some cases, the Court has found that an individual is harmed because the alleged illegal act or unconstitutional action has an impact on the person's well-being.

Example: Law students were allowed to challenge an Interstate Commerce Commission rate-setting policy on the ground that such policies discouraged recycling and thereby diminished the quality of each student's physical environment. If the ICC

rate-setting policy violated congressional statutes, the elimination of those rate-setting policies would have an impact on the students' physical environment. [United States v. SCRAP, 412 U.S. 669 (1973)]

2) **Causation**

There must be a causal connection between the injury and the conduct complained of—*i.e.,* the injury must be traceable to the challenged conduct of the defendant and not be attributable to some independent third party not before the court.

Example: Plaintiffs claiming that a municipality's zoning policies prevented low income persons from finding housing in the municipality were denied standing because they failed to show a substantial probability that they would be able to afford housing in the municipality even absent the zoning policies. [Warth v. Seldin, 422 U.S. 490 (1975)]

3) **Redressability**

In determining whether a litigant has a sufficient injury to establish standing, courts ask whether a ruling favorable to the litigant would eliminate the harm to him. If a court order declaring a government action to be illegal or unconstitutional (and ending that government action) would not eliminate the harm to the litigant, then that individual does not have the type of specific injury that would grant him standing to challenge the government action.

Examples: 1) The Supreme Court held that mothers do not have standing to challenge the government's refusal to enforce criminal laws that would require the fathers of their children to pay child support. The enforcement of the criminal laws against a father who is guilty of nonsupport would not necessarily result in the father's providing support to the mother and her children.

2) Indigents have no standing to challenge an Internal Revenue Service policy that allows hospitals to receive favorable tax treatment even though they refuse to provide free or subsidized care for indigents. The indigents could not demonstrate that a different IRS policy would cause hospitals to provide them with free care.

b. **Common Standing Issues**

1) **Congressional Conferral of Standing**

Congress has no power to completely eliminate the case or controversy requirement, because the requirement is based in the Constitution. [*See* United Food & Commercial Workers Union Local 751 v. Brown Group, Inc., 517 U.S. 544 (1996)] However, a federal statute may create new interests, injury to which may be sufficient for standing.

2) **Standing to Enforce Government Statutes—Zone of Interests**

In some instances a plaintiff may bring suit to force government actors to conform their conduct to the requirements of a specific federal statute. Even in such cases,

the person must have an "injury in fact." Often, the Court asks whether the injury caused to the individual or group seeking to enforce the federal statute is within the "zone of interests" that Congress meant to protect with the statute. If Congress intended the statute to protect such persons, and intended to allow private persons to bring federal court actions to enforce the statute, the courts are likely to be lenient in granting standing to those persons.

Example: Persons who sold data processing services to private businesses had standing to challenge a ruling by the Comptroller of Currency that allowed national banks to make data processing services available to other banks and bank customers. These plaintiffs had an injury in fact because the Comptroller's ruling would hurt their future profits. The plaintiffs were determined to be within the "zone of interests" protected by the federal statutes limiting the authority of the Comptroller and national banks.

3) Standing to Assert Rights of Others

To have standing, the claimant must have suffered or may presently suffer a direct impairment of his ***own*** constitutional rights. A plaintiff may, however, ***assert third-party rights*** where he himself has suffered injury and:

(i) ***Third parties find it difficult to assert their own rights*** (the NAACP was permitted to assert the freedom of association rights of its members in attacking a state law requiring disclosure of membership lists because its members could not file suit without disclosing their identities) [NAACP v. Alabama, 357 U.S. 449 (1958)]; or

(ii) ***The injury suffered by the plaintiff adversely affects his relationship with third parties***, resulting in an indirect violation of their rights (a vendor of beer was granted standing to assert the constitutional rights of males under 21 in attacking a state law prohibiting sale of beer to them but not to females under 21) [Craig v. Boren, 429 U.S. 190 (1976)].

a) Limitation—Family Law Issues

A divorced father sought to challenge on First Amendment grounds, on behalf of his daughter, the saying of the Pledge of Allegiance at her public school because the Pledge includes the words "under God." A state court order gave the girl's mother final authority over decisions regarding the girl's health, education, and welfare. The mother objected to the lawsuit, and neither the mother nor the daughter objected to the Pledge. The Court held that the father lacked standing to bring the claim. [Elk Grove Unified School District v. Newdow, 542 U.S. 1 (2004)]

4) Standing of Organizations

An organization (unincorporated association, corporation, union, etc.) has standing to challenge government action that causes injury to ***the organization itself***. An organization also has standing to challenge government actions that cause an injury in fact to ***its members if*** the organization can demonstrate the following three facts:

(i) There must be an ***injury in fact to the members*** of the organization that would give individual members a right to sue on their own behalf;

(ii) The injury to the members must be ***related to the organization's purpose***; ***and***

(iii) ***Neither the nature of the claim nor the relief requested requires participation of the individual members*** in the lawsuit.

[Hunt v. Washington Apple Advertising Commission, 432 U.S. 333 (1977)]

Example: The All Dentist Association ("ADA") is composed entirely of dentists; its purpose is to promote the professional well-being of dentists. Assume that most ADA members make between $100,000 and $200,000 per year. The ADA would not have standing to challenge a change in the federal income tax rates that will disadvantage all persons making between $100,000 and $200,000 on the basis that the statute deprives all persons (in the income category) of property without due process, because that claim is not related to the organization's purpose—the representation of dentists as such. But the ADA probably could bring a lawsuit challenging a state regulation of dental practices if the regulation injures ADA members, as long as the injury to ADA members does not vary.

5) No Citizenship Standing

As stated above, if an injury is too generalized, there can be no standing. Thus, people have no standing merely "as citizens" to claim that government action violates federal law or the Constitution. Congress cannot change this rule by adopting a statute that would allow persons to have standing merely as citizens (where they otherwise have no direct, personal claim) to bring suit to force the government to observe the Constitution or federal laws. [Lujan v. Defenders of Wildlife, 504 U.S. 555 (1992)]

6) Taxpayer Standing

a) Generally No Standing to Litigate Government Expenditures

A taxpayer, of course, has standing to litigate her tax bill (*e.g.,* whether she really owes X dollars). However, people generally do not have standing as taxpayers to challenge the way tax dollars are spent by the state or federal government, because their interest is too remote.

b) Exception—Congressional Measures Under Taxing and Spending Power that Violate Establishment Clause

There is an exception to the general rule: A federal taxpayer has standing to challenge federal appropriation and spending measures if she can establish that the challenged measure:

(i) Was enacted under ***Congress's*** taxing and spending power (*see* II.A.2., 3., *infra*); and

(ii) Exceeds some specific limitation on the power.

To date, the only limit that the Supreme Court has found on the taxing power is the Establishment Clause. (*See* XXII.D., *infra.*)

Note: The measure challenged must arise under the taxing and spending power. Thus, there was no standing to challenge a federal government transfer of surplus property under the Property Clause that allegedly violated the Establishment Clause. [Valley Forge Christian College v. Americans United for Separation of Church and State, 454 U.S. 464 (1982)] Neither was there standing to challenge expenditures of executive branch general funds that allegedly violated the Establishment Clause. [Hein v. Freedom From Religion Foundation, 551 U.S. 587 (2007)]

7) Legislators' Standing

Legislators may have standing to challenge the constitutionality of government action if they have a sufficient "personal stake" in the dispute and suffer sufficient "concrete injury." [Raines v. Byrd, 521 U.S. 811 (1997)]

Example: A state's lieutenant governor cast the deciding vote to break a tie in the state senate. Legislators who had voted against the prevailing position had standing to challenge the right of the lieutenant governor to vote because his vote completely nullified theirs and caused the specific legislative enactment to go into effect. [Coleman v. Miller, 307 U.S. 433 (1939)]

Compare: Members of Congress had ***no*** standing to challenge the Line Item Veto Act authorizing the President to cancel (veto) certain spending and tax law measures that are part of a bill that he signs into law. *Rationale:* Rather than causing a "personal" and "concrete" injury, the challenged statute caused only a type of "institutional" injury to all members of Congress equally. [Raines v. Byrd, *supra*]

8) Assignee Standing

An assignee of a legal claim has standing even if the assignee has agreed to remit any proceeds recovered from the litigation back to the assignor, if this is done pursuant to an ordinary business agreement made in good faith. [Sprint Communications Co., L.P. v. APCC Services, Inc., 554 U.S. 269 (2008)—a paid collection agent has standing to bring the claims of an assignor even though the collection agent will submit any recovery back to the assignor]

5. Adequate and Independent State Grounds

The Supreme Court will hear a case from a state court only if the state court judgment turned on federal grounds. The Court will refuse jurisdiction if it finds ***adequate and independent*** nonfederal grounds to support the state decision.

a. "Adequate"

The nonfederal grounds must be "adequate" in that they are fully dispositive of the case, so that even if the federal grounds are wrongly decided, it would not affect the outcome of the case. Where that is the case, the Supreme Court's review of the federal law grounds for the state court's decision would have no effect on the judgment rendered

by the state court, so that the Supreme Court, in effect, would be rendering an advisory opinion.

b. **"Independent"**
The nonfederal grounds must also be "independent": If the state court's interpretation of its state provision was based on federal case law interpreting an identical federal provision, the state law grounds for the decision are not independent.

c. **Where Basis Is Unclear**
If it is unclear whether the state court decision turned on federal or state law, the Supreme Court may dismiss the case or remand it to the state court for clarification. However, the Court will usually assume that there is no adequate state ground unless the state court expressly stated that its decision rests on state law. [*See* Michigan v. Long, 463 U.S. 1032 (1983)]

6. **Abstention**

a. **Unsettled State Law**
When a federal constitutional claim is premised on an ***unsettled question of state law***, the federal court should stay its hand ("abstain" temporarily), so as to give state courts a chance to settle the underlying state law question and thus potentially avoid the needless resolution of a federal constitutional issue. [Railroad Commission of Texas v. Pullman, 312 U.S. 496 (1941)]

b. **Pending State Proceedings**
Generally, federal courts will ***not enjoin pending state criminal proceedings***. [Younger v. Harris, 401 U.S. 37 (1971)]

1) **Pending**
State court proceedings are pending if begun before the federal court begins proceedings on the merits. Hence, the order of filing charges is irrelevant. "Proceedings of substance" must occur first in federal court before an injunction will issue. [Hicks v. Miranda, 422 U.S. 332 (1975)]

2) **Civil and Administrative Proceedings**
Federal courts should abstain from enjoining pending state administrative or civil proceedings when those proceedings involve an important state interest.
Examples: 1) A federal court should not enjoin a pending state civil action to remove a child from the child's parents due to alleged child abuse.

2) A federal court should not enjoin: (i) a state court order holding a person or corporation in contempt for failing to pay a civil judgment; or (ii) a state court judgment that permits a plaintiff to execute a lien against a defendant's property. [Judice v. Vail, 430 U.S. 327 (1977); Pennzoil Co. v. Texaco, Inc., 481 U.S. 1 (1987)]

3) **Exception**
An order enjoining state proceedings will be issued in cases of ***proven harassment*** or ***prosecutions taken in bad faith*** (without hope of a valid conviction).

7. Political Questions
The Court will not decide political questions.

a. Definition
Political questions are:

(i) Those issues committed by the Constitution to another branch of government; or

(ii) Those inherently incapable of resolution and enforcement by the judicial process.

Examples: Political questions include:

1) Questions regarding the conduct of foreign relations; or issues as to when hostilities have stopped;

2) Questions relating to which group of delegates should be seated at the Democratic National Convention [O'Brien v. Brown, 409 U.S. 1 (1972)];

3) The procedures used by the Senate to "try" impeachments. Thus, the Court refused to rule on the constitutionality of the Senate's delegation of the duty to take evidence and testimony to a committee of senators prior to the Senate deciding whether to vote for conviction on an impeachment of a federal judge [Nixon v. United States, 506 U.S. 224 (1993)];

4) What constitutes a "republican form of government" guaranteed to the state by Article IV, Section 4 [Pacific States Telephone & Telegraph Co. v. Oregon, 223 U.S. 118 (1912)]; and

5) Whether the number of votes a candidate for Congress received is sufficient to elect him and whether the candidate meets the age and residency requirements for office [Roudebush v. Hartke, 405 U.S. 15 (1972)].

b. Compare—"Nonpolitical Controversies"

1) Legislative Apportionment
Legislative apportionment was considered to be "political" until *Baker v. Carr,* 369 U.S. 186 (1962). The numerous court decisions requiring "one person-one vote" make clear that this is no longer true. [Reynolds v. Sims, 377 U.S. 533 (1964)]

2) Presidential Papers and Communications
These are generally considered to be privileged and protected against disclosure in the exercise of the executive power. But where these documents are necessary to the continuation of criminal proceedings, the question of production is ***justiciable and not political***. [United States v. Nixon, 418 U.S. 683 (1974)]

8. Eleventh Amendment Limits on Federal Courts

The Eleventh Amendment is a jurisdictional bar that modifies the judicial power by prohibiting a federal court from hearing a private party's or foreign government's claims against a state government. [*See* Hans v. Louisiana, 134 U.S. 1 (1890)]

a. What Is Barred?

The Eleventh Amendment's jurisdictional bar extends to the following:

(i) Actions against state governments ***for damages***;

(ii) Actions against state governments for injunctive or declaratory relief ***where the state is named as a party***;

(iii) Actions against state government officers where the effect of the suit will be that ***retroactive damages*** will be paid from the state treasury or where the action is the functional equivalent of a ***quiet title action*** that would divest the state of ownership of land; and

(iv) Actions against state government officers ***for violating state law***.

1) Compare—Sovereign Immunity

The Court has also held that the following are barred by the doctrine of ***sovereign immunity:***

a) Suits against a state government in state court, even on federal claims, without the defendant state's consent [Alden v. Maine, 527 U.S. 706 (1999)—provision in federal Fair Labor Standards Act creating a private cause of action in state courts against state employers who violate the Act violates sovereign immunity]; and

b) Adjudicative actions against states and state agencies before federal administrative agencies [Federal Maritime Commission v. South Carolina State Ports Authority, 535 U.S. 743 (2002)].

b. What Is Not Barred?

1) Actions Against Local Governments

The Eleventh Amendment protects only state governments. Local governments (*e.g.,* cities or counties) are not protected.

2) Actions by the United States Government or Other State Governments

Actions by the United States Government or other state governments are not barred.

3) Bankruptcy Proceedings

The Eleventh Amendment does not apply to federal laws that are exercises of Congress's Article I power to create bankruptcy laws, and thus does not bar actions of the United States bankruptcy courts that have a direct impact on state finances. [Tennessee Student Assistance Corp. v. Hood, 541 U.S. 440 (2004); Central Virginia Community College v. Katz, 546 U.S. 356 (2006)]

c. **Exceptions to Eleventh Amendment**

1) **Certain Actions Against State Officers**
The Supreme Court allows the following actions to be brought against ***state officials*** despite the Eleventh Amendment:

a) **Actions Against State Officers for Injunctions**
A federal court may enjoin a state officer to refrain from future actions that violate federal law or to take prospective actions to comply with constitutional mandates. [*Ex parte* Young, 209 U.S. 123 (1908)]

b) **Actions Against State Officers for Monetary Damages from Officer**
A federal court may hear an action for damages against a state officer for violations of ***federal law if*** the monetary damages are to be paid out of the officer's own pocket. *Rationale:* By acting outside the scope of federal law, the officer is stripped of his representative capacity—the action is not one against a state, but rather is against an individual.

c) **Actions Against State Officers for Prospective Payments from State**
A federal court may hear an action for damages against a state officer where the effect of the action will be to force the state to pay money in the future to comply with the court order. [*Ex parte* Young, *supra*] However, federal court jurisdiction is barred if the action will result in retroactive damages to be paid from the state treasury. [Edelman v. Jordan, 415 U.S. 651 (1984)]

Example: P sues the State Commissioner of the Department of Public Welfare for failing to comply with federal welfare regulations. The federal court can order future compliance with the federal regulations, even if this will result in costing the state a large amount of money in the future. However, the federal court cannot award back payments of amounts previously improperly withheld, because the order would require payment from the state treasury for retroactive relief. [Edelman v. Jordan, *supra*]

2) **Congressional Removal of Immunity Under the Fourteenth Amendment**
Congress can remove the states' Eleventh Amendment immunity under its power to ***prevent discrimination under the Fourteenth Amendment.*** For example, the Equal Pay Act—based on the Fourteenth Amendment—can serve as a basis for federal suits against a state by its employees. [Fitzpatrick v. Bitzer, 427 U.S. 445 (1976)]

a) **Compare—Article I Powers**
Unlike its power under the Fourteenth Amendment, Congress's legislative powers under Article I (*see* II., *infra*) do ***not*** include the power to abrogate state immunity under the Eleventh Amendment. [Seminole Tribe of Florida v. Florida, 517 U.S. 114 (1996)] However, the Supreme Court has held that states may not assert sovereign immunity in proceedings arising under the bankruptcy law. [Central Virginia Community College v. Katz, *supra*]

d. **Summary**
For most bar exam questions, a key principle to remember is this: The Eleventh Amendment will prohibit a federal court from hearing a claim for damages against a state government (although not against state officers) unless:

1) The state has consented to allow the lawsuit in federal court;

2) The plaintiff is the United States or another state; or

3) Congress has clearly granted federal courts the authority to hear a specific type of damage action under the Fourteenth Amendment (*e.g.*, under a civil rights statute).

II. LEGISLATIVE POWER

A. ENUMERATED AND IMPLIED POWERS
The Constitution grants Congress a number of specific powers, many of which are enumerated in Article I, Section 8. It also grants Congress auxiliary power under the Necessary and Proper Clause.

1. **Necessary and Proper "Power"**
The Necessary and Proper Clause grants Congress the power to make all laws necessary and proper (*i.e.,* appropriate) for carrying into execution ***any*** power granted to ***any*** branch of the federal government.
Example: Congress has the power to charter banks since that power is appropriate to executing Congress's enumerated powers to tax, borrow money, regulate commerce, etc. [McCulloch v. Maryland, 17 U.S. 316 (1819)]

Note: The Necessary and Proper Clause is not itself a basis of power; it merely gives Congress power to execute specifically granted powers. Thus, if a bar exam question asks what is the best source of power for a particular act of Congress, the answer should not be the Necessary and Proper Clause, standing alone.

a. **Limitation**
Congress cannot adopt a law that is expressly prohibited by another provision of the Constitution.

2. **Taxing Power**
Congress has the power to lay and collect taxes, imposts, and excises, but they must be uniform throughout the United States. [Art. I, §8] Capitation or other direct taxes must be laid in proportion to the census [Art. I, §9, cl. 4], and direct taxes must be apportioned among the states [Art. I, §2, cl. 3].

a. **Uniformity**
Requirement of uniformity in the levy of indirect taxes (generally, this means any kind of "privilege" tax, including duties and excises) has been interpreted by the Court to mean ***geographical uniformity*** only—*i.e.*, identical taxation of the taxed Article in every state where it is found. [Fernandez v. Wiener, 326 U.S. 340 (1945)]

b. Direct Taxes—Must Be Apportioned

A "direct" tax (imposed directly on property or on the person) has seldom been employed by Congress because of the cumbersome ***apportionment requirement***; taxes on income from real or personal property were initially held "direct" by the Court, but the resulting need for apportioning such taxes was obviated by the Sixteenth Amendment (income tax amendment).

c. Export Taxes Not Permitted

Neither Congress nor the state can tax exports to foreign countries.

d. Taxes Are Generally Valid

Absent a specific restriction such as those above, be very hesitant to rule against a tax measure on the exam. A tax measure will be upheld if it bears some ***reasonable relationship to revenue production*** or if Congress has the ***power to regulate*** the taxed activity.

Example: Special excise tax levied on dealers in illegal narcotics is valid because it raises revenue. [United States v. Doremus, 249 U.S. 86 (1919)]

3. Spending Power

Congress may spend to "provide for the common defense and general welfare." [Art. I, §8] This spending may be for ***any public purpose***—not merely the accomplishment of other enumerated powers. However, nonspending regulations are not authorized. Remember that the Bill of Rights still applies to this power; *i.e.,* the federal government could not condition welfare payments on an agreement not to criticize government policies.

a. Regulation Through Spending

Note that Congress can use its spending power to "regulate" areas, even where it otherwise has no power to regulate the area, by requiring entities that accept government money to act in a certain manner (*i.e.,* attaching "strings" to government grants). (*See* VI.A.2.b., *infra.*)

4. Commerce Power

Article I, Section 8, Clause 3 empowers Congress to "regulate commerce with foreign nations and among the several states, and with the Indian tribes."

a. Definition of Commerce

1) Includes Basically All Activity Affecting Two or More States

Chief Justice Marshall, in *Gibbons v. Ogden,* 22 U.S. 1 (1824), defined commerce as "every species of commercial intercourse . . . which concerns more states than one" and included within the concept virtually every form of activity involving or affecting two or more states.

2) Includes Transportation or Traffic

The Court has consistently regarded transportation or traffic as commerce, whether or not a commercial activity is involved.

Example: Interstate transportation of liquor for personal consumption, women for immoral purposes (not necessarily prostitution), and

interstate transportation of stolen motor vehicles are all interstate commerce.

a) **Vehicular Transportation Not Required**
Any ***transmission across state lines***, such as electricity, gas, telegraph, telephone, TV, radio, and mail transmission (including educational materials and sale of insurance), will constitute interstate commerce.

b. **"Substantial Economic Effect"**
The Supreme Court has sustained congressional power to regulate any activity, local or interstate, that either in itself ***or in combination with other activities*** has a ***"substantial economic effect upon,"*** or ***"effect on movement in,"*** interstate commerce.

Example: The classic case is the Court's holding that Congress can control a farmer's ***production*** of wheat ***for home consumption***. [Wickard v. Filburn, 317 U.S. 111 (1942)] *Rationale:* Cumulative effect of many instances of such production could be felt on the supply and demand of the interstate commodity market.

1) **Power Not Unlimited**
The Supreme Court has recently made clear that the power of Congress to regulate commerce, although very broad, does have limits so as not to obliterate the distinction between what is national and what is local. To be within Congress's power under the Commerce Clause, a federal law must either:

(i) ***Regulate the channels*** of interstate commerce;

(ii) ***Regulate the instrumentalities*** of interstate commerce and persons and things in interstate commerce; or

(iii) ***Regulate activities that have a substantial effect*** on interstate commerce.

a) **Intrastate Activity**
When Congress attempts to regulate ***intrastate*** activity under the third prong, above, the Court will uphold the regulation if it is of ***economic or commercial activity*** and the court can conceive of a ***rational basis*** on which Congress could conclude that the activity ***in aggregate*** substantially affects interstate commerce. [Gonzales v. Raich, 545 U.S. 1 (2005)—upholding regulation of intrastate cultivation and use of marijuana (permitted by state law for medicinal purposes) because it was part of a comprehensive federal program to combat interstate traffic in illicit drugs] However, if the regulated intrastate activity is noncommercial and noneconomic, it cannot be regulated under the Commerce Clause unless Congress can factually show a ***substantial economic effect*** on interstate commerce. [*See, e.g.,* United States v. Lopez, 514 U.S. 549 (1995)—federal statute barring possession of a gun in a school zone is invalid; United States v. Morrison, 529 U.S. 598 (2000)—federal civil remedy for victims of gender-motivated violence is invalid]

5. War and Related Powers

Article I, Section 8 gives Congress the power to declare war, raise and support armies, provide for and maintain a navy, make rules for the government and regulation of the armed forces, and organize, arm, discipline, and call up the militia. Of course, several other congressional powers may have direct or indirect application to military purposes: tax and spending power, commerce power, Senate's treaty consent power, maritime power, investigatory power, etc.

a. Economic Regulation

1) During War

Regulatory power of Congress, especially in economic matters and mobilization of troops, in support of war effort is ***pervasive*** (although theoretically limited by the Bill of Rights); thus, the Court has sustained national price and rent control, as well as conscription and regulation of civilian/military production and services.

2) Postwar

To a considerable extent, this pervasive regulatory power may be validly extended into post-wartime periods both to ***remedy wartime disruptions*** [*e.g.,* Woods v. Miller, 333 U.S. 138 (1948)—rent controls] and to cope with ***"cold war" exigencies***. Legislation in the field of veterans' rights and limitations thereon may be extended indefinitely as long as veterans or their relatives may survive.

b. Military Courts and Tribunals

The constitutional basis of courts of military justice (trial and review of offenses by military personnel, including courts-martial and reviewing agencies and tribunals) is not Article III, but rather Article I, Section 8, Clause 14 (congressional power to make rules for government and regulation of armed forces), buttressed by the Necessary and Proper Clause.

1) Judicial Review

The regular federal (or state) courts have ***no general power to review*** court-martial proceedings. However, in habeas corpus cases, the Article III courts, including the Supreme Court, may make a limited inquiry into the military court's jurisdiction of the person and offense or the validity of the court's legislative creation.

2) Court-Martial of Enemy Civilians and Soldiers Permitted

Military courts may try enemy civilians as well as enemy military personnel, at least during wartime.

a) Suspension of Habeas Corpus for Enemy Combatants

Congress does not have the power to deny habeas corpus review to all aliens detained as enemy combatants absent a meaningful substitute for habeas corpus review. A meaningful substitute would allow prisoners to (i) challenge the President's authority to detain them indefinitely, (ii) contest the military commission's findings of fact, (iii) supplement the record on review with exculpatory evidence discovered after the military commission's proceedings, and (iv) request release. [Boumediene v. Bush, 553 U.S. 723 (2008)]

3) **Court-Martial of American Soldiers Permitted**
Military courts have jurisdiction over ***all*** offenses (not just service connected offenses) committed by persons who are members of the armed services, both when charged and at the time of the offense. [Solorio v. United States, 483 U.S. 435 (1987), *overruling* O'Callahan v. Parker, 395 U.S. 258 (1969)]

4) **Court-Martial of American Civilians Generally Prohibited**
The Supreme Court has denied Congress the power to authorize the court-martial trial of American civilians as long as actual warfare has not forced courts to shut down, even though martial law has been declared [*Ex parte* Milligan, 71 U.S. 2 (1866)]; even though the civilians accused may have been members of the armed forces when committing the alleged offense [Toth v. Quarles, 350 U.S. 11 (1955)] or are dependents of military personnel accompanying the latter overseas [Reid v. Covert, 354 U.S. 1 (1957)] or are civilian employees of the military forces at overseas bases and installations; such trials by court-martial violate the Fifth and Sixth Amendments, particularly the right to trial by jury.

c. **Calling Forth the Militia**
Under the Militia Clauses [Art. I, §8, cl. 15, 16], Congress has the power to authorize the President to order members of National Guard units into federal service—even in circumstances that do not involve a national emergency (*e.g.,* for training outside of the United States). The President need not obtain the consent of the governor of a unit's home state to call it into such service. [Perpich v. Department of Defense, 496 U.S. 334 (1990)]

6. **Investigatory Power**
The power to investigate to secure information as a basis for potential legislation or other official action (such as impeachment or trying impeachments) is a well-established implied power. It is a ***very broad power***, in that an investigation need not be directed toward enactment of particular legislation, but the following limitations on its use do exist.

a. **Authorized Investigation**
The investigatory inquiry must be expressly or impliedly authorized by the congressional house concerned, *i.e.,* by statute or resolution creating or directing the investigating committee or subcommittee.

b. **Witnesses' Rights**

1) **Fifth Amendment**
The privilege against compulsory self-incrimination (the Fifth Amendment) is available to witnesses, whether formal or informal, unless a statutory immunity co-extensive with the constitutional immunity is granted.

2) **Relevance**
Written or oral information elicited by the investigative body must be "pertinent" to the subject of the inquiry.

3) **Procedural Due Process**
Witnesses are generally entitled to procedural due process, such as presence of

counsel and right of cross-examination; but it is not yet clear whether such rights are constitutionally required or whether some of them are required merely by house rule or statute.

c. **Enforcement of Investigatory Powers**
Congress can hold a subpoenaed witness in contempt for refusing to appear or answer before Congress.

7. **Property Power**
Congress has the power to "dispose of and make all needful rules and regulations respecting the territory or other property belonging to the United States." [Art. IV, §3] Many other congressional powers (war, commerce, postal, fiscal, etc.) obviously would be unworkable if the ancillary ***power to acquire and dispose of property of all kinds***—real, personal, and intangible—were not also implied from the main grants.

Example: The Property Clause empowers Congress to even protect wildlife wandering onto federally owned lands. [Kleppe v. New Mexico, 426 U.S. 529 (1976)]

a. **No Limits on Disposition of Property**
There is no express limitation on Congress's power to dispose of property owned by the United States. The power extends to all species of property, such as leasehold interests and electrical energy, as well as ordinary realty and personalty. Moreover, disposal may involve direct competition with private enterprise and has never been invalidated on that ground.

b. **Eminent Domain**
Acquisition of property for a public purpose by eminent domain is indirectly recognized by the Fifth Amendment: ". . . nor shall private property be taken for public use, without just compensation." Federal taking must be for the purpose of ***effectuating an enumerated power*** under some other provision of the Constitution.

8. **No Federal Police Power**
Congress has no general police power (*i.e.,* power to legislate for the health, welfare, morals, etc., of the citizens). Thus, on the bar exam the validity of a federal statute cannot rely on "the police power." However, Congress can exercise police power-type powers as to the District of Columbia pursuant to its power to legislate over the capital [Art. I, §8, cl. 17] and over all United States possessions (*e.g.,* territories, military bases, Indian reservations) pursuant to the property power.

9. **Bankruptcy Power**
Article I, Section 8, Clause 4 empowers Congress "to establish uniform laws on the subject of bankruptcies throughout the United States." This power has been interpreted by the Supreme Court as nonexclusive; *i.e.,* state legislation in the field is superseded only to the extent that it conflicts with federal legislation therein.

10. **Postal Power**
Article I, Section 8, Clause 7 empowers Congress "to establish post offices and post roads."

a. **Exclusive**
The postal power has been interpreted as granting Congress a postal monopoly. Neither

private business nor the states may compete with the Federal Postal Service absent Congress's consent. [Air Courier Conference of America v. American Postal Workers Union, 498 U.S. 517 (1991)]

b. **Scope of Power**
Congress may validly classify and place ***reasonable restrictions*** on use of the mails, ***but may not deprive*** any citizen or group of citizens of the general mail "privilege" or regulate the mail in such a way as to abridge freedom of speech or press (except under valid standards, such as "obscenity") or violate the ban of the Fourth Amendment against unreasonable search and seizure.

11. Power Over Citizenship
Article I, Section 8, Clause 4 empowers Congress "to establish a uniform rule of naturalization."

a. **Exclusion of Aliens**
Congress's power to exclude aliens is broad.

1) **Nonresident Aliens**
Aliens have no right to enter the United States and ***can be refused entry*** because of their political beliefs. [Kleindienst v. Mandel, 408 U.S. 753 (1972)]

2) **Resident Aliens**
Resident aliens are entitled to ***notice and hearing*** before they can be deported.

b. **Naturalization and Denaturalization—Exclusive Control of Congress**
Congress has exclusive power over naturalization and denaturalization. The Supreme Court has held that this grant gives Congress plenary power over aliens (*see* XVIII.D.2.a., *infra*).

1) **No Loss of Citizenship Without Consent**
Under the Fourteenth Amendment, Congress may not take away the citizenship of any citizen—native-born or naturalized—without his consent.

Example: The Court held unconstitutional a statute that provided for loss of citizenship upon voting in a foreign election. [Afroyim v. Rusk, 387 U.S. 253 (1967)]

a) **Proof of Intent**
A citizen's intent to relinquish citizenship may be expressed by words or conduct—and Congress may provide that such intent may be proven by a preponderance of the evidence. [Vance v. Terrazas, 444 U.S. 252 (1980)]

2) **Rights of Children of Citizens**
A person born in another country to United States citizen parents does not have a constitutional right to become a United States citizen. Congress can grant citizenship to children born abroad conditioned on their return to live in the United States within a specified period of time or for a specified number of years. Such a child who fails to return to the United States loses his grant of citizenship because he has failed to meet the statutory condition precedent to his final grant of citizenship.

12. **Admiralty Power**
Although congressional power to legislate in maritime matters is not expressed in the Constitution, the Supreme Court has implied it from the exclusive jurisdiction given the federal courts in this field by Article III, Section 2, supported by the Necessary and Proper Clause of Article I, Section 8.

a. **Exclusive Power**
The congressional power is plenary and exclusive, except to the extent that Congress may leave (and has left) some maritime matters to state jurisdiction.

b. **Navigable Waterways**
The federal admiralty power attaches to all navigable waterways—actually or potentially navigable—and to small tributaries that affect navigable waterways. The federal maritime power is not limited to tidewaters or interstate waters.

13. **Power to Coin Money and Fix Weights and Measures**
Congress has the power to coin money and fix the standard of weights and measures under Article I, Section 8, Clause 5.

14. **Patent/Copyright Power**
Congress has the power to control the issuance of patents and copyrights under Article I, Section 8, Clause 8.

B. DELEGATION OF LEGISLATIVE POWER

1. **Broad Delegation Allowed**
Congress has broad discretion to delegate its legislative power to executive officers and/or administrative agencies [Schechter Poultry Corp. v. United States, 295 U.S. 495 (1935)], and even delegation of rulemaking power to the courts has been upheld [Mistretta v. United States, 488 U.S. 361 (1989)].

Example: Congress can delegate the power to establish sentencing guidelines for criminal cases to a sentencing commission located in the federal courts and made up, in part, of federal judges, as long as the tasks delegated do not undermine the integrity of the judiciary or usurp the powers of the other branches. [Mistretta v. United States, *supra*]

2. **Limitations on Delegation**

a. **Power Cannot Be Uniquely Confined to Congress**
To be delegable, the power must not be uniquely confined to Congress; *e.g.,* the power to declare war cannot be delegated, nor the power to impeach.

b. **Clear Standard**
It is said that delegation will be upheld only if it includes intelligible standards for the delegate to follow. However, as a practical matter almost anything will pass as an "intelligible standard" (*e.g.,* "upholding public interest, convenience, or necessity").

c. **Separation of Powers Limitations**
While Congress has broad power to delegate, the separation of powers doctrine restricts Congress from keeping certain controls over certain delegates. For example, Congress

cannot give itself the power to remove an officer of the executive branch by any means other than impeachment (*e.g.,* if Congress delegates rulemaking power to an executive branch agency (*e.g.,* the FCC), it may not retain the power to fire the agency head). (*See* III.B.1.b.2)a), *infra.*) Similarly, Congress cannot give a government employee who is subject to removal by Congress (other than by impeachment) purely executive powers. (*See* III.B.1.b.2)b), *infra.*)

Example: A federal statute transferred the authority to control two D.C. area airports from the federal government to a local authority. However, the statute reserved to a review board a veto power over the local authority's decisions. The review board was comprised of nine members of Congress. The statute violates the separation of powers doctrine in one of two ways: (i) If the review board's power is considered to be legislative, the statute created an unconstitutional legislative veto (*see* D., *infra*). (ii) If the review board's power is considered to be executive, the separation of powers doctrine prohibits members of Congress from exercising it. [Metropolitan Washington Airports Authority v. Citizens for Abatement of Aircraft Noise, 501 U.S. 252 (1991)]

d. Important Liberty Interests

If the delegate interferes with the exercise of a fundamental liberty or right, the burden falls upon the delegate to show that she has the power to prevent the exercise of the right and her decision was in furtherance of that particular policy.

Example: In *Kent v. Dulles,* 357 U.S. 116 (1958), the Secretary of State was required to issue a passport to a Communist because he could not show that Congress gave him the power to encroach upon the fundamental right to travel simply because the applicant was a Communist.

e. Criminal vs. Civil Punishment

The legislature may delegate its authority to enact regulations, the violation of which are crimes, but prosecution for such violations must be left to the executive and judicial branches. [*See* United States v. Grimaud, 220 U.S. 506 (1911)] However, agencies may enact and impose civil penalties (*i.e.,* fines labeled as civil fines) without prosecution in court. [Helvering v. Mitchell, 303 U.S. 391 (1938)]

C. THE SPEECH OR DEBATE CLAUSE—SPECIAL IMMUNITY FOR FEDERAL LEGISLATORS

Article I, Section 6 provides that "For any speech or debate in either House [members of Congress] shall not be questioned in any other place."

1. Persons Covered

The immunity extends to aides who engage in acts that would be immune if performed by a legislator. [Gravel v. United States, 408 U.S. 606 (1972)]

Note: The Speech or Debate Clause does ***not extend to state legislators*** who are prosecuted for violation of federal law. [United States v. Gillock, 445 U.S. 360 (1980)]

2. Scope of Immunity

Conduct that occurs in the regular course of the legislative process and the motivation behind that conduct are immune from prosecution.

a. **Bribes Excluded**
Taking of a bribe is not an act in the regular course of the legislative process and is therefore actionable. [United States v. Brewster, 408 U.S. 501 (1972)]

b. **Speeches Outside Congress**
Speeches and publications made outside Congress are not protected.

c. **Defamatory Statements**
Republication in a press release or newsletter of a defamatory statement originally made in Congress is not immune. [Hutchinson v. Proxmire, 443 U.S. 111 (1979)]

D. CONGRESSIONAL "VETO" OF EXECUTIVE ACTIONS INVALID

A legislative veto is an attempt by Congress to overturn an executive agency action ***without*** bicameralism (*i.e.,* passage by both houses of Congress) or presentment (*i.e.,* giving the bill to the President for his signature or veto). Legislative vetoes of executive actions are invalid. [Immigration & Naturalization Service v. Chadha, 462 U.S. 919 (1983)] The legislative veto usually arises where Congress delegates discretionary power to the President or an executive agency. In an attempt to control the delegation, Congress requires the President or agency to present any action taken under the discretionary power to certain members of Congress for approval. If they disapprove, they veto the action and that is the final decision on the action. This is unconstitutional, because, to be valid, legislative action (the veto) must be approved by both houses and presented to the President for his approval (*see* III.B.3., *infra*). In *Chadha,* the Court also noted that the legislative veto violates the implied separation of powers requirements of the Constitution.

Examples: 1) Congress granted to the Immigration & Naturalization Service ("INS") the power to deport or suspend from deportation illegal aliens. INS decisions to suspend deportations had to be submitted to Congress. Either house could pass a resolution overriding the decision. This legislative veto provision is unconstitutional. [Immigration & Naturalization Service v. Chadha, *supra*]

2) By statute, Congress grants to the President the power to send military troops into combat, without Congress's prior approval, whenever the United States or its territories are attacked. The statute, however, reserves in Congress the power to force the President to withdraw the troops. The statute does not provide for presidential veto of Congress's decision to withdraw. The decision in *Chadha* suggests that this statute is unconstitutional.

III. THE EXECUTIVE POWER

A. VESTED IN PRESIDENT

The entire "executive power" is vested in the President by Article II, Section 1 of the Constitution. Various executive functions may be and are delegated within the "executive branch" by the President or by Congress.

B. DOMESTIC POWERS

1. Appointment and Removal of Officers

a. Appointment

Under Article II, Section 2, the President is empowered "with the advice and consent of the Senate" to appoint "all ***ambassadors***, other ***public ministers*** and consuls, ***judges of the Supreme Court***, and all ***other officers of the United States***, whose appointments are not herein otherwise provided for . . . but the Congress may by law vest the appointment of such inferior officers, as they think proper, in the President alone, in the courts of law, or in the heads of departments."

1) Appointment of "Independent Counsel" (Special Prosecutor)

A special prosecutor with the limited duties of investigating a narrow range of persons and subjects (*e.g.*, to investigate alleged misconduct of a government employee) is an inferior officer. Therefore, under the Appointment Clause, Congress is free to vest the power to appoint a special prosecutor in the judiciary. [Morrison v. Olson, 487 U.S. 654 (1988)]

2) No Appointments by Congress

Although Congress may appoint its own officers to carry on ***internal legislative tasks*** (*i.e.,* its staff), it may not appoint members of a body with administrative or enforcement powers; such persons are "officers of the United States" and must, pursuant to Article II, Section 2, be appointed by the President with senatorial confirmation unless Congress has vested their appointment in the President alone, in federal courts, or in heads of departments. [Buckley v. Valeo, 424 U.S. 1 (1976)]

b. Removal

As to removal of appointees, the ***Constitution is silent*** except for ensuring tenure of all Article III judges "during good behavior."

1) By President

Under the Court's decisions, the President probably can remove high level, purely executive officers (*e.g.,* Cabinet members) at will, without any interference from Congress. However, after *Morrison v. Olson, supra,* it appears that Congress may provide statutory limitations (*e.g.,* removal for good cause) on the President's power to remove all other executive appointees.

2) By Congress

a) Limitation on Removal Power

Congress cannot give itself the power to remove an officer charged with the execution of laws except through impeachment. A congressional attempt through legislation to remove from government employment specifically named government employees is likely to be held invalid as a bill of attainder.

b) Limitation on Powers of Removable Officers

Congress cannot give a government employee who is subject to removal from office by Congress any powers that are truly executive in nature. For this reason, Congress could not give to the Comptroller General (who could be removed from office not only by impeachment but also by a joint resolution of Congress)

the function of establishing the amount of automatic budget reductions that would be required if Congress failed to make budget reductions necessary to insure that the federal budget deficit did not exceed a legislatively established maximum amount. [Bowsher v. Synar, 478 U.S. 714 (1986)]

2. Pardons

The President is empowered by Article II, Section 2, "to grant reprieves and pardons for offenses against the United States, ***except in cases of impeachment***." This power has been held to apply before, during, or after trial, and to extend to the offense of criminal contempt, but not to civil contempt, inasmuch as the latter involves the rights of third parties. The pardon power ***cannot be limited by Congress***, and includes power to commute a sentence on any conditions the President chooses, as long as they are not independently unconstitutional. [Schick v. Reed, 419 U.S. 256 (1974)]

3. Veto Power

a. Congress May Override Veto by Two-Thirds Vote

Every act of Congress must be approved by the President before taking effect, unless passed over his disapproval by two-thirds vote of ***each house***. [Art. I, §7]

b. President Has Ten Days to Veto

The President has 10 days (excepting Sundays) to exercise his veto power. If he fails to act within that time:

(i) The bill becomes law if Congress is still in session; or

(ii) The bill is automatically vetoed if Congress is not in session (a "***pocket veto***"). [Pocket Veto Case, 279 U.S. 655 (1929)]

Note: Brief recesses during an annual session create no pocket veto opportunity. [Wright v. United States, 302 U.S. 583 (1938)]

c. Line Item Veto Unconstitutional

The veto power allows the President only to approve or reject a bill in toto; he cannot cancel part (through a line item veto) and approve other parts. *Rationale:* The President's veto power does not authorize him to amend or repeal laws passed by Congress. [Clinton v. City of New York, 524 U.S. 417 (1998)]

4. Power as Chief Executive

The President's power over internal (*i.e.*, within the United States) affairs as the chief executive is unclear. Clearly the President has some power to direct subordinate executive officers, and there is a long history of presidents issuing executive orders. Perhaps the best guide for determining the validity of presidential actions regarding internal affairs can be based on Justice Jackson's opinion in *Youngstown Sheet & Tube v. Sawyer*, 343 U.S. 579 (1952):

(i) Where the President acts with the express or implied authority of Congress, his authority is at its maximum and his actions likely are valid;

(ii) Where the President acts where Congress is silent, his action will be upheld as long as the act does not take over the powers of another branch of the government or prevent another branch from carrying out its tasks [*see, e.g.,* United States v. Nixon, I.E.7.b.2), *supra*—President's invocation of executive privilege was invalidated because it kept federal courts from having evidence they needed to conduct a fair criminal trial]; and

(iii) Where the President acts against the express will of Congress, he has little authority and his action likely is invalid.

Example: Hamdan was captured in the Afghanistan war, sent to Guantanamo Bay, and then tried for war crimes by a military commission that had been created by an Executive Order issued after the 9/11 terrorist attack. Citing Justice Jackson's *Youngstown* concurrence, the Court held that the military commission could not proceed, because the executive order authorizing the commission went beyond the limitations that Congress had placed on the President. The Court found that the Executive Order was authorized by an act of Congress that was interpreted as limiting the President's power to convene commissions to those that comply with the Constitution, laws, and rules of war, and that the commission here violated the laws and rules of war in several respects (*e.g.*, it did not require a sufficient showing of the facts justifying the commission's jurisdiction; it did not provide the accused and his attorney sufficient access to the evidence). [Hamdan v. Rumsfeld, 548 U.S. 557 (2006)]

a. No Power to Impound

It follows from the above that the President has no power to refuse to spend appropriated funds when Congress has expressly mandated that they be spent. [Kendall v. United States, 37 U.S. 524 (1838)]

C. POWER OVER EXTERNAL AFFAIRS

1. War

Although lacking the power to declare or initiate a "formal" war, the President has extensive military powers (essentially an external field, although applicable to civil war as well and to many domestic affairs caught up in military necessities).

a. Actual Hostilities

The President may act militarily under his power as ***commander in chief*** of the armed forces and militia (when federalized), under Article II, Section 2, in actual hostilities against the United States without a congressional declaration of war. But ***Congress*** may limit the President under its power to enact a ***military appropriation every two years.*** (A military appropriation may not be for more than two years.)

b. Military Government

This power includes the establishment of military governments in occupied territories, including military tribunals.

2. Foreign Relations

The President's power to represent and act for the United States in day-to-day foreign relations is paramount. He has the power to appoint and receive ambassadors and make treaties (with the advice and consent of the Senate), and to enter into executive agreements. His power is broad even as to foreign affairs that require congressional consent. No significant judicial control has been exercised over this power.

3. **Treaty Power**
The treaty power is granted to the President "by and with the advice and consent of the Senate, provided ***two-thirds of the Senators*** present concur." [Art. II, §2, cl. 2]

a. **Supreme Law**
Like other federal law, treaties are the "supreme law of the land." Any state action or law in conflict with a United States treaty is invalid (regardless of whether it is a state law or a state constitutional provision).

1) **Self-Executing vs. Non-Self-Executing Treaties**
Some treaties are expressly or impliedly self-executing (*i.e.*, they are effective without any implementation by Congress). Others are not effective unless and until Congress passes legislation to effectuate their ends. If a treaty is not self-executing, it is not treated as the supreme law of the land until Congress acts to effectuate it, but the treaty itself can serve as an independent basis for Congress's power to adopt the required legislation (*i.e.*, Congress need not point to one of its enumerated powers, such as the commerce power, as the basis for the legislation).

a) **President Has No Power to Implement Non-Self-Executing Treaties**
Based on the *Youngstown* analysis (B.4., *supra*), the President generally does not have any independent power to issue a "memorandum" ordering compliance with a non-self-executing treaty that has not been the subject of effectuating legislation by Congress. [Medellin v. Texas, 552 U.S. 491—President had no power to enforce provisions of the Vienna Convention (a non-self-executing international treaty) by issuing a memorandum requiring states to grant habeas corpus petitions to reconsider convictions of criminals who are foreign nationals and who were not informed at the time of their arrest of their right to notify their consulate of their detention]

2) **Conflict with Congressional Acts**
Valid treaties are on a "supremacy parity" with acts of Congress; a conflict between an act of Congress and a treaty is resolved by order of adoption—***the last in time prevails***.

3) **Conflict with Constitution**
Treaties are not co-equal with the Constitution. For example, no treaty (or executive agreement) could confer on Congress authority to act in a manner inconsistent with any specific provision of the Constitution. [Reid v. Covert, 354 U.S. 1 (1957)]

b. **Other Limitations**
Other substantive limitations on the treaty power have not been judicially established; but in one case the Court expressed in dictum the view that a treaty could not upset the basic structure of the United States's federalism, or wield a power barred to the national government by the Constitution, or cede any part of a state to a foreign nation without the state's consent. The Court has ***never held a treaty unconstitutional*** (*Reid v. Covert,*

supra, invalidated an executive agreement for violating the Fifth Amendment), but it is conceivable that the treaty power extends only to subjects plausibly bearing on our relations with other countries.

4. Executive Agreements

The President's power to enter into agreements (*i.e.,* executive agreements) with the heads of foreign countries is not expressly provided for in the Constitution; nevertheless, the power has become institutionalized. Executive agreements can probably be on any subject as long as they do not violate the Constitution. They are very similar to treaties, except that they do not require the consent of the Senate.

a. Conflicts with Other Governmental Action

Executive agreements that are not consented to by the Senate are not the "supreme law of the land." Thus, ***conflicting federal statutes and treaties*** will prevail over an executive agreement, regardless of which was adopted first. However, executive agreements prevail over conflicting state laws.

b. Example—Power to Settle Claims of United States Citizens

The President, with the implicit approval of Congress, has power to settle claims of United States citizens against foreign governments through an executive agreement. [Dames & Moore v. Regan, 453 U.S. 654 (1981)]

D. EXECUTIVE PRIVILEGE/IMMUNITY

1. Executive Privilege

The executive privilege is not a constitutional power, but rather is an inherent privilege necessary to protect the confidentiality of presidential communications.

a. Extent of the Privilege

Presidential ***documents and conversations*** are ***presumptively privileged***, but the privilege must yield to the need for such materials as evidence in a criminal case to which they are relevant and otherwise admissible. This determination must be made by the trial judge after hearing the evidence.

1) National Security Secrets

Military, diplomatic, or sensitive national security secrets are given great deference by the courts.

2) Criminal Proceedings

In criminal proceedings, presidential communiques will be available to the prosecution, where a need for such information is demonstrated. [United States v. Nixon, B.4., *supra*]

3) Civil Trials

The Court has avoided ruling on the scope of executive privilege in a civil case. Nevertheless, in *Cheney v. United States District Court*, 542 U.S. 367 (2004), the Court noted that the need for information in a criminal case is "weightier," and the Executive's withholding of information in a civil trial would not impair the judiciary's ability to fulfill its responsibility to resolve cases as much as in a criminal trial. Thus, it appears that an Executive branch decision to withhold information will be given more deference in a civil trial than in a criminal trial.

4) **Screening Papers and Recordings of Former President**
A federal statute requiring the Administrator of General Services to screen presidential papers is valid, notwithstanding the privilege. [Nixon v. Administrator of General Services, 433 U.S. 425 (1977)]

5) **Screening by Judge in Chambers**
The court will determine in an *in-camera* inspection which communications are protected and which are subject to disclosure.

2. Executive Immunity

a. Absolute Immunity for President
The President has ***absolute immunity from civil damages*** based on any action that the President took within his ***official responsibilities*** (even if the action was only arguably within the "outer perimeter" of presidential responsibility). [Nixon v. Fitzgerald, 457 U.S. 731 (1982)] However, the President has ***no*** immunity from private suits in federal courts based on ***conduct that allegedly occurred before taking office***. [Clinton v. Jones, 520 U.S. 681 (1997)] *Rationale:* The immunity is intended only to enable the President to perform his ***designated functions*** without fear of personal liability.

b. Immunity May Extend to Presidential Aides
Presidential aides share in this immunity only if they are exercising discretionary authority for the President in "sensitive" areas of national concern, such as foreign affairs. Other aides are entitled only to a qualified immunity (a "good faith" defense). [Harlow v. Fitzgerald, 457 U.S. 800 (1982)]

Example: The Attorney General does not share the President's absolute immunity for authorizing a warrantless wiretap on "national security" grounds. The Attorney General would have a defense to a lawsuit regarding such a wiretap if it was shown that he was able to act in good faith because his actions were not violating clearly established or well-settled statutory or constitutional rights. [Mitchell v. Forsyth, 472 U.S. 511 (1985)]

E. IMPEACHMENT

1. Persons Subject to Impeachment
The President, Vice President, and all civil officers of the United States are subject to impeachment.

2. Grounds
The grounds for impeachment are treason, bribery, high crimes, and misdemeanors.

3. Impeachment by the House
A ***majority vote*** in the House is necessary to invoke the charges of impeachment.

4. Conviction by the Senate
A ***two-thirds vote*** in the Senate is necessary to convict.

PART TWO: THE FEDERAL SYSTEM

IV. RELATIVE SPHERES OF FEDERAL AND STATE POWER

A. EXCLUSIVE FEDERAL POWERS

1. Power of States Expressly Limited

Some powers are exclusively federal because of express constitutional limitation on or prohibition of the states' exercise thereof—such as the treaty power, coinage of money, and duty on imports.

2. Inherent Federal Powers

Others are exclusively federal in view of their nature—such as declaration of war, federal citizenship, naturalization, and borrowing money on the credit of the United States. Any state exercise of these powers would basically subvert the federal system. On the exam, ***do not*** allow states to take actions that might touch upon ***foreign relations***.

Examples: 1) In *Zschernig v. Miller,* 389 U.S. 429 (1968), the Court held invalid state statutes that sought to withhold the proceeds of local decedents' estates from heirs living in nations that (i) discriminate against Americans in their probate laws, (ii) impede the transmission of funds to the United States, or (iii) confiscate property inherited by their citizens. The Court concluded that such laws are so potentially disruptive of a nationally conducted foreign policy that they are invalid notwithstanding the traditional commitment of probate law to the states.

2) California adopted an act to aid Holocaust victims that, among other things, required any California insurer that sold insurance policies in Europe between 1920 and 1945 to disclose certain information about those policies. The President of the United States also entered into an agreement with Germany regarding Holocaust victims' claims and informed California that its law would impede the effectiveness of that agreement. Nevertheless, California announced that it would enforce its law. Several insurance companies and a trade association brought suit to enjoin enforcement of the act. *Held:* The act interferes with the President's power over foreign affairs and is preempted on that ground. [American Insurance Association v. Garamendi, 539 U.S. 396 (2003)]

B. EXCLUSIVE STATE POWERS

Whereas the federal government has only those powers granted to it by the Constitution, the state governments are governments of "unlimited" powers, having all powers not prohibited to them by the Constitution. This is recognized by the Tenth Amendment, which provides that all powers not delegated to the federal government by the Constitution are reserved to the states (or to the people). However, given the expansive interpretation of federal powers (*e.g.,* the commerce power; *see* II.A.4., *supra*), little state power is exclusive.

C. CONCURRENT FEDERAL AND STATE POWER—SUPREMACY CLAUSE

Most governmental power is concurrent, belonging to both the states and the federal government. Thus, it is possible for states and the federal government to pass legislation on the same subject matter. When this occurs, the Supremacy Clause provides that the federal law is supreme, and the conflicting state law is rendered void.

1. **Actual Conflict Between State and Federal Laws**
A valid act of Congress or federal regulation supersedes any state or local action that actually conflicts with the federal rule—whether by commanding conduct inconsistent with that required by the federal rule, or by forbidding conduct that the federal rule is designed to foster.
Example: Federal law [42 U.S.C. §1983] gives state and federal courts jurisdiction to hear claims for violations of federal rights committed by persons acting under color of state law. New York determined that the majority of suits seeking money damages from corrections officers under section 1983 are frivolous and therefore divested its trial courts of jurisdiction to hear such cases. *Held:* The state's policy of shielding corrections officers from suits under section 1983 violates the Supremacy Clause. State courts must hear federal claims. They may apply their own procedural rules as they do to state claims, but they cannot exclude a class of federal claims from being heard in state court. [Haywood v. Drown, 129 S. Ct. 2108 (2009)]

2. **State Prevents Achievement of Federal Objective**
The conflict need not relate to conduct; it is sufficient if the state or local law interferes with achievement of a federal objective. This is true even if the state or local law was enacted for some valid purpose and not merely to frustrate the federal law.
Example: A purpose of the federal bankruptcy laws is to give bankrupts a fresh start, free of their old debts. A state law providing for suspension of the driver's license of persons who have failed to pay off auto accident judgments, regardless of the judgment debtor's discharge in bankruptcy, interferes with the federal objective and will fail. [Perez v. Campbell, 402 U.S. 637 (1971)]

3. **Preemption**
A state or local law may fail under the Supremacy Clause, even if it does not conflict with federally regulated conduct or objectives, if it appears that Congress intended to "occupy" the entire field, thus precluding ***any*** state or local regulation.

   a. **Express Preemption**
   Federal law may expressly preempt state law. Note, however, that an express preemption clause will be narrowly construed. [*See* Altria Group, Inc. v. Good, 129 S. Ct. 538 (2009)]
   Example: A federal law [15 U.S.C. §1334(b)] provides that: "no requirement or prohibition based on smoking and health shall be imposed under state law with respect to the advertising or promotion of any cigarettes" that are labeled in conformity with federal law. A smoker brought a state law consumer fraud claim against a cigarette company, claiming that the company's advertisements that its cigarettes were "light" and contain less tar and nicotine were fraudulent. The cigarette company argued that its advertisements were in conformity with federal law and, therefore, the state law claim was preempted by the federal law. *Held:* The state law claim is not preempted. The state consumer protection law is based on a duty not to deceive rather than on smoking or health, and the federal law preempts only state laws based on smoking or health. [Altria Group, Inc. v. Good, *supra*]

b. Implied Preemption

If the federal law does not specifically indicate whether state law should be preempted, the courts will try to deduce Congress's intent. For example, if the federal laws are comprehensive or a federal agency is created to oversee the area, preemption will often be found. However, the Supreme Court has stated that in all preemption cases, especially any involving a field traditionally within the power of the states (*e.g.,* regulations involving health, safety, or welfare), it will start with the ***presumption*** that the historic state police powers are ***not*** to be superceded unless that was the ***clear and manifest purpose of Congress.*** [Wyeth v. Levine, 129 S. Ct. 1187 (2009)]

Example: A person who was injured by a prescription drug that was improperly administered brought a state law tort suit against the drug's manufacturer, claiming that the drug's label did not provide adequate warnings. The label was approved by the Food and Drug Administration ("FDA") pursuant to its power to regulate prescription drugs. The drug company claimed that the state tort action was preempted. *Held:* Congress did not intend to preempt the state court action here. The Court held that while Congress enacted the legislation here to protect consumers, it did not provide a remedy for consumers injured by unsafe drugs. Also Congress had not enacted an express preemption provision within the statute for prescription drugs although it did enact an express preemption provision for medical devices. Moreover, there is no conflict between the FDA approval of a warning label and the state tort failure to warn claim here because the FDA regulation allowed companies to strengthen warnings without preapproval and, thus, the company was free to provide stronger warnings. [*See, e.g.,* Wyeth v. Levine, *supra*]

D. ABSENCE OF FEDERAL AND STATE POWERS

Some powers are denied to both Congress and the states. For example, the Supreme Court has held that the Qualifications Clauses [Art. I, §2, cl. 2; §3, cl. 3], setting the qualifications to serve in Congress, are exclusive and cannot be altered by Congress or the states. [United States Term Limits, Inc. v. Thornton, 514 U.S. 779 (1995)—state-imposed term limit for members of Congress invalidated; *and see* Cook v. Gralike, 531 U.S. 510 (2001)—state law instructing each member of its congressional delegation to support a constitutional amendment for term limits, and providing that failure to do so be noted on the ballot, was held invalid because it imposes a substantive qualification rather than regulates the "manner" in which elections are held]

E. INTERSTATE COMPACT CLAUSE

The Constitution provides that states may enter into agreements or compacts with other states upon the consent of Congress. [Art. I, §10, cl. 3] However, not all agreements between states are "compacts" requiring congressional consent. The Compact Clause reaches only interstate agreements that ***increase the political power*** of the states at the expense of federal supremacy (*e.g.,* an agreement whereby one state cedes territory to another state). [*See* United States Steel Corp. v. Multistate Tax Commission, 434 U.S. 452 (1978)—congressional consent not required for multistate tax compact because the compact does not give member states any powers they could not exercise in its absence] The Supreme Court has the power to interpret such compacts—the member states do not have final authority over interpretation. [West Virginia *ex rel.* Dyer v. Sims, 341 U.S. 22 (1951)]

F. FULL FAITH AND CREDIT CLAUSE

The Full Faith and Credit Clause provides that "full faith and credit shall be given in each state to the public acts, records, and judicial proceedings of every other state." By virtue of the Clause, if a judgment is entitled to full faith and credit, it must be recognized in sister states (*i.e.*, a party who loses a case in New York generally may not relitigate it in New Jersey; the New Jersey courts are bound by the New York ruling). However, not every decision is entitled to full faith and credit. There are three requirements:

(i) The court that rendered the judgment must have had ***jurisdiction over the parties and the subject matter***;

(ii) The judgment must have been ***on the merits***; *i.e.,* on the substance of the plaintiff's claim rather than on a procedural issue, such as improper venue or running of the statute of limitations; and

(iii) The judgment must be ***final***.

Although the Clause itself governs only recognition of state judgments in sister states, a federal statute provides for recognition of state judgments in federal courts as well.

V. INTERSOVEREIGN LITIGATION

A. SUITS BY THE UNITED STATES AGAINST A STATE

The United States may sue a state without its consent.

B. SUITS BY STATE AGAINST UNITED STATES—UNITED STATES MUST CONSENT

Public policy forbids a state from suing the United States without its consent. Congress can pass legislation that permits the United States to be sued by a state in given situations.

C. FEDERAL OFFICER AS DEFENDANT

1. Limitation

Suits against a federal officer are ***deemed to be brought against the United States*** itself ***if*** the judgment sought would be satisfied out of the public treasury or would interfere with public administration and, therefore, are not permitted.

2. Specific Relief Against the Individual Officer

Specific relief against an officer as an individual will be granted if the officer acted ultra vires:

a. Beyond his statutory powers; or

b. The valid power was exercised in an unconstitutional manner.

D. SUITS BY ONE STATE AGAINST ANOTHER

One state may sue another state without the latter's consent. The Supreme Court has ***exclusive original jurisdiction***.

VI. INTERGOVERNMENTAL TAX AND REGULATION IMMUNITIES

A. FEDERAL TAXATION AND REGULATION OF STATE OR LOCAL GOVERNMENTS

The Tenth Amendment provides that powers not delegated to the United States by the Constitution, nor prohibited to the states, are reserved to the states. This reservation of power is often cited as a restriction on Congress's power to regulate the states.

1. Tax or Regulation Applying to State and Private Entities—Valid

The Supreme Court will not likely strike down on Tenth Amendment grounds a tax or regulation that subjects states or local governments to regulations or taxes that apply to ***both*** the public sector and the private sector. It has held that in such cases, the states' interests are best protected by the states' representation in Congress. [Garcia v. San Antonio Metropolitan Transit Authority, 469 U.S. 528 (1985)]

Example: Congress can require state and local governments to follow the provisions of the Federal Fair Labor and Standards Act requiring minimum wages for all employees. [Garcia v. San Antonio Metropolitan Transit Authority, *supra*]

2. Tax or Regulation that Applies Only to States

However, the Tenth Amendment does limit Congress's power to regulate the states alone by requiring the states to act in a particular way. Congress may not compel states to enact or enforce a regulatory program. [New York v. United States, 505 U.S. 144 (1992)—federal statute requiring states to either regulate radioactive waste or take title to it is beyond Congress's power] Similarly, if Congress passes a tax that does not apply to private businesses but merely taxes state government entities, there is a possibility that the Court would use the Tenth Amendment to prohibit the tax.

a. Exception—Civil Rights

Congress ***may*** use its power under the Fourteenth and Fifteenth Amendments to restrict state activities that it determines would violate the civil liberties of persons within the state.

Examples: 1) Congress may invalidate state laws establishing a literacy test as a prerequisite to voting in state elections. [Oregon v. Mitchell, 400 U.S. 112 (1970)]

2) Congress may restrict changes in state voting laws that have the effect of diminishing the voting power of racial minorities even though the change in state law was not purposeful racial discrimination that would violate Section 1 of the Fifteenth Amendment. [Rome v. United States, 446 U.S. 156 (1980)]

b. Exception—Spending Power Conditions

Congress may also "regulate" states through the spending power by imposing explicit ***conditions on the grant of money to state or local governments***. Such conditions will not violate the Tenth Amendment merely because Congress lacked the power to directly regulate the activity that is the subject of the spending program.

Example: A federal law that would withhold 5% of the federal highway funds otherwise allocable to a state if the state did not set a 21 years' minimum age for the drinking of alcohol has been upheld. [South Dakota v. Dole, 483 U.S. 203 (1987)]

3. Commandeering State Officials

The Supreme Court has held that the Tenth Amendment prohibits Congress from adopting a statute that "commandeers" state officials by ***requiring states to regulate their own citizens***. [Printz v. United States, 521 U.S. 898 (1997)—striking portions of a federal gun law that required state law enforcement officers to collect from gun dealers reports regarding prospective handgun purchasers and to conduct background checks on them] However, the Court has allowed Congress to ***regulate the states by prohibiting them from performing certain acts***. [*See* Reno v. Condon, 528 U.S. 141 (2000)—upholding federal act that bars states (as well as private resellers) from disclosing personal information required on drivers' license applications]

B. STATE TAXATION AND REGULATION OF FEDERAL GOVERNMENT

1. No Direct Tax on Federal Instrumentalities

A state tax levied directly against the property or operation of the federal government without the consent of Congress is invalid.

2. Nondiscriminatory, Indirect Taxes

Nondiscriminatory, indirect taxes on the federal government or its property are permissible if they ***do not unreasonably burden*** the federal government.

Examples: 1) State income taxes on salaries of federal employees are valid. However, a state tax that imposes a higher tax on federal employees (or retired federal employees) than on state or local government employees (or retired employees) would violate the principle of intergovernmental tax immunity, unless Congress had approved this discriminatory tax. [Davis v. Michigan Department of Treasury, 489 U.S. 803 (1989)]

2) Private contractors, ***acting as purchasing agents*** for the federal government, cannot be compelled to pay state sales or use taxes on materials purchased on behalf of the federal government. However, state sales or use taxes are valid where the contractor is working for the federal government on a "cost-plus" basis. These extra costs are not characterized as direct taxes.

3. State Regulation of Federal Government

The states have no power to regulate the activities of the federal government unless Congress consents to the regulation. Thus, instrumentalities and agents of the federal government are immune from state regulations relating to performance of their federal functions.

Examples: 1) A state may not require a post office employee to obtain a state driver's license in order to drive a mail truck. [Johnson v. Maryland, 254 U.S. 51 (1920)]

2) A state may not require a contractor to obtain a state license to build facilities on an Air Force base, located within the state, pursuant to a government contract. [Leslie Miller, Inc. v. Arkansas, 352 U.S. 187 (1956)]

VII. PRIVILEGES AND IMMUNITIES CLAUSES

A. INTRODUCTION

There are two Privileges and Immunities Clauses: the Fourteenth Amendment Privileges or

Immunities Clause and the Interstate Privileges and Immunities Clause of Article IV. The Fourteenth Amendment clause protects attributes of United States citizenship and is rarely applicable. The Article IV provision prevents some discrimination by states against nonresidents, and is usually more relevant on the bar exam.

B. ARTICLE IV—PRIVILEGES OF STATE CITIZENSHIP

Article IV, Section 2, the Interstate Privileges and Immunities Clause, provides that "[t]he Citizens of each state shall be entitled to all Privileges and Immunities of citizens in the several states." Thus, it prohibits discrimination by a state against nonresidents.

1. Corporations and Aliens Not Protected

Corporations and aliens are ***not citizens*** of a state for purposes of the Privileges and Immunities Clause.

2. Only "Fundamental Rights" Protected

The Interstate Privileges and Immunities Clause does not prohibit all discrimination by a state in favor of its own citizens, but only when the denial concerns "fundamental rights"—*i.e.,* those involving important ***commercial activities*** (such as pursuit of a livelihood) or ***civil liberties***. For example, the following have been struck down:

a. ***Statute charging nonresident commercial fishermen substantially more for commercial fishing license*** than resident commercial fishermen ($2,500 vs. $25) [Toomer v. Witsell, 334 U.S. 385 (1948); *cf.* Baldwin v. Montana Fish & Game Commission, 436 U.S. 371 (1978)—vast difference between resident and nonresident ***recreational*** hunting license constitutional since no essential commercial activity involved];

b. ***Statute giving resident creditors priority*** over nonresident creditors as to assets of foreign corporations in receivership proceedings [Blake v. McClung, 172 U.S. 239 (1898)];

c. ***Statute or court rule requiring state residency to be licensed*** to practice law within the state [Supreme Court of Virginia v. Friedman, 487 U.S. 59 (1988)];

d. ***State income tax only on nonresidents*** who earn money within the state [Austin v. New Hampshire, 420 U.S. 656 (1975)]; and

e. ***State law requiring private sector employers to give hiring preference to residents*** absent a closely related substantial justification (*see* below) [Hicklin v. Orbeck, 437 U.S. 518 (1978)], but states ***may*** require a person to be a resident to hold ***government employment*** [McCarthy v. Philadelphia Civil Service Commission, 424 U.S. 645 (1976) (per curiam)].

3. Substantial Justification Exception

A state law discriminating against nonresidents may be valid if the state has a substantial justification for the different treatment. In effect, it must show that nonresidents either cause or are part of the problem it is attempting to solve, and that there are ***no less restrictive means*** to solve the problem.

Example: The Court held that a city ordinance requiring 40% of employees of contractors and subcontractors working on city construction projects to be city residents was an apparent violation of the Article IV Privileges and Immunities Clause because it gave a preference in private sector employment to city residents. However, the Court found that it could not make a final determination as to ***whether the preference was justified*** in this case because the record from the lower courts did not allow it to evaluate the city's argument that the preference was necessary ***to counteract grave economic and social ills*** in urban environments caused by spiraling unemployment and declines in the population base of such cities. [United Building & Construction Trades Council v. Mayor of Camden, 465 U.S. 208 (1984)]

4. Note—Relationship to Commerce Clause

Although the Article IV Privileges and Immunities Clause and the Commerce Clause may apply different standards and produce different results, they tend to mutually reinforce each other. Consequently, they both have to be considered in analyzing bar exam questions.

C. FOURTEENTH AMENDMENT—PRIVILEGES OF NATIONAL CITIZENSHIP

The Fourteenth Amendment Privileges or Immunities Clause prohibits states from denying their citizens the privileges and immunities of national citizenship, such as the right to petition Congress for redress of grievances, the right to vote for federal officers, the right to enter public lands, the right to interstate travel, and any other right flowing from the distinct relation of a citizen to the United States Government.

1. Corporations Not Protected

Corporations are ***not citizens*** of the United States and are ***not protected***.

2. Bill of Rights Not Included

The *Slaughterhouse Cases,* 83 U.S. 36 (1873), held that the fundamental rights protected against federal abuse (first 10 Amendments) are ***not privileges or immunities of national citizenship*** within the meaning of the Fourteenth Amendment; nor are such other basic rights as the right to live, work, and eat. Thus, the guarantees of the Bill of Rights are protected from state action only by the Due Process and Equal Protection Clauses of the Fourteenth Amendment.

3. Right to Travel and the Privileges and Immunities Clause

The right to travel, which is protected by the Fourteenth Amendment, includes the right of newly arrived citizens to enjoy the same privileges and immunities as are enjoyed by other citizens of the state.

Example: A California statute limiting the welfare benefits of first year residents was held unconstitutional under the Fourteenth Amendment Privileges or Immunities Clause. The statute provided that citizens who had lived in California for less than one year could receive only the benefits they would have received in their prior state of residence. The Court noted that the right to travel includes the right to be treated equally in a new state of residence. [Saenz v. Roe, 526 U.S. 489 (1999)]

PART THREE: STATE REGULATION OR TAXATION OF COMMERCE

VIII. REGULATION OF FOREIGN COMMERCE

A. LIES EXCLUSIVELY WITH CONGRESS

For all practical purposes, the power to regulate foreign commerce lies exclusively with Congress. "Foreign" commerce has been held to include traffic on the high seas, even though both terminal ports are within the United States. [Japan Line, Ltd. v. County of Los Angeles, 441 U.S. 434 (1979)]

B. MINOR EXCEPTIONS WHERE STATE REGULATION PERMITTED

The Supreme Court, however, has recognized a few minor exceptions; thus, the states are free to regulate local aspects of port pilotage and navigation of ships in foreign commerce (*e.g.,* aspects such as safety of handling); and in one case the Court permitted state regulation of excursion boat traffic between Detroit and a Canadian island (state barred racial discrimination among boat passengers) since no Canadians or Canadian products or services were involved. [Bob-Lo Excursion Co. v. Michigan, 333 U.S. 28 (1948)]

IX. REGULATION OF INTERSTATE COMMERCE

A. REGULATION OF COMMERCE BY CONGRESS

As already seen, Congress's power over interstate commerce is "plenary" and pervasive. However, the power is ***nonexclusive***—it is shared with the states to some degree.

1. Power of Congress to Supersede or Preempt State Regulation

Recall that the Supremacy Clause makes federal law supreme. (*See* IV.C., *supra.*) Thus, if a state law regulating commerce conflicts with a federal law, the state law will be void. Moreover, if Congress desires, it may preempt an entire area of regulation, thus preventing states from making any laws concerning the area preempted. (*See* IV.C.3., *supra.*)

2. Power of Congress to Permit or Prohibit State Regulation

Although Congress's commerce power is nonexclusive, the states' power to regulate interstate commerce is restricted by the negative implications of the Commerce Clause, even absent federal legislation—the states generally may ***not*** discriminate against interstate commerce. (*See* below.) Nevertheless, Congress is not so restricted; it may allow the states to adopt legislation that would otherwise violate the Commerce Clause.

Example: A state imposed a 3% tax on out-of-state insurance companies for all premiums received from insuring residents of the state. No similar tax was placed on in-state insurance companies. Although such a tax would ordinarily be held invalid under the Commerce Clause—because it discriminates against interstate commerce—the tax here was upheld because Congress had adopted an act permitting the states to regulate insurance in any manner, as long as the state regulation did not conflict with a federal statute specifically regulating insurance. [Prudential Insurance Co. v. Benjamin, 328 U.S. 408 (1946); *and see* Northeast Bancorp, Inc. v. Board of Governors, 472 U.S. 159 (1985)]

Note: As indicated above, Congress may also prohibit the states from adopting legislation that would otherwise be permitted under the Commerce Clause.

a. **Limitation**
While Congress may permit states to adopt regulations that would otherwise violate the Commerce Clause, such consent will not obviate other constitutional objections to the regulation. Thus, Congress may not give states the power to restrict civil liberties. (*See* X.A.1.b.2)a), *infra.*)

B. STATE REGULATION OF COMMERCE IN THE ABSENCE OF CONGRESSIONAL ACTION

If Congress has not enacted laws regarding the subject, a state or local government may regulate local aspects of interstate commerce if the regulation:

(i) Does ***not discriminate*** against out-of-state competition to benefit local economic interests; and

(ii) Is ***not unduly burdensome*** (*i.e.,* the incidental burden on interstate commerce does not outweigh the legitimate local benefits produced by the regulation).

If either test is not met, the regulation will be held void for violating the Commerce Clause (sometimes called the "***Dormant Commerce Clause***" or "***Negative Commerce Clause***" under such circumstances).

1. Discriminatory Regulations

a. **Generally Invalid**
State or local regulations that discriminate against interstate commerce to protect local economic interests are almost always invalid.

b. **Examples**

1) **Regulations Protecting Local Businesses**
Laws designed to protect local businesses against interstate competition generally will be invalidated.

Examples: 1) A state cannot place a surcharge on out-of-state milk to make that milk as expensive as (or more expensive than) milk produced in the state.

2) A state cannot exempt local businesses or products from taxation or regulation that it seeks to apply to out-of-state businesses or products that come into the state.

3) A law requiring all locally produced solid waste to be processed at a local waste processing business was held to violate the Commerce Clause because it was a trade barrier against competition from out-of-state waste processors. [C&A Carbone, Inc. v. Town of Clarkstown, 511 U.S. 383 (1994)]

2) **Regulations Requiring Local Operations**

If a state law requires a business to perform specific business operations in the state to engage in other business activity within the state, the law will normally be held invalid as an attempt to discriminate against other states where the business operations could be performed more efficiently.

Example: If a state required all businesses that produce melons in the state and all businesses that purchase melons from local producers to wrap or package the melons in the state (before the melons were exported from the state), the law would be invalid as an attempt to force businesses to locate their packaging operations in the state.

3) **Regulations Limiting Access to In-State Products**

A state law that makes it difficult or impossible for out-of-state purchasers to have access to in-state products (other than products owned by the state itself) is likely to be held invalid.

Examples: 1) A state cannot prohibit in-state owners of "ground water" from selling and exporting the water they own to persons in other states.

2) A state cannot require in-state companies to sell products at a lower price to in-state residents than to out-of-state residents.

4) **Regulations Prohibiting Out-of-State Wastes**

A state may not prohibit private landfill or waste disposal facilities from accepting out-of-state garbage or waste or surcharge such waste [Philadelphia v. New Jersey, 437 U.S. 617 (1978); Chemical Waste Management v. Hunt, 504 U.S. 334 (1992)] unless Congress authorizes such discrimination [New York v. United States, VI.A.2., *supra*—federal statute allowing states to impose surcharge on certain out-of-state nuclear wastes upheld]. This rule applies even to hazardous wastes. [Oregon Waste Systems, Inc. v. Department of Environmental Quality, 511 U.S. 93 (1994)]

c. **Exceptions**

1) **Necessary to Important State Interest**

A discriminatory state or local law may be valid if it furthers an important, noneconomic state interest (*e.g.,* health or safety) and there are ***no reasonable alternatives*** available.

Example: A state could prohibit the importation of live baitfish (such as minnows) into the state because the state could demonstrate that it had no other way of effectively avoiding the possibility that such baitfish might bring certain parasites into the state or, in other ways, have a detrimental effect on the state's wild fish population. [Maine v. Taylor, 477 U.S. 1138 (1986)] However, a state could not prohibit the export of live baitfish to out-of-state purchasers because the sale of such fish to out-of-state purchasers would not impair any interest of the state, except the interest of protecting local purchasers of baitfish from competition by out-of-state purchasers. [Hughes v. Oklahoma, 441 U.S. 322 (1979)]

2) **State as Market Participant**

The Commerce Clause does not prevent a state from preferring its own citizens when the state is acting as a market participant (*e.g.,* buying or selling products, hiring labor, giving subsidies).

Examples: 1) A state may purchase scrap automobiles from its citizens at a higher-than-market rate and refuse to pay nonresidents the same amount. [Hughes v. Alexandria Scrap Corp., 426 U.S. 794 (1976)]

2) Under the market participant exception to the Commerce Clause, a city may require that all construction ***projects funded by the city*** be performed by contractors using a workforce composed of at least 50% bona fide residents of the city. [White v. Massachusetts Council of Construction Employers, 460 U.S. 204 (1983)]

a) **Limitation—Interstate Privileges and Immunities Clause**

While a state or local government does not violate the ***Commerce Clause*** by preferring its own citizens while acting as a market participant, there is no market participant exception to the Interstate Privileges and Immunities Clause. Thus, a regulation that interferes with private sector employment, such as the one in example 2), above, may violate the Privileges and Immunities Clause unless the regulating entity can show a substantial justification for the regulation. (*See* VII.B.3., *supra.*)

b) **Limitation—"Downstream" Restrictions**

While a state may choose to sell only to state residents, it may not attach conditions to a sale that would discriminate against interstate commerce.

Example: Alaska violated the Commerce Clause when it imposed a contractual requirement on purchasers of state-owned timber that the timber be processed in Alaska before being shipped out of state. [South-Central Timber Development, Inc. v. Wunnicke, 467 U.S. 82 (1984)—plurality opinion]

3) **Favoring Government Performing Traditional Government Functions**

The Supreme Court applies a more lenient standard when a law favors government action involving the performance of a traditional government function (such as waste disposal). Discrimination against interstate commerce in such a case is permissible because it is likely motivated by legitimate objectives rather than by economic protectionism.

Examples: 1) A county flow control ordinance that favored a state-created public waste facility by requiring waste haulers to bring the wastes to the state facility rather than to private facilities is valid. [United Haulers Association, Inc. v. Oneida-Herkimer Solid Waste Management Authority, 550 U.S. 330 (2007)]

2) A state may exempt from state taxation interest on its own bonds and bonds of its municipalities while taxing bonds of other states and their subdivisions. [Department of Revenue of Kentucky v. Davis, 533 U.S. 328 (2008)—issuing debt securities to pay for

public projects is a "quintessentially public function" with a venerable history]

2. **Nondiscriminatory Laws—Balancing Test**
Sometimes a nondiscriminatory state or local law that regulates commerce may impose a burden on interstate commerce; *e.g.,* a state law regulating the size of trucks within that state may burden interstate commerce because interstate trucking operations will be subject to the law when their trucks enter the state. A nondiscriminatory law will be invalidated only if the burden on interstate commerce outweighs the promotion of legitimate (not discriminatory) local interests. This is a case-by-case balancing test. Thus, some regulations of trucks will be upheld, because they do not impose an undue burden on interstate commerce, whereas other truck regulations will be invalidated, because they would make it extremely difficult for interstate trucking operators to have their trucks travel into or through the state.

a. **Less Restrictive Alternatives**
In determining whether a nondiscriminatory state regulation of interstate commerce violates the Commerce Clause, a court will sometimes consider whether less restrictive alternatives are available.
Example: Although it is legitimate for a city to pass laws designed to ensure that milk products sold within the city are safe, a city cannot require those businesses that wish to sell milk in the city to have the milk processed (purified and placed in bottles) at a processing site close to the city. *Rationale:* The city has a variety of alternatives that impose less burden on interstate commerce.

b. **Absence of Conflict with Other States**
State and local laws regulating commerce are more likely to be upheld when there is little chance that states would have conflicting regulations of the same subject matter.
Example: A state could validly apply a state law prohibiting racial or gender discrimination in the hiring of personnel to an airline doing business in the state because the law was not discriminatory against out-of-state businesses, it promoted a legitimate interest, and no other state could validly require or permit racial or gender discrimination by airlines.

c. **State Control of Corporations**
A different standard may apply to statutes regulating the internal governance of a corporation adopted by the state of incorporation. Because of the states' long history of regulating the internal governance of corporations that they create, and because of their strong interest in doing so, even a statute that heavily impacts interstate commerce may be upheld.
Example: To protect shareholders of corporations incorporated in Indiana from hostile takeovers, the Indiana legislature adopted a "control share acquisition statute." The statute provided that once a person acquires shares that take him across a specified ownership threshold (*e.g.*, one-third ownership of all voting shares), he may not vote those shares unless the other shareholders consent. Even though most hostile takeover bids originate from outside the state, the Supreme Court found that the statute did not violate the Commerce Clause because its aim was to protect current

shareholders, it did not discriminate between takeover bidders based on their state of origin, and there is no chance that the state law would conflict with the laws of other states because the internal governance of a corporation is regulated only by the state in which the corporation is incorporated. [CTS Corp. v. Dynamics Corp. of America, 481 U.S. 69 (1987)]

C. TWENTY-FIRST AMENDMENT—STATE CONTROL OVER INTOXICATING LIQUOR

1. Intrastate Regulations

The Twenty-First Amendment, which repealed prohibition, gives state governments wide latitude over the importation of liquor and the conditions under which liquor is sold or used within the state. However, state liquor regulations that constitute only an economic preference for local liquor manufacturers may violate the Commerce Clause. The Commerce Clause prohibits both outright economic favoritism for local businesses and attempts to regulate out-of-state transactions in order to guarantee the competitive position of in-state businesses.

Examples: 1) A state law that prohibits out-of-state wineries from shipping wine directly to in-state consumers, but permitting in-state wineries to do so if licensed, discriminates against interstate commerce. [Granholm v. Heald, 544 U.S. 460 (2005)]

2) A state law that requires out-of-state distillers or sellers of alcoholic beverages to affirm that the price the distiller/seller is charging liquor retailers or wholesalers in the state is no greater than the price the distiller/seller is charging in other states violates the Commerce Clause. Such a price affirmation law directly interferes with and burdens interstate commerce. The Twenty-First Amendment does not authorize this type of state interference with commerce. [Brown-Forman Distillers Corp. v. New York State Liquor Authority, 476 U.S. 573 (1986); Healy v. The Beer Institute, Inc., 491 U.S. 324 (1989)]

2. Interstate Regulations

Transitory liquor (liquor bound for out-of-state destinations) is subject to the Commerce Clause. Thus, a state prohibition on transporting liquor through the state would probably be held unconstitutional as violating the Commerce Clause.

3. Federal Power

The Twenty-First Amendment does not prohibit Congress from controlling economic transactions involving alcoholic beverages under the federal commerce power. Thus, federal antitrust law can prohibit a practice of liquor dealers that has the effect of fixing minimum prices. [324 Liquor Corp. v. Duffy, 479 U.S. 335 (1987)] Similarly, as mentioned above, Congress may, without violating the Twenty-First Amendment, "regulate" liquor distribution by imposing conditions on the grant of federal funds given under the spending power. [South Dakota v. Dole, VI.A.2.b., *supra*]

D. BAR EXAM APPROACH

Whenever a bar exam question involves a state regulation that affects the free flow of interstate commerce, you should proceed as follows:

First, see if the question refers to ***any federal legislation*** that might be held either to: (i) ***supersede*** the state regulation or ***preempt*** the field, or (ii) ***authorize*** state regulation otherwise impermissible.

Second, if neither of these possibilities is dispositive of the question, ask if the state legislation either ***discriminates*** against interstate or out-of-state commerce or places an ***undue burden*** on the free flow of interstate commerce. If the legislation is discriminatory, it will be invalid unless (i) it furthers an important state interest ***and*** there are no reasonable nondiscriminatory alternatives, or (ii) the state is a market participant. If the legislation does not discriminate but burdens interstate commerce, it will be invalid if the burden on commerce outweighs the state's interest. Consider whether there are less restrictive alternatives.

X. POWER OF STATES TO TAX INTERSTATE COMMERCE

A. GENERAL CONSIDERATIONS

The same general considerations applicable to state regulation of commerce (*supra*) apply to taxation. Pursuant to the Commerce Clause, Congress has complete power to authorize or forbid state taxation affecting interstate commerce. If Congress has not acted, look to see whether the tax ***discriminates*** against interstate commerce. If it does, it is invalid. If it does not, assess whether the burden on interstate commerce outweighs the benefit to the state. Three tests must be met: (i) there must be a ***substantial nexus*** between the taxpayer and the state; (ii) the tax must be ***fairly apportioned***; and (iii) there must be a ***fair relationship*** between the tax and the services or benefits provided by the state.

1. Discriminatory Taxes

Unless authorized by Congress, state taxes that discriminate against interstate commerce violate the Commerce Clause. Such taxes may also be held to violate the Interstate Privileges and Immunities Clause (*see* VII.B., *supra*) if they also discriminate against nonresidents of the state [Austin v. New Hampshire, 420 U.S. 656 (1975)], as well as the Equal Protection Clause if the discrimination is not rationally related to a legitimate state purpose [WHYY, Inc. v. Borough of Glassboro, 393 U.S. 117 (1968)—denial of tax exemption solely because taxpayer was incorporated in another state is invalid].

a. Finding Discrimination

1) Tax Singles Out Interstate Commerce

If a state tax singles out interstate commerce for taxation, the Court ordinarily will not "save" the tax by finding other state taxes imposed only on local commerce (which might arguably eliminate the "apparent" discrimination against interstate commerce).

Example: The Supreme Court invalidated an Ohio statute that gave a tax credit against the Ohio motor vehicle fuel sales tax (paid by fuel dealers) for each gallon of ethanol sold as a component of gasohol if, but only if, the ethanol was produced in Ohio or in a state that granted a similar tax advantage to ethanol produced in Ohio. The Supreme Court found that this tax credit system constituted discrimination against interstate commerce. [New Energy Co. of Indiana v. Limbach, 486 U.S. 269 (1988)]

Note: However, state taxes that single out interstate commerce are considered ***nondiscriminatory*** if the particular statutory section or scheme ***also*** imposes the same type of tax on ***local*** commerce (*e.g.,* sales and use taxes, discussed *infra*).

2) Tax with In-State Subsidy

A seemingly uniform tax may be ruled to be discriminatory if the proceeds from the tax are "earmarked" for subsidies to in-state businesses.

Example: A state imposed a tax on all milk dealers, but the tax law provided that revenue from the tax would be put into a fund that would be used to pay subsidies to in-state dairy farmers. This assessment-subsidy system violates the Commerce Clause because it operates identically to a tax placed only on sales of milk produced outside the state. [West Lynn Creamery, Inc. v. Healy, 512 U.S. 186 (1994)]

b. Choosing the Proper Clause

While a state or local tax that discriminates against interstate commerce generally violates the Commerce Clause, the Clause is not always the strongest argument against the tax.

1) Interstate Privileges and Immunities Clause

If a state or local tax discriminates against a ***natural person who is a nonresident***, the Article IV Interstate Privileges and Immunities Clause is the strongest argument against the tax's validity, because it is more direct than a Commerce Clause argument.

2) Equal Protection

a) Where Congress Approves the Discrimination

Although the Supreme Court normally uses the Commerce Clause to invalidate discriminatory legislation, it may also find that such discrimination violates the Equal Protection Clause. This is important where Congress has given the states the power to do something that would otherwise violate the Commerce Clause: Congress can give states the power to take actions that otherwise would violate the Commerce Clause, but it ***cannot*** approve state actions that would violate equal protection. Thus, if Congress has approved a type of state tax that discriminates against out-of-state businesses, that state tax will not be in violation of the Commerce Clause, but it might be found to be a violation of equal protection.

Example: In *Metropolitan Life Insurance Co. v. Ward,* 470 U.S. 869 (1985), the Court invalidated a state tax on insurance companies that imposed a higher tax on out-of-state insurance companies than was paid by in-state companies. The Court found that federal statutes exempted state regulation of insurance businesses from Commerce Clause restrictions but found that the tax violated equal protection because it did not relate to a legitimate interest of government (*i.e.,* the state does not have a legitimate interest in discriminating against out-of-state businesses simply to protect local economic interests from competition).

b) Taxes Based on Suspect Classifications or Infringing on Fundamental Rights

The Court may use equal protection analysis rather than Commerce Clause analysis to strike state taxes that are imposed on the basis of a ***suspect classification*** or that burden a ***fundamental right***. A state tax system giving tax exemptions only to long-time residents of the state and denying a similar tax exemption to newer residents will be held to violate the Equal Protection Clause.

Example: The Court invalidated a state property tax provision that gave an exemption from the property tax only to those Vietnam-era veterans who had been residents of the state before May 1976. [Hooper v. Bernalillo County Assessor, 472 U.S. 612 (1985)]

2. Nondiscriminatory Taxes

The Court reviews nondiscriminatory state and local taxes affecting interstate commerce and balances the state need to obtain the revenue against the burden the tax imposes on the free flow of commerce—an approach similar to the one used for examining nondiscriminatory regulations to see whether they impose an undue burden on interstate commerce (*see* IX.B.2., *supra*).

a. Factors

The Court generally considers three factors in determining whether the nondiscriminatory tax is valid:

1) Substantial Nexus

A state tax will be valid under the Commerce Clause only if there is a substantial nexus between the activity or property taxed and the taxing state. Substantial nexus requires significant or substantial activity within the taxing state.

Examples: 1) A state in which a sale is made may force the seller to pay a sales tax if the seller has some significant contact with the state (*e.g.,* carries on business in the state). However, the state may not force the seller to pay a sales tax if its only contact with the state is the receipt of orders from sales representatives that may be accepted or rejected by the seller.

2) If an interstate seller solicits sales in a state by mail only, with orders shipped to the state by mail or common carrier, the substantial nexus required by the Commerce Clause is not present—the mere mailing of catalogs to the state and shipment by mail or common carrier is not significant activity within the state. [Quill Corp. v. North Dakota, 504 U.S. 298 (1992)]

2) Fair Apportionment

A state or local tax affecting interstate commerce will be valid under the Commerce Clause only if it is fairly apportioned according to a rational formula (*i.e.,* the tax should be based on the extent of the taxable activity or property in the state). Otherwise the activity or property would be subject to cumulative tax burdens.

Examples: 1) State A imposes a 1% tax on gross receipts of all businesses within the state. Harvester is located in State A but makes a number

of sales out of state. The tax is invalid as to Harvester's out-of-state sales since it potentially subjects those sales to cumulative burdens—the tax by the seller's state and a similar tax by the buyer's state—without apportioning the tax.

2) Chooch is a resident of State A. It owns railroad cars used in interstate commerce. The cars are in State A three months each year and State B three months each year. For a State B property tax on the railroad cars to be valid, it must fairly apportion the tax, so that the cars will not be subjected to a similar tax by State A, thus cumulating Chooch's tax burden.

Note: The taxpayer has the burden of proving an unfair apportionment.

3) **Fair Relationship**

A state or local tax affecting interstate commerce will be valid under the Commerce Clause only if the tax is fairly related to the services or benefits provided by the state.

Example: A state may levy a tax on passengers enplaning at a state airport if the tax is related to the benefits that the passengers receive from the state (*e.g.,* the airport facilities). [*See* Evansville-Vanderburg Airport Authority District v. Delta Airlines, Inc., 405 U.S. 707 (1972)]

B. USE TAX

Use taxes are taxes imposed on the users of goods purchased out of state.

1. Permissible in Buyer's State

Use taxes are not considered to discriminate against interstate commerce even though they single out interstate commerce for taxation (*i.e.,* they are imposed only on goods purchased outside the state), as long as the use tax rate is not higher than the sales tax rate. *Rationale:* The purpose of such a tax is to ***equalize*** the tax on in-state and out-of-state goods rather than to give in-state goods an advantage. [*See* Henneford v. Silas Mason Co., 300 U.S. 577 (1937)]

2. State May Force Seller to Collect Use Tax

Often, states force the user to come forward and pay the state the use tax owed. However, a state may force a nonresident, interstate seller to ***collect*** the use tax from the local buyer and remit it to the state ***if*** the seller has the substantial nexus required by the Commerce Clause. The substantial nexus requirement can be met if the seller engages in some ***significant activity*** in the buyer's state, *e.g.,* maintains offices there. Merely soliciting orders by mail and shipping orders into the state is not sufficient. [Quill Corp. v. North Dakota, A.2.a.1), *supra*]

C. SALES TAXES

Sales taxes are taxes imposed on the seller of goods for sales consummated within the state. They generally do not discriminate against interstate commerce; rather the issue usually involves whether there is a substantial nexus (*see* A.2.a.1), *supra*) between the taxpayer and the taxing state, or whether the tax is properly apportioned.

D. AD VALOREM PROPERTY TAXES

Ad valorem property taxes are taxes based on a percentage of the assessed value of the property in question. Such taxes are generally valid. However, a Commerce Clause issue arises when the property taxed moves in interstate commerce. Goods in transit are ***totally exempt*** from taxation. Once the goods come to a halt in a state (*i.e.,* obtain a ***taxable situs***), they may be taxed. Then, the issue usually revolves around whether the tax imposes an undue cumulative burden (*i.e.,* apportionment).

1. No Tax on Commodities in the Course of Interstate Commerce

Commodities in the course of interstate commerce are ***entirely exempt*** from local taxation—since each state could otherwise exact a toll as the goods passed through, imposing an intolerable burden on interstate commerce. [Standard Oil v. Peck, 342 U.S. 382 (1952)] Thus, states may not levy an ad valorem property tax on commodities being shipped in interstate commerce, even if the goods happen to be in the state on tax day.

a. When Is Property "in the Course of" Interstate Commerce?

Only property "in the course of" interstate commerce is immune from local property taxation.

1) When Does Interstate Transportation Begin?

Interstate transportation begins when (i) the cargo is delivered to an interstate carrier (the shipper thereby relinquishing further control), ***or*** (ii) the cargo actually starts its interstate journey. Goods merely being prepared for transit are ***not*** in the course of interstate commerce.

2) Effect of a "Break" in Transit

Once started, a shipment remains in the course of interstate commerce unless actually diverted. Breaks in the continuity of transit will not destroy the interstate character of the shipment, unless the break was ***intended to end or suspend*** (rather than temporarily interrupt) the shipment.

3) When Does Interstate Shipment End?

The interstate shipment usually ends when it ***reaches its destination***, and thereafter the goods are ***subject to local tax***.

b. No Apportionment Required

The validity of state taxes on goods in interstate commerce is strictly a Commerce Clause question; *i.e.*, either the goods are "in the course of" interstate commerce and exempt from tax or they are not. There is no need for apportionment.

2. Tax on Instrumentalities Used to Transport Goods Interstate

The validity of ad valorem property taxes on instrumentalities of commerce (airplanes, railroad cars, etc.) depends on (i) whether the instrumentality has acquired a ***"taxable situs"*** in the taxing state (*i.e.,* whether there are ***sufficient "contacts" with the taxing state*** to justify the tax), and (ii) since the physical situs of the instrumentalities may change from state to state during the year, whether the ***value*** of the instrumentality has been properly ***apportioned according to the amount of "contacts"*** with each taxing state. (The taxable situs ("nexus") is required by the Due Process Clause to establish the state's power to tax at all, and apportionment is required by the Commerce Clause to prevent an intolerable burden on interstate commerce.)

a. **Taxable Situs ("Nexus")**
In general, an instrumentality has a taxable situs in a state if it receives ***benefits or protection*** from the state. [Braniff Airways v. Nebraska Board of Equalization and Assessment, 347 U.S. 590 (1954)—airplanes have taxable situs in nondomiciliary state where airline company owned no property but made 18 regularly scheduled flights per day from rented depot space, even though same aircraft did not land every day] Note that an instrumentality ***may have more than one taxable situs***, upon each of which states can impose a tax subject to the required apportionment (*infra*).

b. **Apportionment Requirement**
If an instrumentality has only one situs, the domiciliary state can tax at full value. If the instrumentality has more than one taxable situs, a tax apportioned on the value of the instrumentality will be upheld if it fairly approximates the average physical presence of the instrumentality within the taxing state. [Union Tank Line Co. v. Wright, 249 U.S. 275 (1919)] The ***taxpayer has the burden*** of proving that an instrumentality has acquired a taxable situs outside his domiciliary state.

1) **Proper Apportionment**
The following methods have been upheld:

(i) Using the proportion of ***miles traveled*** within the taxing state to the total number of miles traveled by the instrumentalities in the entire operation. [Ott v. Mississippi Valley Barge Line Co., 336 U.S. 169 (1949)]

(ii) Computing the ***average number of instrumentalities*** (tank cars) ***physically present*** in the taxing state on any one day during the tax year and taxing that portion at full value—*i.e.,* as if in the state all year. [Johnson Oil Refining Co. v. Oklahoma, 290 U.S. 158 (1933)]

Note: Because different states may use different apportionment formulas to tax the same property, there may still be some double taxation of the same instrumentalities. However, the double taxation should be minimal if proper apportionment formulas have been used.

E. PRIVILEGE, LICENSE, FRANCHISE, OR OCCUPATION TAXES

Privilege, license, franchise, and occupation taxes are cumulatively known as "doing business" taxes. States generally can impose such taxes—on companies engaged exclusively in interstate commerce, as well as on interstate companies engaged in local commerce—for the privilege of doing business within the state. Such taxes may be measured by a flat amount or by a proportional rate based on revenue derived from the taxing state. In either case, the tax must meet the basic requirements—the activity taxed must have a ***substantial nexus to the taxing state***; and the tax must be ***fairly apportioned***, must ***not discriminate*** against interstate commerce, and must ***fairly relate to services provided*** by the state. [Complete Auto Transit, Inc. v. Brady, 430 U.S. 274 (1977)—*overruling* Spector Motor Service v. O'Connor, 340 U.S. 602 (1951)]

Examples: 1) A privilege tax for doing business, based on the gross income derived from transporting goods within the state, can be applied to a trucking company that delivers goods coming from outside the state. [Complete Auto Transit, Inc. v. Brady, *supra*]

2) An occupation tax on all businesses, based on gross income derived within the state, can be applied to a stevedoring company operating within the state that loads and unloads ships carrying goods in interstate commerce. [Department of Revenue v. Association of Washington Stevedoring Cos., 435 U.S. 734 (1978)—*overruling* Joseph v. Carter & Weekes Stevedoring Co., 330 U.S. 442 (1947)]

1. Taxpayer Has Burden of Proof

The taxpayer has the burden of showing that the state's apportionment formula is unfair. However, a state tax that discriminates against interstate commerce will be held invalid regardless of whether the taxpayer can show that an actual, unfair multiple burden is imposed on his business.

XI. POWER OF STATES TO TAX FOREIGN COMMERCE

A. IMPORT-EXPORT CLAUSE

Article I, Section 10, Clause 2 provides: "No state shall, without the Consent of the Congress, lay any Imposts or Duties on Imports or Exports, except what may be absolutely necessary for executing its inspection Laws . . . ."

1. State Taxation of "Imports" Prohibited Absent Congressional Consent

The Import-Export Clause prohibits the states from imposing any tax on imported goods as such or on commercial activity connected with imported goods ***as such*** (*i.e.,* taxes discriminating against imports), except with congressional consent. [Brown v. Maryland, 25 U.S. 419 (1827)]

2. State Taxation of "Exports" Prohibited

The Import-Export Clause prohibits the states from imposing any tax on goods after they have entered the "export stream."

B. COMMERCE CLAUSE

The Commerce Clause gives Congress the exclusive power to regulate foreign commerce and thus inherently limits a state's power to tax that commerce. Therefore, a state tax applied to foreign commerce must meet all of the Commerce Clause tests that apply to state taxation of interstate commerce. (*See* X.A., *supra.*) And even if a state tax meets those tests, the tax is invalid if it would (i) create a substantial risk of international multiple taxation or (ii) prevent the federal government from "speaking with one voice" regarding international trade or foreign affairs issues. [Barclays Bank PLC v. Franchise Tax Board, 512 U.S. 298 (1994)]

PART FOUR: INDIVIDUAL GUARANTEES AGAINST GOVERNMENTAL OR PRIVATE ACTION

XII. LIMITATIONS ON POWER AND STATE ACTION REQUIREMENT

A. CONSTITUTIONAL RESTRICTIONS ON POWER OVER INDIVIDUALS

The Constitution provides individuals with a number of rights that restrict the power of the government (*e.g.,* the right to speak freely). Some rights/restrictions are applicable only to the federal government, some are applicable only to state and local governments, and some are applicable to all governmental bodies. A few even apply to private action. Several constitutional provisions also give Congress the power to adopt legislation to protect individual rights.

Note: The Constitution sets the ***minimum level*** of protection for individuals. States generally are free to grant broader protections than those granted in the United States Constitution.

1. Bill of Rights

The Bill of Rights (first 10 Amendments to the Constitution) is the most important source of limitations on the federal government's power. By its terms, the Bill is not applicable to the states, although most of its safeguards have been held to be applicable to the states through the Fourteenth Amendment Due Process Clause.

a. Rights Applicable to States

The Supreme Court has stated that only those safeguards in the Bill of Rights that are "essential to liberty" are applicable to the states through the Fourteenth Amendment. Included in this concept are: ***all the First Amendment*** guarantees (speech, press, assembly, right to petition, free exercise, and nonestablishment of religion); the ***Second Amendment*** right to bear arms; the ***Fourth Amendment*** (unreasonable search and seizure); some ***elements of the Fifth Amendment*** (privilege against self-incrimination; compensation for taking of private property for public use); the ***Sixth Amendment*** (speedy and public trial by impartial jury, notice and right of confrontation, compulsory process, and right to legal counsel in all serious criminal proceedings); and the ***Eighth Amendment*** (cruel and unusual punishment, excessive bail, and excessive fine provisions are ***assumed*** to be incorporated but there is no precise ruling).

b. Rights Not Applicable to States

There are four provisions of the Bill of Rights that have not yet been incorporated into the Due Process Clause:

(i) The ***Third Amendment*** prohibition against quartering troops in a person's home;

(ii) The ***Fifth Amendment*** right to a grand jury indictment in criminal cases;

(iii) The ***Seventh Amendment*** right to a jury trial in civil cases; and

(iv) The ***Eighth Amendment*** right against excessive fines.

[*See* McDonald v. Chicago, 130 S. Ct. 3020 (2010)] The ***Tenth Amendment,*** by its terms, limits the federal government's power over states, and so is inapplicable to the states.

2. Thirteenth Amendment

The Thirteenth Amendment provides that slavery shall not exist in the United States.

a. No Requirement of State Action

The amendment contains no language limiting its effect to governmental action (*e.g.,* "no ***state*** shall . . . "); thus, it is applicable even to ***private action***.

b. Congressional Power

The enabling clause of the Thirteenth Amendment gives Congress the power to adopt appropriate legislation, and the Supreme Court apparently will uphold legislation proscribing almost any private racially discriminatory act that can be characterized as a "***badge or incident of slavery.***"

Examples: The Supreme Court has upheld legislation:

1) Prohibiting private parties from refusing to rent or sell housing to a person because of race [Jones v. Alfred H. Mayer Co., 392 U.S. 409 (1968)];

2) Prohibiting private, nonsectarian schools from refusing to admit nonwhite children [Runyon v. McCrary, 427 U.S. 160 (1967)]; and

3) Prohibiting a private employer from discriminating in hiring on the basis of race [Patterson v. McLean Credit Union, 491 U.S. 164 (1989)].

Note: The above are examples of where Congress used its power to adopt statutes prohibiting "badges of slavery"; the proscribed activities would not necessarily be held to violate the Thirteenth Amendment absent the legislation.

3. Fourteenth Amendment

The Fourteenth Amendment ***prohibits states*** (not the federal government or private persons) from depriving any person of life, liberty, or property without due process and equal protection of the law. As discussed above, this amendment is a most important source of limitations on the states' power over individuals, because, through the Due Process Clause, most of the protections of the Bill of Rights are applicable to the states.

Note: The meaning of due process and equal protection will be discussed later in this outline.

a. Requirement of State Action

The Fourteenth Amendment applies only if there is action by a state or local government, government officer, or private individual whose behavior meets the requirements for state action (*see* B., below).

b. Scope of Congressional Power

Section 5 of the Fourteenth Amendment is an enabling clause giving Congress the power to adopt ***appropriate legislation*** to enforce the rights and guarantees

provided by the Fourteenth Amendment. Under Section 5, Congress may ***not*** expand existing constitutional rights or create new ones—it may only enact laws to prevent or remedy violations of rights already recognized by the courts. To adopt a valid law, Congress must point to a history or pattern of state violation of such rights and adopt legislation that is ***congruent and proportional*** (*i.e.*, narrowly tailored) to solving the identified violation. Note, however, that when Congress is dealing with a type of discrimination that the Supreme Court reviews using heightened scrutiny (*i.e.,* race, national origin, or gender—*see* XVIII.D., E., *infra*), Congress will generally have more power to act.

Examples: 1) The Americans With Disabilities Act ("ADA") includes provisions that, among other things, prohibit states from discriminating against disabled persons in hiring practices and requires states to make reasonable accommodations for disabled employees. Under the Fourteenth Amendment Equal Protection Clause, the Court has recognized a right of disabled people to be free from irrational state discrimination. In adopting the ADA, Congress did not identify a history or pattern of irrational employment practices by the states. Even if there were such a pattern, the provisions here were not congruent and proportional to remedying irrational discrimination; they are overinclusive, because they prohibit states from making employment decisions that are constitutional under the rational basis test. [Board of Trustees of University of Alabama v. Garrett, 531 U.S. 356 (2001)] Under similar reasoning, the Supreme Court has held that Congress has no power under Section 5 to broadly restrict ***age discrimination by state employers***. [Kimel v. Florida Board of Regents, 528 U.S. 62 (2000)]

2) The Supreme Court held that there is no violation of the First Amendment, applicable to the states through the Fourteenth Amendment, where a state law incidentally burdens a religious practice. [Employment Division v. Smith, XXII.C.3., *infra*] In response, Congress adopted a statute, purportedly under Section 5, providing that a state may not burden religious practices absent a compelling interest. The statute was held unconstitutional because it sought to expand substantive First Amendment rights beyond those recognized by the Supreme Court. [City of Boerne v. Flores, 521 U.S. 507 (1997)]

Compare: The Court has held that Congress ***has*** power under Section 5 to provide that state governments may be sued for violating Title II of the ADA (which prohibits state and local government discrimination against people with disabilities in government programs, services, or activities) when the discrimination involves access to the courts. *Rationale:* The right of meaningful access to judicial proceedings is a "fundamental right" under the Due Process Clause, and is thus subject to "heightened judicial scrutiny" much more demanding than "rational basis." This heightened scrutiny makes it "easier for Congress to show a pattern of state constitutional violations." [Tennessee v. Lane, 541 U.S. 509 (2004)]

4. **Fifteenth Amendment**
The Fifteenth Amendment is a limitation on both the ***states and the federal government***. It prohibits them from denying any citizen the right to vote on account of race or color. As indicated above, the Fifteenth Amendment contains an enabling clause that allows Congress to adopt legislation protecting the right to vote from discrimination.

5. **Commerce Clause**
The Supreme Court has allowed Congress to use the Commerce Clause to limit the power of individuals over other individuals—by adopting legislation barring private racial discrimination in activities "connected with" interstate commerce. Recall that under the affectation doctrine, almost any activity can be said to be connected with interstate commerce. (*See* II.A.4.a.1), *supra*.)

a. **Civil Rights Act**
Provisions of the Civil Rights Act of 1964 ***barring discrimination in places of public accommodation*** are proper and valid exercises of commerce power.

b. **Extent of Commerce Power**
The reach of the commerce power is broad. Any business that is ***open to interstate travelers*** or that ***uses products shipped in interstate commerce*** is covered. [Daniel v. Paul, 395 U.S. 298 (1969)—private resort held to be a public place of accommodation encompassed within the Act because drinks and entertainment facilities had been purchased and shipped through interstate commerce]

6. **Rights of National Citizenship**
The Supreme Court has also allowed Congress to limit the power of private individuals to infringe upon others' rights of national citizenship (*e.g.,* the right of interstate travel, the right to assemble to petition Congress for redress), without pointing to any specific constitutional source for the power. [Griffin v. Breckenridge, 403 U.S. 88 (1971)]

B. STATE ACTION REQUIREMENT
As indicated above, the Constitution generally prohibits only governmental infringement of constitutional rights. Thus, to find some action unconstitutional, it is generally necessary to attribute the action to the state, which includes government agencies and officials acting under the color of state law. However, this does not mean that the act must be directly by a government actor; "state action" can be found in the actions of seemingly private individuals who (i) perform exclusive public functions, or (ii) have significant state involvement in their activities.

1. **Exclusive Public Functions**
The Supreme Court has found that certain activities are so ***traditionally*** the ***exclusive*** prerogative of the state that they constitute state action even when undertaken by a private individual or organization. To date, only running a town and running an election for public office have been found to be such exclusive public functions.

Examples: 1) The owner of a "company town" with ***all*** of the attributes of a public town (*e.g.,* homes, sidewalks, streets, police and fire protection, etc.) cannot deny a person's First Amendment right to distribute religious literature in the town,

since the company town is equivalent to a town. [Marsh v. Alabama, 326 U.S. 501 (1946)] However, the owner of a shopping mall can deny people their First Amendment right to picket, since a mall does not have all of the attributes of a town. [Hudgens v. NLRB, 424 U.S. 507 (1976)]

2) Running elections is an exclusive public function, so if a private organization runs a preprimary that has a substantial effect on who is ultimately elected, its actions will be state action. [Terry v. Adams, 345 U.S. 461 (1953)—county political group whose candidate almost always runs unopposed in primary and general election cannot discriminate]

a. **Must Be Traditional *and* Exclusive Function**

To be state action, the activity must be ***both*** a ***traditional*** and ***exclusive*** government function. Thus, the Court has held that a warehouseman authorized by statute to sell goods stored with him for unpaid charges is not exercising state action when he makes the sale, because while resolution of private disputes is a traditional public function, it is not exclusive—the bailor had state law remedies to check abuses by the warehouseman. [Flagg Brothers v. Brooks, 436 U.S. 149 (1978)] State action exists, and due process guarantees apply, ***only if*** the creditor uses judicial or executive agencies to secure properties in the possession of the debtor.

2. **Significant State Involvement—Facilitating Private Action**

"State action" also exists whenever a state ***affirmatively*** facilitates, encourages, or authorizes acts of discrimination by its citizens. Note, however, that there must be some sort of affirmative act by the state approving the private action; it is not enough that the state permits the conduct to occur.

a. **Instances of Significant State Involvement**

1) **Official Encouragement**

Purportedly private action will be given state action status if the action is encouraged or sanctioned by the state.

a) **Judicial Approval**

State court enforcement of ***restrictive covenants prohibiting sale or lease of property to blacks*** constitutes state action even in civil proceedings between private parties. [Shelley v. Kraemer, 334 U.S. 1 (1948)]

(1) **Peremptory Challenges**

The use of peremptory challenges, even by a private party, constitutes state action, both because jury selection is a traditional public function and because there is overt, significant participation by the government (the judge) in the jury selection process. Thus, private litigants and defendants are prohibited from using peremptory challenges in a discriminatory manner. [*See* Edmonson v. Leesville Concrete, 500 U.S. 614 (1992); Georgia v. McCollum, 505 U.S. 42 (1992)]

b) Official Acts

State action may be found in the absence of an unconstitutional statute or ordinance if it appears that the state sanctions constitutional violations by its own officers.

(1) Discriminatory Law Enforcement

The Court reversed a conviction of sit-in demonstrators where no statute or ordinance required segregation but the mayor and police had announced publicly that they would invoke trespass and breach of the peace laws to enforce a local custom of racial separation in eating places. [Lombard v. Louisiana, 373 U.S. 267 (1963)]

(2) Apparent Legal Authority

Even if a state forbids officers from acting in a certain way (*e.g.,* depriving persons of their constitutional rights), the forbidden action may still constitute state action if the state puts the actor in a position to commit the unconstitutional act.

Example: A sheriff beat a prisoner to death in an effort to secure a confession. Both the state and the sheriff were held liable. The actions of the sheriff involved "state action" because the sheriff ***acted under "the color of state law***—the state in effect cloaked him with the apparent legal authority." [Screws v. United States, 325 U.S. 91 (1945)]

(3) Public Defenders

A public defender ***does not act for the state*** when he represents an indigent client. Therefore, negligence or malpractice by the public defender is not a denial of due process because the public defender's actions are not "state actions." [Polk County v. Dodson, 454 U.S. 312 (1982)]

2) State Authorization

In *Reitman v. Mulkey,* 387 U.S. 369 (1967), the Court invalidated a state constitutional provision that ***repealed*** all existing ***state laws banning discrimination*** in the sale or lease of property and prohibited reenactment of such laws in the future because such laws "authorize" private discrimination.

3) The State as Lessor for a Racially Discriminatory Lessee

In *Burton v. Wilmington Parking Authority,* 365 U.S. 715 (1961), Delaware was held responsible under the Fourteenth Amendment Equal Protection Clause for the exclusion of blacks from a coffee shop which was located in a public building. The shop was constructed by and leased from the state. The ***maintenance*** of the facility was ***paid for with public funds*** and Delaware was able to charge a higher rent because it allowed the restaurant owner to cater to the prejudices of its white customers.

4) Administration of Private Discriminatory Trust by Public Officials

State action exists where city personnel maintain a park, "open to all except blacks," under a private trust. [Evans v. Newton, 382 U.S. 296 (1966)]

5) **Entwinement of State and Private Entities**
The fact that a state entity helps formulate and adopts the rules of a private entity, and chooses to follow the order of the private entity pursuant to those rules, does not convert the private entity's action into state action. However, a state may be so entwined with a private organization that the organization's actions will be considered state action. [Brentwood Academy v. Tennessee Secondary School Athletic Association, 531 U.S. 288 (2001)]

Example: The National Collegiate Athletic Association ("NCAA") is a voluntary association of public and private universities that establishes rules for its members regarding collegiate sports. Pursuant to its rules, the NCAA urged a member college to suspend its coach for recruiting violations. The coach cannot successfully sue the NCAA for violating his constitutional rights because there is no state action. [National Collegiate Athletic Association v. Tarkanian, 488 U.S. 179 (1988)]

Compare: An association that regulates high school sports within a single state: (i) to which most public high schools belong; (ii) whose governing body is made up mostly of public school officials; (iii) whose meetings are held during regular school hours; (iv) whose employees may join the state retirement system; and (v) which is funded by gate receipts from the regulated sports is so entwined with the state that its action can be considered state action. [Brentwood Academy v. Tennessee Secondary School Athletic Association, *supra*]

b. **Instances of Insignificant State Involvement**

1) **Heavily Regulated Businesses and/or Granting of a Monopoly to a Utility**

a) **Electric Company**
State action will not be found merely because the state has granted a monopoly to a business or heavily regulates it.

Example: In *Jackson v. Metropolitan Edison,* 419 U.S. 345 (1974), ***no state action*** was found where an electric company terminated the user's service without notice and hearing. The state had not directed or ordered the termination and the fact that the company was heavily regulated and the state commission had approved private utility regulations authorizing such termination was not enough.

b) **Nursing Home**
A nursing home operated by a private corporation did ***not exercise state action*** when it discharged Medicaid patients, even though its operation was extensively regulated by the government. [Blum v. Yaretsky, 457 U.S. 991 (1982)]

c) **School**
A school operated by a private corporation did ***not*** exercise state action when it discharged teachers (allegedly in violation of their First Amendment rights) even though the school had contracts with the state to educate or care for many of its students and it received almost all of its operating funds from the government. [Rendell-Baker v. Kohn, 457 U.S. 830 (1982)]

2) **Licensing and Provision of Essential Services**
Granting a liquor license and providing essential services (police, fire, water, power, etc.) to a ***private club*** that imposes racial restrictions on its members and guests are ***not*** sufficient to constitute state action. [Moose Lodge v. Irvis, 407 U.S. 163 (1972)]

3) **Congressional Grant of Corporate Charter and Exclusive Name**
Congressional grant of a corporate charter and exclusive use of a name is not sufficient to constitute state action. [San Francisco Arts & Athletics, Inc. v. United States Olympic Committee, 483 U.S. 522 (1987)—congressional charter and grant of exclusive name "Olympic" does not clothe United States Olympic Committee with state action]

4) **No Government Duty to Protect Individuals from Harm by Private Persons**
The mere refusal of government agents to protect a victim from harm by a private person will not result in a finding that the harm was attributable to "state action," at least when state law does not give the victim a right to government protection. [DeShaney v. Winnebago County Department of Social Services, 489 U.S. 189 (1989)—government not responsible for harm inflicted on a child by his father, even though government social worker had reason to believe the child was being abused and did nothing to protect the child] However, if government employees enter into an agreement or conspiracy with private persons to cause harm to a victim, the victim's injuries are the result of state action; the private persons, as well as the government employees with whom they conspired, will have violated the victim's constitutional rights. [Screws v. United States, a.1)b)(2), *supra*; Dennis v. Sparks, 449 U.S. 24 (1980)]

C. TIPS FOR BAR EXAM

1. **State Must Be "Significantly Involved" in Private Entity**
The state must be "significantly involved" in the private entity. Merely granting a license or providing essential services is insufficient.

2. **No Constitutional Mandate to Outlaw Discrimination**
States are not constitutionally required to outlaw discrimination. The Constitution forbids only their encouraging or authorizing it.

XIII. RETROACTIVE LEGISLATION

A. CONTRACT CLAUSE—IMPAIRMENT OF CONTRACT

The Contract Clause prohibits ***states*** from enacting any law that ***retroactively*** impairs contract rights. It does not affect contracts not yet entered into.

1. **Not Applicable to Federal Government**
There is no comparable clause applicable to the federal government, although a flagrant contract impairment would be forbidden by the Due Process Clause of the Fifth Amendment.

2. **Only Applicable to State Legislation**
The provision applies only to state ***legislation***, not court decisions. [*See* Tidal Oil v. Flanagan, 263 U.S. 444 (1924)]

3. **Basic Impairment Rules**

a. **Private Contracts**
The Contract Clause prevents only ***substantial impairments*** of contract (*i.e.,* destruction of most or all of a party's rights under a contract). However, not all substantial impairments are invalid. In determining whether legislation is valid under the Contract Clause, use a three-part test:

(i) Does the legislation substantially impair a party's rights under an existing contract? If it does not, the legislation is valid under the Contract Clause. If it does, it will be valid ***only if*** it:

(ii) Serves an important and legitimate public interest; and

(iii) Is a reasonable and narrowly tailored means of promoting that interest.

Examples: 1) A Minnesota statute that imposed a moratorium on mortgage foreclosures during a severe depression did not violate the Contract Clause. [Home Building & Loan Association v. Blaisdell, 290 U.S. 398 (1934)]

2) A state statute that restricted underground coal mining to protect a variety of public and private uses of surface land (and buildings) and that left the owners of subsurface mining rights with some reasonable value in, or return from, their investment does not violate the Contract Clause. [Keystone Bituminous Coal Association v. DeBenedictis, 480 U.S. 470 (1987)]

b. **Public Contracts—Stricter Scrutiny**
Public contracts (*i.e.,* those in which the state or political subdivision is a party) are tested by the same basic test detailed above; however, they will likely receive stricter scrutiny, especially if the legislation reduces the contractual burdens on the state. When applying the three-part test, note the following:

(i) There is no substantial impairment if the state has reserved the power to ***revoke, alter, or amend*** either in the contract itself or in a statute or law the terms of which should be considered to be incorporated into the contract [Dartmouth College v. Woodward, 17 U.S. 518 (1819)];

(ii) In determining whether the law serves as a legitimate public interest, note that the state cannot be obligated by contract to refrain from exercising its police powers necessary to protect the health and safety of its residents; and

(iii) To be narrowly tailored, the law should not constitute an unnecessarily broad repudiation of contract obligations.

Example: In *Allied Structural Steel Co. v. Spannaus,* 438 U.S. 234 (1978), the Court invalidated state pension reform legislation which increased the obligation of companies under preexisting pension plans to employees who previously had terminated their work for the company or who previously had retired from employment with the company. Because the legislation constituted a substantial impairment of contract by changing the compensation for work already completed and because it was not necessary to remedy an important social problem in the nature of an emergency, it was held to be a violation of the Contract Clause.

B. EX POST FACTO LAWS

1. Two Ex Post Facto Clauses

Neither the state nor the federal government may pass an ex post facto law. [Art. I, §9—federal prohibition; Art. I, §10—state prohibition] An ex post facto law is ***legislation*** that ***retroactively*** alters the ***criminal law*** (not civil regulation, such as denial of professional licenses) in a ***substantially prejudicial*** manner so as to deprive a person of any right previously enjoyed ***for the purpose of punishing the person for some past activity.***

a. What Is "Criminal"

If a law's ***purpose*** is civil rather than punitive, it is not an ex post facto law unless its ***effect*** is so ***clearly*** punitive as to negate the legislature's intention.

Example: A law requiring any sex offender within the state to register and provide his name, address, place of employment, vehicle information, etc., to law enforcement authorities and authorizing law enforcement authorities to make some of this information public is not an ex post facto law, even if noncompliance can be punished criminally, and even if some of the law is contained in the state's criminal code. The goal of such a law is not to punish or stigmatize. Rather, legislatures have found that sex offenders pose a high risk of reoffending, and the release of the information required under the act is intended to protect the public from sex offenders. [Smith v. Doe, 538 U.S. 84 (2003)]

b. Retroactive Alterations

A statute retroactively alters a law in a substantially prejudicial manner if it:

(i) Makes criminal an act that ***was innocent when done***;

(ii) Prescribes ***greater punishment*** for an act than was prescribed for the act when it was committed; or

(iii) ***Reduces the evidence*** required to convict a person of a crime from what was required at the time that the act was allegedly committed.

Example: A statute of limitations reflects a legislative judgment that after a certain time, no quantum of evidence is sufficient to convict. Thus, a law that revives the possibility of a criminal prosecution after the previously applicable statute of limitations has expired is an unconstitutional ex post facto law. [Stonger v. California, 539 U.S. 607 (2003)]

2. Distinguish—Procedural Changes

Mere procedural changes in state law will not necessarily trigger the Ex Post Facto Clause. A modified law can be applied to a crime committed before the law's modification if the defendant had notice of the possible penalty and the modified law does not increase the burden on the defendant.

Example: Florida had a death penalty statute that was invalidated by the Supreme Court because the statute restricted discretion in sentencing. Before a new statute was enacted, D committed a murder. Florida then passed a new death penalty provision that complied with Supreme Court criteria. The new provision was applied at D's trial, and he was sentenced to death. This was not a prohibited ex post facto law, since the earlier statute (although unconstitutional) gave D notice of the possible penalty and the new provision made it ***less likely*** that the death penalty would be imposed in a given case. [Dobbert v. Florida, 432 U.S. 282 (1977)]

3. Indirect "Application" to Courts

Although the Ex Post Facto Clauses prohibit only retroactive ***legislation***, the Supreme Court has held that due process prohibits courts from retroactively interpreting criminal law in an unexpected and indefensible way. [Rogers v. Tennessee, 532 U.S. 451 (2001)—state supreme court's abolition of common law "year and a day rule" (which prohibits prosecution for murder if the victim dies more than a year after an attack) was not unexpected and indefensible because medical science has undermined the rule's usefulness and the rule has already been abolished in most jurisdictions]

C. BILLS OF ATTAINDER

A bill of attainder is a legislative act that ***inflicts punishment without a judicial trial*** upon individuals who are designated either by name or in terms of past conduct. Past conduct acts to define who those particular persons are.

1. Two Clauses

Both the ***federal and state governments*** are prohibited from passing bills of attainder.

2. Two Requirements Preclude Finding of Bill of Attainder

These provisions ***require both judicial machinery*** for trial and punishment of crime and ***definition of criminal conduct in such general terms*** as not to ensnare within the definition a single individual or small group for punishment because of past behavior.

Example: The Court found a provision in the Landrum-Griffin Act, making it a crime for a member of the Communist Party to act as an officer or employee of a labor union, to be legislative punishment for a party membership, and hence a bill of attainder. [United States v. Brown, 381 U.S. 437 (1965)]

3. *Nixon* Case

In *Nixon v. Administrator of General Services,* 433 U.S. 425 (1977), Congress passed legislation to authorize government control of the presidential papers and tape recordings of former President Nixon. The Supreme Court held that this was ***not a bill of attainder***. The

circumstances of the Nixon resignation made him a unique "class of one" as to the need to control his papers. The act was held "***nonpunitive***" and in pursuance of ***important public policy***.

4. Draft Registration Case

In *Selective Service System v. Minnesota Public Interest Research Group,* 468 U.S. 841 (1984), the Court upheld a federal statute denying financial aid for higher education to male students between the ages of 18 and 26 who had failed to register for the draft. The law required applicants for the aid to file a statement with their institutions of higher learning certifying their compliance. Failure to register within 30 days of one's 18th birthday was a felony, but the regulations allowed men who failed to register in a timely manner to qualify for aid by registering late. The Court found that this was ***not a bill of attainder***. The law reasonably ***promoted nonpunitive goals*** and was ***not a legislative punishment*** taken on the basis of any irreversible act, since aid was awarded to those who registered late. The Court also found that the statute did not violate the Fifth Amendment privilege against self-incrimination.

D. DUE PROCESS CONSIDERATIONS

Under the Due Process Clauses of the Fifth and Fourteenth Amendments, retroactive legislation or other governmental action may be, but is not necessarily, a violation of the Constitution. The question of whether a retroactive law (that does not violate the Contracts, Ex Post Facto, or Bill of Attainder Clauses) violates due process is a ***substantive due process*** issue. If the law does not relate to a fundamental civil right, the retroactive law should be upheld if it is rationally related to a legitimate government interest.

Examples: 1) A retroactive tax law will be upheld as long as the retroactive aspects of the law are rationally related to legitimate government interests. [United States v. Carlton, 512 U.S. 26 (1994)—upholding retroactive modification of the estate tax]

2) Retroactive legislation affecting ***merely a remedy*** does not violate due process (*e.g.,* repealing or extending a statute of limitations), unless it would oust an already vested property interest. [Chase Securities Corp. v. Donaldson, 325 U.S. 304 (1945)—permissible to revive a previously dead cause of action]

XIV. PROCEDURAL DUE PROCESS

A. BASIC PRINCIPLE

The Due Process Clauses of the Fifth Amendment (applicable to the federal government) and the Fourteenth Amendment (applicable to the states) provide that the government shall not take a person's life, liberty, or property without due process of law. Due process contemplates fair process/procedure, which requires at least an opportunity to present objections to the proposed action to a fair, neutral decisionmaker (not necessarily a judge).

1. When Is Individualized Adjudication Required?

There is a right to procedural due process only when the government acts to deprive an ***individual*** of life, liberty, or property (*see* below). There is no right to individualized adjudication when the government acts generally, even if the action will result in burdening individuals' life, liberty, or property interests.

Example: A state legislature need not provide individuals with an opportunity for a hearing when adopting the general requirements for obtaining a driver's license (*e.g.,* age, residence, ability, etc.), but it must provide individualized process to determine whether a particular person meets the requirements.

2. **Intentional Deprivation vs. Negligent Deprivation**
Fair process is required for ***intentional*** acts of the government or its employees. If an injury is caused to a person through the mere ***negligence*** of a government employee, there is no violation of the Due Process Clause. [Daniels v. Williams, 474 U.S. 327 (1986); Davidson v. Cannon, 474 U.S. 344 (1986)]

a. **"Deprivation"**
A "deprivation" of life, liberty, or property requires more than a mere denial of certain kinds of remedies. Only when the government affords ***no*** remedy or ***inadequate*** remedies may a deprivation of life, liberty, or property result. [Florida Prepaid Postsecondary Education Expense Board v. College Savings Bank, 527 U.S. 627 (1999)]

3. **Fair, Neutral Decisionmaker—Judge Bias**
The Due Process Clause requires a judge to recuse himself when he has ***actual bias*** (*e.g.,* he has a direct, personal, substantial, pecuniary interest in a case) or when there is merely a ***serious risk of actual bias***. A serious risk of actual bias exists when "under a realistic appraisal of psychological tendencies and human weakness," the judge's interest poses such a risk of actual bias or prejudice that it must be forbidden. [Caperton v. A. T. Massey Coal Co., 129 S. Ct. 2252 (2009)]
Example: The chairman of a company spent over $3 million to support an attorney's campaign to be elected to the state supreme court after a $50 million verdict was entered against the chairman's company, knowing that the supreme court would eventually hear the appeal of the verdict. The $3 million was more than the total amount spent by all of the other supporters of the attorney, and the attorney won by fewer than 50,000 votes. When the case was appealed, the winner of the verdict asked the newly elected justice to recuse himself. Under these circumstances, recusal was required. [Caperton v. A. T. Massey Coal Co., *supra*]

4. **Protection vs. Creation**
The due process provisions do not create property or liberty interests; their purpose is to provide ***procedural safeguards against arbitrary deprivation***. Hence, the Fourteenth Amendment Due Process Clause does not, for example, give out-of-state attorneys the right to appear in state courts without meeting a state's bar admission requirements. [Leis v. Flynt, 439 U.S. 438 (1979)]

B. IS LIFE, LIBERTY, OR PROPERTY BEING TAKEN?

Older Supreme Court cases indicated that due process protects "rights," but not "privileges." This approach is no longer followed; rather the Court will determine whether a ***legitimate*** liberty or property interest is being taken.

1. **Liberty**
The term "liberty" is not specifically defined. It includes more than just freedom from bodily

restraints (*e.g.,* it includes the right to contract and to engage in gainful employment). A deprivation of liberty occurs if a person:

(i) Loses significant freedom of action; ***or***

(ii) Is denied a freedom provided by the Constitution or a statute.

Examples of liberty interests include:

a. Commitment to Mental Institution

1) Adults
Adults are entitled to an ***adversary hearing*** before they are indefinitely committed to a mental institution against their will. The state must prove the basis for commitment by "clear and convincing" evidence. However, after a person has been acquitted of criminal charges on the basis of an insanity defense, the acquitted defendant can be committed if a court finds by a "preponderance of the evidence" that the person should be committed to a mental health care facility. [Jones v. United States, 463 U.S. 354 (1983)]

2) Minor Children
Minor children have a substantial liberty interest in not being confined unnecessarily for medical treatment. Thus, they are entitled to a ***screening by a "neutral factfinder"*** before commitment to a mental institution. Mere parental consent to commitment is not enough. [Parham v. J.R., 442 U.S. 584 (1979)]

b. Injury to Reputation
Injury to reputation in itself is not a deprivation of liberty or property. [Paul v. Davis, 424 U.S. 693 (1976)] However, if governmental acts (such as a statement of reasons given for termination of public employment) so injure a person's reputation that he will have ***lost significant employment or associational opportunities***, there is a loss of liberty.

c. Exercise of Fundamental Constitutional Rights
The Due Process Clause protects a person's freedom to engage in activities that involve fundamental constitutional rights, such as the right to speak and associate, the right to travel, and the right to vote.

1) Application—Government Employee's Freedom of Speech
A public employee may not be discharged for engaging in ***constitutionally protected speech***. (*See* XXI.C.1., *infra.*) If a government employee is discharged for her speech or writing, a hearing must be held to determine whether the speech was protected. If so, the employee cannot be fired. [*See* Givhan v. Western Line Consolidated School District, 439 U.S. 410 (1979)—Court held that teacher could not be fired for privately communicating her grievances about working conditions or opinions concerning public issues to her employer]

2. Property
"Property" includes more than personal belongings and realty, chattels, or money, but an

abstract need or desire for (or a unilateral expectation of) the benefit is not enough. There must be a ***legitimate claim*** or "***entitlement***" to the benefit under state or federal law. [Board of Regents v. Roth, 408 U.S. 564 (1972); Leis v. Flynt, *supra*] Examples of property interests include:

a. **Public Education**
There is a property interest in public education when school attendance is required. Thus, a significant suspension (*e.g.,* 10 days) requires procedural due process. [Goss v. Lopez, 419 U.S. 565 (1975)]

b. **Welfare Benefits**
One has a property interest in welfare benefits if she has previously been determined to meet the statutory criteria. [Goldberg v. Kelly, 397 U.S. 254 (1970)]

c. **Continued Public Employment**
If there is a state statute or ordinance that creates a public employment contract, or there is some clear practice or mutual understanding that an employee can be terminated only for "cause," then there is a property interest [Arnett v. Kennedy, 416 U.S. 134 (1974)]; but if the employee holds his position only at the "will" of the employer, there is no property interest in continued employment [Bishop v. Wood, 426 U.S. 341 (1976)].

C. WHAT TYPE OF PROCESS IS REQUIRED?

While all intentional governmental deprivations of life, liberty, or property require fair process, what constitutes fair process in terms of the timing and scope of the hearing varies according to the circumstances of the deprivation. The Court will weigh:

(i) The importance of the ***individual interest*** involved;

(ii) The value of specific ***procedural safeguards*** to that interest; and

(iii) The ***governmental interest*** in fiscal and administrative efficiency.

[Mathews v. Eldridge, 424 U.S. 319 (1976)] In all situations, the Court will probably require ***fair procedures*** and an ***unbiased decisionmaker***. Normally, the person whose interest is being deprived should also receive ***notice*** of the government's action and have an ***opportunity to respond before*** termination of the interest. However, the court may allow a post-termination hearing in situations where a pre-termination hearing is highly impracticable. The Court has made the following rulings with regard to specific types of deprivations:

1. **Welfare Benefits**
Due process requires an ***evidentiary hearing prior to termination*** of welfare benefits. It need not be a judicial or quasi-judicial trial if there is adequate post-termination review; but the recipient must have timely and adequate ***notice*** of the reasons for the proposed termination, the right to confront adverse witnesses, and the right to present his own arguments and evidence orally. Counsel need not be provided, but must be permitted. Finally, the decision must be based solely on evidence adduced at the hearing and must be rendered by an impartial decisionmaker (thus disqualifying any participant in the termination proposal under review). [Goldberg v. Kelly, *supra*]

2. Disability Benefits

No prior evidentiary hearing is required for termination of disability benefits, as long as there is ***prior notice*** to the recipient, an opportunity to respond in writing, and a ***subsequent evidentiary hearing*** (with retroactive payment if the recipient prevails). *Rationale*: Disability benefits (unlike welfare benefits) are not based on financial need and hence are not vital. [Mathews v. Eldridge, *supra*]

3. Public Employment

A public employee who is subject to removal only for "cause" (and who, therefore, has a property interest in his job) generally must be given ***notice*** of charges against him that are to be the basis for his job termination, and a ***pre-termination opportunity to respond*** to those charges. The employee does not have to be given a full, formal hearing before his termination, as long as there is a fair system of pre-termination notice, an opportunity to respond (to the person making the termination decision), and a ***subsequent evidentiary hearing*** regarding the termination (with reinstatement if the employee prevails). [Cleveland Board of Education v. Loudermill, 470 U.S. 532 (1985)] *But note:* If there is a ***significant reason*** for not keeping the employee on the job, he may be suspended without pay and without an opportunity to respond, as long as there is a prompt post-suspension hearing with reinstatement and back pay if the employee prevails. [Gilbert v. Homar, 520 U.S. 924 (1997)—police officer suspended after being arrested and formally charged with a felony]

4. Public Education—Disciplinary Suspension

Although no formal evidentiary hearing is required before a student may be temporarily suspended (for 10 days or less), due process usually requires ***notice*** of the charges and an ***opportunity to explain***. However, if the student's presence poses a danger to persons or property, or threatens to disrupt the academic process, such notice and hearing may ***follow*** removal as soon as practicable. [Goss v. Lopez, *supra*]

a. Corporal Punishment in Public School

This may involve constitutionally protected "liberty." However, the traditional common law tort remedies for excessive punishment satisfy procedural due process, and a prior hearing is not required. [Ingraham v. Wright, 430 U.S. 651 (1977)]

5. Public Education—Academic Dismissal

No prior evidentiary hearing is required when a student is dismissed for "academic" deficiencies rather than for "disciplinary" reasons. Due process is satisfied if the student is adequately informed of the deficiency and given an opportunity to respond. [Board of Curators v. Horowitz, 435 U.S. 78 (1978)]

6. Creditors' Remedies

Pretrial remedies, such as attachment of property or garnishment of wages, that are merely designed to provide a plaintiff with some guarantee that there will be assets to satisfy a judgment against the defendant if the plaintiff eventually wins the case ***should not be issued by a court without notice*** to the defendant and a ***hearing prior to the issuance*** of the order. A court may issue a temporary order of this type if: (i) there are exigent circumstances that justify the order; and (ii) the defendant is given a hearing after the order is issued but prior to trial. [Sniadach v. Family Finance Corp., 395 U.S. 337 (1969); Connecticut v. Doehr, 501 U.S. 1 (1991)] However, laws authorizing creditors to garnish assets, or a conditional seller to seize or sequester property, will be upheld ***without prior notice*** to the debtor ***if***:

a. The creditor posts a security bond;

b. The application is made to a judge, is not conclusory, and documents narrowly confined facts susceptible of summary disposition; ***and***

c. Provision is made for an early hearing at which the creditor must show probable cause.

7. Driver's License

The state generally must afford a ***prior hearing*** before a driver's license is suspended or terminated. [Bell v. Burson, 402 U.S. 535 (1971)] However, a post-suspension hearing satisfies due process where a statute mandates suspension of a driver's license for refusing to take a breathalyzer test upon arrest for drunk driving. [Mackey v. Montrym, 443 U.S. 1 (1979)]

8. Parental Status Litigation and Hearing

a. Termination of Parental Status

Due process does ***not require the appointment of counsel*** for indigent parents in every case in which the state seeks to terminate parental status (*i.e.,* take children from their parents), ***but*** only when "fundamental fairness" requires the appointment. [Lassiter v. Department of Social Services, 452 U.S. 18 (1981)] To terminate parental rights, the state must prove its allegations of parental neglect or misconduct by "clear and convincing evidence." [Santosky v. Kramer, 455 U.S. 745 (1982)]

b. Paternity Actions

A state may allow paternity to be established in a support proceeding brought by a mother or child by a ***preponderance of evidence***—no greater burden of proof is required by the Due Process Clause. [Rivera v. Minnich, 483 U.S. 574 (1987)] However, due process requires the state to ***pay for blood tests*** that might exculpate an indigent defendant in a paternity action if the ***state is responsible for the lawsuit*** (the suit is brought by a state agency or the state requires the mother to bring the civil paternity suit). [Little v. Streater, 452 U.S. 1 (1981)]

c. Hearings for Men Who Seek to Establish Paternity

1) Unmarried Father Living with Mother

If the father of an illegitimate child is a part of a "family unit" that includes the child, the relationship between the father and child will be protected by due process. [Stanley v. Illinois, 405 U.S. 645 (1972)—state cannot take child from father after mother dies, unless state has a fair process to determine whether the parental relationship should be severed]

2) Father Who Never Tried to Establish Paternity

The father of an illegitimate child who has never attempted to establish a legal or personal relationship with the child has no right to notice prior to the adoption of the child by other persons. [Lehr v. Robertson, 463 U.S. 248 (1983)]

3) Mother Married to Another Man

The Supreme Court has upheld a statute that presumed that a child born during

wedlock was the husband's child where the statute allowed an alleged biological father to have a hearing regarding visitation rights, but the Court did not rule on whether a biological father could be denied visitation under these circumstances without a hearing. [Michael H. v. Gerald D., 491 U.S. 110 (1989)]

9. Detention of Citizen Enemy Combatants

Due process requires that a ***citizen held in the United States*** as an "enemy combatant" have a meaningful opportunity to contest the factual basis for his detention before a neutral decisionmaker. However, due process does not forbid some tailoring of the proceedings to alleviate burdens that they may impose on Executive authority during an ongoing military conflict. This may include accepting some use of hearsay, permitting government rebuttable presumptions, and ***perhaps*** use of a properly authorized and constituted military tribunal. [Hamdi v. Rumsfeld, 542 U.S. 507 (2004)—effect of views of five Justices in two separate opinions]

Example: Hamdi, an American citizen, was captured in Afghanistan, classified as an "enemy combatant" for allegedly taking up arms with the Taliban, and transported to a naval brig in Charleston, SC. Hamdi's father brought a habeas corpus petition on his behalf. The appellate court held that because Hamdi was caught in a combat zone, he had no right to refute the government's charges. The Supreme Court reversed, holding that Hamdi was at least entitled to some hearing to contest the factual basis for his detention before a neutral decisionmaker. [Hamdi v. Rumsfeld, *supra*]

10. Notice of Adversary Proceedings

When the government seeks to use a judicial or administrative process to take or terminate property interests, it ***must give notice*** to those persons whose property interests may be taken by that process. The form of notice must be reasonably designed to insure that those persons will in fact be notified of the proceedings.

Example: Personal notice or notice by mail must be given to both mortgagor and mortgagee before a "tax sale" of property for unpaid taxes. [Mennonite Board of Missions v. Adams, 462 U.S. 791 (1983)]

11. Civil Forfeitures

Procedural due process limits the government's ability to seize property allegedly subject to forfeiture (which most often occurs when the government claims that the property was connected to, or was the product of, criminal activity). Absent exceptional circumstances, the government must provide the owner of ***real property*** notice and an opportunity for some type of hearing ***prior*** to seizing real property. [United States v. James Daniel Good Real Property, 510 U.S. 43 (1993)] However, the government might be able to seize ***personal property prior*** to providing the owner a hearing, since personal property can be hidden or destroyed. [Calero-Toledo v. Pearson Yacht Leasing Co., 416 U.S. 663 (1974)]

D. DUE PROCESS RIGHTS ARE SUBJECT TO WAIVER

Due process rights are subject to waiver. However, the Supreme Court has not clearly defined the standard for determining whether someone has validly waived the right to a hearing before governmental deprivation of liberty or property. Presumably, any such waiver must be ***voluntary***. Additionally, it is possible that a waiver will be valid only if it is made ***knowingly*** (with an understanding of the nature of the rights being waived).

E. ACCESS TO COURTS—INDIGENT PLAINTIFFS

There may often be a fee for government services, including a fee for use of courts (*e.g.*, a filing fee). Whether the government must waive such fees for indigents depends on the nature of the rights involved.

1. Fundamental Rights—Waiver Required

The Supreme Court has required a waiver of government fees when the imposition of a fee would deny a fundamental right to the indigent. (Fundamental rights are examined in the substantive due process and equal protection sections of this outline.)

Examples: 1) The government cannot deny an indigent the right to marry or divorce because of the indigent's inability to pay a marriage license fee or a divorce court filing fee.

2) The government must waive even a reasonable filing fee for candidates for electoral office if it can be shown that the candidate cannot afford to pay the filing fee. The right to be a candidate is connected to the fundamental right of individuals to vote for candidates of their choice.

3) The government may not require an indigent to pay the cost of a transcript in order to appeal from termination of her parental rights. [M.L.B. v. S.L.J., 519 U.S. 102 (1997)]

2. Nonfundamental Rights—Waiver Not Required

When there is no fundamental right regulated by the imposition of a fee, the government can refuse to grant the service to those persons who cannot pay the required fee.

Examples: 1) The federal government can refuse to grant access to bankruptcy courts to persons who cannot pay a filing fee. There is no fundamental right to receive a bankruptcy discharge from debts.

2) A state can limit judicial review of welfare termination hearings to those persons who pay a $25 fee.

XV. THE "TAKING" CLAUSE

A. IN GENERAL

The Fifth Amendment prohibits governmental taking of private property "for public use without just compensation." The prohibition is applicable to the states through the Fourteenth Amendment [Chicago Burlington & Quincy Railroad v. Chicago, 166 U.S. 226 (1897)], and taking questions often arise in connection with states' exercise of their police power (*i.e.*, the power to legislate for the health, welfare, safety, etc., of the people).

1. Not a Grant of Power

The Fifth Amendment is not a grant of power, but rather is a limitation on power (*i.e.*, a taking must be for a public purpose and compensation must be paid). The power for a taking must arise out of some other source (*e.g.*, the police power).

2. Scope of Taking

The concept of a governmental taking probably originally contemplated only physical appropriations of property. Today, however, the term also encompasses some governmental action

that significantly damages property or impairs its use (*e.g.,* frequent flyovers by airplanes near airport [United States v. Causby, 328 U.S. 256 (1946)]). Moreover, even intangibles may be the subject of a taking. [*See* Ruckelshaus v. Monsanto Co., 467 U.S. 986 (1984)—government requirement that trade secret be disclosed may be a taking where government takes and discloses the secret in such a way that it diminishes the secret's economic value and interferes with reasonable, investment-backed expectations of its holders]

B. "PUBLIC USE" LIMITATION LIBERALLY CONSTRUED

The Court will not review underlying policy decisions, such as general desirability for a particular public use or the extent to which property must be taken therefor. A use will be held to be "public" as long as it is rationally related to a legitimate public purpose, *e.g.,* health, welfare, safety, moral, social, economic, political, or aesthetic ends. The government may even authorize a taking by private enterprise, as long as the taking will redound to the public advantage (*e.g.,* railroads and public utilities).

Example: A city adopted an integrated development plan to revitalize its ailing economy by buying up privately held land in its riverfront area, developing some land into parks, and transferring the rest to developers who would open marinas, stores, etc. Pursuant to the plan, the city bought up land from willing sellers and initiated condemnation proceedings against owners who refused to sell. The recalcitrant owners brought suit against the city, claiming that the use for which the city was condemning the land (*i.e.,* to transfer the land to private developers) was not a public use. The Supreme Court held that a taking is for public use so long as the government acts out of a reasonable belief that the taking will benefit the public, and taking private property to promote economic development has long been accepted as a public use. [Kelo v. City of New London, 545 U.S. 469 (2005)]

C. "TAKING" VS. "REGULATION"

While the government must fairly compensate an owner when her property is taken for public use, it need not pay compensation for mere regulation of property. Thus, whether government action amounts to a taking or is merely regulation is a crucial issue. The question is one of degree; there is no clear cut formula for determining whether there has been a taking. The following guidelines have emerged.

1. Actual Appropriation or Physical Invasion

A taking will almost always be found if there is an actual appropriation or destruction of a person's property or a permanent physical invasion by the government or by authorization of law.

Examples: A taking was found in the following situations:

1) Ordinance requiring landlords to allow installation of cable TV in their rental units but limiting to $1 the fee landlords could charge for this access. [Loretto v. Teleprompter Manhattan CATV Corp., 458 U.S. 419 (1982)]

2) Statute ***abolishing*** rights of descent and devise of property (although government has broad authority to regulate this area). [Hodel v. Irving, 481 U.S. 704 (1987)]

3) Requirement that public be given free access to a privately developed waterway. [Kaiser Aetna v. United States, 444 U.S. 164 (1980)]

a. **Exception—Emergencies**
A taking is less likely to be found in emergency situations, even where there is destruction or actual occupation of private property.

Examples: 1) No compensation was required when the state ordered the destruction of cedar trees that threatened to spread disease to apple orchards. [Miller v. Schoene, 276 U.S. 272 (1928)]

2) No compensation was required when federal troops destroyed oil facilities to prevent them from falling into enemy hands. [United States v. Caltex, Inc., 344 U.S. 149 (1952)]

2. **Use Restrictions**

a. **Denial of *All* Economic Value of Land—Taking**
If a government regulation denies a landowner of ***all*** economic use of his land, the regulation is equivalent to a physical appropriation and is thus a taking unless principles of nuisance or property law that existed when the owner acquired the land make the use prohibitable. [Lucas v. South Carolina Coastal Council, 505 U.S. 1003 (1992)—state's zoning ordinance, adopted after owner purchased lots, amounted to a taking because the ordinance prohibited owner from erecting any permanent structures on his lots]

1) **Temporary Denials of All Economic Use**
Temporarily denying an owner of all economic use of property does not constitute a per se taking. Instead, the Court will carefully examine and weigh all the relevant circumstances—the planners' good faith, the reasonable expectations of the owners, the length of the delay, the delay's actual effect on the value of the property, etc.—in order to determine whether "fairness and justice" require just compensation. [Tahoe-Sierra Preservation Council, Inc. v. Tahoe Regional Planning Agency, 535 U.S. 302 (2002)—finding no taking where there was a 32-month moratorium on land development in the Lake Tahoe Basin while a comprehensive land-use plan was being developed for the area]

b. **Decreasing Economic Value**
Regulations that merely decrease the value of property (*e.g.,* prohibit its most beneficial use) do not necessarily result in a taking, ***as long as they leave an economically viable use for the property***. The Court considers the economic impact of the regulation on the claimant and whether the regulation substantially interferes with distinct, investment-backed expectations of the claimant. [Penn Central Transportation Co. v. New York, 438 U.S. 255 (1978)]

Example: The Court upheld a "landmark" zoning ordinance that prohibited altering the external appearance of Grand Central Station. It found historic preservation to be an important government interest and that certain rights granted to the landmark owners mitigated their loss. [Penn Central Transportation Co. v. New York, *supra*]

1) **Building/Development Permits—Transfer of Occupation Rights**
Municipalities often attempt to condition building or development permits on a landowner's (i) conveying title to part, or all, of the property to the government or (ii)

granting the public access to the property (*e.g.*, an easement across the property). Such conditions constitute an uncompensated taking unless (i) the government can show that the condition relates to a legitimate government interest and (ii) the adverse impact of the proposed building/development on the area is roughly proportional to the loss caused to the property owner from the forced transfer of occupation rights. [Nollan v. California Coastal Commission, 483 U.S. 825 (1987); Dolan v. City of Tigard, 512 U.S. 374 (1994)]

Example: City agreed to approve a permit to expand plaintiff's retail store and pave a parking lot on the condition that plaintiff dedicate land for (i) a public greenway and (ii) a bike path. The Supreme Court found that City did not show a sufficient relationship between the dedications and the impact that the expansion would have on the area. [Dolan v. City of Tigard, *supra*]

2) Utility Rate Regulation

There is no taking where the government sets rates that utility companies can charge, as long as the rates are not set so low that they are unjust and confiscatory. [Duquesne Light Co. v. Barash, 488 U.S. 299 (1989)]

3) Zoning Ordinances

The Court has long held that governments may adopt zoning ordinances that regulate the way real property may be used, pursuant to the police power (*e.g.*, limiting development in a particular area to single-family homes, restricting buildings to a particular height, etc.). Such regulations generally do not amount to a taking—even if they deny an owner the highest and best use of her property—unless they: (i) amount to a physical appropriation, as in *Loretto*, (ii) deny an owner of all economic use, as in *Lucas*, or (iii) unreasonably interfere with distinct, investment-backed expectations as set out in *Penn Central*. [*See* Lingle v. Chevron, 544 U.S. 528 (2005)]

3. Remedy

If a property owner challenges a regulation and the court determines that there was a taking, the government will be required to either:

(i) ***Pay the property owner compensation*** for the taking (*see* below); or

(ii) ***Terminate the regulation and pay the owner for damages*** that occurred while the regulation was in effect (*i.e.*, temporary taking damages).

[First English Evangelical Church v. County of Los Angeles, 482 U.S. 304 (1987)]

a. Who May Sue

The right to claim a "taking" is ***not*** limited to persons who held title to the property at the time a challenged use restriction was imposed. A person who purchases property after a regulation is in place still may bring a taking claim. [Palazzolo v. Rhode Island, 533 U.S. 606 (2001)]

D. "JUST COMPENSATION"

The owner is entitled to the ***reasonable value*** of her property ***at the time of the taking***—fair market value. The test is ordinarily a ***loss to the owner***, not a gain to the taker. Due process guarantees notice and hearing, administrative or judicial, on the amount of compensation, but the hearing need not precede the taking.

1. **"Worthless" Property**

   Because just compensation is measured by the loss to the owner and not by the gain to the taker, property that is "worthless" to the owner can be the subject of a taking, but no compensation need be paid when it is taken.

   Example: A state law required attorneys to keep clients' funds in trust accounts on behalf of their clients and to pay to the client any interest earned on the funds. If a client's funds were too small to earn enough interest to exceed the costs of distributing the interest, the attorneys were required to pay the interest over to a legal aid charity. Although this requirement constitutes a taking, no compensation is due because the clients have not suffered a pecuniary loss. [Brown v. Legal Foundation of Washington, 538 U.S. 216 (2003)]

XVI. INTRODUCTION TO SUBSTANTIVE DUE PROCESS AND EQUAL PROTECTION

A. RELATIONSHIP BETWEEN SUBSTANTIVE DUE PROCESS AND EQUAL PROTECTION

The Due Process Clauses and the Equal Protection Clause guarantee the fairness of laws—substantive due process guarantees that laws will be reasonable and not arbitrary, and equal protection guarantees that similarly situated persons will be treated alike. Both guarantees require the Court to review the ***substance of the law*** rather than the procedures employed.

1. **Substantive Due Process**

   Generally where a law limits the liberty of ***all*** persons to engage in some activity, it is a due process question.

2. **Equal Protection**

   Where a law treats a person or class of persons differently from others, it is an equal protection question. [*See* Village of Willowbrook v. Olech, 528 U.S. 562 (2000)—equal protection claims may be brought by a class with as few as one member] However, an at-will government employee who claims to be a victim of arbitrary discrimination cannot use the "class of one" theory to make an equal protection claim. [Engquist v. Department of Agriculture, 533 U.S. 591 (2008)]

3. **Examples**

   If a law prohibits all persons from purchasing contraceptive devices, there is a due process issue; if the law prohibits only purchases by unmarried persons, there is an equal protection issue. A state's refusal to have any publicly funded schools raises a due process issue; a state law that establishes separate schools for children of different races raises an equal protection issue.

4. **Note—Clauses Not Necessarily Mutually Exclusive**

   Since both clauses protect against unfairness, both may be appropriate challenges to the

same governmental act, and a discussion of both may be appropriate in an essay answer. On the MBE, however, the examiners will probably not include both as alternatives in the same question. The above approaches can be used as a rough guideline of when each clause applies.

B. WHAT STANDARD OF REVIEW WILL THE COURT APPLY?

The Court employs one of three tests in reviewing laws under these clauses, depending on the circumstances.

1. Strict Scrutiny (Maximum Scrutiny)

The Court uses the strict scrutiny standard when a suspect classification or fundamental right (these terms will be discussed *infra*) is involved. Under the strict scrutiny standard, a law will be upheld only if it is ***necessary*** to achieve a ***compelling*** or ***overriding*** government purpose. The Court will always consider whether less burdensome means for accomplishing the legislative goal are available. Most governmental action examined under this test fails.

a. Burden of Proof on Government

When the strict scrutiny standard is applied, the ***government*** will have the burden of proving that the law is necessary. The Court will not allow a loose fitting law (*i.e.,* if a law reaches more people or conduct than is necessary (overinclusive) or does not reach all of the people or conduct sought to be regulated (underinclusive), it will likely be struck down).

2. Intermediate Scrutiny

The Court uses intermediate scrutiny when a classification based on gender or legitimacy is involved. Under the intermediate scrutiny standard, a law will be upheld if it is ***substantially*** related to an ***important*** government purpose.

a. Burden of Proof Probably on Government

It is unclear who has the burden of proof when the Court uses the intermediate standard, but in most cases, it appears to be the government.

3. Rational Basis (Minimal Scrutiny)

The rational basis standard is used whenever the other two standards are not applicable (*i.e.,* most legislation). Under the rational basis standard, a law will be upheld if it is ***rationally related to a legitimate*** interest. It is difficult to fail this test, so most governmental action examined under this standard is upheld unless it is ***arbitrary*** or ***irrational***.

a. Burden of Proof on Challenger

Under the rational basis standard, laws are presumed valid. Therefore, the challenger has the burden of proof. This is a very difficult burden to meet, given the deference the Court gives to legislatures under the rational basis standard. (*See* below.)

b. Deference to Legislature

Under the rational basis standard, the Court will usually defer to a legislature's decision that a law is rational. Loose fitting laws are permissible here: The law need not be the best law that could have been written to achieve the legislative goal. Indeed, it need not go far at all toward a conceivable legislative goal; the Court will uphold a law taking a "first step" toward any legitimate goal, even if the Court thinks the law is unwise.

Example: City decided that advertisements on motor vehicles are traffic hazards, so it banned such advertisements except for those on vehicles advertising the owner's own product. Even though the excepted advertisements were no less distracting than the banned ones, the Court upheld the "first step" law. [Railway Express Agency v. New York, 336 U.S. 106 (1949)]

XVII. SUBSTANTIVE DUE PROCESS

A. CONSTITUTIONAL SOURCE—TWO CLAUSES

There are two separate clauses protecting substantive due process:

(i) The Due Process Clause of the Fifth Amendment (applies to the federal government); and

(ii) The Due Process Clause of the Fourteenth Amendment (applies to state and local governments).

As indicated above, ***the same tests*** are employed under each clause.

B. APPLICABLE STANDARDS

1. Fundamental Right—Strict Scrutiny

Where a law limits a fundamental right, strict scrutiny will be applied, and the law (or other governmental action) will be upheld only if it is necessary to promote a ***compelling or overriding interest***. Fundamental rights include:

a. Right to travel;

b. Privacy;

c. Voting; and

d. All First Amendment rights.

2. All Other Cases—Mere Rationality

In all other cases, the mere rationality test is applied, and the law will be upheld if it is ***rationally related to any conceivable legitimate end of government***. Examples include the following:

a. Business and Labor Regulations

The Court will sustain all varieties of business regulation; *e.g.,* "blue sky" laws, bank controls, insurance regulation, price and wage controls, unfair competition and trade practice controls, etc.

b. Taxation

Taxation is also invariably ***sustained***. However, discriminatory taxes might still be invalidated.

c. **Lifestyle**

There is, as yet, ***no recognized right*** to lead a certain lifestyle. Thus, the Supreme Court will uphold laws: prohibiting drugs ("hard" or "soft"), requiring motorcyclists to wear helmets, or requiring police officers to have short hair. [Kelley v. Johnson, 425 U.S. 238 (1976)]

d. **Zoning**

Regulation of the ownership or use of property has also been liberally tolerated by the Court.

1) **Statutes Forbidding Nuisances or Promoting Community's Preferred Lifestyle**

Statutes forbidding certain uses as nuisances have been sustained, as have all kinds of statutes designed to promote the public's enjoyment of space and safety or to promote a community's preferred lifestyle and character. For example, the Supreme Court held that a Long Island suburb could zone out all groups of three or more persons unrelated by blood, adoption, or marriage. [Village of Belle Terre v. Boraas, 416 U.S. 1 (1974)]

2) **Cannot Prohibit Traditionally Related Families from Living Together**

However, you should know that the Supreme Court held that zoning regulations that prohibit members of traditional families from living together (*i.e.,* zoning excluding cousins or grandchildren) violate due process. [Moore v. City of East Cleveland, 431 U.S. 494 (1977)]

e. **Punitive Damages**

The Supreme Court has held that punitive damages do not necessarily violate due process. However, "grossly excessive" damages—those that are unreasonably high to vindicate the state's interest in punishment—are invalid. [TXO Production Corp. v. Alliance Resources Corp., 509 U.S. 443 (1993)]

1) **Factors Considered**

In assessing whether punitive damages violate due process, the key issue is whether the defendant had ***fair notice of the possible magnitude*** of the punitive damages. In assessing such notice, the Court will look to:

(i) The ***reprehensibility*** of the defendant's conduct (*e.g.,* whether the defendant caused physical harm rather than merely economic harm, whether the defendant acted with reckless disregard for harm, whether the conduct was repeated rather than isolated, and whether the harm resulted from intentional malice or deceit rather than from an accident);

(ii) The ***disparity between*** the actual or potential ***harm suffered*** by the plaintiff and the ***punitive award;*** and

(iii) The ***difference between the punitive damages award and the criminal or civil penalties*** authorized for comparable misconduct.

[BMW of North America, Inc. v. Gore, 517 U.S. 559 (1996)]

2) **Rule of Thumb**
Except for particularly egregious conduct—especially when the conduct resulted in only a small amount of compensatory damages—punitive damages should not exceed ***10 times the compensatory damages.*** [State Farm Mutual Auto Insurance Co. v. Campbell, 538 U.S. 408 (2003)—punitive damages of 145 times compensatory damages violate due process]

f. **Compare—Vagueness Doctrine**
Under the Due Process Clause of the Fourteenth Amendment, a law can be held unconstitutional if it fails to provide minimal guidelines to govern law enforcement officers so as to discourage arbitrary and discriminatory enforcement. [Kolender v. Lawson, 461 U.S. 352 (1983); City of Chicago v. Morales, 527 U.S. 41 (1999)—holding unconstitutional on vagueness grounds an ordinance that allowed officers to disperse suspected gang members when they were "loitering," which was defined as remaining in any one place with no ***apparent purpose***]

C. A FEW IRREBUTTABLE PRESUMPTIONS MAY BE INVALID

If the government "presumes facts" against a person so that she is not qualified for some important benefit or right, the irrebuttable presumption may be unconstitutional. Although the Court often characterizes this as a due process question, it is more accurately an equal protection question because the government is creating an arbitrary classification. In any case, if the presumption affects a fundamental right (*e.g.,* right to travel) or a suspect or quasi-suspect classification (*e.g.,* gender), it will likely be invalid under strict scrutiny or intermediate scrutiny analysis, because the administrative convenience created by the presumption is not an important enough interest to justify the burden on the right or class. If some other classification or right is involved, the presumption will likely be upheld under the rational basis standard.

Examples: 1) A state may not presume a teacher incapable of continuous service in the classroom merely because she is four or five months' pregnant or has a child under age three. [Cleveland Board of Education v. LaFleur, 414 U.S. 632 (1974)]

2) The government may presume that a marriage entered into within nine months of a wage earner's death was simply to secure Social Security benefits. [Weinberger v. Salfi, 422 U.S. 749 (1975)]

XVIII. EQUAL PROTECTION

A. CONSTITUTIONAL SOURCE

The Equal Protection Clause of the Fourteenth Amendment has ***no counterpart in the Constitution applicable to the federal government***; it is limited to state action. Nevertheless, it is clear that grossly unreasonable discrimination by the federal government violates the ***Due Process Clause of the Fifth Amendment***. [Bolling v. Sharpe, 347 U.S. 497 (1954)—racial discrimination in the public schools of the District of Columbia held a violation of due process] Thus, there are really two equal protection guarantees. The Court applies the same standards under either constitutional provision.

B. APPLICABLE STANDARDS

As indicated above, the Court will apply one of three standards when examining governmental

action involving classifications of persons. If a ***suspect classification or fundamental right*** is involved, the strict scrutiny standard will be applied and the action will be struck down unless the government proves that it is necessary to achieve a compelling interest. If a ***quasi-suspect classification*** is involved, the Court will likely require the government to prove that the action is substantially related to an important government interest. If ***any other classification*** is involved, the action will be upheld unless the challenger proves that the action is not rationally related to a legitimate government interest.

C. PROVING DISCRIMINATORY CLASSIFICATION

The mere fact that legislation or governmental action has a discriminatory effect is not sufficient to trigger strict scrutiny or intermediate scrutiny. There must be ***intent*** to discriminate on the part of the government. Intent can be shown in three ways: (i) facial discrimination; (ii) discriminatory application; or (iii) discriminatory motive.

1. Facial Discrimination

A law may include a classification on its face. This type of law, by its own terms, makes an explicit distinction between classes of persons (perhaps by race or gender; *e.g.,* all white males 21 or older may serve as jurors [*see* Strauder v. West Virginia, 100 U.S. 303 (1880)]). In such cases the courts merely have to apply the appropriate standard of review for that classification. (The standards for racial classifications and gender classifications are described below.)

a. Facial Discrimination Absent Racial Language

In a few cases, the Supreme Court has held that a law used a racial classification "on its face" even though the language of the law did not include racial language. In these cases, the Supreme Court found that the law could not be explained except in racial terms.

Example: The Court found that a state law establishing districts for the election of Representatives to the United States Congress should be deemed to use a racial classification on its face because one bizarrely shaped district could not be explained except in terms of establishing a district where minority race voters would control the outcome of the election. The Court did not rule on the question of whether this racial classification was narrowly tailored to a compelling interest, such as remedying proven past discrimination, because that question had not been addressed in the lower courts. [Shaw v. Reno, 509 U.S. 630 (1993)]

Note: If a legislative districting map could be explained in terms other than race, the Court would not find that the law constituted racial discrimination on its face. In such a case, the persons attacking legislative districts as being based on racial classification would have to show that district lines were drawn for a racially discriminatory purpose. [Hunt v. Cromartie, 532 U.S. 234 (2001)—"Hunt II"]

2. Discriminatory Application

In some instances, a law that appears to be neutral on its face will be applied in a different manner to different classes of persons. If the persons challenging the governmental action can prove that the government officials applying the law had a discriminatory purpose (and used discriminatory standards based on traits such as race or gender), the law will be invalidated.

Examples: 1) A law prohibited operating a laundry in wooden buildings, but gave a government agency discretion to grant exemptions. It was shown that most such laundries were owned by people of Chinese descent, but the agency granted exemptions only to non-Asian applicants. The law was deemed to involve racial or national origin classification and was invalidated as applied. [Yick Wo v. Hopkins, 118 U.S. 356 (1886)]

2) Laws allow attorneys to move to strike potential jurors from a jury either for cause or without cause (a peremptory strike). In either case, there is an equal protection violation when it is proved that an attorney excluded a person from a jury on account of the person's race or sex. [*See* Batson v. Kentucky, 476 U.S. 79 (1986); J.E.B. v. Alabama *ex rel.* T.B., 511 U.S. 127 (1994)] Note that because striking potential jurors from a jury significantly involves the state, even attorneys representing private parties are prohibited from discriminatory strikes. (*See* XII.B.2.a.1)a)(1), *supra.*)

3. Discriminatory Motive

Sometimes a government action will appear to be neutral on its face and in its application, but will have disproportionate impact on a particular class of persons (such as a racial minority or women). Such a law will be found to involve a classification (and be subject to the level of scrutiny appropriate to that classification) only if a court finds that the law-making body enacted or maintained the law for a ***discriminatory purpose***. In such cases, the court should admit into evidence statistical proof that the law has a disproportionate impact on one class of persons. However, mere statistical evidence will rarely be sufficient in itself to prove that the government had a discriminatory purpose in passing a law. Statistical evidence may be combined with other evidence of legislative or administrative intent to show that a law or regulation is the product of a discriminatory purpose.

Examples: 1) A police department used results from a written test as a criterion for hiring police officers. Members of identifiable racial minorities consistently got low scores on the test, although there was no proof that the test was written or otherwise employed for the purpose of disadvantaging minority applicants. Because of the absence of nonstatistical proof of discriminatory purpose, there was no equal protection violation. [Washington v. Davis, 426 U.S. 229 (1976)]

2) A state law gave a preference in the hiring and promotion of civil service employees to persons who were honorably discharged from the United States military. The foreseeable and actual impact of this law was to disadvantage the female population of job applicants, because the majority of veterans are men. Because there was no proof (other than the statistical impact of the law) that the legislature enacted the law for the purpose of hurting women (as opposed to the purpose of aiding veterans), the law was upheld.

3) A statistical study showing that black defendants in capital cases are much more likely to receive the death penalty than are white defendants in a state will not in itself establish that a particular black defendant was denied equal protection by being sentenced to death for murder in that state. The statistical study is insufficient to prove purposeful discrimination. [McCleskey v. Kemp, 481 U.S. 279 (1987)]

D. SUSPECT CLASSIFICATIONS

1. Race and National Origin

If governmental action classifies persons based on exercise of a fundamental right or involves a suspect classification (race, national origin, or alienage), strict scrutiny is applied. The result is invalidation of almost every case where the classification would burden a person because of her status as a member of a racial or national origin minority. The only explicit race discrimination upheld despite strict scrutiny was the wartime incarceration of United States citizens of Japanese ancestry on the West Coast. [Korematsu v. United States, 323 U.S. 214 (1944)—found to be necessary to achieve compelling interest of national security]

Example: A state could not deny custody of a child from a previous marriage to a white mother merely because her new husband was black, where the mother was otherwise found to be an appropriate parent. Racial prejudice against mixed race couples does not justify taking a child from his mother. [Palmore v. Sidoti, 466 U.S. 429 (1984)]

a. School Integration

Recall that only intentional discrimination will be found to create discriminatory classifications calling for strict scrutiny (*see* C., *supra*); thus, only intentional segregation in schools will be invalidated under equal protection.

Example: No equal protection violation was found where a school system established attendance zones in a racially neutral manner, but racial imbalance occurred because of housing patterns. [Keyes v. School District No. 1, 413 U.S. 189 (1973)]

1) Remedying Intentional School Segregation

If it is proven that a school board has engaged in the racial districting of schools, the board must take steps to eliminate the effects of that discrimination (*e.g.,* busing students). If the school board refuses to do so, a court may order the school district to take all appropriate steps to eliminate the discrimination.

a) Order Limited

A court may not impose a remedy that goes beyond the purpose of remedying the vestiges of past segregation. Thus, it is impermissible for a court to impose a remedy whose purpose is to attract nonminority students from outside the school district when there is no evidence of past segregation outside the district. [Missouri v. Jenkins, 515 U.S. 70 (1995)—state not required to fund salary increases and remedial programs to create magnet schools to attract suburban students to urban schools]

b. "Benign" Government Discrimination—Affirmative Action

Government action—whether by federal, state, or local governmental bodies—that ***favors*** racial or ethnic minorities is subject to strict scrutiny, as is government action discriminating ***against*** racial or ethnic minorities. [Adarand Constructors, Inc. v. Pena, 515 U.S. 200 (1995)—*overruling* Metro Broadcasting, Inc. v. Federal Communications Commission, 497 U.S. 547 (1990), which applied intermediate standard to federal discrimination]

Note: Prior to its ruling in *Adarand, supra*, the Supreme Court upheld a federal requirement that 10% of federal grants for public works be set aside for minority businesses. [Fullilove v. Klutznick, 448 U.S. 448 (1980)] In *Adarand*, the Court reserved judgment on whether a *Fullilove*-type program would survive strict scrutiny. Some commentators have suggested that it might, because the Court might give Congress more deference than the states based on Congress's power under the Enabling Clause of the Fourteenth Amendment (*see* XII.A.3., *supra*), but the continued validity of *Fullilove* is, at best, uncertain.

1) **Remedying Past Discrimination**

The government has a compelling interest in remedying past discrimination against a racial or ethnic minority. Thus, if a court finds that a governmental agency has engaged in racial discrimination, it may employ a race-conscious remedy tailored to end the discrimination and eliminate its effects. A remedy of this type is permissible under the Equal Protection Clause because it is narrowly tailored to further a compelling interest (the elimination of the illegal or unconstitutional discrimination).

Example: When it has been proven that a public employer engaged in persistent racial discrimination, a court may order relief that establishes a goal for the hiring or promotion of minority persons so as to eliminate the effects of the past discrimination. [United States v. Paradise, 480 U.S. 149 (1987)]

2) **Where There Has Been No Past Discrimination by Government**

Even where a state or local government has not engaged in past discrimination, it may have a compelling interest in affirmative action. However, the governmental action must be ***narrowly tailored*** to that interest. [City of Richmond v. J.A. Croson Co., 488 U.S. 469 (1989)]

a) **Remedial Justifications**

(1) **Local Private Discrimination**

Remedying past private discrimination ***within*** the governmental agency's jurisdiction is a compelling interest, but there is no compelling interest in remedying the general effects of societal discrimination. Thus, for a city to give a preference to minority race applicants for city construction contracts, it must identify the past unconstitutional or illegal discrimination against minority-owned construction businesses that it is now attempting to correct. [City of Richmond v. J.A. Croson Co., *supra*]

Example: In *United Jewish Organizations v. Carey,* 430 U.S. 144 (1977), the Court upheld New York's revised voting district plan, based solely on racial statistics, because the revisions were made to insure that minorities that had previously been discriminated against in New York would be represented in the legislature.

(2) **Diversity in Public Education**

A school board may not assign students to a school on the basis of race unless necessary to achieve a compelling interest, such as remedying past unconstitutional (*i.e.,* intentional) discrimination. A majority of the Court has not found diversity itself to be a sufficiently compelling interest. [*See* Parents Involved in Community Schools v. Seattle School District No. 1, 551 U.S. 701 (2007)] However, the law is different for colleges and universities. Colleges and universities have claimed that they have a compelling interest in having a diverse student body—in its own right—because students with diverse backgrounds enhance classroom discussions and the educational experience both in and outside the classroom, promote cross-racial understanding, and break down racial stereotypes for the workforce. The Court has held that it will defer to a state college or university's good faith judgment that it has such a compelling interest. [Grutter v. Bollinger, 539 U.S. 306 (2003); Gratz v. Bollinger, 539 U.S. 244 (2003)] However, the Court has also held that colleges and universities should consider each applicant as an individual. Although race or ethnicity may be deemed a ***plus,*** as one of a range of factors to consider when making an admissions decision, if race or ethnicity is the defining criterion for admission, the admission policy will not be narrowly tailored to achieving the compelling interest of ensuring a diverse student body.

Example: In its admission process, the University of Michigan's law school required admissions officers to assess an applicant's academic ability and ***all other factors*** about the applicant relevant to whether the student will be an asset to the entering class. The school's policies specifically allowed officers to consider whether an applicant was from a group that has historically been discriminated against, such as African-Americans, Hispanics, and Native Americans. The officers were not told to prescribe any particular weight to this factor, although they were told to include enough applicants from historically underrepresented groups to ensure a "critical mass" of such students—*i.e.,* enough minority students so that they do not feel isolated or become spokespersons for their race. At trial, admissions officers testified that the extent that race factored into an admissions decision varied from applicant to applicant, and statistics showed that, while race was a strong factor in admissions decisions, it was not the predominant factor. The Court held that such a program does not violate the Equal Protection Clause. [Grutter v. Bollinger, *supra*]

Compare: To obtain a critical mass of minority students in its undergraduate admissions process, the University of Michigan allowed admissions officers to give students points for being a member of a historically underrepresented minority group and for a variety of other factors (*e.g.,* academic ability, leadership ability, a good admissions essay, etc.).

Being a member of an underrepresented minority group was worth 20 points, while high school leadership ability, a good admissions essay, etc., were worth less than five points each. Applicants with 100 points or more were guaranteed admission into the school. Under these admissions policies, virtually every academically qualified applicant who was from a group defined as a historically underrepresented minority group was admitted to the school. Such a program violates the Equal Protection Clause because it makes race the predominant factor in making admissions decisions and so is not sufficiently narrowly tailored. [Gratz v. Bollinger, *supra*]

Note: The Court has similarly held that while public schools might have a compelling interest in a racially diverse faculty, a school board may not fire or lay off white teachers with greater seniority than minority race teachers for the sole purpose of maintaining racial balance in a faculty during a period when teacher layoffs are necessary. [Wygant v. Jackson Board of Education, 476 U.S. 267 (1989)]

c. Discriminatory Legislative Apportionment

Race can be considered in drawing up new voting districts, but it ***cannot be the predominant factor***. If a plaintiff can show that a redistricting plan was drawn up predominantly on the basis of racial considerations (as opposed to the more traditional factors, such as compactness, contiguity, and community interest), the plan will violate the Equal Protection Clause ***unless*** the government can show that the plan is ***narrowly tailored*** to serve a ***compelling state interest***. [Miller v. Johnson, 515 U.S. 900 (1995)—while eradicating the effects of past discrimination would be a compelling state interest, the redistricting here was driven by the Justice Department's policy of maximizing the number of districts where racial minority members are the majority, which is not a compelling interest]

d. Private Affirmative Action

Private employers, of course, are not restricted by the Equal Protection Clause, since the Clause applies only to the government, and private employers lack state action. Nevertheless, Congress has adopted statutes regulating private discrimination by employers pursuant to its power under the enabling provisions of the Thirteenth and Fourteenth Amendments and the Commerce Clause. Thus, if an exam question asks whether private employer discrimination is valid, the answer generally cannot be based on equal protection.

2. Alienage Classifications

a. Federal Classifications

The standard for review of federal government classifications based on alienage is not clear, but they never seem to be subject to strict scrutiny. Because of Congress's plenary power over aliens, these classifications are valid if they are ***not arbitrary and unreasonable***. Thus, federal Medicare regulations could establish a five-year residency requirement for benefits that eliminated many resident aliens. [Mathews v. Diaz, 426 U.S. 67 (1976)]

b. State and Local Classifications

State/local laws are ***subject to strict scrutiny*** if based on alienage. A "compelling state interest" must be shown to justify disparate treatment. For example, a state law requiring United States citizenship for welfare benefits, civil service jobs, or a license to practice law will be struck down because there is no compelling interest justifying the requirement.

1) Exception—Participation in Self-Government Process

If a law discriminates against alien participation in the functioning of the state government, the ***rational basis*** standard is applied.

Examples: 1) A state cannot require a notary public to be a citizen. A notary's responsibilities are essentially clerical and do not fall within the exception for positions related to participation in the governmental process, and there is no compelling government interest justifying such a requirement. [Bernal v. Fainter, 467 U.S. 216 (1984)]

2) A state can validly refuse to hire aliens as police officers and ***primary*** and ***secondary*** school teachers (because such teachers influence the attitudes of young minds toward government, the political process, and citizenship, as well as provide an example for civic virtues) and for all other positions that have a direct effect on the functioning of government. [Ambach v. Norwick, 441 U.S. 68 (1979); Cabell v. Chavez-Salido, 454 U.S. 432 (1982)]

c. Undocumented Aliens

1) Punitive Laws Against "Illegal" Alien Adults

The Supreme Court has ***not*** held that undocumented ("illegal") aliens are a suspect classification. Thus, a state law that denies benefits to (or imposes burdens on) persons who are in the United States without the permission of the federal government might be upheld under the rational basis test as long as the law was not totally arbitrary.

2) Education Rights of Alien Children

In *Plyler v. Doe,* 457 U.S. 202 (1982), the Court held that a state denied equal protection to undocumented alien children when it denied them state-supported primary or secondary education. However, the Supreme Court upheld a state statute that permitted a school district to deny tuition-free education to any child (whether or not he was a United States citizen) who lived apart from his parent or lawful guardian if the child's presence in the school district was for the "primary purpose" of attending school in the district. The state does not have to consider such a child to be a bona fide resident of the school district. [Martinez v. Bynum, 461 U.S. 321 (1983)]

E. QUASI-SUSPECT CLASSIFICATIONS

Classifications based on gender or legitimacy are almost always suspect. When analyzing government action based on such classifications, the Court will apply the intermediate standard and strike the action unless it is ***substantially related*** to an ***important*** government interest.

1. Gender

The Court has expressly held that the ***government*** bears the burden of proof in gender discrimination cases and that an ***"exceedingly persuasive justification"*** is required in order to show that gender discrimination is substantially related to an important government interest. [United States v. Virginia, 518 U.S. 515 (1996)]

a. Intentional Discrimination Against Women

Gender classifications that ***intentionally*** discriminate against women will generally be invalid under the intermediate standard, because the government is unable to show the "exceedingly persuasive justification" that is required.

Examples: 1) A statute giving the husband, as head of the household, the right to unilaterally dispose of property jointly owned with his wife violates equal protection. [Kirchberg v. Feenstra, 450 U.S. 455 (1981)]

2) A statute giving preference to males over females to act as administrator of an estate violates equal protection. [Reed v. Reed, 404 U.S. 71 (1971)—ease in determining who should serve is not an important interest]

Compare: 1) A state law that excluded from state disability insurance benefits "disabilities" arising from normal pregnancy and childbirth was upheld on a holding that it did not constitute a gender classification and so did not constitute intentional discrimination. [Geduldig v. Aiello, 417 U.S. 484 (1974)]

2) A state statute granting a hiring preference to veterans was upheld even though the result would disadvantage women since most veterans are men. The Court found that the purpose of the statute was to help veterans, not to discriminate against women. [Personnel Administrator of Massachusetts v. Feeney, 442 U.S. 256 (1979)]

1) Government Interest Must Be Genuine

The "important government interest" advanced to justify categorization on the basis of gender must be ***genuine***—not hypothesized for the purpose of litigation defense. Neither may the government's justification rely on ***overbroad generalizations*** about males and females that will create or perpetuate the legal, social, and economic inferiority of women. [United States v. Virginia, *supra*]

Example: When a state military school's policy of admitting only men was challenged, the state justified the policy, claiming that: (i) offering a diversity of educational approaches within the state (*e.g.,* some schools having men only, some having women only, and some having both) yields important educational benefits, and (ii) females ***generally*** would not be able to meet the school's physical requirements and would not do well under the school's adversative approach to education. The Supreme Court found these arguments unavailing. There was no evidence that the single-sex school in question was established or had been maintained with a view toward fostering a diversity of educational opportunities, and

there was some evidence that ***some*** women could meet the school's physical requirements and thrive under the school's adversative approach. [United States v. Virginia, *supra*]

b. Affirmative Action Benefiting Women

Classifications benefiting women that are designed to ***remedy past discrimination*** against women will generally be upheld.

Examples: 1) Social Security and tax exemptions that entitle women to greater benefits to make up for past discrimination in the workplace are valid. [Califano v. Webster, 430 U.S. 313 (1977)]

2) A Navy rule granting female officers longer tenure than males before mandatory discharge for nonproduction is valid to make up for past discrimination against females in the Navy. [Schlesinger v. Ballard, 419 U.S. 498 (1975)]

c. Intentional Discrimination Against Men

Intentional discrimination against men generally is invalid. However, a number of laws have been held valid as being substantially related to an important government interest.

1) Invalid Discrimination

The following have been held invalid under the Equal Protection Clause:

a) ***Denial to admit males to a state university or nursing school*** [Mississippi University for Women v. Hogan, 458 U.S. 718 (1982)];

b) Law that provides that ***only wives are eligible for alimony*** [Orr v. Orr, 440 U.S. 268 (1979)];

c) Law that permits ***unwed mother, but not unwed father, to stop adoption*** of offspring [Caban v. Mohammed, 441 U.S. 380 (1979)]; and

d) Law providing a ***higher minimum drinking age for men*** than for women [Craig v. Boren, 429 U.S. 190 (1976)].

2) Valid Discrimination

The following have been upheld under the Equal Protection Clause despite their discriminatory intent:

a) Law punishing males but not females for ***statutory rape*** (sexual intercourse with a minor) [Michael M. v. Superior Court, 450 U.S. 464 (1981)—classification was found to be substantially related to important interest of preventing pregnancy of minors];

b) ***Male-only draft registration*** [Rostker v. Goldberg, 453 U.S. 57 (1981)—classification was found to be substantially related to important interest of preparing combat troops]; and

c) A law granting ***automatic United States citizenship to nonmarital children born abroad to American mothers***, but requiring American fathers of children born abroad to take specific steps to establish paternity in order to make such children United States citizens. [Nguyen v. Immigration and Naturalization Service, 533 U.S. 53 (2001)—promotes the important governmental interest of avoiding proof of paternity problems, which are more difficult to resolve for fathers]

2. Legitimacy Classifications

Distinctions drawn between legitimate and illegitimate children are also reviewed under the intermediate scrutiny standard. Such classifications "must be ***substantially related*** to an ***important*** governmental objective." [Clark v. Jeter, 486 U.S. 456 (1988)]

a. No Punitive Purpose

When the Court examines a classification based on illegitimacy, it gives greater attention to the purpose behind the distinction. It will not uphold discriminatory legislation intended to punish the offspring of illicit relationships.

1) Inheritance from Father

A state statute cannot absolutely exclude illegitimate children from inheriting from their intestate fathers. [Trimble v. Gordon, 430 U.S. 762 (1977)]

Note: However, to promote efficient disposition of property at death (an important government interest), a state can require that the paternity of the father be proved before his death, since the requirement is substantially related to the important interest. [Lalli v. Lalli, 439 U.S. 259 (1978)]

2) Statute of Limitations on Paternity Suits May Be Discriminatory

The Supreme Court struck down a state statute that required illegitimate children to bring paternity suits within six years of their birth while allowing legitimate children to seek support from parents at any time. The Court found that the law was not related to the state interest of preventing stale or fraudulent claims. [Clark v. Jeter, *supra*]

b. Immigration Preference to Legitimate Children—Permissible

Due to the plenary power over immigration, the Court upheld a federal law granting immigration preferences to legitimate children. [Fiallo v. Bell, 430 U.S. 787 (1977)]

F. OTHER CLASSIFICATIONS

All other classifications are reviewed under the rational basis standard and will be upheld unless they bear no rational relationship to any conceivable legitimate government interest. Nevertheless, if the government has no interest in denying a benefit or imposing a burden on a group of persons other than a societal fear or dislike of them, the classification will not meet the standard.

Examples: 1) The Court struck down a zoning ordinance that allowed denial of a special use permit to a group of unrelated, mentally retarded persons who wished to share a residential home or apartment building. Retarded persons are not a suspect or quasi-suspect class and the right to housing is not a fundamental right; thus the Court applied the rational basis standard. It found that the sole reason the permit

was denied was the applicants' mental condition and that the government has no legitimate interest in prohibiting mentally retarded persons from living together. [Cleburne v. Cleburne Living Center, Inc., 473 U.S. 432 (1985)]

2) Several municipalities passed ordinances banning discrimination in housing, employment, etc., based on sexual orientation. In response, the state voters adopted a state constitutional amendment prohibiting any state or local action protecting the status of persons based on their homosexual or bisexual orientation. *Held:* A state constitutional provision that identifies persons by a single trait and then denies them the right to seek ***any*** specific protections from the law—no matter how local or widespread the injury—is so unprecedented as to imply animosity toward such persons and is thus not related to any legitimate state interest. [Romer v. Evans, 517 U.S. 620 (1996)]

1. Age Not Suspect

Age is not a suspect class. Thus, government action based on age will be upheld if there is a conceivable rational basis for the classification. [*See, e.g.,* Massachusetts Board of Retirement v. Murgia, 427 U.S. 307 (1976)—police officer can be forced to retire at age 50, even though he is as physically fit as a younger officer; Gregory v. Ashcroft, 501 U.S. 452 (1991)—a state constitution that requires state judges to retire at age 70 does not violate the Equal Protection Clause]

2. Wealth Not Suspect

The Court has never held that wealth alone is a "suspect classification." However, the lack of wealth, or the inability to pay a governmentally required fee, cannot be the sole basis upon which a person is deprived of a ***fundamental*** constitutional right.

Example: The government will be required to waive a marriage license fee or divorce court fee for a person who cannot afford to pay that fee. Marriage and divorce rights are part of the right of privacy.

a. Abortions

The Supreme Court upheld the governmental refusal to pay for abortions. The Court found that a woman did not have a fundamental constitutional right to obtain abortion services, but only a fundamental right to make her decision to have an abortion without government interference.

b. Education

The Supreme Court has not yet held education to be a fundamental right. The Court has not found that children are denied equal protection when the government provides greater educational opportunities for children who can afford to pay for access to the best state-operated schools. In fact, the Court has upheld the use of a property tax to fund local schools where the tax system resulted in children in districts with a high tax base getting a significantly better education than children in tax districts that could not afford significant taxes for education. [San Antonio Independent School District v. Rodriguez, 411 U.S. 1 (1973)] The Court has also upheld a statute that authorizes some school districts in the state to charge user fees for bus transportation to the local public schools. [Kadrmas v. Dickinson Public Schools, 487 U.S. 450 (1988)]

XIX. FUNDAMENTAL RIGHTS

A. INTRODUCTION

Certain fundamental rights are protected under the Constitution. If they are denied to everyone, it is a substantive due process problem. If they are denied to some individuals but not to others, it is an equal protection problem. The applicable standard in either case is strict scrutiny. Thus, to be valid the governmental action must be ***necessary*** to protect a ***compelling interest***.

B. RIGHT OF PRIVACY

Various privacy rights, including marriage, sexual relations, abortion, and childrearing, are fundamental rights. Thus, regulations affecting these rights are reviewed under the ***strict scrutiny*** standard and will be upheld only if they are ***necessary*** to a ***compelling interest***.

1. Marriage

The right of a male and female to enter into (and, probably, to dissolve) a marriage relationship is a fundamental right. Although not all cases examining marriage regulations clearly use the compelling interest standard, a law prohibiting a class of adults from marrying is likely to be invalidated unless the government can demonstrate that the law is narrowly tailored to promote a compelling or overriding or, at least, important interest.

Note: The Court has indicated that there is a "marital zone of privacy" [*see* Griswold v. Connecticut, 381 U.S. 479 (1965)], so it will likely grant broader protection to private sexual relations between married persons than it does concerning nonmarried persons.

a. Special Test in Prisoners' Rights Cases

A statute or regulation that restricts the constitutional rights of prison inmates will be upheld as long as the statute or regulation "is reasonably related to legitimate penological interests."

Example: Even under this lenient standard, a prison regulation that prohibited an adult prisoner from establishing a legal marriage relationship with another adult unless the prison superintendent approved the marriage was held invalid, because the regulation was not reasonably related to any asserted penological interest. [Turner v. Safley, 482 U.S. 78 (1987)]

2. Use of Contraceptives

A state cannot prohibit distribution of nonmedical contraceptives to adults except through licensed pharmacists, nor prohibit sales of such contraceptives to persons under 16 who do not have approval of a licensed physician. [Carey v. Population Services International, 431 U.S. 678 (1977)]

3. Abortion

The Supreme Court has held that the right of privacy includes the right of a woman to have an abortion under certain circumstances without undue interference from the state. [Roe v. Wade, 410 U.S. 113 (1973)] However, because the Court has held that the states have a compelling interest in protecting the health of both the woman and the fetus that may become a child, it is difficult to apply the normal "strict scrutiny" analysis to abortion regulations (since these two compelling interests may conflict with each other and with the woman's privacy right). Moreover, the Supreme Court has actively been changing the rules

regarding abortions and the Justices have not come to agreement on any applicable standard. In the Court's latest announcement, the plurality opinion adopted two rules: a pre-viability rule and a post-viability rule.

a. **Pre-Viability Rule—No Undue Burdens**
Before viability (*i.e.,* a realistic possibility of maintaining the fetus's life outside the womb), a state may adopt regulations protecting the mother's health and the life of the fetus only if the regulation does not impose an "undue burden" or substantial obstacle to the woman's right to have an abortion. The Court has not specifically defined what will constitute an undue burden, stating that a state can adopt a statute designed to persuade a woman to choose childbirth over abortion as long as the statute is reasonably related to that purpose and does not put a ***substantial*** obstacle to abortion in the woman's path. A statute will not impose a substantial obstacle or an undue burden simply because it has the incidental effect of making it more difficult or more expensive to obtain an abortion. [Planned Parenthood of Southeastern Pennsylvania v. Casey, 505 U.S. 833 (1992)]

1) **Informed Consent—No Undue Burden**
States can require abortions to be performed by licensed physicians, and it is not an "undue burden" to require the ***physician*** to provide the woman with truthful information about the nature of the abortion procedure, the health risks of abortion and childbirth, and the probable gestational age of the fetus. [Planned Parenthood of Southeastern Pennsylvania v. Casey, *supra*]

2) **Waiting Period—No Undue Burden**
Requiring a 24-hour waiting period between the time the woman gives her informed consent and the time of the abortion does not amount to an undue burden. [Planned Parenthood of Southeastern Pennsylvania v. Casey, *supra*]

3) **Parental Consent—No Undue Burden**
A state may require a minor to obtain her parents' (one or both) consent to have an abortion (or give notice to them even if their consent is not required) if there is a "bypass procedure" whereby the minor may obtain the abortion (without notice to or consent of her parents) with the consent of a judge. The judge is required to make a prompt decision as to (i) whether the minor is sufficiently mature to make her own abortion decision, and (ii) if she is not sufficiently mature, whether having an abortion without notice to her parents is in her best interests. [Hodgson v. Minnesota, 497 U.S. 417 (1990); Ohio v. Akron Center for Reproductive Health, 497 U.S. 502 (1990); Planned Parenthood of Southeastern Pennsylvania v. Casey, *supra;* Lambert v. Wicklund, 520 U.S. 292 (1997)]

4) **Compare—Spousal Consent Is Undue Burden**
It is an undue burden to require a woman to sign a statement that she has notified her spouse that she is about to undergo an abortion. [Planned Parenthood of Southeastern Pennsylvania v. Casey, *supra*]

5) **"Physician Only" Requirement—No Undue Burden**
A law restricting the performance of abortions to licensed physicians does not impose an undue burden on a woman seeking an abortion. [Mazurek v. Armstrong, 520 U.S. 968 (1997)—*per curiam*]

6) **"Partial-Birth Abortion" Ban—No Undue Burden**
A federal law (the Partial-Birth Abortion Ban Act of 2003) prohibiting "intact D&E" (a type of abortion procedure in which a live fetus is partially delivered, killed, and then fully removed from the woman's body) does not ***on its face*** impose an undue burden where other abortion procedures are available (*e.g.*, a D&E not involving partial live delivery), the law includes specific anatomical standards and an exception to protect the woman's life, and there is uncertainty within the medical profession whether banning the intact D&E procedure creates a significant health risk for women. Although the Court generally upheld the statute, it also held that the statute could not be applied in situations wherein the woman's health would be endangered. [Gonzales v. Carhart, 550 U.S. 124 (2007)—*distinguishing* Stenberg v. Carhart, 530 U.S. 914 (2000)—which invalidated a state partial-birth abortion ban that did not contain clearly defined anatomical standards nor provide any health exception]

7) **Other Regulations Uncertain**
Prior to *Planned Parenthood of Southeastern Pennsylvania v. Casey, supra,* the Supreme Court upheld a requirement that abortions be performed in a clinic or medical facility with all of the basic medical equipment that would be found in a hospital surgery room. The Court also upheld a requirement that tissue from an aborted fetus be sent to a pathologist. These holdings surely are still valid. But the Court struck down certain other regulations (*e.g.,* requiring early term abortions to be approved by another doctor or hospital committee). Whether these regulations would be found to be undue burdens is uncertain.

b. **Post-Viability Rule—May Prohibit Abortion Unless Woman's Health Threatened**
Once the fetus has become viable, the state's interest in the fetus's life can override the woman's right to choose an abortion, but it does not override the state's interest in the woman's health. Thus, after viability the state can prohibit a woman from obtaining an abortion unless an abortion is necessary to protect the mother's life or health. However, viability is itself a medical question, and a state cannot unduly interfere with the attending physician's judgment as to the reasonable likelihood that the fetus can survive outside the womb. [Colautti v. Franklin, 439 U.S. 379 (1979)]

c. **Remedy**
When a court is faced with a statute restricting access to abortions that may be applied in an unconstitutional manner so as to harm the mother's health, it should ***not*** invalidate the statute in its entirety if the statute has valid applications. Instead, the court should attempt to fashion narrower declaratory and injunctive relief against the unconstitutional application. [Ayotte v. Planned Parenthood of Northern New England, 546 U.S. 320 (2006)]

Example: Court should not have invalidated an entire statute requiring minors to give parents notice before obtaining an abortion merely because the statute did not include an exception for cases where the minor's health is at stake; rather, it should be "declared invalid to the extent that it reaches too far, but otherwise left intact." [Ayotte v. Planned Parenthood of Northern New England, *supra*]

d. **Financing Abortions**
Neither federal nor local governments are required to grant medical benefit payments

for abortions to indigent women, even if they grant benefits to indigent women for childbirth services. [Maher v. Roe, 432 U.S. 464 (1977); Harris v. McRae, 448 U.S. 297 (1980)] Moreover, a state may prohibit the public funding of abortions by prohibiting the use of public facilities for abortions and prohibiting any public employee acting within the scope of her public employment from performing or assisting in the performance of abortions. [Webster v. Reproductive Health Services, 492 U.S. 490 (1989)]

4. Obscene Reading Material

The right of privacy encompasses the freedom to read obscene material in your home, except for child pornography. [Stanley v. Georgia, 394 U.S. 557 (1969); Osborne v. Ohio, 495 U.S. 103 (1990)] It does not, however, include the right to sell, purchase, receive, or transport obscene material. [Paris Adult Theatre v. Slayton, 413 U.S. 49 (1973)]

5. Keeping Extended Family Together

The right of privacy includes the right of family members—even extended ones—to live together. Thus, a zoning ordinance cannot prohibit extended families from living in a single household since there is no compelling interest to justify such a rule. [Moore v. City of East Cleveland, 431 U.S. 494 (1977)]

6. Rights of Parents

Parents have a fundamental right to make decisions concerning the care, custody, and control of their children. [Troxel v. Granville, 530 U.S. 57 (2000)]

a. Education

Although the state may prescribe reasonable educational standards, it may ***not*** require that all children be educated in public schools. [Pierce v. Society of Sisters, 268 U.S. 510 (1925)] Neither may the state forbid education in a language other than English. [Meyer v. Nebraska, 262 U.S. 390 (1923)]

b. Visitation

A state law was found to be overbroad and in violation of parents' rights where it (i) authorized the courts to grant "any person" (including grandparents) a right to visit a child upon finding that this would be in the child's best interests, and (ii) did not allow the judge to give significant weight to the parent's offer of meaningful visitation opportunity and the traditional presumption that a fit parent will act in the child's best interests. [Troxel v. Granville, *supra*]

7. Intimate Sexual Conduct

The state has no legitimate interest in making it a crime for ***fully consenting adults*** to engage in ***private*** intimate sexual conduct that is not commercial in nature. [Lawrence v. Texas, 539 U.S. 558 (2003)—a state law making it a crime for members of the same sex to engage in sodomy violates the Due Process Clause]

8. Freedom from Collection and Distribution of Personal Data

The right of privacy does not prevent the state from accumulating and computerizing the names and addresses of patients for whom dangerous drugs are prescribed. [Whalen v. Roe, 429 U.S. 589 (1977)] And the state can republish the recording of an official act, such as an arrest. [Paul v. Davis, 424 U.S. 693 (1976)]

C. RIGHT TO VOTE

The right of all United States citizens over 18 years of age to vote is mentioned in the Fourteenth, Fifteenth, Nineteenth, Twenty-Fourth, and Twenty-Sixth Amendments. It extends to all national and state government elections, including primaries. The right is fundamental; thus, restrictions on voting, other than on the basis of age, residency, or citizenship, are ***invalid*** unless they can pass strict scrutiny.

1. Restrictions on Right to Vote

a. Residency Requirements

Relatively short residency requirements restricting the right to vote (*e.g.,* 30 days) are valid because there is a compelling interest in ensuring that only bona fide residents vote. However, longer residency requirements will probably be held invalid (*e.g.,* one year) because they discriminate against newer residents without a compelling reason, and thus violate the Equal Protection Clause. Such residency requirements might also violate the right to travel interstate. (*See* D.1.b.1), *infra.*) Note also that Congress may override state residency requirements in ***presidential*** elections. [Oregon v. Mitchell, 400 U.S. 112 (1970)]

1) Members of Armed Forces

The right to vote cannot automatically be denied to members of the armed forces stationed at a particular locality. They must be given an opportunity to prove their bona fide residency. [Carrington v. Rash, 380 U.S. 89 (1965)]

2) Compare—Nonresidents

Laws that prohibit nonresidents from voting are generally valid as long as they have a rational basis. [*See* Holt Civic Club v. City of Tuscaloosa, 439 U.S. 60 (1978)—upholding denial of right to vote in city elections to persons outside of city limits, but within the city's police and licensing jurisdiction]

b. Property Ownership

Conditioning the right to vote, to be a candidate, or to hold office on property ownership is usually invalid under the Equal Protection Clause, since property ownership is not necessary to any compelling governmental interest related to voting. [*See, e.g.,* Kramer v. Union Free School District, 395 U.S. 621 (1969)—requirement of owning property or having children in schools to vote in school board elections struck] However, certain special purpose elections (*e.g.,* water storage district elections) can be based on property ownership. (*See* below.)

c. Poll Taxes

Poll taxes are prohibited under the Twenty-Fourth Amendment, and the Supreme Court has held that they also violate equal protection because wealth is not related to the government's interest in having voters vote intelligently. [Harper v. Virginia Board of Elections, 383 U.S. 663 (1966)]

d. Primary Elections

1) State Regulation of Party Primaries

States may exercise some control over primary elections, but such regulation is

subject to restrictions under the First Amendment (freedom of political association) and the Fourteenth Amendment (Equal Protection Clause). Thus, to prevent interparty "raiding," the Supreme Court has held that states can require a person to have been registered with a party for a reasonable time before that party's primary election in order to be eligible to vote in the primary. [Rosario v. Rockefeller, 410 U.S. 752 (1973)—11 months' registration upheld; Kusper v. Pontikes, 414 U.S. 51 (1973)—23 months not upheld] However, if a political party wishes to open its primary elections to anyone, whether or not registered with the party, the state cannot prohibit this because the state interest here is overridden by the right of political association. [Tashjian v. Republican Party of Connecticut, 479 U.S. 208 (1986)]

2) States May Subsidize Primaries of Major Parties

States may subsidize the primaries of major parties without similarly defraying the costs of mechanisms through which minor parties qualify candidates for the general election [American Party of Texas v. White, 415 U.S. 767 (1974)—upholding law requiring new or small parties to proceed by petition or convention at their own expense rather than by publicly funded primary], as long as new or small parties are given some effective way to qualify for the general election [Williams v. Rhodes, 393 U.S. 23 (1968)—unduly burdensome petition requirements for new or small parties struck down as not justified].

2. Dilution of Right to Vote

a. One Person, One Vote Principle

The Equal Protection Clause of the Fourteenth Amendment has been interpreted to prohibit state dilution of the right to vote, and Article I has been interpreted to place the same type of restriction on the federal government.

1) Establishing Voting Districts

Whenever a governmental body establishes voting districts for the election of representatives, the number of persons in each district may not vary significantly. This is commonly referred to as the one person, one vote principle.

a) Congressional Elections—Almost Exactly Equal

States establish the districts for congressional elections. However, the Supreme Court requires ***almost exact mathematical equality*** between the ***congressional*** districts within a state; thus, deviations of even a few percentage points between the congressional districts within a state may result in the invalidation of the congressional district plan.

(1) Compare—Apportionment Among the States

Congress apportions representatives among the states "according to their respective number." [Art. I, §2] Congress's good faith choice of method in so apportioning the representatives commands far more deference than state districting decisions and is ***not*** subject to the same precise mathematical standard as state plans. [United States Department of Commerce v. Montana, 503 U.S. 442 (1992)]

b) **State and Local Elections—Variance Not Unjustifiably Large**
The variance in the number of persons included in districts for the purpose of electing representatives to a ***state or local governmental body*** must not be unjustifiably large, but the districts need not be within a few percentage points of each other: If a state can show that the deviation from mathematical equality between districts is reasonable and tailored to promote a legitimate state interest, the law establishing the districts may be upheld. [Mahan v. Howell, 410 U.S. 315 (1973)—16% variance in district populations was upheld in light of state's interest in preserving political subdivisions, although 30% variance would be excessive]

c) **Scope**
The one person, one vote principle applies to almost every election where a person is being elected to perform normal governmental functions. [Hadley v. Junior College District, 397 U.S. 50 (1970)—trustees for junior college district] However, there are a few exceptions to note:

(1) **Exception—Appointed Officials and Officials Elected "At Large"**
The apportionment requirement is inapplicable to appointed officials. Neither is it applicable in at-large systems of election, because in such a system there are no electoral districts to violate the one person, one vote principle. However, if an at-large voting system were established or maintained for the purpose of suppressing the voting power of minority race voters, it would be unconstitutional.

(2) **Exception—Special Purpose Government Units (Water Storage Districts)**
The government can limit the class of persons who are allowed to vote in an election of persons to serve on a special purpose government unit ***if*** the government unit has a special impact on the class of enfranchised voters. To date, the Supreme Court has found only "water storage districts" to be so specialized that their governing boards are not subject to the one person, one vote principle. [Salyer Land Co. v. Tulane Water District, 410 U.S. 719 (1973); Ball v. James, 451 U.S. 355 (1981)—apportionment rules do not apply to water district even if the district is major supplier of electricity in the state]

2) **Standardless Recount**
Counting uncounted ballots in a presidential election without standards to guide ballot examiners in determining the intent of the voter violates the Fourteenth Amendment Equal Protection Clause. [Bush v. Gore, 531 U.S. 98 (2000)]

b. **Gerrymandering**

1) **Racial Gerrymandering**
As indicated above, race (and presumably other suspect classifications) cannot be the predominant factor in drawing the boundaries of a voting district unless the district plan can pass muster under strict scrutiny. [*See* Miller v. Johnson, XVIII.D.1.c., *supra*] Moreover, a district's bizarre shape can be used to show that

race was the predominant factor in drawing the district's boundaries [*see* Shaw v. Reno, XVIII.C.1.a., *supra*], although a bizarre shape is not necessary to such a finding. Note that the person challenging the reapportionment has the burden of proving the race-based motive. [Shaw v. Hunt, 517 U.S. 899 (1996)]

2) Political Gerrymandering

The Court has ***never*** ruled that a legislative redistricting map should be overturned on the basis of political gerrymandering, and a number of Justices have suggested that political gerrymandering is a nonjusticiable issue. [Vieth v. Jubelirer, 541 U.S. 267 (2004); *and see* League of United Latin American Citizens v. Perry, 548 U.S. 399 (2006)—refusing to find a constitutional violation when there was mid-decade redistricting for partisan political reasons]

c. Multi-Member Districts

A state is generally free to have some multi-member districts together with some single-member districts, as long as the number of members representing a district is proportional to its population. However, single-member or multi-member districts will be held to violate equal protection (even though they meet the one person, one vote principle) if the district lines were drawn on the basis of unconstitutional criteria, such as to suppress the voting power of racial minorities or an identifiable political group.

3. Candidates and Campaigns

a. Candidate Qualifications

1) Fee Must Not Preclude Indigents as Candidates

States may not charge candidates a fee that results in making it impossible for indigents to run for office. An unreasonably high filing fee (which was not tailored to promote a substantial or overriding state interest) might be held totally invalid so that no candidate would have to pay the fee. A reasonable, valid fee would have to be waived for an indigent candidate who could not pay the fee.

2) Restrictions on Ability of Person to Be a Candidate

Restrictions on the ability of persons to be candidates must be examined to see if they violate either the First Amendment right of political association or the Fourteenth Amendment Equal Protection Clause. Such regulations are judged on a sliding scale of scrutiny. (*See* XXI.B., *infra.*)

Example: The Court invalidated a March deadline for filing a nominating petition for independent candidates for a November election where the state allowed the major political parties to name their candidates later in the year. [Anderson v. Celebrezze, 460 U.S. 780 (1983)]

Note: A state may require candidates to show reasonable support (signatures or votes) to qualify to have their names placed on the ballot. [Munro v. Socialist Workers Party, 479 U.S. 189 (1986)—upholding requirement of receipt of at least 1% of the votes cast in the primary election]

3) Required Resignation of Office Is Permissible

A state may require state officials to resign their office if they enter an election for another government office. [Clements v. Fashing, 457 U.S. 957 (1982)]

b. **Campaign Funding, Contributions, and Expenditures**
Government ***may*** allocate more public funds to the two "major" parties than to "minor" parties for political campaigns, and may withhold public funding from candidates who do not accept reciprocal limits on their total campaign expenses; but such expenses cannot otherwise be limited, unlike campaign contributions to political candidates, which may be limited if government chooses. (XXI.B., *infra.*)

4. **Extraordinary Majorities—Referendum Elections**
The government may require a supermajority vote for voter referendums, even though such a requirement might give a minority disproportionate power. [Gordon v. Lance, 403 U.S. 1 (1971)—upholding 60% requirement for referendum approval; Town of Lockport v. Citizens for Community Action, 430 U.S. 259 (1977)—upholding requirement that new county charter be approved by separate majorities of city and noncity voters]

5. **Replacement of Incumbent Legislators**
A state may validly give to a political party the right to name an interim appointee to the legislature to fill out the unexpired term of a legislator from that political party who left office. No voter is denied equal protection by this system. [Rodriguez v. Popular Democratic Party, 457 U.S. 1 (1982)]

D. RIGHT TO TRAVEL

1. Interstate Travel

a. **Nature of the Right**
Individuals have a fundamental right to travel from state to state, which encompasses the right: (i) to leave and enter another state, and (ii) to be treated equally if they become permanent residents of that state. [Saenz v. Roe, VII.C.3., *supra*—striking California law that limited welfare benefits for new residents to what they would have received in their prior state of residence]

b. **Standard of Review**
When a state uses a durational residency requirement (a waiting period) for dispensing benefits, that requirement normally should be subject to the "strict scrutiny" test. This means that the government must show that the waiting period requirement is tailored to promote a compelling or overriding interest. However, in some right to travel cases, the Court has not been clear as to whether it is using this strict scrutiny, compelling interest standard of review. The important point to note for the bar exam is that state residency requirements should not be upheld merely because they have some theoretical rational relationship to an arguably legitimate end of government.

1) **Examples**
Because of the ad hoc nature of these rulings, we will list four examples of Supreme Court decisions in this area:

a) A one-year waiting period before a person may receive subsistence welfare payments is ***invalid***. Similarly, a law providing that persons residing in the state for less than a year may receive welfare benefits no greater than those paid in the state of prior residence is also invalid. [Saenz v. Roe, *supra*]

b) A one-year waiting period for state subsidized medical care is ***invalid***.

c) A one-year waiting period to get a divorce is ***valid***.

d) A state may require a voter to register to vote in a party primary 10 months before the primary election (to avoid interparty "raiding"). However, a 23-month registration period would be ***invalid***.

c. Distinctions Between Old and New Residents

Some state laws that have an adverse impact on new residents do not involve a waiting period. For example, a state may attempt to dispense state benefits on the basis of the length of time a person has resided in the state. A state law that distinguishes between residents of the state on the sole basis of their length of residency will serve no legitimate state interest. This type of law should be ***stricken*** under the rational basis test because it has ***no rational relationship*** to any legitimate state interest.

Examples: 1) A state statute that dispensed differing amounts of state money to residents of the state based on each resident's length of residence was held invalid.

2) A state statute that grants an annual property tax exemption to a veteran of military service only if he resided in the state before a specific date (May 1976) is invalid.

3) A state law that grants a hiring preference (for civil service employment) to a veteran only if he was a resident of the state prior to joining the armed services is invalid.

2. International Travel

The Supreme Court has not yet declared that the right to international travel is fundamental, although the right appears to be ***protected from arbitrary federal interference*** by the Due Process Clause of the Fifth Amendment. The Court has held that this right is not violated when the federal government refuses to pay Social Security benefits to persons who leave the country. The test here is "mere rationality, not strict scrutiny." [Califano v. Aznavorian, 439 U.S. 170 (1978)] Congress may give the executive branch the power to revoke the passport of a person whose conduct in another country presents a danger to United States foreign policy. [Haig v. Agee, 453 U.S. 280 (1981)] The Treasury Department, with congressional authorization, could restrict travel to and from Cuba without violating the Fifth Amendment. [Regan v. Wald, 468 U.S. 222 (1984)]

E. RIGHT TO REFUSE MEDICAL TREATMENT

The Supreme Court had held that the right to refuse medical treatment is a part of an individual's "liberty" that is protected by the Fifth and Fourteenth Amendment Due Process Clauses. However, the Supreme Court has not ruled that this aspect of liberty is a "fundamental right" and ***has not*** explained which standard of review should be used. Nevertheless, the Court has ruled on the validity of several types of legislation.

1. Vaccination

An individual can be made to submit to vaccination against contagious diseases because of the governmental and societal interest in preventing the spread of disease. [Jacobsen v. Massachusetts, 197 U.S. 11 (1905)]

2. **Refusal of Medical Treatment**
The Supreme Court has assumed (without deciding) that a mentally competent adult has the right to refuse lifesaving medical treatment (including lifesaving nutrition). [Cruzan v. Director, Missouri Department of Health, 497 U.S. 261 (1990)]

a. **Compare—No Right to Assisted Suicide**
There is no general right to commit suicide; thus, a state may ban persons from giving individuals assistance in committing suicide. [Washington v. Glucksberg, 521 U.S. 702 (1997)] It is not irrational to permit competent persons to refuse life-sustaining treatment but prohibit physicians to assist in suicide because there is a logical, rational, and well-established distinction between letting someone die and making someone die. [Vacco v. Quill, 521 U.S. 793 (1997)]

b. **Compare—Criminal Defendants**
Under the Due Process Clause, the government may ***involuntarily*** administer antipsychotic drugs to a mentally ill defendant facing serious criminal charges in order to make him competent to stand trial if: (i) the treatment is medically appropriate, (ii) the treatment is substantially unlikely to cause side effects that may undermine the fairness of the trial, and (iii) considering less-intrusive alternatives, the treatment is necessary to further important governmental trial-related interests. [Sell v. United States, 539 U.S. 166 (2003)]

PART FIVE: FIRST AMENDMENT FREEDOMS

The First Amendment prohibits Congress from establishing a religion or interfering with the exercise of religion, abridging the freedom of speech or the press, or interfering with the right of the people to assemble. These prohibitions have been made applicable to the states through the Fourteenth Amendment. The freedoms, however, are not absolute, and exam questions often focus on their boundaries. The following material will outline the scope of each freedom.

XX. FREEDOM OF SPEECH AND ASSEMBLY

A. GENERAL PRINCIPLES
The freedoms of speech and assembly protect the free flow of ideas, a most important function in a democratic society. Thus, whenever the government seeks to regulate these freedoms, the Court will weigh the importance of these rights against the interests or policies sought to be served by the regulation. When analyzing regulations of speech and press, keep the following guidelines in mind:

1. **Government Speech**
The Free Speech Clause restricts government ***regulation of private speech***; it does not require the government to aid private speech nor restrict the government from expressing its views. The government generally is free to voice its opinions and to fund private speech that furthers its views while refusing to fund other private speech, absent some other constitutional

limitation, such as the Establishment Clause or Equal Protection Clause. Because government speech does not implicate the First Amendment, it is not subject to the various levels of scrutiny that apply to government regulation of private speech (*see infra*). [Pleasant Grove City, Utah v. Summum, 129 S. Ct. 1125 (2009)] Generally, government speech and government funding of speech will be upheld if it is ***rationally related to a legitimate state interest.***

Examples: 1) The government may choose to aid a union representing government employees by providing for payroll deductions of general union dues while refusing to allow payroll deductions that will be used by unions to fund political activities. The decision not to collect funds for political activities is rationally related to a legitimate government interest (*i.e.,* avoiding the appearance of favoritism), and thus the refusal to collect such funds is constitutional. [Ysursa v. Pocatello, 129 S. Ct. 1093 (2009)]

2) The government may fund family planning services but except from funding services that provide abortion information. [Rust v. Sullivan, 500 U.S. 173 (1991)]

3) The government may refuse to fund artists whose work it finds offensive. [National Endowment for the Arts v. Finley, 524 U.S. 569 (1998)]

a. Public Monuments

A city's placement of a ***permanent*** monument in a public park is government speech and thus is not subject to Free Speech Clause scrutiny. This is true even if the monument is privately donated. By displaying the monument, the government is disseminating a message, and the message is not necessarily the message of the donor(s). As a corollary, the government cannot be forced to display a permanent monument with a message with which the government disagrees, and the government's refusal to display a proffered monument likewise is not subject to Free Speech Clause scrutiny.

Example: A city with a Ten Commandments monument in its park was not required to display a religious monument of another religion (the "Seven Aphorisms" of the Summum faith). The Ten Commandments monument, although privately donated, was deemed government speech. When the government is the speaker, it may engage in content-based choices. [Pleasant Grove City, Utah v. Summum, *supra*] (*Note:* While an Establishment Clause issue was not raised in *Summum,* a concurring opinion suggested that the Ten Commandments monument did not violate the Establishment Clause because it was one of 15 monuments in the park recognizing the historical roots and morals of the community. [*And see* Van Orden v. Perry, XXII.D.2.a.2), *infra*])

b. Compare—Government Funding of Private Messages

In contrast to government funding of speech for the purpose of promoting its own policies (such as the family planning services involved in *Rust v. Sullivan, supra*), when the government chooses to fund private messages, it generally must do so on a viewpoint neutral basis. [*See* Rosenberger v. Rector and Visitors of the University of Virginia, 515 U.S. 819 (1995)—state university exclusion of religious magazine from program financially supporting many other types of student publications violates the First Amendment]

1) Exception—Funding of the Arts

From a financial standpoint, the government cannot fund all artists, and choosing among those it will fund and those it will not inevitably must be based on the content of the art. [National Endowment for the Arts v. Finley, *supra*]

2. **Content vs. Conduct**
A regulation seeking to forbid communication of specific ideas (*i.e.,* a ***content*** regulation) is less likely to be upheld than a regulation of the ***conduct*** incidental to speech.

a. **Content**
It is presumptively unconstitutional for the government to place burdens on speech because of its content. To justify such content-based regulation of speech, the government must show that the regulation (or tax) is ***necessary*** to serve a ***compelling*** state interest and is narrowly drawn to achieve that end. [Simon & Schuster, Inc. v. Members of the New York State Crime Victims Board, 502 U.S. 105 (1991)—striking a law requiring that proceeds to criminals from books and other productions describing their crimes be placed in escrow for five years to pay claims of victims of the crimes]

1) **Exception—Unprotected Categories of Speech**
The Supreme Court has previously determined that certain categories of speech (*e.g.,* obscenity, defamation, and "fighting words"; *see* C., *infra*) generally are proscribable despite the First Amendment. Even in these cases, however, the Court is less likely to uphold a prior restraint (*i.e.,* a regulation prohibiting speech before it occurs) than a punishment for speech that has already occurred.

2) **Content-Neutral Speech Regulations**
While content-based regulation of speech is subject to strict scrutiny, content-neutral speech regulations generally are subject to ***intermediate scrutiny***—they will be upheld if the government can show that: (i) they advance ***important*** interests unrelated to the suppression of speech, and (ii) they ***do not burden substantially more speech than necessary*** to further those interests. [Turner Broadcasting System, Inc. v. FCC, 512 U.S. 622 (1994)]

b. **Conduct**
The Court has allowed the government more leeway in regulating the conduct related to speech, allowing it to adopt content-neutral, ***time, place, and manner*** regulations. Regulations involving public forums (*i.e.,* forums historically linked with the exercise of First Amendment freedoms) must be ***narrowly tailored*** to achieve an ***important*** government interest (*e.g.,* a prohibition against holding a demonstration in a hospital zone). Regulations involving nonpublic forums must have a reasonable relationship to a legitimate regulatory purpose (*e.g.,* a law prohibiting billboards for purposes of traffic safety).

3. **Reasonableness of Regulation**

a. **Overbroad Regulation Invalid**
Since the purpose of the freedoms of speech and assembly is to encourage the free flow of ideas, a regulation will not be upheld if it is overbroad (*i.e.,* prohibits ***substantially*** more speech than is necessary). If a regulation of speech or speech-related conduct punishes a ***substantial amount of protected speech,*** judged in relation to the regulation's plainly legitimate sweep, the regulation is ***facially invalid*** (*i.e.,* it may not be enforced against anyone—not even a person engaging in activity that is not constitutionally protected) unless a court has limited construction of the regulation so as to remove

the threat to constitutionally protected expression. [Virginia v. Hicks, 539 U.S. 113 (2003)] If a regulation is not substantially overbroad, it can be enforced against persons engaging in activities that are not constitutionally protected.

Examples: 1) The Supreme Court struck down as overbroad an ordinance that prohibited speech that ***"in any manner"*** interrupts a police officer in the performance of her duties. [Houston v. Hill, 482 U.S. 451 (1987)]

2) An airport authority rule that bans "***all*** First Amendment activities" within the "central terminal area" is invalid as being substantially overbroad. [Board of Airport Commissioners v. Jews for Jesus, 482 U.S. 569 (1987)]

3) A law banning ***all*** door-to-door solicitations will be struck as being overbroad [Martin v. City of Struthers, 319 U.S. 141 (1943)], but a law requiring solicitors to obtain a homeowner's consent to solicit is valid [Breard v. City of Alexandria, 341 U.S. 622 (1951)].

4) An ordinance that prohibited ***all*** canvassers from going onto private residential property to promote ***any*** cause without first obtaining a permit was overbroad. While the government may have an interest in preventing fraud from door-to-door solicitation, the permit requirement here went beyond cases where fraud was likely to occur, and applied to religious proselytization, advocacy of political speech, and enlisting support for unpopular causes. [Watchtower Bible and Tract Society of New York, Inc. v. Village of Stratton, 536 U.S. 150 (2002)]

5) A city ordinance that prohibits homeowners from displaying ***any sign*** on their property except "residence identification" or "for sale" signs is invalid because the ordinance bans virtually all residential signs. [Ladue v. Gilleo, 512 U.S. 43 (1994)]

b. Void for Vagueness Doctrine

If a criminal law or regulation fails to give persons reasonable notice of what is prohibited, it may violate the Due Process Clause. This principle is applied somewhat strictly when First Amendment activity is involved in order to avoid the chilling effect a vague law might have on speech (*i.e.*, if it is unclear what speech is regulated, people might refrain from speech that is permissible for fear that they will be violating the law). Vagueness issues most often arise in relation to content regulations, but the same principles would apply to time, place, and manner restrictions.

Examples: 1) A municipal ordinance that prohibited vagrants was held void for vagueness when it defined vagrants as "rogues and vagabonds . . . lewd, wanton, and lascivious persons . . . persons wandering or straying around from place to place without any lawful purpose or object . . . ." [Papachristou v. City of Jacksonville, 405 U.S. 156 (1972)]

2) A statute that prohibits attorneys representing clients in a pending case from making statements that would have a substantial likelihood of prejudicing a trial, but that also allows attorneys to make public statements regarding the "general nature of the defense" they will present at trial, is void for vagueness, because it does not give fair notice of the

types of trial-related statements that are punishable. [Gentile v. State Bar, 501 U.S. 1030 (1991)]

1) **Burden on Challenger**
The person challenging the validity of the regulation has the burden of showing substantial overbreadth. [Virginia v. Hicks, *supra*]

2) **Funding Speech Activity**
Greater imprecision is allowed when the government acts as a patron in funding speech activity than when enacting criminal statutes or regulatory schemes, because speakers are less likely to steer clear of forbidden areas when only a subsidy is at stake. [National Endowment for the Arts v. Finley, 1., *supra*—requirement that NEA consider standards of "decency" and "respect for values of American people" is not invalid on its face]

c. **Cannot Give Officials Unfettered Discretion**
A regulation cannot give officials broad discretion over speech issues; there must be ***defined standards*** for applying the law. The fear, of course, is that the officials will use their discretionary power to prohibit dissemination of ideas that they do not agree with. This issue usually arises under licensing schemes established to regulate the time, place, and manner of speech. To be valid, such licensing schemes must be related to an important government interest, contain procedural safeguards (*see* D.2., *infra*), and not grant officials unbridled discretion.

Example: County required persons desiring to hold a parade, march, or rally to first obtain a permit from the county administrator. The administrator was empowered to charge up to $1,000 for the permit, but could adjust the fee to meet the necessary expenses of administration and police protection. This scheme is invalid because it gives the administrator unbridled discretion despite the $1,000 limit. It also is unconstitutional because it is a content-based restriction (the administrator theoretically would adjust the costs based on the popularity of the subject at issue—an unpopular subject would require greater police protection). [Forsyth County, Georgia v. Nationalist Movement, 505 U.S. 123 (1992)]

1) **Unlimited Discretion—Void on Face**
If a statute gives licensing officials unbridled discretion, it is ***void on its face***, and speakers need not even apply for a permit. They may exercise their First Amendment rights even if they could have been denied a permit under a valid law, and they may not be punished for violating the licensing statute. [Lovell v. City of Griffin, 303 U.S. 444 (1938)]

Examples: 1) An ordinance vesting officials with the power to grant or deny parade permits based on their judgment as to the effect of the parade on community "welfare" or "morals" is unconstitutional on its face. [Shuttlesworth v. Birmingham, 394 U.S. 147 (1969)] Similarly, ordinances giving officials broad discretion as to who may place magazine racks on public property or who may obtain licenses to solicit door to door are invalid. [City of Lakewood v. Plain Dealer Publishing Co., 486 U.S. 750 (1988); Lovell v. City of Griffin, *supra*]

2) A statute prohibiting excessively loud sound trucks is valid [Kovacs v. Cooper, 336 U.S. 77 (1949)], but an ordinance giving officials discretion as to who may use sound trucks is invalid [Saia v. New York, 334 U.S. 558 (1948)].

2) Statutes Valid on Face

If the licensing statute is valid on its face because it contains adequate standards, a speaker may not ignore the statute, but must seek a permit. If he is denied a permit, even if he believes the denial was incorrect, he must then seek reasonably available administrative or judicial relief. Failure to do so precludes later assertion that his actions were protected by the First Amendment. [Poulos v. New Hampshire, 345 U.S. 395 (1953)]

4. Scope of Speech

a. Includes Freedom Not to Speak

The freedom of speech includes not only the right to speak, but also the right to refrain from speaking or endorsing beliefs with which one does not agree—the government may not compel an individual personally to express a message with which he disagrees.

Examples: 1) A state ***cannot force school children to salute*** or say a pledge to the flag. [West Virginia State Board of Education v. Barnette, 319 U.S. 624 (1943)]

2) A motorist ***could not be punished*** for blocking out the portion of his automobile license plate bearing the motto "Live Free or Die"; as long as he left the license plate in a condition that served its auto identification purpose, he did not have to display a slogan endorsed by the state. [Wooley v. Maynard, 430 U.S. 705 (1977)]

3) A state may not require private parade organizers to include in their parade groups with messages with which the organizers disagree. [Hurley v. Irish-American Gay, Lesbian & Bisexual Group of Boston, 515 U.S. 557 (1995)]

1) Mandatory Financial Support

Although the government may not compel a person to express a message, the government may tax people and use the revenue to express a message with which people disagree.

a) Government Speech

The Court has held that compelled support of government speech does ***not*** raise First Amendment concerns. [Johanns v. Livestock Marketing Association, 544 U.S. 550 (2005)—beef producers can be required to pay an assessment to support generic advertising of beef approved by a semi-governmental producers' board and ultimately by the Secretary of Agriculture—even if they think generic advertising is a waste of money—because the advertisements are governmental speech]

b) Compare—Private Speech

On the other hand, it appears that people ***cannot*** be compelled to subsidize ***private*** messages with which they disagree.

Examples: The Court has held that while teachers may be forced to pay union dues to a private union representing a majority of their fellow teachers, and attorneys may be forced to join a mandatory bar association, people may not be forced to pay sums that will be used to support political views that, or candidates whom, they do not endorse. [Abood v. Detroit Board of Education, 431 U.S. 209 (1977); Keller v. State Bar of California, 496 U.S. 1 (1990)]

(1) Exception—University Activity Fees

The government can require public university students to pay a student activity fee even if the fee is used to support political and ideological speech by student groups whose beliefs are offensive to the student, as long as the program is viewpoint neutral (*see* B.2.a., *infra*). [Board of Regents v. Southworth, 529 U.S. 217 (2000)]

2) State Can Require Shopping Center to Permit Persons to Exercise Speech Rights

Note that the freedom not to speak does not prohibit a state's requiring a large shopping center (that is open to the public) to permit persons to exercise their speech rights on shopping center property—at least as long as the particular message is not dictated by the state and is not likely to be identified with the owner of the shopping center. [Pruneyard Shopping Center v. Robins, 447 U.S. 74 (1980)]

b. Includes Symbolic Conduct

Speech includes not only verbal communication, but also conduct that is undertaken to communicate an idea. Of course, not all regulation of symbolic conduct is prohibited. The Court will uphold a conduct regulation if: (i) the regulation is within the constitutional power of the government; (ii) it furthers an important governmental interest; (iii) the governmental interest is ***unrelated to suppression of speech***; and (iv) the incidental burden on speech is no greater than necessary. [United States v. O'Brien, 391 U.S. 367 (1968)—upholding a prohibition against burning draft cards to protect the government's important interest in facilitating the smooth functioning of the draft system] Note, however, that a regulation is ***not*** invalid simply because there is some imaginable alternative that might be less burdensome on speech. [Rumsfeld v. Forum for Academic and Institutional Rights, 547 U.S. 47 (2006)—statute requiring schools of higher education to grant the military access to recruit on campus is not invalid merely because the military could take out ads in newspapers, on television, etc.]

Example: A state may prohibit public nudity, even as applied to nude dancing at bars and places of adult entertainment. Although nude dancing is marginally within the protections of the First Amendment—because it involves the communication of an erotic message—the government has a "substantial" interest in combating crime and other "secondary effects" caused by the presence of adult entertainment establishments that is unrelated to the suppression of free expression. [Barnes v. Glen

Theatre, Inc., 501 U.S. 560 (1991); City of Erie v. Pap's A.M., 529 U.S. 277 (2000)—city council made findings regarding secondary effects]

Compare: 1) A prohibition against students wearing armbands to protest the war in Vietnam was struck because it had no regulatory interest other than prohibiting the communicative impact of the conduct. [Tinker v. Des Moines Independent Community School District, 393 U.S. 503 (1969)]

2) A prohibition against mutilating a United States flag (except in cases of proper disposal of a soiled flag) was held invalid as an attempt to restrain speech; the Court found that no imminent breach of the peace was likely to result, and the government has no other interest in prohibiting such burnings. [United States v. Eichman, 496 U.S. 310 (1990)]

c. **Excludes Freedom to Bar Military Recruitment**
Requiring schools of higher education to allow military recruiters to recruit on campus or risk losing federal funding does not implicate free speech rights. This is so even if the schools disagree with the military's ban against homosexuals. School recruitment receptions are not inherently expressive from the schools' standpoint; they are merely a way to help students obtain jobs. Schools are not being asked to say or refrain from saying anything, and neither are they being asked to associate with the military in any significant way. Moreover, there is little chance that a person would attribute the military's positions to the schools. Therefore, there is no First Amendment violation. [Rumsfeld v. Forum for Academic and Institutional Rights, *supra*]

5. **Prison Speech**
A regulation concerning the activities of prison inmates, including ***any*** First Amendment speech activities, is governed by a different standard in order to facilitate prison order: The regulation will be upheld if it is ***reasonably related to legitimate penological interests.*** [Shaw v. Murphy, 532 U.S. 223 (2001)] Thus, a restriction on ***incoming*** mail will be upheld if it is rational; a restriction on ***outgoing*** mail must be narrowly tailored because there is less of a penological interest involved. [*See* Thornburgh v. Abbott, 490 U.S. 401 (1989)]

B. TIME, PLACE, AND MANNER RESTRICTIONS—REGULATION OF CONDUCT

All speech is conveyed through physical action (*e.g.,* talking, writing, distributing pamphlets, etc.), and while the freedom of belief is absolute, the freedom to convey beliefs cannot be. The extent to which government may regulate speech-related conduct depends on whether the forum involved is a public forum, a designated public forum, a limited public forum, or a nonpublic forum.

1. **Public Forums and Designated Public Forums**
Public property that has historically been open to speech-related activities (*e.g.,* ***streets, sidewalks,*** and ***public parks***) is called a public forum. Public property that has not historically been open to speech-related activities, but which the government has thrown open for such activities on a permanent or temporary basis, by practice or policy (*e.g.,* school rooms that are open for after-school use by social, civic, or recreation groups), is called a designated public forum. The government may regulate speech in public forums and designated public forums with reasonable time, place, and manner regulations.

a. Test

To be valid, government regulations of speech and assembly in public forums and designated public forums must:

(i) Be ***content neutral*** (*i.e.,* subject matter neutral and viewpoint neutral);

(ii) Be ***narrowly tailored*** to serve an ***important*** government interest; and

(iii) Leave open ***alternative channels*** of communication.

Remember: Even if a regulation meets the above conditions, it might still be struck down on other grounds (*e.g.,* overbreadth, vagueness, unfettered discretion; *see* A.3., *supra*).

1) Content Neutral

The regulation cannot be based on the content of the speech, absent substantial justification (*see* C., *infra*).

Examples: 1) The Court held invalid an ordinance allowing peaceful ***labor*** picketing near schools, but prohibiting all other picketing, since it was a content-based restriction. [Chicago Police Department v. Mosely, 408 U.S. 92 (1972)]

2) A law may not forbid only those signs within 500 feet of a foreign embassy that are critical of the foreign government. [Boos v. Barry, 485 U.S. 312 (1988)]

2) Narrowly Tailored

The regulation must be narrowly tailored (*i.e.,* it may not burden ***substantially*** more speech than is necessary to further the significant government interest). However, the regulation need not be the least restrictive means of accomplishing the goal.

Example: A law requiring persons performing at a city's theater to use the city's sound equipment is narrowly tailored to the city's interest in preventing excessive noise. [Ward v. Rock Against Racism, 491 U.S. 781 (1989)]

Compare: An ordinance that prohibited ***all*** canvassers from going onto private residential property to promote ***any*** cause without first obtaining a permit was not narrowly tailored to the interest of preventing fraud because it included too much speech that was not likely to give rise to fraud (*e.g.,* religious proselytization, advocacy of political speech, and enlisting support for unpopular causes). [Watchtower Bible and Tract Society of New York, Inc. v. Village of Stratton, A.3.a., *supra*]

Note: A regulation that is not narrowly tailored might also fail on overbreadth grounds. (*See* A.3.a., *supra.*)

3) Important Interest

The regulation must further an important government interest. Such interests include: traffic safety, orderly crowd movement, personal privacy, noise control, litter control, aesthetics, etc.

Example: The Court upheld the constitutionality of a state law prohibiting persons within 100 feet of a health care facility from approaching within eight feet of those seeking access to the health care facility for purposes of oral protest, education, or counseling. The Court found that the law was a content-neutral regulation of speech and a reasonable time, place, and manner restriction that served the important interest of preserving access to health care facilities. [Hill v. Colorado, 530 U.S. 703 (2000)—statute upheld against challenge by petitioners who wished to "counsel" women as they enter abortion clinics]

4) Alternative Channels Open

The law must leave open alternative channels of communication; *i.e.,* other reasonable means for communicating the idea must be available.

b. Examples—Residential Areas

1) Targeted Picketing

The Supreme Court upheld a statute that prevented focused residential picketing (*i.e.,* picketing in front of a single residence). The street/sidewalk involved was a public forum, but the ordinance passed the three-part test: (i) it was content neutral because it regulated the location and manner of picketing rather than its message; (ii) it was narrowly tailored to the important interest of protecting a homeowner's privacy (because it applied only to focused picketing); and (iii) alternative means of communications were available because the protesters could march ***through*** the neighborhood in protest. [Frisby v. Schultz, 487 U.S. 474 (1988)]

2) Charitable Solicitations

Charitable solicitations for funds in residential areas are within the protection of the First Amendment. However, they are subject to reasonable regulation.

Example: A state cannot require professional fundraisers (before making an appeal for funds) to disclose to potential donors the percentage of contributions collected over the previous year that were actually turned over to the charity. The disclosure is not necessary to promote the state interest of protecting the public from fraud. However, the state can require a fundraiser to disclose her professional status. [Riley v. National Federation of the Blind of North Carolina, 487 U.S. 781 (1988)] In *Riley,* the Court also invalidated a restriction on the fees that professional fundraisers could charge a charity, because the particular statute was not narrowly tailored to protect either the public or the charities.

Compare: States have a significant interest in preventing fraudulent charitable solicitations. This interest justifies charging a telemarketing firm with fraud for telling persons solicited that the firm pays "a significant amount of each donation" to the charity, when in fact the firm keeps 85% of gross receipts. [Illinois *ex rel.* Madigan v. Telemarketing Associates, Inc., 538 U.S. 600 (2003)]

3) **Permits**

A state may not require persons to obtain permits in order to canvass door-to-door for noncommercial or nonfundraising purposes. [Watchtower Bible and Tract Society of New York, Inc., v. Village of Stratton, *supra*]

c. **Example—Designated Public Forum**

Schools generally are not public forums. However, if a public school or university allows private organizations and members of the public to use school property for meetings when school programs or classes are not in session, the property is a designated public forum for that time, and the school cannot deny a religious organization permission to use the property for meetings merely because religious topics will be discussed. Such a restriction would be content discrimination. [Widmar v. Vincent, 454 U.S. 263 (1981); Lamb's Chapel v. Center Moriches Union Free School District, 508 U.S. 384 (1993)]

d. **Injunctions**

Injunctions that restrict First Amendment activity in public forums are treated differently from generally applicable ordinances because injunctions present a greater risk of censorship and discriminatory application. The test to be used to determine whether an injunction that restricts speech or protest is constitutional depends on whether the injunction is content neutral.

1) **Content Based—Necessary to a Compelling Interest**

If the injunction is content based, it will be upheld only if it is necessary to achieve a compelling government interest.

2) **Content Neutral—Burdens No More Speech than Necessary**

If the injunction is content neutral, it will be upheld only if it burdens no more speech than is necessary to achieve an ***important*** government purpose.

Example: Parts of an injunction establishing a 36-foot buffer zone between protesters and abortion clinic entrances were upheld. [Madsen v. Women's Health Center, 512 U.S. 753 (1994)]

Compare: An injunction providing for a "floating buffer zone" of 15 feet between protesters and persons entering and leaving an abortion clinic was held to violate the First Amendment. The floating zone barred all verbal and written communication from a normal conversational distance on public sidewalks, and thus burdened more speech than necessary to ensure ingress and egress from the clinic. [Schenk v. Pro-Choice Network of Western New York, 519 U.S. 357 (1997)]

2. **Limited Public Forums and Nonpublic Forums**

Other than streets, sidewalks, parks, and designated public forums, most public property is

considered to be a limited public forum or a nonpublic forum. The government can regulate speech in such a forum to ***reserve the forum for its intended use***. Regulations will be upheld if they are:

(i) ***Viewpoint neutral***; and

(ii) ***Reasonably related to a legitimate government purpose***.

a. Viewpoint Neutral

Regulations on speech in nonpublic forums need not be content neutral; *i.e.,* the government may allow speech regarding some subjects but not others. However, such regulations must be ***viewpoint*** neutral; *i.e.,* if the government allows an issue to be presented in a nonpublic forum, it may not limit the presentation to only one view.

Example: If a high school newspaper is a nonpublic forum, a school board could decide to prohibit articles in the paper regarding nuclear power. However, it may not allow an article in favor of nuclear power and prohibit an article against nuclear power.

Similarly, the government may discriminate based on the identity of the speaker in nonpublic forums (*e.g.,* a school board might limit speakers to licensed teachers).

b. Reasonableness

Regulation of speech and assembly in nonpublic forums need only be rationally related to a legitimate governmental objective.

Example: A city bus is not a public forum. The city, therefore, may constitutionally sell space for signs on the public buses for commercial and public service advertising while refusing to sell space for political or public issue advertising in order to minimize the appearance of favoritism and the risk of imposing on a captive audience. [Lehman v. Shaker Heights, 418 U.S. 298 (1974)]

c. Significant Cases

1) Military Bases

Military bases are not public forums; thus, on-base speech and assembly may be regulated, even during open houses where the public is invited to visit. [*See* United States v. Albertini, 472 U.S. 675 (1985)] However, if the military leaves its streets open as thoroughfares, they will be treated as public forums. [Flower v. United States, 407 U.S. 197 (1972)]

2) Schools

Generally, schools and school-sponsored activities are not public forums. Thus, speech (and association) in schools may be reasonably regulated to serve the school's educational mission.

Examples: 1) Schools can control the content of student speeches or student newspapers for legitimate pedagogical concerns. [*See, e.g.,* Bethel School District No. 403 v. Fraser, 478 U.S. 675 (1986)—student suspended for sexually explicit speech at school assembly] Similarly, a school may prohibit student speech that may be interpreted as advocating or celebrating the use of illegal drugs ("BONG HiTS

4 JESUS") during a school-supervised activity (*e.g.,* a field trip). [Morse v. Frederick, 551 U.S. 393 (2007)]

2) To be given access to the platform of official school recognition and school funding, a public law school may require extracurricular student groups to accept all students regardless of their "status or beliefs." [Christian Legal Society v. Martinez, 130 S. Ct. 2971 (2010)—school could deny funding to group that limited membership to persons who were willing to sign a statement of faith based on Christianity and excluded persons who supported homosexuality and premarital sex; *and see* XXI.D., *infra*]

3) A state association that regulates interscholastic high school sports of schools that ***voluntarily join*** may prohibit certain recruiting statements to middle-school students for athletic programs. Even if the message involves a matter of public concern, the rule is ***necessary*** for managing an effective high school athletic league. [Tennessee Secondary School Athletic Association v. Brentwood Academy, 551 U.S. 291 (2007)]

Compare: A school was forbidden to prohibit the wearing of black armbands in the school (to protest government policies), because that prohibition was designed to suppress communication, *i.e.,* not related to regulatory interest. [Tinker v. Des Moines Independent Community School District, A.4.b., *supra*]

3) Government Workplace or Charity

Neither a government workplace (including a court building and its grounds) nor a government controlled charity drive constitutes a public forum.

Examples: 1) The government may conduct an annual fundraising drive that includes some charities but excludes others on some ideologically neutral basis (*e.g.,* all charities that lobby). However, it cannot exclude a charity merely because it disagrees with the organization's political views. [Cornelius v. NAACP Legal Defense and Education Fund, Inc., 473 U.S. 788 (1985)]

2) A state may develop a system for meeting with and hearing the views of a select group of its employees (*e.g.,* union representatives) while denying the ability to voice opinions at such restricted meetings to other government employees. [Minnesota State Board v. Knight, 465 U.S. 271 (1984)]

Compare: In a public forum, the government cannot restrict the ability to participate in public speech on the basis of union membership. Thus, the Court has held that a teacher cannot be constitutionally prohibited from speaking at a meeting of the school board that was open to the public. [City of Madison Joint School District No. 8 v. Wisconsin Employment Relations Commission, 429 U.S. 167 (1976)]

4) **Postal Service Property**
Although sidewalks generally are public forums, sidewalks on postal service property are not public forums. [United States v. Kokinda, 497 U.S. 720 (1990)]

5) **Signs on Public Property**
The Supreme Court has upheld a city ordinance prohibiting posting signs on public property (including sidewalks, crosswalks, street lamp posts, fire hydrants, and telephone poles), even if the sign is temporary in nature and could be removed without damage to the public property. [Members of City Council v. Taxpayers for Vincent, 466 U.S. 789 (1984)]

6) **Airport Terminals**
Airport terminals operated by a public authority are ***not*** public forums. Thus, it is reasonable to ban ***solicitation*** within airport terminals, since it presents a risk of fraud to hurrying passengers. [International Society of Krishna Consciousness v. Lee, 505 U.S. 672 (1992)] However, it is ***not*** reasonable to ban ***leafletting*** within multipurpose terminals having qualities similar to a shopping mall [Lee v. International Society of Krishna Consciousness, 505 U.S. 830 (1992)]; although such leafletting can still be subject to reasonable time, place, and manner regulations (*see* B.1., *supra*).

7) **Candidate Debates on Public Television**
A public television station debate for congressional candidates from major parties or who have strong popular support is not a "public forum" because such debates are not open to a class of speakers (*e.g.*, all candidates), but rather to selected members of the class. Exclusion of candidates who are not from a major party and who lack popular support is permissible because these criteria are (i) viewpoint neutral and (ii) reasonable in light of the logistics for an educationally valuable debate. [Arkansas Educational Television Commission v. Forbes, 523 U.S. 666 (1998)]

8) **Mailboxes**
A letter/mailbox at a business or residence is ***not*** a public forum. Thus, the government may prohibit the placing of unstamped items in post boxes to promote efficient mail service. [United States Postal Service v. Council of Greenburgh Civic Association, 453 U.S. 114 (1981)]

C. UNPROTECTED SPEECH—REGULATION OR PUNISHMENT BECAUSE OF CONTENT

Restrictions on the content of speech must be necessary to achieve a compelling government interest. As indicated above, very few restrictions on the content of speech are tolerated. The Court allows them only to prevent grave injury. The following is a list of the only reasons for which the Court has allowed content-based restrictions on speech (*i.e.,* the following are categories of unprotected speech):

(i) It creates a ***clear and present danger*** of imminent lawless action.

(ii) It constitutes ***"fighting words"*** as defined by a narrow, precise statute.

(iii) The speech, film, etc., is ***obscene***. (This category includes "child pornography.")

(iv) The speech constitutes ***defamation***, which may be the subject of a civil "penalty" through a tort action brought by the injured party in conformity with the rules set out *infra*.

(v) The speech violates regulations against ***false or deceptive advertising—commercial speech is protected*** by the First Amendment and it cannot be proscribed simply to help certain private interests.

(vi) The government can demonstrate a ***"compelling interest"*** in limitation of the First Amendment activity.

Recall that even if a regulation falls within one of the above categories, it will not necessarily be held valid; it might still be held to be void for vagueness or overbreadth. (*See* A.3., *supra.*)

1. Clear and Present Danger of Imminent Lawlessness

A state cannot forbid advocating the use of force or of law violation unless such advocacy (i) ***is directed to producing or inciting imminent lawless action,*** and (ii) ***is likely to produce or incite such action***. [Brandenberg v. Ohio, 395 U.S. 444 (1969)]

Example: The "clear and present danger" test has been applied to hold that a state may not punish as contempt out-of-court utterances critical of a judge, absent special circumstances showing an extremely high likelihood of serious interference with the administration of justice. [*See* Wood v. Georgia, 370 U.S. 375 (1962)]

a. Allows for Sanctions Against Speech

The test allows for sanctions against speech causing demonstrable danger to important government interests. Disclosure of United States intelligence operations and personnel is "clearly not protected" speech. [Haig v. Agee, 453 U.S. 280 (1981)]

b. Compelling Justification Test

A similar test—one of "compelling justification"—was employed to hold unconstitutional the Georgia legislature's refusal to seat Julian Bond, an elected black representative, where Bond's speeches, critical of United States policy on Vietnam and the draft, led the legislature to doubt his fitness and his ability to take the oath of office in good faith. [Bond v. Floyd, 385 U.S. 116 (1966)]

2. Fighting Words

a. True Threats

The First Amendment does not protect "true threats"—statements meant to communicate an intent to place an individual or group in fear of bodily harm. [Virginia v. Black, 538 U.S. 343 (2002)—a state may ban cross burning done with an intent to intimidate; because of cross burning's long history as a signal of impending violence, the state may specially regulate this form of threat, which is likely to inspire fear of bodily harm]

b. States May Ban Words Likely to Incite Physical Retaliation

States are free to ban the use of "fighting words," *i.e.,* those personally abusive epithets that, when addressed to the ordinary citizen, are inherently likely to incite immediate physical retaliation. [Chaplinsky v. New Hampshire, 315 U.S. 568 (1942)] *Chaplinsky* has, however, been narrowly read. Thus, in *Cohen v. California,* 403 U.S. 15 (1971), the Court held that the state may not punish the defendant for wearing a jacket bearing the words "Fuck the Draft," pointing out that "while the four-letter word displayed by Cohen in relation to the draft is commonly employed in a personally provocative fashion, in this instance, it was clearly not directed to the person of the hearer."

c. **Statutes Regulating Fighting Words Tend to Be Overbroad or Vague**
While this classification of punishable speech continues to exist ***in theory***, the Court rarely upholds punishments for the use of such words. Statutes that attempt to punish fighting words will tend to be overbroad or vague; the statute will define the punishable speech as "opprobrious words," "annoying conduct," or "abusive language." Such statutes will fail, as their imprecise terms could be applied to protected (nonfighting words) speech. Such a statute could not be used to punish a person for saying to a police officer, "White son of a bitch, I'll kill you." [Gooding v. Wilson, 405 U.S. 518 (1972); Lewis v. City of New Orleans, 415 U.S. 130 (1974)]

d. **Statutes Cannot Be Content-Based—Limits Hate Crime Legislation**
Although the general class of "fighting words" is proscribable under the First Amendment, the Supreme Court generally will not tolerate in fighting words statutes restrictions that are designed to punish only certain viewpoints (*i.e.,* proscribing fighting words only if they convey a particular message). [R.A.V. v. City of St. Paul, 505 U.S. 377 (1992)—ordinance that applies only to those fighting words that insult or provoke violence on the basis of race, religion, or gender is invalid]

1) **Compare—Punishing Racially Motivated Conduct**
The First Amendment does not protect conduct simply because it happens to be motivated by a person's views or beliefs. Thus, a state can increase a convicted defendant's sentence for aggravated battery based on the fact that the defendant selected the victim of his crime because of the victim's race. [Wisconsin v. Mitchell, 508 U.S. 476 (1993)] However, punishment may not be increased merely because of the defendant's abstract beliefs. [Dawson v. Delaware, 503 U.S. 159 (1992)—unconstitutional to increase defendant's sentence merely because it was proved that he belongs to an organization that advocates racism]

3. **Obscenity**
Obscenity is ***not protected*** speech. [Roth v. United States, 354 U.S. 476 (1957)] The Court has defined "obscenity" as a description or depiction of sexual conduct that, taken ***as a whole***, by the ***average person***, applying ***contemporary community standards***:

(i) Appeals to the ***prurient interest*** in sex;

(ii) Portrays sex in a ***patently offensive*** way; and

(iii) ***Does not have serious literary, artistic, political, or scientific value***—using a national, reasonable person standard, rather than the contemporary community standard. [Miller v. California, 413 U.S. 15 (1973); Pope v. Illinois, 481 U.S. 497 (1987)]

a. **Elements**

1) **Appeal to Prurient Interest**
The dominant theme of the material considered as a ***whole*** must appeal to the prurient interest in sex of the average person. The Supreme Court has found this to include that which appeals to ***shameful or morbid interests*** in sex, but not that which incites ***lust*** (insofar as lust may include a ***normal*** interest in sex). [Brockett

v. Spokane Arcades, Inc., 472 U.S. 491 (1985)] For exam purposes, it is probably sufficient merely to know the standard (since its application is a fact determination).

a) **Average Person**
Both sensitive and insensitive adults may be included in determining contemporary community standards, but children may not be considered part of the relevant audience.

b) **Material Designed for Deviant Group**
Where the allegedly obscene material is designed for and primarily disseminated to a clearly defined deviant sexual group (*e.g.,* sadists), rather than to the public at large, the prurient appeal requirement is satisfied if the ***dominant theme*** of the material, taken as a whole, ***appeals to the prurient interest of that group***. [Mishkin v. New York, 383 U.S. 502 (1966)]

2) **Patently Offensive**

a) **Community Standard**
The material must be patently offensive in affronting contemporary community standards regarding the description or portrayal of sexual matters.

b) **National Standard Not Required**
A statewide standard is permissible but not mandatory. A juror may draw on knowledge of the community or vicinity from which he comes, and the court may either direct the jury to apply "community standards" without specifying the "community," or define the standard in more precise geographic terms. [Hamling v. United States, 418 U.S. 87 (1974); Jenkins v. Georgia, 418 U.S. 153 (1974)]

3) **Lacking in Serious Social Value**
The fact that the material may have some redeeming social value will not necessarily immunize it from a finding of obscenity. It must have serious literary, artistic, political, or scientific value, using a national standard. [Pope v. Illinois, *supra*]

4) **Standard May Be Different for Minors**
The state can adopt a specific definition of obscenity applying to materials sold to minors, even though the material might not be obscene in terms of an adult audience. [Ginsberg v. New York, 390 U.S. 629 (1968)] However, government may not prohibit the sale or distribution of material to adults merely because it is inappropriate for children.

Example: Because of the present lack of "gateway" technology that would permit speakers on the Internet to block their communications, a federal statute's bar on transmitting "indecent" or "patently offensive" messages to minors effectively amounts to a total ban and thus violates the First Amendment right of adults to receive such materials. [Reno v. American Civil Liberties Union, 521 U.S. 844 (1997)]

Compare: To prevent minors from getting harmful material, the government ***may*** condition its support of Internet access in public libraries on their installing software to block obscenity and child pornography—at least when the library will unblock filtered material on any adult user's request. [United States v. American Library Association, Inc., 539 U.S. 194 (2003)]

a) **Pictures of Minors**
To protect minors from exploitation, the government may prohibit the sale or distribution of ***visual*** depictions of sexual conduct involving minors, even if the material would not be found obscene if it did not involve children. [New York v. Ferber, 458 U.S. 747 (1982)] The government may also prohibit ***offers*** to provide (and requests to obtain) material depicting children engaged in sexually explicit conduct when the prohibition requires scienter and does not criminalize a substantial amount of protected speech. Such offers of material that is unlawful to possess have no First Amendment protection. [United States v. Williams, 553 U.S. 285 (2008)]

b) **Compare—Simulated Pictures of Minors**
The government may not bar visual material that only appears to depict minors engaged in sexually explicit conduct, but that in fact uses young-looking adults or computer generated images. [Ashcroft v. Free Speech Coalition, 535 U.S. 234 (2002)] A holding otherwise would bar speech that is not obscene under the *Miller* test and that does not involve the exploitation of children as in *Ferber.*

b. **Question of Fact and Law**

1) **Jury Question**
The determination of whether material is obscene is a question of fact for the jury. Of course, the judge can grant a directed verdict if the evidence is such that a reasonable, unprejudiced jury could not find that all parts of the test have been met.

2) **Independent Review by Appellate Court**
Appellate courts will conduct an independent review of constitutional claims, when necessary, to assure that the proscribed materials "depict or describe patently offensive 'hard core' sexual conduct." [Jenkins v. Georgia, *supra*]

3) **Evidence of Pandering**
In close cases, evidence of "pandering"—commercial exploitation for the sake of prurient appeal—by the defendant may be probative on whether the material is obscene. Such evidence may be found in the defendant's advertising, his instructions to authors and illustrators of the material, or his intended audience. In effect, this simply accepts the purveyor's own estimation of the material as relevant. [Ginzburg v. United States, 383 U.S. 463 (1966)]

4) **Evidence—Similar Published Materials Not Automatically Admissible**
The state need not produce expert testimony. Evidence that similar materials are

available on community newsstands, or that the publication has acquired a second-class mailing privilege, does not necessarily show that the material is not obscene and hence is not automatically admissible. Nor is there any automatic right to have other materials held not to be obscene admitted into evidence. [Hamling v. United States, *supra*]

c. **Statutes Must Not Be Vague**

1) **Sweeping Language**
Attempts to define obscenity broadly have encountered difficulties before the Court.

Examples: 1) A statute banning publication of news or stories of "bloodshed or lust so massed as to become vehicle for inciting crime" is unconstitutionally vague and uncertain. [Winters v. New York, 333 U.S. 507 (1948)]

2) The Court held invalid a statute prohibiting the sale of any book "tending to the corruption of the morals of youth." [Butler v. Michigan, 352 U.S. 380 (1957)]

2) **Construction May Save Vague Statute**
A state statute will be upheld if it meets the tests as construed by the courts of the state. Thus, a seemingly vague obscenity statute may be saved by a state supreme court opinion that limits it to a proscription of depictions of specific types of sexual conduct. [Ward v. Illinois, 431 U.S. 767 (1977)]

d. **Land Use Regulations**
A land use (or zoning) regulation may limit the location or size of adult entertainment establishments (*i.e.*, businesses that focus on sexual activities) if the regulation is designed to reduce the secondary effects of such businesses (*e.g.*, rise in crime rates, drop in property values and neighborhood quality, etc.). However, regulations may not ban such establishments altogether. [City of Los Angeles v. Alameda Books, Inc., 535 U.S. 425 (2002)]

Example: A city ordinance limiting adult entertainment establishments to one corner of the city occupying less than 5% of the city's area was deemed constitutional. [City of Renton v. Playtime Theatres, Inc., 475 U.S. 41 (1986)]

e. **Liquor Regulation**
The Twenty-First Amendment grants states more than the usual regulatory authority with respect to intoxicating beverages. Therefore, regulations prohibiting explicit live sexual entertainment and films in establishments licensed to sell liquor by the drink, even though proscribing some forms of visual presentation that would not be obscene under *Miller,* do not violate the First Amendment as long as they are not "irrational."

f. **Display**
The Court has suggested that the state ***may regulate*** the display of certain material, to prevent it from being so obtrusive that an unwilling viewer cannot avoid exposure to it. [Redup v. New York, 386 U.S. 767 (1967)]

g. **Private Possession of Obscenity**
Private possession of obscenity at home cannot be made a crime because of the constitutional right of personal privacy. [Stanley v. Georgia, 394 U.S. 557 (1969)] However, the protection does not extend beyond the home. Thus, importation, distribution, and exhibition of obscene materials can be prohibited.

1) **Exception—Child Pornography**
The state may make private possession of child pornography a crime, even private possession for personal viewing in a residence. [Osborne v. Ohio, 495 U.S. 103 (1990)]

4. **Defamatory Speech**
When a person is sued for making a defamatory statement, the First Amendment places restrictions on the ability of the government (through its tort law and courts) to grant a recovery where the person suing is a ***public official or public figure***, or where the defamatory statement involves an issue of ***public concern***. In these cases, the plaintiff must prove not only the elements of defamation required by state law, but also that the statement was ***false*** and that the person making the statement was at ***fault*** to some degree in not ascertaining the truth of the statement.

a. **Falsity**
At common law, a defamatory statement was presumed to be false; to avoid liability for an otherwise defamatory statement on the ground that it was true, the defendant had to assert truth as an affirmative defense. The Supreme Court has rejected this presumption in all public figure or public concern cases. In these cases, the plaintiff must prove by clear and convincing evidence that the statement was false. [Philadelphia Newspapers, Inc. v. Hepps, 475 U.S. 767 (1986)]

1) **Requirement of Factual Statement**
To be defamatory, the false statement must be viewed by a reasonable person as a statement of fact, rather than as a statement of opinion or a parody. Furthermore, a public figure cannot circumvent the First Amendment restrictions by using a different tort theory to collect damages for a published statement about him that is not a false statement of fact.

Example: Even though a publisher may have intended to cause psychological distress to a public figure by publishing statements about him that were derogatory, the public figure cannot receive a judgment for "emotional distress" damages if a reasonable person who read or viewed the publication would not understand it to contain a statement of fact about that public figure. [Hustler Magazine Inc. v. Falwell, 485 U.S. 46 (1988)]

Note: The fact that a publisher labels a statement as "opinion" will not provide First Amendment protection if the statement would reasonably be understood to be a statement of fact. [Milkovich v. Lorain Journal Co., 497 U.S. 1 (1990)]

b. **Fault**
At common law, a defendant who had no reason to know that the statement he was making was false and defamatory could still be liable for defamation. Now, however,

a plaintiff in a public figure or public concern case must prove fault on the part of the defendant. The degree of fault required is higher when the plaintiff is a public official or public figure than when the plaintiff is a private person suing on a matter of public concern.

1) **Public Official or Public Figure—Malice Required**
A public official may not recover for defamatory words relating to his official conduct or a matter of public concern without clear and convincing evidence that the statement was made with "malice" (defined below). [New York Times v. Sullivan, 376 U.S. 254 (1964)] This rule has since been extended to public figure plaintiffs. (Note that while the Supreme Court has not specifically held that all statements regarding public officials or public figures necessarily involve matters of public concern, a case to the contrary should be rare.)

a) **Malice Defined**
Malice was defined by the Supreme Court in *New York Times v. Sullivan* as:

(i) ***Knowledge*** that the statement was false, ***or***

(ii) ***Reckless disregard*** as to its truth or falsity.

The plaintiff must show that the defendant was subjectively aware that the statement he published was false or that he subjectively ***entertained serious doubts*** as to its truthfulness.

(1) **Malice in False Quotation Cases**
Proof that a defamation plaintiff was inaccurately quoted does not, by itself, prove actual malice, even if the quotation was intentionally altered by the defendant. If the published "quotation" is substantially accurate, the plaintiff may not collect damages. To show malice, the public figure plaintiff must prove that the defendant's alteration of the quotation materially changed the meaning of the actual statements made by the plaintiff. [Masson v. New Yorker Magazine, Inc., 501 U.S. 496 (1991)]

(2) **Permitted Inquiries by Plaintiff**
In attempting to prove knowing or reckless disregard of the truth, the plaintiff may inquire into the state of mind of those who edit, produce, or publish (*i.e.,* conversations with editorial colleagues). [Herbert v. Lando, 441 U.S. 153 (1979)]

(3) **Petition Clause Does Not Protect Defamatory Statement Made with Malice**
The First Amendment guarantees individuals the right to "petition government for a redress of grievances." However, this right to petition the government does not grant absolute immunity to persons who make defamatory statements about public officials or public figures in their communications with government officials. The defamed individual may

prevail by meeting the *New York Times* requirements. [McDonald v. Smith, 472 U.S. 479 (1985)]

b) **Two Ways to Become a Public Figure**

(1) **General Fame or Notoriety**
A person may be a public figure for all purposes and all contexts if he achieves "***general fame or notoriety*** in the community and pervasive involvement in the affairs of society," although "a citizen's participation in community and professional affairs" does not render him a public figure for all purposes.

(2) **Involvement in Particular Controversy**
A person may "***voluntarily inject*** himself or be drawn into a particular controversy to influence the resolution of the issues involved" and thereby become a public figure for a limited range of issues. [Gertz v. Robert Welch, Inc., 418 U.S. 323 (1974)]

Note that *Gertz* appears to allow for the possibility of a person's being an involuntary public figure for a limited range of issues, although such a case would be "exceedingly rare."

c) **Examples of Persons Not Deemed Public Figures**

(1) **Spouse of Wealthy Person**
Marriage to an extremely wealthy person and divorcing such a person does not amount to voluntarily entering the public arena, even though press conferences are held by the plaintiff, because going to court is the only way she could dissolve her marriage. [Time, Inc. v. Firestone, 424 U.S. 448 (1976)]

(2) **Person Engaging in Criminal Conduct**
A person who engages in ***criminal conduct*** does not automatically become a public figure even when the defamatory statements relate solely to his conviction. [Wolston v. Reader's Digest Association, 443 U.S. 157 (1979)]

(3) **Scientist in Federally Funded Program**
A behavioral scientist engaged in ***federally funded*** animal research studies is not a public figure because he applies for federal grants and ***publishes*** in professional journals. [Hutchinson v. Proxmire, 443 U.S. 111 (1979)]

2) **Private Individual Suing on Matter of Public Concern—At Least Negligence Required**
When a private individual is defamed, there is less of a need to protect freedom of speech and press and more of a need to protect private individuals from injury from defamation because they do not have opportunities as effective for rebuttal

as public figures. Accordingly, defamation actions brought by private individuals are subject to constitutional limitations only when the defamatory statement involves a matter of public concern. And even in those cases, the limitations are not as great as those established for public officials and public figures. [Gertz v. Robert Welch, Inc., *supra*] When the defamatory statement involves a matter of public concern, *Gertz* imposes two restrictions on private plaintiffs: (i) it prohibits liability without fault, and (ii) it restricts the recovery of presumed or punitive damages.

a) **No Liability Without Proof of at Least Negligence**
The plaintiff must show that the defendant was negligent in failing to ascertain the truth of the statement. If the plaintiff establishes negligence but not malice, which is a higher degree of fault, he also has to provide competent evidence of "actual" damages. (This changes the common law rule that damages would be presumed by law for injury to reputation and did not need to be proved by the plaintiff.) Actual damages may be awarded not only for economic losses but also for injury to the plaintiff's reputation in the community and for personal humiliation and distress.

b) **Presumed or Punitive Damages Allowed Only If Malice Established**
If the plaintiff establishes that the defendant made the statement with malice, the actual damage requirement is extinguished. The plaintiff can recover whatever damages are permitted under state law (usually presumed damages and even punitive damages in appropriate cases). In other words, there is no constitutional protection for statements made with malice, even though a matter of public concern is involved.

c) **What Is a Matter of Public Concern?**
The courts decide on a case-by-case basis whether the defamatory statement involves a matter of public concern, looking at the content, form, and context of the publication. [Dun & Bradstreet, Inc. v. Greenmoss Builders, Inc., 472 U.S. 749 (1985)]
Example: In *Dun & Bradstreet,* the Court determined that a credit agency's erroneous report of plaintiff's bankruptcy, distributed to five subscribers, was speech solely in the private interest of the speaker and its specific business audience. Therefore, because a matter of public concern was not involved, the First Amendment restrictions did not apply and the state court award of presumed and punitive damages was upheld.

3) **Private Individual Suing on Matter Not of Public Concern**
The Supreme Court has not imposed constitutional restrictions on defamation actions brought by private individuals that do not involve a matter of public concern. Hence, presumed and punitive damages can be recovered even if malice is not established.

c. **Procedural Issues**

1) **Federal Summary Judgment Standard**
When ruling on a motion for summary judgment in a federal court defamation action in a case involving an issue of public concern, a judge must apply the clear and convincing evidence standard (*i.e.,* the judge should grant the motion ***unless*** it appears that the plaintiff could meet his burdens of proving falsity and actual malice at trial by clear and convincing evidence). However, the Supreme Court has not clearly held that state courts must follow this practice under similar circumstances.

2) **Judicial Review**
An appellate court must review a defamation case by conducting an independent review of the record to determine if the finder of fact (the jury) could have found that the malice standard was met in the case. [Harte-Hanks Communications, Inc. v. Connaughton, 491 U.S. 657 (1989)]

d. **Recovery for Depiction in a False Light**
To recover damages for depiction in a false light (as opposed to a defamatory injury to reputation) arising out of comments directed at activities of public interest, an individual must establish ***falsity*** and ***actual malice*** whether or not he qualifies as a public figure under *Time, Inc. v. Hill,* 385 U.S. 374 (1967). However, it is ***assumed*** that the Court would now modify this to mirror the *Gertz* negligence rule for private plaintiffs.

e. **True Privacy Actions**

1) **Publishing True Fact of Public Record**
A newspaper or broadcaster cannot be sued for publishing a true fact once it is lawfully obtained from the public record or otherwise released to the public. [Cox Broadcasting Corp. v. Cohn, 420 U.S. 469 (1975)—rape victim's name already in court records open to the public; The Florida Star v. B.J.F., 491 U.S. 524 (1989)—rape victim's name inadvertently given to the press by police]

2) **Publishing Name of Juvenile Charged with Crime**
A state cannot require judicial approval before the media can print the name of a juvenile charged with murder where the name of the juvenile was obtained through legal means (reporter heard name of defendant over police frequency radio and questioned witnesses to the crime). [Smith v. Daily Mail Publishing Co., 443 U.S. 97 (1979)]

3) **Publishing Information on Judge's Competency**
A state cannot make it a crime to publish information, released in a confidential proceeding, concerning the competency of members of the state judiciary. [Landmark Communications v. Virginia, 435 U.S. 829 (1978)]

f. **Commercial Privacy—Disclosing a Private Performance Can Violate "Right to Publicity"**
In *Zacchini v. Scripps-Howard Broadcasting Co.,* 433 U.S. 562 (1977), the Court held that state law could award damages to an entertainer who attempted to restrict the showing of his act to those who paid admission, when a television station broadcast his entire act. Here the "human cannonball" had his entire 15-second act broadcast over his objection.

g. **Copyright Infringement**
The First Amendment does not require an exception to copyright protection for material written by a former President or other public figures. Magazines have no right to publish such copyrighted material beyond the statutory fair use exception. [Harper & Row Publishers v. Nation Enterprises, 471 U.S. 539 (1985)]

5. **Some Commercial Speech**
False advertising is not protected by the First Amendment, although commercial speech in general does have some First Amendment protection. In determining whether a regulation of commercial speech is valid, the Supreme Court asserts that it uses a four-step process. However, it may be easiest to think about this as an initial question followed by a three-step inquiry. ***First,*** determine whether the commercial speech concerns a lawful activity and is not misleading or fraudulent. Speech proposing an unlawful transaction (*e.g.,* "I will sell you this pound of heroin for X dollars") and fraudulent speech may be outlawed. If the speech regulated concerns a ***lawful activity*** and is ***not misleading or fraudulent***, the regulation will be valid only if it:

(i) Serves a ***"substantial"*** government interest;

(ii) ***"Directly advances"*** the asserted interest; and

(iii) Is ***narrowly tailored*** to serve the substantial interest. This part of the test does ***not*** require that the "least restrictive means" be used. Rather, there must be a ***reasonable fit*** between the legislation's end and the means chosen. [Board of Trustees of State University of New York v. Fox, 492 U.S. 469 (1989)]

[Central Hudson Gas v. Public Service Commission, 447 U.S. 557 (1980)]

Examples: A city could not prohibit the use of newsracks on sidewalks for the distribution of commercial publications (such as free publications advertising products or real estate for sale) if the city allowed sidewalk newsracks for the distribution of newspapers. There is no "reasonable fit" between the category of commercial speech and any substantial interest. Commercial newsracks do not cause any physical or aesthetic harm different from that caused by newspaper newsracks. [Cincinnati v. Discovery Network, Inc., 507 U.S. 410 (1993)] Similarly, a law prohibiting beer bottle labels from displaying alcohol content was held invalid because, although the government has a substantial interest in preventing "strength wars," the government did not show that the label prohibition advanced this interest in a material way. [Rubin v. Coors Brewing Co., 514 U.S. 476 (1995)]

a. **Complete Bans**
Complete bans on truthful advertisement of lawful products are very unlikely to be upheld due to a lack of tailoring. Thus, the Court has ***struck down*** total bans against advertising:

(i) Legal abortions;

(ii) Contraceptives;

(iii) Drug prices;

(iv) Attorneys' services; and

(v) Liquor prices.

Note that the Twenty-First Amendment—giving states the power to regulate liquor commerce within their borders—does not give states power to override First Amendment protections.

1) Commercial Sign Regulation
It is unclear whether billboards may be totally banned from a city. However, they can be regulated for purposes of traffic safety and aesthetics.

a) Blockbusting
A town could not prohibit the use of outdoor "for sale" signs by owners of private homes as a way of reducing the effect of "blockbusting" real estate agents (*i.e.,* encouraging homeowners to sell at reduced prices because of the threat of a sudden influx of minorities). [Linmark Associates v. Willingboro Township, 431 U.S. 85 (1977)]

b. Required Disclosures
Commercial speech is protected largely because of its value to consumers. Thus, the government may require commercial advertisers to make certain disclosures if they are not unduly burdensome and they are reasonably related to the state's interest in preventing deception. [*See, e.g.*, Milavetz, Gallop & Milavetz, P.A. v. United States, 130 S. Ct. 1324 (2010)—advertisements by lawyers (and others) as debt relief agencies may be required to include information about their legal status and the nature of the assistance provided, as well as the possibility of the debtor's filing for bankruptcy]

c. Special Attorney Advertising Rules
The Court has upheld prohibitions against in-person solicitation by attorneys for pecuniary gain [Ohralik v. Ohio State Bar, 436 U.S. 447 (1978)—state interest in protecting lay persons from fraud and overreaching is substantial, and prohibition here is narrowly tailored and directly advances that interest] and sending mail solicitations to accident victims and their relatives within 30 days following an accident [Florida Bar v. Went For It, Inc., 515 U.S. 618 (1995)—state interest in protecting lawyers' reputation is substantial, and ban here is narrowly tailored and directly advances that interest].

D. PRIOR RESTRAINTS

A prior restraint is any governmental action that would prevent a communication from reaching the public (*e.g.,* a licensing system, a prohibition against using mails, an injunction, etc.). Prior restraints are not favored in our political system; the Court would rather allow speech and then punish it if it was unprotected. However, the Court will uphold prior restraints if some special harm would otherwise result. As with other restrictions on speech, a prior restraint must be narrowly tailored to achieve some compelling or, at least, significant governmental interest. The Court has also required that certain procedural safeguards be included in any system of prior restraint.

1. **Sufficiency of Governmental Interest**

The Supreme Court has not adopted a brightline standard for determining when a prior restraint is justified, but it has said that the government's burden is heavy. For exam purposes, you should ask whether there is some ***special societal harm*** that justifies the restraint.

a. **National Security**

National security is certainly a sufficient harm justifying prior restraint. Thus, a newspaper could be prohibited from publishing troop movements in times of war. [Near v. Minnesota, 283 U.S. 697 (1931)] However, the harm must be more than theoretical. Thus, the Court refused to enjoin publication of *The Pentagon Papers* on the basis that publication might possibly have a detrimental effect on the Vietnam War. [New York Times v. United States, 403 U.S. 713 (1971)]

b. **Preserving Fair Trial**

Preserving a fair trial for an accused might be a sufficient basis for prior restraint. However, the restraint will be upheld only if it is the only sure way of preserving a fair trial. [Nebraska Press Association v. Stewart, 427 U.S. 539 (1976)]

1) **Compare—Grand Jury Prior Restraint**

A state law prohibiting a grand jury witness from ever disclosing the testimony he gave to the grand jury (even after the grand jury term had ended) violates the First Amendment. Such a law is not narrowly tailored to a compelling interest, since any such interest that the government may have in protecting the grand jury process can be protected by a nonpermanent prohibition. [Butterworth v. Smith, 494 U.S. 624 (1990)]

c. **Contractual Agreements**

The Supreme Court has held that prior restraint is permissible where the parties have contractually agreed to the restraint. [Snepp v. United States, 444 U.S. 507 (1980)—CIA agent contractually agreed to give agency a prepublication review of any item related to his employment]

d. **Military Circumstances**

The Supreme Court has held that the interests of maintaining discipline among troops and efficiency of operations on a military base justify a requirement that persons on a military base obtain the commander's permission before circulating petitions.

e. **Obscenity**

The Court has held in a number of cases that the government's interest in preventing the dissemination of obscenity is sufficient to justify a system of prior restraint.

2. **Procedural Safeguards**

The Supreme Court has held that no system of prior restraint will be upheld unless it provides the persons whose speech is being restrained certain procedural safeguards. The safeguards arose in the context of movie censorship for obscenity, but the court has held that similar safeguards must be provided in all prior restraint cases:

(i) The standards must be "***narrowly drawn, reasonable, and definite***," so as to include only prohibitable speech (*e.g.,* improper to permanently enjoin witness from disclosing grand jury testimony; government interest can be protected by nonpermanent injunction [Butterworth v. Smith, *supra*]);

(ii) If the restraining body wishes to restrain dissemination of an item, it must ***promptly seek an injunction*** (*e.g.,* improper to allow 50 days before seeking injunction [Teitel Film Corp. v. Cusack, 390 U.S. 139 (1968)]); and

(iii) There must be a ***prompt and final judicial determination*** of the validity of the restraint (*e.g.,* improper to leave an injunction in place pending an appeal that could take up to a year; government must either lift the injunction or expedite the appeal [National Socialist Party v. Village of Skokie, 432 U.S. 43 (1977)]).

A number of other cases, especially in the area of movie censorship, also provide that the ***government bears the burden*** of proving that the speech involved is unprotected. [Freedman v. Maryland, 380 U.S. 51 (1965)]

Example: A federal statute authorized the Postmaster General (i) to deny use of the mails and postal money orders for materials found to be obscene in an administrative hearing, and (ii) to obtain a court order, upon a showing of probable cause, to detain incoming mail pending completion of the administrative hearing. The Court found that this denial of use of the mails violated the First Amendment: The procedures did not require the government to initiate proceedings to obtain a final judicial determination of obscenity, failed to assure prompt judicial review, and failed to limit any restraint in advance of a final judicial determination to preserving the status quo for "the shortest fixed period compatible with sound judicial resolution." [Blount v. Rizzi, 400 U.S. 410 (1971)]

3. Obscenity Cases

Much of the case law in the area of prior restraint has arisen in connection with banning obscenity.

a. Seizure of Books and Films

As with any seizure by the government, seizures of books and films may be made only upon probable cause that they contain obscenity or are otherwise unlawful. (*See* Criminal Procedure outline.)

1) Single Seizures

Seizures of a single book or film (to preserve it as evidence) may be made only with a warrant issued by a neutral and detached magistrate. And even here, a prompt post-seizure determination of obscenity must be available. If other copies of a seized film are not available to the exhibitor, he must be allowed to make a copy so that he may continue showing the film until a final determination has been made. [Heller v. New York, 413 U.S. 483 (1973)] Of course, if the materials are available for sale to the general public, an officer may enter into the establishment and purchase the book or film to use it as evidence in a later prosecution without obtaining a warrant. [Maryland v. Macon, 472 U.S. 463 (1985)]

2) **Large Scale Seizures**
"Large scale" seizures of allegedly obscene books and films—"to destroy them or block their distribution or exhibition"—must be ***preceded*** by a ***full adversary hearing*** and a judicial determination of obscenity. [Fort Wayne Books, Inc. v. Indiana, 489 U.S. 46 (1989)]

3) **Forfeiture of Business**
The First Amendment does not prohibit forfeiture of a defendant's adult entertainment business after the defendant has been found guilty of violating the Racketeer Influenced and Corrupt Organizations Act and criminal obscenity laws, even though the business assets included nonobscene books and magazines, where the entire business was found to be part of the defendant's racketeering activity. [Alexander v. United States, 509 U.S. 544 (1993)]

b. **Injunction**
After seizing material, the government may enjoin its further publication only after it is determined to be obscene in a ***full judicial hearing***. [Kingsley Books, Inc. v. Brown, 354 U.S. 436 (1957)]

c. **Movie Censorship**
The Court has noted that movies are different from other forms of expression, and that time delays incident to censorship are less burdensome for movies than for other forms of expression. Thus, the Court allows governments to establish censorship boards to screen movies ***before*** they are released in the community, as long as the procedural safeguards mentioned above are followed. The censor bears the burden of proving that the movie is unprotected speech.

d. **Burden on Government**
When the government adopts a content-based, prior restraint of speech, the government has the burden of proving that the restriction is the least restrictive alternative to accomplish its goal. [Ashcroft v. American Civil Liberties Union, 542 U.S. 656 (2004)—upholding a preliminary injunction against enforcement of a statute requiring age verification for access to Internet websites with sexually explicit material, and criminalizing the failure to obtain age verification, because less restrictive alternatives (*e.g.,* parents installing filters) are available]

E. FREEDOM OF THE PRESS

As a general rule, the press has no greater freedom to speak than does the public. However, a number of issues have arisen in the freedom of press context.

1. Publication of Truthful Information

Generally, the press has a right to publish information about a matter of public concern, and this right can be restricted only by a sanction that is narrowly tailored to further a state interest of the highest order. The right applies even if the information has been unlawfully obtained in the first instance, as long as (i) the speech relates to a matter of public concern, (ii) the publisher did not obtain it unlawfully or know who did, and (iii) the original speaker's privacy expectations are low. [Bartnicki v. Vopper, 532 U.S. 514 (2001)]

Example: During heated collective bargaining negotiations between a teachers' union and a school board, an unknown person intercepted a cell phone call between

a union negotiator and the union's president. The tape was forwarded to a radio commentator, who played it on the radio. The commentator was sued for damages under civil liability provisions of state and federal wiretap laws that prohibited intentional disclosure of the contents of an electronically transmitted conversation when one has reason to know that the conversation was intercepted unlawfully. The Supreme Court held that the statute violated the First Amendment as applied under these circumstances. [Bartnicki v. Vopper, *supra*]

2. Access to Trials

The First Amendment guarantees the public and press a right to attend criminal trials. But the right may be outweighed by an overriding interest articulated in findings by the trial judge. [Richmond Newspapers v. Virginia, 448 U.S. 555 (1980)—no majority opinion] The right probably applies to civil trials, although the Supreme Court has not conclusively resolved that issue.

a. Access to Voir Dire Examination

The First Amendment guarantee of public and press access to criminal trials also includes access to proceedings involving the voir dire examination of potential jurors. In *Press-Enterprise Co. v. Superior Court,* 464 U.S. 501 (1984), the Court found that a trial court could not constitutionally close voir dire examination of potential jurors without consideration of alternatives to closure even though, in some circumstances, there may be a compelling interest in restricting access to such proceedings to protect the privacy of potential jurors or the fairness of the trial.

b. Access to Other Pretrial Proceedings

Pretrial proceedings are presumptively subject to a First Amendment right of access for the press and public. Thus, a law requiring that all preliminary hearings be closed to the press and public violates the First Amendment. [El Vocero de Puerto Rico (Caribbean International News Corp.) v. Puerto Rico, 508 U.S. 147 (1993)—per curiam] If the prosecution and defense counsel seek to have a judge close pretrial proceedings, the judge would have to make specific findings on the record demonstrating (i) that closure was essential to preserve "higher" or "overriding" values, and (ii) that the closure order was narrowly tailored to serve the higher or overriding value. [Press-Enterprise Co. v. Superior Court, 478 U.S. 1 (1986)]

If the prosecution seeks to have a pretrial hearing or trial closed to the public and the defendant objects to the closure, there will be a Sixth Amendment violation if the judge excludes the public and the press from the hearing or trial without a clear finding that a closure order was necessary to protect an overriding interest.

c. Compelling Interest in Protecting Children

The government has a compelling interest in protecting children who are victims of sex offenses. Portions of trials wherein such children testify may be closed to the public and press, but only if the trial court makes a finding that such closure is necessary to protect the child in the individual case. A state statute, however, violates the First Amendment if it requires closure of the trial during testimony of a child victim of a sex offense without a finding of necessity by the trial judge. [Globe Newspaper Co. v. Superior Court, 457 U.S. 596 (1982)]

d. **Protective Order in Publishing Information Gained in Pretrial Discovery**
The Supreme Court has upheld a state trial court "protective order" prohibiting a newspaper defendant in a defamation suit from publishing, disseminating, or using information gained through pretrial discovery from the plaintiff in any way except where necessary for preparation for trial. [*See* Seattle Times Co. v. Rhinehart, 467 U.S. 20 (1984)]

3. **Requiring Members of the Press to Testify Before Grand Juries**
In *Branzburg v. Hayes,* 408 U.S. 665 (1972), the Court held that requiring a journalist to appear and testify before state or federal grand juries ***does not abridge freedom of speech or press***, despite the claim that such a requirement would so deter the flow of news from confidential sources as to place an unconstitutionally heavy burden on the First Amendment interest in the free flow of information to the public. The Court's opinion refused to create—and even rejected—a conditional privilege not to reveal confidential sources to a grand jury conducting a good faith inquiry. This position was affirmed in *New York Times v. Jascalevich,* 439 U.S. 1331 (1978).

4. **Interviewing Prisoners**
Although the First Amendment protects prisoners, and especially those corresponding with them by mail, from a sweeping program of censorship [Procunier v. Martinez, 416 U.S. 396 (1974)], it does not permit journalists to insist upon either interviewing specified prisoners of their choice [Pell v. Procunier, 417 U.S. 817 (1974)] or inspecting prison grounds [Houchins v. KQED, Inc., 438 U.S. 1 (1978)].

5. **Business Regulations or Taxes**
Press and broadcasting companies can be subject to general business regulations (*e.g.,* antitrust laws) or taxes (*e.g.,* federal or state income taxes). Thus, a tax or regulation applicable to both press and non-press businesses will be upheld, even if it has a special impact on a portion of the press or broadcast media, as long as it is not an attempt to interfere with First Amendment activities. However, no tax or regulation impacting on the press or subpart of the press may be based on the content of the publication absent a compelling justification.

Examples: 1) State tax on publisher's use of more than $100,000 of paper and ink products annually violates the First Amendment. [Minneapolis Star & Tribune v. Minnesota Commissioner of Revenue, 460 U.S. 575 (1983)]

2) State sales tax or "receipts tax" on the sale of general interest magazines that exempts newspapers and religious, professional, trade, and sports journals from the tax violates the First Amendment. [Arkansas Writers' Project, Inc. v. Ragland, 481 U.S. 221 (1987)]

3) A state sales tax that exempted the sales of newspapers and magazines from the tax but did not give a similar exemption to the sale of broadcast services (cable or subscription television) did not violate the First Amendment. The tax was not based on the content of broadcasts and did not target a small category of publishers. The tax was applicable to all cable or satellite television sales. (There is no comparable sale of "free TV" such as network broadcasts.) [Leathers v. Medlock, 499 U.S. 439 (1991)]

6. Monetary Damages for Failure to Keep Identity Confidential

When a reporter or publisher promises a "source person" to keep his identity confidential and then publishes the source person's name, state contract law or promissory estoppel law may allow the source person to recover from the reporter or publisher any damages caused by the publication of his identity. [Cohen v. Cowles Media Co., 501 U.S. 663 (1991)]

7. Broadcasting Regulations

Radio and television broadcasting may be more closely regulated than the press. *Rationale:* Due to the limited number of frequencies available, broadcasters have a special privilege—and, consequently, a special responsibility to give suitable time to matters of public interest and to present a suitable range of programs. The paramount right is the ***right of viewers and listeners*** to receive information of public concern, rather than the right of broadcasters to broadcast what they please.

a. Fairness Doctrine

Accordingly, the Court has upheld, under a regulatory "fairness doctrine" (which is no longer enforced), FCC orders requiring a radio station to offer free broadcasting time (i) to opponents of political candidates or views endorsed by the station, and (ii) to any person who has been personally attacked in the course of a broadcast, for a reply to the attack. [Red Lion Broadcasting Co. v. FCC, 395 U.S. 367 (1969)]

1) Compare—Grant of Equal Newspaper Space

A statute granting political candidates a right to equal space to reply to criticism by the newspaper ***violates*** First Amendment freedom of the press. Decisions respecting size and content of newspaper are forbidden to government. [Miami Herald Publishing Co. v. Tornillo, 418 U.S. 241 (1974)]

b. Newspaper Ownership of Radio or TV Station

Similarly, to promote the diversity of information received by the public, the FCC may forbid ownership of a radio or television station by a daily newspaper located in the same community. [FCC v. National Citizens Committee, 436 U.S. 775 (1978)]

c. Prohibiting Indecent Speech

Because of a broadcast's ability to invade the privacy of the home, the First Amendment does not forbid imposing civil sanctions on a broadcaster for airing a full monologue (in contrast to isolated use of a few such words) of "patently offensive sexual and excretory speech," even though it is not "obscene"—at least at those times when children are likely to be listening. [FCC v. Pacifica Foundation, 438 U.S. 726 (1978)]

d. Political Advertisements

The First Amendment does ***not*** require broadcasters to accept political advertisements.

e. Elimination of Editorial Speech from Stations Receiving Public Grants

Congress violated the First Amendment when it forbade any noncommercial educational station receiving a grant from the Corporation for Public Broadcasting from engaging in "editorializing." [FCC v. League of Women Voters, 468 U.S. 364 (1984)] This was the ***suppression of speech*** because of its content; the elimination of editorial speech from stations receiving public grants of this type was not narrowly tailored to promote an overriding government purpose regarding the regulation of broadcasting in general or noncommercial broadcasters in particular. Congress could deny persons receiving the federal funds the right to use those funds for editorial activities, but it could not condition the receipt of those funds upon a promise not to engage in any such speech.

8. Cable Television Regulation

While generally regulations of newspapers are subject to strict scrutiny, and regulations of the broadcast media are subject to less critical review, regulations of cable television transmissions are subject to review by a standard somewhere between these two. *Rationale:* The physical connection to a viewer's television set makes the cable subscriber a more captive audience than a newspaper reader and distinguishes cable from newspapers, which cannot prevent access to competing newspapers. On the other hand, unlike broadcast media, which is limited to a small number of frequencies (*see* 7., *supra*), there is no practical limitation on the number of cable channels; thus, the government's interest in protecting viewers' rights is weaker with regard to cable. [Turner Broadcasting System, Inc. v. FCC, A.2.a.2), *supra*]

Example: A law requiring cable operators to carry local stations is subject to "intermediate scrutiny" since it is content neutral (*see* A.2.a.2), *supra*). Since a "must carry" provision directly serves the important interest of preserving economic viability of local broadcasters and promotes the dissemination of information to noncable viewers, it is constitutional. [Turner Broadcasting System, Inc. v. FCC, *supra*]

a. Compare—Content-Based Cable Broadcast Regulations

A content-based cable broadcast regulation will be upheld only if it passes muster under the strict scrutiny test. [United States v. Playboy Entertainment Group, Inc., 529 U.S. 803 (2000)—law requiring cable operators to limit "sexually oriented" programs to after 10 p.m. is invalid because of the less restrictive alternative of enabling each household to block undesired channels]

9. Internet Regulation

The strict standard of First Amendment scrutiny, rather than the more relaxed standard applicable to broadcast regulation, applies to regulation of the Internet. *Rationale*: In contrast to broadcasting, there is no scarcity of frequencies (*see* 7., *supra*) on the Internet and little likelihood that the Internet will unexpectedly invade the privacy of the home (*see* 7.c., *supra*). [Reno v. American Civil Liberties Union, C.3.a.4), *supra*]

XXI. FREEDOM OF ASSOCIATION AND BELIEF

A. NATURE OF THE RIGHT

Although the First Amendment does not mention a right of freedom of association, the right to join together with other persons for expressive or political activity is protected by the First Amendment. However, the right to associate for expressive purposes is ***not absolute***. At the very least, the right may be infringed to serve a ***compelling government interest***, unrelated to the suppression of ideas, that cannot be achieved through means significantly less restrictive of associational freedoms. However, in some cases, as noted below, a more lenient standard will apply.

Examples: 1) A state's interest in ending invidious discrimination justifies prohibiting private clubs that are large and basically unselective in their membership, or that are often

used for business contacts, from discriminating on the basis of race, creed, color, national origin, or sex—at least when it is not shown that this would impede the individual members' ability to engage in First Amendment activity. [New York State Club Association, Inc. v. New York City, 487 U.S. 1 (1988); Board of Directors of Rotary Club International v. Rotary Club of Duarte, 481 U.S. 537 (1987); Roberts v. United States Jaycees, 468 U.S. 609 (1984)]

2) A federal statute making it a crime to provide "material ***support*** or resources" of any kind to a ***foreign terrorist*** organization with ***knowledge*** of its being designated a foreign terrorist organization by the federal government does not violate the freedom of association (or speech). The statute does not forbid mere membership or association with the organization, only material support (which was defined in the statute). Moreover, given the difficulty of obtaining information about terrorist threats, any burden that the statute places on a person's freedom of association is justified. [Holder v. Humanitarian Law Project, 130 S. Ct. 2705 (2010)]

Compare: 1) A state antidiscrimination law may not bar the Boy Scouts from excluding an openly gay assistant scoutmaster from membership. Forced inclusion would ***significantly burden*** the right of expressive association of the Boy Scouts, since one of the ***sincerely held*** purposes of the Scouts is to instill certain moral values in young people, including the value that "homosexual conduct is not morally straight." [Boy Scouts of America v. Dale, 530 U.S. 640 (2000)]

2) A city ordinance that restricted admission to certain dance halls to persons between the ages of 14 and 18 was constitutional; it did not have to be justified with a compelling interest because the associational activity of meeting in a dance hall is not an activity within the protection of the First Amendment. [Dallas v. Stanglin, 490 U.S. 19 (1989)]

B. ELECTORAL PROCESS

Laws regulating the electoral process might impact on First Amendment rights of speech, assembly, and association. The Supreme Court uses a ***balancing test*** in determining whether a regulation of the electoral process is valid: if the restriction on First Amendment activities is severe, it will be upheld only if it is narrowly tailored to achieve a compelling interest, but if the restriction is reasonable and nondiscriminatory, it generally will be upheld on the basis of the states' important regulatory interests. [Burdick v. Takushi, 504 U.S. 428 (1992)—upholding prohibition against write-in candidates]

Example: A state may require in-person voters to show a government-issued voter ID. This is an "evenhanded" protection of the integrity of the electoral process and is justified by "sufficiently weighty" interests of detecting voter fraud and protecting public confidence in elections. Thus, the requirement is plainly legitimate and is not ***"facially invalid."*** [Crawford v. Marion County Election Board, 553 U.S. 181 (2008)]

1. Ballot Regulation

a. Signature Requirements

The Court has found that the interest of running an efficient election supports a requirement that candidates obtain a reasonable number of signatures to get on the ballot. [Munro v. Socialist Workers Party, 479 U.S. 189 (1986)—1%] Similarly, a state's interest in promoting transparency and accountability in elections is sufficient to justify public disclosure of the names and addresses of persons who sign ballot petitions. [Doe v. Reed, 130 S. Ct. 2811 (2010)] However, the Court struck down a severe ballot restriction requiring new political parties to collect twice as many signatures to run for county office as for state office. [Norman v. Reed, 502 U.S. 279 (1992)]

b. **Primary Voting Regulations**
A state may enforce a party rule requiring that a person be registered as a member of the party within a reasonable amount of time prior to a primary to be able to vote. [Rosario v. Rockefeller, 410 U.S. 752 (1973)] It may also require that voters in a party's primary be registered either in the party ***or as independents***. *Rationale:* The burden on the party's associational rights is ***not severe***. Thus, strict scrutiny does not apply and the state's important regulatory interests (*e.g.,* in preserving political parties as viable identifiable groups, preventing party raiding, etc.) are sufficient to justify the restriction. [Clingman v. Beaver, 544 U.S. 581 (2005)] However, a state may not prohibit a party from allowing independent voters to vote in the party's primary if the party wishes to allow independent voters to participate; such a requirement constitutes a severe burden on the associational rights of the party and can be justified only if it is narrowly tailored to serve a compelling interest. [Tashjian v. Republican Party of Connecticut, 479 U.S. 208 (1986)]

c. **Single Party Limitation**
A state law that prohibits an individual from appearing on the ballot as the candidate of more than one party does ***not*** impose a severe burden on the association rights of political parties. The state's interest in ballot integrity and political stability are "sufficiently weighty" to justify the law. [Timmons v. Twin Cities Area New Party, 520 U.S. 351 (1997)]

d. **"Nonpartisan" Blanket Primary**
A state primary ballot law providing that candidates ***self-identify*** their party preference and that the two top vote getters advance to the general election does not ***on its face*** violate the association rights of political parties. *Rationale:* (i) The law does not state that any candidate is a party's nominee, (ii) there was no evidence that voters would be confused by the self-identifications, and (iii) the state may design a ballot that will make this clear. [Washington State Grange v. Washington State Republican Party, 552 U.S. 442 (2008)]

2. **Party Regulation**
The state has less interest in governing party activities than in governing elections in general. Thus, the Court has held invalid a statute prohibiting the governing committee of a political party from endorsing or opposing candidates in primary elections. [Eu v. San Francisco County Democratic Central Committee, 489 U.S. 214 (1989); *and see* California Democratic Party v. Jones, 530 U.S. 567 (2000)—state cannot require political parties to allow nonparty members to vote in the party's primary election] Similarly, it has held invalid state regulations concerning the selection of delegates to a national party convention and the selection of candidates at such elections. [Cousins v. Wigoda, 419 U.S. 477 (1975); Democratic Party v. LaFolette, 450 U.S. 107 (1981)]

a. **Judicial Candidate Selection**
A state law that permits political parties to choose nominees for state judgeships at state conventions does not violate the freedom of association rights of candidates for judgeships simply because the historic domination of party leaders results in strongly favoring those that they support. *Rationale:* This process "has been a traditional means of choosing party nominees." [New York State Board of Elections v. Lopez Torres, 552 U.S. 196 (2008)]

3. **Limits on Contributions**
A statute limiting election campaign contributions is not tested under a strict scrutiny standard; rather, it must be "closely drawn" to match a "sufficiently important interest"—an intermediate scrutiny standard. [McConnell v. Federal Election Commission, 540 U.S. 93 (2003)]

a. **To Political Candidate**
Laws limiting the amount of money that a person or group may contribute to a political candidate are ***valid***, since the government has a sufficiently important interest in stopping the fact (or appearance) of corruption that may result from large contributions. Moreover, such laws do not substantially restrict freedom of expression or freedom of association (as long as the contributor may spend his money directly to discuss candidates and issues). [Buckley v. Valeo, 424 U.S. 1 (1976)]

1) **Equalizing Large Expenditures**
A law increasing contribution limits for a candidate whose wealthy opponent achieves an advantage by spending personal funds (exceeding $350,000) violates the First Amendment. *Rationale*: Although Congress may raise contribution limits for both candidates in situations of this kind, "penalizing" a self-financing candidate who robustly expresses the right to advocate his own election cannot be justified by leveling opportunities for candidates of different personal wealth. [Davis v. Federal Election Commission, 128 S. Ct. 2759 (2008)]

b. **To Ballot Referendum Committee**
The government may ***not*** limit contributions to a political committee that supports or opposes a ballot referendum (as opposed to one that supports a political candidate). Such a limitation on contributions to influence referendum elections violates the freedoms of speech and association. [Citizens Against Rent Control v. Berkeley, 454 U.S. 290 (1982)]

c. **Disclosure of Contributors or Recipients of Money**
The government may require a political party or committee to disclose the names of contributors or recipients of money to or from the party or committee. However, if the party or committee can show a "reasonable probability" that disclosure will cause harm to the party, committee, or private individuals, they have a First Amendment right to refuse to make such disclosures. [Brown v. Socialist Workers '74 Campaign Committee, 454 U.S. 1122 (1982)]

4. **Limits on Expenditures**
As discussed above, the government ***may*** limit the amount that a person is permitted to ***contribute*** to another's campaign. However, the government ***may not*** limit the amount that

a person ***expends*** on his own campaign. [Buckley v. Valeo, *supra*] Neither may the government limit the amount that a person spends to get a candidate elected, as long as the expenditures are not contributed directly to the candidate nor coordinated with that of the candidate (*i.e.,* as long as the expenditures are independent of the candidate and are not disguised contributions). Thus, corporations, unions, etc., may spend whatever they desire to get a candidate elected. [*See, e.g.,* Citizens United v. Federal Election Commission, 130 S. Ct. 876 (2010)]

5. Compare—Regulations of Core Political Speech

Regulation of "core political speech" must be distinguished from regulation of the process surrounding elections. Regulation of "core political speech" will be upheld only if it passes muster under strict scrutiny. [McIntyre v. Ohio Elections Commission, 514 U.S. 334 (1995)]

a. Prohibiting Any Election Day Campaigning

A state law prohibiting ***any*** campaigning on election day has been held ***invalid*** as applied to a newspaper urging people to vote in a certain way. The right to comment on political issues is one of the most essential elements of free speech, and such conduct by newspapers would pose little danger to conducting elections. [Mills v. Alabama, 384 U.S. 214 (1966)]

1) Compare—Hundred-Foot Limit

A law prohibiting campaign activity within 100 feet of a polling place is ***valid***. Even though the law is content based and concerns an essential element of free speech, it is ***necessary*** to serve the ***compelling*** interest of preventing voter intimidation and election fraud. [Burson v. Freeman, 504 U.S. 191 (1992)]

b. Prohibiting Anonymous Campaign Literature

Laws prohibiting distribution of anonymous campaign literature involve core political speech and have been stricken because they were not narrowly tailored to a compelling state interest. [McIntyre v. Ohio Elections Commission, *supra*; Buckley v. American Constitutional Law Foundation, 525 U.S. 182 (1999)]

c. Prohibiting Judge Candidates from Announcing Their Views

A rule prohibiting candidates for judicial election from announcing their views on disputed legal and political issues violates the First Amendment. This is both a content-based restriction and a restriction on core political speech. In either case, it can be justified only if it is necessary to a compelling state interest. Two state interests were suggested to support the rule here: It is necessary to maintain an impartial judiciary and it is necessary to preserve the appearance of impartiality. The Court found that the rule is "woefully underinclusive" and so is not tailored at all toward achieving these goals. For example, it allows candidates to show bias toward political parties while it prohibits them from stating an opinion about political issues. The Court also found that finding judges without any preconceptions in favor of particular legal views is not a compelling interest because it would be both impossible to find such a person and undesirable. [Republican Party of Minnesota v. White, 536 U.S. 765 (2002)]

d. Distinguishing Political Speech from Candidate Advocacy

An ad concerning a political issue, even if sponsored by a corporation, run during an election campaign will be considered to be core political speech—rather than candidate

advocacy—unless it is susceptible of no reasonable interpretation other than one as an appeal to vote for or against a particular candidate. [Federal Election Commission v. Wisconsin Right to Life, Inc., 551 U.S. 449 (2007)—ad urging voters to contact their senators to encourage them to end a filibuster of federal judicial nominations was core political speech—and could not be banned—even when one of the senators was running for re-election]

C. BAR MEMBERSHIP AND PUBLIC EMPLOYMENT

The government often requires persons who accept government jobs to submit to loyalty oaths and refrain from certain conduct (*e.g.,* campaigning). Such regulations often impact upon the freedom of speech and association.

1. Restraints on Conduct

If a government employer seeks to fire an employee (or to terminate a relationship with an independent contractor) for speech-related conduct, one of two tests will apply, depending on whether the speech involved a matter of public concern. If a matter of public concern is involved, courts must carefully balance the employee's rights as a citizen to comment on a matter of public concern against the government's interest as an employer in the efficient performance of public service. If the speech did not involve a matter of public concern, the courts should give a wide degree of deference to the government employer's judgment concerning whether the speech was disruptive.

Examples: 1) A teacher cannot be fired for writing a letter to a newspaper attacking school board policies. [Pickering v. Board of Education, 391 U.S. 563 (1968)]

2) The Court held invalid the firing of a clerical employee from a constable's office for expressing her disappointment that an assassination attempt on President Reagan did not succeed, because in context the statement could not be understood to be an actual threat or an action that would interfere with the running of the office; rather, the Court viewed it as a commentary on the public issue of the President's policies. [Rankin v. McPherson, 483 U.S. 378 (1987)]

Compare: The Court upheld the firing of an attorney for circulating in the office a petition regarding transfer policies. [Connick v. Myers, 461 U.S. 138 (1983)]

a. Official Duty Exception

A government employer may punish a public employee's speech whenever the speech is made pursuant to the employee's official duties. This is true even if the speech touches on a matter of public concern. [Garcetti v. Ceballos, 547 U.S. 410 (2006)]

Example: P, a district attorney, reviewed a case, concluded that there were irregularities in an underlying search warrant, contacted his supervisors, and suggested dismissing the case. P's supervisors nevertheless proceeded with the prosecution. At a hearing challenging the warrant, P again raised his concerns about the warrant, but the court rejected the challenge. P claims that he was then subjected to retaliatory employment actions because of his testimony and sued his employer for violating his First Amendment rights. P's employer denied undertaking any retaliatory actions, but even if such actions did occur, no First Amendment violation could occur here because the speech was undertaken as part of P's job—a government employer may evaluate an employee based on any writing or speech that the employee undertakes as part of his official duties. [Garcetti v. Ceballos, *supra*]

b. **Participation in Political Campaigns**
The federal government ***may*** prohibit federal executive branch employees from taking an active part in political campaigns. The rationale is twofold: to further nonpartisanship in administration and to protect employees from being coerced to work for the election of their employers. [United Public Workers v. Mitchell, 330 U.S. 75 (1947)]

c. **Bans on Receiving Honoraria**
A provision of the Ethics in Government Act banning government employees from accepting an honorarium for making speeches, writing articles, or making appearances was held to violate the First Amendment when applied to "rank and file" employees. Such a rule deters speech within a broad category of expression by a massive number of potential speakers and thus can be justified only if the government can show that the employees' and their potential audiences' rights are outweighed by the necessary impact the speech would have on actual operation of the government. The government failed to cite any evidence of misconduct related to honoraria by the rank and file employees, and so failed to meet the burden here. [United States v. National Treasury Employees Union, 513 U.S. 454 (1995)]

d. **Patronage**
The First Amendment freedoms of political belief and association forbid the hiring, promotion, transfer, firing, or recall of a public employee because of political party affiliation unless the hiring authority demonstrates that party affiliation is an appropriate requirement for the effective performance of the public office involved, *e.g.,* "policy-making" or "confidential" nature of work. [Rutan v. Republican Party of Illinois, 497 U.S. 62 (1990)]

2. **Loyalty Oaths**
It is permissible for the federal government to require employees and other public officers to take loyalty oaths. However, such oaths will not be upheld if they are overbroad (*i.e.,* prohibit constitutionally protected activities) or are vague so that they have a chilling effect on First Amendment activities.

a. **Overbreadth**

1) **Knowledge of Organization's Aim Required**
Public employment cannot be denied to persons who are simply members of the Communist Party because only knowing membership with "specific intent to further unlawful aims" is unprotected by the First Amendment. [Keyishian v. Board of Regents, 385 U.S. 589 (1967)]

2) **Advocacy of Doctrine Protected**
A political party may not be denied a place on the ballot for refusing to take a loyalty oath that it does not advocate violent overthrow of the government as an

abstract doctrine. The First Amendment forbids "statutes regulating advocacy that are not limited to advocacy of action." [Communist Party v. Whitcomb, 414 U.S. 441 (1974)]

b. **Vagueness**

1) **Oaths Upheld**
Compare the following oaths that have been upheld:

a) **To Support the Constitution**
An oath that required public employees and bar applicants to "support the Constitution of the United States" and the state constitution has been upheld. [Connell v. Higgenbotham, 403 U.S. 207 (1971)]

b) **To Oppose the Overthrow of the Government**
An oath required of all state employees "to oppose the overthrow of the government . . . by force, violence, or by an illegal or unconstitutional method" has also been upheld. The Court read this oath as akin to those requiring the taker simply to "support" the Constitution, "to commit themselves to live by the constitutional processes of our system." Moreover, the oath provided fair notice, because its violation could be punished only by a prosecution for perjury, which required proof of knowing falsity. [Cole v. Richardson, 405 U.S. 676 (1972)]

2) **Oath Not Upheld**
A loyalty oath for public employees that they "promote respect for the flag and . . . reverence for law and order" is void for vagueness, since a refusal to salute the flag on religious grounds might be found in breach thereof. [Baggett v. Bullitt, 377 U.S. 360 (1964)]

3. **Disclosure of Associations**
Forcing disclosure of First Amendment activities as a condition of public employment, bar membership, or other public benefits may have a chilling effect. Thus, the state cannot force every prospective government employee to disclose ***every*** organizational membership. Such a broad disclosure has ***insufficient relation*** to loyalty and professional competence, and the state has available ***less drastic means*** to achieve its purpose. [Shelton v. Tucker, 364 U.S. 479 (1960)] The state may inquire only into those activities that are relevant to the position. If the candidate fails to answer relevant questions, employment may be denied. [Konigsberg v. State Bar of California, 366 U.S. 36 (1961)]

a. **Fifth Amendment Limitation**
If the job candidate refuses to answer on a claim of the privilege against self-incrimination, denial of the job violates the Fifth and Fourteenth Amendments. [Spevack v. Klein, 385 U.S. 511 (1967)] However, if individuals are ordered by appropriate authorities to answer questions "specifically, directly, and narrowly relating to their official duties," and they refuse to do so by claiming the privilege against self-incrimination, they may be denied the job or discharged without violating the Fifth Amendment, if they were given immunity from the use of their answers or the fruits thereof in a criminal prosecution. [Lefkowitz v. Turley, 414 U.S. 70 (1973); Gardner v. Broderick, 392 U.S. 273 (1968)]

4. **Practice of Law**
Regulation of the legal profession may conflict with the freedom of association rights of certain groups because it may impair their ability to band together to advise each other and utilize counsel in their common interest.

a. **Countervailing State Interest Required**
To overcome a group's right to exercise its First Amendment rights, the state must show a substantial interest, such as evidence of objectionable practices occurring or an actual or clearly threatened conflict of interest between lawyer and client.
Examples: 1) The NAACP encouraged, instructed, and offered to represent parents of black children to litigate against school segregation. This was held to be protected political expression. The state's ban on solicitation of legal business was inapplicable because the NAACP sought no monetary gain. [NAACP v. Button, 371 U.S. 415 (1963)]

2) A railroad labor union recommended a specific lawyer to pursue rights of members injured on the job, and also obtained a fee from a lawyer for performing investigative services. This was held protected. [Brotherhood of Railroad Trainmen v. Virginia, 377 U.S. 1 (1964)]

D. SCHOOL SPONSORSHIP OF EXTRACURRICULAR CLUBS

The Supreme Court has held that the compelling interest test does not apply to infringement cases involving public school sponsorship of extracurricular clubs; instead, the test used in limited-public-forum-speech cases applies—sponsorship of associations can be subject to regulation that is ***viewpoint neutral*** and ***reasonably related to a legitimate government interest.*** (*See* XX.B.2.c.2), *supra.*)
Example: A public law school officially recognized student groups and gave them funding from mandatory student activity fees only if the groups accepted all students regardless of their "status or beliefs" (*i.e.,* the "all comers" policy). A group that required students to sign a statement of faith based on Christian beliefs and denied membership to persons who supported homosexuality and premarital sex sought an exemption from the "all comers" policy and was denied. The group sued the school, claiming that the policy violated members' associational rights. *Held:* The "all comers" policy is constitutional. It is viewpoint neutral in that it draws no distinctions on point of view. Moreover, it is reasonably related to school purposes such as encouraging tolerance and providing leadership, educational, and social opportunities to all students. [Christian Legal Society v. Martinez, XX.B.2.c.2), *supra*]

XXII. FREEDOM OF RELIGION

A. CONSTITUTIONAL PROVISION

The First Amendment provides "Congress shall make no law respecting an establishment of religion, or prohibiting the free exercise thereof."

B. APPLICABILITY TO THE STATES

Both the Establishment and Free Exercise Clauses of the First Amendment apply to the states under the Fourteenth Amendment.

C. FREE EXERCISE CLAUSE

1. No Punishment of Beliefs

The Free Exercise Clause prohibits the government from punishing (denying benefits to, or imposing burdens on) someone on the basis of the person's ***religious beliefs***. It is sometimes said that the government can engage in such activity only if it is necessary to achieve a compelling interest; sometimes the rule is stated as a total prohibition of such government actions. In any case, the Supreme Court has never found an interest that was so "compelling" that it would justify punishing a religious belief.

a. What Constitutes Religious Belief?

The Supreme Court has not defined what constitutes a religious belief. However, it has made clear that religious belief does not require recognition of a supreme being [Torcaso v. Watkins, 367 U.S. 488 (1961)], and need not arise from a traditional, or even an organized, religion [*see* Frazee v. Illinois Department of Employment Security, 489 U.S. 829 (1989)]. One possible definition is that the "belief must occupy a place in the believer's life parallel to that occupied by orthodox religious beliefs." [United States v. Seeger, 380 U.S. 163 (1965)—interpreting statutory, rather than constitutional, provision] In any case, the Court has never held an asserted religious belief to be not religious for First Amendment purposes.

1) Courts May Not Find Religious Beliefs to Be False

The courts may not declare a religious belief to be "false." For example, if a person says he talked to God and that God said the person should solicit money, he cannot be found guilty of fraud on the basis that God never made such a statement. However, the court may determine whether the person is sincerely asserting a belief in the divine statement. [United States v. Ballard, 322 U.S. 78 (1944), *as described in* Employment Division v. Smith, 494 U.S. 872 (1990)]

b. Religious Oaths for Governmental Jobs Prohibited

The ***federal*** government may not require any federal office holder or employee to take an oath based on a religious belief as a condition for receiving the federal office or job, because such a requirement is prohibited by Article VI of the Constitution. State and local governments are prohibited from requiring such oaths by the Free Exercise Clause. [Torcaso v. Watkins, *supra*]

c. States May Not Exclude Clerics from Public Office

A state may not exclude clerics (persons who hold an office or official position in a religious organization) from bcing elected to the state legislature, or from other governmental positions, because that exclusion would impose a disability on these persons based upon the nature of their religious views and their religious status. [McDaniel v. Paty, 435 U.S. 618 (1978)]

2. No Punishment of Religious Conduct Solely Because It Is Religious

The Supreme Court has stated that the Free Exercise Clause prohibits the government from punishing conduct merely because it is religious or displays religious belief (*e.g.*, the state cannot ban the use of peyote only when used in religious ceremonies). [Employment Division v. Smith, *supra*—dicta] A law that is designed to suppress actions only because the actions are religiously motivated is not a neutral law of general applicability. Such a law will be invalid unless it is necessary to promote a compelling interest.

Example: A city law that prohibited the precise type of animal slaughter used in the ritual of a particular religious sect violated the Free Exercise Clause because the Court found that the law was designed solely to exclude the religious sect from the city. The law was not a neutral law of general applicability; nor was the law necessary to promote a compelling interest. [Church of the Lukumi Babalu Aye, Inc. v. Hialeah, 508 U.S. 520 (1993)]

Compare: A state law that excluded pursuit of a degree in ***devotional theology*** from a college scholarship program for all students did ***not*** violate the Free Exercise Clause. Although a school ***could*** provide such scholarships without violating the Establishment Clause (*see infra*), the Free Exercise Clause does not require such scholarships. The exclusion from scholarship eligibility does not show animus toward religion, but rather merely reflects a decision not to fund this activity. Moreover, the burden that the exclusion imposes on religion is modest, and there is substantial historical support against using tax funds to support the ministry. [Locke v. Davey, 540 U.S. 712 (2004)]

3. States Can Regulate General Conduct—Criminal Laws and Other Regulations

Of course, states may prohibit or regulate conduct in general, and this is true even if the prohibition or regulation happens to interfere with a person's religious practices. The Free Exercise Clause cannot be used to challenge a law of general applicability unless it can be shown that the law was motivated by a desire to interfere with religion. [Employment Division v. Smith, *supra*]

a. Generally No Exemptions Required

The Free Exercise Clause does not require exemptions from criminal laws or other governmental regulations for a person whose religious beliefs prevent him from conforming his behavior to the requirements of the law. In other words, a law that regulates the conduct of all persons can be applied to prohibit the conduct of a person despite the fact that his religious beliefs prevent him from complying with the law.

b. Examples

The Supreme Court has held that no religious exemption was required from the following religiously neutral regulations, even though certain groups objected because the regulation interfered with conduct inspired by sincerely held religious beliefs:

1) Prohibition against ***use of peyote*** [Employment Division v. Smith, *supra*—challenged by person whose religious beliefs require use of peyote during religious ceremony];

2) ***Denial of tax exempt status to schools that discriminate*** on the basis of race [Bob Jones University v. United States, 461 U.S. 574 (1983)—challenged by religious school whose tenets require certain separations of races];

3) Requirement that employers comply with ***federal minimum wage laws*** [Tony and Susan Alamo Foundation v. Secretary of Labor, 471 U.S. 290 (1985)—challenged by employer that argued minimum wages interfere with members' religious desires to work without compensation];

4) Requirement that employers pay ***Social Security taxes*** [United States v. Lee, 455 U.S. 252 (1982)—challenged by person whose religious beliefs prohibited payment and receipt of Social Security type payments]; and

5) ***Sales and use taxes*** [Jimmy Swaggart Ministries v. Board of Equalization of California, 493 U.S. 378 (1990)—challenged as applied to sales of goods and literature by religious group].

4. Unemployment Compensation Cases—Some Exemptions Required

Many state unemployment compensation programs make payments only to persons who are involuntarily unemployed (*i.e.,* were fired or laid off rather than resigned), and who are available for work (*i.e.,* willing to accept offered employment). Here, however, unlike other areas of regulation, the Supreme Court has held that the states must grant religious exemptions. Thus, if a person resigns from a job or refuses to accept a job because it conflicts with her religious beliefs, the state must pay her unemployment compensation if she is otherwise entitled.

Examples: 1) A state cannot deny unemployment compensation merely because the applicant quit a job rather than work on a "holy day" on which religious beliefs forbid work. [Sherbert v. Verner, 374 U.S. 398 (1963)]

2) A state cannot deny unemployment compensation merely because the applicant quit his job rather than work on production of military equipment after his factory converted from nonmilitary to military production. [Thomas v. Review Board, 450 U.S. 707 (1981)]

a. Need Not Belong to Formal Religious Organization

A person does not have to be a member of a formal religious organization to receive the above exemptions from unemployment compensation requirements. All that is required is that the person ***sincerely hold*** religious beliefs that prevent him from working on a certain day or on military products. [Frazee v. Illinois Department of Employment Security, 1.a., *supra*]

b. Limitation—Criminal Prohibitions

The unemployment compensation cases do not give individuals a right to disregard criminal laws due to their religious beliefs. Thus, unemployment compensation laws may disqualify persons fired for "misconduct" (which includes any violation of criminal law).

Example: A person was fired from his job as a counselor at a private drug abuse clinic when it was discovered that he used peyote (at times when he was not at work) for religious reasons. All use of peyote was illegal in the state (even if the use was part of a religious ceremony). The Supreme Court held that unemployment compensation could properly be denied here. [Employment Division v. Smith, *supra*]

5. Right of Amish Not to Educate Children

The Supreme Court has required an exemption for the Amish from a neutral law that required school attendance until age 16, because a fundamental tenet of Amish religion forbids secondary education. The Court found that the Amish are productive and law-abiding, and ruled that the right to educate one's children (*see* XIX.B.6., *supra*) and the Free Exercise Clause outweighed the state's interest here. [Wisconsin v. Yoder, 406 U.S. 205 (1972)]

D. ESTABLISHMENT CLAUSE

The Establishment Clause prohibits laws respecting the establishment of religion.

1. Sect Preference

If a law or government program includes a preference for some religious sects over others, it will almost certainly be held invalid because the compelling interest test applies: To be valid, the law or program must be ***narrowly tailored*** to promote a ***compelling interest***.

Example: A state law created a public school district whose boundaries were intentionally set to match the boundaries of a particular Jewish neighborhood (so that several handicapped students would not have to be sent outside their neighborhood to attend special education classes that the state required and which the students' private school could not adequately provide). The Supreme Court found the law unconstitutional. [Board of Education v. Grumet, 512 U.S. 687 (1994)]

2. No Sect Preference—*Lemon* Test

If government action does not involve a sect preference, the compelling interest test is not used; instead, the government action will be valid under the Establishment Clause if it:

(i) Has a ***secular purpose***;

(ii) Has a ***primary effect*** that neither advances nor inhibits religion; ***and***

(iii) Does not produce ***excessive government entanglement*** with religion.

[Lemon v. Kurtzman, 403 U.S. 602 (1971)—the *"Lemon"* test] (Note that some recent cases have simply focused on whether the action is neutral as between the religious and nonreligious when there is no endorsement of a particular religion.) The Establishment Clause cases can be grouped into three categories: (i) a limited group of cases unconnected to financial aid or education; (ii) cases involving financial aid to religiously affiliated institutions; and (iii) cases concerning religious activities in public schools. The details regarding the Supreme Court rulings are given below.

a. Cases Unconnected to Financial Aid or Education

In cases unconnected to financial aid or education, a good rule of thumb is that a law favoring or burdening religion or a specific religious group in particular will be invalid, but a law favoring or burdening a larger segment of society that happens to include religious groups will be upheld.

Example: The government may not delegate governmental power to religious organizations because such action would involve excessive governmental entanglement. [Larkin v. Grendel's Den, Inc., 459 U.S. 116 (1982)—statute gave church-affiliated schools power to veto nearby liquor licenses]

Compare: The IRS may deny tax exemptions claimed for religious donations when the sums were paid to the church ***in exchange for services*** (*e.g.*, classes) since this is a general rule that applies to all charities. [Hernandez v. Commissioner of Internal Revenue, 490 U.S. 680 (1989)]

1) State Legislature Can Employ a Chaplain

Despite the principle of separation of church and state, the Court has held that a

state legislature could employ a chaplain and begin each legislative day with a prayer. [Marsh v. Chambers, 463 U.S. 783 (1983)] This decision was based on the history of legislative prayer in America; it does not modify the "Religious Activities in Public Schools" rulings examined below.

2) Displays of Ten Commandments on Public Property

If a display of the Ten Commandments is shown to have a ***"predominantly religious purpose,"*** it violates the Establishment Clause; otherwise, the Ten Commandments may be displayed. [McCreary County v. ACLU, 545 U.S. 844 (2005)]

Example: Two counties posted large copies of the Ten Commandments in their courthouses. After complaints based on the Establishment Clause, each county adopted a resolution calling for a more extensive exhibit showing that the Commandments are Kentucky's "precedent legal code" and noting the state legislature's acknowledgment of Christ as the "Prince of Ethics." The displays were then modified to add smaller copies of other historic texts with religious references (*e.g.,* the "endowed by their creator" clause of the Declaration of Independence). A district court found the displays invalid under the *Lemon* test because they lacked any secular purpose. The counties again modified the displays—without any guiding resolutions—to include eight equally sized items around the Ten Commandments (including the Bill of Rights and a picture of Lady Justice) and the title "Foundations of American Law and Government." The ACLU moved to enjoin these displays, claiming that their purpose was still religious rather than secular. Given the displays' history, the Supreme Court agreed, finding that the taint from the earlier displays had not been dissipated even though, on their faces, the most current displays appeared not to have a religious purpose. [McCreary County v. ACLU, *supra*]

Compare: A monument of the Ten Commandments on a 22-acre State Capitol ground displaying 17 monuments and 21 historical markers commemorating the state's "people, ideals, and events that compose its identity" communicated not only a religious message but also a secular moral message, and its setting suggested that the state intended the secular message to predominate. [Van Orden v. Perry, 545 U.S. 677 (2005)]

3) Some Holiday Displays Are Permissible

If the ***government*** maintains a holiday-Christmastime display that does not appear to endorse religion, the display will survive review under the three-part Establishment Clause test. If a government's holiday display includes religious symbols (*e.g.,* a nativity scene or a menorah) as well as other holiday decorations (*e.g.,* a Christmas tree or a Santa Claus figure), the courts will hold that the display: (i) has a secular purpose (based on the history of government recognition of holidays); (ii) has a primary nonreligious effect (it does not endorse religion); and (iii) does not create excessive entanglement between government and religion. If the display includes only the religious symbols (*e.g.,* only a nativity scene), it will violate the

Establishment Clause because it has a religious effect (it "endorses" religion). [County of Allegheny v. ACLU, 492 U.S. 573 (1989)]

4) **Absolute Right Not to Work on a Sabbath Impermissible**
The state may not force employers to grant all employees an absolute right to refrain from working on their sabbath, because the primary effect of such a law is to advance religion. [Estate of Thornton v. Caldor, 472 U.S. 703 (1985)] However, a state may require employers to make reasonable efforts to accommodate employee religious practices.

5) **Exemptions from Antidiscrimination Laws**
The federal government may exempt religious organizations from the federal statutory prohibition against discrimination in employment on the basis of religion, at least regarding their nonprofit activities. Thus, a janitor can be discharged from his employment at a gymnasium owned by a religious organization (which was open to the public and run as a nonprofit facility) because he was not a member of that religious organization. [Corporation of the Presiding Bishop of the Church of Jesus Christ of Latter-Day Saints v. Amos, 483 U.S. 327 (1987)]

b. **Cases Involving Financial Benefits to Church-Related Institutions**
A statute authorizing governmental aid to a religiously affiliated institution (hospital, school, etc.) must be tested under the general test detailed above (secular purpose, primary effect, and excessive entanglement). However, the Supreme Court applies these tests with greater strictness when the government aid is going to a religiously affiliated grade school or high school than it does when the aid is going to another type of religiously affiliated institution (such as a college or hospital).

1) **Recipient-Based Aid**
The government may give aid in the form of financial assistance to a defined class of persons as long as the class is defined without reference to religion or religious criteria. Such a program is valid even if persons who receive the financial assistance are thereby enabled to attend a religiously affiliated school.

Examples: 1) The Supreme Court upheld a state program that made education subsidy payments directly to a blind or disabled student even though a student used his aid to study at a Christian college for the purpose of becoming a pastor or missionary. The class of persons who received the aid was defined without reference to any religious criteria; only an incidental benefit would go to the religiously affiliated college or vocational training institution. The aid program thus passed review under the purpose, effect, and entanglement tests. [Witters v. Washington Department of Services, 474 U.S. 481 (1986)]

2) The Court held that the Establishment Clause would not prevent a public school district from paying for a sign language interpreter for a deaf student at a religious high school under a religiously neutral program of aid to all handicapped school children in both public and private schools. [Zobrest v. Catalina Foothills School District, 509 U.S. 1 (1993)]

3) The Supreme Court upheld a program that provided tuition vouchers to parents of poor children in kindergarten through the eighth grade which could be used to pay for attending participating public or private schools of their parents' choice, even though a very high percentage of the recipients chose to attend religiously affiliated schools. The program was part of a larger program that also created publicly funded magnet schools and community schools that were independent from the local school district. The Court found that the program did not have the purpose or effect of advancing religion. Its purpose was secular—to provide educational assistance to poor children in a failing public school system. Its primary effect was to provide poor children with funds to attend other schools. Any benefit to the religious schools resulted from parents choosing to send their children to those schools and was not attributable to the government. [Zelman v. Simmons-Harris, 536 U.S. 639 (2002)]

a) **Compare—Tuition Tax Deductions or Credits Limited to Religious School Tuition**

A state may not use a system of statutory grants, tax credits, or tax deductions to reimburse parents or students for tuition paid ***only to religiously affiliated schools***. However, a tax deduction to all students or parents based on the actual expenditures for attending any public or private school (including religious schools) has been upheld. [Mueller v. Allen, 463 U.S. 388 (1983)]

It would appear that a valid tax deduction statute must allow a deduction for: (i) expenditures for public as well as private schools; and (ii) some expenditures other than tuition (such as expenditures for school supplies or books) so that public school students or their parents may benefit from the deduction.

2) **Aid to Colleges, Hospitals, Etc.**

The Court will uphold a government grant of aid to the secular activity of a religiously affiliated hospital or college (such as a grant to build a new hospital ward or a laboratory-classroom building) as long as the government program requires that the aid be used only for ***nonreligious purposes***, and the recipient so agrees in good faith. [Tilton v. Richardson, 403 U.S. 672 (1971); Bradfield v. Roberts, 175 U.S. 291 (1899)]

Example: The Adolescent Family Life Act—which provides for grants of government funds to a variety of public and private (including religiously affiliated) agencies to provide counseling and educational services to young people regarding sexual activity—has been upheld. The Act has a secular purpose (dealing with problems of teenage pregnancy). The Act does not on its face advance religion because a religiously affiliated organization could contractually be required to use the funds for nonreligious counseling. And the Act does not give rise to excessive entanglement because there is no reason to assume that a significant percentage of the funds would be granted to pervasively sectarian institutions. [Bowen v. Kendrick, 487 U.S. 589 (1988)]

3) Aid to Religiously Affiliated Grade Schools or High Schools

Programs of aid to these institutions are subject to the same three-part test as are all other laws under the Establishment Clause. All government programs examined by the Supreme Court which provide aid for religiously affiliated grade schools or high schools have been found to have a "secular purpose." However, if significant aid is given to the religious school, the program may be deemed to have a primary effect that advances religion. If the government program has detailed administrative or legislative regulations that are designed to ensure that the aid does not result in a primary effect of advancing religion, the law may be stricken as giving rise to an excessive entanglement between government and religion.

a) Aid Upheld

The Supreme Court has upheld state programs that:

(1) Provide state-approved ***textbooks*** to ***all*** students [Board of Education v. Allen, 392 U.S. 236 (1968)] (but note that the state may not loan textbooks to students attending schools that discriminate on the basis of race, since this would violate the Fourteenth Amendment [Norwood v. Harrison, 413 U.S. 455 (1973)]);

(2) Lend religiously neutral instructional materials (*e.g.*, library books, computers) to parochial schools as well as to public and other nonprofit private schools, where the program did not define recipients by reference to religion and the ***challenger did not prove*** that the neutral aid was used for religious indoctrination. [Mitchell v. Helms, 530 U.S. 793 (2000), *overruling* Meek v. Pittenger, 421 U.S. 349 (1975)];

(3) Provide ***transportation to and from school*** to ***all*** students [Everson v. Board of Education, 330 U.S. 1 (1947)];

(4) Reimburse private schools for the expenses of ***compiling state-required data***, such as student attendance records, or administering and grading ***standardized*** state educational achievement tests [Committee for Public Education and Religious Liberty v. Regan, 444 U.S. 646 (1980)]; and

(5) Provide ***"auxiliary services"*** (*e.g.*, remedial education, guidance, or job counseling) to all disadvantaged children at their school, including children at parochial schools [Agostini v. Felton, 521 U.S. 203 (1997)].

b) Aid Invalidated

The Supreme Court has struck down the following state programs, either because they had a primary effect that advanced religion or because they involved excessive entanglement between government and religion:

(1) Programs paying a portion of private school ***teachers' salaries*** (for their secular classes), since the primary effect would be to advance religion and a system to ensure that the money/teachers not be used for religious purposes would involve excessive entanglements. [Lemon v. Kurtzman, 2., *supra*]; and

(2) Programs reimbursing private schools for ***writing achievement tests*** (this would have the primary effect of advancing religion since the schools could write tests advancing their religious mission) [Levitt v. Community for Public Education, 413 U.S. 472 (1973)].

4) Tax Exemption for Religious, Charitable, or Educational Property

An exemption from property taxation for "real or personal property used exclusively for religious, educational, or charitable purposes" does not violate the Establishment Clause. Neither the purpose nor the effect of such an exemption is the advancement or the inhibition of religion, and it constitutes neither sponsorship nor hostility, nor excessive government entanglement with religion. The "government does not transfer part of its revenue to churches but simply abstains from demanding that the church support the state . . . ." [Walz v. Tax Commission, 397 U.S. 664 (1970)]

5) Tax Exemption Available Only to Religions

Although religious schools or religious associations may be included in tax exemptions available to a variety of secular and religious organizations, a tax exemption that is available only for religious organizations or religious activities violates the Establishment Clause. [Texas Monthly, Inc. v. Bullock, 489 U.S. 1 (1989)—an exemption from the sales and use tax for religious magazines or books (but no other publications) violates the Establishment Clause]

c. Religious Activities in Public Schools

1) Prayer and Bible Reading

Prayer and Bible reading in school are invalid as establishments of religion. [Engel v. Vitale, 370 U.S. 421 (1962); Abington School District v. Schempp, 374 U.S. 203 (1963)] It does not matter whether participation is voluntary or involuntary, and neither does it matter that the prayer period is designated as a period of silent prayer or meditation. [Wallace v. Jaffree, 472 U.S. 38 (1985)] This rule extends to prohibit public school officials from having clerics give invocation and benediction prayers at graduation ceremonies. [Lee v. Weisman, 505 U.S. 577 (1992)] Similarly, a school policy authorizing students to elect whether to have a student invocation before varsity games, to select a student to deliver it, and to decide its content ***violates*** the Establishment Clause. Unlike student speeches at an open public forum (*see* 4), below), this policy's purpose is to encourage religious messages. [Santa Fe Independent School District v. Doe, 530 U.S. 290 (2000)]

2) Posting Ten Commandments in Classroom Is Invalid

Posting the Ten Commandments on the walls of public school classrooms plainly serves a religious purpose and is invalid, despite the legislature's statement that it was for a secular purpose. [Stone v. Graham, 449 U.S. 39 (1980)]

3) Released-Time Programs

a) In Public School Building

Programs in which regular classes end an hour early one day a week and

religious instruction is given in public school classrooms to students who request it are invalid. [McCollum v. Board of Education, 333 U.S. 203 (1948)]

b) Nonpublic Building Used

Programs in which participating children go to religious classes conducted at religious centers away from the public school do not violate the Establishment Clause. [Zorach v. Clauson, 343 U.S. 306 (1952)]

4) Accommodation of Religious Students—On-Campus Meetings

As discussed at XX.B.1.c., *supra*, under the Free Speech Clause, if a public school allows members of the public and private organizations to use school property when classes are not in session, it cannot deny a religious organization permission to use the property for meetings merely because religious topics will be discussed. Such an "equal access rule" does not violate the Establishment Clause because the primary purpose of such programs is secular (to accommodate all interests), people are not likely to assume that the government endorses the religious ideas discussed, and there is no excessive government entanglement, at least where the meetings are not run by school personnel. [Good News Club v. Milford Central School, 533 U.S. 98 (2001)]

5) Curriculum Controls

A government statute or regulation that modifies a public school curriculum will violate the Establishment Clause if it fails the secular purpose test, primary effect test, or excessive government entanglement test.

Example: A state statute that prohibited the teaching of human biological evolution in the state's public schools was held to violate the Establishment Clause because the Supreme Court found that the legislature had a religious purpose for enacting the statute. [Epperson v. Arkansas, 393 U.S. 97 (1968)] Similarly, the Court invalidated a state statute that prohibited instruction regarding "evolution science" (the theory of human biological evolution) in the public schools unless that instruction was accompanied by instruction regarding "creation science," because the Court found that the legislature enacted this statute for the purpose of promoting religion. [Edwards v. Aguillard, 482 U.S. 578 (1987)]

ESSAY EXAM QUESTIONS

INTRODUCTORY NOTE

The essay questions that follow have been selected to provide you with an opportunity to experience how the substantive law you have been reviewing may be tested in the hypothetical essay examination question context. These sample essay questions are a valuable self-diagnostic tool designed to enable you to enhance your issue-spotting ability and practice your exam writing skills.

It is suggested that you approach each question as though under actual examination conditions. The time allowed for each question is 60 minutes. You should spend 15 to 20 minutes spotting issues, underlining key facts and phrases, jotting notes in the margins, and outlining your answer. ***If*** you organize your thoughts well, 40 minutes will be more than adequate for writing them down. Should you prefer to forgo the actual writing involved on these questions, be sure to give yourself no more time for issue-spotting than you would on the actual examination.

The BARBRI technique for writing a well-organized essay answer is to (i) spot the issues in a question and then (ii) analyze and discuss each issue using the "CIRAC" method:

C — State your ***conclusion*** first. (In other words, you must think through your answer ***before*** you start writing.)
I — State the ***issue*** involved.
R — Give the ***rule(s)*** of law involved.
A — ***Apply*** the rule(s) of law to the facts.
C — Finally, restate your ***conclusion***.

After completing (or outlining) your own analysis of each question, compare it with the BARBRI model answer provided herein. A passing answer does ***not*** have to match the model one, but it should cover most of the issues presented and the law discussed and should ***apply the law to the facts*** of the question. Use of the CIRAC method results in the best answer you can write.

EXAM QUESTION NO. 1

Sierra Toxics, Inc. ("Sierra"), is a privately owned company engaged in the business of disposing of toxic waste generated by chemical and pharmaceutical plants. Sierra operates pursuant to a license issued by the Commissioner of Ecological Preservation of the state of Alpha. This license authorizes Sierra to contract with such plants to provide the following services: (i) collection of toxic waste at the plant site; and (ii) transportation of that waste to Sierra's disposal station, which is located in Alpha, three miles from the border with the state of Beta.

Pursuant to the authority granted by its license, for the past 10 years Sierra has contracted to provide services to plants in Alpha, and, a few years ago, expanded its business to serve plants just across the border in Beta. The Beta plants that contract with Sierra dispose of approximately one-half their toxic waste output through that company and the remainder of their waste through disposal companies located in Beta.

Shortly after Sierra extended its services to the Beta plants, the residents of the town in which Sierra's disposal station is situated became alarmed at the amount of toxic waste stored there. These residents were concerned about the proximity of such toxic waste, both to their homes and to the reservoir located in their town which supplies water to households in the immediate surrounding area.

The residents petitioned the Commissioner of Ecological Preservation to close Sierra's disposal station. Sierra objected. The Commissioner held an open hearing on the matter at which numerous witnesses testified. After that hearing, the Commissioner resolved the dispute by issuing an order that, effective immediately, use of Sierra's disposal station would be limited to toxic waste removed from chemical and pharmaceutical plants in Alpha only. The Beta plants were barred from disposing of their toxic waste through Sierra.

Both Sierra and the state of Beta have filed suit against the Alpha Commissioner of Ecological Preservation, seeking to rescind that order. The two lawsuits have been consolidated for trial before the judge whom you serve as law clerk. The judge has asked you to prepare a memorandum identifying the claims raised and the defenses asserted, and analyzing the legal bases for all such claims and defenses.

Prepare the memorandum.

EXAM QUESTION NO. 2

State University has had a nationally prominent football program for many years. A recent investigation by the American Athletic Association ("AAA"), consisting of public and private educational institutions nationwide, including State University, uncovered serious violations of the rules and regulations of the Association. These included recruiting infractions which implicated the head football coach. After a hearing conducted by the Association in which State University participated and in which Coach was a witness, the Association placed State University on probation for two years. It ordered that further sanctions will be imposed unless Coach is suspended for the probationary period. The president of State University has notified Coach of his intent to impose the required suspension.

As part of his fight against the suspension, Coach granted an interview to the sports editor of the student newspaper in which he disputed the Association's charges. The president has directed the paper not to publish the resulting article, and the editorial staff has complied.

Frustrated by his inability to tell his side of the story and threatened by loss of his job, Coach has retained your law firm to institute appropriate action.

Prepare a legal memorandum setting forth Coach's causes of action, the legal basis for each, and the defenses to be anticipated.

EXAM QUESTION NO. 3

A bill has been introduced in the legislature of the state of Uphoria which would limit appointment of members of the state police force to male citizens of the United States who are over the age of 20 years.

Senator Strate is chairman of the committee to which this bill has been referred, and he requires a carefully written summary analyzing the legal principles implicated by this bill. He retains you to prepare this summary in clear and concise language so that it may be used by members of his committee in their consideration of the merits of the bill.

Comply with the senator's request.

EXAM QUESTION NO. 4

Irma LaTouce and Lester DeJacques were employed as dancers at a Fun City cocktail lounge. Both dancers received a weekly salary plus commissions on drinks purchased for them by customers between performances. Police officers observed Irma and Lester socializing with lounge patrons and brought charges against them under a local ordinance which provided:

> Entertainers in business premises where alcoholic beverages are sold are prohibited from mingling with customers.

The stated purpose of the ordinance was to prevent disorderly conduct in premises where liquor is sold, to encourage temperance, and to discourage opportunities for the solicitation of prostitution or engaging in any other immoral activity.

At the trial before the local municipal court, the dancers testified that the commissions were earned for socializing with the clientele, which involved conversation and casual companionship with men and women who patronized the club. They both admitted that the main purpose of this activity was to get the customers to buy more drinks. It was stipulated that there had been no disorderly conduct in the lounge and that neither defendant had solicited any act of prostitution or engaged in any other immoral activity. The court found both dancers guilty as charged and imposed a fine as provided in the ordinance.

Irma and Lester have now consulted you. They desire to appeal their convictions. Prepare a brief in support of Irma and Lester as petitioners.

ANSWERS TO ESSAY EXAM QUESTIONS

ANSWER TO EXAM QUESTION NO. 1

To: Judge
From: Law Clerk
Re: Sierra Toxics

Commerce Clause: The Commissioner of Ecological Preservation's ("CEP's") order violates the Commerce Clause. At issue is whether a state may prohibit hazardous waste disposal facilities within the state from accepting hazardous wastes from outside the state.

The Commerce Clause gives Congress plenary power to regulate commerce among the states. This power is not exclusive; the states may also regulate commerce. However, state regulation that discriminates against interstate commerce usually will be stricken as violating the Commerce Clause unless the regulation is necessary to achieve an important state interest.

Here, the CEP's order clearly discriminates against interstate commerce since it prohibits disposal of out-of-state wastes but allows disposal of wastes generated within the state. The Commission would no doubt argue that the state's interest in the safety of residents around Sierra's disposal facility necessitates the limitation, but this argument will fail. A nondiscriminatory regulation (*e.g.,* limiting the amount of hazardous waste that may be disposed of at Sierra's plant, regardless of where the hazardous waste was generated) could provide the same protection as the prohibition here. Thus, the regulation discriminates against interstate commerce without valid justification and so violates the Commerce Clause.

Contracts Clause: The order of the CEP might also violate the Contracts Clause. At issue is whether a state order that prohibits a waste disposal facility from accepting wastes from certain customers violates the Contracts Clause.

The Contracts Clause generally prohibits states from acting to retroactively and substantially impair existing contracts rights. However, the bar is not absolute; even if a state act substantially impairs existing contract rights it still will be upheld if the impairment serves an important public interest and the law is reasonable and narrowly tailored to promote that interest.

Here, it is not clear whether the CEP's order substantially impairs any existing contract rights, although we are told that the order prohibits Sierra from accepting hazardous wastes from outside the state, and that Sierra has contracted with out-of-state customers in the past, we are not told whether Sierra has any continuing contracts that would be impaired by the CEP's order. Assuming such contracts exist, the order would violate the Contracts Clause. Since the CEP is a state agency, there is action by the state. And while safeguarding the community from toxic wastes is clearly an important interest, as discussed above the order here is not reasonable to deal with the problem because it does nothing to prevent wastes generated within the state from jeopardizing the community's safety. Accordingly, the order violates the Contracts Clause.

Privileges and Immunities Clause of Article IV: The CEP order might violate the Privileges and Immunities Clause of Article IV, at least with respect to the citizens of state Beta. At issue is whether a state may prohibit nonresidents from contracting for commercial services in the state.

The Privileges and Immunities Clause of Article IV prohibits states from discriminating against nonresidents in matters concerning fundamental rights, which include important commercial activities and civil liberties. However, even if a state discriminates against nonresidents, the discrimination can be upheld if the state has a substantial justification for the different treatment and there are no less

restrictive means to accomplish the state's goal. In any case, the Privileges and Immunities Clause is available only to natural persons; corporations cannot take advantage of its protections.

Here, we are not told whether any of Sierra's customers are natural persons; they might all be corporations. If Beta is allowed to represent the interests of natural persons who are being discriminated against by the CEP's order, the order probably violates the Privileges and Immunities Clause. Contracting for commercial waste disposal services probably is an important commercial activity, and the CEP's order discriminates against nonresidents by completely prohibiting them from contracting on an equal basis with residents of Alpha. And while there probably is substantial justification for the order (to protect the community from hazardous wastes), as discussed above, the order is not the least restrictive means of protecting that interest. Thus, the order could violate the Privileges and Immunities Clause of Article IV.

Procedural Due Process: Finally, it could be argued that Sierra was denied its right to procedural due process. At issue is whether Sierra had an adequate opportunity to present its case.

The Due Process Clause of the Fifth Amendment, made applicable to the states through the Fourteenth Amendment, provides that the government shall not take a person's life, liberty, or property without due process of law. Due process contemplates fair procedures, which requires at least an opportunity to present objections to the proposed action and a fair and neutral decisionmaker. The timing and scope of the hearing due depend on the circumstances of the deprivation. In most cases, the person being deprived of life, liberty, or property should receive notice of the government's proposed action and have an opportunity to respond before the deprivation.

Here, the CEP has limited Sierra's right to contract, a liberty interest. The facts state that a public hearing was held, but we are not told whether Sierra was given individual notice of the meeting or was given an opportunity to speak. Presumably, sufficient notice and an opportunity to respond were given, and thus Sierra was afforded adequate procedural due process.

ANSWER TO EXAM QUESTION NO. 2

To: Partner
From: Associate
Re: Coach's Causes of Action

Coach v. AAA: AAA has informed State University that it will be subject to sanctions unless Coach is suspended for two years. The first issue is whether the action of AAA constitutes state action.

To find state action, an actor must perform public functions or have significant state involvement. It appears, under this standard, that AAA is not a state actor; regulating sports at public and private institutions nationwide is not a function traditionally reserved to the states and neither are its activities so involved with the state so as to rise to the level of state action. [*Compare:* Brentwood Academy v. Tennessee Secondary School Athletic Association, 531 U.S. 288 (2001)—state action found where, among other things, "private" regulating body operated in a single state, was made up mostly of public school officials, and met during school hours]

Furthermore, AAA has given State University a choice of what to do, albeit a coercive choice. State University does not have to suspend Coach; it could choose to accept further sanctions and not suspend Coach. Therefore, no causes of action will lie against AAA because it merely made findings and left it to State University to decide what actions to take. [*See* National Collegiate Athletic Association v. Tarkanian, 488 U.S. 179 (1988)]

Coach v. State University: The actions of State University through its president, however, do constitute state action. The university is an institution of the state, as indicated by its name, and the president is a state actor. The question, then, is what constitutional rights Coach has, and whether these rights were infringed by the university.

We must ascertain whether Coach was removable for cause. An employee removable only for cause has a property interest in his job, and thus is entitled to due process before the state deprives him of his job.

Assuming Coach is removable only for cause, due process requires that he be given notice of the charges against him, as well as a pretermination opportunity to respond to the charges. An evidentiary hearing regarding the termination decision must be provided either before or after the termination, with reinstatement if he prevails. If no cause is required for removal, Coach is an employee at will and is not due any process before or after termination.

We should move to secure the above procedural safeguards for Coach. While Coach participated in the AAA hearing, he appeared only as a witness, and not as a party. Coach is entitled to a more substantial opportunity to respond to the charges against him. Coach has received notice of the decision to suspend him. He may respond to the president's notification of suspension and is entitled to an evidentiary hearing regarding his termination.

The university may assert that a two-year suspension is not the same as a termination. However, our position is that a two-year loss of job and salary is an infringement of Coach's property rights serious enough to warrant a hearing.

Should we bring this claim, the university may institute a defense of ripeness. They could claim that no action has been taken against Coach and that his claim is premature. However, an action is ripe for review when there is the immediate threat of harm. Here, the president has notified Coach of its intent to suspend him. Thus, Coach's claim will not fail for lack of ripeness.

Coach's First Amendment claim: Coach feels silenced by the refusal of the school newspaper to print the views he expressed in his interview. However, Coach's constitutional rights probably have not been violated. First, the contents of a school-funded newspaper can be regulated because the Supreme Court has found that such papers are not public forums, but merely are educational devices.

Even if the newspaper were a public forum, it would not give rise to a cause of action by Coach. Generally, a party cannot assert the constitutional rights of others. To have standing, the claimant must have suffered a direct impairment of his own constitutional rights. Here, a prior restraint has been placed on the newspaper. This is a burden on the newspaper's rights. And while Coach is affected, it is not a direct impairment of his rights. Thus, he lacks standing to bring a suit based in the First Amendment.

ANSWER TO EXAM QUESTION NO. 3

The state of Uphoria's bill would be valid as to its age and citizenship requirements, but would be unconstitutional due to its gender classification.

Under the Equal Protection Clause of the Fourteenth Amendment, government may not treat similar people in a dissimilar manner without a sufficient reason. The strength of the reason necessary depends on the basis of the classification. There are three tests:

The first test is the strict scrutiny or compelling state interest test. This test is used if the classification is based on a suspect classification, which includes race, national origin, or alienage. Under this test, the law is considered to be invalid unless the government can prove that it is necessary to achieve a compelling state objective.

The second test involves intermediate scrutiny. Under this test, the court will strike down a law unless the government can show that the law bears a substantial relation to an important government interest. This is the test used in situations such as that here, where there is a classification based on gender. Gender classifications will be struck down absent an exceedingly persuasive justification, and the government may not rely on overbroad generalizations about males and females that will perpetuate the legal, social, and economic inferiority of women. [United States v. Virginia, 518 U.S. 515 (1996)—striking state military school's policy of admitting only men]

The third test is the rational basis test (minimum scrutiny). Under this test, the classification is valid if there is any conceivable basis upon which the classification might relate to a legitimate governmental interest. In other words, the person challenging the classification must prove that it is arbitrary or irrational. This is a very "loose" test and it is very difficult for a law to fail it. This test is used for all classifications relating to matters of economics or social welfare.

The gender designation of Uphoria's bill limiting the appointment of state police officers to males would fall under the intermediate scrutiny test due to its inherent gender classification. Therefore, this component will only be upheld if it is substantially related to an important governmental interest.

This gender classification is not related to an important governmental interest. As in *United States v. Virginia, supra,* the government will not be able to show that all women are incapable of performing the duties of a state trooper. If Uphoria claims that its bill is based on ability to do the work, it can design a test of each individual's (male or female) ability to perform the work required of a state police officer, and not unfairly discriminate against women. Accordingly, under the intermediate scrutiny test, this bill would be found invalid due to the fact that it discriminates against women without an exceedingly persuasive justification.

The bill also limits appointment of police officers to citizens of the United States. Since this component of the bill is based on alienage, it ordinarily falls under the strict scrutiny-compelling interest test. However, there is an exception to this rule which provides that if, as here, the law discriminates against alien participation in the functioning of state government, the mere rationality test is applied. Under the mere rationality test, a state can validly refuse to hire aliens as police officers, or for other positions which have direct effect on the function of government. [Ambach v. Norwick, 441 U.S. 68 (1979)] Accordingly, the bill would be valid as far as its citizenship requirement is concerned.

The bill sets the age for appointment of a police officer to be over 20 years. The Court has held that age is not a suspect classification, so a rational basis analysis can be applied. The 20-year-old minimum age requirement in this statute would be held constitutional under the rational basis test because of the state's interest in having police officers who are physically and emotionally mature enough to handle the stress of police work.

ANSWER TO EXAM QUESTION NO. 4

A. FIRST AMENDMENT ISSUES

Under the First Amendment, "Congress shall make no law abridging the freedom of speech, or of the press . . . ." This guarantee has been held applicable to the states by reason of the "liberty" protected by the Due Process Clause of the Fourteenth Amendment.

1. Freedom of Association and Belief: The First Amendment protects freedom of association. Here, it appears that the ordinance impinges on the rights of the entertainers to talk and mingle with the customers. As such, the ordinance has the effect of chilling this vital First Amendment right. Thus, on this ground, the ordinance is unconstitutional.

2. The Ordinance Is Overbroad: If a regulation of speech or speech related conduct punishes a substantial amount of protected speech, judged in relation to the regulation's plainly legitimate sweep, the regulation is facially invalid (*i.e.,* it cannot be enforced against anyone—not even a person engaging in activity that is not constitutionally protected.). Here, the stated purposes of the ordinance are to (i) prevent disorderly conduct; (ii) encourage temperance; (iii) discourage prostitution; and (iv) prevent any other immoral activity. While these purposes are legitimate government interests, the ordinance, as written, restricts expression and conduct that are in no way connected with prostitution, immoral activity, etc. Accordingly, the ordinance chills speech and conduct that are protected under the First Amendment. Certainly, the ordinance could be worded to restrict only the activities that are the focus of its basic purposes, *i.e.,* preventing prostitution and drunkenness. Prohibiting mingling of customers and entertainers goes beyond these legitimate purposes. Therefore, the ordinance is unconstitutionally overbroad and cannot be enforced against anyone.

3. The Ordinance Is Vague: Laws regulating speech-related activities are unconstitutional if they are too vague to make absolutely clear what they forbid. To the extent their vagueness suggests that they prohibit constitutionally protected speech, they have a "chilling effect" on speech. Here, the ordinance prohibits the entertainers from "mingling" with customers. The word "mingling" is too vague to define what conduct is proscribed by the ordinance. Thus, it appears that the entertainers may be forced to refrain from conduct and expression protected by the First Amendment in order not to be considered "mingling" with the customers. Because this ordinance has, in this manner, the effect of "chilling" activity and expression that is protected by the First Amendment, it is unconstitutional.

4. Effect of Twenty-First Amendment on First Amendment Rights: The Twenty-First Amendment gives the states much control over the sale and use of intoxicating liquor within their borders. Thus, Fun City's attorneys could argue that the ordinance is a valid exercise of the state's constitutionally granted powers with respect to intoxicating liquors. However, this argument fails because, as a general rule, individual rights guaranteed by the Bill of Rights and the Fourteenth Amendment outweigh state liquor control laws. Here, the ordinance, which constitutes a liquor control regulation, chills First Amendment rights made applicable, to states under the Fourteenth Amendment. Accordingly, the ordinance is unconstitutional.

B. SUBSTANTIVE DUE PROCESS ISSUES

Substantive due process protects certain fundamental rights not articulated within the text of the Constitution. It is a test of the "reasonableness" of a statute in relation to the government's power to enact such legislation. It prohibits arbitrary government action. The Due Process Clause of the Fourteenth Amendment applies to state and local governments.

Under substantive due process principles, where a fundamental right is limited, the law (or other government action) must be necessary to promote a compelling or overriding state interest. Fundamental rights include interstate travel, privacy, voting, and all rights implied under the First Amendment.

Here the ordinance, as discussed above, chills the entertainers' First Amendment rights of association and speech. From the facts, Fun City has shown no compelling or overriding interest to do so. Accordingly, on this ground, the ordinance violates substantive due process.

C. EQUAL PROTECTION ISSUES

Under the Equal Protection Clause of the Fourteenth Amendment (applicable to the states), and as an implicit guarantee of the Due Process Clause of the Fifth Amendment (applicable to the federal government), governmental acts that classify people improperly may be invalid. It is unconstitutional for the government to treat similar people in a dissimilar manner absent sufficient justification. Under the "strict scrutiny" test, the classification must be necessary to promote a compelling interest. This test is employed when, as here, the classification affects the exercise of a fundamental right.

Here, the ordinance seeks to classify the entertainers as individuals who cannot exercise certain fundamental rights—those granted by the First Amendment. Thus, to sustain the classification, Fun City must show that it has a "compelling interest" to do so. Clearly, Fun City does not have a compelling interest to make such a classification and, therefore, the ordinance violates equal protection.

D. CONCLUSION

For the foregoing reasons, Irma's and Lester's convictions should be reversed. Irma and Lester have been charged with violation of an ordinance which is overbroad and infringes on their guaranteed constitutional rights.

Contracts and Sales

CONTRACTS AND SALES

TABLE OF CONTENTS

I. WHAT IS A CONTRACT?

A. GENERAL DEFINITION

A contract is a promise or set of promises, for the breach of which the law gives a remedy, or the performance of which the law in some way recognizes as a duty.

B. COMMON LAW VS. ARTICLE 2 SALE OF GOODS

Generally, the common law governs contracts. However, special rules have been developed for contracts involving the sale of ***goods***, and those rules are contained in Article 2 of the Uniform Commercial Code ("U.C.C."). Article 2 has adopted much of the common law of contracts, but where the common law and Article 2 differ, Article 2 prevails in a contract for the sale of goods.

1. "Sale" Defined

A sale is a contract in which title to ***goods*** passes from the seller to the buyer for a price. [U.C.C. §2-106(1)]

2. "Goods" Defined

Article 2 defines "goods" as all ***things movable*** at the time they are identified as the goods to be sold under the contract. [U.C.C. §2-105(1)] Thus, Article 2 applies to sales of most tangible things (*e.g.,* cars, horses, hamburgers), but does not apply to the sale of real estate, services (*e.g.,* a health club membership), or intangibles (*e.g.,* a patent), or to construction contracts. Goods associated with real estate (*e.g.,* minerals, growing crops and uncut timber, and fixtures removed from the land) ***may*** fall under Article 2 under certain circumstances.

3. Contracts Involving Goods and Nongoods

If a sale involves both goods and services (*e.g.,* a contract to paint a portrait), a court will determine which aspect is dominant and apply the law governing that aspect to the whole contract. However, if the contract divides payment between goods and services, then Article 2 will apply to the sale portion and the common law will apply to the services portion.

4. Merchants vs. Nonmerchants

A number of the rules in Article 2 depend on whether the seller and/or buyer are merchants. Article 2 generally defines "merchant" as one who regularly deals in goods of the kind sold or who otherwise by his profession holds himself out as having special knowledge or skills as to the practices or goods involved. [U.C.C. §2-104(1)] For many of the Article 2 provisions dealing with general business practices (*e.g.,* Statute of Frauds, confirmatory memos, firm offers, modification), almost anyone in business can be deemed a merchant. However, a few Article 2 provisions (*e.g.,* the implied warranty of merchantability) are narrower and require a person to be a merchant with respect to goods of the kind being sold.

C. TYPES OF CONTRACTS

1. As to Formation

Contracts are frequently described as express, implied, or quasi. Only the first two are actually contracts, and they differ only in the manner in which they are formed.

a. Express Contract

Express contracts are formed ***by language***, oral or written.

b. Implied in Fact Contract
Implied contracts are formed by manifestations of assent other than oral or written language, *i.e.,* ***by conduct*** (*e.g.,* if a person sits in a barber's chair and the barber cuts his hair, a contract has been formed by the parties' conduct).

c. Quasi-Contract or Implied in Law Contract
Quasi-contracts are ***not contracts*** at all. They are constructed by courts to ***avoid unjust enrichment*** by permitting the plaintiff to bring an action in restitution to recover the amount of the benefit conferred on the defendant. (*See* VIII.C., *infra.*) Their only relationship to genuine contracts is historical.

2. As to Acceptance

a. Bilateral Contracts—Exchange of Mutual Promises
The traditional bilateral contract is one consisting of the exchange of mutual promises, *i.e.,* a promise for a promise, in which each party is both a promisor and a promisee.
Example: Sidney promises to sell Blackacre to Bertram for $6,000, and Bertram promises to purchase Blackacre at that price.

b. Unilateral Contracts—Acceptance by Performance
The traditional unilateral contract is one in which the offeror requests performance rather than a promise. Here, the offeror-promisor promises to pay upon the ***completion of the requested act*** by the promisee. Once the act is completed, a contract is formed. In such contracts, there is one promisor and one promisee.
Example: Susan promises to pay Charles $5 if he will deliver a textbook to Rick. Charles is not obligated to deliver the book, but if he does in fact deliver it, Susan is obligated to pay him the $5.

c. Modern View—Most Contracts Are Bilateral

1) Acceptance by Promise or Start of Performance
Under Article 2 and the Restatement (Second) of Contracts, unless clearly indicated otherwise by the language or circumstances, ***all*** offers are "doubtful" or "indifferent" offers, which means that they may be accepted by promising or beginning performance.
Example: Acme Co. orders specifically manufactured goods from Barnes Manufacturing Co. Recognizing the speed with which the order must be filled, Barnes begins to manufacture the ordered item shortly after the order is received. This constitutes an acceptance of the offer if Barnes gives Acme notice of its beginning of performance within a reasonable time, and it creates an implied promise on the part of Barnes to complete manufacture.

2) Unilateral Contracts Limited to Two Circumstances
Under Article 2 and the Second Restatement, a traditional unilateral contract (*i.e.,* a contract that can be formed only by full performance) occurs in only two situations: (i) where the offeror clearly (unambiguously) indicates that ***completion of performance is the only manner of acceptance***—the offeror is the master of the offer and may create the offer in this fashion; and (ii) where there is an ***offer to the***

public, such as a reward offer, which so clearly contemplates acceptance by performance rather than a promise (not to mention the total ineffectiveness of a promise in such a situation) that only the performance requested in the offer will manifest acceptance.

3. As to Validity

a. Void Contract
A void contract is one that is totally ***without any legal effect*** from the beginning (*e.g.*, an agreement to commit a crime). It ***cannot be enforced by either party***.

b. Voidable Contract
A voidable contract is one that one or both parties may ***elect to avoid*** (*e.g.*, by raising a defense that makes it voidable, such as infancy or mental illness).

c. Unenforceable Contract
An unenforceable contract is an agreement that is otherwise valid but which may not be enforceable due to ***various defenses*** extraneous to contract formation, such as the statute of limitations or Statute of Frauds.

D. CREATION OF A CONTRACT
When a suit is brought in which one party seeks to enforce a contract or to obtain damages for breach of contract, a court must first decide whether there was in fact a contract. In making this determination, a court will ask the following three basic questions:

1. Was there ***mutual assent***?

2. Was there ***consideration*** or some substitute for consideration?

3. Are there any ***defenses*** to creation of the contract?

II. MUTUAL ASSENT—OFFER AND ACCEPTANCE

A. IN GENERAL
Mutual assent is often said to be an agreement on the "same bargain at the same time"—"a meeting of the minds." The process by which parties reach this meeting of the minds generally is some form of negotiation, during which, at some point, one party makes a proposal (an offer) and the other agrees to it (an acceptance). An actual subjective meeting of the minds is not necessary. Rather, courts use an ***objective measure***, by which each party is bound to the ***apparent intention*** that he manifested to the other(s).

B. THE OFFER
An offer creates a power of acceptance in the offeree and a corresponding liability on the part of the offeror. For a communication to be an offer, it must create a ***reasonable expectation*** in the offeree that the offeror is willing to enter into a contract on the basis of the offered terms. In deciding whether a communication creates this reasonable expectation, you should ask the following three questions:

(i) Was there an expression of a ***promise, undertaking, or commitment*** to enter into a contract?

(ii) Were there ***certainty and definiteness*** in the essential terms?

(iii) Was there ***communication*** of the above to the offeree?

1. Promise, Undertaking, or Commitment

For a communication to be an offer, it must contain a promise, undertaking, or commitment to enter into a contract, rather than a mere invitation to begin preliminary negotiations; *i.e.,* there must be an ***intent*** to enter into a contract. The criteria used to determine whether a communication is an offer include the following:

a. Language

The language used may show that an offer was or was not intended. Technical language such as "I offer" or "I promise" is useful to show that an offer was made, but it is not necessary. Also, certain language is generally construed as merely contemplating an invitation to deal, preliminary negotiations, or "feelers," rather than being an offer. This includes phrases such as "I quote," "I am asking $30 for," and "I would consider selling for." No mechanical formula is available.

Example: "I quote you . . . for immediate acceptance" will probably be construed as an offer. By coupling words of invitation with words of offer, the offeror has at least created an ***ambiguity***, which will be ***construed in favor of the offeree***.

b. Surrounding Circumstances

The circumstances surrounding the language will be considered by courts in determining whether an offer exists. For example, where the statement is made in jest, anger, or by way of bragging, and the statement is reasonably understood in this context, it will have no legal effect. However, where the statement is subjectively intended to be in jest but reasonably understood by the hearer to have been made seriously, the statement is an offer because it is interpreted objectively (*i.e.,* according to a reasonable person's expectations).

c. Prior Practice and Relationship of the Parties

In determining whether certain remarks constitute an offer rather than preliminary negotiations, a court will look to the prior relationship and practice of the parties involved.

d. Method of Communication

1) Use of Broad Communications Media

The broader the communicating media (*e.g.,* publications), the more likely it is that the courts will view the communication as merely the ***solicitation of an offer***. (Note that there is an exception as to reward offers.)

2) Advertisements, Etc.

Advertisements, catalogs, circular letters, and the like containing price quotations are ***usually*** construed as mere ***invitations for offers***. They are announcements of prices at which the seller is willing to receive offers. However, in certain situations courts have treated advertisements as ***offers*** where the language of the advertisement can be construed as containing a promise, the terms are certain and definite, and the offeree(s) is clearly identified.

Example: Defendant store advertised a particular coat worth $140 for $1 on a "first come, first served" basis. *Held:* Valid offer to first person accepting on this basis as nothing was left open for negotiation.

e. Industry Custom

The courts will also look to generally accepted custom in the industry in determining whether the proposal qualifies as an offer.

2. Definite and Certain Terms

An offer must be definite and certain in its terms. The basic inquiry is whether enough of the essential terms have been provided so that a contract including them would be ***capable of being enforced***. The principle is that the parties make their own contract; the courts do not make it for them. What is essential for the requisite certainty in an offer depends on the kind of contract contemplated. Typically, the following are important: (i) the ***identity of the offeree***; (ii) the ***subject matter***; and (iii) the ***price*** to be paid. However, a promise generally will be enforceable even if it does not spell out every material term, as long as it contains some ***objective standard*** for the court to use to supply the missing terms. (*See* b.2), *infra.*)

a. Identification of the Offeree

To be considered an offer, a statement must sufficiently identify the offeree or a class to which she belongs to justify the inference that the offeror intended to create a power of acceptance.

Examples: 1) In the example above with the $140 coat selling for $1, the "first come, first served" language eliminates any identification problem.

2) Harvey promises a reward to the person who captures a wanted fugitive. Although the offeree is unidentified and indeed unidentifiable at the time the offer is made, the performance of the requested act constitutes both an identification of the offeree and an acceptance.

b. Definiteness of Subject Matter

The subject matter of the deal must be certain, because a court can enforce a promise only if it can tell with reasonable accuracy what the promise is.

1) Requirements for Specific Types of Contracts

a) Real Estate Transactions—Land and Price Terms Required

An offer involving realty must identify the ***land*** and the ***price*** terms. The land must be identified with some particularity but a deed description is not required (*e.g.,* "my house in Erewhon" is sufficient if the seller has only one house in Erewhon). Most courts will ***not*** supply a missing price term.

b) Sale of Goods—Quantity Term Required

In a contract for the sale of goods, the ***quantity*** being offered must be cer or capable of being made certain.

(1) **"Requirements" and "Output" Contracts**
In a requirements contract, a buyer promises to buy from a certain seller all of the goods the buyer requires, and the seller agrees to sell that amount to the buyer. In an output contract, a seller promises to sell to a certain buyer all of the goods the seller produces, and the buyer agrees to buy that amount from the seller. Although no specific quantity is mentioned in offers to make these contracts, the offers are sufficiently definite because the quantity is ***capable*** of being made certain by reference to objective, extrinsic facts (*i.e.,* the buyer's actual requirements or the seller's actual output).

(a) **Quantity Cannot Be Unreasonably Disproportionate**
It is assumed that the parties will act in good faith; hence, there may not be a tender of or a demand for a quantity ***unreasonably disproportionate*** to (i) any stated estimate, or in the absence of a stated estimate (ii) any normal or otherwise comparable prior output or requirements.

(b) **Established Business vs. New Business**
A number of courts have sometimes refused to enforce such agreements if the promisor did not have an established business. The courts in these cases reason that, due to the lack of any basis for estimating quantity, the agreement is illusory or the damages too speculative. Article 2 avoids this problem by reading a "good faith" agreement into the contract; *i.e.,* the promisor must operate his plant or conduct his business in good faith and according to commercial standards of fair dealing in the trade so that his output or requirements will approximate a reasonably foreseeable figure.

(2) **Reasonable Range of Choices**
An offer allowing a person to specify an item within a reasonable range of choices may be sufficiently definite to result in a contract if accepted.

Example: Seller states to Buyer: "I will sell you any of these motorcycles for $1,000. Pick one." These words will result in a contract when Buyer's choice is made and manifested.

c) **Services—Nature of Work Required**
The nature of the work to be performed is required in an offer for services.

2) **Missing Terms**
The fact that one or more terms are left open does ***not prevent the formation*** of a contract if it appears the parties ***intended to make a contract*** and there is a ***reasonably certain basis*** for giving a remedy. In such a case, the majority of jurisdictions and Article 2 hold that the ***court can supply reasonable terms*** for those that are missing. [*See* U.C.C. §§2-204, 2-305] These terms will be supplied, however, only where they are consistent with the parties' intent as otherwise expressed. Note that the more terms the parties leave open, the less likely it is that they intended to enter into a binding agreement.

a) **Price**
Except in contracts for real property, the failure to state the price does not prevent the formation of a contract if the parties intended to form a contract without the price being settled. For example, if parties enter into a contract for services and the price is not included in the offer, a court might imply the service provider's usual price for the services, the normal price for such services in the area, etc.

(1) **Article 2 Gap Filler**
Article 2 includes some very specific "gap fillers" for situations where certain terms are not included in a contract for the sale of goods. Under Article 2, the price will be a ***reasonable price at the time of delivery*** if:

(i) Nothing is said as to price;

(ii) The price is left to be agreed to by the parties and they fail to agree; or

(iii) The price is to be fixed by some external factor or third party and it is not so set.

[U.C.C. §2-305(1)]

(2) **Price Fixed by Party Under Article 2**
Under Article 2, a contract will be formed even if the parties agree that one of the parties will fix the price in the future (*e.g.,* "price to be set by seller at time of delivery"). However, the party to whom the contract gives the right to fix the price must act in ***good faith***. If that party does not fix the price in good faith, the other party may either cancel the contract or fix a reasonable price herself. [U.C.C. §2-305(3)]

3) **Distinguish—Vague Terms**
The presumption that the parties' intent was to include a reasonable term goes to supplying ***missing*** terms. However, the presumption ***cannot*** be made if the parties have ***included*** a term that makes the contract too vague to be enforced. The problem then is that the parties have manifested an intent that cannot be determined.
Examples: 1) An agreement to divide profits "on a liberal basis" is too vague to be enforced.

2) An agreement to purchase a parcel of land for "$8,000 or less" is also too vague.

a) **Vagueness Can Be Cured by Part Performance**
Where part performance supplies the needed clarification of the terms, it can be used to cure vagueness.

b) **Uncertainty Can Be Cured by Acceptance**
If uncertainty results because the offeree is given a choice of alternative performances, the offer becomes definite when the offeree communicates her choice. (*See* previous example about choice of motorcycle for $1,000.)

c) **Focus on Contract**
In short, the ***contract*** (as distinguished from the offer) must be definite and certain in its terms—hence, even if the offer lacks certainty, the problem can be cured if there is some way in which the offer is capable of being made certain, *e.g.,* by part performance or acceptance.

4) **Terms to Be Agreed on Later**
Often, an offer will state that some term is to be agreed on at a future date. If the term is a ***material*** term, the offer is ***too uncertain***. The courts will not supply a reasonable term, as the parties have provided otherwise. However, as discussed above, Article 2 permits a reasonable ***price*** term to be supplied by the court under these circumstances if the other evidence indicates that the parties intended to form a contract.

3. **Communication to Offeree**
To have the power to accept, the offeree must have ***knowledge*** of the offer. Therefore, the proposal must be communicated to her.
Example: Chauncey returned Bowater's lost briefcase unaware that Bowater had placed an advertisement offering a $20 reward for its return. Because the offer had not been communicated to Chauncey, there could not be mutual assent. Hence, there is no contract.

C. TERMINATION OF OFFER
The power of acceptance created by an offer ends when the offer is terminated. The mutual assent requirement obviously cannot be met where the termination occurs before acceptance is effective. Thus, you must establish whether the offer has been terminated, and if so, in what fashion.

1. **Termination by Acts of Parties**

a. **Termination by Offeror—Revocation**
A revocation is the retraction of an offer by the offeror. A revocation terminates the offeree's power of acceptance if it is communicated to her ***before she accepts***.

1) **Methods of Communication**

a) **Revocation by Direct Communication**
Revocation directly communicated to the offeree by the offeror terminates the offer.

(1) **Revocation by Publication**
Offers made by publication may be terminated by publication of revocation ***through comparable means.***
Example: An offer published in *The New York Times* may be revoked by publication in *The New York Times.* It may not be revoked by publication in *Reader's Digest* or by a TV spot.

b) **Revocation by Indirect Communication**
The offer may be effectively terminated if the offeree ***indirectly*** receives: (i)

correct information, (ii) from a reliable source, (iii) of acts of the offeror that would indicate to a reasonable person that the offeror no longer wishes to make the offer.

Example: Offeree, before attempting to accept Offeror's offer to sell Greenacre, was informed by a reliable third party that Offeror had sold Greenacre to another. *Held:* Offeror revoked the offer.

2) **Effective When Received**

A revocation is generally effective when ***received*** by the offeree. Where revocation is by publication, it is effective when ***published.***

3) **Limitations on Offeror's Power to Revoke**

Offers can be revoked at will by the offeror, even if he has promised not to revoke for a certain period, except under certain situations where the offeror's power to terminate the offer is limited.

a) **Options**

An option is a distinct contract in which the ***offeree gives consideration*** for a promise by the offeror not to revoke an outstanding offer.

Example: An offeror offers to sell her farm—Blackacre—to an offeree for $1 million and promises to keep the offer open for 90 days if the offeree pays the offeror $1,000 to keep the offer open. If the offeree pays the offeror the $1,000, an option contract is formed and the offeror must keep the offer open.

Compare: An offeror offers to sell her farm—Blackacre—to an offeree for $1 million and promises to keep the offer open for 90 days. Because there is no consideration (*see infra*) to make enforceable the promise to keep the offer open, the offeror may terminate her offer at any time despite her promise.

b) **Merchant's Firm Offer Under Article 2**

Under Article 2, there are circumstances in which a promise to keep an offer open is enforceable even if no consideration has been paid to keep the offer open. Under Article 2:

(i) If a ***merchant***;

(ii) Offers to sell goods in a ***signed writing***; and

(iii) The writing ***gives assurances that it will be held open*** (*e.g.,* "this offer will be held open for 10 days," "this offer is firm for 10 days," "I shall not revoke this offer for 10 days");

(iv) The offer ***is not revocable*** for lack of consideration during the time stated, or if no time is stated, for a reasonable time (but in no event may such period exceed three months).

[U.C.C. §2-205] *Note:* As with the Statute of Frauds requirements (IV.D., *infra*), the signed writing requirement for a merchant's firm offer may be satisfied by an electronic record (*e.g.*, e-mail, fax) and an electronic signature. [*See* Uniform Electronic Transactions Act §7 (1999)]

c) **Detrimental Reliance**

Where the offeror could reasonably expect that the offeree would rely to her detriment on the offer, and the offeree does so rely, the offer will be held ***irrevocable as an option contract for a reasonable length of time***. At the very least, the offeree would be entitled to relief measured by the extent of any detrimental reliance. [Restatement (Second) of Contracts §87] The case law indicates that this may be limited to those situations in which the offeror would ***reasonably contemplate reliance*** by the offeree in ***using the offer before it is accepted***.

Example: A general contractor solicited bids from various subcontractors before making its own irrevocable offer on a construction project. For the subcontractor to be held to its offer, the subcontractor must reasonably have foreseen the possible use of its subcontracting bid in the making of the general contractor's irrevocable offer.

d) **Part Performance—True Unilateral Contract Offers**

(1) **Implied Contract for Reasonable Time**

Under the First and Second Restatements, as well as Article 2, an offer for a true unilateral contract becomes ***irrevocable once performance has begun.*** Note that the unilateral contract will not be formed until the total act is complete. However, once the offeree begins to perform, she is given a ***reasonable time to complete performance*** during which time the offer is irrevocable. Note also that the offeree is ***not bound*** to complete performance—she may withdraw at any time prior to completion of performance.

Example: Matt offers to pay Lisa $1,000 if she will paint his house, insisting that the acceptance occur only by the act of painting the house rather than through Lisa's promise. Lisa begins to paint the house. Matt attempts to revoke the offer. Matt's attempt at revocation is ineffective because Lisa must have a reasonable time in which to complete the act of painting. If Matt refuses to allow Lisa to continue to paint, Matt will be in breach of contract and will be liable for damages.

(a) **First Restatement**

The First Restatement reaches the above result by holding that a contract is formed at the moment performance is begun, but the offeror's duty of performance is conditional upon completion of the requested act within a reasonable time or within the time stated in the offer. [Restatement (First) of Contracts §45]

(b) **Second Restatement**

Under the Second Restatement, an ***option contract*** is formed upon the start of performance by the offeree, making the offer irrevocable for a reasonable time. It is as if the offeree had paid consideration to keep the offer open for a reasonable time. [Restatement (Second) of Contracts §45]

(2) **What Is Part Performance?**

(a) **Preparations to Perform**

The rules limiting the offeror's power to revoke an offer for a unilateral contract apply only if the offeree has ***embarked*** on performance. They do not apply when the offeree is only preparing to perform. Note, however, that substantial preparations to perform ***may constitute detrimental reliance*** sufficient to make the offeror's promise binding to the extent of the detrimental reliance. [Restatement (Second) of Contracts §§45, 87, 90]

Example: Matt offers to pay Lisa $1,000 if she will paint his house, insisting that the acceptance occur only by the act of painting. Lisa immediately drives to the local hardware store; expends $100 purchasing paint brushes, drop cloths, and masking tape to enable her to paint the house; and returns. On her return, Matt tells Lisa that he has changed his mind and does not want his house painted after all. Matt's revocation of his offer is valid because Lisa's acts did not constitute the beginning of performance, but rather were merely done in preparation to perform. However, Lisa will have an action against Matt to recover the $100 she spent in detrimental reliance on his offer.

(b) **Offeror Refuses to Accept Performance**

What happens if performance is tendered by the offeree but refused by the offeror? If the offeror's cooperation is necessary for performance, his withholding of it upon the tender of part performance is the equivalent of part performance. [Restatement (Second) of Contracts §45]

e) **Part Performance—Offer Indifferent as to Manner of Acceptance**

As noted above, most offers are indifferent as to the manner of acceptance, and thus, a bilateral contract may be formed ***upon the start of performance*** by the offeree. (*See* I.C.2.c.1), *supra.*) Therefore, once the offeree ***begins performance,*** the contract is complete and ***revocation*** becomes ***impossible.*** *But note:* Notification of the start of performance may be necessary. (*See* D.3.b., *infra.*)

b. **Termination by Offeree**

1) **Rejection**

a) **Express Rejection**
An express rejection is a statement by the offeree that she does not intend to accept the offer. Such a rejection will terminate the offer. [Restatement (Second) of Contracts §36]

b) **Counteroffer as Rejection**
A counteroffer is an offer made by the ***offeree*** to the offeror that contains the same subject matter as the original offer, but differs in its terms. A counteroffer serves as a rejection of the original offer ***as well as a new offer***. [Restatement (Second) of Contracts §39] This usually happens in two situations:

(i) Counteroffer combined with express rejection, *e.g.,* "Not at that price, but I'll take it at $200."

(ii) Acceptance conditional upon additional terms, *e.g.,* "I'll take it at that price, but only if it is also equipped with air conditioning."

Note: Article 2 provides for exceptions to the above general treatment in the "battle of forms" provision. (*See* D.4.c.2), *infra.*)

(1) **Distinguish—Mere Inquiry**
Distinguish between a counteroffer (which constitutes a rejection) and a mere inquiry. An inquiry will not terminate the offer when it is consistent with the idea that the offeree is still keeping the original proposal under consideration. The test is whether a ***reasonable person*** would believe that the original offer had been rejected.

Examples: 1) The offeree says to the offeror, "Would you consider lowering your price by $5,000?" This, without more, is merely an inquiry, not a rejection.

2) The offeree says to the offeror, "I couldn't possibly pay your asking price but could pay $5,000 less." This is more than a mere inquiry because of the certitude involved and will be treated as a counteroffer.

c) **Effective When Received**
A rejection is effective when ***received*** by the offeror.

d) **Revival of Offer**
If an offer is rejected, the offeror may restate the same offer and create a new power of acceptance. Some courts refer to this as the revival of the original offer. It is more precise to suggest that a new offer, although the same as the original offer, has been made.

e) **Rejection of Option**
Because an option is a contract to keep an offer open, a rejection of or a counteroffer to an option does ***not*** constitute a termination of the offer. The

offeree is still free to accept the original offer within the option period unless the offeror has ***detrimentally relied*** on the offeree's rejection. [Restatement (Second) of Contracts §37]

2) **Lapse of Time**

a) **Must Accept Within Specified or Reasonable Time**
The offeree must accept the offer within the time period specified or, if no time period is specified, within a reasonable time. If she does not do so, then she will have allowed the offer to terminate. (*Note:* Where the offer's terms are unclear as to time, *e.g.,* "by return mail," the time limit is what a reasonable person in the offeree's position would have assumed.)

b) **Look to When Offer Is Received by Offeree**
If the offer provides that it will expire within a particular time period, that period commences when the offer is received by the offeree. If the offer is delayed in transmission and this fact ***is or should have been apparent to the offeree***, the offer terminates at the time it would have expired had there been no delay. All relevant facts must be considered in determining whether this knowledge is present. These include, *e.g.,* date of letter, postmark, and any subsequent statements made by the offeror.

2. **Termination by Operation of Law**

a. **Termination by Death or Insanity of Parties**
If either of the parties dies or is adjudicated insane prior to acceptance, the offer is terminated. It is ***not*** necessary that the death or insanity be ***communicated*** to the other party. [Restatement (Second) of Contracts §48] (*Compare:* Supervening mental incapacity of the offeror without an adjudication of incapacity will terminate an offer only if the offeree is aware of the incapacity.) Note, however, that the offer will ***not*** terminate in this fashion if the rules limiting an offeror's power to terminate are applicable (*e.g.,* in an option contract, the offer becomes irrevocable because the offeree gives consideration to keep it open).

b. **Termination by Destruction of Subject Matter**
Destruction of the subject matter terminates the offeree's power of acceptance. [Restatement (Second) of Contracts §36]

c. **Termination by Supervening Legal Prohibition of Proposed Contract**
If the subject matter of the proposed contract becomes illegal, the offer will terminate. [Restatement (Second) of Contracts §36]

Example: Lucky Lou offers Vegas Vernon a share in his casino business. Prior to acceptance, a law is passed banning casinos. The offer is automatically terminated.

D. **THE ACCEPTANCE**
An acceptance is a manifestation of assent to the terms of an offer. Through this manifestation of assent, the offeree exercises the power given her by the offeror to create a contract.

1. Who May Accept

a. Party to Whom Offer Is Addressed or Directed

Generally, only the person to whom an offer is addressed has the power of acceptance. This is so even though the offer does not call for personal performance or special financial responsibility on the part of the offeree. One may also have the power of acceptance if she is a member of a class to which an offer has been directed. If the offer is made to the general public, anyone may qualify as an offeree. If the offer requests performance from an unlimited number of persons, performance by anyone knowing of the offer will cut off the power of every other person to accept, provided that the offeror desires only one performance and there is no indication that he is willing to pay more than once.

b. Offeree's Power of Acceptance Cannot Be Assigned

Unlike rights under an existing contract, the offeree's power of acceptance ***cannot be assigned***.

1) Exception—Option Contracts

An exception exists for the right to accept under an option contract, because the power to accept is itself a contract right in these contracts, and contract rights generally are assignable (*see* IX.C.1.b., *infra*).

2. Offeree Must Know of Offer

The offeree must know of the offer in order to accept, and this is true whether the offer is for a bilateral or unilateral contract.

Examples: 1) Alex sends Becky a letter offering to sell her Blackacre for $500,000. That same day, without knowledge of Alex's letter, Becky sends Alex a letter offering to buy Blackacre from him for $500,000. No contract is formed because neither party knew of the other's letter when sending his or her own letter.

2) Cindy offers to pay $1,000 to the person who finds her missing dog. Dee finds a dog in her yard, reads its tags, and returns the dog to Cindy without knowledge of Cindy's offer. Most courts hold that no contract is formed here.

3. Acceptance of Offer for Unilateral Contract

If an offer provides that it may be accepted only by performance (*i.e.*, an offer for a unilateral contract), note the following particular rules.

a. Completion of Performance

Most courts hold that an offer to form a unilateral contract is not accepted until performance is completed. The beginning of performance may create an option so that the offer is irrevocable. (*See* C.1.a.3)d), *supra*.) However, the offeree is not obligated to complete performance merely because he has begun performance, as only complete performance constitutes an acceptance of the offer.

b. Notice

Generally, the offeree is ***not*** required to give the offeror notice that he has begun the requested performance, but is required to notify the offeror within a reasonable time

after performance has been completed. If a required notice is not given, a contract is formed, but the offeror's duties are discharged for failure of an implied condition subsequent (*see* VI.D.2.c., *infra*). However, no notice is required if:

(i) The offeror ***waived notice***; or

(ii) The offeree's ***performance would normally come to the offeror's attention*** within a reasonable time.

Example: Joe tells Susan he will pay her $1,000 if she paints the house that he is living in. Susan need not formally notify Joe that she has painted his house, as her performance would be obvious to him.

Compare: In writing, Joe tells Susan that if she lends Tina $1,000 for one year, he will repay the loan if Tina fails to pay. Joe becomes contractually bound on his promise the instant Susan loans Tina the money, but Joe will be discharged from this contractual obligation unless Susan notifies him of her acceptance (*i.e.,* her making the loan to Tina) within a reasonable time.

1) Compare—Article 2

Article 2 has a slightly different rule regarding notice, although the end result is basically the same. It provides that when a contract is accepted by the beginning of performance, if the offeree fails to notify the offeror of the acceptance (*i.e.,* the ***beginning*** of performance rather than the completion of performance) within a reasonable time, the offeror may treat the offer as having ***lapsed before acceptance*** (*i.e.*, no contract was ever formed, as opposed to the Restatement view that a contract was formed but performance is excused by failure of a condition). [U.C.C. §2-206(2)]

4. Acceptance of Offer for Bilateral Contract

Recall that unless an offer specifically provides that it may be accepted only through performance, it will be construed as an offer to enter into a bilateral contract and may be accepted either by a promise to perform or by the ***beginning of performance*** (compare offers for true unilateral contracts, which may be accepted only by full performance).

a. Generally, Acceptance Must Be Communicated

Generally, acceptance of an offer to enter into a bilateral contract must be communicated to the offeror.

1) Exception—Waiver in Offer

If an offer provides that acceptance need not be communicated, then no communication of the acceptance is required.

Example: Alex applies for life insurance on a form that provides that the policy will become effective immediately upon approval by the insurance company's home office. The insurance contract is formed when the home office approves Alex's application.

2) Silence as Acceptance

Although the offeree cannot be forced to speak under penalty of having her silence treated as an acceptance, if the offeree silently takes offered benefits, the courts will often find an acceptance. This is especially true if prior dealings between the parties, or trade practices known to both, create a commercially reasonable expectation by the offeror that silence represents an acceptance. In such a case, the offeree is under a duty to notify the offeror if she does not intend to accept. [Restatement (Second) of Contracts §69]

b. Method of Acceptance

Unless otherwise provided, an offer is construed as inviting acceptance in ***any reasonable manner*** and by any medium reasonable under the circumstances. Any objective manifestation of the offeree's counterpromise is usually sufficient.

Example: Nikki ***telephones*** an offer to Skip that is to remain open for five days. Two days later, Skip ***e-mails*** an acceptance, or two days later Skip ***mails*** an acceptance. Whether there has been a proper acceptance depends on whether the use of e-mail or mail was reasonable under the circumstances.

1) Act as an Acceptance

The offeror is the master of her offer and may require an act to signify acceptance.

Example: Jennifer offers to purchase Steve's car for $1,000, specifying that Steve accept the offer by wearing a yellow shirt to lunch next Tuesday. Steve can accept the offer only by acting as requested. If Steve simply tenders the automobile, most courts would construe the tender as a rejection and counteroffer. Also, recall that Steve must know of the offer to accept. If he simply wears a yellow shirt without knowing of Jennifer's offer, there is no acceptance and no bilateral contract.

2) Offers to Buy Goods for Current or Prompt Shipment

Under Article 2, an offer to buy goods for current or prompt shipment is construed as inviting acceptance either by a ***promise to ship*** or by ***current or prompt shipment*** of conforming or nonconforming goods.

a) Shipment of Nonconforming Goods

The shipment of nonconforming goods is an acceptance creating a bilateral contract as well as a ***breach*** of the contract unless the seller seasonably notifies the buyer that a shipment of nonconforming goods is offered only as an ***accommodation***. The buyer is not required to accept accommodation goods and may reject them. If he does, the shipper is not in breach and may reclaim the accommodation goods, because her tender does not constitute an acceptance of the buyer's original offer.

Examples: 1) Craig orders 1,500 blue widgets from Susy. Susy ships 1,500 black widgets but does not notify Craig that the goods are offered only as accommodation. Susy's shipment is both an acceptance of Craig's offer and a breach of the resulting contract. Craig may sue for any appropriate damages.

2) In the example above, Susy, before the goods arrive, notifies Craig that black widgets have been sent as an

accommodation. The shipment is a counteroffer and, if Craig accepts delivery, there will be a contract for the purchase of black widgets.

3) Craig orders 1,500 blue widgets from Susy. Susy sends Craig a fax promising to ship the widgets within two days. Upon checking her stock, Susy discovers that she has only 1,000 blue widgets. She ships the 1,000 blue widgets along with 500 black widgets and a letter explaining that the black widgets are offered only as an accommodation. Craig may sue for damages. Susy accepted Craig's order via the fax, promising to ship 1,500 blue widgets. This is not a case of acceptance by shipment.

c. **Acceptance Must Be Unequivocal**

Traditional contract law insisted on an absolute and unequivocal acceptance of each and every term of the offer (the "mirror image rule").

1) **Common Law Rule**

At common law, any different or additional terms in the acceptance make the response a ***rejection and counteroffer***.

Example: Adam offers to lease a warehouse to Jamie by handing Jamie a signed copy of his standard lease agreement. Jamie reads over the lease, adds a clause providing that disputes will be settled by arbitration, signs the lease, and hands it back to Adam. Adam hands the keys over to Jamie. By adding the arbitration clause to the lease, Jamie rejected Adam's offer and made a counteroffer. By handing Jamie the keys to the warehouse, Adam accepted Jamie's counteroffer.

a) **Distinguish—Statements that Make Implicit Terms Explicit**

Statements by the offeree that make implicit terms explicit do not prevent acceptance.

Example: The statement by an offeree, "I accept provided you convey marketable title," is a valid acceptance because the obligation to convey marketable title is implicit in the offer to sell.

b) **Distinguish—"Grumbling Acceptance"**

A "grumbling acceptance" (*i.e.,* an acceptance accompanied by an expression of dissatisfaction) is an effective acceptance as long as it stops short of actual dissent.

Example: "I think it's highway robbery at that price, but I guess I'll have to accept" is a valid acceptance.

c) **Distinguish—Request for Clarification**

A request for clarification does not necessarily amount to a rejection and counteroffer.

Example: "The $1,000 price—that includes shipping, doesn't it?" is not a counteroffer.

2) **Article 2 Rule—Battle of the Forms Provision**
Article 2 has abandoned the mirror image rule, providing instead that the proposal of additional or different terms by the offeree in a definite and timely acceptance does ***not*** constitute a rejection and counteroffer, but rather is ***effective as an acceptance***, unless the acceptance is ***expressly*** made conditional on assent to the additional or different terms. Whether the additional or different terms become part of the contract depends on whether or not both parties are merchants. [U.C.C. §2-207(1); *see* V.D.1., *infra,* for a discussion of what terms are included]

Example: Harry sends Sally an e-mail offering to sell her his car for $1,000. Sally e-mails back, "I accept; deliver it to my house by noon tomorrow." At common law, no contract would be formed here because Sally's acceptance added a delivery term. Under Article 2, a contract is formed and whether or not Harry is required to deliver the car to Sally's house by noon of the next day is determined by the rules discussed at V.D.1., *infra.*

Compare: Same facts as above, but Sally's e-mail says, "I accept, but only if you agree to deliver the car to my house by noon tomorrow." No contract is formed here because Sally's acceptance was expressly conditioned on assent to the new terms.

3) **Bilateral Contracts Formed by Performance**
Sometimes in business, a contract is not formed by the parties' communications, either because: (i) the mirror image rule has not been satisfied; or (ii) in a contract for the sale of goods, the original offeror's form contains a clause objecting in advance to any new or inconsistent term and the offeree sends a response with new or different terms that states it is not an acceptance unless the original offeror agrees to these terms. Clearly, no contract is formed at this point. But, as is sometimes the case, if the parties begin to perform as if they formed a contract, a contract is formed. *Rationale:* At common law, the last communication sent to the party who performed is considered a counteroffer and the performance is considered acceptance of the counteroffer. In contracts for the sale of goods, Article 2 specifically provides that conduct by both parties that recognizes the existence of a contract is sufficient to establish the contract. [U.C.C. §2-207(3)]

d. **When Effective—The Mailbox Rule**
Acceptance by mail or similar means creates a contract at the ***moment of dispatch***, provided that the mail is properly addressed and stamped, ***unless:***

(i) The ***offer stipulates*** that acceptance is not effective until received; or

(ii) An ***option contract*** is involved (an acceptance under an option contract is effective only upon ***receipt*** [Restatement (Second) of Contracts §63]).

Note: Because in most states a revocation is effective only upon receipt (*see* C.1.a.2), *supra*), under the mailbox rule if the offeree dispatches an acceptance ***before he receives a revocation*** sent by the offeror, a contract is formed. This is true even though the acceptance is dispatched after the revocation is dispatched and received after the revocation is received.

1) **Effect of Offeree Sending Both Acceptance and Rejection**
Because a rejection is effective only when received, an offeree sending both an acceptance and rejection could create problems for the offeror if the mailbox rule were applicable; *e.g.,* a contract would be created when the acceptance was dispatched even if the offeror received the rejection and relied on it before receiving the acceptance.

a) **Offeree Sends Rejection, Then Acceptance—Mailbox Rule Does Not Apply**
If the offeree sends a rejection and then sends an acceptance, the mailbox rule does not apply. Whichever one is ***received first*** is effective.

b) **Offeree Sends Acceptance, Then Rejection—Mailbox Rule Generally Applies**
If the offeree sends the acceptance first, the mailbox rule applies; *i.e.,* a contract is created upon dispatch of the acceptance. However, if the offeror received the rejection first and ***changed his position in reliance*** on it, the offeree will be ***estopped*** from enforcing the contract.

2) **Acceptance by Unauthorized Means**
An acceptance transmitted by unauthorized means or improperly transmitted by authorized means may still be ***effective if it is actually received*** by the offeror while the offer is still in existence.

Examples: 1) Bailey makes an offer to Janet specifying that acceptance should be by fax. Janet mails Bailey her acceptance. The acceptance will not be effective upon dispatch of the letter but only upon receipt by Bailey, if the offer is still open.

2) Janet, in a situation where the mailbox rule otherwise applies, incorrectly addressed the envelope in mailing back the acceptance. It will be effective upon receipt if the offer is still open.

E. AUCTION CONTRACTS

The U.C.C. contains some special rules regulating auction sales. [*See* U.C.C. §2-328] They are:

1. Goods Auctioned in Lots

In a sale by auction, if goods are put up in lots, each lot is the subject of a separate sale.

2. When Sale Is Complete

A sale by auction is complete when the auctioneer so announces by the ***fall of the hammer*** or in another customary manner. Where a bid is made while the hammer is falling in acceptance of a prior bid, the auctioneer may, in his discretion, reopen the bidding or declare the goods sold under the bid on which the hammer was falling.

3. Auction With Reserve or Without Reserve

An auction sale is with reserve unless the goods are explicitly put up without reserve. "***With reserve***" means the ***auctioneer may withdraw the goods*** at any time until he announces completion of the sale. In an auction without reserve, once the auctioneer calls for bids on an article or lot, that article or lot cannot be withdrawn unless no bid is made within a reasonable time. In either case, a bidder may retract his bid until the auctioneer announces completion of the sale, but a bidder's retraction does not revive any previous bid.

4. A Bid on Seller's Behalf

Except at a forced sale, if the auctioneer knowingly receives a bid on the seller's behalf, or the seller makes or procures such a bid (in order to drive up the price of the goods), and notice has not been given that liberty for such bidding is reserved, the winning bidder may at his option avoid the sale or take the goods at the price of the ***last good faith bid*** prior to the completion of the sale.

III. CONSIDERATION

A. INTRODUCTION

The majority of agreements that qualify as legally enforceable contracts contain a bargained-for change in legal position between the parties, *i.e.,* valuable consideration. While substitute doctrines may permit enforcement of an agreement, only the presence of ***valuable consideration on both sides*** of the bargain will make an executory bilateral contract fully enforceable from the moment of formation. Simply stated, consideration is the price for enforceability in the courts.

B. ELEMENTS OF CONSIDERATION

Basically, two elements are necessary to constitute consideration: (i) there must be a ***bargained-for exchange*** between the parties; and (ii) that which is bargained for must be considered of ***legal value*** or, as it is traditionally stated, it must constitute a benefit to the promisor ***or*** a detriment to the promisee. At the present time, the ***detriment*** element is emphasized in determining whether an exchange contains legal value.

Example: Jeff promises to sell his used television to Kristen for $100 in exchange for Kristen's promise to pay $100. Both elements of consideration are found in this example. First, Jeff's promise was bargained for. Jeff's promise induced a detriment in the promisee, Kristen. Kristen's detriment induced Jeff to make the promise. Second, both parties suffered detriments. The detriment to Jeff was the transfer of ownership of the television, and the detriment to Kristen was the payment of $100 to Jeff.

1. Bargained-For Exchange

This element of consideration requires that the promise induce the detriment ***and*** the detriment induce the promise (*see* preceding example). Unless both of these elements are present, the "bargained-for exchange" element of consideration is not present.

a. Gift

If either of the parties intended to make a gift, he was not bargaining for consideration, and this requirement will not be met.

1) Act or Forbearance by Promisee Must Be of Benefit to Promisor

It is not enough that the promisee incurs detriment; the detriment must be the ***price*** of the exchange, and not merely fulfillment of certain conditions for making the gift. The test is whether the act or forbearance by the promisee would be of any benefit to the promisor. In other words, if the promisor's motive was to induce the detriment, it will be treated as consideration; if the motive was no more than to state a condition of a promise to make a gift, there is no consideration.

Example: "Come to my house and I will give you my old television." The

promisee suffers a detriment by going to the promisor's house, as she did not have to go there at all. However, the promise of the television was probably not made to induce the promisee to come to the promisor's house. Hence, there is no consideration.

2) Economic Benefit Not Required

The benefit to the promisor need not have economic value. Peace of mind or the gratification of influencing the mind of another may be sufficient to establish bargained-for consideration, provided that the promisee is not already legally obligated to perform the requested act.

Example: Father tells Daughter, "I'll give you $1,000 if you stop smoking." Father's emotional gratification from influencing his daughter's health suffices as consideration.

b. "Past" or "Moral" Consideration

1) General Rule—Not Sufficient Consideration

If something was already given or performed before the promise was made, it will not satisfy the "bargain" requirement. The courts reason that it was not given in exchange for the promise when made.

Example: A loose piece of molding fell from a building and was about to hit Sam. Sherry, seeing this, pushed Sam out of the molding's path and was herself struck by it and seriously injured. Sam later promised Sherry that he would pay her $100 per month for life. There is no consideration because Sherry did not bargain for Sam's promise.

2) Exceptions

There is substantial disagreement with the general rule. Thus, the courts have sought to avoid its application by creating exceptions.

a) Debt Barred by a Technical Defense

If a past obligation would be enforceable except for the fact that a technical defense to enforcement stands in the way (*e.g.,* statute of limitations), the courts will enforce a new promise if it is ***in writing*** or has been ***partially performed***. However, the court will enforce the contract only to the extent of the new promise.

Example: Debtor owed Creditor $2,000, but the statute of limitations had run on the debt. Debtor won some money in her state lottery and wrote to Creditor, explaining that she had just won some money and promising to pay Creditor $1,000. The promise to pay is enforceable—at least to the extent of the $1,000—despite the lack of new consideration.

b) Promise to Pay Arising Out of Past Material Benefit—Material Benefit Rule

Under a modern trend, ***some*** courts will enforce a promise if it is based on a material benefit that was previously conferred by the promisee on the promisor and if the promisee did not intend to confer the benefit as a gift. This includes situations in which the promisee performed an act at the promisor's

request or performed an unrequested act during an emergency (such as in the example in b.1), above). The Second Restatement follows this rule but adds that the promise is unenforceable to the extent it is disproportionate to the benefit conferred. [Restatement (Second) of Contracts §86]

2. Legal Value

a. Adequacy of Consideration

Courts of law normally will ***not*** inquire into the adequacy of consideration (*i.e.,* the relative values exchanged). If a party wishes to contract to sell an item of high market value for a relatively low price, so be it. However, ***courts of equity*** may inquire into the relative values and deny an ***equitable remedy*** (such as an order for specific performance) if they find a contract to be unconscionable.

1) Token Consideration

If the consideration is only token (*i.e.,* something entirely devoid of value), it will usually not be legally sufficient. The courts reason that this indicates a gift rather than bargained-for consideration.

2) Sham Consideration

Parties to a written agreement often recite that it was made in consideration of $1 or some other insignificant sum. Frequently, this recited sum was not in fact paid and, indeed, it was never intended to be paid. Most courts hold that evidence may be introduced to show that the consideration was not paid and no other consideration was given in its stead.

3) Possibility of Value

Where there is a possibility of value in the bargained-for act, adequacy of consideration will be found even though the value never comes into existence.

Example: Harry promises to convey upon his death certain land by quitclaim deed in consideration for a promise to bequeath him money. Consideration will be found even though Harry has already conveyed the land, as there is a possibility of a future interest in his favor coming into effect.

b. Legal Benefit and Legal Detriment Theories

1) Majority Rule

The majority of courts still adhere to the view that ***detriment to the promisee*** in performing an act or making a promise is the exclusive test of consideration. The fact that this act or promise may confer a legal benefit on the other party, taken alone, is not sufficient consideration.

2) Minority and First Restatement

The minority and First Restatement view is stated in the alternative (although the Restatement does not use the benefit/detriment terminology): Either ***detriment or benefit*** to the other party will suffice.

3) Second Restatement

The Second Restatement departs from the use of the benefit/detriment test.

The only question it would ask about consideration is whether something was ***bargained for and given*** (or promised to be given) in exchange.

4) **Detriment and Benefit Defined**

a) **Legal Detriment to Promisee**
Legal detriment will result if the promisee does something he is under no legal obligation to do or refrains from doing something that he has a legal right to do. It is important to remember that the detriment to the promisee need not involve any actual loss to the promisee or benefit to the promisor.

Example: Uncle promises Nephew $5,000 if he will refrain from drinking, smoking, swearing, and gambling until he reaches age 21. Nephew's refraining is a legal detriment, and because it was bargained for, Uncle must pay the $5,000 if Nephew so refrains. [*See* Hamer v. Sidway, 124 N.Y. 538 (1891)]

Note: Remember that the promisor must have primarily sought to induce the detrimental act by his promise. (*See* television set example under B.1.a.1), *supra.*)

b) **Legal Benefit to Promisor**
A legal benefit to the promisor is simply the reverse side of legal detriment. In other words, it is a forbearance or performance of an act by the promisee which the promisor was not legally entitled to expect or demand, but which confers a benefit on the promisor.

c. **Preexisting Legal Duty Not Consideration**
Traditionally the promise to perform, or the performance of, an existing legal duty ***is not consideration***.

Examples: 1) Mike contracts to build a garage for Richard for $15,000. Mike discovers that he cannot make a profit at that price and tells Richard that he will not build the garage unless Richard promises to pay him $16,000. Because Richard does not have time to find a new contractor before winter and he does not want his new car exposed to snow, he agrees to pay Mike the $16,000. When Mike finishes the garage, Richard pays Mike $15,000. Mike cannot enforce the promise for the additional $1,000 because he was under a preexisting duty to build the garage.

2) Smith offers a $10,000 reward for recovery of his kidnapped daughter. Jones, a police officer assigned to this case, recovers the daughter. Jones's performance of her official duty is not sufficient consideration.

1) **Exception—New or Different Consideration Promised**
If the promisee has given something in addition to what she already owes in return for the promise she now seeks to enforce, or has in some way agreed to vary her preexisting duty, such as by accelerating performance, there is consideration. It is important to note that it is usually immaterial how slight the change is, because courts are anxious to avoid the preexisting duty rule.

2) Exception—Voidable Obligation

A promise to perform a voidable obligation (*i.e.,* ratification) is enforceable despite the absence of new consideration. Thus, an infant's (*i.e.*, minor's) ratification of a contract upon reaching the age of majority is enforceable without new consideration, as is a defrauded person's promise to go through with the tainted contract after learning of the fraud.

3) Exception—Preexisting Duty Owed to Third Party

Traditionally, when a preexisting duty was owed to a third party, courts held that the new promise did not constitute consideration. However, the modern view adopted by the Second Restatement and the majority of jurisdictions states that the new promise ***constitutes consideration***. [*See* Restatement (Second) of Contracts §73]

Example: Saul Pimon contracts with Pam Promotor to sing at a concert in New York for $25,000. Later, when Pimon threatens to cancel, Dud Dooright, a Pimon fan, offers to pay Pimon an additional $5,000 if he sings at the concert. Pimon appears and sings as agreed. Under the traditional view, Pimon cannot enforce Dooright's promise to pay the additional $5,000, but under the majority view Pimon can enforce the promise because Pimon did not owe a duty to Dooright under the original contract.

4) Exception—Honest Dispute as to Duty

If the scope of the legal duty owed is the subject of honest dispute, then a modifying agreement relating to it will ordinarily be given effect. The compromise by each party is a detriment.

5) Exception—Unforeseen Circumstances

Under the majority view, mere unforeseen difficulty in performing is ***not*** a substitute for consideration. But if the unforeseen difficulty ***rises to the level of impracticability***, such that the duty of performance would be discharged (*see* VI.E.5., *infra*), most states will hold that the unforeseen difficulty is an exception to the preexisting legal duty rule.

6) Exception—Modification of Contract for the Sale of Goods

At common law, a contract modification generally is ***unenforceable*** unless it is supported by new consideration. Article 2 does not follow this rule. Under Article 2, contract modifications sought in ***good faith*** are binding without consideration. Modifications extorted from the other party are in bad faith and are unenforceable. [*See* U.C.C. §2-209, comment 2]

Example: Paintco has agreed to sell to Retailco 15,000 gallons of paint at a price of $5 per gallon, to be delivered in 500-gallon installments each month for 30 months. After 15 months, the price of materials rises so that Paintco is losing 50¢ per gallon. Paintco had at the inception of the contract made a profit of 25¢ per gallon. Paintco tells Retailco the circumstances and asks if Retailco will agree to pay $5.75 per gallon for the remaining deliveries. Retailco agrees and the proper writing is executed. The modification was no doubt sought in good faith and is binding even though Paintco gave Retailco no new consideration. If Paintco had asked for an increased price because she believed that it was too late for Retailco to purchase elsewhere and Retailco would pay the higher price to get the paint, the modification would be in bad faith and would be unenforceable.

7) **Existing Debts**

One of the recurring problems in the preexisting duty area concerns promises regarding existing debts. When the amount due is undisputed, ***payment of a smaller sum*** than due will ***not*** be sufficient consideration for a promise by the creditor to discharge the debt. Neither a legal detriment nor a benefit would be present.

But again, bear in mind that courts will attempt to avoid this result by application of the above exceptions. Thus, for example, if the consideration is in any way ***new or different*** (*e.g.,* payment before maturity or to one other than the creditor; payment in a different medium, *e.g.,* stock instead of cash; or payment of a debt that is subject to an honest dispute), then sufficient consideration may be found.

d. **Forbearance to Sue**

The promise to refrain from suing on a claim may constitute consideration. If the claim is ***valid***, the forbearance to sue is, of course, sufficient consideration. If the claim is ***invalid*** and the claimant is aware of this fact, he has no such right; his suit is no more than the wrongful exercise of a power. But even if the claim is invalid, in law or in fact, if the claimant reasonably and in good faith believes his claim to be valid, forbearance of the legal right to have his claim adjudicated constitutes detriment and consideration.

C. MUTUAL AND ILLUSORY PROMISES—THE REQUIREMENT OF MUTUALITY

Consideration must exist on both sides of the contract; that is, promises must be mutually obligatory. There are many agreements in which one party has become bound but the other has not. Such agreements lack mutuality, *i.e.,* at least one of the promises is "illusory." If so, consideration fails.

Example: Acme Co. promises to buy from Batcher, Inc. "such ice cream as I may wish to order from Batcher, Inc." Acme's promise is illusory, because it is still free to buy from anyone else it chooses, or not to buy at all.

However, the requisite mutuality will be found to exist in certain situations even though the promisor has some choice or discretion. Notable among these are the following:

1. **Requirements and Output Contracts**

"Requirements" contracts (promises to buy "all that I will require") and "output" contracts (promises to sell "all that I manufacture") are enforceable. (*See* II.B.2.b.1)b)(1), *supra.*) Consideration exists, as the promisor is suffering a legal detriment; he has parted with the legal right to buy (or sell) the goods he may need (or manufacture) from (or to) another source. [U.C.C. §2-306]

2. **Conditional Promises**

Conditional promises are ***enforceable***, no matter how remote the contingency, ***unless*** the "condition" is entirely within the promisor's control.

Example: Alice promises to deliver goods to Charles "only if her son comes into the business." Valid consideration exists. If the promise were "only if I decide to take my son into the business," a court might find no consideration.

a. **Promise Conditioned on Satisfaction**

A promise to buy conditioned on satisfaction with the goods is ***not illusory***, because the buyer cannot reject the goods unless the buyer is truly dissatisfied. The buyer has a duty to act in good faith in such a situation. [U.C.C. §1-304]

3. **Right to Cancel or Withdraw**

Although reservation of an unqualified right to cancel or withdraw at any time may be an illusory promise, the consideration is valid if this right is in ***any way restricted***, *e.g.,* the right to cancel upon 60 days' notice. Note that Article 2 implies a requirement of reasonable notice even if it is not specified in the contract. [U.C.C. §2-309(3)]

4. **Exclusivity Agreements—Best Efforts Implied**

A court may find an implied promise furnishing mutuality in appropriate circumstances (such as exclusive marketing agreements). The courts generally will find an implied promise to use best efforts and sustain agreements that might otherwise appear illusory.

Example: Y Corp. was granted exclusive rights to sell Dominick's dresses in return for one-half the profit. The agreement was silent as to any obligation on the part of Y Corp. *Held:* Y Corp. impliedly promised to use its best efforts to sell Dominick's dresses. [*See* U.C.C. §2-306(2)]

5. **Voidable Promises**

Voidable promises are not held objectionable on "mutuality" grounds. [Restatement (Second) of Contracts §78]

Example: Victor entered into a contract with Baby Jane, an infant. Baby Jane's power to disaffirm her contractual obligation will not prevent her promise from serving as consideration.

6. **Unilateral/Option Contracts**

Unilateral contracts, enforceable because one has begun performance, or option contracts, enforceable because one has purchased time to decide (*e.g.,* whether to purchase land), are not held objectionable on "mutuality" grounds.

7. **Suretyship Promises**

A suretyship contract involves a promise to pay the debt of another. A suretyship contract is not enforceable unless it is supported by consideration. If a surety is compensated, the requirement of consideration is not much of an issue, because the compensation will serve as consideration for the surety's promise. If, however, the surety is gratuitous (*i.e.,* the surety is not paid for his services), the consideration requirement may cause problems. The timing becomes important in determining whether adequate consideration is present in a gratuitous surety situation.

a. **Surety Makes Promise Before (or at the Same Time as) Creditor Performs or Promises to Perform—Consideration Present**

If the gratuitous surety makes his promise to pay ***before*** (or at the ***same time*** as) the creditor performs or promises to perform, the ***creditor's*** performance or promise will

serve as consideration for the surety's promise, because the creditor has incurred a detriment in exchange for the surety's promise.

Example: Beth sees a car on Sam's used car lot that she wants, but she does not have enough money to pay for the car. Sam tells Beth that he will sell her the car for $500 and a two-year promissory note for the remainder if Beth can get her father to co-sign the note with her. Beth's father agrees. The three parties meet, Beth and her father sign the note, and Sam signs over title of the car to Beth. Beth's father is bound as a surety because the consideration passed from Sam at the same time Beth's father made his promise.

b. Surety Makes Promise After Creditor Performs or Promises to Perform—Generally No Consideration to Support Surety's Promise

If a gratuitous surety does not make his promise until ***after*** the creditor has performed or made an absolute promise to perform, there is no consideration to support the surety's promise because of the preexisting legal duty rule—the creditor has not incurred any new detriment in exchange for the surety's promise. Thus, the surety's promise is unenforceable.

Example: Beth sees a car on Sam's used car lot that she wants, but she does not have enough money to pay for the car. Sam tells Beth that she can have the car for $500 and a two-year promissory note for the remainder. Beth agrees. Sam signs the title of the car over to Beth, and Beth gives Sam $500 and a promissory note for the remainder. A few days later, Sam discovers that Beth works only part-time and will likely have trouble making payments on her current income. He calls Beth and asks her to get a surety on the note. Beth's father sends Sam a letter promising to pay whatever Beth owes if she defaults. Beth's father is not bound as surety because there is no consideration to support his promise.

1) Exception—Obtaining Surety Is Condition Precedent

If the contract between the debtor and the creditor makes obtaining a surety a condition precedent to the creditor's performance, so that the creditor would be justified in refusing to perform the contract until a surety is obtained, the surety's promise is binding if the creditor performs in reliance on the surety's promise.

2) Exception—Additional Consideration

As with other contracts, if the creditor gives additional consideration in exchange for the surety's promise, the surety will be bound.

8. Right to Choose Among Alternative Courses

A promise to choose one of several alternative means of performance is illusory unless ***every alternative*** involves ***some legal detriment*** to the promisor. However, if the power to choose rests with the ***promisee*** or some ***third party*** not under the control of the promisor, the promise is enforceable as long as ***at least one alternative*** involves some legal detriment.

Example: Smith, an English professor, tells Jack that in return for Jack's promise to pay $250, Smith will either (i) give Jack swimming lessons, (ii) paint Jack's portrait, or (iii) teach his English class (of which Jack is a member) on a regular basis during the next term, the choice to be entirely Smith's. Because

alternative (iii) represents a ***preexisting duty*** owed by Smith to the university under his contract of employment, it involves no legal detriment, and Smith's promise does not constitute valuable consideration for Jack's promise to pay $250.

Compare: Had Smith allowed Jack's mother (or Jack) to select the performance, there would be a legal detriment and valuable consideration—even if alternative (iii) were selected.

a. Selection of Valuable Alternative Cures Illusory Promise

Even if a promisor retains the power to select an alternative without legal detriment, his ***actual*** selection of an alternative involving legal detriment would cure the illusory promise.

Example: In the above example (in which Smith was allowed to select a means of performance), if Smith had ***actually*** chosen alternative (i) or (ii), his illusory promise would have been cured.

D. PROMISSORY ESTOPPEL OR DETRIMENTAL RELIANCE

Consideration is not necessary if the facts indicate that the promisor should be estopped from not performing. Under section 90 of the First Restatement, a promise is enforceable if necessary to prevent injustice if:

(i) The promisor should reasonably ***expect to induce action or forbearance***;

(ii) ***Of a definite and substantial character***;

(iii) And ***such action or forbearance is in fact induced***.

In the Second Restatement, section 90 no longer requires that the action or forbearance be "of a definite and substantial character." It also provides that the remedy "***may be limited as justice requires***." Typically, if the elements for promissory estoppel are present, a jurisdiction following the First Restatement approach will award expectation damages (*i.e.,* what was promised under the contract), while a jurisdiction following the Second Restatement might award reliance damages (*i.e.,* whatever the promisee spent in reliance on the promise), which usually is something less than expectation damages, but theoretically can exceed them.

Examples: 1) Alberto Alum promises to bequeath State University $5 million for a new School of Management building. State University puts up a plaque announcing the new building and hires an architect to design it. State University may recover the $5 million under the First Restatement approach and at least the cost of the plaque and the architect's fees under the Second Restatement approach.

2) Tom offers to give Betty $15,000 if she will buy herself a new car. Betty buys a car for $13,000. Tom is liable to Betty for $15,000 under the First Restatement approach and $13,000 under the Second Restatement Approach.

IV. REQUIREMENT THAT NO DEFENSES EXIST

A. INTRODUCTION

Even if an agreement is supported by valuable consideration or a recognized substitute, contract rights may still be unenforceable because there is a defense to formation of the contract, because there is a defect in capacity (making the obligations voidable by one of the parties), or because a defense to enforcement of certain terms exists.

B. DEFENSES TO FORMATION

There are three categories of defenses to formation of a contract: (i) absence of mutual assent; (ii) absence of consideration; and (iii) public policy considerations that deny contractual status to the agreement.

1. Absence of Mutual Assent

a. Mutual Mistake as to Existing Facts

When both parties entering into a contract are mistaken ***about existing facts*** (not future happenings) relating to the agreement, the contract may be voidable by the adversely affected party if:

(i) The mistake concerns a ***basic assumption*** on which the contract is made (*e.g.,* the parties think they are contracting for the sale of a diamond but in reality the stone is a cubic zirconia);

(ii) The mistake has a ***material effect*** on the agreed-upon exchange (*e.g.,* the cubic zirconia is worth only a hundredth of what a diamond is worth); and

(iii) The party seeking avoidance ***did not assume the risk*** of the mistake.

1) Assumption of Risk

Mutual mistake is not a defense if the adversely affected party bore the risk that the assumption was mistaken. This commonly occurs when one party is in a position to better know the risks than the other party (*e.g.,* contractor vs. homeowner) or where the parties knew that their assumption was doubtful (*i.e.,* when the parties were consciously aware of their ignorance). In other words, to be a defense it must be a mistake, not a mere uncertainty.

Examples: 1) Homeowner contacts builder regarding the cost of installing an inground pool. Builder bids $15,000 and Homeowner accepts. While digging the hole for the pool, Builder encounters an unexpected slab of granite. Blasting away the granite will add 20% to Builder's costs, making the contract unprofitable. Builder will be held to have assumed the risk.

2) Roger finds a stone that appears to be valuable and shows it to his friend Betsy. The two do not know what the stone is but think it is a topaz. Roger agrees to sell the stone to Betsy for $100. The parties subsequently discover that the stone is a diamond worth $1,000. Roger cannot void the contract on mutual mistake grounds because the parties knew that their assumption about the stone was doubtful.

Compare: Roger finds a stone that appears to be valuable. Because Roger is not an expert as to gems, he takes it to Jeweler. Jeweler, in good faith, tells Roger that the stone is a topaz worth very little and offers to buy it for $100. Roger accepts, but subsequently discovers that the stone actually is a diamond worth $1,000. Roger can rescind the contract on mutual mistake grounds. Roger's reliance on an expert's opinion shows that Roger did not intend to assume the risk of not knowing about the stone.

a) **Mistake in Value Generally Not a Defense**

If the parties to a contract make assumptions as to the value of the subject matter, mistakes in those assumptions will generally not be remedied—even though the value of the subject matter is generally a basic assumption and the mistake creates a material imbalance—because both parties usually assume the risk that their assumption as to value is wrong. However, it is possible for the facts to show that the adversely affected party did not assume the risk in determining value.

Example: Roger finds a stone that appears to be valuable and shows it to his friend Betsy. The two properly determine that the stone is a topaz. Roger believes the topaz is worth $500, and Betsy believes the topaz is worth $50, but Roger agrees to sell it to Betsy for $200. The parties subsequently discover that the topaz is worth $600. Roger cannot void the contract because he knew that the parties did not know the true value of the stone, and so assumed the risk that their valuation was incorrect.

Compare: Same facts as above, but because Roger and Betsy did not know the value of a topaz, they took it to Jeweler, who told them the stone was worth $200. Subsequently, Roger discovers that Jeweler knows nothing about topaz stones and determines that the stone was worth $600. Roger can void the contract for mutual mistake and force Betsy to return the stone because here the facts show that the parties did not intend to assume the risk of determining value (because they sought out an expert to determine the true value).

b. **Compare—Unilateral Mistake**

If only one of the parties is mistaken about facts relating to the agreement, the mistake will ***not*** prevent formation of a contract. However, if the nonmistaken party ***knew or had reason to know of the mistake*** made by the other party, the contract is voidable by the mistaken party.

Examples: 1) Seller advertises a particular dredge for sale. After an employee of Buyer inspects the dredge, Buyer offers $35,000 for it, which Seller accepts. Prior to the delivery of the dredge, Buyer discovers that the dredge will not perform certain operations in shallow water, which was the central purpose Buyer intended for the dredge. Seller was unaware of Buyer's belief and in no way created the belief that the dredge would perform the particular operation that Buyer had in mind. The contract is not voidable by Buyer because Buyer's unilateral mistake about the contract's subject matter was not known by Seller nor should it have been known.

2) Seller agrees to sell Buyer a number of different items of hardware. Seller computes the total price at $15,000, and Buyer agrees to pay this amount. Subsequently, Seller discovers that he made an error in computation and the price should be $17,000. In this situation, the preferred analysis is that there ***is*** a contract at $15,000, assuming that Buyer was ***reasonably unaware of the unilateral computation error***. Note also that the error was not an error in the offer; the mistake was ***antecedent*** to the offer by Seller. When Seller stated the offer at $15,000, he meant $15,000.

Compare: Homeowner asks four contractors to submit bids to build a two-car garage on Homeowner's property. When Homeowner receives the bids they are: $17,000, $19,000, $19,500, and $9,000. The last bid was due to a typographical error. Homeowner will not be able to snap up the $9,000 offer because he should have known, based on the other bids, that the $9,000 bid probably contained an error.

1) Unilateral Mistake May Be Canceled in Equity

There is authority in a number of cases that contracts with errors, such as mistakes in ***computation***, may be canceled in equity, assuming that the nonmistaken party has ***not relied*** on the contract. There is also modern authority indicating that a unilateral mistake that is ***so extreme*** that it outweighs the other party's expectations under the agreement will be a ground for cancellation of the contract.

2) Error in Judgment

An error in judgment by one of the parties as to the value or quality of the work done or goods contracted for will ***not*** prevent formation of a contract, even if the nonmistaken party knows or has reason to know of the mistake made by the other party.

Example: Seller offers to sell her car to Buyer for $500, and Buyer accepts. Buyer knows that Seller's car has a market value of $1,500 and that this fact is unknown to Seller. The contract is enforceable.

c. Mistake by the Intermediary (Transmission)

When there is a mistake in the transmission of an offer or acceptance by an intermediary, the prevailing view is that the message ***as transmitted*** is operative unless the other party knew or should have known of the mistake.

Example: Harry put his home up for sale at the price of $340,000. After viewing the home, Sally called her attorney and asked him to prepare an offer to purchase the home for $313,000. The attorney misunderstood Sally and prepared an offer for $330,000 and transmitted the offer to Harry. Harry accepted. Assuming that the attorney had the power to bind Sally, a contract was formed to buy the house for $330,000, despite the attorney's mistake in transmitting the price.

Compare: Same facts as above, but Sally asked her attorney to prepare an offer for $318,000 and the attorney misunderstood and submitted an offer for $380,000. Here, Sally probably would not be bound because Harry

probably should have known of the error as the offer substantially exceeded his asking price.

d. **Ambiguous Contract Language**
Contract language with at least two possible meanings leads to different results depending on the awareness of the parties.

1) **Neither Party Aware of Ambiguity—No Contract**
If neither party was aware of the ambiguity at the time of contracting, there is ***no contract unless*** both parties happened to intend the same meaning.

Example: Buyer agrees to purchase cotton from Seller when the cotton is delivered by a ship named Peerless. This is the total expression of agreement. It is subsequently determined that Buyer contemplated a ship named Peerless that was to dock in September while Seller contemplated a ship named Peerless that was to dock in December. Neither party was aware that there were two ships named Peerless. Their subsequent expression of the ship each intended indicates that they did not intend the same ship at the time of contracting. Therefore, there is no contract. [*See* Raffles v. Wichelhaus, 159 Eng. Rep. 375 (1864)]

2) **Both Parties Aware of Ambiguity—No Contract**
If both parties were aware of the ambiguity at the time of contracting, there is ***no contract unless*** both parties in fact intended the same meaning.

3) **One Party Aware of Ambiguity—Contract**
If one party was aware of the ambiguity and the other party was not at the time of contracting, a ***contract*** will be enforced according to the intention of the party who was unaware of the ambiguity.

Example: Collector agrees to purchase a Picasso sketch from Gallery. It is subsequently determined that Gallery has two sketches and that Gallery intended to sell one of these to Collector while Collector intended to buy the other one. Collector did not know that Gallery owned two sketches; Gallery, of course, knew that it did. Here, there is a contract for the sketch that Collector had in mind because this is a situation in which one party knew of the ambiguity (Gallery) while the other party did not (Collector).

4) **Subjective Intention of Parties Controls**
While the objective test is used in contract law generally, the latent ambiguity situation is unique in that the courts look to the subjective intention of the parties. This is because the objective test simply does not work in this situation. The objective manifestations of the parties appear to be perfectly clear but subsequent facts indicate the latent ambiguity. It is then necessary to receive evidence of what each party subjectively thought at the time of contracting.

e. **Misrepresentation**

1) **Fraudulent Misrepresentation (Fraud in the Inducement)—Contract Voidable**
If a party induces another to enter into a contract by using ***fraudulent misrepresentation*** (*e.g.,* by asserting information she knows is untrue), the contract is ***voidable*** by the innocent party if she ***justifiably relied*** on the fraudulent misrepresentation. This is a type of ***fraud in the inducement.***

Example: Buyer agreed to buy a painting from Seller because Seller told her that the painting previously had been owned by Bubbles Springfield, a famous rock star. In fact, Seller knew that Springfield had never owned the painting. Buyer's promise is voidable if she justifiably relied on Seller's misrepresentation.

a) **Distinguish—Fraud in the Factum**
If one of the parties was tricked into giving assent to the agreement under circumstances that prevented her from appreciating the significance of her action, the agreement cannot be enforced; it is ***void.***

Example: Joe Rocket, a famous football player, signs autographs after each game. After one game, a fan handed him a paper to sign that was in reality the last page of a contract. The contract is void due to fraud in the factum because Rocket was tricked into signing it.

2) **Nonfraudulent Misrepresentation—Contract Voidable If Material**
Even if a misrepresentation is ***not*** fraudulent, the contract is ***voidable*** by the innocent party if the innocent party ***justifiably relied*** on the misrepresentation and the misrepresentation was ***material.*** A misrepresentation is material if either: (i) the information asserted would induce a reasonable person to agree; or (ii) the maker of the misrepresentation knew the information asserted would cause a particular person to agree.

Example: Same facts as in the painting example in 1), above, except that Seller truly believed that the painting had once belonged to Springfield. Because a famous prior owner would likely make a reasonable person agree to buy a painting, the misrepresentation is material. Therefore, Buyer's promise is voidable if she justifiably relied on Seller's misrepresentation.

3) **Innocent Party May Rescind Agreement**
Note that the innocent party need not wait until she is sued on the contract, but may take affirmative action in equity to ***rescind*** the agreement. This right to void or rescind such a contract may be lost, however, if the party so induced affirms the contract in question.

2. **Absence of Consideration**
If the promises exchanged at the formation stage lack the elements of bargain or legal detriment, ***no contract*** exists. In this situation, one of the promises is always illusory.

3. **Public Policy Defenses to Contract Formation—Illegality**
If either the ***consideration or the subject matter*** of a contract is illegal, this will serve as a defense to enforcement. Contracts may be illegal because they are inconsistent with the Constitution, violate a statute, or are against public policy as declared by the courts.

a. **Some Typical Cases of Illegality**
Some of the most common areas in which problems of illegality have arisen are:

1) Agreements in restraint of trade;

2) Gambling contracts;

3) Usurious contracts;

4) Agreements obstructing administration of justice;

5) Agreements inducing breach of public fiduciary duties; and

6) Agreements relating to torts or crimes.

b. **Effect of Illegality**

1) **Generally Contract Is Void**
Illegal consideration or subject matter renders a contract void and unenforceable. In a close case, a court may sever an illegal clause from the contract rather than striking down the entire contract.

2) **Effect Depends on Timing of Illegality**
If the subject matter or consideration was illegal at the time of the offer, there was ***no valid offer***. If it became illegal after the offer but before acceptance, the supervening illegality operates to ***revoke the offer***. If it became illegal after a valid contract was formed, the supervening illegality operates to ***discharge the contract*** because performance has become impossible (*see* VI.E.5.a., *infra*).

3) **Compare—Illegal Purpose**
If the contract was formed for an illegal ***purpose*** but neither the consideration nor the subject matter is illegal (*e.g.,* a contract to rent a plane when the renter's purpose is to smuggle drugs out of Colombia), the contract is only ***voidable*** (rather than void) by the party who (i) did not know of the purpose; or (ii) knew but did not facilitate the purpose ***and*** the purpose does not involve "serious moral turpitude." If both parties knew of the illegal purpose and facilitated it, or knew and the purpose involves serious moral turpitude, the contract is ***void*** and unenforceable. [Restatement (Second) of Contracts §182]

c. **Limitations on Illegality Defense**

1) **Plaintiff Unaware of Illegality**
If the plaintiff contracted without knowledge that the agreement was illegal and the defendant acted with knowledge of the illegality, the innocent plaintiff may recover on the contract.

2) **Parties Not in Pari Delicto**
A person may successfully seek relief if he was not as culpable as the other.
Example: Punter, a casual bettor, may recover against Booker, a professional

bookie. (Some courts reach this result on the theory that the criminal proscription was designed to protect a class to which Punter belongs.)

3) **Licensing—Revenue Raising vs. Protection**
If a contract is illegal solely because a party does not have a required license, whether the contract will be enforceable depends on the reason for the license:

a) **Revenue Raising—Contract Enforceable**
If the license is required merely to raise revenue (*e.g.,* a city requires all vendors at a fair to pay a $25 license fee), the contract generally is enforceable.

b) **Protection of Public—Contract Not Enforceable**
If the license is required to ensure that the licensee meets minimum requirements to protect the public welfare (*e.g.,* a license to practice law, medicine, accounting, etc.), the contract is void. This means that even if the unlicensed party performs perfectly under the contract, the party cannot collect any damages.

C. DEFENSES BASED ON LACK OF CAPACITY

1. Legal Incapacity to Contract
Individuals in certain protected classes are legally incapable of incurring binding contractual obligations. Timely assertion of this defense by a promisor makes the contract ***voidable*** at his election.

a. Contracts of Infants (Minors)

1) **Who Is an Infant?**
The age of majority in most jurisdictions is 18. However, in many states, married persons under age 18 are considered adults.

2) **Effect of Infant's Contract**
Infants generally lack capacity to enter into a contract binding on themselves. However, contractual promises of an adult made to an infant are binding on the adult. In other words, a contract entered into between an infant and an adult is ***voidable by the infant but binding on the adult.***

3) **Disaffirmance**
An infant may choose to disaffirm a contract any time before (or shortly after) reaching the age of majority. If a minor chooses to disaffirm, she must return anything that she received under the contract ***that still remains*** at the time of disaffirmance. However, there is no obligation to return any part of the consideration that has been squandered, wasted, or negligently destroyed.

4) **Affirmance upon Majority**
An infant may affirm, *i.e.,* choose to be bound by his contract, upon reaching majority. He affirms either expressly or by conduct, *e.g.,* ***failing to disaffirm*** the contract ***within a reasonable time after reaching majority.***

5) **Exceptions**
There are, however, certain situations where the infant cannot choose to avoid the contract entered into by him. These are:

a) **Necessities**
An infant is bound to pay the reasonable value of necessities. What a necessity is depends on the infant's station in life.

b) **Statutory Exceptions**
Some states have statutory exceptions. Such statutes usually encompass insurance contracts, student loan contracts, and the like.

b. **Mental Incapacity**
One whose mental capacity is so deficient that he is incapable of understanding the nature and significance of a contract may disaffirm when lucid or by his legal representative. He may likewise affirm during a lucid interval or upon complete recovery, even without formal restoration by judicial action. In other words, the contract is ***voidable***. As in the case of infants, mentally incompetent persons are liable in quasi-contract for necessities furnished to them.

c. **Intoxicated Persons**
One who is so intoxicated that he does not understand the nature and significance of his promise may be held to have made only a ***voidable*** promise if the other party had reason to know of the intoxication. The intoxicated person may affirm the contract upon recovery. Once again, there may be quasi-contractual recovery for necessities furnished during the period of incapacity.

2. **Duress and Coercion**
Contracts induced by duress (*e.g.,* "sign the contract or I'll break your legs") or coercion are ***voidable*** and may be rescinded as long as not affirmed.

a. **Economic Duress Generally Not a Defense**
Generally, taking advantage of another person's economic needs is not a defense. However, withholding something someone wants or needs will constitute economic duress if:

(i) The party threatens to commit a wrongful act that would seriously threaten the other contracting party's property or finances; and

(ii) There are no adequate means available to prevent the threatened loss.

Example: Barry buys his dream home for $700,000. A few years later, Barry loses his job, stops making mortgage payments, and is threatened with foreclosure. Because of the economy, houses are not selling in Barry's neighborhood, so his friend Freida offers to buy Barry's house for the $500,000 that he owes on it. Before the closing, Barry finds a job and does not want to sell the house. Barry is bound; his economic duress is not a defense.

Compare: Barry buys his dream home for $700,000. A few years later, Barry's boss, Freida, tells Barry that if he will not sell her his house for $500,000, she will fire him from his job. Barry agrees to the sale, but before closing finds a new job. The economic duress here would probably be a defense.

D. DEFENSES TO ENFORCEMENT

Defects in the subject matter of a bargain or in the capacity of one party to a contract arise at the formation stage and make the agreement void or voidable. Other defenses, however, involve failure of the agreement to qualify for judicial relief and may arise at the formation stage or later.

1. Statute of Frauds

In most instances, an oral contract is valid. However, certain agreements, by statute, must be evidenced by a ***writing signed by the parties sought to be bound.***

a. Writing Requirement

The Statute of Frauds does not require that the contract be in writing; it requires only that there be one or more writings signed by the person sought to be held liable on the contract that reflect the ***material terms*** of the contract (*e.g.,* in a land sale contract, a description of the property and the price are required; in a contract for the sale of goods, the quantity is required). Thus, a letter (even to a nonparty) or receipt, or even a check indicating a quantity of goods on the memo line, could be sufficient.

Example: Becky Baker calls Sam Supplier and orders 2,000 pounds of flour for use in her bakery at Sam's price of 70¢ a pound. As will be discussed *infra,* this contract is within the Statute of Frauds and is unenforceable by either party without some writing evidencing the material terms. Later the same day, Becky receives a flyer from another supplier indicating that their price for flour is 65¢ per pound. Becky immediately faxes Sam Supplier the following note: "Please cancel my order for 2,000 pounds of flour. /s/ Becky Baker." Becky's attempted cancelation of the contract is a sufficient writing under the Statute of Frauds to make the contract enforceable, at least against her.

1) Electronic Record Satisfies Writing Requirement

Whenever a law, such as the Statute of Frauds, requires a record to be in writing, an electronic record satisfies that law. [Uniform Electronic Transactions Act ("UETA") §7(c)] Thus, the writing requirement may be satisfied by an e-mail.

b. Signature Requirement

The signature requirement is liberally construed by most courts. It need not be handwritten; it can be printed or typed. A party's initials or letterhead may also be sufficient.

1) Electronic Signature

The signature requirement may be satisfied by an electronic signature. [UETA §7(d)] As with paper signatures, whether a record is "signed" is a question of fact. No specific technology is necessary to create a valid signature. If the requisite intent is present, one's name as part of an e-mail may suffice as a signature, as may the firm name on a facsimile (fax).

c. **Agreements Covered**

1) **Executor or Administrator Promises Personally to Pay Estate Debts**
A promise by an executor or administrator to pay the estate's debts out of his own funds must be evidenced by a writing.

2) **Promises to Pay Debt of Another (Suretyship Promises)**

a) **Must Be a Collateral Promise**
A promise to answer for the debt or default of another must be evidenced by a writing. The promise may arise as a result of a tort or contract, but it must be collateral to another person's promise to pay, and not a primary promise to pay.
Example: "Give him the goods, and if he does not pay, I will." This promise is a collateral promise and must be evidenced by a writing. But if the promise is, "Give him the goods, and I will pay for them," the promise is a primary promise and need not be evidenced by a writing.

b) **Main Purpose Must Not Be Pecuniary Interest of Promisor**
If the main purpose or leading object of the promisor is to serve a pecuniary interest of his own, the contract is ***not within the Statute of Frauds*** even though the effect is still to pay the debt of another.
Example: Ernie contracted with ABC Co. to have some machines custom-made for his factory. He promised ABC Co.'s supplier that if it would continue to deliver materials to ABC, Ernie would guarantee ABC Co.'s payment to the supplier. This promise need not be in writing because Ernie's main purpose in guaranteeing payment was to assure that ABC Co. had adequate supplies to build his machines.

3) **Promises in Consideration of Marriage**
A promise the consideration for which is marriage must be evidenced by a writing. This applies to promises that induce marriage by offering something of value (other than a return promise to marry—*e.g.,* "if you marry my son, I will give the two of you a house").

4) **Interest in Land**
A promise creating an interest in land must be evidenced by a writing. This includes not only agreements for the sale of real property, but also other agreements pertaining to land.

a) **What Is an Interest in Land?**
A problem may exist as to whether the subject matter of a given contract constitutes an interest in land. In addition to agreements for the ***sale of real property***, the following items are among the more important interests in land generally covered by the Statute:

(1) ***Leases for more than one year;***

(2) ***Easements of more than one year;***

(3) ***Fixtures;***

(4) ***Minerals (or the like) or structures*** if they are to be severed by the ***buyer.*** If they are to be severed by the seller, they are not an interest in land but rather are goods. If the subject matter is growing crops, timber to be cut, or other things attached to realty capable of severance without material harm to the realty, it is a contract for the sale of goods (*see* 6), *infra*) [U.C.C. §2-107]; and

(5) ***Mortgages*** and most other security liens.

b) Items Not Within the Statute

Even though the end result of some contracts may be an interest in land, they still do not come within the Statute. For example, a contract to build a building or a contract to buy and sell real estate and divide the profits do not come within the Statute.

c) Effect of Performance on Contracts

If the seller conveys to the purchaser (*i.e.,* fully performs), the seller can enforce the buyer's oral promise to pay. Similarly, the purchaser may be able to specifically enforce a land contract if the "***part performance doctrine***" is applicable. Under the doctrine, conduct (*i.e.,* part performance) that ***unequivocally indicates*** that the parties have contracted for the sale of the land will take the contract out of the Statute of Frauds. What constitutes sufficient part performance varies among the jurisdictions. Most require ***at least two*** of the following: payment (in whole or in part), possession, and/or valuable improvements.

5) Performance Not Within One Year

A promise that by its terms ***cannot*** be performed within one year is subject to the Statute of Frauds. Part performance does not satisfy the Statute of Frauds in this case.

a) Effective Date

The date runs from the ***date of the agreement*** and not from the date of performance.

Example: Maria entered into an employment agreement whereby she was to perform services from April 1, 2010, until March 31, 2011. The agreement was entered into on March 15, 2010. It must be evidenced by a writing.

b) Contracts Not Within the Statute

The following contracts do not fall within this provision of the Statute:

(1) Possibility of Completion Within One Year

If the contract is possible to complete within one year, it is not within the one-year prong of the Statute of Frauds, even though actual performance may extend beyond the one-year period.

Example: Carlo makes the following oral statement to Nellie: "Be my nurse until I recover and I will pay you a small salary

now, but leave you a large estate in my will." The contract need not be evidenced by a writing because Carlo could recover within one year.

(2) **Right to Terminate Within Year**
If a contract that cannot be performed within one year allows both parties the right to terminate within a year, there is a ***split*** as to whether the right to terminate takes the contract out of the one-year prong of the Statute of Frauds. The majority view is that nonperformance is not performance within one year, and so the contract is still within the Statute of Frauds. The minority Second Restatement view suggests that because the contract is terminable by either party within a year, it is outside the Statute.

Example: Susan contracts to employ Linda for two years. Part of their agreement allows either party to terminate on 30 days' notice. Under one view, this contract would be within the Statute of Frauds (excusable nonperformance is still not performance within a year). The Second Restatement view makes this contract enforceable because giving the 30 days' notice is an alternative form of performance that can occur within one year.

(3) **Lifetime Contracts**
A contract measured by a lifetime (*e.g.,* a promise to "employ until I die" or "work until I die") is not within the Statute because it is capable of performance within a year since a person can die at any time.

6) **Goods Priced at $500 or More**
A contract for the sale of goods for a price of $500 or more is within the Statute of Frauds and generally must be evidenced by a signed writing to be enforceable. Note that a writing is sufficient even though it omits or incorrectly states a term, but the contract is ***not enforceable beyond the quantity of goods shown in the writing***.

Examples: 1) To meet the Statute of Frauds requirement, Constructo offers a notation made on Widgetco's office pad and signed by Widgetco's president reading: "Sold to Constructo, widgets." The writing is probably not sufficient because no quantity term is given.

2) Facts the same as above, but the memorandum reads: "Sold to Constructo, 1,500 widgets." The memorandum is sufficient to support a contract for up to 1,500 widgets. If the actual agreement was for 15,000 widgets, the agreement would be enforceable only to the extent of 1,500 widgets. However, if the actual agreement was for only 150 widgets, the actual agreement may be shown.

a) **When Writing Not Required**
There are three situations described in U.C.C. section 2-201(3) in which contracts are enforceable without the writing described above:

(1) **Specially Manufactured Goods**
If goods are to be specially manufactured for the buyer and are not suitable for sale to others by the seller in the ordinary course of his business, the contract is enforceable if the seller has, under circumstances that reasonably indicate that the goods are for the buyer, made ***substantial beginning*** in their manufacture or ***commitments*** for their purchase before notice of repudiation is received. [U.C.C. §2-201(3)(a)]

(2) **Admissions in Pleadings or Court**
If the party against whom enforcement is sought admits in pleadings, testimony, or otherwise in court that the contract for sale was made, the contract is enforceable without a writing (but in such a case the contract is not enforced beyond the quantity of goods admitted). [U.C.C. §2-201(3)(b)]

(3) **Payment or Delivery of Goods**
If goods are either received and accepted or paid for, the contract is enforceable. However, the contract is not enforceable beyond the quantity of goods accepted or paid for. Thus, if only some of the goods called for in the oral contract are accepted or paid for, the contract is only partially enforceable. If an indivisible item is partially paid for, most courts hold that the Statute of Frauds is satisfied for the whole item.

Examples: 1) Ketty and Lydia orally agree that Lydia will purchase 150 widgets from Ketty at a price of $10 each. Lydia gives Ketty a check for $70. The contract is enforceable for seven widgets only.

2) Joe orally contracts to buy a car from Suzette for $15,000. Joe gives her a $1,000 down payment. Although Joe has only partially paid for the car, most courts would hold that the contract is enforceable.

b) **Merchants—Confirmatory Memo Rule**
In contracts between merchants, if one party, within a reasonable time after an oral agreement has been made, sends to the other party a ***written*** confirmation of the understanding that is sufficient under the Statute of Frauds to bind the sender, it will also bind the recipient if: (i) he has reason to know of the confirmation's contents; and (ii) he does not object to it in writing within 10 days of receipt. [U.C.C. §2-201(2)]

d. **Effect of Noncompliance with the Statute**
Under the majority rule, noncompliance with the Statute of Frauds renders the contract unenforceable at the option of the party to be charged (*i.e.,* the party being charged may raise the lack of a sufficient writing as an affirmative defense). If the Statute is not raised as a defense, it is waived.

e. **Promissory Estoppel**
Promissory estoppel (*see* III.D., *supra*) is sometimes applied in cases where it would be inequitable to allow the Statute of Frauds to defeat a meritorious claim. When a defendant falsely and intentionally tells a plaintiff that the contract is not within the Statute or

that a writing will subsequently be executed, or when his conduct foreseeably induces a plaintiff to change his position in reliance on an oral agreement, courts may use the doctrine to remove the contract completely from the Statute of Frauds.

f. Remedies If Contract Is Within Statute

If a contract is within the Statute of Frauds because there is noncompliance with the Statute and no applicable exception, in almost all cases a party can sue for the ***reasonable value*** of the services or part performance rendered, ***or*** the ***restitution*** of any other benefit that has been conferred. (*See* VIII.C., *infra,* for a detailed discussion.) This recovery would be in ***quantum meruit*** rather than a suit on the contract. The rationale is that it would be unjust to permit a party to retain benefits received under the failed contract without paying for them.

1) Part Performance

If the part performance rendered takes the contract out of the Statute of Frauds, the performing party has the option of suing ***on the contract*** for expectation damages, rather than merely in restitution for the value of the benefit conferred.

g. Contract Made by Agent

The problem: A given contract is required under state law to be evidenced by a writing. An agent now purports to enter into such a contract on behalf of her principal. Must the agent's authority also be in writing? Most states would answer no, except for contracts involving interests in real property. A few states would answer yes as to all such contracts pursuant to the states' ***equal dignities*** statutes. However, even where written authority would otherwise be required, written authority may be dispensed with if the agent contracted in the presence and under the direction of the principal or if the principal later ratified the contract in writing.

2. Unconscionability

The concept of unconscionability allows a court to ***refuse to enforce a provision or an entire contract*** (or to modify the contract) to avoid "unfair" terms. It is sometimes said that there are two types of unconscionability: substantive unconscionability (*i.e.,* unconscionability based on price alone) and procedural unconscionability (*i.e.,* unconscionability based on unfair surprise or unequal bargaining power). However, few cases recognize substantive unconscionability based on unfair price alone. Instead, the cases have dealt mostly with procedural unconscionability.

a. Common Instances of Procedural Unconscionability

1) Inconspicuous Risk-Shifting Provisions

Standardized printed form contracts often contain a material provision that seeks to shift a risk normally borne by one party to the other. Examples of such provisions are:

(i) ***Confession of judgment*** clauses, which are illegal in most states;

(ii) ***Disclaimer of warranty*** provisions; and

(iii) ***"Add-on" clauses*** that subject all of the property purchased from a seller to repossession if a newly purchased item is not paid for.

Typically, such clauses are found in the fine print ("boilerplate") in printed form contracts. Courts have invalidated these provisions because they are ***inconspicuous*** or ***incomprehensible*** to the average person, even if brought to his actual attention.

2) **Contracts of Adhesion—"Take It or Leave It"**
Courts will deem a clause unconscionable and unenforceable if the signer is unable to procure necessary goods, such as an automobile, from any seller without agreeing to a similar provision. The buyer has no choice.

3) **Exculpatory Clauses**
An exculpatory clause releasing a contracting party from liability for his own ***intentional*** wrongful acts is usually found to be unconscionable because such a clause is against public policy in most states. Exculpatory clauses for ***negligent*** acts may be found to be unconscionable if they are inconspicuous (as discussed above), but commonly are upheld if they are in contracts for activities that are known to be hazardous (*e.g.,* a contract releasing a ski hill operator for liability for negligence often will be upheld).

4) **Limitations on Remedies**
A contractual clause limiting liability for damages to property generally will ***not*** be found to be unconscionable unless it is inconspicuous. However, if a contract limits a party to a certain remedy and that remedy ***fails of its essential purpose***, a court may find the limitation unconscionable and ignore it. [*See, e.g.,* U.C.C. §2-719(2)]

Example: An automobile dealership sells a car and the contract provides that the dealer's liability for defects in the car is limited to repair or replacement. Generally, such a clause is ***not*** unconscionable. However, if a particular customer brings his car back numerous times for the same problem and the dealer is unable to effectively fix the car, the remedy fails of its essential purpose, and a court may ignore the limiting clause and allow the normal remedies for breach.

b. **Timing**
Unconscionability is determined by the circumstances as they existed ***at the time the contract was formed***.

c. **Effect If Court Finds Unconscionable Clause**
If a court finds as a matter of law that a contract or any clause of the contract was unconscionable ***when made***, the court may: (i) refuse to enforce the contract; (ii) enforce the remainder of the contract ***without*** the unconscionable clause; or (iii) ***limit the application of any clause*** so as to avoid an unconscionable result. [*See, e.g.,* U.C.C. §2-302]

V. DETERMINING THE TERMS OF THE CONTRACT

A. INTRODUCTION

Once you have determined that a contract exists, the next thing you must do is determine what are its terms.

B. GENERAL RULES OF CONTRACT CONSTRUCTION

There are a number of general rules of construction applied by the courts when interpreting contracts. The following are among the more frequently invoked:

1. Construed as a Whole

Contracts will be construed as a "whole"; specific clauses will be subordinated to the contract's general intent.

2. Ordinary Meaning of Words

The courts will construe words according to their "ordinary" meaning unless it is clearly shown that they were meant to be used in a technical sense.

3. Inconsistency Between Provisions

If provisions appear to be inconsistent, written or typed provisions will prevail over printed provisions (which indicate a form contract).

4. Custom and Usage

The courts will generally look to see what custom and usage is in the particular business and in the particular locale where the contract is either made or to be performed. [*See also* U.C.C. §1-303]

5. Preference to Construe Contract as Valid and Enforceable

It is important to note that the courts generally will try to reach a determination that a contract is valid and enforceable. Hence, they will be inclined to construe provisions in such a fashion as to make them operative. Obviously, this general policy will not be carried so far as to contravene the intention of the parties.

6. Ambiguities Construed Against Party Preparing Contract

Ambiguities in a contract are construed against the party preparing the contract, absent evidence of the intention of the parties. This is particularly true when there is no evidence of fraud, mutual mistake, duress, or knowledge by one party of unilateral mistake; and both parties are represented by counsel.

C. PAROL EVIDENCE RULE—SUPPLEMENTING, EXPLAINING, OR CONTRADICTING TERMS

In interpreting and enforcing a contract, questions often arise as to whether the written instrument is the complete embodiment of the parties' intention. Where the parties to a contract express their agreement in a ***writing*** with the ***intent*** that it embody the full and final expression of their bargain (*i.e.,* the writing is an ***"integration"***), any other expressions—written or oral—made ***prior to*** the writing, as well as any oral expressions ***contemporaneous with*** the writing, are ***inadmissible to vary*** the terms of the writing.

Example: Buyer is interested in purchasing a new car from Dealer. He settles on a particular car, and Buyer and Dealer begin to negotiate the terms of the sale. During the negotiations, Dealer tells Buyer that if he agrees to buy the car "today," Dealer will provide free car washes for as long as Buyer owns the car. The two parties finally come to an agreement on price and sign a written contract. The written contract contains a clause providing that it is the full agreement between the parties. However, it does not provide for free car washes. Absent an applicable exception, the parol evidence rule would prevent Buyer from introducing evidence in court

of the oral agreement concerning car washing services that was made prior to the execution of the written contract.

1. **Purpose**
Its name notwithstanding, the parol evidence rule is not generally regarded as a rule of evidence, but rather as a rule of ***substantive contract law***. It is designed to carry out the apparent intention of the parties and to facilitate judicial interpretation by having a single clean source of proof (the writing) on the terms of the bargain.

2. **Is the Writing an "Integration"?**
The question of whether a writing is an "integration" of all agreements between the parties can be broken down into two further subquestions:

(i) Is the writing intended as a ***final*** expression?

(ii) Is the writing a ***complete*** or ***partial*** integration?

a. **Is the Writing Intended as a Final Expression?**
Writings that evidence a purported contract are not necessarily the "final" expression of that contract. Thus, for example, the parties might only have intended such writings to be preliminary to a final draft. If so, the parol evidence rule will not bar introduction of further evidence. One should note that the ***more complete*** the agreement appears to be on its face, the more likely it is that it was intended as an ***integration***.

b. **Is the Writing a Complete or Partial Integration?**
After establishing that the writing was "final," one should determine if the integration was "complete" or only "partial." In the former case, it may not be contradicted or supplemented; in the latter it cannot be contradicted, but may be supplemented by proving up consistent additional terms. *Note:* If the agreement contains a ***merger clause*** reciting that the agreement is complete on its face, this clause strengthens the ***presumption*** that all negotiations were merged in the written document.

c. **Who Makes Decision?**
The ***majority view*** is that the question as to whether an agreement is an integration is one of fact. However, this fact question, unlike others, is decided by the ***judge***, not the jury. If the judge decides that the writing was an integration of all agreements between the parties, he will exclude evidence of prior written or oral terms, or contemporaneous written terms, that seek to vary the terms of the integrated writing. Otherwise, he may admit the offered extrinsic evidence. Then, if there is a jury, it will make its own determination as to whether this extrinsic evidence was part of the agreement.

d. **How Is Determination Made?**
There are two competing tests for determining whether the parties intended the writing to be a complete and final integration: the Corbin test and the Williston test.

1) **Corbin Test**
The Corbin test is followed by most courts. It takes into account the ***specific circumstances of the transaction involved*** (*e.g.,* are the parties related or strangers, was it a large transaction, etc.) and asks whether parties like these

situated as they are would naturally and normally include in their writing the extrinsic matter that is sought to be introduced. If people like these under circumstances like this would normally include the extrinsic matter in their writing, it will be excluded under the parol evidence rule. Otherwise, the evidence will be admissible.

2) **Williston Test**
A minority of courts follow the Williston test. These courts do not take into account the particular circumstances of the transaction; instead they look only at the face of the written agreement and decide whether contracting parties (in general) would include the term sought to be proved. If so, the evidence will be excluded.

3. **Extrinsic Evidence Outside Scope of Rule**
Because the rule prohibits admissibility only of extrinsic evidence that seeks to vary, contradict, or add to an "integration," other forms of extrinsic evidence may be admitted where they will not bring about this result, *i.e.,* they will fall outside the scope of the parol evidence rule.

a. **Attacking Validity**
A party to a written contract can attack the agreement's validity. The party acknowledges (concedes) that the writing reflects the agreement but asserts, most frequently, that the ***agreement never came into being*** because of any of the following:

1) **Formation Defects**
Formation defects (*e.g.,* fraud, duress, mistake, and illegality) may be shown by extrinsic evidence.

2) **Conditions Precedent**
Where a party asserts that there was an oral agreement that the written contract would not become ***effective*** until a condition occurred, all evidence of the understanding may be offered and received. This would be a condition precedent to effectiveness. The rationale is that you are not altering a written agreement by means of parol evidence if the written agreement never came into being. It should be borne in mind that parol evidence of such a condition precedent will not be admitted if it contradicts the express language of the written contract.

Example: Giorgio and Susan sign what appears to be a complete contract, but agree orally that the agreement is not to become binding unless Susan can secure financing, or until her home office approves, or the like. The nonhappening of the stipulated event may be shown because the parol evidence rule does not come into play until a binding contract exists.

a) **Distinguish from Condition Subsequent**
Parol evidence is inadmissible as to conditions subsequent, *i.e.,* an oral agreement that the party would not be obliged to ***perform*** until the happening of an event. This latter type of condition limits or modifies a duty under an existing or formed contract.

b. **Interpretation**

If there is uncertainty or ambiguity in the written agreement's terms or a dispute as to the ***meaning*** of those terms, parol evidence can be received to aid the fact-finder in reaching a correct interpretation of the agreement. If the meaning of the agreement is plain, parol evidence is inadmissible.

c. **Showing of "True Consideration"**

The parol evidence rule will not bar extrinsic evidence showing the "true consideration" paid.

Example: A contract states that $10 has been given as full and complete consideration. Extrinsic evidence will be admitted, by way of a defense, to show that this sum has never been paid.

d. **Reformation**

If a party to a written agreement alleges facts (*e.g.,* mistake) entitling him to reformation of the agreement (*see* VIII.E., *infra*), the parol evidence rule is inapplicable. Why? Because the plaintiff is asserting as a cause of action that despite the apparently unambiguous terms of the written agreement, those terms do not in fact constitute the agreement between the parties.

4. **Collateral Agreements and Naturally Omitted Terms**

Parol evidence is often said to be admissible if the alleged parol agreement is collateral to the written obligation (*i.e.,* related to the subject matter but not part of the primary promise) and does not conflict with it. This "collateral agreement" doctrine is hard to apply because it is conclusory. The Restatements of Contracts include a similar concept with a more definitive approach: the naturally omitted terms doctrine. The doctrine allows evidence of terms that would naturally be omitted from the written agreement. A term would naturally be omitted if:

(i) It ***does not conflict*** with the written integration; and

(ii) It concerns a subject that similarly situated parties ***would not ordinarily be expected to include*** in the written instrument.

[Restatement (First) of Contracts, §240; Restatement (Second) of Contracts, §216]

Example: Seller offered to sell his sister his ranch. The deed gave Seller an option to repurchase, but the parties orally agreed that the option could not be transferred to a third party. Oral evidence of the agreement was not barred by the parol evidence rule. The court held that when family members are contracting, they would not ordinarily be expected to put such a term into the written contract. [*See* Masterson v. Sine, 68 Cal. 2d 222 (1968)]

Compare: Seller offered to sell his farm to Buyer. In connection with the sale, Seller orally promised to tear down an unsightly structure across the road from the farm. The court did not allow evidence of the oral agreement to be presented. *Rationale:* At least between strangers, one would ordinarily expect this type of term to be included in the written integration. [Mitchill v. Lath, 247 N.Y. 377 (1928)]

5. Parol Evidence Rule Not Applicable to Subsequent Modifications
Parol evidence can be offered to show subsequent modifications of a written contract, because the parol evidence rule applies only to prior or contemporaneous negotiations. In short, the parties may show that they have altered the integrated writing after its making.

6. Article 2 Rule
Article 2 generally follows the rules discussed above (including the Corbin test), providing that a party cannot contradict a written contract but he may add ***consistent additional terms*** unless: (i) there is a merger clause, or (ii) the courts find from all of the circumstances that the writing was intended as a complete and exclusive statement of the terms of the agreement. [*See* U.C.C. §2-202] Article 2 also provides that a written contract's terms may be ***explained*** or ***supplemented*** by the following whether or not the writing appears to be ambiguous:

a. Course of Dealing
The parties' course of dealing may be used to explain a contract. A course of dealing is a sequence of conduct concerning ***previous transactions*** between the parties to a particular transaction that may be regarded as establishing a common basis of their understanding. [U.C.C. §1-303(b), (d)]

b. Usage of Trade
A usage of trade may also be used to explain a contract. A usage of trade is a ***practice or method of dealing***, regularly observed in a particular business setting so as to justify an expectation that it will be followed in the transaction in question. [U.C.C. §1-303(c), (d)]

c. Course of Performance
Where a contract involves ***repeated occasions for performance*** by either party and the other party has the opportunity to object to such performance, any course of performance accepted or acquiesced to is relevant in determining the meaning of the contract. [U.C.C. §1-303(a), (d)]

D. OTHER ARTICLE 2 PROVISIONS ON INTERPRETING CONTRACTS

1. Battle of the Forms
Recall that U.C.C. section 2-207 provides that a contract can be formed even though the terms of the acceptance do not match the terms of the offer. (*See* II.D.4.c.2), *supra*.) Article 2 has specific rules for determining what terms are included in the contract in such a case, and these rules are dependent on whether both parties to the transaction are merchants.

a. Contracts Involving a Nonmerchant—Terms of Offer Govern
If any party to the contract is not a merchant, the additional or different terms are considered to be mere proposals to modify the contract that do ***not*** become part of the contract unless the offeror expressly agrees.

Example: Paul sends a letter offering to sell his car to Stephanie for $1,200. Stephanie sends Paul a letter stating: "I accept and want you to put new tires on it." This is a contract, but Paul is not bound to put new tires on the car.

b. Contracts Between Merchants—Additional Terms in Acceptance Usually Included

If ***both*** parties to the contract are merchants, ***additional*** terms in the acceptance will be included in the contract unless:

(i) They ***materially alter*** the original terms of the offer (*e.g.,* they change a party's risk or the remedies available);

(ii) The offer ***expressly limits acceptance*** to the terms of the offer; or

(iii) The ***offeror has already objected*** to the particular terms, or ***objects within a reasonable time*** after notice of them is received.

Example: Widgetco offers to sell Machineco 1,500 widgets at $10 each. Machineco replies, "We accept, 5% discount for paying within 30 days." The parties have formed a contract and it probably includes a 5% discount for payment within 30 days (assuming that the discount is not material).

Compare: Widgetco offers to sell Machineco 1,500 widgets at $10 each. Machineco replies, "We accept. Any disputes will be settled by arbitration." The parties have formed a contract. However, the arbitration provision will be construed by most courts as a material alteration that will not be included in the terms of the contract.

c. Contracts Between Merchants—Different Terms in Acceptance May or May Not Be Included

There is a split of authority over whether terms in the acceptance that are ***different*** from (as opposed to in addition to) the terms in the offer will become part of the contract. Some courts treat different terms like additional terms, and follow the test set out above in determining whether the terms should be part of the contract. Other courts follow the ***"knockout rule,"*** which states that conflicting terms in the offer and acceptance are knocked out of the contract because each party is assumed to object to the inclusion of such terms in the contract. Under the knockout rule, gaps left by knocked out terms are filled by the U.C.C. (*e.g.,* when the date of delivery differs in the offer and the acceptance, the U.C.C. provides that delivery must be made within a reasonable time).

Example: Seller offers to sell to Buyer 1,500 widgets at $10 each ***plus freight***. Buyer replies: "I accept. The price is $10.10 each ***including freight***." There is a contract, assuming that the actual cost of freight is not materially different from $150, as the offer was to sell the widgets for $10 plus (actual) freight costs and the acceptance was to purchase the widgets at $10.10 each including freight costs (the extra 10¢ apparently being to cover freight costs). Under the approach treating different terms like additional terms, the buyer's acceptance will control (*i.e.,* the buyer is obligated to pay $15,150 for the widgets and no additional freight charges) unless Seller objects. If Seller does object, there is a contract on Seller's original terms. However, under the knockout rule, the different freight terms will be knocked out. The price will be $10 plus the reasonable cost of freight at the time of delivery according to the U.C.C.

2. Supplemental ("Gap-Filler") Terms

Recall that the key to forming a contract for the sale of goods is the quantity term (*see* II.B.2.b.1)b), *supra*). If other terms are missing from the agreement, Article 2 has gap-filler provisions to fill in the missing term(s).

a. Price

If: (i) nothing has been said as to price; (ii) the price is left open to be agreed upon by the parties and they fail to agree; or (iii) the price is to be fixed in terms of some standard that is set by a third person or agency and it is not set, then the price is a ***reasonable price at the time for delivery***. [U.C.C. §2-305]

b. Place of Delivery

If the place of delivery is not specified, the place is the ***seller's place of business***, if he has one; otherwise, it is the seller's home. However, if the goods have been identified as the ones to satisfy the contract and the parties know that they are in some other place, then that is the place of delivery. [U.C.C. §2-308]

c. Time for Shipment or Delivery

If the time for shipment or delivery is not specified, shipment/delivery is due in a ***reasonable time***. [U.C.C. §2-309]

d. Time for Payment

If the time for payment is not specified, payment is due at the ***time and place at which the buyer is to receive the goods***. [U.C.C. §2-310]

e. Assortment

If a contract provides that an assortment of goods is to be delivered (*e.g.,* blouses in various colors and sizes) and does not specify which party is to choose, the assortment is to be ***at the buyer's option***. If the party who has the right to specify the assortment does not do so seasonably, the other party is excused from any resulting delay and may either proceed in any reasonable manner (*e.g.,* choose a reasonable assortment) or treat the failure as a breach. [U.C.C. §2-311]

3. Delivery Terms and Risk of Loss

All contracts for the sale of goods require delivery of the goods. Often, delivery consists merely of allowing the buyer to take the goods with him (*e.g.,* a purchase of groceries from the grocery store). However, circumstances often require some other type of delivery (*e.g.,* delivery of 100 cases of cereal to the grocery store requires shipment). A contract's delivery terms are important because they determine when risk of loss passes from the seller to the buyer if the goods are damaged or destroyed.

a. Noncarrier Case

A noncarrier case is a sale in which it appears that the parties did not intend that the goods would be moved by a common carrier (*e.g.,* when you buy groceries). In such a case, if the ***seller is a merchant***, risk of loss passes to the buyer only when she ***takes physical possession*** of the goods. If the ***seller is not a merchant***, risk of loss passes to the buyer upon ***tender of delivery***. [*See* U.C.C. §2-509(3)]

Examples: 1) Merchant Seller sells goods to Buyer who is to pick them up at noon on Monday. Seller has the goods ready for Buyer at that time, but Buyer does not arrive. The goods are destroyed at 1:30 p.m. that day. Risk

of loss falls on the merchant seller because the buyer had not actually picked up the goods.

2) Nonmerchant Seller sells goods to Buyer and the parties agree that the goods will be picked up by Buyer at noon on Monday. Seller has the goods ready for Buyer at that time, but Buyer does not arrive. The goods are destroyed at 1:30 p.m. that day. Risk of loss falls on Buyer because Seller tendered delivery at noon when he had the goods ready for pick-up by Buyer.

b. Carrier Cases

A carrier case is a sale in which it appears that the parties intended the goods to be moved by a carrier (*e.g.,* when you order a book from an Internet website). There are two types of carrier cases: shipment contracts and destination contracts. Whether a contract is a shipment contract or a destination contract depends on the delivery terms used in the contract.

1) Shipment Contract

If the contract authorizes or requires the seller to ship the goods by carrier but does not require him to deliver them at a particular destination, it is a shipment contract and risk of loss passes to the buyer when the goods are ***delivered to the carrier.*** [U.C.C. §2-509(1)(a)]

Example: Seller in New York sells 10,000 tons of steel to Buyer in California. The contract authorizes shipment by carrier but does not require Seller to tender the goods in California. Risk passes to Buyer when the goods are placed in possession of the carrier. If the goods are damaged in transit, the loss falls on Buyer.

2) Destination Contracts

If the contract requires the seller to deliver the goods at a particular destination, the risk of loss passes to the buyer when the goods are ***tendered to the buyer at the destination***. [U.C.C. §2-509(1)(b)]

Example: If in the last example, the contract provided that the goods must be tendered in California, risk of loss during transit to California would have been on Seller.

3) Common Delivery Terms

A number of abbreviations are often used in commercial contracts to set out the shipping terms. When used, these abbreviations determine whether the contract is a shipment or a destination contract. If the contract contemplates delivery by a carrier and no delivery term is used, the contract is a shipment contract.

a) C.I.F. and C. & F.

C.I.F. stands for "cost, insurance, and freight"; and C. & F. stands for "cost and freight." These terms mean that the price in the contract includes the price of the goods, the cost of shipping them to the buyer, and (in C.I.F. contracts) the cost of purchasing insurance for the benefit of the buyer in case the goods are destroyed in transit. These contracts are ***always shipment contracts*** (*i.e.,* the risk of loss passes to the buyer as soon as the goods are turned over to the carrier).

b) **F.A.S.**
F.A.S. stands for "free alongside." The term is generally used only when goods are to be shipped by boat. The risk of loss passes to the buyer once the goods are delivered to the dock.

c) **F.O.B.**
F.O.B. stands for "free on board." The letters F.O.B. are always followed by a location, and the risk of loss passes to the buyer at the named location. The seller bears the risk and expense of getting the goods to the named location. These contracts can be either shipment contracts or destination contracts, depending on the location named.

Examples: 1) Seller in New York sells 10,000 widgets to Buyer in California, "F.O.B. New York," or "F.O.B. Seller's materials yard." This is a shipment contract and risk of loss and expenses of shipment must be borne by the buyer during shipment.

2) Same facts as above, but the contract is "F.O.B. California" or "F.O.B. Buyer's warehouse." This is a destination contract and Seller must bear the risk of loss and expenses of shipping to the named destination.

c. **Effect of Breach on Risk of Loss**

1) **Defective Goods**
If goods are so defective that the buyer has a right to reject them, the risk of loss does not pass to the buyer until the defects are ***cured*** or she ***accepts*** the goods in spite of their defects. [U.C.C. §2-510(1)] Note that a buyer generally has the right to reject for any defect. (*See* VII.C., *infra.*)

Example: Buyer has ordered blue widgets from Seller, F.O.B. Seller's plant. Seller ships blue-black widgets, giving Buyer a right to reject. The widgets are damaged in transit. The risk of loss falls on Seller, although the risk would have been on Buyer if blue widgets had been shipped.

2) **Revocation of Acceptance**
If the buyer rightfully revokes acceptance, the ***risk of loss*** is treated as having rested ***on the seller from the beginning*** to the extent of any deficiency in the buyer's insurance coverage, the risk of loss at issue being that between the time of acceptance and the time of revocation of acceptance. [U.C.C. §2-510(2)] However, revocation of acceptance is rightful only if it occurs "before any substantial change in condition of the goods which is not caused by their own defects." [U.C.C. §2-608(2)] Thus, there can be no revocation of acceptance after a casualty loss to the goods.

d. **Risk in Sale or Return and Sale on Approval Contracts**

1) **Sale or Return**
For the purpose of determining the risk of loss, a sale or return contract (*e.g.*, the buyer takes goods for resale but may return them if she is unable to resell them)

is treated as an ordinary sale and the above rules apply. If the goods are returned to the seller, the ***risk remains on the buyer*** while the goods are in transit. [U.C.C. §2-327(2)]

Example: A magazine distributor delivers 1,000 magazines to a newsstand. The parties agree that the buyer need only pay for any magazines that are not returned to the seller within 40 days. This is a sale or return, and the buyer has the risk of loss until the seller receives any returned magazines.

2) **Sale on Approval**

In a sale on approval (*i.e.,* the buyer takes goods for use but may return them even if they conform to the contract), the risk of loss does not pass to the buyer until she ***accepts***. Acceptance may take place by failure to return or notify the seller of an intention to return within the required time. If the buyer decides not to take the goods, return is ***at the seller's risk***. [U.C.C. §2-327(1)]

Example: A door-to-door vacuum seller offers to leave a vacuum with a homeowner for 30 days on approval—and the homeowner is not obligated to buy unless completely satisfied at the end of the 30-day period. This is a sale on approval. The risk of loss remains with the seller during the approval period. Thus, if the vacuum is destroyed during the trial period, the buyer is not liable to the seller for its price.

4. **Insurable Interest and Identification**

As noted above, a buyer often bears the risk of loss before receiving the goods purchased. In order to aid buyers in this situation (and a few others), Article 2 gives buyers a special property interest in goods as soon as they are identified as the ones that will be used to satisfy the contract (*e.g.,* as soon as the seller sets them aside for the buyer). This special property interest is insurable, so that a buyer may obtain insurance for goods while they are being shipped to prevent loss in case of damage or destruction during shipment. [*See* U.C.C. §2-501]

5. **Bilateral Contracts Formed by Performance**

Recall that a contract may be formed by the parties' performance where the mirror image rule is not satisfied and under certain circumstances under Article 2's "battle of the forms" provision [U.C.C. §2-207]. (*See* II.D.4.c.3), *supra.*) In such cases, under Article 2, the contract includes all of the terms on which the writings of both parties agree. Any necessary missing terms are filled in by the supplemental terms provided for in Article 2. [U.C.C. §2-207(3)]

a. **Compare—Common Law Last Shot Rule**

The rule is different in common law contracts. At common law, the contract will include the terms of the last communication sent to the party who performed. *Rationale:* That communication was a rejection of any prior offer and a counteroffer, and the performance was an acceptance of the terms in that counteroffer.

6. **Warranties**

Contracts for the sale of goods automatically include a warranty of title (in most cases). They also may include certain implied warranties and express warranties.

a. Warranty of Title and Against Infringement

1) Warranty of Title
Any seller of goods warrants that the title transferred is good, that the transfer is rightful, and that there are no liens or encumbrances against the title of which the buyer is unaware at the time of contracting. [U.C.C. §2-312] This warranty arises automatically and need not be mentioned in the contract.

2) Warranty Against Infringement
A ***merchant seller*** regularly dealing in goods of the kind sold also automatically warrants that the goods are delivered free of any patent, trademark, copyright, or similar claims. But a ***buyer who furnishes specifications*** for the goods to the seller must hold the seller harmless against such claims. If this warranty is breached and the buyer is sued, she must give the seller notice of the litigation within a reasonable time or lose her right to any remedy. In such a case, the seller can give the buyer notice of his wish to defend the lawsuit and, if the seller agrees to bear all expenses and satisfy any adverse judgment, the buyer must let him defend or lose any rights against him arising out of the breach. [U.C.C. §2-607(3), (5)]

b. Implied Warranty of Merchantability

1) When Given
Implied in every contract for ***sale by a merchant*** who deals in goods of the kind sold, there is a warranty that the goods are merchantable. The serving of food or drink for consumption on the premises is a sale of goods subject to the warranty of merchantability. [U.C.C. §2-314(1)]

2) Elements of Warranty of Merchantability
To be merchantable, goods must at least:

(i) ***Pass without objection*** in the trade under the contract description;

(ii) In the case of fungible goods, ***be of fair average quality*** within the description;

(iii) ***Be fit for the ordinary purposes*** for which such goods are used;

(iv) Be, within the variations permitted by the agreement, ***of even kind, quality, and quantity*** within each unit and among all units involved;

(v) ***Be adequately contained, packaged, or labeled*** according to the contract; and

(vi) ***Conform to any promises or affirmations of fact made on the label.*** Other warranties of merchantability may arise from the course of dealing or usage of trade.

[U.C.C. §2-314(2)] The most important test is "***fit for the ordinary purposes for which such goods are used***," and a failure to live up to this test is the usual claim in a merchantability suit.

3) Seller's Knowledge of Defect Not Relevant

As in all implied warranty cases, it makes no difference that the seller himself did not know of the defect or that he could not have discovered it. Implied warranties are not based on negligence but rather on ***absolute liability*** that is imposed on certain sellers.

c. Implied Warranty of Fitness for a Particular Purpose

A warranty will also be implied in a contract for the sale of goods whenever (i) ***any seller***, merchant or not, ***has reason to know the particular purpose*** for which the goods are to be used and that the ***buyer is relying*** on the seller's skill and judgment to select suitable goods; and (ii) the ***buyer in fact relies*** on the seller's skill or judgment. [U.C.C. §2-315] The comment to section 2-315 says, "A particular purpose differs from the ordinary purpose for which goods are used in that it envisages a specific use by the buyer which is peculiar to the nature of his business whereas the ordinary purposes for which goods are used are those envisaged in the concept of merchantability."

Examples: 1) Seller, who as a hobby prepared an automobile for dirt track racing, sold it to Buyer for racing purposes. Buyer was a novice in racing. The steering mechanism collapsed in a turn during a race. The mechanism would not have collapsed in ordinary driving. There was a breach of warranty of fitness for "particular purposes" if the seller had reason to know that the buyer was relying on him to provide a suitable racing vehicle.

2) Seller, a law student, sells his used automobile to Buyer. The steering mechanism collapses during an ordinary Sunday afternoon drive. There is no breach of a warranty of fitness for particular purposes because the element of selection based on Seller's purported skill is not present.

3) Note that in both of the above examples, if the seller knew that the automobile had a particular defect and did not disclose this fact to the buyer, he might be subject to liability because of a lack of good faith. Section 1-304 provides that every contract or duty within the U.C.C. imposes an obligation of good faith in its performance or enforcement.

d. Express Warranties

Any affirmation of fact or promise made by the seller to the buyer, any description of the goods, and any sample or model creates an express warranty if the statement, description, sample, or model is part of the ***basis of the bargain***. For the statement, description, sample, or model to be a part of the basis of the bargain, it need only come at such a time that the ***buyer could have relied*** on it when she entered into the contract. The buyer does not need to prove that she actually did rely, although the seller may negate the warranty by proving that the buyer as a matter of fact did not rely. It is not necessary that the seller intended the affirmation of fact, description, model, or sample to create a warranty. [U.C.C. §2-313]

1) Distinguish—Statements of Value or Opinion

A statement relating merely to the value of the goods, or a statement purporting to be only the seller's opinion or commendation of the goods, does not create an express warranty.

Examples: 1) "Chevrolet cars are better." No warranty.

2) "You will like this." No warranty.

Compare: A number of courts have held that such statements as "this tractor is in A-1 condition" or "this automobile is in top mechanical condition" do create express warranties that are breached if the statement is not a proper characterization of the condition of the thing sold.

e. Disclaimer of Warranties

1) Warranty of Title

The title warranty can be disclaimed or modified only by specific language or by circumstances which give the buyer notice that the seller does not claim title or that he is selling only such rights as he or a third party may have (*e.g.,* a sheriff's sale).

2) Implied Warranties

The implied warranties of merchantability and fitness for a particular purpose can be disclaimed by either specific disclaimers or general methods of disclaimer.

a) Specific Disclaimers

Article 2 provides specific methods for disclaiming the implied warranties of merchantability and fitness. Use of these methods is the best way for a seller to ensure that a disclaimer is effective.

(1) Disclaimer of Warranty of Merchantability

The warranty of merchantability can be specifically disclaimed or modified only by ***mentioning merchantability***. If the sales contract is in writing, the disclaimer must be ***conspicuous***. [U.C.C. §2-316(2)]

(2) Disclaimer of Warranty of Fitness for a Particular Purpose

The warranty of fitness for a particular purpose can be specifically disclaimed only by a ***conspicuous writing***. A written disclaimer, according to the statute, is sufficient if it says, for example, "[t]here are no warranties which extend beyond the description on the face hereof." [U.C.C. §2-316(2)]

(3) "Conspicuous" Defined

A term is conspicuous when it is "so written, displayed, or presented that a reasonable person against whom it is to operate ought to have noticed it." Language in the body of a writing is conspicuous if: (i) it is in larger type than surrounding text; (ii) it is in a contrasting type, font, or color; or (iii) it is set off from the text by marks that call attention to it. [U.C.C. §1-201(b)(10)] The court, not the jury, decides any fact question as to conspicuousness.

b) General Disclaimer Methods

The U.C.C. also provides several general methods for disclaiming implied warranties. These methods are more dependent on the circumstances than the specific methods, and so are less certain to be effective than specific disclaimers.

(1) By General Disclaimer Language
Unless the circumstances indicate otherwise, the implied warranties of merchantability and fitness can be disclaimed by expressions such as "***as is***," "with all faults," or other expressions that in common understanding call the buyer's attention to the fact that there are no implied warranties.

(2) By Inspection or Refusal to Inspect
When the buyer, before entering into the contract, has examined the goods or a sample or model as fully as she desires or has refused to examine, there is no warranty as to defects that a reasonable examination would have revealed to her.

(3) By Course of Dealing, Etc.
Implied warranties may also be disclaimed by the course of dealing, course of performance, or usage of trade.

3) Express Warranties

a) In General
As discussed above, any affirmation of fact or promise, description of the goods, model, or sample will create an express warranty. If there are also words or conduct negating the express warranty, problems of interpretation will arise. The U.C.C. provides that words or conduct relevant to the creation of express warranties and words or conduct tending to negate such warranties shall wherever possible be construed as consistent with each other, but "***negation or limitation is inoperative to the extent that such construction is unreasonable***." [U.C.C. §2-316] Practically every sale will involve some description of the goods, and the comment to section 2-313 suggests that the ***basic obligation*** created by this description cannot be read out of the contract by a disclaimer clause.

Example: Seller sells to Buyer something that Seller describes as an "automobile" being sold "as is," and with sufficient disclaimers of all implied warranties. The thing delivered is an automobile body without an engine, a transmission, or wheels. While an automobile with very substantial defects would have fulfilled this contract, what was delivered was not an "automobile" at all. Seller's description "automobile" created an express warranty that an automobile would be delivered, and the disclaimer did not negate this basic obligation.

Of course, the language of disclaimer in the example would substantially reduce the quality of the automobile that must be delivered.

b) Parol Evidence Rule
The parol evidence rule might be an obstacle to a buyer to whom an express

warranty was made when the contract contains a broad disclaimer of warranties. In a typical situation, the seller makes an express warranty verbally, but the written contract contains no such warranty and instead contains a clause disclaiming all warranties not set forth in the contract. Here, the parol evidence rule could prevent the buyer from introducing evidence of the verbal warranty. *But note:* The buyer can often avoid the rule by a showing that he did not intend that the writing be the complete and exclusive expression of the parties' agreement (*see* V.C.2., *supra*) or that the disclaimer is unconscionable under the circumstances (*see* 6), *infra*).

4) Limitations on Damages

Parties may include in their contract a clause limiting the damages available in the case of breach of warranty (*e.g.*, "remedy for breach of warranty is limited to repair or replacement of the defective goods"). Such a limitation generally will be upheld unless the limitation is unconscionable (*e.g.*, causes the remedy to fail of its essential purpose; *see* IV.D.2.a.4) *supra*).

5) Timing—Disclaimers and Limitations in the Box

To be effective, a disclaimer of warranty or limitation on remedies must be agreed to during the bargaining process. Thus, although a few courts hold otherwise, most hold that a warranty disclaimer or limitation on remedy included inside the packaging of goods is not effective against the buyer. However, there are ways around this (*e.g.*, the outside of the box could indicate that the sale is subject to the conditions stated inside the box; a registration card within the box can indicate that by registering, the owner agrees to all of the conditions set out in the documents in the box (modifying the contract), etc.).

a) Compare—"Clickwrap"

Computer software often comes with terms that appear on the user's computer screen during the installation process, and the purchaser must click to agree to the terms before installing. Such limitations and disclaimers typically are upheld on the rationale that the purchaser can return the software if he disagrees with the conditions.

6) Unconscionability and Warranty Disclaimers

Some courts will, in addition to determining whether disclaimers have met the formal requirements discussed above, test warranty disclaimers by the conscionability standards of U.C.C. section 2-302. Such things as lack of bargaining position, lack of choice, and failure to understand would be relevant in determining whether a disclaimer is unconscionable. (*See* IV.D.2., *supra*.) Moreover, warranty disclaimers that limit damages for personal injury caused by a breach of warranty on consumer goods are prima facie unconscionable.

f. Damages for Breach of Warranty

1) In General—Difference Between Goods Tendered and as Warranted

Generally, the measure of damages for breach of any warranty is the difference between the value of the goods accepted and the value of the goods as warranted, measured at the time and place of acceptance. When, however, there are special

circumstances that show proximate damages of a different amount, that amount is the proper measure.[U.C.C. §2-714(2)]

2) **Breach of Warranty of Title**
In the case of a breach of warranty of title, the buyer may rescind the contract, revoke acceptance of the goods, or sue for damages. In these cases, the goods are reclaimed by the true owner or lien holder, thus dispossessing the purchaser. The value of the goods accepted is deemed to be nothing; so the damages are the value of the goods as warranted. Often, but not always, that is the same as the purchase price.

a) **Special Circumstances—Appreciation and Depreciation**
As noted above, damages may be measured differently if there are special circumstances. A great appreciation or depreciation in the value of the goods from the time of delivery until the purchaser is dispossessed of the property is usually considered such a special circumstance. In that case, the value is measured at the time of the dispossession rather than at the time of acceptance.

Examples: 1) Buyer purchases a painting for $10,000 from Seller, who in turn purchased the painting from Gallery. Unbeknownst to any of the parties, the person who sold the painting to Gallery had stolen it. Several years after Buyer's purchase, Owner, the painting's true owner, sues Buyer and recovers the painting, which is now worth $100,000. The appreciation is a special circumstance, so Buyer's damages will be the value of the painting at dispossession—$100,000. [*See* Menzel v. List, 24 N.Y.2d 91 (1969)]

2) Buyer purchases a used truck for $5,000 from Seller's used car dealership. After driving it for one year, Buyer is pulled over in a routine traffic stop. The police inform Buyer the truck is stolen and impound it. When taken by the police, the truck was worth $4,200. Having use and possession of the truck for a substantial period of time is a special circumstance, and Buyer is entitled only to the value of the truck on the date it was impounded. [*See* City Car Sales v. McAlpin, 380 So. 2d 865 (Ala. 1979); Schneidt v. Absey Motors, Inc., 248 N.W.2d 792 (N.D. 1976)]

g. **To Whom Do Warranties Extend?**
Article 2 provides alternative provisions for determining to whom warranty liability extends. [U.C.C. §2-318] Most states have adopted ***Alternative A***, which provides that the seller's warranty liability extends to any natural person who is in the ***family*** or ***household*** of the buyer or who is a ***guest*** in the buyer's home if it is reasonable to expect that the person may use, consume, or be affected by the goods and that person suffers ***personal injury*** because of a breach of warranty. The seller cannot escape the effect of this section by contract. (The comments say that beyond this, the section is neutral and is not intended to enlarge or restrict the developing case law on whether the seller's warranties given to his buyer who resells extend to other persons in the distributive chain.) Alternative B extends a seller's express or implied warranty liability to ***any natural person*** reasonably expected to use, consume, or be affected by the goods and

who suffers ***personal injury*** because of a breach of warranty. The broadest alternative, Alternative C, extends warranty liability to ***any person*** reasonably expected to use, consume, or be affected by the goods and who is ***injured*** by breach of the warranty (this includes property damage). The seller may not exclude or limit the operation of the section with respect to ***personal injury***.

E. MODIFICATION OF CONTRACT TERMS

1. Consideration

Under general contract law, a final contract cannot be modified unless the modification is supported by new consideration. Under the U.C.C., however, promises of new and different terms by the parties to a sales contract are valid without consideration.

2. Writing

A written contract can be modified orally. For sales of goods contracts, however, the modification must be in writing if the contract as modified falls within the Statute of Frauds. Thus, if the contract ***as modified*** is for $500 or more, it must be evidenced by a writing; if the contract ***as modified*** is for less than $500, no writing is necessary. [U.C.C. §2-209]

Examples: 1) Seller agrees to sell Buyer his car for $525 and the parties put the contract in writing to satisfy the Statute of Frauds. Subsequently, Buyer discovers that he can afford to spend only $475 on a car. Buyer calls Seller and tells Seller of his trouble. Seller agrees to lower the price to $475. A writing is no longer necessary, and either party can enforce the oral modification.

2) Mary phones Paul and asks Paul for his price on widgets. Paul informs Mary that he currently is selling widgets for $3 each. Mary asks Paul to send her 150 widgets. Paul agrees, and tells Mary that he will ship them the next day. The contract is enforceable without a writing. A few hours later, Mary phones Paul back and asks Paul whether he could send her 200 widgets instead of 150. Paul agrees. The contract is no longer enforceable absent a written memorandum satisfying the Statute of Frauds.

a. Provisions Prohibiting Oral Modification Not Effective at Common Law

The common law rule is that even if a written contract expressly provides that it may be modified only by a writing, the parties can orally modify the contract.

b. U.C.C. Recognizes No-Modification Clauses

Under the U.C.C., even if a contract is not within the Statute of Frauds, if it explicitly provides that it may not be modified or rescinded except by a signed writing, that provision will be given effect. [U.C.C. §2-209]

1) Contract Between Merchant and Nonmerchant

If a contract is between a merchant and a nonmerchant and the provision requiring written modification is on the merchant's form, it will not be given effect unless it is ***separately signed*** by the nonmerchant.

2) Waiver

If the parties attempt to orally modify a contract that requires written modification, it is technically ineffective as a modification, but can operate as a waiver of the "no

oral modification" clause. Such a waiver will be found whenever the other party has changed position in reliance on the oral modification.

a) **Retraction of Waiver**
A party who makes a waiver affecting an executory (not yet performed) portion of the contract may retract the waiver if she notifies the other party that strict performance of the waived terms is required. The waiver may not be retracted, however, if the other party detrimentally relied on it. [U.C.C. §2-209(5)]

Example: A contract between Buyer and Seller for 800 widgets contains a clause requiring all modifications to be in writing. The parties orally agree to reduce the number to 400 widgets. Buyer later decides he wants 800 widgets after all. If Seller relied on the oral modification in making contracts with other parties for widgets and does not have stock available, Buyer cannot retract the waiver. If, however, Seller did not change his position in reliance on the waiver, Buyer may retract the waiver and enforce the contract for the full 800 widgets.

3. **Parol Evidence Rule Does Not Apply**
As noted above, parol evidence is admissible to show subsequent oral modifications of a written contract.

VI. PERFORMANCE AND EXCUSE OF NONPERFORMANCE

A. INTRODUCTION
Having established that there is a contract and having determined what are the terms of the contract, the next issue to consider is what performance is due and whether any nonperformance is excused.

B. PERFORMANCE AT COMMON LAW
A party's basic duty at common law is to substantially perform all that is called for in the contract.

C. PERFORMANCE UNDER ARTICLE 2
Article 2 generally requires a ***perfect tender***—the delivery and condition of the goods must be exactly as promised in the contract. Note the following:

1. **Obligation of Good Faith**
Article 2 requires all parties to act in good faith, which is defined as "honesty in fact and the observance of reasonable commercial standards of fair dealing." [U.C.C. §1-201(2)]

2. **Seller's Obligation of Tender and Delivery**

a. **Noncarrier Cases**
Recall that a noncarrier case is a sale in which it appears that the parties did not intend that the goods be moved by carrier. (*See* V.D.3.a., *supra*.)

1) **Tender of Delivery**
In a proper tender of delivery, the seller must put and hold conforming goods at the buyer's disposition for a time sufficient for the buyer to take possession. The seller must ***give the buyer notice*** reasonably necessary to enable her to take possession of the goods. The ***tender must be at a reasonable hour***. [U.C.C. §2-503(1)]

2) **Place of Delivery**
In the absence of an agreement otherwise, the place of delivery is the ***seller's place of business***, or if he has none, his residence. However, if at the time of contracting, the goods are, to the knowledge of both parties, at some other place, that place is the place of delivery. [U.C.C. §2-308]

b. **Carrier Cases**
Recall that a carrier case is a sale in which, due either to the circumstances or to the express terms of the agreement, it appears that the parties intended that a carrier be used to move the goods. (*See* V.D.3.b., *supra*.)

1) **Shipment Contracts—Where Seller Has Not Agreed to Tender at Particular Destination**
In the absence of an agreement otherwise, the seller need not see that the goods reach the buyer, but need only:

a) Put the goods into the hands of a reasonable carrier and make a reasonable contract for their transportation to the buyer;

b) Obtain and promptly tender any documents required by the contract or usage of trade or otherwise necessary to enable the buyer to take possession; and

c) Promptly notify the buyer of the shipment.

2) **Destination Contracts—Where Seller Has Agreed to Tender at Particular Destination**
If the contract requires the seller to tender delivery of the goods at a particular destination, the seller must, at the destination, put and hold conforming goods at the buyer's disposition. He must also give the buyer any notice of tender that is reasonably necessary and provide her with any documents of title necessary to obtain delivery. Tender of documents through ordinary banking channels is sufficient. [U.C.C. §2-503]

3. **Buyer's Obligation to Pay—Right to Inspect**

a. **Delivery and Payment Concurrent Conditions**
In ***noncarrier cases***, unless the contract provides otherwise, a sale is for cash and the price is due concurrently with tender of delivery. However, unless otherwise agreed, when goods are shipped ***by carrier***, the price is due only at the time and place at which the buyer receives the goods. Therefore, in a shipment case, the price is due when the goods are put in the hands of the carrier, and in a destination contract, the price is due when the goods reach the named destination.

b. Payment by Check

Tender of payment by check is sufficient unless the seller demands legal tender and gives the buyer time to get cash. If a check is given, the buyer's duty to pay is suspended until the check is either paid or dishonored. If the check is paid, the buyer's duty to pay is discharged. If the check is dishonored, the seller may sue for the price or recover the goods. [U.C.C. §2-511]

c. Installment Contracts

In an installment contract (*i.e.,* one that requires or authorizes delivery in separate installments), the seller may demand payment for each installment if the price can be so apportioned, unless a contrary intent appears. [U.C.C. §2-307]

d. Buyer's Right of Inspection

Unless the contract provides otherwise, the buyer has a right to inspect the goods before she pays. Expenses of inspection must be borne by the buyer but may be recovered from the seller if the goods do not conform and are rejected. A buyer may inspect at any reasonable time and in any reasonable manner. [U.C.C. §2-513]

Note: If the contract between the parties provides for payment C.O.D. or otherwise indicates that the buyer has promised to pay without inspecting the goods, there is no right of inspection prior to payment. If payment is due before inspection, the fact that the goods are defective does not excuse nonpayment unless the defect appears without inspection or there is fraud in the transaction. [U.C.C. §§2-512, 2-513]

Examples: 1) Buyer in California and Seller in New York contract for sale of steel to be shipped to California. Nothing is said as to payment. Buyer has a right to inspect the goods before payment.

2) Same situation as above, except that the contract provides for payment of cash on delivery. Buyer must pay when the steel is delivered, and she does not have a right of inspection prior to payment.

3) Same situation as last example, except that the goods are defective. To put Seller in breach, Buyer must pay, unless the defect appears without inspection.

D. CONDITIONS—HAS THE DUTY TO PERFORM BECOME ABSOLUTE?

A contract may provide that a party does not have a duty to perform unless some condition is fulfilled. In such a case, the party's failure to perform will normally be ***justified*** if the condition was not fulfilled.

1. Distinction Between Promise and Condition

It is important to understand that there is a difference between whether a party is bound under a contract and whether a party who is bound has come under a duty to perform. A person is bound if there has been an offer, an acceptance, and an exchange of consideration. However, the contract may provide (impliedly or explicitly) that a party who is bound does not come under a duty to perform unless or until some specified condition occurs. In looking at the terms of a contract, a distinction has to be drawn between an absolute promise on the one hand and a condition on the other.

a. **Definitions**

1) **Promise**
A promise is a commitment to do or refrain from doing something. If a promise is unconditional, the failure to perform according to its terms is a breach of contract.

2) **Condition**
In this context, the term "condition" normally means ***either***: (i) an event or state of the world that must occur or fail to occur ***before*** a party has a duty to perform under a contract; or (ii) an event or state of the world the occurrence or nonoccurrence of which ***releases*** a party from its duty to perform under a contract. In other words, a condition is a provision the fulfillment of which creates or extinguishes a duty to perform under a contract. A condition is a ***"promise modifier."*** There can be no breach of promise until the promisor is under an immediate duty to perform. He may insert conditions on his promise to prevent that duty of immediate performance from arising until the conditions are met.

a) **Failure of Condition vs. Breach of Contract**
The failure of a contractual provision that is only a condition is ***not a breach of contract***, but it discharges the liability of the promisor whose obligations on the conditional promise never mature.

Example: Gene agrees to sell his horse to Roy, the contract providing that delivery of possession will take place on June 1. On May 25, the horse dies. Was delivery of possession of the horse a condition? If so, its failure to occur will discharge Roy's duty to pay; however, Roy will not have a cause of action against Gene for nondelivery. Or was it a promise by Gene, the breach of which will give to Roy both an action against Gene for breach of contract and release him from his duty to pay?

An unexcused failure to perform a ***promise*** is always a breach of contract and always gives rise to liability, however minimal. On the other hand, nonfulfillment of a ***condition*** is ***not*** a breach of contract and does not give rise to liability.

b) **Excuse of Performance**
Breach of a ***promise*** by one party may or may not excuse the other party's duty to perform under the contract (*see* 6.b., *infra*). Nonfulfillment of a ***condition*** normally will excuse a duty to perform that was subject to the condition.

c) **Interrelation of Conditions and Promises**
If a party's ***promise*** to perform is subject to a condition, there can be no breach of contract by that party until the condition has been fulfilled.

b. **Interpretation of Provision as Promise or Condition**
As the above example indicates, it is of considerable importance whether any given contractual provision is to be interpreted as a promise or condition. The basic test is one of ***"intent of the parties."*** The courts employ several basic criteria in reaching a determination as to intent.

1) **Words of Agreement**
Words such as "provided," "if," and "when" usually indicate that an express condition rather than a promise was intended. Words such as "promise" and "agree" usually indicate a promise. However, words by themselves might not be determinative. Both the specific words of the phrase and the words of the rest of the agreement (thus the context of the entire contract) will be examined by the courts in drawing a conclusion.

2) **Prior Practices**
The prior practices of the contracting parties, particularly with one another, will be taken into consideration.

3) **Custom**
The custom with respect to that business in the community will be examined.

4) **Third-Party Performance**
If performance is to be rendered by a third party, it is more likely to be a condition than an absolute promise.

5) **Courts Prefer Promise in Doubtful Situations**
In doubtful situations, most courts will hold that the provision in question is a ***promise***. The underlying rationale is that this result will serve to support the contract, thereby preserving the expectancy of the parties. This preference is particularly significant in situations where the breaching party has ***substantially performed***, because if the provision is treated as a ***condition***, the nonbreaching party is completely discharged from her obligation; whereas, if the provision is treated as a ***promise***, the nonbreaching party must perform, although she may recover for the damage she has suffered as a result of the breach.

Example: Stan contracts to build a house for Natasha using pipe of Reading manufacture. In return, Natasha agrees to pay Stan $100,000. Without Stan's knowledge, a subcontractor mistakenly uses pipe of Cohoes manufacture, which is identical in quality and is virtually indistinguishable from Reading pipe. The substitution is not discovered until the house is completed, when replacement of the pipe would require substantial destruction of the house. Natasha refuses to pay Stan. The installation of Reading pipe was a promise, not a condition, of the contract; therefore, Stan has a claim against Natasha for $100,000, subject to her claim against him for breach of duty to use Reading pipe. To treat it as a condition would be unfair to Stan, because he would be penalized in an amount far greater than the amount of the damage suffered by Natasha.

Note: When seeking to establish the reasonable expectations of the parties, one should determine whether the performance of the stipulation goes to the "very root" of the contract's consideration. If so, it is probably a condition rather than a promise.

c. **Provision Both Promise and Condition**
In some cases, a provision may be both a promise and a condition—*i.e.*, a party may

commit (promise) to bring about a given state of events, and the contract containing that commitment may also expressly state that the other party's duty to perform under the contract is conditioned on the occurrence of the state of events.

Example: Carrier promises to get Manufacturer's goods to Los Angeles by October 1, and the contract expressly provides that Manufacturer will have no duty to pay Carrier unless the goods arrive by that time. Getting the goods to Los Angeles by June 1 is both a promise by Carrier and a condition to Manufacturer's liability.

2. Classification of Conditions

a. Condition Precedent

A condition precedent is one that must occur ***before*** an absolute duty of immediate performance arises in the other party.

Example: Sal and Mary agree that "in consideration of Mary's promise to repay principal plus 8% interest, Sal hereby promises to loan Mary $50,000 for one year, provided that on July 1, the market value of Mary's country home is not less than $100,000." On July 1, Mary's country home is appraised at a market value of $80,000. Sal refuses to make the loan, and Mary sues. Sal wins because his duty to loan the $50,000 is subject to an express condition precedent. Because the condition was not satisfied, Sal's contingent liability never matured.

b. Conditions Concurrent

Conditions concurrent are those that are capable of occurring ***together***, and that the parties are bound to perform at the same time (*e.g.,* tender of deed for cash). Thus, in effect, each is a condition "precedent" to the other.

Example: Smith and Jones agree that "in consideration of Jones's promise to pay the sum of $500, Smith promises to convey his 1970 Buick." Having signed this agreement, Jones never tenders the $500 and Smith does not tender the car. Neither party is in breach of contract. The contract is silent regarding the time and place of performance, but the promises exchanged as consideration can obviously be performed at the same time and place. Hence, tender of the promised performance by each party is a constructive condition concurrent to liability of the other. Because both parties failed to tender performance, neither obligation matured.

c. Condition Subsequent

A condition subsequent is one the occurrence of which ***cuts off*** an already existing absolute duty of performance.

Example: Will and Grace enter the following contract: In consideration of Will's conveying his painting to her, Grace promises to pay Will $5,000 on July 1. Grace further promises to permit Will to retain the painting for purposes of exhibition during the months of July and August, provided security precautions for the safety of the painting are approved by Captain Smith. On July 1, Grace pays Will $5,000, and Will begins to exhibit the painting. On July 10, Captain Smith inspects security at the exhibition and declares it to be inadequate. Grace immediately asserts her right to possession, but Will refuses to surrender the painting. Grace is entitled to immediate possession of the painting. Her allowing Will to retain the painting for exhibition was subject to an express condition subsequent based on Captain Smith's approval of security precautions. Because the condition subsequent has ripened, Grace's conditional obligation to allow Will to retain the painting is extinguished.

3. **Express Conditions**

The term "express condition" normally refers to an ***explicit contractual provision***. It is an express statement in the contract providing that either (i) a party does not have a duty to perform unless some event occurs or fails to occur; or (ii) if some event occurs or fails to occur, the obligation of a party to perform one or more of his duties under the contract is suspended or terminated. Conditions of satisfaction are common express conditions.

a. **Promisor's Satisfaction as Condition Precedent**

Many contracts include an express condition that a party will pay only if "satisfied" with the other party's performance. Because it is a condition, the promisor is under no duty to pay unless she is satisfied. The issue is how the promisor's satisfaction is to be measured; *i.e.*, whether the performance must meet with promisor's ***actual personal*** satisfaction, or must only be a performance that would meet with the satisfaction of a ***reasonable person***. The provision requiring the promisor's satisfaction is construed according to the ***subject matter*** of the contract.

1) **Mechanical Fitness, Utility, or Marketability**

In contracts involving mechanical fitness, utility, or marketability (*e.g.*, construction or manufacturing contracts), a condition of satisfaction is fulfilled by a performance that would satisfy a ***reasonable person***. It is therefore immaterial that the promisor was not personally satisfied if a reasonable person would have accepted and approved the performance tendered.

2) **Personal Taste or Judgment**

If the contract involves personal taste or personal judgment, a condition of satisfaction is fulfilled only if the promisor is ***personally satisfied***. For example, contracts for portraits, dental work, or tailoring all require the promisor's personal satisfaction.

a) **Lack of Satisfaction Must Be Honest and in Good Faith**

Even if a condition requires personal satisfaction, it will fail to be fulfilled only if the promisor's lack of satisfaction is honest and in good faith. Therefore, if the promisor refuses to examine the promisee's performance, or otherwise rejects the performance in bad faith, the condition of satisfaction will be ***excused***.

b. **Satisfaction of Third Person as Condition**

In many contracts, an express condition requires the satisfaction of a third person rather than a party to the contract. In particular, construction contracts often include a condition requiring the satisfaction of the owner's architect or engineer. When the satisfaction of a third person is a condition, most courts take the position that the condition requires the ***actual personal satisfaction*** of the third person. As in the case where a party's

personal satisfaction is required, however, a condition that requires a third person's personal satisfaction will be excused if the third person's dissatisfaction is not ***honest and in good faith***.

4. Constructive (Implied) Conditions

Sometimes it is implied that the duty to render performance under a contract is conditional upon the occurrence of some event or state of the world, even though the contract does not explicitly so state. In that case, there is said to be an "implied" or "constructive" condition that the relevant event or state of the world must occur before the performance of one or both parties comes due.

a. Constructive Conditions of Performance

By far the most important and common implied condition is that the duty of each party to render performance is conditioned on the ***other party*** either rendering ***his*** performance or making a tender of his performance.

Example: Owen and Pete make a contract under which Pete will paint Owen's house by May 30, and Owen will pay Pete $8,000 on June 1. It is an implied condition to Owen's duty to pay $8,000 that Pete shall have painted the house. If Pete fails to paint Owen's house by June 1, it has a dual effect: (i) it is a breach of contract for which Pete will be liable in damages, and (ii) it is a nonfulfillment of an implied condition to Owen's duty to pay, so Owen does not have a duty to pay Pete.

b. Constructive Conditions of Cooperation and Notice

Constructive conditions of cooperation and notice are common. Under a constructive condition of cooperation, the obligation of one party to render performance is impliedly conditioned on the other party's cooperation in that performance. Also, it is often a condition to one party's performance of a duty under a contract that the other party give him ***notice*** that the performance is due. A condition of notice is most commonly applied where a party could not reasonably be expected to know a fact that triggered the duty to perform unless such notice was given.

Examples: 1) Seller promises to deliver certain goods to the "No. 2 loading dock" of Buyer's factory. It is an implied condition to Seller's duty to deliver the goods that such a loading dock exists, that the dock is reasonably accessible for making a delivery, and that Buyer permits Seller to make the delivery at the dock.

2) Landlord leases a building to Tenant and promises to maintain and repair the interior of the building as necessary. It is an implied condition to Landlord's promise to repair that Tenant will give her reasonable notification of the need for repairs and will permit her to enter to make the repairs. Tenant therefore cannot sue Landlord for failure to make a needed repair unless he has first notified Landlord that the repair is required, and given Landlord an opportunity to make the repair.

c. Order of Performance

The courts will also imply conditions relating to the time for performing under the contract.

1) **Simultaneous Performance Possible—Conditions Concurrent**
If both performances can be rendered at the same time, they are constructively concurrent; thus, each is a condition "precedent" to the other. Hence, absent excuse, each party must first tender his own performance if he wishes to put the other under a duty of immediate performance resulting in breach if he fails to perform.
Example: Lulu agrees to sell Hank her old tractor for $4,000. Because Lulu can sign over title and Hank can hand over money at the same time, the conditions are constructively concurrent.

2) **One Performance Takes Time—Conditions Precedent**
If one performance will take a period of time to complete while the other can be rendered in an instant, completion of the longer performance is a constructive condition precedent to execution of the shorter performance.
Example: Lulu agrees to paint Hank's barn for $400. In absence of a contract provision to the contrary, Lulu must paint the barn before Hank must pay.

5. **Effect of Condition—Equitable Remedy**
If a contract is not enforceable due to the failure or occurrence of a condition, and one of the parties has fully or partially performed, he can usually recover under unjust enrichment theories (*see* VII.C., *infra*), although the measure of damages in that case may be less advantageous than the contract price.

6. **Have the Conditions Been Excused?**
A duty of immediate performance with respect to a conditional promise does not become ***absolute*** until the conditions (i) have been ***performed***, or (ii) have been ***legally excused***. Thus, in analyzing a question, if the facts do not reveal performance of the applicable condition precedent or concurrent, look to see whether the condition has been excused. Excuse of conditions can arise in a variety of ways.

a. **Excuse of Condition by Hindrance or Failure to Cooperate**
If a party having a duty of performance that is subject to a condition (*i.e.,* she is the party protected by the condition) prevents the condition from occurring, the condition will be excused if such prevention is ***wrongful***. Note, however, that it is not necessary to prove bad faith or malice. Courts construe the requirement simply to mean that the other party would not have reasonably contemplated or assumed the risk of this type of conduct.
Example: Franz agrees to paint Worthington's portrait. Worthington's promise to pay for the portrait is conditional upon her being satisfied with it. Worthington refuses to even look at the portrait. Because of her refusal, the condition is excused and her promise to pay becomes absolute.

Note: It appears fairly well settled today that a condition will be excused not only by "active" noncooperation but by "passive" noncooperation as well.

b. **Excuse of Condition by Actual Breach**
An actual breach of the contract when performance is due will excuse the duty of counterperformance. Note, however, that counterperformance will be excused at

common law ***only*** if the ***breach is material***. A minor breach may suspend this duty, but it will not excuse it. Even if the minor breach may be cured, it will not suffice to excuse conditions. Rather, the courts will make the nonbreaching party whole by either giving him damages or otherwise mitigating his promised performance so as to account for the breach. (As to rules determining materiality of breaches, *see* VII.B., *infra.*)

c. **Excuse of Condition by Anticipatory Repudiation**

Anticipatory repudiation occurs if a promisor, prior to the time set for performance of his promise, indicates that he will not perform when the time comes. If the requirements set forth below are met, this anticipatory repudiation will serve to excuse conditions.

1) **Executory Bilateral Contract Requirement**

Anticipatory repudiation applies only if there is a bilateral contract with ***executory (unperformed) duties on both sides***. If the nonrepudiating party has nothing further to do at the moment of repudiation, as in the case of a unilateral contract or a bilateral contract fully performed by the nonrepudiator, the doctrine of anticipatory repudiation does not apply. The nonrepudiator must wait until the time originally set for performance by the repudiating party. Until such time, the repudiator has the option to change his mind and withdraw the repudiation and perform in accordance with the contract. [*Accord:* U.C.C. §2-611]

Example: Winston promises to pay Salem $2,000 on November 15 as consideration for Salem's car, the latter to be delivered on October 20. Salem delivers the car to Winston on October 20; on November 3, Winston repudiates. Because Salem does not have any more duties to perform, he will not have a cause of action until November 15.

2) **Requirement that Anticipatory Repudiation Be Unequivocal**

An anticipatory repudiation stems from the words or conduct of the promisor ***unequivocally*** indicating that he cannot or will not perform when the time comes. This statement must be positive.

Example: Wright states to Jones, "Business has not been going well and I have doubts about whether I will be able to perform my contract with you." This is ***not*** an anticipatory repudiation; mere expressions of doubt or fear will not suffice (although such expressions may establish prospective inability to perform, discussed below).

3) **Effect of Anticipatory Repudiation**

In the case of an anticipatory repudiation, the nonrepudiating party has four alternatives:

(i) Treat the anticipatory repudiation as a total repudiation and ***sue immediately***;

(ii) Suspend his own performance and ***wait to sue*** until the performance date;

(iii) Treat the repudiation as an offer to rescind and ***treat the contract as discharged***; or

(iv) Ignore the repudiation and ***urge the promisor to perform*** (but note that by urging the promisor to perform, the nonrepudiating party is not waiving the repudiation—she can still sue for breach and is excused from performing unless the promisor retracts the repudiation).

Note: U.C.C. section 2-610 provides substantially identical alternatives to a nonrepudiating party when there is an anticipatory repudiation in the case of the sale of goods.

4) Retraction of Repudiation

A repudiating party may at any time before his next performance is due withdraw his repudiation unless the other party has ***canceled, materially changed*** her ***position*** in reliance on the repudiation, or otherwise indicated that she considers the ***repudiation final.*** Withdrawal of the repudiation may be in any manner that clearly indicates intention to perform, but must include any assurances justifiably demanded. [*See* U.C.C. §2-611]

d. Excuse of Condition by Prospective Inability or Unwillingness to Perform

Prospective failure of condition occurs when a party has reasonable grounds to believe that the other party will be unable or unwilling to perform when performance is due.

Example: John contracts with Barbara to buy her house for $150,000. Payment is due on August 1. On July 10, John goes into bankruptcy (or Barbara transfers title to the house to Emily). Prospective inability to perform has occurred.

1) Distinguish from Actual and Anticipatory Repudiation

Prospective inability or unwillingness to perform is not an anticipatory repudiation because such a repudiation must be ***unequivocal***, whereas prospective failure to perform involves conduct or words that merely raise doubts that the party will perform. (In short, the distinction between anticipatory repudiation and prospective inability to perform is one of degree.)

2) What Conduct Will Suffice?

Any conduct may suffice for a finding that there is prospective inability or unwillingness to perform. Note that in judging this conduct, a ***reasonable person*** standard will be applied.

3) Effect of Prospective Failure

The effect of this prospective failure is to allow the innocent party to suspend further performance on her side until she receives ***adequate assurances*** that performance will be forthcoming. If she fails to obtain adequate assurances, she may be excused from her own performance and may treat the failure to provide assurances as a repudiation. (This same basic right is provided in U.C.C. section 2-609—*see* VIII.A.2.c., *infra.*)

4) Retraction of Repudiation

As with anticipatory repudiation, retraction is possible if the defaulting party regains his ability or willingness to perform. However, this fact must be communicated to the other party in order to be effective. If the other party has already changed her position in reliance on the prospective failure, an attempted retraction may be ineffective.

e. **Excuse of Condition by Substantial Performance**

The performance of one contractual promise is usually a condition precedent to the duty of immediate performance of the return promise (*see* 4., *supra*). Technically, if the promise has not been completely performed, the other performance is not yet due. This can cause forfeiture if the breach is minor, because the promisee can receive almost complete performance with no duty to perform in return. To avoid this harsh result, the courts have adopted the "substantial performance" and "divisibility" concepts.

1) **Rule of Substantial Performance**

Generally, the condition of complete performance may be excused if the party has rendered substantial performance. In this case, the other party's duty of counter-performance becomes absolute. It should be noted, however, that courts generally apply this doctrine only where a ***constructive*** (implied in law) condition is involved. They will not apply it where there is an ***express*** condition for fear this would defeat the express intent of the parties.

2) **Substantial Performance Arises If Breach Is Minor**

Rules for determining substantiality of performance are the same as those for determining materiality of breach. (*See* VII.B.2., *infra.*) In other words, the test is whether the breach of contract by the performing party is material or minor. If it is material, then performance ***has not*** been substantial; if it is minor, performance ***has*** been substantial.

3) **Inapplicable Where Breach "Willful"**

Most courts will not apply the substantial performance doctrine if the breach was "willful." (This is so even though willfulness is only one of the six factors usually relied on in determining materiality of a breach. *See* VII.B.2., *infra.*) Trivial defects, however, even if willful, will be ignored by the courts as de minimis.

4) **Damages Offset**

Even though the party who has substantially performed is able to enforce the contract, the other party will be able to mitigate by deducting damages suffered due to the first party's incomplete performance.

5) **Generally Inapplicable to Contracts for the Sale of Goods**

The doctrine of substantial performance was developed in construction contracts cases, and there is considerable doubt as to the application of the doctrine beyond such cases. As to contracts for the sale of goods, the U.C.C. "***perfect tender rule***" gives the buyer the right to reject goods that do not conform to the contract in any manner, with a few exceptions (*see* VII.C., *infra*). [U.C.C. §2-601]

f. **Excuse of Condition by "Divisibility" of Contract**

Divisibility, like the doctrine of substantial performance, is a concept designed to mitigate the harsh result of a potential forfeiture.

1) **Rule of "Divisibility"**

If a party performs one of the units of a divisible contract, he is entitled to the agreed-on equivalent for that unit even if he fails to perform the other units. It is not a condition precedent to the other party's liability that the whole contract be

performed. However, the other party has a cause of action for failure to perform the other units and may withhold his counterperformance for those units.

Example: Cambridge Construction Co. is to build 10 houses for $800,000, at $80,000 per house, for Beth. Because the building takes a long time and payment can be rendered in one instant, the substantial completion of 10 houses would normally be a constructive condition precedent to payment. Completion of seven houses would leave Cambridge without any remedy on the contract itself (whatever rights it might have as a defaulting party would be by way of quasi-contractual relief). The divisibility doctrine allows Cambridge to sue for the pro rata price each time it completes a house.

2) What Is a "Divisible" Contract?

Obviously, the rule applies only if there is a finding that the contract is "divisible" (as compared to "entire"). ***Three tests*** must be ***concurrently*** satisfied in order to make this finding.

(i) The ***performance of each party is divided into two or more parts*** under the contract;

(ii) The ***number of parts due from each party is the same***; and

(iii) The ***performance of each part by one party is agreed on as the equivalent of the corresponding part*** from the other party, *i.e.*, each performance is the quid pro quo of the other.

[Restatement (Second) of Contracts §240]

a) Interpretation

Decisions on divisibility are questions of interpretation. The underlying consideration is one of fairness. Generally, the courts will construe contracts as divisible so as to avoid hardships and forfeitures that might otherwise result.

b) Contract Expressly Indivisible

If the contract by its own terms is expressly indivisible, the court may not construe it as otherwise.

3) Sales of Goods—Installment Contracts

Like the common law, Article 2 assumes that a contract is not divisible unless it authorizes deliveries in several lots, in which case the contract is called an installment contract. In installment contracts, the price, if it can be apportioned, may be demanded for ***each lot*** unless a contrary intent appears. [U.C.C. §§2-307, 2-612]

g. Excuse of Condition by Waiver or Estoppel

One having the benefit of a condition under a contract may indicate by ***words or conduct*** that she will not insist on that condition's being met. Consideration is not required for a valid waiver of condition. The courts, in certain circumstances, will enforce this expression on the basis that the party has "waived" the condition or is "estopped" from asserting it.

1) Estoppel Waiver

Whenever a party indicates that she is "waiving" a condition before it is to happen, or she is "waiving" some performance before it is to be rendered, and the person addressed ***detrimentally relies*** on the waiver, the courts will hold this to be a binding (estoppel) waiver. Note, however, that the promise to waive a condition may be retracted at any time ***before*** the other party has changed his position to his detriment.

2) Election Waiver

When a condition or a duty of performance is broken, the beneficiary of the condition or duty must make an election; she may: (i) terminate her liability, ***or*** (ii) continue under the contract. If she chooses the latter course, she will be deemed to have waived the condition or duty. This election waiver requires neither consideration nor estoppel (although estoppel elements are often present).

Example: Frederick contracted with Karen to sell her a new MP3 player in "perfect working order." In fact, the player when delivered had some minor mechanical troubles that Karen was apprised of at the time. Karen, nonetheless, elects to accept the player. She will be deemed to have waived the "perfect working order" condition.

3) Conditions that May Be Waived

If ***no consideration*** is given for the waiver, the condition must be ***ancillary or collateral*** to the main subject and purpose of the contract for the waiver to be effective. In other words, one cannot "waive" entitlement to the entire or substantially entire return performance. This would amount to a new undertaking that is really a gift in the disguise of a waiver.

Example: Robinson, a contractor, breaches a promise to build a garage for Hortense at a price of $6,000. Hortense says, "Even though you have not built the garage, I shall pay you the $6,000, waiving the constructive condition of performance." This waiver will not be enforceable; Robinson did not give consideration for the waiver, and the condition concerned the main subject and purpose of the contract.

4) Waiver in Installment Contracts

In an ***installment contract***, if a waiver is not supported by consideration, the beneficiary of the waived condition can insist on strict compliance with the terms of the contract for future installments (so long as there has been no detrimental reliance on the waiver) by giving notice that he is revoking the waiver.

Example: Carrie, a boutique owner, entered into an installment contract with Jimmy Shoos. Jimmy was to deliver 20 pairs of shoes to Carrie every week, payment due in cash on delivery ("C.O.D.") of each shipment. Once the deliveries started, Jimmy allowed Carrie to mail him a check one week after delivery for the first three deliveries, rather than demanding payment at the time the shoes were delivered. Jimmy will be held to have waived the C.O.D. term because he did not demand immediate payment for the first three shipments, but Jimmy may insist on compliance with the original terms for any future deliveries (so long as Carrie is given notice and has not detrimentally relied on the waiver).

5) **Right to Damages for Failure of Condition**
It is important to note that a waiver severs only the right to treat the failure of the condition as a total breach excusing counterperformance. However, the waiving party does ***not*** thereby waive her right to damages. Thus, for instance, in the example above involving delivery of the MP3 player in "perfect working order," the waiving party still has her right to damages for the defects in the player—she merely waived her right to treat the failure as a total breach excusing counterperformance.

h. **Excuse of Condition by Impossibility, Impracticability, or Frustration**
Conditions may be excused by impossibility, impracticability, or frustration of purpose. (*See* E.5., *infra.*)

E. HAS THE ABSOLUTE DUTY TO PERFORM BEEN DISCHARGED?

Once it is determined that a party is under an immediate duty to perform, the duty to perform must be discharged.

1. **Discharge by Performance**
The most obvious way to discharge a contractual duty is, of course, by full and complete performance.

2. **Discharge by Tender of Performance**
Good faith tender of performance made in accordance with contractual terms will also discharge contractual duties. Note that the tendering party must possess the ***present ability*** to perform; a mere promise of performance will not suffice.

3. **Discharge by Occurrence of Condition Subsequent**
The occurrence of a condition subsequent will serve to discharge contractual duties.

4. **Discharge by Illegality**
If the subject matter of the contract has become illegal due to a subsequently enacted law or other governmental act, performance will be discharged. This is often referred to as "supervening illegality."

Example: Jim and Beam enter into a partnership contract to operate a tavern in the city of Clover. Subsequently, the Clover legislature enacts a prohibition law. The contract is discharged.

Note: If the illegality existed at the time the agreement was made, no contract was formed because of the illegality. (*See* IV.B.3., *supra.*)

5. **Discharge by Impossibility, Impracticability, or Frustration**
The occurrence of an unanticipated or extraordinary event may make contractual duties impossible or impracticable to perform or may frustrate the purpose of the contract. Where the nonoccurrence of the event was a ***basic assumption*** of the parties in making the contract and ***neither*** party has expressly or impliedly ***assumed the risk*** of the event occurring, contractual duties may be discharged.

Remember that the promisor's duties to perform serve as a condition precedent to the other party's duty to perform. Hence, if these duties should be excused by impossibility, impracticability, or frustration, the other party's contractual duties will also be discharged.

a. **Discharge by Impossibility**
Contractual duties will be discharged if it has become impossible to perform them.

1) **Impossibility Must Be "Objective"**
For this rule to operate, the impossibility must be "objective"; *i.e.,* the duties could not be performed by anyone. "Subjective" impossibility will not suffice, *i.e.,* where the duties could be performed by someone but not the promisor.

2) **Timing of Impossibility**
The impossibility must arise ***after*** the contract has been entered into. If the facts giving rise to impossibility already existed when the contract was formed, the question is not really one of "discharge of contractual duties." Rather, it is a "contract formation" problem, namely, whether the contract is voidable because of mistake.

3) **Effect of Impossibility**
If a contract is discharged because of impossibility, each party is excused from duties arising under the contract that are yet to be fulfilled. Either party may sue for rescission and receive restitution of any goods delivered, payments made, etc.

4) **Partial Impossibility**
If the performance to be rendered under the contract becomes only partially impossible, the duty may be discharged ***only to that extent.*** The remainder of the performance may be required according to the contractual terms. This is so even though this remaining performance might involve added expense or difficulty.

5) **Temporary Impossibility**
Temporary impossibility ***suspends*** contractual duties; it does not discharge them. When performance once more becomes possible, the duty "springs back" into existence. Note, however, that a duty will not "spring back" into existence if the burden on either party to the contract would be substantially increased or different from that originally contemplated.

6) **Part Performance Prior to Impossibility—Quasi-Contractual Recovery**
If part performance has been rendered by either party prior to the existence of the facts leading to impossibility, that party will have a right to recover in quasi-contract at the contract rate or for the reasonable value of his performance if that is a more convenient mode of valuation. (Note that such recovery will also be available when contract duties are discharged by impracticability or frustration, discussed below.)

7) **Specific Situations**

a) **Death or Physical Incapacity**
Death or the physical incapacity of a person ***necessary*** to effectuate the contract serves to discharge it.

Example: Helmut agrees to teach German to Max. Helmut's death or physical incapacity would discharge the contract. Max's death or physical incapacity would similarly discharge the contract.

(The death or physical incapacity may also be that of a third person. Thus, for example, if Helmut had contracted with Max to teach German to Max's son, the death or physical incapacity of the son would also serve to discharge the contract.)

Note: Most fact situations on this point involve personal service contracts. Check to see whether the services involved are ***"unique."*** If the services are the kind that could be delegated (*see* IX.C.2.b., *infra*), the contract is ***not*** discharged by the incapacity of the person who was to perform them.

b) Supervening Illegality

As we have seen, supervening illegality may serve to discharge a contract. Many courts treat such supervening illegality as a form of impossibility.

c) Subsequent Destruction of Contract's Subject Matter or Means of Performance

If the contract's subject matter is destroyed or the designated means for performing the contract are destroyed, contractual duties will be discharged. Note, however, that this destruction must not have been the fault of either party. Substantial damage to the subject matter will generally be construed by the courts as the equivalent of "destruction."

Example: Olivia hires Charlie to replace the shingles on the roof of her house. When Charlie has completed 90% of the work, the house is hit by lightning and is destroyed by fire. The contract will be discharged for impossibility because there no longer is a house needing reshingling. Charlie will be able to recover for the work done in quasi-contract. (*See* VIII.C., *infra*.)

(1) Compare—Contracts to Build

A contractor's duty to ***construct*** a building is ***not*** discharged by destruction of the work in progress. *Rationale:* Construction is not rendered impossible; the contractor can still rebuild. However, if the destruction was not caused by the contractor, most courts will excuse the contractor from meeting the original deadline.

Example: Olivia hires Charlie to build her a garage. When Charlie has completed 90% of the work, the garage is hit by lightning and is destroyed by fire. Charlie will not be discharged from his contractual duty to build the garage because it is not impossible to rebuild the garage.

(2) Specificity Required

(a) Subject Matter

Note that destruction of the subject matter will render a contract impossible only if the very thing destroyed is necessary to fulfill the contract. If the thing destroyed is not actually necessary, impossibility is not a defense.

Example: Linda contracts to sell her car to John. Subsequently, the car is destroyed through no fault of either party.

The contract will be discharged because of impossibility because the only car that could fulfill the obligation no longer exists.

Compare: John orders a new car from his local Kia dealer. While the car that the dealer ordered for John is being delivered from the factory, it is destroyed in a crash. The contract is not discharged for impossibility because it is not impossible for the dealer to get another Kia that will satisfy the contract.

(b) Specificity of Source

As with the destruction of the subject matter, destruction of a source for fulfilling the contract will render the contract impossible only if the source is the one source specified by the parties.

Example: Jackson contracts to sell Daley 100 tons of iron ore from the Blarney Iron Mine, which Jackson owns. A nearby dam breaks and floods the mine. Jackson will be discharged from the contract for impossibility.

Compare: Jackson, who owns the Blarney Iron Mine, contracts to sell Daley 100 tons of iron ore. A nearby dam breaks and floods Jackson's mine. Jackson will not be discharged from the contract because the contract did not specify that the iron ore was to come from Jackson's mine. Thus, iron ore from any other mine can fulfill the contract.

(3) If Risk of Loss Has Already Passed to Buyer

The rules relating to discharge because of destruction of the subject matter ***will not apply*** if the risk of loss has already passed to the buyer. The usual situations involve contracts for the sale of goods under the U.C.C. and contracts for the sale of land where equitable conversion has taken place. In such cases, the seller may enforce the contract and the buyer will have to pay.

b. Discharge by Impracticability

Modern courts will also discharge contractual duties where performance has become impracticable.

1) Test for Impracticability

The test for a finding of impracticability is that the party to perform has encountered:

(i) ***Extreme and unreasonable*** difficulty and/or expense; and

(ii) Its nonoccurrence was a ***basic assumption*** of the parties.

In effect, the courts will allow relief against performance where subjective impossibility is found. It should be noted, however, that a mere change in the degree of difficulty or expense due to such causes as increased wages, prices of raw materials, or costs of construction, unless well beyond the normal range, does ***not*** amount to impracticability, because these are the types of risks that a fixed-price contract is intended to cover. Thus, the fact that something is more expensive—even much more expensive—is not impracticability. [Restatement (Second) of Contracts §261]

2) Contracts for the Sale of Goods

Article 2 generally follows the above rules for impossibility and impracticability. If performance has become impossible or commercially impracticable, the seller will be ***discharged to the extent of the impossibility or impracticability***. [U.C.C. §2-615]

a) Allocation of Risk

Generally, the seller assumes the risk of the occurrence of such unforeseen events and must continue to perform. However, if it is fair to say that the parties would not have placed on the seller the risk of the extraordinary occurrence, the seller will be discharged.

b) Events Sufficient for Discharge

Events sufficient to excuse performance include a ***shortage of raw materials*** or the inability to convert them into the seller's product because of contingencies such as war, strike, embargo, or unforeseen shutdown of a major supplier. Catastrophic local crop failure (as opposed to a mere shortage) also is sufficient for discharge. However, mere increases in costs are rarely sufficient for discharge unless they change the nature of the contract.

Example: Assume StoneOil contracted with Manuco to sell Manuco one million gallons of Persian Gulf crude oil. If a war subsequently breaks out in the Gulf, and supplies of Gulf oil are interrupted, StoneOil is discharged. However, if instead a war breaks out between Israel and Egypt and the Suez Canal is blocked, thus forcing StoneOil to ship the oil around the Cape of Good Hope, StoneOil will probably not be discharged merely because of the increase in the cost of shipping. [*See* Transatlantic Financing Co. v. United States, 363 F.2d 312 (D.C. Cir. 1966)]

Note: There is no bright line test for determining when a rise in price changes the nature of the contract, but increases in costs of more than 50% have been held to be insufficient. [*See, e.g.,* Iowa Light & Power Co. v. Atlas Corp., 467 F. Supp. 129 (N.D. Iowa 1978)]

c) Seller's Partial Inability to Perform

If the seller's inability to perform as a result of the unforeseen circumstance is only partial, he ***must allocate deliveries*** among his customers and, at his option, may include in the allocation regular customers not then under contract. The seller must reasonably notify his buyers of any delay or reduction in

deliveries because of unforeseen circumstances. A buyer who receives such a notification may refuse any particular delivery affected, and if the deficiency substantially impairs the whole contract, she may treat the contract as at an end.

3) Temporary or Partial Impracticability
The rules spelled out above for temporary and partial impossibility are equally applicable to temporary and partial impracticability.

c. Discharge by Frustration
Frustration will exist if the purpose of the contract has become valueless by virtue of some supervening event not the fault of the party seeking discharge. (Recall the *Coronation Cases* if you studied them.) If the purpose has been frustrated, a number of courts will discharge contractual duties even though performance of these duties is still possible. The elements necessary to establish frustration are as follows:

(i) There is some ***supervening act*** or event leading to the frustration;

(ii) At the time of entering into the contract, the parties ***did not reasonably foresee*** the act or event occurring;

(iii) The ***purpose*** of the contract has been completely or almost completely ***destroyed*** by this act or event; and

(iv) The purpose of the contract was realized by ***both parties*** at the time of making the contract.

Example: Sports, Inc. contracted to rent a sports stadium for a boxing match to be held on August 1 in the town of Greensville. On July 31, a sudden hurricane resulted in tremendous damage in Greensville, causing it to be classified as a "disaster area." No one could get in or out of the area. Sports, Inc.'s promise to rent the stadium (which was still intact) was discharged by frustration of purpose (a hurricane was not anticipated by the parties and it completely destroyed the value of the contract).

Note: Article 2's rules on impracticability apply equally to frustration situations.

d. Distinguish Uses of Defenses of Impossibility/Impracticability and Frustration
A seller of land, goods, or services will raise impossibility or impracticability as a defense that discharges performance. By contrast, the party who is supposed to pay (usually the buyer) will raise frustration of purpose as a defense discharging performance. Paying money is never impracticable.

Example: Caretaker is hired to tend to the mansion on Blackacre and signs a three-year employment contract to that effect at a rate of $30,000 per year. In the second year of Caretaker's contract, the mansion is destroyed by fire and the employer stops paying Caretaker. Caretaker sues the employer for breach and the employer countersues Caretaker. Caretaker will raise the defense of discharge by impossibility because the subject matter of the contract was destroyed. The employer will raise the defense of

discharge by frustration of purpose for the same reason. The employer cannot claim impossibility because he is still able to pay money.

6. Discharge by Rescission

Rescission will serve to discharge contractual duties. Rescission may be either mutual or unilateral.

a. Mutual Rescission

The contract may be discharged by an ***express agreement*** between the parties to rescind. The agreement to rescind is itself a binding contract supported by consideration, namely, the giving up by each party of her right to counterperformance from the other. The reasons for entering into such an agreement are immaterial absent duress or fraud.

1) Contract Must Be Executory

For a contract to be effectively discharged by rescission, the duties must be executory on ***both*** sides.

a) Unilateral Contracts

If the contract is unilateral (*i.e.,* only one party owes an absolute duty), a contract to mutually rescind where one party still has a duty to perform will be ineffective. The courts reason that the original promisor, who has not suffered a legal detriment, has not given consideration. Thus, for an effective rescission in a unilateral contract situation where the offeree has already performed, the rescission promise must be supported by one of the following:

(1) An offer of ***new consideration*** by the nonperforming party;

(2) Elements of ***promissory estoppel***, *i.e.,* detrimental reliance; or

(3) Manifestation of an ***intent*** by the original offeree to make a ***gift*** of the obligation owed her.

b) Partially Performed Bilateral Contracts

A mutual agreement to rescind will usually be enforced when a bilateral contract has been partially performed. Whether the party who has partially performed will be entitled to compensation will depend on the terms of the rescission agreement. The party seeking such compensation must affirmatively prove his right to the compensation in order to recover.

2) Formalities

Mutual rescission may be made ***orally***. This is so even though the contract to be rescinded expressly states that it can be rescinded only by a written document. Several ***exceptions*** should be noted, however:

a) Subject Matter Within Statute of Frauds

If the subject matter of the contract to be rescinded falls within the Statute of Frauds (*e.g.,* transfer of land), then the rescission should generally be in writing. Some courts, however, hold that even when the Statute of Frauds

comes into play, the oral rescission will still be enforceable if it is "executed" or promissory estoppel is present.

b) **Contracts for the Sale of Goods**
In addition to the Statute of Frauds requirement with respect to contracts for the sale of goods, Article 2 requires a written rescission or modification if the original contract to be rescinded or modified expressly requires a written rescission. [U.C.C. §2-209(2)]

3) **Contracts Involving Third-Party Beneficiary Rights**
If the rights of third-party beneficiaries have already ***vested*** (*see* IX.B.2., *infra*), the contract may ***not*** be discharged by mutual rescission.

b. **Unilateral Rescission**
Unilateral rescission results when one of the parties to the contract desires to rescind it but the other party desires that the contract be performed according to its terms. For unilateral rescission to be granted, the party desiring rescission must have adequate legal grounds. Most common among these are mistake, misrepresentation, duress, and failure of consideration. If the nonassenting party refuses to voluntarily grant rescission, the other party may file an action in equity to obtain it.

7. **Partial Discharge by Modification of Contract**
If a contract is subsequently modified by the parties, this will serve to discharge those terms of the original contract that are the subject of the modification. It will ***not*** serve to discharge the ***entire contract***. To have such a partial discharge, the following requirements must usually be met.

a. **Mutual Assent**
The modifying agreement must have been mutually assented to. Note, however, that under the doctrine of ***reformation*** (VIII.E., *infra*), either of the parties to the contract may bring an equity action to have a contract's terms modified if the writing, through mistake or misrepresentation, does not incorporate the terms orally agreed on.

b. **Consideration**
Generally, consideration is necessary to modify a contract. However, the courts usually find consideration to be present because each party has limited his right to enforce the original contract as is. Check the facts to see whether the modification would operate to the benefit of one of the parties only. If so, it may be unenforceable without some consideration being given to the other party. (*See* discussion of the preexisting legal duty rule, III.B.2.c., *supra*.)

1) **Requirement Where Modification Is Only "Correction"**
No consideration is necessary where the effect of the modification is merely to correct an error in the original contract.

2) **Contracts for the Sale of Goods**
No consideration is needed for the modification of a contract for the sale of goods under Article 2, as long as the modification is sought in good faith. [U.C.C. §2-209(1)]

8. **Discharge by Novation**
A novation occurs when a new contract substitutes a new party to receive benefits and assume duties that had originally belonged to one of the original parties under the terms of the old contract. A novation will serve to discharge the old contract. The elements for a valid novation are as follows:

(i) A ***previous*** valid contract;

(ii) An ***agreement*** among all parties, including the new party (or parties) to the new contract;

(iii) The ***immediate extinguishment*** of contractual duties as between the original contracting parties; and

(iv) A valid and enforceable ***new*** contract.

Example: John contracts to sell his house to Jane for $150,000. Before the closing date, John, Jane, and Joanna execute a new agreement wherein all rights and duties in connection with the transaction are transferred by Jane to Joanna. The original John-Jane contract will be discharged by novation.

9. **Discharge by Cancellation**
The destruction or surrender of a written contract will not usually by itself discharge the contract. If, however, the parties manifest their ***intent*** to have these acts serve as a discharge, it will usually have this effect if consideration or one of its alternatives is present.

10. **Discharge by Release**
A release and/or contract not to sue will serve to discharge contractual duties. The release or contract not to sue usually must be in ***writing*** and supported by ***new consideration*** or ***promissory estoppel*** elements. [*Compare* U.C.C. §1-306—governing the sale of goods and requiring an authenticated record (such as a writing) but ***not*** requiring consideration]

11. **Discharge by Substituted Contract**
A contract may be discharged by a substituted contract. This occurs when the parties to a contract enter into a second contract that ***immediately revokes*** the first contract.

a. **Revocation May Be Express or Implied**
The second contract may revoke the first contract either expressly or impliedly. The first contract will be impliedly revoked if the second contract's terms are inconsistent with the terms of the first contract.

b. **Intent Governs**
Whether a second contract will constitute a substituted contract depends on whether the parties intend an immediate discharge or a discharge only after performance of the second contract. If an immediate discharge is intended, there is a substituted contract. If the parties intend the first contract to be discharged only after performance of the second contract, there is an executory accord (*see* 12.a., *infra*) rather than a substituted contract.

12. Discharge by Accord and Satisfaction

A contract may be discharged by an accord and satisfaction.

a. Accord

An accord is an agreement in which one party to an existing contract agrees to accept, in lieu of the performance that she is supposed to receive from the other party to the existing contract, some other, different performance.

Example: Mel owes Alice $1,000 under a contract. Mel promises to give his car to Alice in settlement of the debt, and Alice agrees to accept the car in settlement of the debt. This agreement is an accord.

1) Requirement of Consideration

In general, an accord must be supported by consideration. Where the consideration is of a lesser value than the originally bargained-for consideration in the prior contract, it will be sufficient if the new consideration is of a ***different type*** or if the claim is to be paid to a ***third party***.

Example: Fred owes Barney $700 under an existing contract. Fred offers Barney a new TV set worth $500 in lieu of the existing debt. Barney accepts. This new consideration is sufficient to form a valid accord, even though it is worth less than the consideration originally owed, because it is of a different type.

a) Partial Payment of Original Debt

One often encountered problem involves the offer of a smaller amount than the amount due under an existing obligation in satisfaction of the claim, *i.e.,* partial payment of an original debt. The ***majority view*** is that this will suffice for an ***accord and satisfaction*** if there is a ***"bona fide dispute"*** as to the claim or there is otherwise some alteration, even if slight, in the debtor's consideration. (*See* discussion of the preexisting legal duty rule, III.B.2.c., *supra.*)

2) Effect of Accord

The accord, taken alone, will not discharge the prior contract. It merely ***suspends*** the right to enforce it in accordance with the terms of the accord contract.

b. Satisfaction

Satisfaction is the performance of the accord agreement. Its effect is to discharge not only the original contract but also the accord contract as well.

c. Effect of Breach of Accord Agreement Before Satisfaction

What happens when the accord agreement is not followed by an immediate satisfaction, and one of the parties breaches the accord agreement?

1) Breach by Debtor

If the breach is by the debtor, the creditor may sue either on the original undischarged contract ***or*** for breach of the accord agreement.

2) Breach by Creditor

If the accord agreement is breached by the creditor, *i.e.,* he sues on the ***original*** contract, the debtor has two courses of action available:

a) She may raise the accord agreement as an equitable defense and ask that the contract action be dismissed.

b) As an alternative, she may ***wait until she is damaged***, *i.e.*, the creditor is successful in his action on the original contract, and then bring an action at law for damages for breach of the accord contract.

d. Checks Tendered as "Payment in Full"

If a monetary claim is ***uncertain*** or is subject to a ***bona fide dispute***, an accord and satisfaction may be accomplished by a ***good faith*** tender and acceptance of a check when that check (or an accompanying document) ***conspicuously states*** that the check is tendered in ***full satisfaction*** of the debt. [U.C.C. §3-311]

13. Discharge by Account Stated

An account stated is a contract between parties whereby they agree to an amount as a ***final balance due*** from one to the other. This final balance encompasses a number of transactions between the parties and serves to merge all of these transactions by discharging all claims owed. In other words, all rights as to the individual, original transactions are discharged and the new agreement is enforceable. For an agreement to qualify as an account stated, the parties must have had ***more than one prior transaction*** between them.

a. Writing Generally Not Required

It is not necessary that the account stated be in writing. However, if one or more of the original transactions was subject to the Statute of Frauds, a writing will usually be required.

b. Account May Be Implied

It is also not required that an account stated be "express." It may be implied.

Example: Cindy and Dave have entered into a number of transactions. Cindy presents Dave with a bill for $1,000 covering all of these previous transactions. Dave does not object to this amount within a reasonable period of time. It will be held that there is an account stated.

14. Discharge by Lapse

Where the duty of each party is a condition concurrent to the other's duty, it is possible that on the day set for performance, neither party is in breach and their contractual obligations lapse.

a. Time When Lapse Becomes Effective

If the contract states that time is "of the essence," the lapse will occur immediately; otherwise the contract will lapse after a reasonable time.

Example: Sally contracts with Bobby to sell 100 widgets to her for $1,000 on November 15. On November 15, Sally does not tender the widgets and Bobby does not tender the $1,000. Ten months afterward, Sally attempts to put Bobby in breach by tendering the widgets. Sally will not have a claim, as the contractual obligations of both parties have been discharged by lapse.

15. Effect of Running of Statute of Limitations

If the statute of limitations on an action has run, it is generally held that an action for breach

of contract may be barred. Note, however, that only ***judicial remedies*** are barred; the running of the statute ***does not discharge the duties***. (Hence, if the party who has the advantage of the statute of limitations subsequently agrees to perform, new consideration will not be required.)

VII. BREACH

A. WHEN DOES A BREACH OCCUR?

If it is found that (i) the promisor is under an absolute duty to perform, and (ii) this absolute duty of performance has not been discharged, then this failure to perform in accordance with contractual terms will amount to a breach of the contract. The nonbreaching party who sues for breach of contract must show that she is ***willing and able*** to perform but for the breaching party's failure to perform.

B. MATERIAL OR MINOR BREACH—COMMON LAW CONTRACTS

Once you have determined that there is a breach of contract, the next determination to be made in a common law contract situation is whether that breach is material or minor.

1. Effect of Breaches

a. Minor Breach

A breach of contract is minor if the obligee gains the substantial benefit of her bargain despite the obligor's defective performance. Examples would be insignificant delays in completing performance or small deficiencies in the quality or quantity of performance when precision is not critical. The effect of a minor (immaterial) breach is to provide a remedy for the immaterial breach to the aggrieved party. The aggrieved party is ***not relieved*** of her duty of performance under the contract.

b. Material Breach

If the obligee does not receive the ***substantial benefit of her bargain*** as a result of failure to perform or defective performance, the breach is considered material. If the breach is material, the consequences are more severe. The nonbreaching party (i) may treat the contract as at an end, *i.e.,* any duty of counterperformance owed by her will be discharged, and (ii) will have an ***immediate right*** to all remedies for breach of the entire contract, including total damages.

c. Minor Breach Coupled with Anticipatory Repudiation

If a minor breach is coupled with an anticipatory repudiation (*see* VI.D.6.c., *supra*), the nonbreaching party may treat it as a material breach; *i.e.,* she may sue immediately for total damages and is permanently discharged from any duty of further performance. Indeed, the courts hold that the aggrieved party must not continue on, because to do so would be a failure to mitigate damages. The U.C.C. modifies this to permit a party to complete the manufacture of goods to avoid having to sell unfinished goods at the lower salvage value. (*See infra.*)

d. Material Breach of Divisible Contract

In a divisible contract, recovery is available for substantial performance of a divisible part even though there has been a material breach of the entire contract.

2. Determining Materiality of Breach

a. General Rule

Whether a breach is material or minor is a fact question. To make this determination, the courts generally apply the following six criteria [Restatement of Contracts §275]:

1) Amount of Benefit Received

Look to the extent to which the nonbreaching party will receive substantially the benefit she could have anticipated from full performance. The greater the extent, the less material the breach.

2) Adequacy of Damages

Look to the extent to which the injured party may be adequately compensated in damages. The greater the extent, the less material the breach.

3) Extent of Part Performance

Look to the extent the party failing to perform completely has already performed or made preparations to perform. The greater the extent, the less material the breach.

4) Hardship to Breaching Party

Look to the extent of hardship on the breaching party should the contract be terminated. If a finding of materiality and termination of the contract would cause great hardship to the breaching party, the breach is less likely to be found to be material.

5) Negligent or Willful Behavior

Look to the extent of negligent or willful behavior of the party failing to perform. The greater the extent, the more material the breach.

6) Likelihood of Full Performance

Look to the extent of likelihood the party who has failed to perform will perform the remainder of his contract. The greater the extent, the less material the breach.

b. Failure of Timely Performance

The basic question here is whether the parties to the contract must perform on time. Assuming that the defaulting party had a duty of immediate performance when his failure to perform occurred, then his failure to perform on time will always be a breach of contract. There are, however, additional specific rules for determining the materiality of breach by failure of timely performance.

1) As Specified by Nature of Contract

Unless the nature of the contract is such as to make performance on the exact day agreed upon of vital importance, or the contract by its terms provides that time is of the essence, failure by a promisor to perform at the stated time will not be material.

2) When Delay Occurs

Delay at the onset of performance before the delaying party has rendered any part of his agreed-on performance is more likely to be considered material than delay where there has been part performance.

3) **Mercantile Contracts**
In mercantile contracts, timely performance as agreed is important, and unjustified delay is material.

4) **Land Contracts**
More delay in land contracts is required for materiality than in mercantile contracts.

5) **Availability of Equitable Remedy**
In equity, the courts generally are much more lenient in tolerating considerable delay. Hence, they will tend to find the breach immaterial and award compensation for the delay where possible.

c. **Material Breach and Substantial Performance**
Whether performance is "substantial" depends on the quantity and quality of the performance. If the performance is "substantial," the breach is not material.

C. PERFECT TENDER RULE—SALE OF GOODS

Article 2 generally does not follow the common law substantial performance doctrine. Instead, it follows the perfect tender rule—if ***goods or their delivery fail to conform to the contract in any way***, the buyer generally may reject all, accept all, or accept any commercial units and reject the rest.

1. Commercial Unit Defined

A "commercial unit" is one that by commercial usage is treated as a single whole for the purpose of sale, and division of which materially impairs its value (*e.g.*, place setting of dishes). A commercial unit may be a single article (*e.g.*, a machine) or a set of articles (*e.g.*, suite of furniture), a quantity (*e.g.*, a bale, a gross), or any other unit treated in use or in the relevant market as a single whole. [U.C.C. §2-105(6)] The test for "commercial unit" is "not only what unit has been the basis of contract, but also whether the partial acceptance produces so materially an adverse effect upon the remainder as to constitute bad faith." [U.C.C. §2-601, comment 1]

Example: Widgets are always sold in units of 100. Buyer orders 500 widgets. They arrive but are found to be defective. Buyer keeps 25 and rejects 475. Buyer is probably required to reject in units of 100 and the rejection of the 75 above 400 is probably wrongful.

2. Right to Reject Cut Off by Acceptance

A buyer's right to reject under the perfect tender doctrine generally is cut off by acceptance. Under Article 2, a buyer accepts when:

(i) After a reasonable opportunity to inspect the goods, she ***indicates to the seller that they conform*** to requirements or that she will keep them even though they fail to conform;

(ii) She ***fails to reject*** within a reasonable time after tender or delivery of the goods or fails to seasonably notify the seller of her rejection; or

(iii) She does any ***act inconsistent with the seller's ownership.***

[U.C.C. §2-606]

a. **Notice**
If in connection with rejection the buyer fails to state that the goods have a particular defect that is ascertainable by reasonable inspection, she ***cannot rely on that defect*** to justify rejection or to show seller's breach ***if***:

(i) The ***seller could have cured*** the defect if he had been told about it; or

(ii) ***Between merchants*** when the ***seller has***, after rejection, ***made a request*** in writing for a full and final written statement of all defects upon which the buyer proposes to rely.

[U.C.C. §2-605]

Example: Buyer has ordered blue widgets. Buyer rejects because the shipment did not contain the widget wrench that, under the contract, went with each widget. Buyer does not give the reason for rejection. If Seller had known the reason, he could have had the necessary number of widget wrenches at Buyer's business within hours. That probably would have constituted an adequate cure. If so, Buyer's rejection is unjustified; she will not be able to rely on the absence of the wrenches as a reason for rejection or as the basis for a claim for damages.

3. **Buyer's Responsibility for Goods After Rejection**

a. **Buyer Must Hold Goods with Reasonable Care**
After rejecting goods in her physical possession, the buyer has an obligation to hold them with reasonable care at the seller's disposition for a time sufficient to permit the seller to remove them. If the seller has no agent or place of business within the market area where the goods are rejected, a ***merchant*** buyer has an obligation to obey any reasonable instructions as to the rejected goods (*i.e.,* she must arrange to reship the goods to a destination designated by the seller or resell on request of the seller, if reasonable). [U.C.C. §2-602]

b. **When Seller Gives No Instructions on Disposal of Goods**
If a seller gives no instructions within a reasonable time after notification of rejection, the buyer may ***reship*** the goods to the seller, ***store*** them for the seller's account, or ***resell*** them for the seller's account. The buyer has a ***security interest*** in rejected goods in her possession for ***any part of the price already paid*** and for expenses reasonably incurred in connection with handling them after rejection. [U.C.C. §2-604]

c. **When Buyer Resells Goods**
If the buyer does resell rejected goods, she is entitled to have her expenses of selling and any commission ordinarily paid in the trade or, if there is none, a reasonable commission not exceeding 10%. [U.C.C. §2-603(2)]

4. **Buyer's Right to Revoke Acceptance**
Once goods are accepted, the buyer's power to reject the goods generally is terminated and

the buyer is obligated to pay the price less any damages resulting from the seller's breach. However, under limited situations, a buyer may revoke an acceptance already made. A proper revocation of acceptance has the effect of a rejection.

a. **When Acceptance May Be Revoked**
The buyer may revoke her acceptance of goods if the goods have a defect that ***substantially impairs*** their ***value*** to her ***and***:

(i) She accepted them on the ***reasonable belief that the defect would be cured*** and it has not been; or

(ii) She accepted them because of the ***difficulty of discovering defects*** or because of the ***seller's assurance that the goods conformed*** to the contract.

[U.C.C. §2-608]

b. **Other Requirements for Revocation of Acceptance**
Revocation of acceptance must occur:

1) ***Within a reasonable time*** after the buyer discovers or should have discovered the defects; and

2) ***Before any substantial change in the goods occurs*** that is not caused by a defect present at the time the seller relinquished possession. [U.C.C. §2-608(2)]
Example: If the buyer receives defective goods and due to her own fault damages the goods in some other way, she can no longer revoke acceptance, because the damage is a substantial change in the goods not caused by the seller. Similarly, if the buyer receives damaged goods and then resells the goods, she cannot revoke acceptance and her only remedy is to recover damages for the defect (*see* VIII.B.2.a.2), *infra*). If the buyer sells some but not all of the defective units, she can revoke acceptance (within a reasonable time) of any unsold unit.

5. **Exceptions to the Perfect Tender Rule**

a. **Installment Contracts**
The right to reject when a contract is an installment contract (*i.e.,* when there is to be more than one delivery) is much more limited than in a single delivery contract situation. Installment contracts follow a rule akin to the common law substantial performance doctrine. In an installment contract situation, an installment can be rejected only if the nonconformity ***substantially impairs*** the value of that installment ***and cannot be cured*** (*see* below). In addition, the whole contract is breached only if the nonconformity ***substantially impairs*** the value of the ***entire contract***.
Example: Steve and Becky enter into a contract under which Steve is to deliver to Becky 100 blue widgets on the first day of each month, and Becky is to pay Steve $275 by the 10th of each month. Steve makes a perfect delivery the first two months and Becky makes the required payments. On the first day of the third month, Steve sends only 90 widgets. The 10-widget shortfall would be a basis for rejection under the perfect

tender rule, but because this is an installment contract, Becky cannot reject the installment unless she can show that the 10-widget shortfall substantially impairs the value of that installment, and she cannot cancel the entire contract unless she can show that the shortfall substantially impairs the value of the entire contract.

b. Seller's Right to Cure

1) Single Delivery Contracts

a) Seller Can Cure by Notice and New Tender Within Time for Performance

If the buyer has rejected goods because of defects, the seller may within the time originally provided for performance "cure" by giving ***reasonable notice*** of her intention to do so and making a ***new tender of conforming goods*** that the buyer must then accept. [U.C.C. §2-508]

Example: Buyer ordered blue widgets for delivery during the first 15 days of June. The widgets are delivered on June 9, but the widget wrenches required by the contract are missing. Seller can cure this defect by giving reasonable notice of his intention to provide and subsequently providing wrenches for the widgets by June 15. If he does, Buyer must accept, or Buyer will breach the contract.

b) Seller's Right to Cure Beyond Original Contract Time

Ordinarily, the seller has no right to cure beyond the original contract time. However, in cases where the buyer rejects a tender of nonconforming goods that the seller ***reasonably*** believed would be acceptable "with or without money allowance," the seller, upon a reasonable notification to the buyer, has a ***further reasonable time*** beyond the original contract time within which to make a conforming tender. A seller will probably be found to have had reasonable cause to believe that the tender would be acceptable if the seller can show that (i) trade practices or prior dealings with the buyer led the seller to believe that the goods would be acceptable, or (ii) the seller could not have known of the defect despite proper business conduct (*e.g.,* packaged goods purchased from a supplier).

Examples: 1) In the last example above, widgets are delivered without wrenches on June 15. Seller and Buyer have had a number of contracts over the years for the sale of widgets in which the wrench was a part of the contract. On several occasions, Seller has not been able to deliver the wrenches, and on each occasion, Buyer has accepted the widgets with a reduction in price and purchased the wrenches from another source. This time Buyer rejects the widgets. Seller will have a reasonable time after June 15 within which to cure by furnishing the wrenches.

2) Barry ordered 100 barrels of grade A oil from Sonya to be delivered on or before January 1. On January 1, Sonya delivered to Barry 100 barrels of oil that she had purchased from her supplier, Refineco. Upon delivery, Barry opened a barrel and

found that the oil was grade B oil. Barry immediately rejected the delivery. Sonya checked with Refineco and discovered that Refineco had made a packaging error and could replace the oil within two days. Assuming two days is a reasonable time under the circumstances (*e.g.,* if Barry does not need the oil immediately), Sonya will have a right to cure even though the time for performance has passed.

2) **Installment Contracts**

Article 2 provides that a defective shipment in an installment contract cannot be rejected ***if the defect can be cured***. Ordinarily, defects in the particular goods themselves cannot be cured, so the buyer can reject them, but then might be required to accept substitute goods under the provisions discussed above. Note that a deficiency in quantity may be cured by an additional delivery, and a delivery of too much may be cured by acceptance or return of a part. [U.C.C. §2-612]

D. ANTICIPATORY REPUDIATION

Recall that an anticipatory repudiation (*see* VI.D.6.c., *supra*) can be treated as an immediate breach of contract.

E. BREACH OF WARRANTY

At common law, the rule was caveat emptor—let the buyer beware. Once goods were accepted, the seller's obligations were discharged. However, as we have seen, today sellers give warranties as to the condition of the goods that apply even after acceptance. Failure to live up to these warranties constitutes a breach of warranty, for which a remedy is available.

VIII. REMEDIES

A. NONMONETARY REMEDIES

There are two broad branches of remedies available in breach of contract situations: nonmonetary and monetary. The primary nonmonetary remedy for exam purposes is specific performance, but Article 2 has a number of other specific nonmonetary remedies for certain situations involving contracts for the sale of goods.

1. Specific Performance

If the ***legal remedy is inadequate***, the nonbreaching party may seek specific performance, which is essentially an order from the court to the breaching party to perform or face contempt of court charges. The legal remedy (damages) generally is inadequate when the ***subject matter of the contract is rare or unique***. The rationale is that if the subject matter is rare or unique, damages will not put the nonbreaching party in as good a position as performance would have, because even with the damages the nonbreaching party would not be able to purchase substitute performance.

a. Available for Land and Rare or Unique Goods

Specific performance is always available for land sale contracts because all land is considered to be unique. It is also available for goods that are rare or unique at the time performance is due (*e.g.,* rare paintings, gasoline in short supply because of oil embargoes, etc.).

b. Not Available for Service Contracts

Specific performance is not available for breach of a contract to provide services, even if the services are rare or unique. This is because of problems of enforcement (it would be difficult for the court to supervise the performance) and because the courts feel it is tantamount to involuntary servitude, which is prohibited by the Constitution.

1) Injunction as Alternate Remedy

In contrast, a court may ***enjoin*** a breaching employee from working for a competitor throughout the duration of the contract if the services contracted for are rare or unique. This is allowed because less court supervision is required for a negative injunction than for a specific performance decree, and the prohibition against working (as opposed to the requirement of working) does not run afoul of the Constitution. The rationale for this approach is that an employee providing rare or unique services expressly or impliedly covenants that she will not work for a competitor during the contract term.

c. Covenant Not to Compete

Most courts will grant an order of specific performance to enforce a contract not to compete if: (i) the services to be performed are unique (thus rendering money damages inadequate); and (ii) the covenant is reasonable. To be reasonable:

(i) The covenant must be reasonably necessary to protect a ***legitimate interest*** of the person benefited by the covenant (*i.e.,* an employer or the purchaser of the covenantor's business);

(ii) The covenant must be reasonable as to its ***geographic scope and duration*** (*i.e.,* it cannot be broader than the benefited person's customer base and typically cannot be longer than one or two years); and

(iii) The covenant ***must not harm the public***.

Example: A locksmith agrees to sell his shop to a competitor and agrees not to open a new locksmith shop within 75 miles of his old shop within the next year. The covenant not to compete probably will be upheld.

d. Equitable Defenses Available

Because specific performance is an equitable remedy, it is subject to equitable defenses. The most frequently claimed equitable defenses are laches, unclean hands, and sale to a bona fide purchaser.

1) Laches

The equitable defense of laches arises when a party delays in bringing an equitable action and the delay prejudices the defendant (*e.g.,* the delay has substantially increased the cost or difficulty of performance). Note that mere delay itself is not a ground for this defense.

2) Unclean Hands

The unclean hands defense arises when the party seeking specific performance is guilty of some wrongdoing in the transaction being sued upon (*e.g.,* the defendant entered into the contract because of the plaintiff's lies). Note that the wrongdoing must be related to the transaction being sued upon; it is not sufficient that the plaintiff has defrauded other persons in similar transactions.

3) **Sale to a Bona Fide Purchaser**
If the subject matter of a goods or land contract has already been sold to another who purchased for value and in good faith (*i.e.,* a bona fide purchaser), the right to specific performance is cut off.
Example: Store contracts to sell a specific van Gogh painting to Ben. Before Store delivers the painting to Ben, Carla, who is unaware of Ben's contract with Store, offers to buy the same van Gogh from Store. Store accepts Carla's offer and gives the painting to Carla. Ben may not obtain specific performance.

2. **Nonmonetary Remedies Under Article 2**

a. **Buyer's Nonmonetary Remedies**

1) **Cancellation**
If a buyer rightfully rejects goods because they do not conform to the contract, one of her options is simply to cancel the contract.

2) **Buyer's Right to Replevy Identified Goods**

a) **On Buyer's Prepayment**
If a buyer has made at least ***part payment*** of the purchase price of goods that have been identified under a contract and the seller ***has not delivered*** the goods, the buyer may ***replevy*** the goods from the seller in two circumstances:

(i) The seller becomes ***insolvent*** within 10 days after receiving the buyer's first payment; or

(ii) The goods were purchased for ***personal, family, or household purposes.***

In either case, the buyer must ***tender*** any unpaid portion of the purchase price to the seller. [U.C.C. §2-502]

b) **On Buyer's Inability to Cover**
In addition, the buyer may replevy undelivered, identified goods from the seller if the buyer, after reasonable effort, is ***unable to secure adequate substitute goods*** (*i.e.,* cover). [U.C.C. §2-716(3)]
Example: Buyer and Seller enter into a contract for the delivery of 10,000 widgets on December 31. Seller, who has identified goods to the contract (*e.g.,* seller has set aside 10,000 widgets on his loading dock), refuses to deliver. Buyer makes reasonable efforts to find widgets from another source, but the earliest delivery date he can arrange is March 15. The widgets are needed for Buyer's manufacturing operations in February

and March. Buyer can replevy the goods from Seller. However, if the widgets were not to be used by Buyer until June, widgets for March 15 delivery would probably be reasonable substitute goods and Buyer could not recover the widgets from Seller.

3) **Buyer's Right to Specific Performance**
A right closely related to the buyer's right to replevy is her right to specific performance "where the goods are unique or in other proper circumstances." [U.C.C. §2-716(1)] The court may order specific performance ***even where the goods have not yet been identified*** to the contract by the seller. The comments to section 2-716 say that inability to cover is "strong evidence of other circumstances." Thus, buyers in inability-to-cover situations have their choice of replevin or specific performance remedies. Of course, a specific performance remedy is always discretionary with the court, and unclean hands, laches, etc., might bar an equity action but would not affect a replevin recovery. In any case, keep in mind that ***replevin will lie only for identified goods***, while specific performance may be decreed even though the goods have not previously been identified.

b. **Seller's Nonmonetary Remedies**

1) **Seller's Right to Withhold Goods**
If the buyer fails to make a payment due on or before delivery, the seller may withhold delivery of the goods. The seller may also withhold goods when the goods are sold on credit and, before the goods are delivered, the seller discovers that the buyer is insolvent. However, in such a case, the seller must deliver the goods if the buyer tenders cash for their payment. [U.C.C. §2-702]

2) **Seller's Right to Recover Goods**

a) **Right to Recover from Buyer on Buyer's Insolvency**
If a seller learns that a buyer has received delivery of goods on credit while insolvent, the seller may reclaim the goods upon demand made within 10 days after the buyer's receipt of the goods. However, the 10-day limitation does not apply if a misrepresentation of solvency has been ***made in writing*** to the particular seller ***within three months*** before delivery. Note that the seller's right to reclaim the goods is subject to the rights of a buyer in the ordinary course or any other good faith purchaser. [U.C.C. §2-702]

b) **Right to Recover Shipped or Stored Goods from Bailee**

(1) **On Buyer's Insolvency**
The seller may stop delivery of goods in the possession of a carrier or other bailee when he discovers the buyer to be insolvent. Of course, the seller must deliver the goods if the buyer tenders cash for their payment. [U.C.C. §2-705(1)]

(2) **On Buyer's Breach**
The seller may stop delivery of carload, truckload, planeload, or larger

shipments of goods when the buyer breaches the contract or when the seller has a right to withhold performance pending receipt of assurances. (*See* c., *infra,* on the right to demand assurances.) [U.C.C. §2-705(1)]

(3) When Goods May Not Be Stopped
The seller may stop delivery of the goods to the buyer ***until*** the buyer receives: (i) the goods or a negotiable document of title covering the goods; or (ii) an acknowledgment from a bailee other than the carrier that it is holding the goods for the buyer. [U.C.C. §2-705(2)]

(4) Obligation of Carrier or Bailee
The seller's notification must come in time to give the person in possession a ***reasonable time to stop delivery.*** If a negotiable document covers the goods, the carrier or bailee is not obligated to obey a stop order until the document is surrendered.

3) Seller's Ability to Force Goods on Buyer Limited
The seller's ability to force goods on a buyer is limited to an action for price when the seller is unable to resell the goods to others at a reasonable price. (*See* B.2.b.2), *infra.*)

c. Right to Demand Assurances
Under Article 2, actions or circumstances that increase the risk of nonperformance by the other party to the contract, but that do not clearly indicate that performance will not be forthcoming, may ***not*** be treated immediately as an anticipatory repudiation (*see* VI.D.6.c., *supra*). Instead, if the party ***reasonably*** fears that the other party will not perform, he may demand assurances that the performance will be forthcoming at the proper time. Until he receives adequate assurances, he may suspend his own performance. If the proper assurances are not given within a reasonable time (*i.e.,* within 30 days after a justified demand for assurances), he may then treat the contract as repudiated. What constitutes an adequate assurance depends on the facts of the case.

Examples: 1) Seller hears a rumor, in fact false, that Buyer is in financial trouble. Seller reasonably believes that the rumor may have foundation in fact. He is justified in making a demand for assurances and withholding any goods for which he has not been paid. Buyer, within a reasonable time, sends a financial report from her banker showing good financial condition. This is adequate assurance and Seller must resume performance.

2) Same facts as above except that Buyer ***is*** in bad financial condition. Adequate assurance may require a third party of good credit to back up Buyer.

3) Same facts as above. Buyer does not give any assurances. Seller may treat the failure to give assurances as a repudiation of the contract.

B. MONETARY REMEDY—DAMAGES

The most frequently sought remedy for breach of contract is an action at law for damages. In cases of willful breach, courts are more likely to be flexible in determining the plaintiff's damages alternatives

1. Types of Damages

a. Compensatory Damages

The purpose of contract damages is to give compensation for the breach; that is, to ***put the nonbreaching party where she would have been had the promise been performed*** so far as money can do this.

1) "Standard Measure" of Damages—Expectation Damages

In most cases, the plaintiff's standard measure of damages will be based on an "expectation" measure, *i.e.,* sufficient damages for her to buy a ***substitute performance.*** This is also known as ***"benefit of the bargain"*** damages.

2) Reliance Damage Measure

If the plaintiff's expectation damages will be too speculative to measure (*e.g.,* the plaintiff cannot show with sufficient certainty the profits she would have made if the defendant had performed the contract), the plaintiff may elect to recover damages based on a "reliance" measure rather than an expectation measure. Reliance damages award the plaintiff the cost of her performance; *i.e.,* they are designed to ***put the plaintiff in the position she would have been in had the contract never been formed.***

Example: J-Mart gives Sam a "dealer franchise" to sell J-Mart's products in a stated area for one year. In preparation for performance, Sam spends money on advertising, hiring sales personnel, and acquiring premises that cannot be used for other purposes. J-Mart then repudiates before performance begins. If it cannot be established with reasonable certainty what profit Sam would have made if the contract had been performed (*i.e.,* Sam's expectation damages), Sam can recover as reliance damages his expenditures in preparation for performance.

3) Consequential Damages

Consequential damages consist of losses resulting from the breach that any ***reasonable person*** would have ***foreseen*** would occur from a breach at the time of entry into the contract. Note that in contracts for the sale of goods, ***only a buyer*** may recover consequential damages.

4) Incidental Damages—Contracts for the Sale of Goods

In contracts for the sale of goods, compensatory damages may also include incidental damages. Incidental damages include expenses reasonably incurred by the buyer in inspection, receipt, transportation, care, and custody of goods rightfully rejected and other expenses reasonably incident to the seller's breach, and by the seller in storing, shipping, returning, and reselling the goods as a result of the buyer's breach.

b. Punitive Damages

Punitive damages are generally ***not*** awarded in contract cases.

c. Nominal Damages

Nominal (token) damages (*e.g.,* $1) may be awarded where a breach is shown but no actual loss is proven.

d. Liquidated Damages

The parties to a contract may stipulate what damages are to be paid in the event of a breach. These liquidated damages must be in an amount that is reasonable in view of the actual or anticipated harm caused by the breach.

1) Requirements for Enforcement

Liquidated damage clauses will be enforceable if the following two requirements are met:

(i) Damages for contractual breach must have been ***difficult to estimate or ascertain at the time the contract was formed.***

(ii) The amount agreed on must have been a ***reasonable forecast*** of compensatory damages in the case of breach. The test for reasonableness is a comparison between the amount of damages prospectively probable at the time of contract formation and the liquidated damages figure. If the liquidated damages amount is unreasonable, the courts will construe this as a ***penalty*** and will not enforce the provision.

a) U.C.C. Rule

The U.C.C. allows a court to consider actual damages to validate a liquidated damages clause. Even if the clause was not a reasonable forecast of damages at the time of the contract formation, it will be valid if it was reasonable in light of the subsequent actual damages. [U.C.C. §2-718(1)]

2) Recoverable Even If No Actual Damages

If the above requirements are met, the plaintiff will receive the liquidated damages amount. Most courts hold this is so even if no actual money or pecuniary damages have been suffered. Should one or both of the above requirements not be met, the provision fails and the plaintiff will recover only those damages that she can ***prove***.

3) Effect of Electing Liquidated or Actual Damages

Should a contract stipulate that the plaintiff may elect to recover liquidated damages set by a clause or actual damages, the liquidated damage clause may be unenforceable.

2. Contracts for Sale of Goods

a. Buyer's Damages

1) Seller Does Not Deliver or Buyer Rejects Goods or Revokes Acceptance

The buyer's basic damages where the seller does not deliver or the buyer properly rejects or revokes her acceptance of tendered goods consist of the difference between the contract price and either the market price (*i.e.*, ***benefit of the bargain*** damages) or the cost of buying replacement goods (*i.e.*, ***cover***), plus incidental and consequential damages (*see* above), if any, less expenses saved as a result of the seller's breach. In the case of a seller's anticipatory repudiation, the buyer's damages are measured as of the time she learns of the breach.

a) **Difference Between Contract Price and Market Price**
If the buyer measures damages by the difference between contract price and market price, market price usually is determined as of the time the buyer learns of the breach and at the place of tender. [U.C.C. §2-713] Note that the ***buyer's damages*** are measured as of the ***time she learns of the breach***, while the ***seller's damages*** are measured as of the ***time for delivery***. (*See* b.1)a), *infra.*)

b) **Difference Between Contract Price and Cost of Replacement Goods—"Cover"**
Cover is the usual measure of damages for a buyer. Typically, if a buyer is not sent the goods contracted for, he will go out into the marketplace to buy replacement goods. If the buyer chooses the cover measure (*i.e.,* difference between contract price and cost of buying replacement goods), the buyer must make a ***reasonable contract*** for substitute goods ***in good faith*** and ***without unreasonable delay.*** [U.C.C. §2-712]

Example: Seller and Buyer have a contract for the sale of 10,000 widgets at $1 per widget. Seller does not deliver. At the time and place for determining market price, the average price of widgets is $1.05. However, Buyer made a replacement contract within a reasonable time and in good faith at a price of $1.07. Buyer can recover $700 based on her replacement costs. If, on the other hand, Buyer could have bought substitute widgets for $1.03 while the general market price was $1.05, but she chose not to cover, she could recover $500 based on the difference between contract and market prices, rather than being limited to her cover costs.

2) **Seller Delivers Nonconforming Goods that Buyer Accepts**

a) **Warranty Damages**
If the buyer accepts goods that breach one of the seller's warranties, the buyer may recover as damages "loss resulting in the normal course of events from the breach." The basic measure of damages in such a case is the difference between the ***value of the goods as delivered*** and the ***value they would have had if they had been according to contract***, plus incidental and consequential damages. [U.C.C. §2-714] (*See* V.D.6.f., *supra.*)

b) **Notice Requirement**
To recover damages for any defect as to accepted goods, the buyer must, ***within a reasonable time after she discovers or should have discovered the defect***, notify the seller of the defect. If she does not notify the seller within a reasonable time, she loses her right to sue. "Reasonable time" is, of course, a flexible standard.

3) **Seller Anticipatorily Breaches Contract**
Under section 2-713, the measure of damages when the seller anticipatorily breaches the contract is the difference between the ***market price at the time the buyer learned of the breach*** and the ***contract price***.

4) **Consequential Damages**
As noted above, a seller is liable for consequential damages arising from his breach if: (i) he had reason to know of the buyer's general or particular requirements, and (ii) the subsequent loss resulting from those needs could not reasonably be prevented by cover. Particular needs must be made known to the seller, but general requirements usually need not be. [U.C.C. §2-715(2)]

a) **Goods for Resale**
If the buyer is in the business of reselling the goods, the seller is deemed to have knowledge of the resale.

b) **Goods Necessary for Manufacturing**
If a seller knows that the goods he provides are to be used in the manufacturing process, he should know that his breach would cause a disruption in production leading to a loss of profits.

b. **Seller's Damages**

1) **Buyer Refuses to Accept Goods or Anticipatorily Breaches Contract**
The seller's basic damages when the buyer refuses to accept goods or repudiates are either the difference between the contract price and the market price or the difference between the contract price and the resale price of the particular goods, plus incidental (but ***not*** consequential) damages, if any, less expenses saved as a result of the breach. If damages based on the difference between the contract price and market or resale price do not put the seller in as good a position as performance would have, then the seller may recover lost profits plus incidental damages. [U.C.C. §§2-706, 2-708, 2-710] In the case of a buyer's anticipatory breach, the seller's damages are measured as of the actual time for performance, unless the suit comes to trial before the time for performance, in which case damages are measured as the time the seller learned of the breach.

a) **Difference Between Contract Price and Market Price**
The market price is measured as of the time and at the place for ***delivery***.

b) **Difference Between Contract Price and Resale Price**
This is the usual measure of a seller's damages. The seller must resell under the provisions of section 2-706. This section requires a ***good faith, commercially reasonable sale*** that may be either private or public (auction). In the case of a private sale, the breaching buyer must be given reasonable notice of intention to resell. In the case of an auction sale, the sale must be at a usual market for such goods if such a market is reasonably available. Notice of the sale must be given to the breaching buyer unless the goods are perishable or threaten to decline rapidly in value. Only existing and identified goods may be sold, unless there is a market in futures for the particular goods. The seller may buy the goods at an auction sale.

c) **Damages Based on Lost Profits**
The previous two measures of damages might not give adequate compensation for the buyer's breach in situations where the seller can obtain or

manufacture as many goods as he can sell (*e.g.,* a car dealership). In such a case, the seller is known as a ***lost volume seller***, because although he is able to resell the goods for the same or similar price as in the initial contract, he loses ***volume*** of business: But for the buyer's breach, the seller would have made ***two*** sales instead of one. Generally, lost profit is measured by the contract price with the breaching buyer minus cost to the seller.

Example: Seller, a distributor of widgets, can get all of the widgets he needs for sale. He makes a contract to sell 10,000 widgets to Buyer at a price of $1 per widget. Buyer repudiates the contract. Seller resells the widgets he had identified to Buyer's contract to Z for $1 per widget. If damages are measured by the difference between the contract price and resale price, Seller will be denied recovery. However, assuming Seller paid 85¢ per widget for these widgets, his lost profit on the Buyer deal is $1,500 ($10,000 less $8,500), because even if Buyer had not breached, Seller would have been able to supply Z with widgets. Because Buyer's breach did not ***enable*** Seller to make the sale to Z, and because the sale to Z would have been made in any event, the only way to make Seller whole is to allow him to recover his lost profits, *i.e.,* $1,500. If Seller would have incurred sales commissions of $500 and delivery expenses of $100 if Buyer had taken the goods, but does not now incur those expenses, the saved expenses reduce the recovery. Therefore, the recovery would be $900 ($1,500 less saved expenses of $600).

Compare: Seller and Buyer enter into a contract for the sale of a particular painting by van Gogh at a price of $25,000. Seller paid $15,000 for the painting two years earlier. Buyer repudiates. Seller resells to Z at $24,000. Seller's measure of damages is $1,000 plus incidental damages. Seller cannot get the $10,000 lost profit measure (*i.e.,* the difference between the contract price and what Seller paid for the painting) because there is only one painting, and Seller could not have made the sale to Z but for Buyer's repudiation.

2) Action for Price

If the buyer has accepted the goods and has not paid, or has not accepted the goods and the seller is ***unable to resell*** them at any reasonable price, or if the goods have been lost or damaged at a time the risk of loss was on the buyer (*see* V.D.3., *supra*), the seller may maintain an action against the buyer for the full contract price. [U.C.C. §2-709]

3. Contracts for Sale of Land

The standard measure of damages for breach of land sale contracts is the difference between the contract price and the fair market value of the land.

4. **Employment Contracts**
In employment contracts, check to see whether the breach was by the employer or the employee.

a. **Breach by Employer**
Irrespective of when the breach occurs—*i.e.,* before performance, after part performance, or after full performance, the standard measure of the employee's damages is the ***full contract price***.

b. **Breach by Employee**
If the employee is the breaching party, check to see whether the breach is intentional or unintentional.

1) **Intentional Breach**
If the employee's breach is intentional, the employer is entitled to a standard measure of damages computed according to what it ***costs to replace*** the employee, *i.e.,* the difference between the cost incurred to get a second employee to do the work and the cost to the employer had the first breaching employee done the work. The modern view allows the employee to offset any monies due from work done to date.

2) **Unintentional Breach**
The standard measure of damages for unintentional breach is the same as for intentional breach. However, when the breach is unintentional, *e.g.,* personal illness, the employee may have a right to quasi-contractual recovery for work done to date.

5. **Construction Contracts**
If construction contracts are involved, check to see whether the owner or the builder is breaching.

a. **Breach by Owner**
If the owner has breached, check to see when the breach occurred.

1) **Breach Before Construction Started**
If the breach occurred before construction started, the builder is entitled to the ***profits*** he would have derived from the contract.

2) **Breach During Construction**
If the breach occurs during construction, the builder is entitled to any ***profit*** he would have derived from the contract ***plus*** any ***costs*** he has incurred to date. The formula is also stated as the contract price minus the cost of completion. Either formula will give the same result.

3) **Breach After Construction Completed**
If the breach occurs after construction has been completed, the builder is entitled to the full ***contract price plus interest*** thereon.

b. **Breach by Builder**
If the breach is by the builder, check to see when it occurred.

1) **Breach Before Construction Started**
If the builder breaches before construction, the owner's measure of damages is the ***cost of completion***, *i.e.*, the amount above the contract price that it will cost to get the building completed ***plus*** reasonable compensation for any delay in performance.

2) **Breach During Construction**
If the builder breaches after partially performing, the owner is entitled to the ***cost of completion plus reasonable compensation for any delay*** in performance. If, however, completion would involve undue economic waste, the measure of damages will be the difference between the value of what the owner ***would have received*** if the builder had properly performed the contract and the value of what the owner ***actually received***.

Example: Homeowner and Builder enter into a contract to build a house. The contract provides, among other things, that all of the plumbing pipes will be copper. After the plumbing is installed throughout the house, but before construction of the house is completed, Homeowner discovers that the pipes installed were made of polyvinyl chloride ("PVC"), and not copper. Homeowner insists that Builder remove the entire plumbing system and replace the PVC pipes with copper pipes. The house with PVC pipes would be valued at $500 less than it would have been had copper pipes been installed. However, it would cost Builder $10,000 in labor and materials to rip out the PVC pipes and replace them with copper pipes. *Result:* Builder would not be compelled to replace the pipes, and Homeowner's damages would be $500, which may be offset against the amount owed to Builder.

3) **Breach by Late Performance**
If the builder completes performance, but it is late, the owner has a right to damages for any loss incurred by not being able to use the property when performance was due, *e.g.*, loss of reasonable rental value when property could have been leased. However, if damages for this "lost use" are not easily determined or were not foreseeable at the time the contract was entered into, the owner can recover only the ***interest*** on the value of the building as a capital investment.

6. **Contracts Calling for Installment Payments**
If a contract calls for payments in installments and a payment is not made, there is only a partial breach. The aggrieved party is limited to recovering only the missed payment, not the entire contract price. However, the contract may include an ***acceleration clause*** making the entire amount due on any late payment, in which case the aggrieved party may recover the entire amount. [Restatement (Second) of Contracts §243(3)]

7. **Certainty Rule**
The plaintiff must prove that the losses suffered were certain in their nature and ***not speculative***. Traditionally, if the breaching party prevented the nonbreaching party from setting up a new business, courts would not award lost profits from the prospective business as damages, because they were too speculative. However, modern courts may allow lost profits

as damages if they can be made more certain by observing similar businesses in the area or other businesses previously owned by the same party.

8. Avoidable Damages (Mitigation)

The nonbreaching party cannot recover avoidable damages. Thus, she must refrain from piling up losses after she receives notice of the breach; she must not incur further expenditures or costs, and she must make reasonable efforts to cut down her losses by procuring a substitute performance at a fair price. Should she not do so, she will not be allowed to recover those damages that might have been avoided by such mitigation after the breach. Generally, a party may ***recover the expenses of mitigation***. Note the following specific contract situations:

a. Employment Contracts

If the employer breaches, the employee is under a duty to use ***reasonable care*** in finding a position of the same kind, rank, and grade in the same locale (although it does not necessarily have to be at the same exact pay level). However, note that the burden is on the employer to show that such jobs were available.

b. Contracts for Sale of Goods

If the buyer is in breach, recall that the seller generally cannot bring an action against the buyer for the full contract price unless the goods cannot be resold at a reasonable price or were damaged or lost when the risk of loss was on the buyer. (*See* 2.b.1)c), *supra.*)

c. Manufacturing Contracts

Generally, in a contract to manufacture goods, if the person for whom the goods are being manufactured breaches, the manufacturer is under a duty to mitigate by ***not continuing work*** after the breach. However, if the facts are such that completion of the manufacturing project will decrease rather than increase damages, the manufacturer has a right to continue.

Example: Partly manufactured goods may be without value because they cannot be sold. The nonbreaching manufacturer may complete production and recover for his expenses in doing so, because finished goods usually can be resold, and the damages will be decreased as a result.

d. Construction Contracts

A builder does not owe a duty to avoid the consequences of an owner's breach, *e.g.,* by securing other work, but does have a duty to mitigate by ***not continuing work*** after the breach. Again, however, if completion will decrease damages, it will be allowed.

C. RESTITUTION

As an alternative to the contract damages discussed above, restitution may be available in a contract-type situation. Restitution is not really part of contract law, but rather is a distinct concept. Restitution is based on preventing ***unjust enrichment*** when one has conferred a benefit on another without gratuitous intent. Restitution can provide a remedy not only when a contract exists and has been breached, but also when a contract is unenforceable, and in some cases when no contractual relationship exists at all between the parties.

1. **Terminology**
When a contract is unenforceable or no contract between the parties exists, an action to recover restitutionary damages often is referred to as an action for an ***implied in law*** contract or an action in ***quasi-contract***.

2. **Measure of Damages**
Generally, the measure of restitution is the ***value of the benefit conferred***. Although this is usually based on the benefit received by the defendant (*e.g.*, the increase in value of the defendant's property or the value of the goods received), recovery may also be measured by the "detriment" suffered by the plaintiff (*e.g.*, the reasonable value of the work performed or the services rendered) if the benefits are difficult to measure or the "benefit" measure would achieve an unfair result.
Example: Homeowner hires Painter to paint Homeowner's house in exchange for $5,000. When the job is 70% complete, Homeowner orders Painter to stop because Homeowner does not like the new color. The value of the work performed thus far is $4,000. Although the value of Homeowner's house might not have been increased by the partially finished paint job, Painter may recover in a restitutionary action the $4,000 value of the services rendered.

3. **Specific Applications**

a. **When Contract Breached**
When a contract has been breached and the nonbreaching party has not fully performed, he may choose to rescind the contract and sue for restitution to prevent unjust enrichment. Note that if the plaintiff has fully performed, he is ***limited to his damages under the contract.*** This may be less than he would have received in a restitutionary action because a restitutionary remedy is not limited to the contract price (*see* example below).

1) **"Losing" Contracts**
A restitutionary remedy often is desirable in the case of a "losing" contract (*i.e.,* a contract in which the actual value of the services or goods to be provided under the contract is higher than the contract price), because normal contract expectation damages or reliance damages would be for a lesser amount.
Example: Builder hires Architect to design a home and agrees to pay Architect $10,000 for the plans. When the plans are 80% complete, Architect shows them to Builder. Although the plans meet the criteria discussed by the parties, Builder is dissatisfied with them and fires Architect. The fair market value of the work Architect performed is $12,000. In an action for restitution, Architect can recover from Builder the full $12,000, even though, had Architect completed the plans, Architect's remedy would have been limited to the $10,000 contract price.

2) **Breach by Plaintiff**
Typically, the plaintiff will be seeking restitution because the defendant breached the contract. However, under some circumstances, a plaintiff may seek restitution even though the plaintiff is the party who breached. If the breach was intentional, some courts will not grant the breaching party restitution; modern courts, however,

will permit restitutionary recovery but limit it to the contract price less damages incurred as a result of the breach.

Example: Client hires Attorney to represent Client in a contract dispute. Attorney prepares the case, but withdraws without good cause. The case is settled favorably for Client. Modern courts will allow Attorney to recover for the value of the services he rendered to Client, up to the contract price, reduced by the reasonable amount Client had to expend to hire another attorney.

a) **Restitution of Advance Payments or Deposit If Buyer in Breach**

If the buyer has paid part of the purchase price in advance and then breaches the contract, he can usually recover some of the payments.

(1) **General Offset Provision**

When the buyer breaches, the seller may keep advance payments totaling 20% of the purchase price or $500, whichever is less. The balance must be returned to the buyer. [U.C.C. §2-718(2)(b)]

(2) **Effect of Liquidated Damages Provision**

If there is a valid liquidated damages clause, the seller is required to refund only the excess of the buyer's payments over the amount of liquidated damages. [U.C.C. §2-718(2)(a)]

(3) **Seller's Right to Greater Damages**

The general offset rule above applies only if the seller cannot prove greater actual damages. If the seller can prove damages in excess of 20% of the price or $500, he may recover them. Even if he cannot prove actual damages beyond the offset, he is additionally entitled to incidental damages and the value of any benefits received by the buyer. [U.C.C. §2-718(3)]

b. **When Contract Unenforceable—Quasi-Contract Remedy**

Restitution may be available in a ***quasi-contract*** action when a contract was made but is unenforceable and unjust enrichment otherwise would result.

Examples: 1) Aristotle hires Derek to sign autographs in Aristotle's sporting goods store one day next month and gives Derek half of his $1,000 fee upon making the contract. Derek then dies and so is discharged from his obligation to perform. Aristotle can recover the $500 from Derek's estate as restitution in quasi-contract.

2) Owner hires Builder to repair Owner's house. After Builder has completed half of the repair work, the house is destroyed by a tornado. Although the parties will be discharged for impossibility, Builder will be able to recover in restitution for the valuable improvements made to the house before it was destroyed.

3) Landlord promises to sell Tenant five acres of a 1,000-acre tract that Tenant is leasing, but the contract fails to state which five acres. Tenant plants fruit trees on the five acres that he thinks were intended. Tenant

cannot enforce the promise because it does not specify which five acres were intended, but he can recover restitution in a quasi-contract action for the value of the fruit trees.

c. **When No Contract Involved—Quasi-Contract Remedy**
Restitution may also be available in a ***quasi-contract*** action when there is no contractual relationship between the parties if:

(i) The plaintiff has ***conferred a benefit*** on the defendant by rendering services or expending properties;

(ii) The plaintiff conferred the benefit with the ***reasonable expectation of being compensated*** for its value;

(iii) The defendant ***knew or had reason to know*** of the plaintiff's expectation; and

(iv) The defendant would be ***unjustly enriched*** if he were allowed to retain the benefit without compensating the plaintiff.

Example: Doctor witnesses an automobile accident and rushes to aid an unconscious victim. Doctor can recover the reasonable value of his services.

Note: Where the parties are in a ***close relationship*** to one another, it is usually presumed that the benefits were given gratuitously and the party claiming relief bears the burden of showing that they were conferred with an expectation of being paid therefor.

D. RESCISSION

Rescission is a remedy whereby the original contract is considered voidable and rescinded. The parties are left as though a contract had never been made.

1. Grounds

The grounds for rescission must have occurred either before or at the time the contract was entered into. The grounds are:

a. ***Mutual mistake*** of a material fact (*see* IV.B.1.a., *supra*);

b. Unilateral mistake if the ***other party knew*** or should have known of the mistake;

c. Unilateral mistake if ***hardship by the mistaken party is so extreme*** it outweighs the other party's expectations under the contract;

d. ***Misrepresentation of fact or law*** by either party as to a material factor in the negotiations that was relied upon; and

e. ***Other grounds***, such as duress, undue influence, illegality, lack of capacity, and failure of consideration.

2. Defenses

Generally all equitable defenses (*e.g.*, laches, unclean hands) are available in a rescission action. Note that the plaintiff's negligence is not a defense.

3. **Additional Relief**
If the plaintiff has paid money to the defendant, she is entitled to restitution in addition to rescission.

E. REFORMATION

Reformation is the remedy whereby the writing setting forth the agreement between the parties is changed so that it conforms to the original intent of the parties.

1. **Grounds**
A reformation action is usually based on mutual mistake; *i.e.*, the parties agree to a set of terms and unbeknownst to either party the written contract fails to reflect those terms. Reformation is also possible if there is a unilateral mistake and the party who knows of the mistake does not disclose it. Finally, reformation is available when the writing is incorrect because of innocent or fraudulent misrepresentation. In that case, the writing will be reformed to reflect the ***expressed*** intent of the parties.

2. **Clear and Convincing Evidence Standard**
The variance between the antecedent agreement and the writing must be established by clear and convincing evidence.

3. **Parol Evidence Rule and Statute of Frauds Do Not Apply**
The parol evidence rule is not applied in reformation actions. Likewise, the majority rule is that the Statute of Frauds does not apply—but many courts will deny reformation if it would add land to the contract without complying with the Statute of Frauds.

4. **Defenses**
In addition to the general equitable defenses, the existence of a bona fide purchaser for value is also a defense to reformation. If the subject matter of the contract is sold to a bona fide purchaser, reformation will not be allowed. Similarly, reformation is not permitted if the rights of third parties will be unfairly affected.

F. STATUTE OF LIMITATIONS UNDER U.C.C.

States have enacted differing statutes of limitation for contracts actions in general, and some have specific limitations periods for specific types of contracts. For sales contracts, however, the U.C.C. provides for a ***four-year statute*** of limitations. [U.C.C. §2-725]

1. **Parties May Agree to Shorter Period**
The parties to a sales contract may shorten the limitations period by agreement to ***no less than one year***, but they may not lengthen the period.

2. **Accrual of Action**
The statutory period begins to run when the cause of action accrues. The cause of action accrues when a party can bring suit, *i.e.*, when the breach occurs. The statutory period begins to run regardless of whether the aggrieved party knows about the breach. [U.C.C. §2-725(2)]

3. **Breach of Warranty Actions**
For a breach of warranty action, the breach occurs and the limitations period begins to run upon ***delivery*** of the goods. This is true even if the buyer does not discover the breach until much later.

a. **Warranty Extends to Future Performance**
If there is an express warranty that explicitly extends to future performance of the goods, the four-year period does not begin to run until the buyer should have discovered the breach.

Example: Buyer purchases a lawn mower from Seller. In the contract, Seller specifically warrants that all parts will be free from defect for five years. Two years after the sale, one of the blades breaks in two. The four-year period begins to run on the day the blade broke.

b. **Implied Warranties Breached on Delivery**
Because implied warranties cannot "explicitly" extend to future performance, they are breached, if at all, upon delivery.

IX. RIGHTS AND DUTIES OF THIRD PARTIES TO THE CONTRACT

A. INTRODUCTION

The general rule is that a contract operates to confer rights and impose duties only on the parties to the contract and on no other person. However, two important exceptions exist: (i) contractual rights involving third-party beneficiaries, and (ii) contractual rights or duties that are transferred to third parties. In the first situation, the original contract will confer the rights and duties on the third party; in the second situation, the original contract does not confer any rights or obligations on the third party, but subsequently one of the parties has sought to transfer his rights and/or duties under the contract to a third party (*i.e.,* assignment of rights, delegation of duties).

B. THIRD-PARTY BENEFICIARIES

The basic situation to be dealt with here is: A enters into a valid contract with B that provides that B will render some performance to C. A is the promisee, B is the promisor, and C is a third party. Three main problems must be focused on:

(i) Is C a third-party beneficiary?

(ii) Can A and B alter the contract's terms to deprive C of her rights? That is, when do C's rights vest?

(iii) What are the rights of A and C against B; of C against A?

1. **Which Third-Party Beneficiaries Can Sue?**

a. **Categories of Beneficiaries**

1) **Intended vs. Incidental Beneficiaries**
The first line of demarcation to be drawn is between intended beneficiaries, who have rights under the contract, and mere incidental beneficiaries, who do not.

a) **Test**
The best test for determining whether someone is an intended beneficiary is to pose the following question: "To whom is performance to be given ***according to the language of the contract***?" In other words, was the purpose of the promisee, according to the language of the contract, to get the benefit for

herself primarily or to confer a right on another directly? If the purpose was to confer a right on another directly, we have a third-party beneficiary situation.

Example: Alex offers to sell his car to Becky if Becky pays Cindy the $1,000 purchase price. Cindy is a third-party beneficiary because the contract appears to have been intended to directly benefit her.

Compare: Alex promises Becky that he will give her a brand new General Motors car if she will work for him for three months. General Motors probably is not an intended beneficiary even though it is named in the contract (*see* factors to consider, below).

b) Determining Promisee's Intention

The courts generally look at the following ***factors*** in resolving the question of intention:

(1) Is the third party expressly ***designated*** in the contract? If so, it is more likely that it is primarily for her benefit. But note that it is not necessary that the third-party beneficiary be named, or even identifiable, at the time the contract is made; she need only be identifiable at the time performance is due.

(2) Is ***performance to be made directly*** to the third party? If so, it is more likely that the contract is primarily for her benefit.

(3) Does the third party have any ***rights*** under the contract (*e.g.,* the right to designate when and where performance is to be made)? If so, it is more likely that the contract is primarily for her benefit.

(4) Does the third party stand in such a ***relationship*** to the promisee that one could infer that the promisee wished to make an agreement for the third party's benefit? If so, it is more likely that the contract is primarily for her benefit.

2) Creditor or Donee Beneficiary

There are two basic categories of "intended" beneficiaries who may sue on the promise: creditor and donee beneficiaries. The distinction between the two is based on the promisee's purpose in extracting the commitment from the promisor.

a) Creditor Beneficiary

If the promisee's purpose in extracting the promise was to discharge an obligation owed to the third party, the third party is a creditor beneficiary.

b) Donee Beneficiary

If the promisee's purpose in extracting the promise was to confer a gift on the third party, the third party is a donee beneficiary.

2. **When Do the Rights of the Beneficiary Vest?**
An "intended" beneficiary can enforce a contract only after his rights have vested. This becomes important when the original parties to the contract take actions (*e.g.,* rescission, modification, etc.) that affect the third-party beneficiary. The general rule for ***both*** creditor and donee beneficiaries is that their rights vest when the beneficiary:

(i) Manifests ***assent*** to the promise in a manner invited or requested by the parties;

(ii) Brings ***suit*** to enforce the promise; or

(iii) Materially ***changes position*** in justifiable reliance on the promise.

[Restatement (Second) of Contracts §311]

a. **Significance of Vesting**
Before the intended third-party beneficiary's rights vest, the promisor and promisee are free to modify their contract—including removing the third-party beneficiary altogether—without consulting the third party. Once the third-party beneficiary's rights have vested, the promisor and promisee cannot vary his rights without his consent.

3. **What Are the Rights of the Third-Party Beneficiary and the Promisee?**

a. **Third-Party Beneficiary vs. Promisor**
If the promisor fails to perform, the third-party beneficiary may sue the promisor on the contract, subject to defenses as follows:

1) **Promisor's Defenses Against Promisee**
Because the third-party beneficiary's rights are derivative, the promisor may raise any defense against the third-party beneficiary that he would have against the promisee, including: lack of assent, lack of consideration, illegality, impossibility, and failure of a condition.

2) **Promisee's Defenses Against Third-Party Beneficiary If Promise Not Absolute**
Whether the promisor can use any of the defenses that the promisee would have against the third-party beneficiary depends on whether the promisor made an absolute promise to pay (*e.g.,* "I will pay T $500 in exchange for your services") or only a promise to pay what the promisee owes the beneficiary (*e.g.,* "I will pay T whatever you owe him in exchange for your services"). In the former case, the promisor ***cannot*** assert the promisee's defenses; in the latter case, the promisor ***can*** assert the promisee's defenses.

b. **Third-Party Beneficiary vs. Promisee**
If the promisor fails to perform vis-à-vis the third-party beneficiary, whether the third-party beneficiary may sue the promisee depends on whether the third-party beneficiary is a donee beneficiary or a creditor beneficiary. A ***donee beneficiary*** generally may ***not*** sue the promisee because generally there is no right to sue for nondelivery of a gift. (*But see* exception below.) However, a ***creditor beneficiary*** can sue the promisee on the underlying obligation that the promisor's performance was meant to discharge.

Example: Suppose Alex offers to sell his car to Becky if Becky pays Cindy the $1,000 purchase price. Alex informs Cindy of the arrangement and she nods with approval, thus vesting her rights. Alex transfers his car to Becky, but Becky does not pay the $1,000 to Cindy. If Alex intended the $1,000 to be a gift to Cindy, she cannot sue Alex for Becky's failure to pay. But if Alex owed Cindy a debt and the $1,000 was meant to satisfy the debt, Cindy may sue Alex on the unsatisfied obligation that he owed her.

Note: The rights of a creditor beneficiary are cumulative. She need not elect between suing the promisor and suing her own debtor (*i.e.,* the promisee). She may ***sue both***. Of course, she may obtain but ***one satisfaction***.

1) Exception—Detrimental Reliance

If the ***promisee tells*** the donee beneficiary of the contract and should ***foresee reliance*** by the beneficiary, and the beneficiary ***reasonably relies*** to her detriment, the beneficiary can sue the promisee directly under a promissory estoppel/detrimental reliance theory (*see* III.D., *supra*), even though the beneficiary cannot sue the promisee as a third-party beneficiary.

Example: Alex contracts to rent his house to Becky for one year, but the contract provides that Becky is to make the first three payments to Alex's cousin Cindy. Alex then calls Cindy and tells her that she will be able to buy the new furniture that she has wanted because Becky will be making his first three payments to Cindy. Cindy rushes out and buys new furniture. Alex decides not to rent the house to Becky. Cindy can sue Alex under a promissory estoppel/detrimental reliance theory but not as a third-party beneficiary under the contract.

c. Promisee vs. Promisor

1) Donee Beneficiary Situation

If the promisor fails to perform and the contract involves a donee beneficiary, it was once said that the promisee could not sue the promisor at law. The rationale was that because the donee beneficiary had no cause of action against the promisee, there was no damage suffered. Today, however, the ***majority view*** is that the ***promisee has a cause of action***. Because the promisee hardly ever suffers any actual damage, however, she will usually receive only nominal damages. Hence, most courts have resolved this problem by allowing ***specific performance*** in this situation.

2) Creditor Beneficiary Situation

If the promisor fails to perform as to a creditor beneficiary and a promisee has had to pay the beneficiary on the existing debt, the promisee ***may recover*** against the promisor. If the debt has not yet been paid by the promisee to the third party, the promisee can compel the promisor to pay in a ***specific performance*** action.

C. ASSIGNMENT OF RIGHTS AND DELEGATION OF DUTIES

The basic fact situation to be dealt with here is: X enters into a valid contract with Y. This contract does not contemplate performance to or by a third party. Subsequently, one of the parties seeks to transfer her rights and/or duties under the contract to a third party.

1. **Assignment of Rights**
   A transfer of a right under a contract is called an "assignment." The main issues regarding assignments are:

   (i) What rights may be assigned?

   (ii) What is necessary for an effective assignment?

   (iii) Is the assignment revocable or irrevocable?

   (iv) What are the rights and liabilities of the various parties?

   (v) What problems exist if there have been successive assignments of the same rights?

   a. **Terminology**
      X and Y have a contract. Y assigns her rights under the contract to Z. Y is the assignor, Z is the assignee, and X is the obligor.

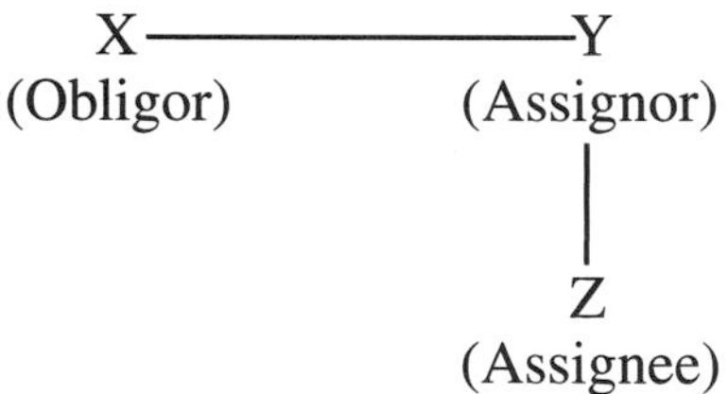

   b. **What Rights May Be Assigned?**

      1) **General Rule**
         Generally, ***all*** contractual rights may be assigned. However, several ***exceptions*** to this rule exist.

      2) **Exceptions**

         a) **Assigned Rights Would Substantially Change Obligor's Duty**
            If an assignment of rights would substantially change the obligor's duty, the assignment will be barred.

            (1) **Personal Service Contracts**
                If the assignment of rights would result in the obligor having to perform personal services for someone other than the original obligee, the attempted assignment will be invalid. This will usually apply, however, only where the nature of personal services is ***unique*** (*e.g.,* services involving lawyers, doctors, authors, etc.) rather than routine.

            (2) **Requirements and Output Contracts**
                At common law, the right to receive goods under a requirements contract

or to sell goods under an output contract generally was not assignable, because the assignment could change the obligation. Article 2 has eliminated this concern by providing that quantity under such contracts must be measured by good faith output or requirements and cannot be unreasonably disproportionate to a stated estimate or, if there is no stated estimate, prior output or requirements. Thus, it would appear that output and requirements contracts are assignable under Article 2 as long as the assignee does not disproportionately alter the contemplated quantity.

(a) **Compare—Duties Under Output and Requirements Contracts**
The buyer's duty to purchase goods under an output contract and the seller's duty to sell goods under a requirements contract can always be delegated, unless they fall within the general restrictions on delegation listed at 2.b., *infra,* because the other party's rights are not affected.

b) **Rights Assigned Would Substantially Alter Obligor's Risk**
When the obligor's risk would be substantially altered by any attempted assignment, the assignment will fail.

Example: Kwan owns a summer home that is insured by Acme Insurance Co. against loss due to fire. Kwan sells the building to Lincoln, who intends to convert it into a restaurant. Kwan may not, without the consent of Acme, assign his rights under the policy to Lincoln.

c) **Assignment of Future Rights**
The assignment of a ***right expected to arise*** under a contract of employment not then existing operates only as a promise to assign the right when it arises, *i.e.,* when the expected future contract is in fact entered into.

Contrast this with ***future rights in existing contracts***, which are generally ***assignable*** even though the right might not yet have vested.

d) **Assignment Prohibited by Law**
A right may not be assigned if the assignment is prohibited by law. Such public policy against assignment may be embodied either in a statute or in case precedent. For example, many states have laws prohibiting, or at least limiting, wage assignments.

e) **Express Contractual Provision Against Assignment**

(1) **Assignment of "the Contract"**
Absent circumstances suggesting otherwise, a clause prohibiting the assignment of "the contract" will be construed as barring ***only the delegation*** of the assignor's ***duties***. [Restatement (Second) of Contracts §322; U.C.C. §2-210(4)]

Example: Sam and Betty enter into a contract wherein Betty will purchase 100 books from Sam, a book collector, for $5,000. The contract provides that "this contract shall not be assigned." Subsequently, Sam assigns to Charlie his right to receive the $5,000 from the contract. Sam has not breached the contract because he merely assigned his right to receive payment; he did not delegate his duty to deliver the books.

(2) **Assignment of Rights Under the Contract**
A clause prohibiting the assignment of ***contractual rights*** generally does not bar assignment, but merely gives the obligor the right to sue for breach if an assignment is made. [Restatement (Second) of Contracts §322] In other words, the assignor has the ***power but not the right*** to assign.

(a) **Factors that Make Assignment Ineffective**
Notwithstanding the general rule, if the clause provides that any attempt to assign will be ***"void,"*** assignment will be ineffective (*i.e.,* the assignor has neither the power nor the right to assign). Also, if the assignee has ***notice*** of the nonassignment clause, assignment will be ineffective.

c. **Effect of Assignment—Real Party in Interest**
The effect of an assignment is to establish privity of contract between the obligor and the assignee while extinguishing privity between the obligor and assignor. The assignee then replaces the assignor as the real party in interest, and she alone is entitled to performance under the contract.

d. **What Is Necessary for an Effective Assignment?**

1) **Requirement of Writing**
A writing is usually ***not required*** to have an effective assignment, so an oral assignment is generally effective. However, there are situations where an assignment ***must*** be in writing:

a) Wage assignments;

b) Assignments of an interest in land;

c) Assignments of choses in action (*see infra* for definition) worth more than $5,000; and

d) Assignments intended as security interests under Article 9 of the U.C.C.

2) **Requirement of Adequate Description**
The right being assigned must be adequately described.

3) **Requirement of Present Words of Assignment**
The assignor must also manifest an intent to transfer his rights under the contract ***completely and immediately*** to the assignee. Whether such intent is present will be determined by looking to the terms of the transfer itself, *i.e.,* the test is objective, not subjective. It is not necessary to use the word "assign"; any generally accepted words of transfer will suffice (*e.g.,* "convey," "sell," "transfer," etc.).

4) **No Requirement of Consideration**
Consideration is ***not required***; a gratuitous assignment is effective.

Note: It is important to remember, however, that even though neither a writing nor consideration is generally required, the lack thereof will affect revocability. (*See* f., *infra.*)

e. **Partial Assignments**
Contract rights may be transferred to one assignee or split up and transferred to two or more. Similarly, the assignor may transfer some rights under the contract and retain others.

f. **Is the Assignment Revocable or Irrevocable?**
When, if ever, do the rights of the assignee "vest" so that the assignment becomes irrevocable? Assignments are divided into two categories: assignments for value and gratuitous assignments.

1) **Assignments for Value Are Irrevocable**
An assignment is for value if it is: (i) done for ***consideration***, or (ii) taken as security for or payment of a ***preexisting debt***. Assignments for value cannot be revoked.

2) **Gratuitous Assignments Are Revocable**
An assignment not for value, *i.e.,* a "gratuitous" assignment, is generally ***revocable***.

a) **Exceptions to Rule of Revocability**
In certain situations, however, a gratuitous assignment will be held irrevocable.

(1) **Performance by Obligor**
If the obligor has already performed, the assignment will be irrevocable.

(2) **Delivery of Token Chose**
If a token chose (tangible claim) involving the rights to be assigned (*e.g.,* stock certificates, savings account passbook, etc.) has been delivered, the assignment will be irrevocable.

(3) **Assignment of Simple Chose in Writing**
If the assignment involves a simple chose, *i.e.,* an intangible claim not embodied by any token (or the great majority of ordinary contract rights), setting it forth in a writing will make the assignment irrevocable.

(4) **Estoppel**
The theory of estoppel may prevent the assignor from revoking a gratuitous assignment if: (i) the assignor should reasonably foresee that the assignee will change her position in reliance on the assignment; and (ii) such detrimental reliance does in fact occur.

b) **Methods of Revocation**
A gratuitous revocable assignment may be terminated in a number of ways:

(1) ***Death*** of the assignor;

(2) ***Bankruptcy*** of the assignor;

(3) ***Notice*** of revocation communicated by the assignor to either the assignee or the obligor;

(4) The ***assignor takes performance*** directly from the obligor; or

(5) ***Subsequent assignment*** of the same right by the assignor to another.

c) **Effect of Revocation**
Once an assignment is revoked, the privity between the assignor and the obligor is restored, and the assignor is once again the real party in interest.

3) **Effect of "Irrevocable" Assignment**
One should note that the term "irrevocable" as applied to an assignment may be misleading. The effect of such irrevocability is to remove from the assignor the right to revoke or make a subsequent assignment of the same right to a third party. However, in many situations, even though the assignor no longer has this ***right***, he still has the ***power*** to do so. He would, of course, be liable for a breach of contract. *Exception:* An exception exists for assignments accompanied by ***delivery of a token chose***. In this case, the assignor loses both the right ***and*** the power to revoke or further assign.

g. **What Are the Rights and Liabilities of the Various Parties?**

1) **Assignee vs. Obligor**
As the assignee is the real party in interest, she may enforce her rights against the obligor ***directly***.

a) **What Defenses Does Obligor Have Against Assignee?**
An assignee's rights against the obligor may be subject to any defenses that the obligor had against the assignor. This rule is similar to the rule discussed *supra* for promisors who are being sued by third-party beneficiaries.
Example: Opie, a mechanic, enters into a contract to purchase a car from Andy for $2,000, payment to be made in 30 days. Opie then performs some repair work for Andy and bills Andy $200. Andy tells Opie to subtract the $200 from the $2,000 that Opie owes Andy. The following week, Andy assigns his right to collect from Opie to his landlord, Lori. If Lori brings suit against Opie to collect the entire $2,000, Opie can raise the $200 set off as a defense.

(1) **Exception—Personal Defenses Arising After Assignment**
If the obligor's defense is unrelated to the contract itself (*i.e.,* it is a

personal defense against the assignor, such as a setoff or counterclaim), the defense is not available against the assignee if it arose ***after*** the obligor had notice of the assignment.

Example: Same facts as in the example in a), above, but Opie performed the work for Andy after Andy asked Opie to pay the $2,000 due under the purchase agreement to Lori. Andy may ***not*** raise the set off as a defense against Lori because it arose too late.

(a) Test

Is the defense ***inherent*** in the contract itself (*e.g.,* failure of consideration) ***or*** is it a defense ***unrelated*** to the contract, the right of which has been assigned? As to defenses inherent in the contract itself, these defenses are always available against the assignee because they came into existence when the contract was made. As to setoffs, counterclaims, and the like, such defenses are good against the assignee only if they came into existence before the obligor had notice or knowledge of the assignment.

(2) Estoppel

The estoppel doctrine may operate to prevent the obligor from asserting a defense that might otherwise exist against the assignor.

Example: Jim and Harold entered into a contract. Subsequently, Harold sought to assign his rights under the contract to Zorba. Zorba inquired of Jim whether he had any defenses against Harold. Jim replied in the negative. Thereupon, Zorba paid Harold valuable consideration for the assigned rights. Jim may be estopped to raise any defenses existing at the time of his statement to Zorba.

b) Modification of the Contract

Suppose that after the obligor has received ***notice*** of the assignment, the obligor and assignor attempt to ***modify*** the contract. Will the modification affect the assignee's rights?

(1) No Effect on Rights of Assignee

Generally, such a modification of the contract will ***not*** affect the rights of the assignee. This is so even when the modification is undertaken in good faith.

(2) U.C.C. Position

The U.C.C. provides that such a modification of an assigned right to payment that ***has not yet been fully earned by performance*** is effective against the assignee if made in ***good faith***. However, the modification will cause a breach of an assignment contract that prohibits such modifications. [U.C.C. §9-405]

c) **Defenses of Assignor Not Available**
The obligor will not be able to raise by way of defense any defenses that the assignor might have against the assignee.

2) **Assignee vs. Assignor**

a) **Implied Warranties**
The assignor is deemed to give several implied warranties to the assignee, the breach of which will give rise to a cause of action.

(1) **Warranty Not to Defeat Assigned Right**
If the assignment is irrevocable, the assignee has the right to enforce the obligation and may proceed against the assignor if he wrongfully exercises his ***power*** to revoke.

(2) **Warranty that Right Is Not Subject to Defenses**
The assignee may also have a cause of action against the assignor where the obligor successfully asserts the defense she had against the assignor in an action brought by the assignee to enforce the obligation, thereby defeating the assigned right. This is so only if the assignee was without notice of the defense at the time of the assignment.

b) **Obligor Incapable of Performance**
The assignor will ***not*** be liable to the assignee if the obligor is incapable of performing, *e.g.*, is insolvent.

c) **Rights of Sub-Assignees**
Sub-assignees do not have any rights against the original assignor. The courts reason that there is no privity of contract. However, the assignee who "sub-assigns" becomes the assignor with respect to that assignment and can be held liable thereon.

3) **Do Third Parties Have Any Equities Relating to Assignment?**
If third parties have any equities in the subject matter of the assignment, the assignee will take subject to them if she has notice; she will not be subject to such equities if she is a bona fide purchaser without notice of the assigned interest.

h. **What Problems Exist If There Have Been Successive Assignments of the Same Rights?**
The problem: X assigns to Y a right to the payment of $500 owed him by Smith. Subsequently, X assigns this same right to Z. Who prevails—Y or Z?

1) **Revocable Assignments**
If the first assignment made is ***revocable***, a subsequent assignment will serve to ***revoke*** it (*i.e.*, the subsequent assignee prevails).

2) **Irrevocable Assignments**

a) **First Assignee Has Priority**
The general rule is that if the assignor makes two assignments of the same right and the first assignment is ***irrevocable***, the ***first*** assignee has priority.

b) **Exceptions**

In certain situations, a second assignee who ***pays value*** and takes ***without notice*** of the earlier irrevocable assignment will prevail.

(1) **Judgment Against Obligor**

If the subsequent assignee gets the ***first judgment*** against the obligor, she will prevail.

(2) **Payment of Claim**

If the later assignee gets ***first payment*** from the obligor on the assigned claim, her rights will be superior.

(3) **Delivery of Token Chose**

If the subsequent assignee gets the ***first delivery of a token chose*** from the assignor, she will prevail.

(4) **Novation**

The second assignee will prevail if she obtains a novation that supersedes the obligation running to the assignor in favor of the new one running to her. This assumes that the obligor had ***no knowledge*** of the prior assignment at the time of the novation.

(5) **Estoppel**

If the subsequent assignee is able to set up an estoppel against the first assignee, she will have priority, *e.g.,* the first assignee permits the assignor to retain a document that would indicate to a reasonable person that the assignor was sole owner of the right. (Estoppel could, of course, operate the other way as well. Thus, if the subsequent assignee has actual knowledge of the earlier assignment, she will be estopped to assert her claim as against the earlier assignee even though she would, under any of the other rules above, normally succeed.)

3) **U.C.C. Rules**

Basically, the U.C.C. has approached the successive assignments problem by imposing ***filing requirements***. [U.C.C. §9-310] If the filing provision is applicable to the transaction, generally the assignee who is the first to file will prevail. [U.C.C. §9-322]

2. **Delegation of Duties**

A transfer of contractual duties is called a "delegation." The main issues regarding delegations are:

(i) What duties may be delegated?

(ii) How does one make a valid delegation?

(iii) What are the rights and liabilities of the various parties where there has been a valid delegation?

a. **Terminology**
X and Y have a contract. Y delegates duties thereunder to Z. Y is the ***obligor*** because Y is the one with the duty to perform the obligation. Y also is the ***delegator*** (sometimes called the delegant) because Y delegated the duty. Z is the ***delegate*** (sometimes called the delegatee) because Z is the one to whom the duty was delegated. X is called the ***obligee***, because X is the one for whom Y or Z is obligated to perform.

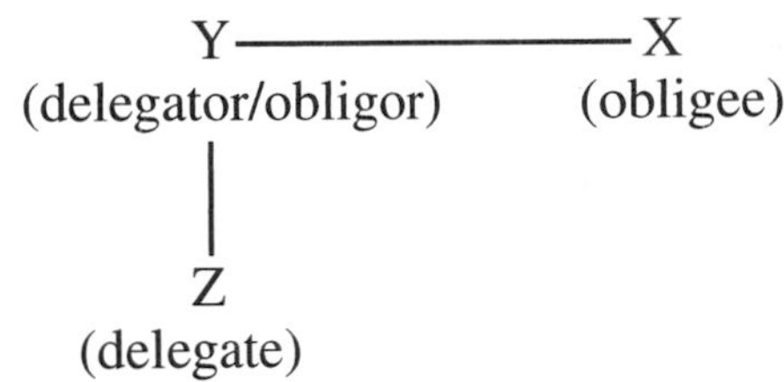

b. **What Duties May Be Delegated?**

1) **General Rule**
As a general rule, ***all contractual duties*** may be delegated to a third person.

2) **Exceptions**
There are several exceptions to the general rule.

a) **Duties Involving Personal Judgment and Skill**
If the duties involve personal judgment and skill, they may not be delegated.
Example: A talent agency cannot delegate its duty to select performers for a certain show to some other agency. It is immaterial that the other agency may have a better reputation and may have more performers under contract than the delegator. A court will not make such inquiries at all.

b) **"Special Trust" in Delegator**
Where a special trust has been reposed in the delegator, he may not delegate his duties (*e.g.,* relationship of attorney and client, physician and patient, etc.).

c) **Change of Obligee's Expectancy**
If performance by the delegate will materially change the obligee's expectancy under the contract, the duty may not be delegated.

d) **Contractual Restriction on Delegation**
If a contract restricts either party's right to delegate duties, such a provision will usually be given ***strict effect***.

c. **What Is Necessary for Effective Delegation?**
In general, no special formalities are required to have a valid delegation. The delegation may be either ***written or oral***. However, the delegator must manifest a ***present intention*** to make the delegation. There is no need that the word "delegate" be used; any generally accepted words of transfer may be used.

d. What Are Rights and Liabilities of Parties?

1) Obligee

The obligee must accept performance from the delegate of all duties that may be delegated. She need not accept performance from the delegate of those duties that may not be delegated.

2) Delegator

The delegator will ***remain liable*** on his contract. This is so even if the delegate expressly assumes the duties. There may be a different result if the obligee expressly consents to this transfer of duties. This could be construed as an offer of novation.

3) Delegate

The liability of a delegate turns largely on the question of whether there is a mere "delegation" or that plus an "assumption of duty."

a) Delegation

Delegation is the creation of a ***power*** in another to perform the delegator's contract duty. The nondelegating party to the contract (the obligee) cannot compel the delegate to perform, as the latter has not promised to perform.

b) Assumption

An assumption occurs when the delegate promises that she will perform the duty delegated and the ***promise*** is ***supported by consideration*** or its equivalent. This creates a third-party beneficiary situation in which the nondelegating party to the contract can compel performance or bring suit for nonperformance.

Example: Tom promises Becky that he will paint her fence for $100. Tom then asks Huck if he would paint the fence for $50 if Tom provides Huck with all of the paint and supplies needed. Huck agrees. Becky is a third-party beneficiary of the contract between Tom and Huck and may enforce Huck's promise to paint.

c) Result When Duties Delegated with Assignment of Rights

What happens if a delegation of duties is made in connection with an assignment of rights under the same contract out of which the duties arise, but the delegate has nonetheless not expressly assumed the duties? The majority of courts, the Restatement, and the U.C.C. hold that unless a contrary intention appears, words assigning "the contract" or "all my rights under the contract" are to be construed as including an ***assumption*** of the duties; *i.e.,* they imply a promise by the assignee to assume the duties of performance.

D. NOVATION DISTINGUISHED FROM OTHER THIRD-PARTY SITUATIONS

Note the difference between novation and the other third-party situations discussed above. Novation ***substitutes a new party*** for an original party to the contract. It requires the ***assent of all parties*** and ***completely releases*** the original party. The consent of the remaining party may be express or by implication of the acceptance of performance by the new party with knowledge that a novation is intended.

E. POWER OF PERSON OTHER THAN OWNER TO TRANSFER GOOD TITLE TO A PURCHASER

1. Entrusting

Entrusting goods to a merchant ***who deals in goods of that kind*** gives him the power (but not the right) to transfer all rights of the entruster to a ***buyer in the ordinary course of business***. [U.C.C. §2-403] Entrusting includes both delivering goods to the merchant and leaving purchased goods with the merchant for later pick-up or delivery. Buying in the ordinary course means buying in good faith from a person who deals in goods of the kind without knowledge that the sale is in violation of the ownership rights of third parties.

Examples: 1) Amy leaves her watch with Jeweler for repairs. Jeweler sells the watch to Zoe, who does not know that Jeweler has no right to sell. Zoe gets good title as against Amy. Amy's only remedy is to sue Jeweler for damages.

2) Amy leaves her watch with Jeweler for repairs. Jeweler borrows money from the bank, giving specific items of inventory, including Amy's watch, as pledged collateral. Amy can recover the watch from the bank. The bank is not a ***buyer***.

2. Voidable Title Concept

The U.C.C. continues the pre-Code concept of voidable title. [*See* U.C.C. §2-403] That is, if a sale is induced by fraud, the seller can rescind the sale and recover the goods from the fraudulent buyer. However, the defrauded seller may not recover the goods from a ***good faith purchaser for value*** who bought from the fraudulent buyer. The U.C.C. specifies four particular situations in which the bona fide purchaser for value cuts off the rights of the true owner; in several of these instances the result under pre-Code law is changed.

Under the U.C.C., the ***good faith purchaser for value cuts off the defrauded seller's rights***, even though:

(i) The seller was deceived as to the identity of the buyer;

(ii) The delivery was in exchange for a check later dishonored;

(iii) The sale was a "cash sale"; or

(iv) The fraudulent conduct of the buyer is punishable as larceny.

The rights of a defrauded seller are cut off both by a buyer and by a person who takes a ***security interest*** in the goods.

3. Thief Generally Cannot Pass Title

If a thief steals goods from the true owner and then sells them to a buyer, the thief is ***unable*** to pass title to the buyer (because his title is ***void***). *Rationale:* A seller can transfer only the title he has or has power to transfer. Therefore, even a good faith purchaser for value generally cannot cut off the rights of the true owner if the seller's title was void. [U.C.C. §2-403(1)]

Example: Thief stole a painting from Owner and sold it to Buyer. Later, Owner discovered that Buyer had her painting. Owner may recover the painting from Buyer, even if Buyer purchased the painting in good faith and for value.

a. **Exceptions**

A thief may pass title in limited circumstances, such as where the buyer has made ***accessions*** (*i.e.,* valuable improvements) to the goods or the true owner is estopped from asserting title (*e.g.,* if the true owner expressly or impliedly represented that the thief had title).

REVIEW QUESTIONS

INTRODUCTORY NOTE

The short-answer questions that follow are intended to serve as both a substantive review and a diagnostic test. Respond to the questions quickly and compare your answers to those found at the end of this section. This will allow you to identify areas in which you may need further review.

FILL IN ANSWER

MUTUAL ASSENT

1. Acceptance of an offer for a unilateral contract is complete when the offeree promises to perform the required act. True or false? ________

2. A says to B, "I have decided to sell my car for $300." B replies that he will buy it at that price. Has a contract been formed? ________

3. The parties' agreement provides that "each is to make a fair profit" from the bargain. Will the court uphold the bargain by determining what would be a "fair" profit to each? ________

4. A offers to purchase a rare gem from B. B accepts, but no price is mentioned. Is there a contract? ________

5. A offers to purchase from B, at an agreed price, all the steel that B will produce in his new manufacturing plant. B accepts. Is there a contract? ________

6. An attempt to revoke an executory offer made to the public (*e.g.,* an offer of reward) is effective only if notice of the revocation comes to the actual attention of all those who have learned of the offer. True or false? ________

7. At common law, a revocation of an offer is effective upon dispatch through a commercially reasonable mode of communication. True or false? ________

8. O promises A that he will hold open his offer for 30 days. One week later, and before A has acted on the offer, O revokes his offer.

   a. Is the revocation effective? ________

   b. Would the result be the same if O and A were merchants dealing in goods? ________

9. The general rule is that an offeror can revoke his offer for a unilateral contract at any time until the offeree has completed the requested act of performance. True or false? ________

10. In most jurisdictions, a rejection is effective upon receipt by the offeror. True or false? ________

11. Is an offer terminated by "operation of law" if the subject matter dies or is destroyed? ________

12. The general rule is that an offer may be accepted only by the person to whom it is made. True or false? ________

13. A offers to employ B as an advertising manager for $1,000 per month. B accepts "provided my salary is payable weekly." Is there an enforceable contract? ________

14. Merchant A offers to sell 200 radios to Merchant B for $1,000. B accepts "provided you make delivery to my plant." Is there a contract? ________

15. Where the offer is for a bilateral contract, notice of acceptance is usually required to form a contract. True or false? ________

16. At common law, an acceptance of an offer for a bilateral contract is effective only when received. True or false? ________

    a. Does the same rule generally apply in contracts for the sale of goods? ________

17. Using an expressly authorized mode of communication, Fox mails an acceptance to the offeror, Brown. On the same day, Fox changes her mind and faxes a rejection of the offer to Brown. Has a contract been formed between the parties if Brown receives the fax of rejection first? ________

18. The general rule is that silence is not an acceptance of an offer. True or false? ________

CONSIDERATION

19. Fox says to Brown, "I'll give you my golf clubs if you will come around to my apartment this evening to claim them." Brown calls on Fox that evening and demands the clubs. Fox refuses, declaring that she has "changed her mind." Brown's best claim to legal title rests on a theory of unilateral contract. True or false? ________

20. D promises to pay P $20 per week for so long as P shall live "in consideration of P's 40 years of continuous service." Can P enforce this executory promise if D fails to pay? ________

21. P nursed and cared for X, who was having financial difficulties. Later, X's son, D, learns of this service and promises to repay P "for all of the expenses that you have incurred in being of such aid to my father." At common law, this executory promise is unenforceable should D change his mind. True or false? ________

22. Debtor's promissory note to Creditor for $1,000 was discharged in bankruptcy. Later, Debtor wrote to Creditor and promised to pay $50 per month until the

full amount of the note was paid. However, Debtor never made any payments and Creditor now sues. Assuming that the Bankruptcy Code presents no bars to enforcement of Debtor's promise, Creditor is entitled to recover: ________

(A) Nothing.
(B) $50 per month until the debt is paid.
(C) The $1,000 debt.

23. John promises to give Mary $10,000 if she names her expected baby "John." When the baby is born, she gives him the name "John." The promise made to the mother is enforceable at common law. True or false? ________

24. In June 2010, Brown borrows $5,000 from the City National Bank. Under the terms of the loan, the sum was to bear interest at the rate of 8% per year. The note was due and payable on July 1, 2011. On June 15, 2011, Brown requests that his obligation to repay be extended for one year. The bank agrees. Two weeks later, the bank changes its mind and demands immediate payment. When Brown refuses, an action to collect the sum of the loan is commenced. Brown will prevail if he asserts the agreement to extend as a defense. True or false? ________

25. O hires C to install sprinklers for $500. Later, during the course of a normal installation, C demands and O agrees to pay $600 for the job. C then completes the installation. O makes a tender of $500 and refuses to pay "one cent more." Can C enforce the promise made to pay the additional $100? ________

26. A claims that he has been defamed by B. B denies it, but offers to pay A $100 to drop his claim. A accepts. Later, B refuses to pay on the ground that he was legally privileged to say the things he said about A, and therefore A had no valid claim against him, so there was no consideration for his promise to pay $100. Is B's promise enforceable by A? ________

27. A promises to sell his car to B "unless I change my mind." Is his promise enforceable? ________

28. A promises to buy goods only from B, but reserves an option to cancel by giving 30 days' notice to B. Is A's promise to buy only from B sufficient consideration to render enforceable B's counterpromise to sell to A? ________

29. S promises to sell, and B, age 17, promises to buy, specific goods. Can B enforce the contract? ________

30. H gratuitously promises his wife, W, that he will devise his farm to W's favorite nephew, N. W tells N about H's promise, and relying thereon, N expends money and time improving H's farm and working the crops. Will N's reliance on H's promise to W be sufficient to invoke promissory estoppel? ________

DEFENSES

31. Walker sold Sherwood a cow for only $80 because both parties believed the cow to be sterile. When Walker discovered that the cow was pregnant and worth between $750 and $1,000, he refused to deliver. Sherwood will win in a suit for recovery. True or false? ________

32. O offers to sell a violin to B for $200, not knowing that it is actually worth $1,000. B accepts, believing it to be worth $1,000. Can B enforce the contract? ________

33. O advertises for bids on a construction job. She receives three bids: $42,000, $50,000, and $57,000, and accepts the lowest one. The low bidder promptly notifies O that he made a mistake in computation and cannot perform at the price bid. O then employs the next highest bidder and sues the low bidder for the $8,000.

    a. Will O recover? ________

    b. Would the result be the same if the low bid were $12,000 instead of $42,000? ________

34. A telegraphs an offer to B to sell butter at 62¢ per pound, but the telegraph company errs in the transmittal and the wire reads 60¢ per pound. B accepts. Is there a contract? ________

35. A accepts O's offer to sell her house on Peck Road. A does not know that O owns two houses on Peck Road. Has a contract been formed? If so, which house is the subject of the contract? ________

36. A statute requires all plumbers to be licensed. P, an unlicensed plumber, contracts with and performs services for O. O refuses to pay. Can P obtain a judgment for the contract price? In quasi-contract for the value of the work done? ________

37. Landlord rents an apartment to Son, age 17 (a minor), for $200 per month.

    a. Can Son enforce the lease against Landlord, even though Landlord could not enforce it against Son? ________

    b. If Son does not pay the agreed rent, can Landlord recover from Son in quasi-contract the reasonable value of the use of the apartment during the time Son lives there (which may be less than the agreed rent)? ________

38. Can "economic duress" be a valid defense to a contract action? ________

39. Which, if any, of the following types of contracts fall within the Statute of Frauds provision applicable to contracts incapable of being performed within one year? ________

(A) Lifetime employment contracts.
(B) Requirements or output contracts.
(C) A lease of personal property terminable at will.
(D) A five-year lease of personal property, terminable by either party giving 90 days' notice to the other.

40. In determining the applicability of the Statute of Frauds to a contract for the sale of goods, it is the ***price,*** not the ***value,*** of the goods that is determinative. True or false? ________

41. Under the majority common law view, failure to comply with the Statute of Frauds renders void a contract that the Statute requires to be memorialized by a writing signed by the person to be charged. True or false? ________

PERFORMANCE OF CONTRACT

42. A and B sign a memorandum as to a contemplated business deal. Is A later permitted to show certain additional oral terms that were not covered in the memorandum? ________

43. A "collateral agreement" may be shown by extrinsic evidence. True or false? ________

44. The occurrence of a condition subsequent extinguishes a previously existing duty of performance. True or false? ________

45. Will constructive (*i.e.,* implied in law) conditions be implied in a contract whenever necessary to the performance of the contract? ________

46. To enforce a contract, a plaintiff must plead and prove that all conditions have been either performed or legally excused. True or false? ________

47. A furnished advertising for B's hotel resort, for which B promised to pay when he "sold the hotel." B made a gift of the hotel to his children. Is B under any duty to A? ________

48. On June 1, Vendor and Vendee entered into a contract for the sale of Blackacre, with Vendor to convey title on September 1. On July 1, Vendor sold Blackacre to T, with an option to repurchase at any time. Vendee learned of the sale to T on July 15. Is Vendee's duty of counterperformance excused? ________

49. The legal effect of prospective inability or unwillingness to perform is to excuse the duty of counterperformance. True or false? ________

50. A has a contract with B to employ B commencing June 1. In April, A tells B, "Unless business improves, I'm afraid I'll be unable to take you on the payroll in June."

    a. Has there been an anticipatory breach? ________

b. Does B have an immediate cause of action for damages against A? ________

51. Notwithstanding the fact that rights and liabilities under an executory contract may be excused by virtue of some unforeseen contingency that renders further performance impossible, if the promisor has conferred benefits on the promisee prior to the supervening contingency, she may have a recovery for their market value in quasi-contract. True or false? ________

52. The death or permanent incapacitation of a party who was to receive performance under a personal services contract will operate to excuse any further liability on the part of either the promisor or the legal representative of the promisee. True or false? ________

53. As a practical matter, the critical difference between the operative effect of a "material" as opposed to a "minor" breach of contract is that in the event of a material breach, the aggrieved party is relieved of any further obligation to render his own promised performance. True or false? ________

54. Faced with a tender of nonconforming goods, a buyer may mitigate his damages by making an immediate cover contract. True or false? ________

THIRD-PARTY RIGHTS

55. A contracts with B to build a road connecting C's farm with the highway.

    a. Can C enforce the contract? ________

    b. Can D, C's adjoining neighbor, enforce the contract? ________

56. Can a donee-beneficiary sue the promisee of a third-party beneficiary contract? ________

57. May a student who is awarded a scholarship assign his right to someone else? ________

58. A owns property on which she carries a policy insuring against loss by fire. On sale of her property to B, A assigns the policy to B.

    a. Is the assignment effective? ________

    b. Assume a fire occurred prior to the sale and A assigns to B her rights to the proceeds. Is this assignment effective? ________

59. B has a contract to purchase Blackacre from A for $50,000, payable $25,000 in cash and the balance secured by a mortgage on Blackacre. Before closing, B assigns the contract to C. Can C enforce the contract? ________

60. For consideration, A assigns to B one-half of any proceeds A will obtain if A sells Blackacre. Is this an effective assignment? ________

61. A contract contains the following provision: "Each party agrees not to assign this contract or any interest herein." Notwithstanding, party A assigns her interest to another. Is the assignment effective? ________

62. Must an assignment be in writing and signed by the assignor to be effective? ________

63. May a ***gratuitous*** assignment be revoked? ________

64. As a gift, A orally assigns to B a $15,000 debt owed by XYZ due within one month. B thereupon contracts to purchase a new car. A is aware of this and also knows that B has no other sources of funds with which to make the payment due for the car. Nonetheless, the day before the debt comes due, A tells B that he has changed his mind and needs the money himself. B is entitled to the payment from XYZ. True or false? ________

65. If a gratuitous assignment of a simple chose is in writing but the assignor makes a subsequent assignment, does the original assignee have an action against the assignor? ________

66. D owes A $1,000. A orally assigns her right to the $1,000 as a gift to B. Later, in writing, A assigns the same right to C. As between B and C, C will prevail. True or false? ________

67. D owes A $1,000. For consideration, A assigns her right to B, who notifies D of the assignment. Later, and also for consideration, A assigns the same right to C. As between B and C, C prevails. True or false? ________

68. A "sells, transfers, and assigns" to B "all of my rights and obligations" in connection with a specified business. B promises nothing but takes over the business operations. Can a creditor of A sue B for payment of A's obligation? ________

ANSWERS TO REVIEW QUESTIONS

Ques. No.	Answer	Explanation
1.	***FALSE***	An offer that looks toward the formation of a true unilateral contract can be accepted only by the offeree's doing the requested performance. A promise to perform is not a valid acceptance.
2.	***PROBABLY NOT***	It is most doubtful that any court would interpret A's statement as the communication of an "offer." It lacks evidence of a present manifestation of a present willingness to enter a contract. If A's words have any significance beyond a mere general declaratory statement, they would probably be held as merely evidencing a willingness to receive offers.
3.	***VERY DOUBTFUL***	Under the common law tests, such an exchange would be simply too indefinite for a court to regard it as the basis for a present contract. Under the U.C.C., in contracts for the sale of goods, there has been some relaxation of this policy (*e.g.,* the parties can leave the determination of the price to be fixed by a third party, some certain event, or a trade journal quotation; or they may leave it to future agreement), but none of the exceptions by which the price term can be made sufficiently certain are incorporated by the vague terms of this agreement.
4.	***NO***	Again, a manifestation of agreement on the essential term (price) is missing, and the agreement by its terms does not set up the machinery by which a court may arrive at a price. Given the unique subject matter, this would not fall under the rule that the court can remedy the omission by supplying a "reasonable price."
5.	***YES***	Here, the essential quantity term is measured by the seller's output. Under the U.C.C., this is specifically authorized as a sufficient basis to create a present contract.
6.	***FALSE***	The revocation is effective if it is given through means comparable to the means used to make the offer. If this requirement is satisfied, then revocation is effective through the constructive notice, even as to individuals who do not actually learn of it.
7.	***FALSE***	Under the common law view, such a revocation is effective upon receipt by the offeree.
8.a.	***YES***	At common law, an offer not supported by consideration or detrimental reliance can be revoked at the will of the offeror, even if he has promised to hold the offer open.

b. ***NOT NECESSARILY*** It depends on whether the promise was in a signed writing. If it was, then under the U.C.C., this would be a "merchant's firm offer," and, as such, it is effective for the stated period of 30 days without the necessity of showing any independent consideration.

9. ***FALSE*** Today nearly all courts hold that once the offeree has begun actual performance of the requested act (as opposed to steps taken in preparation for performance), the offeror's power of revocation is stayed for a reasonable period, thus giving the offeree further time to complete the act of acceptance, at which point the contract is formed.

10. ***TRUE*** In contrast to the rules regarding acceptance, a rejection is effective upon receipt by the offeror.

11. ***YES*** Death or destruction of the subject matter of an offer that is still executory terminates the offer by operation of law.

12. ***TRUE*** To this extent an offer is deemed "personal" to the intended offeree.

13. ***PROBABLY NOT*** Because of the subject matter (personal services), the more liberal U.C.C. provisions would not apply, and B's additional terms will be regarded at common law as a rejection and counteroffer.

14. ***NO*** The contract is for the sale of goods; hence, the U.C.C. rules apply. Under the U.C.C., an acceptance containing additional terms is sufficient to form a contract unless the acceptance is expressly made conditional on assent to the additional terms. Here, there is no contract because the acceptance was made conditional on acceptance of a new term (". . . provided that you make delivery to my plant").

15. ***TRUE*** Because a bilateral agreement is formed by the exchange of promises, notice of the return promise generally must be communicated to the offeror. Any objective manifestation of assent is sufficient for this purpose.

16. ***FALSE*** Ordinarily, acceptance is effective on dispatch. Only if acceptance is attempted by an "unauthorized" mode of communication is acceptance delayed until its receipt by the offeror.

a. ***YES*** But under the U.C.C., the rules have been even further liberalized in favor of the offeree—the offeree obtains the benefit of the "mailbox rule" (acceptance effective upon dispatch) if any mode of communication commercially reasonable under the circumstances is used.

17. ***YES*** This surprising result flows from a strict application of the common law rule—a contract was formed upon dispatch of the acceptance. However, if the offeror relies to his detriment on the rejection, the offeree will be estopped from enforcing the contract.

18. ***TRUE*** The offeror cannot impose upon the offeree the peril of having silence treated as a binding acceptance.

19. ***TRUE*** Brown's case might not, however, survive Fox's defense that she made no offer looking toward performance of a bargained-for act (coming to the apartment), but merely stated a condition, the satisfaction of which would position Brown to receive a gratuity. A gift is revocable absent donative intention plus delivery, here refused.

20. ***NO*** The promise is supported only by past consideration which, at common law, cannot bind a promisor who has changed his mind concerning the terms of an executory obligation.

21. ***TRUE*** It is supported only by "moral consideration" and, like "past consideration," is incapable of binding a now unwilling promisor to an executory obligation.

22. ***(B)*** Here is an example of an exception to the "moral consideration" rule that will be enforced because the new promise to pay the debt, which was discharged in bankruptcy, was in writing (it will be enforced per the terms of the ***new promise***).

23. ***TRUE*** Here is an example of bargained-for valuable consideration. But for this proposal, the mother was free to name the child anything she wished. In response to the offer, she named the infant "John." This is a legal detriment. In such a case, the law will not inquire into the economic equivalency of the promise and the act.

24. ***TRUE*** The bank will raise the objection of failure of consideration because Brown was already under an existing duty to repay the principal. However, the facts strongly imply an obligation on Brown's part to pay the 8% interest for the second year, and this is valuable consideration supporting the bank's extension promise.

25. ***NO*** O's promise of the additional $100 was not supported by an exchange of valuable consideration. All C promised or did was to complete the installation, but this was already his existing duty under the original executory contract. This case cannot, on the facts, qualify for the exception where performance is more onerous than foreseeably anticipated.

26. ***YES*** A bargained-for promise to forbear the prosecution of any claim that is not patently groundless, and that the party in good faith believes to have merit, is another example of "valuable consideration."

27. ***NO*** Given the express reservation, A has given only an "illusion" of a promise.

28. ***YES*** Here, the key is that unless and until A gives the notice, his promise binds him to regard B as an exclusive source of supply for the goods in question.

29. *YES* A contract entered into between a minor and an adult is binding on the adult. Only the minor can void the contract.

30. *YES* Under the trend of modern decisions prompted by section 90 of the Second Restatement, a gratuitous promise made for the benefit of an intended third-party beneficiary, which induces reasonable reliance on the part of the intended beneficiary, may be enforced as against the promisor on a theory of promissory estoppel.

31. *FALSE* There can be no recovery on the contract, because of a mutual mistake concerning a basic assumption of the contract. Here, both parties are held to have contracted for the purchase and sale of a barren cow. Afterwards, this mutual assumption is discovered to be at variance with the fact of the cow's pregnancy. Such a mutual mistake goes to the "essence of the transaction" in that it changes the value of the subject matter approximately tenfold over the contract price. Such circumstances excuse the seller's executory obligation.

32. *YES* Here, there is a mistake as to the value as it is fixed in the mind of the seller. Such a mistake of judgment (as opposed to a unilateral mistake in computation) generally does not prevent the formation of a contract between parties dealing at arm's length, even though the other party is of the well-founded opinion that the offeror is mistaken in his judgment.

33.a. *PROBABLY YES* O can probably recover the $8,000. There is a ***unilateral mistake*** that is unknown to O, who has accepted reasonably and in good faith.

b. *PROBABLY NOT* If the disparity had been $38,000 ($12,000 vs. $50,000 as the next lowest bid), there would still be a unilateral mistake, but here the facts strongly suggest that O could not form a reasonable, good faith belief that the bidder was not mistaken when he submitted such an obviously defective bid. The law protects and rewards only commercially reasonable expectations entertained in good faith.

34. *PROBABLY YES* While there is a division of authority here, most courts hold that there is a contract on the terms actually transmitted to the offeree unless the mistake would be so obvious that no reasonable person in the position of the offeree could have assumed that it represented a correct manifestation of an offeror's intention. Here, the error is 2¢ per pound on a 62¢ per pound item. A minority of courts would hold that no contract was formed on a theory that the error in transmission prevented the minds of the parties from meeting on an offer.

35. *YES* There is a binding contract, and it is for the sale of the house that A knew O to own on Peck Road. O is guilty of using a patently ambiguous term as to her own understanding. A is not chargeable with such negligence; hence, credence is given to A's construction of the term.

36. *NO/NO* No recovery can be had either on the contract or in quasi-contract, because P (the party who violated the statute) is seeking to enforce the contract, and

he is ***not*** an "innocent" party. The courts take the position that activity by an individual who proceeds without a mandatory license to traffic in the affairs of such a calling or profession is "illegal." Moreover, P will not be able to recover in equity under the theory of quasi-contract because he has unclean hands.

37.a. ***YES*** Because the agreement is with a minor, it is voidable at the option of the minor only; it is not voidable by the adult.

b. ***YES*** The landlord may always recover in quasi-contract for necessities had and received. Recovery is measured by the market value and not the contract price.

38. ***MAYBE*** Contracts induced by duress are voidable, but merely taking advantage of another's economic need generally is not duress.

39. ***(D)*** Under the majority view, termination is not the equivalent of performance and so does not take a contract out of the Statute of Frauds. The minority view is contra. The remaining obligations are capable of being discharged within one year. The lifetime employee may die, requirements or output may cease, and the lease may be terminated within a period of one year following the making of these oral promises. Because performance is technically possible (however unlikely), the Statute of Frauds has been held not to apply.

40. ***TRUE*** The price set by the terms of the contract is determinative.

41. ***FALSE*** Under the majority view, such a contract would be voidable at the option of the party to be charged. The party would have to raise the Statute as an affirmative defense.

42. ***DEPENDS*** A can show additional oral terms unless the writing was a complete integration of all the agreements between the parties. Whether a writing represents such an integration is a question of intention. If A and B came to regard the writing as representing the full and final expression of the terms of their agreement, then for purposes of application of the parol evidence rule, the writing is regarded as "integrated."

43. ***TRUE*** Parol evidence may always be offered for the purpose of establishing the terms of a "collateral agreement." Here, the theory is that the parties reached two agreements, only one of which was reduced to an integrated writing. The proffer of parol evidence goes to the establishment of the terms of the second agreement, which the parties intended to "rest in parol."

44. ***TRUE*** The operation of the classic "condition subsequent" is to extinguish a present contract obligation.

45. ***NO*** True "constructive conditions" arise on the theory that they are inserted by operation of law in the interest of preserving fair and equitable dealings between the parties.

46.	***FALSE***	The plaintiff has the burden of pleading and proving that all ***conditions precedent*** to or ***concurrent*** with the ripening of the defendant's duty of performance have either been performed or excused. Once this is established, the defendant, if he would rely on the escape possibility afforded by a ***condition subsequent,*** must allege and prove the happening of the event or contingency that satisfied the condition subsequent as a matter of affirmative defense.
47.	***YES***	Here, it is likely that the condition will be held to have been ***excused*** by B's conduct. The key issue would be whether A can fairly be said to have assumed the risk that B would dispose of the hotel by means that technically were not a "sale." As a business creditor, it is highly unlikely that A would be held to have assumed this risk.
48.	***NO***	The factor that prevents this from being a case of excuse by prospective inability to perform is the fact that in the July 1 conveyance to T, Vendor retained an option to repurchase "at any time." Clearly, such conduct on the part of Vendor, who is under an executory contract duty to convey to Vendee on September 1, would give Vendee reasonable grounds for insecurity and a right to demand of Vendor adequate assurance of performance. Failure of Vendor to respond with such assurances within a commercially reasonable period will ripen into a breach by Vendor that would then excuse the duty of counterperformance.
49.	***TRUE***	It establishes a prospective failure of condition, as much as actual prevention.
50.a.	***NO***	Here, A's statement falls far short of an unconditional present repudiation of his executory contract obligation and thus fails to provide grounds for a present breach by anticipatory repudiation.
b.	***NO***	For the simple reason that there exists ***no present*** breach of the contract on the part of A, B does not have an immediate cause of action against A.
51.	***TRUE***	Nearly all American courts have allowed recovery of the restitution interest in an action premised on a theory of quasi-contract.
52.	***TRUE***	Under such circumstances, performance of the personal services that formed the subject matter of the agreement has been rendered legally impossible.
53.	***TRUE***	If the default on the part of the other party amounts to only a minor breach, the aggrieved party is not relieved of a duty to render performance of his own promise, but, having done so, such a party may recover damages occasioned by the minor breach.
54.	***TRUE***	The U.C.C. provides that the buyer may buy substitute goods and recover the difference between the contract price and the price of the substitute goods.
55.a.	***YES***	C can enforce the obligation of A on the theory that C was an ***intended third-party beneficiary*** of a direct obligation of performance created in the A-B contract.

b. ***NO*** D is only an incidental beneficiary. D might be economically benefited by A's performance, but this is insufficient to vest in D enforceable rights.

56. ***NO*** Such a beneficiary would have an enforceable right to sue for the promisor's performance, but generally has no remedies against the donor-promisee, who is under no existing obligation. The donor-promisee has simply attempted a gift.

57. ***NO*** Such a contract right to scholarship funds would be considered nonassignable in that it would vary the promisor's obligation or undermine the confidence that induced selection of the original promisee as the beneficiary of the scholarship assistance.

58.a. ***NO*** Such an attempted assignment of the insurance coverage would vary the risk of the promisor (insurer) in that the risk of a casualty loss would vary with the habits and practices of the occupant of the insured premises.

b. ***YES*** If the fire has already occurred, the proceeds of A's claim are assignable. Here, there would be no enlargement of the insurer's obligation or risk.

59. ***NO*** Even though the debt in both instances will be secured by a mortgage on the same land, A cannot be forced by this unilateral assignment to accept C's credit risk in lieu of that of B, the original promisee.

60. ***NO*** Here, there is an attempt to make a present assignment of future rights in a nonexisting future contract. For the simple reason that a contract for the sale of Blackacre does not presently exist, there is no operable present assignment. Note that because the assignment was for consideration, courts can treat it as a contract to assign and, under this rationale, impress a constructive trust on any proceeds that A may realize from a sale of Blackacre in the future, thus protecting B's interest.

61. ***YES*** Here, the language of the agreement would be held to destroy only A's ***right*** to make an assignment, but it does not destroy A's ***power*** to do so. The assignment will be effective, and A will be liable for breach of the covenant not to assign.

62. ***NO*** As a general common law rule, no formalities are mandatory to create a present assignment. There is a major exception for assignments of land or an interest in land. Here, the Statute of Frauds would be operable and would require a writing signed by the party to be charged (here, the assignor).

63. ***YES*** Because it is made without consideration, a gratuitous assignment is revocable by the assignor at any time before the promisor of the obligation that has been the subject of the assignment renders performance to the assignee.

64. ***TRUE*** Such detrimental reliance, which is reasonably foreseeable to the assignor, will give rise to a substitute for valuable consideration and will function to cut off the assignor's power of revocation.

65. ***YES*** If a gratuitous assignment of a simple chose is in writing, the assignment is irrevocable.

66. ***TRUE*** The assignment to B, although first in time, was gratuitous and ***oral*** and, hence, revocable. Such revocation was automatically accomplished when A, as assignor, made the second assignment to C.

67. ***FALSE*** The general rule is that where an assignor makes two assignments of the same right and the first assignment is irrevocable, the first assignee has priority.

68. ***YES*** Although some of the old cases required an express assent to the assumption of delegated duties, the prevailing modern view is that acceptance of the rights under an assignment that clearly is coupled with a delegation of duties operates as legally effective assent to receive the delegation of duties as well as assignment of rights.

ESSAY EXAM QUESTIONS

INTRODUCTORY NOTE

The essay questions that follow have been selected to provide you with an opportunity to experience how the substantive law you have been reviewing may be tested in the hypothetical essay examination question context. These sample essay questions are a valuable self-diagnostic tool designed to enable you to enhance your issue-spotting ability and practice your exam writing skills.

It is suggested that you approach each question as though under actual examination conditions. The time allowed for each question is 60 minutes. You should spend 15 to 20 minutes spotting issues, underlining key facts and phrases, jotting notes in the margins, and outlining your answer. ***If*** you organize your thoughts well, 40 minutes will be more than adequate for writing them down. Should you prefer to forgo the actual writing involved on these questions, be sure to give yourself no more time for issue-spotting than you would on the actual examination.

The BARBRI technique for writing a well-organized essay answer is to (i) spot the issues in a question and then (ii) analyze and discuss each issue using the "CIRAC" method:

C — State your ***conclusion*** first. (In other words, you must think through your answer ***before*** you start writing.)
I — State the ***issue*** involved.
R — Give the ***rule(s)*** of law involved.
A — ***Apply*** the rule(s) of law to the facts.
C — Finally, restate your ***conclusion***.

After completing (or outlining) your own analysis of each question, compare it with the BARBRI model answer provided herein. A passing answer does ***not*** have to match the model one, but it should cover most of the issues presented and the law discussed and should ***apply the law to the facts*** of the question. Use of the CIRAC method results in the best answer you can write.

EXAM QUESTION NO. 1

On Thursday, May 14, Tenant received the following letter from Shore: "Dear Tenant, I will let you have my 'Shore House' for this June through August season, same terms under which you occupied it last year. Please reply in a week." Tenant noticed Shore's letter was postmarked May 11.

Earlier in May, Tenant had made inquiry at "The Cliffs," a mountain resort owned by Cliff. In Cliff's absence, Joe, one of Cliff's caretakers, had shown Tenant two available houses, "Hi-Vu" and "Lo-Vu," which Joe stated were listed for rent at $6,000 and $3,000, respectively, for one season.

On May 15, Tenant received a letter from Cliff which read, "This confirms statements by Joe. You may have Hi-Vu at $6,000, or Lo-Vu at $3,000, for the season June through August, all services included, payable in equal monthly installments."

On May 17, Tenant wrote to Cliff as follows, "I think your prices are high. Will you take $5,000 for Hi-Vu? If not, then I'll have to settle for Lo-Vu, and I agree to pay the $3,000 you ask, only I hope you may be willing to consider some concession if I pay the whole $3,000 in advance."

On May 17, Tenant learned that Shore had sold Shore House to Jones for Jones's immediate occupancy.

On May 18, Cliff received Tenant's letter and Cliff immediately telegraphed Tenant, "No change in prices. See my letter of the 16th." Tenant received Cliff's telegram the same day, May 18. Later that day Tenant also received Cliff's letter of May 16, which read, "Our deal is off." Tenant immediately wrote Shore, "I'll take Shore House per your letter of the 11th."

The normal course of post between Tenant and Shore and Tenant and Cliff was one day.

You may assume that all requirements of the Statute of Frauds have been satisfied. What rights, if any, does Tenant have against Shore and against Cliff? Discuss.

EXAM QUESTION NO. 2

Brother brews and sells bottled beer. Ace prints and sells labels for beer bottles. On June 1, Brother called Ace and asked about buying labels for Brother's beer. Ace called Brother back and said: "I'll sell and deliver all the labels you require for $6 per hundred labels." Brother wrote back to Ace: "I accept your offer. I will usually require 10,000 labels delivered on the first of each month, at $5 per hundred. Brother." Ace received Brother's note but did not respond.

(a) Applying only Article 2 of the Uniform Commercial Code, fully discuss whether Ace and Brother have an enforceable contract and, if so, identify the terms.

Assume there is an enforceable contract between Ace and Brother for the sale and delivery of all Brother's label requirements for $5 per hundred labels. On July 1, Ace delivered 10,000 labels to Brother satisfying the July requirement. Brother timely paid Ace $500. Attached to the delivery was a note from Ace stating that he would not be able to supply any more labels until September 1. After reasonable and timely inspection, Brother discovered that 5,000 of the labels were unusable because the printing was smeared. Without additional labels until September 1, Brother will lose a month and a half of beer sales. Additional labels are not available from another source until August 1 and will cost $10 per hundred labels.

(b) Applying only Article 2 of the Uniform Commercial Code, fully discuss Brother's rights and available remedies.

EXAM QUESTION NO. 3

On April 1, Ann Star, a young television personality, signs a contract with Bland Television Network to perform May 1 in a one-hour "live" TV show from 8 to 9 p.m. Bland agrees to pay Star $1,000 for this performance. The contract also provides that if for any reason Star does not appear as scheduled, she will "forfeit the sum of $25,000 to Bland as liquidated damages."

On April 10, Star informs Bland that she is suffering from acute fatigue and that her physician probably will not allow her to appear as scheduled. Bland immediately urges her in writing to fulfill her contractual obligations.

On April 15, Star tells Bland that she has miraculously recovered and will appear as scheduled on the May 1 show.

On April 23, Bland informs Star that, due to her unpredictability, it has hired actress Prima Donna as of that date and will not require Star's services.

On April 28, Prima Donna breaks her leg in an accident. Bland immediately wires Star that it has reconsidered the whole matter and will hold her to the original contract to perform on May 1.

On the evening of May 1, Star appears at the studio ready to perform, but Bland, acting under orders from the Federal Communications Commission, cancels the show in order to broadcast a special address by the President of the United States.

Discuss the legal implications of the foregoing events.

EXAM QUESTION NO. 4

P and D, who were casual acquaintances, resided in communities 100 miles apart. On February 1, P wrote D as follows:

> I have decided to give up my farm, Blackacre, and move to town. I thought you might consider buying it from me because you have often said that you were going to move to a farm after retirement. I will sell you Blackacre for $100,000. I'll let you have 10 days to think about it and to talk it over with your wife. In other words, I'll keep the offer open and will not withdraw it during this time.
>
> Sincerely yours,
>
> /s/P
> February 1, 2010

As a result of a delay in the mails, P's letter did not arrive in the normal course on February 2, but was received on February 4. On February 8, P deposited in the mail a letter addressed to D in which he said, among other things, "Blackacre deal off." This letter was not received by D until February 12, a few hours after D had posted an acceptance of the offer. The letter of acceptance was received in due course on February 13. In the correspondence that followed, P denied that any contract resulted, and D did not tender any money to P. On February 20, D delivered to A a writing that stated, "I hereby transfer to A my right to Blackacre under my contract with P for $100, receipt of which is hereby acknowledged. /s/D." On February 25, D gave a similar instrument to B, who immediately presented it to P. The next day A presented his claim to P.

What are the rights and liabilities of all the parties? Discuss.

ANSWERS TO EXAM QUESTIONS

ANSWER TO EXAM QUESTION NO. 1

Tenant v. Shore

Shore made an offer to Tenant and revoked it prior to Tenant's acceptance. At issue is whether the offer was accepted before it was terminated.

Effect of Shore's Letter to Tenant: Shore's letter to Tenant probably constitutes an effective offer, creating a power of acceptance in Tenant as offeree. This can be inferred from the use of the words, "I will let you have" and from the fact that Shore asks for a "reply in a week"—suggesting a present intent to contract. Although the price is left open, this does not impair the requisite certainty of terms; assuming the letter incorporates by reference the terms of the previous year's occupancy, the past dealings between the parties can be used to make the terms of the offer complete.

Effect of Tenant's Letter to Shore: The issue here is whether a ***timely*** acceptance has been communicated sufficient to form a contract between the parties. An acceptance can create a valid contract only if it takes effect prior to ***termination*** of the offer.

Although Tenant replied unequivocally to Shore that he would take Shore House, this response was not dispatched until May 18. Prior thereto, on May 17, Tenant acquired indirect knowledge that Shore had sold the house to Jones. If the source of this information was reliable (and there is nothing stated in the facts to indicate that it was not), an effective ***revocation*** thereby occurred, extinguishing Tenant's power to accept. Even though Shore requested a reply within a week, he made no promise to hold the offer open for that period (and even if he did, the promise probably would not be enforceable because no consideration was given in exchange for keeping the offer open). Therefore, Tenant's purported acceptance was too late to form an executory contract, and he has ***no rights*** against Shore.

Tenant v. Cliff

There is a contract between Tenant and Cliff to rent Lo-Vu for $3,000. At issue is whether Tenant accepted Cliff's offer before it was revoked.

On May 15, Cliff apparently extended a sufficient offer to rent either of his properties at specified prices. Parol evidence can be received to supply the details incorporated by direct reference.

Effect of Tenant's Letter to Cliff: The problem raised is whether Tenant manifested an unequivocal assent required for a valid acceptance. Arguably, he has made no present commitment in accordance with the terms of Cliff's offer, but is only "haggling" for lower prices and inviting further negotiations with Cliff. However, his "haggling" is accompanied by an agreement to pay the requested $3,000 for Lo-Vu. The request for some concession does not condition the assent; hence, it can be inferred from the language used that Tenant's intent is to accept in any event—whether or not Cliff agrees to the concession.

Thus, the better argument is that Tenant dispatched an operable acceptance—albeit a "grumbling" one.

Effect of Cliff's Letter of May 16: Cliff sent a letter calling the deal off on May 16, thereby attempting a revocation of his offer. However, a revocation is not effective until ***received.*** Here, Tenant did not receive the notice of revocation until one day after he had mailed his acceptance, and since the acceptance was sent via an impliedly authorized mode of communication (letter), it was effective upon dispatch under the mailbox rule. Thus, Cliff's purported rejection was not timely and was of no legal effect. Tenant's acceptance, therefore, effectively formed a ***binding contract*** to rent Lo-Vu for $3,000.

ANSWER TO EXAM QUESTION NO. 2

(a) **Is There a Contract?**

Brother and Ace do have an enforceable contract. At issue is whether Brother's response to Ace's offer was an acceptance or a counteroffer. Both Brother and Ace qualify as "merchants" as defined in the Uniform Commercial Code because they both deal in goods of the kind about which they are negotiating. A contract for the sale of goods may be made in any manner sufficient to show agreement between the parties.

Ace's call to Brother constituted an offer to sell labels to Brother. Brother's writing back to Ace constituted an acceptance because it was a definite expression of acceptance to buy the labels. The fact that Brother's writing included a different price term (*i.e.,* $5 per hundred) does not prevent the writing from constituting an acceptance. The different price term is considered a proposed addition to the contract. Between merchants, a proposed addition to the contract will not automatically become a part of the contract if it is a material alteration. In this case, the proposed change in the price term ***is*** a material alteration, and therefore will not become part of the contract absent an express acceptance of the proposed new term by Ace.

The Statute of Frauds must also be considered because this is a contract for the sale of goods for an amount of $500 or more. There must be a writing that satisfies the Statute of Frauds before a contract will be enforceable. In this case, there are two merchants. Therefore, one of the parties must receive a writing confirming the contract and sufficient against the sender within a reasonable time. If the party receiving the writing has reason to know its contents, and does not object within 10 days after receipt of the writing, the writing will satisfy the Statute of Frauds requirement. In this case, Brother's letter to Ace satisfies the Statute of Frauds requirement, and Ace did not object to the letter. The Statute of Frauds is satisfied.

The price term of this contract is $6 per hundred labels. As discussed above, Brother's indication of $5 per hundred labels is considered only a "proposal" for a different term and it does not become part of the contract unless expressly accepted by the other party, something that did not occur in this case.

This is a "requirements contract" as the term is used in the Uniform Commercial Code, and therefore the ***quantity*** of the labels contracted for is the actual amount of labels required by Brother. However, the quantity Ace is required to deliver cannot be unreasonably disproportionate to the stated estimate of 10,000 labels per month.

The duration of the contract is perpetual so long as Brother has need for the labels.

(b) **Brother's Rights and Remedies**

Ace is in breach, and Brother can recover for costs and losses resulting from anticipatory repudiation regarding the August delivery and for the defective labels in the July delivery. At issue is whether Ace's actions constitute breach, and if so, Brother's measure of recovery.

Ace's note indicating he could not deliver any more labels until September 1 constituted an "anticipatory repudiation" because it will substantially impair the value of the contract for August. The remedies available to Brother for the anticipatory repudiation include: (i) waiting for a commercially reasonable time to see if Ace can perform, (ii) cancelling the entire contract ***if*** the breach goes to the entire contract (which is not the case here), (iii) seeking damages, or (iv) attempting to "cover" the breach by finding labels from another source.

With respect to recovering damages, Brother could seek the difference between the market price ($10 per hundred) and the contract price ($5 per hundred), which is $500. Consequential damages may also be available to Brother. In the context of this case, that would be the lost beer sales for August. This option may not be available, however, because it appears there are substitute goods (cover) available. Brother would also be able to recover any incidental damages reasonably related to the breach by Ace.

In this case, it appears there is cover available in the form of the purchase of 10,000 substitute labels at $10 per hundred. Because the cover price is higher than the contract price, Brother is entitled to recover the difference as damages.

In addition to the anticipatory repudiation, Ace breached the contract by delivering 5,000 labels that were nonconforming. Brother is permitted to accept the labels that are not smeared, and reject the labels that are smeared. Brother must hold the rejected labels for Ace to pick up. Brother is then entitled to seek damages for the improper delivery.

Brother can recover the difference of $250 between the market price ($0) and the contract price ($250) for the unusable labels if he has already paid Ace for those nonconforming labels. If he has not paid Ace yet, Brother can withhold payment for the nonconforming labels.

It appears Brother will be unable to sell 5,000 bottles of beer in July because he does not have labels. Those lost beer sales constitute consequential damages, and Brother can recover those as a remedy for Ace's delivery of the nonconforming labels. Brother would also recover whatever "incidental damages" he incurred that were reasonably related to Ace's delivery of nonconforming labels.

ANSWER TO EXAM QUESTION NO. 3

The major issues raised by this question are whether either Bland or Star can be held in breach of the contract and whether the purported "liquidated damages clause" would be enforceable against Star.

Formation of Contract

There appear to be no problems as to the formation of an executory bilateral contract between Star and Bland on April 1. There was a writing stating the essential terms signed by the parties, and the promise to perform in return for the promise to pay $1,000 represents legally sufficient consideration on both sides of the agreement.

Effect of April 10 Communication

Star's notice to Bland on April 10 that she probably would not be able to appear as scheduled raises the issue of ***breach by anticipatory repudiation.*** Where in advance of the time set for performance either party to an executory bilateral contract manifests an unconditional, unequivocal refusal to perform as promised, there is a present material breach, giving the other party the right to bring immediate suit. Here, however, Star's letter falls short of an express repudiation. The fact that she "probably" would not be able to perform does not approach a notification that she ***will not*** or ***cannot*** perform. Her expression of mere doubt is not enough to constitute the requisite repudiation, and hence, at this juncture, the contract remained intact as to both parties.

Effect of April 15 Communication

Even if it were held that Star's notice amounted to an anticipatory breach, Star's communication to Bland on April 15 would constitute a valid ***retraction*** and "revive" the contract. According to the general view, the repudiator can withdraw a repudiation any time before the other party has changed position in reliance thereon. Because Bland neither commenced suit nor otherwise suffered any detriment in the interim, any threatened breach at this point has been cured.

Effect of April 23 and April 28 Communications

When Bland informed Star that it would not be requiring her services, this amounted to an express repudiation. Having couched its intent in unequivocal language, Bland could have been held liable for

anticipatory breach. However, Star did not bring suit and the facts in no way indicate that she changed her position (*e.g.,* by procuring another job). Thus, the subsequent wire from Bland deciding to hold Star to the original contract was a communication of its firm intention to abide by the agreement and, hence, was a valid retraction of the repudiation. The agreement, therefore, remained in force.

Defense of Discharge by Impossibility of Performance

Where after the formation of a contract either party's performance becomes objectively impossible to fulfill through no fault of his own, the contract is discharged, and neither can be held in breach.

In this case, on May 1 both Star and Bland were apparently ready, willing, and able to perform, yet the supervening F.C.C. orders rendered their performances impossible. Such a development constitutes an act that excuses the obligations of both parties under the doctrine of impossibility of performance. Thus, neither Bland nor Star has any contractual rights against the other.

[*Note:* Arguably, the doctrine of ***frustration of purpose*** also applies to discharge the contract, because the purpose for which Bland entered the agreement was thwarted by the supervening and unforeseeable F.C.C. orders.]

Status of Liquidated Damages Clause

Because neither party can be held in breach, the status of the damages clause in the contract is really a moot question. Briefly, however, its enforceability would depend on whether it is found to be a valid liquidated damages clause or void as an attempted penalty. Two conditions must be met for the clause to be upheld: (i) at the time of contracting, both parties must have recognized that actual damages in the event of breach would be extremely difficult to ascertain; and (ii) the amount adopted must be a reasonable forecast of actual damages. Here, it is likely that the first condition was met, because there are so many variables in the television industry that could affect the consequences to Bland should Star not perform. Whether $25,000 is a reasonable estimate of actual loss would be a jury question (although use of the word "forfeit" is suspect terminology).

ANSWER TO EXAM QUESTION NO. 4

This question raises major formation and assignment issues, both of which will be discussed in the context of the various possible suits between the parties.

D v. P

A suit by D against P for breach of the alleged contract is foreclosed on the ground that D no longer has any ***standing to sue***. Although he was an original party to the contract, as will be discussed below, an operable assignment transpired prior to any tender by D, which extinguished both his right to receive performance from P and his right to pursue a cause of action on the contract.

A v. P

Standing to Sue: A is the proper party to bring suit. At issue is the effect of D's assignment of rights to A. Because A was not a party to the alleged contract, his rights to sue, if any, are as an assignee pursuant to an operable assignment. This requires a showing of a present transfer of an ***assignable right***. Although the right to purchase land is often held too "personal" to assign, this is generally true only with credit transactions (because the obligor should not be subject to variation in risk that he will be paid). Apparently, however, a sale of Blackacre on credit was not contemplated here. Moreover, P in no way indicated in his letter that any attempted assignment would be void. Hence, at this point, A has succeeded to D's rights by way of an operable assignment.

However, the facts state that D subsequently made a similar assignment to B. This poses the problem of whether A thereby lost his standing to sue by virtue of the law of ***successive assignments.*** Under the majority rule, where, as in this case, the equities are equal between the parties (*i.e.,* both A and B paid consideration for delivery of a written assignment), the ***first assignee in time*** prevails. The rationale is that thereafter the assignor had nothing left to transfer. Hence, in most jurisdictions A is now the proper party to bring suit.

Formation of Contract: The issue here is whether the offer ***terminated*** either by its own terms or by notice of revocation prior to the dispatch of a timely acceptance by D.

Termination by Lapse of Time? P's promise to keep the offer open for 10 days could arguably be construed as restricting D's power to accept it within 10 days after the letter was (a) dated, (b) normally would have been received, or (c) actually was received. Moreover, it is also plausible that P meant that he had to be aware of D's acceptance within 10 days. Nevertheless, where, as here, it is not clear what P intended, the interpretation turns on what a reasonable offeree would understand P's statement to mean (objective theory of contracts). According to the facts, D was given 10 days to think over the offer. Because it obviously takes time for mail to travel, P probably intended the offer to remain open for 10 days after receipt in the normal course of post (one day). Thus, because as a reasonable person D would be expected to have read the date on the letter (February 1), thereby realizing it was delayed in transit, he would have only until February 12 to accept the offer. The facts state that D did post an acceptance on February 12; hence, the offer had not yet terminated by lapse of time.

Termination by Revocation? Although P promised to hold his offer open for 10 days, this commitment was not binding because it was not supported by consideration. P therefore retained the power to revoke and in fact attempted to do so in his February 8 letter, received by D on February 12, but after D had dispatched his acceptance. According to the weight of authority, a revocation is not effective until ***received,*** and an acceptance is effective upon ***dispatch*** through an authorized mode of communication. Because the offeree is impliedly authorized to use any means of transmission comparable to that used by the offeror (here, mail), D's acceptance became effective when posted (as discussed above, the offer had not yet terminated). Therefore, being that the revocation was not received until a few hours later, in most jurisdictions a ***valid contract was formed*** for the conveyance of Blackacre. Consequently, P is obligated to follow through with his promise to sell.

B v. D

As indicated above, in most jurisdictions, assignee A is the sole party in possession of the contract right against P. However, B (the losing assignee), having paid consideration for the assignment, can sue D for ***breach of implied warranty*** that the assigned right exists (*i.e.,* that it was not previously transferred). Under the minority rule, where B would prevail over A, A can pursue an action against D for breach of implied warranty that he would not make a subsequent assignment.

Criminal Law

CRIMINAL LAW

TABLE OF CONTENTS

INTRODUCTION: GENERAL APPROACH

The Multistate Examination directs examinees to answer questions according to "the generally accepted view" unless otherwise noted. In Criminal Law, the examiners may tell you the law to apply if there is no prevailing view. For example:

(i) The call of a question might tell you that the common law applies or that the state follows the Model Penal Code ("M.P.C.") approach; hence, you should be familiar with both the common law rules and the important M.P.C. distinctions discussed in this outline.

(ii) A fact pattern may also include a statute that you are to apply to the facts; the outline discusses typical statutes on a variety of topics that may be the subject of examination questions.

(iii) Finally, a question might reference a well-known legal doctrine (*e.g.,* the Wharton rule or the *M'Naghten* test); you should review those doctrines in the outline as well.

Note that if the examiners do not tell you whether the common law or a statutory version of the crime applies, it likely means that specific elements of the crime are not relevant to the question—for example, the question may concern whether voluntary intoxication is a defense to a crime, in which case the relevant factor is what type of mental state the crime requires, not other elements of the crime that may vary from jurisdiction to jurisdiction.

I. JURISDICTION AND GENERAL MATTERS

A. JURISDICTION

As used in this section, jurisdiction means the authority of a sovereign to ***create*** substantive criminal law. The authority of a court to ***enforce*** criminal laws is also an aspect of jurisdiction, but is more properly treated as a matter of criminal procedure.

1. Federal Criminal Jurisdiction

The power of the federal government to create crimes falls into the following broad categories:

a. Power over Federally Owned or Controlled Territory

The federal government has extensive power to enact general criminal codes governing conduct in the District of Columbia, the territories, and federal enclaves (*e.g.,* naval yards, federal courthouses, national parks, etc.).

b. Power over Conduct Occurring Within a State

In contrast, federal power to criminalize conduct within a state is limited by the requirement that each statute be founded upon an express or implied constitutional grant of authority.

c. Power over United States Nationals Abroad

Federal criminal statutes may, by express provision, reach conduct by citizens while on foreign soil.

d. **Power over Conduct on Ships or Airplanes**
Federal "maritime jurisdiction" extends to conduct by all persons aboard American ships or aircraft when on or over the high seas or even in foreign waters or ports.

2. **State Criminal Jurisdiction**
Unlike the federal government, every state has inherent authority by virtue of its "police power" to regulate its internal affairs for the protection or promotion of the health, safety, welfare, and morals of its citizens.

a. **Situs of the Crime**
At common law, and in those states that have not expanded jurisdiction by statute, only the state in which the situs of the crime is located has jurisdiction over the crime. "Situs" is generally defined as the place where the proscribed act (or omission) takes place, if the crime is defined in these terms; or the place of the harmful result, if the crime includes a result as a material element.
Example: A libelous statement may be made a crime where it is published, not where it is written, because the crime of libel proscribes the act of publication rather than the act of writing the libelous statement.

b. **Modern Bases for Jurisdiction**
A person is subject to prosecution in a state for an offense that he commits within or outside that state, by his own conduct or that of another for which he is legally accountable, under the following conditions:

1) When the ***offense is committed wholly or partly within the state*** ("partly within the state" includes occurrences within the state of either (i) conduct that is an element of the offense, or (ii) a result constituting such an element—*e.g.,* in homicide, the "result" is either the physical contact causing death or the death itself); or

2) When there is ***conduct outside the state that constitutes an attempt or conspiracy*** to commit an offense within the state ***plus an act inside the state***; or

3) When there is ***conduct within the state constituting an attempt, solicitation, or conspiracy to commit, in another jurisdiction, an offense*** under the laws of both the state and such other jurisdiction; or

4) When an offense based on the ***omission of performance of a duty*** imposed by the law of a state is committed within that state, regardless of the location of the offender at the time of the omission.

B. SOURCES OF CRIMINAL LAW

1. **Common Law Crimes**
A common law crime is one created and enforced by the judiciary in the absence of a statute defining the offense.

a. **No Federal Common Law Crimes**
Federal criminal law is governed entirely by statute. Although there are no federal

common law crimes, Congress has provided for common law crimes in the District of Columbia.

b. **Majority View—Common Law Crimes Retained**
A majority of the states retain common law crimes either implicitly or by express "retention statutes."

c. **Minority View (Modern Trend)—Common Law Crimes Abolished**
A minority of the states (about 20) have abolished common law crimes either expressly by statute or impliedly by the enactment of comprehensive criminal codes. These states nevertheless retain the various common law defenses such as insanity and self-defense.

2. **Statutory Crimes**
Today, state legislative statutes are the primary source of criminal law. Many states have adopted or are in the process of drafting comprehensive criminal codes.

3. **Constitutional Crimes**
The Constitution defines treason as levying war against the United States, adhering to enemies of the United States, or giving them aid and comfort. No person can be convicted of treason unless two witnesses testify to the same overt act, or unless the defendant confesses.

4. **Administrative Crimes**
A legislature may delegate to an administrative agency the power to prescribe rules, the violation of which may be punishable as a crime. Note, however, that the legislature may not delegate the power to determine which regulations shall carry criminal penalties; nor may it delegate the power of adjudication (*i.e.,* the determination of guilt or innocence). With the proliferation of administrative agencies, this source of criminal law is becoming increasingly important.
Example: Violation of the antifraud rules adopted by the Securities and Exchange Commission may result in severe criminal liability.

5. **The Model Penal Code**
Although not a source of law, the Model Penal Code ("M.P.C.") was a scholarly endeavor to compile a comprehensive and coherent body of criminal law. Since its publication in 1962, the M.P.C. has greatly influenced the drafting of state criminal statutes. Due to its enlightened position on many different issues, the M.P.C. may be the single most important source of general criminal law.

C. THEORIES OF PUNISHMENT
Historically, several theories have been advanced to justify criminal punishment.

1. **Incapacitation (Restraint)**
While imprisoned, a criminal has fewer opportunities to commit acts causing harm to society.

2. **Special Deterrence**
Punishment may ***deter the criminal*** from committing future crimes.

3. General Deterrence
Punishment may ***deter persons other than the criminal*** from committing similar crimes for fear of incurring the same punishment.

4. Retribution
Punishment is imposed to vent society's sense of outrage and need for revenge.

5. Rehabilitation
Imprisonment provides the opportunity to mold or reform the criminal into a person who, upon return to society, will conform her behavior to societal norms.

6. Education
The publicity attending the trial, conviction, and punishment of some criminals serves to educate the public to distinguish good and bad conduct and to develop respect for the law.

D. CLASSIFICATION OF CRIMES

At common law, all crimes were divided into three classes: treason, felonies, and misdemeanors. Several additional means of classifying crimes are now frequently employed either by the courts or by state statutory schemes.

1. Felonies and Misdemeanors
Most states now classify as ***felonies*** all crimes punishable by ***death or imprisonment exceeding one year***. Under such modern schemes, ***misdemeanors*** are crimes punishable by ***imprisonment for less than one year or by a fine*** only. At common law, the only felonies were murder, manslaughter, rape, sodomy, mayhem, robbery, larceny, arson, and burglary; all other crimes were considered misdemeanors.

2. Malum In Se and Malum Prohibitum
A crime ***malum in se*** (wrong in itself) is one that is ***inherently evil***, either because criminal intent is an element of the offense, or because the crime involves "moral turpitude." By contrast, a crime ***malum prohibitum*** is one that is wrong only because it is ***prohibited by legislation***.

Example: Battery, larceny, and drunken driving are mala in se, whereas hunting without a license, failure to comply with the Federal Drug Labeling Act, and driving in excess of the speed limit are mala prohibita.

3. Infamous Crimes
At common law, infamous crimes are all crimes involving fraud, dishonesty, or the obstruction of justice. Under modern law, this concept has been expanded to include most felonies.

4. Crimes Involving Moral Turpitude
The concept of moral turpitude—committing a base or vile act—is often equated with the concept of malum in se. Conviction of a crime involving moral turpitude may result in the deportation of an alien, the disbarment of an attorney, or the impeachment of a trial witness.

E. PRINCIPLE OF LEGALITY—VOID-FOR-VAGUENESS DOCTRINE

The Due Process Clause of the federal Constitution, found in the Fifth and Fourteenth Amendments, has been interpreted by the Supreme Court to require that no criminal penalty be imposed without fair notice that the conduct is forbidden. The "void-for-vagueness" doctrine, which has been held to require particular scrutiny of criminal statutes capable of reaching speech protected by the First Amendment, incorporates two considerations:

1. **Fair Warning**
A statute must give a person of ordinary intelligence fair notice that his contemplated conduct is forbidden by the statute.

2. **Arbitrary and Discriminatory Enforcement Must Be Avoided**
A statute must not encourage arbitrary and erratic arrests and convictions.

F. CONSTITUTIONAL LIMITATIONS ON CRIME CREATION

In addition to the constitutional requirement that a criminal statute be sufficiently specific to provide fair warning and prevent arbitrary enforcement, Article I of the federal Constitution places two substantive limitations on both federal and state legislatures.

1. **No Ex Post Facto Laws**
The Constitution expressly prohibits ex post facto laws. The Supreme Court has defined an ex post facto law as one that operates retroactively to:

   (i) ***Make criminal an act*** that when done was not criminal;

   (ii) ***Aggravate a crime or increase the punishment*** therefor;

   (iii) ***Change the rules of evidence*** to the detriment of criminal defendants as a class; or

   (iv) ***Alter the law of criminal procedure*** to deprive criminal defendants of a substantive right.

   [Calder v. Bull, 3 U.S. (3 Dall.) 386 (1798)]

2. **No Bills of Attainder**
Bills of attainder are also constitutionally prohibited. A bill of attainder is a legislative act that inflicts punishment or denies a privilege ***without a judicial trial***. Although a bill of attainder may also be an ex post facto law, a distinction can be drawn in that an ex post facto law does not deprive the offender of a judicial trial.

G. INTERPRETATIONS OF CRIMINAL STATUTES

1. **Plain Meaning Rule**
When the statutory language is plain and its meaning clear, the court must give effect to it even if the court feels that the law is unwise or undesirable. An exception to this rule exists if the court believes that applying the plain meaning of a statute will lead to injustice, oppression, or an absurd consequence.

2. **Ambiguous Statutes Strictly Construed in Favor of Defendant**
The rule of lenity requires that an ambiguous criminal statute must be strictly construed in favor of the defendant. Ambiguity should be distinguished from vagueness. An ambiguous statute is one susceptible to two or more equally reasonable interpretations. A vague statute is one that is so unclear as to be susceptible to no reasonable interpretation.

3. *Expressio Unius, Exclusio Alterius*

According to this maxim, the expression of one thing impliedly indicates an intention to exclude another.

Example: A criminal statute defines bigamy as the act of remarriage by one who has a living spouse. The statute expressly provides an exception for one whose spouse disappeared more than seven years before. Can a person remarry if the spouse has been gone for less than seven years provided he or she believes in good faith that the spouse is dead? Most jurisdictions answer no. The fact that the statute provides one exception impliedly excludes all others.

4. The Specific Controls the General, the More Recent Controls the Earlier

If two statutes address the same subject matter but dictate different conclusions, the more specific statute will be applied rather than the more general. The more recently enacted statute will control an older statute.

Examples: 1) If one statute prohibits all forms of gambling and another permits charity-sponsored raffles, the latter will control a church raffle.

2) A 1980 statute banning advertising of cigarettes will govern a 1975 statute providing a limit on advertising expenditure by cigarette manufacturers.

5. Effect of Repeal

At common law, in the absence of a saving provision, the repeal or invalidation of a statute operates to bar prosecutions for earlier violations, provided the prosecution is pending or not yet under way at the time of the repeal. However, a repeal will not operate to set free a person who has been prosecuted and convicted and as to whom the judgment has become final.

a. Saving Provision

Many of the new comprehensive codes include a provision to the effect that crimes committed prior to the effective date of the new code are subject to prosecution and punishment under the law as it existed at the time the offense was committed.

H. MERGER

1. Common Law Rule

a. Merger of Misdemeanor into Felony

At common law, if a person engaged in conduct constituting both a felony and a misdemeanor, she could be convicted only of the felony. The misdemeanor was regarded as merged into the felony.

b. No Merger Among Offenses of Same Degree

If the same act or a series of acts that were all part of the same transaction constituted several felonies (or several misdemeanors), there was no merger of any of the offenses into any of the others.

2. Current American Rule—No Merger

There is generally no merger in American law, with the following limited ***exceptions***:

a. **"Merger" of Solicitation or Attempt into Completed Crime**

One who solicits another to commit a crime (where solicitation itself is a crime) cannot be convicted of both the solicitation and the completed crime (if the person solicited does complete it). Similarly, a person who completes a crime after attempting it may not be convicted of both the attempt and the completed crime. Conspiracy, however, does not merge with the completed offense (*e.g.,* one can be convicted of robbery and conspiracy to commit robbery).

b. **"Merger" of Lesser Included Offenses into Greater Offenses**

Lesser included offenses "merge" into greater offenses, in the sense that one placed in jeopardy for either offense may not later be retried for the other. Nor may one be convicted of both the greater offense and a lesser included offense. A lesser included offense is one that consists entirely of some, but not all, elements of the greater crime. This rule is sometimes labeled a rule of merger, but it is also clearly required by the constitutional prohibition against double jeopardy.

Examples: 1) D allegedly possessed certain narcotics. On the basis of this, she is charged with (i) illegal possession of narcotics, (ii) illegal possession of narcotics for sale, and (iii) possession of a drug not in a properly stamped container. May she be convicted of all three offenses? *Held:* No. She may not be convicted of simple possession and possession for sale. She may be convicted of possession for sale and possession in an improper container, because neither is a lesser included offense of the other. Each requires proof of something the other does not, *i.e.,* intent to sell and use of an improper container.

2) D is convicted of operating a motor vehicle without the owner's consent. She is then charged with stealing the vehicle based upon the same incident. Operating the vehicle without the owner's consent is a lesser included offense of theft, because theft requires proof of everything necessary to prove operation of a vehicle without consent of the owner ***plus*** the intent to steal. May D be prosecuted for theft? *Held*: No. Conviction for a lesser included offense bars prosecution for the greater offense. [Brown v. Ohio, 432 U.S. 161 (1977)]

3) D is convicted of felony murder based on proof that his accomplice shot and killed a store clerk during an armed robbery. He is then charged with and convicted of armed robbery based on the same incident. *Held:* Because the armed robbery was the underlying felony for the felony murder conviction, it is a lesser included offense of the felony murder and the subsequent prosecution is barred. [Harris v. Oklahoma, 433 U.S. 682 (1977)]

3. **Developing Rules Against Multiple Convictions for Parts of Same "Transaction"**

Many jurisdictions are developing prohibitions against convicting a defendant for more than one offense where the multiple offenses were all part of the same "criminal transaction." In some states, this is prohibited by statute. In others, courts adopt a rule of merger or of double jeopardy to prohibit it.

a. **No Double Jeopardy If Statute Provides Multiple Punishments for Single Act**
Imposition of cumulative punishments for two or more statutorily defined offenses, specifically intended by the legislature to carry ***separate punishments***, arising from the same transaction, and constituting the same crime, does not violate the Double Jeopardy Clause prohibition against multiple punishments for the same offense when the punishments are imposed at a single trial. [Missouri v. Hunter, 459 U.S. 359 (1983)]
Example: D robs a store at gunpoint. D can be sentenced to cumulative punishments for armed robbery and "armed criminal action" under a "use a gun, go to jail" statute.

II. ESSENTIAL ELEMENTS OF CRIME

A. ELEMENTS OF A CRIME
Culpability under Anglo-American criminal law is founded upon certain basic premises that are more or less strictly observed by legislatures and courts when formulating the substantive law of crimes. Consequently, the prosecution is generally required to prove the following elements of a criminal offense:

(i) ***Actus Reus*** (guilty act): A physical act (or unlawful omission) by the defendant;

(ii) ***Mens Rea*** (guilty mind): The state of mind or intent of the defendant at the time of his act;

(iii) ***Concurrence***: The physical act and the mental state existed at the same time; and

(iv) ***Harmful Result and Causation***: A harmful result caused (both factually and proximately) by the defendant's act.

Virtually all crimes require a physical act and may require some sort of intent. Many crimes also require proof of certain ***attendant circumstances*** without which the same act and intent would not be criminal. For example, the crime of receipt of stolen property requires that the property received has in fact been stolen. If the defendant receives property (the act) that he believes to have been stolen (the mental element), when in fact the property has not been stolen, the absence of this required circumstance renders the defendant not liable for receipt of stolen property. Other crimes require result and causation. Homicide, for example, requires that the victim die and that the defendant's act be the cause of death.

B. PHYSICAL ACT
For there to be criminal liability, the defendant must have either performed a voluntary physical act or failed to act under circumstances imposing a legal duty to act. For this purpose, an act is defined as a ***bodily movement***. A thought is not an act. Therefore, bad thoughts alone cannot constitute a crime. Note, however, that speech, unlike thought, is an act that can cause liability (*e.g.*, perjury, solicitation).

1. **The Act Must Be Voluntary**
The defendant's act must be voluntary in the sense that it must be a ***conscious exercise of the will***. *Rationale:* An involuntary act will not be deterred by punishment. The following acts are ***not*** considered "voluntary" and therefore cannot be the basis for criminal liability:

a. Conduct that is ***not the product of the actor's determination***.
Example: A shoves B into C, with the result that C falls to his death. Can B be held criminally liable for C's death? No.

b. ***Reflexive or convulsive*** acts.

c. Acts performed while the defendant was either ***unconscious or asleep unless*** the defendant knew that she might fall asleep or become unconscious and engaged in dangerous behavior.

2. Omission as an "Act"

Although most crimes are committed by affirmative action rather than by nonaction, a defendant's ***failure to act*** will result in criminal liability provided ***three requirements*** are satisfied.

a. Legal Duty to Act

The defendant must have a legal duty to act under the circumstances. A legal duty to act can arise from the following sources:

1) A ***statute*** (*e.g.,* filing an income tax return or reporting an accident).

2) A ***contract*** obligating the defendant to act, such as one entered into by a lifeguard or a nurse.

3) The ***relationship*** between the defendant and the victim, which may be sufficiently close to create a duty.
Examples: 1) A parent has the duty to prevent physical harm to his or her children.

2) A spouse has the duty to prevent harm to his or her spouse.

4) The ***voluntary assumption of care*** by the defendant of the victim. Although in general there is no common law duty to help someone in distress, once aid is rendered, the Good Samaritan may be held criminally liable for not satisfying a reasonable standard of care.
Examples: 1) A, while hiking, sees B drowning in a river. Although A is a good swimmer, he takes no steps to save B, who drowns. Was A's failure to act an "act" upon which liability could be based? No, because A had no duty to act. Note that the answer would be the same even if A recognized B as a person whom he disliked and took great pleasure in watching B drown.

2) If A began to swim out toward B and only after reaching B decided that B was someone not worth saving, A would have violated his duty to act by unreasonably abandoning a rescue effort that was voluntarily undertaken.

5) The ***creation of peril*** by the defendant.
Example: Believing that B can swim, A pushes B into a pool. It becomes apparent that B cannot swim, but A takes no steps to help B. B

drowns. Was A's failure to attempt a rescue an "act" on which liability can be based? Yes.

b. **Knowledge of Facts Giving Rise to Duty**

As a general rule, the duty to act arises when the defendant is aware of the facts creating the duty to act (*e.g.,* the parent must know that his child is drowning before his failure to rescue the child will make him liable). However, in some situations the law will impose a duty to learn the facts (*e.g.,* a lifeguard asleep at his post would still have a legal duty to aid a drowning swimmer).

c. **Reasonably Possible to Perform**

It must be reasonably possible for the defendant to perform the duty or to obtain the help of others in performing it.

Example: A parent who is unable to swim is under no duty to jump in the water to attempt to save his drowning child.

3. **Possession as an "Act"**

Criminal statutes that penalize the possession of contraband generally require only that the defendant have control of the item for a long enough period to have an opportunity to terminate the possession. Possession need not be exclusive to one person, and possession also may be "constructive," meaning that actual physical control need not be proved when the contraband is located in an area within the defendant's "dominion and control."

a. **State of Mind Requirement**

Absent a state of mind requirement in the statute, the defendant must be aware of his possession of the contraband, but he need not be aware of its illegality or true nature. However, many statutes and the M.P.C. add a "knowingly" state of mind element to possession crimes (*see* C.6., *infra.*). Under such statutes, the defendant ordinarily must know the identity or nature of the item possessed. On the other hand, a defendant may not consciously avoid learning the true nature of the item possessed; knowledge or intent may be inferred from a combination of suspicion and indifference to the truth.

C. MENTAL STATE

1. **Purpose of Mens Rea Requirement**

The reason that mens rea is normally required is to distinguish between inadvertent or accidental acts and acts performed by one with a "guilty mind." The latter type of act is more blameworthy and, arguably, can be deterred. However, in some cases (strict liability crimes), mens rea is not required.

2. **Specific Intent**

If the definition of a crime requires not only the doing of an act, but the doing of it with a specific intent or objective, the crime is a "specific intent" crime.

a. **Significance**

It is necessary to identify specific intent for two reasons:

1) **Need for Proof**

The existence of a specific intent cannot be conclusively imputed from the mere doing of the act, and the prosecution must produce evidence tending to prove the existence of the specific intent. That said, ***the manner*** in which an act was done may provide circumstantial evidence of intent.

Example: A shoots B. The fact that A shot B does not show that A had the intent to shoot and kill B. However, if A bought a revolver and ammunition shortly before shooting B, carefully loaded the revolver, took careful aim at B, and fired several times, that evidence may circumstantially prove A's intent to kill B.

2) **Applicability of Certain Defenses**

Some defenses, such as voluntary intoxication and unreasonable mistake of fact, apply only to specific intent crimes.

b. **Enumeration of Specific Intent Crimes**

The major specific intent crimes and the intent they require are as follows:

1) ***Solicitation***: Intent to have the person solicited commit the crime;

2) ***Attempt***: Intent to complete the crime;

3) ***Conspiracy***: Intent to have the crime completed;

4) ***First degree premeditated murder*** (where so defined by statute): Premeditated intent to kill;

5) ***Assault***: Intent to commit a battery;

6) ***Larceny and robbery***: Intent to permanently deprive another of his interest in the property taken;

7) ***Burglary***: Intent at the time of entry to commit a felony in the dwelling of another;

8) ***Forgery***: Intent to defraud;

9) ***False pretenses***: Intent to defraud; and

10) ***Embezzlement***: Intent to defraud.

3. **Malice—Common Law Murder and Arson**

Although the intents required for the "malice" crimes—common law murder and arson—sound similar to specific intent (*e.g.,* the "intent to kill" for murder), these crimes are ***not*** open to the specific intent defenses. The common law created this special mental state category especially to deny to murder and arson the specific intent defenses. To establish malice in these cases, the prosecution need only show that the defendant recklessly disregarded an obvious or high risk that the particular harmful result would occur.

4. **General Intent—Awareness of Factors Constituting Crime**

Generally, all crimes require "general intent," which is an awareness of all factors constituting the crime; *i.e.,* the defendant must be aware that she is acting in the proscribed way and that any attendant circumstances required by the crime are present. (Note that the defendant need not be certain that these attendant circumstances exist; it is sufficient that she is aware of a high likelihood that they exist.)

Example: To commit the crime of false imprisonment (*see* VII.D., *infra*), the defendant must be aware that she is confining a person, and that the confinement has not been specifically authorized by law or validly consented to by the person confined.

a. **Inference of Intent from Act**

A jury can infer the required general intent merely from the doing of the act. It is not necessary that evidence specifically proving the general intent be offered by the prosecution.

b. **Transferred Intent**

If a defendant intended a harmful result to a particular person or object and, in trying to carry out that intent, caused a similar harmful result to another person or object, her intent will be transferred from the intended person or object to the one actually harmed. Any defenses or mitigating circumstances that the defendant could have asserted against the intended victim (*e.g.,* self-defense, provocation) will also be transferred in most cases. The doctrine of transferred intent most commonly applies to homicide, battery, and arson. It does ***not*** apply to ***attempt***.

Example: A shoots at B, intending to kill him. Because of bad aim, she hits C, killing him. Is A guilty of C's murder? *Held:* Yes. Her intent to kill B will be transferred to C. Note that A may also be guilty of the attempted murder of B.

Compare: A shoots twice at B, thinking that B was C, whom she had wanted to kill. She wounds not only B, but also D, a bystander. Is A guilty of the attempted murder of B and D? *Held:* A is guilty of the attempted murder of B, because her mistake as to B's identity is a mistake of fact that does not negate her intent to kill the person in front of her (B). There is no transferred intent issue in that scenario. However, most courts would hold that she is not guilty of the attempted murder of D.

c. **Motive Distinguished**

The motive for a crime is distinct from the intent to commit it. A motive is the reason or explanation underlying the offense. It is generally held that ***motive is immaterial*** to substantive criminal law. A good motive will not excuse a criminal act. On the other hand, a lawful act done with bad motive will not be punished.

Example: An impoverished woman steals so that her hungry children may eat. Despite her noble ***motive***—feeding her children—the woman could be held criminally liable for her acts because her ***intent*** was to steal.

5. **Strict Liability Offenses**

A strict liability offense is one that does not require awareness of all of the factors constituting the crime. Generally, the requirement of a state of mind is not abandoned with respect to all elements of the offense, but only with regard to one or some of the elements. The major significance of a strict liability offense is that ***certain defenses***, such as mistake of fact, are ***not available***.

a. **Identification of Strict Liability Offenses**

Strict liability offenses, also known as public welfare offenses, are generally "regulatory" offenses, *i.e.,* offenses that are part of a regulatory scheme. They generally involve a relatively low penalty and are not regarded by the community as involving significant moral impropriety. Note that the mere fact that a statute is silent on the question of mental state does not necessarily mean that the offense is a strict liability offense. If no mental state is expressly required by the statute, the courts may still interpret the statute as requiring some mens rea, especially if the statute appears to be a codification of a traditional common law offense or if the statute imposes a severe penalty.

Example: Federal legislation prohibits the transfer of firearms not registered under federal law. Is it a defense that the defendant was ignorant of the fact that a firearm was not registered? *Held:* No, because this is a strict liability offense. Awareness of the fact of nonregistration is not necessary, although it is necessary that the defendant have been aware of the fact that she was possessing a firearm.

Compare: Federal legislation requires registration of any fully automatic machinegun. The statute is silent on the question of mental state and provides a penalty of up to 10 years' imprisonment. *Held:* Defendant may assert as a defense that he was not aware that the weapon in his possession was automatic. The type of statute and the harsh penalty indicate that Congress did not intend to dispense with the mens rea requirement. [Staples v. United States, 511 U.S. 600 (1994)]

b. Constitutionality

The majority view is that strict liability offenses are constitutional. *Exception:* The Supreme Court struck down as a violation of due process a Los Angeles municipal ordinance imposing strict liability for failure to register as a felon. The key factor in the court's decision was the absence of "circumstances which might move one to inquire as to the necessity of registration." *Note:* The scope of this holding is limited to statutes making criminal the failure to register.

6. Model Penal Code Analysis of Fault

The M.P.C. advocates the elimination of the ambiguous common law distinction between general and specific intent. Instead, the M.P.C. proposes four categories into which the mental component of a criminal offense (*i.e.,* the element of fault) can be characterized. Because consistent use of these categories leads to analytical clarity, they have been incorporated into several state criminal codes. They likewise provide a convenient way of analyzing problems on the exam that incorporate statutes.

a. Purposely, Knowingly, or Recklessly

When a statute requires that the defendant act purposely ("intentionally"), knowingly, or recklessly, a subjective standard is being used, *i.e.,* the question is what was actually going on in the defendant's mind.

1) Purposely

A person acts purposely with respect to his conduct when it is his conscious object to engage in certain conduct or cause a certain result, *e.g.,* burglary.

2) Knowingly

A person acts knowingly with respect to the nature of his conduct when he is

aware that his conduct is of that nature or that certain circumstances exist. He acts knowingly with respect to the result of his conduct when he knows that his conduct will necessarily or very likely cause such a result. Conduct performed knowingly also satisfies the mental state of a statute that requires willful conduct.

3) **Recklessly**
A person acts recklessly when he ***consciously disregards a substantial or unjustifiable risk*** that circumstances exist or that a prohibited result will follow, and this disregard constitutes a ***gross deviation from the standard of care*** that a reasonable person would exercise in the situation. An act performed recklessly is also performed wantonly. Recklessness requires that the actor take an unjustifiable risk and that he know of and consciously disregard the risk. Mere realization of the risk is not enough. He must know that injury might result (if he knows that it is ***certain*** to result, he acts ***knowingly***). Thus, recklessness involves both objective ("unjustifiable risk") and subjective ("awareness") elements.

b. **Negligence**
A person acts negligently when he ***fails to be aware of a substantial and unjustifiable risk*** that circumstances exist or a result will follow, and such failure constitutes a ***substantial deviation from the standard of care*** that a reasonable person would exercise under the circumstances. To determine whether a person acted negligently, an ***objective standard*** is used. However, it is not merely the reasonable person standard that is used in torts; the defendant must have taken a ***very unreasonable risk*** in light of the usefulness of his conduct, his knowledge of the facts, and the nature and extent of the harm that may be caused.

Example: D held himself out to the public as a doctor even though he was not a licensed physician. He treated a sick woman by wrapping her in kerosene-soaked flannels for three days. The woman died. *Held:* D is guilty of manslaughter. His good intentions were irrelevant. By objective standards, he took an unjustifiable risk.

1) **Violation of Statute or Ordinance as Evidence of Negligence**
Violation of a state statute, municipal ordinance, or administrative regulation may—as in tort law—be evidence of liability.

Example: A, driving in excess of the speed limit, hits and kills B, a pedestrian. A's speeding violation may be admissible as evidence of his negligence in a prosecution for manslaughter.

c. **Analysis of Statutes Using Fault Standards**

1) **State of Mind Applies to All Material Elements of Offense**
Often a statute will establish a culpable state of mind without indicating whether it is required for all the material elements of the offense. In that case, the specified state of mind applies to all material elements of the offense unless a contrary purpose appears in the statute.

Example: Under a statute imposing criminal liability on anyone who "knowingly makes a sale of an intoxicating beverage to a minor," the M.P.C. would require knowledge for each material element of the offense. Thus, if the defendant can show that she did not know that a sale took place, that the beverage was intoxicating, or that the purchaser was a minor, she will be able to avoid liability.

2) **General State of Mind Requirement—Recklessness**
If the statute defining the offense (other than a strict liability offense) does not include a state of mind requirement, the defendant must have acted with at least recklessness with regard to each material element of the offense.

a) **Higher Degree of Fault Suffices**
Under the M.P.C.'s hierarchy of fault levels, a showing of a higher state of mind automatically satisfies a lower mental state requirement of a statute. Thus, a showing that the defendant acted purposely or knowingly will satisfy the general requirement of recklessness.

b) **Other Levels of Fault Must Be Specified**
Because a standard of recklessness is assumed where the state of mind is not specified, if a lower standard of negligence will satisfy liability, or if a higher standard of knowledge or purpose is required, those standards must be indicated in the language of the statute.
Example: Under a statute creating criminal liability for anyone who "sells intoxicating beverages to one whom he should know to be a minor," the material elements include the act of selling and the attendant circumstances that the beverage be intoxicating and that the purchaser be a minor. Under the M.P.C. formula, a minimum standard for recklessness is required as the state of mind for the first two elements, while the third element of the statute specifies that only a negligence level of fault is required.

7. **Vicarious Liability Offenses**
A vicarious liability offense is one in which a person without personal fault may nevertheless be held vicariously liable for the criminal conduct of another (usually an employee). The criminal law doctrine of vicarious liability is analogous to the tort doctrine of respondeat superior. *Note:* Unlike strict liability, which dispenses with the mens rea requirement but retains the requirement that the defendant have personally engaged in the necessary acts or omissions, vicarious liability dispenses with the personal actus reus requirement but retains the need for ***mental fault on the part of the employee.***

a. **Limitation on Punishment**
Because the imposition of criminal liability for faultless conduct is contrary to the basic premise of criminal justice that crime requires fault on the part of the accused, at least one state court has held that imprisonment in such cases violates the due process guarantees of the state constitution. The current trend in the legislatures is to limit vicarious liability to ***regulatory crimes*** and to limit punishment to ***fines***.

b. **Implying Vicarious Liability from Underlying Strict Liability Offense**
Despite some decisions to the contrary, the mere fact that the underlying offense is clearly a strict liability offense should ***not*** imply a legislative intent to impose vicarious liability.

Example: A statute makes it a crime "for anyone to serve an alcoholic beverage to a minor." Although a bartender may be strictly liable under this statute regardless of her belief that the customer was legally old enough to drink, this statute should not be construed to impose liability on the tavern owner who neither was present at the time the minor was served nor authorized the actions of the bartender.

8. Enterprise Liability—Liability of Corporations and Associations

a. Common Law—No Criminal Liability

At common law, a corporation could not commit a crime because it was unable to form the necessary criminal intent.

b. Modern Statutes—Vicarious Criminal Liability

Modern statutes often provide for the liability of corporations and sometimes even unincorporated associations (*e.g.,* partnerships). This liability is, by necessity, vicarious. Under such provisions, corporations may be held liable under the following conditions:

1) Act Within Scope of Office

Except where the law specifically provides otherwise, the conduct giving rise to corporate liability must be performed by an agent of the corporation acting on behalf of the corporation and within the scope of his office or employment.

2) "Superior Agent Rule"

Some jurisdictions limit corporate criminal liability to situations in which the conduct is performed or participated in by agents sufficiently high in the corporate hierarchy to presume that their acts reflect corporate policy.

c. Model Penal Code

Under the M.P.C., a corporation may be guilty of a criminal offense provided the offense:

1) Consists of the ***failure to discharge a specific duty*** imposed by law on the corporation;

2) Is defined by a statute in which a ***legislative purpose to impose liability*** on corporations plainly appears; or

3) Was "authorized, requested, commanded, performed, or recklessly tolerated ***by the board of directors or by a high managerial agent*** acting on behalf of the corporation within the scope of his office or employment."

d. Individual Liability Independent of Enterprise Liability

The person who, in the name of the corporation, performs (or causes to be performed) the conduct that is an element of the offense is legally accountable and subject to punishment to the same extent as if the conduct were performed in his name or on his own behalf. Similarly, the fact that the corporation is liable does not prevent the conviction of the individual who committed the offense.

D. CONCURRENCE OF MENTAL FAULT WITH PHYSICAL ACT REQUIRED

The defendant must have had the intent necessary for the crime at the time he committed the act constituting the crime. In addition, the intent must have prompted the act.

Example: A decides to kill B. While driving to the store to purchase a gun for this purpose, A negligently runs over B and kills him. Is A guilty of murder? No, because although at the time A caused B's death he had the intent to do so, this intent did not prompt the act resulting in B's death (*i.e.,* A's poor driving).

Compare: With the intent to kill B, A strangles B to the point of unconsciousness, but does not actually kill B. Thinking B is dead, A buries B, and B dies as a result. Is A guilty of murder, even though the death-causing act of burying B was done without the intent to murder? Yes, in a majority of jurisdictions. Most courts would find that the two acts were part of a single transaction with a common intent.

E. CAUSATION

Some crimes (*e.g.,* homicide) require a harmful result and causation. For a full discussion of causation, *see* VII.C.5., *infra.*

III. ACCOMPLICE LIABILITY

A. PARTIES TO A CRIME

1. Common Law

The common law distinguished four types of parties to a felony: ***principals in the first degree*** (persons who actually engage in the act or omission that constitutes the criminal offense); ***principals in the second degree*** (persons who aid, command, or encourage the principal and are present at the crime); ***accessories before the fact*** (persons who aid, abet, or encourage the principal but are ***not*** present at the crime); and ***accessories after the fact*** (persons who assist the principal after the crime).

a. Significance of Common Law Distinctions

At common law, the distinctions between the parties had a great deal of procedural significance. For example, an accessory could not be convicted unless the principal had already been convicted, although both could be convicted in a joint trial if the jury determined the principal's guilt first. Most modern jurisdictions have abandoned this requirement, and an accessory can be convicted even if the principal has evaded apprehension or has been tried and acquitted.

2. Modern Statutes

Most jurisdictions have abolished the distinctions between principals in the first degree, principals in the second degree, and accessories before the fact (accessories after the fact are still treated separately). Under the modern approach, all "parties to the crime" can be found guilty of the criminal offense. For convenience, this section will designate the actual perpetrator of the criminal act as the principal and the other parties to the crime as accomplices.

a. Principal

A principal is one who, with the requisite mental state, ***actually engages in the act or***

omission that causes the criminal result. Also, anyone who acts through an innocent, irresponsible, or unwilling agent is classified as a principal.

Example: A gives a poisonous drink to B to give to C. B does so; C drinks it and dies. If B did not know that the drink was poisonous, or if B was mentally ill or under duress, A, not B, is the principal. Note that the principal need not be present when the harm results.

b. **Accomplice**

An accomplice is one who, with the intent that the crime be committed, aids, counsels, or encourages the principal before or during the commission of the crime.

c. **Accessory After the Fact**

An accessory after the fact is one who receives, relieves, comforts, or assists another, knowing that he has committed a felony, in order to ***help the felon escape arrest, trial, or conviction.*** The crime committed by the principal must be a ***felony*** and it must be ***completed*** at the time the aid is rendered. Today, the crime is usually called "harboring a fugitive," "aiding escape," or "obstructing justice."

1) **Penalty**

Typically the punishment for this crime bears no relationship to the principal offense; five years is the most common maximum sentence. Exemptions are usually provided for close relatives of the principal offender (the common law exempted only the spouse).

B. MENTAL STATE—INTENT REQUIRED

To be convicted as an accomplice under the prevailing common law rule, a person must have given aid, counsel, or encouragement with the ***intent*** to aid or encourage the principal in the commission of the crime charged. In the absence of a statute, most courts would hold that mere ***knowledge*** that a crime would result from the aid provided is insufficient for accomplice liability, at least where the aid involves the sale of ordinary goods at ordinary prices. However, procuring an illegal item or selling at a higher price because of the buyer's purpose may constitute a sufficient "stake in the venture" for a court to find intent to aid.

Example: A tells B that he wants to buy a can of gasoline from B to burn a house down. B sells A the gasoline and A burns down the house. B is not liable as an accomplice to arson (unless it was illegal to sell gasoline in cans or B charged A twice his usual price because of what A was using the gasoline for).

C. SCOPE OF LIABILITY

An accomplice is responsible for the crimes he did or counseled ***and*** for any other crimes committed in the course of committing the crime contemplated, as long as the other crimes were ***probable or foreseeable.***

Example: A commands B to burn C's house, and B does so. The fire spreads to X's house, and it was foreseeable that it would do so. A is an accomplice to the burning of X's house.

1. Inability to Be Principal No Bar to Liability as Accomplice

One who may not be convicted of being a principal may be convicted of being an accomplice.

Example: At common law, a woman may not be convicted of rape as a principal, but may be convicted of that crime as an accomplice.

2. **Exclusions from Liability**

Under some circumstances, a person who would otherwise be liable as an accomplice is not subject to conviction, either because of a legislative intent to exempt him or because he has a special defense.

a. **Members of the Protected Class**

If the statute is intended to protect members of a limited class from exploitation or overbearing, members of that class are presumed to be immune from liability, even if they participate in the crime in a manner that would otherwise make them liable.

Example: A is charged with transporting B, a woman, in interstate commerce for immoral purposes; B is charged as an accomplice, on the ground that she encouraged and assisted A. Is B guilty? *Held:* No. The statute was intended to protect women, and thus the woman transported cannot be convicted.

b. **Necessary Parties Not Provided For**

If a statute defines a crime in a way that necessarily involves more than one participant and provides for the liability of only one participant, it is presumed that the legislative intent was to immunize the other participant from liability as an accomplice. The rule is most often applied to statutes making the sale of certain items a criminal offense.

Example: A asked B to sell her some heroin. B did so. Both were apprehended. B was charged as a principal for the sale of narcotics; A was charged as an accomplice. Is A subject to conviction? *Held:* No. Since the statute prohibiting sale does not mention the liability of the buyer, the presumed legislative intent is to exempt her.

c. **Withdrawal**

One who has rendered encouragement or aid to another may avoid liability as an accomplice if he voluntarily withdraws from the crime before it is actually committed by the principal. What is necessary for an effective withdrawal ***depends upon what the person initially did***.

(i) If the person merely ***encouraged*** the commission of the crime, withdrawal requires that he ***repudiate*** this encouragement.

(ii) If the person assisted by ***providing some material*** to the principal, withdrawal requires at least that the person attempt to ***neutralize this assistance***, *e.g.,* by doing everything possible to retrieve the material provided.

If it is impossible to withdraw by these methods, an alternative means of withdrawing is to ***notify authorities*** or take some other action to prevent the commission of the offense. In any case, the withdrawal must occur ***before*** the chain of events leading to the commission of the crime becomes unstoppable.

Example: B expresses a desire to kill C. A encourages him to do so, and provides him with a gun. Later, A changes his mind. He seeks B out, and tells B that his earlier position was wrong and that B should not kill C. He also gets his gun back. Nevertheless, B obtains another gun and kills C. Is A liable as an accomplice? *Held:* No, since he did all that was possible to render his encouragement and assistance ineffective before B's plan to kill C became unstoppable.

IV. INCHOATE OFFENSES

A. IN GENERAL

The inchoate offenses are solicitation, attempt, and conspiracy. They are quite frequently considered felonies. An inchoate offense is committed prior to and in preparation for what may be a more serious offense. It is a complete offense in itself, even though the act to be done may not have been completed. At common law under the doctrine of merger, inchoate offenses were regarded as misdemeanors; if the principal offense was carried out, they were considered felonies. The doctrine of merger has been abandoned in many jurisdictions in cases involving a conspiracy, allowing an accused to be convicted of ***both*** conspiracy and the principal offense. However, an accused ***cannot*** be convicted of either attempt or solicitation ***and*** the principal offense.

B. SOLICITATION

At common law it was a misdemeanor to solicit another to commit a felony or an act that would breach the peace or obstruct justice. Modern statutes often retain the crime of solicitation, but some restrict it to the solicitation of certain serious felonies.

1. Elements

Solicitation consists of inciting, counseling, advising, inducing, urging, or commanding another to commit a felony with the specific ***intent that the person solicited commit the crime*** (general approval or agreement is insufficient). The offense is complete at the time the solicitation is made. It is not necessary that the person solicited agree to commit the crime or do anything in response. (If the person solicited committed the crime, the solicitor would be liable for the crime as a party; if the person solicited proceeded far enough to be liable for attempt, the solicitor would be a party to that attempt.)

2. Attempt Distinguished

Solicitation generally is not an attempt to commit the crime solicited. This distinction is important in jurisdictions where there is no crime of solicitation or where the crime of solicitation does not extend to as many offenses as does the crime of attempt.

3. Defenses and Potential Defenses

a. Factual Impossibility No Defense

It is not a defense that the solicitation could not have been successful, as where the person solicited was a police undercover agent. The culpability of the solicitor is measured by the circumstances as she believed them to be.

b. Withdrawal or Renunciation No Defense

Once the solicitation has been made, it is generally no defense that the solicitor changed her mind or countermanded her advice or urging. The M.P.C. recognizes renunciation as a defense if the defendant prevents the commission of the crime, such as by persuading the person solicited not to commit the crime.

c. Exemption from Intended Crime Is Defense

If the solicitor could not be guilty of the intended crime because of a legislative intent to exempt her, she would have a defense. For example, a minor female could not be found guilty of solicitation of statutory rape by urging a man to have intercourse with her, because she could not be guilty of the completed crime.

C. CONSPIRACY

1. Introduction

At common law, a conspiracy was defined as a combination or agreement between two or more persons to accomplish some criminal or unlawful purpose, or to accomplish a lawful purpose by unlawful means. Recent state codifications require that the object of the conspiracy be a specifically proscribed offense. Yet many states essentially codify the expansive common law notion by making it a crime to conspire to commit acts injurious to the public welfare. The Supreme Court has indicated that such statutes are unconstitutionally vague unless construed narrowly.

a. No Merger—Conviction for Conspiracy and Completed Crime

Under the old rule, if the conspirators were successful and completed their crime, the crime of conspiracy "merged" into the completed crime. While the members of the agreement could be convicted of the completed crime, they could not be convicted of the conspiracy. This is no longer the law in most jurisdictions. (*See* the discussion of merger in I.H., *supra.*) Now, if the conspirators are successful, they can be convicted of both criminal conspiracy and the crime they committed pursuant to the conspiracy.

b. Liability of One Conspirator for Crimes Committed by Other Conspirators

One conspirator may, by virtue of his participation in the scheme, meet the requirements for "aiding and abetting" the commission of crimes by his co-conspirators and therefore be liable for those crimes as an accomplice. Even if the conspirator did not have the sufficient mental state for accomplice liability, a separate doctrine provides that each conspirator may be liable for the crimes of all other conspirators if ***two requirements*** are met:

(i) The ***crimes were committed in furtherance*** of the objectives of the conspiracy; and

(ii) The crimes were "a natural and probable consequence" of the conspiracy, *i.e.,* ***foreseeable.***

This doctrine applies only if the conspirator has not made a legally effective withdrawal from the conspiracy before the commission of the crime by the co-conspirator. (*See* 4.b., *infra.*)

c. Attempt Distinguished

In attempt cases, the law requires that there be a ***substantial step*** toward commission of the crime. In conspiracy cases, at least at common law, the agreement itself is normally sufficient to constitute the crime. Hence, in common law conspiracy cases the law intervenes at an earlier stage than the planning of the crime. The reason for this is that the secret activity is potentially more dangerous to society and, since a group is involved, it is more difficult for one person to stop the activity once the agreement has been made.

2. Elements

The elements of conspiracy at common law are as follows:

(i) An ***agreement between two or more*** persons;

(ii) An ***intent to enter into an agreement***; and

(iii) An ***intent to achieve the objective*** of the agreement.

Under the traditional definition of conspiracy, the agreement itself was the culpable act (the actus reus). Today, a majority of states require an ***overt act*** in furtherance of the conspiracy, but mere preparation will usually suffice.

a. Agreement Requirement

The parties must agree to accomplish the same objective by mutual action. The agreement need not be express. The existence of an agreement may be shown by a concert of action on the part of the conspirators over a period of time under circumstances showing that they were aware of the purpose and existence of the conspiracy and agreed to participate in the common purpose. Where multiple crimes and multiple parties are involved, there are often problems in deciding whether there is a single conspiracy or several smaller conspiracies.

1) Object of the Agreement

At common law, it was not necessary that there be an agreement to commit a crime in order to find a criminal conspiracy. It was only necessary that the object of the agreement was something "unlawful" or that the parties intended to accomplish something lawful by "unlawful" means. "Unlawful" in this context covered a variety of noncriminal matters that were regarded as contrary to the public welfare. But the modern trend is to limit criminal conspiracies to agreements to ***commit crimes***.

2) Multiple Crimes

Where the same parties perform a number of crimes over an extended period of time, is each individual crime the subject of a separate conspiracy or are all the crimes to be treated as arising out of one overriding conspiracy? If there is an initial agreement among the parties to engage in a ***course of criminal conduct*** constituting all the crimes, then there is only ***one conspiracy***.

Example: A and B agree to commit one bank robbery each month for one year. Even though they plan to rob 12 banks, they are guilty of only one conspiracy.

3) Number of Conspiracies in Multiple Party Situations

In complex situations involving numerous parties, it is sometimes important to determine how many conspiracies existed and who conspired with whom. There are two general ways to characterize situations of this sort.

a) "Chain" Relationship—One Large Conspiracy

If there is a series of agreements, all of which are regarded as part of a single large scheme in which all of the parties to the subagreements are interested, the situation will be regarded as one large conspiracy involving all of the participants. The subagreements will be characterized as "links" in the overall "chain" relationship.

b) **"Hub-and-Spoke" Relationships—Multiple Conspiracies**
One participant may enter into a number of subagreements, each involving ***different persons***. All of the agreements are similar in that they have ***one common member***. However, if it is established that the ***subagreements are reasonably independent of each other***—if, for example, the members of each agreement (other than the common member) have little or no interest in whether the other agreements succeed—the situation will be regarded as involving numerous different and independent conspiracies. The common member can be characterized as the "hub" (as of a wheel) and each subagreement as a "spoke." The common member is, of course, a member of each conspiracy. But the members of each "spoke" conspiracy are not members of the other "spoke" conspiracies and have not conspired with the members of those conspiracies.

Examples: 1) In a large narcotics ring, a smuggler brings heroin into the country and sells it to a wholesaler. The wholesaler sells it to numerous retailers. How many conspiracies? One, because this is a "chain" situation. Because the smuggler-wholesaler agreement and the wholesaler-retailers agreements were all part of a scheme in which all participants were interested, there is only one conspiracy.

2) Brown agreed with A, B, and C to help each of them make fraudulent loan applications. Each application was to be an independent action and the applicants in one situation had no interest in whether the other fraudulent applications were successful. How many conspiracies? Three: Brown with A, Brown with B, and Brown with C. Since the subagreements were not part of an overall scheme in which A, B, and C all were interested, this is a "hub-and-spoke" situation. A has not conspired with B and C, but only with Brown.

4) **Implications of Requirement of Two or More Parties**
A conspiracy must involve a "meeting of the minds" between at least two independent persons. Moreover, at common law there must be a meeting of at least two "guilty minds," *i.e.,* between two persons who are actually committing themselves to the scheme. If one person in a two-party conspiracy is only feigning agreement (*e.g.,* an undercover police officer), the other person cannot be convicted of conspiracy (unless the M.P.C. unilateral approach, discussed below, is followed). This requirement of two guilty parties gives rise to a number of problems.

a) **Husband and Wife**
At common law, a husband and wife could not conspire together because the law viewed them as one person. They could, however, be guilty of conspiracy with a third person. This distinction has been abandoned in virtually all states today.

b) **Corporation and Agent**
Since a corporation can act only through an agent, it has been held that there can be no conspiracy between the corporation and a single agent acting on

behalf of the corporation. There is a split of authority as to whether the agents can be deemed co-conspirators. Note that a corporation may be a party to a conspiracy with other corporations or individuals who are not agents of the corporation.

c) **Wharton-Type Problems**

(1) **Wharton Rule**
Where two or more people are necessary for the commission of the substantive offense (*e.g.,* adultery, dueling, sale of contraband), the "Wharton rule" (named after its author) states that there is ***no crime of conspiracy unless more parties participate in the agreement than are necessary for the crime***. Some courts hold that if the Wharton rule applies, there can never be a conviction for conspiracy. Others hold that if the rule applies, it prohibits conviction for both conspiracy and the crime that the parties agreed to commit.

Example: A and B agree to meet at dawn to engage in a duel. They are apprehended before daybreak, however. Dueling is a crime in the jurisdiction, and A is charged with conspiracy to commit dueling. Does A have a defense? Yes. The Wharton rule applies and prevents liability.

Compare: The Wharton rule does not apply to agreements with "***necessary parties not provided for***" (*see* III.C.2.b., *supra*). Thus, where a state statute prohibiting the sale of narcotics imposes criminal liability only on the seller and not on the buyer, both the buyer and seller may be guilty of conspiracy to sell narcotics (even though both parties are necessary for commission of the substantive offense).

(2) **Agreement with Person in "Protected Class"**
If members of a conspiracy agree to commit an act that violates a statute that was designed to protect persons within a given class, ***a person within that class*** cannot be guilty of the crime itself. (*See* III.C.2.a., *supra.*) Moreover, she ***cannot be guilty of a conspiracy*** to commit that crime. It follows, then, that between two people, the person ***not*** in the protected class cannot be guilty of criminal conspiracy on the basis of an agreement with the person in the protected class.

Example: A, a woman, and B, a man, agreed on a scheme in which A would be transported over state lines for purposes of prostitution. Is B guilty of criminal conspiracy? No. The act of transporting women over state lines for immoral purposes violates a statute (the Mann Act) that was designed to protect women; thus, A could not be guilty of a violation of the Act and cannot be guilty of conspiracy to violate the Act. Therefore, B cannot be guilty of criminal conspiracy because there were not two guilty parties to the agreement.

d) **Effect of Acquittal of Other Conspirators**
A conspiracy requires two guilty parties at common law. Thus, in most courts, the acquittal of ***all*** persons with whom a defendant is alleged to have conspired precludes conviction of the remaining defendant. This rule does ***not*** apply where the other parties are not apprehended, are charged with lesser offenses, or are no longer being prosecuted (*nolle prosequi*).

e) **Compare Unilateral (Model Penal Code) Approach**
Under the M.P.C.'s unilateral approach, conspiracy is established by showing that the defendant "agreed" with another to commit the crime (regardless of whether the other person shared in that commitment); it is not necessary to show an actual agreement between two or more persons. Thus, the fact that all the other parties to the conspiracy have been acquitted or were only feigning agreement will ***not*** prevent the defendant's conviction.

b. **Mental State—Specific Intent**
Conspiracy is a ***specific intent*** crime. There are two different intents that are necessary: intent to agree and intent to achieve the objective of the conspiracy.

1) **Intent to Agree**
It is very difficult to separate the intent to agree from the act of agreement. Hence, most courts do not even try. For bar exam purposes, the only thing that is important to remember is that the intent to agree can be ***inferred*** from conduct.

2) **Intent to Achieve Objective**
The defendant must intend to achieve the objective of the conspiracy. This intent must be established as to ***each*** individual defendant. Under the common law approach, a minimum of two persons must intend to achieve the same purpose; *i.e.,* there must be a "meeting of guilty minds."
Example: A, B, and C agree to steal D's car, but only A and B intend to keep it permanently; C intends to return it to D. Only A and B are guilty of conspiracy to commit larceny, because only they had the intent to permanently deprive D of his car. If only A so intended, and both B and C intended to return the car, then A could not be liable for conspiracy to commit larceny.

3) **Intent to Facilitate a Conspiracy**
A person who acts with the intent to facilitate a conspiracy may thereby become a member of the conspiracy. However, ***intent cannot be inferred from mere knowledge***. Therefore, a merchant who sells a good in the ordinary course of business that he knows will be used to further a conspiracy does not thereby join the conspiracy. On the other hand, a merchant may be held to have joined the conspiracy if the good sold is a specialty item that cannot easily be obtained elsewhere or if the merchant otherwise has a stake in the criminal venture (*e.g.,* by raising the price of the good because of the buyer's purpose).

4) **"Corrupt Motive" Not Required**
The majority rule is that the parties to a conspiracy need not have been aware that their plan was an illegal one. A minority of courts have held to the contrary,

however, reasoning that a requirement of evil motive flows implicitly from the word conspiracy. According to the "corrupt motive" doctrine, which operates as an exception to the general rule that ignorance of the law will not excuse criminal liability, the parties to a conspiracy must have known that their objective was criminal. The corrupt motive doctrine is usually limited to offenses that are malum prohibitum (*see* I.D.2., *supra*).

5) **Conspiracy to Commit "Strict Liability" Crimes**
Conspiracy is a specific intent crime. Therefore, in most jurisdictions, a conspiracy to commit a "strict liability" crime (for which intent is not required) requires intent.

Example: A and B agree on a scheme to persuade C, a 12-year-old girl, to have intercourse with one of them. They believe she is 21, but this would not be a defense to the completed crime of statutory rape. Can they be convicted of conspiracy to commit statutory rape? No, because conspiracy to commit statutory rape requires knowledge of the victim's age even though the completed crime does not.

c. **Overt Act**
At common law, the conspiracy was complete when the agreement with the requisite intent was reached. This is still the law in some states. Most states, however, require that an ***act in furtherance of the conspiracy*** be performed. If an overt act is required, any act in pursuit of the conspiracy will suffice, even an act of mere preparation. The act may be performed by any one of the conspirators.

Example: A, B, and C agreed to rob a bank. A, unbeknownst to B and C, rents a car to be used in the getaway. If an overt act is required, the renting of a car is sufficient.

3. **Termination of Conspiracy**
Since acts or declarations of co-conspirators are admissible only if made in furtherance of the conspiracy, it becomes critically important to determine when the conspiracy ends. This is also important for statute of limitations purposes.

a. **Acts of Concealment**
Since most criminals attempt to conceal the fact that they have committed a crime, courts have generally taken the view that ***evidence of overt acts of concealment is not sufficient to make the act of concealment part of the conspiracy***. In other words, there must be direct evidence that the parties specifically agreed, prior to commission of the crime, that they would act in a certain way to conceal the fact that they had committed the crime.

Example: Suppose the statute of limitations for tax evasion is six years. If A and B conspire to commit tax evasion, does their conspiracy end at the time of the commission of the fraud, or does it extend for the six years during which time A and B presumably endeavor to keep their crime a secret? The answer depends upon whether at the time of the agreement to commit tax evasion there was also a specific subsidiary agreement to conceal the crime until the statute of limitations had run. If there was no such specific agreement, as, for example, if A and B were not aware of the statute of limitations, then the conspiracy does not extend beyond the completion of the act of evasion.

b. Government Frustration of Conspiracy's Objective

The government's defeat of the conspiracy's ultimate objective does not automatically terminate the conspiracy. [United States v. Jimenez-Recio, 537 U.S. 270 (2003)]

Example: Police stop A, who was transporting illegal drugs in his vehicle. Instead of simply arresting A, the police instead decide to set up a "sting" operation. They drive the vehicle to a preset location, and instruct A to contact B, a drug dealer, in accordance with A and B's original plan. B tells A that he will call C and D and have them pick up the vehicle with the drugs. C and D do so. C and D can be convicted of conspiracy to distribute illegal drugs. The fact that the government defeated the conspiracy's objective does not terminate the conspiracy, and impossibility is no defense to a charge of conspiracy (*see* below).

4. Defenses

a. Factual Impossibility—No Defense

Factual impossibility is ***not a defense*** to conspiracy. Even if it was factually impossible to achieve the ultimate objective of the conspiracy, the defendants can be found guilty of the conspiracy itself.

Example: A and B agree to rape a woman whom they believe is asleep. In fact, she is dead. A and B may be convicted of conspiracy to rape.

b. Withdrawal—No Defense to Conspiracy Charge

The general rule is that withdrawal from a conspiracy is ***not a defense*** to a charge of conspiracy, because the conspiracy is complete as soon as the agreement is made and an overt act is committed. The M.P.C. recognizes voluntary withdrawal as a defense if the defendant thwarts the success of the conspiracy (*e.g.,* by informing the police).

1) Defense to Subsequent Crimes of Co-Conspirators

A person may limit his liability for subsequent acts of the other members of the conspiracy, including the target crime for which the conspiracy was formed, if he withdraws. To withdraw, he must perform an affirmative act that ***notifies all members*** of the conspiracy, and such notice must be given in time for them to have the opportunity to abandon their plans. (Note that if he has also provided material assistance so as to be liable as an accomplice, he must attempt to neutralize the assistance (*see* III.C.2.c., *supra*).)

5. Punishment

Because a defendant may be convicted of both conspiracy and the completed crime, most jurisdictions have enacted express penalty provisions for conspiracies. Some statutes make conspiracy a misdemeanor regardless of its objective; some provide a permissible maximum sentence regardless of the objective; and still others provide different maximums depending upon the objective. Note that because the punishment for conspiracy usually is not expressed as a fraction of the punishment for the completed crime, the punishment for conspiracy may be more severe than the punishment for the completed crime.

D. ATTEMPT

A criminal attempt is an act that, although done with the intention of committing a crime, falls short of completing the crime. An attempt therefore consists of two elements: (i) a specific intent to commit the crime, and (ii) an overt act in furtherance of that intent.

1. Intent

The defendant must have the intent to perform an act and obtain a result that, if achieved, would constitute a crime.

a. Attempt Requires Specific Intent

Regardless of the intent required for a completed offense, an attempt always requires a ***specific intent***. For example, attempted murder requires the specific ***intent to kill*** another person, even though the mens rea for murder itself does not necessarily require a specific intent to kill (*see* VII.C.2.a.1), *infra*).

b. Attempt to Commit Negligent Crimes Is Logically Impossible

A crime defined as the negligent production of a result cannot be attempted, because if there were an intent to cause such a result, the appropriate offense would be attempt to intentionally commit the crime rather than attempt to negligently cause the harm.

c. Attempt to Commit Strict Liability Crimes Requires Intent

Although a strict liability crime does not require criminal intent, to attempt a strict liability crime the defendant must act with the intent to bring about the proscribed result.

2. Overt Act

The defendant must have committed an act ***beyond mere preparation*** for the offense. Several tests have been used to determine whether the act requirement for attempt liability has been satisfied:

a. Traditional Rule—Proximity Test

Traditionally, courts used a proximity approach; *i.e.,* they have evaluated the act based on how close the defendant came to completing the offense. Under the typical proximity test, attempt requires an act that is dangerously close to success.

Example: Pointing a loaded gun at an intended victim and pulling the trigger is sufficient under the proximity test, but going to the store to purchase bullets or even driving to the intended victim's house is insufficient. [*See* People v. Rizzo, 246 N.Y. 334 (1927)]

b. Majority Rule—Model Penal Code Test

The M.P.C. and most state criminal codes require that the act or omission constitute a "substantial step in a course of conduct planned to culminate in the commission of the crime." In addition, an act will not qualify as a substantial step unless it is strong corroboration of the actor's criminal purpose.

3. Defenses to Liability for Attempt

a. Impossibility of Success

Factual impossibility traditionally has been distinguished from legal impossibility, and should be distinguished for exam purposes.

1) **Legal Impossibility Is Always a Defense**
Legal impossibility arises only when the defendant did, or intended to do, acts that would not constitute a crime under any circumstances. So defined, ***all*** states (and the M.P.C.) will recognize this type of legal impossibility.
Example: To celebrate the Fourth of July, D drives to a neighboring state to purchase his favorite type of fireworks and brings them back into his state, which he believes is illegal. In fact, there is no law against bringing that particular type of fireworks into the state. May D be charged or convicted with an attempt to bring illegal fireworks into the state? No. None of the acts that D committed and intended to commit constitutes a crime, so he cannot be charged with an attempt based on those acts.

a) **Effect of Statute or Case Abolishing Impossibility Defenses**
Even a jurisdiction with a statute or case law purporting to do away with impossibility defenses will recognize the above type of legal impossibility. Such statutes ordinarily contain a provision that the defendant must be charged with the attempt ***of a crime***, thus implicitly recognizing a true legal impossibility defense. Such statutes or cases generally have the effect of preventing factual impossibility from becoming a good defense by its being labeled as legal impossibility.

2) **Factual Impossibility Is No Defense**
It is no defense to attempt that it would have been factually impossible for the defendant to complete her plan, *i.e.,* do all of those things that she intended to do. This is factual impossibility.
Example: A stops B on the street, points a gun at her, and asks her to hand over her money. Unbeknownst to A, B has no money. Is A guilty of attempted robbery? Yes.

a) **Includes Impossibility Due to Attendant Circumstances**
Impossibility is also no defense when the defendant engages in conduct while mistaken about certain attendant circumstances: Had the circumstances been as she believed they were, what she set out to do would be a crime. However, because the circumstances were otherwise, what she has set out to do will not be a crime. Courts traditionally have split on whether this is legal or factual impossibility, but the ***better view*** is that it is factual impossibility and not a defense.
Example: Goods are stolen from A by B. B is apprehended and the goods are recovered. Police secure A's permission to use the goods to trap C, a suspected fence. On police orders, B takes the goods to C and offers to sell them, telling C that they are stolen. C buys them. Since the goods are no longer stolen (they are being used with the owner's permission), C is not guilty of receipt of stolen goods. Is C guilty of attempt to receive stolen goods? In most states and under the M.P.C., yes, because C, with the requisite culpability, has engaged in conduct that would constitute receipt of stolen property if the circumstances were as he believed them to be.

3) **Distinguishing Between Factual and Legal Impossibility**
The bright-line division between legal and factual impossibility above is a bit of an artifice; courts are not as consistent in distinguishing the two. However, for exam purposes, you should use the "better view" outlined above and define legal impossibility narrowly. Ask yourself: "If the defendant were able to complete all of the acts that he intended to do, and if all of the attendant circumstances actually were as the defendant believed them to be, would the defendant have committed a crime?" The answer usually will be yes, in which case the impossibility is factual and not a defense. In the unusual case where the answer is no, the defendant most likely has a legal impossibility defense.

b. **Abandonment**
If a defendant has, with the required intent, gone beyond preparation, may she escape liability by abandoning her plans? The majority rule is that abandonment is ***never a defense***. The M.P.C. approach is that ***withdrawal will be a defense but only if:***

1) It is ***fully voluntary*** and not made because of the difficulty of completing the crime or because of an increased risk of apprehension; and

2) It is a ***complete abandonment*** of the plan made under circumstances manifesting a renunciation of criminal purpose, not just a decision to postpone committing it or to find another victim.

4. **Prosecution for Attempt**
A defendant charged with a completed crime may be found guilty of either the completed crime or an attempt to commit the crime as long as the evidence presented supports such a verdict. The reverse is not true. A defendant charged only with attempt may not be convicted of the completed crime.

5. **Punishment for Attempt**
Most states punish attempt less severely than the crime attempted. The most common statutory scheme permits a penalty up to one-half the maximum penalty for the completed crime, with a specific maximum set for attempts to commit crimes punishable by death or life imprisonment. Under the M.P.C. and some state statutes, an attempt may be punished to the same extent as the completed crime, except for capital crimes and the most serious felonies.

V. RESPONSIBILITY AND CRIMINAL CAPACITY

A. INSANITY
The insanity defense exempts certain defendants because of the existence of an abnormal mental condition at the time of the crime. The various formulations differ significantly on what effects a mental illness must have had to entitle the defendant to an acquittal. Note that insanity is a ***legal term*** rather than a psychiatric one. Furthermore, insanity is a generic term comprising many possible mental abnormalities, all of which have only one thing in common: they are recognized by law as dictating certain legal consequences. Usually, the cause of a defendant's mental illness or insanity is irrelevant in determining the legal consequences.

1. **Formulations of Insanity Defense**

a. ***M'Naghten* Rule**

1) **Elements**
The traditional *M'Naghten* rule provides that a defendant is entitled to an acquittal if the proof establishes that:

a) A ***disease*** of the mind

b) ***Caused a defect*** of reason

c) Such that the defendant ***lacked the ability at the time*** of his actions to either:

(1) Know the ***wrongfulness*** of his actions; or

(2) Understand the ***nature and quality*** of his actions.

2) **Application**

a) **Defendant with Delusions**
If the defendant suffered from delusions (false beliefs), it is necessary to determine whether his actions would have been criminal if the facts had been as he believed them to be.
Example: A, because of a mental illness, believed B wanted to kill him. A killed B. Is A entitled to an acquittal on insanity grounds under the *M'Naghten* rule? *Held:* No. Even if A's delusion had been accurate, he would not have been legally entitled to kill B simply because B wanted to kill him.

b) **Belief that Acts Are Morally Right**
A defendant is not entitled to an acquittal merely because he believes his acts are morally right, unless he has lost the capacity to recognize that they are regarded by society as wrong.

c) **Inability to Control Oneself**
Under the traditional interpretation given to the *M'Naghten* rule, it is irrelevant that the defendant may have been unable to control himself and avoid committing the crime. Loss of control because of mental illness is ***no defense***.

3) **Evidence Admissible**
In practice, the *M'Naghten* rule does not unduly restrict the evidence heard by juries. Most jurisdictions admit any evidence that reasonably tends to show the mental condition of the defendant at the time of the crime.

b. **Irresistible Impulse Test**
Under the irresistible impulse test, a defendant is entitled to an acquittal if the proof establishes that because of mental illness he was ***unable to control his actions or to conform his conduct to the law***. Contrary to what the name irresistible impulse might

imply, this inability need not come upon the defendant suddenly. Some jurisdictions apply both *M'Naghten* and the irresistible impulse test. Thus, a person is entitled to an acquittal if he meets either test.

c. ***Durham* (or New Hampshire) Test**
Under the *Durham* rule, a defendant is entitled to an acquittal if the proof establishes that his crime was the "***product of mental disease or defect.***" A crime is a "product of" the disease if it would not have been committed ***but for*** the disease. In this way, the *Durham* test is broader than either the *M'Naghten* or irresistible impulse tests; it was intended primarily to give psychiatrists greater liberty to testify concerning the defendant's mental condition. Although severely criticized for being unduly vague, the *Durham* rule was followed in the District of Columbia from 1954 until 1972, at which time the court of appeals replaced it with the A.L.I. test. (*See* below.) It remains the law in a few jurisdictions.

d. **American Law Institute ("A.L.I.") or Model Penal Code Test**
Under this test, the defendant is entitled to an acquittal if the proof shows that he suffered from a ***mental disease*** or defect and as a result ***lacked substantial capacity*** to either:

(i) ***Appreciate the criminality*** (wrongfulness) of his conduct; or

(ii) ***Conform his conduct*** to the requirements of law.

This test combines the *M'Naghten* and the irresistible impulse tests by allowing for the impairment of both cognitive and volitional capacity.

2. **Exclusion of "Psychopaths"**
Many formulations (including the A.L.I. test) expressly exclude the psychopathic criminal—the person who repeatedly commits crimes without experiencing guilt. This is usually accomplished by defining "mental illness" so as to exclude any abnormality evidenced only by repeated antisocial conduct. "Sociopathic" and "psychopathic" are synonymous.

3. **Refusal to Participate in Psychiatric Examination**
If the defendant does not put his mental state in issue and does not plan to use an insanity defense, he may refuse to participate in a court-ordered psychiatric examination to determine competency to stand trial. If he does not refuse, he is entitled to the *Miranda* warnings prior to such an examination.

4. **Procedural Issues Related to Insanity Defense**
Several important procedural matters are raised by the insanity defense.

a. **Burdens of Proof**

1) **Presumption of Sanity and Burden of Producing Evidence**
All defendants are presumed sane. The insanity issue is not raised, then, until the defendant comes forward with some evidence tending to show that he was insane under the applicable test. Depending upon the jurisdiction, this burden is carried either by a mere shred (or scintilla) of evidence, or by evidence sufficient to raise a reasonable doubt as to sanity.

2) **Burden of Persuasion**
In some jurisdictions and under the M.P.C., once the issue has been raised, the prosecution must prove the defendant was sane beyond a reasonable doubt. In others, the defendant must prove his insanity, generally by a preponderance of the evidence. Federal courts require the defendant to prove insanity by clear and convincing evidence.

b. **When Defense May Be Raised and Who May Raise It**

1) **Defense May Be Raised After Arraignment**
The insanity defense may be raised at the arraignment when the plea is taken, but the defendant need not raise it then. A simple "not guilty" at that time does not waive the right to raise the defense at some future time. A minority of jurisdictions, however, require that the defendant give reasonable notice to the prosecution of an intent to raise the defense at trial.

2) **Neither Prosecutor Nor Judge May Raise Defense for Competent Defendant**
Neither a prosecutor nor a judge can assert the insanity defense when a competent defendant, who is adequately represented, has elected not to do so.

c. **Pretrial Psychiatric Examination**

1) **Right to Support Services for Defense**
Where a defendant has made a preliminary showing that it is likely he will be able to use the insanity defense, the state must provide a psychiatrist for the preparation of the defense. Where the state presents evidence that the defendant is likely to be dangerous in the future, the defendant is entitled to psychiatric examination and testimony in the sentencing proceeding. [Ake v. Oklahoma, 470 U.S. 68 (1985)]

2) **No Privilege Against Self-Incrimination**
At the present time, a defendant has no right to refuse to be examined by a psychiatrist appointed to aid the court in the resolution of his insanity plea. However, a defendant who does not put his mental state in issue is entitled to the *Miranda* warnings before he may be compelled to undergo a court-ordered competency examination; the defendant may then refuse to be examined.

5. **Post-Acquittal Commitment to Mental Institution**

a. **Committed Until Cured**
In most jurisdictions, acquittal by reason of insanity puts into operation a procedure by which the acquitted defendant may be committed to a mental institution until cured. In some jurisdictions, such commitment is possible only if it is proven that the defendant is presently mentally ill and dangerous. In others, commitment follows automatically.

b. **Confinement May Exceed Maximum Period of Incarceration Carried by Offense**
The confinement of an insanity acquittee in a mental hospital, based solely on the trial court's finding of insanity by a preponderance of the evidence, may last until he has regained his sanity or is no longer dangerous. This ***does not deny due process*** even if the result is confinement for a period longer than the maximum period of incarceration

carried by his offense. Nor is the insanity acquittee entitled, at the end of the statutory maximum incarceration period, to a civil commitment hearing at which proof of his insanity would have to be established by clear and convincing evidence. [Jones v. United States, 463 U.S. 354 (1983)]

6. Mental Condition During Criminal Proceedings

In addition to being a defense to criminal liability, the abnormal mental condition of a defendant is relevant at two other stages of the legal proceeding.

a. Incompetency to Stand Trial

Under the Due Process Clause of the United States Constitution, a defendant may not be tried, convicted, or sentenced if, as a result of a mental disease or defect, he is ***unable***:

(i) ***To understand the nature of the proceedings*** being brought against him; or

(ii) ***To assist his lawyer*** in the preparation of his defense.

The Due Process Clause prevents a defendant from being declared incompetent without notice and a hearing. Many jurisdictions grant a right to a jury determination of competence. A finding of incompetence will suspend the criminal proceedings and invariably ***result in commitment*** until such time as the defendant regains competence. The Constitution may demand that the defendant's hospitalization be limited to a reasonable period of time necessary to decide whether there is a likelihood of recovery in the near future.

b. Incompetency at Time of Execution

A defendant may not be executed if he is incapable of understanding the nature and purpose of the punishment. Modern statutes often permit only the warden to raise this issue. Some expressly provide for a jury determination.

7. Limits on Testimony Regarding Sanity Issue

About half the states limit evidence on the issue of insanity to expert psychiatric testimony. The M.P.C. rejects this approach, and would allow any type of evidence relevant to the issue of whether the defendant had the mental state required for the particular crime charged.

8. Diminished Capacity

Some states recognize the defense of "diminished capacity," under which the defendant may assert that as a result of a mental defect (*e.g.,* neurosis, obsessive compulsiveness, or dependent personality) short of insanity, he did not have the particular mental state (purpose, knowledge, recklessness, or negligence) required for the crime charged. Most states recognizing this defense limit it to specific intent crimes.

9. Bifurcated Trial

Some states, such as California, employ a two-stage trial process whenever the defense of insanity is raised. The first stage determines ***guilt*** (did the defendant actually perform the criminal act?); the second stage (which may be tried before a new jury at the judge's discretion) determines ***insanity*** (was the defendant legally insane at the time he performed the act?).

B. INTOXICATION

Intoxication may be caused by ***any substance***. Alcohol, drugs, and medicine are the most frequent.

Evidence of intoxication may be raised whenever the intoxication negates the existence of an element of a crime. The law generally distinguishes between voluntary and involuntary intoxication.

1. **Voluntary Intoxication**
Intoxication is voluntary (self-induced) if it is the result of the intentional taking without duress of a substance known to be intoxicating. The person need not have intended to become intoxicated.

a. **Defense to Specific Intent Crimes**
Voluntary intoxication evidence may be offered, when the defendant is charged with a crime that requires ***purpose*** (***intent***) ***or knowledge***, to establish that the intoxication prevented the defendant from formulating the requisite intent. Thus, it may be a good defense to ***specific intent*** crimes, but usually will not be a sufficient defense to general intent crimes. The defense is not available if the defendant purposely becomes intoxicated in order to establish the defense.

b. **No Defense to Crimes Requiring Malice or Recklessness**
Voluntary intoxication is not a defense to crimes requiring malice, recklessness, or negligence, or crimes of strict liability. Thus, voluntary intoxication is not a defense to common law murder, which requires a mens rea of "malice aforethought" (*see* VII.C.2.a.1), *infra*).

Example: After drinking heavily, A breaks into a house, wrongly thinking it is her own. When surprised by B, the owner, A reacts with force, beating B with her fists. While driving home A is cited for speeding. Will A have a defense of intoxication: (i) to burglary? (Yes, if as a result she did not know that the house belonged to B or did not have the intent to commit a felony therein); (ii) to battery? (No, because as defined battery may be the result of recklessness); or (iii) to speeding? (No, because speeding is a strict liability offense).

c. **Defense to First Degree Murder, But Not Second Degree Murder**
It is generally held that voluntary intoxication may reduce first degree (premeditated) murder to second degree murder, but it will not reduce second degree murder to manslaughter. *Rationale:* In a jurisdiction that divides murder into degrees (*see* VII.C.3. *infra*), all murders are second degree murder unless the prosecution proves, *e.g.*, deliberation and premeditation. Common law "depraved heart" murders would fall into the second degree category. Although voluntary intoxication may negate the defendant's ability to deliberate and premeditate (first degree murder), it cannot negate the criminal recklessness required for depraved heart murder (second degree murder).

2. **Involuntary Intoxication**
Intoxication is involuntary only if it results from the taking of an intoxicating substance (i) ***without knowledge*** of its nature, (ii) ***under direct duress*** imposed by another, or (iii) ***pursuant to medical advice*** while unaware of the substance's intoxicating effect.

Involuntary intoxication may be ***treated as mental illness,*** in which case a defendant is entitled to acquittal if, because of the intoxication, she meets whatever test the jurisdiction has adopted for insanity.

3. **Relationship to Insanity**
Intoxication and insanity are two separate defenses. However, continuous, excessive drinking

or drug use may bring on actual insanity (*e.g.,* delirium tremens). Thus, a defendant may be able to claim both an intoxication defense and an insanity defense.

C. INFANCY

1. Common Law

At common law, the defense of lack of capacity to commit a crime by reason of infancy gave rise to three presumptions. ***Physical age*** (not mental age) ***at the time of the crime*** (not at the time of the trial) governs.

a. Under Seven—No Criminal Liability

Under the age of seven, a child could not be held responsible for any crime (conclusive presumption of incapability of knowing wrongfulness of acts).

b. Under Fourteen—Rebuttable Presumption of No Criminal Liability

Children between the ages of seven and 14 were presumed incapable of knowing the wrongfulness of their acts, but this presumption was rebuttable by clear proof that the defendant appreciated the nature and quality of his act (*e.g.,* conduct undertaken to conceal the crime). Note, however, that children under 14 were ***conclusively*** presumed incapable of committing ***rape***.

c. Over Fourteen—Adult

Children age 14 or older were treated as adults.

2. Modern Statutes

a. Some Have Abolished Presumptions

A number of modern statutes have abolished the presumptions of the common law and have provided that no child can be convicted of a crime until a stated age is reached, usually 13 or 14. Other states, however, retain the common law presumptions.

b. Juvenile Delinquency

All states have enacted some type of juvenile delinquency laws or have set up special juvenile or family courts. These laws ordinarily provide that with respect to conduct that would be deemed criminal if committed by an adult, the juvenile court has exclusive jurisdiction over children under a certain age, and concurrent jurisdiction (with the criminal courts) over older children. In the "concurrent jurisdiction" situation, the child must be "charged" with delinquency in juvenile court unless the juvenile court waives jurisdiction and authorizes the trial of the child as an adult in criminal court. In most jurisdictions, the common law immunity rules for infants do not apply in juvenile court because the primary goal is rehabilitation rather than punishment. The M.P.C. follows this approach, providing that the juvenile court has exclusive jurisdiction over minors younger than 16 and concurrent jurisdiction over 16- and 17-year-old minors.

VI. PRINCIPLES OF EXCULPATION

A. JUSTIFICATION

Under certain circumstances, the commission of a proscribed act is viewed by society as justified and hence not appropriate for criminal punishment. Generally, the defendant must raise the issue of justifiable use of force by introducing ***some*** evidence ("more than a scintilla") tending to show justification as an affirmative defense. Once she has done this, the state may require the prosecution to prove that the use of force was not justified, or it may impose on the defendant the burden of proving this affirmative defense by a preponderance of the evidence.

1. Self-Defense

a. Nondeadly Force

As a general rule, an individual who is without fault may use ***such force as reasonably appears necessary*** to protect herself from the imminent use of unlawful force upon herself. (*See* discussion *infra* on reasonableness and unlawful force.) There is ***no duty to retreat*** before using nondeadly force, even if retreat would result in no further harm to either party.

b. Deadly Force

A person may use deadly force in self-defense if (i) she is without fault, (ii) she is confronted with unlawful force, and (iii) she is threatened with imminent death or great bodily harm.

1) Without Fault

A person who has initiated an assault or provoked the other party will be considered the aggressor. (*See* discussion *infra.*)

2) Unlawful Force

The attacker must be using unlawful force (*i.e.,* force that constitutes a crime or a tort).

3) Threat of Imminent Death or Great Bodily Harm

The defendant must ***reasonably*** believe that she is faced with imminent death or great bodily harm if she does not respond with deadly force. The danger of harm must be a present one. There is no right to use deadly force if harm is merely threatened at a future time or the "attacker" has no present ability to carry out the threat.

Example: A, who has his arms tied behind his back, says to D, "I am going to kill you." D pulls out a gun and shoots A. No self-defense.

4) Retreat

Must a person retreat as far as possible before using deadly force, if such retreat is possible without the person endangering himself? For purposes of the examination, the ***majority rule*** is that there is ***no duty to retreat***. A person (other than the initial aggressor) may use deadly force in self-defense even if this could be avoided by retreating. Even in the minority of courts that follow a common law rule and impose a duty to retreat, retreat is only sometimes necessary. First, no retreat is necessary unless it can be made in complete safety. Second, no retreat is necessary in several special situations: (i) where the attack occurs in the victim's home; (ii) where the attack occurs while the victim is making a lawful arrest; and (iii) where the assailant is in the process of robbing the victim.

Example: A is standing in a public park feeding the birds. B walks up to A, pulls a knife from his pocket, and—as he comes closer to A—says, "I am going to kill you." A pulls a gun from her pocket and shoots B, killing him. Does A have a defense of self-defense? Under the majority rule the answer would be yes, because A had no duty to retreat before using deadly force, as long as the force was necessary to defend herself against imminent attack. Even under the minority approach the answer might be yes, because even if A was under a general duty to retreat before using deadly force, here it did not appear that such retreat could have been done in complete safety.

c. **Right of Aggressor to Use Self-Defense**
Generally, one who begins a fight has no right to use force in her own defense during that fight. But an aggressor can "regain" her right to use self-defense in two ways:

1) **Withdrawal**
An aggressor who, in good faith, effectively removes herself from the fight, and communicates to the other person her desire to remove herself, regains her right to use self-defense.

2) **Sudden Escalation**
If the victim of the initial aggression suddenly escalates a "minor" fight into one involving deadly force and does so without giving the aggressor the chance to withdraw, the aggressor may use force in her own defense.

2. **Defense of Others**
There are two issues in determining whether a person who has used force to defend another person is criminally liable for her acts.

a. **Relationship with Person Aided**
Must there be some special relationship between the defendant and the person in whose defense she acted? The majority rule is no. One may use force in defense of any other person if the other requirements of the defense are met. A few jurisdictions require that the person whom the defendant aided must either have been a member of the defendant's family or the defendant's servant or employer.

b. **Status of Person Aided**
A defendant has the defense of defense of others only if she reasonably believed that the person she assisted had the legal right to use force in his own defense. If in fact that person had no such legal right, does the defendant still have a defense? The better view is yes, because all that is necessary for the defense is the ***reasonable appearance of the right to use force***. In a minority of jurisdictions, however, the answer is no, because the defendant "steps into the shoes of the person she defends" and therefore has no defense if that person had no legal right to use force in self-defense.

3. **Defense of a Dwelling**

a. **Nondeadly Force**
A person is justified in the use of nondeadly force in defense of her dwelling when, and

to the extent that, she reasonably believes that such conduct is necessary to prevent or terminate another's unlawful entry into or attack upon her dwelling.

b. **Deadly Force**
One is generally justified in the use of deadly force in two situations.

1) **Tumultuous Entry Plus Personal Danger**
Use of deadly force is justifiable where the entry was made or attempted in a riotous, violent, or tumultuous manner ***and*** the person reasonably believes that the use of force is necessary to prevent a personal attack upon herself or another in the dwelling.

2) **Felony**
Use of deadly force is also justifiable where the person reasonably believes that such force is necessary to prevent the entry into the dwelling by a person who intends to commit a felony in the dwelling.

4. **Defense of Other Property**

a. **Nondeadly Force**
Nondeadly force may be used to defend property in one's possession from unlawful interference. In the case of real property, this means entry or trespass; in the case of personal property, this means removal or damage. The need to use force must reasonably appear imminent. Thus, force may not be used if a request to desist or refrain from the activity would suffice. In addition, the right is limited to property in one's possession. Force cannot be used to regain possession of property wrongfully taken, unless the person using it is in "immediate pursuit" of the taker.

b. **Deadly Force May Not Be Used**
Defense of property alone can never justify the use of deadly force. A person may use deadly force in the defense of property generally only in conjunction with another privileged use of force, *e.g.,* self-defense, defense of others, or to effectuate an arrest.

5. **Crime Prevention**

a. **Nondeadly Force**
Generally, one is privileged to use force to the extent that it reasonably appears necessary to prevent a felony, riot, or other serious breach of the peace, although some states (*e.g.,* California) have extended this to the prevention of any crime.

b. **Deadly Force**
The traditional rule was that deadly force could be used to prevent the commission of any felony, but the modern view is that deadly force may be used only if the crime is a "dangerous felony" involving risk to human life. This would include robbery, arson, burglary of a dwelling, etc.

6. **Use of Force to Effectuate Arrest**

a. **By Police Officer**
The use of deadly force to apprehend a fleeing felon constitutes a seizure. The force

used to effect a seizure must be reasonable. Deadly force is reasonable only when the felon threatens death or serious bodily harm and deadly force is necessary to prevent his escape. [Tennessee v. Garner, 471 U.S. 1 (1985)] Thus, a police officer cannot use deadly force to apprehend an unarmed, nondangerous felon; but an officer may use deadly force to prevent a felon from escaping if the felon poses a threat of serious bodily harm to the officer or others.

b. By Private Person

A private person has the same right to use force to make an arrest as a police officer or one acting at the direction of a police officer, except that the private person has a defense to the use of ***deadly force only if*** the person harmed was ***actually guilty*** of the offense (*i.e.,* felony) for which the arrest was made. It is not enough that it reasonably appeared that the person was guilty. A private person has a privilege to use ***nondeadly force*** to make an arrest if a crime was in fact committed and the private person has ***reasonable grounds to believe*** the person arrested has in fact committed the crime.

7. Resisting Arrest

a. Right to Resist Person Not Known to Be Police Officer

An individual may lawfully repel, with deadly force if necessary, an attack made by a police officer trying to arrest her if the individual does not know that the person is a police officer.

b. Right to Resist Known Police Officer

May a person resist arrest if the person attempting to make the arrest is known to be a police officer? The majority rule is that ***nondeadly force*** may be used to resist an improper arrest even if a known officer is making that arrest. A minority of courts and the M.P.C. take the position that force may not be used to resist one known to be a police officer.

8. Necessity

Conduct otherwise criminal is justifiable if, as a result of pressure from natural forces, the defendant reasonably believed that the conduct was necessary to avoid some harm to society that would exceed the harm caused by the conduct. The ***test is objective***; a good faith belief in the necessity of one's conduct is insufficient. Causing the death of another person to protect property is never justified. The defense of necessity is not available if the defendant is at fault in creating a situation which requires that she choose between two evils.

Example: Throwing cargo overboard during a violent storm, if necessary to save the lives of the crew and other people on board a ship, would not constitute criminal damage to property. On the other hand, throwing some members of the crew overboard to save the cargo would never be justifiable.

a. Duress Distinguished

While duress (discussed below) involves a human threat, necessity involves pressure from physical or natural forces.

Example: A points a gun at B and threatens to kill B if she does not break into C's house and steal food. B does as she is told. B may raise the defense of duress. If, however, B is a starving victim of a plane crash in a desolate area and commits the same act, she has the defense of necessity.

9. **Public Policy**
A police officer (or one assisting her) is justified in using reasonable force against another, or taking property, provided the officer acts pursuant to a law, court order, or process requiring or authorizing her to so act.
Example: The public executioner is not guilty of murder when she carries out a lawfully imposed sentence of execution. If the sentence was not lawful, the executioner is still immunized from criminal liability by a reasonable belief that her conduct was required by law.

10. **Domestic Authority**
The parents of a minor child, or any person "in loco parentis" with respect to that child, may lawfully use reasonable force upon the child for the purpose of promoting the child's welfare. Whether or not the force is "reasonable" is judged by the totality of the circumstances, including the age, sex, and health of the child.

B. THE EXCUSE OF DURESS (ALSO CALLED COMPULSION OR COERCION)

A person is not guilty of an offense, ***other than homicide***, if he performs an otherwise criminal act under the threat of imminent infliction of death or great bodily harm, provided that he reasonably believes death or great bodily harm will be inflicted on himself or on a member of his immediate family if he does not perform such conduct. Threats to harm any third person may also suffice to establish the defense of duress. Note that an act committed under duress is termed excusable rather than justifiable. The subtle distinction stems from the fact that criminal acts performed under duress are condoned by society rather than encouraged.

C. OTHER DEFENSES

1. Mistake or Ignorance of Fact

a. Mistake Must Negate State of Mind

Ignorance or mistake as to a matter of fact will affect criminal guilt only if it shows that the defendant did not have the state of mind required for the crime.
Example: A, hunting in the woods, shoots at what he reasonably believes to be a deer. In fact, it is B, who is killed. A's mistake of fact establishes that he did not have the state of mind required for murder.

Compare: A, hunting in the woods, shoots through the trees at a figure he believes to be his enemy B, intending to kill him. In fact, the figure is C, who is killed. A is guilty of murdering C despite his mistake of fact as to C's identity, because A's mistake does not negate his intent to kill a person.

b. Requirement that Mistake Be Reasonable

1) **Malice and General Intent Crimes—Reasonableness Required**
If the mistake or ignorance is offered to negate the existence of general intent or malice, it must be a reasonable mistake or ignorance, *i.e.,* the type of mistake or ignorance that a reasonable person would have made under the circumstances.

2) **Specific Intent Crimes—Reasonableness Not Required**
Any mistake of fact, reasonable or unreasonable, is a defense to a specific intent crime.

Example: A, leaving a restaurant, takes an umbrella, believing that it was the one she had left there a week ago. In fact, it belongs to B. Is A guilty of larceny? *Held:* No; since A believed the umbrella was hers, she could not have intended to deprive B of his right to it. Therefore, she lacked the state of mind necessary for larceny. Since her mistake negates a specific intent, it is not material whether it was a reasonable mistake or not.

c. **Strict Liability Crimes—Mistake No Defense**

Since strict liability crimes require no state of mind, mistake or ignorance of fact is no defense to them.

2. **Mistake or Ignorance of Law**

a. **General Rule—No Defense**

It is not a defense to a crime that the defendant was unaware that her acts were prohibited by the criminal law or that she mistakenly believed that her acts were not prohibited. This is true even if her ignorance or mistake was reasonable.

b. **Mistake or Ignorance of Law May Negate Intent**

If the mental state for a crime requires a certain belief concerning a collateral aspect of the law, ignorance or mistake as to that aspect of the law ***will negate the requisite state of mind***. This situation involves ignorance of some aspect of the ***elements*** of a crime rather than the ***existence*** of the statute making the act criminal.

Examples: 1) A is charged with violating a statute prohibiting the sale of a pistol to one known to be a convicted felon. A was unaware of the statute prohibiting this, but was aware that the person to whom the pistol was sold had been convicted of assault. A mistakenly believed, however, that assault was a misdemeanor; in fact, it was a felony. Is A guilty? *Held:* No. A's ignorance of the statute prohibiting the sale does not affect her liability, but the statute requires awareness that the buyer was a convicted felon. Since A believed the buyer to be only a convicted misdemeanant, she lacked the state of mind required for the crime.

2) B, who has had her car repossessed by a loan company, honestly believes she is still the lawful owner of the vehicle and is lawfully entitled to possession of it. She sees it sitting in a parking space in front of the loan company office and takes it. Even if B is wrong about her right to take the automobile, she is not guilty of larceny because she lacks the requisite intent to deprive another of his property.

c. **Exceptions**

1) **Statute Not Reasonably Available**

The defendant has a defense if the statute proscribing her conduct was not published or made reasonably available prior to the conduct.

2) **Reasonable Reliance on Statute or Judicial Decision**

The defendant has a defense if she acted in reasonable reliance on a statute or

judicial decision, even though the statute is later declared unconstitutional or the decision is overruled. The defense is strongest when the decision relied on was rendered by the highest court in the jurisdiction.

3) **Reasonable Reliance on Official Interpretation or Advice**
At common law, it was no defense that the defendant relied on an erroneous official statement of the law contained in an administrative order or grant, or in an official interpretation by the public officer or body responsible for the interpretation, administration, or enforcement of the law. The emerging rule, advocated by the M.P.C., provides a defense when the statement is obtained from one "charged by law with responsibility for the interpretation, administration, or enforcement of the law."

4) **Compare—Reasonable Reliance on Advice of Private Counsel**
Unlike reasonable reliance on an official interpretation of the law (*e.g.,* an opinion of the Attorney General), relying on the advice of one's own counsel is normally not allowed as a true affirmative defense to a crime. If, however, the reliance on the attorney negates an otherwise necessary mental state element (*e.g.,* knowingly violating the law), such reliance can demonstrate that the government has not proved its case beyond a reasonable doubt.

3. Consent

a. May Negate Element of Offense
Consent of the victim is generally no defense. However, if it negates an element of the offense, consent is a complete defense.

Examples: 1) Showing that the victim consented to intercourse is a defense to a charge of forcible rape.

2) Showing that an adult person consented to traveling with the defendant is a defense to kidnapping.

For some crimes, the consent of the victim is of no relevance (*e.g.,* consent of a victim of statutory rape has no legal significance). For other offenses, consent may be of limited effect (*e.g.,* within limits, victim may consent to infliction of physical violence, and one inflicting it will therefore not be guilty of assault or battery).

b. Requirements of Consent as Defense
Whenever consent may be a defense, it must be established that:

1) The consent was voluntarily and ***freely given*** (without compulsion or duress);

2) The party was ***legally capable*** of consenting; and

3) ***No fraud*** was involved in obtaining the consent.

4. Condonation by Injured Party No Defense
Forgiveness by the injured party after the crime has been committed ordinarily does not operate as a defense to the commission of a crime, unless a statute establishes such a defense.

Example: Forgiveness by an assault victim would not bar a criminal prosecution of the perpetrator.

Compare: Some statutes provide that marriage of the parties will bar a prosecution for seduction.

5. Criminality of Victim No Defense

The nearly universal rule is that illegal conduct by the victim of a crime is no defense.

Example: A, knowing that B has amassed a fortune through illegal gambling, defrauds B in a real estate deal. Does B's unlawful gambling activity provide A with a defense to fraud? No.

6. Entrapment

Entrapment occurs if the intent to commit the crime originated not with the defendant, but rather with the creative activities of law enforcement officers. If this is the case, it is presumed that the legislature did not intend to cover the conduct and so it is not criminal. The defense of entrapment consists of two elements:

(i) The ***criminal design*** must have ***originated with law enforcement*** officers; and

(ii) The defendant must ***not*** have been ***predisposed*** to commit the crime prior to the initial contact by the government.

If the defendant offers credible evidence on these two elements, in most jurisdictions the government must then show predisposition beyond a reasonable doubt.

a. Offering Opportunity to Commit Crime Distinguished

It is not entrapment if the police officer merely provides the opportunity for the commission of a crime by one otherwise ready and willing to commit it.

Example: A, an undercover police agent, poses as a narcotics addict in need of a fix. B sells narcotics to A. Does B have the defense of entrapment? No. By posing as an addict, A merely provided an opportunity for B to commit the criminal sale.

b. Inapplicable to Private Inducements

A person cannot be entrapped by a private citizen. Inducement constitutes entrapment only if performed by an officer of the government or one working for him or under his control or direction.

c. Availability If Offense Denied

If a defendant denies her participation in the offense, she has elected not to pursue entrapment and is not entitled to raise the issue, even if the facts would otherwise permit her to do so. Under the modern trend, however, a defendant may raise the defense of entrapment even while denying participation in the offense. The Supreme Court has adopted this rule for federal offenses. [Mathews v. United States, 485 U.S. 58 (1988)]

d. Practical Difficulties of Entrapment

In cases where there is extended inducement by the government, the issue becomes

whether the defendant was predisposed to commit the offense or whether the intent to commit it was instilled by the officers. Predisposition must exist prior to the government's initial contact with the defendant. A mere "inclination" to engage in the illegal activity is not adequate proof of predisposition. [Jacobson v. United States, 503 U.S. 540 (1992)] However, even if predisposition is not proved, the introduction by the prosecution of potentially damaging evidence on the issue of the defendant's predisposition may cause a jury to convict on the basis of the extensive evidence of the defendant's culpable state of mind.

e. **Minority Rule—Objective Test**
The minority rule would replace the entrapment elements set out above with a test based entirely on the nature of the police activity. Under this test, a defendant would be entitled to acquittal if the police activity was reasonably likely to cause an innocent (*i.e.,* unpredisposed) person to commit the crime. The defendant's innocence or predisposition is irrelevant. Under this approach, the issue is decided by the judge rather than the jury.

f. **Provision of Material for Crime by Government Agent Not Entrapment**
The Supreme Court has held that under federal law an entrapment defense cannot be based upon the fact that a government agent provided material for commission of the crime, even if the material provided was contraband. [United States v. Russell, 411 U.S. 423 (1973); Hampton v. United States, 425 U.S. 484 (1976)] A few states, however, make the provision of essential material—such as ingredients for drugs or the drugs themselves—entrapment.

VII. OFFENSES AGAINST THE PERSON

A. ASSAULT AND BATTERY

1. **Battery**
Battery is an unlawful application of force to the person of another resulting in either bodily injury or an offensive touching. Simple battery is a misdemeanor.

a. **State of Mind—Intent Not Required**
A battery need not be intentional. It is sufficient that the defendant caused the application of force with criminal negligence.

b. **Indirect Application of Force Sufficient**
The force need not be applied directly. Thus, it is sufficient if the force is applied by a force or substance put in motion by the defendant. For example, battery may be committed by causing a dog to attack the victim or by causing the victim to take a poisonous substance.

c. **Aggravated Battery**
Most statutes define certain acts as aggravated batteries and punish them as felonies. Among the most common are batteries in which:

1) A ***deadly weapon*** is used (any ordinary object may become a deadly weapon depending upon how it is used);

2) ***Serious bodily injury*** is caused; or

3) The ***victim is a child, woman, or police officer.***

d. Consent as a Defense
Contrary to the general rule that consent of the victim is not a valid defense, some jurisdictions recognize consent as a defense to simple battery and/or certain specified batteries, *e.g.,* a medical operation, or reasonable injuries incurred in consensual athletic contests.

2. Assault
In a majority of jurisdictions, an assault is either:

(i) An ***attempt to commit a battery***; or

(ii) The ***intentional creation***—other than by mere words—of a ***reasonable apprehension*** in the mind of the victim of imminent bodily harm.

A minority of jurisdictions limit assault to an attempt to commit a battery. Simple assault is a misdemeanor.

a. Present Ability to Succeed
Some statutes define assault as an unlawful attempt to commit a battery coupled with a present ability to succeed. Lack of an ability to succeed precludes liability under such statutes.

Example: A points an unloaded gun at B. A pulls the trigger, thereby frightening B. Is A guilty of assault under a statute defining assault as "an attempt to commit a battery, coupled with the present ability to succeed"? No. Because the gun was unloaded, A could not have succeeded in committing a battery.

b. Battery Distinguished
If there has been an actual touching of the victim, the crime can only be battery. If there has been no such touching, the act may or may not constitute an assault, depending on the circumstances.

c. Statutory Aggravated Assault
All jurisdictions treat certain "aggravated assaults" more severely than simple assault. Such aggravated assaults include, but are not limited to, assaults:

1) With a ***dangerous (or deadly) weapon***;

2) With ***intent to rape, maim, or murder.***

B. MAYHEM

1. **Common Law**
At common law, the felony of mayhem required either dismemberment (the removal of some bodily part) or disablement of a bodily part. The crime was enforced to preserve the King's right to his subjects' military service.

2. **Modern Statutes**
Most states retain the crime of mayhem in some form, although the recent trend is to abolish mayhem as a separate offense and to treat it instead as a form of aggravated battery. Modern statutes have expanded the scope of mayhem to include permanent disfigurement. A few states require a specific intent to maim or disfigure.

C. HOMICIDE

1. **Classifications of Homicides**
At common law, homicides were divided into three classifications:

   a. ***Justifiable*** homicides (those commanded or authorized by law);

   b. ***Excusable*** homicides (those for which there was a defense to criminal liability); and

   c. ***Criminal*** homicides.

2. **Common Law Criminal Homicides**
At common law, criminal homicides were subdivided into three different offenses.

   a. **Murder**
   Murder is the unlawful killing of another human being with malice aforethought. Malice aforethought may be express or implied.

   1) **Malice Aforethought**
   In the absence of facts excusing the homicide or reducing it to voluntary manslaughter, malice aforethought exists if the defendant has any of the following states of mind:

   (i) Intent to kill (express malice);

   (ii) Intent to inflict great bodily injury;

   (iii) Reckless indifference to an unjustifiably high risk to human life ("abandoned and malignant heart"); or

   (iv) Intent to commit a felony (felony murder; *see infra*).

   In the case of (ii), (iii), or (iv), the malice is "implied."

   2) **Deadly Weapon Rule**
   Intentional use of a deadly weapon authorizes a permissive inference of intent to kill. A deadly weapon is any instrument—or in some limited circumstances, any part of the body—used in a manner calculated or likely to produce death or serious bodily injury.

Example: The following persons may be held guilty of murder under the deadly weapon rule: (i) one who pilots a speedboat through a group of bathers; (ii) one who fires a bullet into a crowded room; and (iii) a professional boxer who beats up and kills a belligerent tavern owner.

b. Voluntary Manslaughter

Voluntary manslaughter is a killing that would otherwise be murder but is distinguishable from murder by the existence of adequate provocation—*i.e.,* a killing in the heat of passion.

1) Elements of Adequate Provocation

At common law, provocation would reduce a killing to voluntary manslaughter only if it met four tests:

a) The provocation must have been one that would arouse ***sudden and intense passion*** in the mind of an ***ordinary person*** such as to cause him to lose his self-control;

b) The defendant must have ***in fact*** been ***provoked***;

c) There ***must not have been a sufficient time*** between the provocation and the killing for the passions of a reasonable person to cool. (This is a factual question that depends upon the nature of the provocation and the attendant circumstances, including any earlier altercations between the defendant and the victim); and

d) The defendant ***in fact*** did not cool off between the provocation and the killing.

2) When Provocation Is Adequate

Adequate provocation is most frequently recognized in cases of:

a) Being subjected to a ***serious battery*** or a threat of ***deadly force***; and

b) Discovering one's ***spouse in bed with another person***.

3) Provocation Inadequate as a Matter of Law

At common law, some provocations were defined as inadequate as a matter of law. The most significant was "***mere words***." Modern courts tend to be more reluctant to take such cases from juries and are more likely to submit to the jury the question of whether "mere words" or similar matters constitute adequate provocation.

4) Recent Expansion—Imperfect Self-Defense

Some states recognize an "imperfect self-defense" doctrine under which a murder may be reduced to manslaughter even though:

a) The ***defendant was at fault*** in starting the altercation; or

b) The defendant ***unreasonably but honestly believed*** in the necessity of responding with deadly force.

c. **Involuntary Manslaughter**
Involuntary manslaughter is of two types.

1) **Criminal Negligence**
If death is caused by criminal negligence (or by "recklessness" under the M.P.C.), the killing is involuntary manslaughter. Criminal negligence requires a greater deviation from the "reasonable person" standard than is required for civil liability. (Some states require that the defendant have had a subjective awareness of the risk.)

2) **"Unlawful Act" Manslaughter**
A killing caused by an unlawful act is involuntary manslaughter. There are two subcategories of such acts:

a) **"Misdemeanor-Manslaughter" Rule**
A killing in the course of the commission of a misdemeanor is manslaughter, although most courts would require either that the misdemeanor be malum in se (*i.e.,* an inherently wrongful act), or if malum prohibitum, that the death be the foreseeable or natural consequence of the unlawful conduct.

b) **Felonies Not Included in Felony Murder**
If a killing was caused during the commission of a felony but does not qualify as a felony murder case, the killing will be involuntary manslaughter. The death also must be a foreseeable consequence of the felony. (*See* 4.c.3), *infra.*)

3. **Statutory Modification of Common Law Classification**
Modern statutes often divide murder into degrees, and the bar examination often contains questions based on statutes similar to them. Under such schemes, all murders are ***second degree*** murders unless the prosecution proves any of the following, which would make the murder ***first degree*** murder:

a. **Deliberate and Premeditated Killing**
"Deliberate" means that the defendant made the decision to kill in a cool and dispassionate manner. "Premeditated" means that the defendant actually reflected on the idea of killing, if only for a very brief period.

b. **First Degree Felony Murder**
Many state statutes list specific felonies that may serve as the basis for felony murder. If a killing is committed during the commission of one of these enumerated felonies, the killing is usually first degree murder without the prosecution needing to show that the killing was either deliberate or premeditated. The felonies most commonly listed are burglary, arson, rape, robbery, and kidnapping, but other felonies that are inherently dangerous to human life are often specifically added.

1) **Second Degree Felony Murder**
Even if the state lists the felonies to be included under the doctrine, a separate statute (or case) may provide for criminal liability for a killing committed during the course of a felony that is ***not*** listed. Such killings typically will be classified as second degree murder.

2) **Other State Variations**
Some states may not list the felonies to be included under felony murder doctrine at all. Other states that permit felony murder liability based on a felony that is not listed sometimes include the additional requirement that the felony be inherently dangerous to human life or that the felony be dangerous to human life as committed.

c. **Others**
Some statutes make killings performed in certain ways first degree murder. Thus, killing by lying in wait, poison, or torture may be first degree murder.

4. **Felony Murder (and Related Matters)**
As the definition of malice aforethought above makes clear, a killing—even an accidental one—committed during the course of a felony is murder. Malice is implied from the intent to commit the underlying felony.

a. **What Felonies Are Included?**
Under the common law, there were only a handful of felonies (*see* I.D.1., *supra*). Today, the criminal codes of states have created many more.

b. **Scope of the Doctrine**
When the felony murder doctrine is combined with conspiracy law, the scope of liability becomes very broad. If, in the course of a conspiracy to commit a felony, a death is caused, all members of the conspiracy are liable for murder if the death was caused in furtherance of the conspiracy and was a foreseeable consequence of the conspiracy.

c. **Limitations on Liability**
There are some limitations on liability under the broad felony murder doctrine.

1) **Commission of Underlying Felony**
To convict a defendant of felony murder, the prosecution must prove that he committed the underlying felony. Thus, if the defendant has a ***substantive defense*** that negates an element of the underlying felony, he has a defense to felony murder. However, procedural defenses (such as a statute of limitations defense to the underlying felony) will not be a defense to felony murder in most states.

2) **Felony Must Be Independent of Killing**
The felony murder rule can be applied only where the underlying felony is independent of the killing. Thus, a felony such as manslaughter or aggravated battery will not qualify as the underlying felony for purposes of felony murder liability.

3) **Foreseeability of Death**
The majority rule is that death must have been a foreseeable result of the commission of the felony. However, it is important to note that ***courts have been willing to find most deaths foreseeable.*** A minority of courts do not apply a foreseeability requirement, requiring only that the felony be malum in se.

Example: A intentionally sets fire to a dwelling. B, a firefighter, dies in an effort to extinguish the blaze. C, the owner of the dwelling, dies of a heart attack while watching his largest possession being destroyed.

Is A guilty of felony murder? Of B, yes. The death of a firefighter is a foreseeable consequence of setting a fire. Of C, no. The heart attack was unforeseeable.

4) **During the Commission of a Felony—Termination of Felony**
The death must have been "caused during" the commission or attempted commission of the felony, but the fact that the felony was technically completed before death was caused does not prevent the killing from being felony murder. Deaths caused while fleeing from the crime are felony murder. But once the felon has reached a ***place of "temporary safety,"*** the impact of the felony murder rule ceases and deaths subsequently caused are not felony murder.

5) **Killing of Co-Felon by Victims of Felonies or Pursuing Police Officers**
Is the defendant liable for a co-felon's death caused by resistance of the victim or police? The majority view is no. The so-called *Redline* view (the majority position) is that ***liability for murder cannot be based upon the death of a co-felon*** from resistance by the victim or police pursuit.

a) **Compare—Killing of Innocent Party by Victim or Police**
Courts are split when resistance by the victim or police pursuit causes the death of an innocent party rather than a co-felon. In states following the "agency theory" of felony murder, the killing must have been caused by the defendant or someone acting as the defendant's "agent" (*i.e.*, an accomplice); hence, the defendant is not liable for felony murder when someone is killed by the victim or police. In states following the "proximate cause" theory, the defendant ***can*** be liable when an innocent party is killed by resistance from the victim or police because the death is a direct consequence of the felony.

d. **Related Limits on Misdemeanor Manslaughter**
Limits similar to those placed on felony murder are placed on involuntary misdemeanor manslaughter. If the misdemeanor involved is not malum in se, *i.e.,* one that involves conduct that is inherently wrong, a death caused during the commission of a misdemeanor is manslaughter only if death was a foreseeable result of the commission of the misdemeanor. A minority of courts limit the doctrine to malum in se misdemeanors.

Example: K is driving on a good road in excellent weather, but is slightly exceeding the posted speed limit. V dashes from behind a bush into the street and is struck by K's car. V dies. Is K guilty of involuntary manslaughter, assuming that speeding is a misdemeanor? The best answer is no, because the misdemeanor was not malum in se and death was not a foreseeable result of its commission.

5. **Causation**

a. **General Requirement—Must Be Cause-in-Fact and Proximate Cause**
When a crime is defined to require not merely conduct but also a specified result of that conduct, the defendant's conduct must be both the cause-in-fact and the proximate cause of the specified result.

1) Cause-in-Fact

The defendant's conduct must be the cause-in-fact of the result; *i.e.,* the result would not have occurred "***but for***" the defendant's conduct.

2) Common Law Requirement—"Year and a Day" Rule

The death of the victim must occur within one year and one day from the infliction of the injury or wound. If it does not occur within this period of time, there can be no prosecution for homicide, even if it can be shown that "but for" the defendant's actions, the victim would not have died as and when he did. The rule has been sharply criticized by the United States Supreme Court as "an outdated relic of the common law," and most of the states that have recently reviewed the rule have abolished it.

3) "Proximate" Causation

Problems of proximate causation arise only when the victim's death occurs because of the defendant's acts, but in a manner not intended or anticipated by the defendant. The question in such cases is whether the difference in the way death was intended or anticipated and the way in which it actually occurred breaks the chain of "proximate cause" causation.

a) All "Natural and Probable" Results Are Proximately Caused

The general rule is that a defendant is responsible for all results that occur as a "natural and probable" consequence of his conduct, even if he did not anticipate the precise manner in which they would occur. All such results are "proximately caused" by the defendant's act. This chain of proximate causation is broken only by the intervention of a "superseding factor."

b. Rules of Causation

1) Hastening Inevitable Result

An act that hastens an inevitable result is nevertheless a legal cause of that result.

Example: A terminates the life support system of B, resulting in B's death. B had only 24 hours to live. Can A be held liable for B's death? Yes. Note that society may not wish to condemn such an "act of mercy." Nevertheless, for purposes of causation analysis, A's act caused B's death.

2) Simultaneous Acts

Simultaneous acts by two or more persons may be considered independently sufficient causes of a single result.

3) Preexisting Condition

A victim's preexisting condition that makes him more susceptible to death does not break the chain of causation; *i.e.,* the defendant "takes the victim as he finds him."

Example: A, with malice aforethought, shoots B in the leg. B bleeds to death before he can receive medical attention because he is a hemophiliac. A is liable for murder despite the fact that a person without hemophilia would not have died from the shooting.

c. **Intervening Acts**

As a general rule, an intervening act will shield the defendant from liability if the act is a mere coincidence or is outside the foreseeable sphere of risk created by the defendant's act.

Examples: 1) ***Act of Nature:*** A is driving negligently. To avoid A's swerving car, B takes an unaccustomed route home. B's car is struck by lightning, and B dies. Can A be charged with manslaughter? No. The fact that lightning struck B was a mere coincidence.

2) ***Act by Third Party:*** A, intending to kill B, merely wounds him. B receives negligent medical treatment at a nearby hospital. B dies. Can A be held liable for B's death? Yes. Despite improvements in medical care, negligent care remains a ***foreseeable risk.*** A contrary result would follow if B died due to gross negligence or intentional mistreatment.

3) ***Acts by the Victim:*** A, intending to kill B, merely wounds him. B refuses medical treatment for religious reasons and dies. If modern medical knowledge could have saved B, can A be held liable for B's death? Most jurisdictions have held yes, because A's act directly created the risk of death and because the refusal of medical care may be found to be foreseeable. This rule may apply even if the victim acts affirmatively to harm himself. Suppose B, in unbearable pain, commits suicide. The suicide may be found to be a foreseeable consequence of A's actions. Thus, A would be liable for B's death.

6. **Summary—Analytical Approach**

In analyzing any homicide situation, the following questions must be asked and answered:

a. Did the defendant have any of the ***states of mind*** sufficient to constitute malice aforethought?

b. If the answer to a. is yes, is there proof of anything that will, under any applicable statute, raise the homicide to ***first degree murder***?

c. If the answer to a. is yes, is there evidence to reduce the killing to ***voluntary manslaughter***, *i.e.*, adequate provocation?

d. If the answer to a. is no, is there a sufficient basis for holding the crime to be ***involuntary manslaughter,*** *i.e.*, criminal negligence or misdemeanor manslaughter?

e. Is there ***adequate causation*** between the defendant's acts and the victim's death? Did the victim ***die within a year and one day***? Was the defendant's act the ***factual cause*** of death? Is there anything to break the chain of ***proximate causation*** between the defendant's act and the victim's death?

Example: A came upon B, who was letting the air out of a tire on A's car. When A shouted at B, B picked up a rock and threw it at A, shouting obscenities. B ran off, but A went to his car, pulled a gun out, and shot at B, hitting him in the leg. B was taken to a hospital where he underwent surgery;

the wrong gas was used as an anesthetic, and B died. Generally, wounds of this sort are not deadly. A testifies under oath that he merely intended to wound B as revenge for causing A the inconvenience of the flat tire. What is A's liability?

1) Even if A intended only to wound B with a bullet, this is intent to inflict great bodily injury and is sufficient for malice aforethought.

2) If the statute makes premeditated killings first degree murder, A almost certainly did not premeditate.

3) While B's shouted obscenities might not be adequate provocation, a jury could certainly find that throwing the rock was such provocation.

4) If the answer to inquiry a. had been no, A's actions would have constituted criminal negligence.

5) There is causation. B died within a year and one day. But for A's shot, B would not have died. Negligent medical care is not a superseding intervening factor that will break the chain of proximate causation, unless it is "gross" negligence or intentional malpractice.

D. FALSE IMPRISONMENT

The common law misdemeanor of false imprisonment consisted of:

(i) Unlawful

(ii) Confinement of a person

(iii) Without his valid consent.

1. Confinement

Confinement requires that the victim be compelled either to go where he does not wish to go or to remain where he does not wish to remain. It is not confinement to simply prevent a person from going where he desires to go, as long as alternative routes are available to him. The confinement may be accomplished by actual force, by threats, or by a show of force. The M.P.C. takes a similar approach in that the confinement must "interfere substantially" with the victim's liberty.

2. "Unlawfulness"

Confinement is unlawful unless it is specifically authorized by law or by the consent of the person.

3. Lack of Consent

Consent to the confinement precludes it from constituting false imprisonment, but the consent must be ***freely given*** by one with ***capacity*** to give such consent. Thus, consent is invalidated by coercion, threats, deception, or incapacity due to mental illness, retardation, or youth.

E. KIDNAPPING

At common law, the misdemeanor of kidnapping was the forcible abduction or stealing away of a person from his own country and sending him into another. Modern statutes and the M.P.C. generally expand the definition of kidnapping far beyond the common law definition, although it usually remains a form of aggravated false imprisonment.

1. General Pattern

Kidnapping is often defined as confinement of a person that involves either:

a. Some ***movement*** (*i.e.*, "asportation") of the victim; ***or***

b. ***Concealment*** of the victim in a "secret" place.

2. Aggravated Kidnapping

Modern statutes often contain as a separate offense an aggravated kidnapping crime. Among the more common forms of this offense are:

a. Kidnapping for Ransom

The abduction or secretion of a person for the purpose of obtaining anything of value for the return of the person is often defined as aggravated kidnapping.

b. Kidnapping for Purpose of Commission of Other Crimes

Abduction or secretion for the purpose of committing other offenses, such as robbery, is sometimes defined as aggravated kidnapping.

c. Kidnapping for Offensive Purpose

Abduction or secretion with the intent of harming the person or of committing some sexual crime with him is sometimes defined as aggravated kidnapping.

d. Child Stealing

Leading, taking, enticing, or detaining a child with the intent to keep or conceal the child from a guardian or parent is often defined as aggravated kidnapping. Use of "enticement" covers the situation in which a child is persuaded by promises or rewards to come with the defendant or remain. The consent of a child to his detention or movement is not of importance, because the child is incapacitated by age from giving valid consent.

3. Required Movement

Although at common law extreme movement was required, most modern statutes require only some movement of the person; if such movement occurs, the extent of the movement is not material. Other statutes require no movement, making confinement (as used in false imprisonment) sufficient.

4. Secrecy

Generally, it is not necessary that kidnapping involve secrecy. Some statutes, however, require secrecy when the kidnapping is based on confinement rather than movement of the victim.

5. Consent

As with false imprisonment, free consent given by a person competent to give it precludes the confinement or movement of a person from being kidnapping. But a person may be incompetent to give such consent by reason of age (*see* above) or mental condition.

6. **Relationship to Other Offenses**
Statutes that define kidnapping as detention involving movement of the victim mean that it is arguable that kidnapping often occurs incident to the commission of other crimes, such as robbery or rape. Some courts—but not all—have held that in such situations kidnapping (in addition to the robbery or rape) is committed only if the movement of the victim substantially increases the risk to the victim over and above that necessarily involved in the other crime. If no such increased risk is involved, the defendant will be held to have committed only the robbery or rape.

VIII. SEX OFFENSES

A. RAPE

Traditionally, rape (a felony) was the unlawful carnal knowledge of a woman by a man, not her husband, without her effective consent. Today, a number of states have renamed "rape" as "sexual assault" and have made such statutes gender neutral.

1. **Penetration Sufficient**
Rape requires only the penetration of the female sex organ by the male sex organ. Emission is not necessary to complete the crime.

2. **Absence of Marital Relationship**
At common law and under the M.P.C., the woman must not have been married to the man who committed the act. Today, however, most states have either dropped this requirement where the parties are estranged or separated, or abolished it entirely.

3. **Lack of Effective Consent**
The intercourse must be without the victim's effective consent. Consent, even if given, may be ineffective in several situations.

   a. **Intercourse Accomplished by Force**
   If the intercourse is accomplished by actual force, no question concerning consent is raised.

   b. **Intercourse Accomplished by Threats**
   If intercourse is accomplished by placing the victim in fear of great and immediate bodily harm, it constitutes rape. Any consent obtained by such threats is ineffective. The failure of the victim to "resist to the utmost" does not prevent the intercourse from being rape if resistance is prevented by such threats.

   c. **Woman Incapable of Consenting**
   If the victim is incapable of consenting, the intercourse is rape. Inability to consent may be caused by unconsciousness, by the effect of drugs or intoxicating substances, or by the victim's mental condition. If the victim is so insane or retarded as to be incapable of giving consent, intercourse with her constitutes rape.

d. **Consent Obtained by Fraud**
Only in limited circumstances will intercourse with consent obtained by fraud constitute rape.

1) **Fraud as to Whether Act Constitutes Sexual Intercourse**
If the victim is fraudulently caused to believe that the act is not sexual intercourse, the act of intercourse constitutes rape.
Example: D persuaded V that what was actually an act of intercourse was medical treatment accomplished by surgical instruments. Was D guilty of rape? Yes.

2) **Fraud as to Whether Defendant Is Victim's Husband**
If the defendant fraudulently persuades the victim that he is her husband, is the intercourse rape? The best answer is no.
Example: D arranges for X to pretend to marry D and V. In fact, X has no authority to marry persons and there is no marriage. After the sham marriage, D has intercourse with V. Is D guilty of rape? The best answer is no because there was consent.

3) **Other Fraud**
Other kinds of fraud will not make the intercourse rape.
Example: D promises to marry V at a later time and thereby induces V to consent to intercourse. D never intended to marry V. Is D guilty of rape? No. (But D may be guilty of seduction (*see* F., below).)

B. STATUTORY RAPE

1. **Victim Below Age of Consent**
Statutory rape is the crime of carnal knowledge of a person under the age of consent. Even if the victim willingly participated, the offense is nevertheless committed because consent is irrelevant. The age of consent varies from state to state, generally from 16 to 18.

2. **Mistake as to Age**
Will a defendant's reasonable mistake as to the victim's age prevent liability for statutory rape? For purposes of the examination, the best answer is no, since statutory rape is a ***strict liability crime***. A second best answer, to be used only if no alternative making use of the best position is presented, is that a reasonable mistake as to age will prevent conviction if the defendant reasonably believed the victim was old enough to give an effective consent.

C. CRIMES AGAINST NATURE

An early (1533) English statute made sodomy—a generic term encompassing many different acts—a felony, so that it became part of the American common law of crime. However, because of recent court decisions, it is unlikely that a defendant could be successfully prosecuted for most of these crimes. Bestiality, which is the carnal copulation with an animal by a human being (male or female), is probably the only crime that survives.

D. ADULTERY AND FORNICATION

Adultery and fornication were not common law crimes in England, but were punished by the church as ecclesiastical offenses. They are made misdemeanor offenses by statute in some states.

1. **Adultery**
Under modern statutes, any person who cohabits or has sexual intercourse with another not his spouse commits the misdemeanor offense of adultery if:

a. The behavior is ***open and notorious; and***

b. The person is ***married*** and the other person involved in such intercourse is not his spouse; or

c. The person is not married and knows the ***other person*** in such intercourse is ***married***.

2. **Fornication**
Fornication is sexual intercourse between or open and notorious cohabitation by unmarried persons.

E. INCEST
Incest is a statutory offense, usually a felony, that consists of either marriage or a sexual act (intercourse or deviate sexual conduct) between persons who are too closely related.

1. **Degree of Relationship**
No uniformity exists among the states. A majority restricts the crime to blood relations, although a significant number of states include some nonblood relatives.

2. **Degree of Responsibility**
Some states make a distinction in penalties depending on the parties involved.

F. SEDUCTION OR CARNAL KNOWLEDGE
A statutory felony in many states, the crime of seduction is committed when a male person induces an unmarried female of previously chaste character to engage in an act of intercourse on promise of marriage. The M.P.C. includes a section on seduction; it requires only that there be a false promise of marriage and does not require chastity or that the female be unmarried.

In many states, subsequent marriage of the parties is a defense, but there is no uniformity as to whether the marriage must be entered into before indictment, after sentence, or anywhere in between.

G. BIGAMY
Bigamy is a traditional strict liability offense that consists of marrying someone while having another living spouse. At common law, a defendant is guilty of bigamy even if she reasonably believes that a purported divorce is valid or that her spouse is dead.

IX. PROPERTY OFFENSES

This section deals with a number of property offenses. But for purposes of the examination, the greatest challenge is in distinguishing among three of these: larceny, embezzlement, and false pretenses. There is no difference among the intents required for the three crimes. The major differences among these crimes are in the kind of misappropriation of the property. They are discussed in detail below and can be summarized as follows:

	activity	***method***	***intent***	***title***
larceny	taking and asportation of property from possession of another person	without consent or with consent obtained by fraud	with intent to steal	title does not pass
embezzlement	conversion of property held pursuant to a trust agreement	use of property in a way inconsistent with terms of trust	with intent to defraud	title does not pass
false pretenses	obtaining title to property	by consent induced by fraudulent misrepresentation	with intent to defraud	title passes

A. LARCENY

Larceny was the basic common law property offense. It has been significantly modified by statute in many American jurisdictions. Larceny consists of:

(i) A taking (caption);

(ii) And carrying away (asportation);

(iii) Of tangible personal property;

(iv) Of another;

(v) By trespass;

(vi) With intent to permanently (or for an unreasonable time) deprive the person of his interest in the property.

1. Property that May Be the Subject of Larceny

Larceny can be committed only by the acquisition of ***personal property*** capable of being possessed and of some value.

a. Realty and Severed Material

Realty and its fixtures are ***not*** subjects of larceny. If something is severed from the realty and taken before it comes into possession of the landowner as personal property, larceny is not committed. If, however, the landowner gains possession of the severed material as personalty, a subsequent taking of it is larceny.

Example: A went onto land owned by B and cut down 15 trees. She loaded 10 into her truck and drove off. B came onto the land, found the remaining five trees, and placed them in his shed. A returned and took them. Is A guilty of larceny of 15, 10, five, or no trees? *Held:* A is guilty of larceny of the five trees that came into B's possession after their severance from the realty.

b. Services

Traditionally, obtaining services wrongfully cannot give rise to larceny.

c. **Intangibles**

Intangibles cannot give rise to larceny.

Example: A wrongfully obtains entrance to B's theater and observes a performance of a play. Has A committed larceny of that performance? *Held:* No. The right or ability to observe a play is intangible.

Note that gas and electricity are considered to be personal property that may be stolen.

d. **Documents and Instruments**

Documents and instruments were, at common law, regarded as merged with the matter they represented. Thus, unless they had monetary value in themselves, they could not be the subject of larceny.

Example: A takes a deed to certain realty and a contract for the sale of cattle from B's desk. Is A guilty of larceny? *Held:* No. The deed "merged" with the realty and the contract merged with the intangible contract right; thus, there was no larceny.

Modern statutes have expanded larceny to include written instruments embodying intangible rights.

2. **Property "Of Another"**

Larceny is a crime against possession. Therefore, all that is necessary is that the property be taken from someone who has a possessory interest superior to that of the defendant.

a. **Requirement that Taking Be from One with "Possession"**

The property must be taken from someone with possession other than the defendant. If the defendant had possession at the time of the taking (*e.g.,* defendant is a bailee of the property), the resulting offense is not larceny, although it may be embezzlement. However, if the defendant has "custody" rather than "possession," her misappropriation of the property is larceny.

1) **Custody vs. Possession**

Possession involves much greater scope of authority to deal with the property than does custody.

Example: A, while in a store, asks B, the clerk, if she may take a certain suit of clothing home on approval. B consents. A then asks to see a watch to examine it; B gives it to her. A then absconds with both items. Have either of them been taken from B's possession? *Held:* The watch was taken from B's possession, because A had only the authority to look at it. The suit, on the other hand, was in A's possession at the time it was misappropriated, because of the extent of control B had given A over it.

2) **Employees**

Low level employees generally have only custody of their employers' property. They have possession, however, if the employer gives them especially broad powers over it or if the property is given directly to them by a third person, without the employer having intermediate possession.

3) **Bailee and "Breaking Bulk"**
Generally, a ***bailee has possession***. If, however, she opens closed containers in which the property has been placed by the bailor (*i.e.,* she "breaks bulk"), the possession is regarded by use of a fiction as returning to the bailor. If a bailee misappropriates property ***after breaking bulk***, she takes it from the possession of the bailor and is guilty of ***larceny*** if she has the intent to steal.

b. **Possession Is All that Is Needed**
The person from whom the property is taken only needs to have possession. Thus, it is larceny if property is taken from a thief, as he has a possessory interest superior to the person who takes the property from him.
Example: A takes her car to be repaired in B's garage. B does the repairs and as a result has a mechanic's lien on the car. A takes the car without paying for the repairs. Has A taken the property of another from the other's possession? *Held:* Yes. B had a possessory interest in the car and it was in his possession. It is not material that A had title to the car.

c. **Joint Property**
At common law, larceny could not be committed by the taking of jointly held property by one of the joint owners.

d. **Lost, Mislaid, and Abandoned Property**
Lost or mislaid property is regarded as constructively in the possession of the owner, and thus if it is found and taken, it is taken from his possession and larceny might be committed. Abandoned property, however, has no owner and larceny cannot be committed by appropriating it.

3. **Taking**
It is essential that the defendant actually obtain control of the property.

a. **Destruction or Movement Is Not Sufficient**
Mere destruction or movement of the property is not sufficient to constitute a taking.
Example: D knocked a glass from X's hand. It fell and broke. Is D guilty of larceny? No. Although X may have lost possession, D never obtained control. The damage to the item is irrelevant.

b. **Sufficient If Caused to Occur by Innocent Agent**
Even if a defendant obtains control of the property through the act of an innocent agent, it is a taking.
Example: D, pointing out a cow in a nearby field, offers to sell it to X for $10. X gives D the money and then takes the cow. In fact, the cow belonged to Y. Is D guilty of larceny of the cow? Yes. She obtained control of it by virtue of X, an innocent agent of hers.

4. **Asportation**
Larceny requires asportation, *i.e.,* that all parts or portions of the property be moved and that this movement—which need only be slight—be part of the carrying away process.
Example: A came upon two upside-down wheelbarrows in B's yard. She turned them both right side up, and moved one six inches toward the gate. Was she guilty

of larceny of one, two, or no wheelbarrows? *Held:* Guilty of larceny of one. Merely turning the wheelbarrows over is not part of the carrying away movement; thus, it is not asportation. But merely moving the other wheelbarrow a short distance is enough, because that movement is part of carrying it away.

5. Taking Must Be "Trespassory"

The defendant must take the property from the possession of another in a trespassory manner, *i.e.,* without the consent of the person in possession of the property.

a. Taking by Consent Induced by Misrepresentations—"Larceny by Trick"

If the victim consents to the defendant's taking possession of the property but this consent has been induced by a misrepresentation, the consent is not valid. The resulting larceny is often called "larceny by trick." A major difficulty is in distinguishing larceny by trick from false pretenses. (*See* C.1., *infra.*)

6. State of Mind Required—Intent to Permanently Deprive

Generally, larceny requires that at the time of the taking the defendant must have the intent to permanently deprive the person from whom the property is taken of his interest in the property. The intent has to exist at the moment of the taking of the property.

a. Sufficient Intent

1) Intent to Create Substantial Risk of Loss

If the defendant intends to deal with the property in a manner that involves a substantial risk of loss, this is sufficient for larceny.

2) Intent to Pledge Goods or Sell Them to Owner

It is larceny to take goods with the intent to sell them back to the owner or to pledge them, because this involves the substantial equivalent of permanent loss or the high risk of permanent loss.

b. Insufficient Intent

1) Intent to Borrow

If the defendant intends to return the property within a reasonable time and at the time of the taking has a substantial ability to do so, the unauthorized borrowing does not constitute larceny. Note that many states make it a crime to borrow a motor vehicle, even when the borrower fully intends to return it ("joyriding").

2) Intent to Obtain Repayment of Debt

It is not larceny to take money or goods of another if the defendant honestly believes that she is entitled to them as repayment for a debt of the other (although the goods must not be worth more than the amount of the debt). In these situations, the defendant believes the property is "hers" and therefore lacks an intent to deprive someone else of "his" property.

c. Possibly Sufficient

1) **Intent to Pay for Property**
If the property taken is not for sale, the fact that the defendant intends to pay the other for it does not negate the larceny. If the property is for sale and the defendant has a specific and realistic intent to repay the person, the taking is not larceny.

2) **Intent to Claim Reward**
If the defendant takes goods, intending to return them and hoping for a reward, this is not larceny. However, if she takes them not intending to return them unless she is assured of a reward, this is larceny because it creates a substantial risk of loss.

7. **Specialized Application of Larceny Doctrine**
There are several situations in which the application of the requirements for larceny is highly technical.

a. **Abandoned or Lost Property**
Property abandoned by its owner, *i.e.,* discarded with the intent of giving up all rights in it, cannot be the subject of larceny. One who finds property that has merely been lost by its owner can, however, commit larceny of it. Two requirements exist:

(i) The finder must know or have reason to believe she ***can find*** out the ***identity of the owner***; and

(ii) The finder must, at the moment she takes possession of the lost property, have the ***intent*** necessary for larceny.

If the finder takes possession of the lost property without the intent to steal but later formulates this intent, she has not committed larceny. Nor has she committed embezzlement, since no trust relationship between the finder and the owner has been created. (*See* below.)

b. **Misdelivered Property**
One to whom property is delivered by mistake may, by accepting the property, commit larceny of it. Two requirements must be met:

1) The recipient must, at the time of the misdelivery, ***realize the mistake*** that is being made; and

2) The recipient must, at the time she accepts the delivery, have the ***intent*** required for larceny.

c. **"Container" Situations**

1) **Issue Is Whether Defendant Already Has Possession**
One subcategory of "misdelivery" cases presents special problems: The "container" cases, in which the defendant is charged with larceny of an item that she discovers within another item after she has legitimately taken possession of the larger item—or the container—from the victim. The difficult question is whether, at the time she appropriates the item, does she already have possession? If so,

larceny is not committed because the property is not taken from the possession of another.

2) **Larceny May Depend on Whether Parties Intended to Transfer Container**
One solution to this problem is to distinguish among cases according to whether or not the parties intended the original transfer to be the transfer of a container, *i.e.,* an item containing other items. If the parties intended to transfer a container, the recipient is regarded as taking immediate possession of both the container and its contents. Her later misappropriation of the contents is not larceny, because it occurs at a time when she already has possession. If, however, both parties did not intend to transfer a container but rather regarded the items transferred as empty (or otherwise not involving a transfer of contained items), the recipient does not obtain possession of the contents until she discovers them. If at the time she discovers and appropriates them she has the intent to steal, she is guilty of larceny.

d. **"Continuing Trespass" Situations**
A trespassory taking of property without the intent required for larceny is not, of course, larceny. However, if a defendant takes property with a wrongful state of mind but without the intent to steal, and later, while still in possession of it, forms the intent to steal it, the trespass involved in the initial wrongful taking is regarded as "continuing" and the defendant is guilty of larceny. This doctrine has no application if the defendant's initial taking of the property, although trespassory, was not motivated by a wrongful state of mind.

Example: A took X's umbrella from X's possession without X's permission, intending to use the umbrella and return it the next day. The next morning when A awoke, she examined the umbrella carefully and decided to keep it. Is A guilty of larceny of the umbrella? Yes. The larceny took place when A formed the intent to steal it. Since her initial possession was wrongful, the trespass continued until she formed the intent to steal. On the other hand, if A had taken X's umbrella by mistake, and later decided to keep it after discovering her mistake, the doctrine would not apply because her initial taking was done with an innocent state of mind.

B. EMBEZZLEMENT

Embezzlement was not originally a common law crime. Intended to plug the gaps in the law of larceny, it was made a misdemeanor by statute in 1799 and is regarded as part of American common law. Modern statutes often distinguish between grand embezzlement (a felony) and petit embezzlement (a misdemeanor) based upon the value of the property embezzled. Although variously defined in different jurisdictions, embezzlement generally requires:

(i) The fraudulent;

(ii) Conversion;

(iii) Of property;

(iv) Of another;

(v) By a person in lawful possession of that property.

1. Distinguished from Larceny

a. Manner of Obtaining Property

In embezzlement, the misappropriation of the property occurs while the defendant has lawful possession of it. In larceny, it occurs generally at the time the defendant obtains wrongful possession of the property.

Example: A was foreman of a construction crew. One day, he took a tool used by the crew to his home. The next day, he was fired. On his way out, he took another tool. Was he guilty of embezzlement of one, two, or no tools? *Held:* Only of the first tool, which he converted while it was in his possession by virtue of his employment. He had no right to possession of the tools at the time he took the second.

b. Manner of Misappropriation

Larceny requires caption and asportation with the intent to permanently deprive. Embezzlement requires intentional conversion. (*See* below.)

2. Conversion

The conversion required by embezzlement requires only that the defendant deal with the property in a manner inconsistent with the trust arrangement pursuant to which he holds it. No movement or carrying away of the property is required. The conversion need not result in direct personal gain to the defendant.

Example: A trustee who siphons off trust fund money in order to donate to a favorite charity is as guilty of embezzlement as the trustee who uses the converted funds to pay his overdue gambling debts.

3. Property

Embezzlement statutes are often worded in terms of "property that may be subject to larceny"; *i.e.,* real property and services may not be embezzled. Some relatively expansive statutes, however, make embezzlement of real property a crime.

Example: A, an agent with apparent authority to sell B's real estate, fraudulently transfers the title to a bona fide purchaser. Is A guilty of embezzlement? No, under the traditional embezzlement statute. Yes, under the more expansive statute.

4. Requirement that Property Be that "Of Another"

Embezzlement requires that the property converted be that of someone other than the converter. Therefore, a person who borrows money, converts the sum to his own use, and subsequently fails to repay it is not guilty of embezzlement.

5. Fraudulent Intent

A defendant must intend to defraud for a conversion to become embezzlement. This appears to be the functional equivalent of larceny's specific intent to permanently deprive.

a. Intent to Restore

If the defendant intended to restore the ***exact*** property taken, it is not embezzlement. But if he intended to restore ***similar or substantially identical*** property, it is embezzlement, even if it was money that was initially taken and other money—of identical value—that he intended to return.

b. **Claim of Right**
As in larceny, embezzlement is not committed if the conversion is pursuant to a claim of right to the property, as where it is retained for payment of a debt honestly believed to be owed. The fact that the defendant retained the property openly tends to establish a claim of right.

6. **Necessity for Demand for Return**
If it is clear that there has been a conversion of the property, the victim need not make a demand that it be returned. If, however, there is doubt as to the existence of a conversion, a demand by the owner for return and a refusal to return by the defendant may be necessary.

7. **Limitation to Property Entrusted**
Some states limit embezzlement to the fraudulent conversion of property "entrusted" or "delivered" to the embezzler. These states would not punish one who finds lost property and, while in lawful possession of it, fraudulently converts it.

C. FALSE PRETENSES

The offense of false pretenses was created by English statute in 1757, and consequently is part of the common law in those American states that use 1776 as the determining date. Like larceny and embezzlement, most jurisdictions distinguish grand false pretenses (a felony) from petit false pretenses (a misdemeanor). The offense of false pretenses generally consists of:

(i) Obtaining title;

(ii) To the property of another;

(iii) By an intentional (or, in some states, knowing) false statement of past or existing fact;

(iv) With intent to defraud the other.

1. **"Larceny by Trick" Distinguished**
False pretenses differs from larceny by trick in what is obtained. If only ***possession*** of the property is obtained by the defendant, the offense is larceny by trick. If ***title*** is obtained, the offense is false pretenses. What is obtained depends upon what the victim intended to convey to the defendant.

Example: D asked X if X would sell a car and offered as payment what was purported to be a demand note signed by Y. D falsely represented that the note was one executed by Y; in fact, D himself had forged it. X agreed to sell the car but told D that the sale would not be final until she had collected the amount of the note from Y. X then permitted D to use the car until Y could be located. D drove off in the car. Has he committed larceny or false pretenses? Larceny, because X did not intend to transfer title to D. X intended only to transfer possession pending collection on the note.

Compare: Same facts as above, except the note purportedly signed by Y is due in 30 days rather than on demand. Based on Y's good credit, X agreed to convey

full title to the car in exchange for the note. D drove off in the car. D has committed false pretenses rather than larceny.

2. Misrepresentation Required

There are several limits upon the misrepresentations required for false pretenses. (These also apply to larceny by trick.)

a. False Representation Concerning Matter of Fact

The defendant must have created a false impression as to the matter of fact. If his statements reasonably construed constitute only an opinion or a "puffing," they are not representations. It is not misrepresentation to fail to correct what is known to be a mistaken belief that the victim holds, ***if*** the defendant was not responsible for creating that belief, or the defendant has no fiduciary duty to the aggrieved party.

b. Misrepresentation Must Relate to Present or Past Facts

The misrepresentation must concern past facts or the present situation. A misrepresentation as to what will occur in the future is not sufficient. A false promise, even if made without the present intent to perform, is also not sufficient.

3. Requirement that Representation Be the "Cause" of Obtaining Property

The victim must actually be deceived by, or act in reliance on, the misrepresentation, and this must be a major factor (or the sole cause) of the victim passing title to the defendant.

4. Intent to Defraud

Depending on the statute involved, the defendant must either have known the statement to be false or have intended that the victim rely upon the misrepresentation. Subjecting the victim to a risk of loss will suffice.

Example: A obtained money from B by representing that he was securing it by a first mortgage on certain property. He intended to pay back the loan. The mortgage actually given was, as A knew, only a second mortgage. Is A guilty of false pretenses? *Held:* Yes. He knowingly subjected B to a substantially greater risk of loss of the money than B was aware of. This was a sufficient intent to defraud.

5. Related Crimes

Many states have enacted specific legislation covering certain conduct that resembles the crime of false pretenses but is sufficiently different to warrant separate consideration.

a. Bad Check Legislation

Almost all jurisdictions have created a new and separate statutory crime prohibiting the giving of a no-account or insufficient funds check with the intent to defraud.

b. Abuse or Misuse of Credit Card

Most jurisdictions have enacted legislation making it a misdemeanor to knowingly obtain property by means of a stolen, forged, canceled, revoked, or otherwise unauthorized credit card.

D. ROBBERY

Robbery, a felony in all jurisdictions, consists of the following:

(i) A taking;

(ii) Of personal property of another;

(iii) From the other's person or presence;

(iv) By force or intimidation;

(v) With the intent to permanently deprive him of it.

Thus, robbery is basically an aggravated form of larceny in which the taking is accomplished by force or threats of force.

1. **Force or Threats Necessary**
If force is used, it obviously must be sufficient to overcome the victim's resistance. If threats are used, they must be threats of immediate death or serious physical injury to the victim, a member of her family, a relative, or a person in her presence at the time. A threat to do damage to property will not suffice, with the exception of a threat to destroy the victim's dwelling house.

2. **Property Must Be Taken from Person or Presence of Victim**
The property must be taken from some location reasonably close to the victim, but it need not be taken from her person. Property is in the victim's presence if it is in her vicinity. Property in other rooms of the house in which the victim is located is in her presence.

3. **Force or Threats Must Be Used to Obtain Property or Immediately Retain It**
The force or threats must be used either to gain possession of the property or to retain possession ***immediately*** after such possession has been accomplished.
Example: A reached into B's pocket without B's knowledge and removed B's wallet. B felt the wallet slip out, turned around, and grabbed A as he moved away. A struck B, rendering her unconscious, and ran. Is A guilty of robbery? *Held:* Yes. The force was used to prevent the victim from immediately apprehending A and regaining the property. Thus, it is sufficiently related to the taking.

4. **Aggravated Robbery**
Statutes often create a form of aggravated robbery, usually defined as robbery accomplished with a deadly weapon.

E. EXTORTION

Extortion is an offense that generally has been expanded by modern statutes far beyond its initial common law definition.

1. **Common Law Definition—Collection of Unlawful Fee**
The common law misdemeanor of extortion consisted of the corrupt collection of an unlawful fee by an officer under color of his office.

2. **Modern Definition—Blackmail**
In many modern statutes, extortion (or blackmail) is defined as obtaining property from another by means of certain oral or written threats. The prohibited threats often include

threats to do physical harm to the victim or others, or threats to damage the victim's property. Under some statutes, the crime is completed when the threats are made with the intent to obtain money or something of value; the threat is the essence of the offense. Under other statutes, the money or property must actually be obtained by means of the threats.

a. **Threats Need Not Involve Immediate or Physical Harm**
Extortion may be committed by threats that are not sufficient for robbery. To constitute extortion, the threats do not need to involve immediate or physical harm.

b. **Property Need Not Be in Victim's Presence**
To constitute extortion, it is generally not necessary that the property be obtained from the victim's person or presence (as is necessary for robbery).

F. RECEIPT OF STOLEN PROPERTY

The common law misdemeanor of receipt of stolen property is substantially identical to the modern offense. The elements of the crime are:

(i) Receiving possession and control;

(ii) Of "stolen" personal property;

(iii) Known to have been obtained in a manner constituting a criminal offense;

(iv) By another person;

(v) With the intent to permanently deprive the owner of his interest in the property.

1. Possession

Manual possession of the property, while sufficient for "receiving," is not necessary. It is also receiving if: (i) the thief places the stolen property in a place that the defendant has designated; or (ii) for profit, the defendant arranges for a sale of the property by the thief to a third person.

2. "Stolen" Property

Most jurisdictions define "stolen" property broadly to include property obtained by commission of any of the property offenses. However, the property must have "stolen" status at the time it is received by the defendant. Thus, if stolen goods have been recovered by the police and are used in an undercover operation with the owner's permission, the goods are not stolen and the defendant cannot be guilty of receipt of stolen property; however, the defendant may be guilty of attempt to receive stolen goods (*see* IV.D.3.a.1)a), *supra*).

G. STATUTORY CHANGES IN PROPERTY ACQUISITION OFFENSES

Modern criminal codes and the M.P.C. have substantially altered the common law. Among the major changes are the following:

1. Consolidation of Offenses into Theft

There is a growing tendency to consolidate larceny, embezzlement, false pretenses, and receipt of stolen goods under the single heading: Theft. It is important to note that theft is a modern statutory crime, not a traditional common law offense.

2. **Expansion of Property Subject to Larceny (and Other Offenses)**
The things subject to the offenses have often been expanded to cover services, documents, and intangibles, as well as joint property.

3. **Rejection of Asportation for Larceny**
Some jurisdictions have rejected the requirement of asportation and require only that "control" of property be obtained.

4. **Rejection of Technicalities of Trespass Requirement**
A number of jurisdictions have replaced the detailed technicalities of the trespass requirement by a simplified requirement that the defendant have obtained unauthorized "control" over the property.

H. FORGERY

At common law, forgery and uttering a forged instrument are separate offenses.

1. **Forgery**
Forgery consists of the following:

   a. Making or altering;

   b. Of a false writing;

   c. With intent to defraud.

2. **Uttering a Forged Instrument**
Uttering consists of:

   a. Offering as genuine;

   b. An instrument that may be the subject of forgery and is false;

   c. With intent to defraud.

3. **Writings that Are Possible Subjects of Forgery**
Any writing that has ***apparent legal significance*** is a potential subject of forgery. Writing includes typewritten, printed, engraved, and similar material.

Example: A drafts and signs what purports to be a letter of introduction from a local physician and a letter of recommendation from a firm represented as a former employer. Both are false. Has A committed one, two, or no forgeries? *Held:* One forgery. The recommendation has apparent legal significance, because one who recommends another may incur legal liability if his recommendation is false. Thus, it can be the subject of forgery. But the letter of introduction has only social significance, and cannot be the subject of forgery.

Writings that derive their value from the mere fact of their existence—historical or artistic value—cannot be the subject of forgery.

Example: A painted a picture and signed it "Rembrandt." She then sold it to X, representing it as an original "Rembrandt." Is A guilty of forgery? No, because the picture and signature derive their value from the fact of their existence. (*Note:* A did commit false pretenses by the sale.)

4. **Required Falsity—Writing Itself Must "Be a Lie"**
It is not sufficient that the writing contains a false statement. The writing must represent itself to be something that it is not.
Examples: 1) A, in charge of a warehouse, issues a warehouse receipt that represents that the warehouse has received certain grain. It has not. Is this forgery? *Held:* No. The warehouse receipt contains a misrepresentation. But it is what it purports to be, *i.e.,* a warehouse receipt issued by one with authority to issue it.

2) B obtains blank receipts from A's warehouse, fills them in so they represent that certain grain has been received, and signs A's name. Is this forgery? *Held:* Yes. The instruments purport to be what they are not, *i.e.,* warehouse receipts issued by one with authority to do so.

5. **Required "Making"**

a. **Entire Instrument or Material Alteration**
Forgery can be committed by the "making" of an entire instrument. It can also, however, be committed by altering an existing instrument, if the alteration is "material," that is, if it affects a legal right. Alteration may be in the form of changing some of the writing, adding to the existing writing, removing some of the existing writing, or improperly filling in blanks left by the signer.

b. **Fraudulently Obtaining Signature of Another**
If the defendant fraudulently causes a third person to sign a document that the third person does not realize he is signing, forgery has been committed. But if the third person realizes he is signing the document, forgery has not been committed even if the third person was induced by fraud to sign it.

6. **Required Intent—Intent to Defraud**
The defendant must have had the intent to defraud, although no one need actually have been defrauded. It is not necessary that she intended to do pecuniary harm; it is sufficient if she intended to harm another in any way.

I. MALICIOUS MISCHIEF
The common law misdemeanor of malicious mischief consists of:

(i) Malicious;

(ii) Destruction of, or damage to;

(iii) Property of another.

1. **Damage Required**
Destruction of the property is not required for malicious mischief. All that is necessary is that some physical damage be done that impairs the utility of the property or materially diminishes its value.

2. **State of Mind Required—Malice**
Malice requires no ill will or hatred. It does, however, require that the damage or destruction have been intended or contemplated by the defendant.

X. OFFENSES AGAINST THE HABITATION

A. BURGLARY
At common law, the elements of burglary are:

(i) A breaking;

(ii) And entry;

(iii) Of the dwelling;

(iv) Of another;

(v) At nighttime;

(vi) With the intent of committing a felony therein.

1. **Breaking Required**

a. **Actual Breaking—Minimal Force Sufficient**
Actual breaking requires some use of force to gain entry, but minimal force is sufficient; opening a closed but unlocked door constitutes a breaking. If force is used to enlarge an opening so that entry can be made, the traditional rule was that this did not constitute a breaking. Under the better view, however, a breaking has occurred because force was used to gain entry.

Example: D, intending to steal a valuable painting inside V's house, approaches V's door. The door is open about six inches. D pushes it fully open and enters. Is D guilty of burglary? The best answer is yes, since force—although only minor force—was used to gain entry.

b. **Constructive Breaking**
Constructive breaking consists of gaining entry by means of fraud, threat, or intimidation, or by use of the chimney.

Example: P wants to get into V's apartment to commit a felonious assault on V, but V's door is securely locked. P knocks and when V asks who it is, P responds, "I am a friend of your brother and he asked me to deliver this message to you." V then unlocks the door and invites P in. P enters. P has never met V's brother. Is P guilty of burglary? Yes. Since entry was obtained by fraud, this is constructive breaking.

c. **Requirement of Trespass—Consent to Enter**
A breaking requires a trespass, so that if the defendant had the consent of the resident to enter, his use of force to gain entry is not a breaking. The existence of consent to enter during limited periods, however, will not prevent entry by force at other times from

being a breaking. Moreover, if the consent was procured by fraud or threats, this is a constructive breaking.

d. **Requirement that Breaking Be "Of the House"**
The breaking must be to effect entry into the structure or some separately secured subportion of it. Thus, it is sufficient that the defendant broke to enter a closed closet or wall safe within a dwelling, but it is not enough if he merely breaks open a box or trunk within the dwelling.

e. **Breaking to Exit Insufficient**
The breaking ***must be to gain entry***. It is not burglary to hide in a dwelling, with the intent to commit a felony, and then break to get out of the dwelling.

2. **Entry Required**
Entry is made by placing any portion of the body inside the structure, even momentarily. Insertion of a tool or inanimate object into the structure is entry if it is inserted for the purpose of accomplishing the felony. It is not sufficient if it is inserted for purposes of gaining entry.

Examples: 1) A approached B's dwelling and shot a bullet through his window, intending to kill B. Has A committed burglary? *Held:* Yes. He has inserted an inanimate object into the dwelling by breaking for the purpose of committing the felony.

2) Z intends to go into V's house and steal valuable jewels from a safe. He carefully cuts out a small portion of glass from a window and reaches in with his hand to unlock the window. At that point he is apprehended. Is Z guilty of burglary? Yes. His hand had "entered" the dwelling.

3. **"Dwelling"—Used for Sleeping Purposes**
A structure is a dwelling if it is used with regularity for sleeping purposes.

a. **Used for Other Purposes—Still a Dwelling**
A structure remains a dwelling even if it is also used for other purposes, such as conducting a business.

b. **Temporary Absence of Inhabitants—Still a Dwelling**
Temporary absence of those dwelling in a structure will not deprive it of its character as a dwelling. It is not a dwelling, however, before anyone has moved in, even if it was built for use as a dwelling, nor does it remain a dwelling after the last dweller has moved out with no intent to return.

4. **"Of Another"—Occupancy Is Determinative**
The requirement is that the structure be used as a dwelling by someone other than the defendant. Occupancy rather than ownership is material. An owner can commit burglary of his own structure if it is rented and used as a dwelling by others.

5. **Requirement of Nighttime**
Burglary could be committed only during the nighttime, defined as that period during which the countenance of a person could not be discerned by natural light.

6. Required Intent—Intent to Commit a Felony at Time of Entry
The defendant must have intended to commit a felony. It is not necessary that this be carried out. It is, however, essential that the intent exist at the time of entry; if the intent is formed after entry is completed, burglary is not committed.

7. Modern Statutory Changes
Modern statutes have modified the common law definition of burglary in a variety of ways that differ among jurisdictions. Some of the most common are as follows:

a. Abandonment of Requirement of Breaking
In many jurisdictions, it is sufficient that the defendant entered the structure, even if he did not break to gain entry.

b. Remaining in a Structure
It is often made burglary to remain concealed in a structure with the intent to commit an offense.

c. Broadening Structures that Can Be Burglarized
The description of structures that can be burglarized is often expanded beyond dwellings and sometimes beyond structures to include yards and cars.

d. Elimination of Nighttime Requirement
The requirement that entry be at nighttime is often abandoned, although burglary at nighttime is often assigned a more severe penalty than other burglaries. Nighttime is often defined by statute in terms of sunset and sunrise.

e. Intent to Commit Misdemeanor Theft
The intent necessary is often expanded to make it sufficient that the defendant intended to commit any theft, even if it was misdemeanor theft.

B. ARSON
At common law, arson consists of:

(i) The malicious;

(ii) Burning;

(iii) Of the dwelling;

(iv) Of another.

1. Requirement of a "Burning"

a. Necessity of Fire
At common law, the required damage (*see* below) must be caused by ***fire***; damage caused by an explosion does not constitute arson.

b. Damage Required—"Scorching" (Insufficient) vs. "Charring" (Sufficient)
Traditionally, destruction of the structure or even significant damage to it is not required

to complete the crime of arson. But mere blackening by smoke or discoloration by heat (scorching) is not sufficient. There must be some damage to the fiber of the wood or other combustible material; this is generally stated as the rule that "mere charring is sufficient."

2. "Dwelling"

At common law, dwelling was defined for arson as it was for burglary. (*See* above.) Most states by statute extend arson to structures other than dwellings. (*Note:* Questions on the Multistate Exam that are testing on other arson issues (*e.g.,* malice) will often assume without saying that the jurisdiction's arson law applies to structures other than dwellings.)

3. "Of Another"—Ownership Immaterial

Arson, like burglary, is a crime against the habitation. Thus, the structure had to be used as a dwelling by another; ownership was not material, even if the defendant himself was the owner. (*Note:* At common law, the burning of one's house was the misdemeanor of "house-burning" if other dwellings were nearby.)

4. State of Mind Required—Malice

The burning does not have to be with ill will or for any particular motive. No specific intent is required. On the other hand, it is not sufficient that the burning was accidental, even if the defendant was negligent. All that malice requires is that the defendant have acted with the intent or knowledge that the structure would burn, or with ***reckless disregard*** of an obvious risk that the structure would burn.

5. Related Offenses

a. Houseburning

The common law misdemeanor of houseburning consists of:

1) Malicious (as defined in arson);

2) Burning;

3) Of one's own dwelling;

4) If the structure is situated either:

   a) In a city or town; or

   b) So near to other houses as to create a danger to them.

b. Arson with Intent to Defraud an Insurer

At common law, it was not arson to burn one's own dwelling for purposes of fraudulently collecting the insurance on it. But this is often made an offense by modern statutes.

6. Modern Statutory Changes

Like statutory changes for burglary, modern arson statutes (including the M.P.C.) have modified the common law rules, usually to expand potential criminal liability. Most states

have expanded the definition of arson to include damage caused by explosion, and expanded the types of property that may be destroyed to include commercial structures, cars, trains, etc.

XI. OFFENSES INVOLVING JUDICIAL PROCEDURE

A. PERJURY

A misdemeanor at common law, perjury consisted of the willful and corrupt taking of a false oath in regard to a material matter in a judicial proceeding.

1. Materiality

Materiality is an element of this offense, which must be alleged in the indictment and proved by the prosecution. The statement is material if it might affect some phase or detail of the trial, hearing, declaration, etc.

2. Contradictory Statements

If a witness has made two contradictory statements at the same proceeding and admits, before the end of the proceeding, that one of the statements is false, he cannot be prosecuted for having made the false statement. This is to encourage witnesses to correct any false statements they may have made before substantial damage is caused.

3. Civil Liability

In litigation brought under 42 U.S.C. section 1983 (Civil Rights Act), all witnesses—including police officers—are absolutely immune from civil liability based on their testimony (*i.e.,* alleged perjury) in judicial proceedings. [Briscoe v. LaHue, 460 U.S. 325 (1983)]

B. SUBORNATION OF PERJURY

A separate offense at common law, subornation of perjury consists of procuring or inducing another to commit perjury. In some states, this is not part of the perjury statute.

C. BRIBERY

The common law misdemeanor of bribery consisted of the corrupt payment or receipt of anything of value in return for official action. Under modern statutes, it can be a felony, and it may be extended to classes of persons who are not public officials (*e.g.,* athletes). Either the offering of a bribe or the taking of a bribe may constitute the crime.

1. Mutual Criminal Intent Unnecessary

It is not necessary that there be mutual criminal intent on the part of both the person tendering the bribe and the recipient.

2. Failure to Report a Bribe

Some statutes also make it a misdemeanor offense to fail to report a bribe.

D. COMPOUNDING A CRIME

At common law, the misdemeanor of compounding a crime consisted of entering into an agreement ***for valuable consideration*** to not prosecute another for a felony or to conceal the commission of a felony or whereabouts of a felon.

Under modern statutes, the definition remains essentially the same, except that it refers to ***any crime*** (not only felonies). A few states make it a felony offense.

E. MISPRISION OF A FELONY

At common law, the misdemeanor of misprision of a felony consisted of the failure—by someone other than a principal or accessory before the fact—to disclose or report knowledge of the commission of a felony. Misprision was distinguished from compounding a crime in that no passage of consideration was required for the former. Today most jurisdictions do not recognize the crime of misprision of a felony. In these jurisdictions, therefore, a person is under ***no obligation to report a crime***.

REVIEW QUESTIONS

INTRODUCTORY NOTE

The questions that follow are intended to serve as both a substantive review and a diagnostic test. Respond to the questions quickly and compare your answers with those found at the end of this section. This will allow you to identify areas in which you may need further review.

FILL IN ANSWER

MERGER

1. Defendant offers Hitman $1,000 to murder Victim, and Hitman does so. Can Defendant be convicted of either solicitation or criminal homicide? ________

PHYSICAL ACT

2. To save himself from falling, Defendant grabs at a passerby, Victim, causing her severe injury. Has Defendant "acted" so as to be guilty of any crime? ________

3. After a quarrel with Husband, Wife takes a fatal overdose of sleeping pills. Husband observes this, and decides to let the pills take their effect although he knows that he could save her by calling a doctor.

   a. Has Husband "acted" so as to be guilty of any crime? ________

   b. If he has, is his "act" a proximate cause of Wife's death? ________

   c. If Husband is otherwise liable for Wife's death, would it be a defense that Wife herself was guilty of a crime (suicide)? ________

   d. Would it be a defense that Wife had in effect ***consented*** to die? ________

4. Defendant assaults Victim with intent to rape her. In an attempt to escape, Victim falls into the river, is overcome by the current, and drowns.

   a. If Defendant could have rescued her, but chose not to, has he "acted" so that her death is attributable to him? ________

   b. Would Defendant have committed a homicide if he ***lacked the ability*** to save Victim (*e.g.*, Defendant could not swim and there was no other way of saving Victim)? ________

   c. Would Defendant have committed a homicide if he was ***unaware*** of Victim's predicament (*e.g.*, Defendant had turned away just before Victim fell into the river)? ________

5. Same facts as in previous question. But assume now that before Victim drowned, her predicament was observed by Witness, who was an expert swimmer.

a. If Witness failed to go to Victim's assistance because he "didn't want to get involved," is Witness guilty of homicide? ________

b. Suppose Witness knew Victim, hated her, and purposefully refrained from assisting her in order that she would drown. Would Witness now be guilty of homicide? ________

c. Suppose Witness had been hired by the city as a lifeguard to patrol the swimming area in question. Would Witness now be guilty of homicide if he failed to go to Victim's aid? ________

MENTAL STATE

6. If Defendant is charged with "assault with intent to commit murder," the prosecution must prove, among other things, that Defendant acted with a ***specific intent*** to kill. True or false? ________

7. If a statute fails to specify any particular mental state, the crime is automatically classified as a "strict liability offense." True or false? ________

8. Defendant puts poison in Victim's drink, intending to kill him.

   a. If Bystander drinks the poison instead of Victim, and Bystander dies, is Defendant guilty of an ***intentional*** killing of Bystander? ________

   b. If Bystander merely became ill from the poison, could Defendant be prosecuted for a ***battery*** upon Bystander? ________

9. If a crime is a "strict liability" offense, can Defendant be convicted on the basis of acts that result from ***ordinary*** negligence? ________

10. Defendant sets off a charge of dynamite in a building, which he had been employed to demolish for highway construction purposes. A drunk had entered the building the night before and was still asleep therein when the blast went off, and was killed in the blast. If Defendant knew that drunks had occasionally used the building for sleeping in the past, and made no effort to find out whether there were any drunks asleep therein at the time of the blast, Defendant's mental state would be classified as "wanton." True or false? ________

11. If Defendant is charged with "receiving stolen property," it is sufficient if the prosecution proves that a reasonable person in Defendant's shoes would have known that the merchandise was stolen. True or false? ________

ACCOMPLICE LIABILITY

12. Defendant procures poison for Actor to poison Victim. Actor does so and Victim dies. Actor is arrested but is acquitted at trial. May Defendant now be convicted of first degree murder? ________

13. Defendant leases an apartment to Madam, knowing that she intends to use the apartment for purposes of prostitution, a misdemeanor.

    a. If Defendant does nothing more, Defendant cannot be held criminally liable for Madam's activities. True or false? ________

    b. If Defendant charges Madam a percentage of the "take" as rental for the apartment, Defendant cannot be held criminally liable for Madam's activities. True or false? ________

    c. If Defendant "screens" all callers, and puts in a special buzzer to alert Madam in the event the police arrive, Defendant cannot be held criminally liable for Madam's activities. True or false? ________

14. Defendant works in a drugstore and tells Thief that he will leave the door unlatched so that Thief can enter the store after it closes and take some drugs. That night, Defendant leaves the door unlatched, and Thief enters and takes the drugs. If Thief is an undercover police agent who takes the drugs in order to implicate Defendant, Defendant cannot be prosecuted as an accessory before the fact to theft of the drugs. True or false? ________

15. Defendant hires Thief to steal a car for Defendant. Thief kills the night watchman of an auto dealer when he steals the car. Is Defendant criminally liable for the homicide? ________

SOLICITATION

16. Defendant observes Actor in the process of beating Victim. Defendant shouts, "Good hit!" The beating continues, resulting in Victim's death. Is Defendant guilty of solicitation? ________

17. Defendant hires Actor to murder Victim. Actor is an undercover police officer, who arrests Defendant on the spot. Can Defendant be convicted of solicitation? ________

18. Defendant offers Madam $100 to engage in an act of prostitution. Madam refuses. Can Defendant be convicted of solicitation at common law? ________

CONSPIRACY

19. Pete and Joe agree to "fix" a basketball game to take advantage of the betting odds. Can they be convicted of conspiracy? ________

20. Abel and Baker publicly announce plans to blow up the state capitol as part of a protest movement. Charlie reads about their plans and sends them a wire: "It's a great idea! I support what you plan to do!" Is Charlie guilty of conspiracy? ________

21. Jesse and Billy agree to hold up a liquor store. Billy buys a map of the area in order to plan the job. If nothing further happens, can Jesse and Billy be convicted of conspiracy? ________

22. Wyatt hires Jesse and Billy to hold up a liquor store, with the understanding that only toy guns will be used, and Wyatt will remain outside the store. Jesse enters the store and uses a real gun, killing the owner. On leaving, Billy throws a firebomb into the store, burning it down.

    a. Can Wyatt be convicted of a homicide? ________

    b. Can Wyatt be convicted of burning down the store? ________

23. Abel tells Baker and Charlie, separately, about his plans to blow up the state capitol. Baker agrees to furnish the getaway car, and Charlie agrees to furnish a hiding place for Abel. Can Baker and Charlie be convicted of conspiracy if they never met each other and neither realized that anyone else was involved in Abel's scheme? ________

24. Jesse and Wyatt agree to hold up a liquor store. However, Wyatt is an undercover police officer, and he immediately arrests Jesse. Can Jesse be convicted of conspiracy under common law? ________

25. John agrees with a woman, Trixie, to cross state lines to have her engage in prostitution in violation of the Mann Act. Can ***both*** be prosecuted for conspiracy under common law? Can ***either*** be prosecuted? ________

26. Wanda, a married woman, is having an affair with her secretary, Sam. They agree to spend the night together at the Bijou Motel. Can they be prosecuted for conspiracy to commit adultery? ________

27. Abel and Baker agree to attempt to "corner the market" on pork bellies, unaware that such activities are illegal under a state statute. Is their ignorance of the law a defense to a conspiracy charge? ________

28. Jesse and Billy agree to rob a liquor store. On the way to the store, Jesse tells Billy that he has changed his mind and leaves; Billy decides to carry on by himself and completes the crime.

    a. Can Jesse be convicted of conspiracy? ________

    b. Can Jesse be convicted as an accomplice to Billy's robbery? ________

29. Can a person be convicted of ***both*** conspiracy ***and*** the completed crime? ________

ATTEMPT

30. Defendant is beneficiary of an insurance policy on Victim's life. He decides to murder Victim. Does Defendant become guilty of attempted murder when:

a. Defendant hires Hitman to shoot Victim? ________

b. Hitman rigs a bomb under Victim's car, unaware that Victim is out of town? ________

c. Dissatisfied with Hitman's performance, Defendant decides to kill Victim himself, buys a gun, and lies in wait outside Victim's house? ________

d. While lying in wait outside Victim's house, Defendant fires at (but misses) a figure that he thinks is Victim, but turns out to be a large dog? ________

31. Assuming Defendant has committed a preparatory act, could he be convicted of attempted murder if it was shown that Victim had been in a traffic accident on the way home, and was ***already dead*** at the time Defendant reached his ambush site? ________

32. Defendant throws a firebomb into a passing freight train, unaware that a hobo is riding inside one of the cars. The hobo almost dies from the burns inflicted. Is Defendant guilty of either attempted murder or attempted manslaughter? ________

33. Defendant decides to blow up the state capitol. She plants the bomb and lights the fuse. Just before the bomb explodes, she snuffs out the fuse and deactivates the bomb. Can Defendant be convicted of criminal attempt? ________

34. Suppose the bomb actually went off. Could Defendant be ***convicted*** of ***both*** the attempt ***and*** the completed crime? ________

RESPONSIBILITY AND CRIMINAL CAPACITY

35. Can an accused claim insanity as a defense if his mental illness has been caused by prolonged and excessive use of drugs? ________

36. In states retaining the *M'Naghten* test of insanity, must it be shown that the accused ***both*** did not know the "nature or quality" of his act, ***and*** did not know that it was "morally wrong"? ________

37. In states retaining the *M'Naghten* test, the accused's capacity to "know" the nature of his act or its "wrongfulness" is measured by his level of ***emotional*** maturity, rather than strictly ***intellectual*** capacity. True or false? ________

38. Suppose the evidence shows that the accused's mental illness ***had not completely*** deprived him of the capacity to know and understand what he was doing or its "wrongfulness" or to control his acts. The fact that he had ***some limited*** capacity would allow him to establish "insanity" as a defense under which, if any, of the following tests? ________

a. *M'Naghten* test.

b. The "irresistible impulse" test.

c. The American Law Institute "substantial capacity" test.

39. At a party, Defendant drinks a "punch" which, through no fault of his, he mistakenly believes is nonalcoholic, but which in fact intoxicates him. His intoxication is a possible defense to ***any*** crime requiring a mens rea. True or false? ________

40. At a party, Defendant drinks a "punch" which he ***knows*** contains alcohol, and becomes quite intoxicated, although he wishes to remain sober. His intoxication is a possible defense to burglary, but not to battery. True or false? ________

EXCULPATION

41. Is Defendant's killing Victim justified where it appears that—

   a. Victim struck Defendant first with a rubber hose, and Defendant responded with a knife? ________

   b. Defendant started the fight by punching Victim in the nose, and Victim suddenly retaliated with a knife, whereupon Defendant "stood his ground" and shot Victim? ________

   c. Defendant was seated in his car when Victim drew a knife on him, whereupon Defendant shot Victim? ________

   d. Victim was attempting to rape a woman when Defendant shot him? ________

   e. Victim was attempting to steal Defendant's car when Defendant shot him? ________

42. Father attempts to lightly spank Son to punish him for lying. Son moves away at the last minute, and Father hits Friend instead. Is Father guilty of a battery on Friend? ________

43. Plainclothes police officer Pete was attempting to arrest Betty on a drunk and disorderly charge, and she was struggling to escape. Defendant saw this, and mistakenly thought Pete was attempting to rape Betty. Defendant drew a gun and killed Pete. If Defendant's mistake was reasonable, is the homicide excusable? ________

44. At gunpoint, Art forces Betty to drive him away from the scene of a larceny.

   a. Does Betty thereby become an accessory after the fact to Art's crime? ________

   b. If Art forced Betty to run down a police officer at a police roadblock, killing the police officer, would she be guilty of a criminal homicide? ________

   c. Suppose Art was ***not*** armed when he jumped in the car, but threatened Betty that if she did not do exactly as told, he would return later and kill her family. Under these circumstances, could Betty be convicted as an accessory after the fact to Art's larceny? ________

45. Defendant drives away in Victim's car and is promptly arrested for grand theft auto. His defense is that he thought the car was his own. Which of the following must Defendant prove? _________

    a. That he ***reasonably*** believed the car was his.

    b. That he ***honestly*** believed the car was his.

    c. That his belief was ***both honest and reasonable.***

46. Defendant, for no good reason, menaces Victim with a gun, which he thinks is unloaded. Expecting only to frighten Victim, Defendant pulls the trigger, but the gun fires and kills Victim. If Defendant was both "honestly" and "reasonably" mistaken, his mistake of fact is a defense to a criminal prosecution. True or false? _________

47. Wife married Husband in the mistaken belief that her earlier Mexican divorce decree was valid.

    a. Is her reasonable mistake as to the validity of the Mexican decree by itself a valid defense to a bigamy charge? _________

    b. Would her mistake of law be a valid defense if it was based on erroneous advice that Wife had received from a reputable attorney? _________

    c. Would her mistake of law be a valid defense if based on erroneous advice given to her by the chief clerk at the marriage license bureau? _________

48. On Father's death intestate, Son takes all of Father's cash and squanders it. He is prosecuted for theft. His defense is that he thought that he was Father's sole heir under intestate laws (whereas in fact he is not). Son loses, because "mistake of law is no defense." True or false? _________

49. Defendant drives off in Victim's car, intending to keep it permanently. Victim calls the police and Defendant is arrested and charged with grand theft auto. Which, if any, of the following would constitute a valid defense? _________

    a. Victim had told Defendant that he could use Victim's car to drive Defendant's "sick wife" to the hospital. (Later, Victim found out that Defendant had no wife.)

    b. After Defendant had misappropriated the car, Victim told him it was "o.k." and that he would not file charges against Defendant.

    c. Victim recaptured the auto and accepted $1,000 from Defendant in return for his agreement not to report the matter to the police.

    d. Victim had left the keys in the ignition, in violation of a state law specifically designed to prevent car theft.

    e. Victim didn't even own the car, but had stolen it from Owner; moreover, Victim was using the car for the illegal transport of narcotics.

50. Narcotics agents arrest Informant for possession of heroin. They tell him that if he will help them gather evidence against Defendant, a suspected "pusher," they will drop the charges against Informant. Informant approaches Defendant suffering from what appear to be withdrawal symptoms and begs for a "fix"; after several refusals, Defendant goes out and later returns with some heroin, which he sells to Informant. Defendant is promptly arrested.

    a. Defendant cannot successfully claim entrapment as a defense because Informant was not a government officer. True or false? ________

    b. If Defendant was in fact already engaged in selling heroin, he cannot claim entrapment, and it makes no difference that he was deceived by Informant. True or false? ________

ASSAULT AND BATTERY

51. Which of the following acts would constitute a battery? ________

    a. Defendant puts poison in Victim's drink, and Victim drinks it.

    b. Defendant kisses Victim while she is asleep, knowing that she would not consent if awake.

    c. At gunpoint, Defendant forces Victim to jump from a second-story window.

    d. Defendant intentionally spits on Victim's shoes.

52. Suppose Defendant was criminally negligent in driving his car, and it struck Victim. Would Defendant be guilty of a battery? ________

53. Defendant points a gun at Victim and pulls the trigger, but the gun does not go off.

    a. Suppose Defendant thought the gun was loaded, but it was not. Is Defendant guilty of an assault? ________

    b. Suppose Defendant ***knew*** the gun was unloaded, and she only intended to frighten Victim (who was frightened). Is Defendant guilty of an assault? ________

54. Defendant intended to punch Victim in the mouth, but missed, and only barely touched Victim's shoulder. Can Defendant be convicted of ***both*** an assault ***and*** a battery? ________

MAYHEM

55. Defendant slashes at Victim with a knife, intending to cut off his ear, but she misses and cuts Victim's face, which leaves a large scar. Is Defendant guilty of mayhem? ________

HOMICIDE

56. Wife is suffering from an incurable disease causing her great pain, and begs Husband to kill her. He complies reluctantly.

    a. Is this killing a homicide? ________

    b. If it is, is it murder? ________

57. Which, if any, of the following acts could result in a ***murder*** conviction? ________

    a. Defendant slashes at Victim with a knife for the purpose of inflicting a slight wound, but an infection sets in and Victim dies.

    b. Defendant throws a bottle in Victim's general direction; it shatters and a piece of glass cuts Victim, a hemophiliac, and he eventually bleeds to death.

    c. Defendant intentionally drops a heavy rock from a bridge onto a freeway; the rock causes Victim to lose control of his car, and he is killed in the crash.

    d. Defendant is engaged in an illegal "drag race" on a public highway when his car goes out of control, killing Victim.

58. Assuming an adequate provocation, an intentional killing is murder rather than manslaughter if sufficient time elapsed between the provocation and killing that a ***reasonable person*** would have regained control of himself, even though the defendant may not have. True or false? ________

59. Defendant intentionally kills Victim. Which, if any, of the following facts would be sufficient to reduce the homicide from murder to manslaughter at common law? ________

    a. Defendant had been drinking all night, and had no recollection of his acts.

    b. Defendant is emotionally unstable (although not insane).

    c. A third person held a gun on Defendant and forced him to shoot Victim.

    d. Victim had called Defendant a coward in front of a crowd of people.

    e. Victim had bragged, in front of a crowd of people, about having an affair with Defendant's wife.

60. If a killing is felony murder, is it necessarily first degree murder? ________

61. Which, if any, of the following killings should be charged as ***involuntary manslaughter?*** ________

a. Defendant intentionally dropped a large rock from a freeway overpass, which caused Victim to lose control of his car on the freeway, and to be killed in a crash.

b. In a drunken rage, Defendant threw a kerosene lamp at Victim, which missed Victim but crashed into a wall, starting a fire in which Victim was killed.

c. Defendant was attempting to commit suicide. Victim attempted to disarm Defendant, but in the ensuing struggle, the gun went off, killing Victim.

62. In determining whether a killing is first degree murder, will the court consider evidence that the accused was ***voluntarily*** intoxicated? ________

63. Defendant beats Victim with his fists (a battery). Victim trips and falls, hitting his head, and death results. Does the felony murder rule apply? ________

64. Moe, Larry, and Curly rob a store. In the course of the robbery, Larry accidentally shoots the store owner and kills him.

a. Are all three of the robbers liable for the store owner's death under the felony murder rule? ________

b. If Moe became enraged at Larry for shooting the victim, and therefore shot Larry, would both Moe and Curly be guilty of the felony murder of Larry? ________

c. If the police arrive during the robbery and shoot Curly, who was attempting to escape, is Moe guilty of the felony murder of Curly? ________

65. Butch and Sundance are in the process of robbing a bank. Sundance becomes attracted to one of the tellers and forces his attentions upon her, notwithstanding Butch's repeated admonitions to stop this conduct. Finally, Butch strikes Sundance with the butt of Butch's gun, but the gun discharges accidentally, and kills Sundance. Is Butch guilty of felony murder of Sundance? ________

66. Defendant is in the process of holding up a liquor store with a toy pistol which appears to be real. The police arrive and order Defendant to throw down his weapon. Instead, he attempts to run. The police fire, but their bullets miss Defendant and kill an innocent bystander, Victim. Is Defendant guilty of felony murder? ________

67. Defendant stabs Victim. The wound itself is not fatal, but Victim goes into shock, which causes a fatal heart attack. Has Defendant committed a criminal homicide? ________

68. Defendant stabs Victim. The wound itself is not fatal, but surgery is required. The surgeon negligently performs the operation, causing Victim to die. Has Defendant committed a homicide? ________

69. Defendant stabs Victim. The wound itself is not fatal, but Victim refuses medical care and consequently bleeds to death. Has Defendant committed a homicide? ________

SEX OFFENSES

70. Defendant picks up a woman in a bar, who agrees to have sexual relations with him for $20. Later, she changes her mind and refuses, even though Defendant has already paid her the $20.

    a. Defendant then forces her to submit. Is Defendant guilty of rape? ________

    b. What if, when Victim refused, Defendant threatened to tell the police that Victim was a prostitute. If Victim submitted only as a result of such threat, would Defendant be guilty of rape? ________

71. Defendant picks up a woman in a bar, who willingly accompanies him to his apartment and drinks a great deal of the liquor he offers her. She passes out, and thinking she would not mind, Defendant commits the physical act upon her. Is Defendant guilty of rape? ________

72. Defendant picks up a woman in a bar, who agrees to have sexual relations with him for $20. After completing sexual intercourse, Defendant refuses to pay the $20. Is Defendant guilty of rape? ________

LARCENY AND RELATED OFFENSES

73. Which of the following items can be the subject of common law larceny? ________

    a. Avocados growing on the tree.

    b. Heroin.

    c. Stolen goods.

    d. Lost goods.

74. Which of the following acts are punishable as larceny at common law? ________

    a. Defendant takes Victim's horse for a ride without Victim's consent, later returning it to its stall.

    b. Defendant leaves his TV set with Victim for repairs. After finishing repairs, Victim demands $100. Defendant takes his TV set without Victim's knowledge, and without having paid for the repairs.

    c. Defendant and Partner own a business as partners. Defendant takes the business car without Partner's consent and refuses to return it.

d. Defendant sneaks into Victim's plant and photographs secret formulas belonging to Victim.

e. Defendant sneaks into Victim's plant and uses Victim's computer without Victim's knowledge or consent.

75. Victim asks his chauffeur, Defendant, to drive Victim's car to the garage for service. Instead, Defendant absconds with Victim's car.

a. If Defendant decided to steal the car on the way to the garage, is he guilty of common law larceny? ________

b. Would it be common law larceny if Defendant was employed in some supervisory or managerial capacity, rather than as a mere chauffeur? ________

c. Would it be common law larceny if Defendant had been given the car to drive on his day off? ________

76. Defendant promises to take Victim's car to an "auto auction" and sell it on Victim's behalf. Instead, Defendant steals Victim's car. Is Defendant guilty of common law larceny? ________

77. On payday, an employer leaves his clerk in the store without paying him his wages. The clerk takes his pay out of the employer's cash register, intending to put the money back when paid his wages. Is the clerk guilty of common law larceny? ________

78. Defendant takes a shopping cart from the parking lot outside Victim's market, and notifies Victim that he will return it on payment of $10. Is Defendant guilty of common law larceny? ________

79. Employer sends her employee to car dealer to pick up a new car that Employer has ordered. Employee decides to steal the car and drives off with it. Is Employee guilty of common law larceny? ________

80. Defendant picks up a briefcase in a public restroom at the airport. Later, he opens it up and finds that it contains $100,000, which he decides to keep. Is Defendant guilty of common law larceny if—

a. He mistakenly believed that it was his own briefcase when he picked it up? ________

b. He knew it wasn't his when he picked it up, but there was no identification on it, so he decided to take it for himself? ________

c. He knew it wasn't his when he picked it up, but thought it belonged to a friend who had just left, and took it intending to return it to this friend? ________

d. He knew it wasn't his own when he picked it up, but honestly believed that the law was "finders-keepers" so that he was entitled to keep it? ________

81. Victim sells his car to Defendant, having forgotten to remove his golf clubs from the trunk. A week later, Defendant finds the golf clubs and decides to keep them. Is Defendant guilty of common law larceny? ________

82. Victim takes his car to Defendant's garage for service. After he fixes the car, Defendant decides to keep it for himself, and takes off in Victim's car. Is Defendant guilty of common law larceny? ________

83. Defendant borrows $5,000 from the Victim Bank. Defendant later decides to abscond with the $5,000 without repaying the loan. Is Defendant guilty of common law larceny? Of embezzlement? Of false pretenses? ________

84. Defendant borrows $500 from his employer's cash drawer, putting in its place a signed "I.O.U." for $500. Is Defendant guilty of common law larceny? Of embezzlement? ________

85. Defendant buys a car for $5,000, paying for it with a check that he knows to be worthless. Is Defendant guilty of common law larceny? Of false pretenses? ________

86. Car dealer Defendant sets back the odometer on a car he sells to Victim, from 90,000 miles to 9,000 miles, but makes no other representation regarding the car's mileage. Victim purchased in reliance on the mileage shown on the odometer.

    a. Is Defendant guilty of false pretenses? ________

    b. Could Defendant successfully defend on the ground that no reasonable person would have relied on the mileage shown, because of the condition of the car, etc.? ________

87. Which, if any, of the following thefts constitute ***robbery*** at common law? ________

    a. Defendant "lifts" Victim's wallet without Victim's feeling it.

    b. Defendant attempts to rape Victim; she flees, leaving her purse behind, which Defendant then finds and takes.

    c. Victim pays over $500 to Defendant, after Defendant has threatened to accuse Victim of committing arson.

    d. Victim is killed in a traffic accident. Defendant clips and takes a valuable necklace from around Victim's neck.

88. Witness sees Defendant commit robbery. Witness demands $1,000 from Defendant to "keep quiet" about what he saw, and Defendant pays. Is Witness guilty of ***extortion?*** ________

89. If the police have in fact recovered the "stolen" property, and thereafter use it in a plan to catch the "fence," can the "fence" be convicted for receiving "stolen" property? ________

90. If a pawnbroker buys goods from one whom he ***suspects*** is a thief (but does not know for sure), and purposefully makes no further inquiry regarding the source of the goods, is he guilty of receiving stolen property? ________

91. Which of the following acts, if done with fraudulent intent, would constitute ***forgery?*** ________

   a. Defendant signs Victim's name to a will while Victim is still alive.

   b. Defendant signs his own name to a deed of property that he knows he does not own.

   c. Defendant signs the name "Picasso" to a painting that is a copy of a real Picasso.

   d. Defendant scratches out Victim's name on Victim's driver's license and inserts his own.

   e. Defendant obtains Victim's signature on a promissory note by telling Victim that it is only an application for credit.

BURGLARY

92. Defendant crawls into Victim's home at night through an open window for the purpose of raping her, but Victim is not at home.

   a. Would Defendant's entry be common law burglary? ________

   b. Would it be common law burglary if the window was left open by Victim's maid, who was working in collusion with Defendant? ________

   c. If Defendant opened Victim's bedroom door and entered, looking for her, would Defendant be guilty of common law burglary? ________

93. Landlord uses a passkey to enter Tenant's house at night to steal Tenant's jewelry. Is Landlord guilty of common law burglary? ________

94. Which, if any, of the following factors would ***by itself*** constitute a defense to a common law burglary charge? ________

   a. The owners were out of town when Defendant broke in, and no one was at home.

   b. Once inside, Defendant abandoned whatever felonious intent he had and left without causing any harm.

   c. Defendant was only looking for shelter from a storm when he broke in; later he decided to steal whatever he could.

d. Defendant had been drinking before he broke in.

e. Defendant intended no harm to the occupants when he broke in; he was only looking for some food to eat.

ARSON

95. Defendant throws a firebomb into Victim's house. The bomb lands on a sofa and burns the fabric and then goes out. Is Defendant guilty of arson? ________

96. Tenant in Apartment House sets fire to his own apartment to protest Landlord's failure to repair the premises as agreed. The fire accidentally spreads to other apartments in the building. Is Tenant guilty of common law arson? ________

97. While burglarizing Victim's home, Defendant unintentionally leaves a burning cigarette, and a fire results, destroying the house. Is Defendant guilty of common law arson? ________

98. While burglarizing a building filled with high explosives, Defendant unintentionally leaves a burning cigarette, and the resulting fire and explosion destroy the building. Is Defendant guilty of arson (under a statute expanding it to include any building)? ________

ANSWERS TO REVIEW QUESTIONS

Ques. No.	Answer	Explanation
1.	***YES***	Under modern law, Defendant ***can*** be prosecuted and convicted for either; instigating makes him an accomplice to the homicide. However, Defendant cannot be convicted of ***both***, since solicitation merges into the liability he incurs as an accomplice to Hitman's criminal homicide.
2.	***YES***	Defendant is guilty if his grabbing resulted from conscious exercise of will, rather than pure reflex. (But Defendant may be able to invoke necessity as a justification for his actions.)
3.a.	***YES***	Because of their special relationship, if Husband has the ability to save Wife (even from consequences of her own act), he has a duty to do so. His breach of that duty is a form of negative act.
b.	***YES***	Husband's negative act would be a concurrent direct cause of Wife's death.
c.	***NO***	Wife's own criminal conduct is no excuse. Her death is the combined result of her own affirmative act and Husband's negative act. She has committed a suicide, but Husband has simultaneously committed a homicide because his negative act contributed directly to the death of another human being, *i.e.*, his wife.
d.	***NO***	Wife cannot give effective consent to a homicide.
4.a.	***YES***	Having caused her to be in a position of peril, his failure to rescue is an act of homicide.
b.	***YES***	He did not commit a homicide by his failure to rescue, as it is stipulated that he lacked the ability to do so. He has committed a homicide because his effort to rape has indirectly led to Victim's drowning. Her own intervening act of falling into the river is a ***dependent*** intervening force, which is not a totally abnormal response to what Defendant did.
c.	***YES***	This is the same causation theory as in b., above. Moreover, a purely accidental and unintended killing may be felony murder.
5.a.	***NO***	Witness had no duty to act, because Witness had no relationship with Victim.
b.	***NO***	Witness still had no duty; he did not cause her predicament.
c.	***YES***	A duty arises from the contractual relationship.
6.	***TRUE***	An "assault with intent to commit murder" is a specific intent crime; Defendant must have the intent to kill.

7.	***FALSE***	Often a general criminal intent will be an implied requirement.
8.a.	***YES***	This is an example of the transferred intent doctrine.
b.	***YES***	The same type of criminal act and intent is present in either case. (Poisoning another is battery.)
9.	***YES***	These are offenses to which a lesser standard of culpability applies.
10.	***FALSE***	"Occasional" use indicates that Defendant's act is not creating the "***very high*** probability" of death or serious bodily harm required for "wanton conduct." Defendant's acts would be criminally negligent, making him guilty of involuntary manslaughter.
11.	***FALSE***	Negligence is not equivalent to "knowledge." However, such facts would be circumstantial evidence that Defendant might have had actual knowledge or might have willfully remained ignorant of the true facts.
12.	***DEPENDS***	At common law, an accessory could not be convicted unless and until the principal had been convicted. This rule has been changed by statute in most states.
13.a.	***TRUE***	Merely leasing an apartment would ***not*** be sufficient to constitute "aiding and abetting" the crime.
b.	***FALSE***	The terms of the rent give him a sufficient "stake in the venture."
c.	***FALSE***	This is sufficient special assistance to constitute "aiding and abetting" the crime.
14.	***TRUE***	Since Thief has committed no crime, there is no possibility of holding Defendant ***vicariously*** liable for Thief's conduct. However, Defendant ***could*** be prosecuted for solicitation.
15.	***YES***	The abettor is liable for any foreseeable crime committed in the course of the crime abetted.
16.	***NO***	This is not solicitation because Defendant's words were not an incitement; Actor was apparently already bent on committing the crime and Defendant's words were merely an expression of general approval.
17.	***YES***	The person solicited need not accept.
18.	***NO***	At common law, the crime involved must be a serious felony or involve a breach of peace.
19.	***YES***	Even if the "fix" is not in itself a crime, it is sufficiently immoral and unlawful to be the object of a conspiracy in most states. (But in some states only conspiracy to commit major crimes is punishable.) However, many states woul require an "overt act" in furtherance of the criminal goal.

20.	***NO***	Charlie's expression of support falls short of an actual agreement to work with Abel and Baker toward the illegal end.
21.	***YES***	An "overt act" generally is required, but any preparatory act is generally held sufficient.
22.a.	***YES***	The killing was in furtherance of the robbery, even though it was contrary to the agreement.
b.	***NO***	The firebombing would not seem to be in furtherance of the robbery, or a foreseeable consequence. It was more a "personal frolic" of Billy's, unless it was done to conceal the homicide of the proprietor.
23.	***YES***	It is ***not*** required that all conspirators know each other. Such knowledge is a mere detail. It is enough that each agreed to render some aid to the unlawful act.
24.	***NO***	Where only two parties are involved, ***both*** must have guilty mens rea at common law; Wyatt has only pretended to accept. (Consider Jesse as guilty of solicitation and attempted conspiracy.)
25.	***NO (as to both questions).***	Conspiracy requires two guilty parties at common law; Trixie is exempt from prosecution for conspiring to violate a law enacted for her protection.
26.	***NO***	If two or more people are required for the commission of the substantive offense, no separate conspiracy charge lies unless more parties participate in the agreement than are necessary for the crime. (Wharton rule.)
27.	***NO***	The best view is that conspirators need not have been aware that their plan was illegal. However, some states follow the "corrupt motive doctrine," which requires that the parties know their objective is criminal.
28.a.	***YES***	Withdrawal does not absolve the illegal agreement.
b.	***NO***	Withdrawal terminates a co-conspirator's liability for later acts.
29.	***YES***	There is no merger of the crime of conspiracy into its target offense.
30.a.	***NO***	Hitman's activities are still "in preparation." (But Defendant would be guilty of solicitation.)
b.	***YES***	Hitman has committed an act beyond mere preparation under any of the tests for attempt liability. Factual impossibility does not change this and is not a defense. Defendant is an accomplice.
c.	***YES***	Defendant has committed an act beyond mere preparation under any of the tests for attempt currently in use.
d.	***YES***	Defendant would be guilty under one of two alternate theories: (i) this should be classed as factual, not legal, impossibility; (ii) Defendant's acts prior

to shooting at the dog had been sufficient preparation to make him already guilty of attempt.

31. ***YES*** — Courts would treat this as "factual impossibility"; it would not be the same as shooting a corpse.

32. ***NO*** — Attempt requires a specific intent (even though Defendant's act, if wanton, would have made him guilty of murder if the hobo had died).

33. ***YES (most courts)*** — Abandonment is not a defense once the perpetrating act is committed. The minority view is contra, if she is voluntarily abandoning the plan, not merely postponing.

34. ***NO*** — This is an example of the doctrine of merger.

35. ***YES*** — The cause of mental illness is immaterial.

36. ***NO*** — The test is in the alternative.

37. ***FALSE*** — The *M'Naghten* test focuses exclusively on cognitive (intellectual) capacity.

38. ***"c"*** — The *M'Naghten* and irresistible impulse tests require ***total*** loss of cognitive or volitional power; the A.L.I. test does not.

39. ***TRUE*** — Intoxication as a result of mistake of fact is ***involuntary*** intoxication, which is treated the same as insanity.

40. ***TRUE*** — Voluntary intoxication is a defense only to crimes requiring a specific intent (*e.g.*, burglary). Where only general intent is required, voluntary intoxication is a form of gross negligence.

41.a. ***NO*** — Excessive force is not privileged.

b. ***PROBABLY YES*** — If the victim of the initial aggression suddenly escalates a minor fight into one involving deadly force, without giving the aggressor a chance to withdraw, the aggressor regains his right to self-defense.

c. ***YES*** — There is no duty to retreat in such circumstances (most courts).

d. ***YES*** — Deadly force is justified if necessary to prevent commission of the act.

e. ***NO*** — There is generally no right to use deadly force solely in defense of property or for prevention of a nondangerous felony such as larceny.

42. ***PROBABLY NOT*** — Father's act as to Son was justified ("domestic authority"), and since not criminal as to Son, not criminal as to Friend (unless the risk to Friend was so clear that the act is criminally negligent).

43. ***YES (better view)*** — Deadly force is justified in defense of others: Reasonable mistake of fact doctrine applies.

44.a.	***NO***	Duress excuses that which would otherwise be a criminal act.
b.	***YES***	Duress does ***not*** excuse a criminal homicide (but it may mitigate the killing to no more than manslaughter).
c.	***YES***	Threats of ***future*** harm to Betty or her family do not constitute sufficient duress to excuse a present criminal act.
45.	***"b"***	Larceny is a specific intent crime. Even an unreasonable mistake of fact may negate such intent.
46.	***FALSE***	Even under the facts Defendant believed, his conduct was at least ***"malum in se,"*** and, in many states, itself constitutes an assault. Thus, it is an instance of misdemeanor-manslaughter or involuntary manslaughter via criminal negligence.
47.a.	***MAYBE***	Assuming that bigamy is treated as a strict liability offense, as it has traditionally been, a mistake of law or fact would not be a defense. A mistake of law or fact must negate the criminal state of mind; because a strict liability offense does not require a criminal state of mind, mistake of law or fact is not a defense to a strict liability crime. However, under another approach, bigamy is sometimes treated as requiring some criminal intent, in which case the mistaken belief as to the validity of the Mexican divorce decree might become a defense.
b.	***NO (most courts)***	To allow such would encourage advice from incompetent attorneys.
c.	***NO***	A marriage license clerk is not charged with the responsibility of enforcing bigamy laws, and hence does not fall within the "executive or administrative officials" exception.
48.	***FALSE***	Mistake of law (even if unreasonable) other than the law violated (theft) here prevents Son from having the specific intent required for larceny or embezzlement.
49.	***NONE***	Choice "a" is incorrect because Defendant's fraud vitiated the consent to the taking. Choice "b" is incorrect because condonation does not bar prosecution. Choice "c" likewise is incorrect (and Victim would be guilty of compounding). Choices "d" and "e" are incorrect because Victim's guilt or negligence is no defense; it is nonetheless larceny to steal from a thief.
50.a.	***FALSE***	It is enough that Informant was acting in cooperation with the police.
b.	***TRUE***	Merely providing an opportunity for commission of a crime to which Defendant is predisposed is not entrapment. Defendant would stand a better chance

in a jurisdiction following the "objective standards" for entrapment, but more details as to the level of Informant's pressure would be required to make this judgment.

51. ***ALL*** Force may be directly or indirectly applied; the slightest offensive touching is sufficient.

52. ***YES*** It is sufficient that the defendant caused the application of force with criminal negligence.

53.a. ***YES (most courts)*** This would be an "attempted battery" assault; however, a minority holds contra, because there is no "actual" ability to cause a battery. (A few courts hold this to be attempted assault, however.)

b. ***YES (most states)*** The minority does not recognize this type of assault.

54. ***NO*** Since the battery was completed (shoulder), the attempt (assault) is merged.

55. ***YES*** A scar on the face is a permanent disfigurement, recognized by modern statutes as included in the definition of mayhem; it is sufficient if Defendant intended one mayhem-type injury and another resulted.

56.a. ***YES*** Any killing of a human being is homicide.

b. ***YES*** Any intentional killing is murder, unless a legally recognized factor of justification, excuse, or mitigation exists. Consent has never been so recognized in a homicide situation.

57. ***"c" and "d"*** Only choices "c" and "d" involve the creation of the very high probability of death or grave bodily harm required for "wanton" conduct.

58. ***TRUE*** The "cooling down" period is measured objectively.

59. ***NONE*** Choice "c" (coercion) ***might*** be sufficient if absolutely necessary to save one's own life. But voluntary intoxication (a) or emotional instability (b) ***does not*** mitigate in most states; nor would insults (d), or hearing about spouse's adultery (e) at common law.

60. ***NO*** Under most statutes, a felony murder is first degree murder only if certain felonies are involved (rape, robbery, arson, burglary).

61. ***"c" only*** Choices "a" and "b" involve a sufficient level of risk (wantonness) to be classified as murder. Choice "c" involves a malum in se act (suicide).

62. ***YES*** Voluntary intoxication bears on the absence of premeditation and deliberation.

63.	***NO***	Battery is only a misdemeanor. However, this would be a classic instance of "misdemeanor manslaughter."
64.a.	***YES***	All are accomplices to a felony murder.
b.	***NO***	Serious question as to whether the felony would be the ***proximate*** cause of Larry's death. It is more likely a "totally abnormal" response to the felony. However, Moe himself could be found guilty of murder without resort to the felony murder rule.
c.	***NO (most courts)***	The majority view is that liability for murder cannot be based on the death of a co-felon from police pursuit.
65.	***NO***	It is doubtful that Sundance's death proximately resulted from commission of the felony. More likely, it was a totally unforeseeable result thereof. *But note:* The killing might still be murder; *i.e.*, if Butch's striking Sundance with the butt of the gun is an act in "wanton disregard for a risk to human life."
66.	***YES (most courts)***	Although liability for murder cannot be based on the death of a co-felon from resistance by the victim or police pursuit, murder liability can be based on the death of an innocent bystander from such causes.
67.	***YES***	Every direct cause that produces death is a "proximate cause" for homicide purposes.
68.	***YES***	Negligence in medical treatment is not a superseding cause; it is a dependent intervening force which is not a totally abnormal response to what Defendant did (*i.e.*, it is foreseeable).
69.	***PROBABLY YES***	Most courts hold that a victim's refusal of medical care is foreseeable and thus is not a superseding cause.
70.a.	***YES***	Basically, this is a case of no consent by the victim.
b.	***NO***	Threats must be of immediate physical force; threats of criminal charges are not enough.
71.	***YES***	There is no valid consent; the mens rea requirement is satisfied by criminal negligence as to lack of consent.
72.	***NO***	Consent was given, even though procured by mistake or fraud.
73.	***"b," "c," and "d"***	Growing crops (a) could not be the subject of a larceny at common law (modern law contra).
74.	***"b"***	The right to ***possession*** (not ownership) is determinative; the repair shop had a possessory lien for its services.

Choice "a" is incorrect, because Defendant has no intent to "permanently" deprive owner of possession of horse.

Choice "c" is incorrect, because Defendant is considered an owner of the car; it is not the property "of another."

Choice "d" is incorrect, because there is no caption or asportation (modern law contra).

Choice "e" is incorrect, because mere ***use*** of another's property is not deemed a taking and carrying away.

75.a. ***YES*** Ordinarily employees get custody, not possession, of employer's goods; hence the taking is trespassory.

b. ***PROBABLY YES*** High-ranking employees are more likely to get "possession," rather than mere "custody"; hence, ***no*** trespassory taking. However, here the instructions are so specific and the use so restricted that it is likely even a managerial employee would get only "custody."

c. ***NO*** Defendant, an employee, is a bailee (this would be embezzlement, however).

76. ***MAYBE*** Defendant would be guilty of larceny if he intended to steal it ***when Victim turned it over to him;*** Defendant never got rightful possession. This is "larceny by trick." However, if Defendant formed such intent later, this is embezzlement.

77. ***NO*** If the clerk intended to reimburse from his salary when paid, he had no intent to permanently deprive employer of the money.

78. ***YES*** There was sufficient mens rea (permanent deprivation), because the offer to return was conditioned on payment.

79. ***NO*** Employee got possession from a third person; hence there was no trespassory taking. This is embezzlement.

80.a. ***NO*** An innocent taking is not larceny because the "continuing trespass" doctrine does not apply.

b. ***NO*** This is not larceny unless Defendant knows or has reason to believe he can discover the owner's identity and Defendant had the necessary intent for larceny at the time he took possession of the briefcase.

c. ***NO*** There was no wrongful intent at time of taking (and note this would ***not*** be embezzlement either because the owner had not entrusted it to Defendant).

d. ***NO*** An ***honest*** mistake, even a quite stupid one, of law as to some law other than the law of theft may prevent intent.

81.	***YES (most courts)***	Since the parties did not intend to transfer a container, Defendant did not obtain possession of the clubs until he discovered them. If at the time he discovered and appropriated the clubs he had intent to steal (it appears that he did), Defendant is guilty of larceny.
82.	***NO***	Defendant got possession rightfully, and only ***subsequently*** formed the intent to appropriate; hence no trespassory taking. (But this would be embezzlement.)
83.	***NO***	The defendant is not guilty of common law larceny because the money was freely given to him by the bank; hence, there is no trespass, nor would there be any larceny by trick both because he used no fraud in getting the money and because he was given title as well as possession of the money. There would be no embezzlement because he had not only possession but also title to the money, and there would be no false pretenses because while he did obtain title to the money, there is no indication that he made any false statement in order to get it. This is nothing more than a breach of loan agreement; it is a civil matter, not a crime.
84.	***NO, as to larceny; YES, as to embezzlement***	If Defendant was custodian of the money, there is no larceny because Defendant apparently had no intent to ***permanently*** deprive the employer; but if Defendant was in possession of the money, it is embezzlement because the "loan" was unauthorized and the intent to restore was still "fraudulent."
85.	***YES, as to larceny; NO as to false pretenses***	Most courts hold Seller ***did not intend*** to pass title or possession unless the check cleared; hence this is larceny by trick.
86.a.	***YES***	This constitutes a form of implied affirmative representation as to a material fact.
b.	***NO***	Reliance is measured ***subjectively*** (not on a reasonable person basis).
87.	***NONE***	Choice "a" is incorrect because the taking must be by force. Choice "b" is incorrect because the taking was ***neither*** from her person ***nor*** in her presence. Choice "c" is incorrect because a threat to Victim's reputation is not enough to qualify for robbery. (This, however, would be extortion.) Choice "d" is incorrect because taking from a corpse is not from a ***person*** (unless Defendant is responsible for Victim's death).
88.	***YES***	Threats to accuse a person of a crime, even when the person is guilty, constitute extortion.

89. ***NO*** Once recovered, the property is no longer "stolen"; but most courts allow prosecution for ***attempt.***

90. ***YES*** Suspicion coupled with failure to make inquiry lest the suspicion be confirmed is sufficient.

91. ***"a," "d," and "e"*** Choice "a" is a forgery, because if Victim dies the court may rely on the forged will as a basis for determining rights to Victim's estate.

Choice "b" is not a forgery, because the writing itself is not false (falsity relates to contents); this could lead to false pretenses.

Choice "c" is not a forgery, because the signature on the painting is of no legal efficacy; again, it could lead to false pretenses.

Choice "d" is a forgery, because even a driver's license has apparent legal efficacy (right to drive).

Choice "e" is a forgery, because he obtained the signature by deception as to the ***nature*** of the instrument.

92.a. ***NO*** There was no "breaking" since the window was open.

b. ***YES*** A "constructive breaking" would occur in such a case.

c. ***YES*** Opening of inner doors (locked or not) with felonious intent constitutes burglary.

93. ***YES*** Occupancy (not ownership) determines whether a dwelling is property of "another."

94. ***"c" only*** Felonious intent must exist at time of entry.

Choice "a" is incorrect because temporary absence of occupants does not change status of dwelling house.

Choice "b" is incorrect because abandonment of felonious intent after breaking and entering is immaterial. The burglary has already occurred.

Choice "d" is incorrect because voluntary intoxication would not automatically disprove the requisite mens rea, the specific intent to commit a felony inside. It would depend on how drunk Defendant was.

Choice "e" is incorrect because even petit theft (of food) is considered a felony, for burglary. (Although if Defendant was starving, he might urge necessity as a defense.)

95. ***NO*** There must be some burning of the ***structure***, rather than only its contents. Defendant would be guilty of attempted arson.

96. *YES* Apartment House is the dwelling of all.

97. *NO* "Malice" is required. There is no "felony arson" rule as there is a felony murder rule.

98. *NO* The presence of high explosives and flammables might render Defendant's conduct "grossly" or "criminally" negligent, but that still is not "malice." Wantonness (intentional exposure to risk), at least, is required.

ESSAY EXAM QUESTIONS

INTRODUCTORY NOTE

The essay questions that follow have been selected to provide you with an opportunity to experience how the substantive law you have been reviewing may be tested in the hypothetical essay examination question context. These sample essay questions are a valuable self-diagnostic tool designed to enable you to enhance your issue-spotting ability and practice your exam writing skills.

It is suggested that you approach each question as though under actual examination conditions. The time allowed for each question is 60 minutes. You should spend 15 to 20 minutes spotting issues, underlining key facts and phrases, jotting notes in the margins, and outlining your answer. ***If*** you organize your thoughts well, 40 minutes will be more than adequate for writing them down. Should you prefer to forgo the actual writing involved on these questions, be sure to give yourself no more time for issue-spotting than you would on the actual examination.

The BARBRI technique for writing a well-organized essay answer is to (i) spot the issues in a question and then (ii) analyze and discuss each issue using the "CIRAC" method:

C — State your ***conclusion*** first. (In other words, you must think through your answer ***before*** you start writing.)
I — State the ***issue*** involved.
R — Give the ***rule(s)*** of law involved.
A — ***Apply*** the rule(s) of law to the facts.
C — Finally, restate your ***conclusion***.

After completing (or outlining) your own analysis of each question, compare it with the BARBRI model answer provided herein. A passing answer does ***not*** have to match the model one, but it should cover most of the issues presented and the law discussed and should ***apply the law to the facts*** of the question. Use of the CIRAC method results in the best answer you can write.

EXAM QUESTION NO. 1

Bob, age 13, and Hal, age 16, bored by the prospect of another long summer afternoon, set out on their favorite pastime—rummaging through the garages and toolsheds of neighbors. In the past they had sometimes merely used, but had sometimes also taken, tools kept there. Hal's younger brother Jim, age six, tagged along for the first time.

The boys entered Smith's garage, which was attached to the rear of his home, through the closed but unlocked garage door. Bob and Hal rummaged through the toolboxes and practiced cutting wood on the table saw. Jim, alone near a corner shelf in the garage, saw a gold watch that had been left there inadvertently by Smith. Jim picked up the watch, put it in his pocket, and without a word left for home.

After about an hour in the garage Bob and Hal also left and continued to Jones's toolshed for the stated purpose of taking a large screwdriver that had, on a prior occasion, caught Bob's fancy. Jones's shed was detached and about 50 yards from her house. Although the door was always locked, the boys had never had difficulty in prying open the door, and on this occasion they again broke the lock. As Hal pushed the door open and stepped into the shed, he was shot in the head, suffering a fatal wound.

On the prior evening Jones had mounted a loaded pistol in the shed, aimed at the door and connected so that the pistol would discharge if the door were pushed open. Jones told the police she mounted the gun to protect her property from thieves, that she intended to scare them away and did not intend to kill anyone. No statute prohibited the use of spring guns.

(1) Bob and Jim are charged with burglary of Smith's garage and larceny of Smith's watch.

(2) Bob is charged with burglary of Jones's toolshed.

(3) Jones is charged with the murder of Hal.

What result as to each charge? Discuss.

EXAM QUESTION NO. 2

John, Max, Rip, and Dopey, all engaged in the illegal numbers racket, planned to burn down the home of another numbers bookie. Pursuant to the plan, Dopey was given $2 and sent to a nearby gas station to buy a can of gasoline to start the fire.

On the way, Dopey stopped in a tavern and spent the money on whiskey. Afraid to return without the gasoline, Dopey went to the station and attempted to fill the can from the pump while the operator wasn't looking. When he was spotted, Dopey ran across the highway carrying the full can with the operator chasing him. The operator, intent on catching Dopey, ran into the path of an oncoming automobile and was killed instantly. John, Max, Rip, and Dopey were arrested before the planned burning took place.

What crimes were committed by John, Max, Rip, and Dopey? Discuss.

EXAM QUESTION NO. 3

Adams suspected that his girlfriend, Kitty, was unfaithful to him. He told Barlow that he needed his help to test Kitty. Adams's plan was that he would bring a box of chocolates laced with a fatal dose of LSD to Barlow at the pool hall they frequented; Barlow was then to offer the chocolates to Kitty. If Kitty accepted the chocolates from Barlow, who was a stranger to her, this would satisfy Adams that she was unfaithful to him and deserved to die.

Barlow entertained excessive and irrational suspicions and distrust of others. For this reason and because he feared what Adams would do to him if he refused, he was afraid to refuse to join in the plan.

Adams brought the chocolates to the pool hall, laid the box beside his coat on a bench, and went off to shoot pool while waiting for Barlow to show up. Cox, the proprietor, opened the box and sampled the candy. He soon became unconscious. Adams discovered Cox and thought he was dead, although in fact the dose of LSD taken by Cox was not sufficient to kill him. Adams dragged the unconscious Cox out of the pool hall, put him in a car, and drove to a secluded spot and left him there. Shortly thereafter, Cox died from exposure without regaining consciousness.

Adams is charged with the attempted murder of Kitty. Is he guilty? Is he guilty of any other crime or crimes? Is Barlow? Discuss.

EXAM QUESTION NO. 4

Don, in need of funds, approached Oscar, a friend who sold stereo equipment. Oscar told Don that he had no ready cash to give him, but that he owned thousands of dollars worth of readily saleable and fully insured stereo equipment stored in a nearby warehouse that he also owned. Don replied that if this were the case Oscar would not lose any money if some of the equipment "disappeared" and Don sold it. Oscar then said he would give Don a duplicate key to the warehouse so that Don, with Don's brother Allen, could remove the equipment, on condition that Don reimburse him for any loss for which he could not recover from his insurance company. Don said, "That's great," and left with the key.

Don told Allen about the plan and Allen agreed to help him. Don and Allen entered the warehouse with the key, and the two men loaded Don's truck with $50,000 worth of equipment. After the items were removed and the warehouse locked, it was agreed that Allen would immediately drive the truck and equipment to Mexico, to be joined later by Don. It was also agreed that Don should go home by means of an automobile that the two had observed in an enclosed parking area to the rear of the warehouse.

Allen drove away and Don reentered the warehouse to reach the parking area. He took the automobile and with it rammed through the locked gate of the fence that enclosed the parking area and proceeded to his apartment.

Allen was driving in excess of the speed limit when a highway patrol officer attempted to stop him. Allen, believing the theft had been discovered, attempted to escape by driving at over 100 miles per hour. In the ensuing chase the highway patrol officer lost control of his patrol car and was killed when it overturned.

(A) Has Don committed burglary (i) in the removal of the stereo equipment, or (ii) in the theft of the vehicle? Discuss.

(B) Is Don guilty of either murder or manslaughter in the death of the highway patrol officer? Discuss.

(C) Is Oscar criminally liable for any crime or crimes committed by Don? Discuss.

ANSWERS TO ESSAY EXAM QUESTIONS

ANSWER TO EXAM QUESTION NO. 1

Are Bob and Jim Guilty of Burglary of Smith's Garage?

At common law, burglary is defined as the breaking and entering by trespass of the dwelling house of another, at night, with the intention of committing a felony therein. The facts stipulate that Bob and Jim "entered"; and, since their entry was unauthorized, it was "trespassory." The "breaking" element does not require damage to the structure, but simply the putting aside of some barrier to entry, no matter how flimsy. Hence, the boys' act in opening the garage door is a sufficient "breaking"; it makes no difference that the door was unlocked.

At common law, burglary was a nocturnal offense. Since the boys' activity occurred during the afternoon, they would ***not*** be guilty of burglary under the common law. However, most jurisdictions have eliminated the "nighttime" requirement, and for purposes of this answer, it will be assumed that such a change has been made.

The "dwelling house" element, even at common law, embraced outbuildings, such as a stable, within the curtilage or fenced area around the main house. A garage would be the modern equivalent of a stable. In any event, the scope of burglary has been expanded almost everywhere to include most types of enclosed structures, no matter where they are located.

The difficult issue is whether the boys had an intention to commit a felony ***when they entered*** the garage. Arguably, they had only a contingent intent to steal—the contingency being to take anything that might strike their fancy. However, there is no reason to treat this sort of intent any less seriously han a clear determination to steal.

As to Bob (age 13), there was at common law a ***rebuttable*** presumption that one between seven and 14 is too immature to form the mens rea for a crime. However, that presumption weakens as one nears 14, and would be overcome by a showing that Bob did in fact know that what he was doing was morally wrong.

As to Jim, at common law one under the age of seven was "conclusively presumed" too immature to form any mens rea. Therefore, Jim did not commit burglary.

Are Bob and Jim Guilty of Larceny?

Jim is not guilty of larceny because of his age. Even though he may have trespassorily taken and carried away Smith's watch, Jim is under age seven, and therefore ***conclusively presumed*** incapable of formulating the requisite criminal intent for larceny. His otherwise criminal act is therefore excused.

Bob is not guilty of larceny either, because it appears that Jim was acting solely on his own when he took Smith's watch. Even assuming that Hal and Bob's purpose was to take whatever they might find in Smith's garage (not merely tools, as they have taken from other neighbors in the past), and even assuming further that by "tagging along" Jim joined such plan, the fact remains that Jim apparently took the watch for himself, and ***not*** in furtherance of any common purpose with the other boys. Consequently, Jim's act cannot be imputed to Bob.

Is Bob Guilty of the Burglary of Jones's Toolshed?

The activities directed at the toolshed were clearly without the consent of the owner, and hence trespassory. As noted above, the opening of an ***unlocked*** door is a sufficient "breaking," and the opening of a ***locked*** door is all the more so. Since Hal "stepped into the shed" before he was shot, the requisite "entering" had occurred, thus taking Hal's acts beyond the category of ***attempted*** burglary. The specific intent requirement was satisfied by the boys' intent to take Jones's screwdriver; the intent

to commit ***any*** larceny (grand or petit) is sufficient. The burglary was complete upon the entry. It is immaterial whether the target felony or larceny was accomplished.

As noted above, the boys' activities would not constitute burglary at common law because they occurred during the day. Furthermore, the toolshed was probably too far away from the main house (50 yards) to be considered "within the curtilage." However, modern burglary statutes generally cover entries of any structure at any time; and under such statutes, Hal's acts would be burglary. Although Bob himself did not enter, he was an ***accomplice*** of Hal (indeed, he was a co-principal in the first degree), and thus is chargeable with Hal's actions. Again, Bob might be able to avoid this accomplice liability because of his age (13), unless it is shown that he was mature enough to know that his acts were wrong.

Is Jones Guilty of the Murder of Hal?

Jones clearly has committed a homicide. The spring gun she set was an actual cause of Hal's death—*i.e.,* ***but for*** Jones's setting the trap, Hal would not have died when, where, and as he did. True, Jones's trap was not the ***direct*** cause of Hal's death because the gun would not have gone off except for Hal's ***independent, intervening act*** of opening the door. However, an independent, intervening force "breaks the chain of causation" only if it was not foreseen or foreseeable. Here, Jones clearly foresaw that someone might try to open the door; indeed, that is why she set the gun. Her act, therefore, is the proximate (legally recognized) cause of Hal's death.

If this homicide was committed with "malice," it will be murder at common law. Whether Jones had "malice" depends on her state of mind when she set the trap. Even if the jury believes Jones's claim that she intended only to scare away intruders and not to kill anyone, she must have been ***aware*** that her setting of the gun, aimed as it was at the door, created a ***plain and serious risk*** of killing or seriously injuring humans. Such awareness would constitute a wanton or reckless state of mind, which is one form of "malice."

Moreover, since Jones intentionally pointed a deadly weapon so that it would hit a vital part of the human body should the door be opened, a jury could infer that she actually ***did*** intend to kill or to inflict serious bodily harm upon anyone who opened the door—regardless of her protestations to the contrary.

In the absence of any factor of justification, excuse, or mitigation, either of the above mental states is sufficient "malice" for murder.

Arguably, Jones's use of deadly force may be justified as ***prevention of a felony***. Jones's purpose in setting the spring gun was to prevent criminal acts directed against her toolshed and its contents. Here, Hal (who has no "youthfulness" defense since he is over 14 years of age) ***was*** committing statutory burglary. The common law permitted the use of deadly force only to prevent "dangerous" or "atrocious" felonies, of which burglary was one. In many jurisdictions today, statutory burglary is similarly treated. In such jurisdictions, Jones's homicide of Hal would be deemed justified, and hence the killing was without the requisite malice.

However, other jurisdictions hold (and this is deemed the better view) that using deadly force for the prevention of burglary is justified only when there is ***actually*** a human being within, or in the general vicinity of, the structure burglarized. Otherwise, the particular burglary is not "dangerous" or "atrocious." In these jurisdictions, Jones would be guilty of common law murder—unless the court accepted "imperfect crime prevention" as a form of ***mitigation***, which would reduce the homicide from murder to ***voluntary manslaughter***. If the court rejects such an argument, Jones is guilty of common law murder because the killing is not otherwise justified, excused, or mitigated.

By statute, most jurisdictions today divide murder into two degrees. One form of first degree murder is an intentional murder with "premeditation and deliberation." Another form is a murder committed by means of poison, torture, bomb, or ambush. If Jones is found to have ***intended*** to kill, she would

be guilty of first degree murder, because she clearly premeditated and deliberated with respect to this intention. This inference is compelling in a spring gun situation, which by its very nature shows that the idea of killing was considered for an appreciable time, and then calmly acted upon.

ANSWER TO EXAM QUESTION NO. 2

Conspiracy

All four are guilty of conspiracy to commit arson. Conspiracy consists of an intentional agreement between two or more persons to commit an offense and (in most jurisdictions) an overt act by any member of the conspiracy in furtherance of the agreement. The four clearly intended and agreed to commit arson. The overt act requirement was satisfied when they sent Dopey to buy gas to start the fire. An act of preparation, even one innocent in itself, is sufficient.

Attempted Arson

The four are ***not*** guilty of attempted arson. The mens rea of attempt is specific intent to commit the crime, and the four clearly intended to perpetrate an act that would be arson. But the actus reus of attempt requires an act beyond mere preparation: an act that comes very "close" to completing the crime and/or that "unequivocally" displays an intent to commit the crime. The four were a long way from actually burning their competitor's home. They still had to go there, spread the gas around, and set it on fire. Nor did the acts already accomplished unequivocally demonstrate an intent to commit arson. Obtaining a can of gas is a common act not ordinarily limited to arsonists. Although arson is a very heinous crime, so that one will be deemed to enter its zone of perpetration sooner than would be true as to some other crimes, this act was "preparatory" in the fullest meaning of the term.

Theft of $2

Dopey is guilty of either petty larceny or petty embezzlement of the $2, depending on whether he formed the intent to spend the money on whiskey before or after he received it. The others gave Dopey possession of the $2 for the sole purpose of buying gas. If a bailee receives property, intending at that time to spend it on himself, and he does so, he is guilty of larceny. On the other hand, if a bailee receives property, and only later forms the intent to misappropriate it, when he does so, he is guilty of embezzlement. (In many jurisdictions both crimes would now be denominated simply as "theft," so that the timing of Dopey's intention to steal would not be important.) Theft of property worth less than $200 (or in some jurisdictions as little as $50) is petty theft. The $2 Dopey stole is clearly in the petty category. It would be no defense to Dopey that the victims of his theft were themselves criminals.

Theft of Gasoline

Dopey is also guilty of petty larceny of the gasoline. Larceny includes taking and carrying away the personal property of another without her consent (*i.e.,* trespassorily) and with intent to deprive her of it permanently. All of these conditions were met here. The gas Dopey stole could not have been worth more than a few dollars and is clearly in the petty category. To move Dopey's actions from attempted larceny to larceny itself, it is necessary only that he "carry away," not that he "get away."

Involuntary Manslaughter

Criminal Negligence Theory: Dopey may also be guilty of involuntary manslaughter, which consists of causing the death of another person through criminal negligence. To establish "criminal negligence," it must be shown that the accused's conduct created a ***serious risk of harm*** to another of which a reasonable person would have been aware (a higher probability of such harm than in "ordinary" or civil negligence).

Here, a reasonable person may well have realized that in attempting to escape across a busy highway, it was foreseeable that the gas station operator would give chase and thereby be placed in danger from cars on the highway.

As for the causation requirement, Dopey's acts must be shown to be both an actual and proximate cause of the operator's death. They clearly were an actual cause, because "but for" the theft and attempted escape the operator would not have been killed. They were a proximate cause as well. It is true that two other events intervened to cause the death, but neither operates to "break the chain" of causation leading back to Dopey's act. The act of the station operator in heedlessly pursuing Dopey out into the highway was a dependent or responsive cause, one generated by what Dopey did, and it cannot be said to be a totally abnormal response, especially from the vantage point of hindsight. The act of the driver in running down the station operator was an independent or coincidental intervening force, but it should have been foreseen by Dopey. Neither a normal ***dependent*** intervening force nor a foreseeable independent intervening force will "break the chain" of proximate causation between Dopey's act and the operator's death.

Misdemeanor Manslaughter Theory: Manslaughter (involuntary) can also be committed by killing another person in the course of committing a misdemeanor. As discussed above, Dopey perpetrated the misdemeanor of petty larceny against the operator, and this crime was a cause of the operator's death. Even though the operator was killed after the larceny itself was consummated, in most jurisdictions flight ***following*** a crime (especially where there is immediate pursuit) is considered part of the crime for purposes of the misdemeanor manslaughter rule. An additional requirement is that the misdemeanor be malum in se, which means inherently wrong by common moral standards. Larceny falls within this category. Consequently, Dopey could be convicted of involuntary manslaughter. (Unlike the modern view with respect to felony murder, there is no requirement under the misdemeanor manslaughter rule that the direct cause of the killing be the misdemeanant.)

Vicarious Liability

John, Max, and Rip are ***not*** liable for Dopey's substantive crimes. Conspirators are liable for acts of their co-conspirator that take place within the foreseeable scope of the conspiracy. However, Dopey's theft of the gasoline and his subsequent acts in escaping therefrom were ***not*** foreseeable to the other three; indeed, they had given him money to ***buy*** the gasoline. Therefore, his subsequent loss of the money and decision to steal the gasoline cannot be regarded as within the foreseeable scope of the criminal conspiracy. It was really a side excursion of his own to cover up the misappropriation of the money. Accordingly, John, Max, and Rip are not liable for the larceny of the gas or the death of the gas station operator. Since they neither advised nor aided the larceny of the gas, they were not accomplices to Dopey's theft.

ANSWER TO EXAM QUESTION NO. 3

Is Adams Guilty of the Attempted Murder of Kitty?

A criminal attempt consists of two elements: (i) a specific intent to cause a result that would be a crime; and (ii) an act beyond mere preparation for the offense.

Intent: That Adams had the requisite intent for murder seems clear enough. He intended to kill Kitty if she failed his "test" for faithfulness; and no legally recognized justification, excuse, or mitigation appears.

Act: Whether Adams's acts were beyond mere preparation depends on the test adopted by the jurisdiction for making such determinations. Under the abandoned common law approach, the act had to be the final step necessary to complete the crime. Under the proximity test, the act must be dangerously close to success. Under either test, Adams's acts were insufficient—all he did was purchase chocolates, poison them, and go to the place where he was to pass them to his accomplice. Such acts are far from the last acts necessary for commission of the crime (he had yet to meet with Barlow to give him the chocolates).

The question is closer under the equivocality test, which requires the act to demonstrate that the defendant had an unequivocal intent to commit the crime. Here, Adams's procuring poisoned chocolates and waiting for Barlow demonstrates a criminal purpose as to someone, but not necessarily as to Kitty, the intended victim. Thus, the act is probably insufficient under the equivocality test.

Adams's act was probably sufficient under the Model Penal Code test, which requires that the act constitute a substantial step toward commission of the crime. Buying poisoned chocolates and taking them to pass them on to an accomplice are certainly substantial steps toward commission of the murder plan here; so Adams could be found guilty under this test.

If the court concludes that Adams's acts were sufficient for an indictable attempt, it is not a defense that Adams was mistaken as to the lethality of the candy. An accused need be shown only to have had the ***apparent*** ability to carry out his plan; therefore, as long as a reasonable person in Adams's shoes would have thought the candy contained enough LSD to kill Kitty, the crime would be complete even though the candy was, in fact, not lethal.

Is Adams Guilty of Solicitation?

Solicitation consists of counseling, inciting, and inducing another person to commit a crime, with the intention of procuring its commission. Adams's statements to Barlow fit within this definition, as he was in substance proposing that Barlow aid him in poisoning Kitty if she accepted the chocolates.

The crime was complete when the plan was proposed by Adams. It is immaterial whether Barlow agreed thereto, or intended to carry it out. (However, if Barlow did in fact agree thereto, and such agreement constituted a criminal conspiracy, *see* below, most courts hold that the solicitation is ***merged*** with the conspiracy.)

Are Adams and Barlow Guilty of Conspiracy?

A conspiracy is the combination or agreement of two or more persons for the purpose of committing an unlawful act; and, in most jurisdictions, an overt act committed in furtherance of the agreement.

Overt Act: Insofar as an "overt act" is required, Adams's procuring the LSD-laced chocolates would clearly suffice, since a mere act of preparation satisfies this requirement (even though such an act may ***not*** be enough for a criminal attempt; *see* above).

Barlow's Intent: There is no conspiracy at common law unless at least two persons have the requisite criminal intent. Barlow's assent to Adams's plan is inferred (we are told that he was afraid to refuse), but it is not clear whether Barlow really intended to carry out the plan or was merely feigning agreement. The fact that he entertained "excessive and irrational suspicions and distrust of others" and was afraid of Adams, and that he apparently did not show up at the pool hall, suggests that he was merely pretending to go along with Adams. If so, Barlow lacked the requisite criminal intent, so that neither he nor Adams could be prosecuted for conspiracy. (Adams could still be prosecuted for solicitation, however; *see* above.)

If, on the other hand, Barlow really intended to offer the chocolates to Kitty as per Adams's plan, there would be an indictable conspiracy.

Insanity: Barlow's "excessive and irrational" fears would ***not*** constitute insanity so as to excuse criminal liability. Even though "irrational" fears may indicate some mental disorder, there apparently was no impairment of his ability to realize that killing Kitty was wrongful. Hence, Barlow cannot be considered legally insane.

Coercion: The only other possible theory of exculpation would be coercion or duress. However, this too would fail because (i) coercion does not excuse a criminal homicide, and the same result should follow where a conspiracy to commit a criminal homicide is involved; and (ii) in any event, the coercion defense operates only where one person is making a threat to immediately kill or inflict serious injury upon another, and no such threat was made or is reasonably inferable from Adams's conduct.

Is Adams Guilty of the Criminal Homicide of Cox?

Adams's acts were both the actual and proximate cause of Cox's death. Cox would not have died but for Adams's having dumped him in the woods. Moreover, Adams's abandoning Cox in a helpless condition, exposed to the elements, was the direct cause of Cox's death (no intervening forces); every direct cause that takes effect within one year is recognized by the common law as a proximate cause for homicide purposes. Therefore, Cox's death is a homicide attributable to Adams.

Murder: Cox's death would be murder only if Adams acted with "malice aforethought." Since Adams did not intend to kill or injure Cox at all, "malice aforethought" can be established only if Adams's acts were so wanton and willful as to fall within the "abandoned and malignant heart" category. This would require a showing that Adams intentionally performed acts that he (subjectively) was aware created a plain and serious risk (a very high probability) that another would die. Nothing in the facts lends support to this theory. First, Adams was apparently unaware that anyone would open and sample the box of poisoned candy that he had laid on the bench. Second, when Adams later dumped Cox in the woods, he clearly had no awareness of the risk to human life involved, because he thought the body was already lifeless. Consequently, Adams lacked the requisite mens rea for murder.

Manslaughter: Adams is apparently guilty of involuntary manslaughter, which is a criminal homicide committed without malice aforethought, as a result of ***criminal negligence, or*** in the commission of an ***unlawful***, ***malum in se act***.

The "unlawful act" category is clearly involved in this case. In dumping what he thought to be a lifeless body in the woods, Adams was apparently attempting to conceal evidence of what he thought was a crime. This attempt to conceal evidence is probably itself a crime; but even if it is not, it is clearly an attempt to interfere with the processes of justice and hence an inherently evil ("malum in se") act. Consequently, any death resulting from the commission of such an act, even though accidental, is involuntary manslaughter.

It is also possible to argue that Adams is guilty of manslaughter on a "criminal negligence" theory—*i.e.,* that he was grossly negligent ***in determining whether Cox was still alive***, and it was this negligence that led to his dumping the body in the woods and Cox's subsequent death. There was certainly no social utility whatsoever in Adams's conduct, and he apparently made no effort whatsoever to seek medical aid or diagnosis, so that his acts would move quickly from the "ordinary" to the "criminal" negligence category. (*Comment:* It is tempting to discuss "criminal negligence" on the theory that Adams was negligent in leaving a box of LSD-laced chocolates lying around where others could eat them. However, this would be an erroneous analysis because leaving the box of chocolates was ***not*** the ***cause of Cox's death.*** Cox died from exposure to the elements, not from consuming the chocolates.)

Is Barlow Guilty of the Criminal Homicide of Cox?

The only conceivable theory on which Barlow might be held criminally liable for Cox's death is to impute to him Adams's acts on the theory that they were co-conspirators (*see* above).

A conspirator is criminally liable (as a principal in the second degree at common law) for acts of his co-conspirator committed ***in furtherance*** of the conspiracy. Basically, this includes all acts undertaken to promote the common goal, and which are a natural and probable consequence of the illegal combination or agreement.

However, it is highly unlikely that Adams's acts and the results thereof would be held within the foreseeable scope of the Adams-Barlow conspiracy. The crime planned was to poison Kitty (murder), while the crime that resulted was the accidental killing of a third person through ***other means***—being abandoned and exposed to the elements.

Under such circumstances, even assuming there was a conspiracy, Adams's abandoning Cox in the woods was not in furtherance of the conspiracy, and hence Barlow is not vicariously liable for Cox's death.

ANSWER TO EXAM QUESTION NO. 4

Burglary

The Stereo Equipment: Under the common law, the felony of burglary involved the trespassory breaking and entering of the dwelling house of another at night for the purpose of committing a felony therein. We are told that Don "entered" the warehouse. Furthermore, his use of a key to do so means that he opened a closed door—a sufficient physical act to constitute the element of "breaking." Although at common law a commercial building, such as a warehouse, was not considered a "dwelling house" within the definition of burglary, this element has been universally expanded by statute; hence, in modern times many sorts of structures, including a warehouse, can be burglarized.

We are not told whether Don's activity at the warehouse took place at night, as is required at common law; nor are we told whether, if it took place in the daytime, the jurisdiction involved is one that has abandoned the nighttime requirement for burglary, as many states have done. But in any event, Don's activity does not constitute burglary because Oscar's ***consent*** to the entry of the warehouse and the taking of the stereo equipment operates to eliminate the "trespass" element of this crime. Since Oscar authorized Don to do precisely what he did do, his entering of the structure was not trespassory, and his taking of the stereo equipment was not larcenous.

The Vehicle in the Parking Lot: This fact pattern raises a number of problems regarding the elements of the crime of burglary. First, there are the same "dwelling house" and "nighttime" issues discussed above. Second, burglary usually occurs when one enters a building in order to commit a felony "therein." Where, as here, it is necessary to go through a closed building in order to commit a felony in an open area, it is possible that the entering of that building will be a burglary. Nevertheless, the problem remains that although we are told Don "reentered the warehouse," we are left to infer whether he reopened a door to do so, or whether he opened any door in order to exit.

The question of consent also arises. Since the warehouse and the parking lot were owned and possessed by Oscar, presumably he would have authorized Don, his cohort in crime, to act as he did in the warehouse and in the parking lot area. If this were the case, there was no "trespass" by Don.

Finally, there is a problem as to whether Don's actions in taking the automobile constituted larceny, since we are not told whether he intended to keep the automobile permanently or to use it temporarily and then abandon it. If his intent was to abandon the car, under the circumstances here the intent to steal for larceny would be missing. Thus, if his plan for the auto was not larcenous, then he lacked the "felonious intent" required for burglary at the time of his reentry.

Criminal Homicide of Police Officer

Before Don's liability can be determined, it is necessary to assess the liability of his accomplice, Allen, who was driving the speeding truck the officer was chasing at the time of his death. The first issue is whether Allen was a proximate cause of the officer's death. There is no question that Allen was an ***actual*** cause of the death, because had he not done what he did, the officer would not have died when, where, and as he did. The difficulty is that Allen was not the ***direct*** cause of the officer's death,

because another causative factor—namely, the decision of the patrol officer to pursue Allen—intervened between Allen's driving at over 100 m.p.h. and the actual death of the officer.

Nonetheless, this intervening force was a dependent or responsive one—that is, it was generated by Allen's speeding in the first place. Therefore, since the officer's action was not abnormal or extraordinary, its presence as an intervening force does not "break the chain of causation" so as to prevent Allen from being a "proximate" cause of the officer's death.

Intent is a problem to finding Don guilty of murder in that Allen did not intend to kill or to inflict serious bodily injury upon the police officer. Moreover, since Don's activities with respect to the stereo equipment and the warehouse were not larcenous because of Oscar's consent (discussed above), the felony murder rule probably would not be operative (even if one assumes that at this time and place the felony was still being "perpetrated" as required by that rule) unless the jurisdiction treated the attempt to defraud the insurance company as a felony, but this is not indicated by the facts. However, it is possible to be guilty of murder even without committing a felony, and without intending harm. If one intentionally does an act with an awareness that it creates a plain and serious risk of death or grave bodily harm, and there is no factor of justification, excuse, or mitigation, the act is "wanton conduct" (sometimes called the act of one with a "depraved" or "abandoned and malignant heart"). One who unintentionally but proximately causes the death of another human being while engaging in "wanton conduct" is guilty of murder under the common law. Under modern statutes, such murder is second degree murder. Furthermore, even if a jury did not consider Allen's conduct to be wanton, driving an automobile at that rate of speed would at least be considered criminally negligent, in which event the homicide would be involuntary manslaughter.

Returning to Don's liability as an accomplice and a co-conspirator of Allen, Don is chargeable with any crimes that Allen foreseeably committed for the purpose of accomplishing the underlying criminal goals. Since it could be anticipated that Allen, hurrying with the truck toward Mexico, would drive in excess of the speed limit, and that if a police car tried to stop him, Allen would think that the "theft" had been discovered and try to escape the officer, the murder or manslaughter committed by Allen would be imputable to Don, his accomplice.

Oscar's Liability

The agreement between Don and Oscar to cause a phony "disappearance" of Oscar's insured stereo equipment, and thereby defraud Oscar's insurance carrier, amounts to the crime of conspiracy. This conspiracy expanded when Allen agreed to join it. An "overt act" occurred when Oscar handed Don the duplicate key.

In addition to being liable for the conspiracy itself, one who participates in a conspiracy is vicariously liable for a crime committed by the co-conspirators, either if the crime was the goal of the conspiracy, or if its commission could reasonably have been foreseen in the furtherance of that goal. Therefore, any liability that Don or Allen incurred would be imputable to Oscar. Overlapping the rule of vicarious liability in conspiracy situations is the concept of accomplice liability, which, again, would make Oscar liable for the activities of Don. Don and Oscar may be guilty of an attempt to defraud the insurance carrier under the Model Penal Code substantial step test, but would probably not be guilty of attempt under the other tests mentioned above because the loss had not yet been reported to the insurance carrier.

Personal Property

PERSONAL PROPERTY

TABLE OF CONTENTS

I. REAL AND PERSONAL PROPERTY DISTINCTIONS

A. GENERAL DISTINCTIONS

Real property is ***immovable*** property and consists of land, things fixed to land, and things incidental or appurtenant to land. Personal property is ***movable*** property, which includes every kind that is not real property. Real property may be converted into personalty by severance and vice versa by an annexation intended to be permanent.

B. LEASEHOLDS

Leases of land for a term of years, no matter of what length, are classified with personal property as ***chattels.***

C. CROPS

1. Fructus Naturales vs. Fructus Industriales

Fructus naturales are crops that grow spontaneously on the land (*e.g.*, trees, bushes, grass), while fructus industriales are the result of cultivation (*e.g.*, grain, vegetables). Title to fructus naturales passes with the land, and such crops are ***real property.*** Fructus industriales are ***personalty.***

2. Conveyance

A conveyance of land includes annual crops, unless a reservation in the deed (or provision in the operative will) is made to the contrary. This result is based upon the presumed intention of the parties; however, a contrary intent may be shown.

3. Mortgage

In general, the prior mortgage of the land will prevail over the subsequent mortgage of the crops. Similarly, the prior mortgage of the crops will prevail over the subsequent mortgage of the land. In other words, the ***first mortgage in time prevails.***

4. Doctrine of Emblements

Emblements is the well-established right of a ***former tenant*** (or her personal representative) to enter upon property to cultivate, harvest, and ***remove crops*** planted by her prior to the termination of her estate. The right of emblements exists where two requirements are fulfilled: (i) the tenancy was for an uncertain duration (*i.e.,* life estate or tenancy at will); and (ii) the tenancy terminated without fault on the part of the tenant.

D. FIXTURES

Under the concept of fixtures, a chattel that has been annexed to real property is ***converted from personalty to realty.*** The former chattel becomes an accessory to the land (*i.e.,* a fixture) and passes with ownership of the land. Section 9-334 of the Uniform Commercial Code governs priorities of conflicting security interests in fixtures and real estate. For a more detailed discussion of fixtures, *see* Real Property outline.

II. ACQUISITION AND LOSS OF RIGHT OR TITLE TO PERSONAL PROPERTY

A. PRINCIPAL MODES

Rights and title to personal property are acquired or lost by occupancy, adverse possession, accession, confusion, judgment, gift, or when the chattel is lost, mislaid, or abandoned. In general,

an owner of personal property cannot be divested of title without her consent. A purchaser of a chattel or of a chose in action acquires title by voluntary act or by operation of law (such as conduct creating an estoppel). The intent of the parties is controlling in determining which goods pass and when title passes in a sale.

B. OWNERSHIP

A thing capable of ownership but not then owned belongs to the person who acquires actual or constructive ***dominion and control*** over it and has the ***intent*** to assert ownership over it.

1. Wild Animals

Wild animals (ferae naturae) in their natural state are ***unowned***. They become private property upon being reduced to possession.

a. Acquisition of Title

1) Possession

The first person to exercise ***dominion and control*** over such an animal becomes, with possession, the owner of the animal.

2) Constructive Possession

Animals caught in a ***trap or net*** belong to the one who owns and has set the trap or net. By setting such a trap, one is said to ***constructively*** possess those animals snared.

3) Mere Pursuit

Mere pursuit does ***not*** constitute the exercise of dominion and control sufficient to give the hunter a property right in the animal. However, where an animal has been ***mortally wounded*** so that actual possession is practically inevitable, a ***vested*** property right in the animal accrues that cannot be divested by another's act in intervening and killing the animal.

4) Trespass

While a landowner is not regarded as the owner of all wild animals found on his property, a ***trespasser*** who kills game on another's land ***forfeits*** her ***title*** in favor of the landowner. This is to prevent the act of trespassing from benefiting the trespasser.

5) Violation of Statute

One who violates a statute (*e.g.,* failure to have a hunting license) forfeits her title in animals caught pursuant thereto.

b. Loss of Title

1) Escape

If a wild animal, captured and held in private ownership, escapes and resumes its natural liberty, the former owner loses his property right in it. The animal once again is ***unowned***, and the first person thereafter to capture it becomes the new owner.

2) Habit of Return

If a wild animal escapes and, though wandering about without restraint, ***periodically returns*** to its owner's home, or if, though endeavoring to escape, it is still pursued by the owner or is by other means liable to be recaptured by the owner, title is not lost.

3) **Marked Animals**
When certain animals, such as furbearing animals, have been captured and reduced to private ownership, it is common for the owner to mark or brand them for purposes of identification. If the animal escapes and resumes its natural liberty, the question becomes whether title is lost. Normally, modern courts will allow title to be retained in the former possessor as long as the animal is ***marked*** and the owner exercises all possible ***effort to recapture*** the animal.

2. **Literary Property**
The author of a book or literary composition has, by copyright, the exclusive right to continue to reproduce and sell her "original work of authorship" as expressed and "fixed" in a tangible medium of expression. Protection of this right exists solely under federal statute. [*See* 17 U.S.C. §301(a)]

a. **Requirements for Protection**
Certain requirements must be met before one is entitled to copyright protection.

1) **Concrete Form**
The work must have already taken on concrete form in order to be entitled to protection, *e.g.,* an abstract idea for a future work is not entitled to protection.

2) **Work Must Be New**
The material involved must be new and original.

3) **Must Be "Fixed"**
The work must be "fixed" in a tangible medium of expression. A work is "fixed" when its embodiment in a copy or phonorecord (terms of art broadly defined) is sufficiently permanent to permit it to be perceived or reproduced, for a period of more than transitory duration, with or without the aid of a machine or device. [*See* 17 U.S.C. §101]

b. **Extent of Protection**
This protection securing the author's exclusive rights to reproduction, display, etc., is limited to her ***lifetime plus 70 years***, or if the author was anonymous or working for hire (*e.g.,* an employee of a corporation), 95 years from publication or 120 years from creation, whichever expires first. [17 U.S.C. §302]

c. **Copyright Enforcement**
A claim of copyright ownership must be properly registered with the United States Copyright Office in order to enforce the author's rights, even though a copyright is deemed to be present from the time a work is created. Until a work is preregistered or registered, an author cannot bring an action for copyright infringement. [17 U.S.C. §411(a)] Once a work is properly registered, an infringement action may be brought even for infringement occurring before registration. Note that if an author does not register the copyright, his protection is limited to any contractual or quasi-contractual theories available under state law (*e.g.,* recovery in implied contract for misappropriation of sketched idea for a movie).

d. **Limitation on Protection**
The protection is not good as against any individual who ***independently creates*** the identical or similar work product.

e. **Letters**
Letters are "literary works," which are "works of authorship" under 17 U.S.C. section 102(a)(1). The ***sender*** of a letter has the ***exclusive right*** to sell, publish, or reproduce the ***contents*** of the letter. Ownership of the ***document*** itself lies in the receiver of the letter.

f. **Rights in an Idea**
Although ideas receive no copyright protection, a person has a property right in her own idea that is ***original, concrete, and useful*** and is disclosed in circumstances that, reasonably construed, clearly indicate that ***compensation is contemplated*** if the idea is accepted and used. Damages may be recovered for the use or appropriation of the idea by another.

3. **Persona**
A celebrity's right of publicity (*i.e.*, the right to control the commercial value of his name, likeness, or personality) is tangible personal property. This protects people from losing the benefit of their work in creating a recognizable persona or identity. This right exists both at common law and by statute.

4. **Human Tissue**
While a person has a property right to his own tissue, that right evaporates once a sample is voluntarily given to a third party. [*See* Moore v. Regents of the University of California, 51 Cal. 3d 120 (1990)—patient did not have property right to spleen following its removal by doctors who then used it to create a cell line of great commercial value]

5. **Tortious Conversion**
Tortious conversion of personal property ***does not deprive the true owner of her title***. Moreover, one who does not have title to goods cannot pass title to even a bona fide purchaser, ***except*** in the following circumstances:

a. **Money and Negotiable Instruments**
Transfers of money and of negotiable instruments will pass title to a bona fide purchaser.

b. **Owner Intended to Transfer Title**
Where the owner of goods is induced by fraud or misrepresentation to sell the goods and the vendee subsequently transfers the goods to a bona fide purchaser, the latter retains the goods as against the original owner where the original owner ***intended*** to transfer title to the goods to the defrauder.

c. **Owner Represented that Possessor Has Authority to Sell**
The owner of goods may be estopped from asserting title if she has expressly or impliedly represented that the possessor of the goods is the owner or has authority to sell them and a bona fide purchaser has relied in good faith upon such representations.
Examples: 1) Owner delivers the goods to a retailer of similar items.

2) Owner delivers indicia of title to a third party.

6. **Burden of Showing Title**

One attempting to divest another of personal property has the burden of showing title and the right to do so. Any evidence is admissible, and ownership may be established by proof of acts of ownership as well as by direct testimony. Possession plus a claim of title is prima facie evidence of title and ownership.

C. LOST, MISLAID, AND ABANDONED PROPERTY

1. **Concept**

The fact that the owner has either ***lost or mislaid*** his property does not lead to the divestiture of his title. Title to such property persists despite the fact that it has been lost or mislaid. The owner relinquishes title when he ***abandons*** the property.

a. **Lost Property**

Property is "lost" when the owner has ***accidentally and involuntarily*** parted with his possession and does not know where to find it. To determine whether property is lost, the key factor is the place ***where it is found***: judging from the place where found, would a reasonable person conclude that the owner had accidentally and involuntarily parted with possession of it and does not know where to find it?

Example: A wristwatch found on the floor in a public place will likely be regarded as lost property. Judging from the place where found, it is reasonable to conclude that one would not intentionally place a wristwatch on the floor.

b. **Mislaid Property**

Property is "mislaid" when, judging from the place where found, it can reasonably be determined that it was ***intentionally placed*** there and ***thereafter forgotten***.

Example: A briefcase found on a desk, table, or counter will likely be regarded as mislaid property. Judging from the place where found, it is reasonable to conclude that the item was intentionally placed there and thereafter forgotten.

c. **Abandoned Property**

Abandoned property is property that the owner has voluntarily relinquished all ownership of without reference to any particular person or purpose. It is necessary to show an ***intent to give up both title and possession***.

Examples: 1) Allowing refrigerators to remain in a building that the owner of the refrigerators knew was to be destroyed was held to be an act of abandonment.

2) A tenant's act of leaving her apartment for one week and being in arrears for one week's rent was held to be not enough to constitute abandonment of the property in the apartment. The landlord padlocked the tenant's door and attempted to charge an extra fee before allowing the tenant to enter again. It was held that the tenant had not abandoned her property and so the landlord had converted the property.

1) **Distinguish from Lost**

A chattel is not abandoned merely because the owner has parted with its possession.

If the owner of a chattel ***involuntarily*** parts with possession of goods, they should be categorized as either lost or mislaid. Lost or mislaid goods are treated differently from abandoned chattels. To show that a chattel has been abandoned, one must show that the former owner ***voluntarily*** gave up and relinquished his ownership in the chattel.

2) **Acquisition of Title**
If a chattel can be categorized as abandoned, it becomes, by virtue of the abandonment, unowned. As with wild animals, ownership of an abandoned chattel is acquired by reducing it to possession. Title to abandoned chattel is acquired by: (i) ***actual or constructive dominion and control*** over the thing, and (ii) an ***intent to assert ownership*** over it.

3) **Escheat**
Where abandoned property is held by an intermediary with no property interest in the property (*e.g.,* unclaimed funds held by banks or other depositories), the state may assume title to the property through a process called ***escheat***. Property may be escheated only by the state in which the property is located. Intangible property is considered to be located at the domicile of the property owner. [Delaware v. New York, 507 U.S. 490 (1993)—state of owner's last known address is state with right to escheat unclaimed securities funds]

2. **General Rules for Lost or Mislaid Property**
Once you have established that property is lost or mislaid, you must discuss who has the right to possess the property as against the whole world—except the true owner.

a. **Finder of Lost Property**

1) **General Rule—Finder Entitled to Possession Except Against True Owner**
If property is categorized as "lost," the one who reduces it to possession becomes its finder. Possession is ***physical control*** coupled with an ***intention to assume dominion*** over the object. The intent may be manifested by an effort to keep others away, or may be implied, as in the case of an article discovered on the land of an owner. Generally, the finder of lost property is entitled to possession of it as against all except the true owner.

Examples: 1) A boy who discovered a sock and threw it among his friends was held not to have the requisite intent to assert control over the sock or the money found in it.

2) The act of placing markers over the spot where a wrecked steamboat was located was held not to be a sufficient exercise of dominion and control by the plaintiff to allow him to claim title to the abandoned property.

2) **Exceptions to General Rule**

a) **Trespasser**
To penalize one who trespasses onto private property, most courts would hold that a trespasser-finder will not be allowed to secure possessory rights in the lost property. The right of possession will therefore fall to the owner of the place where the item of property is found (locus in quo).

b) **Highly Private Locus**

Where a chattel is found in a highly private locus, the owner of the locus in quo, and not the finder, will acquire the possessory rights. Several explanations have been given for this rule. One is that the owner of a highly private locus possesses, by definition, everything within the locus, and therefore possesses the item that has been lost. Another reason set forth is that the true owner, having lost property in such a private locus, will more likely return to the place to recoup his property.

(1) **Private Place**

For the finder to be deprived of his possessory right in the lost article, the place of discovery must be ***highly private***. The rule is generally applicable only to locations wherein the public is not invited, *e.g.,* a home.

(2) **Public Place**

If the place of discovery is open to the public, then the finder becomes entitled to the right of possession. The mere fact that the place of discovery is ***privately owned*** is not sufficient to render it a highly private locus.

c) **Employer-Employee**

There is some authority that holds that an employee who finds an article in the course of his employment should surrender the right of possession to his employer. Within the employer-employee relationship, the basic concept is that the employer has the right to direct the employee in his activities. On this basis, if the employee found the article by virtue of an act specifically directed by the employer, the employer should acquire the rights of possession in the article.

d) **Buried Articles**

On a theory of constructive possession, it can be held that the owner of real property possesses all that which lies beneath the surface of his land. On this basis, if one finds an article buried beneath the surface, the right of possession ought to belong to the owner of the locus rather than the finder.

b. **Finder of Mislaid Property**

The finder of mislaid property does not acquire the right to possession. The ***owner*** of the ***locus in quo*** becomes entitled to possess the mislaid property against all the world except the true owner. *Rationale:* Since, by definition, mislaid property is that which has been intentionally placed where found and thereafter forgotten, when the true owner realizes where he has mislaid his property he will return to that location to retrieve his property. On this basis, in an effort to return property to its owner, the right of possession is given to the owner of the locus in quo and not the finder.

Example: A maid found a valuable brooch in the slats of a hotel bed. The possessor of the room at the time claimed the brooch as finder (the maid having put the brooch on his dresser). *Held:* The brooch must have been placed in the slats on purpose and not by inadvertence. Therefore, the brooch was mislaid property and possession was awarded to the hotel as owner of the premises.

c. **Rights and Duties of Possessor**

The foregoing rules, applicable under the common law, describe who acquires the right of possession as against the whole world except the true owner. Under these rules, however, neither the finder (as to lost goods) nor the owner of the locus in quo (as to mislaid goods) becomes the title owner of the property; he merely acquires the right of possession, and as possessor has the following rights and duties.

1) **Possessor as Quasi-Bailee**

The possessor is a quasi-bailee. His title is good as against all the world except the true owner, even to the point of suing for the return of the property if wrongfully taken from him.

Example: A lost ring belonging to O was found by X, who then lost it himself. It was then found by Y. X may recover possession from Y or anyone else but O.

2) **Duty to Find Owner**

Should the finder know or have reasonable means of discovering the true owner, he must do so, or he may be guilty of larceny, and he may be held liable in tort for conversion.

Example: X finds a wallet containing identification papers, including the telephone number of its owner, Y. X does not attempt to contact Y, but holds the wallet (including contents) with intent to return it to Y should Y ever ask for it. X has converted the wallet and its contents.

3) **Duty of Due Care**

The possessor must keep the goods with due care, considering that he is a gratuitous bailee and considering the nature of the goods. Failure to adhere to this standard will render him liable in negligence.

4) **Extent of Obligations**

These obligations persist until sufficient time has passed for the true owner to be deemed to have abandoned her goods (which will depend upon the character of the goods and circumstances of the case) or until the statute of limitations has run.

5) **Acquiring Title**

As a general rule, after a sufficient time has run for the goods to be deemed abandoned, or after the statute of limitations has run, the possessor becomes the new owner of the goods.

d. **Treasure Trove**

Treasure trove is any gold or silver in coin, plate, or bullion found concealed (*e.g.,* in the earth, in a house, in a bureau, etc.), the owner of which is unknown. Treasure trove has been held to include paper representatives of gold and silver.

1) **Right of Finder**

Treasure trove, according to the common law, belonged to the finder as against everyone in the world except the true owner. In addition, the fact that the finder was a trespasser would not deprive him of his possessory rights.

2) **Modern View**
Today, many states apply the usual rules applicable to lost property in dealing with treasure trove. No exception is made today for the handling of treasure trove problems.

3. **Uniform Unclaimed Property Act**
Most states have adopted a version of the Uniform Unclaimed Property Act (the "Act"), which provides for the disposition of intangible property (such as money, checks, and stock) and property in safe deposit boxes. Under the Act, such property is ***presumed abandoned*** if the owner does not claim it or otherwise demonstrate an interest in it for the statutory period, generally five years. The Act provides a procedure for turning the property over to a state administrator, who sells it if unable to locate the owner. A holder who disposes of unclaimed property pursuant to the Act is ***relieved of liability*** to the owner.

A minority of states use the older ***Uniform Disposition of Unclaimed Property Act***, which differs primarily in fixing the basic statutory period at seven years.

D. ACCESSION

Accession is the addition of value to property by the expenditure of labor or the addition of new materials. If the addition can be detached from the principal chattel, this will be ordered and each party will be put in status quo ante. If the addition cannot be detached from the principal chattel, the issue is one of ownership: Who is the owner of the chattel in its enhanced state? The answer depends upon whether the trespasser acted in good faith or was a willful trespasser.

1. **Accession by Innocent Trespasser**

a. **General Rule—Trespasser Cannot Recover**
Where a trespasser adds value to the original owner's chattel, the original owner retains title, and the trespasser cannot sue for compensation for the value of his labor or materials added to the chattel.

b. **Original Owner's Remedies**

1) **Damages for Conversion**
The original owner may sue the trespasser and obtain conversion damages—the value of the original materials plus any consequential damages.

2) **Replevin**
Alternatively, the original owner may seek replevin—return of the chattel.

c. **When Original Owner Is Limited to Damages**
In some cases the original owner is limited to a cause of action for damages; she may not sue in replevin because the act of accession divested her of title.

1) **Complete Change**
When the species of property has been completely changed by the addition of value to the property by the expenditure of labor or new materials, the original owner may not recoup the chattel.

2) **Great Increase in Value**
A similar exception is made when the increase in value is so great that it would be unfair to permit the original owner to reclaim her property.

Examples: 1) The owner of clay used by another in making bricks has no title to the bricks because the identity of the clay has been lost in the creation of a new species.

2) Where trees originally worth $25 are converted by a person in good faith into barrel hoops worth $700, the original owner cannot recover the hoops.

2. **Accession by Willful Trespasser**
A willful trespasser cannot gain any rights of ownership in the property he has enhanced in value under the rules of accession. The original owner of the chattel is entitled to the property in its improved state regardless of the degree of augmentation in value made by the trespasser.

a. **Complete Change**
The original owner's title persists even though there has been a complete change in the form of the chattel.

b. **Original Owner's Remedy**
The owner of the chattel subject to willful trespass may elect to sue the trespasser for ***damages for conversion*** (*i.e.,* the full present value of the property in its improved state) ***or*** for ***replevin*** (*i.e.,* the return of the chattel as now changed or improved).

E. **CONFUSION**
Confusion is an ***intermixture*** of goods owned by different persons such that the property of each can no longer be distinguished, *i.e.,* fungible goods. If the property can be identified and returned, there is no confusion.

1. **Known Contributions**
Where goods are of the same kind and quality, the parties are ***tenants in common*** of the mass ***in proportion*** to their respective interests, regardless of how the confusion took place, and even regardless of whether the confusion was fraudulent or willful.

Example: Where wheat of the same grade belonging to different persons is wrongfully and fraudulently mingled by one of them and ground into flour, the wrongdoer is entitled to his proportionate share of the mass.

2. **Unknown Contributions**

a. **Innocent Confusion**
If the confusion was innocent (*e.g.,* by an act of God, act of a third party, or consent), the owners are ***tenants in common*** of the mass. If the amount of contribution is unknown, the parties share equally.

b. **Wrongful Confusion**
If the confusion was caused wrongfully by one of the owners, her agent, bailee, or

trustee, the burden is upon such owner to identify her portion. If she cannot do so, the ***entire mass belongs to the innocent owner***.

Example: Where the owner of bales of cotton fraudulently mingles them with bales belonging to another so that they become indistinguishable, the wrongdoer is entitled to no part of the goods unless she identifies it as her property.

c. **Negligent Confusion**

Cases are split as to whether negligent confusion is innocent or wrongful; most say it is wrongful.

F. ADVERSE POSSESSION—STATUTE OF LIMITATIONS

Title to personal property by adverse possession results from the running of a statute of limitations, which requires that the cause of action for recovery of the property be brought within a specified period after it accrues. When the period specified has run, the presumption that the person in possession has the right to possession cannot be overcome by the former owner; the party in possession thereafter has an enforceable right to possession superior to everyone and thus becomes the true owner. In an action for recovery of the property, the defendant must plead the statute of limitations as an affirmative defense.

1. Requirements

As with real estate, the cause of action does not accrue and, therefore, the statute of limitations does not run unless the possession relied on is: (i) actual; (ii) open and notorious; (iii) hostile and adverse, under a claim of right; and (iv) exclusive and continuous.

a. **Actual**

The property has not been given to another.

b. **Open and Notorious**

There must be some visible ***act of dominion or use*** on the part of the possessor that is inconsistent with the absolute right of property in the owner, so as to give reasonable notice to the owner. In the case of thieves, a secret holding is presumed. A ***finder*** of lost or mislaid property is presumed to hold openly.

c. **Hostile and Adverse**

Possession must not be by consent and not in subordination to the rights of the true owner.

d. **Exclusive and Continuous**

Possession must be exclusive to the adverse possessor (except for tacking—*see* below). Since the possession must be continuous for the statutory period, interrupted periods that together total the required time are insufficient.

2. Statute of Limitations

Title passes when the statutory limitation period has run.

a. **Accruing of Claim**

The accruing of the claim or cause of action is often a crucial question. Demand

and refusal may be required, *e.g.,* when possession passed originally as a gratuitous bailment.

b. Tacking

Successive possessors of the property may "tack" or combine their respective periods of possession ***as long as they are in privity***, *e.g.,* the property is sold, given, or bequeathed to the subsequent possessor.

c. Tolling the Statute

Tolling the statute means that the time during which the following conditions are met is not counted in the time period, or that the period, which has otherwise expired, is extended beyond a certain event.

1) Disability of Plaintiff

When a person entitled to maintain an action is a minor, mentally incompetent, or imprisoned on the date the action accrues, she may bring the action ***after*** removal of the disability within a period permitted by statute.

2) Defendant Out of Jurisdiction

When the wrongdoer, who is a ***resident*** of this jurisdiction, is outside the jurisdiction, the statute is tolled until the wrongdoer returns.

3) Fraudulent Concealment

When a potential defendant fraudulently conceals himself after the action accrues, so as to avoid service, the statute is tolled until the concealment has ended.

3. Bona Fide Purchaser of Stolen Goods

A bona fide purchaser of stolen goods is not protected against the claim of the owner unless the statute of limitations has run on the owner. Since a secret (rather than open and notorious) holding is presumed in the case of stolen goods, the running of the statute is unlikely. The risk is on the purchaser.

G. TITLE BY JUDGMENT

1. Election of Remedies

One who destroys, misuses, misdelivers, or otherwise wrongfully deprives the owner of a chattel of her possessory rights may be liable to the owner under various theories of recovery.

a. Replevin

Replevin is an action to ***recover the chattel itself.***

Example: A bailed her automobile to B. Upon A's making proper demand for its return, B refused to redeliver possession of the car. A may sue B in replevin to have the subject matter of the bailment returned to her in specie.

b. Trespass

The action in trespass is to ***recover money damages*** incurred by reason of the dispossession.

c. **Trover**
The action in trover is to ***recover the value of the chattel*** along with damages for dispossession.

2. **Conversion**
An owner may allege conversion and sue the wrongdoer in trover. The substance of the action is that from and after the time the property was converted (*i.e.,* wrongfully dealt with, misdelivered, or damaged), the wrongdoer by her action "purchased the chattel." By proceeding on the theory of conversion, the court in substance forces a sale of the chattel for the value as of the date of conversion.

a. **Effect of Suing in Trover**
Should the owner proceed under a trover theory, title to the chattel, by virtue of the forced sale, becomes ***vested in the converter*** by operation of law.

1) **Merger**
If the remedy elected is trover, the right to possession, which is the basis of the cause of action and which is necessarily proved if the plaintiff prevails, is merged in the judgment awarding damages. It is not extinguished, however, until the judgment is satisfied, and the plaintiff ***may elect to sue in replevin*** until that time.

2) **Relation Back**
When the judgment is satisfied by the tortfeasor, title to the converted property passes to him but relates back to the date of conversion. Thus, if the property is destroyed after conversion but before satisfaction of the judgment, the loss falls on the converter. Likewise, if the property fluctuates in value once the judgment has been satisfied, the tortfeasor recoups the benefits or the burdens of the fluctuation in value.

b. **Who Can Sue?**
Anyone who is in actual possession of the chattel in question or who is entitled to immediate possession of the chattel can maintain an action for trover. On this basis, a bailee who has the right of possession or who is entitled to the right of possession may elect trover as the action when faced with the wrongful conduct of another.

c. **Who Can Be Sued?**
Obviously, the tortfeasor-converter can be sued in trover. However, a situation frequently arises in which the converter sells the subject matter of the tort before the action is brought. In such cases, the ***purchaser*** (even a bona fide purchaser) ***is liable*** as a converter.

H. GIFT
A gift is a ***voluntary transfer*** of property by one to another without any consideration or compensation. To be valid, a gift ***must be executed or actually made***. A gratuitous promise to make a gift in the future is not binding.

1. **Gifts Inter Vivos**
An inter vivos gift, once made, is irrevocable. There are three requirements for an inter vivos gift: (i) donative intent, (ii) delivery, and (iii) acceptance of the gift.

a. **Donative Intent**

1) **Intent to Make a Present Gift**

The donor must have a present mental capacity and must intend to make an effective gift of her property.

Example: Where the donor intended to retain use of so much of her bank account as she desired during her life and to give the balance remaining at her death to the donee, there was ***no valid gift***, even though the bank book had been delivered to the donee. There being ***no intent to make an immediate gift***, and the transfer not being effective until the donor's death, the transaction was testamentary.

2) **Promise to Make a Gift in the Future**

If, by the act of the donor, it can be determined that the donor manifested her intention to have title pass to the donee at some future date, the requisite ***mental state is not present*** and no gift follows.

Example: A mother tells her daughter, "I shall make a gift of this wristwatch to you tomorrow." The requisite mental state is not present. The mother, the would-be donor, has not indicated that she wishes to vest title in the daughter ***at that moment***. The mother has made a mere gratuitous promise to make a gift in the future.

3) **Donative Intent Applies to Title**

The requirement of donative intent should not be construed to require that the donor intends the donee to obtain full and complete rights of use and enjoyment in the subject matter of the gift. The donor may intend to immediately vest title in the donee, and yet reserve right of possession until some future date. Notwithstanding this intention, a ***gift may be effective***.

Example: A father tells his son, "This wristwatch is now yours; however, I wish to use it until my new one arrives." As long as all other requirements for the valid execution of the gift are complied with, the gift is effective even though the donor has retained possessory rights in the subject matter of the gift.

b. **Delivery**

In addition to the requirement that the donor possess the requisite donative intent, delivery in one form or another must be made in order to effect a valid gift inter vivos.

1) **Types of Delivery**

The basic ways of accomplishing the delivery requirement are: (i) actual physical delivery, (ii) constructive delivery, (iii) delivery by written instrument, and (iv) symbolic delivery.

a) **Actual Physical Delivery**

If the donor physically vests the donee with possession of the subject matter of the gift, the delivery requirement is satisfied. To show that delivery has been accomplished in this manner, there must be a showing that the ***donee has received dominion and control*** over the subject matter of the gift.

Example: A husband places certain securities in an envelope. The envelope bears the following inscription: "The enclosed are for my wife, Mary." The envelope is then placed with its contents into the husband's safe deposit box. There would be no valid gift. The delivery requirement is not satisfied because the husband has not physically transferred the securities to his wife, and has retained dominion and control over his own safe deposit box.

b) **Constructive Delivery**

When an item, because of its size or location, would be impossible or impracticable to manually deliver, substitute delivery may be sufficient. In such cases, the delivery requirement will be satisfied if the donor ***surrenders as much control*** over the subject matter of the gift as he presently possesses.

Examples: 1) If A declares that he gives an antique desk and all its contents to B and hands B the key to the desk, the delivery requirement may have been satisfied because A has given control over the desk.

2) Since a passbook to a savings account is evidence of control of that account, delivery of the passbook with the requisite donative intent is sufficient delivery.

c) **Delivery by Written Instrument**

Since delivery has been established as a fraud-prevention device, most courts will accept a written document evidencing the gift. The execution and subsequent delivery of this written "deed of gift" should be sufficient to accomplish the gift.

(1) **Requirements**

To be sufficient, the writing should manifest the donative intent, describe the subject matter of the gift, be signed by the donor, and be delivered.

(2) **Physical Delivery Possible**

One may accomplish delivery by written instrument even though the subject matter of the gift was capable of being manually transferred. Note that some courts that do not recognize the validity of delivery by written instrument may still treat the writing as a form of ***symbolic delivery*** (*see* below) if manual delivery is impossible or impracticable.

d) **Symbolic Delivery**

When manual delivery is impossible or impracticable, symbolic delivery is permitted. Symbolic delivery occurs when the donor hands over some ***object***, other than the item given, ***that is symbolic*** of the item. Symbolic delivery is most commonly effectuated by delivering a written instrument, as described above.

2) **Donee Already in Possession**

If the donee is already in possession of the article, the donor need not repossess the

article and then return it to the donee, because the law will not require a useless act. But the donor must do something to make his intent objectively clear.

3) **Gift Through Agent**

a) **If Agent of Donee**
If a gift is given through an agent of the donee, the gift is effective when the ***donor delivers*** to the agent.

b) **If Agent of Donor**
If a gift is given through the agent of the donor, the gift is effective when the ***agent delivers*** to the donee, unless the agent has assented to hold the property for the donee. Thus, where such assent is missing and the donor delivers the item to his agent for delivery to the donee, if the donor dies before delivery is made, there is no gift. The agent's authority to deliver terminated upon the donor's death, and no delivery was made.

4) **Special Problems in Delivery**

a) **Checks**

(1) **Check of Donor**
The mere manual delivery of a check made by the donor does not fulfill the delivery requirement. Since the check simply orders the bank to perform the delivery of the real subject matter (*i.e.,* the money), there is ***no delivery until*** such time as the ***bank makes payment.***

(2) **Check of Another**
Since the check of another is not the directive of the donor to have complete delivery made by his agent, but rather a contract right given by another, its ***transfer fulfills the delivery requirement.*** It is important to note that even where a check must be indorsed by the donor for proper negotiation, the manual delivery of the unindorsed check (coupled with the requisite donative intent) completes the gift.

b) **Promissory Notes**
Because a promissory note, drawn by the donor, is merely a promise to deliver money in the future, the execution and manual delivery of a promissory note is not a valid gift. However, if a promissory note has been drawn in favor of the donor, and thereafter the donor transfers it to a third person (*i.e.,* the donee), the gift is valid.

c) **Stock Certificates**
Delivery of shares of stock with the requisite donative intent constitutes a valid gift. This may be true though the donor continues to receive the dividends thereon up to the time of his death. In addition, indorsement of the stock certificate is not a prerequisite to valid and complete delivery. Also, it is not necessary that the donee's name be entered on the corporate books in order to complete delivery.

d) **Life Insurance Policy**
The rules for delivery of life insurance policies are similar to those for delivery of stock certificates.

e) **Bank Savings Deposits**
Delivering a bank book to the donee with intent to make a gift is a sufficient symbolic delivery. Since withdrawals may be made from a savings account only upon presentation of the bank book, the savings bank book represents dominion over the amount on deposit.

f) **Joint Checking Account**

(1) **Rebuttable Presumption of No Gift**
In some jurisdictions, where a joint checking account is opened and one party puts in all or most of the money, there is a presumption that this is done for the convenience of that party and not as a gift, particularly where the person whose money is involved is an invalid or is otherwise unable to get to the bank easily. The presumption may be rebutted by clear proof of donative intent. It may also be rebutted by showing that convenience was not the reason; *i.e.,* the person whose money was involved had ready access to the joint account.

(2) **Survivor Becomes Owner**
Other jurisdictions do not allow such a rebuttable presumption to be raised in the case of a joint checking account. If statutory formalities are complied with, the survivor of a joint account will automatically become the owner of the account (absent fraud, undue influence, mental incapacity, or mistake). [*See In re* LaGarce's Estate, 487 S.W.2d 493 (Mo. 1972)]

c. **Acceptance of Donee**
When the gift is beneficial to the donee, acceptance by her is presumed. However, the donee may refuse to accept a gift by an affirmative act.

d. **Gifts in Contemplation of Marriage**
Most jurisdictions hold that engagement gifts are made in contemplation of marriage and are conditioned on the subsequent ceremonial marriage taking place. If the marriage does not occur, engagement gifts must be returned. While an engagement ring by definition is given in contemplation of marriage, this may not be the case with other gifts given during the engagement period. Courts consider factors such as the type of property given, fraud, conditions attached to the gift, and the intent of the donor to determine whether the gift will be deemed to be given in contemplation of marriage (and thus recoverable by the donor if the marriage does not occur).

2. **Gifts Causa Mortis**

a. **Concept and Essential Elements**
A gift causa mortis is one ***given in contemplation of death***. For the gift to be valid, the following elements must exist:

1) **Present Mental Capacity**
The donor must have the same present mental capacity to make the gift as is required for a gift inter vivos.

2) **Gift Must Be Personal Property**
Real property cannot be conveyed as a gift causa mortis.

3) **Delivery and Acceptance**
The delivery and acceptance requirements that are essential to the validity of a gift inter vivos are also required for gifts causa mortis.

a) **Identical Test**
To accomplish a gift causa mortis, the requisite ***donative intent***, in addition to ***delivery*** and ***acceptance*** of the subject matter of the gift, is required. The rules relating to delivery and acceptance are identical for both gifts inter vivos and gifts causa mortis, with one exception.

b) **Exception—Delivery by Deed of Gift (Symbolic Delivery)**
There are a significant number of states that hold that the donor may not accomplish a gift causa mortis by virtue of symbolic delivery. The rationale given is that execution of a written document that acts as a testamentary device should be sufficient to vest title in a donee only if drawn in compliance with the Statute of Wills. All other forms of delivery previously indicated as being acceptable for the valid accomplishment of a gift inter vivos will be sufficient and acceptable for the valid accomplishment of a gift causa mortis.

4) **Anticipation of Death**
The definition of a gift causa mortis includes the requisite that the donor be in contemplation of imminent death. As originally envisioned, the donor must have been suffering from an illness that realistically confronted her with a fear of death.

a) **Imminence**
There is recognition of a valid gift causa mortis as long as the donor was suffering from an actual illness that threatened her life. The mere abstract fear of death from a future cause (*e.g.*, fear of flying, fear of death in war, etc.) is not sufficient.

b) **Death as Anticipated**
To validate a gift causa mortis, older cases held that the donor had to die as anticipated. If she died from some other cause, some early decisions indicated that the gift was revoked. There has been, however, considerable liberality given to this concept in more recent decisions.

Example: A victim of an automobile accident is placed in an ambulance. In fear of death from the injuries sustained in the accident, she attempts to make a gift causa mortis. En route to the hospital the ambulance is struck by a train and the donor is killed. Can it be said that the donor died "as anticipated"? The more modern authorities would say yes.

c) **Recovery**

(1) **Gift Is Revoked by Operation of Law**
An important ingredient in determining the validity of the gift causa mortis is the failure of the donor to recover from the illness that placed her in contemplation of death. Once it can be said that the donor "recovered," the gift is revoked by operation of law. As long as the donor has failed to recover, the gift is not revoked. The concept of "recovery" predominates in most modern cases. As in the example given above, the donor did not recover from the illness that prompted the attempted gift causa mortis. Therefore, one who attempts a gift causa mortis in contemplation of death will have made a valid gift as long as she fails to recover, though the precise cause of death is different.

(2) **Compare—Deed to Real Property Not Revoked**
Because the property given must be personal property, a deed to real property executed and delivered in contemplation of death is not revoked as a gift causa mortis when the donor recovers.

5) **Absence of Revocation**
In addition to the failure of the donor to recover, a requirement of a valid gift causa mortis is that it ***not be revoked***.

a) **Affirmatively by Donor**
The definition of the gift causa mortis contemplates that the donor has passed title to the donee. However, it is a revocable transaction. The donor reserves the right, as a condition subsequent, to revest ownership in herself by any affirmative act manifesting such intention.

b) **Failure of Donee to Survive**
The gift causa mortis is given on the essential condition that the donee survive the donor. Should the donee fail to survive the donor, the gift is revoked by operation of law.

b. **Creditor Claims**
A gift causa mortis is always ***subject to the claims*** of creditors of the donor's estate.

I. UNIFORM TRANSFERS TO MINORS ACT

1. **Purpose of Act**
While at common law a minor may legally receive a gift, a gift to a minor may be troublesome because of uncertainty over who will manage or care for the property until the donee reaches majority. There may also be questions about the donor's eligibility for the annual $13,000 gift tax exclusion provided by the Internal Revenue Code. A donor who gives property in a manner prescribed by the Uniform Transfers to Minors Act ("UTMA") makes a completed gift to the minor donee and qualifies for the gift tax exclusion.

2. **Subject Matter of Gift**
The UTMA applies to ***all kinds of property*** whether real or personal, tangible or intangible.

3. **Types of Transfers**
The UTMA applies to ***all types of transfers***, not just lifetime outright gifts. It includes transfers from trusts, estates, guardianships, and the minor's debtors.

4. **Title**
The ***gift is irrevocable***. The custodial property is indefeasibly vested in the minor, subject to the rights, powers, duties, and authority of the custodian.

5. **Possession of Gift**
The donor must place the custodian in control of the property as soon as practicable. However, the donor's failure to comply with this requirement, his designation of an ineligible person as custodian, or the death or incapacity of the person designated as custodian does ***not*** affect a consummation of the gift.

6. **Creation of Custodial Property**
Custodial property is created when:

(i) A ***security*** is registered in the name of the donor, other adult, or trust company as custodian for a minor, or delivered with endorsements to someone other than the donor.

(ii) ***Money*** is paid or delivered to a broker or financial institution for credit to account in the custodian's name, as custodian for the minor.

(iii) A ***life insurance policy or annuity*** is registered or assigned and delivered.

(iv) An interest in ***real property*** is recorded.

(v) ***Other property*** interests are transferred to a trust company or adult other than the donor, and the custodian signs the receipt.

(vi) A ***certificate of title*** is issued by state or federal government (*e.g.,* for aircraft, boats, automobiles).

[UTMA §9]

7. **One Minor**
Each gift may be to only one minor.

8. **Custodian**

a. **Who Is Custodian?**
Only one person may be the custodian. The custodian may be the donor, another adult, an adult member of the minor's family, the guardian of a minor, or a trust company.

b. **Duties of Custodian**

1) **Preservation of Property**
The custodian must take control of custodial property, register or record title if appropriate, and collect, hold, manage, invest, and reinvest it as would a prudent person dealing with the property of another.

2) **Payment to Minor**
The custodian pays to the minor for expenditure by him, or expends for the minor's benefit, so much of the custodial property as the custodian deems advisable.

c. **Compensation**
The custodian is entitled to reasonable compensation and reasonable expenses, but may act without compensation.

d. **Successors**
The custodian, should he resign, designates a successor custodian, or a successor may be appointed by the court upon petition.

e. **Removal**
The custodian may be removed by the court upon petition of the minor (if age 14 or older), the donor, an adult member of the minor's family, or the guardian of the minor.

9. **Final Distribution**
Final distribution to the minor should be made when the minor reaches the age of ***majority***. If the minor dies before reaching majority, distribution should be made to the minor's estate.

10. **Uniform Gifts to Minors Act**
Two states, Vermont and South Carolina, continue to use the Uniform Gifts to Minors Act ("UGMA"), which the UTMA was designed to replace. The UGMA differs from the UTMA primarily in that it covers fewer types of property and transfers.

a. **Subject Matter of Gift**
The UGMA applies only to gifts of securities, money, life insurance, or annuity contracts.

b. **Types of Transfers**
The UGMA applies only to lifetime outright gifts. It does not include transfers from trusts, estates, guardianships, or the minor's debtors.

III. LIENS

A. IN GENERAL

1. **Concept**
A lien is the right of one (the lienor) to possess and retain personal property that she has improved or enhanced in value, or otherwise serviced, as security for the payment by the person claiming the property (the lienee) of all charges for the improvement or service.

a. **Conditions for Lienor's Right to Possess**
The lienor has a right to possess for a period of time only if the following conditions are present:

1) A debt that arises from services performed on the thing;

2) Title to the thing is in the debtor (lienee); and

3) Possession of the thing is with the creditor (lienor).

b. Pawn Distinguished

The pawn is held to secure the performance of a promise or other obligation. There may or may not be improvements to or services upon the pawned article.

c. Mortgage Distinguished

In a mortgage there is a transfer of legal title to the mortgagee as security for the performance of the mortgagor's obligations. Upon the failure of the mortgagor to perform, the mortgagee's title becomes absolute, subject to the equity of redemption.

2. Classes of Liens

a. General Lien

A general lien is the right to retain ***all of the property*** of another as security for a general balance due from that person. It exists only when (i) ***separately contracted*** for, (ii) conferred ***by statute***, or (iii) (most commonly) according to the ***usage or custom*** of a particular trade, a general lien is so well established that the parties to a particular transaction must be taken to have made their contracts in relation to the usage or custom. This custom is well established for certain professions, *e.g.,* attorney, banker, factor, universal agent, and innkeeper.

b. Special Lien

A special lien is the right to retain ***specific property*** as security for payment of charges for work done on or services rendered concerning that specific piece of property.

1) Lienor Has Possession

For the special lien, the article must be in possession of the lienor. Thus, if work is done on the owner's premises, no lien will attach unless the parties intended that the lienor should possess the chattels, *e.g.,* materials used in a building on the owner's land.

2) Lienor Must Add Value

For the special lien, the lienor generally must add value to the chattel. It is not enough that the chattel be used to produce a valuable result.

Examples: 1) The local gas station washes Smith's car. Value is added, no matter how infinitesimal. (A clean car is worth more than a dirty car.) There is a lien.

2) Owner sent type to a printer, who used the type to produce a printed work for Owner. There is no lien in the type, for no value was added to it.

a) Exception—Special Lienors

The special lien may exist for a common or private carrier, a warehouser, an ordinary bailee, a trustee, an arbitrator, a general agent, or a special agent (*see* B.1., below). They are entitled to a lien without having added value to the chattel. Furthermore, if a person performs labor on the chattel which does not increase the value of the chattel, she should have a special lien for the reasonable value of the services performed.

c. **Consequence of Classification**

The classification of liens is important only when the lienholder releases a portion of the chattels held as security.

1) **General Lien**

If the lienor has a general lien and releases some of the chattels, the chattels released are freed from the lien, but the lienor may hold the unreleased portion until the ***entire*** lien charge is paid.

2) **Special Lien**

If the lienor has a special lien and releases some of the chattels held, he thereby waives his lien to the extent of the chattels released.

3) **Ambiguous—Construe as Special**

In case of doubt, a lien is ***construed as special*** rather than general, because the law does not favor general liens.

B. RIGHTS OF DIFFERENT LIENORS

As a rule, the lien is given by the owner of the property. In exceptional circumstances, a lien may be given by one who is not the owner of the chattel.

1. Lienors Under the General Rule

a. **Attorney**

Attorneys have a lien on all papers, securities, money, and documents in their possession for the general balance of accounts with their clients.

b. **Cleaner and Launderer**

Cleaners, launderers, dyers, and pressers have a lien on clothing for the value of the services performed.

c. **Mechanic or Artisan**

A mechanic or artisan who makes, alters, or repairs any article of personal property at the request of the owner has a statutory lien on that property for her just and reasonable charges for work done and materials furnished.

d. **Motor Vehicles, Including Trailers**

Any person who stores, repairs, or furnishes supplies of or concerning motor vehicles has a lien for the agreed or reasonable charges when the charges are incurred by the owner, the conditional vendee, or the chattel mortgagor.

e. **Warehouser**

A warehouser has a lien to secure him for the time and labor expended upon the chattel and for his storage charge.

f. **Landlord**

A landlord has a lien for rent upon the tenant's personal chattels on the premises, from the time of execution of the lease and the bringing of a chattel onto the premises.

g. **Common Carrier**

A common carrier has a lien for charges on the theory that the common carrier is

compelled by law to accept all persons who present themselves. However, it has no lien on the goods that it receives from persons other than the owner, such as goods stolen by the shipper. The reason for this rule is that the carrier may demand transportation charges in advance, or in the alternative, proof from the shipper that she is acting with authority from the owner. This bailee for hire should be particularly distinguished from the innkeeper (*see* below).

2. Exceptions to Rule

a. Innkeepers

The lien of an innkeeper is peculiar in that it attaches to any property brought into the inn by the guest. It is not essential in all cases that the guest is the owner of the property. The property may be that of a third person, or even stolen. As long as the innkeeper has no knowledge that the property is not rightfully in the possession of the guest, his lien will attach generally to all the property to the extent of a reasonable charge for the services rendered.

Example: The samples of a traveling salesman are subject to a lien for an innkeeper's charges and may be sold, after proper notice, to satisfy the charges, even though the innkeeper has full knowledge that they are owned by the guest's employer.

b. Other Bailees for Hire

Other bailees for hire acquire no lien on goods received from someone not the owner, for there is no similar duty to accept all goods offered. Therefore, the situation is governed by the general rule that "a lien is a proprietary interest," a qualified ownership, and, in general, can be created only by the owner or by some person authorized by her.

Example: A person in possession of a truck with the owner's permission cannot create a lien for repairs. That the repairs are of benefit to the owner is immaterial.

C. WAIVER OF LIEN

1. By Contract

Although a lien is conferred by law, it may be waived by any contract inconsistent with the existence of the lien. Such contracts usually occur when the artisan agrees to deliver the goods before payment for his services is to be made.

Example: If a person delivers cloth to a tailor to be made into a garment, under agreement by which the tailor is to be paid for his services 30 days after the completion and delivery of the garment, the tailor has no lien on the goods.

2. By Acceptance of Other Security

So too, where a lienor accepts security for payment, the security eliminates the common law lien. The acceptance of the security indicates an intention to regard it as a substitute for the lien.

3. Demand for Excess Charges

A lienor who in good faith demands charges in excess of the original amount of the lien does not waive the lien. However, if the lienee tendered the original amount due under the lien before the lienor demanded the excess amount, the lienor must discharge the lien. If the lienor does not discharge the lien, he may be subject to statutory penalties or liable in an action for replevin or trover.

4. Reservation of Lien or Temporary Use by Bailor

The lien is not lost if the lienholder surrenders the goods to the bailor, specially reserving his lien, or if the bailor is permitted to make temporary use of the property. Therefore, a garage proprietor does not lose his lien on automobiles stored in his garage where the owners are permitted to use their cars daily. In the case of the surrender of temporary possession, the lien enjoys priority over the claims of the bailor's subsequent creditors.

D. MECHANIC'S LIEN VS. PERFECTED SECURITY INTEREST

In many states, the ***mechanic*** who performs labor at the request of the mortgagor ***has priority*** as against the holder of a perfected security interest. This is true even though the mechanic performs her work at a time when the security interest exists. The rationale is that the mechanic has enhanced the value of the article.

E. ENFORCEMENT OF LIEN

A common law possessory lien is merely a right to hold possession until the debt is paid. The lienor has no right to sell the goods to reimburse himself unless this right is conferred by statute or special agreement. Statutes in practically all states give the lienor the power to enforce the lien ***by sale***, either by notice or by judicial foreclosure.

IV. BAILMENTS

A. DEFINITION

A bailment is the relationship created by the transfer of possession of an item of personal property by one called the bailor to another called the bailee for the accomplishment of a certain purpose.

Example: If a coat is delivered to a tailor to be repaired, she acquires a right to its possession as against all the world except for the owner, who, as bailor, retains an unconditional title to the coat with the right to its return.

1. No Transfer of Title

The bailment relationship involves the transfer of possession of an item of personal property to the bailee ***without a transfer of title***. The bailee acquires the right to possess the property in accordance with the terms of the bailment. A bailment obligates the bailee to return the item of personal property to the bailor or otherwise dispose of it according to the terms of the bailment.

2. Contract Aspect

The bailment arises where one possesses the property of another. This relationship may be part of an express contractual arrangement between the parties; however, an ***express contract is not necessary***.

Example: If one finds a lost article and takes it into her possession, she is a bailee for the unknown owner, although she made no contract with that owner.

B. ELEMENTS OF BAILMENT

1. Possession of the Property

There is no bailment unless the bailee obtains ***physical custody*** over the property coupled with ***intent to exercise control***.

Example: Plaintiff's overcoat disappeared after he hung it on a hook on the wall immediately behind, and within two feet of, the table at which plaintiff sat in defendant's restaurant. Plaintiff did not notice a placard stating: "Not responsible for hats, overcoats, umbrellas, etc." Neither defendant nor any of her employees ever saw the coat. It was held that there was no bailment for the overcoat since the facts are inconsistent with the hypothesis that plaintiff intended to transfer to defendant or her employees such possession of the coat as would exclude plaintiff's possession.

2. Bailee's Consent Required

Possession cannot be thrust upon the bailee without her consent. Therefore, a delivery without acceptance by the bailee will not create a bailment and the ***mere custody*** of a chattel is ***not sufficient*** in law to constitute possession.

Example: B, who has bought goods from S, claims that they are defective. He takes them back to S's shop. S asserts that they are perfect and refuses to accept a return of them. Thereupon B walks out of the shop, leaving the goods there. S is not a bailee, although she is now in possession of goods belonging to another. S cannot be made a bailee except with her consent. Therefore, S is under no duty to exercise care of the goods. She may even remove them from her shop.

3. Knowledge of Presence

It cannot be said that a person is in possession of an article as a bailee unless she has knowledge or can be charged with knowledge of the presence of the article.

Example: Where a customer, while trying on garments, lays her coat on the counter in the presence of a clerk, the store is liable for the loss of the coat. In such a situation, the clerk (and the store) impliedly invite customers to remove their coats and lay them aside. Therefore, the removal of the coat in the presence of a clerk who has an opportunity to watch it constitutes a transfer of possession to the store with the consequent duty of caring for it as a bailee. A contrary conclusion has been reached in a case where neither the store nor its employee was aware of the fact that a customer had placed her coat on a counter.

4. Property Concealed in Bailed Property

If a bailment exists with respect to an article, it does not follow that a bailment exists with respect to something that is concealed within that article.

Examples: 1) Where a coat with a fur piece concealed in it is deposited in a coat check room, and the fur piece is not returned, the owner of the coat check room is not liable, because she was not a bailee for the fur piece. Although she had custody of the fur, she could not have intended to assume control over it, because it was concealed and she did not know of its existence.

2) The articles in a car stored in a garage, parking lot, etc., are considered the subject of a bailment only if the bailee has actual or imputed knowledge of them. For example, there would not be a bailment with respect to musical instruments left in the trunk of a car without notice to the garage.

C. BAILMENT DISTINGUISHED FROM OTHER TRANSACTIONS

1. Renting

a. Parking Lots

1) Examine Surrender of Control Over Car

Parking a car in a parking lot may constitute a renting of parking space or it may constitute a bailment. Whether a particular transaction amounts to a bailment or to a mere renting of parking space depends on whether the owner surrenders control over the car to the operator of the lot. Thus, the turning over of the keys by the owner to the operator or use by the operator of a checking system would indicate a bailment. Where the owner parks her own car, selecting her own space, locking the car, and taking the keys, she leases the space, and the operator of the parking lot or garage is not a bailee.

2) Where Lot Owner Is Deemed a Lessor

Where the parking lot owner is held to be a lessor, the lessor must still exercise ordinary care. The lessor is therefore liable to a car owner for damage done to the car where the attendant was on actual notice of tampering.

b. Safe Deposit Boxes

The relationship existing between a bank and the one who rents a safe deposit box in the bank is that of bailor and bailee. Usually, the bank and the "renter" of the box have duplicate keys, but the renter cannot have access to the box except with consent and use of the bank's key. This type of almost ***absolute control by the bank*** of the box and its contents makes the bank a bailee.

2. Employer and Employee Relationship

a. Employee Cannot Be Bailee of Employer's Goods

The ordinary possession by an employee of his employer's goods does not constitute a bailment. The employee merely has custody of the goods. Possession and control of the goods remain with the employer. In a bailment, the bailee has the right of possession and control of the goods, for the term of bailment, against all the world including the bailor. Because an employee is at all times subject to the orders and control of his employer, he cannot, as an employee, be a bailee of his employer's goods.

Example: A truck driver, while using his employer's truck in the course of his employment, is not a bailee of the truck. If, however, the employer permits the truck driver to use the truck over the weekend for his pleasure or convenience, a bailment results.

b. **Negligence of Bailee Not Imputed to Bailor**
As to liability, the negligence of the employee is imputed to the employer if the tort is committed in the course and scope of the employment. In contrast, the negligence of a bailee is not usually imputed to the bailor because the possession and control is in the bailee and the act of the bailee is usually in her own interest.

3. **Consignment**
A consignee differs from an ordinary bailee in that she is authorized to sell the goods in the ordinary course of trade. Hence, a ***consignment*** may be described as a ***special bailment*** for the purpose of sale. In a true consignment for sale, the consignee is not only a bailee, but also an agent of the consignor to sell the goods. In such cases the consignor's right to the goods will be sustained as against: (i) the consignee's creditors, and (ii) the trustee in bankruptcy of the consignee.

4. **Sale**

a. **In General**

1) **Distinction Is Relevant as to Risk of Loss**
A sale involves a transfer of title to the vendee. A bailment involves merely a transfer of possession to the bailee, the title to the goods remaining in the bailor. The importance of this distinction appears whenever it is necessary to determine which party undertook the risk of loss. In a sale, the loss of goods is sustained by the vendee because she is the owner. In a bailment, the loss of goods falls upon the bailor because he has title.

2) **Test for Bailment vs. Sale**
A fairly workable rule to determine the nature of the transaction, whether bailment or sale, is the following: When the identical thing delivered is to be restored in the same or an altered form, the contract is one of bailment, and the title to the property is not changed; but when there is ***no obligation to restore*** the specific article, and the receiver is at liberty to return another thing of equal value or the money value, the title to the property is changed—it is a ***sale***.

Examples: 1) When the article, however altered in form (*e.g.,* wheat into flour, grapes into wine, or milk into butter), is to be returned, the transaction is a bailment and the title remains in the bailor.

2) But if a farm and cattle are leased with a stipulation that the lessee is to return an equal number of cattle of the same quality at the expiration of the tenancy, the transaction is a sale because it does not call for the redelivery of the same property.

b. **Sale on Approval vs. Sale or Return**

1) **Sale on Approval**
Where goods are delivered on "approval" or "on trial," the transaction constitutes a ***bailment***, the bailee having an option to purchase. Title to the goods does not pass until the option is exercised by an indicated approval or until the expiration of a reasonable time, when a time for approval is not otherwise fixed. This should be distinguished from a "sale or return."

2) **Sale or Return**

A "sale or return" transaction is a sale with the privilege on the part of the vendee to reinvest title in the vendor upon notice to him. Thus, where goods are shipped to a vendee on a "sale or return" and the vendee gives notice of her election to reinvest title in the vendor, the vendee becomes a bailee while the goods remain in her possession. Thus, in a "sale or return," the transaction ***may end as a bailment***, although it begins as a sale.

5. **Pledge**

A pledge is a particular type of bailment by which the bailor delivers property to the bailee to secure an obligation owed by the bailor to the bailee.

6. ***Intra Hospitum***

A hotel or innkeeper is an ***insurer*** of the goods of a guest taken into custody and control of the establishment. It is therefore liable for any loss or damage, except where it can be shown that it was caused by an act of God, a public enemy, or the fault of the guest.

Examples: 1) Guest gives his car to a doorman for parking in the garage of a hotel. The hotel is an insurer of the car and all of its contents (regardless of notice) unless it can show the loss or damage is due to an act of God, a public enemy, or the fault of the guest.

2) Guest leaves his car with the doorman for parking in a nearby garage, knowing that it is an independent establishment. The garage is liable only as a bailee.

D. BAILEE'S RIGHTS IN BAILED CHATTEL

1. **Possession**

The bailee has the exclusive right to possession of the property during the bailment, provided she is exercising this right according to the terms and conditions of the bailment. This right is operative not only against third persons, but also against the owner of the property.

a. **Rights of Action**

The bailee may maintain a trover, trespass, or replevin action against third parties interfering with her possession, or even against the bailor. Unless she is a gratuitous bailee, she may replevy even as against the bailor to recover her possession if, for example, the bailor takes the object bailed before the termination of the term.

b. **Attachment by Bailor's Creditor**

A creditor of the bailor has no greater rights than the bailor himself and no right to take the bailed goods by attachment.

2. **Use of Bailed Goods**

Ordinarily, the bailee has no right to use the subject matter of the bailment. However, she may acquire this right by express contract with the bailor. But, even where there is no such contract, the circumstances may indicate a presumed intention that the bailee make some use of the property.

Example: It has been held that a stablekeeper has presumed authority to exercise a horse and milk a cow in order to preserve the health of the animals.

a. **Agreed Use**

In bailments for the hired use of personal property, as where A rents his horse, car, or launch to B for B's use, the bailee (B) obviously has the right to make the agreed use of the property bailed. The same is true of the gratuitous loan of an article for use. In such cases, however, the bailee's use of the bailed article is limited by the terms of the agreement. Any ***intentional, unauthorized use*** of the goods that results in loss or damage ***renders the bailee absolutely liable*** to the bailor, irrespective of the question of care or negligence. (*See* F.4., below.) However, if the departure from the terms of the contract is unintentional, no liability ensues unless the bailee has been negligent.

b. **Incidental Use**

In bailments for storage, repair, or transportation, the bailee is under a duty not to make any use of the goods except such use as is incidental to the performance of her services.

Example: A stores his car in B's garage. B, without A's knowledge or consent, uses A's car on the highway. While the car is being so used, and without any negligence on B's part, it is damaged or wrecked. B is absolutely liable to A for the damage or loss.

E. BAILOR'S RIGHTS IN BAILED CHATTEL

1. Actions Against Bailee

Where, due to the wrongful act of the bailee, the goods bailed have been lost or damaged, the bailor can maintain an action against the bailee.

a. **Action for Damages for Breach of Contract**

For example, a bailor can maintain an action against a bailee for money paid to the bailee for work improperly done on the bailed goods.

b. **Tort Action for Damages**

A bailor can maintain an action for damages against a bailee who by her wrongful act has destroyed or injured the goods bailed.

c. **Conversion Action**

Where the bailee's wrongful conduct constitutes or amounts to a conversion of the bailed goods, the bailor can maintain trover (conversion) against the bailee.

d. **Replevin**

A bailor entitled to immediate possession can maintain replevin against the bailee to recover the bailed goods.

2. Actions Against Third Parties

a. **Bailment of Definite Duration**

Where the bailment is for a definite time, a bailor ***cannot*** maintain trover or replevin during the life of the bailment against a person who converts the bailed property from the bailee because, although he has the general property right in the thing, he has neither the possession nor the right to possession. Trover and replevin are predicated upon the immediate right to possession. However, he may bring an action for damages that he has suffered on the theory of the common law action of trespass on the case. (*See* 2.c., below.)

Example: X rents a book to Y for one year and Z wrongfully takes the book from Y on the second day. X may not bring, until the year has passed, replevin against Z for recovery of the book, nor may he bring an action in trover for its value when taken, for he is not entitled to possession during the term of the bailment. He may bring replevin after the term of the bailment has expired.

b. **Terminable Bailment**

Where the bailor may treat the bailment as ended by reason of a gratuitous bailment, a bailment terminable at will, or the bailee's unauthorized act, he may maintain the actions of conversion or replevin against a third party.

Example: Where a bailee of a sewing machine sells it to a third party, the bailor may replevy it from him, as the bailee's conversion terminates the bailment contract and gives the bailor an immediate right to possession.

c. **Actions for Damage to Future Right of Possession**

A bailor may sue a third party who injures the bailed property for damages for injury to his reversionary interest, even though he may not maintain trover or replevin for lack of the immediate right to possession. In such an action it is ***immaterial*** that the bailee may have been contributorily negligent, as the negligence of a bailee is not imputed to her bailor. The sole issue in the case is whether or not the third party was negligent. The reason for this rule is that the use and care of the chattel is in the control of the bailee and subject to her exclusive control. The bailor has relinquished all control.

Example: A husband who gratuitously lent his automobile to his wife, a physician, to enable her to make professional calls, was permitted to recover from a third party for injury to his car caused by the concurring negligence of his wife and the third party, since the bailee's negligence is not imputed to the bailor.

F. BAILEE'S DUTY WITH RESPECT TO BAILED GOODS

1. Bailee's Duty of Care

a. **Bailee Is Not Insurer of Goods**

A bailee must exercise due care with respect to the bailed goods; she is not an insurer of their safety. If the goods are damaged or lost through no fault of the bailee (*e.g.,* theft, earthquake), the loss falls on the bailor.

b. **Type of Bailment May Determine Degree of Care**

The specific degree of negligence upon which liability will rest is said to vary with the type of bailment. Generally, where the bailment is for the ***sole benefit of the bailor*** (the bailee is uncompensated), only slight diligence is required and liability is said to rest on gross negligence. Where the bailment is for the ***sole benefit of the bailee*** (*e.g.,* where the bailor gratuitously loans his property), great diligence is required and liability will result from slight negligence. Bailments for hire and pledges are for the ***mutual benefit*** of bailor and bailee and ordinary due care is required. Today, the trend is away from such classifications and toward a rule that considers whether the bailee exercises ordinary care under all circumstances. These circumstances include the value of the goods, the type of bailment, any custom of a trade, etc.

2. Burden of Proof as to Bailee's Negligence

Where goods have been lost, destroyed, or damaged during the bailment, the burden is on the bailee to prove that the loss, etc., was caused ***despite*** her due care. Consequently, when the bailor has shown a delivery of the goods to the bailee and that the latter has failed on proper demand to return the goods, or has returned them in a damaged state, he has made out a prima facie case for recovery. The burden is then on the bailee to explain why the goods were not returned or why they were returned in a damaged condition. The reason for this rule is that the bailee has in her possession the means of ascertaining the exact cause of the damage or the nonreturn of the goods.

3. Contractual Provisions on Bailee's Duty of Care

The parties may prescribe the extent of the bailee's liability by contract and may impose either a lesser or a greater obligation than the law ordinarily requires.

a. Waiver of Liability for Negligence

Such contracts are ***not generally favored*** and are therefore strictly construed. Thus, a bailee may not, by contract, exempt herself from liability created by her own negligence. This rule is founded on public policy, which opposes a complete exoneration from the consequences of one's own negligence.

b. Liability May Be Limited

An ***ordinary*** bailee (*e.g.,* a neighbor who borrows an item) may exempt herself from liability for her own negligence. On the other hand, public policy prevents a ***professional*** bailee from exempting herself from liability for her own negligence, although she may, under proper circumstances, limit her liability. However, a professional bailee's limitation is not valid unless the bailor knows or should know of the limitation and assents to it.

1) Posted Signs

It is the customary practice of check room proprietors, warehousers, and garagekeepers to post public notices limiting their liability. It is held, however, that such a limitation is not binding on the bailor in the absence of proof that the bailor ***read the notice*** or, considering its size and location, should have read the sign.

2) Claim Check

It is also a customary practice for check room proprietors, garages, and warehousers to place a limitation of liability on the claim check. Most courts hold that a claim check ***does not evidence a contract*** between the parties. A claim check is generally issued for purposes of identification, and the mere fact that a would-be contract provision is contained on the claim check is not sufficient proof that the bailor actually knew, or should have known, of this term.

3) Hotels

a) May Limit Liability

By statute, hotels may limit their liability for articles placed in their care by providing notice thereof. The hotel is limited to a certain sum in liability for items placed in a safe provided for that purpose, unless it specifically contracted for higher liability. Also, by providing a safe and such notice, the hotel's liability for loss of goods from the hotel room is limited to such amount of money and jewelry or other articles of value as it is usually common or prudent for guests to retain in their rooms.

b) **Compliance with Posted Notice Required**
If a hotel posts a notice requiring guests to bolt the door and deposit their key with the desk when leaving, the hotel is not liable for lost luggage or other articles should it appear that the door was not locked or bolted or that the key was not deposited, unless the loss is directly or indirectly caused by, or attributable to, the proprietor or his employees.

4) **Warehouses**
A warehouseman may limit the amount of his liability in case of loss or damage to stored goods by including a limitation provision in the warehouse receipt or storage agreement. On the other hand, at the time of signing the storage agreement or within a reasonable time after receiving the warehouse receipt, the bailor may request in writing that the warehouseman increase the amount of his liability. In this event, the warehouseman may charge increased rates based on the increased valuation of the goods. A limitation with respect to the warehouseman's liability for conversion to his own use is not effective.

4. **Absolute Liability**
The bailee is absolutely liable for loss or damage without regard to her care under the following circumstances.

a. **Departure from Terms of Bailment**
The bailee is rendered absolutely liable as a converter when she departs from the terms of the bailment, as by using the goods for a different purpose than the one agreed upon. In addition, absolute liability attaches if the bailee removes the goods from an agreed place of storage to another without the bailor's knowledge or consent.

Examples: 1) B rents a car and agrees to use it only within City M. On impulse, she drives the car to City P, and while it is legally parked on the street, a car driven by X totally demolishes it. B is liable for the damage since the use was unauthorized and outside the scope of the bailment.

2) A stores his car in B's garage. B, without A's knowledge or consent, uses A's car on the highway. While the car is being so used, and without any negligence on B's part, it is damaged or wrecked. B is absolutely liable to A for the damage or loss.

b. **Breach of Agreement to Insure**
When the bailee expressly agrees, or by custom or previous course of dealing impliedly agrees, to insure the goods against hazards, but fails to do so and the goods are damaged or destroyed by such hazard, the bailee is rendered absolutely liable.

5. **Duty to Redeliver**
Upon the termination of the bailment, the bailee owes a duty to redeliver or account for the thing bailed in its original or agreed-upon, altered form. Delivery must be made to the bailor or someone claiming under him.

a. **Absolute Liability**
Although a bailee is held only to a standard of reasonable care with respect to protection and preservation of the bailed chattel, she is absolutely liable for improperly delivering the bailed chattel to someone other than the bailor. Such misdelivery is a breach of the bailment and a conversion of the bailed chattel. Therefore, the liability is absolute and not based upon negligence.

Example: A bailee who in good faith delivers the bailed chattel to the wrong person under an expertly forged order is held liable to the bailor for the value of the goods.

b. **Exception—Indispensable Instrument**
An ***exception to the rule of absolute liability*** for misdelivery has been made by some courts when the bailee delivers the chattel to one holding an indispensable instrument (*e.g.,* claim check) as long as the bailee had no notice or knowledge that the one presenting the instrument was not the original bailor.

Example: A bails his car to a parking garage and receives a numbered claim check, which he then loses. B finds the claim check and presents it to the bailee garage. The garage delivers the car to B in reliance upon the indispensable instrument (*i.e.,* the claim check). As long as the garage had no knowledge or notice that B was not the original bailor, it will not be held to a standard of strict liability for delivering the car to B.

c. **Exception—Involuntary Bailee**
An involuntary bailee is liable only if the bailee was negligent in delivering the goods to the wrong person. Courts impose strict liability on an ordinary bailee because he is in breach of contract when he misdelivers. An involuntary bailee has no contract.

Example: A hotel guest leaves her purse in the hotel restaurant. The hotel is liable for delivering the purse to the wrong person only if it was negligent in doing so.

d. **Adverse Claimants**
When a bailee has notice of, or reason to know of, an adverse claim to the bailed property, the bailee will be absolutely liable for delivery to the original bailor if the original bailor is not the true owner. The appropriate action to be taken by the bailee is to ***interplead all claimants*** of the property.

e. **Excuses for Nondelivery**
However, the bailee is excused from making delivery to the bailor in the following cases:

1) Where, during the life of the bailment, the bailor has sold the property to the bailee or to a third party with notice given to the bailee;

2) Where there is title paramount in a third party and such party claims the article; or

3) Where the property is taken from the bailee by judicial process.

6. **Estoppel of Bailee to Deny Bailor's Title**
Since the bailee acquires possession by means of the bailment contract, she is thereafter

estopped to deny or dispute the bailor's title, because one of the provisions of the contract is to return the article after the purpose of the bailment is accomplished. Thus, the bailee of an article cannot excuse her failure to return it by asserting a claim to it herself or on behalf of another.

7. Conversion by Bailee

A conversion is an unauthorized act over the property of another of such nature as is inconsistent with the rights of the owner. If the bailee has authority to use a chattel in a particular way, the use of it in another manner, or in the same manner but to a greater extent than authorized, is a conversion for which the bailor may maintain trover. Moreover, and very importantly, a ***conversion makes a bailee an insurer*** and therefore liable without reference to the question of negligence. In the case of a bailment, a demand and refusal is a condition precedent to an action in trover.

8. Bailee's Liability to Third Parties

If the bailee's use of the bailor's chattel results in harm to a third person, the bailor is not liable. The liability is the bailee's alone, for she wields possession and control of the article.

Example: X was the administrator of an estate and, as such, had M, a mechanic, repair a car preparatory to its being sold at an administrator's sale. While M was returning the repaired car to X, he negligently injured P. P sues X for damages. Judgment for X. *Held:* No cause of action as against X. M was a bailee; hence, X exercised no control over him.

G. COMPENSATION AND REIMBURSEMENT

1. Compensation

In a bailment for the mutual benefit of the bailor and the bailee, the bailee is entitled to receive the agreed compensation for her services or, in the absence of such agreement, the reasonable value of such services. (For recovery of compensation, follow the rules for enforcement of liens.) In a bailment for the sole benefit of the bailor or for the sole benefit of the bailee, the bailee is entitled to ***no compensation***.

2. Reimbursement

The general rule is that ***ordinary expenses*** must be borne by the bailee and ***extraordinary expenses*** by the bailor. Consequently, if the bailee pays an extraordinary expense, not incurred through her own fault, she is entitled to reimbursement from the bailor for such expense. For example, in the rental of a car, the cost of gasoline and oil and such minor repairs as fixing a flat tire would be ordinary expenses. The cost of a new tire, necessitated by a blowout (there being no spare tire), or the repair of a broken axle, would be extraordinary expenses.

3. Bailee's Lien

A bailee's lien is ***not a general lien***; it extends only to the property bailed. The right to a lien is waived by a previous agreement to give credit, *i.e.,* by an agreement made in advance to deliver or redeliver the goods without receiving contemporaneous compensation for services expended upon them. The lien is forfeited by the lienor's refusal to accept a proper tender of the charges due. The lien is lost by voluntarily parting with possession of the property.

H. BAILEE'S RIGHTS OF ACTION

1. Against Bailor

Where the bailor wrongfully takes from the bailee's possession and converts the subject matter of the bailment, the bailee can maintain an action against the bailor for such ***conversion***.

2. Against Third Parties

The bailee may maintain an action against third persons for damage, destruction, or interference with the bailed goods, and may replevy them from third persons who have wrongfully taken them from her possession. Any recovery by the bailee beyond her interest in the bailed goods is for the benefit of the bailor. Full recovery by either the bailor or bailee against a third person bars the action of the other toward the third party.

I. DEFECTS IN SUBJECT OF BAILMENT

A bailor must exercise care so that the bailee is not harmed through a defect existing in the bailed chattel.

1. Gratuitous Bailments

Where the bailment is gratuitous, the bailor must inform the bailee of any defect that he knows exists in the chattel that might cause injury to the bailee. There is no duty to disclose unknown defects.

2. Bailments for Hire

Where the bailment is for hire, the bailor is bound to inform the bailee of defects that are known to him, or of which he could have known by exercising reasonable diligence.

J. TERMINATION OF BAILMENT

Generally, a bailment may be terminated by agreement or conduct of the parties.

1. By Agreement

Mere lapse of the specified time or accomplishment of the purpose terminates a bailment.

2. By Conduct of Parties

Notice to the other party (where the bailment is for an indefinite period), resumption of possession by the bailor, mutual agreement, destruction of the property, or misconduct of the bailee (at the election of the bailor) will terminate a bailment.

V. COMMON CARRIERS

A. CONCEPT

A common carrier is one who undertakes for hire to transport persons or goods from place to place. Three requirements must be met: (i) there must be a holding out to perform service for all those who apply, (ii) the carriage must be for hire, and (iii) the service must be one for carriage.

B. LIABILITY FOR LOSS OR DAMAGE OF GOODS SHIPPED

The common carrier is an ***insurer of the goods*** given to it by the shipper and is liable for any loss or damage to the goods under any circumstances other than the following: (i) an act of God; (ii) an act of a public enemy; (iii) an act of state—*e.g.,* legal process; (iv) an act of a shipper—*e.g.,* defective packaging of goods by the shipper; or (v) the inherent nature of the goods—*e.g.,* perishable fruit damaged due to natural causes.

1. **Commencement of Liability**
A carrier's liability as a common carrier commences when the goods are expressly or impliedly ***delivered*** to, ***and accepted*** by, the carrier ***for immediate transportation***. Where the goods are stored in a warehouse and immediate transportation is not contemplated, the carrier is merely liable as a warehouser.

2. **Limitation of Liability at Common Law Allowed**

   a. **Cannot Limit Liability Due to Negligence**
   By contract with the shipper, the common carrier may limit its liability for loss of the shipped goods. Such a contract is binding even though the shipper has not read the contract. Since the shipper is entitled to demand that the carrier accept and carry its goods at a reasonable rate and subject to full responsibility, the carrier must offer some additional consideration for the shipper's agreement to a limitation of liability—*e.g.,* a lower rate to the shipper. A contract that relieves the carrier from all liability for damage to the shipper's goods due to the ***negligence*** of the carrier is void as against public policy.

   b. **Effect of Posted Notice**
   Posted notices limiting liability, even though brought to the attention of the shipper, are not effective to relieve the carrier of liability.

3. **Limitation of Liability Forbidden by Statute**
The Interstate Commerce Act, and more particularly the Carmack Amendment, forbids carriers operating in interstate commerce from limiting the liability imposed on them by the Act (inapplicable to passengers' baggage). [49 U.S.C. §11706(c)(1)]

C. PASSENGER BAGGAGE

Baggage is goods that a passenger carries with him on a trip for his personal use, convenience, or enjoyment, that are suitable to his station in life.

1. **Delivery**
A common carrier is liable as an insurer for baggage delivered to it. A carrier is not liable for goods that are not baggage unless the carrier, knowing the nature of the goods, accepts them anyway.

2. **Nondelivery**
A carrier is ***not liable as an insurer*** for goods retained in the possession or control of the passenger. However, the carrier may be ***liable in a negligence action*** for failure to properly protect its passengers.

REVIEW QUESTIONS

INTRODUCTORY NOTE

The true/false questions that follow are intended to serve as both a substantive review and a diagnostic test. Respond to the questions quickly and compare your answers with those found at the end of this section. This will allow you to identify areas in which you may need further review.

		FILL IN ANSWER
1.	Farm crops, such as corn, are personal property.	________
2.	Wheat stored by farmers in a grain elevator is an example of confused goods.	________
3.	Replevin is an action to recover damages for an injury to a chattel.	________
4.	There are two requirements for a valid inter vivos gift: donative intent and delivery.	________
5.	A deed to real property executed and delivered in contemplation of death is revoked as a gift causa mortis if the donor recovers.	________
6.	A bailment can be accomplished without the transfer of possession to the bailee.	________
7.	A bailee may maintain an action for conversion against the bailor for interference with the bailee's right of possession.	________
8.	A bailor cannot maintain an action for money against a bailee for payments already made to the bailee for work improperly done on the bailed goods.	________
9.	A bailee expressly agrees to insure bailed goods. The goods are destroyed by fire. The bailor must prove negligence against the bailee to recover the value of the goods.	________
10.	Generally, a common carrier is an insurer of the goods given to it.	________

ANSWERS TO REVIEW QUESTIONS

Ques. No.	Answer	Explanation
1.	***TRUE***	Farm crops are considered fructus industriales and are personalty.
2.	***TRUE***	Confusion is an intermixture of goods owned by different persons.
3.	***FALSE***	Replevin is an action to recover the chattel itself.
4.	***FALSE***	Acceptance of the gift is also required.
5.	***FALSE***	Real property cannot be conveyed as a gift causa mortis; therefore, a deed to real property is not revoked in these circumstances.
6.	***FALSE***	There is no bailment unless the bailee obtains possession of the property.
7.	***TRUE***	The bailee has the exclusive right of possession during the bailment; this right is operative against the owner as well as against third persons.
8.	***FALSE***	A bailor may maintain such an action for damages for breach of contract.
9.	***FALSE***	In this circumstance, the bailee is rendered absolutely liable.
10.	***TRUE***	A common carrier is generally an insurer of goods given to it.

ESSAY EXAM QUESTIONS

INTRODUCTORY NOTE

The essay questions that follow have been selected to provide you with an opportunity to experience how the substantive law you have been reviewing may be tested in the hypothetical essay examination question context. These sample essay questions are a valuable self-diagnostic tool designed to enable you to enhance your issue-spotting ability and practice your exam writing skills.

It is suggested that you approach each question as though under actual examination conditions. The time allowed for each question is 60 minutes. You should spend 15 to 20 minutes spotting issues, underlining key facts and phrases, jotting notes in the margins, and outlining your answer. ***If*** you organize your thoughts well, 40 minutes will be more than adequate for writing them down. Should you prefer to forgo the actual writing involved on these questions, be sure to give yourself no more time for issue-spotting than you would on the actual examination.

The BAR/BRI technique for writing a well-organized essay answer is to (i) spot the issues in a question and then (ii) analyze and discuss each issue using the "CIRAC" method:

C — State your ***conclusion*** first. (In other words, you must think through your answer ***before*** you start writing.)
I — State the ***issue*** involved.
R — Give the ***rule(s)*** of law involved.
A — ***Apply*** the rule(s) of law to the facts.
C — Finally, restate your ***conclusion***.

After completing (or outlining) your own analysis of each question, compare it with the BAR/BRI model answer provided herein. A passing answer does ***not*** have to match the model one, but it should cover most of the issues presented and the law discussed and should ***apply the law to the facts*** of the question. Use of the CIRAC method results in the best answer you can write.

EXAM QUESTION NO. 1

John Adams of Chicago owned a late-model, customized Volkswagen van in which he had installed carpeting and a folding bed. The windows on each side of the van were custom-made for him in the shape of the letter "J." In the summer of 2010, while vacationing in Atlantic City, New Jersey, Adams's van was stolen. A few months later, the van was abandoned on a street in New York City, completely stripped of its engine, battery, seats, bed, carpeting, wheels, fenders, and radiator. The transmission was damaged beyond repair. The license plates had been removed, and only part of the van's vehicle identification number remained.

In early 2011, the New York City Police impounded the van and, being unable to trace its ownership, sold it as "junk" at an auction sale to Dan Smith for $250, which was market value at the time. Smith, who lived in New York, was a weekend mechanic who wanted to own a recreational van. Smith proceeded to restore the van. He used approximately $3,000 of his own savings to buy replacement parts and completely restore the van to running condition. In June 2011, John Adams was visiting New York City and happened to pass Smith's home. The van with windows in the shape of a "J" was parked outside. After carefully checking the van and the circumstances surrounding Smith's purchase of the vehicle, Adams was able to establish that the van Smith bought at the auction was in fact the van stolen from Adams in 2010. Adams's insurer, the Holy Grail Insurance Company, having paid the loss and taken assignment of Adams's right in the van, sued in the supreme court of New York County to replevy the van or, in the alternative, for the value of the vehicle as fully restored and equipped by Smith at the time of the suit (value was alleged to be $5,500), and for the value of the use of the van at the rate of $20 per day from the time Smith acquired it from the New York City Police. The case is charged before you as a trial judge without a jury.

How would you rule on the respective rights of the Holy Grail Insurance Company and Smith? State your reasons and discuss all issues fully.

EXAM QUESTION NO. 2

Mary Smith, a 50-year-old resident of New Jersey, became ill while visiting friends in California. The doctor who examined her strongly recommended that Mary undergo exploratory surgery while she was still in California to ascertain whether a small growth on her thyroid gland was malignant. On March 1, 2011, a few days before the scheduled surgery, Mary called Wendy Lloyd, her long-time close friend and neighbor in New Jersey. Mary told Wendy that, since the doctor told her about the need for surgery, she had been giving a great deal of thought to certain things she had planned to do since the beginning of the year but had not done. Mary said, "Wendy, I want you to have the grand piano in my living room. I know how much you have admired it over the years, and since my husband died, I have not played it. You would get a lot of pleasure from it. Since I am away from the house, why don't you use the spare house key I left with you a couple of years ago and move the piano over to your house?"

Mary also told Wendy that she had a strange premonition about not surviving the surgery and she wanted Wendy to take care of two matters for her. Mary told Wendy that she had planned to send a letter to her nephew, Tom Smith, before she left for California. An envelope addressed to Tom containing the letter was in her wall safe in the house, and Mary gave Wendy the combination to the safe. Mary asked Wendy to put a stamp on the envelope and mail it to Tom. Also, she wanted Wendy to take Mary's diamond bracelet from the wall safe and "if I don't come through the surgery, I want you to give the bracelet to my niece, Susan Smith."

The envelope contained the following letter signed by Mary Smith:

> New Jersey Atlantic Bank
> 100 Commerce Street
> Newark, New Jersey 07751
>
> Dear Sir:
>
> Please give to the presenter of this letter the two $5,000 bearer bonds you are holding under my name for the purpose of collecting the semiannual interest payments. He is my nephew, Tom Smith, and the bonds now belong to him.
>
> Sincerely,
>
> /s/ Mary Smith

On March 3, 2011, Wendy and her husband went to Mary Smith's house. They decided that professional movers would be necessary to move the piano because of its size. Wendy opened the wall safe and removed the envelope addressed to Tom and the diamond bracelet. The same day, Wendy mailed the envelope to Tom Smith and placed the diamond bracelet in her own strongbox. Wendy's husband arranged with Ace Moving Company to come by on March 11, 2011, and move the piano.

On March 6, 2011, Wendy received a call from Mary's friend in California, who told Wendy that while Mary was walking into the hospital for her surgery that morning, she slipped on a wet floor and struck her head, causing a fatal concussion. The next day, Wendy called Susan Smith and told her that her aunt Mary had died and that Mary wanted Susan to have her diamond bracelet if she did not survive the surgery scheduled for the preceding day. Susan came over to Wendy's the following day and picked up the bracelet. On March 11, 2011, Ace Moving Company moved the piano from Mary's house to Wendy's house. On March 5, 2011, Tom Smith received the letter mailed by Wendy. On March 9, 2011, Tom went to the New Jersey Atlantic Bank and was given the two bonds.

The administrator of Mary Smith's estate, which is being probated in New Jersey, seeks to recover for the estate the piano, the bracelet, and the two bearer bonds. How would you rule on the administrator's request for each item of personalty? State your reasons.

ANSWERS TO ESSAY EXAM QUESTIONS

ANSWER TO EXAM QUESTION NO. 1

An analysis of the question necessarily involves a consideration of the rights of the Holy Grail Insurance Company and Smith. Considering each in turn:

The Holy Grail Insurance Company

Any analysis of the right of the Holy Grail Insurance Company necessarily involves an analysis of the rights of Adams because the insurance company is subrogated to Adams's rights and can properly assert any claim that Adams would have against Smith. Although title never passed to Smith, he was entitled to possession of the van. The New York City Police had possession of the van but would not acquire title until the statutory period for adverse possession had elapsed. There is no basis for assuming that Adams abandoned the van, as the facts clearly state that the van was stolen from him. Therefore, Adams retained title. However, because Smith will almost certainly be deemed an innocent converter who greatly enhanced the value of the converted chattel through no known wrongdoing on his part, the insurance company's claim is limited to a suit for conversion damages in the amount of the fair market value of the vehicle at the time of the innocent conversion. Hence, the Holy Grail Insurance Company is entitled to recover $250 from Smith.

Dan Smith

As previously noted, although Smith never received title to the van as a result of its being stolen, he is nonetheless entitled to retain possession. He was an innocent converter of Adams's property and should not be charged as having been on notice of any defects in title. The general rule is that accession in the value to property by labor of an innocent converter does not prevent the rightful owner from retaining title. However, an exception to the general rule of accession applies when an innocent converter of property in good faith through his labor or through the addition of new materials greatly increases the value of the chattel converted or changes its essential nature. Here, although the refurbished van is similar in nature to the van at the time it was stolen from Adams, Smith received only a stripped frame. Therefore, Smith's labor greatly enhanced and increased the value of what he had converted. He cannot be held liable for the original destruction of the van and should be entitled to retain possession. Smith is, however, liable to Adams as the original owner for the fair market value of the chattel at the time of the innocent conversion, which is stated as being $250. The van was unusable at the time it was impounded by the police; therefore, there is no basis on which to assess a daily rental charge. However, because the Holy Grail Insurance Company is asserting Adams's claim in his place, Smith has no additional liability to Adams.

ANSWER TO EXAM QUESTION NO. 2

A valid gift inter vivos or gift causa mortis requires donative intent, delivery, and acceptance by the donee. Delivery can be actual, constructive, or symbolic, and the donor must completely surrender dominion and control over the item intended to be conveyed. Generally, most problems occur in determining whether delivery has been effected. Acceptance poses few problems and is generally presumed.

Gift of the Piano to Wendy

The gift of the piano to Wendy was a valid inter vivos gift. Mary had the intent to transfer the

possession and control of the piano to Wendy immediately, and her intent was not conditioned upon fear of her death. Because Mary was physically away from her home, she could not manually deliver the piano. However, because of its size, even if Mary were at home, she could not have made physical delivery. Mary instructed Wendy to take delivery and authorized her to use a key to enter the house. The following day, Wendy went to Mary's house and, solely because of the size of the piano, Wendy was unable to take actual possession at that time. If a gift is not readily susceptible to manual transfer because of its size, delivery can be accomplished if the donative words are accompanied by express authority or license to take the property. In such cases, the delivery requirement will be satisfied if the donor surrenders as much control over the subject matter of the gift as she presently possesses. Although Wendy already had the key to Mary's home, the express authorization to use the key, enter the house, and remove the piano amounted to constructive delivery. The fact that professional movers, as agents of Wendy, did not transfer the piano to Wendy until after Mary had died will not affect the validity of the gift.

Bracelet to Susan Smith

This was an attempted gift causa mortis. A gift causa mortis is one given in contemplation of imminent death. Mary wanted Wendy to take Mary's bracelet and give it to Susan if Mary did not survive the surgery, but there is a question as to whether Mary believed that her death was imminent. She had been told that she might have cancer, and she also had a premonition about not surviving the surgery. Courts have held that a subjective apprehension of death is not in and of itself sufficient, absent objective evidence to support the belief. Susan could try to argue that the likelihood of Mary having cancer would provide the objective support for her premonition.

Mary died from a cause other than that which gave rise to her apprehension. In the past, a gift causa mortis would generally be upheld only if the donor died as a result of the event that gave rise to the making of the gift. However, the weight of authority now follows the rule that it is not essential that the sole cause of the donor's death be from that peril giving rise to the apprehension.

Nevertheless, the gift will fail because of improper delivery. Although delivery may be accomplished through a third party, if the third party is the agent of the donor, the gift is not effective until the agent delivers it to the donee. If the donor dies before delivery is made, there is no gift; the agent's authority terminates on the donor's death. The rationale behind this is that, since the donor can control her agent, she has not parted with dominion and control. On the other hand, if the third party is the agent of the donee, the gift is effective on delivery to the donee's agent. As Mary's longtime close friend, Wendy would likely be considered Mary's agent. The bracelet was in Wendy's strongbox when Mary died and therefore was not effectively delivered to Susan so as to complete the gift. Therefore, the gift to Susan would be invalid.

Bonds to Tom Smith

The gift of the bearer bonds to Tom was a valid inter vivos gift. Where actual manual delivery is impracticable because the situation of the parties will not permit it, symbolic delivery is permitted. Symbolic delivery is most commonly effectuated by delivering a written instrument. To be sufficient, the writing should manifest the donative intent, describe the subject matter of the gift, be signed by the donor, and be delivered to the donee. If the gift is in the possession of a custodian, the gift may be perfected when the donor gives the donee the means of obtaining possession of the contemplated gift, accompanied by declarations clearly showing a present intent to give the gift and to divest the donor of possession.

Here, the bonds were in the possession of a custodian (the bank). The letter to the bank, when delivered to Tom, was tantamount to symbolic delivery of the bonds themselves. In her letter to the bank, Mary expressed her intent that the bonds belong to Tom immediately. She signed the letter, and it was delivered to Tom through the mail.

The letter to the bank was sufficient to transfer complete control and possession of the bearer bonds to Tom.

Real Property

REAL PROPERTY

TABLE OF CONTENTS

I. ESTATES IN LAND

A. IN GENERAL

"Estates in land" are ***possessory interests*** in land. These interests may be ***presently*** possessory (present estates), or they may become possessory in the ***future*** (future interests). They may be "freeholds," which give possession under some legal title or right to hold (*e.g.,* fees or life estates), or they may be "nonfreeholds," which give mere possession (*i.e.,* leases). Estates in land may be of potentially infinite duration, as in the case of a fee simple, or they may be of limited duration, as in the case of an estate for years. But whatever their characteristics, "estates in land" must be distinguished from ***nonpossessory*** interests such as easements, profits, covenants, and servitudes.

This section of the outline will examine various estates in land. It divides the interests into two classes: present interests and future interests. However, some future interests (those following defeasible fees) will be considered with the present interests to which they are attached.

B. PRESENT POSSESSORY ESTATES

1. Fee Simple Absolute

An estate in fee simple absolute is the largest estate permitted by law. It invests the holder of the fee with full possessory rights, now and in the future. The holder can sell it, divide it, or devise it; and if she dies intestate, her heirs will inherit it. The fee simple has an indefinite and potentially infinite duration. The common law rule requiring technical words of inheritance ("and his heirs") has been abolished by statute in nearly all jurisdictions. Typically, such statutes provide: "A fee simple title is presumed to be intended to pass by a grant of real property unless it appears from the grant that a lesser estate was intended."

Example: A conveyance from "O to A" is presumed to pass a fee simple interest if O owned one. At common law, absent the words of inheritance, even a conveyance "to A in fee simple" would convey only a life estate to A.

2. Defeasible Fees

Defeasible fees are fee simple estates of ***potentially*** infinite duration that can be terminated by the happening of a specified event. Because defeasible fees can result in forfeitures, courts will construe, where possible, a purported limitation as a mere declaration of the grantor's purpose or motive for making the grant (*i.e.,* as precatory language). (*See* b.1)a), *infra.*)

a. Fee Simple Determinable (and Possibility of Reverter)

A fee simple determinable, also called a determinable fee, is an estate that ***automatically terminates*** on the happening of a stated event and goes back to the grantor. (It must be distinguished from the fee simple subject to a condition subsequent, where the grantor must take affirmative steps to terminate the estate of the grantee if the stated event occurs.) It is created by the use of durational, adverbial language, such as "for so long as," "while," "during," or "until." A fee simple determinable can be conveyed by the owner thereof, but his grantee takes the land subject to the termination of the estate by the happening of the event.

Example: O conveys land "to A for so long as no alcoholic beverages are consumed on the premises." This gives A a fee simple because the estate may last forever if no one ever quaffs a brew. If A conveys his fee simple

determinable estate to B, B will own the "for so long as" estate. If A does not convey his estate, on A's death it will pass by will or intestacy to his successors, and so on. If, however, someone ever consumes an alcoholic beverage on the premises, the estate will automatically come to an end according to its own terms; and O will immediately and automatically become the owner of the fee simple, without taking any steps to terminate A's interest.

1) **Correlative Future Interest in Grantor—Possibility of Reverter**
Because the grantee's estate may end upon the happening of the stated event, there is a possibility that the land may revert back to the grantor. The interest that is left in a grantor who conveys an estate in fee simple determinable is called a "possibility of reverter." It is a future interest because it becomes possessory only upon the occurrence of the stated event.

a) **Possibility of Reverter Need Not Be Expressly Retained**
At common law and in nearly all states today, the grantor does not have to expressly retain a possibility of reverter. It arises ***automatically*** in the grantor as a consequence of his conveying a fee simple determinable estate, with its built-in time limitation.

b) **Transferability of Possibility of Reverter**
At early common law, the possibility of reverter could not be transferred inter vivos or devised by will. An attempted transfer of the interest was invalid; but the possibility of reverter was not extinguished by the attempted transfer and would still descend to the heirs of the owner. Today, in most jurisdictions, the possibility of reverter can be transferred inter vivos or devised by will, and descends to the owner's heirs if she dies intestate.

2) **Correlative Future Interest in Third Party—Executory Interest**
A possibility of reverter arises only in the grantor, not in a third party. If a comparable interest is created in a third party, it is an executory interest. (*See* C.3., *infra*.)

b. **Fee Simple Subject to Condition Subsequent (and Right of Entry)**
A fee simple subject to a condition subsequent is created when the grantor retains the power to terminate the estate of the grantee upon the happening of a specified event. Upon the happening of the event stated in the conveyance, the estate of the grantee ***continues until the grantor exercises her power of termination*** (right of entry) by bringing suit or making reentry. The following words are usually held to create conditions subsequent: "upon condition that," "provided that," "but if," and "if it happens that."

Example: O, owning Blackacre in fee simple, conveys it "to A and his heirs, on the express condition that the premises are never to be used by A for the sale of liquor, and in the event that they are so used, then O or her heirs may enter and terminate the estate hereby conveyed." A has a fee simple subject to a condition subsequent. O has a right of entry. If the condition is broken, O has a power to terminate the estate of A by asserting her ***right of entry***.

1) **Correlative Future Interest in Grantor—Right of Entry**
A right of entry (also known as "right of reentry" or "power of termination") is the future interest retained by the transferor who conveys an estate on condition subsequent. It is necessary to ***expressly*** reserve the right of entry in the grantor; this retained interest does not automatically arise as in the case of a fee simple determinable and possibility of reverter.

a) **Failure to Reserve Right of Entry**
Courts often hold that words of condition, standing alone, create only covenants, easements, or trusts, or are mere precatory terms.

Example: O conveys land "to A and his heirs, provided that liquor is not sold on the premises." O has not used words indicating the estate will terminate if liquor is sold on the premises. Nor has O retained a right to reenter. Because a statement of the grantor's wishes as to how the property should be used does not ordinarily imply a right retained by the grantor to enforce the purpose, a court may construe the deed as giving A a fee simple absolute. [Wood v. Board of County Commissioners, 759 P.2d 1250 (Wyo. 1988)]

b) **Waiver of Right of Entry**
Because the grantor can elect whether or not to terminate the grantee's estate, she may waive her right or power to enforce a forfeiture by express agreement or by her conduct. (Such is not the case with a fee simple determinable, where the forfeiture is automatic.)

(1) **Inaction by Itself Not a Waiver**
The general rule is that when there is a breach of the condition and the grantor simply does nothing about it, the power of termination is not waived. However, where there is any element of ***detrimental reliance*** by the fee holder, many courts treat inaction as a waiver on an estoppel or laches theory.

c) **Transferability of Right of Entry**
At common law, a right of entry was ***not devisable or transferable inter vivos*** to a third person. The right of entry did, however, descend to the heirs of the grantor on her death. Today, in most jurisdictions, a right of entry is still ***not*** alienable inter vivos. (Indeed, in a handful of states, an attempted transfer destroys it.) But in most states, rights of entry are devisable; and in all states, they descend to the owner's heirs.

2) **Correlative Future Interest in Third Party—Executory Interest**
A right of entry can be created only in favor of the grantor and her heirs. If a similar interest is created in favor of a third party, the interest is called an executory interest (*e.g.,* "if the property is ever used for other than church purposes, then to B and his heirs"). Unlike a right of entry, an executory interest is subject to the ***Rule Against Perpetuities***. (*See* E., *infra.*)

3) Compare—Fee Simple Determinable

This estate is distinguished from a determinable fee in that the breach of the condition does ***not*** itself terminate the estate and immediately revest the fee in the grantor or her successor. The estate continues in the grantee or his successor unless or until the grantor or her successor affirmatively elects to terminate it.

a) Construction of Ambiguous Language

The general policy of courts is to avoid forfeiture of estates. Thus, a conveyance that contains both durational language and a power of termination may be construed as creating a ***fee simple subject to a condition subsequent***, because the forfeiture is ***optional*** at the grantor's election rather than automatic.

Example: O conveys land "to A so long as liquor is not sold on the premises, and if liquor is sold, O has a right to reenter." The words "so long as" point to a fee simple determinable. The retained right of entry points to a fee simple subject to a condition subsequent. The court can classify the language to create either estate, but the fee simple subject to a condition subsequent is preferred.

c. Fee Simple Subject to an Executory Interest

A fee simple subject to an executory interest is an estate that, upon the happening of a stated event, is ***automatically divested in favor of a third person*** rather than the grantor.

Examples: 1) O conveys land "to Church; provided, however, that if the premises shall ever cease to be used for church purposes, title shall pass to the American Heart Association." Church has a fee simple subject to an executory interest in favor of the Heart Association. O does not have a right of entry because no such interest was reserved in the conveyance. The Heart Association's interest is not a right of entry because that future interest can be reserved only in favor of a grantor. The Heart Association's future interest is not a remainder because it divests a fee simple. Therefore, it is an executory interest.

Note: Executory interests are subject to the Rule Against Perpetuities, but the Heart Association's interest is valid because of the "charity-to-charity" exception to the Rule. (*See* E.1.e.1), *infra.*)

2) O conveys land "to Church for so long as the premises are used for church purposes, and if they shall ever cease to be so used, then and in that event to the American Red Cross." Church has a fee simple determinable subject to an executory interest in favor of the Red Cross. O has no possibility of reverter because he has not retained any interest; he has conveyed away his entire estate in the property. The future interest in the Red Cross cannot be a possibility of reverter because that interest arises only in a grantor, and the Red Cross is a grantee. It is an executory interest and not a remainder because it divests a fee simple. (Further discussion of these points will come later.)

Note: Were it not for the "charity-to-charity" exception to the Rule Against Perpetuities, the executory interest in favor of the Red Cross would violate the Rule.

d. Limitations on Possibilities of Reverter and Rights of Entry

In a few states, statutes limit the permissible duration of possibilities of reverter and rights of entry to a certain number of years (usually 30) in order to foster marketability of title. Other statutes (usually called "marketable title acts") require the rerecording of various future interests (including possibilities of reverter and rights of entry) every 20 to 40 years or they become unenforceable.

3. Fee Tail

The fee tail, typically created by the words "to A and the heirs of his body," limited inheritance to ***lineal descendants*** of the grantee. If no lineal descendants survived at the grantee's death, the property either reverted to the grantor or her successors or passed to a designated remainderman. Today, most United States jurisdictions have abolished the fee tail and have enacted statutes under which any attempt to create a fee tail results in the creation of a fee simple.

4. Life Estate

An estate for life is an estate that is not terminable at any fixed or computable period of time, but cannot last longer than the life or lives of one or more persons. It may arise by operation of law or may be created by an act or agreement of the parties.

a. Life Estates by Marital Right (Legal Life Estates)

Such estates arise under ***dower*** and ***curtesy***, the common law interests of wife and husband, respectively, in real property of which the other spouse was seised during marriage (including property acquired before marriage). At common law, a surviving wife's dower right entitled her to a life estate in an undivided one-third of her husband's lands. A surviving husband's right of curtesy gave him a life estate in all of his wife's lands if issue were born. For exam purposes, it is important to remember that a conveyance by a husband to a bona fide purchaser does not defeat dower unless the wife joins in the conveyance. Likewise, a husband's creditors cannot defeat a wife's dower rights. Most states have abolished both dower and curtesy and have instead given the surviving spouse a statutory right to take a portion of the deceased spouse's estate. Community property states do not recognize either dower or curtesy.

b. Conventional Life Estate

1) For Life of Grantee

The usual life estate is measured by the life of the grantee and is called simply a life estate. It may be indefeasible (so that it will end ***only*** when the life tenant dies), or it ***may be made defeasible*** in the same ways that fee estates can be defeasible (*e.g.,* determinable, subject to a condition subsequent, subject to an executory interest). In such a case, the estate may end ***before*** the life tenant dies if the limiting condition occurs. (*See* Example 5), below.)

Examples: 1) O conveys "to A for life." In this case, A has an estate in the land for as long as he lives. On his death, the land reverts to O, the grantor.

2) "To A for life, then to B." This is a life estate because it is measured by the life of A and is not terminable at a fixed period of time.

3) "To A for life, but in no event for more than 10 years." This is an estate for years and not a life estate because the estate in A will end in 10 years (*i.e.,* a fixed time period).

4) "To A for 10 years if he lives so long." This is also an estate for years and not a life estate because the estate in A will end in 10 years.

5) "To A for life or until she remarries." This is a life estate subject to a limitation, but nevertheless a life estate. The estate in A will not end at any fixed or computable time period. It can be termed a "life estate determinable," and is analogous to the fee simple determinable discussed above.

6) "To B and C after the life of A." A has an implied life estate.

2) Life Estate Pur Autre Vie (Life of Another)

A life estate pur autre vie is a life estate measured by the life of someone other than the life tenant. Such an estate can be created ***directly*** by the grantor, *e.g.,* "to A for the life of B." A's estate ends when B dies. It can also be created ***indirectly***, as where the grantor conveys "to B for life," and B later conveys his interest to A. A owns an estate measured by B's life; it ends when B dies.

a) Inheritability

At common law, if A died before B, the property was regarded as without an owner until B died. Today, statutes provide that such estates are devisable and inheritable if no special occupant is named in the original grant. (A "special occupant" is a person named by the grantor to take the balance of the term, if any.)

c. Rights and Duties of Life Tenant—Doctrine of Waste

A tenant for life is entitled to all the ordinary uses and profits of the land; but he cannot lawfully do any act that would injure the interests of the person who owns the remainder or the reversion. If he does, the future interest holder may sue for ***damages and/or to enjoin*** such acts.

1) Affirmative (Voluntary) Waste—Natural Resources

As a general rule, a life tenant may not consume or exploit natural resources on the property (*e.g.,* timber, minerals, oil). ***Exceptions*** to this rule allow exploitation in the following circumstances:

(i) In reasonable amounts where necessary ***for repair and maintenance*** of the land;

(ii) When the life tenant is ***expressly given the right to exploit*** such resources in the grant;

(iii) When ***prior to the grant, the land was used in exploitation*** of such natural resources, so that in granting the life estate the grantor most likely intended the life tenant to have the right to exploit (*but see* "open mines doctrine," below); and

(iv) In many states, where the ***land is suitable only for such exploitation*** (*e.g.,* a mine).

Note: There is a vague "reasonableness" limit on the amount of oil or coal a life tenant can remove from the property.

a) Open Mines Doctrine
If mining (extraction of minerals) was done on the land before the life estate began, the life tenant may continue to mine the property—but is limited to the mines ***already open***. The life tenant may not open any new mines. There is a trend away from this limitation, applying instead the rule in (iii), above, to all natural resources, including minerals.

2) Permissive Waste
Permissive waste occurs when the life tenant allows the land to fall into disrepair or fails to take reasonable measures to protect the land.

a) Obligation to Repair
A life tenant is obligated to preserve the land and structures in a ***reasonable state of repair***, to the extent of the income or profits derived from the land (or if the life tenant is using the property himself and receiving no rent, then to the extent of the reasonable rental value of the land). But the tenant is under no obligation to make permanent improvements on the land, no matter how wise it might seem to do so.

b) Obligation to Pay Interest on Encumbrances
A life tenant is obligated to pay interest on any encumbrances on the land to the extent of the income or profits from the land (or in their absence to the extent of the reasonable rental value of the land). However, he does not have to pay anything on the principal of the debt; reversioners or remaindermen must pay the principal in order to protect their interests.

The foregoing applies to encumbrances on the entire fee simple estate. Of course, a life tenant could place a mortgage on the life estate alone, and would then be liable for both principal and interest payments.

c) Obligation to Pay Taxes
The life tenant is obligated to pay ***all ordinary taxes*** on the land to the extent of the income or profits from the land (or in their absence to the extent of the reasonable rental value of the land).

d) Special Assessments for Public Improvements
If the life of a public improvement on the land is shorter than the expected duration of the life estate, the life tenant is obligated to pay all of the assessment. However, if the improvement is likely to outlast the life estate (*e.g.,*

curbing, sewers, water mains, a change in grade of a street), taxes and assessments are ***apportioned*** equitably between the life tenant and the holders of all future interests.

(1) Apportionment of Costs
Costs are usually apportioned by using the ratio produced by the market value of the life estate over the market value of the property.

e) No Obligation to Insure Premises
The life tenant is under no obligation to insure the premises for the benefit of a remainderman. However, both the life tenant and the remainderman have an insurable interest.

f) No Liability for Third Party's Torts
Under the modern view, life tenants are not responsible to remaindermen (as they were at common law) for damages caused by third-party tortfeasors. The life tenant's action against such third parties is limited to the damages to the life estate.

3) Ameliorative Waste
Ameliorative waste consists of acts that economically benefit the property. Ameliorative waste occurs when the use of the property is substantially changed, but the change increases the value of the property. At common law, any change to existing buildings or other improvements was always actionable waste, even if it improved the value of the property. Under modern authorities, however, a life tenant can substantially alter or even demolish existing buildings if:

(i) The market value of the future (or other nonpossessory) interests is not diminished; and ***either***

(ii) The remaindermen do not object; ***or***

(iii) A substantial and permanent change in the neighborhood conditions has deprived the property in its current form of reasonable productivity or usefulness.

Example: A holds a life estate in Blackacre, and B holds the remainder. The premises consist of an old and somewhat shabby apartment building that is nearly fully rented and produces a consistent income. The surrounding neighborhood includes many similar buildings. A proposes to demolish the building and construct a new shopping center on the land, which will produce much higher income. B objects to the change and brings an action to enjoin the demolition. B will prevail even though A's proposed changes would increase the value of the property. Because the existing building is economically productive and consistent with the neighborhood, A's commission of waste would not be justified.

a) **Compare—Leasehold Tenant**
Leasehold tenants are treated differently from life tenants. Most leasehold tenants remain liable for ameliorative waste even if the neighborhood has changed and the market value of the premises is increased. (*See* II.C.1.a.3), *infra.*)

b) **Compare—Worthless Property**
Under modern authority, a life tenant may ask for a judicial sale in a partition proceeding if it appears that the land is practically worthless in its present state. The proceeds are put in trust with income to the life tenant.

d. **Renunciation of Life Estates**
A life tenant who receives the estate by will or intestacy may renounce it, perhaps because owning it would be burdensome. If this occurs, the courts generally ***accelerate*** the future interest that follows the life estate, allowing it to become possessory immediately.

5. **Estates for Years, Periodic Estates, Estates at Will, Tenancies at Sufferance**
These nonfreehold present estates in land are considered in the Landlord and Tenant section of this outline (*see* II.A., *infra*).

C. FUTURE INTERESTS

A future interest is an estate that does not entitle the owner thereof to possession immediately, but will or may give the owner possession in the future. A future interest is a ***present***, legally protected right in property; it is not an expectancy.

Examples: 1) O conveys land "to A for life, and on A's death to B in fee simple." A has a present possessory life estate. B has a future interest. (B's future interest is an indefeasibly vested remainder.) Upon the termination of A's possessory life estate, B's remainder in fee simple will become a present possessory estate in fee simple.

2) O conveys land "to A for life, and on A's death to B in fee simple if B survives A." A has a present possessory life estate. B has a future interest. (It is a contingent remainder.) Upon the termination of A's life estate, B's remainder in fee simple ***may*** become a present possessory estate in fee simple. B must survive A in order to take. (In this example, O also has a future interest. He has not conveyed away the interest represented by the contingency that B may predecease A. If B does predecease A, on the termination of A's life estate title to the land will ***revert*** to O. O's retained future interest is called a reversion.)

3) After the conveyance "to A for life, and on A's death to B," B can transfer his remainder interest to another person. Alternatively, if B dies during A's lifetime, his vested remainder will pass to the devisees under his will or (if B left no will) to his intestate heirs.

1. **Reversionary Interests—Future Interests in Transferor**

a. **Possibilities of Reverter and Rights of Entry**
These future interests are discussed above in connection with the present estates to which they are attached.

b. **Reversions**

A person owning an estate in real property can create and transfer a lesser estate (in the durational sense). The residue left in the grantor, which ***arises by operation of law***, is a reversion.

Examples: 1) O, owning land in fee simple, conveys it (i) "to A for life," or (ii) "to A for 99 years." In each case, O has a reversion in fee simple. She (or her successors) will be entitled to present possession of the land when the granted estate terminates.

2) O, owning a life estate in land, leases it "to A for 20 years." O has a reversion in a life estate. If O is still alive when A's lease expires, title will revert to O for life. What happens if, 10 years after this transfer, O dies? A's lease will come to an end, for he was given a lease by one holding only a life estate. O cannot convey a greater interest than she has.

3) O, owning land in fee simple, conveys it "to A for life, and on A's death to B if B survives A." A has a life estate, B has a contingent remainder, and O has a reversion that will take in present possession at A's death if B predeceases A.

Reversions are transferable, devisable by will, and descendible by inheritance. The holder of a reversion may sue a possessory owner for waste and may recover against third-party wrongdoers for damages to the property (to the extent of the injury to the reversion).

c. **All Reversionary Interests Are "Vested"**

Although a reversionary interest becomes possessory in the future, it is a vested interest, not a contingent interest, because both the owner and the event upon which it will become possessory are certain. This is true even if the reversionary interest is determinable or defeasible. Because it is a vested interest, a reversionary interest is ***not subject to the Rule Against Perpetuities***.

2. **Remainders**

A remainder is a future interest created in a transferee that is ***capable of taking*** in present possession and enjoyment (*i.e.,* capable of becoming a present interest) ***upon the natural termination of the preceding estates*** created in the same disposition. Unlike a reversion, which arises by operation of law from the fact that the transferor has not made a complete disposition of his interest, a remainder ***must be expressly created in the instrument creating the intermediate possessory estate***. At common law, the only preceding estates that could support a remainder were life estates and fee tails. Because nearly all American jurisdictions have abolished the fee tail estate, a safe rule of thumb is that remainders ***always follow life estates***. (*Note:* According to the Restatement of Property, under modern law, a remainder can also follow a term of years. However, there is very little case law on the point, and it is so rare that it is extremely unlikely to be tested.)

Examples: 1) "To A for life, and on A's death to B and his heirs." A has a present possessory life estate. B has a remainder in fee simple. It is a remainder because upon the expiration of A's life estate (natural termination of the preceding

estate), B will be entitled to present possession and enjoyment of the property. The term "remainder" derives from the consequence that when A's life estate comes to an end, title "remains away" from the transferor instead of reverting back to him.

2) On Monday, O conveys Blackacre "to A for life." On Wednesday, O conveys "all of my right, title, and interest in Blackacre" to B. B holds a reversion, not a remainder. B's future interest was not created in the same disposition that gave A a life estate. The Monday conveyance gave A a life estate and raised a reversion in O. The Wednesday conveyance transferred O's reversion to B. "Once a reversion, always a reversion."

A remainder cannot "cut short" or divest a preceding estate prior to its normal expiration. Therefore, a remainder can ***never follow a fee simple***, which has a potentially infinite duration. Future interests that cut short a preceding estate or follow a gap after it are called executory interests. (*See* 3., *infra.*)

a. Indefeasibly Vested Remainder

An indefeasibly vested remainder is a remainder that:

(i) Can be created in and held only by an ***ascertained person or persons*** in being;

(ii) ***Must be certain to become possessory on termination of the prior estates*** (*i.e.*, there is no condition that may operate to prevent the remainder from someday becoming a present interest);

(iii) ***Must not be subject to being defeated or divested*** (compare the vested remainder subject to total divestment, c., *infra*); and

(iv) ***Must not be subject to being diminished in size*** (compare the vested remainder subject to open, b., *infra*).

Examples: 1) "To A for life, and on A's death to B." A has a life estate; B has an indefeasibly vested remainder which is certain to take in possession on the termination of A's life estate.

What if B dies in A's lifetime? There is no stated condition that B survive A in order to take, and the courts do not imply such a condition. B's indefeasibly vested remainder passes by will or intestacy to his successors, who own an indefeasibly vested remainder.

2) "To A for life, then to A's first-born son in fee." At the time of this disposition, A has no children. The state of title: life estate in A, contingent remainder in the first son to be born to A, reversion in fee simple in the transferor. (The reversion will take in present possession if A never has a son.) The remainder is not vested because it is not created in an ascertained person in being. Also, it is subject to the condition that A have a child.

Two years later A has a son, John. The state of title: life estate in A, indefeasibly vested remainder in fee simple in John.

b. Vested Remainder Subject to Open

This is a vested remainder created in a class of persons (*e.g.,* "children," "brothers and sisters") that is certain to take on the termination of the preceding estates, but is ***subject to diminution*** by reason of other persons becoming entitled to share in the remainder. It is also called a "vested remainder subject to partial divestment."

Examples: 1) "To A for life, and on A's death to her children in equal shares." If at the time of this disposition A has no children, the state of title is: life estate in A; contingent remainder in the unborn children of A; reversion in fee in the transferor, which will take in possession if A never has any children.

Suppose two years later a child, Bob, is born to A. The state of title is: life estate in A, vested remainder subject to open in Bob. Bob's remainder is vested because he is in existence and ascertained and his taking is not subject to any contingency. But it is vested subject to open because A may have more children.

Two years later another child, Ray, is born to A. Bob's remainder has been partially divested in favor of Ray, who also meets the description "children of A." Bob and Ray now hold the vested remainder as tenants in common (each with an undivided one-half share) ***subject to open****—i.e.,* their vested remainders will be partially divested if more children are born to A.

Two years later Bob dies; shortly thereafter, A dies. Bob's successors (by will or intestacy) and Ray are entitled to present possession and enjoyment of the property. Bob's share of the remainder was subject to partial divestment, but it was not subject to being totally defeated. No condition of survival was attached to Bob's interest. Bob (or his successors) was certain to take; the only question was the size of his share.

2) Gift by will "to my wife, Rowena, for life, and on her death to ***my*** children in equal shares." T is survived by Rowena and by three children. At first blush this looks like a vested remainder subject to open because it is a remainder to someone's children. In reality, though, it is ***indefeasibly vested***. T, being dead, can have no more children. (Slight qualification of answer: If Rowena is pregnant with T's child at T's death, the posthumous child, if born alive, will share in the gift.)

1) Divesting Interests Are Executory Interests

Once the remainder vests in one existing member of the class, the divesting interest in the unborn members of the class is called an executory interest.

2) Effect on Marketability of Title

Note that where there are outstanding interests in the unborn children, the vested remainderman and the life tenant cannot jointly convey good title.

Example: O "to A for life, remainder to B's children." C wants to buy the land, and desires to know if he can get good title if he purchases from A and all of B's living children. The answer is no, as long as B is alive, because it is possible for B to have more children (no matter what B's age). Thus, there would be outstanding interests in the unborn children of B, and C would not get good title.

c. Vested Remainder Subject to Total Divestment

A vested remainder subject to total divestment arises when the remainderman is in existence and ascertained and his interest is not subject to any condition precedent, but his right to possession and enjoyment is subject to being defeated by the happening of some ***condition subsequent***.

Examples: 1) "To A for life, remainder to B and his heirs, but if at B's death he is not survived by issue, to C and his heirs." Here, B has a vested remainder in fee simple, but his fee simple interest is subject to being divested if at his death he is not survived by issue. (C has a shifting executory interest.)

2) "To A for life, then to B for life." A has a life estate. B has a vested remainder in a life estate subject to total divestment. The transferor has a reversion in fee. B's remainder is vested even though (as a practical matter) he must survive A in order to take. But this practical requirement does not make B's remainder contingent. The only condition to B's taking is the natural termination of A's life estate, and this "condition" is inherent in any remainder life estate. There is no other condition precedent. However, B's remainder life estate is not indefeasibly vested, for it will be ***defeated if he dies in A's lifetime***. Therefore, it is a vested remainder subject to total divestment.

3) "To A for life, and on A's death to B; but if B predeceases A, on A's death to C." A has a life estate. B has a vested remainder subject to total divestment. Although B's taking is ***contingent on his surviving A***, that contingency is expressed as a condition subsequent—meaning that B's remainder is vested subject to total divestment. (C has a shifting executory interest.)

d. Contingent Remainder

There are two ways to create a contingent remainder.

1) Subject to Condition Precedent

A remainder will be classified as contingent if its taking in possession is subject to a condition precedent ("contingent as to ***event***").

Examples: 1) "To A for life, and on A's death to B if B survives A." A has a life estate; B has a contingent remainder in fee simple. The transferor has a reversion, which will become a possessory estate on the termination of A's life estate if B predeceases A. Here, B's taking is subject to a contingency, stated as a condition precedent, that he must survive A in order to take.

Compare this with Example 3) in the preceding section. In that example, B's taking is also subject to a contingency: he must survive A in order to take. Thus in substance, this example and Example 3) are quite similar. But in classifying future interests, the general rule is that ***it is form and not substance that counts***. In Example 3), the contingency of survival is expressed as a ***condition subsequent***; therefore, B's remainder is vested subject to total divestment. But in this example, the contingency of survival is expressed as a ***condition precedent***; therefore, B's remainder is a contingent remainder.

2) "To A for life, and on A's death to B if B marries C." Here, B is an ascertained person, but there is a condition precedent to B's taking: he must marry C. If B marries C in A's lifetime, his remainder will become indefeasibly vested.

3) O conveys "to A for life, then to B and his heirs if B survives A; if B does not survive A, then to C and his heirs." Each remainder is contingent because each is subject to a condition precedent. They are mutually exclusive and exhaustive; *i.e.,* only one can come into possession, and when it does the other can never do so. These are called ***alternative contingent remainders***.

Compare: O conveys "to A for life, then to B and his heirs, but if B marries C, then to D and his heirs." Here B, an ascertained person, takes a vested remainder because it is not limited on a condition precedent. B's remainder is ready to come into possession whenever A dies. But the marriage condition is subsequent—B's marriage to C will forfeit his estate. D's interest is called an executory interest.

2) Unborn or Unascertained Persons

A remainder is contingent if it is created in favor of unborn or unascertained persons ("contingent as to ***person***"), because until the remainderman is ascertained, there is no one ready to take possession should the preceding estate come to an end.

Examples: 1) "To A for life, and on A's death, per stirpes to such of A's descendants as survive her." At the time of this disposition, A is in poor health and she has two adult children (B and C) who are very healthy. State of title: A has a life estate; there is a contingent remainder in such of A's descendants as survive A; the transferor has a reversion (for A may not be survived by any descendants).

While the odds are in B and C's favor that they will take the remainder upon A's death, they are not named as the remaindermen. The remainder is in such of A's descendants as survive A, and we will not be able to identify the remaindermen until A dies and we can see which of A's descendants survived her.

2) O transfers securities in trust "to pay the income to A for life, and on A's death to distribute the trust corpus to A's heirs." There is a contingent remainder in A's heirs. It is true that A's heirs will be determined the moment A dies and A's life estate terminates. But at the time O makes the transfer, the remaindermen are not ascertained, for "*nemo est haeres viventis*" (no one is heir of the living). The persons who turn out to be A's heirs will not be ascertained until A dies.

3) Destructibility of Contingent Remainders

At common law, a contingent remainder had to vest prior to or upon termination of the preceding freehold estate or it was destroyed.

Examples: 1) O conveyed "to A for life, then to the heirs of B." If A predeceased B, there were no heirs of B to take possession so the remainder was destroyed and O or his estate retook possession.

2) O conveyed "to A for life, to B if she reaches age 21." If A died before B reached 21, the remainder was destroyed. (Note that whenever a grantor created a contingent remainder, he retained a reversion, which was normally defeasible.)

Analysis: Why are the interests in the above examples remainders and not executory interests? In each instance it is possible that the future interest will take effect at the natural expiration of A's life estate (as remainders do), or that it will take effect following a gap after A's estate (as executory interests do). The rule is that if an interest may operate as either a remainder or an executory interest (depending on the circumstances at A's death), it is a remainder. Thus, at common law, if such a remainder was then called upon to act as an executory interest, it could not do so and was destroyed.

a) Rule Abolished

Today, the rule of destructibility has been abolished in all but a few states. Thus, in the two examples given above, on A's death, O's ***reversion*** would take over, and would then give way to a springing executory interest on B's death in the first example, and on B's attaining age 21 in the second. (Note that the contingent remainders are not destroyed when the preceding estate ends, but instead become executory interests because they will divest the transferor's estate.)

b) Related Doctrine of Merger

Whenever the same person acquires all of the existing interests in land, present and future, a merger occurs. That person then holds a fee simple absolute. For example, suppose O conveys by deed "to A for life." O now has a reversion. Subsequently, by a later deed, O conveys his reversion interest to A. A will have a fee simple absolute by merger. (A similar result would follow if A conveyed her life estate to O.) Moreover, the common law held (as an aspect of the destructibility doctrine) that if a person acquired all of the interests in land ***except*** a contingent remainder, the merger would occur anyway,

and the contingent remainder would be destroyed! Contingent remainders were considered to be such flimsy, ephemeral interests that they would not keep the merger from occurring. Note that this is still the rule in those few states retaining the common law rule of destructibility.

Example: In Example 1), above (O "to A for life, then to the heirs of B"), title stands as a life estate in A, a contingent remainder in the as yet unascertained heirs of B, and a reversion (if B is still alive at the death of A) in O. If O then purchased A's interest, O would hold a life estate pur autre vie (for the life of A) and a reversion. At common law, O's two interests on either side of the contingent remainder ***merged***, wiping out the contingent remainder and giving O a fee simple.

(1) Compare—Interests Created Simultaneously

If a life estate and the next vested interest were created simultaneously (by the same instrument), there would be no merger at that time because that would defeat the grantor's obvious intent to create a contingent remainder. However, if the life tenant subsequently conveyed his interest to the holder of the next vested estate, the contingent remainder would then be destroyed.

e. Rule in Shelley's Case (Rule Against Remainders in Grantee's Heirs)

At common law, where a freehold estate (usually a life estate) was given to A (by will or inter vivos transfer), and in the same instrument a ***remainder was limited to the "heirs" or to the "heirs of the body" of A***, and the freehold estate and the remainder were both legal or both equitable, the purported remainder in the heirs was not recognized, and A took both the freehold estate and the remainder. The Rule operated (regardless of the grantor's intent) to convert what would otherwise have been a contingent remainder in the heirs into a remainder in the ancestor.

Examples: 1) O grants or devises land "to A for life, and then to the heirs of A." Apart from the Rule in Shelley's Case, the title would be: life estate in A, contingent remainder in fee simple in A's heirs. But by virtue of the Rule, the title is: life estate in A, vested remainder in A in fee simple. (Here, the law of merger causes A's life estate to merge with his remainder so that A gets a present estate in fee simple.)

2) O "to A for life, then to B for life, then to the heirs of A." A has a life estate, and the Rule in Shelley's Case transforms the contingent remainder in the heirs of A into a vested remainder in fee simple in A. But merger does not occur because of the intervening ***vested*** remainder limited to B.

3) O "to A for life, then to B for life, then to the heirs of B." The Rule in Shelley's Case operates, as does merger, and B has a vested remainder in fee simple.

4) O "to A for life, then one day after A's death to the heirs of A." The Rule in Shelley's Case does not operate because the interest limited to

the heirs of A is not a remainder (it can never take over immediately at the termination of the prior freehold estate), but rather is an executory interest.

Compare: O conveys land "to A and his heirs." A takes a fee simple—not by operation of the Rule in Shelley's Case, but because the words "and his heirs" are words of limitation denoting that a fee simple estate has been conveyed. (*See* I.B.1., *supra*.) (It is a common student error to conclude, in this case, that "A takes a fee simple because of the Rule in Shelley's Case." This rule is triggered ***only*** by the attempted creation of a remainder in the grantee's heirs.)

Note: This Rule has been ***abolished in most states today***, but arises occasionally where a conveyance was executed prior to abolition of the Rule.

f. Doctrine of Worthier Title (Rule Against Remainders in Grantor's Heirs)

Under the Doctrine of Worthier Title ("DOWT"), a remainder limited to the grantor's heirs is invalid, and the grantor retains a reversion in the property. This doctrine is still applied to inter vivos transfers in a majority of states, but most states treat it only as a ***rule of construction*** (*i.e.,* it does not apply if the grantor has clearly manifested an intent to create a future interest in his heirs).

Example: O deeds property "to A for life, and on A's death to my heirs at law," or ". . . and on A's death to my next of kin." In most states, the disposition gives A a life estate and presumptively leaves a reversion in fee simple in O. The burden of establishing that O really intended to create a remainder in his heirs (or next of kin) would be on the parties so contending. The litigation would arise after O's death, and would be between (i) the persons designated as O's heirs under the state's intestacy laws, claiming that they take on A's death by remainder; and (ii) the devisees under O's will, contending that O died owning a reversion.

In a state that has abolished the doctrine, the state of title is: life estate in A; contingent remainder in O's heirs; reversion in O.

Compare: 1) O deeds property "to A for life, and on A's death to my children in equal shares." On O's death, his children, X and Y, are O's sole heirs. DOWT does not apply. The doctrine applies only when there is a disposition, following a life estate, to the transferor's ***"heirs"*** or ***"next of kin,"*** or words of like effect.

2) O deeds property "to A for life, and on A's death to the heirs born to my wife Martha and me." DOWT does not apply; the disposition creates a life estate in A and a vested remainder subject to open in the children of O and Martha. Although O used the term "heirs," it is clear from the context that he was not using the term in its technical sense, but was referring to his children by his wife Martha.

3. Executory Interests

Here is a good shorthand rule for classifying executory interests. Remember that there are

two and only two future interests that can be created in a transferee: remainders and executory interests. ***If it is not a remainder because the preceding estate is not a life estate, then it must be an executory interest.*** Thus, an executory interest is any future interest in a transferee that does not have the characteristics of a remainder, *i.e.,* it is not capable of taking on the natural termination of the preceding life estate. More specifically, an executory interest is an interest that ***divests*** the interest of another.

a. Shifting Executory Interest—Divests a Transferee

A shifting executory interest is one that divests the interest of another transferee; *i.e.,* it cuts short a prior estate created by the same conveyance.

Examples: 1) "To A and her heirs; but if B returns from Canada, then and in that event to B and his heirs." A has a fee simple subject to an executory interest. Because the future interest is created in a transferee, it has to be either a remainder or an executory interest. B's future interest is not a remainder because it does not follow the natural termination of the preceding estate (here, A's fee simple estate). If B's interest does take in present possession, it will divest A's fee simple, and title will ***shift*** to B.

2) O conveys "to A for life, remainder to B and his heirs, ***but if B predeceases A***, to C and his heirs." C's interest does not await the expiration of B's vested remainder, but instead may cut it short.

b. Springing Executory Interest—"Follows a Gap" or Divests a Transferor

A springing executory interest is an interest that follows a gap in possession or divests the estate of the transferor.

Examples: 1) O conveys property "to A when and if A marries B." State of title: fee simple subject to an executory interest in O; springing executory interest in fee simple in A. A's interest is not a remainder because if A's future interest becomes a present interest (if A marries B), it will divest O's fee simple. Because it ***divests the estate of a transferor***, it is a springing executory interest.

2) O conveys property "to A for life, and one year after A's death to B." A has a life estate. O has a reversion. B has a springing executory interest in fee simple. B's interest cannot be a remainder because of the one-year gap; it is not capable of taking on the natural termination of the preceding estate (A's life estate). It is therefore an executory interest. It is a springing executory interest because it ***springs out of the transferor's reversion***.

c. Executory Interest Follows a Fee

A ***remainder cannot follow a fee simple interest*** of any kind. Therefore, any interest that follows a fee and is held by a third person is an executory interest.

Examples: 1) O conveys land "to Church for so long as the premises are used for church purposes, and if they shall ever cease to be so used, then and in that event to the American Red Cross." Church has a fee simple determinable subject to an executory interest; the Red Cross has an executory interest that is valid under the charity-to-charity exception to the Rule Against Perpetuities.

2) O conveys "to Church; provided, however, that if the premises shall ever cease to be used for church purposes, then and in that event to the American Red Cross." Church has a fee simple subject to an executory interest; the Red Cross has an executory interest that is valid under the charity-to-charity exception to the Rule Against Perpetuities.

d. Differences Between Executory Interests and Remainders

It is important to be able to distinguish between executory interests and remainders for the following reasons: (i) executory interests are not destructible, while contingent remainders are still destructible in a few jurisdictions; (ii) executory interests are not considered vested, whereas contingent remainders can become vested; and (iii) the Rule in Shelley's Case does not apply to executory interests, but it does apply to remainders limited to the heirs of the grantee.

4. Importance of Classifying Interests "In Order"

Future interests are classified clause by clause—which will often mean that the label appended to the first future interest created in a disposition will determine the label to be appended to a second future interest created in the same disposition. For instance, if the first future interest is a contingent remainder, subsequent future interests must also be contingent remainders. Similarly, if the first future interest is a vested remainder subject to divestment, the following future interests will be executory interests.

Examples: 1) O conveys land "to A for life, and on A's death to B if B survives A; but if B does not survive A, on A's death to C." A has a life estate. B has a contingent remainder because B's taking is subject to a contingency (expressed in condition precedent form) that B must survive A in order to take. C has an alternative contingent remainder.

Because the contingency of B's survival is expressed both as a condition precedent and (in the next clause) as a condition subsequent, why is B's remainder classified as contingent rather than as vested subject to total divestment? The explanation is that interests are classified "in order." Looking first at the clause giving an interest to B, here the contingency is expressed as a condition precedent; therefore, B's remainder is contingent. Then, having classified B's interest, we turn to C's interest. But because B's interest has already been determined to be a contingent remainder, C's interest is necessarily an alternative contingent remainder.

2) O conveys land "to A for life, and on A's death to B. But if B predeceases A, on A's death to C." Watch this one carefully, for the answer turns on the principle that we classify interests "in order." First of all, A has a life estate. Next we classify B's interest. It is a remainder, for it is capable of taking on the natural termination of the preceding estate (A's life estate). It is a vested remainder in fee simple because B is an ascertained person and there is ***no condition precedent*** to B's taking other than the termination of A's life estate. Having classified it as a vested remainder, we read on ("but if") and see that B's estate will be defeated if he predeceases A. Therefore, it is a vested remainder subject to total divestment upon the happening of this condition, which is expressed in ***condition subsequent*** form.

Having classified B's remainder as vested subject to total divestment, we turn to C's interest. It cannot be a remainder, for a remainder follows the natural termination of the preceding estate—B's estate, which is a vested remainder in fee simple. But ***no remainder can follow a fee simple***, for a fee simple is an estate of potentially infinite duration. If C does take, it will cut short B's vested remainder in fee simple some time short of infinity. Therefore, C's interest is an executory interest—a ***shifting executory interest***, because it divests a transferee.

But isn't C's interest capable of taking on the natural termination of A's life estate (if B predeceases A)? Yes, but that does not affect our classification. A remainder is a future interest capable of taking on the termination of the ***preceding*** estate, and here the preceding estate is B's.

Suppose, some years after this disposition, B dies during A's lifetime. What is the state of title? The answer: life estate in A, indefeasibly vested ***remainder*** in C. Now that B's estate is out of the way, the preceding estate is A's life estate, and so now we can change the label and call C's interest a remainder.

5. Transferability of Remainders and Executory Interests

a. Vested Remainders Are Transferable, Devisable, and Descendible

At common law and in all jurisdictions today, vested remainders are fully transferable during life, devisable by will, and descendible by inheritance. This is true of all types of vested remainders: indefeasibly vested, vested subject to open, and vested subject to total divestment.

b. Contingent Remainders and Executory Interests Are Transferable Inter Vivos

At common law, contingent remainders and executory interests were not assignable. While this is still the rule in a few states, most American courts hold that these interests are freely transferable.

c. Contingent Remainders and Executory Interests Are Usually Devisable and Descendible

Whereas the rule at common law was that contingent remainders and executory interests were not transferable inter vivos, it has always been held that these interests are devisable and descendible—***unless***, of course, the holder's ***survival is a condition*** to the interest's taking.

Example: "To A for life, and on A's death to B; but if B does not survive A, on A's death to C." State of title: life estate in A, vested remainder subject to total divestment in B, and shifting executory interest in C. Suppose B dies in A's lifetime, leaving a will that devises "all my property" to Mrs. B. B's remainder interest does not pass under his will because, by the terms of the disposition, that interest failed when B died in A's lifetime.

d. Any Transferable Future Interest Is Reachable by Creditors

The rule followed in nearly all states is this: If a future interest can, under the laws of the state, be transferred voluntarily by its owner, it is also subject to involuntary transfer; *i.e.,* it can be reached by the owner's creditors by appropriate process.

e. **Practical Ability to Transfer Marketable Title**
Technically, most states consider all types of future interests transferable, but in practice those interests held by unborn or unascertained persons are not transferable because courts will not appoint a guardian for purposes of conveying land. (*See* VI.A.3.a.1)b), *infra*.)

6. **Class Gifts**
A "class" is a group of persons having a common characteristic. Typically, they stand in the same relation to each other or to some other person (*e.g.,* children, grandchildren, descendants, nephews and nieces). In a gift to a class, the share of each member of the class is determined by the number of persons in the class.

a. **Definitional Problems**

1) **Dispositions to "Children"**
A gift to a person's "children" generally includes that person's children from all marriages as well as adopted and nonmarital children. That person's stepchildren and grandchildren are generally not included in the class.

2) **Dispositions to "Heirs"**
A disposition to the "heirs" of someone presumptively includes those persons who would take the named person's estate according to the laws of descent and distribution if she were to die without a will.

3) **Dispositions to "Issue" or "Descendants"**
The terms "issue" and "descendants" refer to the lineal offspring of the designated person, whatever the degree of relationship (children, grandchildren, great-grandchildren, etc.). As a general principle, the issue or descendants take per stirpes.

4) **Class Members in Gestation**
Persons in gestation at the time set for distribution are included in a class. The common law presumption is that a child born within 10 lunar months or 280 calendar days after the necessary point in time was in gestation at that time.

b. **When the Class Closes—The Rule of Convenience**
When a gift is made to a group of persons generically described as a class, such as to someone's "children," there is the possibility that other persons may be born who meet the class description. This raises the question, when does the class "close"; *i.e.,* when is the maximum membership of the class determined, such that persons born thereafter are excluded from sharing in the gift? In resolving this problem, the common law courts developed the rule of convenience. This is a rule of construction, not a rule of law. It is applicable in the absence of an expression of intent to include all persons who meet the class description regardless of when they are born. Under the rule, a ***class closes when some member of the class can call for a distribution of her share of the class gift.*** It is presumed that the ordinary transferor intends to include all members of the class, whenever born, ***provided*** that this would ***not cause any undue inconvenience***. Thus, the rule of convenience is based on a policy of including as many persons in the class as possible, consistent with permitting a distribution of the property at the first opportunity without the necessity of a future rebate.

1) Outright Gift—Class Closes at Time Gift Is Made

When a ***will*** makes an outright gift to a class, if any class members are alive at the testator's death, the class closes as of the ***date of the testator's death***.

Example: T's will devises property "to the children of my good friend, John Brown." John has three children (A, B, and C) at the time of T's death; another child (D) is born two years later. The class closes at T's death; A, B, and C share the gift. D is excluded by the rule of convenience.

Here, additional members of the class are included up to the time of T's death because there is no inconvenience in doing so. But we close the class at T's death because it is assumed that T would want an immediate distribution, rather than postponing distribution until John Brown's death, which is the only time we will be sure that John Brown will have no more children. If we were to include D, we would also have to include E, F, and G, who might be born later. Moreover, if we distributed one-third shares to A, B, and C at T's death, but required them to make rebates if more children should be born later to their father, John, all sorts of practical problems would arise. To avoid these problems, there is a strong constructional preference to close the class at T's death.

a) No Class Members Alive at Testator's Death—Class Stays Open

If there are no members of the class living at the testator's death, all after-born persons who come within the class designation are included. Thus, if T had bequeathed $100,000 "to the children of John," and John had no children living at T's death or born within the period of gestation thereafter, then all of John's children, whenever born, are included, regardless of any possible inconvenience in keeping the class open this long.

2) Postponed Gift—Class Closes at Time Fixed for Distribution

When possession and enjoyment of a gift are postponed, as where the gift follows a life estate, the class remains open until the time fixed for distribution (*e.g.,* death of the life tenant).

Example: T's will creates a trust to pay the income to W for life, and on W's death to pay the principal to the children of John. At the time T executes his will, John has two children (A and B). After the will is executed but before T dies, another child (C) is born to John. After T's death but during W's lifetime, another child (D) is born to John. W dies; two years later John has another child (E).

The class closes at W's death; A, B, C, and D each take a one-fourth share. E is excluded by the rule of convenience. There was no inconvenience in leaving the class open until W's death, for the time had not yet come to distribute the corpus. But when W dies, it is time to make a distribution; the class is closed in order to determine the minimum shares going to each class member.

3) Dispositions Subject to Condition of Reaching Given Age

When there is a gift to a class conditioned upon the members attaining a certain age, the class closes when (i) the preceding estate, if any, terminates, and (ii) the first class member reaches the specified age. That class member's minimum share should be determined and distributed to her when she reaches the specified age.

Examples: 1) T's will devises his residuary estate "to the children of John who live to attain the age of 21." At T's death, John has three children: A (age 22), B (age 16), and C (age 10). The class closes at T's death. A is entitled to immediate distribution of her share, and the minimum size of that share must be fixed as of T's death, at one-third. If B lives to attain age 21, but C dies before attaining that age, on C's death, A and B's shares will be increased to one-half.

Two years after T's death, another child (D) is born to John. D is excluded by the rule of convenience. The class was closed at T's death in order to determine the minimum size of A's share so that this share could be distributed to her.

Suppose none of John's children is 21 at T's death. The class remains open until a child of John reaches the designated age, at which time the class closes.

2) T's will devises his residuary estate "to Wanda for life, and on Wanda's death to such of John's children as live to attain the age of 21." Here, the class will close, and the remaindermen who share in the disposition will be determined, when two things occur: (i) Wanda dies; ***and*** (ii) a child of John reaches age 21. If at T's death one of John's children is over age 21, it does not matter; the class remains open until Wanda's life estate terminates. Likewise, if at Wanda's death no child of John has attained age 21, the class remains open until one of John's children reaches that age. If at Wanda's death a child has attained age 21, the class will close at that time.

4) Rule of Convenience Is a Rule of Construction Only

The rule of convenience is a rule of construction only. If the transferor explicitly sets forth the time when membership of the class is to be determined, or if he provides that all members of the class, whenever born, are to share in the gift, then his directions will govern. However, courts have a strong preference for application of the rule of convenience unless there is a fairly clear indication that it is not to govern.

7. Survival

As a general rule, all future interests can pass at death by will or inheritance; *i.e.,* they are descendible and devisable. This is true ***unless*** the interest's taking is subject to an expressed or implied contingency of survival.

Examples: 1) T's will devises his residuary estate "to my sister Sue for life, and on Sue's death to her children in equal shares." At the time of T's death, Sue has

three children: A, B, and C. C dies, then Sue dies survived by A and B. The remainder is shared by A, B, and the estate of C (*i.e.,* the estate takes under C's will or by intestacy), each with one-third shares. *Analysis:* A, B, and C had vested remainders subject to open, but their interests were not in terms conditioned on surviving the life beneficiary—and the law does not imply such a condition of survival. On C's death, his vested remainder subject to open passes via his will or by intestacy. (*Note:* This example does ***not*** invoke the lapsed gift doctrine of Wills law, for C was alive at the testator's death.)

2) "To A for life, and on A's death to B if B is then living; but if B is not then living, to C." C dies, then B dies, then A dies. Who takes? Answer: The takers under C's will or by intestacy. B and C were given alternative contingent remainders. B's remainder was contingent on his surviving A, and B did not meet the condition; his estate was defeated. C's remainder was contingent on B's not surviving A; it was not in terms contingent on C's surviving A, and the law does not imply such a condition.

a. **Express Words of Survival**
In each of the following examples, the italicized language imposes a condition precedent that the remaindermen must survive the life tenant in order to take.
Examples: 1) "To A for life, remainder to his ***surviving children***."

2) "To A for life, and should he ***die leaving children***, to such children."

3) "To A for life, and after the death of A, remainder to the children of A ***then living***."

b. **Implied Contingency of Survival—Gifts to "Issue," "Descendants," or "Heirs"**
Gifts to a person's "issue," "descendants," or "heirs" imply a condition of surviving the named ancestor.

D. TRUSTS

An express trust involves the holding of title to property by a trustee, who has an equitable fiduciary duty to deal with it for the benefit of other persons (the beneficiaries).

1. Private Trust Concepts and Parties

a. **Settlor**
The settlor is the person who ***creates the trust*** by manifesting an intent to do so. While a trust of personal property may be expressed orally, the Statute of Frauds requires a writing to create a trust of real property. The settlor must own the property at the time the trust is created and must intend to make the trust effective immediately.

b. **Trustee**
The trustee ***holds legal title to the property***, but must act under the instructions of the settlor who created the trust. The trustee has a fiduciary duty to use the highest care and skill for the beneficiaries. If the trustee has no duties at all, the trust will fail, and legal title will vest immediately in the beneficiaries. However, if the trustee dies, resigns, or refuses to serve, the trust will not fail; a court of equity will appoint a substitute trustee.

c. **Beneficiaries**

The beneficiaries are the ***persons for whose benefit the trust is created and held***; they hold ***equitable title*** to the property. Every private trust must have at least one beneficiary, and the beneficiaries must be definitely identifiable by the time their interest comes into enjoyment and, in all events, within the period of the Rule Against Perpetuities. Acceptance of the benefits of the trust is normally presumed, but a beneficiary may renounce his rights under the trust within a reasonable time after learning of its creation. A trust may be for a class of beneficiaries (*e.g.*, "all the living descendants of Mary Jones"), provided that the class is small enough to be "reasonably definite."

d. **Res**

The res is ***the property that is the subject of the trust***. If there is no res, the trust fails. The res may be real property or personal property (tangible or intangible), and it may be either a present interest or a future interest (vested or contingent). The trust res must be segregated from other property of the settlor, but this does not preclude a trust of a fractional share interest, such as a trust of "an undivided one-half interest in Blackacre," where the settlor owns all of Blackacre.

e. **Application of Rule Against Perpetuities**

The Rule Against Perpetuities (*see* E., *infra*) applies to the equitable future interests of the beneficiaries in a private trust just as it does to "legal" future interests.

Example: O conveys land to T "in trust for the benefit of A so long as the existing house on the land remains standing, and then for the benefit of the then living descendants of A." The equitable interest of the descendants of A is void because it is not certain to vest or fail within 21 years after the life of any person living at the time the trust is created.

2. **Creation of Trusts**

a. **Inter Vivos Conveyance**

An inter vivos trust can be created by the settlor's conveyance of the trust res to the trustee while the settlor is alive. For real property, this must be done by a writing to satisfy the Statute of Frauds; this is usually accomplished by delivery of a deed.

b. **Inter Vivos Declaration**

The settlor may declare that he is now holding certain property (previously held outright by the settlor) in trust for certain beneficiaries. No deed or delivery is necessary, but if the res is real property, the declaration must be in writing and signed by the settlor.

c. **Testamentary Conveyance**

The settlor may create the trust by language in his will, and may also transfer the res to the trustee by a devise in the will. The trust will come into existence only upon the death of the settlor.

d. **Pour-Over into Existing Trust**

The settlor may create an inter vivos trust before death. The settlor's will may then bequeath property to the trust—"pouring it over" into the trust.

3. Charitable Trusts

a. Beneficiaries

A charitable trust, unlike the private trusts described above, must have an ***indefinite*** group of beneficiaries. The beneficiaries must be reasonably numerous and not individually identified. The trust may be for the benefit of an established charity (*e.g.*, the American Red Cross) or for a group of persons (*e.g.*, the victims of Hurricane Katrina).

b. Application of Rule Against Perpetuities

The Rule Against Perpetuities does not apply to trusts that are ***entirely charitable***. Such trusts may have infinite life. This is true even if the trust benefits two charities, one with a present interest and the other with a future interest that would normally violate the Rule Against Perpetuities. Note, however, that if either the first or second interest is noncharitable, the exemption from the Rule Against Perpetuities does not apply and the second gift is void.

Examples: 1) O conveys land to T in trust "for the benefit of the victims of Hurricane Katrina, and when all houses destroyed by the hurricane have been rebuilt, then for the benefit of the American Red Cross." The interest of the Red Cross may not vest until more than 21 years after the death of any person living when the trust is created, but it is still a valid interest.

2) O conveys land to T in trust "for the benefit of my son John, whose house was destroyed by Hurricane Katrina, and when his house has been rebuilt, then for the benefit of the American Red Cross." The interest of the Red Cross may not vest until more than 21 years after the death of any person living when the trust is created, and it is void.

c. Cy Pres Doctrine

If the purposes of a charitable trust are impossible to fulfill, are illegal, or have been completely fulfilled, a court may redirect the trust to a different purpose that is "as near as may be" (a translation of the Latin "cy pres") to the settlor's original intent.

d. Enforcement of Charitable Trusts

Charitable trusts may be enforced by an action of the attorney general of the state.

E. THE RULE AGAINST PERPETUITIES

The Rule Against Perpetuities may be stated as follows: "No interest in property is valid unless it must vest, if at all, not later than 21 years after one or more lives in being at the creation of the interest." The Rule might be more easily understood if it had been expressed as an affirmative proposition: "An interest is void if there is any possibility, however remote, that the interest may vest more than 21 years after some life in being at the creation of the interest." This paraphrase of the Rule properly places the emphasis on the ***possibility*** of remote vesting, the test by which the invalidity of an interest is shown. If a situation can be imagined in which the interest might not vest within the perpetuities period, the interest is void. This is the result even though the circumstances that might bring about the remote vesting are unlikely to occur or are unrealistic. (All kinds of unlikely things are considered capable of happening under the Rule.) The Rule applies to the following legal and equitable future interests in personal or real property:

(i) Contingent remainders;

(ii) Executory interests;

(iii) Class gifts (even if vested remainders);

(iv) Options and rights of first refusal; and

(v) Powers of appointment.

1. Analysis of the Rule

a. When the Perpetuities Period Begins to Run

The validity of interests under the Rule is determined ***at the time the interests are created***, taking into account the facts then existing. The "lives in being plus 21 years" period begins to run, and the measuring lives used to show the validity of an interest must be in existence, at that time.

1) Wills—Date of Testator's Death

The perpetuities period in the case of a will begins to run on the date of the testator's death.

2) Revocable Trusts—Date Trust Becomes Irrevocable

In the case of revocable trusts, the perpetuities period begins to run on the date the trust becomes irrevocable. This will be at the settlor's death unless the settlor amends the trust, making it irrevocable, during his lifetime.

3) Irrevocable Trusts—Date Trust Is Created

The perpetuities period for irrevocable trusts begins to run on the date the trust is created.

4) Deeds—Date Deed Is Delivered with Intent to Pass Title

In the case of a deed, the perpetuities period begins to run on the date the deed is delivered with the intent to pass title.

b. "Must Vest"

To be valid under the Rule, it must be shown that the interest created in the transferee must vest, regardless of what might happen, within lives in being plus 21 years. An interest becomes "vested" for purposes of the Rule when: (i) it becomes a present possessory estate, or (ii) it becomes an indefeasibly vested remainder or a vested remainder subject to total divestment. Remember that the Rule is applicable only to future interests created in third persons; consequently, the Rule generally applies only to contingent remainders, executory interests, and vested remainders subject to open.

Examples: 1) "To A for life, then to A's children for their lives, and on the death of the last survivor of A's children, to B in fee simple." At the time of this disposition, A has two very young children and is quite capable of having more children in the future. (i) A has a present possessory life estate. A's present children have vested remainders in life estates that are subject to open in favor of any future children born to A. There is

a contingent remainder in a life estate in A's unborn children—but this interest is valid under the Rule because the children's life estates will vest at their birth, which will be in A's lifetime. B has an indefeasibly vested remainder in fee simple. (ii) B's interest is valid under the Rule even though it may be years before B (or her successors) is entitled to present possession and enjoyment of the property, and even though B (or her successors) may not succeed to present possession and enjoyment until the death of some person not now in being (*i.e.,* a future-born child of A may be the last survivor of A's children). Despite all this, B's interest is valid under the Rule because it is an ***indefeasibly vested remainder from the time of its creation***.

2) "To A for life, then to B; but if at B's death she is not survived by children, then in that event to C." (i) A has a present possessory life estate. B has a vested remainder subject to total divestment in fee simple. C has a shifting executory interest in fee simple. (ii) C's interest is valid under the Rule. B's is the relevant life that can be used to show that C's interest will vest within the perpetuities period. If B dies in A's lifetime not survived by children, C's interest will become an indefeasibly vested remainder. If B survives A and thereafter dies not survived by children, C's executory interest will become a present possessory estate. Of course, B may die in A's lifetime (or after A's death) leaving children surviving her, in which case C's interest is extinguished. But that does not matter; the Rule requires that an interest must vest, ***if it does vest*** ("if at all"), within lives in being plus 21 years.

3) "To A for life, and on her death to such of her children as attain the age of 35." At the time this disposition takes effect, A is a 60-year-old woman who has had a hysterectomy. She has two children, ages 30 and 25. Under the common law Rule, here is what might happen: A ***might*** give birth to a child (defying medical science in the process). Then A's other two children might die before attaining age 35; then A might die before the afterborn attained his 14th birthday. (Key: 35 minus 21 is 14.) The afterborn child lives on to attain age 35. If these events were to occur, the remainder to such of A's children as attain age 35 would vest remotely. Because these events ***might*** occur, the remainder violates the Rule; it is stricken.

1) "Wait and See" Rule

A majority of states have modified the "must vest, if at all" rule above. Under the modified approach, these states suspend judgment as to whether the interest in question is good or void. Potentially, they wait until the end of the perpetuities period. If the interest in question ***actually*** vests during the period, it is good; if it does not vest or fail during that period, it is void. Until the end of the perpetuities period, it is impossible to know for sure whether the interest is good or not.

Example: Consider Example 3), above: "To A for life, and on her death to such of her children as attain the age of 35." Under the "wait and see" approach, the courts would inquire as to whether ***in fact*** any child of A reaches the age of 35 within 21 years after A's death. If one or more of A's children does so, the remainder is valid; if none does so, the remainder is void.

c. "If at All"

This simply means that the interest does not have to vest within the perpetuities period in order to be valid; after all, many contingent remainders never vest because the condition precedent to their taking is not satisfied.

Examples: 1) "To A for life, and on A's death to B if B is then living." A has a life estate, B has a contingent remainder, and the transferor has a reversion. B may never take, for she may predecease A. But if B does take ("if at all"), her interest will vest—here, will become a possessory estate—on A's death, when we will know whether B has survived A. In this case, B is "her own life in being," for the condition precedent to B's taking must occur, if it does occur, within B's lifetime. B's interest is valid under the Rule.

2) "To A in fee, but on the express condition that if marijuana is ever smoked on the premises during B's lifetime or within 21 years after B's death, then and in that event to B in fee." A has a fee simple subject to an executory interest; B has an executory interest in fee simple. B's interest might not take, for marijuana might not be smoked on the premises during B's lifetime or within 21 years thereafter. But if B's interest does take, by the terms of the disposition it must take during B's lifetime or within 21 years thereafter. B's interest is valid under the Rule.

d. "Lives in Being"

The law allows any lives to be used to show the validity or invalidity of an interest, but no lives are of any help unless they are somehow ***connected with the vesting of an interest***. The measuring lives need not be given a beneficial interest in the property, and they need not even be expressly referred to in the instrument, but there must be some connection that insures vesting or failure of the interest within the perpetuities period.

Examples: 1) "To A for life, then to such of A's children as attain the age of 21." Here, the relevant measuring life is A. All of A's children are going to attain age 21, ***if at all***, within 21 years after A's death. (This includes a child in the mother's womb at A's death, for the perpetuities period includes any period of gestation actually involved.)

2) T's will devises her residuary estate "to such of my nephews and nieces as attain the age of 21." At the time of T's death, she has two brothers and six nephews and nieces, all of whom are under age 21. Is the gift valid under the Rule? The answer: It depends. Specifically, it depends on whether T's parents are living. The ***relevant measuring lives*** are T's brothers and sisters, because all of T's nephews and nieces will attain age 21, if at all, within 21 years after their parents' deaths. If T's parents are dead, her two brothers are all the brothers she is ever going to have; and T's nephews and nieces will be the children of these brothers. The disposition is valid.

But if T's parents are alive, they ***might*** have another child (call him Excelsior), a brother or sister of T not alive at T's death. Then T's two brothers and six nephews and nieces who were alive at T's death might die. Then Excelsior might have a child who lives to attain age 21—more than 21 years after any life in being. Because this might happen, the disposition is invalid under the Rule.

1) Who Can Be Used as Measuring Lives

In all the examples in this chapter, the measuring lives used to show the validity or invalidity of interests are referred to or are indirectly involved in the disposition itself. It is a common drafting practice to use a ***"perpetuities saving clause"*** (i) to make sure that the Rule has not been accidentally violated, for the Rule is difficult to master; and (ii) sometimes to extend the duration of trusts to the maximum extent permitted under the Rule. The clause reads something like this: "Notwithstanding anything herein to the contrary, any trust created hereunder shall terminate, if it has not previously terminated, 21 years after the death of the survivor of the following named persons: ____________; and the remaining principal and undistributed income of such trusts shall be distributed to . . . ."

In the blanks are inserted the names of the persons to be used as "artificial" measuring lives. Most commonly, the descendants then living of the transferor are specifically named. Alternatively, the clause might provide: "after the death of the survivor of all my descendants who shall be living at the time of my death"—this clause works in a will but does not work in an irrevocable trust. A few more aggressive draftsmen will name 10 healthy babies born in some local hospital on the day the instrument is executed—the probability is that this will permit the trust to run for 100 years.

2) Reasonable Number of Human Lives Can Be Used

Animals and organizations cannot be used as measuring lives; only humans can be used as measuring lives. Also, the number of measuring lives must be reasonable.

Examples: 1) "The trust will terminate 21 years after the death of the survivor of all persons listed in the Manhattan telephone directory." Clearly impermissible.

2) "The trust will terminate 21 years after the death of the survivor of all the descendants of Queen Victoria who are alive at the time of my death." This "royal lives" clause was widely used in England shortly after the turn of the century, and the English courts grudgingly sustained it. If the name of some currently famous person were used in this fashion, it is highly questionable whether American courts would sustain the disposition.

e. Interests Exempt from Rule

1) Gift Over to Second Charity

A charitable trust may last forever (*i.e.,* neither the Rule Against Perpetuities nor any analogous rule applies). However, like any other gift, a gift for charitable purposes is void for remoteness if it is contingent upon the happening of an event that may not occur within the perpetuity period. The only exception to this rule is that if there is a gift to Charity A, followed by a gift over to Charity B upon a possibly remote event, the gift over is valid. Remember, this is the charity-to-charity exception. The Rule Against Perpetuities applies to dispositions over from a ***charity to an individual*** on a remote condition, ***and*** to dispositions over from an ***individual to a charity*** on a remote condition.

Examples: 1) "To the Georgetown YMCA for so long as the premises are used for YMCA purposes; and when they shall cease to be so used, then and in that event to the American Cancer Society." The YMCA has a fee simple subject to an executory interest; the Cancer Society has a shifting executory interest. The gift over to the Cancer Society is valid under the charity-to-charity exception to the Rule.

2) "To the Georgetown YMCA for so long as the premises are used for YMCA purposes; and when they shall cease to be so used, then and in that event to John Hancock, his heirs, successors, and assigns." Classifying the interests without regard to the Rule, the YMCA would have a fee simple subject to an executory interest; Hancock would have a shifting executory interest—which is stricken because it violates the Rule. The YMCA has a fee simple determinable, and the transferor has a possibility of reverter.

3) "To John Hancock, his heirs, successors, and assigns, provided that no marijuana is ever smoked on the premises; and if marijuana is ever smoked on the premises, to the Georgetown YMCA." Classifying interests without regard to the Rule, Hancock would have a fee simple subject to an executory interest; the YMCA would have a shifting executory interest—which is stricken because it violates the Rule. Thus, Hancock has a fee simple absolute.

2) Vested Interests

A vested remainder in an individual is not subject to the Rule. Thus, a devise "to A for life, then to A's children for life, then to B in fee simple" is wholly valid. B has a presently vested remainder. It may vest in ***possession*** long after lives in being if A leaves some surviving children born after the testator's death, but the remainder to B is presently vested in interest, and that is what counts.

a) Compare—Class Gifts Are Subject to Rule

Vested remainders in a class, however, are subject to the Rule ***so long as the class remains open***.

3) Reversionary Interests

Reversions, possibilities of reverter, and rights of entry are all vested in interest and hence are ***not subject to the Rule Against Perpetuities***. (Even so, in many states, there are statutes expressly limiting the duration of possibilities of reverter or rights of entry.)

a) **Compare—Executory Interests Are Subject to Rule**

Possibilities of reverter and rights of entry, which are exempt from the Rule, must be carefully distinguished from executory interests, which are subject to the Rule. Remember that executory interests are created in ***transferees***; possibilities of reverter and rights of entry are created only in the ***grantor*** (or the ***testator's heirs*** if a will is involved). An understanding of this distinction has frequently been tested by the bar examiners.

Example: O conveys Blackacre "to School so long as it is used for educational purposes, and when it is no longer so used, to A." A has an executory interest that violates the Rule because it may vest in possession many years after all lives in being are dead. Because any interest that violates the Rule is void and is stricken from the instrument, this leaves a determinable fee in the school and a possibility of reverter in O. O can now, by a second deed, transfer her possibility of reverter to A (if possibilities of reverter have been made transferable by statute in the jurisdiction). To get a possibility of reverter in A, two pieces of paper are required: one creating the possibility of reverter in O; the second transferring it to A.

f. **Consequence of Violating the Rule—Interest Is Stricken**

An interest that violates the Rule is void and is stricken (subject to the possible application of a perpetuities reform statute). However, all other interests created in the instrument of transfer that are valid under the Rule are given effect.

1) **Exception—"Infectious Invalidity"**

There is an important exception to the preceding statement. Under the principle of "infectious invalidity," if the invalid gift is an essential part of the transferor's dispositive scheme, such that to strike this interest and give effect to the remaining interests would be to subvert the transferor's intent—if it is determined that the transferor would prefer that the entire disposition fail—then the entire disposition is void.

Example: Irrevocable Trust A directs the trustee "to pay the income to my brother's children for life, and on the death of my brother's last surviving child, to pay the principal to the issue of my brother's children." The gift to "the issue of my brother's children" is void because the brother might have a child born ***after the creation of the trust*** (who would thus not be a life in being). That child might not die within 21 years after the death of the last child living at the time the trust was created. After the invalid interest is stricken, the brother's children have a life estate in the income, and the settlor has a reversion in the principal. However, Trust B provides that if any provision of Trust A is invalid, any income and principal from Trust A should be held in trust for the benefit of the brother's children and their issue. By striking out all the gifts in Trust A, valid and invalid, and by giving effect to Trust B, the settlor's presumed intent to benefit his brother's children and their issue may be substantially carried out. [New England Trust Co. v. Sanger, 149 N.E.2d 598 (Mass. 1958)]

2. The Rule in Operation—Common Pitfall Cases

a. Executory Interest Following Defeasible Fee Violates the Rule

An executory interest that follows a defeasible fee, with no limit on the time within which it must vest, violates the Rule Against Perpetuities and is stricken. The effect on the remaining fee estate depends on whether the estate is determinable or subject to a condition subsequent. If the defeasible fee is phrased in durational terms (*e.g.,* "for so long as," "until"), the estate will still terminate upon the happening of the stated event and the grantor will have a possibility of reverter. In contrast, if the fee is subject to a condition subsequent, the condition is also stricken and the estate becomes a fee simple absolute.

Examples: 1) "To John Brown for so long as no marijuana is smoked on the premises; and if marijuana is ever smoked on the premises, then to Candy Barr." (i) John Brown has a fee simple subject to an executory interest; Candy Barr has an executory interest in fee simple. (ii) Candy's interest violates the Rule. Things may stay quiet for generations, long beyond 21 years after the deaths of John and Candy (the only relevant lives in this case). Then someone might light up, triggering the executory interest. Because this ***might*** happen, the executory interest might vest (*i.e.,* might become a possessory estate) long after lives in being plus 21 years. Candy's interest violates the Rule, and it is stricken. This leaves a fee simple determinable in John Brown, and a possibility of reverter in the transferor. The possibility of reverter is valid; retained interests in the transferor are not subject to the Rule.

What if marijuana is smoked on the premises within five years after the transfer, well within lives in being plus 21 years, meaning that in actuality there was no remote vesting? It does not matter. Under the Rule we do not "wait and see." (*But see* 1.b.1), *supra.*) It is ***what might happen*** that counts, viewing the facts as they exist ***at the time the interest is created***. What actually happens is irrelevant.

2) "To John Brown; provided, however, that if marijuana is ever smoked on the premises, then to Candy Barr." (i) John Brown has a fee simple subject to an executory interest; Candy Barr has an executory interest in fee simple. (ii) Candy's interest violates the Rule, under the analysis given in Example 1). Again we strike Candy's interest—leaving John Brown with a fee simple absolute. (Contrast this with the result in Example 1), where the transferor had a possibility of reverter. This is the result of two different forms of expressing the gift to John Brown. Whenever a fee simple determinable is created ("so long as"), the transferor automatically has a possibility of reverter. But when a fee on a condition subsequent is created, the transferor does not have a right of entry unless the right of entry is expressly raised.)

b. Age Contingency Beyond Age Twenty-One in Open Class

A gift to an open class conditioned upon the members surviving to an age beyond 21 violates the Rule Against Perpetuities.

Example: "To A for life, then to such of A's children as live to attain the age of 25." At the time of this disposition, A has two children: X (age 12) and Y (age nine). (i) A has a life estate; there is a contingent remainder in A's children who live to attain age 25, and a reversion in the transferor (for none of A's children may ever reach age 25). (ii) The remainder to A's children violates the Rule. After this transfer, A ***might have another child*** (Z); before this afterborn child (who cannot be used as a life in being) attains age four, A, X, and Y might die; then Z might live on to age 25, at which time the remainder to A's children would vest in Z. But if this were to happen (and it might), the remainder would vest beyond lives in being plus 21 years. Because the interest might vest remotely, it is stricken.

c. **The Fertile Octogenarian**

A woman is ***conclusively presumed*** to be capable of bearing children regardless of her age or medical condition.

Example: Suppose, in the preceding example, X and Y were age 24 and 22, respectively, and A was a 60-year-old woman who has undergone a hysterectomy. Under the "remote possibilities" test, it is ***possible*** for a woman, of whatever age and medical condition, to bear children. Thus, A might have another child, Z. The remainder to A's children violates the Rule.

d. **The Unborn Widow or Widower**

The problem is that the term "widow" (and "widower"), like "heir," is a technical word with a technical meaning: You do not know who a person's widow (or widower) is until he dies and you can determine to whom he was married at his death.

Example: "To A for life, then to his widow for life; and on the death of A's widow, to such of A's descendants as are then living." (i) A has a life estate; there is a contingent remainder in a life estate in his widow; there is a contingent remainder in fee simple in A's descendants; and the transferor has a reversion. (ii) The remainder in the descendants violates the Rule. Although A is now happily married, he might divorce his wife (or she might die), and A might marry someone who was not alive at the time the interest was created. A might have a child by this widow; then everyone now on the scene might die; the ***widow might live for more than 21 years after the death of all lives in being***, then die—leaving the afterborn child or children as "A's descendants then living."

e. **The Administrative Contingency**

A gift that is conditioned on an administrative contingency (*e.g.,* admission of will to probate) violates the Rule. The key question is "under the facts as they existed at the time of the gift, what might happen?"

Example: Disposition of residuary estate "per stirpes to such of my descendants as are living at the time my will is admitted to probate." Alternatively, a will of a German national written during World War II: "to such of my relations in Germany as are living at the time World War II is officially declared at an end." Under the "what might happen" approach of the common law Rule, wills are not probated, wars do not come to an end,

decrees of distribution are never entered, etc. Moreover, because no person's lifetime is connected to the condition attached to this type of gift, we cannot use a life in being; we must use the "period in gross" of 21 years. And because the will "might not" be probated within 21 years, the gift is void.

The fact that the testator's will is in fact probated three weeks after her death does not matter. We do not wait and see. (*But see* 1.b.1), *supra.*) Rather, looking from the time of the testator's death, and taking into account facts as they existed at that time, the question is what might happen.

f. Options and Rights of First Refusal

An ***option*** creates in the optionee a right to purchase the property on terms provided in the option. A ***right of first refusal*** (or "preemptive right") gives the optionee the right to purchase the property only if the seller accepts a third party's offer to purchase, and usually on the same terms as that offer. Options and rights of first refusal are treated as if they were executory interests. If the option is structured so that it ***might*** be exercised later than the end of the Rule's period, it is usually held void.

Examples: 1) A is a subdivision developer and gives B an option to purchase a lot in the subdivision "to be exercised within 60 days after the City Council grants approval for the filing of a subdivision plat." While the parties may expect this to occur soon, it is ***possible*** that it will not occur within 21 years after any life in being at the creation of the option. Hence, the option may be held void.

2) O conveys "to A and her heirs an option to purchase Blackacre for $25,000." This option is not limited to A's life, but can be exercised by A's heirs and their heirs long after A's death. Thus, the option is void.

1) Reasonable Time Limit May Be Inferred

A significant minority of courts, in applying the Rule to these interests, will construe the option as lasting only for a reasonable time, which is invariably less than 21 years, and thus will uphold it. Under this view, the option in the example above would be sustained on the ground that the parties intended it to expire if the City Council failed to act within a reasonable time, less than 21 years. Similarly, if the parties to the option are natural persons, some courts construe the option as lasting only for their lifetimes; hence, it is valid under the Rule. Furthermore, the Uniform Statutory Rule Against Perpetuities (*infra*, 4.d.) excludes options in commercial transactions from the Rule's application.

2) Options Connected to Leaseholds

If a tenant under a lease has an option to purchase the leased premises during the lease term, the Rule is not applied, no matter how long the term. If a tenant assigns the leasehold, the option generally is considered a running covenant, exercisable by the assignee in the absence of contrary intent. However, a tenant may attempt to transfer the option to some other party, thereby separating it from the leasehold estate. While some courts do not permit the option to be transferred separately, most courts hold that the transferability of the option depends on the original

parties' intent when they entered into the lease and option agreement. If the court finds that the option has been separated from the leasehold estate, so that it is no longer exercisable by the tenant, the option becomes subject to the Rule Against Perpetuities.

3. Application of the Rule to Class Gifts

a. "Bad-as-to-One, Bad-as-to-All" Rule

The general principle that the Rule does not invalidate interests that "vest" within the perpetuities period ***does not apply to vested remainders subject to open***. The class gift rule, sometimes called the "all-or-nothing" rule, requires that:

(i) The ***class must close*** within the perpetuities period; and

(ii) All conditions precedent for ***every*** member of the class must be satisfied, if at all, within the perpetuities period.

If it is possible that a disposition might vest remotely with respect to any member of the class, the ***entire class gift is invalid***.

Examples: 1) "To A for life, then to such of A's children as live to attain the age of 35." At the time of this disposition, A has two children: X (age 38) and Y (age 33). (i) A has a life estate. X has a vested remainder subject to open. There is a contingent remainder in such of A's other children as live to attain the age of 35. (ii) The remainder to A's children violates the Rule; the transferor has a reversion in fee. While X's remainder is vested subject to open, it is not vested for purposes of the Rule. Here is what might happen: A might have another child (Z); before Z attains age 14, A, X, and Y might die, etc. The ***gift with respect to any afterborn child of A clearly violates the Rule***; under the "bad-as-to-one, bad-as-to-all" class gift rule, ***the entire class gift is void***.

Why does the "class closing" rule not save the gift? Because X is already age 35, doesn't this mean that the class will close on the life tenant's death? The answer is: yes it does, but this does not help. Although we will close the class at that point, the class as closed might include the afterborn Z, who might be under age 14 at that time; and it still might be more than lives in being plus 21 years before Z's interest might vest.

2) "To A for life, then to A's children for their lives, and on the death of the last survivor of A's children, to A's grandchildren in fee." At the time this disposition takes effect, A is alive and has two children and three grandchildren. A has a life estate, the two children have vested remainders subject to open in a life estate, and the three grandchildren have vested remainders subject to open in fee. The remainder to A's grandchildren is void because every member of the class will not be ascertained until the death of the survivor of A's children; and that surviving child might be born to A after the date of this disposition. Then all of A's children and grandchildren who are lives in being might die and 21 years after their deaths, this afterborn child might give birth to a child

(GC-4); although GC-4's interest would vest at birth, under the hypothesized facts it would vest remotely.

b. Class Closing Rules May Save Disposition

In some cases, the "rule of convenience" applicable to class gifts can be relied on to save a gift from the Rule.

Example: "To A for life, and on her death to A's grandchildren in fee." At the time of this disposition, A has two children and three grandchildren. A has a life estate and the grandchildren have vested remainders subject to open. As in the preceding example, A might have an afterborn child who might produce afterborn grandchildren—but there is one difference. Under the "rule of convenience" the ***class will be closed at the time any member of the class can demand a distribution***—here the death of A, a life in being. Consequently, all members of the class who will be permitted to share in the remainder will be determined on A's death.

c. "Gift to Subclass" Exception

Separate gifts vest at different times. Each gift to a subclass may be treated as a separate gift under the Rule.

Example: "To pay the income to A for life, then to A's children for their lives, and as each child of A dies, to distribute the corpus to such child's issue then living, per stirpes." A has two children at the time of this disposition. In this case, the remainder to issue has been made by a gift to subclasses; as each child dies his issue are to take the share on which he was receiving income. With respect to A's two children now alive, the class of "issue then living" will be determined on their deaths; the gift is good. If A should have another child after the date of this disposition, the ***remainder to such afterborn child's issue is void*** because it might vest beyond the lives in being plus 21 years.

d. Per Capita Gift Exception

When there is a separate gift of a fixed sum to each class member, each gift is tested separately under the Rule.

Example: T's will bequeaths "$1,000 each to such of A's grandchildren as live to attain the age of 21, whether alive at my death or born thereafter." At T's death, A has two children and five grandchildren. Here, we have a per capita gift to each member of the class; there is no problem of knowing within the perpetuities period the number of class members who share in an aggregate gift, and thus the size of each share. Here, the amount to be received by each member is ascertainable without reference to the number of persons in the class. The bequest is valid for all grandchildren by A's two children who were alive at T's death. (This includes all future-born grandchildren as well as the five now on the scene, for all such grandchildren will reach 21, if at all, within 21 years after their parent's death.)

However, the ***bequest is void for any grandchildren by a child born to A after T's death***. Such an afterborn child cannot be used as a life in being.

4. **Perpetuities Reform Legislation**
Most states have enacted one of the following types of statutes designed to eliminate some of the harsh results of the common law Rule Against Perpetuities:

a. A ***"wait and see"*** statute, under which the validity of an interest following one or more life estates is determined on the basis of facts existing at the end of the life estate rather than at the creation of the interest (*see* 1.b.1), *supra*);

b. A ***cy pres*** approach, borrowed from Trusts law, under which an invalid interest is reformed to comply with the Rule and carry out the grantor's intent as nearly as possible;

c. A statute dealing with ***specific perpetuities problems*** (*e.g.,* age contingencies reduced to age 21, women over age 55 presumed incapable of childbearing, gift to widow presumed to mean the person who was the spouse on the date the gift was created); or

d. The ***Uniform Statutory Rule Against Perpetuities***, which provides an alternative 90-year vesting period. The Uniform Rule takes a "wait and see" approach in determining whether an interest actually vests within 90 years.

5. **Technique for Analysis of Perpetuities Problems**
In applying the Rule Against Perpetuities, these three steps should be followed:

a. Determine What Interests Are Created
First, determine what interests are created, applying the proper future interests labels, as though there were no Rule Against Perpetuities.

b. Apply the Rule
Determine the measuring life or lives that can be used to show either that the interest must vest within lives in being plus 21 years ***or*** that the interest might not vest within that period. At this step, assume that there is no such thing as a perpetuities reform statute, for the statute is not brought into play unless there is a perpetuities problem.

c. Apply Reform Statute
If the particular jurisdiction has a perpetuities reform statute that is triggered by the perpetuities violation, apply the statute to reform or save the gift.

F. THE RULE AGAINST RESTRAINTS ON ALIENATION

As a general rule, any restriction on the transferability of a legal (as distinguished from an equitable) interest in property is void: The restriction violates the common law Rule Against Restraints on Alienation. "Restraint on alienation" means an express restriction on the transferability of property. Like the Rule Against Perpetuities, this is a rule of public policy that is designed to prevent property from being tied up and taken out of commerce.

1. **Types of Restraints on Alienation**
There are three types of restraints on alienation: (i) ***disabling*** restraints, under which any attempted transfer is ineffective; (ii) ***forfeiture*** restraints, under which an attempted transfer results in a forfeiture of the interest; and (iii) ***promissory*** restraints, under which an attempted transfer breaches a covenant.

Examples: 1) Property is transferred to A in fee simple, with the added proviso that "neither A nor any of her children shall have the right to transfer the land or any interest therein." Under this restriction, if given effect (***it is not***), any attempted transfer would simply be ineffective. This is a ***disabling restraint***.

2) Property is transferred to A in fee simple, with the added proviso that "if A shall attempt to transfer the land or any interest therein during her lifetime, her estate shall cease, and title therein shall vest in B." This is a ***forfeiture restraint***.

3) Property is transferred to A in fee simple, with the added proviso that "A hereby covenants that she will not transfer the land or any interest therein without [the transferor's] prior written consent." Under this ***promissory restraint***, if given effect, the remedy is injunction or damages for breach of contract.

2. Restraints on a Fee Simple

a. Total Restraints

Any total restraint on a fee simple—either forfeiture, disabling, or promissory—is ***void***. The grantee may ignore the restraint and freely transfer the property.

b. Partial Restraints

A partial restraint is one that purports to restrict the power to transfer to specific persons, or by a specific method, or until a specific time.

1) Reasonable Restraints Doctrine

Although absolute restraints on fee simple estates are void, a restraint ***for a limited time*** and ***for a reasonable purpose*** is likely to be upheld.

Example: A owns and resides in a house. He conveys a one-half interest in the house to his brother, B, including in the deed a covenant that "during their joint lifetimes, each party promises not to convey his interest to any other person without the consent of the other party." This promissory restraint is limited to the joint lifetimes of the parties and is a reasonable way to ensure that neither party will be faced with the prospect of residing with a stranger. The restraint would probably be upheld.

2) Discriminatory Restraints

Restraints prohibiting the transfer or use of property to or by a person of a specified racial, religious, or ethnic group are ***not enforceable***.

a) Fourteenth Amendment

Judicial enforcement of a covenant forbidding use of property by persons of a particular race is ***discriminatory state action*** forbidden by the Fourteenth Amendment to the United States Constitution. [Shelley v. Kraemer, 334 U.S. 1 (1948)]

Example: O conveys Blackacre "to A and his heirs, and A promises that Blackacre will never be used or occupied by nonwhite persons." Thereafter A sells to B, a black man, who moves onto Blackacre. O sues for an injunction prohibiting B from

using Blackacre, and sues A for damages for having sold to B. Injunction and damages are judicial remedies ordinarily available for breach of a covenant. The court cannot grant O either an injunction or damages, because such judicial action would be state action interfering with B's right to enjoy property free of racial discrimination. [Barrows v. Jackson, 346 U.S. 249 (1953)]

b) **Fair Housing Act**
Discriminatory restrictions may also violate the Fair Housing Act of 1968. Recording a deed with a racial restriction is prohibited by the Act. [42 U.S.C. §3604(c)]

3. **Restraints on a Life Estate**

a. **Legal Life Estate**
Forfeiture and promissory restraints on life estates are valid. A life estate is inalienable as a practical matter because few would be willing to pay full value for an estate of uncertain duration; thus, little is lost by giving effect to the transferor's intention to restrict the estate's transferability. (However, ***disabling*** restraints on legal life estates are void.)

b. **Equitable Life Estate**
The rule applicable to restrictions on equitable interests (*i.e.,* those held in trust) is the exact opposite of the rule applicable to legal interests. Spendthrift clauses, which are true disabling restraints, are given effect in the great majority of American jurisdictions. (*See* Trusts outline.)

4. **Other Valid Restraints on Alienation**

a. **Forfeiture Restraint on Transferability of a Future Interest**
A forfeiture restraint on the transferability of a future interest, during the period when the interest is a future interest, is valid.

b. **Reasonable Restrictions in Commercial Transactions**
The courts tend to uphold restrictions on transferability that arise in the context of a commercial transaction on the theory that the restriction appears in an agreement entered into by the parties, it is a product of their bargaining, and presumably serves a useful purpose in facilitating the parties' objectives. Thus, restrictions on transferability that are part of a bargained-for agreement, as distinguished from a donative transaction, are valid.

Examples: 1) O borrows money from M Bank and gives the bank a mortgage on land. The mortgage provides that the land shall not be transferable by O without M's consent, and that if the land is transferred without consent, the entire indebtedness shall be accelerated and shall become immediately due and payable. This "due on sale" restriction on transferability is reasonable because M has an interest in approving who shall be the transferee of the land in which it has a security interest.

2) A, B, C, and D each own 25% of the stock in a closely held corporation. The articles of incorporation provide that no shareholder shall transfer her stock without the consent of a majority of the other shareholders. This restriction on transferability is valid because, due to the closely held nature of the business, the shareholders have a legitimate concern over the identity of their associates.

c. **Right of First Refusal**

The right to have the first opportunity to purchase real estate when it becomes available, or the right to meet any offer, is valid if ***reasonable*** (*e.g.,* by specifying fair market value or other reasonable price). [Restatement (Third) of Property: Servitudes §3.4]

d. **Restrictions on Transferability of Leaseholds**

A provision in a lease prohibiting the lessee's assignment or subletting of her leasehold interest without the consent of the landlord is given effect in all jurisdictions. (*See* II.E.3., *infra.*)

G. CONCURRENT ESTATES

Any of the estates in land previously discussed can be held concurrently by several persons. These persons all have the right to the enjoyment and possession of the land at the same time. Three of the chief forms of concurrent ownership in land are discussed here: joint tenancy, tenancy by the entirety, and tenancy in common.

1. Joint Tenancy

A joint tenancy can be created between two or more co-tenants. Its distinguishing feature is the ***right of survivorship***. Conceptually, when one joint tenant dies, the property is freed from his concurrent interest; the survivor or survivors retain an undivided right in the property, which is no longer subject to the interest of the deceased co-tenant. The survivors do not succeed to the decedent's interest; they hold free of it.

a. **Creation**

1) **Four Unities Required**

At common law, four unities are required to create a joint tenancy:

a) Unity of ***time*** (interests vested at the same time);

b) Unity of ***title*** (interests acquired by the same instrument);

c) Unity of ***interest*** (interests of the same ***type*** and ***duration***); and

d) Unity of ***possession*** (interests give identical rights to enjoyment).

2) **Modern Law**

The above requirements have been eroded in some jurisdictions; *e.g.,* by statute in some states, an owner can create a joint tenancy in herself and another by a single deed (she need not use a "strawman" conveyance), even though the unities of "time" and "title" are not satisfied. Similarly, as indicated below, a number

of transactions are no longer found to sever a joint tenancy despite the seeming absence of continued unities.

3) **Express Language Required**
Under modern law, ***joint tenancies are disfavored***. Hence, there must be a clear expression of intent to create this estate, or it will not be recognized. The usual language required is "to A and B as ***joint tenants with right of survivorship***." Today, when two or more persons take property by a single conveyance, a tenancy in common, not a joint tenancy, is presumed. A joint tenancy results only when an intention to create a right of survivorship is clearly expressed.

b. **Severance**
A joint tenancy can be terminated by a suit for ***partition***, which can be brought by any joint tenant. It may also be terminated by various acts by any joint tenant.

1) **Inter Vivos Conveyance by One Joint Tenant**
An inter vivos conveyance by one joint tenant of her undivided interest destroys the joint tenancy so that the transferee takes the interest as a tenant in common and not as a joint tenant. This rule applies to both ***voluntary and involuntary*** conveyances (even secret conveyances).

a) **When More than Two Joint Tenants**
When property is held in joint tenancy by three or more joint tenants, a conveyance by one of them destroys the joint tenancy ***only as to the conveyor's interest***. The other joint tenants continue to hold in joint tenancy as between themselves, while the grantee holds her interest as a tenant in common with them.

b) **Transactions that May Not Result in Severance**

(1) **Judgment Liens**
In most jurisdictions, when a plaintiff obtains a money judgment against a defendant, that judgment becomes a lien on the defendant's real estate in the county where the judgment is docketed. (This is automatic in some states; in others, the lien must be recorded in the real estate records.) The lien then "runs with the land," burdening it until the judgment is paid or until the lien expires under a statute of limitations (*e.g.,* 10 years). Suppose such a lien is obtained against one of several joint tenants but not against the others. Does it sever the joint tenancy, converting it into a tenancy in common? The majority view is that it does not; a lien is not considered a sufficiently substantial "conveyance" to destroy the unities of time and title. However, if the plaintiff who obtained the judgment then proceeds to enforce it by ***foreclosure*** (often termed a "judgment sale"), the sheriff's deed issued to the buyer at that sale ***will sever*** the joint tenancy. That follows from the fact that the sheriff's deed conveys the defendant's full title.

Example: A and B own land as joint tenants with right of survivorship. P sues A on a tort claim, and obtains and records a judgment. If A dies at that point, B owns the entire land (by virtue of the right of survivorship), and P has a lien on nothing. However, assume that P has a judgment sale, and a sheriff's deed is issued to X, who buys at the sale. Then A dies. B and X each own a one-half interest in the land as tenants in common.

(2) **Mortgages**

In the majority of states, a mortgage is regarded as a lien on title, and one joint tenant's execution of a mortgage on her interest does not by itself cause a severance. (Rather, the severance occurs only if the mortgage is foreclosed and the property sold.) But in the minority of states, which regard a mortgage as a transfer of title, the transfer destroys the unity of title and severs the joint tenancy.

Example: A, B, and C are joint tenants. A mortgages her interest to Lender, who records. Thereafter, A dies and Lender seeks to enforce her mortgage on an undivided one-third interest in the property. In a state following the "lien theory" of mortgages, Lender loses. A's mortgage did not sever the joint tenancy. Lender's rights were lost when A died prior to foreclosure. A's interest evaporated, and with it Lender's security interest.

(3) **Leases**

Theoretically, when one joint tenant leases her interest in jointly held property, the lease destroys the unity of interest and thereby should effect a severance (which is the view taken by some states). But other states hold that the joint tenancy is not destroyed but is merely temporarily suspended (for the length of the lease).

(a) **Death of Lessor**

There is a split among the states following the latter view, on what happens if the lessor/joint tenant dies before the end of the lease. Some courts hold that because the lessor's own right to possession would cease on her death, so must the right of any lessee (*i.e.,* the lessor could not convey more than she had). Others hold that the lease operates as a "temporary severance," and the remaining joint tenant's survivorship rights are therefore postponed until the end of the lease.

2) **Contract to Convey by One Joint Tenant**

In most states, a severance also results where one joint tenant executes a valid contract to convey her interest to another, even though no actual transfer of title has yet been made. The contract to convey is enforceable in equity, and hence is treated as an effective transfer of an equitable interest. Thus, if the vendor dies before the title is transferred, the purchaser is entitled to a deed from the vendor's estate and becomes a tenant in common with the original joint tenant or tenants.

a) **Compare—Executory Contract by All Joint Tenants**

There is a split as to whether an executory contract to sell, entered into by all the joint tenants, will terminate the joint tenancy. Suppose that on January 1, A and B, joint tenants, contract with X to sell and deliver title to Blackacre to X on February 1. A dies on January 15. Two questions arise: (i) On February 1, is B entitled to the full sales proceeds as surviving joint tenant, or is A's estate entitled to one-half (on the theory that the January 1 contract worked an equitable conversion, which created in the vendors a contract right to receive money that was held in tenancy in common)? And, (ii) will X have to obtain a deed not only from B but also from A's administrator on the theory that the retained legal title (for security purposes) was held in tenancy in common?

(1) **Common Law View—Joint Tenancy Continues**
The common law view, still followed by many courts, is that a joint tenancy continues in both the right to the proceeds and the retained legal title, meaning that B gets the full sales proceeds and can give good title.

(2) **Other Courts—Tenancy in Common**
Other jurisdictions, however, proceed on the doctrine of equitable conversion and hold that the executory contract converts A and B's land ownership rights to a mere contract right to receive the purchase price (which they hold as tenants in common because of the statutory presumption favoring such tenancies). Further, the legal title to the land, retained for security purposes, is also held to be in tenancy in common.

3) **Testamentary Disposition by One Joint Tenant Has No Effect**
A joint tenancy is not terminated where a joint tenant executes a will devising her interest to another or dies with such a will in effect. The reason is that a will is ambulatory (effective only at death) and hence is inoperative as to joint tenancy property, because at the instant of death the decedent's rights in the property evaporate. (The result would be contra if all joint tenants had agreed that the decedent could devise her interest; but in such a case, the agreement itself would cause the severance.)

a) **Compare—"Secret" Deeds**
As indicated above, an inter vivos conveyance severs a joint tenancy. This is true even though the deed is kept "secret" and the interest transferred is to take effect only upon the death of the grantor. However, if the grantee does not know about the deed, the grantee's acceptance ***after*** the death of the grantor does not relate back to defeat the right of survivorship. (*See* VI.C.4.b., *infra*.)

4) **Effect of One Joint Tenant's Murdering Another**
Some states have passed statutes under which the felonious and intentional killing of one joint tenant by another joint tenant operates as a severance. In other states, the surviving joint tenant holds the ill-gained portion on a constructive trust for the decedent's estate. Thus, the homicidal survivor keeps her original share but does not profit from her felony.

2. **Tenancy by the Entirety**
A tenancy by the entirety is a marital estate akin to a joint tenancy between husband and

wife. It is not recognized in community property states, but in some common law jurisdictions, it arises presumptively in any conveyance made to husband and wife.

a. **Right of Survivorship**
The estate carries a right of survivorship, which operates in the same manner as the right of survivorship incident to a joint tenancy.

b. **Severance Limited**
The major distinction between a joint tenancy and a tenancy by the entirety concerns severance. A tenancy by the entirety cannot be terminated by involuntary partition. It can be terminated only by: (i) the death of either spouse (leaving the survivor sole owner of the fee); (ii) divorce (in most states leaving the parties as tenants in common with no right of survivorship); (iii) mutual agreement; or (iv) execution by a joint creditor of ***both*** husband and wife (a creditor of one or the other cannot execute).

c. **Individual Spouse Cannot Convey or Encumber**
In most states, an individual spouse may not convey or encumber tenancy by the entirety property. A deed or mortgage executed by only one spouse is ineffective.

3. **Tenancy in Common**
A tenancy in common is a concurrent estate with no right of survivorship. Each owner has a distinct, proportionate, undivided interest in the property. This interest is freely alienable by inter vivos and testamentary transfer, is inheritable, and is subject to claims of the tenant's creditors. The only "unity" involved is possession: Each tenant is entitled to possession of the whole estate. Today, by statute, multiple grantees are presumed to take as tenants in common. The same is true where multiple transferees take by descent.

4. **Incidents of Co-Ownership**

a. **Possession**
Each co-tenant has the right to possess all portions of the property; no co-tenant has the right to exclusive possession of any part. A co-tenant out of possession cannot bring a possessory action unless there has been an "ouster" by the tenant in possession. A claim of right to exclusive possession can constitute an ouster.

b. **Rents and Profits**
In most jurisdictions (but not all), a co-tenant in possession has the right to retain profits gained by her use of the property. A co-tenant in possession need not share such profits with co-tenants out of possession, nor reimburse them for the rental value of her use of the land, unless there has been an ouster or an agreement to the contrary. However, a co-tenant out of possession has a right to share in ***rents from third parties*** and in ***profits*** derived from a use of the land that reduces its value (*e.g.,* removal of minerals, etc.).

c. **Effect of One Concurrent Owner's Encumbering the Property**
A joint tenant or tenant in common may place a mortgage on her interest, but may not, of course, encumber the other co-tenant's interest. If a tenancy in common is involved, the mortgagee can foreclose only on the mortgaging co-tenant's interest. Likewise, if

a joint tenancy is involved and the mortgage itself does not sever the joint tenancy (*see* 1.b.1)b)(2), *supra*), the mortgagee can foreclose on the mortgagor/co-tenant's interest and the foreclosure sale itself will cause a severance. But in the case of a joint tenancy, the mortgagee runs the risk that the mortgaging co-tenant will die before foreclosure, extinguishing the mortgagee's interest. The same principles apply to judgment liens obtained against an individual co-tenant.

Example: A and B are joint tenants with right of survivorship. A injures P in an accident, and P sues A, obtaining a personal injury judgment against A for $1,000. This judgment is, by statute, a lien on A's one-half interest in the land, but it does not cause a severance. If A dies before the lien is foreclosed and is survived by B, B owns the land free and clear of the lien. But if P forecloses the lien before A's death, the foreclosure sale will cause a severance, and the buyer at the sale will own a one-half interest in the land as a tenant in common with B.

d. Ouster

Under the unity of possession, each co-tenant is entitled to possess and enjoy the whole of the property subject to the equal right of her co-tenant. If one tenant ***wrongfully excludes*** another co-tenant from possession of the whole or any part of the whole of the premises, there is an ouster. The ousted co-tenant is entitled to receive his share of the fair rental value of the property for the time he was wrongfully deprived of possession.

e. Remedy of Partition

A joint tenant or tenant in common has a right to judicial partition, either ***in kind*** (division of the tract into parcels) or ***by sale and division of the proceeds*** (in accordance with the ownership interests as modified by permitted recoupments for improvements, repairs, taxes, and the like). Although partition in kind is generally preferred, partition by sale and division of the proceeds is permitted when a fair and equitable physical division of the property cannot be made. [Nordhausen v. Christner, 338 N.W.2d 754 (Neb. 1983)]

Examples: 1) A and B own a single-family home as joint tenants. A brings an appropriate action to partition the land. Because physical division of the home is not feasible, the court will order a sale of the home and division of the proceeds equally between A and B.

2) A owns a three-fourths interest and B owns a one-fourth interest in a four-acre undeveloped parcel of land as tenants in common. The applicable zoning ordinance requires that a buildable lot contain at least two acres. A seeks to partition the land into a three-acre lot for himself and a one-acre lot for B. B argues that the land should be sold and the proceeds divided between A and B according to their respective shares. B will prevail, because the zoning ordinance makes it impossible to divide the land fairly.

1) Restraint on Partition by Co-Tenants

Although in general, a co-tenant has the right to demand a partition by judicial sale at any time, courts give effect to a provision prohibiting partition by any one co-tenant, provided that the restriction is to ***last for only a reasonable time.***

The restriction is not considered to be an invalid restraint on alienation because (i) any co-tenant can transfer her interest to a third person at any time, and (ii) the restraint can be eliminated if the co-tenants join in a deed to a third person, thereby terminating the co-tenancy relationship.

f. Expenses for Preservation of Property—Contribution

Under certain circumstances, equity courts will compel contribution between concurrent owners.

1) Repairs—Contribution May Be Compelled for Necessary Repairs

A co-tenant who pays more than her pro rata share of the cost of necessary repairs is entitled to contribution from the other co-tenants in actions for accounting or partition. Although the courts are split on whether a co-tenant who makes necessary repairs can maintain an independent action for contribution against the other co-tenants, the majority view is that she can compel contribution, provided she has notified the other co-tenants of the need for repairs. Moreover, several recent decisions authorize contribution even without such notice.

The common law view was that because no co-tenant has a duty to make necessary repairs, a co-tenant who makes such repairs cannot bring an action to compel contribution from the other co-tenants. This is now the minority view.

2) Improvements—No Contribution or Setoff

Generally, there is no right of contribution for the cost of improvements, nor can they be set off in an action for accounting. Only in an action for partition can the value of improvements be recouped.

3) Taxes and Mortgages—Contribution Can Be Compelled

Each co-tenant has a duty to pay her share of taxes and payments due on mortgages on the entire property. A tenant who is not in sole possession can pay the taxes and mortgage payments and then compel contribution from the other co-tenants. However, a co-tenant in sole possession will receive reimbursement only for the amount that exceeds the rental value of the property.

g. Duty of Fair Dealing Among Co-Tenants

A confidential relationship exists among co-tenants. Accordingly, the acquisition by one co-tenant of any outstanding title or lien that might affect the estate held by all the co-tenants is deemed to be an acquisition on behalf of all the other co-tenants as well. Thus, when one co-tenant purchases or otherwise acquires a lienholder's (mortgagee's) claim against the co-tenancy property, she must give the other co-tenants a reasonable time to pay their share and acquire a proportionate interest. Courts carefully scrutinize the fairness of transactions between co-tenants. Lastly, it is difficult for one co-tenant to ***adversely possess*** against other co-tenants. (*See* V.B.5.b., *infra.*)

Example: A and B own land as co-tenants. Neither pays the annual property taxes. The county conducts a tax sale and A buys the property for $10,000. If B is willing to pay A $5,000, many courts will compel A to put the property in co-tenancy again.

II. LANDLORD AND TENANT

A. NATURE OF LEASEHOLD

A leasehold is an estate in land. The tenant has a present possessory interest in the leased premises, and the landlord has a future interest (reversion). Certain rights and liabilities flow from this property relationship between landlord and tenant. The three major types of leasehold estates are ***tenancies for years***, ***periodic tenancies***, and ***tenancies at will***. There is a fourth category called ***tenancies at sufferance***.

1. Tenancies for Years

a. Fixed Period of Time

A tenancy for years is one that is to continue for a fixed period of time. It may be for ***more or less*** than a year (*e.g.,* 10 days or 10 years); it may be determinable (similar to a fee simple determinable) or on condition subsequent. The termination date of a tenancy for years is usually certain. As a result, the tenancy expires at the end of the stated period ***without either party giving notice to the other***. Even if the date of termination is uncertain (*e.g.,* L leases the premises to T "until the end of the war"), ***most courts*** hold that if the parties have attempted to state some period of duration, the lease creates a tenancy for years.

b. Creation

Tenancies for years are normally created by written leases. In most states, the Statute of Frauds requires that a lease creating a tenancy for more than one year be in writing. In addition, most states have statutes that restrict the number of years for which a leasehold estate may be created (*e.g.,* 51 years for farm property and 99 years for urban property). When the lease term exceeds the statutory maximum, most courts hold that the lease is ***entirely*** void. Likewise, where the lease contains an ***option to renew*** for a period beyond the permitted maximum, most courts hold the entire lease void.

c. Termination

A tenancy for years ends ***automatically*** on its termination date.

1) Breach of Covenants

In most tenancy for years leases, the landlord reserves the right to terminate if the tenant breaches any of the leasehold covenants. This reserved power is called the landlord's ***right of entry***.

a) Failure to Pay Rent

In many jurisdictions, if the tenant fails to pay the promised rent, the landlord has the right to terminate the lease ***even in the absence of a reserved right of entry***.

2) Surrender

A tenancy for years also terminates upon surrender. Surrender consists of the tenant giving up his leasehold interest to the landlord and the landlord accepting. Usually the same ***formalities*** are required for the surrender of a leasehold as are necessary for its creation. Thus, a writing is necessary for the surrender of a leasehold if the unexpired term is more than one year.

2. **Periodic Tenancies**
A periodic tenancy is a tenancy that continues from year to year or for successive fractions of a year (*e.g.,* weekly or monthly) until terminated by proper notice by either party. The beginning date must be certain, but the ***termination date is always uncertain*** until notice is given.

All conditions and terms of the tenancy are carried over from one period to the next unless there is a lease provision to the contrary. Periodic tenancies do not violate the rules limiting the length of leaseholds because each party retains the power to terminate upon giving notice.

a. **Creation**
Periodic tenancies can be created in three ways:

1) **By Express Agreement**
Periodic tenancies can be created by express agreement (*e.g.,* "Landlord leases to Tenant from month to month").

2) **By Implication**
A periodic tenancy will be implied if the lease has no set termination but does provide for the payment of rent at specific periods.
Example: "Landlord leases to Tenant at a rent of $1,000 ***payable monthly*** in advance." The reservation of monthly rent will give rise to a periodic tenancy from ***month to month***.

Note: If the lease reserves an annual rent, payable monthly (*e.g.,* "$12,000 per annum, payable $1,000 on the first day of every month commencing January 1"), the majority view is that the periodic tenancy is from ***year to year***.

3) **By Operation of Law**
A periodic tenancy may arise even without an express or implied agreement between the parties.

a) **Tenant Holds Over**
If a tenant for years remains in possession after the termination of his tenancy period, the landlord may elect to treat the tenant as a periodic tenant on the same terms as the original lease. (*See* 5.b., *infra.*)

b) **Lease Invalid**
If a lease is invalid (*e.g.,* because of failure to satisfy the Statute of Frauds) and the tenant nonetheless goes into possession, the tenant's periodic payment of rent will convert what would otherwise be a tenancy at will into a periodic tenancy. The period of the tenancy coincides with the period for which the rent is paid.

b. **Termination—Notice Required**
A periodic tenancy is ***automatically renewed***, from period to period, until proper notice of termination is given by either party. Many jurisdictions have statutorily prescribed the notice required to terminate a periodic tenancy. In general, the guidelines are as follows:

(i) The tenancy must end at the ***end of a "natural" lease period***.

(ii) For a tenancy from year to year, ***six months' notice*** is required.

(iii) For tenancies less than one year in duration, a ***full period in advance*** of the period in question is required by way of notice (*e.g.,* for a month-to-month periodic tenancy, one full month's notice is required).

In general, the notice required to terminate a periodic tenancy must be in ***writing*** and must actually be ***delivered*** to the party in question or deposited at his residence in a manner similar to that required for service of process.

3. Tenancies at Will

A tenancy at will is an estate in land that is terminable at the will of either the landlord or the tenant. To be a tenancy at will, both the landlord and the tenant must have the right to terminate the lease at will.

(i) If the lease gives ***only the landlord*** the right to terminate at will, a ***similar right*** will generally be ***implied in favor of the tenant*** so that the lease creates a tenancy at will.

(ii) If the lease is only at the will of the ***tenant*** (*e.g.,* "for so long as the tenant wishes"), courts usually ***do not imply a right to terminate in favor of the landlord***. Rather, most courts interpret the conveyance as creating a life estate or fee simple, either of which is terminable by the tenant. (If the Statute of Frauds is not satisfied, the conveyance is a tenancy at will.)

a. Creation

A tenancy at will generally arises from a specific understanding between the parties that ***either party may terminate*** the tenancy at any time. Note that unless the parties ***expressly agree*** to a tenancy at will, the payment of regular rent (*e.g.,* monthly, quarterly, etc.) will cause a court to treat the tenancy as a periodic tenancy. Thus, tenancies at will are quite rare. Although a tenancy at will can also arise when the lease is for an indefinite period (one that does not satisfy the requirements for creating a tenancy for years), or when a tenant goes into possession under a lease that does not satisfy the requisite formalities (usually the Statute of Frauds), rent payments will usually convert it to a periodic tenancy.

b. Termination

A tenancy at will may be terminated by ***either party without notice***. However, a reasonable demand to quit the premises is required. A tenancy at will terminates by ***operation of law*** if:

1) Either party ***dies***;

2) The tenant commits ***waste***;

3) The tenant attempts to ***assign*** his tenancy;

4) The ***landlord transfers his interest*** in the property; or

5) The ***landlord executes a term lease*** to a third person.

4. **Tenancies at Sufferance**
A tenancy at sufferance (sometimes called "occupancy at sufferance") arises when a tenant ***wrongfully*** remains in possession after the expiration of a lawful tenancy (*e.g.,* after the stipulated date for the termination of a tenancy for years; or after the landlord has exercised a power of termination). Such a tenant is a wrongdoer and is ***liable for rent***. The tenancy at sufferance lasts only until the landlord takes steps to evict the tenant. No notice is required to end the tenancy, and authorities are divided as to whether this is even an estate in land.

5. **The Hold-Over Doctrine**
When a tenant continues in possession after the termination of his right to possession, the landlord has two choices of action:

a. **Eviction**
The landlord may treat the hold-over tenant as a trespasser and evict him under an unlawful detainer statute.

b. **Creation of Periodic Tenancy**
The landlord may, in his sole discretion, bind the tenant to a new periodic tenancy.

1) **Terms**
The terms and conditions of the expired tenancy (*e.g.,* rent, covenants, etc.) apply to the new tenancy. In ***commercial leases***, if the original lease term was for ***one year or more***, a year-to-year tenancy results from holding over. If the original term was for ***less than one year***, the periodic term is determined by the manner in which the rent was due and payable under the prior tenancy. In ***residential*** leases, however, most courts would rule the tenant a month-to-month tenant (or a week-to-week tenant if the tenant was a roomer paying weekly rent), irrespective of the term of the original lease.
Example: A nonresidential tenant was holding under a six-month term tenancy with rent payable monthly. The tenant holds over and the landlord binds him to a new tenancy. The new periodic tenancy is a month-to-month tenancy.

2) **Altered Terms**
If the landlord notifies the tenant before termination of the tenancy that occupancy after termination will be at an increased rent, the tenant will be held to have acquiesced to the new terms if he does not surrender. The tenant will be held to the new terms ***even if he objects*** to the increased rent, provided that the rent increase is reasonable.

c. **What Does Not Constitute Holding Over**
The landlord cannot bind the tenant to a new tenancy under the hold-over doctrine if: (i) the tenant remains in possession for only a ***few hours*** after termination of the lease, or leaves a few articles of personal property on the premises; (ii) the delay is ***not the tenant's fault*** (*e.g.,* because of severe illness); or (iii) it is a ***seasonal lease*** (*e.g.,* summer cottage).

d. **Double Rent Jeopardy**
Many state statutes provide that if a tenant ***willfully*** remains in possession after his term

expires and after the landlord makes a ***written demand for possession***, the landlord may collect double rent for the time the tenant in fact remains in possession.

e. **Forcible Entry Statutes**
Most states by statute prohibit forcible entry, *i.e.,* entry against the will of the possessor. Under such statutes, a landlord must not use force or self-help to remove a hold-over tenant. Some states also bar the landlord from more subtle methods of regaining possession, *e.g.,* changing the locks and locking out the tenant.

The statutes allow the landlord to ***evict*** a tenant who has remained in possession after his right to possession has terminated. The sole issue is "who has the right to possession"; questions of title must be litigated in ejectment actions rather than in eviction actions.

B. LEASES

A lease is a contract containing the promises of the parties. It governs the relationship between the landlord and tenant over the term of the lease. In general, covenants in a lease are ***independent*** of each other; *i.e.,* one party's performance of his promise does not depend on the other party's performance of his promise. Thus, if one party breaches a covenant, the other party can recover ***damages***, but must still perform his promises and ***cannot terminate*** the landlord-tenant relationship.

Example: L leases an office space to T for five years. T covenants to pay $1,250 per month, and L covenants to paint the office once each year. At the beginning of the second year, L refuses to paint the office. T may recover damages from L (the decrease in fair rental value or the cost of painting), but T may not terminate the lease or refuse to pay his rent because of L's breach.

Note that the doctrines of actual and constructive eviction (D.2., *infra*) and implied warranty of habitability (D.3., *infra*) are exceptions to this rule of independence of covenants. An exception also exists in nearly all states for nonpayment of rent; under these statutes, if a tenant fails to pay, the landlord may terminate the lease.

C. TENANT DUTIES AND LANDLORD REMEDIES

1. Tenant's Duty to Repair (Doctrine of Waste)

A tenant cannot damage—commit waste on—the leased premises. The rules governing waste in the leasehold context are very much like those governing waste in the context of the life estate.

a. Types of Waste

1) Voluntary (Affirmative) Waste

A tenant is liable to the landlord for voluntary waste. Voluntary waste results when the tenant intentionally or negligently damages the premises. It also includes exploiting minerals on the property unless the property was previously so used, or unless the lease provides that the tenant may do so.

2) Permissive Waste

Unless the lease provides otherwise, the tenant has no duty to the landlord to make any ***substantial*** repairs (*i.e.,* to keep the premises in good repair). However, the tenant has a duty to make ***ordinary*** repairs to keep the property in the same condition as at the commencement of the lease term, excluding ordinary wear and tear (unless the tenant ***covenanted*** to repair ordinary wear and tear; *see* c.2), *infra*). For example, it is the tenant's duty to repair broken windows or a leaking roof and to take such other steps as are needed to prevent damage from the elements (*i.e.,* keep the premises "wind and water tight"). If the tenant fails to do so, he is liable to the landlord for any resulting damage, but not for the cost of repair. By statute in a growing minority of states, residential tenants have additional duties: (i) not to cause housing code violations; (ii) to keep the premises clean and free of vermin; and (iii) to use plumbing, appliances, etc., in a reasonable manner. Note that even when the burden of repair is on the landlord, the tenant does have a duty to report deficiencies promptly to the landlord.

3) Ameliorative Waste

A tenant is under an obligation to return the premises in the same nature and character as received. Therefore, a tenant is not permitted to make substantial alterations to leased structures even if the alteration increases the value of the property.

a) Liability—Cost of Restoration

The tenant is liable for the cost of restoration should he commit ameliorative waste.

b) Modern Exception—Value of Premises Decreasing

When, through the passage of time, the demised premises have been significantly reduced in value, courts will permit a change in the character of the premises as long as:

(1) The change ***increases the value*** of the premises;

(2) The change ***is performed by a long-term tenant*** (*e.g.,* 25 years); and

(3) The change ***reflects a change*** in the nature and character of the neighborhood.

b. Destruction of the Premises Without Fault

If the leased premises are destroyed (*e.g.,* by fire) without the fault of either the landlord or the tenant, no waste is involved. In this situation, the common law held that the lease continues in effect. In the absence of lease language, neither party has a duty to restore the premises, but the tenant has a duty to continue paying the rent.

1) Majority View—Tenant Can Terminate Lease

In most states, statutes or case law now give the tenant an option to terminate the lease if the premises are destroyed without the tenant's fault, even in the presence of an explicit covenant to repair (*see* below).

c. Tenant's Liability for Covenants to Repair

In ***residential*** leases, even if the tenant covenants to repair, the landlord will usually

be obligated to repair (except for damages caused by the tenant) under the "implied warranty of habitability" (*see* D.3., *infra*), because the landlord's obligations under that warranty are usually held not to be waivable. However, in ***nonresidential*** leases, the tenant's covenant to repair is enforceable, and a landlord's claim that the tenant breached the covenant will be assessed by comparing the property's condition when the lease terminates with its condition when the lease commenced.

1) Rebuilding After Structural Damage or Casualty Destruction

A covenant requiring the tenant to repair is ***not*** usually construed by the modern cases to include rebuilding of structural damage or destruction due to a casualty, structural defects, or a third party's acts, unless the covenant ***expressly includes*** these types of repairs.

Example: L leases greenhouses to T, and the lease contains a covenant by T to "maintain said (greenhouses); and, upon expiration of the term hereof surrender in as good a condition as it shall be when lessee takes possession thereof." The greenhouses are destroyed by fire, and L sues T for the cost of rebuilding them. *Held:* "Maintain" or "repair" does not include an obligation to rebuild after destruction by fire. [Washington Hydroculture, Inc. v. Payne, 635 P.2d 138 (Wash. 1981)]

2) Repairing Ordinary Wear and Tear

A covenant requiring the tenant to repair is usually construed to ***include*** even repair of ordinary wear and tear ***if*** the covenant in the lease makes no specific mention of ordinary wear and tear. However, repair covenants frequently ***exclude*** repair of ordinary wear and tear, and such an exclusion is enforceable.

Example: L leases a restaurant to T. T covenants to "maintain, repair and keep in good order the interior of the building." The covenant does not contain the usual exclusion for ordinary wear and tear. Thus, T is held liable for all needed repairs, including tears in booths and chairs, worn flooring, and a damaged ceiling. [Santillanes v. Property Management Services, Inc., 716 P.2d 1360 (Idaho 1986)]

2. Duty to Not Use Premises for Illegal Purpose

If the tenant uses the premises for an illegal purpose, and the landlord is not a party to the illegal use, the landlord may terminate the lease or obtain damages and injunctive relief.

a. Occasional Unlawful Conduct Does Not Breach Duty

Occasional unlawful conduct of the tenant does not breach this duty. The duty is breached only when the illegal conduct is continuous (*e.g.,* if the tenant operates a gambling ring out of the leased premises).

b. Landlord Remedies—Terminate Lease, Recover Damages

If the conduct is continuous, the landlord may terminate the lease and recover the damages. If the conduct has first been stopped by a public authority, the landlord may terminate and recover damages, but only if she acts within a reasonable time after the use has been stopped. Alternatively, the landlord faced with unlawful tenant conduct may keep the lease in force and seek injunctive or monetary relief.

3. Duty to Pay Rent

At common law, rent is due at the end of the leasehold term. However, leases usually contain a provision making the rent payable at some other time (*e.g.,* "monthly in advance").

a. When Rent Accrues

At common law, rent is not apportionable; *i.e.,* it does not accrue from day to day, but rather accrues all at once at the end of the term. However, most states today have statutes that provide that if a leasehold terminates before the term originally agreed on, the tenant must pay a ***proportionate amount*** of the agreed rent.

b. Rent Deposits

Landlords often require a deposit by the tenant at the outset of the lease. If the money is considered a ***security deposit***, the landlord will not be permitted to retain it beyond the extent of his recoverable damages. But if the deposit is denominated a ***"bonus"*** or a future rent payment (*e.g.,* the last month's rent), then most courts permit the landlord to retain it after the tenant has been evicted.

c. Termination of Rent Liability—Surrender

If a tenant effectively conveys back (surrenders) his leasehold to the landlord, the tenant's liability for future rent ends. Normally, this occurs when there is an agreement between the landlord and tenant that the tenant's interest in the demised premises will end. If the unexpired term of the lease is more than one year, the surrender must be in writing to satisfy the Statute of Frauds.

4. Landlord Remedies

a. Tenant on Premises But Fails to Pay Rent—Evict or Sue for Rent

At common law, a breach, such as failure to pay rent, resulted only in a cause of action for money damages; a breach by either party did not give rise to a right to terminate the lease. Most leases, however, grant the nonbreaching party the right to terminate. Furthermore, nearly all states have enacted an ***unlawful detainer statute***, which permits the landlord to evict a defaulting tenant. These statutes provide for a quick hearing, but severely limit the issues that may be raised. Under most statutes, the only issue properly before the court is the landlord's right to rent and possession. The tenant cannot raise counterclaims.

b. Tenant Abandons—Do Nothing or Repossess

If the tenant ***unjustifiably*** abandons the property, the landlord has two options: she may do nothing, or she may repossess.

1) Landlord Does Nothing—Tenant Remains Liable

By the traditional view, the landlord may let the premises lie idle and collect the rent from the abandoning tenant, unless the tenant tenders an acceptable substituting tenant. However, the majority view requires the landlord to make reasonable efforts to ***mitigate*** his damages by reletting to a new tenant. Under this view, if he could have done so but does not attempt to relet, his recovery against the tenant will be reduced accordingly.

2) Landlord Repossesses—Tenant's Liability Depends on Surrender

If the landlord repossesses and/or relets the premises, the tenant's liability will

depend on whether the landlord has accepted a surrender of the premises. If surrender is not found, the tenant remains liable for the difference between the promised rent and the fair rental value of the property (or, in the case of reletting, between the promised rent and the rent received from the reletting). However, if the landlord's reletting or use of the premises for her own profit constitutes acceptance of surrender, the abandoning tenant is free from any rent liability accruing after abandonment.

a) **Acts that Constitute Acceptance of Surrender**
If the landlord resumes possession of the demised premises for himself, this conduct usually constitutes acceptance of the surrender, and the tenant will be relieved of any further liability.

b) **Acts that Do Not Constitute Acceptance of Surrender**
The fact that the landlord enters the premises after abandonment to make repairs, receives back the keys, or offers to attempt to relet the premises on behalf of the tenant, does not by itself constitute an acceptance of the offered surrender.

D. LANDLORD DUTIES AND TENANT REMEDIES

Subject to modification by the lease, a statute, or the implied warranty of habitability, the general rule is that a landlord has ***no duty to repair or maintain*** the premises. Leases, however, commonly prescribe landlord liability to the tenant in several areas. If a lease does not expressly prescribe landlord duties, some duties will be implied.

1. Duty to Deliver Possession of Premises

a. Landlord Duty—Must Deliver Actual Possession

Statutes in most states require the landlord to put the tenant in actual possession of the premises at the beginning of the leasehold term. In a minority of states, the landlord's obligation is merely to give the tenant the legal right to possession. The difference can be important if the leased premises are occupied by a prior, hold-over tenant who has not moved out. Under the majority view, the landlord is in breach if she has not evicted the hold-over tenant by the beginning of the new tenant's term. Under the minority view, it is up to the new tenant to bring eviction proceedings against the hold-over tenant.

b. Tenant Remedy—Damages

In states following the majority rule, a tenant is entitled to damages against a landlord in breach of the duty to deliver possession. If, *e.g.,* the tenant had to find more expensive housing during the interim or suffered business losses as a consequence of the landlord's breach, he may recover for these items.

2. Quiet Enjoyment

There is implied in every lease a covenant that neither the landlord nor someone with paramount title (*e.g.,* a prior mortgagee of the landlord who forecloses) will interfere with the tenant's quiet enjoyment and possession of the premises. The covenant of quiet enjoyment may be breached in any one of three ways: actual eviction, partial actual eviction, or constructive eviction.

a. **Actual Eviction**
Actual eviction occurs when the landlord or paramount title holder, or a hold-over tenant, excludes the tenant from the ***entire*** leased premises. Actual eviction ***terminates*** the tenant's obligation to pay rent.

b. **Partial Actual Eviction**
Partial actual eviction occurs when the tenant is physically excluded from only ***part*** of the leased premises. (The part from which the tenant is excluded need not be a substantial part of the premises for breach to occur.) The tenant's remedies for breach will differ depending on whether the partial eviction was caused by the landlord or by one with paramount title.

1) **Partial Eviction by Landlord—Entire Rent Obligation Relieved**
Partial eviction by the landlord relieves the tenant of the obligation to pay rent for the ***entire*** premises, even though the tenant continues in possession of the remainder of the premises.

2) **Partial Eviction by Third Person—Rent Apportioned**
Partial eviction by a third person with paramount title results in an apportionment of rent; *i.e.,* the tenant is liable for the reasonable rental value of the portion that he continues to possess.

c. **Constructive Eviction**
If the landlord does an act or fails to provide some service that he has a legal duty to provide, and thereby makes the property uninhabitable, the tenant may ***terminate the lease*** and may also seek ***damages***. The following conditions must be met:

1) The acts that cause the injury must be by the ***landlord*** or by persons acting for him. Acts of neighbors or strangers will not suffice.

2) The resulting conditions must be very bad, so that the court can conclude that the ***premises are uninhabitable***. Typical examples are flooding, absence of heat in winter, loss of elevator service in a warehouse, etc.

3) The tenant must move out, thereby showing that the premises were uninhabitable. If he does not ***vacate within a reasonable time***, he has waived the right to do so.

3. **Implied Warranty of Habitability**
More than half the states have now adopted by court decision or statute the implied warranty of habitability for residential tenancies; it is clearly a growing trend. (It is rarely applied to nonresidential cases, unlike constructive eviction.) The standards are more favorable to tenants than in constructive eviction, and the range of remedies is much broader.

a. **Standard—Reasonably Suitable for Human Residence**
The standard usually applied is the local housing code if one exists; if there is none, the court asks whether the conditions are reasonably suitable for human residence.

b. **Remedies**
The following remedies have been adopted by various courts for violation of the implied warranty (although few courts have adopted all):

1) Tenant may move out and ***terminate lease*** (as in a constructive eviction).

2) Tenant may ***make repairs*** directly, and ***offset the cost*** against future rent obligations. (Some states limit this remedy by statute to a fixed amount, such as one month's rent, or to only one occasion each year.)

3) Tenant may reduce or ***abate rent*** to an amount equal to the fair rental value in view of the defects in the property. (In many jurisdictions, the tenant may withhold all rent until the court determines the amount of this fair rental value, and may then pay it without risk of the landlord's terminating the lease for rent delinquency.)

4) Tenant may remain in possession, pay full rent, and seek ***damages*** against the landlord.

4. Retaliatory Eviction

If a tenant exercises the legal right to report housing or building code violations or other rights provided by statute (*e.g.,* a residential landlord-tenant act), the landlord is not permitted to terminate the tenant's lease in retaliation. The landlord is also barred from penalizing the tenant in other ways, such as raising the rent or reducing tenant services. This protection is recognized by residential landlord-tenant acts in nearly half the states. These statutes usually ***presume*** a retaliatory motive if the landlord acts within, say, 90 to 180 days after the tenant exercises his rights. In other states, the same conclusion is reached by judicial construction of the eviction and code statutes. The protection generally applies to tenants under both periodic leases when the landlord gives notice to terminate and fixed-term leases when the landlord refuses to renew. To overcome the presumption, the landlord must show a valid, nonretaliatory reason for his actions.

5. Discrimination

The ***Civil Rights Act*** of 1866 bars racial or ethnic discrimination in the sale or rental of all property. The ***Fair Housing Act*** bars discrimination based on race, ethnicity, religion, national origin, gender, and disability in the sale or rental of a dwelling. Discrimination against families with children is also barred except in senior citizen housing. The Act does not apply to religious organizations, private clubs, and owners who have no more than three single-family dwellings or who have an owner-occupied apartment with no more than four units.

E. ASSIGNMENTS AND SUBLEASES

Absent an express restriction in the lease, a tenant may freely transfer his leasehold interest, in whole or in part. If he makes a ***complete transfer of the entire remaining term***, he has made an ***assignment***. If he ***retains any part*** of the remaining term, the transfer is a ***sublease***.

Example: L leases property to T for a 10-year term. One month later, T transfers his interest to T1 for nine years, retaining the right to retake the premises (reversion) after nine years. The effect of his transfer is to create a sublease between T (sublessor) and T1 (sublessee).

If, on the other hand, T had transferred to T1 for the remaining period of the lease, reserving no rights, the transfer would constitute an assignment of the lease from T (assignor) to T1 (assignee). (*Note:* It is not controlling that the parties denominate the transfer an "assignment" or "sublease." The court still examines what interest, if any, is retained by T to determine the nature of the transaction.)

1. Consequences of Assignment

The label given to a transfer—an assignment or sublease—determines whether the landlord can proceed directly against the transferee or only against the transferor. To be an assignment, the transfer must be on the same terms as the original lease ***except that the tenant may reserve a right of termination (reentry) for breach of the terms of the original lease*** that has been assigned; *e.g.,* "to A for the balance of the leasehold term. However, should A fail to make the rental payments to the landlord, the right to reenter and reclaim the premises is reserved." If the transfer is an assignment, the assignee stands in the shoes of the original tenant in a direct relationship with the landlord. The assignee and the landlord are in ***"privity of estate,"*** and each is liable to the other on all covenants in the lease that "run with the land."

a. Covenants that Run with the Land

A covenant "runs" if the original parties to the lease so intend, and if the covenant ***"touches and concerns"*** the leased land; *i.e.,* it benefits the landlord and burdens the tenant (or vice versa) with respect to their interests in the property. (These requirements are discussed in detail at IV.D., *infra.*) Covenants held to run with the land (unless the parties specify otherwise) include: covenants to ***do or not do a physical act*** (*e.g.,* to repair, to conduct a business on the land in a specified manner, to supply heat); covenants to ***pay money*** (*e.g.,* rent, taxes, etc.); and covenants regarding the ***duration*** of the lease (*e.g.,* termination clauses).

b. Rent Covenant Runs with the Land

Because the covenant to pay rent runs with the land, an assignee owes the rent ***directly*** to the landlord. He does not owe rent for the period before the assignment, but only for the time that he is in "privity of estate," *i.e.,* from the time of assignment until the end of the lease or until the assignee himself reassigns.

1) Reassignment by Assignee—Privity of Estate with Landlord Ends

If the assignee reassigns the leasehold interest, his privity of estate with the landlord ends, and he is not liable for the subsequent assignee's failure to pay rent. However, if the first assignee specifically promised the landlord that he would be liable for the rent for the remainder of the lease term, he may be obligated to pay based on ***privity of contract***, even though his reassignment ended the privity of estate.

a) Effect of Assignee Assuming Rent Obligation

If the assignee made no promise to the landlord but did promise the original tenant that he would pay all future rent, the landlord may be able to sue the assignee as a ***third-party beneficiary*** of the contract between the original tenant and the assignee.

2) Original Tenant Remains Liable

After assignment, the original tenant is no longer in privity of estate with the landlord. However, if (as is likely) the tenant promised to pay rent in his lease with the landlord, he can still be held liable on his original contractual obligation to pay,

i.e., on privity of contract. This allows the landlord to sue the original tenant where the assignee has disappeared, is judgment-proof, etc.

Example: L rents to T for three years at $9,400 per year. After one year, T assigns to T1. T1 pays the rent for one year, and then assigns to T2. T2 fails to pay rent. L can collect from T or T2 but not from T1 (unless T1 made some ***promise*** on the basis of which L can sue him).

2. Consequences of Sublease

In a sublease, the sublessee is considered the tenant of the original lessee, and usually pays rent directly to the original lessee, who in turn pays rent to the landlord under the main lease.

a. Liability of Sublessee for Rent and Other Covenants

The sublessee is liable to the original lessee for whatever rent the two of them agreed to in the sublease. However, the sublessee is ***not personally liable to the landlord*** for rent or for the performance of any other covenants made by the original lessee in the main lease. The reason is that the sublessee has no contractual relationship with the landlord (no privity of contract), and does not hold the tenant's full estate in the land (no privity of estate); therefore, the covenants in the main lease do not "run with the land" and bind the sublessee.

1) Termination for Breach of Covenants

Even though the sublessee is not personally liable to the landlord, the landlord can still terminate the main lease for nonpayment of rent or, if so stated in the lease, breach of other tenant covenants. If this occurs, the sublease will automatically terminate at the same time.

2) Distress—Landlord's Lien

In many states (especially in nonresidential leases), the landlord who does not receive rent when due can assert a lien on the personal property found on the leased premises. This applies to property owned by sublessees as well as that owned by the original tenant.

b. Assumption by Sublessee

It is possible for the sublessee to assume the rent covenant and other covenants in the main lease. An assumption is not implied, but must be expressed. If this occurs, the sublessee is bound by the assumption agreement and becomes personally liable to the landlord on the covenants assumed. The landlord is considered a third-party beneficiary of the assumption agreement.

c. Rights of Sublessee

The sublessee can enforce all covenants made by the original lessee in the sublease, but has no direct right to enforce any covenants made by the landlord in the main lease. However, it is likely (although there is very little case law on point) that a sublessee in a residential lease would be permitted to enforce the implied warranty of habitability against the landlord.

3. Covenants Against Assignment or Sublease

a. **Strictly Construed Against Landlord**
Many leases contain covenants on the part of the tenant not to assign or sublease without the consent of the landlord. These are strictly construed against the landlord. Thus, a covenant prohibiting assignment does not prohibit subleasing and vice versa.

b. **Waiver of Covenant**
Even if the lease has a valid covenant against assignment, the covenant may be held waived if the landlord knows of the assignment and does not object. This often occurs when the landlord knowingly accepts rent from the assignee.

c. **Continuing Waiver**
If the landlord grants consent to one transfer, the Rule in *Dumpor's Case* provides that he waives his right to avoid future transfers unless he expressly reserves the right to do so. Reservation of right must take place at the time of granting consent.

d. **Transfer in Violation of Lease Not Void**
If a tenant transfers (assigns or sublets) in violation of a prohibition in the lease against transfers, the transfer is not void. However, the landlord usually may terminate the lease under either the lease terms or a statute. Alternatively, he may sue for damages if he can prove any.

e. **Reasonableness**
In a minority of states, the landlord may not unreasonably withhold consent to transfers by the tenant. The majority imposes no such limitation.

4. **Assignments by Landlords**

a. **Right to Assign**
A landlord may assign the rents and reversion interest that he owns. This is usually done by an ordinary deed from the landlord to the new owner of the building. Unless required by the lease (which is very unlikely), the consent of the tenants is not required.

b. **Rights of Assignee Against Tenants**
Once the tenants are given reasonable evidence that the assignment has occurred, they are legally obligated to recognize and pay rent to the new owner as their landlord. This is called ***attornment***. The benefits of all other tenant covenants (*e.g.,* to repair, to pay taxes) also run with the landlord's estate and benefit the new landlord, provided that they touch and concern the land.

c. **Liabilities of Assignee to Tenants**
The assignee is liable to the tenants for performance of all covenants made by the original landlord in the lease, provided that those covenants touch and concern the land. The burdens of those covenants run with the landlord's estate and become the burdens of the new landlord. The ***original landlord also remains liable*** on all of the covenants he made in the lease.

Example: L leases to T, and in the lease covenants to repair and maintain the premises. L then sells the building to L2, subject to the lease. Because a covenant to repair and maintain touches and concerns the land, L2 is personally liable to T if L2 fails to perform the covenant. L also remains liable.

F. CONDEMNATION OF LEASEHOLDS

1. Entire Leasehold Taken by Eminent Domain—Rent Liability Extinguished

If all of the leased land is condemned for the full balance of the lease term, the tenant's liability for rent is extinguished because both the leasehold and the reversion have merged in the condemnor and there is no longer a leasehold estate. Absent a lease provision to the contrary, the lessee is entitled to compensation for the taking of the leasehold estate (*i.e.,* fair market value of the lease).

2. Temporary or Partial Taking—Tenant Entitled to Compensation Only

If the taking is temporary (*i.e.,* for a period less than the remaining term), or if only a portion of the leased property is condemned, the tenant is ***not*** discharged from the rent obligation but is entitled to compensation (*i.e.,* a share of the condemnation award) for the taking.

G. TORT LIABILITY OF LANDLORD AND TENANT

1. Landlord's Liability

At common law, subject to a few exceptions, a landlord had ***no duty*** to make the premises safe. Today there are six exceptions to this rule:

a. Concealed Dangerous Condition (Latent Defect)

If, at the time the lease is entered into, the landlord knows (or should know) of a dangerous condition that the tenant could not discover upon reasonable inspection, the landlord has a ***duty to disclose*** the dangerous condition. Failure to disclose results in liability for any injury resulting from the condition.

Once disclosure is made, if the tenant accepts the premises, she is considered to have assumed the risk of injuries to herself or her guests (*e.g.,* family members, invitees, licensees); the landlord is no longer liable.

b. Common Areas

The landlord has a duty to exercise ***reasonable care*** over common areas, such as halls, walks, elevators, etc., that remain under his control. The landlord is liable for any injury resulting from a dangerous condition that could reasonably have been discovered and made safe. This duty is the same as the duty an owner-occupier owes his guests (*see* Multistate Torts outline).

c. Public Use

A landlord is liable for injuries to members of the public if, at the time of the lease, he: (i) knows or should know of a dangerous condition, (ii) has reason to believe that the tenant may admit the public before repairing the condition (*e.g.,* because of short lease term), and (iii) fails to repair the condition. The landlord's liability extends only to people who enter the premises for the purpose for which the public is invited. Note that the tenant's promise to repair does not relieve the landlord of liability if the landlord has reason to suspect that the tenant will admit the public before making the repair.

d. Furnished Short-Term Residence

When a furnished house or apartment is leased for a short term (*i.e.*, three months or less) for immediate occupancy, many jurisdictions hold that the landlord is liable if the premises are defective and cause injury to a tenant.

e. **Negligent Repairs by Landlord**
Even if a landlord has no duty to make repairs, a landlord who actually attempts to repair is liable if an injury results because the repairs are done ***negligently***, or because they give a ***deceptive appearance of safety***. [Restatement (Second) of Property: Landlord & Tenant §17.7]

Example: L leases an apartment to T. Without obligation, L agrees to repair sagging, rotted boards in the kitchen floor. The work appears to be done correctly, but in fact is structurally unsound. T relies on the deceptive appearance of safety thereby created and walks on the floor. L is subject to liability for injuries to T when the floor collapses.

f. **Landlord Contracts to Repair**
If a landlord covenants to repair, most courts hold that he is liable in tort for an injury to the tenant or the tenant's guests resulting from his failure to repair or negligent repair.

2. **Modern Trend—General Duty of Reasonable Care**
Increasingly, the courts are simply holding that landlords have a ***general duty of reasonable care*** with respect to residential tenants, and that they will be held liable for personal injuries of tenants and their guests resulting from the landlord's ***ordinary negligence***, without regard to the exceptions discussed above. This duty is ordinarily not imposed until the landlord has ***notice*** of a particular defect and a reasonable opportunity to repair it.

a. **Defects Arising After Tenant Takes Possession**
A landlord will generally be held to have notice of defects that existed before the tenant took possession. However, the landlord will ***not be liable*** for defects arising after the tenant takes possession ***unless*** there is evidence that the landlord actually knew or should have known of them.

b. **Legal Duty to Repair**
If the landlord has a statutory duty to repair (*e.g.*, under the housing code), he may be liable to the tenant or the tenant's guests for injuries resulting from his failure to repair. Some courts hold that violation of the housing code (or similar statute) is negligence per se, but most courts hold that it is merely ***evidence of negligence***, which the jury may or may not find conclusive. The same analysis probably applies to a violation of the implied warranty of habitability, but there are very few cases on point.

c. **Security**
Some recent cases have held landlords liable for injuries inflicted on tenants by third-party criminals, where the landlord failed to comply with ***housing code*** provisions dealing with security, or failed to maintain ***ordinary security*** measures (*e.g.*, working locks on apartment doors), or where he ***advertised extraordinary security*** measures (*e.g.*, television surveillance, doormen, security patrols) and then failed to provide them.

3. **Tenant's Liability**
The tenant, as occupier of the premises, may be liable in tort to third persons for dangerous

conditions or activities on the leased property. The duty of care owed by the tenant as an occupier of land is discussed in the Multistate Torts outline.

III. FIXTURES

A. IN GENERAL

A "fixture" is a chattel that has been so affixed to land that it has ceased being personal property and has become part of the realty. For example, S and B contract to sell and buy a house. Before vacating, S removes a "built-in" refrigerator. B claims that the item was "part of the house." Is the refrigerator a "fixture"? If so, B is entitled to its return or appropriate compensation.

It is important in dealing with "fixture" problems to distinguish between ***common ownership*** cases and ***divided ownership*** cases. Courts treat them differently even though they often purport to apply the same tests. "Common ownership" cases are those in which the person who brings the chattel onto the land owns both the chattel and the realty (*e.g.*, X installs a furnace in her own home). "Divided ownership" cases are either ones where the person who owns and installs the chattel does not own the land (*e.g.*, T installs a furnace in her rented home, which belongs to L); or the person owns the land but does not own the chattel (*e.g.*, it is subject to a security interest held by the seller). In addition, there are cases involving more than two persons (*e.g.*, conflicting claims are made by the person having a security interest in the chattel and the mortgagee of the land).

B. CHATTELS INCORPORATED INTO STRUCTURE ALWAYS BECOME FIXTURES

In both common ownership and divided ownership cases, where the items become incorporated into the realty so that they lose their identity, they become part of the realty. Examples include bricks built into a building or concrete poured into a foundation. Similarly, where identification is possible, but removal would occasion considerable loss or destruction, the items are considered fixtures, *e.g.*, heating pipes embedded in the wall or floor of a house.

C. COMMON OWNERSHIP CASES

1. Annexor's Intent Controls in Common Ownership Cases

In all common ownership cases where a chattel is not incorporated into a structure, whether an item is a "fixture" (*i.e.*, part of the realty) depends upon the ***objective intention*** of the party who made the "annexation." This intention is determined by considering:

(i) The ***nature of the article*** (*i.e.*, how essential the item is to normal use of the premises);

(ii) The ***manner in which it is attached*** to the realty (the more substantially attached, the more likely it was intended to be permanent);

(iii) The ***amount of damage*** that would be caused by its removal; and

(iv) The ***adaptation*** of the item to the use of the realty (*e.g.*, custom window treatments, wall-to-wall carpet).

a. Constructive Annexation

In some cases, an article of personal property is considered a fixture even though it is not physically annexed to the real estate at all. This is because it is so ***uniquely adapted*** to the real estate that it makes no sense to separate it. Examples include the keys to the doors of a house; curtain rods that have been cut and sized to the brackets on the walls of a house, even if the rods themselves are not presently installed; and a carpet that has been cut to fit an unusually shaped room, even if the carpet is not nailed or glued in place.

b. **Vendor-Purchaser Cases**
The typical situation is where the owner of land affixes chattels to the land and subsequently conveys the land without expressly providing whether the chattels are to pass with the realty. The intention test works fairly well. The question boils down to whether an owner bringing the disputed chattel to the realty would intend that it become part of the realty. Or to put it another way, ***whether a reasonable purchaser would expect*** that the disputed item was part of the realty.

c. **Mortgagor-Mortgagee Cases**
The intention test is universally applied to determine whether the owner (mortgagor) intended the chattels to become "part of the realty." Where the mortgagor has made the annexation ***prior*** to the giving of the mortgage, the question is what the "reasonably objective" lender expects to come within the security of her lien. However, where the annexation is made ***after*** the giving of the mortgage, the same considerations arguably should ***not*** apply because each item that is "added" to the lien of the mortgage represents a ***windfall*** to the mortgagee should foreclosure occur. Nevertheless, courts universally apply the same intention test regardless of when the annexation was made. (Courts also usually apply the intention test where items are annexed by one in possession of land under an ***executory contract*** to purchase.)

2. **Effect of Fixture Classification**

a. **Conveyance**
If a chattel has been categorized as a fixture, it is part of the real estate. A conveyance of the real estate, in the absence of any specific agreement to the contrary, passes the fixture with it. The fixture, as part of the realty, passes to the new owner of the real estate.

b. **Mortgage**
To the extent that the owner of the real estate mortgages the realty, in the absence of an agreement to the contrary, the mortgage attaches to all fixtures on the real estate.

c. **Agreement to Contrary**
Even though the concept of fixtures may apply and a chattel becomes a fixture, an agreement between a buyer and seller (similarly, between a mortgagor and mortgagee) can cause a severance of title. For example, a buyer and seller may agree that the seller will retain the right to remove fixtures. Similarly, a mortgagor and mortgagee can agree that the mortgage lien shall not attach to specified fixtures. The effect of such an agreement is to de-annex, so far as relevant, the chattel from the realty and reconvert the fixture into a chattel.

D. DIVIDED OWNERSHIP CASES

In divided ownership cases, unlike the ones just discussed, the chattel is owned and brought to the

realty by someone who is not the landowner (*e.g.*, a tenant, a licensee, or a trespasser). The question is whether the ownership of the chattel has passed to the landowner. Courts often say that the intention test (C.1., *supra*) is to be applied in these cases too. But the exceptions disprove the rule.

1. Landlord-Tenant

Early English law favored the landlord. However, American law created a ***trade fixtures*** exception under which tradesmen-tenants could remove an item used in their trade or business, that otherwise would have been a "fixture," unless its removal would cause substantial damage to the premises. Later, this exception was expanded to include all tenants generally. Some courts have treated the trade fixtures exception as consistent with the annexor's-intention test; *i.e.*, a tenant's annexations are removable because "it was not the intention of the tenant to make them permanent annexations to the freehold and thereby donations to the owner of it."

a. Agreement

An agreement between the landlord and tenant is controlling on whether the chattel annexed to the premises was intended to become a fixture. To the extent that the landlord and tenant specifically agree that such annexation is not to be deemed a fixture, the agreement controls.

b. No Intent If Removal Does Not Cause Damage

In the absence of an express agreement to the contrary, a tenant may remove a chattel that he has attached to the demised premises as long as the removal does not cause substantial damage to the demised premises or the virtual destruction of the chattel. In other words, the tenant will ***not*** have manifested an intention to permanently improve the freehold (and the concept of fixtures will be inapplicable) as long as the removal of the chattel does not cause substantial damage to the premises or the destruction of the chattel.

c. Removal Must Occur Before End of Lease Term

Generally, a tenant must remove his annexed chattels before the termination of his tenancy or they become the property of the landlord. If the duration of the tenancy is indefinite (*e.g.*, tenancy at will), the removal must occur within a reasonable time after the tenancy terminates. Similarly, a tenant has a reasonable time for removal if he holds over during unsuccessful negotiations for a new lease.

d. Tenant Has Duty to Repair Damages Resulting from Removal

Tenants are responsible for repairing damages caused by removal of "fixtures."

2. Life Tenant and Remainderman

The same rules should apply here as in the landlord-tenant cases. Historically, however, results have been more favorable to the remaindermen (or reversioners). Apart from statute, the removal privilege has been unrealistically limited to the duration of the term.

3. Licensee and Landowner

Licenses to bring items onto land usually contain agreements respecting removal. In the absence of an agreement, licensees are permitted to remove the items subject to a duty to repair damages caused thereby.

4. **Trespasser and Landowner**
Trespassers (*e.g.*, adverse possessors before the running of the statute of limitations) normally lose their annexations whether installed in good faith or not. Moreover, the trespasser can be held liable for the reasonable rental value of the property on which she annexed the item.

a. **Trespasser's Recovery Limited to Value Added to Land**
Some courts allow a good faith trespasser to recover for the improvement, but the recovery is measured by the value added to the land, not the cost to construct the improvement.

E. THIRD-PARTY CASES

Any of the foregoing cases is complicated by the addition of third-person claimants. The situations can be classified under two headings.

1. **Third Person Claims Lien on Land to Which Chattels Affixed**
Suppose Landowner mortgages her land to Mortgagee. Landowner then leases the land to Tenant, who annexes an item (*e.g.*, a machine) that is a "trade fixture" and thus removable at the end of the term. Landowner defaults before the end of the term, and Mortgagee forecloses. Is the item subject to the lien of the mortgage?

(i) Generally, no. In this situation, the mortgagee has no greater rights than the mortgagor, provided only that the original sufficiency of the security is not impaired (*e.g.*, removal would not substantially damage a building in existence when the mortgage was given).

(ii) The same result occurs where a buyer under an installment land contract leases to a tenant, the tenant makes annexations, and the buyer then defaults. The seller is treated in the same manner as the mortgagee in the first example.

If, in the above example, the land mortgage is made ***after*** the lease and after the tenant has annexed an item that is a "trade fixture" as against the landlord-mortgagor, and, as is usual, the land mortgagee has ***notice*** of the tenant's rights, the mortgagee is in no better position than the landlord-mortgagor. If the mortgagee does not have notice, he wins if the item would have been considered a fixture as between the mortgagee and the mortgagor. (The same result pertains in cases where the landlord ***sells*** the property after the making of a lease.)

2. **Third Person Claims Lien on Chattel Affixed to Land**
Suppose Landowner purchases a furnace from Seller and installs it in her house. She owes a balance on the purchase price of the furnace, and therefore grants Seller a ***security interest*** in the furnace (in accordance with Article 9 of the Uniform Commercial Code ("U.C.C.")). Suppose further that Landowner also executes a ***mortgage*** on her house, to Mortgagee. If Landowner subsequently defaults on her payments, both on the furnace and the house, is Seller or Mortgagee entitled to priority? (Same issue where Landowner ***sells*** the house without mentioning the security interest.)

a. **U.C.C. Rules**
Normally, the rule is that whichever interest is ***first recorded*** in the local ***real estate***

records wins. (Thus, if the chattel security interest was recorded first, it constitutes "constructive notice" to all subsequent lenders or purchasers.) However, an ***exception*** allows a ***"purchase money security interest"*** in an affixed chattel (here, the interest given Seller to secure payment on the furnace) to prevail even over a ***prior recorded*** mortgage on the land, as long as the chattel interest is recorded ***within 20 days*** after the chattel is affixed to the land. [U.C.C. §9-334]

The document used to record the chattel security interest is known as a ***"fixture filing."*** (This is a separate instrument from the "financing statement," which is required to be filed to perfect the chattel security interest in the first place.)

b. Liability for Damages Caused by Removal

In the above example, if Seller were entitled to priority, she would be entitled to remove the furnace. However, she would have to reimburse Mortgagee for any ***damages or repair*** necessitated by the removal (but ***not*** for diminution in value of the property due to the lack of a furnace).

IV. RIGHTS IN THE LAND OF ANOTHER—EASEMENTS, PROFITS, COVENANTS, AND SERVITUDES

A. IN GENERAL

Easements, profits, covenants, and servitudes are ***nonpossessory*** interests in land. They create a right to ***use land possessed by someone else***. For example, A, the owner of Blackacre, grants to B, the owner of an adjacent parcel, Whiteacre, the right to use a path over Blackacre connecting Whiteacre to a public road. An easement has been created, giving B the right to use—but ***not*** to possess—the pathway over Blackacre. Easements, profits, covenants, and servitudes have many similarities in operation, coverage, creation, and termination. They also have important differences, mainly in the requirements that must be met for their enforcement.

B. EASEMENTS

1. Introduction

The holder of an easement has the ***right to use*** a tract of land (called the servient tenement) for a special purpose, but has ***no right to possess and enjoy*** the tract of land. The owner of the servient tenement continues to have the right of full possession and enjoyment subject only to the limitation that he cannot interfere with the right of special use created in the easement holder. Typically, easements are created in order to give their holder the right of access across a tract of land, *e.g.,* the privilege of laying utility lines, or installing sewer pipes and the like. Easements are either affirmative or negative, appurtenant or in gross.

a. Types of Easements

1) Affirmative Easements

Affirmative easements entitle the holder ***to enter upon the servient tenement and make an affirmative use of it*** for such purposes as laying and maintaining utility lines, draining waters, and polluting the air over the servient estate. The ***right-of-way*** easement is another instance of an affirmative easement. Thus, an affirmative easement privileges the holder of the benefit to make a use of the servient estate that, absent the easement, would be an unlawful trespass or nuisance.

2) Negative Easements

A negative easement does not grant to its owner the right to enter upon the servient tenement. It does, however, entitle the privilege holder to compel the possessor of the servient tenement to ***refrain from engaging in activity*** upon the servient tenement that, were it not for the existence of the easement, he would be privileged to do. In reality, a negative easement is simply a restrictive covenant. (*See* D.1.e.1), *infra.*)

Example: A owns Lot 6. By written instrument, he stipulates to B that he will not build any structure upon Lot 6 within 35 feet of the lot line. B has acquired a negative easement in Lot 6.

Courts hesitate to recognize new forms of negative easements and generally have confined them to a traditional handful: easements for ***light, air, subjacent or lateral support,*** and for the ***flow of an artificial stream***.

b. Easement Appurtenant

An easement is deemed appurtenant when the right of special use benefits the holder of the easement in his physical use or enjoyment of another tract of land. For an easement appurtenant to exist, there must be ***two tracts*** of land. One is called the ***dominant tenement***, which has the benefit of the easement. The second tract is the ***servient tenement***, which is subject to the easement right. One consequence of appurtenance is that the benefit passes with transfers of the benefited land, regardless of whether the easement is mentioned in the conveyance.

Example: A owns Lot 6 and B owns Lot 7, which are adjoining tracts of land. By a written instrument, B grants to A the right to cross B's tract (Lot 7). A's use and enjoyment of Lot 6 is benefited by virtue of the acquisition of the right to use Lot 7 for this special purpose. The right is an easement appurtenant. B remains the owner of Lot 7. A has only a right to use Lot 7 for a special purpose, *i.e.,* the right to cross the tract.

1) Use and Enjoyment

In an easement appurtenant, the benefits to be realized by the easement must be directly beneficial to the possessor of the ***dominant tenement*** in his physical use and enjoyment of that tract of land. It is not sufficient that the easement makes use of the land more profitable.

Example: A owns Lot 6 and B owns adjacent Lot 7. A grants to B the right to use part of Lot 6 to mine coal. The right is not an easement appurtenant because the benefit granted is not related to B's physical use and enjoyment of Lot 7.

2) Benefit Attached to Possession

The benefit of an easement appurtenant becomes an incident of the possession of the dominant tenement. All who possess or subsequently succeed to title to the dominant tenement become, by virtue of the fact of possession, entitled to the benefit of the easement. There can be no conveyance of the easement right apart from possession of the dominant tenement, except that the easement holder may

convey the easement to the owner of the servient tenement in order to extinguish the easement (*see* 4.b., *infra*).

3) Transfer of Dominant and Servient Estates

Both the dominant and servient parcels can be transferred. As discussed above, if the dominant parcel is transferred, the benefit of the easement goes with it automatically—even if it is not mentioned in the deed—and becomes the property of the new owner. If the servient parcel is transferred, its new owner takes it ***subject to*** the burden of the easement, ***unless*** she is a bona fide purchaser (*see* VI.E.3., *infra*) with no notice of the easement. There are three ways the person who acquires the servient land might have notice of the easement: (i) actual knowledge, (ii) notice from the visible appearance of the easement on the land, and (iii) notice from the fact that the document creating the easement is recorded in the public records. Everyone who buys land is expected to inspect the land physically and to examine the public records.

Example: A owns Lot 6 and grants B (the owner of Lot 7) an easement for a driveway across Lot 6 to benefit adjacent Lot 7. The easement is not recorded. Then A sells Lot 6 to X. The tire tracks of the driveway are plainly visible at the time of the sale. X is therefore not a bona fide purchaser, and takes Lot 6 subject to the easement.

c. Easement in Gross

An easement in gross is created where the holder of the easement interest acquires a right of special use in the servient tenement independent of his ownership or possession of another tract of land. In an easement in gross, the easement holder is not benefited in his use and enjoyment of a possessory estate by virtue of the acquisition of that privilege. There is no dominant tenement. An easement in gross passes entirely apart from any transfer of land.

Example: A owns Lot 6. By a written instrument, she grants to B the right to build a pipeline across Lot 6. B receives the privilege independent of his ownership or possession of a separate tract of land. B has acquired an easement in gross.

Easements in gross can be either personal (*e.g.*, O gives friend right to swim and boat on lake) or commercial (*e.g.*, utility or railroad track easements). Generally, an easement in gross is transferable only if the easement is for a commercial or economic purpose.

d. Judicial Preference for Easements Appurtenant

If an easement interest is created and its owner holds a corporeal (possessory) estate that is or could be benefited in physical use or enjoyment by the acquisition of the privilege, the easement will be deemed appurtenant. This is true even though the deed creating the easement makes no reference to a dominant tenement.

Example: A conveys to "B, her heirs, successors, and assigns, the right to use a strip 20 feet wide on the north edge of Blackacre for ingress and egress to Whiteacre." Because there is ambiguity as to whether the benefit was intended to attach to B's land, Whiteacre, or to B personally, a court will apply the constructional preference and hold that the benefit was intended to be appurtenant, with the consequence that any conveyance of Whiteacre by B will carry with it the right to use the strip across Blackacre.

2. Creation of Easements

The basic methods of creating an easement are: express grant or reservation, implication, and prescription.

a. Express Grant

Because an easement is an interest in land, the Statute of Frauds applies. Therefore, any easement must be ***in writing*** and signed by the grantor (the holder of the servient tenement) unless its duration is brief enough (commonly one year or less) to be outside a particular state's Statute of Frauds' coverage. An easement can be created by conveyance. A grant of an easement must comply with all the formal requisites of a deed. An easement is presumed to be of perpetual duration unless the grant specifically limits the interest (*e.g.,* for life, for 10 years).

b. Express Reservation

An easement by reservation arises when the owner (of a present possessory interest) of a tract of land conveys title but reserves the right to continue to use the tract for a special purpose after the conveyance. In effect, the grantor passes title to the land but reserves unto himself an easement interest. Note that, under the majority view, the easement can be reserved ***only for the grantor***; an attempt by the grantor to reserve an easement for anyone else is void. (There is a growing trend to permit reservations in third parties, but it remains a minority view.)

Example: G owns Lot 6 and Lot 7, which are adjacent. G sells Lot 7 to B. Later, when G is about to sell Lot 6 to A, B asks G to reserve an easement over Lot 6 in favor of B. G agrees to do so, and executes a deed of Lot 6 to A that contains the following language: "Reserving an easement for a driveway in favor of Lot 7, which is owned by B." The reservation clause is void and no easement is created.

c. Implication

An easement by implication is created by ***operation of law*** rather than by written instrument. It is an exception to the Statute of Frauds. There are only three types of implied easements: (i) an intended easement based on a use that existed when the dominant and servient estates were severed, (ii) an easement implied from a recorded subdivision plat or profit a prendre, and (iii) an easement by necessity.

1) Easement Implied from Existing Use ("Quasi-Easement")

An easement may be implied if, prior to the time the tract is divided, a use exists on the "servient part" that is reasonably necessary for the enjoyment of the "dominant part" and a court determines that the parties intended the use to continue after division of the property. It is sometimes called a "quasi-easement" before the tract is divided because an owner cannot hold an easement on his own land.

a) Existing Use at Time Tract Divided

For a use to give rise to an easement, it must be apparent and continuous at the time the tract is divided. "Apparent" means that a grantee could discover the existence of the use upon reasonable inspection. A nonvisible use may still be "apparent" if surface connections or the like would put a reasonable person on notice of its existence.

b) **Reasonable Necessity**
Whether a use is reasonably necessary to the enjoyment of the dominant parcel depends on many factors, including the cost and difficulty of the alternatives and whether the price paid reflects the expected continued use of the servient portion of the tract.

c) **Grant or Reservation**
An easement implied in favor of the grantee is said to be created by implied grant, while an easement implied in favor of the grantor is said to be created by implied reservation.

2) **Easements Implied Without Any Existing Use**
In two limited situations, easements are implied in a conveyance even though there is no preexisting use.

a) **Subdivision Plat**
When lots are sold in a subdivision with reference to a recorded plat or map that also shows streets leading to the lots, buyers of the lots have implied easements to use the streets in order to gain access to their lots. These easements continue to exist even if the ***public*** easements held by the city or county in the streets are later vacated.

b) **Profit a Prendre**
When a landowner grants a profit a prendre to a person to remove a valuable product of the soil (*e.g.,* grass, asphalt, ore, etc.), the holder of the profit also has an implied easement to pass over the surface of the land and to use it as reasonably necessary to extract the product.

3) **Easement by Necessity**
When the owner of a tract of land sells a part of the tract and by this division deprives one lot of access to a public road or utility line, a right-of-way by absolute necessity is created by implied grant or reservation over the lot with access to the public road or utility line. The owner of the servient parcel has the right to locate the easement, provided the location is reasonably convenient. An easement by necessity terminates when the necessity ceases.

d. **Prescription**
Acquiring an easement by prescription is analogous to acquiring property by adverse possession. (*See* V., *infra.*) Many of the requirements are the same: To acquire a prescriptive easement, the use must be ***open and notorious, adverse, and continuous and uninterrupted for the statutory period***. Note that the public at large can acquire an easement in private land if members of the public use the land in a way that meets the requirements for prescription.

1) **Open and Notorious**
The user must not attempt to conceal his use. Underground or other nonvisible uses, such as pipes and electric lines, are considered open and notorious if the use could be discovered (*e.g.,* through surface connections) upon inspection.

2) **Adverse**
The use must not be with the owner's permission. Unlike adverse possession, the use ***need not be exclusive***. The user of a common driveway, *e.g.*, may acquire a prescriptive easement even though the owner uses it too.

3) **Continuous Use**
Continuous adverse use does not mean constant use. A continuous claim of right with periodic acts that put the owner on notice of the claimed easement fulfills the requirement. Note that tacking is permitted for prescriptive easements, just as for adverse possession (*see* V.B.5.b., *infra*).

4) **When Prescriptive Easements Cannot Be Acquired**
Negative easements cannot arise by prescription, nor generally may easements in public lands. An easement by necessity cannot give rise to an easement by prescription. However, if the necessity ends, so does the easement, and the use is adverse from that point forward.

3. **Scope**
Courts enforcing easements are often called upon to interpret the arrangement in order to determine the ***scope*** and ***intended beneficiaries*** of the interest. The key to interpretation employed in all these cases is the ***reasonable intent of the original parties***. What would the parties reasonably have provided had they contemplated the situation now before the court? What result would reasonably serve the purposes of the arrangement?

a. **General Rules of Construction**
If, as typically happens, the language used is general (*e.g.,* "a right-of-way over Blackacre"), the following rules of construction usually apply: (i) ambiguities are resolved in favor of the grantee (unless the conveyance is gratuitous); (ii) subsequent conduct of the parties respecting the arrangement is relevant; (iii) the parties are assumed to have intended a scope that would reasonably serve the purposes of the grant and to have foreseen reasonable changes in the use of the dominant estate. The rule of reasonableness will be applied only to the extent that the governing language is general. If the location or scope of the permitted use is spelled out in detail, the specifics will govern, and reasonable interpretation will be excluded.

Examples: 1) In 1890, A, the owner of Blackacre, granted to B, the owner of Whiteacre, a "right-of-way" over Blackacre for purposes of ingress and egress to Whiteacre from the public highway running along the western boundary of Blackacre. At the time of the grant, there were only horses and buggies, no automobiles. Applying a "rule of reasonableness" to the general language creating the right-of-way, a court would probably find that the right-of-way could today be used for cars. If, however, the use of cars would impose a ***substantially*** greater burden on Blackacre, the court would probably find against this use on grounds that it was outside the scope reasonably contemplated by A and B.

2) If, in the example just given, the right-of-way was specifically dedicated ("only to the use of horses and carriages"), automobile use would be excluded. Similarly, if the right-of-way was specifically located

(*e.g.*, "over the southern 10 feet of Blackacre"), the rule of reasonableness could not be invoked to change or enlarge the location.

b. Absence of Location

If an easement is created but not specifically located on the servient tenement, an easement of sufficient width, height, and direction to make the intended use reasonably convenient will be implied. The owner of the servient tenement may select the location of the easement so long as her selection is reasonable.

c. Changes in Use

In the absence of specific limitations in the deed creating an easement, the courts will assume that the easement is intended by the parties to meet both present and future reasonable needs of the dominant tenement.

Examples: 1) A roadway easement of unspecified width was created in 1920, when cars were only six feet wide. Today, however, cars are considerably wider. Because the original roadway easement was not specifically limited in width, the easement will expand in size to accommodate the changing and expanding needs of the owner of the dominant tenement.

2) But a basic change in the nature of the use is not allowed. Thus, a telephone or power line may not be added on the roadway. (Many courts are more liberal in allowing such additions if the roadway easement is public rather than private.)

d. Easements by Necessity or Implication

In the case of easements by necessity, the ***extent of the necessity determines the scope*** of the easement. Because there is no underlying written instrument to interpret, courts will look instead to the circumstances giving rise to the easement. Similarly, with other implied easements, the ***quasi-easement*** will provide the starting point for the court's construction of the scope of the easement. Modifications in the easement will be enforced to the extent that they are necessary for reasonably foreseeable changes in the use of the dominant parcel.

e. Use of Servient Estate

Absent an express restriction in the original agreement, the owner of the servient estate may use her land in any way she wishes so long as her conduct does not interfere with performance of the easement, profit, covenant, or servitude.

Example: A grants to B Water Company the right to lay water pipes in a specified five-foot right-of-way. A is not by this grant necessarily precluded from granting similar rights in the same right-of-way to a competing company, so long as the second grant does not interfere with the use made by B, the original grantee. A may also build over the right-of-way so long as the structure does not unreasonably interfere with B's use.

1) Duty to Repair

If the holder of the benefit is the only party making use of the easement, that party has the duty to make repairs (*e.g.*, fill in potholes on a right-of-way) and, absent a special agreement, the servient owner has no duty to do so. If the easement is

nonexclusive and ***both*** the holder of the benefit and the servient owner are making use of the easement, the court will ***apportion*** the repair costs between them on the basis of their relative use.

f. **Intended Beneficiaries—Subdivision of Dominant Parcel**
When an easement is created for the benefit of a landowner, and the landowner later subdivides the parcel, there is a question whether each subdivision grantee will succeed to the original benefit. The answer will turn on whether the extension of the benefit to each of the subdivided parcels will burden the servient estate to a greater extent than was contemplated by the original parties. Absent any other evidence on intent, a court will not find an intent to allow an extension if extending the benefit to each parcel in the subdivision will unreasonably overburden the servient estate. Weighing all the circumstances, a court could find subdivision into four lots reasonable, but subdivision into 50 lots unreasonable; it is determined on a case-by-case basis.

Example: A, the owner of Blackacre, grants to B, the owner of Whiteacre, a right-of-way easement of ingress and egress over Blackacre. B then subdivides Whiteacre into 150 lots. If A and B had not contemplated the subdivision of Whiteacre, and if use of the right-of-way by all 150 lot owners would substantially interfere with A's use of Blackacre (in a way that B's use alone would not), a court would probably not find an intent that the benefit of the right-of-way easement attach to each of the 150 parcels.

g. **Effect of Use Outside Scope of Easement**
When the owner of an easement uses it in a way that exceeds its legal scope, the easement is said to be ***surcharged***. The remedy of the servient landowner is an ***injunction*** of the excess use, and possibly damages if the servient land has been harmed. However, the excess use ***does not terminate*** the easement or give the servient landowner a power of termination.

4. **Termination of Easements**
An easement, like any other property interest, may be created to last in perpetuity or for a limited period of time. To the extent the parties to its original creation provide for the natural termination of the interest, such limitations will control.

a. **Stated Conditions**
If the parties to the original creation of an easement set forth specific conditions upon the happening of which the easement right will terminate, the conditions will be recognized. On this basis, the following conditions are valid: an easement granted "so long as repairs are maintained," an easement granted "so long as X is the holder of the dominant tenement," an easement granted "until the dominant tenement is used for commercial purposes," etc.

b. **Unity of Ownership**
By definition, an easement is the right to use the lands of another for a special purpose. On this basis, the ownership of the easement and of the servient tenement must be in different persons. If ownership of the two comes together in one person, the easement is extinguished.

1) **Complete Unity Required**

For an easement to be extinguished, there must be complete unity of ownership as between the interest held in the easement and that held in the servient tenement. In other words, if the holder of an easement acquires an interest in the servient tenement, the easement is extinguished only if he acquires an interest in the servient tenement of ***equal or greater duration*** than the duration of the easement privilege. Conversely, if the holder of the servient tenement acquires the easement interests, the title acquired must be ***equal to or greater than her interest*** or estate in the servient tenement. If there is incomplete acquisition of title, the easement will not be extinguished.

Example: A is the owner of the servient tenement in fee simple. B has an access easement across the servient tenement and the duration of the easement is in fee simple. A conveys a 10-year term tenancy in the servient tenement to B. There is no complete unity of ownership. The easement right is of longer duration than is the estate acquired by B in the servient tenement. Therefore, the easement is not extinguished.

2) **No Revival**

If complete unity of title is acquired, the easement is extinguished. Even though there may be later separation, the easement will not be automatically revived.

Example: A owns Lot 6, the servient tenement. B owns adjacent Lot 7. A grants to B the privilege of crossing Lot 6, *i.e.,* grants an easement appurtenant to B. Assume A conveys Lot 6 to B in fee simple. The easement would be extinguished because B then holds both the easement and title to the servient tenement. If, thereafter, B conveys Lot 6 to C, the easement is not revived. Of course, it could be created anew.

c. **Release**

An easement may be terminated by a release given by the owner of the easement interest to the owner of the servient tenement. A release requires the ***concurrence of both owners*** and is, in effect, a conveyance. The release must be executed with all the formalities that are required for the valid creation of an easement.

1) **Easement Appurtenant**

The basic characteristic of an easement appurtenant is that it becomes, for the purpose of succession, an incident of possession of the dominant tenement. This basic characteristic requires that the easement interest not be conveyed independently of a conveyance of the dominant tenement. However, an easement appurtenant may be conveyed to the owner of the servient tenement without a conveyance (to the same grantee) of the dominant tenement. This is an exception to the general alienability characteristics of an easement appurtenant (*see* 1.b., *supra*).

2) **Easement in Gross**

The basic characteristic of an easement in gross is that unless it is for a commercial purpose, it is inalienable. However, an easement in gross can be released; *i.e.,*

can be conveyed to the owner of the servient tenement. This is an exception to the general characteristics of an easement in gross.

3) **Statute of Frauds**
The Statute of Frauds requires that every conveyance of an interest in land that has a duration long enough to bring into play a particular state's Statute of Frauds (typically one year) must be evidenced by a writing. This writing requirement is also applicable to a release of an easement interest. If the easement interest that is being conveyed has a duration of greater than one year, it must be in writing in order to satisfy the Statute of Frauds. An oral release is ineffective, although it may become effective by estoppel.

d. **Abandonment**
It has become an established rule that an easement can be extinguished without conveyance where the owner of the privilege demonstrates by physical action an intention to ***permanently*** abandon the easement. To work as an abandonment, the owner must have manifested an intention never to make use of the easement again.

Example: A owns Lot 6 and B owns Lot 7, which are immediately adjacent. A grants to B an easement across Lot 6. This easement is specifically located on the servient tenement and is a walkway. Subsequently, B constructs a house on Lot 7 that completely blocks his access to the walkway. By the physical action of constructing the house in such a way that access to the walkway (*i.e.,* the easement) is denied, B has physically indicated an intent not to use the easement again. The easement is extinguished by abandonment.

1) **Physical Act Required**
An abandonment of an easement occurs when the easement holder physically manifests an intention to permanently abandon the easement. Such physical action brings about a termination of the easement by operation of law and therefore no writing is required; *i.e.,* the Statute of Frauds need not be complied with.

2) **Mere Words Insufficient**
The oral expressions of the owner of the easement that he does not intend to use the easement again (*i.e.,* wishes to abandon) are insufficient to constitute an abandonment of the easement. For words to operate as a termination, such expression will only be effective if it qualifies as a release. In other words, the Statute of Frauds must be complied with.

3) **Mere Nonuse Insufficient**
An easement is not terminated merely because it is not used for a long period by its owner. To terminate the easement, the nonuse must be combined with other evidence of intent to abandon it. Nonuse itself is not considered sufficient evidence of that intent.

e. **Estoppel**
While the assertions of the holder of the easement are insufficient to work a termination unless there is valid compliance with the requirements of a release, an easement may be

extinguished by virtue of the reasonable reliance and change of position of the owner of the servient tenement, based on assertions or conduct of the easement holder.

Example: The owner of a right-of-way tells the owner of the servient tenement that the owner of the servient tenement may build a building on the servient tenement in such a way as to make the right-of-way no longer usable, and the servient owner does in fact build the building. There will be an extinguishment of the easement by estoppel.

For an easement to be extinguished by estoppel, three requirements must be satisfied. Namely, there must be (i) some ***conduct or assertion*** by the owner of the easement, (ii) a ***reasonable reliance*** by the owner of the servient tenement, (iii) coupled with a ***change of position***. Even though there is an assertion by the easement holder, if the owner of the servient tenement does not change her position based upon the assertion, the easement will not be terminated.

f. Prescription

An easement may be extinguished, as well as created, by prescription. Long continued possession and enjoyment of the servient tenement in a way that would indicate to the public that no easement right existed will end the easement right. Such long continued use works as a statute of limitations precluding the whole world, including the easement holder, from asserting that his privilege exists.

The termination of an easement by prescription is fixed by analogy to the creation of an easement by prescription. The owner of the servient tenement must so ***interfere with the easement*** as to create a cause of action in favor of the easement holder. The interference must be open, notorious, continuous, and nonpermissive for the statutory period (*e.g.,* 20 years).

g. Necessity

Easements created by necessity ***expire as soon as the necessity ends***.

Example: A, the owner of a tract of land, sells a portion of it that has no access to a highway except over the remaining lands of A. B, the purchaser, acquires by necessity a right-of-way over the remaining lands of A. Some years later, a highway is built so that B no longer needs the right-of-way across A's property. The easement ends because the necessity has disappeared.

h. Condemnation

Condemnation of the servient estate will extinguish the nonpossessory interest. Courts are split, however, on whether the holder of the benefit is entitled to compensation for the value lost.

i. Destruction of Servient Estate

If the easement is in a structure (*e.g.,* a staircase), involuntary destruction of the structure (*e.g.,* by fire or flood) will extinguish the easement. Voluntary destruction (*e.g.,* tearing down a building to erect a new one) will not, however, terminate the easement.

5. Compare—Licenses

Licenses, like affirmative easements, privilege their holder to go upon the land of another (the licensor). Unlike an affirmative easement, the license is ***not an interest in land***. It is merely a ***privilege***, revocable at the will of the licensor. (Although licenses may acquire some of the characteristics of easements through estoppel or by being coupled with an interest.) The Statute of Frauds does not apply to licenses, and licensees are not entitled to compensation if the land is taken by eminent domain. Licenses are quite common; examples of licensees include delivery persons, plumbers, party guests, etc.

a. Assignability

An essential characteristic of a license is that it is ***personal to the licensee*** and therefore ***not alienable***. The holder of a license privilege cannot convey such right. In fact, most courts have held that the license privilege is so closely tied to the individual parties that it is revoked, by operation of law, upon an attempted transfer by the licensee.

b. Revocation and Termination

Another essential characteristic of a license is that it is revocable by nature. It may be revoked at any time by a manifestation of the licensor's intent to end it. This manifestation may be by a formal notice of revocation or it may consist of conduct that obstructs the licensee's continued use. Similarly, the licensee can surrender the privilege whenever he desires to do so. A license ends by operation of law upon the death of the licensor. In addition, a conveyance of the servient tenement by the licensor terminates the licensee's privilege.

1) Public Amusement Cases

Tickets issued by theaters, race courses, and other places of amusement have given rise to some controversy. The traditional rule is that such tickets create a license. Once describing the tickets as granting a license, the essential characteristic of a license applies; *i.e.,* it is revocable by nature. On this basis, the licensor may terminate the licensee's privilege at will.

2) Breach of Contract

A license may be granted pursuant to an express or implied contract between the licensor and licensee. On this basis, the termination of the licensee's privilege may constitute a breach of contract. While many courts may grant a cause of action for money damages for a revocation of a license in breach of contract, they continue to sustain the licensor's right to terminate the licensee's privilege to continue to remain on the servient tenement.

Example: A pays a $70 greens fee to play 18 holes of golf on B's property. After A has played only nine holes, B terminates A's right to be on B's property. Because A acquired a license and it is revocable by its very nature, B's action is not, in property terms, wrongful. However, A may have a cause of action against B to recoup part or all of A's $70.

c. Failure to Create an Easement

The Statute of Frauds requires that any conveyance of an interest in land (including an easement interest) of duration greater than one year must be in writing to be enforceable. If a party attempts to create an easement orally, the result is the creation of a license, *i.e.,* a revocable privilege. Note, however, that if an oral attempt to create an

easement is subsequently "executed," to the extent that it would be inequitable to permit its revocation (*e.g.,* the licensee has expended substantial funds in reliance on the license), the licensor may be estopped to revoke the license.

d. **Irrevocable Licenses**

1) **Estoppel Theory**
If a licensee invests substantial amounts of money or labor in reliance on a license, the licensor may be estopped to revoke the license, and the license will thus become the equivalent of an affirmative easement.
Example: A orally licenses B to come onto Blackacre to excavate a drainage ditch connected to B's parcel, Whiteacre. B does so at substantial expense. A will probably be estopped to revoke the license and prevent B from using the ditch.

Under the majority view, such irrevocable licenses or easements by estoppel last until the owner receives sufficient benefit to reimburse himself for the expenditures made in reliance on the license. A minority of courts treat easements by estoppel like any other affirmative easements and give them a potentially infinite duration.

2) **License Coupled with an Interest**
If a license is coupled with an interest, it will be irrevocable as long as the interest lasts.

a) **Vendee of a Chattel**
The purchaser of a chattel located upon the seller's land is, in the absence of an express stipulation to the contrary, given the privilege to enter upon the seller's land for the purpose of removing the chattel. The purchaser's right is irrevocable. He must, however, enter at reasonable times and in a reasonable manner.
Example: A, the owner of Blackacre, sells 100 crates of oranges stored in a shed on Blackacre and at the same time licenses B to come onto Blackacre to remove the crates of oranges. B has an irrevocable license to enter Blackacre and remove the crates within a reasonable time.

b) **Termination of Tenancy**
If a tenant's right to possess land has been lawfully terminated, the tenant may still reenter the land at reasonable times and in a reasonable manner for the purpose of removing his chattels. This is an irrevocable privilege.

c) **Inspection for Waste**
The owner of a future interest in land (*e.g.,* a landlord, holder of a reversionary interest, or remainderman) is privileged to enter upon the land, at reasonable times and in a reasonable manner, for the purpose of determining whether waste is being committed by the holder of the present possessory estate.

C. **PROFITS**
Like an easement, a profit (profit a prendre) is a ***nonpossessory*** interest in land. The holder of the

profit is entitled to enter upon the servient tenement and take the soil or a substance of the soil (*e.g.,* minerals, timber, oil, or game). Also, like an easement, a profit may be appurtenant or in gross. In contrast to easements, however, there is a constructional preference for profits in gross rather than appurtenant.

1. Creation
Profits are created in the same way as easements.

2. Alienability
A profit appurtenant follows the ownership of the dominant tenement. A profit in gross may be assigned or transferred by the holder.

3. Exclusive and Nonexclusive Profits Distinguished
When an owner grants the ***sole right*** to take a resource from her land, the grantee takes an exclusive profit and is solely entitled to the resources, even to the exclusion of the owner of the servient estate. By contrast, when a profit is nonexclusive, the owner of the servient estate may grant similar rights to others or may take the resources herself. Ordinarily, profits (like easements) are construed as nonexclusive.

4. Scope
The extent and nature of the profit is determined by the words of the ***express grant*** (if there was a grant), or by ***the nature of the use*** (if the profit was acquired by prescription). Note that implied in every profit is an easement entitling the profit holder to enter the servient estate to remove the resource.

Example: A, the owner of Blackacre, grants B the right to come onto Blackacre to carry off gravel from a pit on Blackacre. B has a profit with respect to the gravel and also the benefit of an implied affirmative easement to go onto Blackacre by reasonable means to remove the gravel.

a. Apportionment of Profits Appurtenant
Courts treat the subdivision of land with a profit appurtenant just as they treat the subdivision of land with an easement appurtenant. The ***benefit of the profit*** will attach to each parcel in a subdivision ***only*** if the burden on the servient estate is not as a result ***overly increased.***

Example: A, the owner of Blackacre, grants B, the owner of adjacent Whiteacre, the right to remove rock from Blackacre. If the profit was to take the rock for purposes of maintaining a boat launch on Whiteacre, then an increase in use from one to 50 boat launches when Whiteacre is subdivided will probably be viewed as overburdensome to Blackacre.

If, however, the profit was to take rock for purposes of reinforcing Whiteacre's coastline to prevent erosion, apportionment would likely be allowed because subdivision would not increase the number of acres to be reinforced and consequently would not impose a greater burden on Blackacre.

b. Apportionment of Profits in Gross
Because profits are freely alienable, a question frequently arises as to whether the holder of a profit can convey it to several people. If a profit is ***exclusive***, the holder may transfer

the profit to as many transferees as he likes. Likewise, if the grant of the profit specifies a limit on the profit (less than all), the right can be transferred to multiple transferees. If, however, the profit is ***nonexclusive*** and not limited as to amount, it is generally not divisible. Undue burden to the servient estate is again the benchmark, however, and a nonexclusive profit may be assigned to a single person or to several persons jointly if the multiple assignees work together and take no more resources than would have been taken by the original benefit holder.

5. Termination

Profits are terminated in the same way as easements. In addition, ***misuse*** of a profit, unduly increasing the burden (typically through an improper apportionment), will be held to ***surcharge*** the servient estate. The result of surcharge in this case is to extinguish the profit. (Contrast this with the result when the benefit of an ***affirmative easement*** is misused: Improper or excessive use increasing the burden on the servient estate is ***enjoinable*** but, in most jurisdictions, does not extinguish the easement; *see* B.3.g., *supra.*)

D. COVENANTS RUNNING WITH THE LAND AT LAW (REAL COVENANTS)

A real covenant, normally found in deeds, is a ***written promise*** to do something on the land (*e.g.,* maintain a fence) or a promise not to do something on the land (*e.g.,* conduct commercial business). Real covenants run with the land at law, which means that subsequent owners of the land may enforce or be burdened by the covenant. To run with the land, however, the benefit and burden of the covenant must be analyzed separately to determine whether they meet the requirements for running.

1. Requirements for Burden to Run

If all requirements are met for the burden to run, the successor in interest to the burdened estate will be bound by the arrangement entered into by her predecessor as effectively as if she had herself expressly agreed to be bound.

a. Intent

The covenanting parties must have intended that successors in interest to the covenantor be bound by the terms of the covenant. The requisite intent may be inferred from circumstances surrounding creation of the covenant, or it may be evidenced by language in the conveyance creating the covenant (*e.g.,* "this covenant runs with the land," or "grantee covenants for herself, her heirs, successors, and assigns").

b. Notice

Under the common law, a subsequent purchaser of land that was subject to a covenant took the land burdened by the covenant, whether or not she had notice. However, under American recording statutes (*see* VI.E., *infra*), if the covenant is not recorded, a bona fide purchaser who has no notice of the covenant and who records her own deed ***will take free*** of the covenant. Hence, as a practical matter, if the subsequent purchaser pays value and records (as will nearly always be true), she is not bound by covenants of which she has no actual or constructive notice.

c. Horizontal Privity

This requirement rests on the relationship between the ***original covenanting parties***. Specifically, horizontal privity requires that, at the time the promisor entered into the covenant with the promisee, the two shared ***some interest in the land independent of the covenant*** (*e.g.,* grantor-grantee, landlord-tenant, mortgagor-mortgagee).

Examples: 1) A and B are neighboring landowners, neither having any rights in the other's land. For good consideration, A promises B, "for herself, her heirs, successors, and assigns," that A's parcel "will never be used for other than residential purposes." The horizontal privity requirement is ***not*** met, and successors in interest to A will ***not*** be bound because at the time A made this covenant, she and B shared no interest in land independent of the covenant.

2) A, the owner of Blackacre in fee, promised B, the holder of a right-of-way easement over Blackacre, "always to keep the right-of-way free of snow or other impediment to B's use of the right-of-way." Horizontal privity is met because, at the time the covenant was made, A owned the parcel in fee and B held the benefit of an easement in it.

3) A, the owner of Blackacre and Whiteacre, deeds Whiteacre to B, promising "not to use Blackacre for other than residential purposes." Horizontal privity exists here by virtue of the grantor-grantee relationship between A and B.

d. Vertical Privity

To be bound, the successor in interest to the covenanting party must hold the ***entire durational interest*** held by the covenantor at the time she made the covenant.

Example: A, who owns Blackacre and Whiteacre in fee simple absolute, sells Whiteacre to B and, in the deed, covenants for herself, her heirs, successors, and assigns to contribute one-half the expense of maintaining a common driveway between Blackacre and Whiteacre. A then transfers Blackacre to C "for life," retaining a reversionary interest for herself. B ***cannot*** enforce the covenant against C because C does not possess the entire interest (fee simple absolute) held by her predecessor in interest, A, at the time A made the promise.

e. Touch and Concern

The covenant must be of the type that "touches and concerns" the land. The phrase "touch and concern the land" is not susceptible to easy definition. It generally means that the effect of the covenant is to make the land itself more useful or valuable to the benefited party. The covenant must affect the legal relationship of the parties as landowners and not merely as members of the community at large. Therefore, as a general matter, for the burden of a covenant to run, performance of the burden must diminish the landowner's rights, privileges, and powers in connection with her enjoyment of the land.

1) Negative Covenants

For the burden of a negative covenant to touch and concern the land, the covenant must restrict the holder of the servient estate in his ***use of that parcel*** of land.

Examples: 1) A, who owned Blackacre and Whiteacre, covenanted with B, the grantee of Whiteacre, that she would not erect a building of over two stories on Blackacre. The burden of the covenant touches and

concerns Blackacre because it diminishes A's rights in connection with her enjoyment of Blackacre.

2) A, who owned Blackacre and Whiteacre, covenanted with B, the grantee of Whiteacre, that she would never operate a shoe store within a radius of one mile of Whiteacre. The covenant does not touch and concern Blackacre because its performance is unconnected to the enjoyment of Blackacre.

Note the similarity of negative covenants and negative easements. The primary difference between them is that negative easements are limited to a few traditional categories, but there are no limits on negative covenants.

2) Affirmative Covenants

For the burden of an affirmative covenant to touch and concern the land, the covenant must require the holder of the servient estate ***to do something***, increasing her obligations in connection with enjoyment of the land.

Examples: 1) A, who owned Blackacre and Whiteacre, covenanted with B, the grantee of Whiteacre, to keep the building on Blackacre in good repair. The covenant touches and concerns Blackacre because it increases A's obligations in connection with her enjoyment of Blackacre.

2) A owned Blackacre and Whiteacre, which were several miles apart. A covenanted with B, the grantee of Whiteacre, to keep the building on Whiteacre in good repair. The covenant does not touch and concern Blackacre because its performance is unconnected to the use and enjoyment of Blackacre.

3) A, the grantee of a parcel in a residential subdivision, covenants to pay an annual fee to a homeowners' association for the maintenance of common ways, parks, and other facilities in the subdivision. At one time, it was thought that such covenants, because physically unconnected to the land, did not touch and concern. The prevailing view today is that the burden will run because the fees are a charge on the land, increasing A's obligations in connection with the use and enjoyment of it. (*See* 3.a., *infra.*)

2. Requirements for Benefit to Run

If all requirements for the benefit to run are met, the successor in interest to the promisee will be allowed to enjoy the benefit (*i.e.,* enforce the covenant).

a. Intent

The covenanting parties must have intended that the successors in interest to the covenantee be able to enforce the covenant. Surrounding evidence of intent, as well as language in the instrument of conveyance, is admissible.

b. Vertical Privity

The benefit of a covenant runs to the assignees of the original estate or of any lesser estate (*e.g.,* a life estate). The owner of ***any*** succeeding possessory estate can enforce the benefit at law. In the majority of states today, horizontal privity is not required for the benefit to run. As a consequence, if horizontal privity is missing, the benefit may run to the successor in interest to the covenantee even though the burden is not enforceable against the successor in interest of the covenantor.

Example: A, who owns Blackacre, covenants with her neighbor, B, who owns Whiteacre, that "A, her successors, and assigns will keep the building on Blackacre in good repair." Horizontal privity is missing. B then conveys Whiteacre, the dominant estate, to C. C can enforce the benefit of the affirmative covenant against A because horizontal privity is not needed for the benefit to run. If, however, A conveys Blackacre to D, neither B nor C could enforce the covenant against D, for horizontal privity is required for the burden to run.

c. Touch and Concern

For the benefit of a covenant to touch and concern the land, the promised performance must benefit the covenantee and her successors ***in their use and enjoyment of the benefited land***.

Examples: 1) A, who owns Blackacre and Whiteacre, covenants with B, the grantee of Whiteacre, not to erect a building over two stories on Blackacre. The benefit of the covenant touches and concerns Whiteacre because, by securing B's view, it increases his enjoyment of Whiteacre.

2) A, who owns Blackacre and Whiteacre, covenants with B, the grantee of Whiteacre, to keep the building on Blackacre freshly painted and in good repair. The benefit of the covenant touches and concerns Whiteacre because, by assuring the view of an attractive house, it increases the value of Whiteacre.

Compare: A, who owns Blackacre, covenants with B, a supermarket operator owning no adjacent land, to erect and maintain on Blackacre a billboard advertising B's supermarkets. The benefit of the covenant does ***not*** touch and concern because it is not connected to and does not operate to increase B's enjoyment of any piece of land.

3. Modern Status of Running of Burden and Benefit

a. Horizontal and Vertical Privity

The Restatement of Property provides that horizontal privity is not required for running of the burden, and further discards the requirement of vertical privity for running of both the burden and the benefit. Instead, the Restatement draws a distinction between ***affirmative*** and ***negative*** covenants. Negative covenants are treated like easements, which run to successors because they are interests in land. The burdens and benefits of affirmative covenants run to persons who succeed to an ***estate of the same duration*** as owned by the original parties, including in most cases an adverse possessor. But affirmative covenants do not run to persons who hold lesser estates than those held by the original parties to the covenant. Special rules are set forth for when affirmative burdens run to lessees and life tenants, and when they can enforce the benefits. [Restatement (Third) of Property: Servitudes §§5.2 - 5.5]

b. Touch and Concern

The Restatement of Property also supersedes the touch and concern requirement by providing that real covenants are ***presumed valid*** unless they are illegal, unconstitutional, or violate public policy. [Restatement (Third) of Property: Servitudes §§3.1, 3.2]

4. Specific Situations Involving Real Covenants

a. Promises to Pay Money

The majority rule is that if the money is to be used in a way connected with the land, the burden will run with the land. The most common example is a covenant to pay a homeowners' association an annual fee for maintenance of common ways, parks, etc., in a subdivision.

b. Covenants Not to Compete

Covenants not to compete have created several problems. Clearly, the burden of the covenant—restricting the use to which the land may be put—"touches and concerns" the land. However, the benefited land, while "commercially enhanced," is not affected in its physical use. Thus, some courts have refused to permit the benefit of such covenants to run with the land.

c. Racially Restrictive Covenants

If a covenant purports to prohibit an owner from transferring land to persons of a given race, no court (state or federal) is permitted to enforce the covenant. To do so would involve the court in a violation of the Equal Protection Clause of the Fourteenth Amendment (*see* I.F.2.b.2), *supra*).

5. Remedies—Damages Only

A breach of a real covenant is remedied by an award of money damages, not an injunction. If equitable relief, such as an injunction, is sought, the promise must be enforced as an equitable servitude rather than a real covenant (*see* below). Note that a real covenant gives rise to personal liability only. The damages are collectible out of the defendant's general assets.

6. Termination

As with all other nonpossessory interests in land, a real covenant may be terminated by: (i) the holder of the benefit executing a ***release in writing***; (ii) ***merger*** (fee simple title to both the benefited and burdened land comes into the hands of a single owner); and (iii) ***condemnation*** of the burdened property. (*See* B.4.b., c., h., *supra.*)

E. EQUITABLE SERVITUDES

If a plaintiff wants an injunction or specific performance, he must show that the covenant qualifies as an equitable servitude. An equitable servitude is a covenant that, regardless of whether it runs with the land at law, equity will enforce against the assignees of the burdened land who have ***notice*** of the covenant. The usual remedy is an injunction against violation of the covenant.

1. Creation

Generally, equitable servitudes are created by covenants contained ***in a writing*** that satisfies the Statute of Frauds. As with real covenants, acceptance of a deed signed only by the grantor is sufficient to bind the grantee as promisor. There is ***one exception*** to the writing requirement: Negative equitable servitudes may be implied from a common scheme for development of a residential subdivision.

a. Servitudes Implied from Common Scheme

When a developer subdivides land into several parcels and some of the deeds contain negative covenants but some do not, negative covenants or equitable servitudes binding ***all*** the parcels in the subdivision may be implied under the doctrine of "reciprocal negative servitudes." The doctrine applies only to negative covenants and equitable servitudes and not to affirmative covenants. Two requirements must be met before reciprocal negative covenants and servitudes will be implied: (i) a common scheme for development, and (ii) notice of the covenants.

Example: A subdivides her parcel into lots 1 through 50. She conveys lots 1 through 45 by deeds containing express covenants by the respective grantees that they will use their lots only for residential purposes. A orally assures the 45 grantees that ***all*** 50 lots will be used for residential purposes. Some time later, after the 45 lots have been developed as residences, A conveys lot 46 to an oil company, which plans to operate a service station on it. The deed to lot 46 contains no express residential restriction. A court will nonetheless imply a negative covenant, prohibiting use for other than residential purposes on lot 46 because both requirements have been met for an implied reciprocal negative servitude. First, there was a ***common scheme***, here evidenced by A's statements to the first 45 buyers. Second, the oil company was on ***inquiry notice*** of the negative covenant because of the uniform residential character of the other lots in the subdivision development.

1) Common Scheme

Reciprocal negative covenants will be implied only if at the time that sales of parcels in the subdivision began, the developer had a plan that all parcels in the subdivision be developed within the terms of the negative covenant. If the scheme arises after some lots are sold, it cannot impose burdens on the lots previously sold without the express covenants. The developer's common scheme may be evidenced by a ***recorded plat***, by a ***general pattern*** of prior restrictions, or by ***oral representations***, typically in the form of statements to early buyers that all parcels in the development will be restricted by the same covenants that appear in their deeds. On the basis of this scheme, it is inferred that purchasers bought their lots relying on the fact that they would be able to enforce subsequently created equitable servitudes similar to the restrictions imposed in their deeds.

2) Notice

To be bound by the terms of a covenant that does not appear in his deed, a grantee must, at the time he acquired his parcel, have had notice of the covenants contained in the deeds of other buyers in the subdivision. The requisite notice may be acquired through ***actual notice*** (direct knowledge of the covenants in the prior deeds); ***inquiry notice*** (the neighborhood appears to conform to common restrictions); or ***record notice*** (if the prior deeds are in the grantee's chain of title he will, under the recording acts, have constructive notice of their contents).

2. Enforcement

For successors of the original promisee and promisor to enforce an equitable servitude, certain requirements must be met.

a. **Requirements for Burden to Run**

1) **Intent**
The covenanting parties must have intended that the servitude be enforceable by and against assignees. No technical words are required to express this intent. In fact, the intent may be ascertained from the purpose of the covenant and the surrounding circumstances.

2) **Notice**
A subsequent purchaser of land burdened by a covenant is not bound by it in equity unless she had actual or constructive notice of it when she acquired the land. This rule is part of the law of equitable servitudes, and exists apart from the recording acts.

3) **Touch and Concern**
This is the same requirement as applies to real covenants (*see* D.1.e., *supra*).

b. **Requirements for Benefit to Run**
The benefit of the equitable servitude will run with the land (and thus to successors in interest of the original parties) if the original parties so ***intended*** and the servitude ***touches and concerns*** the benefited property.

c. **Privity Not Required**
The majority of courts enforce the servitude not as an in personam right against the owner of the servient tenement, but as an equitable property interest in the land itself. There is, therefore, no need for privity of estate.

Examples: 1) A acquires title to Blackacre by adverse possession. Even though he is not in privity of estate with the original owner, he is subject to the equitable servitude because the servitude is an interest in the land.

2) A and B are neighboring landowners, neither having any rights in the other's land. A promises B, "for herself, her heirs, successors, and assigns," that A's parcel "will never be used for other than residential purposes." B records the agreement. A sells Blackacre to C. The burden created by this promise would ***not run at law*** as a negative covenant because horizontal privity is missing. However, under an equitable servitude theory, the burden ***will run***, and an injunction will issue against other than residential uses.

3) Same as above, but A transfers only a life estate to C. Again, the burden would not run at law because of the absence of vertical privity. The burden would, however, be enforceable as an equitable servitude.

d. **Implied Beneficiaries of Covenants—General Scheme**
If a covenant in a subdivision deed is silent as to who holds its benefit, any neighbor in the subdivision will be entitled to enforce the covenant if a general scheme or plan is found to have existed at the time he purchased his lot.

Example: A subdivides her parcel into Lots 1 through 10. She conveys Lot 1 to B, who covenants to use the lot for residential purposes only. A then conveys Lot 2 to C, who makes a similar covenant. Thereafter, A conveys the balance of the lots to other grantees by deeds containing the residential restriction. Can C enforce the restrictions against B? Can B enforce against C?

Subsequent purchaser versus prior purchaser (C v. B): In most jurisdictions, C (the later grantee) can enforce the restriction against B if the court finds a common plan of residential restrictions at the very outset of A's sales. (Evidence would be the similar covenant restrictions in all the deeds.) The rationale is that B's promise was made for the benefit of the land at that time retained by A, the grantor. Such land, Lots 2 through 10, became the dominant estate. When A thereafter conveyed Lot 2 to C, the benefit of B's promise passed to C with the land.

Prior purchaser versus subsequent purchaser (B v. C): In most jurisdictions, B could likewise enforce the restriction against C, even though A made no covenant in her deed to B that A's retained land would be subject to the residential restrictions.

There are two theories on which a prior purchaser can enforce a restriction in a subsequent deed from a common grantor. One theory is that B is a third-party beneficiary of C's promise to A. The other theory is that an implied reciprocal servitude attached to A's retained land at the moment she deeded Lot 1 to B. Under this theory, B is enforcing an ***implied*** servitude on Lot 2 and ***not*** the express covenant later made by C.

3. **Equitable Defenses to Enforcement**

A court in equity is not bound to enforce a servitude if it cannot in good conscience do so.

a. **Unclean Hands**

A court will not enforce a servitude if the person seeking enforcement is violating a similar restriction on his own land. This defense will apply even if the violation on the complainant's land is less serious, as long as it is of the same general nature.

b. **Acquiescence**

If a benefited party acquiesces in a violation of the servitude by one burdened party, he may be deemed to have abandoned the servitude as to other burdened parties. (Equitable servitudes, like easements, may be abandoned.) Note that this defense will not apply if the prior violation occurred in a location so distant from the complainant that it did not really affect his property.

c. **Estoppel**

If the benefited party has acted in such a way that a reasonable person would believe that the covenant was abandoned, and the burdened party acts in reliance thereon, the benefited party will be estopped to enforce the covenant. Similarly, if the benefited party fails to bring suit against a violator within a reasonable time, the action may be barred by ***laches***.

d. **Changed Neighborhood Conditions**

Changed neighborhood conditions may also operate to end an equitable servitude. If the

neighborhood has changed significantly since the time the servitude was created, with the result that it would be inequitable to enforce the restriction, injunctive relief will be withheld. (Many courts, however, will allow the holder of the benefit to bring an action at law for damages.)

Example: A, the owner of Blackacre and Whiteacre, adjacent parcels in an undeveloped area, sells Blackacre to B, extracting a promise that Blackacre "will always be used only for residential purposes." Fifteen years later, the neighborhood has developed as a commercial and industrial center. If B or her successors in interest to Blackacre now wish to use the parcel for a store, an injunction will probably ***not*** issue. A may, however, recover from B or her successors any damages that she may suffer from termination of the residential restriction.

1) **Zoning**

Zoning plays an important role in determining whether changed conditions will be allowed as a defense to enforcement of an equitable servitude. Zoning that is inconsistent with the private restriction imposed by the equitable servitude will not of itself bar the injunction, but it will provide good evidence that neighborhood conditions have changed sufficiently to make the injunction unjust. Thus, in the example above, the position of B or her successors would be fortified by a showing that the area in which Blackacre is situated is presently zoned for commercial uses.

2) **Concept of the "Entering Wedge"**

The concept of the "entering wedge" also plays an important role in changed condition cases. If the equitable servitude is part of a general plan of restrictions in a subdivision, and if the parcel in question is located somewhere at the ***outer edge*** of the subdivision, changed conditions outside of the subdivision will not bar the injunction if it is shown that lifting the restriction on one parcel will produce changed conditions for surrounding parcels, requiring that their restrictions also be lifted, and so on (the "domino effect"). Thus, in the example above, if removing the restriction and allowing commercial development of Blackacre would produce changed conditions for the neighboring, similarly restricted parcel—Whiteacre—with the consequence that its servitude could not be equitably enforced, the injunction against commercial use on Blackacre will probably be allowed, notwithstanding the changed conditions. Note that injunctive relief may be granted if the substantial change occurs ***within*** the subdivision.

4. **Termination**

Like other nonpossessory interests in land, an equitable servitude may be terminated by a ***written release*** from the benefit holder(s), ***merger*** of the benefited and burdened estates, or ***condemnation*** of the burdened property. (*See* B.4.b., c., h., *supra*.)

F. RELATIONSHIP OF COVENANTS TO ZONING ORDINANCES

Both restrictive covenants and zoning ordinances (*see* IX.C., *infra*) may affect legally permissible uses of land. Both must be complied with, and neither provides any excuse for violating the other. For example, if the zoning permits both residential and commercial use but an applicable covenant allows only residential use, the covenant will control.

These two forms of land use restrictions are enforced differently. As discussed above, covenants (if they meet the relevant requirements) can be enforced by nearby property owners at law or in equity. Zoning, on the other hand, is not subject to enforcement by private suit, but can be enforced only by local governmental officials.

G. PARTY WALLS AND COMMON DRIVEWAYS

Often, a single wall or driveway will be built partly on the property of each of two adjoining landowners. Absent an agreement between the owners to the contrary, courts will treat the wall as belonging to each owner to the extent that it rests upon her land. Courts will also imply mutual cross-easements of support, with the result that each party has the right to use the wall or driveway, and neither party can unilaterally destroy it.

1. Creation

While a ***written agreement*** is required by the Statute of Frauds for the express creation of a party wall or common driveway agreement, an "irrevocable license" can arise if there has been detrimental reliance on a parol agreement. Party walls and common driveways can also result from ***implication*** or ***prescription***.

2. Running of Covenants

If party wall or common driveway owners agree to be mutually responsible for maintaining the wall or driveway, the burdens and benefits of these covenants will run to successive owners of each parcel. The ***cross-easements for support*** satisfy the requirement of horizontal privity because they are mutual interests in the same property. And each promise touches and concerns the adjoining parcels.

V. ADVERSE POSSESSION

A. IN GENERAL

Title to real property may be acquired by adverse possession. (Easements may also be acquired by prescription.) Gaining title by adverse possession results from the operation of the statute of limitations for trespass to real property. If an owner does not, within the statutory period, take legal action to eject a possessor who claims adversely to the owner, the owner is thereafter barred from bringing suit for ejectment. Moreover, title to the property vests in the possessor.

B. REQUIREMENTS

To establish title by adverse possession, the possessor must show (i) an ***actual entry*** giving ***exclusive possession*** that is (ii) ***open and notorious***, (iii) ***adverse*** (hostile), and (iv) ***continuous*** throughout the statutory period.

1. Running of Statute

The statute of limitations begins to run when the claimant goes adversely into possession of the true owner's land (*i.e.,* the point at which the true owner could first bring suit). The filing of suit by the true owner is not sufficient to stop the period from running; the suit must be pursued to judgment. However, if the true owner files suit before the statutory period (*e.g.,* 20 years) runs out and the judgment is rendered after the statutory period, the judgment will relate back to the time that the complaint was filed.

2. Actual and Exclusive Possession

a. Actual Possession Gives Notice

The requirement of actual possession is designed to give the true owner notice that a trespass is occurring. It is also designed to give her notice of the ***extent*** of the adverse possessor's claim. As a general rule, the adverse possessor will gain title only to the land that she actually occupies.

1) Constructive Possession of Part

Actual possession of a portion of a unitary tract of land is sufficient adverse possession as to give title to the whole of the tract of land after the statutory period, as long as there is a ***reasonable proportion*** between the portion actually possessed and the whole of the unitary tract, and the possessor has color of title (*i.e.,* a document purporting to give him title) to the whole tract. Usually, the proportion will be held reasonable if possession of the portion was sufficient to put the owner or community on notice of the fact of possession.

b. Exclusive Possession—No Sharing with Owner

"Exclusive" merely means that the possessor is not sharing with the true owner or the public at large. This requirement does not prevent two or more individuals from working ***together*** to obtain title by adverse possession. If they do so, they will obtain the title as tenants in common.

Example: A and B are next door neighbors. They decide to plant a vegetable garden on the vacant lot behind both of their homes. A and B share expenses and profits from the garden. If all other elements for adverse possession are present, at the end of the statutory period, A and B will own the lot as tenants in common.

3. Open and Notorious Possession

Possession is open and notorious when it is the kind of use the usual owner would make of the land. The adverse possessor's occupation must be ***sufficiently apparent*** to put the true owner on ***notice*** that a trespass is occurring. If, *e.g.,* Water Company ran a pipe under Owner's land and there was no indication of the pipe's existence from the surface of the land, Water Company could not gain title by adverse possession because there was nothing to put Owner on notice of the trespass.

Example: A's use of B's farmland for an occasional family picnic will not satisfy the open and notorious requirement because picnicking is not necessarily an act consistent with the ownership of farmland.

4. Hostile

The possessor's occupation of the property must be hostile (adverse). This means merely that the possessor does ***not have the true owner's permission*** to be on the land. It does not mean anger or animosity. The state of mind of the adverse possessor is irrelevant. By the large majority view, it does not matter whether the possessor believes she is on her own land, knows she is trespassing on someone else's land, or has no idea who owns the land.

a. If Possession Starts Permissively—Must Communicate Hostility

If the possessor enters with permission of the true owner (*e.g.,* under a lease or license), the possession does not become adverse until the possessor makes clear to the true owner the fact that she is claiming "hostilely." This can be done by explicit notification, by refusing to permit the true owner to come onto the land, or by other acts inconsistent with the original permission.

b. **Co-Tenants—Ouster Required**
Possession by one co-tenant is not ordinarily adverse to her co-tenants because each co-tenant has a right to the possession of all the property. Thus, sole possession or use by one co-tenant is not adverse, unless there is a clear repudiation of the co-tenancy; *e.g.,* one co-tenant ousts the others or makes an explicit declaration that he is claiming exclusive dominion over the property.

c. **If Grantor Stays in Possession—Permission Presumed**
If a grantor remains in possession of land after her conveyance, she is presumed to be there with the permission of her grantee. Only the grantor's open repudiation of the conveyance will start the limitation period running against the grantee. Likewise, if the tenant remains in possession after the expiration of her lease, she is presumed to have the permission of the landlord.

d. **Compare—Boundary Line Agreements**
There is a separate but related doctrine that may be helpful here. It operates where a boundary line (usually a fence) is fixed by agreement of the adjoining landowners, but later turns out not to be the "true" line. Most courts will fix ownership ***as per the agreed line***, provided it is shown that: (i) there was original ***uncertainty*** as to the true line; (ii) the agreed line was ***established*** (*i.e.,* agreed upon); and (iii) there has been ***lengthy acquiescence*** in the agreed line by the adjoining owners and/or their successors.

1) **Establishment Requirement**
The establishment requirement can be implied by acquiescence. A past dispute is not necessary to show uncertainty, although it can be good evidence of it. But a showing of original uncertainty is required; otherwise, in a court's view, a parol transfer of land would result.

5. **Continuous Possession**
The adverse claimant's possession must be continuous throughout the statutory period. Continuous possession requires only the degree of occupancy and use that the average owner would make of the property.

a. **Intermittent Periods of Occupancy Not Sufficient**
Intermittent periods of occupancy generally are not sufficient. However, constant use by the claimant is not required so long as the possession is of the type that the usual owner would make of the property. For example, the fact that the adverse possessor is using the land for the intermittent grazing of cattle will probably not defeat continuity if the land is ***normally*** used in this manner.

b. **Tacking Permitted**
There need not be continuous possession by the same person. Ordinarily, an adverse possessor can take advantage of the periods of adverse possession by her predecessor. Separate periods of adverse possession may be "tacked" together to make up the full

statutory period with the result that the final adverse possessor gets title, provided there is privity between the successive adverse holders.

1) **"Privity"**
Privity is satisfied if the subsequent possessor takes by descent, by devise, or by deed purporting to convey title. Tacking is not permitted where one adverse claimant ousts a preceding adverse claimant or where one adverse claimant abandons and a new adverse claimant then goes into possession.

2) **Formalities on Transfer**
Even an oral transfer of possession is sufficient to satisfy the privity requirement.
Example: A received a deed describing Blackacre, but by mistake built a house on an adjacent parcel, Whiteacre. A, after pointing the house out to B and orally agreeing to sell the house and land to her, conveyed to B, by a deed copied from her own deed, describing the property as Blackacre. The true owner of Whiteacre argues that there was no privity between A and B because the deed made no reference to Whiteacre, the land actually possessed. Nonetheless, the agreed oral transfer of actual possession is sufficient to permit tacking.

6. **Payment of Property Taxes Generally Not Required**
Only a minority of states require the adverse possessor to pay taxes on the property. However, in all states, payment of property taxes is good evidence of a claim of right.

C. DISABILITY

1. **Effect of Disabilities—Statute Tolled**
The statute of limitations does not begin to run for adverse possession (or easements by prescription) if the true owner was under some disability to sue ***when the cause of action first accrued*** (*i.e.,* the inception of the adverse possession). Typical disabilities are: minority, imprisonment, and insanity.
Example: O, the true owner, is five years old when A goes into adverse possession. The statute will not begin to run until O reaches the age of majority.

Compare: O, the true owner, is declared insane six months after A begins using a pathway adversely. The statute is ***not*** tolled because O's disability arose ***after*** the statute began to run.

2. **No Tacking of Disabilities**
Only a disability of the ***owner*** existing at the time the cause of action arose is considered. Thus, disabilities of successors in interest or subsequent additional disabilities of the owner have no effect on the statute.
Examples: 1) O is a minor at the time A goes into adverse possession of O's land. One year before O reaches the age of majority, O is declared insane. The statute is not tolled by reason of O's insanity (a subsequent disability). Thus, the statute begins to run from the date O reaches the age of majority, whether she is then sane or insane.

2) O, the true owner, is insane when A begins an adverse use. Ten years later, O dies intestate and the land goes to her heir, H, who is then 10 years old. The statute of limitations begins to run upon O's death and is not tolled by H's minority. H's minority is a "supervening" disability and cannot be tacked to O's.

3. Maximum Tolling Periods

In some states, the maximum tolling period is 20 years; thus, the maximum period of the statute of limitations would be the regular statute of limitations period plus the maximum 20-year tolling period.

D. ADVERSE POSSESSION AND FUTURE INTERESTS

The statute of limitations does not run against the holder of a future interest (*e.g.,* a remainder) until that interest becomes possessory. Until the prior present estate terminates, the holder of the future interest has no right to possession, and thus no cause of action against a wrongful possessor.

Examples: 1) O devises Blackacre to A for life and then to B. Thereafter, X goes into possession and possesses adversely for the statutory period. X has acquired A's life estate by adverse possession, but has not acquired any interests against B. Of course, if following A's death, X or her successor stays in possession for the statutory period, X will have acquired B's rights also.

2) X enters into adverse possession of Blackacre. Four years later, O devises Blackacre to A for life and then to B. X continues her adverse possession for seven more years. The statute of limitations is 10 years. In this case, X has acquired the whole title by adverse possession. An adverse possession begun against the owner of the fee simple absolute cannot be interrupted by a subsequent division of the estate.

1. Possibility of Reverter—Statute of Limitations Runs on Happening of Event

In a conveyance "to A for so long as" some event occurs or fails to occur, on the happening of the event the fee simple determinable automatically comes to an end and the grantor (or his successors) is entitled to present possession. At that point, the grantor has a cause of action to recover possession of the property. If he does not bring the action within the period specified by the applicable statute of limitations (and if A or her successors have the requisite open, notorious, continuous, and adverse possession), his action will be barred.

2. Right of Entry—Happening of Event *Does Not* Trigger Statute of Limitations

In the case of a right of entry, on the happening of the stated event the grantor (or his successors) has only a right to reenter the property, a power to terminate the grantee's estate. Until the grantor asserts his right of entry, no cause of action arises because the grantee's continued possession of the land is proper: her fee simple estate has not been terminated. Thus (in most states), the statute of limitations does not operate to bar assertion of a right of entry even though the condition triggering the right of entry has been breached.

a. Grantor Must Act Within Reasonable Time to Avoid Laches

However, to avoid the title problems that might otherwise be presented, most courts hold that the holder of the right of entry must bring his action within a reasonable time

after the event occurs. If he fails to do so, his action is barred by laches. As for what constitutes a reasonable time, many courts look to the statute of limitations governing actions for possession of real property.

E. EFFECT OF COVENANTS IN TRUE OWNER'S DEED

The exact nature of the title obtained depends on the possessor's activities on the land. For example, assume there is a recorded restrictive covenant limiting use of the land to a single-family residence. If the possessor uses the land in violation of that covenant for the limitations period, she takes title free of the covenant. But if she complies with the covenant, she takes title subject to it, and it remains enforceable against her (at least in an equitable action).

F. LAND THAT CANNOT BE ADVERSELY POSSESSED

The statute of limitations does not run against government-owned land (federal, state, or local) or land registered under a Torrens system.

VI. CONVEYANCING

A. LAND SALE CONTRACTS

Most transfers of land are preceded by contracts of sale. These normally contemplate escrows (delivery of deed to a third person to be held until purchase price paid) before closing (exchange of purchase price and deed).

1. Statute of Frauds Applicable

To be enforceable, a land contract must be in writing and signed by the party to be charged. The writing need not be a formal contract; a memorandum suffices—*e.g.,* escrow instructions can be the contract of sale. The Statute of Frauds requires that the writing contain all "essential terms" of the contract. These are: (i) a ***description*** of the property (*see* B.3., *infra*), (ii) identification of ***the parties*** to the contract, and (iii) the ***price*** and manner of payment (if agreed upon). Incidental matters (*e.g.,* prorating of taxes, furnishing of deeds, title insurance, etc.) can be determined by custom; they need not appear in the writing nor even have been agreed upon.

a. Doctrine of Part Performance

A court may give specific performance of a contract (though not damages) despite the absence of a writing if additional facts are present.

1) Theories to Support the Doctrine

a) Evidentiary Theory

Courts state that if acts done by a party can be explained only by reference to an agreement, these acts unequivocally establish the existence of an oral contract.

b) Hardship or Estoppel Theory

If acts done by a party in reliance on the contract would result in hardship to such an extent that it would be a fraud on that party were the contract not specifically enforced, the other party will be estopped from asserting the Statute of Frauds as a defense.

2) **Acts of Part Performance**
In most states, two of the following are required:

(i) ***Possession*** of the land by the purchaser;

(ii) Making of substantial ***improvements***; and/or

(iii) ***Payment*** of all or part of the purchase price by the purchaser.

Some state courts will go beyond this list and will accept as "part performance" other types of detrimental reliance by the purchaser, such as performance of services or sale of other land.

3) **Can Seller Obtain Specific Performance Based on Buyer's Acts?**

a) **Evidentiary Theory**
Under the evidentiary theory, it is immaterial who performed the acts constituting the part performance. Because they refer unequivocally to a contract, the seller may obtain specific performance based on the buyer's acts.

b) **Hardship or Estoppel Theory**
Under the hardship or estoppel theory, however, the ***plaintiff*** must be the one whose action would result in hardship if the Statute of Frauds were invoked. Consequently, the seller normally ***cannot*** rely on the buyer's acts. Even so, make sure that you ascertain whether the ***seller*** has done anything that would cause him a hardship if the Statute of Frauds were successfully asserted by the buyer.

2. **Doctrine of Equitable Conversion**
Under the doctrine of equitable conversion, once a contract is signed and each party is entitled to specific performance, equity regards the purchaser as the owner of the ***real property***. The seller's interest, which consists of the right to the proceeds of sale, is considered to be ***personal property***. The bare legal title that remains in the seller is considered to be held in trust for the purchaser as security for the debt owed the seller. But note that possession follows the legal title; so even though the buyer is regarded as owning the property, the seller is entitled to possession until the closing.

a. **Risk of Loss**
If the property is destroyed (without fault of either party) before the date set for closing, the majority rule is that, because the buyer is deemed the owner of the property, the ***risk of loss is on the buyer***. Thus, the buyer must pay the contract price despite a loss due to fire or other casualty, unless the contract provides otherwise. Some states, however, have adopted the Uniform Vendor and Purchaser Risk Act, which places the risk on the ***seller*** unless the buyer has either legal title or possession of the property at the time of the loss.

1) **Casualty Insurance**
Suppose the buyer has the risk of loss, as is true under the majority view, but

the seller has fire or casualty insurance that covers the loss. In the event of loss, allowing the seller to recover the full purchase price on the contract and to collect the insurance proceeds would be unjust enrichment. Hence, the courts require the seller to give the buyer credit, against the purchase price, in the amount of the insurance proceeds.

b. Passage of Title upon Death

The doctrine of equitable conversion also affects the passage of title when a party to a contract of sale dies before the contract has been completed. In general, it holds that a deceased seller's interest passes as personal property and a deceased buyer's interest as real property.

1) Death of Seller

If the seller dies, the "bare" legal title passes to the takers of his real property, but they must give up the title to the buyer when the contract closes. When the purchase price is paid, the money passes as personal property to those who take the seller's personal property. Note that if the property is ***specifically*** devised, the specific devisee will probably take the proceeds of the sale. (*See* F.1.b., *infra.*)

2) Death of Buyer

If the buyer dies, the takers of his real property can demand a conveyance of the land at the closing of the contract. Moreover, they are entitled to exoneration out of the personal property estate; thus, the takers of his personal property will have to pay the purchase price out of their share of the buyer's estate.

3. Marketable Title

There is an implied warranty in ***every*** land sale contract that at closing the seller will provide the buyer with a title that is "marketable."

a. "Marketability" Defined—Title Reasonably Free from Doubt

Marketable title is title reasonably free from doubt, *i.e.,* title that a reasonably prudent buyer would be willing to accept. It need not be a "perfect" title, but the title must be free from questions that might present an unreasonable risk of litigation. Generally, this means an unencumbered fee simple with good record title.

1) Defects in Record Chain of Title

Title may be unmarketable because of a defect in the chain of title. Examples include: a significant ***variation in the description*** of the land from one deed to the next, a deed in the chain that was ***defectively executed*** and thus fails to meet the requirements for recordation, and evidence that a prior grantor ***lacked capacity*** to convey the property. Many courts hold that an ancient lien or mortgage on the record will not render title unmarketable if the seller has proof of its satisfaction or the statute of limitations on the claim would have run under any possible circumstance, including tolling for disabilities.

a) Adverse Possession

Historically, a title acquired by adverse possession was not considered marketable because the purchaser might be later forced to defend in court the facts that gave rise to the adverse possession against the record owner. On the bar exam, ***title acquired by adverse possession is unmarketable***, despite the fact that most modern cases are contra. Most of the modern cases hold adverse possession titles to be marketable if: (i) the possession has been for a very lengthy period; (ii) the risk that the record owner will sue appears to be very remote; and (iii) the probability of the record owner's success in such a suit appears to be minimal. Because the bar examiners have yet to recognize this line of cases, the modern view should be considered only as a fallback position on the bar exam.

b) Future Interest Held by Unborn or Unascertained Parties

Even though most states consider all types of future interests to be transferable, it is often impossible for the owners of the present and future interests, acting together, to transfer a marketable fee simple absolute title. This is because the future interests are often held by persons who are unborn or unascertainable.

Example: "To A for life, and upon A's death to A's eldest surviving daughter." Assume that at the time of this conveyance A has one daughter, B. State of title: A has a life estate, and B has a contingent remainder. A and B together can transfer the land to a purchaser, such as C, but the title is not marketable. It may turn out that, upon A's death, B will have predeceased A, and some other daughter (perhaps not even yet born when A and B transferred to C) will be "A's eldest surviving daughter." Because that daughter did not join in the conveyance to C, she is not bound by it, and she owns the land. On the other hand, if B does turn out to be A's eldest surviving daughter (which cannot be determined until A's death), then C's title will become a marketable fee simple at that time.

While most courts will appoint a guardian ad litem to represent unborn or unascertained persons in ***litigation***, the majority will not appoint such a guardian for purposes of ***conveying*** the land.

2) Encumbrances

Generally, mortgages, liens, easements, and covenants render title unmarketable unless the buyer waives them.

a) Mortgages and Liens

A seller has the right to satisfy a mortgage or lien ***at the closing*** with the proceeds from the sale. Therefore, as long as the purchase price is sufficient and this is accomplished simultaneously with the transfer of title (usually through the use of escrows), the buyer cannot claim that the title is unmarketable; the closing will result in a marketable title.

b) Easements

An easement that reduces the value of the property (*e.g.,* an easement of way for the benefit of a neighbor) renders title unmarketable. The majority of courts, however, have held that a beneficial easement (*e.g.,* utility easement to service property) that was visible or known to the buyer does not constitute

an encumbrance. Some courts go so far as to hold that the buyer is deemed to have agreed to take subject to any easement that was notorious or known to the buyer when she entered into the contract.

c) **Covenants**
Restrictive covenants render title unmarketable.

d) **Encroachments**
A significant encroachment constitutes a title defect, regardless of whether an adjacent landowner is encroaching on the seller's land or vice versa. However, the encroachment will not render title unmarketable if: (i) it is very slight (only a few inches) and does not inconvenience the owner on whose land it encroaches; (ii) the owner encroached upon has indicated that he will not sue on it; or (iii) it has existed for so long (many decades) that it has become legal by adverse possession, provided that the state recognizes adverse possession titles as being marketable (*see* 1)a), *supra*).

3) **Zoning Restrictions**
Generally, zoning restrictions do not affect the marketability of title; they are not considered encumbrances. An ***existing violation*** of a zoning ordinance, however, does render title unmarketable.

4) **Waiver**
Any of the above-mentioned title defects can be waived in the contract of sale.

b. **Quitclaim Deed—No Effect**
The fact that a contract calls for a quitclaim deed, which does not contain any covenants for title, does not affect the warranty to provide marketable title (unless so provided in the contract).

c. **Time of Marketability**
If, as is usual, the seller has agreed to furnish title "at date of closing," the buyer cannot rescind prior to that date on grounds that the seller's title is not marketable.

1) **Installment Land Contract**
Similarly, where an installment land contract is used, the seller's obligation is to furnish marketable title ***when delivery is to occur***, *e.g.,* when the buyer has made his final payment. Therefore, a buyer cannot withhold payments or seek other remedies (*e.g.,* rescission) on grounds that the seller's title is unmarketable prior to the date of promised delivery. The buyer might get rescissionary relief before the date of delivery by showing that the seller cannot possibly cure the defects in time. Or, under compelling circumstances, a court might require the seller to quiet title during the contract period.

d. **Remedy If Title Not Marketable**
If the buyer determines that the seller's title is unmarketable, he must notify the seller and give a reasonable time to cure the defects, even if this requires extension of the closing date. The notice must specify the nature of the defects. If the seller fails to cure the defects, the buyer may pursue several remedies.

1) **Rescission, Damages, Specific Performance**
In the absence of a contractual stipulation to the contrary, if title is not marketable, the buyer can rescind, sue for damages for breach, get specific performance with an abatement of the purchase price, or, in some jurisdictions, require the seller to quiet title. The seller cannot sue successfully for damages or specific performance.

2) **Merger**
If the buyer permits the closing to occur, the contract is said to merge with the deed (*i.e.,* it disappears) and, in the absence of fraud, the seller is ***no longer liable*** on the implied contractual warranty of marketable title. However, the buyer may have an action for violation of promises made in the deed, if any (*see* D., *infra*). *Note:* The merger rule does not apply to most nontitle matters, such as covenants regarding the physical condition of the property. [Campbell v. Rawls, 381 So. 2d 744 (Fla. 1980)]

4. **Time of Performance**

a. **Presumption—Time Not of the Essence**
In general, the courts assume that time is not "of the essence" in real estate contracts. This means that the closing date stated in the contract is not absolutely binding in equity, and that a party, even though late in tendering her own performance, can still enforce the contract if she tenders within a reasonable time after the date. (A month or two is typically considered a reasonable time.)

b. **When Presumption Overcome**
Time will be considered "of the essence" if:

1) The ***contract*** so states; or

2) The ***circumstances*** indicate it was the parties' intention; *e.g.,* the land is rapidly fluctuating in value or a party must move from out of town and has no other place to go; or

3) One party gives the other ***notice*** that she desires to make time of the essence, and does so within a reasonable time prior to the date designated for closing.

c. **Effect of Time of the Essence Construction**
If time is of the essence, a party who fails to tender performance on the date set for closing is in total breach and loses her right to enforce the contract.

d. **Liability When Time Not of the Essence**
Even if time is not of the essence, a party who is late in tendering performance is liable in damages for the incidental losses she has caused, such as additional mortgage interest, taxes, etc.

5. **Tender of Performance**
In general, the buyer's obligation to pay the purchase price and the seller's obligation to convey the title are deemed to be ***concurrent conditions***. This means that neither party is in

breach of the contract until the other party tenders her performance, even if the date designated for the closing has passed.

a. **When Party's Tender Excused**
A party's tender is unnecessary and is excused if the party has repudiated the contract, or if it is impossible for the other party to perform (*e.g.,* if the seller does not have marketable title and cannot get it).

b. **Neither Party Tenders Performance**
If neither party tenders performance, the closing date is automatically extended indefinitely until one of them does so.

c. **Buyer Finds Seller's Title Unmarketable**
If the buyer determines that the seller's title is unmarketable, the buyer must give the seller a reasonable time to cure title defects.

6. **Remedies for Breach of the Sales Contract**

a. **Damages**
The usual measure of damages is the difference between the contract price and the market value of the land on the date of the breach. Incidental damages, such as title examination and moving or storage costs, can also be recovered.

1) **Liquidated Damages**
Sales contracts usually require the buyer to deposit "earnest money" with the seller, and provide that if the buyer defaults in performance, the seller may retain this money as liquidated damages. The courts routinely uphold the seller's retention of the deposit if the amount appears to be reasonable in light of the seller's anticipated and actual damages. Many courts will uphold a retention of a deposit of up to 10% of the sales price without further inquiry into its reasonableness. Even without a liquidated damages clause, many courts will uphold retention of the deposit, on the ground that giving restitution of the funds to the buyer would unjustly reward a party in breach.

b. **Specific Performance**

1) **Buyer's Remedy**
A court of equity will order a seller to convey the title if the buyer tenders the purchase price. The remedy at law (damages) is deemed inadequate because the buyer is getting land and land is unique.

If the seller cannot give marketable title, but the buyer wishes to proceed with the transaction, she can usually get specific performance with an ***abatement of the purchase price*** in an amount reflecting the title defect.

2) **Seller's Remedy**
Somewhat illogically, the courts also generally will give a specific performance decree for the seller if the buyer is in breach. This is sometimes explained as necessary to have "mutuality of remedy." A few courts in recent years have refused

to award specific performance to sellers if the property is not unique (*e.g.,* if a developer is selling a house in a large subdivision of similar houses).

c. **Special Rules for Unmarketable Title**
If the seller's title is unmarketable for reasons that do not indicate the seller's bad faith (*i.e.,* he did not realize that his title was defective when he signed the contract), about half of the courts limit the buyer's recovery of damages to incidental out-of-pocket costs (title examination, etc.) and return of the buyer's earnest money deposit. The other half of the courts give the buyer the standard measure of contract damages mentioned above.

7. **Seller's Liability for Defects on Property**

a. **Warranty of Fitness or Quality—New Construction Only**
The common law rule is that contracts of sale and deeds of real property, unlike conveyances of personal property, carry no implied warranties of quality or fitness for the purpose intended. One exception is a contract for the sale of a building under construction or to be constructed, on the ground that the buyer has no opportunity to inspect. A majority of courts have now extended the implied warranty of fitness or quality to the sale of any ***new house by the builder***. The warranty implied is that the new house is designed and constructed in a reasonably workmanlike manner and suitable for human habitation. A few courts have gone further, allowing a later owner of the house to recover from the original builder despite lack of privity.

b. **Negligence of Builder**
A person who contracts for construction may always sue a builder for negligence in performing a building contract. Moreover, many courts now permit the ultimate vendee (*e.g.,* a subdivision buyer) to sue the builder despite the fact that the seller hired the builder and the buyer thus lacks "privity."

c. **Liability for Sale of Existing Land and Buildings**
A seller of existing land and buildings (not new construction) may be liable to the purchaser for defects in the improvements (*e.g.*, a leaky roof or basement, termite infestation, a nonfunctioning septic system) on any of several different theories.

1) **Misrepresentation (Fraud)**
This theory requires proof that the seller made a ***false statement of fact*** (oral or written) to the buyer, that the buyer ***relied*** on the statement, and that it ***materially affected*** the value of the property. The seller must either have known that the statement was false, or have made it negligently (without taking reasonable care to determine its truth).

2) **Active Concealment**
The seller is liable as above, even without making any statement, if the seller took steps to conceal a defect in the property (*e.g.*, paneling over a wall to conceal cracks).

3) **Failure to Disclose**
A majority of states now hold sellers liable for failure to disclose defects if the following factors are present:

(i) The seller ***knows or has reason to know*** of the defect;

(ii) The defect is ***not obvious*** or apparent, and the seller realizes that the buyer is unlikely to discover it by ordinary inspection; ***and***

(iii) The defect is ***serious*** and would probably cause the buyer to reconsider the purchase if it were known.

These decisions are more likely to impose liability on the seller if the property is a personal residence, if the defect is dangerous, and if the seller personally created the defect or previously attempted to repair it and failed to do so.

d. Disclaimers of Liability

Sellers sometimes attempt to avoid liability for property defects by inserting clauses in sales contracts exculpating the seller.

1) "As Is" Clauses

A general clause, such as "property sold as is" or "with all defects," is ***not*** sufficient to overcome a seller's liability for fraud, concealment, or (in the states that recognize it) failure to disclose.

2) Specific Disclaimers

If the exculpatory clause identifies and disclaims liability for specific types of defects (*e.g.*, "seller is not liable for leaks in the roof"), it is likely to be upheld.

8. Real Estate Brokers

Most real estate sales contracts are negotiated by real estate brokers. The broker who obtains the "listing" from the seller is the ***seller's agent***. Other agents who participate in the sale (*e.g.*, through a multiple listing service) are also the seller's agents, unless they specifically agree to serve as the buyer's agent. While these agents owe a fiduciary duty to the seller, they also have a duty to the buyer to disclose material information about the property if they have actual knowledge of it. Traditionally, the agent's commission was earned when she found a buyer who was "ready, willing, and able" to purchase the property, even if the buyer later backed out of the contract. But the growing trend of the cases is to award the commission only if the sale actually closes, or if it fails to close because of the seller's fault.

9. Title Insurance

A title insurance policy insures that a good record title of the property exists as of the policy's date and agrees to defend the record title if litigated. The insurance can be taken out by either the owner of the property or the mortgage lender. It protects ***only the person who owns the policy*** and does not run with the land to subsequent purchasers.

B. DEEDS—FORM AND CONTENT

Transfer of title to an interest in real property occasionally occurs through operation of law; but in most circumstances, transfer can be accomplished only by a deed that satisfies various formalities required by statute.

1. Formalities

a. **Statute of Frauds**
The Statute of Frauds requires that a deed be in ***writing*** and signed by the grantor.

b. **Description of Land and Parties**
A deed must identify the land. The description need not be formal, and it may incorporate extrinsic information, but it ***must be unambiguous***. The parties (grantor and grantee) must also be identified. This may be done by name, or by describing them in some other way (*e.g.*, "I grant this land to my eldest daughter," or "I convey this land to the present members of the law review at State University"). If the deed is delivered with the identity of the grantee left blank, the courts will presume that the person taking delivery has authority to fill in the name of the grantee, and if she does so, the deed is valid. But if the land description is left blank, no such authority is presumed, and the deed is void unless the grantee was explicitly given authority to fill in the description, and did so. The grantee must actually exist; hence, a deed delivered to a grantee who is in fact dead at the time of the delivery is void.

c. **Words of Intent**
The deed must evidence an intention to transfer realty, but technical words are unnecessary. The word "grant" by itself is sufficient in many states.

d. **Consideration Not Required**
The deed need not recite any consideration, nor must any consideration pass in order to make a deed valid. A deed may validly convey real property by ***inter vivos gift*** so long as the following requirements are met: (i) donative intent, (ii) delivery, and (iii) acceptance (*see* C., *infra*).

e. **Seal Is Unnecessary**
A seal is unnecessary.

f. **Attestation and Acknowledgment Generally Unnecessary**
Attestation by witnesses is generally unnecessary, as is an acknowledgment. *But note:* Either or both might be required for the deed to be recorded.

g. **Signature**
A deed must be signed by the grantor. The grantor may designate an agent to sign on the grantor's behalf, but if the signing is not done in the grantor's presence, the Statute of Frauds generally requires that the agent's authority be written. In the case of deeds by corporations, statutes usually provide for execution by two officers of the corporation and the affixing of the corporation's seal. If the deed represents a conveyance of all or a substantial part of the corporation's assets, a resolution of the board of directors approving the transfer may be necessary. (The ***grantee's signature is not necessary*** even if the deed contains covenants on her part. Her acceptance of the deed is sufficient to make the covenants enforceable.)

2. **Defective Deeds and Fraudulent Conveyances**

a. **Void and Voidable Deeds**
A deed that is defective may be either void or voidable. "Void" implies that the deed will be set aside by the court even if the property has passed to a bona fide purchaser.

"Voidable" implies that the deed will be set aside only if the property has ***not*** passed to a bona fide purchaser.

1) **Void Deeds**
Deeds considered void include those that are forged, were never delivered, or were obtained by fraud in the factum (*i.e.*, the grantor was deceived and did not realize that he was executing a deed).

2) **Voidable Deeds**
Deeds considered voidable include those executed by persons younger than the age of majority or who otherwise lack capacity (*e.g.*, because of insanity), and deeds obtained through fraud in the inducement, duress, undue influence, mistake, and breach of fiduciary duty.

b. **Fraudulent Conveyances**
Even when a deed complies with the required formalities mentioned above, it may be set aside by the grantor's creditors if it is a fraudulent conveyance. Under the Uniform Fraudulent Transfers Act, which nearly all states have adopted, a conveyance is fraudulent if it was made: (i) with actual intent to hinder, delay, or defraud any creditor of the grantor; or (ii) without receiving a reasonably equivalent value in exchange for the transfer, and the debtor was insolvent or became insolvent as a result of the transfer. However, the deed will not be set aside as against any grantee who took in good faith and paid reasonably equivalent value.

3. **Description of Land Conveyed**
In ***land contracts and deeds***, property may be described in various ways; *i.e.,* by reference to a government survey, by metes and bounds, by courses and angles, by references to a recorded plat, by reference to adjacent properties, by the name of the property, or by a street and number system.

a. **Sufficient Description Provides a Good Lead**
A description is sufficient if it provides a good lead as to the identity of the property sought to be conveyed.
Example: A conveyance of "all my land," or "all my land in Alameda County," provides a sufficient lead. The intention of the grantor is clear and the meaning of this intention can be proved without difficulty (by checking the land records of Alameda County).

b. **Insufficient Description—Title Remains in Grantor**
If the description is too indefinite, title remains in the grantor, subject to the possibility of a suit for reformation of the deed.
Example: A conveyance of "one acre off the western end of my 30-acre tract" (the 30-acre tract being adequately described) would probably fail for uncertainty. "Off the western end" is too vague to ascertain ***which*** acre, and the admission of parol evidence here would be considered a violation of the Statute of Frauds.

c. **Parol Evidence Admissible to Clear Up Ambiguity**
The general rule is that parol evidence is admissible to explain or supplement a written

description or to clear up an ambiguity. If there is a ***patent ambiguity***—one appearing on the face of the deed—parol evidence is normally admissible to ascertain the parties' intent. For example, one part of the deed states that it is conveying "Blackacre" but later it purports to convey an interest in "Whiteacre." Parol evidence is admissible to show which property the grantor intended to convey. Where the ambiguity is ***latent***—not apparent on the face of the deed—parol evidence is generally admissible. For example, if A grants to B "my house in San Francisco," parol evidence is admissible to show which house A owns.

1) Compare—Inadequate Description

If, however, A grants to B "my house in San Francisco," and it turns out that A owns ***three*** houses in that city, the conveyance would probably fail for lack of adequate description. (*But note:* If there is an underlying original agreement in which there was no mistake or ambiguity, and the only mistake was in the ***writing*** of the instrument, relief might be available by way of ***reformation*** of the deed.)

d. Rules of Construction

Where there is a mistake or inconsistency in the description (as where the deed leaves in doubt the exact location of a property line, or measurements give two different locations for the line), the following rules of construction are applied to carry out the parties' probable intent. (These are not "rules of law" and will not be applied where there is clear evidence showing a contrary intent.)

1) Natural monuments prevail over other methods of description; *i.e.,* artificial monuments, courses and distances, surfaces, acreage, or general descriptions (*e.g.,* a call from "Point X to the old oak tree," prevails over a call from "Point X south 100 feet").

2) Artificial monuments (*e.g.,* stakes, buildings, etc.) prevail over all but natural monuments.

3) Courses (*e.g.,* angles) prevail over distances (*e.g.,* "west 90 degrees to Main St." prevails over "west 100 feet to Main St.").

4) All of the foregoing prevail over general descriptions such as name (*e.g.,* "Walker's Island") or quantity (*e.g.,* "being 300 acres").

e. Land Bounded by Right-of-Way

1) Title Presumed to Extend to Center of Right-of-Way

If land is described as being bounded by a street, highway, or other right-of-way, or if the land conveyed is otherwise described but actually is bounded by such, there is a rebuttable presumption that the title of the grantee extends to the center of the right-of-way (assuming that the grantor owns to the center), or to the full width of it if the grantor retains no adjoining land. This presumption accords with (i) the presumed intention of the parties, and (ii) the public policy that disfavors a grantor's retention of thin strips of land.

a) **Evidence to Rebut Presumption**
In many jurisdictions, a description such as "running ***along*** the street" has been held sufficient to rebut the presumption that the grantee took title to the center. (This is to be distinguished from the language "***bounded*** on the west by the highway" to which the presumption applies.)

But when the monument involved is a ***body of water***, more definite language is necessary to rebut the presumption that the grantee takes title to the center. This is because, unlike streets, there are no public rights in most bodies of water abutting on land (except possible navigation easements), and because a grantee of land adjoining water normally expects a right of access to the water.

b) **Measuring from Monument**
Notwithstanding the general rule, and unless a contrary intention is expressed, measurements ***"from"*** a right-of-way are presumed to start from the ***side*** and not the center. Again, this is based on the parties' presumed intent.

2) **Variable Boundary Line Cases**

a) **Slow Change in Course Changes Property Rights**
The ***slow and imperceptible*** change in course of a river or stream serving as a boundary operates to change the legal boundary. Where land is described as abutting upon a body of water, any slow and imperceptible deposit of soil ("accretion") belongs to the owner of the abutting land (the riparian owner). Where accretion builds up in an irregular pattern over the lands of several adjacent property owners, courts determine title to it in a "just and equitable manner," either by (i) merely extending the property lines out into the water with each landowner getting the property that falls within the lines as extended; or (ii) dividing up the newly formed land in proportion to the owners' interests in the adjoining lands. Similarly, slow erosion of a stream's bank results in the owner losing title to the affected area.

b) **Avulsion Does Not Change Property Rights**
A ***sudden***, perceptible change of a watercourse ("avulsion") does not change property rights. Thus, if a river changes course suddenly, boundaries remain where they were, even if someone who formerly had river access now finds himself landlocked.

c) **Encroachment of Water Does Not Change Fixed Boundary Lines**
According to the majority view, where property is encroached upon by a body of water (*e.g.,* lake enlarges), previously fixed boundary lines do not change and ownership rights are not affected. Indeed, the boundary lines can still be proven even though the land is completely under water.

f. **Reformation of Deeds**
Reformation is an equitable action in which the court rewrites the deed to make it

conform to the intention of the parties. It will be granted if the deed does not express what the parties agreed to, either because of their ***mutual mistake*** or a ***scrivener's*** (drafter's) ***error***. It will also be granted for ***unilateral mistake***, but only if the party who is not mistaken induced the mistake by ***misrepresentation*** or some other inequitable conduct. If the property has passed to a bona fide purchaser who relied on the original language of the deed, the court will not reform it.

C. DELIVERY AND ACCEPTANCE

1. Delivery—In General

A deed is not effective to transfer an interest in realty unless it has been delivered. Physical transfer of a deed is not necessary for a valid delivery. Nor does physical transfer alone establish delivery (although it might raise a presumption thereof). Rather, "delivery" refers to the ***grantor's intent***; it is satisfied by ***words or conduct*** evidencing the grantor's intention that the deed have ***some present operative effect***; *i.e.,* that ***title*** pass immediately and irrevocably, even though the right of possession may be postponed until some future time.

Examples: 1) O drafts an instrument conveying Blackacre to A and hands the instrument to A "for safekeeping." Although handed to the named grantee, this is not a valid delivery. There is no evidence that O intended the instrument to have any ***present*** operative effect.

2) O drafts an instrument conveying Blackacre to A. O attempts to give the instrument to A personally but is unable to find A; nevertheless, O quits possession of Blackacre and thereafter treats A as the owner thereof. Nearly all courts would hold that there has been a sufficient delivery.

Under some circumstances (*i.e.,* when a third party is involved), conditional delivery is permissible. This type of delivery becomes effective only upon the occurrence of a condition, but the transfer then ***relates back*** to the time of the conditional delivery. The grantor has only limited rights to revoke prior to the occurrence of the condition. (*See* further discussion of conditional deliveries, 3., *infra.*)

a. Manual Delivery

The delivery requirement will be satisfied where the grantor physically or manually delivers the deed to the grantee. Manual delivery may be accomplished by means of the mails, by the grantor's agent or messenger, or by physical transfer by the grantor's attorney in the grantor's presence.

b. Presumptions Relating to Delivery

As a matter of theory, a deed may be delivered by words without an act of physical transfer. Delivery is presumed if the deed is: (i) ***handed*** to the grantee, (ii) ***acknowledged*** by the grantor before a notary, or (iii) ***recorded***. Unless there is some clear expression of intent that the grantor envisioned the passage of title to the grantee without physical delivery, the continued possession of the deed by the grantor raises a presumption of nondelivery and therefore no passage of title. Conversely, possession by a grantee of a properly executed deed raises a presumption that the delivery requirement has been satisfied. Note, however, that the presumptions involved are rebuttable.

c. **Delivery Cannot Be Canceled**
Title passes to the grantee upon effective delivery. Therefore, returning the deed to the grantor has no effect; it constitutes neither a cancellation nor a reconveyance.

d. **Parol Evidence**

1) **Admissible to Prove Grantor's Intent**
The ***majority rule*** is that any type of parol evidence, including conduct or statements made by the grantor ***before or after*** the alleged delivery, is admissible to prove her intent.

2) **Not Admissible to Show Delivery to Grantee Was Conditional**
If a deed is ***unconditional on its face*** and is given ***directly to the grantee***, in most jurisdictions parol evidence is not admissible to show that the delivery was subject to a condition.

Example: O delivers an absolute deed of Blackacre to A, but ***tells*** A that the deed is effective only if A pays off the encumbrance on the property, or only if O does not return from the hospital. Under the above rule, even if A never pays off the encumbrance or if O returns from the hospital, A is the owner of Blackacre and O cannot claim that there was no valid delivery. *Rationale:* The rule is designed to avoid unsettling of land titles which appear to be in the grantee's name, and to protect both innocent third parties and grantees from testimony fabricated by grantors.

3) **Admissible to Show No Delivery Intended**
But while parol evidence is not admitted to prove that a delivery was subject to a condition, parol evidence ***is*** admissible to prove that the grantor did not intend the deed to have any present effect at all.

Example: O tells A, "I want you to have Blackacre when I die, and I'm giving you this deed to Blackacre so that you can have it ***at that time***." Most courts would hold that O's statements are admissible, and that despite the unconditional nature of the deed itself, they show that O did not intend the deed to have any present effect.

a) **Deed Intended as Mortgage**
Parol evidence is ***always*** admissible to show that a deed absolute on its face was intended by the parties to be a mortgage; *i.e.,* there was no intent to convey title outright. (*See* VII.A.4., *infra.*)

b) **Transfer of Deed to Bona Fide Purchaser**
Suppose O gives A a deed for examination by A's attorney (deed not intended to be effective at this point). A wrongfully records it and sells to B, a bona fide purchaser ("BFP"). On these facts, O would prevail against B unless estopped to assert lack of delivery (*see* below). In other words, absent estoppel, a subsequent BFP is not protected; if there was no delivery, the BFP's grantor had no power to convey.

(1) **Estoppel in Favor of Innocent Purchaser**
Even though the grantor is allowed to show that no delivery at all was intended as against the grantee, he often is estopped to assert lack of delivery against an innocent purchaser.

Example: O gives A a deed but does not intend the deed to be presently effective. A shows the deed to an innocent purchaser, B, who buys the land in reliance thereon. B will prevail in litigation with O, the original grantor, if it appears that O ***negligently permitted*** A to have possession of the deed. *Rationale:* As between two innocent parties, the one who contributed most directly to the loss must bear the burden of it, and in many cases O must be deemed responsible for entrusting A with a deed absolute on its face. The same result occurs where the grantee records the deed and an innocent purchaser relies on the recordation.

4) **Comment**
Obviously, the above rules give the courts flexibility to find either delivery or nondelivery in many situations. It is also evident that there exists a theoretical inconsistency in admitting parol evidence to show that no delivery was intended, but not to show that delivery was "conditional." This inconsistency has been criticized by numerous commentators.

2. **Retention of Interest by Grantor or Conditional Delivery**
Problems arise when the grantor attempts to retain an interest in the property (*e.g.,* a life estate) or when he attempts to make the passage of title dependent upon the happening of a condition or event other than delivery.

a. **No Delivery—Title Does Not Pass**
If the grantor executes a deed but fails to deliver it during his lifetime, no conveyance of title takes place. Without adequate delivery, the title does not pass to the intended grantee.

b. **No Recording—Title Passes**
If the grantor executes and delivers a deed but fails to have it recorded, title passes even though the parties thought the deed would be ineffective until recording. Therefore, an agreement between the grantor and grantee to the effect that the deed will not be recorded until some event takes place in the future does not affect the passage of title.

c. **Express Condition of Death of Grantor Creates Future Interest**
When a deed, otherwise properly executed and delivered, contains an express provision that the title will not pass until the grantor's death, the effect is to create a present possessory life estate in the grantor and a future estate in the grantee. Note, however, that this result follows only when the deed expressly contains such a provision.

d. **Conditions Not Contained in Deed**
If a deed is absolute on its face, but is delivered to the grantee with an ***oral*** condition (*e.g.,*

"title is not to pass until I return from the Orient"), the traditional view was that the condition dropped out and the delivery became absolute. A growing minority of cases enforces the condition. Where the condition is the grantor's death, the deed is usually held "testamentary" and therefore void (unless executed with testamentary formalities).

e. **Test—Relinquishment of Control**
To make an effective delivery, the grantor must relinquish absolute and unconditional control.

3. **Where Grantor Gives Deed to Third Party**
In this situation, the rules are quite different; ***conditional delivery is permissible***. Three situations should be distinguished: (i) where the grantor gives the deed to a third party, there being ***no conditions*** appended; (ii) where the grantor in a ***commercial*** context gives such a deed to a third party, there being conditions appended; and (iii) where the situation is the same as in (ii), but the transaction is ***donative***.

a. **Transfer to Third Party with No Conditions**
If O (the grantor) gives B a deed naming A as grantee and instructs B to give the deed to A, has a delivery occurred? Most courts say yes. Because O indicated an intent to make the deed presently operative, A has a right to the deed and O should not be able to get it back. However, if O told B to retain the deed and give it to A upon O's later instructions, no delivery would have occurred.

When there are no specific instructions regarding delivery, the question is one of O's intent. If B is A's attorney, delivery seems clear. But if B is O's attorney, a court might infer that B was merely O's ***agent*** and that O thus retained the power to recall the deed. (A few courts hold that B is to be treated as O's agent ***in all circumstances***, even if O manifests a clear intention of present effectiveness, and consequently no delivery occurs.)

b. **Transfer to Third Party with Conditions (Commercial Transaction)**
Suppose that O gives B a deed naming A as grantee and tells B to transfer the deed to A when A has paid $5,000 on O's account on or before September 1. This is the ***true escrow*** situation—the true conditional delivery. Under the circumstances outlined below, a valid conditional delivery has occurred. The deed has a present operative effect in that title will transfer automatically upon the occurrence of the condition. O will retain title only if the condition does not occur.

1) **Parol Evidence Admissible to Show Conditions**
Even though a deed is unconditional, the general rule is that parol evidence is admissible to show the conditions and terms upon which a deed was deposited with the escrow. (This is contrary to the rule excluding parol evidence where transfer is directly to the grantee.) If the escrow custodian has violated parol conditions, there will be no valid delivery. Once the condition occurs, whether parol or not, title automatically vests in the grantee and the escrow holds the deed as the grantee's agent.

2) **Grantor's Right to Recover Deed**

a) **Majority View—Can Recover Only If No Written Contract**
Under the majority view, if the grantor seeks to recover the deed prior to the occurrence of the condition, the grantee can object only if there is an enforceable written contract to convey. (On the other hand, once the condition occurs, title passes even in the absence of an enforceable contract.)

(1) The requirement of a written contract is based on the Statute of Frauds' consideration that oral contracts to convey realty should not become enforceable simply because the deed has been deposited with a third party.

(2) Ordinarily, the contract to convey will be a buy-sell land contract. However, written escrow instructions are often a sufficient memorandum of the contract to satisfy the Statute of Frauds.

b) **Minority View—No Right to Recover**
A strong minority prohibits revocation even in the absence of an enforceable underlying contract. Deposit of the deed with a third party on stated conditions is seen to obviate most possibilities of fraud.

3) **Breach of Escrow Conditions—Title Does Not Pass**
When the grantee wrongfully acquires the deed from the escrow holder prior to performance of the conditions of the escrow, title does not pass. Therefore, even though the grantee is in possession of the deed, she cannot convey any interest in the land to a subsequent transferee, even a BFP.

a) **Estoppel Cases**
A ***few*** cases have held that where the escrow holder was chosen by the grantor, the grantor is bound by the escrow holder's acts and is estopped to deny a valid delivery and passage of title to the grantee. Thus, an innocent purchaser (BFP) from the grantee may acquire good title. An important factor is whether the grantor has allowed the grantee to take possession of the property prior to completion of the conditions of the escrow. If the grantor has remained in possession, the purchaser may be held to have notice of the grantor's interest and cannot be a BFP.

4) **"Relation Back" Doctrine**
In an escrow transaction, title does not pass to the grantee until performance of the named conditions. However, where justice requires, the title of the grantee will "relate back" to the ***time of the deposit of the deed in escrow***. Generally, the relation back doctrine will be applied if:

(i) The ***grantor dies*** (doctrine applied to avoid the rule that title must pass before death if instrument is not a will);

(ii) The grantor ***becomes incompetent*** (doctrine applied to avoid the rule that an incompetent cannot convey title); or

(iii) A ***creditor*** of the grantor (who is not a BFP or mortgagee) ***attaches the grantor's title*** (doctrine applied to cut off the creditor's claim).

a) **Not Applied If Intervening Party Is BFP or Mortgagee**
The relation back doctrine is not applied where the intervening third party is a BFP or mortgagee. However, if the sales contract is recorded, there can be no intervening BFPs because its recordation gives constructive notice.

b) **Not Applied in Favor of Escrow Grantee with Knowledge**
The relation back doctrine will not be applied in favor of an escrow grantee who, at the time she performs the terms and conditions of the escrow, has actual or constructive knowledge of prior equities of other persons (*e.g.,* that the grantor conveyed to another). But if the escrow grantee has performed part of the conditions when she acquires such knowledge, she will be protected against all but BFPs or mortgagees.

c. **Transfer to Third Party with Conditions (Donative Transactions)**
If the grantor gives a deed to a third party with instructions to turn it over to the named donee only when certain conditions occur, is there a valid delivery or can the grantor change her mind and demand the deed back before the conditions occur?

1) **Condition Unrelated to Grantor's Death—Delivery Irrevocable**
When O gives to B a deed naming A as grantee, and instructs B to give it to A "when A marries," etc., many courts find a valid conditional delivery despite the absence of any enforceable contract to convey. In such cases, the courts have held that O's intent at ***the time of the transfer to B*** was to create a "springing future interest" in A. Such a finding makes the delivery irrevocable.

2) **Where Condition Is Grantor's Death**
When O executes a deed to A and hands the deed to B with instructions to give it to A upon the death of O, most courts hold that the grantor ***cannot*** get her deed back because her intent was to presently convey a future interest to the grantee (either a remainder, with a life estate reserved in the grantor, or an executory interest). Note that this analysis also makes the gift inter vivos, not testamentary, and thus not in conflict with the Statute of Wills. *Caution:* In dealing with death cases, make sure that it was the grantor's intent that the deed be operative immediately to convey a future interest.

a) **Limitation—No Delivery If Conditioned on Survival**
When O's instructions to B are to deliver the deed to A only if A survives O, it is generally held that there is no valid delivery because it was O's intent to retain title and possession until her death.

4. **Acceptance**

a. **Usually Presumed**
There must be an acceptance by the grantee in order to complete a conveyance. In most states, acceptance is presumed if the conveyance is beneficial to the grantee (whether or not the grantee knows of it). In other states, acceptance is presumed only where the grantee is shown to have knowledge of the grant and fails to indicate rejection of it. Acceptance is presumed in all states if the grantee is an infant or an incompetent.

b. Usually "Relates Back"

Acceptance (presumed or otherwise) usually "relates back" to the date of "delivery" of the deed in escrow. However, many courts refuse to "relate back" an acceptance where it would defeat the rights of ***intervening third parties*** such as BFPs, attaching creditors of the grantor, or surviving joint tenants. A few states will not even "relate back" an acceptance if doing so defeats the devisees of the grantor.

5. Dedication

Land may be transferred to a public body (*e.g.,* a city or county) by dedication. An ***offer*** of dedication may be made by written or oral statement, submission of a map or plat showing the dedication, or opening the land to public use. An ***acceptance*** by the public agency is necessary. This may be accomplished by a formal resolution, approval of thc map or plat, or actual assumption of maintenance or construction of improvements by the agency.

D. COVENANTS FOR TITLE AND ESTOPPEL BY DEED

There are three types of deeds characteristically used to convey property interests other than leaseholds: the ***general warranty*** deed, the ***special warranty*** deed (usually statutory), and the ***quitclaim*** deed. The major difference between these deeds is the scope of assurances (covenants for title) they give to the grantee and the grantee's successors regarding the title being conveyed. The general warranty deed normally contains five covenants for title (*see* 1.a.1)-5), *infra*). The special warranty deed contains fewer and more limited assurances. The quitclaim deed usually contains no assurances; it releases to the grantee whatever interest the grantor happens to own. Covenants for title must be distinguished from covenants for other than title (*i.e.,* covenants running with the land used for private land regulation). "Covenants for title" is a self-contained topic.

1. Covenants for Title in a General Warranty Deed

In this day of recording acts and title insurance, covenants for title are not much relied upon for title assurance. A general warranty deed is one in which the grantor covenants against title defects created both by himself and by ***all prior titleholders***. In a special warranty deed, however, the grantor covenants only that he himself did not create title defects; he represents nothing about what prior owners might have done. General warranty deeds are a rarity in a number of states where many conveyances are made with statutory form special warranty deeds.

a. Usual Covenants

A grantor may give any or all of the following covenants, which are classified as the "usual covenants for title." A deed containing such covenants is called a "general warranty deed."

1) Covenant of Seisin

The covenant of seisin is a covenant that the grantor has the estate or interest that she purports to convey. Both title and possession at the time of the grant are necessary to satisfy the covenant.

2) Covenant of Right to Convey

The covenant of the right to convey is a covenant that the grantor has the power and authority to make the grant. Title alone will ordinarily satisfy this covenant, as will proof that the grantor was acting as the authorized agent of the titleholder.

3) **Covenant Against Encumbrances**
The covenant against encumbrances is a covenant assuring that there are neither visible encumbrances (easements, profits, etc.) nor invisible encumbrances (mortgages, etc.) against the title or interest conveyed.

4) **Covenant for Quiet Enjoyment**
The covenant for quiet enjoyment is a covenant that the grantee will not be disturbed in her possession or enjoyment of the property by a third party's ***lawful*** claim of title.

5) **Covenant of Warranty**
The covenant of warranty is a covenant wherein the grantor agrees to defend on behalf of the grantee any lawful or reasonable claims of title by a third party, and to compensate the grantee for any loss sustained by the claim of superior title. This covenant and the covenant for quiet enjoyment are generally considered to be identical.

6) **Covenant for Further Assurances**
The covenant for further assurances is a covenant to perform whatever acts are reasonably necessary to perfect the title conveyed if it turns out to be imperfect. This is not one of the "usual covenants" but is frequently given in addition thereto.

7) **No Implied Warranties or Covenants**
In the absence of a statute, no covenants of title are implied in deeds. Moreover, the implied (or express) covenant of marketable title found in contracts of sale of real estate is no longer assertable once a deed has been delivered, unless fraud or mistake is shown.

b. **Breach of Covenants**
Three of the covenants (seisin, right to convey, against encumbrances) are ***present covenants*** and are breached, if at all, ***at the time of conveyance***. Quiet enjoyment, warranty, and further assurances are ***future covenants*** and are breached ***only upon interference with the possession*** of the grantee or her successors. This distinction is important in that it determines when the statute of limitations begins running and whether a remote grantee of the covenantor can sue.

1) **Covenants of Seisin and Right to Convey**
The covenants of seisin and right to convey are breached at the time of conveyance ***if the grantor is not the owner*** of the interest she purports to convey (or has not been authorized to so convey). If there is a breach, the grantee has a cause of action against which the statute of limitations begins to run at the time of conveyance. If the grantee reconveys, the general rule is that the subsequent grantee has no right of action against the covenantor. In a few jurisdictions, it is implied that the original grantee assigned the cause of action to the subsequent grantee, thus permitting suit against the original grantor-covenantor. (The latter is probably the better rule because the subsequent grantee most likely paid the original grantee the market value.)

Example: O conveys Blackacre to A by a deed containing a covenant of seisin. O purports to convey a fee simple, but in fact X was the owner of Blackacre. Soon thereafter, A conveys to B. Under the usual view, A, but not B, may recover from O. In a few jurisdictions, it is implied that A assigned her cause of action to B.

2) **Covenant Against Encumbrances**
The covenant against encumbrances is breached and a cause of action arises at the time of conveyance if the property is encumbered. Most jurisdictions hold that the covenant is breached even if the grantee knew of the encumbrance, whether it be an encumbrance on title (*e.g.,* a mortgage) or a physical encumbrance (*e.g.,* an easement or servitude), but others hold there is no breach if the grantee knew of a physical encumbrance.

These jurisdictions charge grantees with constructive notice of visible physical encumbrances (*e.g.,* right-of-way). Several cases go so far as to hold that a covenant against encumbrances is not breached where the encumbrance ("visible" or not) is a benefit to the land involved (*e.g.,* an easement for a sewer or for an adjacent street).

3) **Covenants for Quiet Enjoyment, Warranty, and Further Assurances**
Covenants for quiet enjoyment, warranty, and further assurances are not breached until a ***third party interferes with the possession*** of the grantee or her successors. (*But note:* A covenant for quiet enjoyment or of warranty is not breached by the covenantor's refusal to defend title against a ***wrongful*** claim or eviction by a third party.)

a) **Covenant Runs to Successive Grantees**
These covenants are viewed as "continuous"; *i.e.,* they can be breached a number of times. Their benefit "runs" with the grantee's estate (unlike covenants of seisin and against encumbrances).

Example: O conveys to A by a deed containing a covenant of warranty. A thereafter conveys to B and B to C, and then C is evicted by a third party with title that was paramount when O conveyed to A. C can successfully sue O.

b) **Requirement of Notice**
The covenantor is not liable on her covenant of warranty or of further assurances unless the party seeking to hold her liable gives her notice of the claim against the title she conveyed.

c) **Any Disturbance of Possession**
Most courts hold that any disturbance of possession suffices to constitute a breach. Thus, if the covenantee cannot obtain complete possession or pays off an adverse, paramount claim in order to retain possession, this is a sufficient disturbance of possession. *Compare:* A disturbance of the covenantee's possession is not required as a prerequisite to recovery for breach of covenants of seisin, right to convey, or against encumbrances.

c. **Damages and Remote Grantees**
Suppose successive conveyances from O to A to B to C, each conveyance containing full covenants. C is evicted by X, who was the true owner when O conveyed to A. C may sue O, A, or B because each gave a covenant of warranty the benefit of which "ran" with the land. But what is the measure of C's recovery? Is it the consideration the defendant (*i.e.,* O, A, or B) received? Is it the consideration C paid (an indemnity theory) so that if C was a donee, she gets nothing?

Many states permit C to recover to the extent of the ***consideration received*** by the defendant-covenantor (even though it exceeds the consideration paid by C). Under this view, defendant-shopping is advisable (to sue whomever received most). The defendant who is held liable then has a cause of action against any prior covenantor, until ultimately O is held liable. In other states, C can recover only the ***actual consideration she paid*** (but not to exceed the amount received by the defendant-covenantor).

2. **Statutory Special Warranty Deed**
Statutes in many states provide that (unless expressly negated) the use of the word "grant" in a conveyance creates ***by implication*** the following two limited assurances against ***acts of the grantor*** (not her predecessors): (i) that prior to the time of the execution of such conveyance, the ***grantor has not conveyed the same estate*** or any interest therein to any person other than the grantee; and (ii) that the estate conveyed is free from encumbrances made ***by the grantor***.

3. **Quitclaim Deeds**
A quitclaim deed is basically a ***release of whatever interest***, if any, the grantor has in the property. Hence, the use of covenants warranting the grantor's title is basically inconsistent with this type of deed; *i.e.,* if the deed contains warranties, it is not a quitclaim deed.

4. **Estoppel by Deed**
If a grantor purports to convey an estate in property that she does not then own, her ***subsequent acquisition of title to the property will automatically inure to the benefit of the grantee***. In other words, the grantor impliedly covenants that she will convey title immediately upon its acquisition.

Example: On Day 1, A, who does not own Blackacre, purports to convey Blackacre to B by general warranty deed. On Day 1, B has no interest in Blackacre. On Day 3, A acquires Blackacre from O. That interest automatically passes to B, so that on Day 3 B owns Blackacre. A's warranties will prevent her from denying ownership when she executed the deed on Day 1.

a. **Applies to Warranty Deeds**
The doctrine is most frequently applied where the conveyance is by warranty deed. Regardless of covenants for title, many courts hold that if the deed expressly purports to convey a fee simple or other ***particular estate***, the grantee is entitled to that estate if later acquired by the grantor. In most states, however, the doctrine will not be applied when the conveyance is by a quitclaim deed.

b. **Rights of Subsequent Purchasers**
The majority of courts hold that title inures to the benefit of the grantee only ***as against the grantor*** (who is estopped to deny that she acquired title on behalf of the grantee).

This is a personal estoppel only. Consequently, if the grantor transfers her after-acquired title to an innocent purchaser for value, the BFP gets good title. (There is no basis for invoking an estoppel against an innocent purchaser without notice.)

1) **Effect of Recordation by Original Grantee**
If the original grantee records the deed she receives from the grantor, the question arises as to whether this recordation imparts sufficient notice of the grantee's interest, so as to prevent a subsequent purchaser from being a BFP. This depends on the subsequent grantee's ***burden of searching the title***. (*See* E.4., *infra*.)

c. **Remedies of Grantee**
In jurisdictions following the estoppel rationale, the original grantee, at her election, may ***accept title*** to the land ***or sue for damages for breach of covenants*** for title. However, if an innocent purchaser of the after-acquired title is involved, the grantee has no rights against the BFP.

E. RECORDING

At common law, in nearly all cases priority was given to the grantee ***first in time***. Thus, if O conveyed Blackacre to A and then made an identical conveyance to B, A prevailed over B on the theory that after the first conveyance O had no interest left to convey.

1. Recording Acts—In General

Statutes known as "recording acts" require a grantee to make some sort of recordation so as to give "notice to the world" that title to certain property has already been conveyed, and thus to put subsequent purchasers on guard. These statutes are in effect in some form in every state. Basically, recording acts set up a system by which any instrument affecting title to property located in a certain county can be recorded in that county. These acts seek to protect all subsequent BFPs from secret, unrecorded interests of others.

a. **Purpose of Recordation—Notice**
Recordation is not essential to the validity of a deed, as between the grantor and grantee. However, if a grantee does not record her instrument, she may lose out against a subsequent BFP. By recording, the grantee gives constructive (or "record") ***notice to everyone***. Hence, as stated earlier, proper recording prevents anyone from becoming a subsequent BFP.

b. **Requirements for Recordation**

1) **What Can Be Recorded—Instrument Affecting an Interest in Land**
Practically every kind of ***deed, mortgage, contract to convey***, or other instrument creating or affecting an interest in land can be recorded. *Note:* A judgment or decree affecting title to property can also be recorded. And, even before judgment, where a ***lawsuit is pending that may affect title*** to property, any party to the action can record a ***lis pendens*** (notice of pending action), which will effectively put third parties on notice of all claims pending in the lawsuit.

2) **Grantor Must Acknowledge Deed**
Most recording statutes provide that, in order to be recorded, a deed must be

acknowledged by the grantor before a notary public. This requirement offers some protection against forgery. Problems may arise if the recorder records a deed that has not been acknowledged or has been improperly acknowledged.

c. **Mechanics of Recording**

1) **Filing Copy**
The grantee or her agent normally presents the deed to the county recorder, who photographs it and files the copy in the official records. These records are kept chronologically.

2) **Indexing**
The recorder also indexes the deed to permit title searches. The usual indexes are the grantor-grantee and grantee-grantor indexes, which are arranged by reference to the parties to the conveyance. Tract indexes, which index the property by location, exist in some urban localities.

2. **Types of Recording Acts**
There are three major types of recording acts, classified as "notice," "race-notice," and "race" statutes. Note that the burden is on the subsequent taker to prove that he qualifies for protection under the statute.

a. **Notice Statutes**
Under a notice statute, a subsequent BFP (*i.e.,* a person who gives valuable consideration and has no notice of the prior instrument) prevails over a prior grantee who failed to record. The important fact under a notice statute is that the subsequent purchaser ***had no actual or constructive notice*** at the time of the conveyance. Constructive notice includes both record notice and inquiry notice (*see* 3.b.3), *infra*). A typical notice statute provides:

> A conveyance of an interest in land, other than a lease for less than one year, shall not be valid against any subsequent purchaser for value, ***without notice thereof***, unless the conveyance is recorded.

Note also that the subsequent bona fide purchaser is protected, regardless of whether she records at all.

Example: On January 1, O conveys Blackacre to A. A does not record. On January 15, O conveys Blackacre to B, who gives valuable consideration and has no notice of the deed from O to A. B prevails over A.

What if A records before B? Suppose in the example above that A recorded on January 18, and B never recorded. This is ***irrelevant*** under a "notice" statute, because B had no notice ***at the time of her conveyance*** from O. B is protected against a ***prior*** purchaser even though B does not record her deed (this is the difference between "notice" and "race-notice" statutes). Of course, if B does not record, she runs the risk that a subsequent purchaser will prevail over her, just as she prevailed over A.

b. **Race-Notice Statutes**

Under a race-notice statute, a subsequent BFP is protected only if she records ***before*** the prior grantee. *Rationale:* The best evidence of which deed was ***delivered*** first is to determine who recorded first. To obviate questions about the time of delivery and to add an inducement to record promptly, race-notice statutes impose on the BFP the additional requirement that she record first. A typical race-notice statute provides:

> Any conveyance of an interest in land, other than a lease for less than one year, shall not be valid against any subsequent purchaser for value, ***without notice thereof***, whose conveyance is ***first recorded***.

Example: On January 1, O conveys Blackacre to A. A does not record. On January 15, O conveys Blackacre to B. On January 18, A records. On January 20, B records. A prevails over B because B did not record first.

c. **Race Statutes**

Under a pure race statute, whoever records first wins. Actual notice is irrelevant. The rationale is that actual notice depends upon extrinsic evidence, which may be unreliable. ***Very few states*** have race statutes.

Example: On January 1, O conveys Blackacre to A. A does not record. On January 15, O conveys Blackacre to B. B ***knows*** of the deed to A. B records. Then A records. B prevails over A because she recorded first. It is immaterial that she had actual notice of A's interest.

3. **Who Is Protected by Recording Acts**

Only ***bona fide purchasers*** ("BFPs") are entitled to prevail against a prior transferee under "notice" and "race-notice" statutes. To attain this status, a person must satisfy three requirements (each of which is discussed in detail below). The person must:

(i) Be a ***purchaser*** (or mortgagee or creditor if the statute so allows; *see* below);

(ii) Take ***without notice*** (actual, constructive, or inquiry) of the prior instrument; and

(iii) Pay ***valuable consideration***.

Note: If these requirements are not met, the person is not protected by the recording acts, so that the common law rule of first in time prevails.

Example: O, the owner of Blackacre, executes a contract of sale of the land to A on Monday. A immediately ***records the contract***. On Tuesday, O deeds the land to B. B pays valuable consideration for the land, but is not a BFP because B is held to have constructive notice of A's rights. *Result:* A is entitled to enforce the contract against B, paying B the rest of the price and compelling B to deliver a deed to A. (If A had failed to record the contract, and B had no other notice of it, B would have taken free of A's contract rights. A would have an action in damages against O for breach of contract, but would not have a claim for specific performance against B.)

a. **Purchasers**

All recording acts protect purchasers (of the fee or any lesser estate).

1) **Donees, Heirs, and Devisees Not Protected**
Donees, heirs, and devisees are not protected because they do not give value for their interests.
Example: O, the owner of Blackacre, conveys it to A on Monday. A fails to record. O dies on Tuesday and his heirs/devisees succeed to his property interests. Even though O's heirs/devisees may be unaware of the prior conveyance of Blackacre to A, A prevails.

2) **Purchaser from Donee, Heir, or Devisee**
A person who buys land from the donee, heir, or devisee of the record owner is protected against a prior unrecorded conveyance from the record owner.
Example: O conveys Blackacre to A, who does not record. O dies, leaving H as her heir. (H does not prevail over A because he is not a purchaser.) H conveys to B, a BFP, who records. B prevails over A in nearly all jurisdictions.

An heir who purchases the interests of her co-heirs, without notice of the prior unrecorded conveyance, is entitled to the same protection as any other purchaser to the extent of her purchase.

3) **Mortgagees**
Mortgagees for value are treated as "purchasers," either expressly by the recording act or by judicial classification.
Example: O, the owner of a parcel in State X known as Blackacre, deeds the parcel to A on Monday, but A fails to record the deed. On Tuesday, O executes a mortgage to Bank. State X has a race-notice recording statute. Bank is a good faith purchaser for value, and immediately records its mortgage. *Result:* Bank has a valid mortgage on the land, while the title to the land is held by A. (If Bank had not been a BFP, or had failed to record, A would hold the title free of Bank's mortgage.)

4) **Judgment Creditors**
In nearly all states, a plaintiff who obtains a money judgment can obtain, by statute, a judgment lien on the defendant's real estate. A typical statute reads as follows:

> Any judgment properly filed shall, for 10 years from filing, be a lien on the real property then owned or subsequently acquired by any person against whom the judgment is rendered.

Is a plaintiff who obtains a judgment lien under such a statute protected by the recording acts from a prior unrecorded conveyance made by the defendant? The cases are split, but the majority holds that the judgment lienor is ***not*** protected. These courts usually reason either (i) the plaintiff is not a BFP because he did not pay value for the judgment, or (ii) the judgment attaches only to property "owned" by the defendant, and not to property the defendant has previously conveyed away, even if that conveyance was not recorded.

Example: On January 1, O grants a mortgage on Blackacre to A. A does not record the mortgage. On January 15, B, who had previously sued O on a tort claim, obtains and properly files a judgment against O. B has no knowledge of the mortgage from O to A. Which lien has priority, A's mortgage or B's judgment lien? By the majority view, A has priority despite A's failure to record the mortgage. B is not protected by the recording act.

5) **Transferees from Bona Fide Purchaser—Shelter Rule**

A person who takes from a BFP will prevail against any interest that the transferor-BFP would have prevailed against. This is true even where the transferee had ***actual knowledge*** of the prior unrecorded interest.

Example: O conveys to A, who fails to record. O then conveys to B, a BFP, who records. B then conveys to C, who has actual knowledge of the O to A deed. C prevails over A. (And this is true whether C is a donee or purchaser.)

a) **Rationale**

If the rule were otherwise, a BFP might not be able to convey an interest in the land. The transferee is not protected for her own sake, but rather for the sake of the BFP from whom she received title.

b) **Exception—No "Shipping Through"**

This rule will not help someone who ***previously*** held title and had notice of the unrecorded interest. In the example above, if O repurchased from B, O would have notice of A's interest and could not claim the benefit of the "shelter rule."

6) **Purchaser Under Installment Land Contract**

In most states, a purchaser who has paid only part of the purchase price under an installment land contract (*see* VII.A.3., *infra*) is protected by the recording acts only to the extent of payment made. In a dispute between the contract purchaser and a prior claimant, the court may:

(i) Award the contract purchaser a share of the property as a tenant in common equal to the proportion of ***payments made***;

(ii) Award the land to the prior claimant, but give the contract purchaser a lien on the property to the extent of the ***amount paid*** [Westpark, Inc. v. Seaton Land Co., 171 A.2d 736 (Md. 1961)]; or

(iii) Award the land to the contract purchaser, but give the prior claimant a lien on the property to the extent of the ***balance still owed*** [Sparks v. Taylor, 90 S.W. 485 (Tex. 1906)].

Example: O conveys Blackacre to A, who does not record. O then conveys Blackacre to B as a gift. B, knowing nothing of the O-A conveyance, records her deed. B then sells Blackacre to C for $100,000 via an installment land contract. C is to make four payments of $25,000. C makes the first payment and records his deed. A learns

of the B-C conveyance and files suit against C to quiet title. *Result:* The court may (i) award C a one-fourth interest in Blackacre as a tenant in common; (ii) award Blackacre to A, but order A to pay C $25,000; or (iii) award Blackacre to C, but order C to pay the remaining $75,000 to A.

a) **Exception—Shelter Rule**

If B in the example above were a BFP, the shelter rule would apply and C would be fully protected even though C had notice of the O-A conveyance partway through C's payments.

b. **Without Notice**

"Without notice" means that the purchaser had no actual, record, or inquiry notice of the prior conveyance at the time she paid the consideration and received her interest in the land. While ***no one has a legal duty to perform a title search***, a subsequent purchaser will be charged with the notice that such a search ***would*** provide, whether or not she actually searches. However, the fact that the purchaser obtains knowledge of the adverse claim after the conveyance but before she records it is immaterial; she only has to be "without notice" ***at the time of the conveyance***.

1) **Actual Notice**

The subsequent purchaser must show that she did not actually know of any prior unrecorded conveyance. Actual notice includes knowledge obtained from any source (*e.g.,* newspaper, word-of-mouth, etc.).

2) **Record Notice—Chain of Title**

The fact that a deed has been recorded does not always mean that a purchaser will be charged with notice of it. A subsequent purchaser will be held to have record notice only if the deed in question is recorded "in the chain of title," which means that it is recorded in a fashion that a searcher could reasonably find it. There are several situations in which a deed might be recorded, but very difficult or impossible for a search to locate.

a) **"Wild Deeds"**

A "wild deed" is a recorded deed that is not connected to the chain of title. It does not give constructive notice because the subsequent bona fide purchaser cannot feasibly find it.

Example: O owns Blackacre, which she contracts to sell to A. The contract is not recorded, and O remains in possession. A thereupon conveys Blackacre by deed to B, and B records. O then conveys Blackacre by deed to C. Did B's recordation charge C with constructive notice of B's claim to equitable title to Blackacre derived through A? ***No.*** C is not charged with notice because there was no way for him to find the A-B deed. Nothing related it to O. It was not in O's chain of title; it was a "wild deed."

Compare: If the jurisdiction maintained a tract index, it would not be hard to find that A-B deed. It would be indexed under Blackacre's

block and lot number. But it is impossible to find in a grantor-grantee index without looking at the descriptions of all the recorded properties.

b) **Deeds Recorded Late**

A deed recorded after the grantor therein is shown by the record to have parted with title through another (subsequent) instrument is not constructive notice in most states.

Example: O conveys to A on May 1. O conveys to B, a donee, on May 15. B records on June 1. A records on June 15. B conveys to C on July 1. C has no actual notice of the O-A deed.

B v. A: As between A and B, A would win because B (a donee) was not a bona fide purchaser.

C v. A: In ***notice*** statute jurisdictions, most courts hold that C will prevail over A because the O-A deed was recorded "late" and is not in C's chain of title; *i.e.,* the search burden is too great if C is required to search "down" the grantor index to the present time for each grantor in the chain.

In several ***race-notice*** jurisdictions, however, A's recordation is treated as giving constructive notice to any purchaser ***subsequent to*** such recordation. In these states, the title searcher must search to the present date under the name of each person who ever owned the property in order to pick up deeds recorded late.

(1) **Exception—Shelter Rule**

If B in the example above were a BFP, C would win in any event, for she would "shelter" under B. This result would be the same even if C had actual knowledge of the O-A deed; otherwise B's power to transfer would be restricted.

(2) **Lis Pendens Protection**

What can A do to protect herself when she records her deed and finds the O-B deed on record? She can bring suit against B to expunge B's deed and file a lis pendens (litigation pending) notice under B's name, so any purchaser from B will have notice of A's claim.

c) **Deeds Recorded Before Grantor Obtained Title**

There is a split of authority on whether a recorded deed, obtained from a grantor who had no title at that time but who afterwards obtains title, is constructive notice to a subsequent purchaser from the same grantor.

Example: Suppose that on June 1, O owns Blackacre, but on that same day, A conveys Blackacre by warranty deed to B who promptly records. On July 2, O conveys Blackacre to A, and this deed is also promptly recorded. On August 3, A conveys Blackacre to C, a bona fide purchaser who has no actual notice of the prior A-B deed.

Majority view: Most courts protect C over B on the theory that a deed from A that was recorded prior to the time title came to A is not in the chain of title and so does not give C constructive notice of B's claim to Blackacre. *Rationale:* It would put an excessive burden on the title searcher to have to search the index under each grantor's name ***prior*** to the date the grantor acquired title.

Minority view: However, a minority of courts protect B over C on the basis that as soon as A acquired title from O, it transferred automatically to B by virtue of A's earlier deed to B. Therefore, A had nothing to transfer to C. (*Criticism:* The minority view sharply increases the costs of title search.)

d) Deed in Chain Referring to Instrument Outside Chain

If a recorded document in the chain of title refers to another instrument, such reference may be sufficient to impart constructive notice of the other instrument, even if it is unrecorded or is not itself in the chain of title.

Example: O mortgages Blackacre to A, who does not record. Later, O sells Blackacre to B by deed which recites that title is subject to A's mortgage. This deed is recorded. B then sells to C. C takes subject to A's mortgage, even though it was never recorded, because of the reference to it in the O-B deed.

e) Restrictive Covenants—Deeds from Common Grantor

(1) Subdivision Restrictions

Suppose that O, a subdivider, is developing a residential subdivision. She sells lot #1 to A, and the deed provides that lot #1 is restricted to residential use. The deed also provides that "O on behalf of herself, her heirs, and assigns promises to use her remaining lots (#2, #3, etc.) for residential purposes only." A records the deed. O then sells lot #2 to B. The deed to B contains no restrictions. B wishes to erect a gas station. Is B bound by the restrictions in the O-A deed of which he had no actual notice? The courts are split.

(a) Some charge B with reading ***all*** deeds given by a common grantor, not just the deeds to his particular tract. Hence, B has constructive notice and is bound by the restriction.

(b) However, the ***better view*** is contra; *i.e.,* because the burden of title search would be excessive, deeds to other lots given by a common grantor are not in B's chain of title.

(2) Adjacent Lots

Suppose that O owns lot #1 and lot #2. She grants lot #2 to A with an easement of way over lot #1. The deed to A is indexed as a deed to lot #2; no mention is made of lot #1. Subsequently, O conveys lot #1 to B

without mentioning the easement. As with subdivision restrictions, the courts are split as to whether B is required to read O's deeds of adjoining lots.

f) **Merchantable Title Act**
In some states, a ***search cut-off date*** is established by statute; *e.g.,* defects of title reaching back further than 40 years are barred (a title searcher need only check the chain of title back 40 years). The exact cut-off point varies from state to state.

3) **Inquiry Notice**
Inquiry notice means that if the subsequent grantee is bound to make reasonable inquiry, she will be held to have knowledge of any facts that such inquiry ***would have revealed*** (even though she made none).

a) **Generally No Inquiry from Quitclaim Deed**
In a ***majority*** of states, quitclaim grantees are treated under the recording system the same as warranty deed grantees; *i.e.,* they are not charged with inquiry notice from the mere fact that a quitclaim deed was used.

b) **Inquiry from References in Recorded Instruments**
If a recorded instrument makes reference to an unrecorded transaction, the grantee is bound to make inquiry to discover the nature and character of the unrecorded transaction.

Example: O grants an easement in Blackacre to A, who does not record. O thereafter conveys the fee to B and in the deed states that the property is "subject to an easement." B records. C purchases Blackacre from B without any knowledge of the easement. The reference to the easement in the O-B deed creates a ***duty to inquire*** concerning the easement. If a reasonable inquiry would have informed C of the easement, she has notice of it even though the deed of the easement was never recorded. (Remember the grantee is charged with constructive knowledge of the fruits of a reasonable inquiry even though she made no inquiry.) Thus, C will take subject to A's unrecorded interest in Blackacre.

c) **Inquiry from Unrecorded Instruments in Chain of Title**
Suppose O, the record owner, conveys a life estate to A by a deed that is not recorded. Thereafter, A purports to convey a fee simple to B, a purchaser for valuable consideration, without actual notice that A merely has a life estate. O would prevail over B with respect to the remainder interest because B is "required" (at her peril) to demand a viewing of A's title documents at the time of the purchase when they are unrecorded.

d) **Inquiry from Possession**
A title search is not complete without an examination of possession. If the possession is unexplained by the record, the subsequent purchaser is obligated to make inquiry. The subsequent purchaser is charged with knowledge of

whatever an inspection of the property would have disclosed ***and*** anything that would have been disclosed by inquiring of the possessor.

Example: O, the owner of Blackacre, conveys it to A, who fails to record. However, A goes into possession of Blackacre. Thereafter, O executes an identical conveyance of Blackacre to B, who purchases for valuable consideration and without actual notice of the prior unrecorded conveyance to A. A majority of states hold that B is placed on constructive notice of A's interest. An examination of possession would have revealed A's presence, and A's possession is inconsistent with O's ownership.

Similarly, the physical appearance of the land may give notice of an adverse interest. For example, tire tracks passing over the land to an adjacent parcel may give notice of an easement.

c. Valuable Consideration

A person is protected by the recording statute only from the time that valuable consideration was given. Thus, if a deed was delivered before the consideration was paid, the purchaser will not prevail over deeds recorded before the consideration was given. Valuable consideration must be more than merely nominal. A person who claims to be a BFP must prove that ***real*** consideration was paid.

1) Test—Substantial Pecuniary Value

The test is different from that of contract law, where any consideration suffices to support a contract. Here, the claimant must show that he is not a donee but a purchaser. The consideration need not be adequate, nor the market value of the property, but it must be of substantial pecuniary value. ("Love and affection" is not valuable consideration.)

2) Property Received as Security for Antecedent Debts Is Insufficient

One who receives a deed or mortgage only as security for a preexisting debt has not given valuable consideration.

Example: O becomes indebted to A. O conveys Blackacre to B, who does not record. O then gives A a mortgage on Blackacre to secure the indebtedness, and A records. A did not give valuable consideration, and B prevails over A.

4. Title Search

Suppose O has contracted to sell Blackacre to A. Prior to closing, A, the buyer, will have a title search performed to assure herself that O really owns Blackacre and to determine if there are any encumbrances on O's title. How will A's title searcher(s) proceed?

a. Tract Index Search

In a tract index jurisdiction, the job is comparatively easy. The searcher looks at the page indexed by block and/or lot describing Blackacre and at a glance can see prior recorded instruments conveying, mortgaging, or otherwise dealing with Blackacre.

b. Grantor and Grantee Index Search

The search is much more complicated in a grantor and grantee index jurisdiction.

Examples: 1) V owned Blackacre in 1935. In 1965, V conveyed Blackacre to W. In 1990, W conveyed Blackacre to X. In 1995, X gave B Bank a mortgage on the property. In 2005, X conveyed Blackacre to O. O contracts to sell the land to A. A's title searcher will look in the ***grantee*** index under O's name from the present back to 2005, when she finds the deed from X, then under X's name from 2005 to 1990, when she finds the deed from W to X, then under W's name from 1990 to 1965, then under V's name from 1965 backward. The searcher will then look in the ***grantor*** index under V's name from 1935 to 1965, under W's name from 1965 to 1990, under X's name from 1990 to 2005, and under O's name from 2005 to the present. In this manner, she will pick up the mortgage to B Bank, which was recorded in 1995 in the grantor index under X's name.

2)

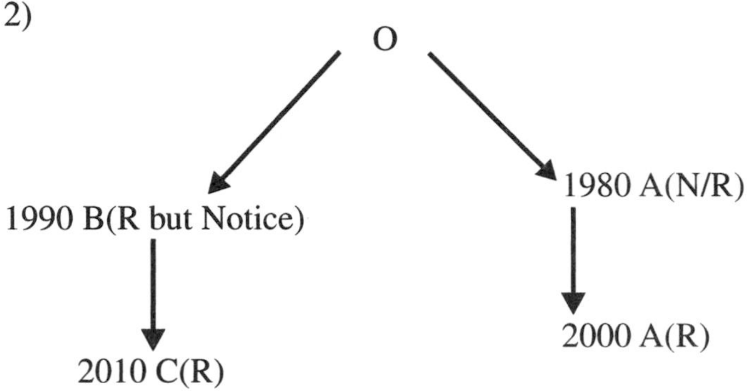

1980	O conveys to A.
1990	O executes an identical conveyance of Blackacre to B. B pays valuable consideration, but B has actual knowledge of the prior unrecorded conveyance to A. B records.
2000	A records.
2010	B conveys his interest in Blackacre to C, who purchases without notice of the conveyance to A and who pays valuable consideration.

In searching the title, C will first look in the grantee index under B's name to discover if his seller, B, ever acquired title. He will find that B acquired title in 1990 from O. Next, he will look in the grantor index under B's name to discover if B made any prior conveyances, and then will look in the grantee index once again, this time under O's name, to discover if O ever acquired title. C will find that O acquired title in 1970. Then he will look in the grantor index under O's name to discover if O made a conveyance prior to his conveyance to B. Under the majority rule, C is required to look under O's name in the grantor index only through 1990. C will find no conveyances. In 1990, C will find the

recorded conveyance to B and he need look no further. On this basis, C will not find the recorded conveyance to A because A recorded after 1990. A's recording is "out of the chain of title," and therefore C is not charged with notice.

Under a ***pure notice or race-notice statute***, as between A and B, A will prevail because B, having knowledge of A's unrecorded conveyance, is not a protected party. However, as between A and C, many courts hold that C should prevail because A's recording is out of the chain of title. The cases are split. Because notice is irrelevant under ***pure race*** statutes, B would prevail over A because B recorded first. Once it is established that B prevails over A, C obviously takes good title.

c. Other Instruments and Events Affecting Title

The title searcher's job may be complicated by marriages and divorces (*e.g.,* a woman's name may have changed between her appearance as grantee and her reappearance as grantor) and by the fact that a number of interests in the land may be filed and indexed elsewhere than in the recording office (*e.g.,* judgment liens may appear in the trial court's judgment docket, and tax liens may be filed only in the tax assessor's office). Similarly, discovering whether land has passed by will or intestacy rather than by conveyance may require a search of probate records.

5. Effect of Recordation

Proper recordation gives all prospective subsequent grantees constructive notice of the existence and contents of the recorded instruments; *i.e.,* there can be no subsequent BFPs. Recordation also raises ***presumptions*** that the instrument has been validly delivered and that it is authentic. These presumptions are rebuttable, not conclusive.

a. Does Not Validate Invalid Deed

As stated earlier, recordation is not necessary for a valid conveyance. Nor does recordation validate an invalid conveyance, such as a forged or undelivered deed.

b. Does Not Protect Against Interests Arising by Operation of Law

Furthermore, recordation does not protect a subsequent purchaser against interests that arise by operation of law, rather than from a recordable document (*e.g.,* dower rights; prescriptive and implied easements; title by adverse possession). Because there is no instrument to record in order to perfect such interests, the recording acts do not apply, and subsequent purchasers take subject to the interests. (*Remember:* If the recording act is inapplicable, the common law priority rules apply.)

Example: O is the record owner of Blackacre. X adversely possesses Blackacre for the period of the statute of limitations. O then conveys Blackacre to A, a BFP. Even though X's interest has never been recorded, X prevails against A.

1) Exception

A court ***may*** protect a subsequent BFP from an unrecorded ***implied easement*** that is ***not visible*** upon inspection of the premises (*e.g.,* an underground sewer).

c. Recorder's Mistakes

An instrument is considered recorded from and after the time it is filed at the recorder's office, irrespective of whether it is actually listed on the indexes. If the recorder's office has made an error in recording, the subsequent purchaser has an action against the recorder's office. There is a strong minority view that protects the searcher.

d. **Effect of Recording Unacknowledged Instrument**
As discussed above, the recording acts require that before an instrument can be recorded, it must be acknowledged by the grantor before a notary. What happens if the recorder, by oversight, records a deed that has not been acknowledged or has been defectively acknowledged?

1) **No Acknowledgment—No Constructive Notice**
Because an unacknowledged deed does not qualify for recordation, it does not give constructive notice to subsequent purchasers. Hence, unless the subsequent purchaser has other notice of the earlier deed, the subsequent purchaser will prevail.
Example: O conveys Blackacre to A by a deed that is not acknowledged, but the recorder nevertheless records it. Later, O conveys to B by an acknowledged deed, which B records. B prevails over A unless B had ***actual*** notice of the deed from O to A (which she might have if she searched the title records) or ***inquiry*** notice (as she would have if A was in possession of Blackacre).

2) **Compare—Defective Acknowledgment**
When a recorded instrument has been acknowledged, but the acknowledgment is defective for some reason ***not apparent on the face*** of the instrument, the better view is that the recordation does impart constructive notice. *Rationale:* A hidden defect in the acknowledgment should not be allowed to destroy the constructive notice that the document otherwise clearly imparts. Purchasers should be entitled to rely on what ***appears*** to be a perfectly recorded document.
Example: A deed bears what appears to be a valid acknowledgment but is in fact invalid because the notary was disqualified to act or because the grantor did not appear personally in front of the notary to acknowledge her signature, as required by law.

F. CONVEYANCE BY WILL

A will is a conveyance that is prepared and executed by the property owner during life, but which does not "speak" or operate until the date of the owner's death. Thus, a will is "ambulatory," meaning that it can be revoked or modified so long as the testator is alive. Some special situations arise when there is a change in the status of the property or beneficiaries between the time the will is executed and the testator's death.

1. **Ademption**
If property is specifically devised or bequeathed in the testator's will, but the testator no longer owns that property at the time of death, the gift is adeemed. This means that the gift ***fails*** and is not replaced by other property. The reason that the property is no longer owned by the testator generally does not matter; *i.e.*, it does not matter whether the testator sold the property or it was accidentally destroyed.
Example: T owns Blackacre and executes a will devising "Blackacre to my daughter Mary." Prior to his death, T sells Blackacre to A and deposits the proceeds of the sale in a bank account. Upon T's death, Mary is not entitled to Blackacre

or to its proceeds. Note that if the will had provided for T's executor to sell Blackacre and distribute the proceeds to Mary, she would be entitled to the proceeds even though the sale occurred before T's death.

a. **Not Applicable to General Devises**
Ademption does not apply unless the gift mentioned specific property. A specific devise or legacy is one that can be satisfied only by the delivery of a particular item; it cannot be satisfied by money. Thus, a bequest of "$10,000," or even of "$10,000 to be paid out of the sale of my IBM stock" cannot be adeemed.

b. **Not Applicable to Land Under Executory Contract**
If the testator enters into an enforceable contract of sale of property after making a specific devise of it by will, the doctrine of ***equitable conversion*** holds that the testator's interest is converted into personal property. Logically, an ademption has occurred, and the proceeds of sale when the closing occurs should not pass to the specific devisee of the property. The traditional case law agrees, but the Uniform Probate Code and statutes in most states have reversed this result. Thus, when property subject to a specific devise is placed under contract of sale before the decedent's death, the proceeds of the sale will pass to the specific devisee.

Example: T owns Blackacre and executes a will devising "Blackacre to my daughter Mary." Prior to his death, T enters into a contract to sell Blackacre to A. After T's death the contract is completed, and A pays the purchase price for the land. Mary is entitled to the purchase price in substitution of the land itself.

1) **No Ademption If Decedent Incompetent When Contract Formed**
If the decedent is unable to enter into the contract, and instead it is entered into by a guardian, attorney in fact, or other representative, courts usually do not apply the equitable doctrine, and they allow the proceeds of the sale to pass to the specific devisee.

c. **Other Proceeds Not Subject to Ademption**
When property is damaged or destroyed before the testator's death but the casualty insurance proceeds are not paid until after the testator's death, ademption does not usually apply. The beneficiary of the specific bequest takes the insurance proceeds. Similarly, ademption usually does not apply to property condemned by the government when the taking was before death but the condemnation award was paid after death.

d. **Partial Ademption**
If the testator specifically devises property and then sells or gives away a part of that property, only that portion is adeemed; the remainder passes to the devisee.

2. **Exoneration**
In many states, if a testator makes a specific devise of real estate that is subject to a mortgage or other lien, the devisee is entitled to have the land "exonerated" by the payment of the lien from the testator's residuary estate. Thus, the property will pass to the devisee free of encumbrances. However, there is a growing trend toward abolition of the exoneration doctrine. In states that have abolished it, the property will pass to the devisee subject to a preexisting mortgage or other lien unless the will expressly provides for a payoff of the lien.

3. Lapse and Anti-Lapse Statutes

A lapse occurs when the beneficiary of a gift in a will ***dies before the testator***. Under the common law, if a lapse occurred, the gift was ***void***. However, nearly all states now have statutes that prevent lapse by permitting the gift to pass to the predeceasing beneficiary's living descendants under certain circumstances. These statutes vary as to the scope of beneficiaries covered.

a. Degree of Relationship to Testator

Many of the anti-lapse statutes apply only when the named beneficiary is a descendant of the testator. Others apply if the beneficiary is more remotely related, such as a descendant of the testator's grandparent. Others apply to any relative, and still others apply to any beneficiary at all.

1) Descendants Are Substituted

The anti-lapse statute does not save the gift for the predeceasing beneficiary's estate; rather it substitutes the beneficiary's descendants for the beneficiary. Thus, property will never pass under the anti-lapse statute to a predeceasing beneficiary's spouse. The property passes to the beneficiary's descendants under the method of distribution (*e.g.,* per stirpes, per capita) used by the state's intestate succession (inheritance) statute.

b. Inapplicable If Beneficiary Dead When Will Executed

If the beneficiary is already dead when the will is executed, the anti-lapse statute usually does not apply, and the gift will lapse and fail.

c. Application to Class Gifts

Ordinarily, if a gift is made by will to a class (*e.g.*, "to my children," or "to the descendants of my brother Bob"), and some members of the class die before the testator, the gift is simply given to the surviving members of the class. However, if class members within the coverage of an anti-lapse statute predecease the testator leaving surviving issue, the statute will apply, and the issue will take the deceased class member's share of the gift.

d. Anti-Lapse Statute Does Not Apply If Contrary Will Provision

The anti-lapse statute does not apply if there is a contrary will provision—*e.g.,* if the gift is contingent on the beneficiary's surviving the testator.

4. Abatement

If the estate assets are not sufficient to pay all claims against the estate and satisfy all devises and bequests, the gifts are abated (*i.e.*, reduced). Absent a contrary will provision, estates in most jurisdictions abate in the following order: (i) property passing by intestacy; (ii) the residuary estate; (iii) general legacies, which abate pro rata; and (iv) specific devises and bequests. Some states provide that within each category personal property abates before real property.

G. CROPS (EMBLEMENTS)

The law recognizes two types of crops: ***Fructus naturales*** are crops that grow spontaneously on the land; *i.e.*, they are produced by nature alone and are perennial (they do not require planting). ***Fructus industriales (emblements)*** are annual crops produced through cultivation. Fructus

naturales are real property and title to them passes automatically with the land. Fructus industriales are personalty.

1. Conveyance of Land Includes Crops

Generally, the owner of the land is presumed to be the owner of both types of crops, and a conveyance of land carries with it all the crops growing on it. This presumption is based on the presumed intent of the parties, but a contrary intent may be shown.

2. Exception—Harvested Crops

An exception to the general rule is recognized for crops that have already been harvested or severed from the land. Such crops do not pass with the conveyance of the land, and the former owner has the right to reenter the land to remove them.

a. Ripened But Unharvested Crops

Some jurisdictions hold that ripened fructus industriales (annual crops) likewise do not pass with a conveyance of the land. These courts treat the ripened crops as having been "constructively severed" upon ripening, because they no longer need to draw sustenance from the soil.

3. Exception—Crops Planted by Tenant

Under the doctrine of emblements, title to crops planted by a tenant during the term of his tenancy remains in the tenant unless there is a contrary provision in the lease. A conveyance of the land by the landlord does not pass title to the tenant's crops. The tenant retains his right to enter upon the property to cultivate, harvest, and remove crops planted prior to the termination of his estate. For this doctrine to apply, the tenancy must have: (i) been for an ***uncertain duration***, and (ii) terminated ***without fault*** on the part of the tenant.

a. Compare—Trespasser

The doctrine of emblements is limited to tenants. One who planted crops while on the land as a trespasser has no title to the crops and has no right of entry to remove them. Crops planted by an adverse possessor acting under a ***claim of right***, however, are generally held to belong to him.

VII. SECURITY INTERESTS IN REAL ESTATE

A. TYPES OF SECURITY INTERESTS

A security interest in real estate operates to secure some other obligation, usually a promise to repay a loan, which is represented by a promissory note. If the loan is not paid when due, the holder of the security interest can either take title to the real estate or have it sold and use the proceeds to pay the debt with accrued interest and any legal and court costs. Of the five types of security interests, the first three are most important.

1. Mortgage

The debtor/notemaker is the mortgagor; he gives the mortgage (along with the note) to the lender, who is the mortgagee. Most states require that a lender realize on the real estate to satisfy the debt only by having a judicial (court-ordered) foreclosure sale conducted by the sheriff.

2. **Deed of Trust**
The debtor/notemaker is the trustor. The trustor gives the deed of trust to a third-party trustee, who is usually closely connected with the lender (*e.g.,* the lender's lawyer, affiliated corporation, or officer). In the event of default, the lender (termed the beneficiary) instructs the trustee to proceed with foreclosing the deed of trust by sale. Many states allow the sale to be either judicial (as with a mortgage) or nonjudicial, under a "power of sale" clause that authorizes the trustee to advertise, give appropriate notices, and conduct the sale personally.

3. **Installment Land Contract**
In an installment land contract, the debtor is the purchaser of the land who signs a contract with the vendor, agreeing to make regular installment payments until the full contract price (including accruing interest) has been paid. Only at that time will the vendor give a deed transferring legal title to the purchaser. In case of default, the contract usually contains a forfeiture clause providing that the vendor may cancel the contract, retain all money paid to date, and retake possession of the land.

4. **Absolute Deed—Equitable Mortgage**
A landowner needing to raise money may "sell" the land to a person who will pay cash and may give the "buyer" an absolute deed rather than a mortgage. This may seem to be safer than a mortgage loan to the creditor and may seem to have tax advantages. However, if the court concludes, by clear and convincing evidence, that the deed was really given for security purposes, they will treat it as an "equitable" mortgage and require that the creditor ***foreclose*** it by judicial action, like any other mortgage. This result will be indicated by the following factors: (i) the existence of a ***debt or promise of payment*** by the deed's grantor; (ii) the grantee's ***promise to return the land*** if the debt is paid; (iii) the fact that the amount advanced to the grantor/debtor was much ***lower than the value of the property***; (iv) the degree of the grantor's ***financial distress***; and (v) the parties' ***prior negotiations***.

5. **Sale-Leaseback**
A landowner needing to raise money may sell her land to another for cash and may then lease the land back for a long period of time. As in the case of the absolute deed, the grantor/lessee may attack such a transaction later as a disguised mortgage. Factors that will lead the court to such a result are: (i) the fact that the regular rent payments on the lease are virtually identical to payments that would be due on a mortgage loan; (ii) the existence of an option to repurchase by the grantor/lessee; and (iii) the fact that the repurchase option could be exercised for much less than the probable value of the property at that time, so that the repurchase would be very likely to occur.

B. TRANSFERS BY MORTGAGEE AND MORTGAGOR

All parties to a mortgage or deed of trust can transfer their interests. Ordinarily, the mortgagor transfers by deeding the property, while the mortgagee usually transfers by indorsing the note and executing a separate assignment of the mortgage. The note and mortgage must pass to ***the same person*** for the transfer to be complete.

1. **Transfer by Mortgagee**

a. **Transfer of Mortgage Without Note**
The case law is divided, with some states holding that the transfer of the mortgage automatically transfers the note as well, unless the mortgagee-transferor expressly

reserves the rights to the note (which there would rarely be any reason for the mortgagee to do). In these states, the transferee of the mortgage can then file an equitable action and compel a transfer of the note as well. Other states hold that, because the note is the principal evidence of the debt, a transfer of the mortgage without the note is a nullity and is void.

b. Transfer of Note Without Mortgage

The ***note can be transferred without the mortgage***, but the mortgage will automatically follow the properly transferred note, unless the mortgagee-transferor expressly reserves the rights to the mortgage (which there would rarely be any reason for the mortgagee to do). No separate written assignment of the mortgage is necessary, although it is customary for the transferee to obtain and record an assignment of the mortgage.

1) Methods of Transferring the Note

The note may be transferred either by indorsing it and delivering it to the transferee, or by a separate document of assignment. Only if the former method is used can the transferee become a holder in due course under U.C.C. Article 3.

a) Holder in Due Course Status

To be a holder in due course of the note, the following requirements must be met:

(1) The note must be ***negotiable in form***, which means that it must be payable "to bearer" or "to the order of" the named payee. It must contain a promise to pay a fixed amount of money (although an adjustable interest rate is permitted), and no other promises, except that it may contain an acceleration clause and an attorneys' fee clause.

(2) The original note must be ***indorsed*** (*i.e.,* signed) by the named payee. Indorsement on a photocopy or some other document is not acceptable.

(3) The original note must be ***delivered*** to the transferee. Delivery of a photocopy is not acceptable.

(4) The transferee must take the note in ***good faith*** and must pay ***value*** for it. ("Value" implies an amount that is more than nominal, although it need not be as great as the note's fair market value.) The transferee ***must not have any notice*** that the note is overdue or has been dishonored, or that the maker has any defense to the duty to pay it.

b) Benefits of Holder in Due Course Status

A holder in due course will take the note free of any personal defenses that the maker might raise. "Personal defenses" include failure of consideration, fraud in the inducement, waiver, estoppel, and payment. The holder in due course is, however, still subject to "real" defenses that the maker might raise. These include infancy, other incapacity, duress, illegality, fraud in the execution, forgery, discharge in insolvency, and any other insolvency.

2) **When Payment to One Without Note Counts**
If the original mortgagee transfers possession of the note ***without giving notice of the transfer*** to the mortgagor, the mortgagor's payment to the original mortgagee is effective even though it is not made to the person entitled to enforce the instrument. [Restatement (Third) of Property: Mortgages §5.5]

Example: A borrows $50,000 from B and gives B a note for that amount, secured by a mortgage on Blackacre. One year later, B assigns the note and mortgage to C, transferring actual possession of the note to C. Two years thereafter, A, who does not realize that B no longer holds the note, pays $50,000 plus interest to B. This payment is effective against C. C's recourse is against B.

2. **Transfer by Mortgagor—Grantee Takes Subject to Mortgage**
If the mortgagor sells the property and conveys a deed, the grantee takes subject to the mortgage, which remains on the land. Unless there is a specific clause in the mortgage, the mortgagee has no power to object to the transfer.

a. **Assumption**
Often the grantee signs an assumption agreement, promising to pay the mortgage loan. If she does so, she becomes ***primarily*** liable to the lender (usually considered a third-party beneficiary), while the ***original*** mortgagor becomes secondarily liable as a ***surety***. If the mortgagee and grantee modify the obligation, the original mortgagor is completely discharged of liability.

b. **Nonassuming Grantee**
A grantee who does not sign an assumption agreement does not become personally liable on the loan. Instead, the original mortgagor remains primarily and personally liable. However, if the grantee does not pay, the mortgage may be foreclosed, thus wiping out the grantee's investment in the land.

c. **Due-on-Sale Clauses**
Most modern mortgages contain "due-on-sale" clauses, which purport to allow the lender to demand full payment of the loan if the mortgagor transfers any interest in the property without the lender's consent. Such clauses are designed to both: (i) protect the lender from sale by the mortgagor to a poor credit risk or to a person likely to commit waste; and (ii) allow the lender to raise the interest rate or charge an "assumption fee" when the property is sold. Federal law preempts state law and makes due-on-sale clauses enforceable for all types of institutional mortgage lenders on all types of real estate. The preemption does not apply to mortgage loans made by private parties.

C. DEFENSES AND DISCHARGE OF THE MORTGAGE

1. **Defenses to Underlying Obligation**
Because a mortgage is granted to secure an obligation, if the obligation is unenforceable so is the mortgage. Therefore, defenses in an action on the underlying obligation are defenses against an action on the mortgage, including: (i) failure of consideration, (ii) duress, (iii) mistake, or (iv) fraud.

2. Discharge of the Mortgage

A mortgagee's right to foreclose is precluded by anything amounting to a discharge of the mortgage, such as payment of the debt secured, merger of the legal and equitable interests, or the acceptance by the mortgagee of a deed in lieu of foreclosure tendered by the mortgagor.

a. Payment

Generally, full payment of the note discharges the mortgage lien. The agreement in the note, however, will normally govern whether the mortgagor may prepay the obligation. If the note or mortgage does not provide for prepayment, the mortgagor has ***no right to prepayment***. The mortgage may also provide for a prepayment fee or a total prohibition of prepayment for part or all of the mortgage term.

b. Merger

A mortgage lien vests the mortgagee with either an equitable interest (lien theory) or a legal interest (title theory), while the mortgagor retains the other interest (*see* D.1., *infra*). If the mortgagee subsequently acquires the mortgagor's interest, the mortgage is said to merge with the title, and the mortgagor's personal liability on the underlying debt is discharged up to the value of the land.

c. Deed in Lieu of Foreclosure

The mortgagor may also tender to the mortgagee a deed in lieu of foreclosure. In effect, the mortgagor simply turns over her equity of redemption (*see* E.1.a., *infra*) to the mortgagee. Acceptance of a deed in lieu of foreclosure permits the mortgagee to take immediate possession without the formalities of a foreclosure sale. Although it is common to negotiate a complete release from the debt, the parties also have the option to negotiate a mortgagor's agreement to remain liable on some portion of the debt. Mortgagors cannot be compelled to tender such a deed, and mortgagees have the right to refuse the deed and proceed to foreclosure.

D. POSSESSION BEFORE FORECLOSURE

When a mortgagor defaults on his debt, the mortgagee can sue on the debt or foreclose on the mortgage. A mortgagee may wish to take possession of the property, or begin receiving the rents from the property, before foreclosure. This is especially important in states where foreclosure is a lengthy process.

1. Theories of Title

The mortgagee may have a right to take possession before foreclosure, depending on the theory the state follows.

a. The Lien Theory

According to the lien theory, the mortgagee is considered the holder of a ***security interest only*** and the mortgagor is deemed the owner of the land until foreclosure. A majority of the states follow this theory, which provides that the mortgagee may not have possession before foreclosure.

b. The Title Theory

Under the title theory, legal ***title is in the mortgagee*** until the mortgage has been satisfied or foreclosed. A minority of states follow this theory, which provides that the mortgagee is entitled to possession upon demand at any time. In practice, this means that as soon as a default occurs, the mortgagee can take possession.

c. **The Intermediate Theory**
The intermediate theory is a compromise position in which legal ***title is in the mortgagor until default***, and upon default, legal title is in the mortgagee. Only a handful of states follow this theory, which provides that the mortgagee may demand possession when a default occurs. There is little practical difference between this theory and the title theory.

2. **Mortgagor Consent and Abandonment**
All states agree that the mortgagee may take possession if the mortgagor gives consent to do so, or if the mortgagor abandons the property.

3. **Risks of Mortgagee in Possession**
The mortgagee who takes possession prior to foreclosure can intercept the rents, prevent waste, make repairs, and lease out vacant space. However, despite these advantages, most mortgagees do not wish to take possession because of the liability risks it presents. These risks include a very strict duty to account for all rents received, a duty to manage the property in a careful and prudent manner, and potential liability in tort to anyone injured on the property.

4. **Receiverships**
Instead of becoming a "mortgagee in possession," most mortgagees attempt to intercept the rents before foreclosure by getting a receiver appointed by the court to manage the property. Courts will generally appoint receivers for rental property upon a showing of some combination of three factors: (i) that waste is occurring, (ii) that the value of the property is inadequate to secure the debt, and (iii) that the mortgagor is insolvent.

E. **FORECLOSURE**
Foreclosure is a process by which the mortgagor's interest in the property is terminated. The property is generally sold to satisfy the debt in whole or in part (foreclosure by sale). Almost all states ***require*** foreclosure by sale. All states allow ***judicial sale***, while about one-half also allow nonjudicial sale under a ***power of sale***. The nonjudicial sale is often permitted with deeds of trust but not with mortgages. Foreclosure sales are conducted by auction, with the highest bidder taking the property. The lender may bid at the sale, and in many cases the lender is the sole bidder. (*Note:* For convenience, the discussion below speaks of mortgagors and mortgagees, but the same principles apply to deed-of-trust trustors and beneficiaries.)

1. **Redemption**

a. **Redemption in Equity**
At any time ***prior to the foreclosure sale***, the mortgagor has the right to redeem the land or free it of the mortgage by paying off the amount due, together with any accrued interest. If the mortgagor has defaulted on a mortgage or note that contains an "acceleration clause" permitting the mortgagee to declare the full balance due in the event of default, the full balance must be paid in order to redeem. A mortgagor's right to redeem her own mortgage cannot be waived in the mortgage itself; this is known as "clogging

the equity of redemption" and is prohibited. However, the right can be waived later for consideration.

b. **Statutory Redemption**

About half the states give the mortgagor (and sometimes junior lienors) a statutory right to redeem for some fixed period after the foreclosure sale has occurred; this period is usually six months or one year. The amount to be paid is usually the foreclosure sale price, rather than the amount of the original debt. Be careful to distinguish equitable redemption, which is universally recognized (but only up to the date of the sale), from statutory redemption, which is only recognized by about half the states and applies only ***after*** foreclosure has occurred.

2. **Priorities**

Generally, the priority of a mortgage is determined by the time it was placed on the property. When a mortgage is foreclosed, the buyer at the sale will take title as it existed when the mortgage was placed on the property. Thus, foreclosure will terminate interests junior to the mortgage being foreclosed but will not affect senior interests.

a. **Effect of Foreclosure on Various Interests**

1) **Junior Interests Destroyed by Foreclosure**

Foreclosure destroys all interests junior to the mortgage being foreclosed. In other words, junior mortgages, liens, leases, easements, and all other types of interests will be wiped out. If a lien senior to that of the mortgagee is in default, the junior mortgagee has the right to pay it off (*i.e.,* redeem it) in order to avoid being wiped out by its foreclosure. Thus, those with interests subordinate to those of the foreclosing party are ***necessary parties*** to the foreclosure action. Failure to include a necessary party results in the preservation of that party's interest despite foreclosure and sale.

2) **Senior Interests Not Affected**

Foreclosure does not affect any interest senior to the mortgage being foreclosed. ***The buyer at the sale takes subject to such interest.*** She does not become personally liable on such senior interests, but she will be forced to pay them in order to prevent their foreclosure in the future.

b. **Modification of Priority**

As noted above, priorities among mortgages on the same real estate are normally determined simply by ***chronology***: the earliest mortgage placed on the property is first in priority, the next mortgage is second, and so on. However, the chronological priority may be changed in the following ways:

1) **Failure to Record**

If the first mortgagee fails to record, and the second mortgagee records, gives value, and takes without notice of the first, the second mortgagee will have priority over the first by virtue of the normal operation of the recording acts.

2) **Subordination Agreement**

A first mortgagee may enter into an agreement with a junior mortgagee, subordinating its priority to the junior mortgagee. Such agreements are generally enforced. However, a broad promise to subordinate to any mortgage (or a vaguely described mortgage) to be placed on the property in the future may be considered too inequitable to enforce.

3) Purchase Money Mortgages

A purchase money mortgage ("PMM") is:

(i) A mortgage given to the vendor of the property as a part of the purchase price; or

(ii) A mortgage given to a third-party lender, who is lending the funds to allow the buyer to purchase the property.

A PMM is considered to have priority over ***prior*** non-PMMs on the property, even if such mortgages or liens are recorded first. However, PMM priority is subject to being defeated by ***subsequent*** mortgages or liens by operation of the recording acts.

Example: A properly records a judgment lien against O (which will attach to any after-acquired property of O). O finances the purchase of Blackacre with a $250,000 loan from B. B does not record its mortgage. A few months later, O borrows $10,000 from C in exchange for a mortgage on Blackacre. C records her mortgage. B's PMM has priority over A's lien because of the general priority rules governing PMMs, but is junior to C's mortgage under any recording act because C had no notice of B's interest and recorded first.

a) Vendor PMM vs. Third-Party PMM

As between two PMMs, one to the vendor and one to a third-party lender, the vendor's mortgage is usually given priority over the third-party lender's.

b) Third-Party PMM vs. Third-Party PMM

If two PMMs are given to two third-party lenders, their priority is determined by the chronological order in which the mortgages were placed on the property, the recording act, and a subordination agreement (if any). Note that in these cases, the recording acts are often of no use because two purchase money mortgagees will almost always know of each other's existence and, thus, have notice.

4) Modification of Senior Mortgage

Suppose there are two mortgages on the land. The landowner enters into a modification agreement with the senior mortgagee, raising its interest rate or otherwise making it more burdensome. The junior mortgage will be given ***priority over the modification***. For example, if the first mortgage debt is larger because of the modification, the second mortgage gains priority over the increase in the debt.

5) Optional Future Advances

In general, a mortgage may obligate the lender to make further advances of funds

after the mortgage is executed, and such advances will have the same priority as the original mortgage. However, if a junior mortgage is placed on the property and the senior lender later makes an "optional" advance while having notice of the junior lien, the advance will lose priority to the junior lien. An optional advance is one that the senior lender is not contractually bound to make. Numerous states have reversed this rule by statute, but it remains the majority view.

3. Proceeds of Sale

The proceeds of the foreclosure sale are used first to pay expenses of the sale, attorneys' fees, and court costs; then to pay the principal and accrued interest on the ***loan that was foreclosed***; next to pay off any ***junior liens*** or other junior interests in the order of their priority; and finally, any remaining proceeds are distributed to the ***mortgagor***. In many cases, there is no surplus remaining after the principal debt is paid off.

4. Deficiency Judgments

If the proceeds of the sale are insufficient to satisfy the mortgage debt, the mortgagee can bring a personal action against the mortgagor/debtor for the deficiency. However, a number of states limit the deficiency that can be recovered to the difference between the debt and the property's fair market value when the fair market value is higher than the foreclosure price. Other states prohibit deficiency judgments entirely on PMMs and on deeds of trust that are foreclosed by power of sale.

Examples: 1) Assume that land has a fair market value of $50,000 and is subject to three mortgages executed by its owner, whose name is MR. The mortgages have priorities and secure outstanding debts in the amounts shown below, which are owed to three different creditors, ME1, ME2, and ME3:

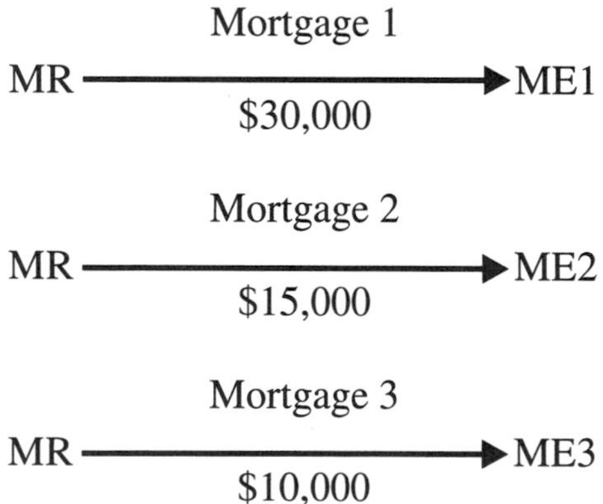

Assume that Mortgage 1 is foreclosed, and the bid at the sale is $50,000 (the fair value of the land). How will the funds be distributed?

In an actual case, the funds would first be used to pay any attorneys' fees and expenses of the foreclosure, and then to any accrued interest on Mortgage 1. However, we will assume that these items are zero.

The $50,000 in funds from the sale will then be used to pay off the mortgages in the order of their priority. Thus, $30,000 is applied to fully pay off Mortgage 1. Then, $15,000 is applied to fully pay off Mortgage 2. There is a remaining balance from the foreclosure sale of $5,000, which is applied toward payment of Mortgage 3. Because this is not enough to discharge Mortgage 3 fully, ME3 is left with a deficiency of $5,000, and may sue MR for a personal judgment in this amount unless state anti-deficiency statutes prohibit it.

2) Assume the same facts as above, except that the bid at the sale is $60,000 rather than $50,000. This will allow full payment of Mortgage 1 ($30,000), Mortgage 2 ($15,000), and Mortgage 3 ($10,000), and will leave a surplus of $5,000. Assuming there are no further liens or encumbrances on the property, this $5,000 will be paid over to MR, the mortgagor.

3) Now assume the same facts as in the original problem, except that it is Mortgage 2 that is being foreclosed. Mortgage 1 exists, but it is either not in default or its holder has not yet taken action to foreclose it.

Recall from the outline above that ***foreclosure does not affect any interest senior to the mortgage being foreclosed***. Thus, foreclosure of Mortgage 2 will not affect Mortgage 1, which will continue to exist on the property in the hands of the foreclosure sale purchaser. Such a purchaser will not be personally liable to pay Mortgage 1 off, but as a practical matter, if Mortgage 1 is not paid, sooner or later ME1 will foreclose it. Hence, the buyer at the foreclosure sale of Mortgage 2 will have a strong economic incentive to pay Mortgage 1; otherwise, she will be subjected to the foreclosure action of ME1, and may well lose much or all of her investment in the property.

What will a wise bidder at the foreclosure sale on Mortgage 2 bid? The maximum is $20,000, which is the fair value of the land ($50,000) minus the amount the successful bidder will subsequently have to pay to discharge Mortgage 1 ($30,000).

If the bid at the foreclosure sale of Mortgage 2 is $20,000, how will the money be distributed? None of it will go to ME1, because he still has his mortgage on the property. $15,000 of the funds will be applied to fully pay off Mortgage 2, and $5,000 will remain to be applied against the $10,000 balance owed on Mortgage 3 (which is, of course, wiped out by the foreclosure of Mortgage 2). ME3 will still have a $5,000 deficiency, as in the first example above.

F. INSTALLMENT LAND CONTRACTS

Installment contracts usually provide for forfeiture rather than foreclosure as the vendor's remedy in the event of default. However, because forfeiture is often a harsh remedy, the courts have tended to resist enforcing forfeiture clauses and in doing so have developed the following theories:

1. Equity of Redemption

Several states allow the contract purchaser who is in default to pay off the accelerated full balance of the contract and to keep the land. In other words, they grant the purchaser a grace period. This is roughly analogous to the equity of redemption in mortgage law. A few states have statutory schedules of grace periods, which often provide for a longer time if a greater percentage of the total price has been paid.

2. **Restitution**
A number of decisions allow actions by the vendor for forfeiture of the land but require her to refund to the purchaser any amount by which his payments exceed the vendor's damages. The court may measure these damages by the property's fair rental value while the purchaser was in possession or by any drop in market value since the contract was executed.

3. **Treat as a Mortgage**
A few states, by statute or case law, now treat installment contracts like mortgages, at least for purposes of the vendor's remedies. In effect, the vendor must foreclose the contract by judicial sale in order to realize on the real estate, and she cannot simply reclaim the land.

4. **Waiver**
Many cases hold that where a vendor has established a pattern of accepting late payments from the purchaser, she cannot suddenly insist on strict on-time payment and declare a forfeiture if such payment is not forthcoming. Such a pattern is said to constitute a waiver of strict performance. To reinstate strict performance, the vendor must send the purchaser a notice of her intention to do so and must allow a reasonable time for the purchaser to make up any late payments and to get back "on stream."

5. **Election of Remedies**
It is commonly held that the vendor who elects to pursue a forfeiture cannot also bring an action for damages or for specific performance. The vendor must choose only one remedy and forgo all others.

VIII. RIGHTS INCIDENTAL TO OWNERSHIP OF LAND (NATURAL RIGHTS)

A. IN GENERAL

The owner of real property has the exclusive right to use and possess the surface, the airspace, and the soil of the property. This right is subject to restrictions in the chain of title (*e.g.*, easements and covenants), to the law of nuisance, and to any valid laws or regulations that restrict the use of the land (*e.g.*, zoning ordinances).

B. RIGHT TO LATERAL AND SUBJACENT SUPPORT OF LAND

1. **Right to Lateral Support**
Ownership of land carries with it the right to have the land supported in its ***natural state*** by adjoining land. This normally means a right to have one's land undisturbed by withdrawal of support (*e.g.*, by excavations on adjoining land).

   a. **Support of Land in Natural State**
   A landowner is ***strictly liable*** if his excavation causes adjacent land to subside (*i.e.*, slip or cave in). Thus, he will be liable even if he used the utmost care.

   b. **Support of Buildings on Land**
   If land is improved by buildings and an adjacent landowner's excavation causes subsidence, the adjacent landowner will be ***strictly liable*** for damages to the land and buildings

caused by the excavation only if it is shown that the land would have collapsed in its natural state (*i.e.*, that it would have collapsed in the absence of the buildings and improvements). Even if the land would not have collapsed in its natural state (*i.e.*, the collapse would not have occurred except for the weight of the buildings), the excavating landowner is liable for loss or damage to the land and buildings if his excavation is found to have been done ***negligently***. (Tort rules apply here.)

2. **Right to Subjacent Support**
When a landowner conveys to a grantee the right to take minerals from beneath the land, the grantor retains the right to have the surface supported unless the conveyance expressly includes authority to destroy the surface if "reasonably necessary" to extract the mineral.

a. **Support of Land and Buildings**
This right of support extends not only to the land in its natural state but also to all buildings existing on the date when the subjacent estate is severed from the surface. However, the underground occupant is liable for damages to subsequently erected buildings only if he was ***negligent***.

b. **Interference with Underground Waters**
Note that an underground occupant is liable for negligently damaging springs and wells, whereas an adjoining landowner is not liable for interfering with underground percolating waters.

C. **WATER RIGHTS**
Different rules apply depending on whether the water rights claimed involve (i) water in watercourses (*e.g.*, streams, rivers, and lakes, including underground watercourses); (ii) ground or percolating water (*e.g.*, water normally pumped or drawn from wells); or (iii) surface water (*e.g.*, rainfall, seepage). Exam questions normally concern who has priority to use the water from watercourses and from the ground, and to what extent a landowner may obstruct or divert the flow of surface water.

1. **Watercourses**
There are two major systems for allocation of water in watercourses: (i) the ***riparian doctrine*** (generally applied in the eastern states where water is or was relatively abundant), and (ii) the ***prior appropriation doctrine*** (generally used in the 17 western states where water is relatively scarce).

a. **Riparian Doctrine**
Under the riparian doctrine, water does not belong to the public generally or to the state (with certain exceptions) but rather to the "riparian" proprietors who own land bordering on the watercourse. All of these landowners have "riparian rights" and none can use the water so as to deprive the others of these rights.

1) **What Land Is Riparian**
Under the ***majority rule***, all tracts held under unity of ownership are riparian if the tracts are contiguous and ***any*** of them front on the water. Thus, if a riparian owner purchases a parcel which is contiguous to the riparian parcel, riparian rights attach to the newly acquired parcel. The ***minority rule*** limits riparian rights to

the smallest tract of land ever owned abutting the water. Under this view, if a back portion of a riparian tract is sold, it becomes nonriparian and can never regain riparian rights.

a) **Riparian Owner**
Riparian owners include the fee owner of the abutting land and, to the extent of their title, lessees and easement owners of such land.

b) **Doctrine Applies Only to Riparian Parcel**
The riparian doctrine permits use of water only in connection with activities carried out on the riparian parcel. Riparian rights cannot be conveyed for the use of nonriparian land nor can they be lost by nonuse.

2) **Nature of Riparian Right**

a) **Natural Flow Theory**
Under the "natural flow" theory, a riparian owner is entitled to the water in the bordering stream or lake subject to the limitation that ***he may not substantially or materially diminish its quantity, quality, or velocity***. Thus, a downstream owner can enjoin an upstream owner's use even though the downstream owner has plenty of water for his own use. No state appears to adhere strictly to this theory because it operates to limit beneficial upstream use and leads to "waste" of the resource.

b) **Reasonable Use Theory**
Under the more common theory, all riparian owners share the right of "reasonable use." The general idea is that the right of each riparian owner to use the stream (*e.g.,* to divert for irrigation, to pollute, etc.) is subject to a like reasonable right in other riparian owners. ***Each riparian owner must submit to reasonable use*** by other riparian owners, and a downstream owner cannot enjoin such use by an upstream owner unless it substantially interferes with the needs of those who have a like right (*i.e.,* unless actual damage is shown).

(1) **Factors to Consider**
In determining whether an owner's use of water is "reasonable," courts generally balance the utility of the use against the gravity of the harm. (Note the analogy to nuisance law.) Six factors are helpful in this balancing process: (i) the ***purpose*** of the questioned use; (ii) the ***destination*** to which the water is taken for use; (iii) the ***extent*** of the use; (iv) the ***pollution*** of water by use; (v) whether the use involves an ***alteration*** in the manner of flow; and (vi) ***miscellaneous*** types of conduct that may give rise to litigation. (These factors may be remembered more easily by using the acronym MAPPED.)

c) **Natural vs. Artificial Use**
Under either of the above theories, water use is categorized as "natural" or "artificial." Natural uses include those necessary for the daily sustenance of human beings (*e.g.,* household consumption, gardening, minimal number of livestock). All other uses, including irrigation and manufacturing, are artificial.

Natural uses prevail over artificial. Upper riparians can take all that they need for natural uses. However, they cannot take for artificial purposes unless there is enough water for the domestic wants of all.

b. **Prior Appropriation Doctrine**
Under the prior appropriation doctrine, the water belongs initially to the state, but the right to divert and use it can be acquired by an individual whether or not he is a riparian owner. Initially, individual rights were established by actual use; thus, each appropriator acquired a vested property right "to divert a given quantity of water, at given times from a given place, to use at a given place for a given purpose."

1) **Factors to Note for Bar Exam**
Present day acquisition and governance of rights under this doctrine are largely dealt with under complex state-administered permit systems that are too detailed for coverage here. However, it is sufficient for bar examination purposes to note that: (i) appropriative rights were originally determined simply by priority of beneficial use; (ii) if there is a decrease in stream flow, priority is accorded in terms of time of appropriation (*i.e.*, the junior appropriators in descending order of priority must suffer); (iii) in many states, an appropriative right can be severed from the land it serviced when acquired and transferred (*i.e.*, can be sold to another for use on other land), provided no injury is caused to existing uses; and (iv) an appropriative right (unlike a riparian one) can be lost by abandonment (intent and nonuse).

2. **Groundwater**
If water comes from an underground watercourse (*e.g.*, a defined stream or river), the riparian or prior appropriation doctrines apply. However, the presumption is that underground water is percolating (*i.e.*, the water moves through the ground diffusely and is usually withdrawn by wells from the underground water table). There are four different rules for determining rights in underground water.

a. **Absolute Ownership Doctrine**
The absolute ownership doctrine is followed by approximately 12 eastern states. The owner of the land overlying the source basin may extract as much water as she wishes and use it for whatever purpose she desires (including export). There is no firmly established system for allocation among overlying owners.

b. **Reasonable Use Doctrine**
The majority view, followed by about 25 states, allows the surface owner to make "reasonable use" of the groundwater. This rule differs from the absolute ownership rule mainly with respect to exporting water off site: Exporting is allowed only to the extent that it does not harm other owners who have rights in the same aquifer. On the other hand, virtually all beneficial uses of water ***on the land*** are considered reasonable and are allowed.

c. **Correlative Rights Doctrine**
In California, the owners of overlying land own the underground water basin as joint tenants, and each is allowed a reasonable amount for her own use.

d. **Appropriative Rights Doctrine**
In some western states, the prior appropriation doctrine applies to groundwater as well as watercourses. Priority of use determines appropriative rights. In most western states, rights to percolating water are now determined by a state water board which controls annual yield, prohibits water waste, etc.

3. **Surface Waters**
Diffused surface waters are those that have no channel but pass over the surface of the land. The source may be rainfall, melting snow, seepage, etc. A landowner can use surface waters within her boundaries for any purpose she desires. Problems concern the right of a lower owner to restrict a flow that would naturally cross his land (*e.g.*, by dikes) and the right of an upper owner to alter or divert a natural flow onto other lands (*e.g.*, by drains, channels, or sloughs). The acting landowner's liability to other landowners depends upon which doctrine the state follows.

a. **Natural Flow Theory**
Under the natural flow theory, followed by about half the states, a landowner cannot refuse to take natural drainage, cannot divert surface water onto the land of another, and cannot alter the rate or manner of natural flow where such actions would injure others above or below him. Because this theory imposes substantial impediments on development (*e.g.*, no paving, large roofs, culverts, etc.), most states have "softened" the rule to permit ***reasonable*** changes in natural flow. And a few states have held the doctrine inapplicable to urban property (because development would otherwise be hindered).

b. **Common Enemy Theory**
Under the common enemy theory, followed by half the states, surface water is a common enemy and any owner can build dikes or change drainage to get rid of it. However, many courts have modified the doctrine and have held landowners to a standard of ordinary care to avoid unnecessary and negligent injury to the land of others.

c. **Reasonable Use Theory**
The growing trend is to apply the reasonable use doctrine which, as in nuisance and watercourse cases, requires balancing the utility of the use against the gravity of the harm. Judicial mitigation of both the natural flow and common enemy doctrines often results in an approximation of the reasonable use theory.

d. **Compare—Capture of Surface Water**
A landowner can capture (*e.g.*, by dam, rain barrels) as much surface water as he wishes. It can be diverted to any purpose on or off the land. Owners below have no cause of action unless the diversion is malicious.

D. RIGHTS IN AIRSPACE
The right to the airspace above a parcel is not exclusive, but the owner is entitled to freedom from excessive noise and transit by aircraft. If flights are so low as to be unreasonably disturbing, they constitute a trespass or (if the airport is government-owned) a taking by inverse condemnation.

E. RIGHT TO EXCLUDE—REMEDIES OF POSSESSOR

1. **Trespass**
If the land is invaded by a ***tangible*** physical object that interferes with the right of exclusive possession, there is a trespass.

2. **Private Nuisance**
If the land is invaded by ***intangibles*** (*e.g.*, odors or noises) that substantially and unreasonably interfere with a private individual's use or enjoyment of her property, the possessor may bring an action for private nuisance.

    a. **Compare—Public Nuisance**
    Public nuisance is an invasion by intangibles that unreasonably interfere with the health, safety, or property rights of the ***public***—*i.e.,* a broad segment of the community, rather than one or a few individuals.

3. **Continuing Trespass**
If the land is repeatedly invaded by a trespasser (*e.g.*, the invader repeatedly swings a crane over the property), the possessor may sue for either trespass or nuisance.

4. **Law or Equity**
If the possessor wants to force the invader to stop the invasion of the property, the remedy is an injunction in equity. If the possessor wants damages, the remedy is an action at law.

    a. **Ejectment**
    The remedy at common law to remove a trespasser from the property is ejectment.

    b. **Unlawful Detainer**
    In the landlord-tenant situation, the landlord may force the tenant to vacate the premises by the statutory remedy of unlawful detainer. (In some states, the term used to describe this action is forcible detainer or summary ejectment.) The action may be joined with a demand for money damages in rent due.

IX. COOPERATIVES, CONDOMINIUMS, AND ZONING

A. COOPERATIVES

In the most common form of housing cooperative, title to the land and buildings is held by a corporation that leases the individual apartments to its shareholders. Thus, the residents in a cooperative are both tenants of the cooperative (by virtue of their occupancy leases) and owners of the cooperative (by virtue of their stock interests). Stock interests in the cooperative are not transferable apart from the occupancy lease to which they are attached.

1. **Restriction on Transfer of Interests**
Because the members of a cooperative are tenants, the cooperative may retain the same controls over assignment and sublease of the apartments as may be exercised by any other landlord.

2. **Mortgages**
Permanent financing is provided through a blanket mortgage on the entire property owned

by the cooperative corporation (land and buildings). This mortgage has priority over the occupancy leases. Failure to meet the payments on the blanket mortgage may result in the termination of the leases through foreclosure of the mortgage. Thus, each cooperative tenant is vitally concerned that the other tenants pay their shares of the blanket mortgage.

3. Maintenance Expenses

Ordinarily, cooperative tenants are not personally liable on the note or bond of the blanket mortgage. However, under their occupancy leases, each tenant is liable for her proportionate share of all of the expenses of the cooperative (including payments on the mortgage as well as other operating expenses).

B. CONDOMINIUMS

In a condominium, each owner owns the interior of her individual unit plus an undivided interest in the exterior and common elements.

1. Restriction on Transfer of Interests

Because condominium unit ownership is treated as fee ownership, the ordinary rules against restraints on alienation apply. A few jurisdictions (*e.g.*, New York) by statute allow reasonable restraints on transfer of condominium units.

2. Mortgages

Each unit owner finances the purchase of her unit by a separate mortgage on her unit. Consequently, unit owners need not be as concerned about defaults by others as they must be in a cooperative.

3. Maintenance Expenses

Each unit owner is personally liable on her own mortgage and each pays her own taxes (unlike the cooperative situation, but like any other homeowner). In addition, each unit owner is liable to contribute her proportionate share to the common expenses of maintaining the common elements, including insurance thereon.

C. ZONING

The state may enact statutes to reasonably control the use of land for the protection of the ***health, safety, morals, and welfare*** of its citizens. Zoning is the division of a jurisdiction into districts in which certain uses and developments are permitted or prohibited. The zoning power is based on the state's police power and is limited by the Due Process Clause of the Fourteenth Amendment. Other limitations are imposed by the Equal Protection Clause of the Fourteenth Amendment and the "no taking without just compensation" clause of the Fifth Amendment. (*See* Multistate Constitutional Law outline.) Cities and counties can exercise zoning power only if authorized to do so by state enabling acts. Ordinances that do not conform to such acts are "ultra vires" (beyond the authority of the local body) and void.

1. Nonconforming Use

A use that exists at the time of passage of a zoning act and that does not conform to the statute cannot be eliminated at once. Some statutes provide for the gradual elimination of such nonconforming uses (*e.g.*, the use must end in 10 years).

2. Special Use Permits

Some unusual uses (*e.g.*, hospitals, funeral homes, etc.) require issuance of a special permit even though the zoning of the particular district (*e.g.*, commercial) allows that type of use.

3. Variance

A variance from the literal restrictions of a zoning ordinance may be granted by administrative action. The property owner must show that the ordinance imposes a unique hardship on him and that the variance will not be contrary to the public welfare.

4. Unconstitutional Takings and Exactions

A zoning ordinance may so reduce the value of real property that it constitutes a taking under the Fifth and Fourteenth Amendments. If an ordinance constitutes a taking, the local government must pay damages to the landowner equal to the value reduction. If the ordinance regulates activity that would be considered a nuisance under common law principles, it will not be a taking even if it leaves the land with no economic value.

a. Denial of *All* Economic Value of Land—Taking

If a government regulation denies a landowner ***all*** economic use of his land, the regulation is equivalent to a physical appropriation and is thus a taking (unless the use was prohibited by nuisance or property law when the owner acquired the land). [Lucas v. South Carolina Coastal Council, 505 U.S. 1003 (1992)—state's zoning ordinance, adopted after owner purchased lots, was a taking because it prohibited owner from erecting any permanent structures on the lots]

b. Denial of *Nearly All* Economic Value—Balancing Test

If a regulation so decreases the value of the property that there is very little economic value, the court will balance the following factors to determine whether there has been a taking:

(i) The ***social goals*** sought to be promoted;

(ii) The ***diminution*** in value to the owner; and

(iii) The owner's ***reasonable expectations*** regarding use of the property.

Generally, the regulation will be found to be a taking only if it ***unjustly*** reduces the economic value of the property (*e.g.,* greatly reduces the property value and only slightly promotes the public welfare). [Pennsylvania Coal Co. v. Mahon, 260 U.S. 393 (1922); Keystone Bituminous Coal Association v. DeBenedictis, 480 U.S. 470 (1987)]

c. Unconstitutional Exactions

Local governments often demand, in exchange for zoning approval for a new project, that the landowner give up some land for a public purpose, such as street widening. However, such demands are unconstitutional under the Fifth and Fourteenth Amendments unless they meet the tests set out below. [Nollan v. California Coastal Commission, 483 U.S. 825 (1987); Dolan v. City of Tigard, 512 U.S. 374 (1994)]

1) Essential Nexus

The local government's demand must be ***rationally connected*** to some additional burden that the proposed project will place on public facilities or rights. Thus, a city could demand land for a street widening upon a showing that the proposed project would otherwise increase traffic congestion and pollution along the street in question.

2) **Rough Proportionality**
Even if the "essential nexus" test above is met, the local government must not demand too much. The required dedication must be ***reasonably related***, both in ***nature*** (the essential nexus) and extent (the amount of the exaction), to the impact of the proposed development.

3) **Burden of Proof**
The local government has the burden of showing that both the essential nexus and rough proportionality tests are met.

d. **Remedy**
If a property owner challenges a regulation and the court determines that there was a taking, the government will be required to either: (i) compensate the owner for the taking, or (ii) terminate the regulation and pay the owner for any damages that occurred while the regulation was in effect. [First English Evangelical Lutheran Church v. County of Los Angeles, 482 U.S. 304 (1987)]

REVIEW QUESTIONS

INTRODUCTORY NOTE

The questions that follow are intended to serve as both a substantive review and a diagnostic test. Respond to the questions quickly and compare your answers with those found at the end of this section. This will allow you to identify areas in which you may need further review.

FILL IN ANSWER

PRESENT POSSESSORY ESTATES

1. Under modern law, a conveyance from "O to A" is presumed to vest in A all of O's right, title, and interest in the property. True or false? ________

2. O conveys Blackacre "to A to have and to hold during the life of B." If A dies before B, does the property revert to O? ________

3. O conveys Blackacre "to A for so long as he may choose to live on the property." Does this create a life estate in A? ________

4. Which of the following acts by a life tenant constitute waste at common law? ________

   (A) Clearing the land of timber and plowing the soil for farm purposes.

   (B) Tearing down an old house on the property and erecting a gasoline station, greatly enhancing the value of the property.

   (C) Failing to cover a hole in the roof, causing damage to the hardwood floors when it rains.

5. O devises an apartment house "to A for life, remainder to B." Assuming there is adequate rental income received by A, which of the following expenses is A obligated to pay? ________

   (A) Principal and interest payments on mortgage.

   (B) Property taxes.

   (C) Insurance premiums on the full value of the land and building.

   (D) Repairs and maintenance.

   (E) Cost of replacing a worn-out furnace.

FUTURE INTERESTS

6. O conveys Blackacre "to A for life." When A is 80 years old, A leases Blackacre to his son, S, for 50 years.

a. After making the lease, A has no remaining interest in Blackacre. True or false? ________

b. If A dies before the end of the 50-year lease period, S's leasehold terminates automatically. True or false? ________

c. After making the lease, A's interest is contingent because there is little likelihood of it ever becoming possessory. True or false? ________

7. Can a remainder follow a term of years (*e.g.*, "to A for 10 years, then to B and her heirs")? ________

8. Any interest in a third party that follows a fee interest is necessarily an executory interest (*e.g.*, "O to A and his heirs, but if A ever becomes bankrupt, to B and her heirs"). True or false? ________

9. O conveys Blackacre "to A for life, remainder to B and her heirs, unless B dies before reaching age 21, in which event to C and his heirs."

a. Most courts would construe B's interest as a contingent remainder. True or false? ________

b. If B's interest is construed as a contingent remainder, C's interest would be classified as an executory interest. True or false? ________

c. If B's interest is construed as a ***vested*** remainder, C's interest would be classified as an executory interest. True or false? ________

d. B's interest cannot be construed as a vested remainder because it is not certain that B will outlive A. True or false? ________

10. O conveys "to A for life, then to B, but if B does not marry, to C." Is B's interest vested or contingent? ________

11. O conveys Blackacre "to A for life and then to B and her heirs, except that if B ever becomes bankrupt, then to C and his heirs." The preferred construction is that ***C's interest*** is an executory interest, rather than an alternative contingent remainder. True or false? ________

12. O conveys Blackacre "to A for life, remainder to A's children."

a. If A has ***no*** children at the time of the conveyance, is the remainder valid? ________

b. If A later has one child, can A and this child (through a guardian) convey good title to Blackacre? ________

c. If A has three children, but two predecease A, does the surviving child take the entire property on A's death? ________

13. O conveys Blackacre "to A for life, remainder to the heirs of B."

    a. The remainder would probably be construed as vested in B's prospective heirs (children, etc.) subject to divestment if they fail to survive her. True or false? ________

    b. Following the conveyance, does O have a reversion in Blackacre? ________

    c. Under modern law, if A predeceases B, is the remainder destroyed? ________

14. O conveys Blackacre "to A for life, remainder to A's first-born child." ***Before*** A has any children, O transfers to A her entire remaining interest in Blackacre. Can A now convey full title to Blackacre? ________

15. O conveys Blackacre "to A for life, remainder to A's heirs." Under modern law, a valid interest is created in A's heirs. True or false? ________

16. O deeds Blackacre "to A for life, remainder to O's heirs."

    a. Under modern law, is it possible for O later to ***sell*** Blackacre (subject to A's life estate), and thereby cut off any interest in "O's heirs"? ________

    b. In construing this deed, would the court have to reject any evidence offered by O's prospective heirs that O intended a present gift to them at the time of the conveyance? ________

    c. If the conveyance was by ***will*** (rather than inter vivos deed), would it be held to create a valid interest in "O's heirs"? ________

17. O conveys "to A and his heirs ***if and when*** A marries X." Is A's interest an executory interest? ________

18. O devised Lot 12 "to A for life, and if A leaves surviving children, then to A's children, but if A has no surviving children, then to B and her heirs." B predeceased A and A died childless. C, O's only heir, and D, B's only heir, each claim an interest in Lot 12. Who is entitled to the land, C, D, or none of the above? ________

19. O devises Blackacre "to the children of A." Suppose A had one child (A1) at the time the will was executed; and another (A2) was born after the will was executed but before O's death; and still another (A3) was born after O's death; and A then died.

    a. Assuming this is a class gift, are all three children entitled to share? ________

    b. If A1 had died before O, would A1 be entitled to share? ________

    c. If A had ***no*** children at the time of O's death, would the gift fail entirely? ________

THE RULE AGAINST PERPETUITIES

20. An executory interest is subject to the Rule Against Perpetuities, whereas a contingent remainder is not. True or false? ________

21. O "to A for life, remainder to such of my relatives who are living when Communist rule in Cuba ends." Is the remainder valid under the Rule? ________

22. O owned an oil well that was expected to run dry within the year. O transferred the oil well to Trustee, instructing her to distribute the income to O's children, and to distribute the proceeds from the sale of the well to O's children when the well ran dry. Six months after the transfer, the well went dry and was sold. Do the children of O get the proceeds from the sale of the well under the Rule Against Perpetuities? ________

23. O "to A for life, remainder in equal shares to A's brothers and sisters reaching age 21." Is the remainder valid under the Rule? ________

24. O "to A for life, remainder in equal shares to ***each of*** A's brothers and sisters reaching age 21." Is the remainder valid under the Rule? ________

25. O died leaving a will that devised Blackacre "to my children for life, then to my grandchildren." Is the remainder valid under the Rule Against Perpetuities? ________

26. O "to A for 99 years and then to B and her heirs." Is B's interest subject to the Rule Against Perpetuities? ________

27. O "to A for life, remainder to B and her heirs upon condition that the property be used only for church purposes."

    a. Is B's interest subject to the Rule? ________

    b. Is O's interest subject to the Rule? ________

28. O "to A and his heirs, but if liquor is ever sold on the premises, to B and her heirs."

    a. Is B's interest valid under the Rule? ________

    b. Would B's interest be valid if the conveyance was O "to A and his heirs, so long as liquor is never sold on these premises"; and then, ***the next day***, O conveyed to B her remaining interest in the property? ________

THE RULE AGAINST RESTRAINTS ON ALIENATION

29. T devises Blackacre "to Wife on condition that she not sell it until our son, S, reaches age 21; and if she does sell prior to that time, her estate shall terminate and the property shall go to X and his heirs." If Wife attempts to sell prior to S's 21st birthday, is the restraint enforceable? ________

30. A restraint on alienation will be upheld as long as it does not result in forfeiture of the estate. True or false? _________

31. In general, a restraint on the right of a life tenant to transfer his estate will be upheld. True or false? _________

CONCURRENT ESTATES

32. O conveys Blackacre "to O (herself) and A, as joint tenants." Was this effective to create a joint tenancy at common law? _________

33. O conveys Blackacre "to A and B." Under modern law, this will be ***presumed*** to create a tenancy in common between A and B, rather than a joint tenancy. True or false? _________

34. Is a conveyance "to A and B as joint tenants" sufficient to create a joint tenancy, without express mention of survivorship rights? _________

35. A, B, and C own Blackacre as joint tenants.

    a. If A ***mortgages*** her interest in Blackacre, does this terminate the joint tenancy as to A? _________

    b. If B ***leases*** Blackacre to a stranger, does this terminate the joint tenancy as to B? _________

    c. If A executes a ***will*** devising her interest in Blackacre to her son, does this terminate the joint tenancy as to A? _________

    d. If C transfers her interest to a ***"strawman"*** who transfers it right back to C, does this terminate the joint tenancy as to C? _________

36. A, B, and C own Blackacre as joint tenants.

    a. If A goes onto the land, farms it, and produces a crop, is she obligated to split the proceeds with B and C, or to pay B and C rent? _________

    b. If A rents the land to a stranger who farms it and pays rent in the form of a share of the crops, is A obligated to split the crop proceeds with B and C? _________

    c. If A builds a barn on the land at her own expense, enhancing its value, can she recover a share of the cost from B and C? _________

LANDLORD AND TENANT

37. L leases Blackacre to T for 15 days at a rent of $100. Is T a tenant for years? _________

38. A periodic tenancy will continue forever unless terminated by proper notice. True or false? _________

39. L leases Blackacre to T at a rental of "$6,000 per year, payable at $500 per month." T has a tenancy for one year in most states today. True or false? ________

40. L leases Blackacre to T for one year, with rent payable at $500 per month. If T remains in possession of the premises after the expiration of his one-year lease, does T automatically become a tenant for a new one-year term in most states? ________

41. L leases a store to T for one year. The store is located in an old neighborhood, where all buildings are of Spanish design. T wishes to tear out the store front and replace it with a new, modern design. L objects. Nothing is said in the lease about any right to make changes or improvements.

    a. Can L prevent T from making the changes? ________

    b. Would the answer be the same if the lease was for 50 years instead of one year? ________

42. L leases a store to T for one year. Nothing is said about insurance, and neither L nor T insures the premises. During the year, the store building is struck by lightning and burns down. Can L recover the value of the destroyed premises from T for failing to obtain insurance? ________

43. If a lease stipulates a monthly rental, but does ***not*** reserve a power of termination for failure to pay rent, can L terminate for nonpayment of rent? ________

44. L leases an office to T for one year, at a rent of $500 per month.

    a. If T fails to pay the rent after the first month, and L therefore evicts T, is T personally liable for the rent for the remainder of the one-year lease? ________

    b. If T ***abandons*** the premises, can L hold him personally liable for the rent for the balance of the term, even though L made no effort whatsoever to relet the premises? ________

    c. If T abandons the premises and L ***resumes possession*** thereof herself, will L be held to have automatically waived any right to hold T liable for the remaining rent under the lease? ________

45. L leases Blackacre to T. L promises to provide heat during the term. During the winter, L fails to provide any heat. Can T remain on Blackacre and withhold rent because this is a "constructive eviction"? ________

46. L leases Blackacre to T for a term of one year. Two months later, T transfers the balance of his term to X for the same rental. T stipulates, however, that if X fails to pay rent he, T, will be entitled to reenter and reclaim the premises. The transfer to X is a sublease because T did not convey his entire interest. True or false? ________

47. L leased a natural gas well on Blackacre to T. T covenanted to pay $1,000 annual rent, and also to furnish L, at her home on Whiteacre, a sufficient amount of gas for L's needs.

    a. T assigns his lease to T-1. T-1 refuses to supply gas to L on Whiteacre. L sues T-1 for breach. Will L win? ________

    b. L sells Blackacre to L-1. T-1 fails to pay rent. L-1 sues T-1. Will L-1 win? ________

    c. If instead of assigning the lease to T-1, T had only subleased to T-1, could T-1 be held liable on the rent covenant? ________

48. L leases Blackacre to T for one year. T promises to keep the premises insured, but T is not obligated to use the proceeds to rebuild. T assigns the lease to T-1. T-1 fails to maintain the insurance, and the premises are destroyed by fire. Even though T-1 is in privity of estate with L, he is not liable to L because the covenant did not run with the land. True or false? ________

49. L leases Blackacre to T in writing for 10 years. Later, T transfers his entire leasehold to T-1.

    a. In the absence of any agreement by T-1 to pay the rent due under the L-T lease, is T-1 personally liable to L for the rent while he is in possession? ________

    b. If T-1 later transfers his entire interest to T-2, and T-2 then defaults in rent, does L have any direct action against T (original tenant) or T-1? ________

50. L leases Blackacre to T in writing for 10 years. The next day, T transfers possession to T-1 for nine years.

    a. In the absence of any agreement by T-1 to pay the rent due under the L-T lease, is T-1 personally liable to L for the rent while he is in possession? ________

    b. If T or T-1 fails to pay the rent, can L evict T-1? ________

51. If a valid covenant against assignment is contained in a lease, is any attempted transfer by T automatically void? ________

52. L, the owner of a large supermarket, gives T a written lease for the butcher shop therein for 10 years, at $1,000 per month. If the property is taken in eminent domain proceedings and the market is torn down, is T entitled to any share of the eminent domain proceeds? ________

53. L leases Blackacre to T for a term of two years. At the inception of the lease, L discloses to T that the stairway to the apartment, though appearing safe, is in dangerous condition. Subsequently, T is injured by the collapse of the stairs. Is L liable to T for failing to repair this latent defect? ________

54. Because of the basic principle that a landlord has no common law duty to make repairs, if L attempts to repair a defective condition, she is not liable for resulting injuries because she was under no duty to do so. True or false? ________

55. L leases Blackacre to T for two years. In the lease, L covenants to maintain Blackacre in good repair during the term. The premises are in a defective condition, and T notifies L to repair them. L fails to do so, and T is injured as a result. Can T recover from L for his injuries? ________

56. L leases Blackacre to T for two years. In the lease, L covenants to keep the premises in good repair. Even though notified by T, L fails to repair and I, an invitee, is injured due to the defective condition. I sues T for his injuries. In this case T is not liable because L promised to repair the premises. True or false? ________

FIXTURES

57. When a mortgage is foreclosed, is the landowner (mortgagor) entitled to remove any chattels that she affixed to the land ***after*** executing the mortgage? ________

58. Are things a tenant installs on premises he rents from another more likely to be held fixtures than things a landowner installs on her own premises? ________

59. Can the seller of an air conditioning system installed in a house obtain an interest in the system (as security for the purchase price) that will prevail even against an existing mortgage on the house? ________

EASEMENTS, PROFITS, COVENANTS, AND SERVITUDES

60. As owner of Blackacre, A conveys to B, the owner of adjoining Whiteacre, the right to use a road on Blackacre to get to the main highway. If B later sells Whiteacre to C, and no mention is made of the easement, does C have the right to use the road? ________

61. A owns Lot 1 and B owns adjoining Lot 2. A grants B the right to use a paved path across Lot 1 to reach Lot 2. A conveys Lot 1 to C. C can prevent B from crossing Lot 1 because the deed to C was silent and therefore the easement was extinguished. True or false? ________

62. The holder of an easement in gross must own or have a possessory interest in the dominant tenement. True or false? ________

63. An easement in gross, being purely personal to the owner of the easement, cannot be transferred by him to another. True or false? ________

64. A conveys to B the back half of A's farm. To enter or leave the property, B has to use a narrow country road, instead of the main highway in front of A's farm. No mention is made of any roadway or access.

    a. Is B entitled to an easement by necessity across the front half of A's farm to the main highway? ________

b. If prior to the sale to B, A had been using a dirt road across the front half of her farm to reach the back half, might B be entitled to an implied easement across A's land? _________

65. A owns a parcel of land that is completely landlocked. She has asked B for permission to drive over B's land to the public highway, but B has refused. Is A entitled to an easement by necessity across B's land? _________

66. The scope of use permitted under an easement may be affected by whether the easement was acquired by express agreement, implication, or prescription. True or false? _________

67. A grants to B an easement of right-of-way across A's land to reach Blackacre, an undeveloped tract owned by B. Subsequently B subdivides Blackacre and sells the lots. A objects to the increased number of cars using the right-of-way on the grounds that the easement was limited to the use made of Blackacre when the easement was created. Will A win in court? _________

68. B owns an easement of right-of-way across Lot 1, owned by A, to reach Lot 2, which B owns. A conveys Lot 1 to B. Shortly thereafter, B conveys Lot 1 to C. Has B lost his easement? _________

69. A conveys to her neighbor, B, a right-of-way over A's land. Which of the following events will cause a termination of B's right-of-way? _________

(A) Excessive and improper use of the right-of-way by B.

(B) B's nonuse of the right-of-way for more than 20 years.

(C) A's placing a fence across the right-of-way.

(D) A's purchasing B's property.

(E) A's selling her property to a bona fide purchaser who had no actual or constructive notice of B's right-of-way.

70. B has an easement of right-of-way across Lot 1, owned by A, to reach Lot 2, owned by B. B tells A he no longer needs the easement. Is the easement terminated? _________

71. A operates a nightclub on Blackacre. She agrees in writing that B shall have the right to install a jukebox in the club in return for 40% of the receipts.

a. Does the agreement create in B an interest in Blackacre? _________

b. Once B installs the jukebox, does he have the right to maintain it on Blackacre as long as A operates the nightclub? _________

72. A and B are neighbors. When B's well runs dry, A conveys to B "the right to take as much water as he needs or wants" from the lake on A's land.

a. B cannot enforce his right to take water from the lake unless the conveyance complies with the Statute of Frauds. True or false? _________

b. B's rights are revocable by A at any time, because no consideration was paid. True or false? _________

c. If B's interest was determined to be a profit in gross, it could not be sold or transferred by him to another. True or false? _________

73. If the benefit of a covenant does not "touch and concern" land, is the ***burden*** enforceable against the heirs and assigns of the covenantor in an action at law? _________

74. A and B own neighboring lands. They sign an agreement in which each agrees to restrict building on his property within 10 feet of their common boundary line, and that this shall bind heirs and assigns. Later, B sells his house to C who proposes to build closer than 10 feet to the boundary line. Can A enforce the covenant against C? _________

75. All homes in Shadyacres residential tract are set back 50 feet from the public highway. Will a purchaser of a lot in the tract be deemed to have notice of a set-back restriction even if it is ***not*** contained in his deed or chain of title? _________

76. Does a person who acquires title by ***adverse possession*** take subject to restrictive covenants concerning the use of the acquired land contained in a recorded instrument executed by the prior owner? _________

77. A owns Blackacre and Whiteacre. She sells Blackacre to B by deed reciting that the land shall be used for residential purposes only. A later leases Whiteacre to C for 50 years. B now proposes to construct a gasoline station on Blackacre. Can C obtain injunctive relief? _________

78. Privity of estate is essential to enforcement of a restriction as an equitable servitude. True or false? _________

79. Will an equitable servitude be enforced so as to prevent land uses permitted by applicable zoning laws? _________

ADVERSE POSSESSION

80. A goes into possession of Blackacre, a farm, under a deed from B, who is not the true owner. A occupies the dwelling located on the northeast corner of Blackacre for the statutory period.

a. Is this sufficient to make A the owner of all of Blackacre? _________

b. Would the result be the same if the true owner occupies the southwest corner of Blackacre? _________

81. A and B own Blackacre as tenants in common. While B is living in Europe, A lives on Blackacre for 20 years (the statutory period), paying taxes, etc. A now has sole title to Blackacre by adverse possession. True or false? ________

82. A adversely possesses Blackacre for 10 years, until she is ousted by B, another adverse possessor. If B remained in possession for 10 years, could he "tack" his possession onto A's? ________

83. A goes into possession of Blackacre, mistakenly thinking it is Whiteacre, which she has just inherited from her aunt. Is A's possession sufficiently hostile for purposes of adverse possession? ________

84. O owns Blackacre. A enters and lives on Blackacre for 10 years, paying taxes, etc. A then leaves for one year, but returns and remains for an additional 10 years. In a state with a 20-year statute of limitations, has A acquired title to Blackacre by adverse possession? ________

85. Possession by one co-tenant of property owned jointly with another is presumed to be hostile and adverse as to the other co-tenant. True or false? ________

86. A goes into adverse possession of O's property. O discovers this and becomes so infuriated that he suffers a stroke and becomes mentally impaired. If this results in O's being adjudicated insane, will the statute of limitations then be tolled? ________

87. Is the statute tolled if O was a minor when adverse possession starts, and before majority, O becomes insane? ________

88. Would a reversioner or remainderman be permitted to file suit to evict an adverse possessor? ________

CONVEYANCING AND RECORDING

89. O contracts to convey Blackacre to A on June 1, closing and transfer of possession to be on August 1. On July 15, the house on Blackacre is destroyed by fire without fault of either party. In the absence of a statute, who bears the loss? ________

90. O executes a written contract to sell Blackacre to A, title to pass on closing of escrow 90 days hence.

    a. Unless expressly provided in the contract, there is no warranty that O has or will deliver marketable title to the property. True or false? ________

    b. A will be entitled to cancel the escrow if the title search discloses a mortgage on the house. True or false? ________

91. O contracts to sell to A her house at 315 Water Street, San Francisco. The deed that O executes conveys "my house in the City and County of San Francisco,"

but, through mistake, omits the address or legal description. Is the deed effective to convey title to the house at 315 Water Street if O owns several other parcels in San Francisco? ________

92. O contracts to sell to A her house at 315 Water Street, San Francisco. The deed conveys "my house at 315 Water Street" (but omits city or county). Is the deed effective to convey title to the house in question? ________

93. O conveys property to A, describing one boundary as running "from Point X south 1,200 feet to the County Road." If it is shown that the County Road is actually 1,250 feet south of Point X, does A get the full 1,250 feet? ________

94. Is physical transfer of a deed essential to a valid delivery? ________

95. O executes an unconditional deed to Blackacre to A. She hands the deed to A's mother, who agrees to give the deed to A. Does this constitute a valid delivery of the deed? ________

96. Does the fact that a deed has been recorded satisfy the delivery requirement? ________

97. O executes and hands a deed of Blackacre to A, telling A that the land will be hers when A stops smoking. A stops smoking. Title to Blackacre remains in O. True or false? ________

98. O hands a deed to Blackacre to the named grantee, A. The deed is unconditional, but O tells A that it will not be effective if O comes back from the Middle East. Later, A sells the property to an innocent purchaser, B, and O returns from the Middle East. O sues to quiet title. Does O win? ________

99. O contracts in writing to sell her house to A, and deposits a deed in escrow.

    a. If A steals the deed from the escrow holder, records it, and then sells the property to a bona fide purchaser ("BFP"), title passes to the BFP. True or false? ________

    b. If before the time set for the closing of escrow, O changes her mind and demands the return of her deed, is she entitled to it? ________

    c. If A performs the contract and the escrow holder duly records O's deed to A, but O had earlier secretly recorded a deed to her mother, M, does this vitiate title in A? ________

    d. If before the time set for the closing of escrow, O dies, does this terminate the escrow holder's authority? ________

100. O executes a deed to her favorite nephew, A. She hands the deed to her attorney, instructing him to deliver the deed to A on O's death. If O later changes her mind and seeks to recover possession of the deed from the attorney, has there been an effective delivery to A? ________

101. Does a warranty deed include a covenant that the property is fit for its intended use? ________

102. A covenant of seisin runs with the grantee's estate and can be enforced by his successors in interest. True or false? ________

103. There is no breach of the covenant for quiet enjoyment unless and until the grantee or his successor has been disturbed in his possession of the premises. True or false? ________

104. A covenant of warranty is continuous in nature, and it is breached ***whenever*** a rightful adverse claim of title arises. True or false? ________

105. None of the "usual covenants for title" are implied in a quitclaim deed. True or false? ________

106. Blackacre is owned by A's father. A conveys Blackacre to B, who records the deed. Later, the father dies and A inherits Blackacre. Is A's deed to B in the chain of title to Blackacre? ________

107. O owns Blackacre. On June 1, O conveys Blackacre to A. On June 2, O conveys Blackacre to B.

    a. In the absence of any recording acts, who owns Blackacre? ________

    b. If the state has a notice-type recording act, does A own Blackacre if she records first? ________

    c. If the state has a race-notice recording act, does A own Blackacre if B does not record first? ________

108. On January 1, O delivers to A a gift deed to Blackacre, which A records on January 10. However, on January 5, O conveyed Blackacre to BFP, who recorded his deed on January 20.

    a. Under a notice statute, BFP prevails over A. True or false? ________

    b. Under a race-notice statute, A prevails. True or false? ________

    c. Under a pure race statute, A prevails. True or false? ________

109. O executes a deed to Blackacre to A, as a gift; A does not record the deed. Later, O executes a deed to Blackacre to B as a gift; B records. In a quiet title suit between A and B, in a jurisdiction with a notice or race-notice recording act, who wins? ________

110. O deeds Blackacre to A as a gift on January 1, but A does not then record the deed. O dies on February 1, and her heirs make a valid sale of the property to BFP, who records immediately. In a quiet title suit between A and BFP, who wins? ________

111. Which of the following factors would by themselves prevent a grantee from attaining the status of a "subsequent bona fide purchaser"? ________

(A) The deed to her was given as security for an antecedent debt.

(B) She paid less than the market value for the property.

(C) The grantor told her of the prior unrecorded deed, but assured her that it was unenforceable because it was not recorded.

(D) The grantor conveyed title to her by a quitclaim deed.

(E) An adverse possessor was in possession of the property at the time of the conveyance (unbeknownst to the grantee).

112. O owns three adjoining parcels. She deeds Parcel #1 to A, the deed containing building restrictions applicable to all three parcels. Is the deed to A in the chain of title of Parcels #2 and #3? ________

SECURITY INTERESTS IN REAL ESTATE

113. A gives O $10,000 in exchange for a deed to O's land, but agrees to return the deed to O upon full payment of the debt. O does not repay A. Does A own the land? ________

114. O borrows $10,000 from a bank, secured by a mortgage on his property. Subsequently, O sells the property to A. If A takes subject to the mortgage, is she liable on the loan? ________

115. O defaults on her mortgage and the lender institutes foreclosure proceedings. If a statute permits, O can redeem the property before the sale. True or false? ________

116. O mortgages her land to M1, M2, and M3 in that order. Subsequently, O defaults on all three mortgages, and M2 institutes foreclosure proceedings. If the land is sold for $20,000 (after expenses and fees) and the outstanding debt on each mortgage is $10,000, which of the following is correct? ________

(A) M1 gets $10,000 and M2 gets $10,000.

(B) M2 gets $10,000 and M3 gets $10,000.

(C) M1 gets $5,000, M2 gets $10,000, and M3 gets $5,000.

SUPPORT AND WATER RIGHTS

117. A builds a swimming pool on her land, close to B's property line. The excavation for the pool causes subsidence on B's parcel. Which, if any, of the following statements is correct? ________

(A) A is absolutely liable for damage to both land and buildings on B's parcel.

(B) A is liable for damage to B's land and buildings only if A was negligent in excavating.

(C) A owes a duty only to support B's land in its natural state and, provided A was not negligent, A is not liable for damages to any building on B's land if the land would not have collapsed in its natural state.

118. A riparian owner's right to take water is limited to uses reasonably necessary for the parcel abutting the watercourse, plus any other parcels owned by him. True or false? ________

119. In most states, a downstream owner can enjoin any interference by an upstream owner with the natural flow of the watercourse. True or false? ________

120. If the elevation of A's lot is the lowest in the neighborhood, and she therefore builds a dike on her lot to divert surface waters onto her neighbors' lots, she is liable for damage to her neighbors' lots caused thereby. True or false? ________

ANSWERS TO REVIEW QUESTIONS

Ques. No.	Answer	Explanation
1.	***TRUE***	Technical words of inheritance are no longer necessary.
2.	***NO***	A's heirs will inherit a possessory estate for the remainder of B's life.
3.	***YES***	Determinable on A's deciding to live elsewhere.
4.	***ALL***	(B) might not be actionable, however, under modern law.
5.	***(B) and (D)***	(A) is incorrect because a life tenant is only obligated to pay ***interest*** on a mortgage debt, not principal; (C) is incorrect because a life tenant is not obligated to insure a remainder interest; (E) is incorrect because replacing the furnace would be a permanent improvement, rather than just a repair.
6.a.	***FALSE***	A has a reversion for life.
b.	***TRUE***	Because A had only a life estate, S's leasehold ends on A's death.
c.	***FALSE***	A's interest is a reversion, which is a vested interest even though the probability of its coming into possession is slight.
7.	***YES***	Like a life estate, a term of years terminates naturally. Thus, an interest following a term of years would be a remainder.
8.	***TRUE***	A remainder ***never*** follows a fee simple estate.
9.a.	***FALSE***	The preferred construction would be a vested remainder subject to total divestment.
b.	***FALSE***	It would be an alternative contingent remainder.
c.	***TRUE***	Under this construction, B's interest would be subject to a condition subsequent and thus terminable by the executory limitation.
d.	***FALSE***	The fact that the interest is defeasible does not prevent it from being vested.
10.	***VESTED***	B has a vested remainder subject to total divestment.
11.	***TRUE***	B's interest is a vested remainder subject to total divestment. C's interest is viewed as arising after B's interest, so it must be an executory interest because it does not follow a life estate.
12.a.	***YES***	As a contingent remainder.

b.	***NO***	A's "children" cannot be ascertained until the death of A; hence, a guardian would have to represent ***all*** children living and unborn.
c.	***NO***	Once born, A's children had vested remainders subject to open, but not conditioned on surviving the life tenant. (The result would be different if the remainder had been to "A's ***surviving*** children.")
13.a.	***FALSE***	B's heirs cannot be ascertained until her death, so they have contingent remainders.
b.	***YES***	If B dies without heirs, Blackacre reverts to O or her estate.
c.	***NO***	O's reversion would take effect until B's death. The result was different at common law under the rule of destructibility of contingent remainders.
14.	***NO (under modern law)***	But the result was different at common law (contingent remainder in A's "first-born" was destroyed by merger of life estate and reversion).
15.	***TRUE***	A's heirs have a contingent remainder. The Rule in Shelley's Case has been abolished in most jurisdictions.
16.a.	***YES***	Under the Doctrine of Worthier Title, O would be deemed to retain a reversion in fee; the contingent remainder in "O's heirs" is void.
b.	***NO***	The Doctrine of Worthier Title is retained today only as a rule of construction; it should not be applied if evidence of O's contrary intent is shown.
c.	***YES***	The Doctrine of Worthier Title is retained today only as to inter vivos conveyances.
17.	***YES***	A has a springing executory interest.
18.	***D***	All future interests are descendible unless a requirement of survival is expressed or implied. No such requirement is implied here.
19.a.	***NO***	The class closed on O's death when a distribution could be made under the rule of convenience. Hence A3 is out.
b.	***DEPENDS***	If a will makes a class gift and a class member predeceases the testator, the surviving class members share the gift ***unless*** the predeceasing class member was within the coverage of an anti-lapse statute and left surviving issue.
c.	***NO***	If there are no class members living at the testator's death, all afterborn persons within the class are included. Thus, the class stays open for A's life.
20.	***FALSE***	To be valid, a contingent remainder must vest within the period of the Rule Against Perpetuities.
21.	***NO***	There is no certainty that Communist rule will end within the period of the Rule.

22. ***NO*** At the time the interest was created, it was possible that the well "might not" run dry within the perpetuities period (even though it did).

23. ***YES*** The measuring lives are A's parents—even though they are not even mentioned! The remainder must vest in the children (A's brothers and sisters), if at all, within 21 years after their parents' deaths.

24. ***YES*** As in question 23.

25. ***YES*** The remainder to O's grandchildren will vest in each grandchild at birth, and each grandchild will be born in his parent's lifetime (or will be in gestation at that time). All of O's children are lives in being at O's death (when the will is operative).

26. ***NO*** Because B presently has an indefeasibly ***vested*** remainder (assuming that B is alive when the conveyance is made).

27.a. ***NO*** Again, B's interest is vested (a remainder in fee subject to total divestment).

b. ***NO*** O has a reversionary interest (and such interests are not subject to the Rule).

28.a. ***NO*** A future interest that follows a defeasible fee violates the Rule. Here, B has the executory interest that follows a fee simple subject to an executory interest (defeasible fee). The contingency (selling liquor) might occur beyond the perpetuities period.

b. ***YES*** O's interest following the conveyance was a possibility of reverter—a vested interest, not subject to the Rule. And because it is alienable under modern law, it could be transferred to B.

29. ***PROBABLY*** Partial restraints on fee simple estates are likely to be upheld as long as they are for a limited time and for a reasonable purpose.

30. ***FALSE*** Forfeiture restraints may be upheld in proper cases—*e.g.,* restraints that limit permissible transferees.

31. ***TRUE*** Unless imposed by disabling rather than promissory or forfeiture devices.

32. ***NO*** This transfer lacks the unities of ***time*** and ***title***. (O would have to convey to a "strawman," who would then convey back to O and A as joint tenants.)

33. ***TRUE*** Modern law disfavors joint tenancies. Joint tenancies arise only when the intention to create a right of survivorship is clear.

34. ***POSSIBLY*** Although many states require more specific language to overcome the presumption of a tenancy in common (*e.g.,* "as joint tenants with right of survivorship" or "as joint tenants and not as tenants in common"), some states

hold that use of the technical term "joint tenants" is sufficient. Remember, no express mention of survivorship is necessary, as long as the intention is clear.

35.a.	***YES (title theory states) NO (lien theory states)***	In a title theory state, the execution of a mortgage passes title interest, thereby severing the joint tenancy. A mortgage in a lien theory state does not pass title interest.
b.	***SPLIT***	A lease conceptually disturbs unities of interest and possession, but some courts hold the opposite.
c.	***NO***	Testamentary conveyance of a joint tenancy interest is ineffective.
d.	***YES***	Even a secret conveyance of title works a severance.
36.a.	***NO as to both questions***	Assuming A has done nothing to exclude B and C from farming the land, A owes them nothing. A has the right to possess and enjoy the whole property.
b.	***YES***	Co-tenants out of possession have the right to share in rent from third parties.
c.	***NO***	There is no right of contribution for the cost of improvements, but the costs would be recovered by A on partition.
37.	***YES***	An estate for years is any estate measured by time, no matter how long or short the period may be.
38.	***TRUE***	A periodic estate continues from period to period until terminated by appropriate notice.
39.	***FALSE***	Because the duration of the tenancy is not fixed and the rent is expressed in an annual amount, a year-to-year ***periodic*** tenancy is created.
40.	***NO***	L has the ***option*** of treating him as such or evicting him. (Note that if this is a ***residential*** tenancy and the landlord elects to bind the tenant for another period, most courts would rule the tenant a month-to-month tenant irrespective of the term of the original lease. Thus, in this case, if it is a residential tenancy, L can elect to bind T to a new month-to-month—rather than a year-to-year—tenancy.)
41.a.	***YES***	Short-term tenants cannot commit even ameliorative waste.
b.	***YES***	While the modern view permits long-term tenants to make ameliorative changes, generally the change must increase the value of the property and reflect a change in the nature and character of the neighborhood. Here, there is no mention of neighborhood change or that the change will increase the value of the property.

42. ***NO*** Unless the tenant has expressly covenanted to the contrary, the tenant has no duty to replace buildings destroyed other than by his negligence. (Note, however, that T may remain liable for the rent.)

43. ***NO*** Absent a statute or a clause in the lease, a breach, such as nonpayment of rent, results in a cause of action for money damages—not a right to terminate.

44.a. ***NO*** Absent an agreement or statute, eviction terminates the landlord-tenant relationship and excuses the tenant from further performance under the lease.

b. ***YES*** T remains liable, but because the landlord made no efforts to mitigate, L's recovery against T will be reduced accordingly. Note that under the traditional view, which is followed by a minority of states, the landlord has no duty to attempt to relet and the tenant remains liable for rent for the balance of the lease term.

c. ***YES*** This usually is considered an acceptance of a surrender, and T will be relieved of further liability.

45. ***NO*** Constructive eviction is a defense to nonpayment only if T abandons the premises within a reasonable time after the "substantial interference."

46. ***FALSE*** The test for determining whether the transfer is an assignment or a sublease is whether T has transferred the entire remaining estate. Even though a right of reentry is permitted, the entire estate was transferred; therefore, this is an assignment.

47.a. ***YES*** The covenant touches and concerns Blackacre.

b. ***YES*** The rent covenant touches and concerns Blackacre, and privity of estate between the original parties to the lease extends to their assignees.

c. ***NO*** There is no privity of estate and, absent an assumption agreement, no privity of contract.

48. ***TRUE*** T-1, although in privity of estate with L, is liable only for covenants that run with the land. A covenant to insure without obligation to rebuild does not sufficiently touch and concern the land.

49.a. ***YES*** L and T-1 are in privity of estate.

b. ***YES as to T; NO as to T-1*** L and T are in privity of contract. Privity of estate ends when T-1 assigns.

50.a. ***NO*** This is only a sublease; hence, there is no privity of estate or privity of contract between T-1 and L.

b.	***YES***	T remains in privity of estate and privity of contract with L, and T-1 can be evicted when T is evicted.
51.	***NO***	The assignment is ***voidable***, and T may be liable for damages for breach of the covenant, but the assignment is not automatically void.
52.	***YES***	Permanent condemnation of the entire property extinguishes the lease. Absent a contrary agreement, the lessee is therefore entitled to compensation for the value of the leasehold.
53.	***NO***	The latent defect exception to the general rule of no landlord responsibility to maintain the premises in good repair is merely a duty to disclose the defect, not to repair it.
54.	***FALSE***	An exception to the "no duty" principle is where the landlord undertakes repairs. Even though she had no duty to act, once she does so, she must act in a reasonable manner and is liable for negligent repairs.
55.	***YES***	Most states now hold that a landlord who covenants to repair and fails to do so is liable for consequential damages.
56.	***FALSE***	The tenant, as occupier, has primary liability to third-party invitees. He is always under a duty to maintain the premises in good repair regardless of what L has promised. However, L may also be liable.
57.	***NO***	Authorities urge this, but the rule is to the contrary.
58.	***NO***	It is less likely that the tenant intended permanent annexation.
59.	***YES***	If proper Uniform Commercial Code "fixture filing" procedures are complied with.
60.	***YES***	Even if not mentioned, easements appurtenant pass with grants of the dominant estate.
61.	***FALSE***	C is not a bona fide purchaser because the easement is plainly visible. Thus, the burden of the easement passes automatically with a transfer of Lot 1 to C.
62.	***FALSE***	An easement in gross is a right of special use in the servient tenement independent of the holder's ownership or possession of another tract of land. There is no dominant tenement.
63.	***FALSE***	An easement in gross, if the use is commercial or impersonal, is transferable unless the parties express a contrary intention.
64.a.	***NO***	The use is not absolutely necessary for the enjoyment of the parcel conveyed.
b.	***YES***	The prior use was apparent and continuous, so B would be entitled to the implied easement if a substitute could not be obtained without unreasonable expense.

65. ***NO*** A is not entitled to an easement unless A's and B's parcels were formerly one and the division caused A's parcel to be landlocked.

66. ***TRUE*** If express, the language determines the scope; if implied, the extent of the necessity or quasi-easement determines the scope; if prescriptive, the character of the use during the period determines the scope.

67. ***DEPENDS*** The law presumes a normal development of the dominant estate. If the dominant estate is subdivided, the easement appurtenant attaches to each separate parcel unless this extension would overburden the servient estate.

68. ***YES*** One of the means of terminating an easement is by merger (unity of ownership of easement and servient estate). When the servient estate is reconveyed, the easement is not automatically revived.

69. ***(D) and (E)*** Neither surcharge (A) nor nonuse (B) will terminate an easement. (C) does not terminate unless continued for the statutory period. However, merger (D) will terminate it, as will a sale to a bona fide purchaser (E).

70. ***NO*** A termination by release requires an instrument in writing. Termination by abandonment requires some action preventing further use of the easement. Mere nonuse or oral expression of intent does not work a termination.

71.a. ***NO*** The writing appears to create no more than a license, which is a revocable privilege.

b. ***NO*** A license may be revoked at any time by a manifestation of the licensor's intent to end it. B may, however, have an action for contract damages.

72.a. ***TRUE*** A profit is an interest in land and therefore must comply with the Statute of Frauds.

b. ***FALSE*** Consideration is unnecessary to support the conveyance of an interest in land. Profits are terminated in the same way as easements.

c. ***FALSE*** Profits in gross can be freely transferred.

73. ***YES by the original promisee; NO by successors of promisee*** The benefit must touch and concern the land in order to run with the land. Thus, if the benefit does not touch and concern the land, it cannot be enforced by the promisee's successors in interest. But a covenant need not run with the land to be enforceable by the covenanting party. Therefore, regardless of whether the benefit runs with the land, the original promisee may enforce the covenant against the promisor's successors, provided the burden runs with the land.

74. ***MAYBE*** Not as a covenant running with the land (no horizontal privity between A and B), but it may be enforceable as an ***equitable servitude*** if C had notice.

75.	***YES***	Absent recordation, many courts charge the taker with notice if a common restriction is apparent from inspection of the neighborhood.
76.	***YES***	Under the servitude theory, notice (not privity) is the crucial element, and the recordation constitutes constructive notice.
77.	***YES***	Privity is not necessary to support an ***equitable servitude*** (C is suing for an injunction). Even if C were suing on the covenant at law, most courts would find adequate privity between A and B through the recital in the grant deed, and between A and C as lessor-lessee.
78.	***FALSE***	Privity is not required to enforce the restriction.
79.	***YES***	However, inconsistent zoning may indicate changed circumstances so that the covenant may be discharged.
80.a.	***YES***	A owns all of Blackacre according to the doctrine of constructive possession under color of title.
b.	***NO***	In this case, A would be the owner only of the portion she ***actually*** occupied.
81.	***FALSE***	To acquire sole title by adverse possession against a co-tenant, there must be an ouster. Otherwise, A is only doing that which she has a right to do.
82.	***NO***	To tack separate periods of adverse possession, the parties must be in privity, which means the subsequent possessor must take from the former by descent, devise, or deed. There is no privity when, as here, one adverse claimant ousts another.
83.	***YES***	A's acts must objectively indicate her intent to claim title hostile (adverse) to the true owner.
84.	***NO***	To acquire title by adverse possession, the hostile possession must be uninterrupted. Here, upon A's reentry, the statute of limitations begins to run all over again.
85.	***FALSE***	Possession is adverse only if there is an explicit ouster or exclusion.
86.	***NO***	Disabilities arising ***after*** the adverse possession commenced do not toll the statute.
87.	***NO***	Only the original disability counts. There is no tacking of disabilities.
88.	***NO***	The statute of limitations does not begin to run against a future interest holder until her interest becomes possessory.
89.	***A***	Under the doctrine of equitable conversion, the interests of the parties are converted from the time the ***contract*** is signed, not the deed. In most states, absent a statute to the contrary, A (the buyer) bears the risk of loss.

90.a.	***FALSE***	All contracts for the sale of land include an implied warranty that the seller will deliver marketable title at closing.
b.	***FALSE***	Title need be marketable only at the ***close*** of escrow. It is permissible to use the proceeds of the sale to pay off and eliminate title defects, such as mortgages.
91.	***NO***	The deed and contract must identify the land precisely enough for anyone to locate it.
92.	***YES***	If necessary, parol evidence will be received to clarify the patent ambiguity.
93.	***YES***	Description by monuments generally prevails over distances.
94.	***NO***	The grantor need only intend that the deed have some present operative effect.
95.	***YES***	Most courts hold that a deed delivered to a third party with no conditions constitutes a valid delivery.
96.	***YES***	If the grantor intends the recording to be the final act vesting title, the recording satisfies the delivery requirement.
97.	***FALSE***	The deed, absolute on its face and delivered, would be effective under the traditional view (condition drops out) and also under the growing minority view (condition is enforced) because A has stopped smoking.
98.	***NO***	The traditional and majority view is that oral conditions drop out, and delivery becomes absolute.
99.a.	***FALSE (absent estoppel)***	Delivery in escrow is conditional; until the conditions occur, no title passes under the deed.
b.	***NO***	There is an enforceable written contract to convey.
c.	***NO***	The relation back doctrine would apply here, and A's title prevails as against a donee.
d.	***NO***	The relation back doctrine applies.
100.	***YES (most courts)***	Some states require an enforceable contract for the deed to be irrevocable, but most treat the delivery as creating a future interest in A.
101.	***NO***	A warranty deed warrants good title and includes covenants of seisin, right to convey, freedom from encumbrances, and quiet enjoyment.
102.	***FALSE***	It is a present covenant and is breached at the time of conveyance, if at all.

103.	***TRUE***	The disturbance can be actual or constructive eviction, and a justified ***threat*** of eviction will also suffice.
104.	***TRUE***	It can be breached a number of times.
105.	***TRUE***	Warranting the grantor's title is inconsistent with this type of deed.
106.	***NO (most courts)***	Between A and B, B wins because of estoppel by deed. But most courts protect future BFPs against B.
107.a.	***A***	At common law, in the absence of any recording statute, the rule of priority is "first in time is first in right."
b.	***DEPENDS***	A notice statute protects B if he buys without notice, regardless of who records first. Therefore, unless A's deed was recorded (thus giving notice) before the conveyance to B, B would prevail provided he had no other notice.
c.	***YES***	In a race-notice jurisdiction, in order for B to be protected by the statute, he must buy without notice ***and*** he must also record first.
108.a.	***TRUE***	BFP had no notice at the time of his conveyance from O.
b.	***TRUE***	BFP must be without notice when he takes ***and*** must record first. (*Note:* A's status as donee is irrelevant.)
c.	***TRUE***	Notice is irrelevant; whoever records first wins.
109.	***A***	Recording acts protect only bona fide purchasers, not donees.
110.	***BFP***	But between A and the heirs, A would win because the heirs stand in O's shoes. (*Note:* The type of recording act is immaterial.)
111.	***(A), (C), and (E)***	While antecedent debt is generally considered to be valuable consideration, a person is not a BFP if the property was conveyed merely as ***security*** for such a debt, rather than in satisfaction of it. Paying less than fair market value (B) does not prevent BFP status. Nor does acquisition of title by a quitclaim deed (D). However, a purchaser is disqualified by actual knowledge (C), or inquiry notice from possession (E).
112.	***SPLIT***	The better view is that the purchasers of Parcels #2 and #3 are not obliged to search the title of Parcel #1, and if they have no notice of the restrictive covenants, they take free of the restrictions. But some courts charge a purchaser with reading ***all*** deeds from a common grantor.
113.	***PROBABLY NOT***	A court will likely treat this as an equitable mortgage and require A to foreclose it like any other mortgage.
114.	***NO***	A nonassuming grantee does not become personally liable on the loan.

115. ***FALSE*** Equitable redemption allows the mortgagor to redeem the property at any time prior to the foreclosure sale, even in the absence of a statute. ***Statutory*** redemption allows the mortgagor to redeem the property some time ***after*** the foreclosure sale.

116. ***(B)*** After expenses and fees, the proceeds of a foreclosure sale are used first to pay the loan that was foreclosed and then to pay off any junior liens in order of their priority. Senior interests are not affected by foreclosure; the buyer at the sale takes subject to them.

117. ***(C)*** A is absolutely liable only for withdrawal of support of the land in its natural state. Hence, A may avoid liability altogether by showing that her excavation was not negligent, and that the land would not have subsided ***but for*** the weight of the buildings thereon.

118. ***FALSE*** Riparian rights attach only to the parcel abutting the watercourse and parcels contiguous thereto.

119. ***FALSE*** Under the more common "reasonable use" theory, a downstream owner cannot enjoin an upstream owner's use unless he is ***substantially*** interfering with her needs.

120. ***SPLIT*** False under the "common enemy theory." But true in states following the "natural flow theory."

ESSAY EXAM QUESTIONS

INTRODUCTORY NOTE

The essay questions that follow have been selected to provide you with an opportunity to experience how the substantive law you have been reviewing may be tested in the hypothetical essay examination question context. These sample essay questions are a valuable self-diagnostic tool designed to enable you to enhance your issue-spotting ability and practice your exam writing skills.

It is suggested that you approach each question as though under actual examination conditions. The time allowed for each question is 60 minutes. You should spend 15 to 20 minutes spotting issues, underlining key facts and phrases, jotting notes in the margins, and outlining your answer. ***If*** you organize your thoughts well, 40 minutes will be more than adequate for writing them down. Should you prefer to forgo the actual writing involved on these questions, be sure to give yourself no more time for issue-spotting than you would on the actual examination.

The BARBRI technique for writing a well-organized essay answer is to (i) spot the issues in a question and then (ii) analyze and discuss each issue using the "CIRAC" method:

C — State your ***conclusion*** first. (In other words, you must think through your answer ***before*** you start writing.)
I — State the ***issue*** involved.
R — Give the ***rule(s)*** of law involved.
A — ***Apply*** the rule(s) of law to the facts.
C — Finally, restate your ***conclusion***.

After completing (or outlining) your own analysis of each question, compare it with the BARBRI model answer provided herein. A passing answer does ***not*** have to match the model one, but it should cover most of the issues presented and the law discussed and should ***apply the law to the facts*** of the question. Use of the CIRAC method results in the best answer you can write.

EXAM QUESTION NO. 1

Sixteen years ago, Olivia, owner of Blackacre, an 80-acre parcel, executed and delivered a deed transferring two acres of Blackacre to X County. The relevant language of this deed stated:

> Olivia hereby grants two acres of Blackacre [adequately described] to X County to be used as the site of a highway weighing station. This deed is on the condition that if said use does not commence within six months from this date, or, having commenced, ceases, the conveyance is to be null and void.

Five years ago, Olivia executed a deed to Blackacre and delivered it to David. This deed described Blackacre as it had been described in the deed by which Olivia had acquired Blackacre. It made no mention of the deed to X County. The following year, Olivia died intestate survived by Henry, her sole heir.

The two-acre parcel conveyed to X County was improved as a highway weighing station site within 60 days from the date of the Olivia-X County deed. It was continually used as such until last year, when X County removed the weighing equipment and sold its interest in the land to Paul. David learned of the county's action before Paul took possession. David removed the fences that had separated the two-acre parcel from David's land and fenced around the outside boundaries of Blackacre, including the two-acre parcel with his land.

Who is entitled to the two-acre parcel and why?

EXAM QUESTION NO. 2

Landlord rented an apartment in his building to Tenant for one year beginning June 1. On June 1, Tenant was unable to move in because the apartment was still occupied by Betty, whose lease had expired on May 31. Betty eventually moved out on June 30, and Tenant moved in on July 1.

During July, a hailstorm caused two broken windowpanes in Tenant's apartment. Tenant demanded that Landlord replace the windowpanes. Landlord replied that Tenant had to do it. Rain coming in through the broken panes caused considerable damage to the wallpaper and floors.

The apartment directly above Tenant's was occupied by Charlie, a member of the famous rock group, "The Charles River." The daily rehearsals of his group interfered with Tenant's law studies and sleep so much that she complained repeatedly to Landlord. On July 15, three of Charlie's friends were arrested in his apartment and charged with possession of narcotics. On August 31, Tenant moved out without ever having paid any rent to Landlord.

What are Landlord's rights, if any, against Tenant? His liabilities? Discuss.

EXAM QUESTION NO. 3

Adams owned Lot 1 on Azure Lake and lived in a house located on the west half. Baker owned Lot 2 behind Adams's lot, and his one-story house overlooked the east half of Lot 1.

Adams and Baker entered into a written agreement under which Baker paid Adams $2,000, and Adams covenanted not to build a house or other structure on the east half of Lot 1. The agreement recited that "Baker has derived much pleasure from the view over Adams's land" and that the parties "intend to assure an unobstructed view from Baker's house." The agreement was never recorded.

Five years later, fire swept through Lot 2 and burned down Baker's house.

Two years after the fire, Adams sold her house and lot to Down. Before committing himself to the purchase, Down had a conversation with Baker in which Baker told Down that Adams's lot is subject to a building restriction on the east side. Down asked Adams about the restriction, and Adams said, "Don't worry about it. It won't be binding on you."

Four years later, Baker sold his lot to Park, telling her of the restriction on Lot 1 and handing her the original agreement signed by Adams and Baker.

While Park was out of the state, Down started building a two-story residence on the east half of his lot. Upon her return, Park consulted you.

Advise Park as to her rights and remedies.

EXAM QUESTION NO. 4

Ollie owned Goldacre, an oil-rich ranch in the state of Lotus. Five years ago in January, Ollie summoned his foreman, Art, handed Art a deed transferring Goldacre to Art, and said, "I want you to have Goldacre if I die before you."

In July that same year, Ollie's accountant, Christy, reported that Art had been embezzling. Ollie immediately discharged Art and, while Christy looked on, called in his bookkeeper, Bill, showed Bill a deed to Goldacre and said: "I am now giving Goldacre to you. You have the combination to my safe. When I die, get this deed out of my safe and record it."

A month later, Ollie discharged Bill for incompetence. Before leaving, Bill removed his deed to Goldacre from the safe and took it with him.

The following January, Ollie told Christy he had revoked his deeds to Art and Bill and that he wanted to retire. On January 15, Ollie conveyed Goldacre to Christy for a valuable consideration. Christy recorded the deed immediately.

Ollie died on February 22 of this year. Art recorded his deed on February 23. Bill recorded his deed on February 24. At Ollie's funeral, on February 25, Bill and Art informed Christy of their respective recordations.

Christy mortgaged Goldacre on May 4 to Elk Mortgage Co., which recorded the same day. Lotus has a recording act of the race-notice type.

Elk Mortgage Co. has brought an action in declaratory relief to determine the rights of Art, Bill, Christy, and Elk Mortgage Co. in the property. What are their rights? Discuss.

EXAM QUESTION NO. 5

Buyer and Seller entered into a written contract by which Seller agreed to sell, and Buyer agreed to buy, a parcel of land improved with a dwelling for a stipulated price, 10% of which was paid on signing the agreement. The agreement stipulated that Seller would convey by quitclaim deed. Buyer intended to raze the house and build a public garage on the land, but this may not have been known to Seller and was not mentioned in the written contract.

In the process of examining title, Buyer learned that the area was restricted to residential uses both by a municipal zoning ordinance and by covenants in the chain of title. Buyer also learned that, until three weeks before the signing of the agreement, the land had been in possession of Possessor, who had held possession for at least five years and had made some improvements. Possessor had originally taken possession under a contract with Seller to purchase the land for a price to be paid in monthly installments over a period of 10 years. Title was to be conveyed when the final payment was made. The contract with Possessor was not recorded, but Seller has offered to certify a copy of the contract, which provided that Seller was entitled to take possession after any default in any installment of the purchase price continuing for more than 60 days, to terminate the rights of Possessor, and to retain all payments received in compensation for the use and occupancy of the land. Seller has also shown Buyer a letter that he received two days previously from Possessor in which Possessor admitted that he was in arrears on his payments for six months and that he would not make any further payments for another six months.

Would Buyer be entitled to terminate her contract with Seller, secure the return of the earnest money, and recover the reasonable value of her title examination? Discuss.

ANSWERS TO ESSAY EXAM QUESTIONS

ANSWER TO EXAM QUESTION NO. 1

David, Henry, and Paul each have plausible claims, which will be explored separately. At issue is whether Olivia retained an interest in the two-acre parcel and, if so, whether she effectively conveyed that interest to David.

David's Claim: Olivia conveyed to X County either a fee simple determinable or a fee simple subject to a condition subsequent. The conveyance is ambiguous because it uses both the phrase "on the condition that" (indicating a condition subsequent) and the phrase "conveyance is to be null and void" (indicating the automatic termination characteristic of a fee simple determinable). In cases of ambiguity, courts will usually hold the interest to be a fee simple subject to a condition subsequent because it does not involve an automatic forfeiture and also permits greater judicial control of the result. However, a court might not do so here because no right of entry was expressly reserved to the grantor by the terms of the grant. Generally, a right of entry must be raised expressly. There is a strong constructional preference against finding a fee simple subject to a condition subsequent and a right of entry if the right of entry is not explicitly provided for.

The conditions in the conveyance were (i) that the site be used for a weighing station within six months of the conveyance (which was fulfilled), and (ii) that the land continue to be so used (which was not fulfilled). The interest retained by Olivia was either a right of entry (if the conveyance is construed to create a fee simple subject to a condition subsequent) or a possibility of reverter (if it is construed as a fee simple determinable). In either case, Olivia's retained interest was not subject to the Rule Against Perpetuities because future interests retained by the grantor are considered to be vested and thus exempt from the Rule.

When Olivia later conveyed Blackacre to David, she evidently intended to convey her reversionary interest in the two-acre parcel to David. Under the majority rules in force today, the possibility of reverter is transferable inter vivos, but the right of entry is not. Thus, David received Olivia's future interest only if (i) Olivia's transfer to X County is held to be a fee simple determinable, or (ii) in the event the court holds it to be a fee simple subject to a condition subsequent, the jurisdiction follows the modern, but still minority, rule that rights of entry are transferable inter vivos.

If David's interest is characterized as a possibility of reverter, title reverted immediately to David when X County violated the condition of continued use. Alternatively, if David took a right of entry (as he could in only a minority of jurisdictions), he properly exercised that right by removing the fences around the two-acre parcel.

David has no "recording act" argument because the county's possession of the two acres was sufficiently obvious to put him on notice of its interest. And David has no claim to the two acres through adverse possession, even though he held color of title to the parcel for more than five years, because he did not actually occupy any part of the two acres.

Henry's Claim: Henry has two arguments. First, he would claim that David's deed did not include Olivia's reversionary interest in the two-acre parcel and that the interest descended to Henry as Olivia's sole heir when Olivia died intestate. Henry would argue that Olivia did not show an intent to convey the reversionary interest merely by repeating the old description, and that David did not expect to receive an interest in view of the obvious presence of the weighing station at the time of the conveyance.

Henry's best argument, however, is that Olivia's conveyance to X County created a fee simple subject to a condition subsequent (because of the "on condition that" language) and that, under the

majority rule, the right of entry retained by Olivia could not be transferred inter vivos to David. As a result, the interest still arguably belonged to Olivia at her death and then passed by descent to Henry.

Paul's Claim: Paul also has two possible arguments. His first would be that Olivia's conveyance to X County created neither a fee simple determinable nor a fee simple subject to a condition subsequent, but rather a fee simple absolute with an affirmative covenant to use the two acres for a weighing station. As a consequence, he would argue that X County's transfer to Paul would not result in forfeiture of the land, but only in an action for damages against Paul for breach of covenant. While courts will, in cases of substantial ambiguity, find a covenant rather than a forfeitable interest, Paul will probably lose on this argument because the "condition" and "null and void" language indicates that forfeiture was clearly intended.

Alternatively, Paul would argue that Olivia's conveyance created a fee simple subject to condition subsequent, but failed to reserve a right of entry, resulting in a fee simple absolute in X County and, consequently, a valid fee simple absolute in Paul. If, however, the court chooses to imply a right of entry, Paul could then argue that the court should apply the common law rule, now in force in a small number of states, that any attempt to transfer a right of entry inter vivos destroys the interest. As a result, X County's interest would be enlarged to a fee simple absolute because of the removal of the condition subsequent, and Paul would now be the owner of a fee simple absolute.

Conclusions

David is entitled to the parcel if rights of entry and/or possibilities of reverter are transferable ***inter vivos*** in the jurisdiction.

Henry wins if Olivia's deed to David is construed not to transfer the reversionary interest (which is a doubtful interpretation), or if the retained interest was a right of entry which, although descendible, is not transferable inter vivos in a majority of states.

Paul wins if the condition in Olivia's conveyance to X County is held to be a covenant (unlikely) or if the retained interest was a right of entry and the common law rule barring transfer destroyed it (not likely), thereby enlarging X County's fee.

ANSWER TO EXAM QUESTION NO. 2

Landlord's rights and liabilities with respect to Tenant can be analyzed in terms of three relevant periods:

June 1 (When Tenant's Term Began) to July 1 (When Tenant's Occupancy Began)

Landlord has no right to receive rent from Tenant for this month. At issue is whether a tenant's duty to pay rent is suspended by the landlord's failure to deliver actual possession of the premises to the tenant at the beginning of the leasehold term. Under the majority rule, Landlord must deliver actual possession of the premises to Tenant. Because Landlord failed to remove the hold-over tenant to make room for Tenant, Landlord is subject to liability for any damages Tenant may have suffered. Tenant may have waived her right to damages by failing to request reimbursement for any expenses incurred during the month; but, because she did not pay rent to Landlord for June, she has not waived her defense to Landlord's action for rent for this month.

July 1 (When Tenant Went into Possession) to August 31 (When Tenant Moved Out)

Hailstorm: Landlord's rights and liabilities as to the broken windowpane and subsequent damages will be governed by the lease and/or statute. At issue is who has the duty to make ordinary repairs

to the leased premises. If common law governs, Tenant's failure to repair the windows constitutes permissive waste, making her liable to Landlord for the value of the windows and any consequential damages. If, however, Tenant's duty has been shifted to Landlord by the lease or by a "repair and deduct" statute, Landlord will be liable to Tenant for the damages flowing from the broken windowpanes. Tenant has met the requirement of giving Landlord timely notice of damage. Unless the lease provides otherwise, Landlord's only liability to Tenant will be for damages, and Tenant will not be excused from paying rent because the covenant to repair is independent of the covenant to pay rent.

Tenant will fail in an argument that the broken window constitutes constructive eviction, because Landlord was not responsible for the damage. Tenant will also fail in an argument that the covenant of habitability has been breached, because the broken window did not represent a substantial threat to her health or safety.

Rehearsals: Landlord will not be liable to Tenant for Charlie's rehearsals, and Tenant will have no defense to an action for rent during this period. At issue is whether a landlord breaches the implied covenant of quiet enjoyment or warranty of habitability by permitting another tenant to conduct daily rehearsals in his apartment.

(1) **Constructive Eviction:** If the landlord does an act or fails to provide some service that he has a legal duty to provide, and thereby makes the premises uninhabitable, the tenant may terminate the lease and seek damages if she vacates within a reasonable time. While the rehearsals probably constituted a substantial interference with Tenant's use and enjoyment of her apartment, they were not caused by Landlord. Although a small handful of courts have taken the position that, by ***permitting*** one tenant to interfere with another's enjoyment, the landlord is himself responsible for that interference, this is not the majority rule. And, even if the requirement of landlord conduct were met, Tenant did not vacate the premises quickly enough to take advantage of the constructive eviction defense.

(2) **Warranty of Habitability:** If the premises become unsuitable for human residence, the tenant may: (i) move out and terminate the lease, (ii) make repairs and offset the cost against future rent, (iii) abate rent, or (iv) seek damages. The rehearsals probably did not represent a sufficient threat to Tenant's health for a breach of this warranty to be found. If, however, a court finds that loss of sleep constitutes a sufficient injury to health, Tenant may collect damages from Landlord, or possibly have a defense to an action for nonpayment of rent.

Narcotics Arrests: Landlord will not be liable to Tenant for Charlie's friends' possession of narcotics on the premises. At issue is whether a landlord has a duty to prevent unlawful conduct on the premises. As with the rehearsals, Tenant will encounter difficulties in pursuing constructive eviction and warranty of habitability claims. She might, in arguing constructive eviction, claim that the unlawful conduct in Charlie's apartment gave Landlord the right to terminate Charlie's lease and thus causally connected Landlord to the narcotics arrests. The two problems with this argument are that a landlord cannot terminate a lease when the unlawful conduct is only occasional, as it was here, and the conduct was not that of his tenant, Charlie, but rather of Charlie's friends.

August 31 (When Tenant Moved Out) to May 31 (When Tenant's Lease Expires)

Landlord has a right to recover rent from Tenant. At issue are a landlord's rights and liabilities when a tenant abandons the premises. Because no defenses are available to Tenant, Landlord can recover rent for two months, July 1 to August 31. For the remainder of the lease term, Landlord can:

(1) Relet the premises on Tenant's account, holding Tenant liable for any difference between the rental payment under her lease and the rental paid by the new tenant; or

(2) If the jurisdiction follows the traditional rule, let the premises remain vacant, recovering rent from Tenant as it becomes due.

ANSWER TO EXAM QUESTION NO. 3

Park will probably be held to have the right to an unimpaired view over the east half of Lot 1. At issue is whether the benefit of the agreement runs to Park as successor to the original promisee, and whether the burden runs against Down as a successor to the promisor. The requirements for benefit and burden to run will be met for purposes of enforcing the agreement as an equitable servitude or a negative easement, but not as a negative covenant.

Intent that Lot 2 Enjoy the Benefit of an Unimpaired View: The Adams-Baker agreement raises a threshold issue of who is to enjoy the benefit of the view. The recital's statement that "Baker has derived much pleasure from the view" might suggest that the benefit was to be held by Baker personally, in which case Park would not succeed to it and would be unable to enforce it. Similarly, the recital's statement that the parties intended "to assure an unobstructed view from Baker's house" might suggest an intent that the benefit attach to the house rather than to the land, with the consequence that, because the house has been destroyed, the benefit cannot be enforced by Park.

However, the general constructional preference is for ***appurtenant*** benefits, rather than benefits in gross. Because either of the above two interpretations would create a benefit in gross, they will give way to the third possible interpretation, under which the benefit would be appurtenant: that Adams and Baker intended that the benefit attach neither to Baker nor to his house, but to Lot 2. Under this interpretation, the successor in interest to Lot 2 (Park) is in a position to enforce the benefit.

The Adams-Baker Agreement Is Enforceable as an Equitable Servitude: In order for the benefit and burden of an equitable servitude to run, the covenant must ***touch and concern*** the land. This requirement is met because the agreement increases the value and enjoyment of Lot 2. The one other requirement for the benefit to run—that Adams and Baker ***intended*** that Baker's successor enjoy the benefit in connection with Lot 2—is met on the basis of the assumption made above, that the parties intended that the benefit attach to Lot 2.

The two other requirements for the burden to run have also been met. ***Intent*** is met—even though the traditional formula, "heirs, successors, and assigns," is missing—because successors to Adams would have to be bound if the purpose of the agreement, assuring an "unobstructed view," is to be met. Further, Baker's subsequent statement to Down about the building restriction provides some evidence of an original intent to bind Adams's successors. The ***notice*** requirement is met by Baker's statement to Down, putting Down at least on inquiry notice, and possibly on actual notice, of the existence of the restriction.

Three possible ***equitable defenses*** may be asserted by Down—abandonment, acquiescence, and estoppel—all premised on Park's absence from the state at the time Down started building the two-story residence. However, because Park was unaware of Down's investment of labor, none of these defenses is likely to be upheld.

The Adams-Baker Agreement Is Not Enforceable as a Negative Covenant: All requirements are met for the benefit of a negative covenant to run: ***intent*** (as in the equitable servitude); ***vertical privity*** (because Park holds the complete interest in land held by Baker at the time the covenant was made); and ***touch and concern*** (because the covenant increases the value and enjoyment of Lot 2). However, the ***burden*** of the covenant ***does not run*** against Down. Although ***intent***, ***notice*** (as in the equitable servitude), ***vertical privity***, and ***touch and concern*** are all met, the ***horizontal privity*** requirement is not met. At the time Adams and Baker entered into the agreement, no independent interest in the land passed between them—*e.g.*, there was no grantor-grantee or landlord-tenant relationship.

Alternatively, this Agreement Might Be Enforceable as a Negative Easement: Under the analysis already pursued, the easement would be appurtenant and, because the ***intent*** and ***notice*** requirements are met, Park would be entitled to enforce the easement against Down. However, a court is not likely to characterize this as a negative easement. First, promissory language was used in the agreement ("Adams covenanted")—suggesting a covenant rather than an easement, which would have been created by grant or reservation. Second, negative easements have traditionally been limited to only four types of arrangements (for light, air, subjacent or lateral support, or flow of an artificial stream), none of which is exactly like the one in dispute. The type of negative easement that this arrangement comes closest to is the easement for light and air. If a court were to characterize this easement for view as a negative easement, it would have to be on an analogy to the negative easement for light and air.

Thus, Park can probably obtain an injunction against Down on an equitable servitude theory. She is less likely to recover damages, on either a negative covenant or negative easement theory, because there appear to be no provable damages as of yet and, more important, the burden of the negative covenant will be held not to run against Down, and the arrangement will not be construed as creating a negative easement.

ANSWER TO EXAM QUESTION NO. 4

Bill owns Goldacre subject to Elk Mortgage Co.'s ("Elk's") mortgage. At issue are (i) whether Ollie ***delivered*** the deed to Art and/or Bill, and (ii) the effect of the ***recording act***.

Delivery: A deed is not effective unless it has been delivered. Delivery is satisfied by words or conduct evidencing the grantor's intention that the deed have some present operative effect; *i.e.*, that title pass immediately and irrevocably, although the right to possession may be postponed until some future time. Ollie did not deliver the deed to Art and, as a result, Art has no interest in Goldacre. While Ollie's physical transfer of the deed to Art creates a presumption of delivery, the presumption is rebutted by Ollie's statement at the time. Although the statement, being parol, is not admissible to prove that the delivery was conditional, it is admissible to show that no delivery (*i.e.,* no present effect) was intended. Ollie's transfer to Art may also be ineffective because it is an invalid testamentary transfer, possessing none of the formalities required for a testamentary instrument under the Statute of Wills.

Ollie did deliver the deed to Bill, giving Bill a valid interest in Goldacre. There is, to be sure, a presumption against delivery arising from the fact that Ollie retained the deed in his possession. However, this presumption is rebutted by two facts. First, Ollie's statement, "I am now giving Goldacre to you," clearly reflects an intent to transfer an interest at once (and, because it bears on intent, the statement is provable by parol). Second, while Ollie retained possession of the deed, it was kept in a place to which Bill had ready access; as a result, the presumption arising from lack of physical transfer is not particularly strong.

Bill was privileged to remove the deed from the safe, for the language restricting him was merely precatory. Even if the statement is viewed as a condition, it is of no effect because conditions cannot be proved by parol. Thus, Ollie could not revoke his transfer to Bill.

Recording Act: Because Art has no interest as a result of the ineffective transfer to him, the conflict here is between Bill, Christy, and Elk.

As between Bill and Christy, Bill will prevail under the recording act. Under a race-notice statute, a subsequent bona fide purchaser (*i.e.*, a person who gives valuable consideration and has no notice of the prior instrument) prevails over a prior grantee only if she records first. Although Christy was a purchaser for value (having paid consideration) and recorded before Bill, she was not a ***bona fide*** purchaser because, at the time she purchased, she had actual notice of Bill's interest. Christy obtained this actual notice by being present when Ollie conveyed Goldacre to Bill. She might try to argue that the deed to Bill was invalid because it was not supported by consideration. This argument would fail because a deed does not require consideration and because, under a race-notice statute, it is only the ***subsequent*** purchaser's status as a purchaser for value that matters.

As between Bill and Elk, Elk will prevail under the recording act. Presumably Elk gave value for its mortgage interest (although the facts do not state this); if no value was given, Elk will lose to Bill. Also, although Elk took its interest after Bill recorded, it will not lose out to Bill under a race-notice statute, because Bill's recorded instrument appeared outside the chain of title and thus would not have shown up in the course of a reasonable title search by Elk. Thus, under the majority "chain-of-title" doctrine, Elk would prevail over Bill.

Thus, Elk has first rights to Goldacre, Bill is second in priority, Christy is third, and Art has no interest at all.

ANSWER TO EXAM QUESTION NO. 5

Buyer would be entitled to terminate her contract with Possessor and secure the return of the earnest money and expenses of the title examination. At issue are (i) whether Seller's title is ***unmarketable***, and (ii) whether the contract can be rescinded based on ***mutual mistake***.

Marketability of Title: There is generally implied in all land sale contracts a condition that the seller will deliver marketable title at closing. Although in some states this condition is not implied where the conveyance is to be by quitclaim deed, the majority rule is to the contrary.

Zoning regulations such as the one involved here do ***not*** affect marketability unless a violation of the zoning ordinance exists at the time the land sale contract is first entered into. No such violation is indicated by the facts.

Enforceable restrictive covenants affect marketability. Restrictive covenants, such as the one in this case, limiting use of the land to residential purposes, if enforceable, constitute encumbrances that render title unmarketable.

The ***installment land contract*** does seriously impair marketability. Although the contract was not recorded, Buyer had actual notice of it and so would take subject to any rights possessed by Possessor.

In many states, Seller could not enforce a forfeiture pursuant to his contract with Possessor, and would have to "foreclose" Possessor's equitable interest by a quiet title action and by paying restitution. Moreover, because Possessor has apparently paid more than 50% of the purchase price and has erected improvements on the property, ***most*** courts today would permit foreclosure of Possessor's equitable interest only by judicial decree and would condition relief upon restitution by Seller of the payments received in excess of the reasonable value of Possessor's use of the land and the cost of resale. Therefore, until Seller obtained such a decree, Possessor's outstanding equitable interest would make Seller's title unmarketable.

Marketable title will also be impaired by the ***possibility*** of litigation, even in those states in which Seller could enforce the forfeiture without the necessity of judicial action. Such a possibility exists here. Possessor's letter would be good, but not conclusive, evidence upon which Buyer could rely in any future litigation. Further, the possibility of litigation exists with respect to other defenses that may be available to Possessor.

Buyer's Intended Use: The facts are ambiguous as to whether Seller was aware of Buyer's purposes in purchasing the land. If Seller was or should have been aware of Buyer's plan to erect a public garage, Buyer would for this reason be entitled to equitable relief—rescission and restitution. On the other hand, if Seller was not aware of Buyer's plans in purchasing the land, Buyer's unilateral mistake by itself would not be a sufficient basis for such relief.

Remedies: If Seller's title is not marketable, or if Seller was aware of Buyer's purpose for purchasing the land, Buyer can get restitution of her earnest money and out-of-pocket costs.

Torts

TORTS

TABLE OF CONTENTS

I. INTENTIONAL TORTS

A. PRIMA FACIE CASE

To establish a prima facie case for intentional tort liability, it is generally necessary that plaintiff prove the following:

(i) ***Act*** by defendant;

(ii) ***Intent***; and

(iii) ***Causation***.

1. Act by Defendant

The "act" requirement for intentional tort liability refers to a ***volitional movement*** on defendant's part.

Examples: 1) Chauncey tripped and was falling. To break the fall, Chauncey stretched out his hand, which struck Darby. Even though the movement was reflexive, it nonetheless was one dictated by the mind, and hence will be characterized as volitional.

2) Lulu suffered an epileptic attack. During the course of it, she struck Darby. This is not a volitional act.

3) Chauncey pushed Lulu into Darby. Chauncey has committed a volitional act; Lulu has not.

2. Intent

The requisite intent for this type of tort liability may be either specific or general.

a. Specific Intent

An actor "intends" the consequences of his conduct if his ***goal*** in acting is to bring about these consequences.

b. General Intent

An actor "intends" the consequences of his conduct if he ***knows with substantial certainty*** that these consequences will result.

Example: D, five years old, pulls a chair out from under P as she is sitting down. Even if D did not desire that she hit the ground, if he knew with substantial certainty that she was trying to sit and would hit the ground, he will have the intent necessary for battery. [Garratt v. Dailey, 279 P.2d 1091 (Wash. 1955)]

c. Actor Need Not Intend Injury

The intent of the actor that is relevant for purposes of intentional torts is the intent to bring about the consequences that are the basis of the tort. Thus, a person may be liable even for an unintended injury if he intended to bring about such "basis of the tort" consequences.

Example: A intends to push B and does so. B falls and breaks his arm. This conduct gives rise to a cause of action for battery. The "consequences"

that are the basis of this tort are harmful or offensive contact to the plaintiff's person. In this case, the actor intended to bring about harmful or offensive contact to B. Hence, he will be liable even though it was not intended that B break his arm.

d. Transferred Intent

1) General Rule

The transferred intent doctrine applies where the defendant intends to commit a tort against one person but instead (i) commits a different tort against that person, (ii) commits the same tort as intended but against a different person, or (iii) commits a different tort against a different person. In such cases, the ***intent to commit a tort against one person is transferred to the other tort or to the injured person*** for purposes of establishing a prima facie case.

Example: A swings at B, intending only to frighten him. A's blow lands on C. A's intent to commit assault on B is transferred to C, and A's act constitutes a battery on C.

2) Limitations on Use of Transferred Intent

Transferred intent may be invoked only where the tort intended and the tort that results are both within the following list:

a) Assault;

b) Battery;

c) False imprisonment;

d) Trespass to land; and

e) Trespass to chattels.

e. Motive Distinguished

Motive impels a person to act to achieve a result. ***Intent*** denotes the purpose to use a particular means to effect that result. ***Only the intent is relevant*** for purposes of establishing the prima facie case. Thus, for example, even though defendant acts without a hostile motive or desire to do any harm, or even where he is seeking to aid the plaintiff, he may be liable.

Note: Evil motive is not an essential element of most torts, but ***malice*** or ulterior purpose is an essential element of some (*e.g.,* malicious prosecution, abuse of process). Further, malice may sometimes negate a privilege that the defendant might have, and it may permit the recovery of ***punitive damages***.

f. Minors and Incompetents Can Have Requisite Intent

Under the majority view, both minors and incompetents will be ***liable*** for their intentional torts; *i.e.,* they are held to possess the requisite intent.

3. Causation

The result giving rise to liability must have been legally caused by the defendant's act or something set in motion thereby. The causation requirement will be satisfied where the ***conduct of defendant is a substantial factor*** in bringing about the injury.

B. PRIMA FACIE CASE—INTENTIONAL TORTS TO THE PERSON

1. Battery

a. Prima Facie Case

To establish a prima facie case for battery, the following elements must be proved:

1) An act by the defendant which brings about ***harmful*** or ***offensive contact*** to the plaintiff's person;

2) ***Intent*** on the part of the defendant to bring about harmful or offensive contact to the plaintiff's person; and

3) ***Causation***.

b. Harmful or Offensive Contact

Whether any given contact is to be construed as harmful or offensive is judged by whether it would be considered harmful or offensive by a ***reasonable person*** of ordinary sensibilities. Contact is deemed "offensive" if the plaintiff has not expressly or impliedly consented to it (*see* D.1., *infra*).

c. Meaning of "Plaintiff's Person"

For purposes of a battery, anything ***connected*** to the plaintiff's person is viewed as part of the plaintiff's person.

Example: Chauncey grabbed Lulu's purse, which was hanging from her shoulder. He may be liable for a battery. (He would also be liable if he had grabbed an article of clothing she was wearing, a cane she was holding, etc.)

d. Causation

The defendant is liable not only for "direct" contact, but also for "indirect" contact; *i.e.,* it will be sufficient if he ***sets in motion a force*** that brings about harmful or offensive contact to the plaintiff's person.

Examples: 1) Chauncey, intending to set a trap, dug a hole in the road upon which Lulu was going to walk. Lulu fell in. Causation exists.

2) Horace struck a glass door so that the breaking glass cut Bowater. Causation exists.

e. Apprehension Not Necessary

A person may recover for battery even though he is not conscious of the harmful or offensive contact when it occurs (*e.g.,* unauthorized surgery performed on unconscious patient).

f. Transferred Intent

The doctrine of transferred intent ***applies*** in battery cases.

g. **Actual Damages Not Required**
It is not necessary to sustain a prima facie case for battery that plaintiff prove actual damages. Plaintiff can recover at least ***nominal damages*** even though he suffered no severe actual damage. In a majority of jurisdictions, ***punitive damages*** may be recovered where defendant acted with ***malice***.

2. Assault

a. **Prima Facie Case**
To establish a prima facie case for assault, the following elements must be proved:

1) An act by the defendant creating a ***reasonable apprehension*** in plaintiff of ***immediate harmful*** or ***offensive contact*** to plaintiff's person;

2) ***Intent*** on the part of the defendant to bring about in the plaintiff apprehension of immediate harmful or offensive contact with the plaintiff's person; and

3) ***Causation***.

b. **Construction of "Apprehension"**

1) **Requirement of Reasonableness**
The apprehension of harmful or offensive contact must be a reasonable one. Courts generally will not protect a plaintiff against exaggerated fears of contact (unless defendant knows of the unreasonable fear and uses it to put plaintiff in apprehension). In determining whether the apprehension in a given case is reasonable, the courts will usually apply a ***reasonable person test***.

a) **Fear, Intimidation, etc., Distinguished**
Apprehension is not the same as fear or intimidation. Note that "apprehension" here is used in the sense of ***expectation***. Thus, one may reasonably apprehend an immediate contact although he believes he can defend himself or otherwise avoid it.

b) **Knowledge of Act Required**
Obviously, for there to be an apprehension, the plaintiff must have been aware of the defendant's act. Contrast this with battery (above), in which the plaintiff need not be aware of the contact at the time thereof.

c) **Knowledge of Defendant's Identity Not Required**
In contrast, it is not necessary that the plaintiff know who the defendant is at the time of the act; *i.e.*, one only need apprehend an immediate harmful or offensive contact, not the identity of the person who is directing this unpermitted force at him.

d) **Defendant's Apparent Ability to Act Is Sufficient**
A person may be placed in reasonable apprehension of immediate harmful or offensive contact even though the defendant is ***not actually capable*** of causing injury to the plaintiff's person. For such apprehension to be reasonable,

however, it is necessary that the defendant have the apparent ability to bring about such contact.

Example: Jan points an unloaded gun at Myron. Myron does not know that the gun is not loaded. Myron's apprehension of immediate harmful or offensive contact is reasonable.

e) **Effect of Words**

(1) **Overt Act Required**

Some overt act is necessary. Words alone, however violent, generally do not constitute an assault because they cannot create a reasonable apprehension of immediate harmful or offensive contact. A different result might occur when such words are accompanied by some overt act, *e.g.,* a clenching of the fist. Moreover, ***words may negate an assault*** by making unreasonable any apprehension of immediate contact, even though the defendant commits a hostile act.

Example: James shakes a clenched fist while talking to Myron, and says, "If I weren't such a good guy, I'd hit you." There is no reasonable apprehension of harmful or offensive contact.

(2) **Conditional Threat Is Sufficient**

Note that if the words and act combine to form a conditional threat, an assault will result.

Example: Robber points a gun at Plaintiff and says, "Your money or your life." Robber is liable for an assault.

2) **Requirement of Immediacy**

The apprehension must be of immediate harmful or offensive contact. Threats of future contact are insufficient. Similarly, there is no assault if the defendant is too far away to do any harm or is merely preparing for a future harmful act.

c. **Causation**

Plaintiff's apprehension must have been legally caused by the defendant's act or something set in motion thereby, either directly or indirectly.

d. **Transferred Intent**

The doctrine of transferred intent ***applies*** to assault cases.

e. **No Requirement of Damages**

It is not necessary to prove actual damages to sustain a prima facie case for assault. If the case is otherwise made out, plaintiff can recover ***nominal damages***. Most states allow ***punitive damages*** to be awarded where defendant's actions have been malicious.

3. **False Imprisonment**

a. **Prima Facie Case**

To establish a prima facie case for false imprisonment, the following elements must be proved:

1) An act or omission to act on the part of the defendant that ***confines*** or ***restrains*** the plaintiff to a ***bounded*** area;

2) ***Intent*** on the part of the defendant to confine or restrain the plaintiff to a bounded area; and

3) ***Causation***.

b. Sufficient Methods of Confinement or Restraint

Actionable confinement or restraint may result in a variety of ways. The following should be noted:

1) Physical Barriers

Defendant may falsely imprison plaintiff by confining him through the use of physical barriers.

2) Physical Force

False imprisonment will result where plaintiff is restrained by the use of physical force directed at ***him*** or a member of his ***immediate family***. An action may also lie if the force is directed against ***plaintiff's property***.

Example: Lulu remained in a building because her purse had been confiscated by Chauncey. She could have left the building but that would have necessitated leaving the purse behind. False imprisonment could result if the purse was wrongfully withheld.

3) Direct Threats of Force

Direct threats of force by the defendant to the plaintiff's person or property or against persons of the plaintiff's immediate family can constitute false imprisonment.

4) Indirect Threats of Force

False imprisonment can also arise from indirect threats of force, *i.e.,* acts or words that ***reasonably*** imply that the defendant will use force against plaintiff's person or property or persons of plaintiff's immediate family.

5) Failure to Provide Means of Escape

Where plaintiff has lawfully come under defendant's control and it would be impossible to leave without defendant's assistance (and it was understood between the parties that such assistance would be forthcoming), the withholding of such assistance with the intent to detain plaintiff will make defendant liable. In short, the courts impose an ***affirmative duty*** on the defendant to take steps to release the plaintiff. If defendant intentionally breaches this duty, this is sufficient for false imprisonment. But, of course, it must first be established that defendant owes such a duty.

Examples: 1) Jailer refused to release a prisoner at the end of his jail sentence. Jailer may be liable for false imprisonment.

2) Plaintiff is imprisoned for failing to produce corporate records. Defendant has the records but is under no legal duty to produce them and refuses to do so. There is no false imprisonment.

6) **Invalid Use of Legal Authority**
The invalid use of legal authority amounts to false imprisonment if it results in a confinement of plaintiff.

a) **False Arrests**
An action for false imprisonment does ***not*** lie for an arrest or a detention made by virtue of legal process duly issued by a court or official having jurisdiction to issue it. However, where an arrest by a police officer or private citizen for a criminal offense ***without a warrant*** is unlawful (*i.e.,* not privileged), it may constitute false imprisonment.

(1) **When Arrests Are Privileged**

(a) **Felony Arrests Without Warrant**
A felony arrest without a warrant by a ***police officer*** (or a private citizen acting at the officer's direction) is valid if the officer has ***reasonable grounds*** to believe that a felony has been committed and that the person arrested has committed it. Such an arrest by a ***private person*** will be privileged only if a felony has ***in fact*** been committed and the private person has reasonable grounds for believing that the person arrested has committed it.

(b) **Misdemeanor Arrests Without Warrant**
Both police officers and private citizens are privileged for misdemeanor arrests without a warrant if the misdemeanor was a ***breach of the peace*** and was committed in the presence of the arresting party. (Note that in most states, police officers have a broader statutory privilege of arrest for ***any*** misdemeanor committed in their presence.)

(c) **Arrests to Prevent a Crime Without a Warrant**
Where a felony or breach of the peace is in the process of being, or reasonably appears about to be, committed, both police officers and private citizens are privileged to make an arrest.

(2) **Amount of Force Allowable**

(a) **Felony Arrest**
For felony arrests, both police officers and private citizens may use that degree of force reasonably necessary to make the arrest; however, deadly force is permissible only when the suspect poses a threat of serious harm to the arresting party or others.

(b) **Misdemeanor Arrest**
For misdemeanor arrests, both police officers and private citizens are privileged to use only that degree of force necessary to effect the arrest, but never deadly force.

b) **"Shoplifting" Detentions Are Privileged**
What if a shopkeeper suspects someone of shoplifting and detains that

individual to ascertain whether this is the case? He may be liable for false imprisonment. But if he does nothing and permits the suspect to simply leave the premises, the merchandise and all possibilities of proving theft will be lost. Hence, by statute in some states and case law in others, shopkeepers have been given a privilege to detain for investigation. For the privilege to apply, the following conditions must be satisfied:

(1) There must be a ***reasonable belief*** as to the fact of theft;

(2) The detention must be conducted in a ***reasonable manner*** and only nondeadly force can be used; and

(3) The detention must be only for a ***reasonable period of time*** and only for the purpose of making an investigation.

c. Insufficient Forms of Confinement or Restraint

As stated above, restraints or confinements produced by requiring the plaintiff to choose between injury to his person or property and his freedom of motion are generally actionable. However, a cause of action will not be sustained for all forms of restraint or confinement.

1) Moral Pressure

A cause of action will not be sustained if a person remains in the area merely because he is responding to the exertion of moral pressure.

2) Future Threats

Similarly, a cause of action will not be sustained if a person remains in the area in response to future threats against person or property.

d. No Need to Resist

Plaintiff is not under any obligation to resist physical force that is being applied to confine him. Similarly, where there is a threat of force, he is not obligated to test the threat where the defendant has the apparent ability to carry it out.

e. Time of Confinement

It is ***immaterial***, except as to the extent of damages, how short the time period of the confinement is.

f. Awareness of Imprisonment

Most American cases hold that awareness of confinement is a necessary element of the tort. The Restatement provides an exception to this requirement where the person confined is actually injured by the confinement (*e.g.,* an infant locked in a bank vault for several days).

g. What Is a Bounded Area?

For an area to be "bounded," the plaintiff's freedom of movement in ***all directions*** must be limited; *e.g.,* merely blocking plaintiff's access to a portion of a park does not constitute false imprisonment. The area will ***not*** be characterized as "bounded" if there is a ***reasonable means of escape*** of which plaintiff is aware.

h. **Causation**
Plaintiff's confinement must have been legally caused by the defendant's act or something set in motion thereby, either directly or indirectly.

i. **Transferred Intent**
The doctrine of transferred intent ***applies*** to false imprisonment.

j. **No Requirement of Damages**
It is not necessary to prove actual damages to sustain a prima facie case for false imprisonment. Again, if defendant's conduct was motivated by malice, plaintiff may also be entitled to punitive damages.

k. **False Imprisonment and Malicious Prosecution Distinguished**
One who participates in, procures, or instigates an unlawful arrest without proper authority may be liable for false arrest. Note that merely giving information to the police about the commission of a crime, leaving to the police the decision whether to make an arrest, does not constitute false imprisonment, as long as one stops short of instigating the arrest. Whether the defendant instigated the arrest or merely furnished information to the police is a question for the trier of fact. Where information only is given, there may be liability for malicious prosecution (*see* II.E.1., *infra*), if not for false imprisonment.

4. **Intentional Infliction of Emotional Distress**

a. **Prima Facie Case**
To establish a prima facie case for intentional infliction of emotional distress, the following elements must be proved:

1) An act by defendant amounting to ***extreme*** and ***outrageous conduct***;

2) Intent on part of defendant to cause plaintiff to suffer ***severe*** emotional distress, or ***recklessness*** as to the effect of defendant's conduct;

3) ***Causation***; and

4) ***Damages—severe*** emotional distress.

b. **Extreme and Outrageous Conduct**

1) **Some Courts Reluctant to Recognize Tort**
This tort covers those situations where the defendant intentionally "shocks" the plaintiff but there is ***no physical injury*** or threat thereof. Some states have been reluctant to recognize this as a cause of action because of the difficulty of proving "shock" (and the ease with which it could be falsified), the speculative nature of the damage, and fear of a flood of litigation.

2) **Liability Limited by Requiring Proof of Outrageous Conduct**
To protect against potential abuses, the courts will limit liability for this tort to those situations where "outrageous conduct" on the part of the defendant is

proved. "Outrageous conduct" is ***conduct that transcends all bounds of decency*** tolerated by society. In the absence of such conduct by the defendant, it is generally held that an average person of ordinary sensibilities would not suffer the kind of severe mental injury that is contemplated by the tort.

3) Examples of Outrageous Conduct

a) Extreme Business Conduct
Certain extreme methods of business conduct may be construed as outrageous conduct, *e.g.,* use of extreme methods of collection, if repeated, may be actionable.

b) Misuse of Authority
Misuse of authority in some circumstances may be actionable, *e.g.,* school authorities threatening and bullying pupils.

c) Offensive or Insulting Language
Generally, offensive or insulting language will ***not*** be characterized as "outrageous conduct." This result could change if there is a ***special relationship*** between plaintiff and defendant or a ***sensitivity*** on plaintiff's part of which defendant is aware. (*See* below.)

4) Special Relationship Situations
Common carriers and ***innkeepers*** owe special duties to their patrons that will be a basis for liability even when the act is something less than outrageous, *e.g.,* bus driver making insulting remarks to passenger.

5) Known Sensitivity
If defendant knows that plaintiff is more sensitive and thus more susceptible to emotional distress than the average person, liability will follow if the defendant uses extreme and outrageous conduct intentionally to cause such distress and succeeds. These rules may also apply where defendant's conduct is directed at individuals in certain groups such as children, pregnant women, and elderly people.

c. Intent
Defendant will be liable not only for intentional conduct but also for ***reckless*** conduct, *i.e.,* acting in reckless disregard of a high probability that emotional distress will result.

d. Causation
The defendant's conduct must have proximately caused the plaintiff's emotional distress.

1) Intent/Causation Requirements in Bystander Cases
When the defendant intentionally causes severe, ***physical*** harm to a third person and the plaintiff suffers severe ***emotional*** distress because of her relationship to the injured person, the elements of intent and causation may be harder to prove. To establish these elements in such cases, the plaintiff is generally required to show the following:

(i) The plaintiff was ***present*** when the injury occurred to the other person;

(ii) The plaintiff was a ***close relative*** of the injured person; and

(iii) The ***defendant knew*** that the plaintiff was present and a close relative of the injured person.

Note: The plaintiff does not need to establish presence or a family relationship if she shows that the defendant had a ***design or purpose*** to cause severe distress to plaintiff.

Example: Defendant called Susan and threatened to kill Mike, with whom Defendant knew Susan was living. Defendant then made good his threat. Liability will attach when Susan suffers severe emotional distress by showing that Defendant's ***purpose*** was to cause her severe distress, even though she was not a relative of Mike and was not present when he was murdered.

2) **Special Liability for Mishandling Corpses**

In an analogous situation, many courts have allowed recovery where the mental distress resulted from the intentional or reckless mishandling of a relative's corpse. Although this cause of action is almost always for emotional distress arising from action directed toward another (the corpse), the courts have created a special category of liability for such conduct.

e. **Actual Damages Required**

Actual damages are required (nominal damages will not suffice). But it is ***not*** necessary to prove ***physical injuries*** to recover. It is, however, necessary to establish ***severe*** emotional distress (*i.e.,* more than a reasonable person could be expected to endure). Punitive damages are allowable where defendant's conduct was improperly motivated.

C. PRIMA FACIE CASE—INTENTIONAL TORTS TO PROPERTY

1. Trespass to Land

a. Prima Facie Case

To establish a prima facie case for trespass to land, the following elements must be proved:

1) An act of ***physical invasion*** of plaintiff's real property by defendant;

2) ***Intent*** on defendant's part to bring about a physical invasion of plaintiff's real property; and

3) ***Causation***.

b. Physical Invasion of Plaintiff's Land

1) **What Constitutes "Physical Invasion"?**

The interest protected by this tort is the interest in exclusive possession of realty.

Hence, all that is necessary to satisfy this element is that there be a physical invasion of plaintiff's land.

a) **Defendant Need Not Enter onto Land**
It is not necessary that the defendant personally come onto the land; *e.g.,* trespass exists where defendant floods plaintiff's land, throws rocks onto it, or chases third persons onto it.

b) **Lawful Right of Entry Expires**
A trespass to land may also exist where defendant remains on plaintiff's land after an otherwise lawful right of entry has lapsed.

2) **If No Physical Object Enters Land**
If no physical object has entered onto plaintiff's land, *e.g.,* damage resulted from blasting concussions, the courts generally do not treat the controversy as a trespass case. Rather, they treat it as a ***nuisance*** case or as a case of ***strict liability*** if ultra-hazardous activities are involved.

3) **What Constitutes "Land"?**
The trespass may occur on the surface of the land, below the surface, or above it.

Courts generally construe plaintiff's "land" to include air space and subsurface space to the height or depth plaintiff can make beneficial use of such space. Thus, for example, one could commit a trespass by stringing wires over the land, flying an airplane at low altitudes over it, tunneling under it, etc.

c. **Intent Required**
Mistake as to the lawfulness of the entry is ***no defense*** as long as defendant intended the entry upon that particular piece of land. Intent to trespass is not required—***intent to enter onto the land*** is sufficient.

Example: Relying on boundary markers fixed by a reputable surveyor, Farmer clears land for cultivation that he believes to be his. In fact, the survey was in error and Farmer cleared a portion of Neighbor's land. Farmer is liable to Neighbor for trespass to land.

d. **Who May Bring Action?**
An action for trespass may be maintained by ***anyone in actual or constructive possession*** of the land. This is so even if that possession is without title. If no one is in possession, the ***true owner*** is presumed in possession and may maintain the action.

If the action is maintained by a ***lessee***, some decisions allow him to recover only to the extent that the trespass damages the leasehold interest. Other cases allow a full recovery for all damage done to the property, but require the lessee to account to the lessor for excess over damages to the leasehold.

e. **Causation**
The physical invasion of plaintiff's property must have been legally caused by the defendant's act or something set in motion thereby.

f. **Transferred Intent**
The doctrine of transferred intent ***applies*** to trespass to land.

g. **No Requirement of Damages**
As with most other intentional torts, damage is presumed; *i.e.,* actual injury to the land is ***not*** an essential element of the cause of action.

Example: Tom intentionally bounced a tennis ball against the side of a building owned by Owen. Although no damage was done to Owen's building, Tom is liable for trespass. In contrast, if Tom had accidentally but negligently hit Owen's building with the ball, Tom would not be liable unless Owen established damages as part of the negligence prima facie case.

2. **Trespass to Chattels**

a. **Prima Facie Case**
To establish a prima facie case of trespass to chattels, the following elements must be proved:

1) An act of defendant that ***interferes with plaintiff's right of possession*** in the chattel;

2) ***Intent to perform the act*** bringing about the interference with plaintiff's right of possession;

3) ***Causation***; and

4) ***Damages***.

b. **Act by Defendant**
Trespass to chattels is designed to protect a person against interferences with his ***right to possess*** his chattels. Hence, any act of interference will suffice. These generally take two forms:

1) **Intermeddling**
An intermeddling is conduct by defendant that in some way serves to directly damage plaintiff's chattels, *e.g.,* denting plaintiff's car, striking plaintiff's dog.

2) **Dispossession**
A dispossession is conduct on defendant's part serving to dispossess plaintiff of his lawful right of possession.

c. **Intent Required**
Mistake as to the lawfulness of defendant's actions (*e.g.*, a mistaken belief that defendant owns the chattel) is ***no defense*** to an action for trespass to chattels. Again, as with trespass to land, the intent to trespass is not required—***intent to do the act of interference*** with the chattel is sufficient.

d. **Who May Bring Trespass to Chattels Action?**
Anyone with possession or the immediate ***right to possession*** may maintain an action for trespass to chattels.

e. **Causation**
The interference with plaintiff's possessory interests in the chattel must have been caused by defendant's act or something set in motion thereby.

f. **Actual Damages Required**
As a general rule, nominal damages will not be awarded for trespass to chattels; *i.e.,* in the absence of any actual damages, an action will not lie. However, if the trespass amounts to a dispossession, the loss of possession itself is deemed to be an actual harm.

g. **Transferred Intent**
The doctrine of transferred intent ***applies*** to trespass to chattels.

h. **Trespass to Chattels and Conversion Distinguished**
As discussed below, conversion grants relief for interferences with a chattel so serious in nature, or so serious in consequences, as to warrant requiring the defendant to pay its full value in damages. For those interferences not so serious in nature or consequences, trespass to chattels is the appropriate action.

3. **Conversion**

a. **Prima Facie Case**
To establish a prima facie case for conversion, the following elements must be proved:

1) An act by defendant ***interfering*** with plaintiff's right of possession in the chattel that is ***serious enough*** in nature or consequence to warrant that the defendant ***pay the full value*** of the chattel;

2) ***Intent*** to perform the act bringing about the interference with plaintiff's right of possession; and

3) ***Causation***.

b. **Acts of Conversion**
One can act in such a way as to seriously invade another's chattel interest in a variety of ways. These include:

1) Wrongful acquisition, *e.g.,* theft, embezzlement.

2) Wrongful transfer, *e.g.,* selling, misdelivering, pledging.

3) Wrongful detention, *e.g.,* refusing to return to owner.

4) Substantially changing.

5) Severely damaging or destroying.

6) Misusing the chattel.

c. **Mere Intent to Perform Act Required**
The only intent required is the intent to perform the act that interferes with the plaintiff's right of possession. Even if the conduct is wholly innocent, liability may attach where the interference is serious in nature.

1) **Bona Fide Purchaser May Be Liable**
Under this principle, even a bona fide purchaser of chattel may become a converter if the chattel had been stolen from the true owner.

2) **Accidental Conduct Insufficient**
Accidentally causing damage to or loss of another's chattel does not amount to conversion unless the actor was using the chattel without permission when the accident occurred. (Note that the actor may be liable in negligence for accidental damage.)

d. **Seriousness of Interference or Consequence**
Usually, where the interference with possessory rights is insubstantial (*e.g.,* where a person momentarily takes another person's property or merely moves it for her own convenience), the actor is not viewed as asserting sufficient interference for conversion (although it may suffice for trespass to chattels). However, such interference with the possessory rights of another in the chattel, if serious enough, may amount to conversion. Thus, for example, if this person ***refuses to return*** the chattel when asked, or ***alters*** it, she may be liable for conversion because her action so seriously interferes with another's chattel rights that it amounts to a claim of dominion and control on the actor's part. No specific rule can be stated for these situations; however, the ***longer the withholding period*** and the ***more extensive the use*** of the chattel during this time, the more likely it is that conversion has resulted.

e. **Special Situation of Bailees Receiving Stolen Property**
A bailee receiving goods from a thief without notice of the improper taking may return the goods to the thief without liability to the real owner. However, if the bailee has notice and the real owner makes a demand for his goods, the bailee is liable for conversion if she returns the goods to the thief.

f. **Subject Matter of Conversion**
Property subject to conversion is limited to tangible ***personal property*** and ***intangibles*** that have been ***reduced to physical form*** (*e.g.,* a promissory note), and documents in which title to a chattel is merged (*e.g.,* a bill of lading or a warehouse receipt). Intangibles such as a bakery route, customer lists, or the goodwill of a business may not be the subject of conversion. Neither may real property be converted.

g. **Who May Bring Action for Conversion?**
Anyone with ***possession*** or the ***immediate right to possession*** may maintain an action for conversion. Possession is viewed as sufficient title against a wrongdoer. However, if the person in possession is not the true owner, she is accountable to the true owner for any recovery to the extent of the owner's interest.

h. **Causation**
The interference with plaintiff's chattel interests must have been legally caused by the defendant's act or something set in motion thereby.

i. **Remedies**
The basic conversion remedies are:

1) **Damages**
The plaintiff is entitled to damages for the ***fair market value*** of the chattel. This value is generally computed as of the ***time and place of conversion***. The defendant is given title upon satisfaction of the judgment so that, in effect, there is a forced sale of the chattel. Note that even if the defendant wishes to return the item, the plaintiff is not obligated to take it back once it has been converted.

2) **Replevin**
If the plaintiff wishes to have the chattel returned, he may get it by availing himself of the remedy of replevin.

D. DEFENSES TO THE INTENTIONAL TORTS

1. Consent
A defendant is not liable for an otherwise tortious act if the plaintiff consented to the defendant's act. Consent may be given expressly; it may also be implied from custom, conduct, or words, or by law.

a. **Express (Actual) Consent**
Express (actual) consent exists where the plaintiff has expressly shown a willingness to submit to defendant's conduct.

1) **Consent by Mistake**
Where a plaintiff expressly consents by mistake, the consent is still a valid defense unless the defendant caused the mistake or knows of the mistake and takes advantage of it.

2) **Consent Induced by Fraud**
If the expressly given consent has been induced by fraud, the consent generally is ***not a defense***. The fraud must, however, go to an essential matter; if it is only with respect to a collateral matter, the consent remains effective.

Examples: 1) Charles expressly consents to balance an apple on his head for Roberta to attempt to shoot it off from 50 yards. She told him she was a professional trick-shot artist, which was not true. Fraud goes to an essential matter; consent is ineffective.

2) Same as above, except that Roberta was in fact a professional trick-shot artist. However, she gave him a $10 bill she knew to be counterfeit. This is a collateral matter; consent is effective.

3) **Consent Obtained by Duress**
Consent obtained by duress may be held ***invalid***. Note, however, that threats of future action or of some future economic deprivation do not constitute legal duress sufficient to invalidate the express consent.

b. **Implied Consent**
Plaintiff's consent may also be implied in a given case. There are two basic kinds of implied consent, apparent consent and consent implied by law.

1) **Apparent Consent**
Apparent consent is that which a ***reasonable person would infer*** from plaintiff's conduct. Thus, for example, somebody who voluntarily engages in a body contact sport impliedly consents to the normal contacts inherent in playing it.

a) **Inferred from Usage and Custom**
Such consent may also be inferred as a matter of usage or custom. Thus, for example, a person is presumed to consent to the ordinary contacts of daily life, *e.g.,* minor bumping in a crowd.

2) **Consent Implied by Law**
In some situations, consent may be implied by law where action is necessary to save a person's life or some other important interest in person or property. Thus, for example, consent will be implied in an ***emergency*** situation where the plaintiff is incapable of consenting and a reasonable person would conclude that some contact is necessary to prevent death or serious bodily harm, *e.g.,* a surgical operation where a person is unconscious after an automobile accident.

c. **Capacity Required**
Incompetents, drunken persons, and very young children are deemed incapable of consent to tortious conduct. Consent of parent or guardian is necessary to constitute a defense in such a case.

d. **Criminal Acts**
For purposes of tort liability, the ***majority*** view is that a person ***cannot consent*** to a criminal act. A minority and the Restatement of Torts take the contrary position and view consent to a criminal act as a valid defense in a civil action for an intentional tort.

1) **Modern Trend**
The modern tendency has been to differentiate between illegal acts that are ***breaches of the peace***, *e.g.,* a street fight (consent ineffective), and those that are not a breach of the peace, *e.g.,* an act of prostitution (consent effective).

2) **Consent Invalid Where Law Seeks to Protect Members of Victim's Class**
Where the act is made criminal to protect a limited class against its own lack of judgment (*e.g.,* statutory rape), consent is not a good defense in an action by a member of that class.

e. **Exceeding Consent Given**
If the defendant goes beyond the act consented to and does something substantially different, he is ***liable***; *e.g.,* consent to perform a tonsillectomy is not consent to perform an appendectomy (unless, of course, an emergency situation is present).

2. **Self-Defense**
When a person has reasonable grounds to believe that he is being, or is about to be, attacked, he may use such force as is reasonably necessary for protection against the potential injury.

a. **When Is Defense Available?**

1) **Reasonable Belief**
The actor need only have a reasonable belief as to the other party's actions; *i.e.,* apparent necessity, not actual necessity, is sufficient. Hence, reasonable mistake as to the existence of the danger does not vitiate the defense.

2) **Retaliation Not Allowed**
Self-defense is limited to the right to use force to prevent the commission of a tort. Thus, one may never use force in retaliation (where there is no longer any threat of injury).

3) **Retreat Not Necessary**
A substantial majority of the courts hold that one need not attempt to escape, but may stand his ground (and even use deadly force when necessary to prevent death or serious bodily harm to himself). A growing modern trend would impose a duty to retreat before using deadly force where this can be done safely ***unless*** the actor is in his own home.

4) **Not Available to Aggressor**
The initial aggressor is not privileged to defend himself against the other party's reasonable use of force in self-defense. However, if the other uses deadly force against an aggressor who had only used nondeadly force, the aggressor may defend himself with deadly force.

b. **How Much Force May Be Used?**
One may use only that force that ***reasonably*** appears to be ***necessary to prevent the harm***. One may not use force likely to cause death or serious bodily injury unless he reasonably believes that he is in danger of serious bodily injury. If more force than necessary is used, the actor loses the privilege of self-defense.

c. **Extends to Third-Party Injuries**
If, in the course of reasonably defending himself, one ***accidentally*** injures a bystander, he is nevertheless protected by the defense. (He might, however, be liable to the bystander on a negligence theory if his conduct warranted it.) If the actor ***deliberately*** injures a bystander in trying to protect himself, he probably cannot raise the privilege of self-defense.

3. **Defense of Others**

a. **When Is Defense Available?**
The actor need only have a ***reasonable belief*** that the person being aided would have the right of self-defense. Thus, even if the person aided has no defense (*e.g.,* if he were the initial aggressor), his defender is not liable as long as he reasonably believed that the person aided could have used force to protect himself.

b. **How Much Force May Be Used?**
The defender, assuming he is justified, may use as much force as he could have used in self-defense if the injury were threatened to him (*see* above).

4. **Defense of Property**

a. **When Is Defense Available?**
Generally, one may use reasonable force to prevent the commission of a tort against her property.

1) **Request to Desist Usually Required**
A request to desist must precede the use of force, unless the circumstances make it clear that the request would be futile or dangerous.

2) **Effect of Mistake**
Reasonable mistake is allowed as to the property owner's right to use force in defense of property where the mistake involves whether an intrusion has occurred or whether a request to desist is required. However, mistake is not allowed where the entrant has a privilege to enter the property that supersedes the defense of property right (*see* 4), below). In such a case the property owner is liable for mistakenly using force against a privileged entrant unless the entrant himself intentionally or negligently caused the mistake (*e.g.,* by refusing to tell the property owner the reason for the intrusion).

3) **Limited to Preventing Commission of Tort**
Defense of property is limited to ***preventing the commission of a tort*** against the defendant's property. Thus, once the defendant has been permanently dispossessed of the property and the commission of the tort is complete, she may not use force to recapture it. However, where one is in ***"hot pursuit"*** of someone who wrongfully dispossessed her of her property, the defense still operates because the other is viewed as still in the process of committing the tort against the property.

4) **Superseded by Other Privileges**
Whenever an actor has a privilege to enter upon the land of another because of necessity, right of reentry, right to enter upon another's land to recapture chattels, etc. (discussed below), that privilege supersedes the privilege of the land possessor to defend her property.

b. **How Much Force May Be Used?**
One may use ***reasonable*** force to defend property. However, she may ***not*** use force that will cause death or serious bodily harm. (Of course, if the invasion of property also entails a serious threat of bodily harm to the owner, she may then invoke the defense of self-defense and use deadly force.) Further, one may not use indirect deadly force such as a trap, spring gun, or vicious dog when such force could not lawfully be directly used, *e.g.,* against a mere trespasser.

5. **Reentry onto Land**

a. **Common Law Privilege**
In former years, it was held that a person who had been ***tortiously dispossessed*** from

her land (by fraud or force) could use ***reasonable force*** to regain possession if she acted promptly upon discovering the dispossession. (Note that this did not apply to a tenant merely overstaying her lease.)

b. No Such Privilege Under Modern Law

However, in most states today there are ***summary procedures*** for recovering possession of real property. Hence, resort to "self-help" is no longer allowed; the owner who uses force to retake possession is thus liable for whatever injury she inflicts.

6. Recapture of Chattels

a. When Is Defense Available?

The basic rule is the same as that for land: where another's possession began lawfully (*e.g.*, a conditional sale), one may use only peaceful means to recover the chattel. ***Force*** may be used to recapture a chattel only when in ***"hot pursuit"*** of one who has obtained possession wrongfully, *e.g.*, by theft.

1) Timely Demand Required

A demand to return the chattel must precede the use of force, unless the circumstances make it clear that the demand would be futile or dangerous.

2) Recovery Only from Wrongdoer

The recapture may only be from a tortfeasor or some third person who knows or should know that the chattels were tortiously obtained. If the chattels have come to rest in the hands of an innocent party, this will cut off the actor's privilege to use force to effect recapture.

b. How Much Force May Be Used?

Reasonable force, ***not*** including force sufficient to cause death or serious bodily harm, may be used to recapture chattels.

c. Entry upon Land to Remove Chattel

1) On Wrongdoer's Land

Where chattels are located on the land of the wrongdoer, the owner is privileged to enter upon the land and reclaim them at a ***reasonable time*** and in a ***reasonable manner***. It is generally required that there be a demand for the return of the chattels before any such entry.

2) On Land of Innocent Party

Similarly, when the chattels are on the land of an innocent party, the owner may enter and reclaim her chattel at a ***reasonable time*** and in a ***peaceful manner*** when the landowner has been given ***notice*** of the presence of the chattel and refuses to return it. In this case, the chattel owner will be liable for any actual damage caused by entry.

3) On Land Through Owner's Fault

If the chattels are on the land of another through the owner's fault, there is ***no*** *privilege* to enter upon the land. They may be recovered only through legal process.

d. **Shopkeeper's Privilege**
Shopkeepers may have a privilege to reasonably detain individuals whom they reasonably believe to be in possession of "shoplifted" goods. (*See* B.3.b.6)b), *supra.*)

7. **Privilege of Arrest**
Depending on the facts of the particular case, one may have a privilege to make an arrest of a third person.

a. **Invasion of Land**
The privilege of arrest carries with it the privilege to enter another's land for the purpose of effecting the arrest.

b. **Subsequent Misconduct**
Although the arrest itself may be privileged, the actor may still be liable for subsequent misconduct, *e.g.,* failing to bring the arrested party before a magistrate, unduly detaining the party in jail, etc.

c. **Mistake**
One who makes an arrest under the mistaken belief that it is privileged may be liable for false imprisonment. (*See* B.3.b.6)a)(1), *supra.*)

8. **Necessity**
A person may interfere with the real or personal property of another where the interference is reasonably and apparently necessary to avoid threatened injury from a natural or other force and where the threatened injury is substantially more serious than the invasion that is undertaken to avert it.

a. **Public Necessity**
Where the act is for the public good (*e.g.,* shooting a rabid dog), the defense is absolute.

b. **Private Necessity**
Where the act is solely to benefit a limited number of people (*e.g.,* the actor ties up his boat to another's dock in a storm), the defense is qualified; *i.e.,* the actor must pay for any injury he causes. *Exception:* The defense is absolute if the act is to benefit the owner of the land.

9. **Discipline**
A parent or teacher may use reasonable force in disciplining children, taking into account the age and sex of the child and the seriousness of the behavior.

II. HARM TO ECONOMIC AND DIGNITARY INTERESTS

In contrast to the intentional torts, the torts in this section involve less tangible harms to a person's relational interests with other persons in society.

Depending on the tort involved, the level of fault required for the prima facie case may range from intent to strict liability.

A. DEFAMATION

1. Prima Facie Case

To establish a prima facie case for defamation, the following elements must be proved:

(i) ***Defamatory language*** on the part of the defendant;

(ii) The defamatory language must be ***"of or concerning" the plaintiff***—*i.e.,* it must identify the plaintiff to a reasonable reader, listener, or viewer;

(iii) ***Publication*** of the defamatory language by the defendant to a third person; and

(iv) ***Damage to the reputation*** of the plaintiff.

Where the defamation refers to a public figure or involves a matter of public concern, two additional elements must be proved as part of the prima facie case:

(v) ***Falsity*** of the defamatory language; and

(vi) ***Fault*** on defendant's part.

2. Defamatory Language

Defamatory language is language that tends to adversely affect one's reputation. This may result from impeaching the individual's honesty, integrity, virtue, sanity, or the like.

a. Inducement and Innuendo

If the statement standing alone is defamatory, it is defamatory "on its face." However, a statement is also actionable if the defamatory meaning becomes apparent only by adding extrinsic facts. The plaintiff pleads and proves such additional facts as inducement and establishes the defamatory meaning by innuendo. Inducement and innuendo identify to the courts and the parties that extrinsic facts are being introduced to the court by the plaintiff to establish the first element of a prima facie case.

Example: Defendant publishes an erroneous report that Plaintiff has given birth to twins. This is defamatory because Plaintiff pleads and establishes that she had been married only one month.

b. Methods of Defamation

Not all defamation consists of direct remarks. Pictures, satire, drama, etc., may convey an actionable defamatory meaning.

c. Statements of Opinion

While a statement of fact may always be defamatory, a statement of opinion is actionable only if it appears to be based on specific facts, ***and*** an express allegation of those facts would be defamatory.

Example: The statement "I don't think Robert can be trusted with a key to the cash register" implies personal knowledge of dishonest conduct by Robert, and thus may be actionable.

1) **Distinguishing Fact and Opinion**
Whether a published statement is one of "fact" or "opinion" depends on the circumstances surrounding the publication and the nature of the words used. Generally, the broader the language used, the less likely that it will be reasonably interpreted as a statement of fact or an opinion based on specific facts.

d. **Who May Be Defamed?**

1) **Individual**
Any ***living*** person may be defamed. Defamation of a deceased person is not actionable.

2) **Corporation, Unincorporated Association, and Partnership**
In a limited sense, a corporation, unincorporated association, or partnership may also be defamed, *e.g.*, by remarks as to its financial condition, honesty, integrity, etc.

3. **"Of or Concerning" the Plaintiff**
The plaintiff must establish that a ***reasonable*** reader, listener, or viewer would understand that the defamatory statement referred to the plaintiff.

a. **Colloquium**
A statement may be actionable even though no clear reference to the plaintiff is contained on the face of the statement. In such a case, however, the plaintiff is required to introduce additional extrinsic facts that would lead a reasonable reader, listener, or viewer to perceive the defamatory statement as referring to the plaintiff. Pleading and proving such extrinsic facts to show that the plaintiff was, in fact, intended is called "colloquium."

b. **Group Defamation**
A significant issue is presented in respect to this prima facie case element when the defamatory language refers to a group without identifying any particular individual within that group. In such cases, the following rules operate:

1) **All Members of Small Group**
Where the defamatory language refers to all members of a small group, each member may establish that the defamatory statement was made of and concerning him by alleging that he is a member of the group.

2) **All Members of Large Group**
If, however, the defamatory statement refers to all members of a large group, no member of that group may establish this element of the cause of action.

3) **Some Members of Small Group**
Where the defamatory language refers to some members of a small group, plaintiff can recover if a reasonable person would view the statement as referring to the plaintiff.

4. **Publication**
A statement is not actionable until there has been a "publication." The publication requirement is satisfied when there is a ***communication to a third person who understood it.***

Example: Libby saw a defamatory statement about Jeffrey printed in Russian. The publication requirement is not met unless it is shown that Libby understood the foreign words.

The communication to the third person may be made either ***intentionally or negligently***.

a. **Only Intent to Publish Required**
Once publication is established, it is no defense that defendant had no idea that she was defaming plaintiff because she neither knew nor had reason to know that plaintiff existed (use of fictional name), nor knew that the publication was defamatory. It is the intent to publish, not the intent to defame, that is the requisite intent.
Example: Defendant published a false statement that Plaintiff had given birth to twins. If Defendant neither knew nor had reason to know that Plaintiff had been married only one month, Defendant is nonetheless liable.

b. **Repetition**
Each repetition of the defamatory statement is a separate publication for which the plaintiff may recover damages.

c. **"Single Publication" Rule—Statute of Limitations**
However, as to publication of a defamatory statement in a number of copies of the same newspaper, magazine, or book, most American courts have adopted the "single publication" rule. Under this rule, all copies of a newspaper, magazine, or book edition are treated as only one publication. The publication is deemed to occur when the finished product is released by the publisher for sale (a matter which is, obviously, most important for the running of the statute of limitations). Damages are still calculated on the total effect of the story on all of the readers.

d. **Who May Be Liable?**

1) **Primary Publisher**
Each individual who takes part in making the publication is charged with the publication as a primary publisher; *e.g.,* a newspaper or TV station carrying a defamatory message would be viewed as a primary publisher and held responsible for that message to the same extent as the author or speaker.

2) **Republisher**
A republisher (*i.e.,* one who repeats a defamatory statement) will be held ***liable*** on the same general basis as a primary publisher. This is so even if the repeater states the source or makes it clear that she does not believe the defamation.

Note: Where there has been a republication, the original defamer's liability may be increased to encompass any new harm caused by the repetition if the republication was either (i) intended by the original defamer or (ii) reasonably foreseeable to her.

3) **Secondary Publishers**
One who is responsible only for disseminating materials that might contain

defamatory matter (*e.g.,* a vendor of newspapers, a player of a tape) is viewed as a secondary publisher. Such individuals are liable only ***if they know or should know*** of the defamatory content.

5. Damage to Plaintiff's Reputation

In ascertaining whether this element of the plaintiff's prima facie case has been satisfied, it may be necessary to distinguish between libel and slander. As will be seen below, the burden of proof as to damages (to plaintiff's reputation) may depend on this distinction.

a. General and Special Damages

1) General or Presumed Damages

General damages are presumed by law and need not be proved by the plaintiff. They are intended to compensate the plaintiff for the general injury to her reputation caused by the defamation.

Note: Constitutional free speech and press considerations may restrict an award of presumed damages when the defamation involves matters of "public concern." [Dun & Bradstreet, Inc. v. Greenmoss Builders, Inc., 472 U.S. 749 (1985)] (*See* 7.d.3), *infra.*)

2) Special Damages

Special damages in a defamation law context means that the plaintiff must specifically prove that she suffered ***pecuniary loss*** as a result of the defamatory statement's effect on her reputation, and are not proved merely by evidence of actual injury—such as the loss of friends, humiliation, or wounded feelings. The loss of a job, a prospective gift or inheritance, an advantageous business relationship, or customers are pecuniary losses such as those contemplated by the special damages requirement.

b. Libel

1) Definition

Libel is a defamatory statement recorded in ***writing or*** some ***other permanent form***. A libel may also be recorded by radio or television in some circumstances. (*See* below.)

2) Damages Rules for Libel

a) General Damages Presumed

In most jurisdictions, general damages are ***presumed by law*** for all libels; *i.e.,* special damages need not be established.

b) Libel Distinction—Minority Position

A substantial minority of courts distinguish between libel per se and libel per quod in determining whether a libel is actionable without proof of special damages.

(1) **Libel Per Se—Presumed Damages**
These courts take the position that injury to the reputation of the plaintiff is presumed by law only if the statement is libelous and defamatory on its face (libel per se). Thus, such libels are actionable without pleading or proving special damages.

(2) **Libel Per Quod—Special Damages Usually Required**
The libelous statement that is not defamatory on its face, but that requires reference to extrinsic facts to establish its defamatory content, is characterized as libel per quod by these courts. These courts generally require special damages to be pleaded and proved for such libels.

c. **Slander**

1) **Definition**
Slander is ***spoken defamation***. It is to be distinguished from libel in that the defamation is in less permanent and less physical form.

a) **Characterization of Repetitions**
Where the original defamation is libel, any repetition, even if oral, is also libel. On the other hand, the written repetition of a slander will be characterized as libel.

b) **Radio and Television Broadcasts Generally Libel**
Most courts today treat defamation in radio and television broadcasts as libel, regardless of whether it was scripted. [*See* Restatement (Third) of Torts §568A]

2) **Damages Rules for Slander**

a) **Special Damages Usually Required**
In slander, injury to reputation is ***not presumed***. Thus, ordinary slander is not actionable in the absence of pleading and proof of special damages.

b) **Slander Per Se—Injury Presumed**
If, however, the spoken defamation falls within one of four categories, characterized as slander per se, an injury to reputation is presumed without proof of special damages. These four categories are:

(1) **Business or Profession**
A defamatory statement adversely reflecting on plaintiff's abilities in his business, trade, or profession is actionable without pleading or proof of special damages. Statements that the plaintiff is dishonest or lacks the basic skill to perform his profession or carry out his office are examples of this slander per se category. The statement must, however, directly relate to plaintiff's profession, trade, or business.

Example: Statement about an engineer stating "he is a Communist" is not directly related to his trade.

(2) **Loathsome Disease**
A defamatory statement that the plaintiff is presently suffering from a foul and loathsome disease is actionable without pleading or proof of special damages. Historically, this slander per se category has been limited to venereal disease and leprosy.

(3) **Crime Involving Moral Turpitude**
A defamatory statement that the plaintiff is or was guilty of a crime involving moral turpitude is actionable without pleading or proof of special damages. Because common law crimes generally are deemed to involve moral turpitude (*e.g.,* assault, larceny, perjury), this category of slander per se incorporates a large number of statements. Thus, the allegation that a married man has a mistress implies that he is guilty of the crimes of fornication and adultery.

(4) **Unchastity of a Woman**
A defamatory statement imputing unchaste behavior to a woman is actionable without pleading or proof of special damages.

d. **"Per Se"**
"Per se" means defamatory on its face when used in libel actions and means slander within one of the four categories when used in slander actions.

6. **Falsity**
At common law, a defamatory statement was presumed to be false. The Supreme Court, however, has rejected this presumption in all cases in which the plaintiff is constitutionally required to prove some type of fault (*see* below). In these cases, the plaintiff must prove as an element of the prima facie case that the statement was false. [Philadelphia Newspapers, Inc. v. Hepps, 475 U.S. 767 (1986)]

a. **Exam Approach**
Even where the statement is true, it may nonetheless give rise to liability if it is uttered under circumstances sufficient to constitute intentional infliction of severe emotional distress or invasion of the right to privacy; hence, consider these torts as well when your exam question presents potentially defamatory statements. However, where plaintiff is a public figure who would be barred on First Amendment grounds from recovering for defamation, he will not be allowed to rely on these other tort theories. [Hustler Magazine, Inc. v. Falwell, 485 U.S. 46 (1988)]

7. **Fault on Defendant's Part**
Although at common law defamation liability could be strict, a number of Supreme Court decisions based on the First Amendment now impose a fault requirement in cases involving public figures or matters of public concern. The degree of fault to be established depends on the type of plaintiff, *i.e.,* whether he is a public official or public figure as compared with a private person involved in a matter of public concern.

a. **Public Officials—Malice Required**
A public official may not recover for defamatory words relating to his official conduct in the absence of "clear and convincing" proof that the statement was made with "malice." (*See* below.) [New York Times v. Sullivan, 376 U.S. 254 (1964)]

b. **Public Figures—Malice Required**
The rule of *New York Times v. Sullivan* has been extended to cover litigation where the plaintiff is a public figure. [Associated Press v. Walker, 388 U.S. 130 (1967); Curtis Publishing Co. v. Butts, 388 U.S. 130 (1967)]

1) **What Constitutes a Public Figure?**
A person may be deemed a "public figure" on one of two grounds: (i) where he has achieved ***such pervasive fame or notoriety*** that he becomes a public figure for all purposes and contexts (*e.g.,* celebrity sports figure); or (ii) where he voluntarily assumes a ***central role*** in a particular ***public controversy*** (*e.g.,* prominent community activist) and thereby becomes a "public figure" for that limited range of issues. [Gertz v. Robert Welch, Inc., 418 U.S. 323 (1974)]

In *Gertz,* the Court indicated that it might be possible for a person to become a public figure through no purposeful action of his own, but considered such instances to be "exceedingly rare." Subsequent cases support this interpretation. [Time, Inc. v. Firestone, 424 U.S. 448 (1976); Hutchinson v. Proxmire, 443 U.S. 111 (1979); Wolston v. Reader's Digest Association, 443 U.S. 157 (1979)]

c. **What Is Malice?**

1) **Test**

Malice was defined by the Supreme Court in *New York Times v. Sullivan* as:

a) ***Knowledge*** that the statement was false, ***or***

b) ***Reckless disregard*** as to its truth or falsity.

2) **What Constitutes "Knowledge or Reckless Falsity"?**
It must be shown that the defendant was subjectively aware that the statement he published was false or that he was subjectively reckless in making the statement. [New York Times v. Sullivan, *supra*]

a) **Reckless Conduct—Subjective Standard**
"Reckless" conduct is ***not*** measured by a reasonable person standard or by whether a reasonable person would have investigated before publishing. There must be a showing that the defendant in fact (subjectively) ***entertained serious doubts*** as to the truthfulness of his publication.

b) **Spite, etc., Not Enough**
It is not enough that the defendant is shown to have acted with spite, hatred, ill will, or intent to injure the plaintiff.

3) **Alteration of Quotation as Malice**
A journalist deliberately altering a quotation attributed to a public figure can be found to have "knowledge of falsity" if it can be established that the alteration results in a ***material change in the meaning conveyed by the statement.*** [Masson v. New Yorker Magazine, 501 U.S. 496 (1991)]

d. Private Persons Need Not Prove Malice

Where the defamatory statement relates to a ***nonpublic*** personage, there is less concern for freedom of speech and press. In addition, private individuals are more vulnerable to injury from defamation because they usually do not have as effective opportunities for rebuttal as public personages. Accordingly, defamation actions brought by private individuals are subject to constitutional limitations only when the defamatory statement involves a matter of "public concern." And even in those cases, the limitations are not as great as those established for public officials and public figures. [Gertz v. Robert Welch, Inc., *supra*]

1) Matters of Public Concern—At Least Negligence Required

When the defamatory statement involves a matter of public concern, *Gertz* imposes two restrictions on private plaintiffs: (i) it prohibits liability without fault, and (ii) it restricts the recovery of presumed or punitive damages.

a) No Liability Without Fault

Where the statement published is such that its defamatory potential was ***apparent*** to a reasonably prudent person, the plaintiff must show that the defendant permitted the false statement to appear, if not through malice, at least through ***negligence*** as to its truth or falsity.

(1) The Supreme Court has left open the question of what the fault standard would be where the statement published involved ***no*** apparent defamatory potential (*i.e.,* factual misstatements that are innocent on their face and require proof of extrinsic facts to be defamatory, such as libel per quod).

b) Damages Limited to "Actual Injury"

Assuming the defendant was in fact negligent in ascertaining the truth of what it published—but still it had no actual knowledge of the falsity, nor was it guilty of reckless disregard for the truth—damages can be recovered but are limited to the ***"actual injury"*** sustained by the plaintiff; *i.e.,* presumed damages are prohibited.

(1) "Actual Injury"

The Supreme Court has deliberately chosen not to define this term, but has stated that it is ***not limited to out-of-pocket loss***. It may include impairment of reputation and standing in the community, personal humiliation, and mental anguish and suffering (*i.e.,* an injury to reputation not resulting in special damages may still be actionable). The important point is that there must be ***competent evidence*** of "actual" injury (no presumed damages), although there need be no evidence that assigns an actual dollar value to the injury.

(2) Presumed Damages or Punitive Damages Allowable Where Malice Found

It follows that if the plaintiff cannot prove "actual injury," he cannot recover any damages, ***unless*** he can show that the publication was made with knowledge of its falsity or with reckless disregard for the

truth. There is no constitutional protection for publications made with "knowledge or reckless falsity," and hence, the plaintiff is entitled to whatever recovery is permitted under state law in such cases (*i.e.,* "presumed" or general damages and even punitive damages in appropriate cases). Note that this approach is simply a restatement of the general rule in torts that damages must be proved in negligence actions (*see infra,* III.E.) but usually are not required where the defendant is more culpable, such as for intentional torts.

2) **Matters of Purely Private Concern—No Constitutional Limitations**
When the defamatory statement involves a matter of purely private concern, the constitutional limitations established by *Gertz* do ***not*** apply; only the four elements of the common law prima facie case are required. Thus, presumed and punitive damages might be recoverable even if malice is not established.

3) **What Is a Matter of Public Concern?**
To determine whether the matter is a public or private concern, the courts will look to the content, form, and context of the publication. [Dun & Bradstreet, Inc. v. Greenmoss Builders, Inc., *supra*]

Example: In *Dun & Bradstreet,* the Court determined that a credit agency's erroneous report of plaintiff's bankruptcy, distributed to five subscribers, was speech solely in the private interest of the speaker and its specific business audience. The content (the bankruptcy of a small business), the form (a credit agency report), and the context (a communication to only five subscribers) established that a matter of public concern was not involved.

8. Defenses to Defamation

a. Consent
As with all torts, consent is a complete defense to a defamation action. (The rules relating to consent discussed under intentional torts, *supra,* also apply here.)

b. Truth
In cases of purely private concern where plaintiff is not required to prove falsity (*see* A.6., *supra*), defendant may establish the truth of the statement as a complete defense.

c. Absolute Privilege
Under certain circumstances, the speaker is not liable for defamatory statements because he enjoys an absolute privilege. Such absolute privileges are ***not*** affected by a showing of malice, abuse, or excessive provocation, as in the case of qualified privileges (*see* below). Absolute privilege exists in the following cases:

1) **Judicial Proceedings**
All statements made by the judge, jurors, counsel, witnesses, or parties in judicial proceedings are absolutely privileged. The privilege attaches to ***all*** aspects of the proceedings, *e.g.,* statements made in open court, pretrial hearing, deposition, or in any of the pleadings or other papers in the case.

There is a requirement that the statement bear some ***reasonable relationship*** to the proceedings.

2) **Legislative Proceedings**
All remarks made by either federal or state legislators in their official capacity during legislative proceedings are likewise absolutely privileged.

There is ***no requirement of a reasonable relationship*** to any matter at hand.

3) **Executive Proceedings**
A governmental executive official is absolutely privileged with respect to any statement made by her while exercising the functions of her office.

There is a requirement that the statement have some ***reasonable relationship*** to the executive matter or proceeding in which she is acting.

4) **"Compelled" Broadcast or Publication**
A radio or TV station compelled to allow a speaker the use of the air, a newspaper compelled to print public notices, etc., is absolutely privileged in an action based on the content of the compelled publication. [Farmers Educational Cooperative v. WDAY, 360 U.S. 525 (1959)]

Example: Radio station gave time to one candidate for public office and hence came under obligation to extend similar treatment to other candidates for the same office. Station had no right to censor these later speeches. Thus, no liability attaches for defamation they might contain.

5) **Communications Between Spouses**
Communications from one spouse to another are generally treated as being absolutely privileged.

Note: Some states have dealt with communications between spouses on the basis that there is no publication. This is not the preferred view.

d. **Qualified Privilege**
In certain situations, a speaker may say something defamatory without being liable because of the existence of a qualified privilege.

1) **Qualified Privilege Situations**
Included within the category of qualified privilege situations are the following:

a) **Reports of Public Proceedings**
There is a qualified privilege for reports of public hearings or meetings. This includes judicial, legislative, or executive proceedings as well as other proceedings of sufficient public interest, *e.g.,* political convention, trade association meeting, etc.

The privilege ***excuses accurate reports*** of statements that were false when made, but it ***does not excuse inaccuracies*** in the reporting of statements.

b) **Public Interest**

(1) **Publication to One Acting in Public Interest**
Statements made to those who are to take official action of some kind are qualifiedly privileged.
Example: Statements made to a parole board about a prisoner by one who opposed the grant of parole are privileged.

(2) **Fair Comment and Criticism**
One is permitted to make remarks that disparage another's acts in the course of a critique of public interest, *e.g.,* book reviews, articles on public institutions, etc. The matter commented upon must be of ***general public interest***.

Note: Obviously, the "qualified privilege" areas of subsections a) and b) have generally been preempted by the constitutional requirements imposed by *New York Times v. Sullivan* and its progeny, *supra.*

c) **Interest of Publisher**
Where defendant's statement is made to defend her own actions, property, or reputation, it may be privileged.
Example: A statement by a debtor explaining to a collection agency her reason for not paying a bill is qualifiedly privileged even if defamatory statements are contained therein.

d) **Interest of Recipient**
A qualified privilege is recognized when the recipient has an interest in the information and it is reasonable for the defendant to make the publication, *i.e.,* when she is not a mere intermeddler.
Examples: 1) A statement by a credit bureau to a customer is qualifiedly privileged.

2) A statement made by a former employer to a prospective employer about a job applicant is qualifiedly privileged.

e) **Common Interest of Publisher and Recipient**
Where there is a common interest between the publisher and the recipient, there is a qualified privilege.
Example: A statement by one board member of a charitable foundation, relating to the foundation's business, to another board member is qualifiedly privileged.

2) **Loss of Qualified Privilege Through Abuse**
A qualified privilege exists only if exercised in a reasonable manner and for a proper purpose. Thus, even though the facts might otherwise give rise to a qualified privilege situation, the actor may have lost this privilege by virtue of his conduct. There are two basic ways in which this generally occurs:

a) **Statement Not Within Scope of Privilege**
The allegedly protected statement must fall within the scope of the privilege. Hence, the privilege does not encompass the publication of irrelevant defamatory matter unconnected with the public or private interest entitled to protection.

Similarly, the privilege does not cover publication to any person whose hearing or reading of the statement could not reasonably be believed to be necessary for the furtherance of that interest.

b) **Malice**
A qualified privilege will be lost if it is shown that the speaker acted with malice. "Malice" here means that the statement was made with (i) ***knowledge*** that it was untrue or (ii) a ***reckless disregard*** as to its truth or falsity.

Note: At common law, many courts held that malice in the sense of ill will of defendant toward plaintiff would result in loss of the qualified privilege. Most courts no longer define malice in this way, however. As long as the defendant is using a proper occasion for a qualified privilege in a proper way, she will not lose this privilege simply because she bears ill will toward plaintiff.

3) **Qualified Privilege—Burden of Proof**
The ***defendant bears the burden*** of proving that a privilege exists. If the privilege is qualified, the plaintiff then bears the burden of proving that the privilege has been lost through excessive publication or malice.

9. **Mitigating Factors**
Several matters, while not defenses to an action, may be considered by the trier of fact on the issue of damages. These include:

a. **No Actual Malice**
Malice may be inferred from some statements, but if the jury is shown that there was no actual malice, such evidence is admissible to mitigate damages. To this end, defendant may prove the source of her information and grounds for her belief.

b. **Retraction**
Unless made immediately after publication so as to negate the defamatory effect of a statement, retraction does not undo the wrong. But the court may consider it to show ***lack of actual malice*** in mitigation of damages. A failure to retract after a request to do so is often allowed as evidence to the opposite effect.

c. **Anger**
Anger of the speaker may be a mitigating circumstance ***if provoked*** by the plaintiff.

B. **INVASION OF RIGHT TO PRIVACY**
The right to protection against unreasonable interferences with an individual's solitude is well recognized. The tort of invasion of privacy as it has developed, however, includes protection of

"personality" as well as protection against interference with solitude. In all, the tort includes the following four kinds of wrongs:

(i) ***Appropriation*** by defendant of plaintiff's picture or name for defendant's ***commercial advantage***;

(ii) ***Intrusion*** by the defendant upon plaintiff's ***affairs*** or ***seclusion***;

(iii) Publication by the defendant of facts placing the plaintiff in a ***false light***; and

(iv) Public disclosures of ***private facts*** about the plaintiff by the defendant.

1. Appropriation of Plaintiff's Picture or Name

a. Prima Facie Case

To establish a prima facie case for invasion of privacy—appropriation of plaintiff's picture or name—only one element need be proved:

1) ***Unauthorized use*** by defendant of plaintiff's picture or name for defendant's ***commercial advantage***.

b. Limited to Advertisement or Promotion of Product or Services

Liability is generally limited to the use of plaintiff's picture or name in connection with the promotion or advertisement of a product or service, *e.g.,* use of plaintiff's picture to advertise an automobile.

The mere fact that defendant is using plaintiff's picture or name for his own personal profit may not, by itself, be sufficient. Thus, for example, the use of a personality's name in a magazine story, even if motivated by profit, may not be actionable.

2. Intrusion on Plaintiff's Affairs or Seclusion

a. Prima Facie Case

To establish a prima facie case for invasion of privacy—intrusion on the plaintiff's affairs or seclusion—the following elements must be proved:

1) ***Act of prying or intruding*** on the affairs or seclusion of the plaintiff by the defendant;

2) The intrusion is something that would be ***highly offensive to a reasonable person***; and

3) The thing to which there is an intrusion or prying is ***"private."***

b. Invasion of Plaintiff's Private Affairs or Seclusion

For liability to attach, there must be an invasion of the plaintiff's private affairs or seclusion; *e.g.,* defendant puts a microphone in plaintiff's bedroom.

c. **Intrusion Highly Offensive to a Reasonable Person**
For liability to attach, the intrusion by defendant must be something that would be highly offensive to a reasonable person.

d. **Intrusion Must Be into Something "Private"**
For liability to attach, the intrusion by defendant must be into something within the plaintiff's own private domain. Thus, for example, taking pictures of a person in a public place is not actionable.

3. **Publication of Facts Placing Plaintiff in False Light**

a. **Prima Facie Case**
To establish a prima facie case for invasion of privacy—publication by defendant of facts placing plaintiff in a false light—the following elements must be proved:

1) Publication of ***facts*** about plaintiff by defendant placing plaintiff in a ***false light*** in the public eye;

2) The "false light" is something that would be ***highly offensive to a reasonable person*** under the circumstances; and

3) ***Malice*** on the part of defendant where the published matter is in the ***public interest***.

b. **Publication or Public Disclosure**
For liability to attach, there must be ***publicity*** concerning the "false light" facts; this requires ***more*** than "publication" in the defamation sense.

c. **What Is "False Light"?**
A fact will be deemed to present plaintiff in a false light if it attributes to him:

(i) Views that he does not hold, or

(ii) Actions that he did not take.

Note: This element involves falsity and, as such, may also involve defamation if the falsity affects reputation.

d. **Highly Offensive to Reasonable Person**
To be actionable, this "false light" must be something that would be highly offensive to a reasonable person under the circumstances.

e. **Malice Necessary Where in Public Interest**
In *Time, Inc. v. Hill*, 385 U.S. 374 (1967), a case involving this particular invasion of privacy branch, the Supreme Court held that the First Amendment prohibits recovery for invasion of privacy in cases where the published matter is in the public interest, unless the plaintiff establishes that the defendant acted with malice. Malice here, as in *New York Times v. Sullivan*, goes to knowledge of falsity or reckless disregard for the truth.

After *Gertz* and *Dun & Bradstreet* (discussed *supra* under Defamation), the Supreme Court may be expected to give the states a slightly larger scope in which to protect privacy where a public figure is not involved. Thus, where the public interest in the information is not overriding and where the risks to the privacy interests of the private person are clear on the face of the material to a reasonably prudent publisher, the Supreme Court may choose in the future to permit an action in privacy without proof of malice in the *New York Times* sense. However, at least in public figure cases, the *Time, Inc. v. Hill* requirement of malice still holds. [*See* Hustler Magazine, Inc. v. Falwell, A.6., *supra*]

4. Public Disclosure of Private Facts About Plaintiff

a. Prima Facie Case

To establish a prima facie case for invasion of privacy—public disclosure of private facts about plaintiff—the following elements must be proved:

1) Publication or public disclosure by defendant of ***private*** information about the plaintiff; and

2) The matter made public is such that its disclosure would be ***highly offensive to a reasonable person***.

b. Publication or Public Disclosure

For liability to attach, there must be publicity concerning a private fact; *i.e.,* the disclosure must be a public disclosure, not a private one.

c. Facts Must Be Private

The facts disclosed must be "private." For example, there is no liability for matters of public record, since these facts are not private.

d. Disclosure Highly Offensive to Reasonable Person

To be actionable, the disclosure of private facts must be such that a reasonable person would find it highly offensive.

Example: Barbara showed, in a public exhibition, a movie of Sandy's cesarean operation. This may be actionable.

e. Facts May Be True

Liability may attach under this privacy branch if the elements of a prima facie case are satisfied even though the factual statement about the plaintiff is true.

f. Constitutional Privilege

The rationale of *Time, Inc. v. Hill* appears to encompass this branch of the invasion of privacy tort as well. In other words, if the matter is one of ***legitimate public interest***, the publication is privileged if made without malice.

1) Effect of Passage of Time

The mere passage of time does not preclude the "public interest" characterization of a publication. Hence, it has frequently been held that the life of one ***formerly*** in the public eye has become public property, even though that person is no longer in the public eye.

Example: A magazine published the life history of a former child prodigy. This may be construed to be a matter in the public interest.

2) **Absolute Privilege with Regard to Matters of Public Record**
Where the matters republished are taken from official public records, there is an absolute constitutional privilege (*e.g.*, rape victim's name obtained from police records or court proceedings used in newspaper article).

5. **Causation**
The invasion of plaintiff's interest in privacy must have been ***proximately caused*** by defendant's conduct.

6. **Proof of Special Damages Unnecessary**
In an action for invasion of right to privacy, the plaintiff need not plead and prove special damages, provided the elements of a prima facie case are present. In other words, emotional distress and mental anguish ***are*** sufficient damages.

7. **Basis of Liability**
The basis for liability in a privacy action may rest upon an ***intentional*** or ***negligent*** invasion. It also appears that ***strict liability*** may be a sufficient basis (as in defamation).

8. **Defenses to Invasions of Privacy**

a. **Consent**
Consent is a defense to an action for invasion of the right to privacy. Some states, by statute, require that the consent be in writing. Here, as in all consent defense situations, the defendant may nonetheless be liable if the consent granted has been exceeded.
Example: Plaintiff consents to be interviewed, and a picture taken during the interview is used in conjunction with an advertisement for a product. Liability may attach.

Note that mistake, even if reasonable, as to whether consent was given (which in fact it was not) is ***not*** a valid defense.

b. **Defamation Defenses**
Those defenses to actions for defamation that are based on ***absolute and qualified privileges*** appear applicable to those invasion of right to privacy actions predicated on publication grounds, *i.e.,* "false light" and "public disclosure of private facts" actions. Thus, for example, one may have an absolute privilege to comment as a participant in judicial proceedings or a qualified privilege to report public proceedings.

Note: Truth is ***not*** a good defense to most invasion of privacy actions. Similarly, inadvertence, good faith, and lack of malice generally are ***not*** good defenses.

9. **Right of Privacy—Miscellaneous**

a. **Right Is Personal**
The right of privacy is a personal right and does not extend to members of a family. The right of privacy does not survive the death of plaintiff and is not assignable.

b. **Not Applicable to Corporations**
Only individuals may avail themselves of a right to privacy action; it does not apply to corporations.

C. MISREPRESENTATION

1. Intentional Misrepresentation (Fraud, Deceit)

a. **Prima Facie Case**
To establish a prima facie case of intentional misrepresentation, fraud, or deceit, the following elements must be proved:

1) ***Misrepresentation*** made by defendant;

2) ***Scienter***;

3) An ***intent to induce*** plaintiff's ***reliance*** on the misrepresentation;

4) ***Causation*** (*i.e.,* actual reliance on the misrepresentation);

5) ***Justifiable reliance*** by plaintiff on the misrepresentation; and

6) ***Damages***.

b. **The Misrepresentation**
Usually, there is a requirement that the false representation be of a ***material past or present fact***. In certain cases, however, a misrepresentation of opinion may be actionable. (This is really a justifiable reliance question. *See* below.)

1) **No General Duty to Disclose**
No general duty to disclose a material fact or opinion to one is imposed upon another. Thus, simple failure to disclose a material fact or opinion does not generally satisfy the first element of this cause of action. A few general ***exceptions*** exist, however:

a) Defendant stands in such a ***fiduciary relationship*** to plaintiff as would call for a duty of disclosure.

b) Defendant selling real property knows that plaintiff is unaware of, and cannot reasonably discover, material information about the transaction (*e.g.,* builder does not tell buyer that the house was built on a landfill).

c) Where defendant speaks and her ***utterance deceives plaintiff,*** she will be under a duty to inform plaintiff of the true facts.

2) **Active Concealment Actionable**
Where a person actively conceals a material fact, she is under a duty to disclose this fact, and failure to do so satisfies the first element of a prima facie case (*e.g.,* salesperson turns back odometer on an automobile).

c. **Scienter**

To establish a prima facie case, plaintiff must prove that defendant made the representation knowing it to be false or, alternatively, that it was made with reckless disregard as to its truth or falsity. This element of the prima facie case is often given the technical name of "scienter."

Example: A corporation's president stated falsely that last year's profits were $100,000 without having looked at a profit and loss statement. Scienter is present.

Note: If scienter is not present, defendant may still be liable for negligent misrepresentation (discussed below).

d. **Intent to Induce Reliance**

The defendant must have intended to induce plaintiff or a class of persons to which plaintiff belongs to act or refrain from acting in reliance on the misrepresentation.

1) **Continuous Deception Exception**

An exception exists where the misrepresentation is a "continuous deception," *e.g.,* mislabeling of product by manufacturer, misrepresentation in negotiable instrument. In such cases, it is not necessary that the reliance of a particular plaintiff be intended. Anyone into whose possession the product or instrument has come may bring an action.

2) **Third-Party Reliance Problem**

One recurring problem is where the defendant communicates directly to one person and another relies upon the misrepresentation. In such cases, the defendant is viewed as intending to deceive the person who relies upon the misrepresentation ***if the defendant could reasonably foresee that the plaintiff will have such reliance.***

Example: Chauncey sends an intentionally false profit statement to a stockbroker, and a customer of the stockbroker relies on this statement to his detriment. Liability exists.

e. **Causation**

Plaintiff must prove that the misrepresentation played a substantial part in inducing him to act as he did. In short, plaintiff must prove "actual reliance."

f. **Justifiable Reliance**

1) **Reliance on Fact Almost Always Justified**

Even though it may have been intended by defendant that plaintiff rely on the representation, plaintiff must nonetheless prove that such reliance was "justified." As a practical matter, the reliance of plaintiff on representations of fact is almost always justified. Only where the facts are obviously false is such reliance not justified.

a) **No Duty to Investigate**

Courts do not impose a duty on plaintiff to investigate the veracity of defendant's representation of fact. This is so even though it would be easy for

plaintiff to do this. If, however, plaintiff does in fact investigate, he may not rely on representations by defendant inconsistent with the facts reasonably ascertainable from such investigation.

2) Reliance on Opinion Usually Not Justifiable

As a general matter, reliance on false statements of opinion, value, or quality will be viewed as unjustified. Some exceptions to this general rule do exist, however.

a) Superior Knowledge of Defendant

If the defendant making a false representation of opinion has a superior knowledge of the subject matter, then reliance by a person without such knowledge may be viewed as justified.

b) Statements of Law

Statements of law are treated as statements of opinion if they are merely predictions as to the legal consequences of facts; they may not be justifiably relied upon unless the statement is made by a lawyer to a layperson, in which case the "superior knowledge" rule operates. On the other hand, a statement of law that includes an express or implied misrepresentation of fact is actionable.

Example: Defendant falsely states that the house she is offering for sale conforms to the city plumbing and electrical requirements. Liability exists.

c) Statements of Future Events

Statements of future events are viewed as statements of opinion and may not be justifiably relied upon. An exception exists if the statement of future events may be characterized as a statement of "present intent," which is viewed as a statement of fact.

Example: Defendant promises to pay plaintiff $50 per month installments for the next two years. This may be viewed as a statement of "fact." (Characterization of statements of future events as "present intent" statements is generally limited to those cases where the defendant has control over the future event, as in this example.)

g. Damages

In an action for intentional misrepresentation, plaintiff may recover ***only*** if he has suffered ***actual pecuniary loss*** as a result of the reliance on the false statement. Most courts use a contract measure of damages—plaintiff may recover the "benefit of the bargain," *i.e.,* the value of the property as represented less the value of the property as it actually is.

2. Negligent Misrepresentation

a. Prima Facie Case

The prima facie case for negligent misrepresentation is similar to that for intentional misrepresentation. The following elements must be proved:

1) ***Misrepresentation*** made by defendant in ***business or professional capacity***;

2) ***Breach of duty*** toward ***particular plaintiff***;

3) ***Causation***;

4) ***Justifiable reliance*** by plaintiff upon the misrepresentation; and

5) ***Damages***.

b. Liability Confined to Commercial Transactions
The ambit of liability for negligent misrepresentation is much more confined than that for deceit. Generally, the action is confined to only those misrepresentations made in a commercial setting, *i.e.,* made by the defendant in a business or professional capacity.

c. Duty Owed Only to Particular Plaintiff Whose Reliance Contemplated
Liability attaches for a negligent misrepresentation only if reliance by the particular plaintiff could be contemplated. In other words, defendant is under a duty of care only to those persons to whom the representation was made or to specific persons who defendant ***knew*** would rely on it. Foreseeability that the statement will be communicated to third persons may be sufficient to impose liability for deceit (above), but it does ***not*** suffice for negligent misrepresentation in most states.

Example: Chauncey sends a negligently prepared profit statement to a stockbroker, and a customer of the stockbroker relies upon this statement to her detriment. Liability does not exist. (*Compare* example in section 1.d.2), *supra*.)

d. Other Elements
The elements of causation, justifiable reliance, and damages are analyzed the same as under intentional misrepresentation.

D. INTERFERENCE WITH BUSINESS RELATIONS

To establish a prima facie case for interference with contract or prospective economic advantage, the following elements must be proved:

(i) Existence of a ***valid contractual relationship*** between plaintiff and a third party or a ***valid business expectancy*** of plaintiff;

(ii) ***Defendant's knowledge*** of the relationship or expectancy;

(iii) ***Intentional interference*** by defendant that induces a breach or termination of the relationship or expectancy; and

(iv) ***Damage*** to plaintiff.

1. Not Limited to Existing Contracts
Plaintiff has a cause of action not only for interference with existing contracts but also for interference with probable future business relationships for which plaintiff has a reasonable expectation of financial benefit.

Example: A real estate broker may have a cause of action against one who improperly diverts potential buyers of the property that the broker was selling.

2. Intent Required
Defendant must have ***intended*** to interfere with the existing or prospective contractual relationships of plaintiff. Most courts do not permit recovery for negligent interference

with contract in the absence of some independent tort, such as negligent misrepresentation (*supra*).

3. Damages

Plaintiff must prove actual damage from the interference, but may also recover mental distress damages and punitive damages in appropriate cases.

4. Privileges

An interferor's conduct may be privileged where it is a proper attempt to obtain business for the interferor or protect its interests.

Example: A bank collecting on an existing promissory note is privileged to induce the debtor to pay it off, even if that will cause the debtor to fail to satisfy obligations owing to other parties.

Several factors will determine whether a privilege exists:

a. Type of Business Relationship Involved

Interference with a prospective business relationship that the plaintiff is pursuing is more likely to be privileged than interference with the plaintiff's existing contract with a third party.

b. Means of Persuasion Used

Interference using legitimate and commercially acceptable means of persuasion is more likely to be privileged than interference using illegal or threatening tactics.

c. Whether Defendant Is a Competitor of Plaintiff

Interference with the plaintiff's prospective business relationships is likely to be privileged if the defendant is a competitor of the plaintiff pursuing those same prospective customers.

d. Defendant's Relationship with the Third Party

Interference may be privileged if the defendant has responsibility for, or a financial interest in, the third party, or if the third party has sought the business advice of the defendant.

E. WRONGFUL INSTITUTION OF LEGAL PROCEEDINGS

1. Malicious Prosecution

a. Prima Facie Case

To establish a prima facie case for malicious prosecution, the following elements must be proved:

1) ***Institution of criminal proceedings*** against plaintiff;

2) Termination ***favorable to plaintiff***;

3) ***Absence of probable cause*** for prosecution;

4) ***Improper purpose*** of defendant; and

5) ***Damages***.

b. **Institution of Criminal Proceedings**
For liability to attach for malicious prosecution, the defendant must have initiated a ***criminal*** proceeding against the plaintiff, such as by filing a police report to procure the plaintiff's arrest. The "initiation" of the proceeding can be by warrant, arrest, indictment, etc.

1) **Defendant Must Initiate Proceedings**
Remember, the defendant must have initiated the proceedings himself. Simply giving the full story to the prosecutor, whereupon the prosecutor decides to prosecute, is not sufficient for a later malicious prosecution action against the informer in most states.

2) **Prosecuting Attorneys Privileged**
Prosecuting attorneys are absolutely privileged and cannot be sued for malicious prosecution (even when they act in bad faith and without probable cause).

c. **Termination of Proceedings in Plaintiff's Favor**
The plaintiff may bring such an action only if the prior proceedings were terminated in her favor; *e.g.,* she was acquitted, the case was dismissed, charges were dropped, etc. The termination must demonstrate the ***innocence*** of the accused.

d. **Absence of Probable Cause for Prior Proceedings**
To recover, the plaintiff must establish that the defendant initiated the prior proceedings without probable cause. She may do so by showing ***either*** (i) that there were insufficient facts for a reasonable person to believe that plaintiff was guilty; ***or*** (ii) that the defendant did not actually believe the plaintiff to be guilty.

1) **Effect of Indictment**
Note that indictment by a grand jury is prima facie evidence of probable cause. However, failure of a grand jury to indict is ***not*** evidence that there was no probable cause.

2) **Prior Action Based on Advice**
If defendant instituted the prior proceedings on advice of counsel after full disclosure of the facts, this establishes probable cause.

e. **Improper Purpose in Bringing Suit**
For purposes of malicious prosecution, the malice or improper purpose element of the prima facie case is satisfied when it is shown that defendant's primary purpose in instituting the prior action was something other than bringing a person to justice.

f. **Damages**
Damages must be ***proved.*** Plaintiff may recover damages for all harms that are the proximate result of defendant's wrong, *e.g.,* expenses in defending criminal suit, embarrassment, etc. Punitive damages are often awarded, since defendant's improper purpose is, of course, already proved to establish the case.

g. **False Arrest Distinguished**
In a false arrest situation, the false arrest itself is illegal, *e.g.,* made without a valid warrant. In a malicious prosecution situation, the arrest itself is carried out in a lawful manner, but is pursuant to a maliciously instituted prosecution.

2. **Wrongful Civil Proceedings**
Most jurisdictions have extended the malicious prosecution action to encompass wrongfully instituted civil cases. The same general rules govern as apply in malicious prosecution. However, lack of probable cause is harder to show in civil actions because reasonable people would more readily file a doubtful case where the only consequences to the person sued are civil.

3. **Abuse of Process**
It is a tort to use any form of process—civil or criminal—to bring about a result other than that for which the form of process was intended; *e.g.,* defendant garnished an account to force plaintiff to sign a lease. The prima facie elements of the action are (i) the wrongful use of the process for an ulterior purpose, and (ii) some definite act or threat against plaintiff to accomplish the ulterior purpose.

   a. **Malicious Prosecution Distinguished**
   If the defendant uses the particular machinery of the law for the immediate purpose for which it was designed, he is not liable for abuse of process notwithstanding any malicious intent. Abuse of process is not the wrongful institution of the action or proceeding, but rather the improper use of process in connection therewith. Hence, the merits of the action itself are of no relevance. In contrast to malicious prosecution, therefore, neither want of probable cause nor favorable termination are elements of the tort.

III. NEGLIGENCE

A. PRIMA FACIE CASE

To establish a prima facie case for negligence, the following elements must be proved:

1. The existence of a ***duty*** on the part of the defendant ***to conform to a specific standard of conduct*** for the protection of the plaintiff against an unreasonable risk of injury;
2. ***Breach*** of that duty by the defendant;
3. That the breach of duty by the defendant was the ***actual and proximate cause*** of the plaintiff's injury; and
4. ***Damage*** to the plaintiff's person or property.

B. THE DUTY OF CARE

1. **Introduction—General Duty of Care**
A general duty of care is imposed on all human activity. When a person engages in an activity, he is under a legal duty to act as an ***ordinary, prudent, reasonable person***. It is presumed that an ordinary, prudent, reasonable person will take precautions against creating unreasonable risks of injury to other persons. Thus, if the defendant's conduct creates an unreasonable risk of injury to persons in the position of the plaintiff, the general duty of care extends from the defendant to the plaintiff. No duty is imposed on a person to take precautions against events that cannot reasonably be foreseen. Therefore, if at the time of the negligent conduct, no foreseeable risk of injury to a person in the position of the plaintiff is created by the defendant's act, the general duty of care does not extend from the defendant to the plaintiff.

In addition, certain other factors such as the status of the parties (*e.g.,* owners or occupiers of land) or statutes may limit or extend this general duty.

2. To Whom Is the Duty of Care Owed?

a. General Rule—Foreseeable Plaintiffs
A duty of care is owed only to foreseeable plaintiffs.

b. The "Unforeseeable" Plaintiff Problem

1) The Problem
The "unforeseeable" plaintiff problem arises when defendant breaches a duty to one plaintiff (P1) and also causes injury thereby to a second plaintiff (P2) to whom a foreseeable risk of injury might or might not have been created at the time of the original negligent act.

Example: An employee of Defendant negligently aided a passenger boarding the train, causing the passenger to drop a package. The package exploded, causing a scale a substantial distance away to fall upon a second passenger. Is the second passenger a foreseeable plaintiff?

2) The Solution(s)
Defendant's liability to P2 will depend upon whether the Andrews or Cardozo view in *Palsgraf* is adopted. [Palsgraf v. Long Island Railroad, 248 N.Y. 339 (1928)] Most courts considering this issue have followed the Cardozo view.

a) Andrews View
According to the Andrews view in *Palsgraf,* the second plaintiff (P2) may establish the existence of a duty extending from the defendant to her by showing that the defendant has breached a duty he owed P1. In short, defendant owes a duty of care to ***anyone*** who suffers injuries as a proximate result of his breach of duty to ***someone***.

b) Cardozo View
According to the Cardozo view in *Palsgraf,* the second plaintiff (P2) can recover only if she can establish that a reasonable person would have foreseen a risk of injury to her in the circumstances, *i.e.,* that she was located in a foreseeable ***"zone of danger."***

c. Specific Situations

1) Rescuers
A rescuer is a foreseeable plaintiff as long as the rescue is not wanton; hence, defendant is liable if he negligently puts himself or a third person in peril and plaintiff is injured in attempting a rescue. Note, however, that the "firefighter's rule" (*infra*, 3.d.2)c)(2)(c)) may bar firefighters and police officers, on public policy or assumption of risk grounds, from recovering for injuries caused by the risks of a rescue.

2) Prenatal Injuries
Prenatal injuries are actionable; *i.e.,* a duty of care is owed toward a fetus. The

fetus must have been ***viable*** at the time of injury. (Most states also permit a wrongful death action (VII.C.2., *infra*) if the fetus dies from the injuries.)

a) **"Wrongful Life" Action Not Recognized**
In most states, the failure to diagnose a congenital defect of the fetus or to properly perform a contraceptive procedure does ***not*** permit the unwanted child to recover damages for "wrongful life," even if the child is born handicapped.

b) **Compare—"Wrongful Birth" and "Wrongful Pregnancy"**
The child's parents, however, ***do*** have an action: either for failure to diagnose the defect ("wrongful birth") or for failure to properly perform a contraceptive procedure ("wrongful pregnancy"). The mother can recover damages for the unwanted labor (medical expenses and pain and suffering). If the child has a defect, parents may recover the additional medical expenses to care for the child and, in some states, damages for emotional distress. If the child is born healthy in a wrongful pregnancy case, most cases do ***not*** permit the parents to recover child-rearing expenses, just damages for the unwanted labor.

3) **Intended Beneficiaries of Economic Transactions**
A third party for whose economic benefit a legal or business transaction is made (*e.g.*, the beneficiary of a will) is owed a duty of care if the defendant could reasonably foresee harm to that party if the transaction is done negligently.

3. What Is Applicable Standard of Care?

a. Basic Standard—The Reasonable Person
Defendant's conduct is measured against the reasonable, ordinary, prudent person. This reasonable person has the following characteristics, measured by an ***objective*** standard:

1) **Physical Characteristics—Same as Defendant's**
Notwithstanding application of the objective standard, the "reasonable person" is considered to have the ***same physical characteristics as the defendant***. However, a person is expected to know his physical handicaps and is under a duty to exercise the care of a person with such knowledge; *e.g.,* it may be negligent for an epileptic to drive a car.

2) **Average Mental Ability**
Defendant must act as would a person with average mental ability. Unlike the rule as to physical characteristics, ***individual mental handicaps are not considered***; *i.e.,* low IQ is no excuse. Likewise, insanity is no defense, and the defendant is held to the standard of a reasonable person under the circumstances.

3) **Same Knowledge as Average Member of Community**
Defendant is deemed to have knowledge of things known by the average member of the community, *e.g.,* that fire is hot. Again, the individual shortcomings of the particular defendant are ***not*** considered. On the other hand, a defendant with knowledge superior to that of the average person is required to use that knowledge.

b. **Particular Standards of Conduct**

Some persons are held to a standard of conduct different from that of the ordinary person.

1) **Professionals**

A person who is a professional or has special skills (*e.g.,* doctor, lawyer, airplane mechanic, etc.) is required to possess and exercise the knowledge and skill of a member of the profession or occupation in good standing in similar communities.

The professional must also use such superior judgment, skill, and knowledge as he actually possesses. Thus, a specialist might be held liable where a general practitioner would not. For medical specialists, a "national" standard of care applies.

a) **Duty to Disclose Risks of Treatment**

A doctor proposing a course of treatment or a surgical procedure has a duty to provide the patient with enough information about its risks to enable the patient to make an ***informed consent*** to the treatment. If an undisclosed risk was serious enough that a reasonable person in the patient's position would have withheld consent to the treatment, the doctor has breached this duty.

Example: Patient consents to an operation not necessary to save his life. Patient is not informed that there is a 40% probability of paralysis in such operations, and paralysis results. Since a reasonable person would not have consented to the operation had the risks been disclosed, Doctor has breached his duty of disclosure.

2) **Children**

A majority of courts take the view that a child is required to conform to the standard of care of a child of ***like age, education, intelligence, and experience***. This permits a ***subjective*** evaluation of these factors.

a) **Minimum Age for Capacity to Be Negligent**

There is a minimum age for which it is meaningful to speak of a child being capable of conforming his conduct to a standard of care. Most courts, however, do not fix this age at any arbitrary figure. Each case is dealt with in terms of whether there is evidence that the individual child—plaintiff or defendant—has the experience, intelligence, maturity, training, or capacity to conform his conduct to a standard of care. It is unlikely, nonetheless, that a court would view a child ***below the age of four*** as having the capacity to be negligent. Or, to put it another way, it is unlikely that a court would impose a legal duty to avoid injuries to others or himself upon a child who is under four.

b) **Children Engaged in Adult Activities**

Where a child engages in an activity that is normally one that only adults engage in, most cases hold that he will be required to conform to the same standard of care as an adult in such an activity, *e.g.,* driving an automobile, flying an airplane, driving a motorboat.

3) **Common Carriers and Innkeepers**
Common carriers and innkeepers are required to exercise a very high degree of care toward their passengers and guests; *i.e.,* they are ***liable for slight negligence***.

4) **Automobile Driver to Guest**
In most jurisdictions today, the duty owed by the driver of an automobile to a rider is one of ordinary care.

a) **Guest Statutes**
A few states have guest statutes. Under these statutes, the driver's only duty to a nonpaying rider is to ***refrain from gross or wanton and willful misconduct***. Note that guest statutes do not apply to "passengers," *i.e.,* riders who contribute toward the expense of the ride; they are owed a duty of ordinary care.

5) **Bailment Duties**
In a bailment relationship, the bailor transfers physical possession of an item of personal property to the bailee without a transfer of title. The bailee acquires the right to possess the property in accordance with the terms of the bailment. A bailment obligates the bailee to return the item of personal property to the bailor or otherwise dispose of it according to the bailment terms.

Example: When the owner of a computer delivers it to a technician to be repaired, the technician becomes a bailee of the computer and the owner is the bailor.

a) **Duties Owed by Bailee**

(1) **Sole Benefit of Bailor Bailment**
If the bailment is for the sole benefit of the bailor (*e.g.,* the bailor asks his neighbor (the bailee) to take in the bailor's mail while he is on vacation), the bailee is liable only for ***gross negligence***.

(2) **Sole Benefit of Bailee Bailment**
If the bailment is for the sole benefit of the bailee (*e.g.,* the bailor gratuitously loans her lawnmower to the bailee), the bailee is liable even for ***slight negligence.***

(3) **Mutual Benefit Bailments**
If the bailment is for the mutual benefit of the bailor and bailee (typically a bailment for hire such as in the computer example above), the bailee must exercise ***ordinary due care***.

(4) **Modern Trend**
Today the trend is away from such classifications and toward a rule that considers whether the bailee exercised ordinary care under all the circumstances. These circumstances include, *e.g.,* value of the goods, type of bailment, custom of a trade, etc.

b) **Duties Owed by Bailor**

(1) **Sole Benefit of Bailee Bailments**
If the bailment is for the sole benefit of the bailee (*e.g.*, a gratuitous loan), the bailor need only inform the bailee of known dangerous defects in the chattel. There is no duty with regard to unknown defects.

(2) **Bailments for Hire**
If the bailment is for hire, the bailor owes a duty to inform the bailee of defects known to him, or of which he would have known by the exercise of reasonable diligence.

c. **Standard of Care in Emergency Situations**
The existence of an emergency, presenting little time for reflection, may be considered as among the circumstances under which the defendant acted; *i.e.,* he must act as the reasonable person would under the same emergency. The emergency may ***not*** be considered, however, if it is of the defendant's own making.

d. **Standard of Care Owed by Owners and/or Occupiers of Land**
In this section, duty problems are resolved by application of special rules that have been developed imposing duties on individuals because of their relationship to property. In some cases, the duty of the owner or occupier depends on whether the injury occurred on or off his premises; in others it depends on the legal status of the plaintiff in regard to the property, *i.e.,* trespasser, licensee, or invitee.

1) **Duty of Possessor to Those Off the Premises**

a) **Natural Conditions**
The general rule is that a landowner owes ***no duty*** to protect one outside the premises from natural conditions on the land.
Example: One is not liable for bugs that live in trees on one's land but that "visit" the neighbors from time to time.

Note: An exception exists for decaying trees next to sidewalks or streets in urban areas.

b) **Artificial Conditions**
As a general rule, there is also ***no duty*** owing for artificial conditions. Two major ***exceptions*** exist, however.

(1) **Unreasonably Dangerous Conditions**
A landowner is liable for damage caused by unreasonably dangerous artificial conditions or structures abutting adjacent land.
Example: While one would not be liable for natural collections of ice on the sidewalk, he might be liable for negligently permitting water to drain off his roof and form ice on the sidewalk.

(2) **Duty to Protect Passersby**
A landowner also has a duty to ***take due precautions*** to protect persons passing by from dangerous conditions, *e.g.,* by erecting a barricade to keep people from falling into an excavation at the edge of the property.

c) **Conduct of Persons on Property**
An owner of land has a duty to exercise reasonable care with respect to his own activities on the land and to control the conduct of others on his property so as to avoid unreasonable risk of harm to others outside the property.

2) **Duties of Possessor to Those on the Premises**
In most jurisdictions, the nature of a duty owed by an owner or occupier of land to those on the premises for dangerous conditions on the land depends on the legal status of the plaintiff in regard to the property, *i.e.,* trespasser, licensee, or invitee.

a) **Duty Owed to a Trespasser**

(1) **Definition of Trespasser**
A trespasser is one who comes onto the land without permission or privilege.

(2) **Duty Owed Undiscovered Trespassers**
A landowner owes ***no duty*** to an undiscovered trespasser. He has no duty to inspect in order to ascertain whether persons are coming onto his property.

(3) **Duty Owed Discovered Trespassers**
Once a landowner discovers the presence of a trespasser, he is under a duty to exercise ordinary care to ***warn*** the trespasser of, or to ***make safe, artificial conditions*** known to the landowner that involve a ***risk of death or serious bodily harm*** and that the trespasser is unlikely to discover. There is no duty owed for natural conditions and less dangerous artificial conditions.

The owner or occupier also has a duty to exercise reasonable care in the exercise of ***"active operations"*** on the property.

(a) **When Is a Trespasser "Discovered"?**
A trespasser is discovered, of course, when she is actually noticed on the property by the owner or occupier. But in addition, a trespasser is viewed as discovered if the owner or occupier is notified by information sufficient for a reasonable person to conclude that someone is on the property.

(4) **Duty Owed Anticipated Trespassers**
The majority of states now treat anticipated trespassers on generally the same basis as discovered trespassers in terms of the duty owed them by the landowner.

(a) **When Is a Trespasser "Anticipated"?**
An "anticipated trespasser" situation arises where the landowner knows or should reasonably know of the presence of trespassers who constantly cross over a section of his land. (Although note that

if the owner has posted "no trespassing" signs, this might serve to convert these "anticipated" trespassers into "undiscovered" trespassers.)

(5) "Attractive Nuisance" Doctrine

Most courts impose upon a landowner the duty to exercise ***ordinary care*** to avoid reasonably foreseeable risk of harm to children caused by artificial conditions on his property. Under the general rule, to assess this special duty upon the owner or occupier of land in regard to children on his property, the plaintiff must show the following:

(i) There is a dangerous condition present on the land of which the owner is or should be aware;

(ii) The owner knows or should know that young persons frequent the vicinity of this dangerous condition;

(iii) The condition is likely to cause injury, *i.e.,* is dangerous, because of the child's inability to appreciate the risk; and

(iv) The expense of remedying the situation is slight compared with the magnitude of the risk.

(a) What Is a Dangerous Condition?

As noted above, a dangerous condition exists where something on the land is likely to cause injury to children because of their inability to appreciate the risk. This usually is an artificial condition, but in some circumstances a natural condition might suffice.

1] Where Applied

The attractive nuisance doctrine has been applied to abandoned automobiles, lumber piles, sand bins, and elevators. Bodies of water are generally not dangerous conditions because the dangers are viewed as obvious and well-known. If, however, a body of water contains elements of unusual danger to children, it may be characterized as a dangerous condition, *e.g.,* logs or plants floating in water, or a thick scum that appears to be a path on the water.

(b) Foreseeability of Harm Is True Basis of Liability

Under the traditional "attractive nuisance" doctrine, it was necessary for the child/plaintiff to establish that she was lured onto the property by the attractive nuisance/dangerous condition. This no longer is the case. Most jurisdictions have substantially revised their attractive nuisance doctrines to bring them within general negligence concepts. Foreseeability of harm to a child is the true basis of liability and the element of attraction is important only insofar as it indicates that the presence of children should have been anticipated by the landowner.

(6) **Duty of Easement and License Holders to Trespassers**
While employees and independent contractors acting on behalf of the landowner have the status of the landowner, persons with an easement or license to use the land do not; they must exercise reasonable care to protect the trespasser.

Example: Power Company obtains an easement from Leonard to run high-tension wires across Leonard's land. Because of Power Company's negligent failure to maintain the wires, one of them falls and injures Plaintiff, an undiscovered trespasser on Leonard's land. Power Company is liable to Plaintiff.

b) **Duty Owed to a Licensee**

(1) **Definition of Licensee**
A licensee is one who enters on the land with the landowner's permission, express or implied, for her ***own purpose or business*** rather than for the landowner's benefit.

(2) **Duty Owed**
The owner or occupier has a ***duty to warn*** the licensee of a dangerous condition ***known*** to the owner or occupier that creates an unreasonable risk of harm to the licensee and that the licensee is unlikely to discover.

(a) **No Duty to Inspect**
The owner or occupier has ***no duty*** to a licensee ***to inspect*** for defects ***nor to repair*** known defects.

(b) **Duty of Care for Active Operations**
The owner or occupier also has a duty to ***exercise reasonable care*** in the conduct of "active operations" for the protection of the licensee whom he knows to be on the property.

(3) **Social Guests Are Licensees**
The social guest is a licensee. Performance of minor services for the host does not make the guest an invitee.

c) **Duty Owed to an Invitee**

(1) **Definition of Invitee**
An invitee is a person who enters onto the premises in response to an express or implied invitation of the landowner. Basically, there are two classes of invitees:

(a) Those who enter as members of the public for a purpose for which the land is ***held open to the public,*** *e.g.,* museums, churches, airports; and

(b) Those who enter for a purpose ***connected with the business*** or other interests of the landowner or occupier, *e.g.,* store customers

and persons accompanying them, employees, persons making deliveries, etc.

(2) **Characterization of Privileged Entrants**
There may be a problem of characterization regarding persons entering the premises in exercise of a privilege, *e.g.*, police, firefighters, census takers, etc. In some situations, they are characterized as licensees, in others as invitees. The following rules should be noted:

(a) An entrant serving some ***purpose of the possessor*** generally is treated as an invitee, *e.g.*, garbage collectors, mail carriers, etc.

(b) One who comes ***under normal circumstances during working hours*** generally is treated as an invitee, *e.g.*, census takers, health inspectors, etc.

(c) Under the ***"firefighter's rule,"*** police officers and firefighters are generally treated like licensees rather than invitees, based on public policy or assumption of risk grounds. They cannot recover for a landowner's failure to inspect or repair dangerous conditions that are an inherent risk of their law enforcement or firefighting activity.

(3) **Scope of Invitation**
A person loses her status as an invitee if she exceeds the scope of the invitation—if she goes into a portion of the premises where her invitation cannot reasonably be said to extend. (Note that the invitation normally does extend to the entrance and steps of a building.)

Example: Gas station customer, buying gas, loses status as invitee when she leaves pumps and falls into grease pit inside station. (Reversion to licensee, perhaps even trespasser, status.)

(4) **Duty Owed**
The landowner owes an invitee a general duty to use reasonable and ordinary care in keeping the property reasonably safe for the benefit of the invitee. This general duty includes the ***duties owed to licensees*** (to warn of nonobvious, dangerous conditions known to the landowner and to use ordinary care in active operations on the property) ***plus*** a ***duty to make reasonable inspections*** to discover dangerous conditions and, thereafter, make them safe.

(a) **Warning May Suffice**
The requirement to "make safe" dangerous conditions usually is satisfied if a reasonable warning has been given.

(b) **Obviousness of Danger**
A duty to warn usually does not exist where the dangerous condition is so obvious that the invitee should reasonably have been aware of it. "Obviousness" is determined by all of the surrounding circumstances.

Example: A banana peel visible on the floor of a supermarket might not be considered obvious if a shopper's attention would likely be diverted by shelf displays.

d) **Users of Recreational Land**
In almost all states, a different standard applies by statute to users of recreational land. If an owner or occupier of open land permits the public to use the land for recreational purposes ***without charging a fee***, the landowner is not liable for injuries suffered by a recreational user unless the landowner ***willfully and maliciously*** failed to guard against or warn of a dangerous condition or activity.

Example: The owner of a large tract of undeveloped rural land who permits the general public to use a pond on the land for swimming and fishing would be covered by this type of statute, whereas the owner of a swimming pool who permits his house guests to swim whenever they visit would not be covered by the statute (he would owe his guests the usual duties owed to licensees).

e) **Modern Trend—Rejection of Rules Based on Entrant's Legal Status**
A strong minority of states have abolished the distinction between licensees and invitees and simply apply a reasonable person standard to dangerous conditions on the land. A few of these states have gone even further and abolished the trespasser distinction as well.

3) **Duties of a Lessor of Realty**

a) **General Duty Rule**
Ordinarily, tort liability in regard to conditions on the property is an ***incident of occupation and control***. Thus, when the owner leases the entire premises to another, the lessee, coming into occupation and control, becomes burdened with the duty to maintain the premises in such a way as to avoid unreasonable risk of harm to others. Similarly, where the owner leases ***portions*** of the premises to tenants, the owner continues to be subject to liability for unreasonably dangerous conditions in those portions of the premises such as corridors, entry lobby, elevators, etc., used in common by all tenants, or by third persons, and over which the owner has retained occupation and control.

b) **Exceptions**
This basic duty, however, is subject to certain exceptions and extensions, as set forth below.

(1) **Duty of Lessor to Lessee**
The lessor is obligated to give ***warning*** to the lessee of ***existing defects*** in the premises of which the lessor is aware, or has reason to know, and which he knows the lessee is not likely to discover on reasonable inspection.

(2) **Effect of Lessor's Covenant to Repair**
If the lessor has covenanted to make repairs and reserves the right to

enter the leased premises for the purpose of inspecting for defects and repairing them, he is subject to ***liability for unreasonably dangerous conditions***.

(3) **Effect of Voluntary Repairs by Lessor**
If the lessor, though under no obligation to make repairs, does so, he is subject to liability if he does so ***negligently***, failing to cure the defect; it is not necessary that his negligent repairs make the condition worse.

(4) **Effect of Admission of the Public**
If the lessor leases the premises knowing that the lessee intends to admit the public, the lessor is subject to ***liability for unreasonably dangerous conditions existing at the time he transfers possession*** where the nature of the defect and length and nature of the lease indicate that the tenant will not repair (*e.g.,* lessor rents convention hall to tenant for three-day period). This liability continues until the defect is actually remedied. A mere warning to the lessee concerning the defect is ***not*** sufficient.

(The duty of care of tenants and lessors is also covered in the Real Property outline.)

c) **Tenant Remains Liable to Invitees and Licensees**
Keep in mind that the potential liability of the lessor for dangerous conditions on the premises does not relieve the tenant, as occupier of the land, of liability for injuries to third persons from the dangerous conditions within the tenant's control.

4) **Duties of Vendor of Realty**
The vendor, at the time of transfer of possession to the vendee, has the ***duty to disclose*** concealed, unreasonably dangerous conditions of which the vendor knows or has reason to know, and of which he knows the vendee is ignorant and is not likely to discover on reasonable inspection. The vendor's responsibility continues until the vendee should have, in the exercise of reasonable care in inspection and maintenance, discovered and remedied the defect.

e. **Statutory Standards of Care**

1) **When Statutory Standard Applicable**
The precise standard of care in a common law negligence case may be established by proving the applicability to that case of a statute providing for a ***criminal*** penalty. If this is done, the statute's specific duty will replace the more general common law duty of due care. In proving the availability of the statutory standard, plaintiff must show the following:

a) **Plaintiff Within Protected Class**
The plaintiff must show that she is in the class intended to be protected by the statute.

Example: A statute requiring a landowner to keep a building in safe condition is meant to protect only those rightfully on the premises and not trespassers.

b) **Particular Harm to Be Avoided**

The plaintiff must show that the statute was designed to prevent the type of harm that the plaintiff suffered.

Example: Violation of a Sunday closing law is not evidence of negligence in the case of an accident in a store on Sunday.

c) **Standards Clearly Defined**

The statute must be clear as to what standard of conduct is expected, where and when it is expected, and of whom it is expected.

2) **Excuse for Violation**

Violation of some statutes may be excused:

a) Where ***compliance would cause more danger*** than violation; *e.g.,* defendant drives onto wrong side of road to avoid hitting children who dart into his path; or

b) Where ***compliance would be beyond defendant's control***; *e.g.,* blind pedestrian crosses against light.

3) **Effect of Establishing Violation of Statute**

Most courts still adhere to the rule that violation of a statute is "negligence per se." This means that plaintiff will have established a ***conclusive presumption of duty and breach of duty.*** (Plaintiff still must establish causation and damages to complete the prima facie case for negligence.)

A significant ***minority*** of courts, however, are unwilling to go this far. They hold either that (i) a rebuttable presumption as to duty and breach thereof arises, or (ii) the statutory violation is only prima facie evidence of negligence.

4) **Effect of Compliance with Statute**

Even though the violation of an applicable criminal statute may be negligence, compliance with it will ***not necessarily establish due care***. If there are unusual circumstances or increased danger beyond the minimum that the statute was designed to meet, it may be found that there is negligence in not doing more.

5) **Violation of a Civil Remedy Statute**

Where the statute in question provides for a civil remedy, plaintiff will sue directly under the statute; *i.e.,* it is not a common law negligence case.

f. **Duty Regarding Negligent Infliction of Emotional Distress**

A duty to avoid negligent infliction of emotional distress may be breached when the defendant creates a foreseeable risk of physical injury to the plaintiff. The plaintiff usually must satisfy two requirements to prevail: (i) plaintiff must be within the "zone of danger"; and (ii) plaintiff must suffer physical symptoms from the distress.

1) **Plaintiff Must Be Within the "Zone of Danger"**
The plaintiff usually must show that her distress has been caused by a threat of physical impact; *i.e.*, she was within the "zone of danger."

Example: Driver negligently ran a red light and skidded to a stop inches away from Pedestrian, who was properly crossing the street in a crosswalk. Pedestrian's shock from nearly being run over caused her to suffer a heart attack. Pedestrian can recover for negligent infliction of emotional distress because she was in the zone of danger.

2) **Plaintiff Must Suffer Physical Symptoms from the Distress**
For the plaintiff to recover damages, most courts usually require that the defendant's conduct cause the plaintiff emotional distress that manifests itself in ***physical symptoms*** (*e.g.*, a nervous breakdown, miscarriage, or heart attack, but note that severe shock to the nervous system that causes physical symptoms will satisfy this requirement). Emotional distress without physical symptoms is insufficient in most jurisdictions.

3) **Special Situations Where Requirements Not Always Necessary**

a) **Bystander Not in Zone of Danger Seeing Injury to Another**
Traditionally, a bystander outside the "zone of danger" of physical injury who sees the defendant negligently injuring another could not recover damages for her own distress. A majority of courts now allow recovery in these cases as long as (i) the plaintiff and the person injured by the defendant are ***closely related***, (ii) ***the plaintiff was present*** at the scene of the injury, and (iii) the plaintiff ***personally observed or perceived*** the event.

Example: Mother sees her child struck by negligently driven automobile on the other side of the street and goes into shock. Most courts would allow recovery.

b) **Special Relationship Between Plaintiff and Defendant**
The defendant may be liable for directly causing the plaintiff severe emotional distress that leads to physical symptoms when a duty arises from the relationship between the plaintiff and the defendant, such that the defendant's negligence has great potential to cause emotional distress.

Example: Doctor negligently confused Patient's file with another and told Patient he had a terminal illness. Patient, who in fact did not have the illness, was shocked and suffered a heart attack as a result. Patient can recover for negligent infliction of emotional distress. Although there was no threat of physical impact from Doctor's negligence, negligently providing a false diagnosis of a terminal illness creates a foreseeable risk of physical injury solely from the severe emotional distress that is caused.

c) **Other Situations**
The plaintiff may be able to recover without proving the two requirements for this tort in special situations where the defendant's negligence creates a great likelihood of emotional distress. These include a defendant providing an erroneous report that a relative of the plaintiff has died or a defendant mishandling a relative's corpse.

g. Affirmative Duties to Act

1) General Rule—No Duty to Act

As a general matter, no legal duty is imposed on any person to affirmatively act for the benefit of others. This general rule is, however, subject to exception, as indicated below.

2) Assumption of Duty to Act by Acting

One who gratuitously acts for the benefit of another, although under no duty to do so in the first instance, is then under a duty to act like an ordinary, prudent, reasonable person and continue the assistance.

Example: Defendant, under no duty to aid Plaintiff who has been injured, picks her up and carries her into a room. He then leaves her there unattended for seven hours and Plaintiff's condition is worsened. Defendant, having acted, may be considered to have breached his duty to act reasonably.

a) "Good Samaritan" Statutes

A number of states have enacted statutes exempting licensed doctors, nurses, etc., who voluntarily and gratuitously render emergency treatment, from liability for ordinary negligence. Liability still exists, however, for gross negligence.

3) Peril Due to Defendant's Conduct

One whose conduct (whether negligent or innocent) places another in a position of peril is under a duty to use reasonable care to aid or assist that person.

4) Special Relationship Between Parties

A defendant having a special relationship to the plaintiff (*e.g.,* parent-child, employer-employee) may be liable for failure to act if the plaintiff is in peril.

a) Duty of Common Carriers

Common carriers are under a duty to use reasonable care to aid or assist passengers.

b) Duty of Places of Public Accommodation

Innkeepers, restaurateurs, shopkeepers, and others who gather the public for profit have a duty to use reasonable care to aid or assist their patrons and to prevent injury to them from third persons.

5) Role of Contract in Creating Duty

a) Nonfeasance—No Duty

In general, for mere nonfeasance, there is no tort duty of care, regardless of whether the defendant promises to undertake action gratuitously or for consideration. Liability for breach of contract extends only to parties in privity.

b) Misfeasance—Due Care Required

However, for misfeasance, failure to perform with due care contractual obligations owed to one may give rise to violation of a legal duty.

Example: Pursuant to a contract with the building owner, Defendant inspected and repaired the elevator, and did so carelessly. The elevator operator is injured as a result. Defendant is liable to the operator.

6) **Duty to Control Third Persons**

Generally, there is no duty to prevent a third person from injuring another. In some situations, however, such an affirmative duty might be imposed. In such cases, it must appear that the defendant had the ***actual ability*** and ***authority*** to control the third person's action. Thus, for example, bailors may be liable for the acts of their bailees, parents may be liable for the acts of their children, employers may be liable for the acts of their employees, etc.

It is generally required for imposition of such a duty that the defendant ***knows*** or ***should know*** that the third person is likely to commit such acts as would require the exercise of control by the defendant.

C. BREACH OF DUTY

Where the defendant's conduct falls short of that level required by the applicable standard of care owed to the plaintiff, she has breached her duty. Whether the duty of care is breached in an individual case is a question for the trier of fact.

Proof of breach is twofold: ***First***, it must be shown what in fact happened. ***Second***, it must be shown from these facts that the defendant acted unreasonably. Proof of what happened may be established by either direct or circumstantial evidence. Other matters may also be offered into evidence to establish the standard by which defendant's conduct is to be measured, *e.g.,* custom or usage, applicability of a statute, etc.

1. Custom or Usage

Custom or usage may be introduced to establish the standard of care in a given case. However, customary methods of conduct do not furnish a test that is conclusive for controlling the question of whether certain conduct amounted to negligence.

2. Violation of Statute

As we have seen above, the existence of a duty owed to plaintiff and breach thereof may be established by proof that defendant violated an applicable statute.

3. Res Ipsa Loquitur

The circumstantial evidence doctrine of res ipsa loquitur ("the thing speaks for itself") deals with those situations where the fact that a particular injury occurred may itself establish or tend to establish a breach of duty owed. Where the facts are such as to strongly indicate that plaintiff's injuries resulted from defendant's negligence, the trier of fact may be permitted to infer defendant's liability. Res ipsa loquitur requires the plaintiff to show the following:

a. Inference of Negligence

Plaintiff must establish that the accident causing his injury is the type that would not normally occur unless someone was negligent.

Example: A windowpane fell from a second story window in Defendant's building, landing on Plaintiff. Res ipsa loquitur may apply.

b. Negligence Attributable to Defendant

Plaintiff must establish evidence connecting defendant with the negligence in order to support a finding of liability, *i.e.,* evidence that this type of accident ordinarily happens because of the negligence of someone in defendant's position. This requirement often can be satisfied by showing that the instrumentality that caused the injury was in the exclusive control of defendant, although actual possession of the instrumentality is not necessary.

1) Multiple Defendants Problem

Where more than one person may have been in control of the instrumentality, res ipsa loquitur generally may ***not*** be used to establish a prima facie case of negligence against any individual party.

Example: Plaintiff left the operating room with an injury to part of her body that was healthy prior to entering the operating room. The injury was not in the zone of the original operation. Res ipsa loquitur may not be available to establish that any individual in that room was negligent. This is so despite the fact that, clearly, someone was negligent. (A substantial ***minority*** of courts in such cases where defendants have control of the evidence require each defendant to establish that his negligence did not cause the injury. [*See, e.g.,* Ybarra v. Spangard, 25 Cal. 2d 486 (1944)])

Compare: The doctrine would be available where a particular defendant had the power of control over the site of the injury. For example, Plaintiff sues Surgeon after a sponge was left in his body at the site of the surgery. Even though Surgeon left it to her assistants to remove the sponges and close up the wound, her responsibility and power of control over the surgery itself allows Plaintiff to use res ipsa loquitur against her.

c. Plaintiff's Freedom from Negligence

Plaintiff must also establish that the injury was not attributable to him, but may do so by his own testimony.

d. Effect of Res Ipsa Loquitur

1) No Directed Verdict for Defendant

The doctrine, where applicable, does not change the burden of proof, nor does it create a presumption of negligence. Where the res ipsa element has been proved, the plaintiff has made a prima facie case and no directed verdict may be given for the defendant.

2) Effect of Defendant's Evidence of Due Care

However, the effect of defendant's evidence that due care was exercised has the same effect in a res ipsa case as in all other cases. If the jury rejects the defendant's evidence and draws the permissible inference of negligence, it will find for the plaintiff. If defendant's evidence overcomes the permissible inference that may be drawn from the res ipsa proof, the jury may find for the defendant. Such a finding for the defendant may result even where defendant rests without offering evidence on the issue if the jury elects not to infer negligence.

D. CAUSATION

1. Actual Cause (Causation in Fact)

Before the defendant's conduct can be considered a proximate cause of plaintiff's injury, it must first be a ***cause in fact*** of the injury. Several tests exist:

a. "But For" Test

An act or omission to act is the cause in fact of an injury when the injury would not have occurred ***but for*** the act.

Example: Failure to provide a fire escape is a cause of death of one who is thereby unable to flee a fire, but it is not a cause of death of one who suffocated in bed.

1) Concurrent Causes

The "but for" test applies where several acts combine to cause the injury, but none of the acts standing alone would have been sufficient (*e.g.,* two negligently driven cars collide, injuring a passenger). But for any of the acts, the injury would not have occurred.

b. Additional Tests

Under certain circumstances, the "but for" test is inadequate to determine causation in fact. The courts must rely upon other tests.

1) Joint Causes—Substantial Factor Test

Where several causes concur to bring about an injury—and any one alone would have been sufficient to cause the injury—it is sufficient if defendant's conduct was a "substantial factor" in causing the injury.

Example: Two fires meet and burn a farm. Either fire alone would have done the damage without the other. Under the "but for" test, neither was the "cause," since, looking at either fire alone, the loss would have occurred without it. Rather than reach this result, the courts consider as causes all those things that were a "substantial factor" in causing injury.

2) Alternative Causes Approach

a) Burden of Proof Shifts to Defendants

A problem of causation exists where two or more persons have been negligent, but uncertainty exists as to which one caused plaintiff's injury. Under the alternative causes approach, plaintiff must prove that harm has been caused to him by one of them (with uncertainty as to which one). The burden of proof then shifts to defendants, and each must show that his negligence is not the actual cause.

Example: Alex and Basil both negligently fire shotguns in Clara's direction. Clara is hit by one pellet, but she cannot tell which gun fired the shot. Under the alternative causes approach, Alex and Basil will have to prove that the pellet was not theirs. If unable

to do this, they may both be liable. [Summers v. Tice, 33 Cal. 2d 80 (1948)]

b) **Applied in Enterprise Liability Cases**
This concept has been extended in some cases to encompass industry groups.
Example: Daughters of women who took the anti-miscarriage drug diethylstilbestrol ("DES") contracted cancer as a result of the drug manufacturer's negligence. However, because the cancer appeared many years after the DES was ingested, it was usually impossible to determine which manufacturer of DES had supplied the drug taken by any particular plaintiff. Several courts have required all producers of DES unable to prove their noninvolvement to pay in proportion to their percentage of the market share. [*See* Sindell v. Abbott Laboratories, 26 Cal. 3d 588, *cert. denied,* 449 U.S. 912 (1980)]

2. **Proximate Cause (Legal Causation)**
In addition to being a cause in fact, the defendant's conduct must also be a proximate cause of the injury. Not all injuries "actually" caused by defendant will be deemed to have been proximately caused by his acts. Thus, the doctrine of proximate causation is a ***limitation of liability*** and deals with liability or nonliability for unforeseeable or unusual consequences of one's acts.

a. **General Rule of Liability**
The general rule of proximate cause is that the defendant is liable for all harmful results that are ***the normal incidents of and within the increased risk caused by*** his acts. In other words, if one of the reasons that make defendant's act negligent is a greater risk of a particular harmful result occurring, and that harmful result does occur, defendant generally is liable. This test is based on ***foreseeability***.

b. **Direct Cause Cases**
A direct cause case is one where the facts present an ***uninterrupted chain*** of events from the time of the defendant's negligent act to the time of plaintiff's injury. In short, there is no external intervening force of any kind.

1) **Foreseeable Harmful Results—Defendant Liable**
If a particular harmful result was at all foreseeable from defendant's negligent conduct, the unusual manner in which the injury occurred or the unusual timing of cause and effect is irrelevant to defendant's liability.
Example: D is driving her sports car down a busy street at a high rate of speed when a pedestrian steps out into the crosswalk in front of her. D has no time to stop, so she swerves to one side. Her car hits a parked truck and bounces to the other side of the street, where it hits another parked vehicle, propelling it into the street and breaking the pedestrian's leg. D is liable despite the unusual way in which she caused the injury to the pedestrian.

2) **Unforeseeable Harmful Results—Defendant Not Liable**
In the rare case where defendant's negligent conduct creates a risk of a harmful

result, but an entirely different and totally unforeseeable type of harmful result occurs, most courts hold that defendant is not liable for that harm.

Example: D, a cabdriver, is driving too fast on a busy elevated highway, threatening P, his passenger, with injury. Without warning, the section of highway that D is on collapses because its support beams had deteriorated with age. P is seriously injured. Even if D's negligent conduct was an actual cause of P's injury (because the cab would not have been on that section of the highway but for D's speeding), courts would not hold D liable for the injury to P.

c. **Indirect Cause Cases**

An indirect cause case is one where the facts indicate that a force came into motion ***after*** the time of defendant's negligent act and combined with the negligent act to cause injury to plaintiff. In short, indirect cause cases are those where ***intervening forces*** are present. Whether an intervening force will cut off defendant's liability for plaintiff's injury is determined by foreseeability.

1) **Foreseeable Results Caused by Foreseeable Intervening Forces—Defendant Liable**

Where defendant's negligence caused a foreseeable harmful response or reaction from an intervening force or created a foreseeable risk that an intervening force would harm plaintiff, defendant is liable for the harm caused.

a) **Dependent Intervening Forces**

Dependent intervening forces are normal responses or reactions to the situation created by defendant's negligent act. ***Dependent intervening forces are almost always foreseeable.***

The following are common dependent intervening forces:

(1) **Subsequent Medical Malpractice**

The original tortfeasor is usually liable for the aggravation of plaintiff's condition caused by the malpractice of plaintiff's treating physician.

(2) **Negligence of Rescuers**

Generally, rescuers are viewed as foreseeable intervening forces, and so the original tortfeasor usually is liable for their negligence.

(3) **Efforts to Protect Person or Property**

Defendant usually is liable for negligent efforts on the part of persons to protect life or property of themselves or third persons endangered by defendant's negligence.

(4) **"Reaction" Forces**

Where defendant's actions cause another to "react" (*e.g.,* negligently firing a gun at another's feet), liability generally attaches for any harm inflicted by the "reacting" person on another.

(5) **Subsequent Disease**

The original tortfeasor usually is liable for diseases caused in part by the

weakened condition in which defendant has placed the plaintiff by negligently injuring her; *e.g.,* injury caused by defendant weakens plaintiff, making her susceptible to pneumonia.

(6) Subsequent Accident

Where the plaintiff suffers a subsequent injury following her original injury, and the original injury was a substantial factor in causing the second accident, the original tortfeasor is usually liable for damages arising from the second accident. For example, as a result of defendant's negligence, plaintiff's leg is broken. Walking on crutches, plaintiff falls and breaks her other leg.

b) Independent Intervening Forces

Independent intervening forces also operate on the situation created by defendant's negligence but are independent actions rather than natural responses or reactions to the situation. Independent intervening forces may be foreseeable where ***defendant's negligence increased the risk that these forces would cause harm*** to the plaintiff.

The following are common fact situations involving independent intervening forces:

(1) Negligent Acts of Third Persons

Defendant is liable for harm caused by the negligence of third persons where such negligence was a foreseeable risk created by defendant's conduct.

Example: D negligently blocked a sidewalk, forcing P to walk in the roadway, where he is struck by a negligently driven car. D is liable to P.

(2) Criminal Acts and Intentional Torts of Third Persons

If defendant's negligence created a foreseeable risk that a third person would commit a crime or intentional tort, defendant's liability will not be cut off by the crime or tort.

Example: D, a parking lot attendant, negligently left the keys in P's car and the doors unlocked when he parked it, allowing a thief to steal it. D is liable to P.

(3) Acts of God

Acts of God will not cut off defendant's liability if they are foreseeable.

Example: D, a roofer, negligently left a hammer on P's roof at the end of the day. P is struck by the hammer when a strong wind blows it off the roof. D is liable to P.

2) Foreseeable Results Caused by Unforeseeable Intervening Forces—Defendant Usually Liable

The problem: Defendant is negligent because his conduct threatens a result of a particular kind that will injure plaintiff. This result is ultimately produced by an ***unforeseeable*** intervening force. Most courts would generally find liability here because they give greater weight to foreseeability of result than to foreseeability of the intervening force. An exception exists, however, where the intervening force is an unforeseeable ***crime*** or ***intentional tort*** of a third party; it will be deemed a "superseding force" that cuts off defendant's liability (*see* discussion below).

Examples: 1) Defendant failed to clean residue out of an oil barge, leaving it full of explosive gas. Negligence, of course, exists since an explosion resulting in harm to any person in the vicinity was foreseeable from any one of several possible sources. An unforeseeable bolt of lightning struck the barge, exploding the gas and injuring workers on the premises. Defendant is liable.

2) Same facts as above example, except that an arsonist caused the explosion. Most courts would not hold Defendant liable here. They think it unfair to make him responsible for such malevolent conduct. The important point here is that an unforeseeable intervening force may still relieve the defendant of liability if it is an unforeseeable crime or intentional tort of a third party.

3) Unforeseeable Results Caused by Foreseeable Intervening Forces—Defendant Not Liable

Most intervening forces that produce unforeseeable results are considered to be unforeseeable intervening forces (*see* below). Similarly, most results caused by foreseeable intervening forces are treated as foreseeable results. In the rare case where a foreseeable intervening force causes a totally unforeseeable result, most courts would not hold the defendant liable.

Example: D, a cabdriver, was driving recklessly during a violent windstorm that was blowing large branches and other debris onto the road, creating a risk to P, his passenger, that D would not be able to stop the cab in time to avoid an accident. D slammed on his brakes to avoid a large branch in the road, causing his cab to swerve sideways onto the shoulder of the road. Before he could proceed, another branch crashed onto the roof of the cab, breaking a window and causing P to be cut by flying glass. D is not liable to P even though his negligent driving was the actual (but for) cause of P's injury and the wind that was blowing the branches down was a foreseeable intervening force.

4) Unforeseeable Results Caused by Unforeseeable Intervening Forces—Defendant Not Liable

As a general rule, intervening forces that produce unforeseeable results (*i.e.,* results that were not within the increased risk created by defendant's negligence) will be deemed to be unforeseeable and ***superseding***. A superseding force is one that serves to ***break the causal connection*** between defendant's initial negligent act and the ultimate injury, and itself becomes a direct, immediate cause of the injury. Thus, defendant will be relieved of liability for the consequences of his antecedent conduct.

Example: D negligently blocks a road, forcing P to take an alternate road. Another driver negligently collides with P on this road, injuring him. Even though D is an actual (but for) cause of P's injury, the other driver's conduct is an unforeseeable intervening force because D's negligence did not increase the risk of its occurrence. Thus, the other driver is a superseding force that cuts off D's liability for his original negligent act.

d. Unforeseeable Extent or Severity of Harm—Defendant Liable

In both direct cause and indirect cause cases, the fact that the extent or severity of the harm was not foreseeable does not relieve defendant of liability; *i.e.,* the tortfeasor takes his victim as he finds him. Thus, where defendant's negligence causes an aggravation of plaintiff's existing physical or mental illness, defendant is liable for the damages caused by the aggravation.

Example: A car negligently driven by D collides with a car driven by P. P suffers a slight concussion, which was foreseeable, and also suffers a relapse of an existing mental illness, which was not foreseeable. D is liable for all of P's damages.

E. DAMAGES

Damage is an essential element of plaintiff's prima facie case for negligence. This means ***actual*** harm or injury. Unlike the situation for some of the intentional torts, damage will not be presumed. Thus, nominal damages are not available in an action in negligence; some proof of harm must be offered.

1. Damages Recoverable in the Action

a. Personal Injury

Plaintiff is to be compensated for ***all*** his damages (past, present, and prospective), both special and general. This includes fair and adequate compensation for ***economic damages***, such as medical expenses and lost earnings, and ***noneconomic damages***, such as pain and suffering. Plaintiff is also entitled to compensation for impaired future earning capacity, discounted to present value so as to avoid an excess award; *i.e.,* plaintiff receives an amount that, if securely invested, would produce the income that the jury wishes him to have.

1) Foreseeability Irrelevant

As noted above in the proximate cause section, it is generally not necessary to foresee the extent of the harm. In other words, a tortfeasor takes the victim as he finds him.

2) Emotional Distress Damages

Plaintiff's noneconomic damages include damages for any emotional distress suffered as a result of the physical injury.

Example: Plaintiff was struck by a piece of metal when the engine blew on a defectively manufactured lawn mower. The piece of metal lodged in his spine at an inoperable location, significantly increasing his risk of future paralysis. In plaintiff's products liability action against the manufacturer of the lawn mower, plaintiff can recover damages not only for his physical injury but also for the emotional distress he suffers from his knowledge of the risk of paralysis, because it arises out of the physical injury caused by the defective product.

b. **Property Damage**
The measure of damages for property damage is the reasonable ***cost of repair***, or, if the property has been almost or completely destroyed, its ***fair market value*** at the time of the accident.

c. **Punitive Damages**
In addition to the various types of compensatory damages discussed above, plaintiff may also be able to recover punitive damages in most jurisdictions if defendant's conduct was "wanton and willful," reckless, or malicious.

d. **Nonrecoverable Items**
Certain items are not recoverable as damages in negligence actions. These include:

1) Interest from date of damage in personal injury action; and

2) Attorneys' fees.

2. **Duty to Mitigate Damages**
As in all cases, the plaintiff has a duty to take reasonable steps to mitigate damages—in property damage cases to preserve and safeguard the property, and in personal injury cases to seek appropriate treatment to effect a cure or healing and to prevent aggravation. Failure to mitigate precludes recovery of any additional damages caused by aggravation of the injury.

3. **Collateral Source Rule**
As a general rule, damages are not reduced or mitigated by reason of benefits received by plaintiff from other sources, *e.g.*, health insurance, sick pay from employer. Hence, at trial, defendants may not introduce evidence relating to any such financial aid from other sources. A growing number of states have made exceptions to this rule in certain types of actions (*e.g.*, medical malpractice actions), allowing defendants to introduce evidence of insurance awards or disability benefits.

Note: These damages rules also are generally applicable to actions based on intentional torts.

F. DEFENSES TO NEGLIGENCE

1. Contributory Negligence

a. Standard of Care for Contributory Negligence

1) **General Rule**
The standard of care required is the same as that for ordinary negligence.

2) **Rescuers**
A plaintiff may take extraordinary risks when attempting a rescue without being

considered contributorily negligent. The emergency situation is one of the factors taken into account when evaluating the plaintiff's conduct.

3) **Remaining in Danger**
It may be contributorily negligent to fail to remove oneself from danger, *e.g.,* remaining in a car with a drunk driver.

4) **Violation of Statute by Plaintiff**
Plaintiff's contributory negligence may be established by his violation of a statute under the same rules that govern whether a statute can establish defendant's negligence (*see* B.3.e., *supra*).

5) **As Defense to Violation of Statute by Defendant**
Contributory negligence is ordinarily a defense to negligence proved by defendant's violation of an applicable statute. But where the defendant's negligence arose from violation of a statute designed to protect this particular class of plaintiffs from their own incapacity and lack of judgment, then plaintiff's contributory negligence is ***not*** a defense.

Example: D is exceeding the speed limit in a school zone when a child on his way to school darts into the street without looking. Because of her speed, D is unable to stop and hits the child. Any contributory negligence on the child's part is not a defense to D's violation of the statute, because the statute was designed to protect children on their way to school.

b. **Avoidable Consequences Distinguished**
As we have seen, plaintiff owes a duty to mitigate damages to person or property after the damage is inflicted. If he does not properly do this, then damages will be reduced. Failure to do this, however, is an avoidable consequence, not contributory negligence.

c. **No Defense to Intentional Torts**
Contributory negligence is never a defense to an action for an intentional tort or for willful or wanton misconduct.

d. **Effect of Contributory Negligence**
At common law, plaintiff's contributory negligence completely barred his right to recover. This was so even though the degree of defendant's negligence was much greater than that of plaintiff.

The severe consequences of strict application of contributory negligence rules initially caused courts to develop "escape" doctrines, such as ***last clear chance*** (below). More recently, however, most jurisdictions have rejected entirely the "all or nothing" approach of contributory negligence in favor of a ***comparative negligence*** system (discussed *infra*).

e. **Last Clear Chance**
The doctrine of last clear chance, sometimes called "the humanitarian doctrine," permits the plaintiff to recover ***despite*** his own contributory negligence. Under this rule,

the person with the last clear chance to avoid an accident who fails to do so is liable for negligence. (In effect, last clear chance is plaintiff's rebuttal against the defense of contributory negligence.)

Example: Bowater negligently parked his car on the railroad tracks. The train engineer saw him in time to stop but failed to do so. The engineer had the last clear chance, and thus the railroad will be liable for the accident.

1) **"Helpless" vs. "Inattentive" Peril**
Many cases distinguish between "helpless" and "inattentive" peril situations in applying last clear chance rules.

a) **Helpless Peril**
Helpless peril exists where plaintiff, through his contributory negligence, puts himself in a position of actual peril from which he cannot extricate himself. In many states, defendant is liable under these circumstances if she had either ***actual*** knowledge of plaintiff's predicament or if she ***should have known*** of plaintiff's predicament. Other states require actual knowledge.

b) **Inattentive Peril**
Inattentive peril exists where plaintiff, through his own negligence, is in a position of actual peril from which he could extricate himself if he were attentive. Almost all courts require ***actual*** knowledge of plaintiff's predicament on defendant's part.

2) **Prior Negligence Cases**
For last clear chance to operate, defendant must have been able to avoid harming plaintiff ***at the time of the accident***. In short, defendant must have had the "last clear chance" to avoid the accident. Hence, if defendant's only negligence had occurred earlier, *e.g.,* she negligently failed to have the steering wheel fixed, the courts will not apply last clear chance.

f. **Imputed Contributory Negligence**
Driver and Passenger are involved in an automobile accident with Cyclist. Driver is negligent; Cyclist is also negligent. Passenger, who is injured, brings an action against Cyclist. Cyclist argues that liability should be denied because of Driver's negligence to the same extent as if Passenger had been negligent himself. This is the concept of "imputed contributory negligence."

1) **General Rule—Plaintiff May Proceed Against Both Negligent Parties**
As a general rule, a plaintiff's action for his damages is ***not*** barred by imputed contributory negligence. He may proceed against both negligent parties as joint tortfeasors to the extent that each is a legal cause of the harm.

2) **When Contributory Negligence Is Imputed**
Contributory negligence will be imputed ***only*** where the plaintiff and the negligent person stand in such a relationship to each other that the courts find it proper to charge plaintiff with that person's negligence, *i.e.,* where plaintiff would be found ***vicariously*** liable for the negligent person's conduct if a third party had brought the action. (*See also* Vicarious Liability, VII.A., *infra.*)

3) **Common Fact Situations**
The following situations should be noted for bar examination purposes:

a) **Employer and Employee**
The contributory negligence of the employee or agent acting within the scope of employment will be imputed to the employer or principal when the latter is a plaintiff suing a third person.

b) **Partners and Joint Venturers**
The contributory negligence of one partner or joint venturer will be imputed to the other when the other is a plaintiff suing a third person.

c) **Husband and Wife**
The contributory negligence of one spouse will ***not*** be imputed to the other when the other is a plaintiff suing a third person.

d) **Parent and Child**
The contributory negligence of the parent or guardian is ***not*** imputed to the child, nor is the contributory negligence of the child imputed to the parent in actions against a third party.

Note: As to sections c) and d) above, note that in a spouse's action for loss of the other spouse's services, or a parent's action for loss of a child's services or recovery of his medical expenses, the contributory negligence of the injured spouse or child ***will*** bar recovery by the other spouse or by the parent. This is not because negligence is imputed, but because the loss of services action is derivative and cannot succeed unless the main action succeeds (*see* VII.D.3., *infra*). This result would also be obtained in a wrongful death action.

e) **Automobile Owner and Driver**
Unless the automobile owner would be vicariously liable for the driver's negligence (because, *e.g.,* the driver was an employee within the scope of employment), the contributory negligence of the driver will ***not*** be imputed to her. (Remember, in situations where the owner is a passenger, she may be liable for her ***own negligence*** in not preventing the accident.)

2. **Assumption of Risk**
The plaintiff may be denied recovery if he assumed the risk of any damage caused by the defendant's acts. This assumption may be expressed or implied. To have assumed risk, either expressly or impliedly, the plaintiff must have ***known of the risk*** and ***voluntarily*** assumed it. It is irrelevant that plaintiff's choice is unreasonable.

a. **Implied Assumption of Risk**
Implied assumption of risk situations are harder to resolve as, of course, the fact issues are difficult to prove.

1) **Knowledge of Risk**
Plaintiff must have known of the risk. Knowledge may be implied where the risk

is one that the average person would clearly appreciate, *e.g.,* risk of being hit by a foul ball in a baseball game.

2) **Voluntary Assumption**
The plaintiff must voluntarily go ahead in the face of the risk. However, plaintiff may not be said to have assumed the risk where there is no available alternative to proceeding in the face of the risk, *e.g.,* the only exit from a building is unsafe.

3) **Certain Risks May Not Be Assumed**
Because of public policy considerations, the courts uniformly hold that some risks may not be assumed. These include:

a) Common carriers and public utilities are not permitted to limit their liability for personal injury by a disclaimer on, *e.g.,* a ticket, a posted sign, etc.

b) When a statute is enacted to protect a class, members of that class will not be deemed to have assumed any risk.
Example: When a statute imposes safety regulations on an employer, the employee is held not to have assumed the risk where the statute is violated.

c) Risks will not be assumed in situations involving fraud, force, or an emergency. Thus, for example, one could take action to save his person or property without assuming a risk unless his actions involve an unreasonable risk out of proportion to the value of those rights.

b. **Express Assumption of Risk**
The risk may be assumed by express agreement. Such exculpatory clauses in a contract, intended to insulate one of the parties from liability resulting from his own negligence, are closely scrutinized but are generally enforceable. (Note that it is more difficult to uphold such an exculpatory clause in an adhesion contract.)

c. **No Defense to Intentional Torts**
Assumption of risk is not a defense to intentional torts. It is, however, a defense to wanton or reckless conduct.

3. **Comparative Negligence**
A substantial ***majority*** of states now permit a contributorily negligent plaintiff to recover a percentage of his damages under some type of ***comparative negligence*** system. In every case where contributory negligence is shown, the trier of fact weighs plaintiff's negligence against that of defendant and reduces plaintiff's damages accordingly.
Example: Defendant negligently drove through a stop sign and collided with Plaintiff, who was contributorily negligent by driving inattentively. Plaintiff suffers damages of $100,000. If a jury finds that Plaintiff was 30% negligent and Defendant was 70% negligent, Plaintiff will recover $70,000.

a. **Types of Comparative Negligence**

1) **"Partial" Comparative Negligence**
Most comparative negligence jurisdictions will still bar the plaintiff's recovery

if his negligence passes a threshold level. In some of these states, a plaintiff will be barred if his negligence was ***more serious*** than that of the defendant (*i.e.*, the plaintiff will recover nothing if he was more than 50% at fault). In the other states, a plaintiff will be barred from recovering if his negligence was ***at least as serious*** as that of the defendant (*i.e.*, the plaintiff will recover nothing if he was 50% or more at fault).

a) Multiple Defendants

If several defendants have contributed to plaintiff's injury, most of these states use a "combined comparison" approach to determine the threshold level (*i.e.*, plaintiff's negligence is compared with the total negligence of all the defendants combined).

2) "Pure" Comparative Negligence

The "pure" variety of comparative negligence, adopted in a third of the comparative negligence states, allows recovery no matter how great plaintiff's negligence is (*e.g.*, if plaintiff is 90% at fault and defendant 10%, plaintiff may still recover 10% of his damages). On the MBE, pure comparative negligence is the applicable rule unless the question specifies otherwise.

b. Comparative Negligence Illustrations

1) Partial Comparative Negligence Jurisdiction—Single Defendant

Plaintiff is 30% negligent and Defendant is 70% negligent in causing the accident. Each party suffers $100,000 in damages. Plaintiff will recover $70,000 from Defendant—$100,000 minus 30% ($30,000). Defendant will recover nothing from Plaintiff because Defendant was more than 50% at fault.

2) Partial Comparative Negligence Jurisdiction—Multiple Defendants

Plaintiff is 40% negligent in causing the accident and suffers $100,000 in damages. D1 is 35% negligent and D2 is 25% negligent. Plaintiff can recover $60,000 from either D1 or D2 under joint and several liability rules (*infra*, VII.B.1.). (The paying defendant can then go against the nonpaying defendant for contribution, discussed *infra* at VII.B.3.) Note that if D1 or D2 also suffered damages, each of them would have a claim against the other two negligent parties because each one's negligence is less than the total negligence of the other two.

3) Pure Comparative Negligence Jurisdiction

Same facts as in illustration 1). Plaintiff has a right to recover $70,000 from Defendant, and Defendant has a right to recover $30,000 from Plaintiff. Defendant's damages will be offset against Plaintiff's damages, and Plaintiff will have a net recovery of $40,000.

c. Effect on Other Doctrines

1) Last Clear Chance

Last clear chance is ***not*** used in most comparative negligence jurisdictions.

2) Assumption of Risk

a) **Implied Assumption of Risk**
Most comparative negligence jurisdictions have abolished entirely the defense of implied assumption of risk. In these jurisdictions, traditional assumption of risk situations must be broken down into two categories:

(1) When the defendant has only a ***limited duty*** to the plaintiff because of plaintiff's knowledge of the risks (*e.g.,* being hit by a foul ball at a baseball game), a court may protect the defendant simply by holding that the defendant did not breach his limited duty of care.

(2) More common is the situation that is a ***variant of contributory negligence,*** in that defendant's initial breach of duty to plaintiff is superseded by plaintiff's assumption of a risk (*e.g.,* builder is negligent in not barricading torn-up sidewalk, but pedestrian chooses to use it despite availability of reasonable alternate route). Here, the ***reasonableness*** of plaintiff's conduct is relevant: If the plaintiff has behaved unreasonably, plaintiff is contributorily negligent and damages will be apportioned under the state's comparative negligence statute.

b) **Express Assumption of Risk**
Most comparative negligence jurisdictions retain the defense of express assumption of risk.

3) **Wanton and Willful Conduct**
In most comparative negligence jurisdictions, plaintiff's negligence ***will*** be taken into account even though the defendant's conduct was "wanton and willful" or "reckless." However, plaintiff's negligence is still not a defense to intentional tortious conduct by the defendant.

IV. LIABILITY WITHOUT FAULT (STRICT LIABILITY)

A. PRIMA FACIE CASE

To establish a prima facie case for strict liability, the following elements must be shown:

1. The nature of the defendant's activity imposes an ***absolute duty*** to ***make safe***;

2. The dangerous aspect of the activity is the ***actual*** and ***proximate cause*** of the plaintiff's injury; and

3. The plaintiff suffered ***damage*** to person or property.

B. LIABILITY FOR ANIMALS

1. Trespassing Animals

The owner is strictly liable for the damage done by the trespass of his animals (other than household pets) as long as it was ***reasonably foreseeable***.

2. **Personal Injuries**

a. **Wild Animals—Strict Liability**
The owner is strictly liable for injuries caused by wild animals (*e.g.,* lion or bear), as long as the person injured did nothing, voluntarily or consciously, to bring about the injury.

b. **Domestic Animals—Knowledge Required**
The owner of a domestic animal (including farm animals) is ***not*** strictly liable for injuries it causes. Such liability does, however, attach if the owner has knowledge of that particular animal's dangerous propensities (*i.e.,* propensities more dangerous than normal for that species). This rule applies even if the animal has never actually injured anyone. Some states have "dog bite" statutes, applicable only to dogs, which impose strict liability in personal injury actions even without prior knowledge of dangerous characteristics.

c. **Persons Protected**

1) **Licensees and Invitees—Landowner Strictly Liable**
Strict liability for injuries inflicted by wild animals or abnormally dangerous domestic animals kept by the landowner on his land will usually be imposed where the person injured came onto the land as an invitee or licensee.

a) **Public Duty Exception**
An exception is recognized where the landowner is under a ***public duty to keep the animals*** (*e.g.,* as a public zookeeper); in such cases, negligence must be shown.

2) **Trespassers Must Prove Negligence**
Strict liability in such cases generally is ***not*** imposed in favor of undiscovered trespassers against landowners. Trespassers cannot recover for injuries inflicted by the landowner's wild animals or abnormally dangerous domestic animals in the absence of ***negligence***, *e.g.,* as where the landowner knows that trespassers are on the land and fails to warn them of the animal.

a) **Compare—Intentional Use of Vicious Watchdogs**
A landowner who protects his property from intruders by keeping a vicious watchdog that he knows is likely to cause ***serious bodily harm*** may be liable even to trespassers for injuries caused by the animal. This liability is based on intentional tort principles: Because the landowner is not entitled to use deadly force in person to protect only property, he also may not use such force indirectly. (*See* I.D.4.b., *supra.*)

C. ABNORMALLY DANGEROUS ACTIVITIES

1. **Definition**
An activity may be characterized as abnormally dangerous if it involves a substantial risk of serious harm to person or property no matter how much care is exercised. Whether an activity is abnormally dangerous is a question of law that the court can decide on a motion for directed verdict.

2. **Test**

The courts generally impose two requirements for finding an activity to be abnormally dangerous:

(i) The activity must create a foreseeable risk of ***serious harm even when reasonable care is exercised*** by all actors; and

(ii) The activity is ***not a matter of common usage*** in the community.

Example: In *Rylands v. Fletcher,* 3 H.L. 330 (1868), the House of Lords held a mill owner strictly liable when a neighbor's mines were flooded by water escaping from the mill owner's reservoir. This was considered an abnormal use in "mining country." (Other examples of abnormally dangerous activities include blasting, manufacturing explosives, crop dusting, and fumigating.)

3. **Products Liability**

There may be strict liability imposed for damage caused by products, depending on the theory used by a court in resolving such problems. (*See* V.D., *infra.*)

D. **EXTENT OF LIABILITY**

1. **Scope of Duty Owed**

As contrasted with negligence, the duty owed is an ***absolute duty to make safe*** the animal, activity, or condition that is classified as "abnormally dangerous," and liability is imposed for any injuries to persons or property resulting therefrom.

a. **To Whom Is the Duty Owed?**

In most states, the duty is owed only to ***"foreseeable plaintiffs"***—persons to whom a reasonable person would have foreseen a risk of harm under the circumstances. (Generally, strict liability is not imposed on a defendant's blasting that hurled rock onto a person so far away that no reasonable person would have foreseen a danger. Note, however, that some courts find liability for all blasting harm because of the intrinsic danger of defendant's activity.)

b. **Duty Limited to "Normally Dangerous Propensity"**

The harm must result from the kind of danger to be anticipated from the dangerous animal or abnormally dangerous activity; *i.e.,* it must flow from the "normally dangerous propensity" of the condition or thing involved.

Example: D's toothless pet leopard escapes from its cage without fault on D's part and wanders into a park, causing P to break her arm while trying to flee. D is strictly liable to P.

Compare: D's dynamite truck blows a tire without warning and hits Pedestrian. D is not strictly liable to Pedestrian. However, if the truck then crashed and exploded, and the explosion injured Bystander, D would be strictly liable to Bystander.

2. **Proximate Cause**

The majority view is that the same rules of direct and indirect causation govern in strict

liability as they do in negligence—defendant's liability can be cut off by unforeseeable intervening forces. In fact, the courts tend to hold more intervening forces "unforeseeable."

3. Defenses

a. Contributory Negligence States

In contributory negligence states, plaintiff's contributory negligence is ***no*** defense if the plaintiff simply failed to realize the danger or guard against its existence (unknowing contributory negligence). It ***is*** a defense, however, if plaintiff ***knew*** of the danger and his unreasonable conduct was the very cause of the abnormally dangerous activity miscarrying. Courts call this conduct "knowing" contributory negligence or a type of assumption of risk. Furthermore, assumption of risk of any type is a good defense to strict liability in contributory negligence states.

Example: P knowingly and unreasonably tries to pass D's dynamite truck on a sharp curve, causing it to turn over and explode. Regardless of whether P's conduct is called contributory negligence or assumption of risk, P cannot recover.

b. Comparative Negligence States

Most comparative negligence states will now simply apply the same comparative negligence rules that they apply to negligence cases.

V. PRODUCTS LIABILITY

A. BASIC PRINCIPLES

In this context, "products liability" is the generic phrase used to describe the liability of a supplier of a product to one injured by the product.

1. Theories of Liability

Plaintiffs in products liability cases may have one of five possible theories of liability available to them:

(i) ***Intent***;

(ii) ***Negligence***;

(iii) ***Strict liability***;

(iv) ***Implied warranties of merchantability and fitness for a particular purpose***; and

(v) ***Representation theories (express warranty and misrepresentation)***.

In an exam question, always consider a defendant's potential liability under each of the theories unless the call of the question indicates the theory that the plaintiff is using.

2. Existence of a Defect

To find liability under any products liability theory, plaintiff must show that the product was "defective" when the product left defendant's control.

a. **Types of Defects**

1) **Manufacturing Defects**
When a product emerges from a manufacturing process not only different from the other products, but also more dangerous than if it had been made the way it should have been, the product may be so "unreasonably dangerous" as to be defective because of the manufacturing process.

2) **Design Defects**
When all the products of a line are made identically according to manufacturing specifications, but have dangerous propensities because of their mechanical features or packaging, the entire line may be found to be defective because of poor design.

a) **Inadequate Warnings**
Inadequate warnings can be analyzed as a type of design defect. A product must have clear and complete warnings of any dangers that may not be apparent to users. For prescription drugs and medical devices, warnings need not be supplied to the patient; a warning to the prescribing physician usually will suffice (the "learned intermediary" rule).

b. **What Is a "Defective Product"?**
In most jurisdictions, a product can be the basis for a products liability action if it is in a "defective condition unreasonably dangerous" to users.

1) **Manufacturing Defects**
For a manufacturing defect, the plaintiff will prevail if the product was ***dangerous beyond the expectation of the ordinary consumer*** because of a departure from its intended design.

a) **Defective Food Products**
Defects in food products are treated the same as manufacturing defects—the "consumer expectation" approach is used.

2) **Design Defects**
For design defects, the plaintiff usually must show a reasonable alternative design, *i.e.*, that a ***less dangerous modification or alternative was economically feasible***.

The factors that the courts consider under the "feasible alternative" approach are the following:

(i) Usefulness and desirability of the product;

(ii) Availability of safer alternative products;

(iii) The dangers of the product that have been identified by the time of trial;

(iv) Likelihood and probable seriousness of injury;

(v) Obviousness of the danger;

(vi) Normal public expectation of danger (especially for established products);

(vii) Avoidability of injury by care in use of product (including role of instructions and warnings); and

(viii) Feasibility of eliminating the danger without seriously impairing the product's function or making it unduly expensive.

Examples: 1) Although people often cut themselves on sharp knives, knives are of great utility. Since there is no way to avoid the harm without destroying the utility of the product, and the danger is apparent to users, the product is not ***unreasonably*** dangerous and the supplier would not be liable for injuries.

2) A power lawn mower that is marketed with no guard over the opening from which cut grass is blown may be unreasonably dangerous even though the product carries several warnings that hands and feet should be kept away from the opening and that rocks may be ejected from the opening. While the product's danger is within the expectations of the user, a court will ***compare the harm caused*** by the product with what it would ***cost*** to put a guard on the opening and consider whether the guard would impair the machine's operation in order to determine whether the product is "defective."

a) Effect of Government Safety Standards

A product is deemed to be defective in design or warnings if it fails to comply with applicable government safety standards. On the other hand, a product's ***compliance*** with applicable government safety standards (including labeling requirements) is evidence—but not conclusive—that the product is ***not*** defective. [Restatement (Third) of Torts—Products Liability §4] Note also that federal labeling requirements ***do not preempt*** state products liability law on defective warnings. [Wyeth v. Levine 129 S. Ct. 1187 (2009)—product may comply with FDA labeling requirements but still be defective due to inadequate warnings]

c. Common Defect Problems

1) Misuse

Some products may be safe if used as intended, but may involve serious dangers if used in other ways. Courts have required suppliers to ***anticipate reasonably foreseeable uses*** even if they are "misuses" of the product.

Examples: 1) Although a screwdriver is intended only for turning screws, a manufacturer must anticipate that screwdrivers are commonly used to pry up lids of cans and must make screwdrivers reasonably safe for that use as well as for their intended use.

2) Liquid furniture polish provided for home use may be fit for its intended use, but the manufacturer must anticipate that it will be used around small children who may play with the bottle and spill or drink its contents. Thus, the manufacturer may have to design a product that is either safe when drunk or that has a child-proof top. A simple warning of danger may not suffice in most states under the "feasible alternative" approach if a child-proof top would cost little to install.

2) **Scientifically Unknowable Risks**
Occasionally, totally unpredictable hazards of a product do not become apparent until after the product has been marketed. This situation arises most frequently with new drugs that yield unpredictable side effects. Even though these drugs might be dangerous beyond consumer expectations, courts have generally refused to find the drugs unreasonably dangerous where it was impossible to anticipate the problem and make the product safer or provide warnings.

3) **Allergies**
Some products affect different users differently—the problem of allergic reaction. If the allergic group is significant in number, the product is defective unless adequate warnings are conveyed. The modern trend requires such ***warnings*** whenever the manufacturer knows that there is a danger of allergic reaction, even though the number affected may be very small.

3. **No Requirement of Contractual Privity Between Plaintiff and Defendant**
Whether the parties to the suit are in privity with each other is generally irrelevant under current law except for some of the warranty theories of liability.

a. **Defined**
The parties are in privity when a contractual relationship exists between them, such as a ***direct sale*** by the defendant retailer to the plaintiff buyer or the buyer's agent.

b. **Vertical Privity Absent**
Privity does not exist where the injured plaintiff, usually the buyer, is in the direct distribution chain but is suing a remote party—the wholesaler or the manufacturer—rather than the retailer who sold the product to the plaintiff.

c. **Horizontal Privity Absent**
Privity is also absent where the defendant, usually the retailer, is in the direct distribution chain with the buyer, but the plaintiff injured by the product is not the buyer, but rather the buyer's friend, neighbor, or a complete stranger.

B. **LIABILITY BASED ON INTENT**
A defendant will be liable to anyone injured by an unsafe product if the defendant intended the consequences or knew that they were substantially certain to occur. Liability based on an intentional tort is ***not very common*** in products liability cases.

1. **Tort Involved**
If the requisite intent on the part of the defendant is established, the intentional tort on which the cause of action most likely will be based is ***battery***.

2. Privity Not Required
The presence or absence of privity is irrelevant where liability is based on an intentional tort.

3. Damages
In addition to compensatory damages, punitive damages are available in a products liability case based on intent, to the same extent as with intentional torts in general.

4. Defenses
The usual defenses available in intentional torts cases, such as consent, would be applicable. Negligence defenses, such as contributory negligence and assumption of risk, are not applicable.

C. LIABILITY BASED ON NEGLIGENCE

1. Prima Facie Case
To establish a prima facie case for negligence in a products liability case, the following elements must be proved:

a. The existence of a ***legal duty*** owed by the defendant to that particular plaintiff;

b. ***Breach*** of that duty;

c. ***Actual*** and ***proximate cause***; and

d. ***Damages***.

2. Defendant with Duty of Care to Plaintiff

a. Commercial Suppliers
In the usual case, the duty of due care arises when the defendant engages in the affirmative conduct associated with being a commercial supplier of products. "Suppliers" include: the manufacturer of a chattel or a component part thereof, assembler, wholesaler, retailer, or even a used car dealer who sells reconditioned or rebuilt cars. Those who repair a product owe a general duty of care, but are not usually "suppliers" for purposes of products liability cases.

1) Labeling Another's Product
A retailer who ***labels*** a product as the retailer's own or assembles a product from components manufactured by others is liable for the negligence of the actual manufacturer, even though the retailer is not personally negligent.

b. Privity Not Required
Since the case of *MacPherson v. Buick,* 217 N.Y. 382 (1916), and its extensions, absence of privity is ***not*** a defense. The duty of due care is owed to ***any foreseeable plaintiff***—user, consumer, or bystander (such as a pedestrian injured when struck by an automobile with defective brakes).

3. Breach of Duty
To prove breach of duty, the plaintiff must show (i) ***negligent conduct*** by the defendant leading to (ii) the supplying of a ***"defective product"*** by the defendant.

a. **Negligence**
The defendant's conduct must fall below the standard of care expected of a reasonable person under like circumstances, considering such superior skill or training as defendant has or purports to have.

1) **Proof of Negligence in Manufacturing Defect Case**

a) **Liability of Manufacturer**
To show negligence in a manufacturing defect case, the plaintiff may invoke ***res ipsa loquitur*** against the manufacturer if the error is usually something that does not occur without the negligence of the manufacturer.

b) **Liability of Dealer**
Retailers and wholesalers owe a duty of due care to their customers and foreseeable victims. But the majority view is that a dealer who buys from a reputable supplier or manufacturer with no reason to anticipate that the product is dangerous need make only a cursory inspection of the goods to avoid liability for manufacturing defects.

2) **Proof of Negligence in Design Defect Case**
To establish that a manufacturer's negligence has resulted in a design defect, the plaintiff must show that those designing the product ***knew or should have known*** of enough facts to put a reasonable manufacturer on notice about the dangers of marketing the product as designed. Negligence is ***not*** shown if the danger of the product becomes apparent to the reasonable manufacturer only after the product has reached the public.

b. **Defective Product**
The analysis of whether a product is so "unreasonably dangerous" as to be defective, discussed *supra,* applies equally to products liability actions based on negligence and to those based on strict tort liability.

4. **Causation**
The standard negligence analysis for both actual causation and proximate cause applies to products liability cases based on negligence.

a. **Intermediary's Negligence**
An intermediary's negligent failure to discover a defect is ***not*** a superseding cause, and the defendant whose original negligence created the defect will be held liable along with the intermediary. But when the intermediary's conduct becomes something more than ordinary foreseeable negligence, it becomes a superseding cause.

Example: P buys a defective product from Retailer who bought it from D. D would still be liable to P if Retailer had negligently failed to notice a serious defect attributable to D. But if Retailer had in fact discovered the defect but failed to warn P of it, D would not be liable.

5. **Nature of Damages Recoverable**
A plaintiff may recover for personal injury and property damages as under the usual negligence analysis. However, if the plaintiff suffers ***only*** economic loss (the product does not

work as well as expected or requires repairs), most courts do not permit recovery under a negligence theory, requiring the plaintiff to bring an action for breach of warranty to recover such damages.

6. Defenses

The standard negligence defenses are applicable to any products liability case predicated on negligence. Thus, in comparative negligence states, plaintiff's contributory negligence may be used to reduce his recovery in an action against a negligent supplier of defective chattels.

D. LIABILITY BASED ON STRICT TORT LIABILITY

For those products liability cases where negligence on the part of the supplier would be difficult to prove, plaintiffs formerly attempted to bring their claims under traditional breach of warranty law as an alternative to using a negligence theory. Gradually, courts began to discard the privity requirement in warranty cases so that an increasing number of victims could recover without proof of negligence. This development has led to strict liability in tort for products liability cases.

1. Prima Facie Case

To establish a prima facie case in products liability based on strict liability in tort, the following elements must be proved:

a. Absolute duty owed by a ***commercial supplier***;

b. Production or sale of a ***defective product***;

c. ***Actual*** and ***proximate cause***; and

d. ***Damages***.

2. Defendant Must Be "Commercial Supplier"

Plaintiff must prove that defendant is a ***commercial*** supplier of the product in question, as distinguished from a casual seller (*e.g.,* a homemaker who sells a jar of jam to a neighbor). Thus, strict liability applies when the defendant is a manufacturer (including the manufacturer of a defective component part), retailer, assembler, or wholesaler.

Examples: 1) A theater may be held strictly liable for selling rotten candy. Even though the theater is not in the primary business of selling candy and similar products, it is a retail supplier of those products.

2) If the boiler in use on a shoe manufacturer's land explodes, the shoe manufacturer's liability is ***not*** analyzed in terms of products liability because the manufacturer is not a commercial supplier of boilers.

Most courts have expanded strict liability to include mass producers of new homes, commercial lessors, and sellers of used products that have been reconditioned or rebuilt.

a. Distinction Between Product and Service

Strict liability is imposed only on one who supplies a product, as opposed to one primarily performing a service. Restaurants are treated as suppliers of products, while most courts treat a transfusion of infected blood (*e.g.,* that gives the recipient hepatitis) as the rendition of a service.

Example: If an airplane crashes due to defective piloting of the plane, a passenger must prove negligence in order to sue the airline company. However, if the passenger sues the manufacturer for a defect in the plane itself, strict liability in tort may be used.

3. **Product Not Substantially Altered**
To hold the commercial supplier strictly liable for a product defect, the product must be expected to, and must in fact, reach the user or consumer without substantial change in the condition in which it is supplied.

4. **Privity Not Required**
As with liability based on negligence, a majority of courts extend this strict duty ***to any supplier in the chain of distribution*** and extend the protection not only to buyers, but also to members of the buyer's family, guests, friends, and employees of the buyer, and foreseeable bystanders.

5. **Production or Sale of Defective Product**
For a strict liability action, the plaintiff need not prove that the defendant was at fault in selling or producing a defective product—only that the product in fact is "defective" (*see* A.2.b., *supra*). As with products liability based on negligence, the two main categories of defects are manufacturing defects and design defects. The only difference in analysis is that the element of ***negligence need not be proved*** in a strict liability case. Thus, in contrast to a negligence action, a retailer in a strict liability action may be liable for a manufacturing or design defect simply because it was a commercial supplier of a defective product—***even if it had no opportunity to inspect the manufacturer's product before selling it***.

6. **Causation**

a. **Actual Cause**
To prove actual cause, the plaintiff must trace the harm suffered to a defect in the product that existed ***when the product left the defendant's control***. However, if the defect is difficult to trace (such as if the product is destroyed), the plaintiff may rely on an inference that this type of product failure ordinarily would occur only as a result of a product defect. If the plaintiff claims that one of the defective conditions was the lack of an adequate warning, plaintiff is entitled to a presumption that an adequate warning would have been read and heeded.

b. **Proximate Cause**
The same concepts of proximate cause governing general negligence and strict liability actions are applicable to strict liability actions for defective products. As with products liability cases based on negligence, the negligent failure of an intermediary to discover the defect does not cut off the supplier's strict liability.

7. **Nature of Damages Recoverable**
The types of damages recoverable in strict liability actions for defective products are the same as those recoverable in negligence actions, namely personal injury and property damages. Once again, most states ***deny*** recovery under strict liability when the sole claim is for ***economic loss***.

8. **Defenses**

a. Contributory Negligence States
According to Restatement (Second) section 402A, ordinary contributory negligence is not a defense in a strict products liability action where the plaintiff merely ***failed to discover the defect or guard against its existence***, or where plaintiff's misuse was reasonably foreseeable (*supra,* A.2.c.1)). On the other hand, other types of unreasonable conduct, such as voluntarily and unreasonably encountering a known risk (*i.e.,* assumption of risk), are defenses.

b. Comparative Negligence States
As with other strict liability actions, most comparative negligence states apply their comparative negligence rules to strict products liability actions. [*See* Restatement (Third) of Torts—Products Liability §17]

c. Disclaimers of Liability Ineffective
Disclaimers of liability are ***irrelevant*** in negligence or strict liability cases if personal injury or property damage has occurred.

E. IMPLIED WARRANTIES OF MERCHANTABILITY AND FITNESS

1. Proof of Fault Unnecessary
If a product fails to live up to the standards imposed by an implied warranty, the warranty is breached and the defendant will be liable. Plaintiff need not prove any fault on defendant's part.

2. Scope of Coverage
Although the Uniform Commercial Code ("U.C.C.") provisions apply only to the ***sale of goods***, the modern trend is to apply implied warranties to ***bailment*** and ***lease*** cases by analogizing to the sales provisions.

3. Implied Warranty of Merchantability
When a merchant who deals in a certain kind of goods sells such goods, there is an implied warranty that they are ***merchantable***. [U.C.C. §2-314] "Merchantable" means that the goods are of a quality equal to that ***generally acceptable*** among those who deal in similar goods and are ***generally fit for the ordinary purposes*** for which such goods are used.

4. Implied Warranty of Fitness for Particular Purpose
An implied warranty of fitness for a particular purpose arises when the seller knows or has reason to know:

(i) The particular purpose for which the goods are required; ***and***

(ii) That the buyer is relying on the seller's skill or judgment to select or furnish suitable goods.

[U.C.C. §2-315] Usually the seller will be a merchant of the type of goods in question, but this is not essential.

5. Privity

a. **Vertical Privity No Longer Required**
Although in the early period of warranty law, courts held strictly to the requirement of complete privity between the plaintiff and defendant, a trend developed with courts finding the needed privity between remote parties on various fictions and theories—*e.g.*, the warranty ran with the goods, or the retailer was the manufacturer's agent. As a result, most courts no longer require vertical privity between the buyer and the manufacturer in implied warranty actions.

b. **U.C.C. Alternatives on Horizontal Privity**
Although U.C.C. section 2-318 is silent on the issue of vertical privity, it offers the states three alternative versions on the issue of horizontal privity: Alternative A extends implied warranty protection to a ***buyer's family, household, and guests*** who suffer personal injury; Alternative B extends protection to any natural person who suffers personal injury; and Alternative C covers any person who suffers any injury. ***Most states have adopted Alternative A***, the narrowest modification of the privity requirement.

6. **Effect of Disclaimers**
Disclaimers of liability for breach of implied warranty ***must be specific*** and are narrowly construed. [U.C.C. §2-316] Contractual limitations on ***personal injury*** damages resulting from a breach of warranty for consumer goods are prima facie ***unconscionable***. [U.C.C. §2-719]

7. **Causation**
Issues of actual cause and proximate cause are treated as in an ordinary negligence case.

8. **Damages**
In addition to personal injury and property damages, purely ***economic losses*** are recoverable in implied warranty actions.

9. **Defenses**

a. **Assumption of Risk**
U.C.C. section 2-715 indicates that when the plaintiff assumes the risk by using a product while knowing of the breach of warranty, any resulting injuries are not proximately caused by the breach.

b. **Contributory Negligence**
Courts in contributory negligence jurisdictions have adopted an approach similar to that used in strict liability in tort—that unreasonable failure to discover the defect does not bar recovery but that unreasonable conduct ***after*** discovery does bar recovery.

c. **Comparative Negligence**
So also, courts in comparative negligence jurisdictions use comparative fault notions in warranty cases to reduce the damage award in the same way as in strict liability cases.

d. **Notice of Breach**
U.C.C. section 2-607 requires the buyer to give the seller notice ***within a reasonable time*** after the buyer discovers or should have discovered the breach. Most courts have

held that the requirement applies even in personal injury cases and where there is no privity between the parties.

F. REPRESENTATION THEORIES (EXPRESS WARRANTY AND MISREPRESENTATION OF FACT)

The two theories discussed in this section differ from those previously discussed because they involve some affirmative representation by the defendant beyond the act of distributing a product. When the product does not live up to the representation, both contract and tort problems are created.

1. Express Warranty

An express warranty arises where a seller or supplier makes any affirmation of fact or promise to the buyer relating to the goods that becomes part of the "basis of the bargain." [U.C.C. §2-313]

a. Scope of Coverage

As with implied warranties, the trend is to extend express warranties to bailments and other nonsales transactions by analogy.

b. Privity Not Required

Although U.C.C. section 2-318 declares that its privity alternatives apply to express as well as implied warranties, most courts have held privity to be irrelevant in express warranty cases.

c. "Basis of the Bargain"

If the buyer is suing, the warranty must have been "part of the basis of the bargain." This is probably less difficult to show than a buyer's subjective "reliance" on the representation. If someone not in privity is permitted to sue, this remote person need ***not*** have known about the affirmation as long as it became part of the basis of the bargain for someone else in the chain of distribution.

d. Basis of Liability—Breach of Warranty

As with implied warranties, the plaintiff need ***not*** show that the breach occurred through the fault of the defendant, but only that a breach of the warranty did in fact occur.

Example: The defendant advertises its hand lotion as "completely safe" and "harmless." Even if there is nothing wrong with the product itself, a buyer who suffers an allergic reaction may bring a successful warranty action.

e. Effect of Disclaimers

U.C.C. section 2-316 provides that a disclaimer will be effective only to the extent that it can be read consistently with any express warranties made. This has the effect of making it practically impossible to disclaim an express warranty.

f. Causation, Damages, and Defenses

These elements are analyzed the same as under implied warranties, *supra*.

2. Misrepresentation of Fact

Liability for misrepresentation may arise when a representation by the seller about a product induces reliance by the buyer. In products cases, liability for misrepresentation is usually based on strict liability, but may also arise for intentional and negligent misrepresentations.

a. **Defendant's State of Mind**

1) **Strict Liability**
As long as the defendant is a seller engaged in the business of selling such products, there is no need to show fault on the defendant's part. The plaintiff need only show that the representation proved false, without regard to the defendant's state of mind.

2) **Intentional Misrepresentation**
For intentional misrepresentations, the plaintiff must show that the misrepresentation was made ***knowingly*** or with ***reckless*** disregard for the facts.

3) **Negligent Misrepresentation**
For negligence liability, knowledge of the misrepresentation on the part of the defendant need not be proved. The plaintiff need only show that a reasonable person should have known such representations to be false when making them.

b. **Material Fact Required**
The misrepresentation must be of a material fact, *i.e.,* a fact concerning the quality, nature, or appropriate use of the product on which a normal buyer may be expected to rely. "Puffing" and statements of opinion are not sufficient.

c. **Intent to Induce Reliance of Particular Buyer**
The defendant must have intended to induce the reliance of the buyer, or a class of persons to which the buyer belongs, in a particular transaction. Evidence of a representation made to the public by label, advertisement, or otherwise is sufficient to show an intent to induce reliance by anyone into whose hands the product may come.

d. **Justifiable Reliance**
There is no liability if the misrepresentation is not known or does not influence the transaction. Reliance may be found if the representation was a ***substantial factor*** in inducing the purchase, even though not the sole inducement.

1) **Reliance Need Not Be Victim's**
As with express warranties, ***privity is irrelevant*** for misrepresentation and the required reliance may be shown to be that of a prior purchaser who passed the product on to the victim.

Example: D, a manufacturer of automobiles, advertises that its cars contain "shatterproof" glass. H reads this advertisement and, partly in reliance on it, buys one of D's cars. While H's friend, F, is driving the car, a stone is thrown through the windshield, shattering the glass. F, hurt by flying glass, has a strict liability action against D for misrepresentation even though F is not in privity with D and knows nothing of the "shatterproof" representation.

e. **Actual Cause**
Reliance by the purchaser serves to show actual cause.

f. **Proximate Cause and Damages**
Both elements are analyzed in the same manner as for products liability cases based on negligence or strict liability, *supra*. If the plaintiff can show that the misrepresentation was intentional, some courts will allow punitive damages to be claimed.

g. **Defenses**

1) **Assumption of Risk**
If the plaintiff is entitled to rely on the representation, a defense of assumption of risk does not apply.
Example: D markets a mace pen to be used against attackers. The product's label says that it instantly renders attackers helpless when sprayed in their faces. When holdup men demanded money from P, P shot his mace pen in their faces but it had no effect—except that the attackers got angry and shot P. D's claim that P assumed the risk of injury by not complying with the attackers' demands fails, since P reasonably relied on the product to achieve its stated results.

2) **Contributory Negligence (Fault)**
Whether contributory negligence is a defense depends on the type of misrepresentation. For negligent misrepresentations, contributory negligence is a valid defense. In strict liability actions, the plaintiff's unreasonable behavior is analyzed as in other strict liability actions for defective products, *supra*. If the plaintiff can show that the defendant's misrepresentation was intentional, contributory negligence would be no defense.

VI. NUISANCE

A. BASIS OF LIABILITY
Nuisance is ***not*** a separate tort in itself, subject to rules of its own. Nuisances are types of harm—the invasion of either private property rights or public rights by conduct that is tortious because it falls into the usual categories of tort liability. In other words, the defendant's conduct may have been intentional or negligent or subjected to liability on a strict liability basis. As a practical matter, nuisances generally are ***intentional*** interferences because defendant has been made aware that his conduct is interfering with plaintiff's use of her land. (If strict liability is the basis for redressing a nuisance, courts sometimes refer to this as an "absolute" nuisance or "nuisance per se.")

B. PRIVATE NUISANCE
Private nuisance is a ***substantial, unreasonable interference*** with another private individual's ***use or enjoyment*** of property he actually possesses or to which he has a right of immediate possession.

1. **Substantial Interference**
The interference with plaintiff's right in his land must be substantial. This means that it must be ***offensive, inconvenient, or annoying to an average person in the community***. It will

not be characterized as substantial if it is merely the result of plaintiff's hypersensitivity or specialized use of his own property.

2. **Unreasonable Interference**
For a nuisance based on intent or negligence, the interference with plaintiff's use of his land must be unreasonable. To be characterized as unreasonable, the severity of the inflicted ***injury must outweigh the utility*** of defendant's conduct. In balancing these respective interests, courts take into account that every person is entitled to use his own land in a reasonable way, considering the neighborhood, land values, and existence of any alternative courses of conduct open to defendant.

3. **Trespass to Land Distinguished**
Trespass to land is to be distinguished from private nuisance. In the former, there is an interference with the landowner's ***exclusive possession*** by a physical invasion of the land; in the latter, there is an interference with ***use or enjoyment***.

C. **PUBLIC NUISANCE**
Public nuisance is an act that unreasonably interferes with the ***health, safety, or property rights of the community***, *e.g.,* blocking a highway or using a building to commit criminal activities such as prostitution, bookmaking, etc. Recovery is available for public nuisance only if a private party has suffered some unique damage not suffered by the public at large.
Example: Pedestrians generally are inconvenienced by having to walk around an obstruction maintained by defendant on the sidewalk. Plaintiff, however, has tripped and fallen. This unique damage permits plaintiff to recover for the public nuisance.

D. **REMEDIES**

1. **Damages**
For a private nuisance, or for a public nuisance where plaintiff has suffered some unique damage, the usual remedy is damages.

2. **Injunctive Relief**
Where the ***legal remedy*** of damages is ***unavailable or inadequate***, injunctive relief may be granted. The legal remedy may be inadequate for a variety of reasons, *e.g.,* the nuisance is a continuing wrong, the nuisance is of the kind that will cause irreparable injury, etc. In deciding whether an injunction should issue, the courts take into consideration the relative hardships that will result to the parties from the grant or denial of the injunction. Hardships will not be balanced, however, where defendant's conduct was willful.

3. **Abatement by Self-Help**

a. **Abatement of Private Nuisance**
One has the privilege to enter upon defendant's land and personally abate the nuisance after notice to defendant and defendant's refusal to act. The force used may be only that necessary to accomplish the abatement, and the plaintiff is liable for additional harm done.

b. **Abatement of Public Nuisance**
One who has suffered some unique damage has a similar privilege to abate a public

nuisance by self-help. In the absence of such unique damage, however, a public nuisance may be abated or enjoined only by public authority.

E. DEFENSES

1. Legislative Authority

Conduct consistent with what a zoning ordinance or other legislative license permits is relevant but not conclusive evidence that the use is not a nuisance.

2. Conduct of Others

No one actor is liable for all the damage caused by the concurrence of his acts and others.

Example: Ten steel mills are polluting a stream. Each steel mill is responsible only for the pollution it causes.

3. Contributory Negligence

Contributory negligence is not ordinarily a defense to the tort of nuisance. However, when a nuisance is based on a negligence theory, one may not avert the consequences of his own contributory negligence by affixing to the negligence of the wrongdoer the label of a nuisance. In such a case, a plaintiff, though pleading nuisance, may have to show his freedom from contributory negligence.

4. "Coming to the Nuisance"

The problem: Has plaintiff assumed the risk, thereby being barred from recovery by the fact that he has "come to the nuisance," by purchasing land and moving in next to the nuisance after it is already in existence or operation? The prevailing rule is that, in the absence of a prescriptive right, the defendant may not condemn surrounding premises to endure the nuisance; *i.e.*, the ***purchaser is entitled to reasonable use or enjoyment of his land*** to the same extent as any other owner as long as he buys in good faith and not for the sole purpose of a harassing lawsuit.

VII. GENERAL CONSIDERATIONS FOR ALL TORT CASES

A. VICARIOUS LIABILITY

Vicarious liability is liability that is derivatively imposed. In short, this means that one person commits a tortious act against a third party, and another person is liable to the third party for this act. This may be so even though the other person has played no part in it, has done nothing whatever to aid or encourage it, or indeed has done everything possible to prevent it. This liability rests upon a special relationship between the tortfeasor and the person to whom his tortious conduct is ultimately imputed.

The basic situations that you should note for bar examination purposes are set out below.

1. Doctrine of Respondeat Superior

A master/employer will be vicariously liable for tortious acts committed by her servant/employee if the tortious acts occur ***within the scope of the employment relationship***.

a. Frolic and Detour

An employee on a delivery or on a business trip for his employer may commit a tort while deviating from the employer's business to run a personal errand. If the deviation was minor in time and geographic area, the employee will still be considered to be acting within the scope of employment rather than on a "frolic" of his own (for which the employer would not be liable).

b. **Intentional Torts**
It is usually held that intentional tortious conduct by employees is ***not*** within the scope of employment. In some circumstances, however, courts find intentional tortious conduct to be within the ambit of this relationship, such as when:

1) Force is authorized in the employment, *e.g.,* bouncer.

2) Friction is generated by the employment, *e.g.,* bill collector.

3) The employee is furthering the business of the employer, *e.g.,* removing customers from the premises because they are rowdy.

c. **Liability for Own Negligence**
Employers may be liable for their ***own negligence*** by negligently selecting or supervising their employees. This is ***not*** vicarious liability, however.

2. **Independent Contractor Situations**
In general, a principal will ***not*** be vicariously liable for tortious acts of her agent if the latter is an independent contractor. Two ***broad exceptions*** exist, however:

(i) The independent contractor is engaged in ***inherently dangerous activities***, *e.g.,* excavating next to a public sidewalk, blasting.

(ii) The duty, because of ***public policy*** considerations, is simply nondelegable, *e.g.,* the duty of a business to keep its premises safe for customers.

a. **Liability for Own Negligence**
An employer may be liable for her ***own negligence*** in selecting or supervising the independent contractor (*e.g.,* hospital liable for contracting with unqualified and incompetent physician who negligently treats hospital's patient). (This is ***not*** vicarious liability.)

3. **Partners and Joint Venturers**
Each member of a partnership or joint venture is vicariously liable for the tortious conduct of another member committed in the scope and course of the affairs of the partnership or joint venture.

a. **What Is a Joint Venture?**
A joint venture, although similar to a partnership, is for a more limited time period and more limited purpose. It is generally an undertaking to execute a small number of acts or objectives. A joint venture exists when two or more people enter into an activity if two elements are present:

1) **Common Purpose**
The test is not precise, but it would appear that the majority of courts would now

look for a "business purpose." The sharing of expenses between individuals is often highly persuasive.

Examples: 1) Two roommates were driving to a store to get decorating materials for their apartment when an accident occurred. *Held:* Joint venture.

2) Two parents were driving child to hospital. *Held:* No joint venture.

2) Mutual Right of Control

It is not crucial that the party does or does not give directions; it is sufficient if there is an understanding between the parties that each has a right to have her desires respected on the same basis as the others.

4. Automobile Owner for Driver

The general rule is that an automobile owner is ***not vicariously liable*** for the tortious conduct of another driving his automobile. However, many states by statute or judicial precedent have adopted the "***family car***" doctrine, by which the owner is liable for tortious conduct of ***immediate family or household members*** who are driving with the owner's express or implied permission. A number of states have now gone further by enacting "***permissive use***" statutes imposing liability for damage caused by ***anyone*** driving with such consent.

a. Liability for Owner's Negligence

Remember that the owner may be liable for her ***own negligence*** in entrusting the car to a driver. Some states have also imposed liability upon the owner if she was present in the car at the time of the accident, upon the theory that she could have prevented the negligent driving, and hence was negligent herself in not doing so. (This is not vicarious liability.)

5. Bailor for Bailee

Under the general rule, the bailor is ***not vicariously liable*** for the tortious conduct of his bailee. As above, the bailor may be liable for her ***own negligence*** in entrusting the bailed object. (This is not vicarious liability.)

6. Parent for Child

A parent is ***not vicariously liable*** for the tortious conduct of the child at common law. Note, however, that most states, by statute, make parents liable for the willful and intentional torts of their minor children up to a certain dollar amount (*e.g.,* $5,000).

a. Child Acting as Agent for Parents

Courts may impose vicarious liability if the child commits a tort while acting as the agent for the parents.

Example: Parent vicariously liable if child is in an accident while running an errand for his mother, or driving his sister to school, but not while on a date.

b. Parent Liable for Own Negligence

The parent may be held liable for her ***own negligence*** in allowing the child to do something, *e.g.,* use a dangerous object without proper instruction. Further, if the parent is apprised of the child's conduct on past occasions showing a tendency to injure another's person or property, she may be liable for not using due care in exercising control to mitigate such conduct, *e.g.,* by allowing the child to play with other children he has a history of attacking.

7. **Tavernkeepers**
At common law, no liability was imposed on vendors of intoxicating beverages for injuries resulting from the vendee's intoxication, whether the injuries were sustained by the vendee or by a third person as a result of the vendee's conduct. Many states, to avoid this common law rule, have enacted ***"Dramshop Acts."*** Such acts usually create a ***cause of action in favor of any third person injured*** by the intoxicated vendee. Several courts have imposed liability on tavernkeepers even in the absence of a Dramshop Act. This liability is based on ordinary negligence principles (the foreseeable risk of serving a minor or obviously intoxicated adult) rather than vicarious liability.

B. PARTIES—MULTIPLE DEFENDANT ISSUES

1. **Joint and Several Liability**
When two or more tortious acts combine to proximately cause an ***indivisible*** injury to a plaintiff, each tortfeasor is jointly and severally liable for that injury. This means that ***each is liable*** to the plaintiff for the ***entire damage*** incurred. Joint and several liability applies even though each tortfeasor acted entirely independently. However, if the actions are independent, plaintiff's injury is divisible, and it is possible to identify the portion of injuries caused by each defendant (*e.g.,* Car 1 breaks plaintiff's leg, and Car 2 breaks plaintiff's arm), then each will only be liable for the identifiable portion.

   a. **Tortfeasors Acting in Concert**
   When two or more tortfeasors act in concert (*i.e.,* by agreement) and injure plaintiff, then each will be jointly and severally liable for the entire injury. This is so even though the injury is divisible and one could identify what each tortfeasor has done alone.

   b. **Statutory Limitations**
   Many states have limited the joint liability doctrine by statute. Two of the most common types of statutes abolish joint liability either (i) for those tortfeasors judged to be less at fault than the plaintiff, or (ii) for all tortfeasors with regard to noneconomic damages (*e.g.,* pain and suffering). The liability of a tortfeasor in these situations is proportional to his fault.

2. **Satisfaction and Release**

   a. **Satisfaction**
   If plaintiff recovers full payment from one tortfeasor, either by settlement or payment of a judgment, there is a "satisfaction." She may not recover further against any other joint tortfeasor. Until there is a satisfaction, however, she may proceed against other jointly liable parties.

   b. **Release**
   A release is a surrender of plaintiff's cause of action against the party to whom the

release is given. Such a release to one of two tortfeasors at common law necessarily released the other. A majority of the states have now rejected the common law rule and provide that a release of one tortfeasor does ***not*** discharge other tortfeasors unless expressly provided in the release agreement. Rather, the claim against the others is reduced to the extent of the amount stipulated in the agreement or the amount of consideration paid, whichever is greater.

3. Contribution and Indemnity

a. Contribution

As stated above, where joint and several tort liability exists, it permits plaintiff to recover the entire judgment amount from any tortfeasor. The rule of contribution, adopted in some form in most states, allows any tortfeasor required to pay more than his share of damages to have a claim against the other jointly liable parties for the excess. Thus, contribution is a device whereby responsibility is ***apportioned*** among those who are at fault.

1) Methods of Apportionment

a) Comparative Contribution

Most states have a comparative contribution system (discussed below), whereby contribution is imposed ***in proportion to the relative fault*** of the various tortfeasors.

b) Equal Shares

A minority of states require all tortfeasors to pay ***equal shares*** regardless of their respective degrees of fault.

2) Contribution Tortfeasor Must Have Liability

The tortfeasor from whom contribution is sought must be originally liable to the plaintiff. If the contribution tortfeasor has a defense that would bar liability, such as intra-family tort immunity, he is not liable for contribution.

3) Not Applicable to Intentional Torts

Contribution is not allowed in favor of those who committed intentional torts. This is so even though each of the tortfeasors was equally culpable.

b. Indemnity

Indemnity involves ***shifting the entire loss*** between or among tortfeasors, in contrast to apportioning it as in contribution. Indemnity is available in the following circumstances:

1) Right to Indemnity by Contract

Contracts in which one person promises to indemnify another against consequences of his own negligence are generally upheld. The right to indemnification will not be read into an agreement unless there is evidence that the right was clearly intended.

2) Vicarious Liability

When one is held for damages caused by another simply because of his relationship to that person (*e.g.,* employer for employee's torts, landowner with nondelegable duty breached by an independent contractor, etc.), this party may seek indemnification from the person whose conduct actually caused the damage.

3) **Indemnity Under Strict Products Liability**
Each supplier of a defective product, where strict liability rules apply, is liable to an injured customer, but each supplier has a right of indemnification against all previous suppliers in the distribution chain. The manufacturer is ultimately liable if the product was defective when it left its control.

4) **Identifiable Difference in Degree of Fault**
A number of jurisdictions extend the principle of indemnity to allow one joint tortfeasor to recover against a co-joint tortfeasor where there is a considerable difference in degree of fault. In other words, he who is least at fault may be able to recover indemnification from the "more wrongful" tortfeasor.

a) **Examples**
The most common examples of such indemnification are:

(1) **Retailers Who Negligently Rely on Product's Condition**
Retailers who negligently fail to discover a product's defect may receive indemnification from the manufacturer who negligently manufactured it.

(2) **Where Liability Imposed Under Secondary Duty**
One whose liability is based on a secondary duty may recover indemnification from the person who had a primary duty.
Example: Municipal corporation under duty to keep streets safe may recover from a person who creates the unsafe condition causing an accident.

(3) **Active/Passive Negligence Doctrine**
Some jurisdictions allow a joint tortfeasor who is passively negligent to recover indemnification from a joint tortfeasor who is actively negligent.
Example: Charles parked his car in a no-parking zone, blocking the view of drivers approaching the intersection. Bowater, driving at 70 m.p.h., hits a pedestrian who could not be seen until it was too late to stop. If the pedestrian sues Charles and recovers, Charles may seek full reimbursement from Bowater by way of indemnification.

b) **Effect of Comparative Negligence System**
Most states with comparative negligence systems ***reject*** indemnity in degree of fault situations, instead applying a general comparative contribution system and apportioning damages based upon relative fault (*see* discussion below). These states continue to permit indemnity where indemnity rules are not based on differences in degree of fault, *e.g.,* vicarious liability cases.

c. **Comparative Contribution**
A ***majority*** of states have now adopted a comparative contribution system based on the ***relative fault*** of the various tortfeasors. Comparative contribution changes the traditional method of apportionment in contribution cases (*supra*) and supplants indemnification rules based on identifiable differences in degree of fault. In both situations, nonpaying tortfeasors are required to contribute only in proportion to their relative fault.

C. SURVIVAL AND WRONGFUL DEATH

1. **Survival of Tort Actions**
At common law, a tort action abated at the death of either the tortfeasor or the victim. Most states have changed this by statute, *i.e.,* the "survival acts." Thus, a victim's cause of action will survive to permit recovery of all damages from the time of injury to the time of death. In the majority of states, these acts apply to both torts to ***property*** and torts resulting in ***personal injury***.

a. **Torts that Expire on Victim's Death**
Exceptions exist in most jurisdictions for those torts that invade an ***intangible personal interest,*** *e.g.,* defamation, malicious prosecution, etc. These torts are felt to be so personal as to expire upon the victim's death.

2. **Wrongful Death**
Every state has now enacted some form of wrongful death act.

a. **Who May Bring Action?**
In some jurisdictions, the personal representative is the proper party to bring the action; in others, the surviving spouse or next of kin herself might be the proper party.

b. **Measure of Recovery**
The measure of recovery in wrongful death actions under most statutes is for the pecuniary injury resulting to the spouse and next of kin. Basically, this allows recovery for loss of support, loss of consortium, etc. It does ***not*** allow any recovery for decedent's pain and suffering; those damages would be an element of a personal injury survival action (*see* above) brought on behalf of the decedent.

1) **Deaths of Children, Elderly People**
Even though the actual loss of support may be very small where decedent is a child or elderly person, most states, nonetheless, allow recovery. Usually, the judgment is quite modest.

2) **Rights of Creditors**
Creditors of the decedent have no claim against the amount awarded.

c. **Effect of Defenses**

1) **Defenses Against Deceased**
Recovery is allowed ***only*** to the extent that the deceased could have recovered in

the action if he had lived. Thus, for example, his contributory negligence would reduce a wrongful death recovery in comparative negligence states.

2) **Defenses Against Beneficiary**
Defenses against potential beneficiaries do not bar the action. However, that particular beneficiary's recovery will be reduced or barred under the state's comparative negligence rules. The total damage award assessed by the jury will be reduced by the amount withheld from the beneficiary.

D. TORTIOUS INTERFERENCES WITH FAMILY RELATIONSHIPS

1. Husband-Wife

In most jurisdictions, both husbands and wives may recover damages for loss of their spouse's consortium or services because of injuries to the spouse from defendant's tortious conduct, whether intentional, negligent, or based on strict liability.

Example: Chauncey hits Husband on the head with a lead pipe, leaving him in a coma for several months and permanently disabled. Wife can recover from Chauncey for loss of consortium and services.

2. Parent-Child

a. Parent's Actions

A parent may maintain an action for loss of the child's services when the child is injured as a result of defendant's tortious conduct, whether such conduct is intentional, negligent, or based on strict liability.

b. Child's Action

A child has ***no*** action in most jurisdictions against one who tortiously injures his parent.

3. Nature of Action for Family Relationship Interference

The action for interference with family relationships is ***derivative.*** Recovery in the derivative action depends on the potential success of the injured family member's own action. Thus, any defense that would prevent recovery by the injured family member, *e.g.,* her own contributory negligence, will also prevent recovery in the derivative action for interference with family relationships.

Further, a defense against a family member seeking such a derivative recovery may also defeat the action.

Example: Husband and Wife, while driving, collide with Chauncey's car. Wife is severely injured; Husband and Chauncey are both negligent. Husband's derivative action for loss of Wife's consortium and services will be defeated by his own contributory negligence.

E. TORT IMMUNITIES

1. Intra-Family Tort Immunities

a. Injury to Person

Under the traditional view, one member of a family unit (*i.e.,* husband, wife, or

unemancipated child) could ***not*** sue another in tort for personal injury. This view has undergone substantial change in most states.

1) **Husband-Wife Immunity Abolished**
Most states have abolished interspousal immunity. Either spouse may now maintain a tort action against the other.

2) **Parent-Child Immunity Limited**
A slight majority of states have abolished parent-child immunity; however, these states generally grant parents broad discretion in the parent's exercise of parental authority or supervision. The remaining states retain parent-child immunity but do not apply it in cases of ***intentional*** tortious conduct and, in many of these states, in ***automobile accident*** cases (at least to the extent of insurance coverage).

b. **Injury to Property**
A suit for property damage may usually be maintained by any family member against any other family member. In short, to the extent that intra-family tort immunity exists, it applies to personal, not property, injuries.

2. **Governmental Tort Immunity**
Under the doctrine of sovereign immunity, governmental units were traditionally not subject to tort actions unless they had consented to the suit. Now, by statute and judicial decision, that immunity is considerably limited. Note, however, that a waiver of sovereign immunity does not create any new tort duties; it only waives immunity for existing statutory or common law duties of care.

a. **Federal Government**
By virtue of the Federal Tort Claims Act, Title 28 U.S.C., the United States has ***waived immunity*** for tortious acts. Under its provisions, the federal government may now be held liable to the same extent as a private individual. However, the Act spells out several situations where this immunity will still attach:

1) **United States Still Immune for Certain Enumerated Torts**
Immunity still attaches for (i) assault, (ii) battery, (iii) false imprisonment, (iv) false arrest, (v) malicious prosecution, (vi) abuse of process, (vii) libel and slander, (viii) misrepresentation and deceit, and (ix) interference with contract rights.

2) **Discretionary Acts Distinguished from Ministerial Acts**
The immunity is not waived for acts characterized as "discretionary," as distinguished from those acts termed "ministerial." In general, discretionary activity is that which takes place at the ***planning or decisionmaking level***, while ministerial acts are performed at the ***operational level*** of government (*e.g.,* repairing traffic signals, driving a vehicle).

3) **Government Contractors**
A government contractor may assert the federal government's immunity defense in a products liability case if the contractor conformed to reasonable, precise specifications approved by the government and warned the government about any known dangers in the product.

b. State Governments
Most states have substantially waived their immunity from tort actions to the same extent as the federal government. Thus, immunity still attaches for discretionary acts and for legislative and judicial decisionmaking.

Note: Where federal or state sovereign immunity still attaches, it also, as a general rule, covers not only "the government" but the various federal and state agencies as well, *e.g.*, schools, hospitals, etc.

c. Municipalities
About half of the states have abolished municipal tort immunity by statute or judicial decision to the same extent that they have waived their own immunity. Hence, immunity is abolished for everything but discretionary acts and policy decisions.

1) Immunity Abolished—Public Duty Rule Limitation
Where municipal immunity has been abolished, many courts apply the "public duty" doctrine to limit the scope of government liability. A duty that is owed to the public at large, such as the duty of police to protect citizens, is not owed to any particular citizen, and no liability exists for failure to provide police protection in the absence of a ***special relationship*** between the municipality and the citizen that gives rise to a special duty. A special relationship can be shown by: (i) an assumption by the municipality, through promises or actions, of an affirmative duty to act on behalf of the party who was injured; (ii) knowledge on the part of the municipality's agents that inaction could lead to harm; (iii) some form of direct contact between the municipality's agents and the injured party; and (iv) that party's justifiable reliance on the municipality's affirmative undertaking.

2) Immunity Retained—Limited to Governmental Functions
Where municipal immunity still exists in its traditional form, the courts have sought in many instances to avoid its consequences. This has primarily been accomplished by differentiating between "governmental" and "proprietary" functions of the municipality. Immunity attaches to the former but not to the latter.

a) Governmental Functions
Certain functions historically have been construed such that they could only be performed adequately by the government, and thus they are held to be "governmental" in character, *e.g.,* police, fire, courts, etc. As stated above, ***tort immunity attaches*** to those functions.

b) Proprietary Functions
If the municipality is performing a function that might as well have been provided by a private corporation, the function is construed as a "proprietary" one (*e.g.,* utility companies, maintaining airport parking lot, etc.). ***No tort immunity*** attaches here.

The inference that a function is "proprietary" is strengthened where the city collects ***revenues*** by virtue of providing the service.

d. Immunity of Public Officials

In addition to the immunity conferred on the government entity, government officials may also have immunity from tort liability. Immunity applies to a public officer carrying out his official duties where they involve ***discretionary*** acts (*supra*) done without malice or improper purpose. On the other hand, for acts that are construed as ***ministerial*** (which generally involve lower-level officials), no tort immunity applies.

3. Charitable Immunity

The majority of jurisdictions have abrogated the common law rule of charitable immunity either by statute or decision. Even where such immunity still exists, it is riddled with exceptions.

REVIEW QUESTIONS

INTRODUCTORY NOTE

The true/false questions that follow are intended to serve as both a substantive review and a diagnostic test. Respond to the questions quickly and compare your answers with those found at the end of this section. This will allow you to identify areas in which you may need further review.

FILL IN ANSWER

1. As a joke, and intending only to frighten his golf companion B, A swings a golf club at B's head, but stops his swing when the head of the club is still six inches from B's head. Nevertheless, due to a defective shaft, the head of the club flies off and strikes B in the eye, causing serious injury.

   a. A cannot be liable for an assault since the injury was an accident. ________

   b. A cannot be liable for a battery. ________

   c. If the head of the club had not flown off, no tort would have been committed. ________

2. Same facts as in previous paragraph, but suppose B ducked and the club head struck C, whom A did not even know was there.

   a. A is liable for a battery upon C, even though his intent was only to frighten B. ________

   b. A is not liable for a battery upon B, because there was no actual touching of B. ________

   c. A is liable for an assault upon B, if B was aware that the club head was aimed at her, and ducked to avoid it; but if she ducked for some other reason, then A would not be liable even for an assault as to B. ________

3. If A, at a dignified social function and for the purpose of making B appear ridiculous, pulls a chair out from under him as B is about to sit down, A commits a battery only if B suffers physical injury. ________

4. Words alone cannot constitute an assault. ________

5. A points a gun at B, his brother, and says, "If you weren't my brother, I'd kill you now!" B is in terror for his life. This is an assault. ________

6. Schoolmaster at a boarding school, A, refuses to permit pupil, B, to go home for the holidays, although B's father has asked A that B be permitted to come home. B is unaware of the discussion between A and her father.

a. A is not guilty of false imprisonment of B, because force is an essential element. ________

b. A is not guilty of false imprisonment of B, because B was not aware of her father's request that she be permitted to leave. ________

7. A, a private citizen, sees B and C bending over a dead person, D. B and C accuse each other of murdering D. A is not sure who killed D, but he has a reasonable suspicion that either B or C did it.

   a. If A arrests B, A will be liable if it turns out C was the murderer. ________

   b. A is privileged to arrest both B and C, even if it turns out F was the real murderer. ________

8. If D's car rolls onto P's land, some further facts might make the entry a trespass. ________

9. The owner of stolen property can maintain an action against one who innocently purchased it from the thief and who will not honor a demand for it. ________

10. Implied consent as a defense to the commission of a battery will not be available if the plaintiff subjectively feared the contact. ________

11. Consent is no defense if the battery also constitutes a crime. ________

12. An actor is not privileged to use any force in protecting his home or possessions without first demanding that the intruder leave, unless it reasonably appears that the demand would be futile or would further endanger the actor's property. ________

13. A person is never privileged to use mechanical devices in protecting his home or property. ________

14. T, a tenant of L's apartment building, remains in possession after termination of the lease. L may use reasonable force to evict T. ________

15. A is completely privileged to enter B's land to escape a dangerous blizzard. ________

16. A is incompletely privileged for the entry in 15., above. ________

17. If a reasonable person would not foresee a possibility of harm to anyone by what D was doing, no duty of due care is owed to anyone who is hurt. ________

18. D negligently sets fire to his own home, and it burns so fiercely that a risk of serious harm to anyone entering the building is apparent. P, a neighbor, sees the fire and dashes into the burning building, thereby sustaining injuries.

a. D may be liable to P if P entered the burning building after hearing cries for help from inside. ________

b. D may be liable to P if P entered the building to save some of her own property which she had previously loaned to D. ________

19. A invites her friend B to dinner. The private road leading to A's house has been dangerously undermined by recent storms, but this cannot be observed by a person driving along the road. While B is driving along the road, it collapses, causing him serious injuries.

a. A should have inspected the road over which she knew her guest, B, would have to drive in order to reach the house and, if such inspection would have revealed the danger, A is liable for B's injuries. ________

b. A is not liable for B's injuries unless she had actual knowledge of the dangerous condition and failed to warn B thereof. ________

c. A is not liable for B's injuries, because a person coming onto another's land assumes the risk of any dangerous condition thereon. ________

20. A land occupier owes no duty to persons outside his property with respect to:

a. Tree limbs growing over the boundary line and overhanging a public road. ________

b. Electric fence located entirely inside property lines. ________

c. Irrigation trenches, several feet deep, running alongside a public highway. ________

21. On a part of her land previously free from trespassers, A sees B, a trespasser, about to come in contact with moving machinery maintained by A on her land. A has time to shut off the power but fails to do so and B is injured. A is liable to B. ________

22. Large piles of slag accumulate on A's mining property, which is unfenced. Neighbor children play on these piles, although A has posted a "DANGER—NO TRESPASSING" sign. One of these children, B, age seven, is injured when she cuts herself on the slag. A is liable for B's injuries. ________

23. In the middle of the night, police officer P is summoned to D's house for the purpose of breaking up a riotous party. P is hurt by a condition unknown to D but about which D should have known. Most courts would hold D liable to P. ________

24. Door-to-door sales solicitors are generally entitled only to the status of a licensee on another's property, while garbage collectors are generally treated as invitees. ________

25. If a lessor has not agreed to keep the leased premises in repair, he is under no duty to anyone. ________

26. D's clear proof that she complied with the statute's safety requirements will entitle D to a directed verdict. ________

27. If one person has the authority and actual ability to control the acts of another in his presence, and fails to do so, he may be held liable for the negligent acts of that other person. ________

28. Such liability (in 27., above) is an example of vicarious liability. ________

29. In determining whether D's conduct was negligent, evidence is never admissible as to what conduct was customary in the community under the same circumstances. ________

30. A and B are both driving carelessly along a lonely road. A collision occurs and B is thrown out of the car into the middle of the road, bleeding profusely and unconscious. A drives on without giving B any attention, although she could have checked the bleeding. B bleeds to death.

    a. A is liable for B's death even if B was contributorily negligent in causing the accident. ________

    b. A would be liable for the death even if she had not been at fault in the collision. ________

31. If the negligent acts of two defendants, D and X, have concurred in causing P's injuries, and, but for the concurrence, P would not have been injured at all, D and X are both liable. ________

32. If P would have sustained the same injury from the act of either defendant acting alone, D and X are both liable. ________

33. If D negligently causes such serious injury to X that X becomes violently insane, and, while in this condition, X attacks and injures P, D is liable for P's injuries on the rationale that a tortfeasor takes his victim as he finds him. ________

34. Direct causation is another name for actual causation. ________

35. The intentional or criminal intervening act of a third party will be held to cut off a defendant's liability if that act is violent. ________

36. Druggist erroneously fills a prescription with a poisonous drug and delivers it to Patient. Nurse, employed by Patient, discovers the poison in the prescription, but negligently fails to alert Patient or Doctor. Patient thereafter consumes the poison and is hurt.

    a. Druggist is liable. ________

    b. Nurse is liable. ________

37. "Contributory negligence" and "avoidable consequences" are different ways of describing the same idea. ________

38. Contributory negligence is a defense to recklessness in a comparative negligence jurisdiction. ________

39. Pedestrian P is negligent in attempting to cross a busy highway at night in the face of oncoming traffic and is struck by D's auto in a traditional contributory negligence jurisdiction. Which of the following facts, if any, might help P in establishing liability against D?

    a. D would have seen P in plenty of time to avoid striking P, but was talking to a passenger in the car and was not looking at the road. ________

    b. D saw P the instant before impact and attempted to slam on his brakes but instead hit the accelerator. P would not have been injured if D had hit his brakes. ________

    c. D in fact saw P in time to avoid the accident, but D's brakes failed. ________

40. A purchases a car from B Auto Co. under a conditional sales contract. Only a few payments have been made on the contract when the car is totally demolished in an accident with C, in which A is contributorily negligent. B Auto Co. can recover from C for its interest in the car, even though A was contributorily negligent. ________

41. Plaintiff's assumption of the risk is never a good defense when defendant's conduct violates a statute. ________

42. Every contract whereby one party waives a cause of action against another for negligence is invalid as against public policy. In other words, a defendant can never be permitted to insulate himself by contract from the results of his own negligent conduct. ________

43. Under the general view, one who blasts in a desolate area is liable if the blast harms a cave dweller whose presence was unknown and not reasonably discoverable. ________

44. A purchases a new truck manufactured by D Co., from a dealer, B. The steering shaft of the truck has an imperceptible crack. While A is driving carefully along a crowded street, the shaft breaks, causing A to lose control of the vehicle. The truck jumps the curb and crashes into a store, injuring A, his son S, who is a passenger in the truck, P, a pedestrian, and T, who is the owner of the store.

    a. A may sue D on a strict liability theory. ________

    b. A may sue B on a strict liability theory. ________

c. S may sue D on a strict liability theory. ________

d. S may sue B on a strict liability theory. ________

e. T may sue D on a strict liability theory. ________

f. T may sue B on a strict liability theory. ________

g. P may sue D on a strict liability theory. ________

h. Actions for negligence against D may be brought by A and S but not by P and T. ________

i. None of the four plaintiffs can bring an action against D for a breach of implied warranty. ________

j. None of the four plaintiffs can bring an action against B for a breach of implied warranty. ________

45. There is a trespass if D causes smoke from his property to drift onto P's property. ________

46. An action for nuisance cannot be maintained unless P is able to show that D's conduct was either intentional or negligent. ________

47. A parks his car on a highway so as to completely obstruct B's egress from her land to the street. B is unable to locate A and therefore carefully pushes A's car out of the way. In so doing, a tire is accidentally punctured. B is liable to A. ________

48. The owner of a saloon is liable for injuries to a customer, resulting from:

a. A bouncer hitting a patron. ________

b. A waiter negligently spilling a hot drink on a customer. ________

49. If A was slandered during his lifetime, his executor can pursue A's cause of action after his death. ________

50. D utters a defamatory remark regarding "Paul Smith" to T. D intended his comment to apply to an individual whose full name is Paul J. Smith (whom T did not even know), but T reasonably thought D was referring to T's friend, Paul M. Smith. Paul M. Smith can sue for defamation. ________

51. P, a noted singer, is currently appearing at a local nightclub. D's newspaper publishes a report that a singer currently appearing in town "has been secretly working with the Mafia." P cannot sue for libel because he was not named. ________

52. A writes and mails to B a letter that is full of defamatory comments about B, all of which are untrue. B reads the letter and shows it to his friends, who tell him to consult an attorney. An attorney is most likely to advise B that he has no cause of action against A for defamation because there was no publication. ________

53. D newspaper publishes a story that the ABC Aluminum Co. is polluting the city's water supply and that to avoid city action against the company for violating an ordinance, ABC is giving large gifts to C, a city council member. The newspaper has based its story on rumors that are false. C sues D for libel. D newspaper has no plausible defenses. ________

54. Truth is a complete defense to defamation, even if the publisher did not believe the statement to be true when she made it. ________

55. D solicits funds for a worthwhile charity by advertising lists of donors but mistakenly includes P's name as one of the donors. P is a community leader who has not donated to this particular charity.

    a. This might be an "invasion" of P's privacy. ________

    b. This might be defamation. ________

    c. If P had given to the charity but wanted her gift to be anonymous, D's disclosure might be an invasion of privacy. ________

56. P asked D, an expert, to drill test holes to determine the depth of the fill of specific land that P contemplated purchasing from T. P explained that he would not purchase the land if the fill went deeper than 16 inches. After making five test holes, D submitted her report that the fill was only 12 inches and presented P with her bill for $25. P purchased the land but, because the fill was actually four feet deep in most places, P had to expend $5,000 more for the foundation.

    a. P may recover from D for negligent misrepresentation. ________

    b. P may recover from D for intentional misrepresentation. ________

57. A person is justified in relying absolutely on the assertions of fact of another and is under no duty to investigate their accuracy. ________

58. A person is never justified in relying on a representation of opinion, value, or quality. ________

59. The defendant in a malicious prosecution action will prevail if he can show that, although the plaintiff was later proved innocent, he had sufficient grounds to reasonably believe the plaintiff to be guilty. ________

60. Malicious prosecution actions can never be maintained against public prosecutors. ________

61. D negligently injures a child in the street. The injury was seen by the child's friend, standing next to her, and by the child's mother, standing across the street. Both suffer emotional distress resulting in physical injury. Photographs of the accident were also published in the newspaper.

a. Friend can recover from D for the harm she suffered. ________

b. Mother can recover from D for the harm she suffered. ________

c. Child can recover from newspaper for invasion of privacy. ________

ANSWERS TO REVIEW QUESTIONS

Ques. No.	Answer	Explanation
1.a.	*FALSE*	A intended to cause apprehension and that intent will suffice.
b.	*FALSE*	Transferred intent will apply.
c.	*FALSE*	All elements of assault are present.
2.a.	*TRUE*	The intent to frighten B is transferred to A's infliction of harm on C.
b.	*TRUE*	Apprehension is insufficient for battery.
c.	*TRUE*	Even telling B afterwards what a close call she had would not make this an assault unless B was apprehensive at the time of the danger.
3.	*FALSE*	An offensive touching will suffice and nominal damages are available.
4.	*TRUE*	Some overt act is necessary.
5.	*FALSE*	Because A has not imposed a danger of imminent harm. The fact that B is afraid is not enough to warrant liability. The words negate the assault.
6.a.	*FALSE*	Force is not an essential element of false imprisonment.
b.	*TRUE*	According to the Restatement, awareness is a requirement unless B has suffered physical harm during the confinement.
7.a.	*FALSE*	A reasonably could suspect both of them since they had accused each other. Since a felony was in fact committed, A will be protected if he reasonably believes he has the correct person, even if he is wrong.
b.	*TRUE*	Reasonable belief that both B and C committed the murder is also possible.
8.	*TRUE*	But only if D intended the entry. Otherwise, try negligence or strict liability.
9.	*TRUE*	This is a classic case of the harshness of the conversion doctrine.
10.	*FALSE*	D is protected if he acts on what he believes a reasonable person would consent to, whatever the victim's unexpressed subjective desires.
11.	*FALSE*	Although there is a split on this, the modern view is that consent will be a defense—except perhaps if the crime also involves a breach of the peace.
12.	*TRUE*	This is an essential element of the privilege of defense of property.

13.	***FALSE***	A person is privileged to use mechanical devices wherever he would be privileged to use such force in person.
14.	***FALSE***	Generally, force may not be used to recover land that is peacefully occupied by someone thereon without authority.
15.	***FALSE***	This is a case of incomplete privilege.
16.	***TRUE***	And A must pay for whatever actual harm he does as a result of the entry.
17.	***TRUE***	Under both the Andrews and Cardozo views, the foreseeability of harm is a prerequisite to any finding of negligence.
18.a.	***TRUE***	A rescuer may recover if her behavior is reasonable and here it appears that she is trying to save a human life. She will recover unless her attempt was foolhardy.
b.	***FALSE***	The danger is apparently much too great to justify attempted rescue of property.
19.a.	***FALSE***	A guest is treated as a licensee and there is no duty to inspect or make conditions safe for that guest.
b.	***TRUE***	The duty is only one to warn of ***known*** dangerous conditions.
c.	***FALSE***	The reason is incorrect. Persons coming onto land do not assume the risk of "any dangerous condition" but only of certain ones—depending on the status of the person entering the land and the knowledge of the occupier.
20.a.	***TRUE***	As a general rule there is no such duty, but there is an exception for decaying trees in urban areas.
b.	***FALSE***	This is an artificial condition as to which he does owe a duty of care if it is reasonably foreseeable that harm might be suffered by those outside the land. The location "inside" the land is not entirely dispositive—especially since persons may stray from the road.
c.	***FALSE***	Again, there is a problem of those who may stray from the road and thus a duty is owed.
21.	***TRUE***	The trespasser has been discovered and a duty is owed even though there was no duty to look out for him in the first place.
22.	***TRUE***	A sign is inadequate if there is reason to know that young children unable to read or appreciate the sign are playing in an area of danger.
23.	***FALSE***	Under the "firefighter's rule," firefighters and police officers are generally treated like licensees (for whom there is no duty of prior inspection).

24.	***TRUE***	These are the rules of status.
25.	***FALSE***	As to existing dangers, there is a continuing duty of care owed to the lessee until the lessee has an opportunity to discover such problems and dangers himself. If the land is leased on a short-term basis for public activities, the lessor owes users of the land a duty to repair existing dangerous conditions.
26.	***FALSE***	Compliance with statutes is rarely enough to establish nonnegligence since statutes usually set only minimum standards of care.
27.	***TRUE***	As a general principle of duty of care by those in authority.
28.	***FALSE***	This is an example of primary negligence and not of vicarious liability.
29.	***FALSE***	Evidence is often admissible as to custom, but it is rarely controlling.
30.a.	***TRUE***	One whose negligence imperils another has a duty to use reasonable care to aid that person.
b.	***TRUE***	Even one whose conduct was not tortious has a duty to act affirmatively for the benefit of another if the conduct has caused the other bodily harm.
31.	***TRUE***	Multiple causation does not defeat the plaintiff's case.
32.	***TRUE***	If both are substantial factors in P's harm, P may recover from both.
33.	***FALSE***	X is the person who became insane and he is not the victim. If D is liable here, it is not because of the rule that a tortfeasor takes his victim as he finds him but rather on a proximate cause analysis, which in turn will depend on how the court treats the intervening insanity.
34.	***FALSE***	Direct causation is sometimes relevant in considering questions of proximate cause. It has no relevance whatsoever to issues of actual causation.
35.	***FALSE***	The test is reasonable foreseeability of the intervening act, not whether it is criminal or violent.
36.a.	***TRUE***	Another party's subsequent intervening negligent conduct does not cut off the original party's liability for negligence.
b.	***TRUE***	Nurse was negligent and Nurse's negligence was the proximate cause of Patient's harm.
37.	***FALSE***	Contributory negligence deals with unreasonable behavior that contributes to the harm, while "avoidable consequences" deals with whether the plaintiff behaves reasonably in mitigating damages after having been injured.
38.	***TRUE***	In contrast to the traditional rule, in most comparative negligence jurisdictions contributory negligence is a defense to willful or wanton misconduct and will reduce the plaintiff's recovery.

39.a.	*FALSE*	This appears to be a case in which P was inattentive, and the fact that D was also inattentive will not help in avoiding the defense of contributory negligence.
b.	*TRUE*	If D's failure to hit the brakes was negligence, it might be viewed as last clear chance negligence and thus avoid the effect of P's contributory negligence.
c.	*FALSE*	Because of the bad brakes, D did not in fact have the last clear chance, and contributory negligence will bar recovery in a traditional contributory negligence jurisdiction.
40.	*TRUE*	Contributory negligence is not imputed in this situation.
41.	*FALSE*	Unless the statute was designed to protect a particular class of people and plaintiff is a member of that class.
42.	*FALSE*	Unless the contract is affecting a public interest (*e.g.,* contracts by public utilities), disclaimers of negligence liability are generally upheld if freely bargained for.
43.	*FALSE*	There is a "foreseeable plaintiff" notion in most states.
44.a.	*TRUE*	Even though there is no privity, most courts will treat the action under a tort analysis.
b.	*TRUE*	The retailer is generally liable on a strict liability theory.
c.	*TRUE*	S is a user who is entitled to invoke strict liability under most theories.
d.	*TRUE*	A user may also sue the retailer on strict liability.
e.	*TRUE*	T is a bystander and, in most states that have ruled on the question, may sue in strict liability.
f.	*TRUE*	T is a bystander. (*See* answer in e., above.)
g.	*TRUE*	P is a bystander.
h.	*FALSE*	All parties may sue for negligence because privity requirements have been abolished.
i.	*FALSE*	Most states now find privity at least where the buyer (A), his family (S), or his household or guests suffer personal injury.
j.	*FALSE*	At the least, A has a legitimate breach of warranty claim because he was in privity of contract with B.
45.	*FALSE*	This is generally treated as a nuisance action and goes to use and enjoyment rather than possession.
46.	*FALSE*	Sometimes a nuisance may be found on the basis of strict liability.

47. *FALSE* B has behaved reasonably, and that reasonable use of force will be a defense even if an injury is suffered. This is an abatement of a nuisance and is comparable to a reasonable use of force in a personal injury case that somehow leads to actual harm.

48.a. *TRUE* As long as the act was in the scope of the bouncer's employment.

b. *TRUE* Under the general rules of employer-employee liability.

49. *FALSE* Defamation is one of those actions that dies with the plaintiff and does not survive.

50. *TRUE* If Paul can show that he was reasonably understood to be the one referred to.

51. *FALSE* One need not actually be named if he can prove he has been defamed by use of colloquium or as a member of a small group.

52. *TRUE* B is apparently an adult and his showing of the letter to friends and the attorney is voluntary and is no basis for finding the necessary publication element.

53. *FALSE* This is a classic case for the expanded *New York Times* privilege, and the question would then be whether the newspaper's reliance on the rumors was reckless behavior.

54. *TRUE* The test is at the trial and not at the time of speaking or writing.

55.a. *FALSE* This would probably not be a false light variety invasion of privacy, unless it would be highly offensive to a reasonable person under the circumstances and was made with malice.

b. *TRUE* But only if there are peculiar conditions in which members of the public could reasonably find it defamatory to have given to this particular charity.

c. *TRUE* Though this might be more of a breach of contract than a classic tort invasion.

56.a. *TRUE* There is a direct contract relationship present here and no privity problem.

b. *TRUE* If P can ***prove*** either deliberate misrepresentation or recklessness in the conduct of the test.

57. *TRUE* A person need not investigate, but if he does know of error he may not blindly rush ahead.

58. *FALSE* Although ***generally true***, the statement is too broad; if the relationship of the parties is such that the speaker knows a lot about the product or is in some fiduciary relation to the recipient, the recipient may rely on the opinions as to value or quality.

59.	***TRUE***	Lack of probable cause is one of the essential elements of malicious prosecution.
60.	***TRUE***	Public prosecutors are absolutely privileged in their behavior in bringing prosecutions.
61.a.	***TRUE***	She was in the zone of physical danger, so she can recover for her distress from the threat of physical impact.
b.	***TRUE***	Even though standing across the street is probably outside the zone of physical danger, a majority of courts now allow recovery because the mother was closely related to the child, was present at the scene, and observed the accident as it happened.
c.	***FALSE***	Photographs of accidents are generally deemed newsworthy.

ESSAY EXAM QUESTIONS

INTRODUCTORY NOTE

The essay questions that follow have been selected to provide you with an opportunity to experience how the substantive law you have been reviewing may be tested in the hypothetical essay examination question context. These sample essay questions are a valuable self-diagnostic tool designed to enable you to enhance your issue-spotting ability and practice your exam writing skills.

It is suggested that you approach each question as though under actual examination conditions. The time allowed for each question is 60 minutes. You should spend 15 to 20 minutes spotting issues, underlining key facts and phrases, jotting notes in the margins, and outlining your answer. ***If*** you organize your thoughts well, 40 minutes will be more than adequate for writing them down. Should you prefer to forgo the actual writing involved on these questions, be sure to give yourself no more time for issue-spotting than you would on the actual examination.

The BARBRI technique for writing a well-organized essay answer is to (i) spot the issues in a question and then (ii) analyze and discuss each issue using the "CIRAC" method:

C — State your ***conclusion*** first. (In other words, you must think through your answer ***before*** you start writing.)

I — State the ***issue*** involved.

R — Give the ***rule(s)*** of law involved.

A — ***Apply*** the rule(s) of law to the facts.

C — Finally, restate your ***conclusion***.

After completing (or outlining) your own analysis of each question, compare it with the BARBRI model answer provided herein. A passing answer does ***not*** have to match the model one, but it should cover most of the issues presented and the law discussed and should ***apply the law to the facts*** of the question. Use of the CIRAC method results in the best answer you can write.

EXAM QUESTION NO. 1

In an outlying, sparsely settled area, Doe's car collided one evening with a car driven by Crane, resulting in damage to Crane's car. Crane was blameless. Doe had been driving at 30 miles per hour in an area where the traffic law prescribes a maximum speed of 15 miles per hour. Doe is prepared to show that, in the area in question, this legal requirement is pretty universally ignored by motorists.

When Doe started out again, he forgot to turn on his lights. He soon ran into another car which, in the darkness, he had failed to see in time. The car thus hit belonged to Smith, who had negligently parked on the highway with his lights out and had gone to sleep in his car. In this accident, Doe's passenger, Jones, suffered a deep cut from which she bled profusely.

Doe's car was heavily damaged and rendered inoperable. Smith's car was damaged but remained operable, although in testing it Smith reported that the brakes were "soft" and untrustworthy as a result of the collision. No houses or other cars were in sight. After a hurried discussion, all three agreed that, despite the known condition of the brakes, it would be best to take Jones in Smith's car to the hospital about two miles down the road. On the way, the brakes failed, and in the resulting accident Jones suffered a fracture and the car was further damaged.

Discuss possible recoveries by Crane, Smith, and Jones.

EXAM QUESTION NO. 2

Mistkill, Inc. manufactured and distributed a weed-killing spray for use by growers of narrow-leaved plants. It was very effective on broad-leaved weeds—and any other broad-leaved plants—but imaginative research and a rigorous system of quality control had eliminated all toxicity to human or animal life. Mistkill sold to Upwind a barrel of its spray that had become contaminated with strychnine. There is no evidence that the contamination was due to any lack of care in the manufacturing process or that it should have been detected by Mistkill or Upwind. Upwind sprayed the contents of the barrel on his crop of rye grass from an airplane in a manner recommended by the Department of Agriculture. A gentle breeze carried a small quantity onto his neighbor Potter's land. Fortunately, this missed Potter's broad-leaved tobacco crop but, unfortunately, some of it was inhaled by Eagle Scout, Potter's valuable stud horse. The inhalation would have caused no more than a mild stomach upset in a normal horse, but Eagle Scout had a very acute, very rare, and hitherto unsuspected susceptibility to strychnine and died as a result of inhaling the spray.

Potter sued Mistkill and Upwind for the loss of her horse, and (as permitted by local procedure) Upwind cross-claimed for recovery from Mistkill in the event that he should be held liable. The case was tried without a jury and all of the above facts, and the horse's value, were proved without substantial contradiction.

What judgments? Discuss.

EXAM QUESTION NO. 3

Andrew took his car to Bob's Repair Shop and directed him to lubricate the car and adjust the steering mechanism. While so doing, Bob noticed that an important steel pin connecting the braking mechanism was worn nearly through, although it was still holding. Bob said nothing about it to Andrew.

Several days thereafter Andrew was driving at a high rate of speed on the highway. About 100 feet ahead of him and standing on the curb was Peter, who was obviously inattentive and was preparing to walk into the street in the face of dangerous oncoming traffic. Andrew, at this time, had glanced away from the road. If he had been looking, he would have had plenty of time to bring the car to a halt, or to slow it down sufficiently so there would have been no risk of striking an inattentive pedestrian such as Peter. As it was, Andrew first saw Peter when Peter was only a short distance directly ahead of him in the street. By the time Peter looked up and saw Andrew's vehicle, he was unable to get out of the way. Andrew jammed on his brakes with great force and would have stopped in time but for the fact that the defective pin in the braking mechanism snapped under the heavy pressure, and the brakes failed to function. Peter was struck by Andrew's car and seriously injured.

Discuss Peter's rights, if any, against Andrew and against Bob.

EXAM QUESTION NO. 4

A town ordinance prohibited the parking of cars so as to block driveways. In violation of this ordinance, Jones parked his car blocking Dr. Paul's driveway.

Smith, who resided in a nearby rural area, telephoned Dr. Paul to come right out because her son, Tom, had been bitten by a snake. Dr. Paul said he would come, started to go, but was unable to back his car out because of Jones's car. Seeing no one around, Dr. Paul released the brake on Jones's car and attempted to push it away. However, in so doing, he suddenly developed a hernia, suffered excruciating pain, and returned with difficulty to his office, where he made several phone calls trying to get another doctor to go see Tom. Due to unavoidable circumstances, he was unable for a long time to contact another doctor, but finally reached Dr. White, who said she would go.

When Dr. White arrived at Smith's home, she found the poison had spread so far that she was unable to save Tom's life. It is agreed that had Dr. Paul been able to respond to Smith's call without delay, he would in all probability have arrived in sufficient time to save Tom's life. (A statute in the jurisdiction gives an action for wrongful death to the parent of a deceased child.)

As Dr. White was driving back to her office, she negligently took her eyes off the road to examine her appointment book. Because of this, she failed to notice Adams, who was staggering on the highway in a helpless, drunken condition, until it was too late to avoid striking and injuring him.

What are the rights of Dr. Paul, Smith, and Adams? Discuss.

ANSWERS TO ESSAY EXAM QUESTIONS

ANSWER TO EXAM QUESTION NO. 1

First Crash

Crane v. Doe: Doe will be liable to Crane. At issue is whether Doe's violation of the speed limit will establish the requisite standard of care.

The prima facie case for negligence consists of: (i) a duty owed by the plaintiff to the defendant to act as a reasonably prudent person under the same or similar circumstances; (ii) breach of such duty; (iii) such breach actually and proximately caused the plaintiff's injuries; and (iv) damages. A court has discretion whether to use a criminal statute to set the applicable standard of care. The statute will establish the standard if: (i) the conduct it requires is clear; (ii) it was designed to prevent the harm that occurred; and (iii) its purpose is to protect a class including the person injured.

The procedural effect of a statutory violation takes one of three forms. A majority of courts holds that the violation constitutes negligence per se; *i.e.,* duty and breach thereof are established. In a "presumption" state, the jury is charged that negligence is presumed from the violation, but the jury may find the violator not negligent if he persuades them that he acted reasonably. In an "evidence" state, the jury is instructed that the violation is mere evidence of negligence. Whichever approach is used, the plaintiff must still establish causation and damages.

The collision between Doe's car and Crane's car is the type of occurrence meant to be prevented by the speed limit law, and Crane, as the driver of another car, is among the class of persons intended to be protected by the law. Thus, the speed limit statute will be used to establish the standard of care. The fact that the speed limit is ignored by motorists will not provide a defense. It makes no difference that the area is sparsely settled. The speed limit is in effect and it cannot be negated by the public's failure to obey it.

As noted above, the violation will have a different procedural effect depending on a particular state's approach. Under any of the three approaches, it appears that Doe was negligent.

Crane will then have to show a causal connection between Doe's violation and Crane's property damage. Actual cause is established if the injury would not have occurred but for the act. Proximate cause is established if the injury was a foreseeable consequence of the defendant's negligence. The facts do not reveal how the accident occurred, but given that Crane was blameless, he likely can establish that, but for Doe's speeding, the collision could have been avoided. The collision also was a foreseeable result of Doe's speeding, so causation likely can be established. Crane suffered damage to his car, completing the prima facie case of negligence against Doe.

Second Crash

Smith v. Doe: Smith will recover against Doe. At issue is whether Smith's negligent parking of his car will preclude his recovery.

Applying the elements for a negligence action discussed above, Doe breached his duty of care to others on the road by driving without his lights on. The collision appears to have occurred because of the darkness, thus establishing causation. Smith's damaged car completes the prima facie case.

Smith was also negligent in parking on the highway with his lights off. Such negligence may have contributed to the collision. In a traditional contributory negligence state, Smith's negligence would defeat his case. Smith can avoid this defense by invoking the doctrine of last clear chance, which provides that the person with the last clear chance of avoiding the accident is liable. At the time of the collision, Smith's negligence was complete and he was asleep, thus putting him in a position of helpless peril. Doe should have been aware of Smith's peril, and would have been aware had Doe turned on his lights. Thus, last clear chance would counteract Smith's contributory negligence in a traditional contributory negligence state.

Most states have rejected the "all or nothing" approach of contributory negligence and have adopted some form of comparative negligence. In states with "partial" comparative negligence, the plaintiff's damages will be reduced by his percentage of fault unless it passes a threshold level (in which case it is barred). States with "pure" comparative negligence allow some recovery no matter how great the plaintiff's fault is. Hence, if the accident occurred in a comparative negligence state, Smith's negligence would bar or reduce his recovery, depending on the version adopted and on Smith's degree of fault relative to that of Doe. Last clear chance does not apply in a comparative negligence state.

Smith v. Jones: Smith likely will not recover against Jones. At issue is whether Jones, as a passenger in Doe's car, breached a duty owed to Smith.

Smith may claim that Jones was negligent in not reminding Doe to turn on his lights. He may argue that, as a passenger, Jones owed a duty to the drivers of other cars. However, any duty she may have owed is minimal compared to the duty of the driver. As a passenger, Jones did not have a duty to pay attention to the road, so she may not have been aware that Doe's lights were off (or she even may have been disoriented by the first crash). Hence, it is doubtful that Jones would be found to have acted negligently. If Jones were found to have been negligent, Smith's contributory negligence (as discussed above) could be a defense.

Jones v. Doe: Jones may recover from Doe. Doe's negligence relative to the second crash is discussed above. Doe owed his passenger the duty to refrain from active negligence in the operation of his car. This duty was clearly breached, which actually and proximately caused Jones's injury (the deep cut). As noted above, it is possible that Jones's failure to warn of the absence of lights was negligent. If so, the effect of her contributory negligence will be taken into account.

Jones v. Smith: Jones may recover from Smith. The facts establish Smith's negligence. Once again, it is possible that Jones will be found to have contributed to her injury. On the other hand, the negligence of Doe will not be imputed to his passenger. The general rule is that another person's contributory negligence will be imputed to the plaintiff only when the parties are in a relationship that would suffice for vicarious liability. It does not appear that Doe and Jones were engaged in a joint enterprise or that any other applicable relationship was present, so Jones's recovery will not be reduced by Doe's negligence.

Because Doe's and Smith's negligence combined to cause Jones's indivisible injury, Doe and Smith may be jointly and severally liable to Jones. If a state applies joint and several liability, each defendant is liable to Jones for the entire amount of the damages from that injury. In states that do not apply that rule, each defendant will be liable only for the amount of damages that correspond to his degree of fault.

Third Crash

Jones v. Smith: Jones may recover from Smith. At issue is whether Jones's fracture was proximately caused by Smith's original negligence.

Given the emergency presented by Jones's profuse bleeding, it was not unreasonable to use Smith's untrustworthy car in an attempt to reach a hospital. Hence, no new negligence is established by the facts. However, when the defendant's original negligence creates a foreseeable risk that an intervening force would harm the plaintiff, the defendant remains liable for the harm caused. Here, because Smith's original negligence caused damage to his brakes, it was foreseeable that Jones's injuries could be aggravated on the way to seeking medical attention. Thus, Smith is liable for the fracture. Note that Jones will not be deemed to have assumed the risk or to have been contributorily negligent, because her decision to ride in the car resulted from the joint negligence of Smith and Doe, and was reasonable in light of her need for medical care.

Jones v. Doe: The analysis applied above against Smith also applies against Doe; *i.e.,* the fracture can be traced to the earlier cut and the damage to Smith's car, for which Doe is jointly liable.

Smith v. Doe: Smith's action for further damage to his car is based on the previously described theory of negligence on the part of Doe; *i.e.,* Smith will claim this as damage proximately flowing from the second crash. As before, Doe may argue that Smith's negligence contributed to the second crash. The effect of Smith's negligence will depend on the jurisdiction.

Note to Students

The first crash raises one point and is worth about 25%. The second crash is major, with its issues of contributory negligence; duty owed to and by a guest; and joint and several liability. The analysis of the second crash controls the treatment of the third one since no new negligence appears. Proximate cause analysis becomes central. The second and third crashes are worth equal credit. This is a very long and complex question in which some credit should be given for sensible organization and consistent analysis. Organization by crash, rather than by parties, greatly facilitates discussion of the second and third crashes.

ANSWER TO EXAM QUESTION NO. 2

Potter v. Mistkill: Two theories of action may be available to Potter: negligence and strict liability.

Negligence:

A prima facie case for negligence consists of (i) a duty of care owed by the defendant, (ii) breach of that duty, (iii) actual and proximate causation, and (iv) damages suffered by the plaintiff. Under the modern common law rule, a manufacturer owes a duty of due care to all persons who may foreseeably be damaged by negligence in manufacturing the product. Virtually all states extend that duty to claims for property damage.

Even though there is no direct evidence of negligence, Mistkill's breach of duty may be established inferentially under the doctrine of ***res ipsa loquitur.*** The doctrine should apply here because the three prerequisites to its application are present:

(i) It is more likely than not that the injury or damage would not have occurred but for someone's negligence (permitting the spray to become adulterated with strychnine).

(ii) The negligence is attributable to the defendant (*i.e.,* this type of accident ordinarily happens because of the negligence of someone in the defendant's position); this can often be established by showing that the instrumentality causing the injury (the spray) was in the exclusive control of the defendant (Mistkill) when the force causing the injury (the adulteration of the spray) was set into motion.

(iii) The plaintiff in no way contributed to the damage to her property (the poisoning of her horse).

These elements being present, Mistkill may be found negligent by the judge in her capacity as trier of fact. In some states, the application of ***res ipsa loquitur*** creates a presumption of negligence that will result in a judgment for the plaintiff in the absence of facts that would tend to rebut the

presumption. No such facts appear here. In other states, the operation of the doctrine raises only an ***inference*** of negligence, which the trier of fact is free to draw or reject.

Mistkill's negligence is a cause in fact of the death of Potter's horse because, but for the adulteration of the spray, the spray would not have resulted in the horse's death.

All of the intervening forces were arguably foreseeable. Aerial spraying is a common method of applying weed-killing sprays in farming areas. It must be expected that a breeze may be blowing when the activity takes place, and that some of the spray may blow over into neighboring lands where valuable farm animals may be present. Furthermore, it should be foreseeable that an animal exposed to spray adulterated with strychnine would be physically injured thereby.

An additional question of proximate cause is presented by Eagle Scout's abnormal susceptibility to strychnine. This situation would seem close to that of the personal injury cases in which courts hold that one must "take his victim as he finds him." But the question is whether that doctrine is applicable only to human life. It is arguable that in negligence cases the party at fault should always be liable for the unforeseeable weaknesses of his innocent victim—even a horse. If this argument is accepted, Mistkill's negligence should be held to be a proximate cause of Eagle Scout's death, and Mistkill should therefore be liable to Potter for the value of Potter's horse.

Strict Liability: Most states now extend a manufacturer's strict liability in tort to a ***bystander*** for damages (either personal injury or property damage) proximately resulting from a defect in a product, if the damage occurred while the product was being used in the manner for which it was designed.

To prove strict liability, the plaintiff must show (i) an absolute duty owed by a commercial supplier; (ii) production or sale of a defective product; (iii) actual and proximate cause; and (iv) damages.

If the strict liability doctrine is applied to the case at bar, it would eliminate the necessity of proving Mistkill's negligence directly or inferentially. Here, Mistkill is a commercial supplier of the spray. That there was a defect is stated in the facts—whether it occurred in the manufacture or in the design. The same considerations of proximate cause discussed above would be equally applicable here. Although it was unlikely to cause death, some damage from the poison was to be expected and liability should follow—as in the negligence discussion.

Potter v. Upwind

Negligence: Upwind's liability, if any, is based on his act of spraying his crop from an airplane. Although this activity took place on his own land, Upwind had a landowner's duty to exercise due care not to expose the property of adjoining landowners to unreasonable risk of harm. Compliance with the Department of Agriculture's recommendations might be evidence of compliance with a standard required by law (depending upon the purpose of the recommendations), but would not conclusively establish due care. The breeze may have come up after the spraying started, in which case there is no actionable negligence by Upwind at all.

Even if negligence can be established, the breach of duty would have been toward the broad-leaved tobacco, since Upwind could not have known about the poison. While it is true that, but for the spraying, Eagle Scout would not have been killed, the risk of injury to the horse was not within the scope of the risk created by the defendant's negligence. Hence, inasmuch as most jurisdictions now apply "scope of the risk" analysis, Upwind would not be found liable for Eagle Scout's death on this theory.

Strict Liability: If an activity not a matter of common usage involves substantial risk of damage to the person or property of others despite the actor's exercise of due care, it is classified as an abnormally dangerous activity, and the actor may be held liable, even in the absence of negligence, for the proximate results of that activity. In some jurisdictions, aerial spraying has been classified among those activities considered abnormally dangerous—because of both the risk of crashes and the risk to others' crops. Whether it would be so considered in this case would depend upon the trier of fact's determination of two factors: first, whether in the present state of the art the exercise of due care can eliminate the serious risk of damage to the property of adjoining landowners; and second, whether the activity is so common in the community in which it took place that the imposition of absolute liability would be impracticable. Inasmuch as aerial spraying is common in many agricultural communities, it may well be classed as an activity which, although dangerous, is too common for the law to impose strict liability for damages resulting therefrom.

If strict liability were imposed, the danger of poisoning animals would probably be found well within the scope of the risk created, since it is the result of the normally dangerous propensity of aerial spraying. The other proximate cause considerations discussed in the section dealing with Upwind's liability for negligence are equally applicable here.

Upwind v. Mistkill

Upwind could base his cross-complaint on an indemnity theory. As between Upwind and Mistkill, Mistkill is primarily liable because the defect occurred while the product was in Mistkill's hands. Therefore, if Upwind is held liable to Potter on any extended negligence or strict liability theory, the entire liability should fall on Mistkill, who was primarily responsible.

ANSWER TO EXAM QUESTION NO. 3

Peter's Rights Against Andrew

In a jurisdiction that retains contributory negligence, Peter may not be able to recover against Andrew. In a jurisdiction that applies principles of comparative negligence, Peter will recover a portion of his damages.

On the facts, negligence provides the only basis for potential tort liability on the part of Andrew. The prima facie case for negligence consists of: (i) a duty on the part of the defendant to conform to a specific standard of conduct for the protection of the plaintiff against an unreasonable risk of injury; (ii) breach of that duty by the defendant; (iii) actual and proximate causation; and (iv) damage to the plaintiff's person or property.

While Andrew was driving his car, he owed a duty to other drivers and pedestrians in the vicinity (such as Peter) to refrain from creating an unreasonable risk of injury to them. Andrew breached this duty by glancing away from the road while driving at a high rate of speed.

The breach of duty was an actual cause of the accident. The plaintiff can show actual cause by proving that, but for the defendant's negligence, the harm would not have occurred. The facts state that if Andrew had been looking, he would have had plenty of time to stop or slow down the car so as to avoid striking a pedestrian. Although Andrew could have stopped in time to avoid the accident had the steel pin not been defective, the pin snapped under the heavy pressure of jamming the brakes with great force. Thus, the injuries would not have occurred but for Andrew's breach of duty, making the breach an actual cause of the injuries.

Andrew's breach was also a proximate cause of Peter's injuries. Under the rule of proximate cause, a defendant is liable for harmful results that are the normal incidents of and within the increased risk caused by his acts, *i.e.,* a test based on foreseeability. Although Andrew was unaware of the defective pin, it was certainly foreseeable that inattentive driving at a high rate of speed posed a risk of harm to a pedestrian such as Peter.

The final element of the prima facie case, damages, is established by the fact that Peter was seriously injured. Peter can claim damages arising from his medical expenses, lost earnings, pain and suffering, and impaired future earning capacity.

A plaintiff has a duty to exercise reasonable care for his own safety. Under a traditional contributory negligence scheme, the plaintiff's contributory negligence completely bars his right to recover. Peter's inattentiveness, as exemplified by his walking into the street in the face of traffic, constituted contributory negligence. However, Peter may be able to recover under the doctrine of last clear chance. This doctrine allows a plaintiff to recover despite his own negligence if the defendant had the last clear chance to avoid the accident. It can be argued that Andrew had the last clear chance to avoid the accident, because he could have avoided the accident if he had been looking at the road.

Most states have adopted some type of comparative negligence system, whereby the trier of fact weighs the plaintiff's negligence against that of the defendant and reduces the plaintiff's damages accordingly. Under a partial comparative negligence system, the plaintiff's recovery is barred if his negligence exceeds a threshold of 49% or 50%; otherwise his recovery is reduced by the percentage of his fault. Under a pure comparative negligence system, the plaintiff will recover something as long as he is not 100% at fault. As stated above, Peter was negligent with regard to his own safety. Thus, in a comparative negligence jurisdiction, his recovery will be reduced, rather than barred, unless his negligence crosses whatever threshold applies under a scheme of partial comparative negligence.

Peter's Rights Against Bob

Peter has a cause of action against Bob based on negligence. As is the case regarding Peter's negligence action against Andrew, principles of contributory negligence or comparative negligence may affect the outcome.

Applying the elements of the prima facie case for negligence set forth above, Bob owed a duty of ordinary reasonable care in his job as a mechanic, pursuant to which he was required to exercise the knowledge and skill of a member of his occupation in good standing in the same or similar community. When Bob noticed that an important steel pin connecting the braking mechanism was worn nearly through, ordinary reasonable care would have required him to report his discovery to Andrew, the car's owner, so as to alert him to the potential seriousness of the problem. Bob owed this duty not just to Andrew but to all foreseeable plaintiffs, which would encompass anyone who might be on the road when Andrew is driving the car. Bob should have reasonably foreseen a risk of injury to pedestrians or people riding in other cars arising from his failure to mention the defective pin. Thus, Bob breached a duty of care owed to Peter.

Peter is entitled to a presumption that, had Bob told Andrew about the pin's defective condition, Andrew would have had the condition repaired or refrained from driving until it was repaired. If the pin had been in proper working condition, Andrew would have been able to stop the car in time to avoid the accident. Thus, Bob's breach of duty was an actual cause of Peter's injuries.

Regarding proximate cause, the accident and the injuries that befell Peter were well within the range of foreseeable risks caused by Bob's failure to disclose the condition of the pin. Andrew's negligence in glancing away from the road was an intervening force; *i.e.,* a force that came into motion after Bob's negligent act that combined with it to cause the injury to the plaintiff. Intervening forces will not cut off the defendant's liability for his own negligence if the intervening force was foreseeable. Here, Andrew's negligence in driving inattentively was ordinary foreseeable negligence; thus, it will not cut off Bob's liability for the foreseeable consequences of his negligence.

As explained in the previous section, Peter's negligently stepping into the street, without which he would not have been injured, would defeat his cause of action in a contributory negligence jurisdiction; however, unlike Andrew, Bob did not have the last clear chance to avoid the accident. In a state that has adopted some form of comparative negligence, Peter's recovery will be reduced (or in some states barred altogether if his negligence exceeds the designated threshold of 49% or 50%).

ANSWER TO EXAM QUESTION NO. 4

Any potential causes of action would be based on negligence. The prima facie case for negligence consists of the following: (i) a duty on the part of the defendant to conform to a specific standard of conduct for the protection of the plaintiff against an unreasonable risk of injury; (ii) breach of duty; (iii) actual and proximate causation; and (iv) damage to the plaintiff's person or property.

Smith's Rights: Smith may have a viable cause of action against Jones for her son's wrongful death. Under the principle of negligence per se, the requirements of a criminal statute, including a municipal ordinance, can establish the applicable duty if: (i) the plaintiff is in the class intended to be protected by the statute; (ii) the statute was designed to prevent the type of harm suffered by the plaintiff; and (iii) the standard of conduct is clearly defined.

The ordinance at issue was probably enacted to promote free access to the street, both for purposes of convenience and for safety in case of emergencies, and a patient in need of emergency treatment by a doctor would likely be in the class intended to be protected by the statute. Jones breached his duty under the ordinance by blocking the doctor's driveway. Absent this breach, the doctor would have reached Tom in time to save his life. This establishes actual causation. Regarding proximate cause, it will be a question of fact for the jury whether it was foreseeable that the doctor would be unable to obtain alternative emergency assistance after he determined that he could not get out. The recoverable damages by the mother in a wrongful death action would include loss of support and loss of companionship.

Note that Smith does not have a viable cause of action against Dr. Paul. The doctor did all that he could reasonably have been expected to do in his efforts to help Smith's son. It was not the doctor's fault that his driveway was blocked, and he tried to push the car out of the way. When those efforts failed, he did his best to reach another doctor.

Dr. Paul's Rights: Dr. Paul has a claim against Jones for his personal injuries. It is likely that the doctor will have to establish a common law negligence duty, because it is doubtful that the harm he suffered was the type of harm that the ordinance was designed to prevent. Jones owed a duty to the doctor to park his vehicle so as to avoid creating an unreasonable risk of injury. Jones breached this duty by blocking the doctor's driveway. This breach actually caused the doctor to suffer injury when he tried to push the car to provide emergency treatment. While again a question for the jury, it was probably foreseeable that the owner of the driveway might be injured in trying to move the car, thus establishing proximate cause. The doctor's hernia and pain constitute his injuries. Because the doctor was attempting to respond to an emergency, he will not be found to have been contributorily negligent in trying to push the car.

Adams's Rights: Adams has a strong case against Dr. White, but does not have a good case against Jones.

Dr. White negligently took her eyes off the road, so she breached her duty to drive in a manner so as to avoid an unreasonable risk of injury to pedestrians. Actual causation is clear, and the clear foreseeability of what happened establishes proximate cause. Finally, the facts indicate that Adams suffered injuries.

Dr. White can raise the issue of Adams's contributory negligence, because he was staggering on the highway in a helpless drunken condition. Absent such conduct, the accident would not have happened, and the injury was a foreseeable result of such conduct. In a contributory negligence jurisdiction, this would defeat the plaintiff's cause of action. However, because Adams was in a helpless situation, the court may find that Dr. White had the last clear chance to avoid the accident, allowing Adams to recover despite his contributory negligence. In a state that has adopted some form of comparative negligence, the fault of Adams will be weighed against that of Dr. White, and will reduce Adams's recovery or bar it altogether in a state applying partial comparative negligence if it exceeds the specified threshold in that state.

A suit by Adams against Jones will fail because proximate cause is absent. Although it is true that but for Jones's negligent blocking of Dr. Paul's driveway, Dr. White would probably not have been at the scene of the accident with Adams, this type of harm was not within the scope of reasonably foreseeable consequences that might occur as a result of blocking the driveway.

barbri®

Chart Supplement

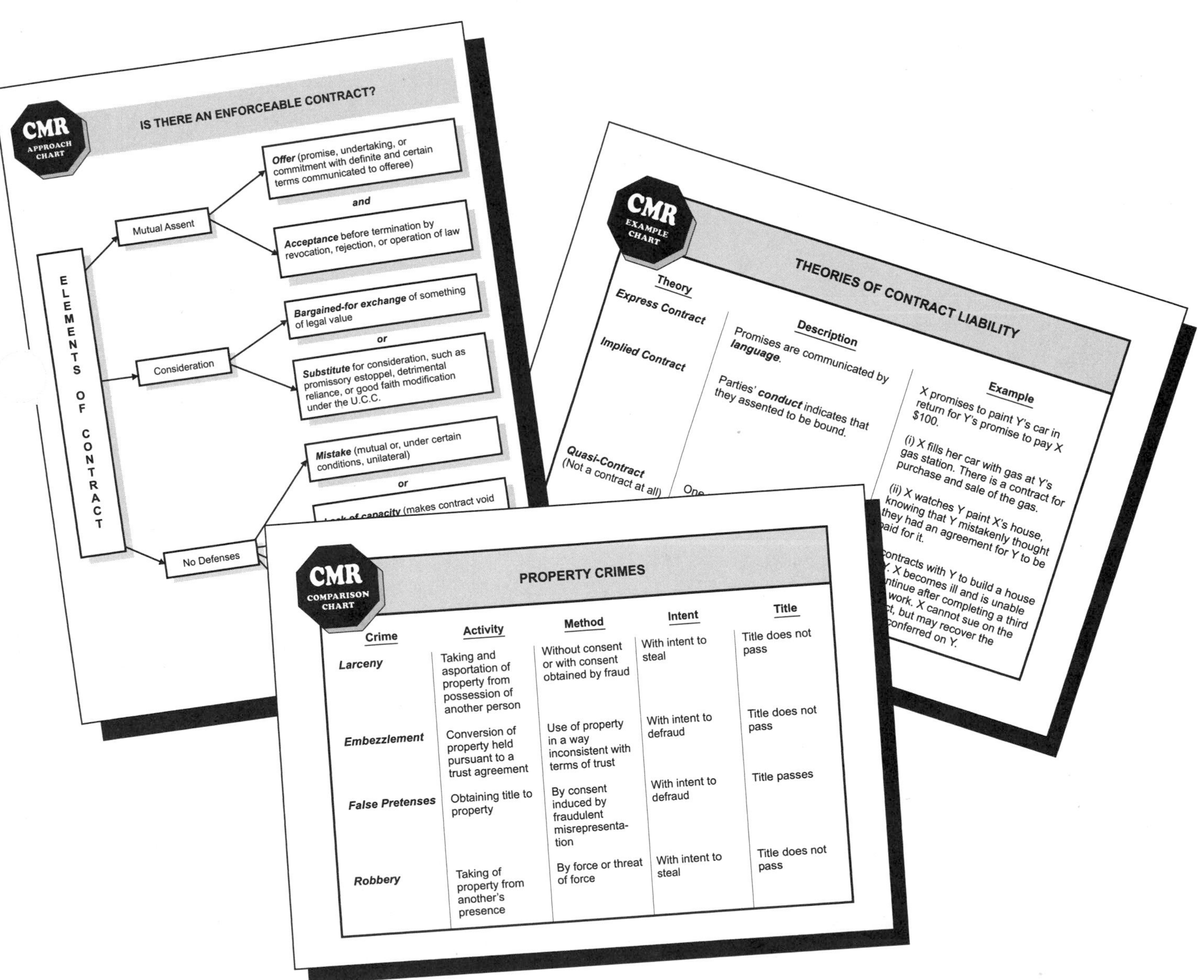

Maximize Your First Year Grades!

Charts Your Course™

REMOVAL ISSUES

The key points to remember are:

☑ A ***federal court must have jurisdiction*** over the case; ***jurisdiction need not have been proper in the state court***.

☑ Removal is to the federal district court ***whose territory encompasses the state court***.

☑ ***Only defendants can remove***; ***all*** defendants must join in the removal.

☑ A case ***based on diversity*** may ***not be removed*** if ***any defendant*** is a ***citizen of the forum*** state.

☑ Notice of removal must be ***filed within 30 days*** of the date defendant receives a copy of the initial pleading.

☑ If a case later becomes removable (as by dismissal of a nondiverse defendant), the case may be removed ***within 30 days of the date it becomes removable, but (for diversity cases) not more than one year after it was brought in state court***.

☑ If the case contains a ***separate and independent claim based on a federal question,*** defendant may remove the ***whole case***.

Charts Your Course™

CMR SUMMARY CHART

TIMING OF RULE 12 DEFENSES

Defense	Timing
1. Lack of jurisdiction over the ***subject matter***	May be raised anytime, even on appeal
2. Lack of jurisdiction over the ***person***	Waived if not raised by motion or answer, whichever is first
3. Improper ***venue***	Waived if not raised by motion or answer, whichever is first
4. Insufficiency of ***process***	Waived if not raised by motion or answer, whichever is first
5. Insufficiency of ***service of process***	Waived if not raised by motion or answer, whichever is first
6. Failure to ***state a claim*** upon which relief can be granted	May be raised anytime before trial or at trial
7. Failure to ***join a party*** under Rule 19 (indispensable party)	May be raised anytime before trial or at trial

FEDERAL CLASS ACTION REQUIREMENTS

A federal class action must meet all four requirements on the left side of the chart and one of the requirements on the right. The three alternatives on the right determine the type of federal class action. Only the third type, *i.e.,* the common question type, ***requires*** notice to all class members and allows opting out.

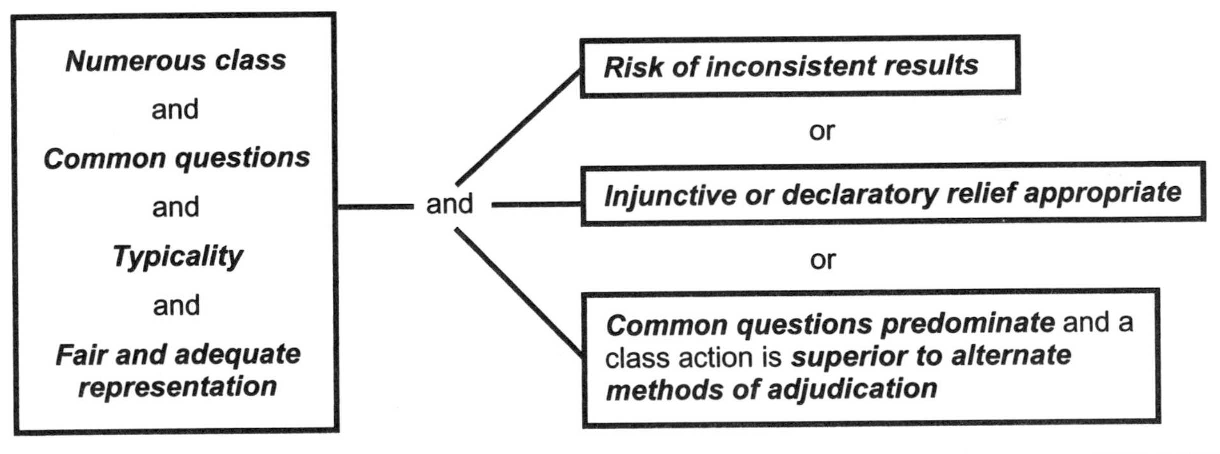

Charts Your Course™

CMR SUMMARY CHART

PROCEDURAL DEVICES THAT MAY TERMINATE CASE

Method	Circumstances	Timing
Pre-Answer Motion [Rule 12(b)]	Addresses the following preliminary matters: defects in subject matter jurisdiction, personal jurisdiction, venue, process, and service of process; failure to state claim; failure to join needed party.	(*See* summary chart *supra* for timing of Rule 12 defenses.)
Voluntary Dismissal by Plaintiff [Rule 41(a)]	Without prejudice once as a matter of right; also possible by stipulation or court order.	If dismissed as a matter of right without prejudice, must be done before defendant files answer or motion for summary judgment.
Involuntary Dismissal [Rule 41(b)]	Plaintiff fails to prosecute the case or to comply with the Rules or a court order.	Anytime.
Motion for Judgment on the Pleadings [Rule 12(c)]	On the face of the pleadings (without considering matters outside the pleadings), the moving party is entitled to judgment. Treated as motion for summary judgment if accompanied by outside matters.	After pleadings are closed but not so late as to delay trial.
Summary Judgment [Rule 56]	No genuine dispute of material fact and moving party is entitled to judgment as a matter of law. May support by pleadings, affidavits, discovery materials.	Unless local rule or court order dictates otherwise, a party may file a motion for summary judgment at any time until 30 days after close of discovery. If a motion is premature, the court may defer ruling on it.
Judgment on Partial Findings [Rule 52]	In a nonjury trial, the judge may enter a judgment as a matter of law if she makes dispositive partial findings on the claim.	During trial, once the judge has heard sufficient evidence to make dispositive findings and all parties have been fully heard on the issue.
Motion for Judgment as a Matter of Law (Directed Verdict) [Rule 50(a)]	Evidence viewed in light most favorable to motion's opponent leads reasonable person to conclusion in favor of moving party.	After opponent has presented case but before submission of case to jury.
Renewed Motion for Judgment as a Matter of Law ("JNOV") [Rule 50(b)]	The verdict returned could not have been reached by reasonable persons. Moving party must have previously sought judgment as a matter of law sometime during the trial.	Within 28 days after entry of judgment.

SOURCES OF CONGRESSIONAL POWER

Government Action	Source of Power
1. Congress enacts divorce laws for the District of Columbia.	General federal police power for D.C. (as well as military bases and federal lands).
2. Congress pays for highways.	Spending Power and Commerce Clause.
3. Federal income tax.	Taxing Power.
4. Congress conditions aid to states for medical programs on state funding of AIDS research.	Spending Power.
5. Congress adopts a tax to regulate banknotes rather than to raise revenue.	Power to coin money.
6. Congress prohibits hunting on federal lands.	Property Power.
7. Congress bars racial discrimination at places of public accommodation.	Commerce Clause.
8. Congress requires all employers, including state governments, to comply with federal minimum wage and overtime provisions.	Commerce Clause.

Note: The Amendments to the Constitution may also be a source of power (*e.g.,* the Thirteenth Amendment gives Congress power to outlaw badges of slavery; thus Congress may require a private seller to sell land to blacks as well as whites). (*See infra.*)

Charts Your Course™

CMR APPROACH CHART

STATE REGULATION OF INTERSTATE COMMERCE

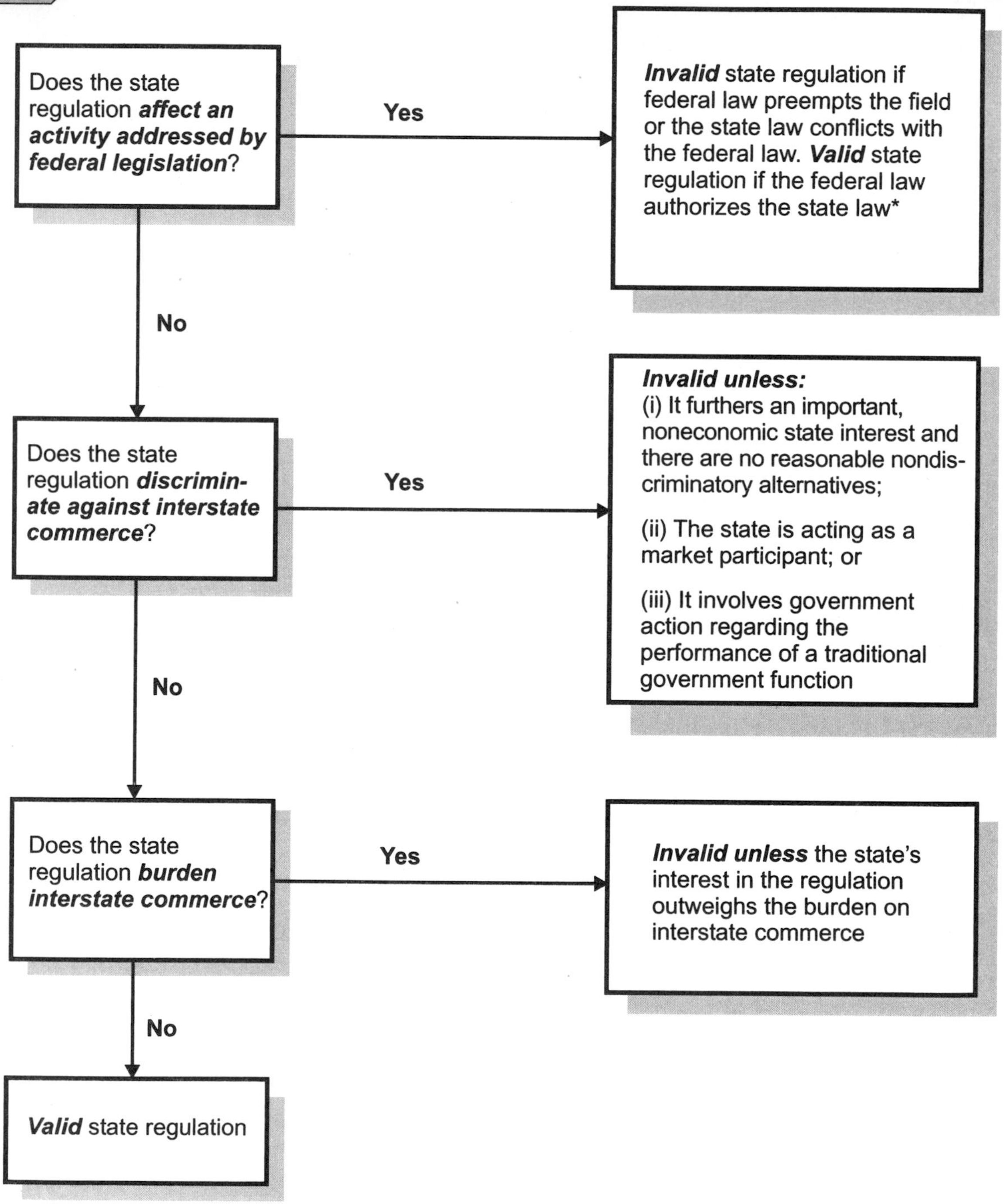

Does the state regulation ***affect an activity addressed by federal legislation***?

Yes → ***Invalid*** state regulation if federal law preempts the field or the state law conflicts with the federal law. ***Valid*** state regulation if the federal law authorizes the state law*

No ↓

Does the state regulation ***discriminate against interstate commerce***?

Yes → ***Invalid unless:***
(i) It furthers an important, noneconomic state interest and there are no reasonable nondiscriminatory alternatives;

(ii) The state is acting as a market participant; or

(iii) It involves government action regarding the performance of a traditional government function

No ↓

Does the state regulation ***burden interstate commerce***?

Yes → ***Invalid unless*** the state's interest in the regulation outweighs the burden on interstate commerce

No ↓

Valid state regulation

*Of course, Congress has no power to authorize legislation that would violate other constitutional provisions, such as the Privileges and Immunities Clause of Article IV.

STATE ACTION VS. NO STATE ACTION

State Action	No State Action
Public Function	
Running a town	Running a shopping mall (does not have all the attributes of a town)
Conducting an election	Holding a warehouseman's lien sale
Significant State Involvement	
Enforcing restrictive covenants prohibiting sale or lease of property through use of state courts	Granting a license and providing essential services to a private club
Leasing premises to a discriminatory lessee where state derives extra benefit from the discrimination (*i.e.,* symbiotic relationship exists)	Granting a monopoly to a utility
Allowing state official to act in discriminatory manner under "color of state law"	Heavily regulating an industry
Administering a private discriminatory trust by public officials	Granting a corporation its charter and exclusive name

CMR APPROACH CHART

SUBSTANTIVE DUE PROCESS OR EQUAL PROTECTION QUESTIONS

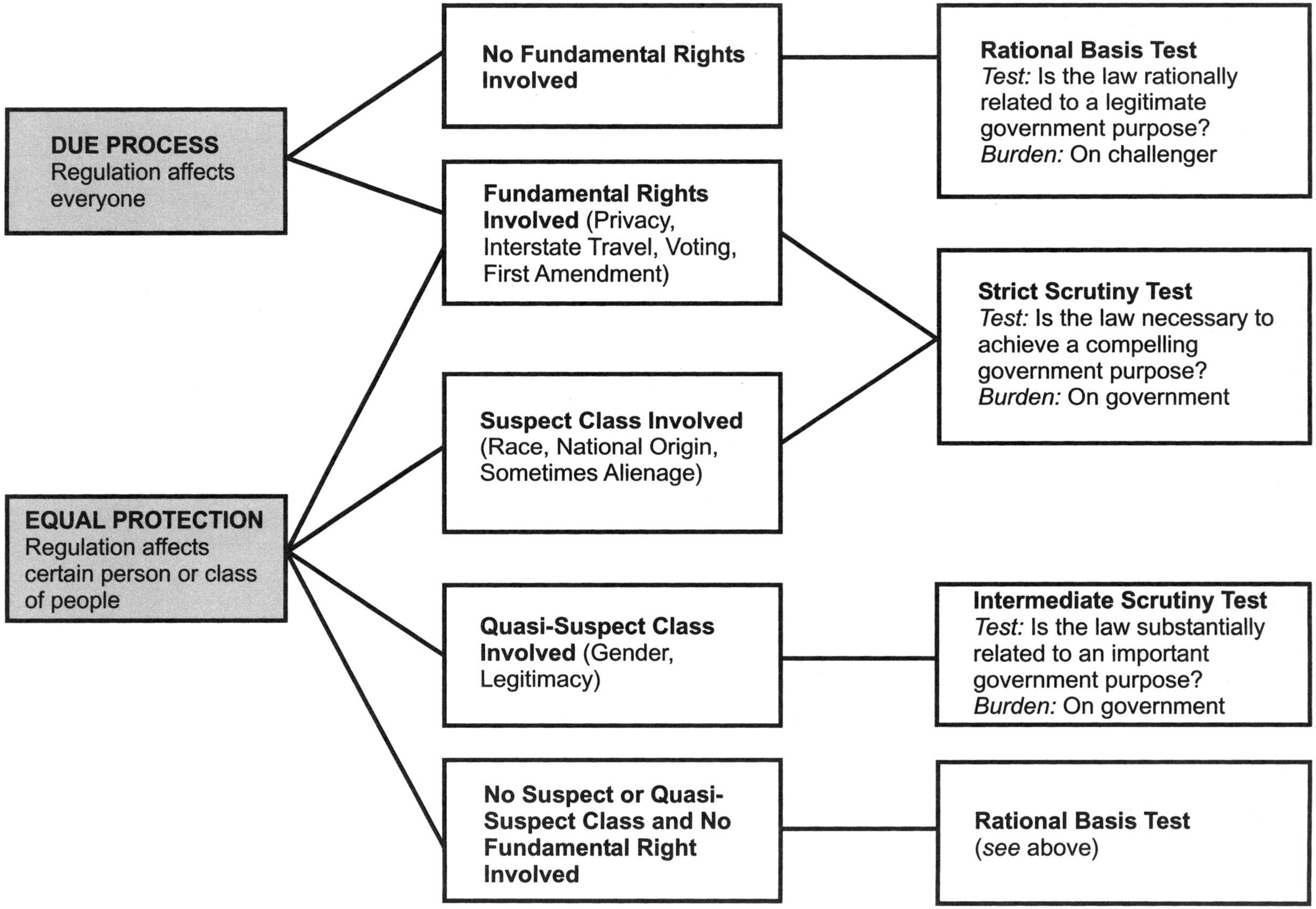

DUE PROCESS
Regulation affects everyone

- **No Fundamental Rights Involved** → **Rational Basis Test** *Test:* Is the law rationally related to a legitimate government purpose? *Burden:* On challenger
- **Fundamental Rights Involved** (Privacy, Interstate Travel, Voting, First Amendment) → **Strict Scrutiny Test**

EQUAL PROTECTION
Regulation affects certain person or class of people

- **Fundamental Rights Involved** (Privacy, Interstate Travel, Voting, First Amendment) → **Strict Scrutiny Test** *Test:* Is the law necessary to achieve a compelling government purpose? *Burden:* On government
- **Suspect Class Involved** (Race, National Origin, Sometimes Alienage) → **Strict Scrutiny Test**
- **Quasi-Suspect Class Involved** (Gender, Legitimacy) → **Intermediate Scrutiny Test** *Test:* Is the law substantially related to an important government purpose? *Burden:* On government
- **No Suspect or Quasi-Suspect Class and No Fundamental Right Involved** → **Rational Basis Test** (*see* above)

Charts Your Course™

CMR APPROACH CHART

IS THERE AN ENFORCEABLE CONTRACT?

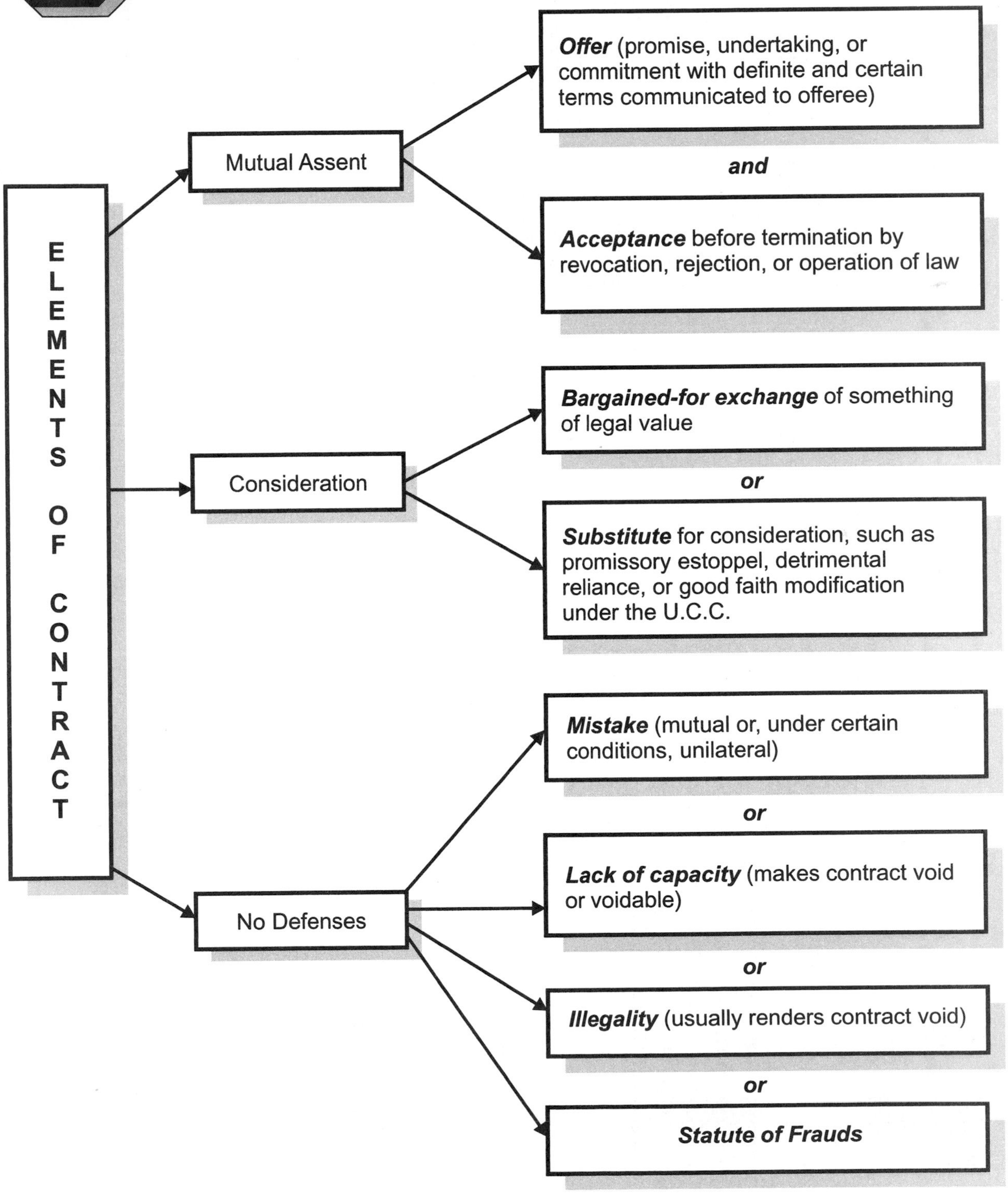

ELEMENTS OF CONTRACT

- Mutual Assent
  - ***Offer*** (promise, undertaking, or commitment with definite and certain terms communicated to offeree)
  - ***and***
  - ***Acceptance*** before termination by revocation, rejection, or operation of law
- Consideration
  - ***Bargained-for exchange*** of something of legal value
  - ***or***
  - ***Substitute*** for consideration, such as promissory estoppel, detrimental reliance, or good faith modification under the U.C.C.
- No Defenses
  - ***Mistake*** (mutual or, under certain conditions, unilateral)
  - ***or***
  - ***Lack of capacity*** (makes contract void or voidable)
  - ***or***
  - ***Illegality*** (usually renders contract void)
  - ***or***
  - ***Statute of Frauds***

barbri®

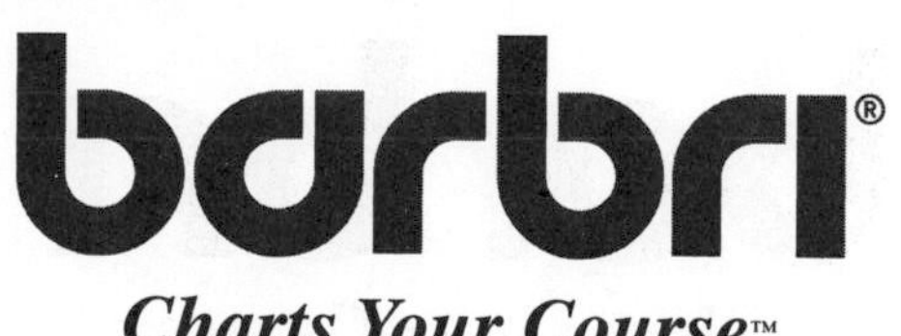

Charts Your Course™

CMR EXAMPLE CHART

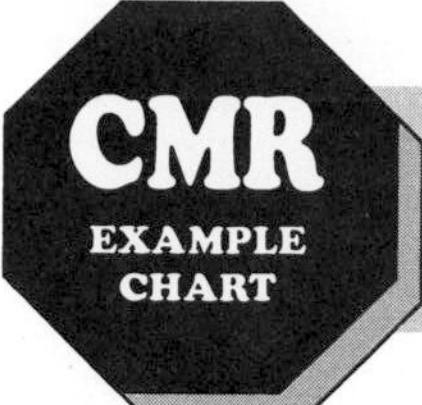

EFFECT OF REJECTION OR REVOCATION ON OFFER

OFFEREE SENDS ACCEPTANCE, THEN REJECTION

CASE 1

- **Offeror:** sends offer — receives acceptance — receives rejection
- timeline
- **Offeree:** sends acceptance — sends rejection

CONTRACT
Mailbox Rule applies

CASE 2

- **Offeror:** sends offer — receives rejection ***and*** detrimentally relies on it — receives acceptance
- timeline
- **Offeree:** sends acceptance — sends rejection

NO CONTRACT
Exception to Mailbox Rule

OFFEREE SENDS REJECTION, THEN ACCEPTANCE

CASE 1

- **Offeror:** sends offer — receives rejection — receives acceptance
- timeline
- **Offeree:** sends rejection — sends acceptance

NO CONTRACT
Mailbox Rule does not apply (whichever received first controls)

CASE 2

- **Offeror:** sends offer — receives acceptance — receives rejection
- timeline
- **Offeree:** sends rejection — sends acceptance

CONTRACT
Mailbox Rule does not apply; whichever received first controls

OFFEROR SENDS OFFER, THEN REVOCATION

CASE 1

- **Offeror:** sends offer — sends revocation
- timeline
- **Offeree:** sends acceptance — receives revocation

CONTRACT
Mailbox Rule applies; revocation effective only on receipt

CASE 2

- **Offeror:** sends offer — sends revocation
- timeline
- **Offeree:** receives revocation — sends acceptance

NO CONTRACT
Receipt of revocation terminates power of acceptance

Charts Your Course™

PERFORMANCE OF CONTRACT

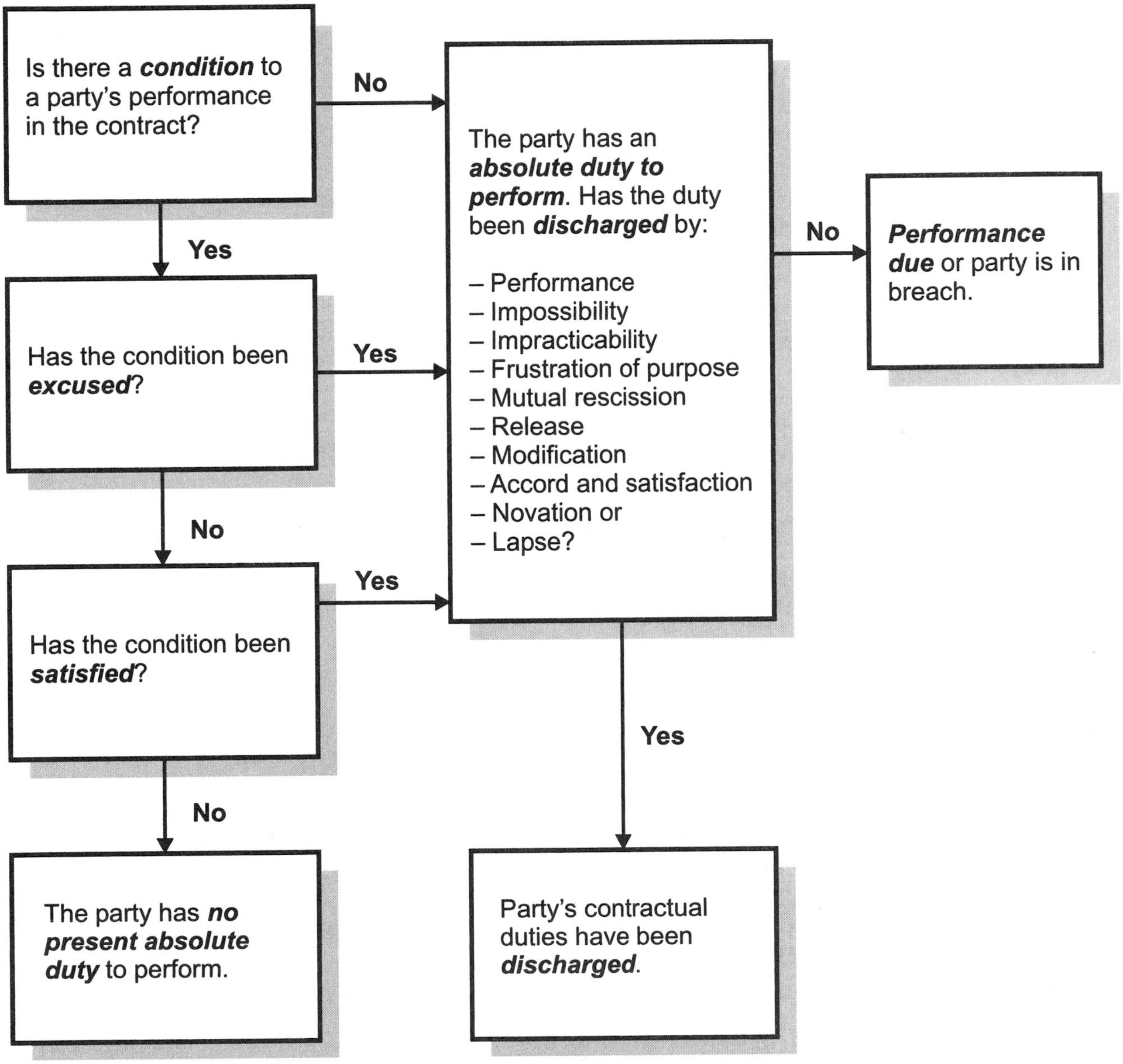

Is there a ***condition*** to a party's performance in the contract?

- **No** → The party has an ***absolute duty to perform***. Has the duty been ***discharged*** by:
  - – Performance
  - – Impossibility
  - – Impracticability
  - – Frustration of purpose
  - – Mutual rescission
  - – Release
  - – Modification
  - – Accord and satisfaction
  - – Novation or
  - – Lapse?
    - **No** → ***Performance due*** or party is in breach.
    - **Yes** → Party's contractual duties have been ***discharged***.
- **Yes** → Has the condition been ***excused***?
  - **Yes** → The party has an ***absolute duty to perform*** (see above).
  - **No** → Has the condition been ***satisfied***?
    - **Yes** → The party has an ***absolute duty to perform*** (see above).
    - **No** → The party has ***no present absolute duty*** to perform.

Charts Your Course™

ACCEPTANCE WITH ADDITIONAL TERMS

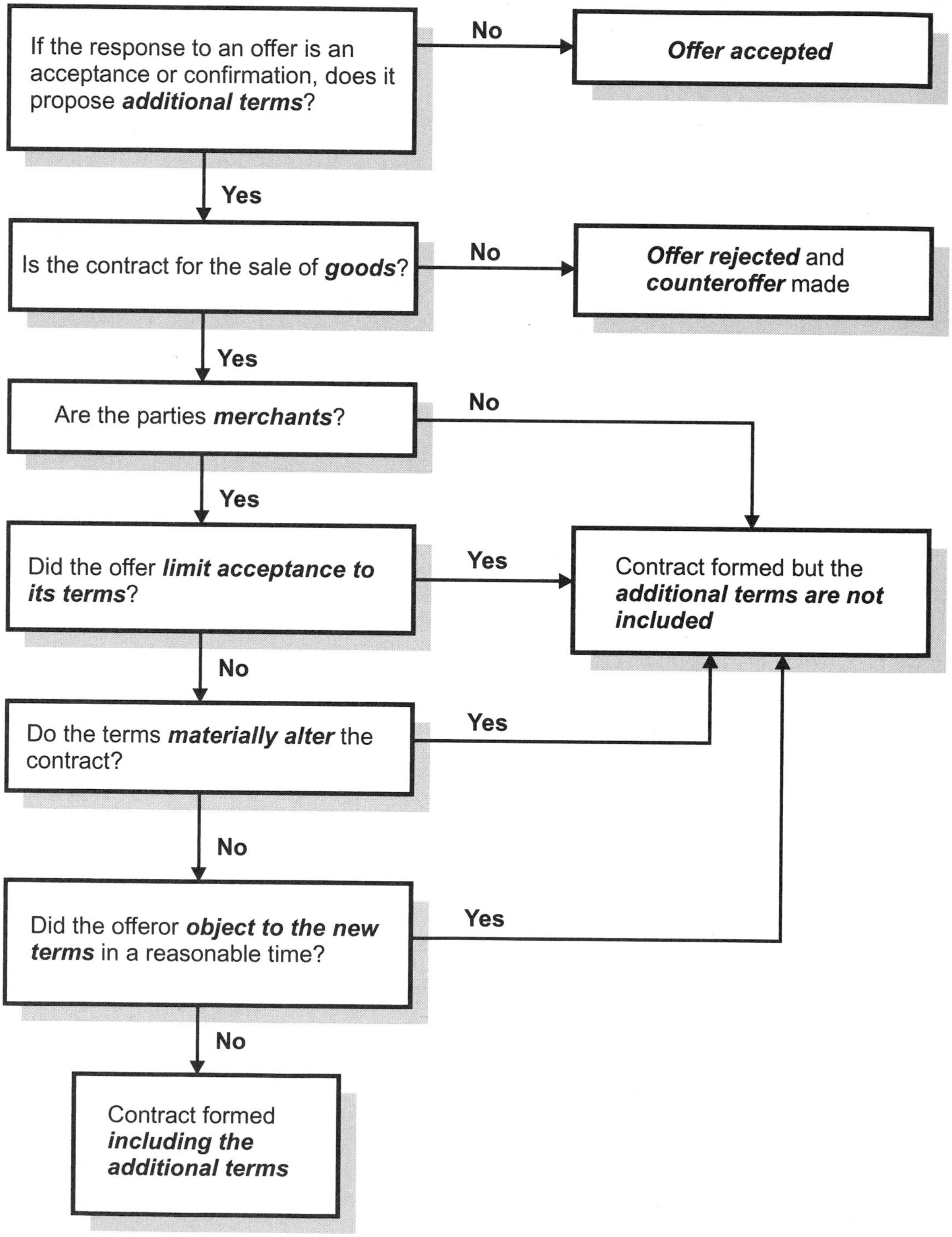

1. If the response to an offer is an acceptance or confirmation, does it propose ***additional terms***?
   - No → ***Offer accepted***
   - Yes → 2
2. Is the contract for the sale of ***goods***?
   - No → ***Offer rejected*** and ***counteroffer*** made
   - Yes → 3
3. Are the parties ***merchants***?
   - No → Contract formed but the ***additional terms are not included***
   - Yes → 4
4. Did the offer ***limit acceptance to its terms***?
   - Yes → Contract formed but the ***additional terms are not included***
   - No → 5
5. Do the terms ***materially alter*** the contract?
   - Yes → Contract formed but the ***additional terms are not included***
   - No → 6
6. Did the offeror ***object to the new terms*** in a reasonable time?
   - Yes → Contract formed but the ***additional terms are not included***
   - No → Contract formed ***including the additional terms***

CMR APPROACH CHART

CLASSIFICATION OF CRIMES

Was the crime committed prior to or in preparation for a more serious offense?

- **Yes** → solicitation, attempt, conspiracy
- **No** → Was the crime committed against property or against a person?
  - **Property** → Was the crime against the habitation or against personal property?
    - **Habitation** → burglary, arson
    - **Personal Property** → larceny, embezzlement, false pretenses, robbery
  - **Person** → Did a death result?
    - **Yes** → murder, manslaughter, felony murder (*see* homicide crimes chart)
    - **No** → battery, assault, false imprisonment, kidnapping, rape

CMR SUMMARY CHART

DEFENSES NEGATING CRIMINAL CAPACITY

Defense	Elements	Applicable Crimes
Insanity	Meet applicable ***insanity test*** (*M'Naghten*, irresistible impulse, *Durham*, or M.P.C.)	Defense to ***all*** crimes
Intoxication		
-voluntary	***Voluntary, intentional taking*** of a substance ***known to be*** intoxicating	Defense to ***specific intent*** crime if intoxication prevents formation of required intent
-involuntary	Taking intoxicating substance ***without knowledge*** of its nature, ***under duress***, or pursuant to ***medical advice***	Treated as mental illness (*i.e.,* apply appropriate insanity test); may be a defense to ***all*** crimes
Infancy	Defendant under age 14 ***at common law***; under ***modern statutes***, defendant under age 13 or 14	*Common law:* Under age seven, absolute defense to ***all*** crimes; under 14, rebuttable presumption of defense. *Modern statutes:* Defense to adult crimes but may still be delinquent
Diminished Capacity (some states)	As a result of mental defect ***short of insanity***, defendant did not have the required mental state to commit the crime	Most states with this defense limit it to ***specific intent*** crimes

Charts Your Course™

CMR SUMMARY CHART

JUSTIFICATION DEFENSES

Defense	Amount of Force Allowed: Nondeadly Force	Amount of Force Allowed: Deadly Force
Self-Defense	If reasonably necessary to protect self	Only if threatened with death or great bodily harm
Defense of Others	If reasonably necessary to protect person	Only if threatened with death or great bodily harm
Defense of Dwelling	If reasonably necessary to prevent or end unlawful entry	Only if person inside is threatened or to prevent felony inside
Defense of Other Property	If reasonably necessary to defend property in one's possession (but if request to desist would suffice, force ***not*** allowed)	Never
Crime Prevention	If reasonably necessary to prevent felony or serious breach of peace	Only to prevent or end felony risking human life
Effectuate Arrest		
– Police	If reasonably necessary to arrest	Only to prevent escape of felon who threatens human life
– Private Person	If crime in fact committed and reasonable belief that this person committed it	Only to prevent escape of person who actually committed felony and who threatens human life
Resisting Arrest	If improper arrest	Only if improper arrest and defendant does not know arrester is a police officer
Necessity	If reasonably necessary to avoid greater harm	Never

CMR
APPROACH CHART

HOMICIDE CRIMES

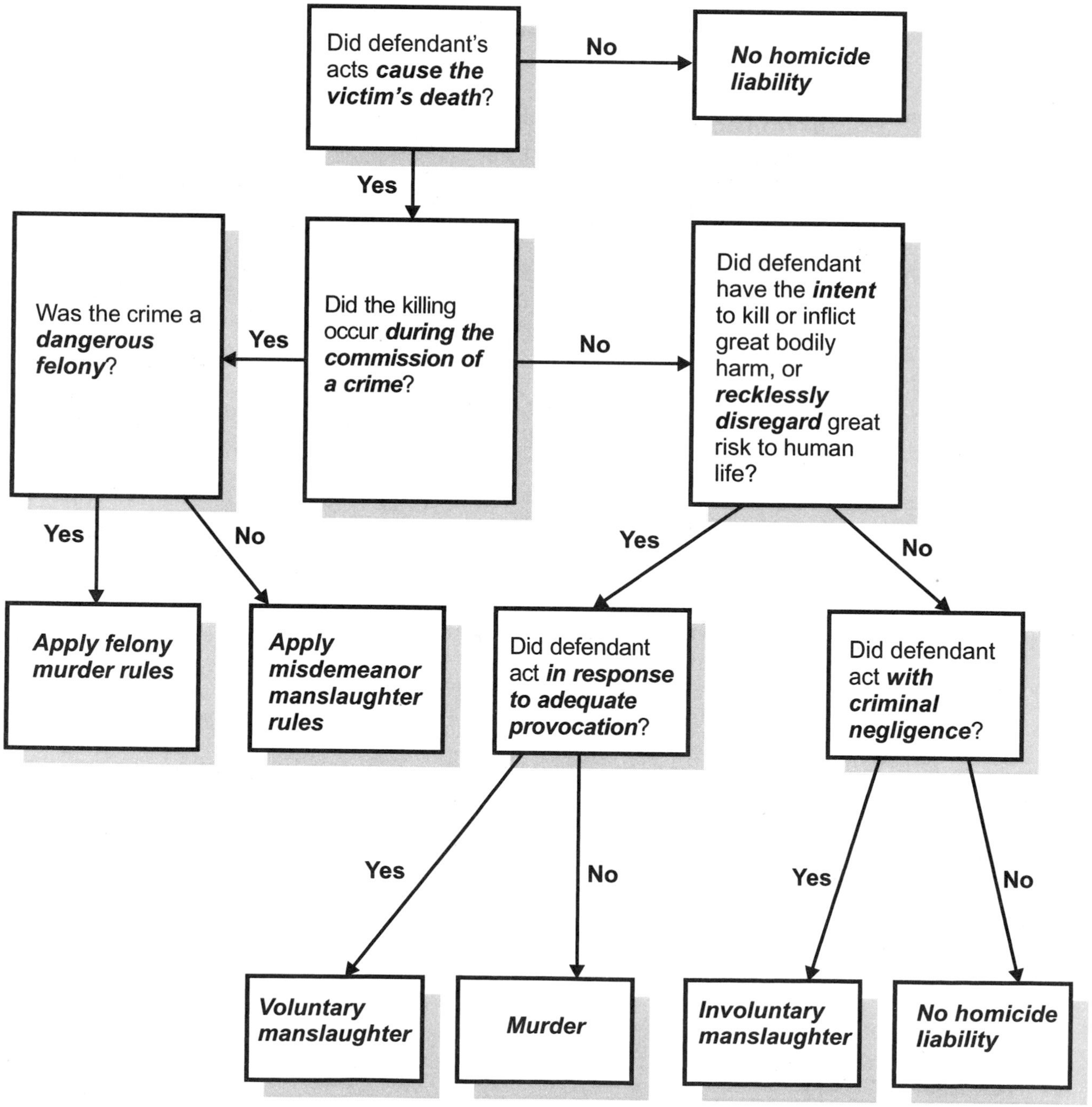

- Did defendant's acts ***cause the victim's death***?
  - **No** → ***No homicide liability***
  - **Yes** → Did the killing occur ***during the commission of a crime***?
    - **Yes** → Was the crime a ***dangerous felony***?
      - **Yes** → ***Apply felony murder rules***
      - **No** → ***Apply misdemeanor manslaughter rules***
    - **No** → Did defendant have the ***intent*** to kill or inflict great bodily harm, or ***recklessly disregard*** great risk to human life?
      - **Yes** → Did defendant act ***in response to adequate provocation***?
        - **Yes** → ***Voluntary manslaughter***
        - **No** → ***Murder***
      - **No** → Did defendant act ***with criminal negligence***?
        - **Yes** → ***Involuntary manslaughter***
        - **No** → ***No homicide liability***

Note: This chart will lead you to the prima facie homicide that defendant committed. You must then decide whether any defenses apply.

Charts Your Course™

CMR
COMPARISON CHART

CONCURRENT OWNERSHIP

Type of Tenancy	Definition	Creation	Termination
Joint Tenancy	Each tenant has an undivided interest in the whole estate, and the surviving co-tenant has a right to the whole estate (***right of survivorship***).	"To A and B as joint tenants with the right of survivorship." (Without survivorship language, it may be construed as a tenancy in common.) Joint tenants must take: (i) identical interests; (ii) from the same instrument; (iii) at the same time; (iv) with an equal right to possess (the four unities).	The right of survivorship may be severed, and the estate converted to a tenancy in common, by: a conveyance by one joint tenant, agreement of joint tenants, murder of one co-tenant by another, or simultaneous deaths of co-tenants. A joint tenancy can be terminated by partition (voluntary or involuntary).
Tenancy by the Entirety	Husband and wife each has an undivided interest in the whole estate and a ***right of survivorship***.	"To H and W." Some states presume a tenancy by the entirety in any joint conveyance to husband and wife where the four unities (above) are present.	The right of survivorship may be severed by death, divorce, mutual agreement, or execution by a joint creditor. Tenancy by the entirety cannot be terminated by involuntary partition.
Tenancy in Common	Each tenant has a distinct, proportionate, undivided interest in the property. There is ***no right of survivorship***.	"To A and B" or, sometimes, "To A and B as joint tenants." Only unity required is possession.	May be terminated by partition.

Charts Your Course™

CMR COMPARISON CHART

ASSIGNMENT VS. SUBLEASE

	Assignment by Landlord	Assignment by Tenant	Sublease by Tenant
Consent	Tenant's consent not required.	Landlord's consent may be required by lease.	Landlord's consent may be required by lease.
Privity of Estate	Assignee and tenant are in privity of estate.	Assignee and landlord are in privity of estate.	Sublessee and landlord are not in privity of estate. Original tenant remains in privity of estate with landlord.
Privity of Contract	Assignee and tenant are not in privity of contract. Original landlord and tenant remain in privity of contract.	Assignee and landlord are not in privity of contract. Original tenant and landlord remain in privity of contract.	Sublessee and landlord are not in privity of contract. Original tenant and landlord remain in privity of contract.
Liability for Covenants in Lease	Assignee liable to tenant on all covenants that run with the land.	Assignee liable to landlord on all covenants that run with the land.	Sublessee is not personally liable on any covenants in the original lease and cannot enforce the landlord's covenants.
	Original landlord remains liable on ***all*** covenants in the lease.	Original tenant remains liable for rent and ***all*** other covenants in the lease.	Original tenant remains liable for rent and ***all*** other covenants in the lease and can enforce the landlord's covenants.

Charts Your Course™

LEASEHOLD ESTATES

Type of Leasehold	Definition	Creation	Termination
Tenancy for Years	Tenancy that lasts for some fixed period of time.	"To T for 10 years."	Terminates at the end of the stated period without either party giving notice.
Periodic Tenancy	Tenancy for some fixed period that continues for succeeding periods until either party gives notice of termination.	"To T from month to month." ***or*** "To T, with rent payable on the first day of every month." ***or*** L elects to bind hold-over T for an additional term.	Terminates by notice from one party at least equal to the length of the time period (*e.g.,* one full month for a month-to-month tenancy). *Exception:* Only six months' notice is required to terminate a year-to-year tenancy.
Tenancy at Will	Tenancy of no stated duration that lasts as long as both parties desire.	"To T for and during the pleasure of L." (Even though the language gives only L the right to terminate, L or T may terminate at any time.) ***or*** "To T for as many years as T desires." (Only T may terminate.)	Usually terminates after one party displays an intention that the tenancy should come to an end. May also end by operation of law (*e.g.,* death of a party, attempt to transfer interest).
Tenancy at Sufferance	Tenant wrongfully holds over after termination of the tenancy.	T's lease expires, but T continues to occupy the premises.	Terminates when landlord evicts tenant or elects to hold tenant to another term.

NONPOSSESSORY INTERESTS

	Easement	License	Profit	Real Covenant/ Equitable Servitude
Definition	A grant of an interest in land that allows someone to use another's land	Permission to go onto another's land	Right to take resources from another's land	Promise to do or not to do something on the land
Example	Owner of parcel A grants owner of parcel B the right to drive across parcel A	O allows the electrician to come onto his land to fix an outlet	O allows A to come onto O's land to cut and remove timber	O conveys an adjoining parcel to A. A promises not to build a swimming pool on the property
Writing	Generally required. *Exceptions:* Less than one year Implication Necessity Prescription	Not required. *Note:* An invalid oral easement is a license	Required	Required. *Exception:* Equitable servitude may be implied from common scheme of development of residential subdivision
Termination	Stated conditions Release Merger Abandonment Estoppel Prescription End of necessity	Usually revocable at will. May be irrevocable if coupled with an interest or if licensor estopped by licensee's expenditures	Same as easement	Release Merger Condemnation Also equitable defenses may apply to enforcement of servitude

Charts Your Course™

CONSTITUTIONAL DEFAMATION

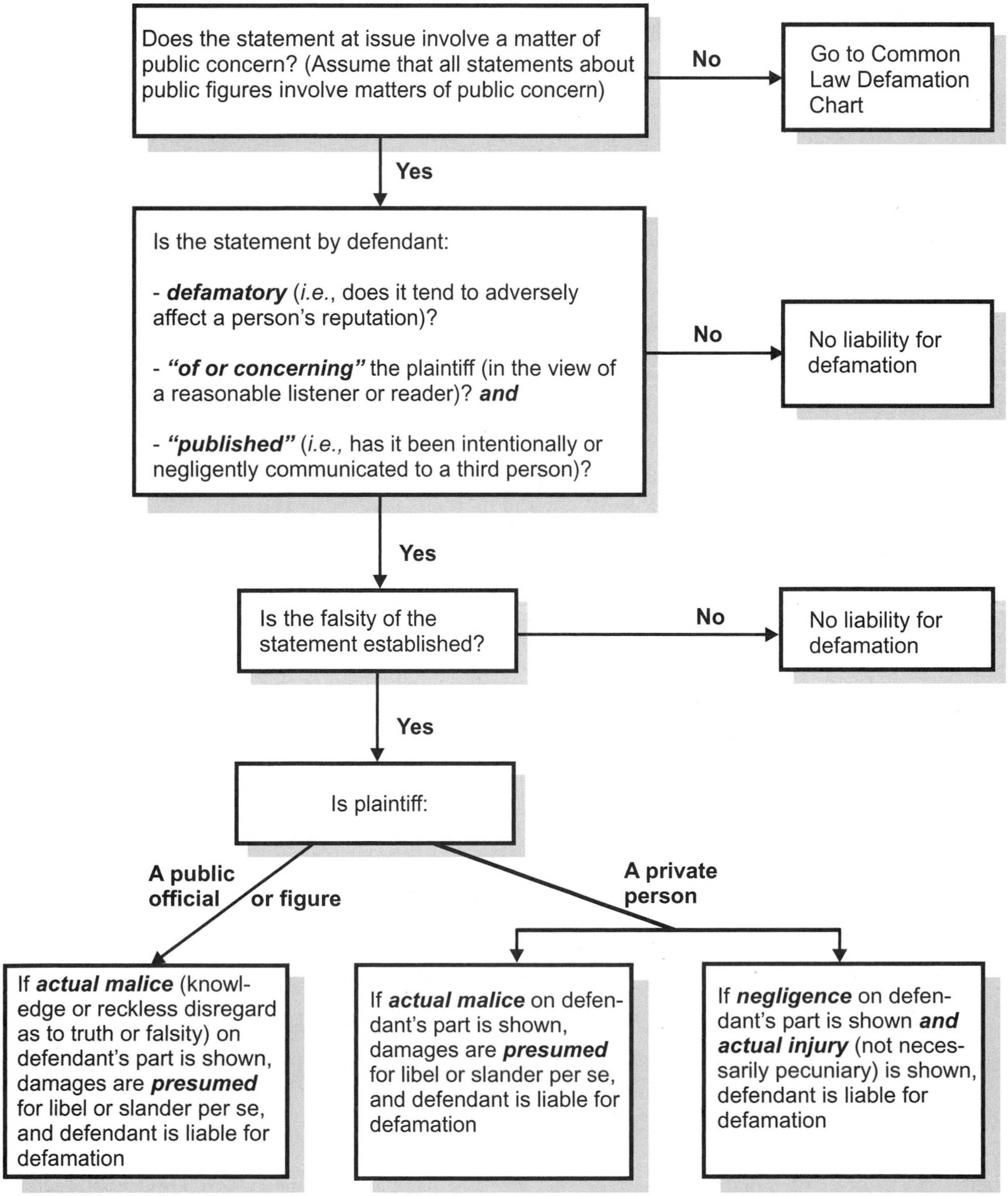

Does the statement at issue involve a matter of public concern? (Assume that all statements about public figures involve matters of public concern)

No → Go to Common Law Defamation Chart

Yes ↓

Is the statement by defendant:

- ***defamatory*** (*i.e.*, does it tend to adversely affect a person's reputation)?

- ***"of or concerning"*** the plaintiff (in the view of a reasonable listener or reader)? ***and***

- ***"published"*** (*i.e.,* has it been intentionally or negligently communicated to a third person)?

No → No liability for defamation

Yes ↓

Is the falsity of the statement established?

No → No liability for defamation

Yes ↓

Is plaintiff:

A public official or figure → If ***actual malice*** (knowledge or reckless disregard as to truth or falsity) on defendant's part is shown, damages are ***presumed*** for libel or slander per se, and defendant is liable for defamation

A private person →

- If ***actual malice*** on defendant's part is shown, damages are ***presumed*** for libel or slander per se, and defendant is liable for defamation
- If ***negligence*** on defendant's part is shown ***and actual injury*** (not necessarily pecuniary) is shown, defendant is liable for defamation

COMMON LAW DEFAMATION

Does the statement at issue involve a matter of public concern? (Assume that all statements about public figures involve matters of public concern)

→ **Yes**: Go to Constitutional Defamation Chart

↓ **No**

Is the statement by defendant:

- ***defamatory*** (*i.e.,* does it tend to adversely affect a person's reputation)?

- ***"of or concerning"*** the plaintiff (in the view of a reasonable listener or reader)? ***and***

- ***"published"*** (*i.e.,* has it been intentionally or negligently communicated to a third person)?

→ **No**: No liability for defamation

↓ **Yes**

Is the statement:

Libel or slander per se → Damages are presumed; defendant is liable for defamation

Slander not within per se categories → If plaintiff shows special (*i.e.,* pecuniary) damages, defendant is liable for defamation

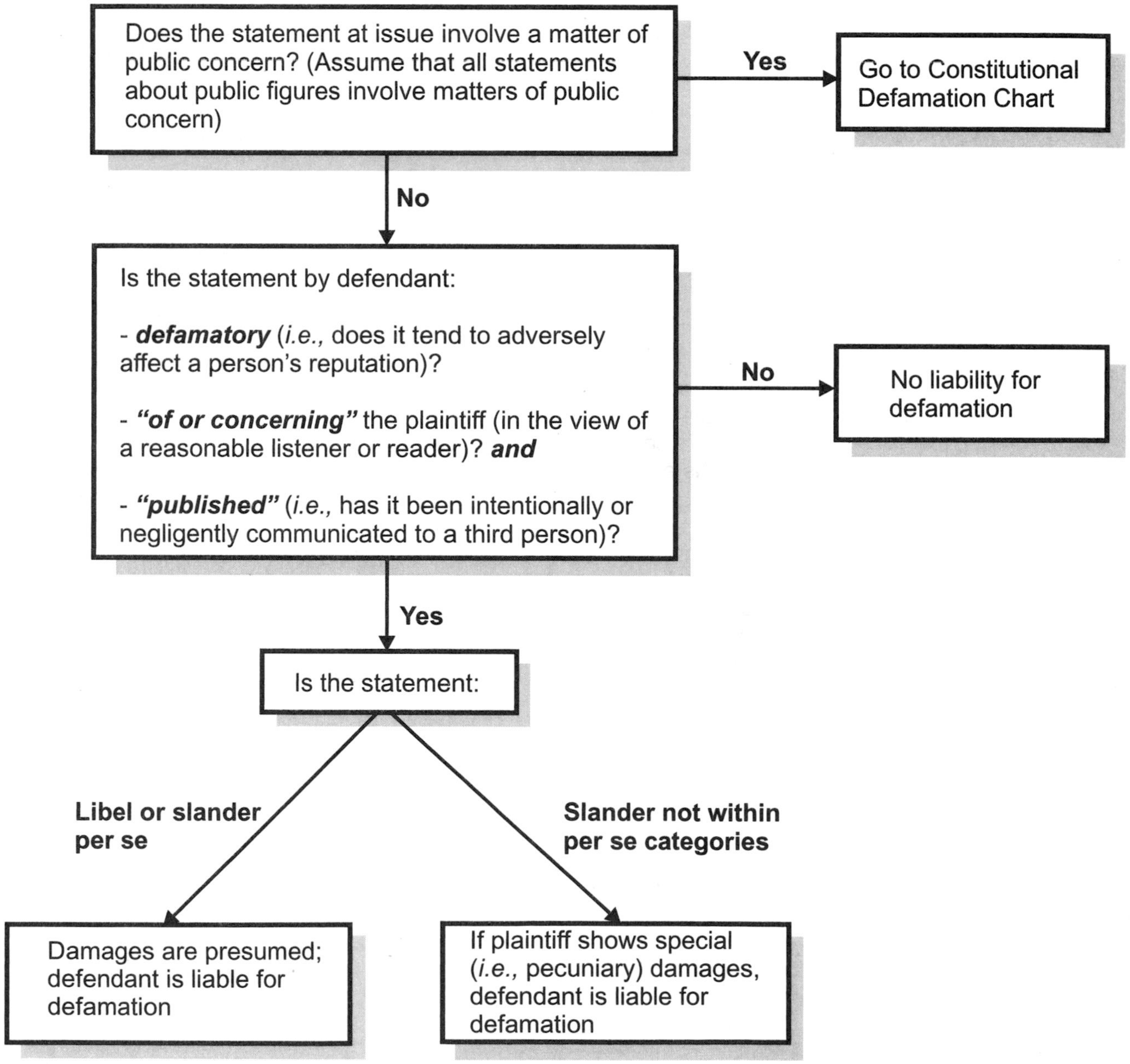

Charts Your Course™

CMR SUMMARY CHART

DUTY OF POSSESSOR OF LAND TO THOSE ON THE PREMISES

Status of Entrant	Duties Owed: *Artificial Conditions*	Duties Owed: *Natural Conditions*	Duties Owed: *Active Operations*
Undiscovered Trespasser	No duty	No duty	No duty
Discovered or Anticipated Trespasser	Duty to warn of or make safe known conditions if non-obvious and ***highly*** dangerous	No duty	Duty of reasonable care
Child (if presence on land foreseeable—attractive nuisance doctrine)	Duty to warn of or make safe if foreseeable risk to child outweighs expense of eliminating danger	No duty (unless child also qualifies as licensee or invitee)	Duty of reasonable care
Licensee (including social guest)	Duty to warn of or make safe known conditions if nonobvious and dangerous	Duty to warn of or make safe known conditions if nonobvious and dangerous	Duty of reasonable care
Invitee (*e.g.,* member of public, business visitor)	Duty to make reasonable inspections to discover nonobvious dangerous conditions and warn of or make them safe	Duty to make reasonable inspections to discover nonobvious dangerous conditions and warn of or make them safe	Duty of reasonable care

Charts Your Course™

INFLICTION OF EMOTIONAL DISTRESS

	Intentional	Negligent
Conduct Required	Extreme and outrageous conduct by defendant	Subjecting plaintiff to threat of physical impact or severe emotional distress likely to cause physical symptoms
Fault Required	Intent to cause severe emotional distress or recklessness as to the effect of conduct	Negligence in creating risk of physical injury to plaintiff
Causation and Damages	Defendant's conduct must cause severe emotional distress	Defendant's conduct generally must cause physical symptoms from the distress
Bystander Recovery When Another Is Physically Injured	Plaintiff bystander must be present when injury occurs and be a close relative of the injured person, and defendant must know these facts when he intentionally injures the other person (or defendant must have intent to cause plaintiff distress)	Plaintiff bystander must (i) be closely related to the injured person, (ii) be present at the scene, and (iii) observe or perceive the injury